# CASES AND MATERIALS ON CORPORATIONS

# CASES AND MATERIALS ON CORPORATIONS

## THIRD EDITION

**Thomas R. Hurst**
*Professor Emeritus*
*University of Florida Levin College of Law*

**William A. Gregory**
*Professor of Law Emeritus*
*Georgia State University College of Law*

**Jack F. Williams**
*Professor of Law*
*Georgia State University College of Law*

**B. Ellen Taylor**
*Associate Professor of Law*
*Georgia State University College of Law*

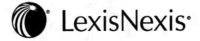

ISBN: 978-0-7698-4912-6
Looseleaf ISBN: 978-0-7698-4913-3
eBook ISBN: 978-0-3271-7994-8

**Library of Congress Cataloging-in-Publication Data**

Hurst, Thomas R., author.

Cases and materials on corporations / Thomas R. Hurst, Professor Emeritus, University of Florida Levin College of Law; William A. Gregory, Professor of Law Emeritus, Georgia State University College of Law; Jack F. Williams, Professor of Law, Georgia State University College of Law; B. Ellen Taylor, Associate Professor of Law, Georgia State University College of Law. -- Third Edition.

pages cm.

Includes index.

ISBN 978-0-7698-4912-6

1. Corporation law--United States--Cases. I. Gregory, William A., 1943- author. II. Williams, Jack F., author. III. Taylor, B. Ellen, author. IV. Title.

KF1413.H87 2014

346.73'066--dc23

2014021815

NOTE TO USERS

To ensure that you are using the latest materials available in this area, please be sure to periodically check the LexisNexis Law School web site for downloadable updates and supplements at www.lexisnexis.com/lawschool.

Editorial Offices

121 Chanlon Rd., New Providence, NJ 07974 (908) 464-6800

201 Mission St., San Francisco, CA 94105-1831 (415) 908-3200

www.lexisnexis.com

MATTHEW◆BENDER

# *Acknowledgments*

---

JFW would like to thank Kenneth P. Brockman (Georgia State Law Class of 2013) for his valuable assistance in the careful research and painstaking review of those chapters he wrote. JFW would further like to thank his family and friends for putting up with him, or more often, his empty chair at home and events, as he worked on this and related projects. Thank you all for your kindness, thoughtfulness, and patience.

BET is grateful for the fine help provided by Georgia State College of Law students Reid Peacock (class of 2013) and Joseph H. Saul (class of 2015), and the consistently excellent work of my assistant, Christine Nwakamma. I also greatly appreciate the love and support of my family — Susan, Adam, Ben, and Callan.

# Table of Contents

# Table of Contents

# Table of Contents

# Table of Contents

# Table of Contents

# Table of Contents

# Table of Contents

# Table of Contents

## Table of Contents

# Table of Contents

# Table of Contents

# Chapter 1

# THE CORPORATION AND OTHER BUSINESS ORGANIZATIONS: CHOICE OF FORM

This book deals primarily with the general business corporation. In order to put the corporation in perspective, however, it is necessary to discuss other forms of business organization as well. The primary alternatives to the corporation today include the general partnership, limited partnership, and more recently, the limited liability company (LLC) and limited liability partnership (LLP). In discussing the relative advantages and disadvantages of the corporation, then, our primary focus will be on comparing it with these entities. (Some forms of business organization, such as the joint stock company and Massachusetts Trust, are no longer in general use for the operation of a business dealing in goods or services and will not be discussed here.) It is also necessary for the student to become familiar with the fundamentals of agency law, as the work of virtually all business organizations, corporation or otherwise, is performed by agents. This is particularly true of the corporation since, as an intangible legal entity, it cannot act other than through its agents.

The corporation in the late 20th Century is the predominant form of business organization as measured by gross receipts. In a recent year, there were about three million active corporations in the United States compared to 13 million sole proprietorships and one million partnerships. In examining the corporation and the reasons for its popularity, we will examine the major characteristics of the corporation.

## A. THE CORPORATION

### 1. Limited Liability of Investors

Perhaps the best known characteristic of the corporation is the limited liability of its investors, or shareholders as they are more properly known. That is, absent special circumstances, which we will explore later, purchasers of stock in a corporation stand to lose, at most, only the money which they paid for their stock in the corporation. If the corporation suffers losses and becomes insolvent, judgment creditors of the corporation cannot look to the stockholders to satisfy their judgment. Surprisingly, this was not always true. Early 19th Century general corporate acts did not provide for the limited liability of shareholders. This is in contrast to the general partnership, where each individual is liable for all obligations of the partnership, whether arising in tort or in contract.

## 2. Centralized Management

In the corporation, managerial power is, by law, concentrated in a group of individuals known as the board of directors. The board is elected, in most cases annually, by the shareholders but until recently the shareholders have not had the power to direct the day to day business affairs of the corporation. Rather, the main benefit of the corporation was seen as its ability to provide for centralized management of the funds of hundreds of investors. Traditionally, the shareholders have been given a voice only in certain major transactions such as amendment of the articles of incorporation, dissolution of the corporation or approval of mergers, or the sale of substantially all of the assets of the corporation. Similarly, all employees of the corporation, even its top officers, act only subject to the authority given to them by the board. This centralization of management is one of the reasons given by historians for the growth in popularity of the corporation in the late 19th Century; the demands of big business for large amounts of capital required the pooling of the investments of thousands of individuals coupled with the right to control the investment of that capital by a handful of individuals. The corporation was ideally suited for this purpose. In contrast, in a general partnership each one of the partners is by law an agent of the partnership and can act on its behalf, unless the partnership agreement provides to the contrary. Thus, the partnership makes no distinction between investors and managers. This failure to distinguish between ownership interests and the right of control would be unworkable in a large organization where specialization is a necessity. There may be many individuals who have the money but not the time or inclination to manage a business and others who have the entrepreneurial ability but not the funds to invest. The corporation is ideally suited to such combinations. Although it is also possible to create a partnership in which managerial authority is delegated to a few of the partners, this requires a carefully drafted written partnership agreement.

## 3. Free Transferability of Interests

The ownership interest in a corporation is represented by shares of stock of one or more classes. The corporate code in every state authorizes the corporation to issue different classes of stock which have such rights, preferences and benefits as are designated, usually in the articles of incorporation. The rights of shares generally include, but are not limited to, the right to receive dividend payments or to share in the liquidation of the enterprise on a pro rata basis with other shareholders of the same class, the right to vote for the board of directors and on certain other major corporate changes such as mergers or liquidations and the right to inspect certain corporate records.

The holder of shares of stock does not have an interest in any specific property of the corporation; as a legal entity in its own right, all property, real and personal, tangible and intangible is held in the name of the corporation. Thus, a shareholder wishing to liquidate her investment cannot direct the sale of specific corporate property. However, absent a provision to the contrary in the articles of incorporation she is free to sell her shares of stock at any time and to anyone whom she wishes for whatever price she may obtain. This right to sell her shares of stock is a major benefit of the corporate form of ownership since it provides liquidity to the investor, at least if the corporation is large enough so that shares of stock are regularly traded on the New York Stock Exchange or some other organized market. Furthermore, because the corporation is a legal entity, the transfer of some or all of its stock from one person to another does not affect the conduct of its business. The board of directors remains in place until the next shareholders meeting when an election is scheduled and all contracts between the corporation and third parties remain unchanged. This combination of stability in business relationships coupled with liquidity for shareholders (investors) is a significant benefit to both the corporation and its owners.

In contrast, in a partnership, the death or withdrawal of any single partner operates as dissolution of the partnership and requires a winding up of the business of the partnership as expeditiously as possible. As a practical matter, what usually happens is that the remaining partners agree to buy out the interest of the partner who wishes to withdraw, since this preserves the valuable contracts and going concern value of the partnership. Nonetheless, the process is disruptive to the normal business of the partnership and may cause problems maintaining the cash flow needed to operate the business. If a partner wishes to sell her interest in the partnership to a third party, this presents difficulties. First, it requires the consent of all of the remaining partners. Second, it requires appraisals since there is no organized market for partnership interests and a buyer must be found. Thus, there is no liquid market for general partnership interests; its sale will be a one-on-one negotiated transaction.

## 4. The Corporation Is a Legal Entity

Some of the consequences of the corporation's status as a legal entity have been discussed above. Specifically, changes in the identity or number of shareholders do not affect the corporation's legal existence. Nor do they affect the validity of its contracts with third parties. Since the corporation holds property in its own name, changes in the identity of its shareholders or of membership in the board of directors do not affect this status at all. This also means that the corporation can pursue litigation in the courts or enter into contracts in its own name and these lawsuits or contracts are unaffected by changes in the board of directors or the shareholders. Only the liquidation or, in some cases, the bankruptcy of the corporation can affect such contracts. Modern corporate statutes typically give the corporation perpetual existence unless the articles of incorporation state otherwise.

Again, the partnership at common law had no right to sue or hold property in its own name. The result was that transactional costs and delay were greater in the partnership; since the withdrawal or entry of a partner dissolved the old partnership and created a new one, it would be necessary to change the description of the holders of real property following the withdrawal of a partner or substitute the name of parties involved in litigation to conform to the identity of the new partnership. Modern statutes have eliminated many of these burdens but others still remain.

## B.  THE CLOSE CORPORATION

There is no uniformly accepted definition of the closely held corporation or "close" corporation. Many federal and state securities laws draw the line at a corporation with 35 or fewer shareholders while other commentators have placed the dividing line at 20 to 25 shareholders. Modern state corporate codes generally treat the large publicly held corporation the same as the small business corporation. However, a number of states do have separate subchapters which contain a handful of special provisions applicable only to the close corporation. Generally, these subchapters are elective, i.e., the drafters of the articles of incorporation may elect to be governed by the close corporation provisions or they may choose to be governed only by those provision applicable to all corporations regardless of size. Nonetheless, even where special statutory rules do not apply, the courts increasingly recognize that the nature of the small incorporated family business is fundamentally different than the large public corporation with tens of thousands of shareholders, justifying a difference in treatment.

We will have much to say in a later chapter about problems peculiar to the close corporation. For the present time, though, it is important to emphasize that the distinguishing characteristics of the corporation mentioned above, which have been presented as generally advantageous in the public corporation, may be a mixed blessing in the close corporation.

The free transferability of ownership interest in a corporation generally raises few policy issues in a corporation the size of General Electric or Microsoft, where the identity of shareholders is generally of little consequence to management. In a close corporation, where all of the shareholders are family members or close friends, the sale of shares, particularly where the block is sizeable enough to elect one or more directors, may be of great concern to the remaining shareholders if the purchaser is someone who is incompatible with the other shareholders. For this reason, the shareholders in a close corporation often place restrictions on the transfer of shares, such as giving existing shareholders a "right of first refusal," which effectively gives shareholders in a close corporation control over their co-shareholders similar to the rights of partners in a partnership.

Second, the perpetual existence of a corporation may pose serious problems with the small family owned business. The most frequent problem occurs with the death of an individual who is actively involved in the business, owns a sizeable block of stock, and is taking most of the profits from the business in the form of a salary as opposed to dividends. If the surviving spouse, who may not have participated in the corporation's affairs, looks to the corporation as the major source of financial security, the perpetual existence poses serious problems. The decedent's salary is no longer available and, if dividends have not been paid and the remaining directors refuse to declare dividends for her benefit, she finds herself receiving no financial remuneration from the largest asset in the estate. Worse yet, because there is no established liquid market for stock in a close corporation she cannot easily dispose of her interest to create the liquidity needed to purchase income-producing investments. In a partnership, the survivors are in a much better bargaining position because death automatically dissolves the partnership. Thus, if the business is to continue, the survivors must buy out the decedent's interest in the partnership; it can only continue with the decedent's survivor as a partner with the mutual consent of all parties. This places the decedent's survivors in a much stronger position in the partnership as opposed to the close corporation. For this reason, buy-sell agreements triggered by the death of one of the principals in the corporation are well nigh essential in the close corporation to protect the financial security of the survivors. Furthermore, limited liability of shareholders is not likely to be as significant an advantage in the close corporation. While limited liability serves to protect shareholders from a variety of unexpected tort claims, those arising from motor vehicle accidents or on the job injuries to employees or customers will be covered by insurance anyway. As for contract claims, most creditors will demand a personal guarantee from shareholders of the close corporation, particularly in the case of a small, start-up business. Such a guarantee effectively negates the limited liability of the all shareholders who sign it. Finally, the centralized management of the corporation may create problems in the close corporation. Typically most of the major stockholders are active participants in the business; to the extent that there are passive stockholders this situation may have arisen due to the death of one or more of the principals in the business and the inheritance of their interest in the business. Because of this, a feeling may arise among those actively working in the business that they are entitled to a majority of the financial returns from the business and they may resent giving up any corporate income to the passive shareholders. Thus, there may be a tendency to "zero out" the corporate income by taking it mostly in the form of salaries or other fringe benefits, such as luxury automobiles or generous expense accounts and declaring no or only small dividends.

Unless the passive shareholders are able to sell their shares at a reasonable price, this raises the real possibility that they will not receive a fair return on their investment. While there may be "passive partners" in a partnership who are not heavily involved in operating the business, every partner has equal rights to manage the partnership business and by law can dissolve the partnership if he or she is not satisfied with the division of the partnership profits, so exploitation of passive investors is less likely to occur.

## C.  THE RELEVANCE OF TAXATION IN CHOICE OF BUSINESS ENTITY

While the above mentioned characteristics have some significance in choosing the form of business organization, they are rarely decisive. This is partly because many of the supposed disadvantages of a partnership can be eliminated by a written partnership agreement. The partnership agreement may provide for centralized management by delegating specified managerial authority to a few partners. Also, written provisions dealing with the transfer of partnership interests may smooth the transition when a partner dies or retires, effectively giving the partnership continuity of life similar to the close corporation. Furthermore, the absence of limited liability in a partnership can largely be overcome by purchasing insurance against foreseeable tort liabilities. Thus, at least prior to 1997, the tax consequences of the choice of business entity undoubtedly had been the major factor influencing the choice of business entity. Traditionally, the corporation has been treated as a taxable entity separate and distinct from its shareholders and taxed under a separate "corporate income tax" with a rate schedule different from personal income tax. A partnership, although required to file a tax return for informational purposes, was not viewed as a separate taxable entity and its income (or losses as the case may be) "flowed through" and were taxed to the individual partners or, in the case of losses could be used by the partner to offset income from other sources. A full discussion of the consequences of these differences is beyond the scope of an introductory course in Corporations. However, a few illustrations may serve to illustrate the types of issues that are involved.

1. If a business expects to experience losses for the first few years, the partnership may be the preferred form, at least for individuals with a substantial earned income from other sources, because these losses "flow through" to the individual partners in proportion to their partnership interests. Such losses may be deducted from the income the partners have earned from other sources and thus reduce the personal income taxes payable by the individual partners. While a corporation may "carry forward" those losses and use them to offset future earned income, thus reducing future corporate income taxes, the losses are not of any use in reducing the personal income taxes of the individual shareholders in the year they were incurred.

2. In years prior to 1986 when corporate income tax rates were significantly lower than personal income tax rates, the corporate form was advantageous to many individuals since it reduced income taxes payable. However, this was only true if the corporation retained the income and did not pay it out in the form of dividends. If the corporation chose to pay out its income in the form of dividends, the situation was significantly changed since the dividends paid were taxable to the individual receiving them. Thus, corporate income actually paid out is subject to "double taxation" once at the corporate level and once at the personal level as taxable dividends. In most cases, this more than offsets the benefits of the lower corporate income tax rates. Owners of close corporations typically tend to avoid this by taking the corporate income in the form of generous salaries and fringe benefits, rather than a dividend, in effect "zeroing out" the corporate income, avoiding not only a tax on dividends but also the corporate income tax as well since if such expenses qualify as "ordinary and necessary business expenses" they are deductible from corporate earned income.

3. In some cases, it is possible to have the best of both the corporate and partnership worlds by qualifying the corporation for subchapter "S" treatment under the Internal Revenue Code. Corporations which elect to qualify for taxation as "S" corporations are treated in most respects as partnerships for federal income tax purposes and thus are not subject to the corporate income tax. Corporate income is taxed to the individual shareholders in much the same manner as partnership income is taxed to partners. Subchapter "S" treatment is not automatic; it requires an affirmative election by a small business corporation which must meet certain qualifications.

Among the more important qualifications are: (1) there must no more than 100 shareholders, (2) all shareholders must be natural persons or their trusts or estates, i.e., no another business entity, (3) no shareholder may be a nonresident alien and

(4) only one class of stock may be issued. In past years, a large number of small business corporations opted for the "S" election since in many ways it allowed for small businesses to have the advantages of both the general partnership and the corporation.

4. Effective January 1, 1997, the Internal Revenue Service (IRS) adopted new regulations, popularly known as "check the box," which dramatically changed and simplified the taxation of small business entities. In previous years, it was often difficult to determine in advance whether the IRS would allow a partnership or other unincorporated organization to qualify for "pass through" taxation or instead would argue that it possessed so many characteristics of a corporation that it should be taxed as a separate entity, i.e., be treated as if it were a corporation for federal income tax purposes. This determination was made under an elaborate set of rules known as the Kintner Regulations. The rules were highly complex and, in the case of many limited partnerships and LLCs, it was often difficult to determine in advance what position the IRS would take. The new rules, known colloquially as "check the box," generally allow any business entity, whether limited partnership, LLC or LLP, to elect either to be taxed as a corporation or as a partnership simply by "checking the box." (An entity created under a corporate statute, however, must be taxed as a corporation although, if it qualifies, it can still make the subchapter "S" election.) Any entity with only one member can elect to be taxed as a corporation or elect to not be taxed at all, as with a sole proprietorship. In conclusion, it is probably safe to say that most small business today will find it advantageous to adopt a business form which will not be taxed as a separate entity but will allow the net income or losses to flow through to the individual owners, be they partners, members (as LLC owners are called) or shareholders.

# Chapter 2

# AGENCY CONCEPTS

Virtually all business organizations employ agents to carry on all or a substantial part of their work. Even a modest sole proprietorship will most likely find the need to employ an agent of some sort, such as a secretary, bookkeeper, sales clerk, etc. The Uniform Partnership Act provides that, unless otherwise provided, every partner is an agent of the partnership and is authorized to bind the partnership in transactions with third parties. Most significantly for our purposes, the corporation, being an intangible legal entity, can function only through the efforts of agents, whether officers, directors or other employees. Thus an understanding of the fundamental concepts of agency is essential to a study of corporate law. In this brief introduction to the law of agency, we will focus on two important concepts, first, what is an agent and what characteristics distinguish the principal-agent relationship from other relationships between the business entity and third parties? Second, when does the agent have the authority to bind her principal to transactions with third parties?

## A. GAY JENSON FARMS CO. v. CARGILL, INC.
Supreme Court of Minnesota
309 N.W.2d 285 (1981)

PETERSON, J.

Plaintiffs, 86 individual, partnership or corporate farmers, brought this action against defendant Cargill, Inc. (Cargill) and defendant Warren Grain & Seed Co. (Warren) to recover losses sustained when Warren defaulted on the contracts made with plaintiffs for the sale of grain. After a trial by jury, judgment was entered in favor of plaintiffs, and Cargill brought this appeal. We affirm.

This case arose out of the financial collapse of defendant Warren Seed & Grain Co., and its failure to satisfy its indebtedness to plaintiffs. Warren, which was located in Warren, Minnesota, was operated by Lloyd Hill and his son, Gary Hill. Warren operated a grain elevator and as a result was involved in the purchase of cash or market grain from local farmers. The cash grain would be resold through the Minneapolis Grain Exchange or to the terminal grain companies directly. Warren also stored grain for farmers and sold chemicals, fertilizer and steel storage bins. In addition, it operated a seed business which involved buying seed grain from farmers, processing it and reselling it for seed to farmers and local elevators.

Lloyd Hill decided in 1964 to apply for financing from Cargill.[1] Cargill's officials

---

[1] [1] Prior to this time, Atwood Larson had provided working capital for Warren, and Warren had

from the Moorhead regional office investigated Warren's operations and recommended that Cargill finance Warren.

Warren and Cargill thereafter entered into a security agreement which provided that Cargill would loan money for working capital to Warren on "open account" financing up to a stated limit, which was originally set as $175,000.[2] Under this contract, Warren would receive funds and pay its expenses by issuing drafts drawn on Cargill through Minneapolis banks. The drafts were imprinted with both Warren's and Cargill's names. Proceeds from Warren's sales would be deposited with Cargill and credited to its account. In return for this financing, Warren appointed Cargill as its grain agent for transaction with the Commodity Credit Corporation. Cargill was also given a right of first refusal to purchase market grain sold by Warren to the terminal market. A new contract was negotiated in 1967, extending Warren's credit line to $300,000 and incorporating the provisions of the original contract. It was also stated in the contract that Warren would provide Cargill with annual financial statements and that either Cargill would keep the books for Warren or an audit would be conducted by an independent firm. Cargill was given the right of access to Warren's books for inspection.

In addition, the agreement provided that Warren was not to make capital improvements or repairs in excess of $5,000 without Cargill's prior consent. Further, it was not to become liable as guarantor on another's indebtedness, or encumber its assets except with Cargill's permission. Consent by Cargill was required before Warren would be allowed to declare a dividend or sell and purchase stock.

Officials from Cargill's regional office made a brief visit to Warren shortly after the agreement was executed. They examined the annual statement and the accounts receivable, expenses, inventory, seed, machinery and other financial matters. Warren was informed that it would be reminded periodically to make the improvements recommended by Cargill.[3] At approximately this time, a memo was given to the Cargill official in charge of the Warren account, Erhart Becker, which stated in part: "This organization [Warren] needs very strong paternal guidance."

In 1970, Cargill contracted with Warren and other elevators to act as its agent to seek growers for a new type of wheat called Bounty 208. Warren, as Cargill's agent for this project, entered into contracts for the growing of the wheat seed, with Cargill named as the contracting party. Farmers were paid directly by Cargill for the seed and all contracts were performed in full. In 1971, pursuant to an agency contract, Warren contracted on Cargill's behalf with various farmers for the growing of sunflower seeds for Cargill. The arrangements were similar to those made in the Bounty 208 contracts, and all those contracts were also completed. Both

---

used Atwood Larson as its commission agent for the sale of market grain on the grain exchange.

   **2** [2] Loans were secured by a second mortgage on Warren's real estate and a first chattel mortgage on its inventories of grain and merchandise in the sum of $175,000 with 7% interest. Warren was to use the $175,000 to pay off the debt that it owed to Atwood Larson.

   **3** [3] Cargill headquarters suggested that the regional office check Warren monthly. Also, it was requested that Warren be given an explanation for the relatively large withdrawals from undistributed earnings made by the Hills, since Cargill hoped that Warren's profits would be used to decrease its debt balance. Cargill asked for written requests for withdrawals from undistributed earnings in the future.

these agreements were unrelated to the open account financing contract. In addition, Warren, as Cargill's agent in the sunflower seed business, cleaned and packaged the seed in Cargill bags.

During this period, Cargill continued to review Warren's operations and expenses and recommend that certain actions should be taken.[4] Warren purchased from Cargill various business forms printed by Cargill and received sample forms from Cargill which Warren used to develop its own business forms.

Cargill wrote to its regional office in 1970 expressing its concern that the pattern of increased use of funds allowed to develop at Warren was similar to that involved in two other cases in which Cargill experienced severe losses. Cargill did not refuse to honor drafts or call the loan, however. A new security agreement which increased the credit line to $750,000 was executed in 1972, and a subsequent agreement which raised the limit to $1,250,000 was entered into in 1976.

Warren was at that time shipping Cargill 90% of its cash grain. When Cargill's facilities were full, Warren shipped its grain to other companies. Approximately 25% of Warren's total sales was seed grain which was sold directly by Warren to its customers. As Warren's indebtedness continued to be in excess of its credit line, Cargill began to contact Warren daily regarding its financial affairs. Cargill headquarters informed its regional office in 1973 that, since Cargill money was being used, Warren should realize that Cargill had the right to make some critical decisions regarding the use of the funds. Cargill headquarters also told Warren that a regional manager would be working with Warren on a day-to-day basis as well as in monthly planning meetings.

In 1975, Cargill's regional office began to keep a daily debit position on Warren. A bank account was opened in Warren's name on which Warren could draw checks in 1976. The account was to be funded by drafts drawn on Cargill by the local bank.

In early 1977, it became evident that Warren had serious financial problems. Several farmers, who had heard that Warren's checks were not being paid, inquired or had their agents inquire at Cargill regarding Warren's status and were initially told that there would be no problem with payment. In April 1977, an audit of Warren revealed that Warren was $4 million in debt. After Cargill was informed that Warren's financial statements had been deliberately falsified, Warren's request for additional financing was refused. In the final days of Warren's operation, Cargill sent an official to supervise the elevator, including disbursement of funds and income generated by the elevator. After Warren ceased operations, it was found to be indebted to Cargill in the amount of $3.6 million. Warren was also determined to be indebted to plaintiffs in the amount of $2 million, and plaintiffs brought this action in 1977 to seek recovery of that sum. Plaintiffs alleged that Cargill was jointly liable for Warren's indebtedness as it had acted as principal for the grain elevator.

---

[4] Between 1967 and 1973, Cargill suggested that Warren take a number of steps, including: (1) a reduction of seed grain and cash grain inventories; (2) improved collection of accounts receivable; (3) reduction or elimination of its wholesale seed business and its specialty grain operation; (4) marketing fertilizer and steel bins on consignment; (5) a reduction in withdrawals made by officers; (6) a suggestion that Warren's bookkeeper not issue her own salary checks; and (7) cooperation with Cargill in implementing the recommendations. These ideas were apparently never implemented, however.

The matter was bifurcated for trial in Marshall County District Court. In the first phase, the amount of damages sustained by each farmer was determined by the court. The second phase of the action, dealing with the issue of Cargill's liability for the indebtedness of Warren, was tried before a jury.

The jury found that Cargill's conduct between 1973 and 1977 had made it Warren's principal. Warren was found to be the agent of Cargill with regard to contracts for:

1. The purchase and sale of grain for market.

2. The purchase and sale of seed grain.

3. The storage of grain.

The court determined that Cargill was the disclosed principal of Warren. It was concluded that Cargill was jointly liable with Warren for plaintiffs' losses, and judgment was entered for plaintiffs.

Cargill seeks a reversal of the jury's findings or, if the jury findings are upheld, a reversal of the trial court's determination that Cargill was a disclosed principal. . . .

1. The major issue in this case is whether Cargill, by its course of dealing with Warren, became liable as a principal on contracts made by Warren with plaintiffs. Cargill contends that no agency relationship was established with Warren, notwithstanding its financing of Warren's operation and its purchase of the majority of Warren's grain. However, we conclude that Cargill, by its control and influence over Warren, became a principal with liability for the transactions entered into by its agent Warren.

Agency is the fiduciary relationship that results from the manifestation of consent by one person to another that the other shall act on his behalf and subject to his control, and consent by the other so to act. *Jurek v. Thompson*, 308 Minn. 191, 241 N.W.2d 788 (1976); *Lee v. Peoples Cooperative Sales Agency*, 201 Minn. 266, 276 N.W. 214 (1937); RESTATEMENT (SECOND) OF AGENCY § 1 (1958). In order to create an agency there must be an agreement, but not necessarily a contract between the parties. RESTATEMENT (SECOND) OF AGENCY § 1, comment b (1958). An agreement may result in the creation of an agency relationship although the parties did not call it an agency and did not intend the legal consequences of the relation to follow. *Id*. The existence of the agency may be proved by circumstantial evidence which shows a course of dealing between the two parties. *Rausch v. Aronson*, 211 Minn. 272, 1 N.W.2d 371 (1941). When an agency relationship is to be proven by circumstantial evidence, the principal must be shown to have consented to the agency since one cannot be the agent of another except by consent of the latter. *Larkin v. McCabe*, 211 Minn. 11, 299 N.W. 649 (1941).

Cargill contends that the prerequisites of an agency relationship did not exist because Cargill never consented to the agency, Warren did not act on behalf of Cargill, and Cargill did not exercise control over Warren. We hold that all three elements of agency could be found in the particular circumstances of this case. By directing Warren to implement its recommendations, Cargill manifested its consent that Warren would be its agent. Warren acted on Cargill's behalf in procuring grain for Cargill as the part of its normal operations which were totally financed by Cargill.[5] Further, an agency relationship was established by Cargill's interference with the internal affairs of Warren, which constituted de facto control of the elevator.

A creditor who assumes control of his debtor's business may become liable as principal for the acts of the debtor in connection with the business. RESTATEMENT (SECOND) OF AGENCY § 14 O (1958). It is noted in comment a to section 14 O that:

> A security holder who merely exercises a veto power over the business acts of his debtor by preventing purchases or sales above specified amounts does not thereby become a principal. However, if he takes over the management of the debtor's business either in person or through an agent, and directs what contracts may or may not be made, he becomes a principal, liable as a principal for the obligations incurred thereafter in the normal course of business by the debtor who has now become his general agent. The point at which the creditor becomes a principal is that at which he assumes de facto control over the conduct of his debtor, whatever the terms of the formal contract with his debtor may be.

*[handwritten margin note: Creditor becomes principal]*

A number of factors indicate Cargill's control over Warren, including the following:

(1) Cargill's constant recommendations to Warren by telephone;

(2) Cargill's right of first refusal on grain;

(3) Warren's inability to enter into mortgages, to purchase stock or to pay dividends without Cargill's approval;

(4) Cargill's right of entry onto Warren's premises to carry on periodic checks and audits;

(5) Cargill's correspondence and criticism regarding Warren's finances, officers salaries and inventory;

(6) Cargill's determination that Warren needed "strong paternal guidance";

(7) Provision of drafts and forms to Warren upon which Cargill's name was imprinted;

(8) Financing of all Warren's purchases of grain and operating expenses; and

(9) Cargill's power to discontinue the financing of Warren's operations.

We recognize that some of these elements, as Cargill contends, are found in an ordinary debtor-creditor relationship. However, these factors cannot be considered in isolation, but, rather, they must be viewed in light of all the circumstances surrounding Cargill's aggressive financing of Warren.

It is also Cargill's position that the relationship between Cargill and Warren was that of buyer-supplier rather than principal-agent. RESTATEMENT (SECOND) OF AGENCY § 14K (1958) compares an agent with a supplier as follows:

---

[5] [7] Although the contracts with the farmers were executed by Warren, Warren paid for the grain with drafts drawn on Cargill. While this is not in itself significant see *Lee v. Peoples Cooperative Sales Agency*, 201 Minn. 266, 276 N.W. 214 (1937) — it is one factor to be taken into account in analyzing the relationship between Warren and Cargill.

One who contracts to acquire property from a third person and convey it to another is the agent of the other only if it is agreed that he is to act primarily for the benefit of the other and not for himself.

Factors indicating that one is a supplier, rather than an agent, are: (1) That he is to receive a fixed price for the property irrespective of price paid by him. This is the most important. (2) That he acts in his own name and receives the title to the property which he thereafter is to transfer. (3) That he has an independent business in buying and selling similar property.

RESTATEMENT (SECOND) OF AGENCY § 14K, Comment a (1958).

Under the RESTATEMENT approach, it must be shown that the supplier has an independent business before it can be concluded that he is not an agent. The record establishes that all portions of Warren's operation were financed by Cargill and that Warren sold almost all of its market grain to Cargill. Thus, the relationship which existed between the parties was not merely that of buyer and supplier. * * *

In this case, as in Butler, Cargill furnished substantially all funds received by the elevator. Cargill did have a right of entry on Warren's premises, and it, like Bunge, required maintenance of insurance against hazards of operation. Warren's activities, like Bayles' operations, formed a substantial part of Cargill's business that was developed in that area. In addition, Cargill did not think of Warren as an operator who was free to become Cargill's competitor, but rather conceded that it believed that Warren owed a duty of loyalty to Cargill. The decisions made by Warren were not independent of Cargill's interest or its control.

Further, we are not persuaded by the fact that Warren was not one of the "line" elevators that Cargill operated in its own name. The Warren operation, like the line elevator, was financially dependent on Cargill's continual infusion of capital. The arrangement with Warren presented a convenient alternative to the establishment of a line elevator. Cargill became, in essence, the owner of the operation without the accompanying legal indicia.

The amici curiae assert that, if the jury verdict is upheld, firms and banks which have provided business loans to county elevators will decline to make further loans. The decision in this case should give no cause for such concern. We deal here with a business enterprise markedly different from an ordinary bank financing, since Cargill was an active participant in Warren's operations rather than simply a financier. Cargill's course of dealing with Warren was, by its own admission, a paternalistic relationship in which Cargill made the key economic decisions and kept Warren in existence.

Although considerable interest was paid by Warren on the loan, the reason for Cargill's financing of Warren was not to make money as a lender but, rather, to establish a source of market grain for its business. As one Cargill manager noted, "We were staying in there because we wanted the grain." For this reason, Cargill was willing to extend the credit line far beyond the amount originally allocated to Warren. It is noteworthy that Cargill was receiving significant amounts of grain and that, notwithstanding the risk that was recognized by Cargill, the operation was considered profitable.

On the whole, there was a unique fabric in the relationship between Cargill and Warren which varies from that found in normal debtor-creditor situations. We conclude that, on the facts of this case, there was sufficient evidence from which the jury could find that Cargill was the principal of Warren within the definitions of agency set forth in RESTATEMENT (SECOND) OF AGENCY §§ 1 and 140.

## NOTES

1. The definition of agency in *Cargill*, taken from the RESTATEMENT (SECOND) OF AGENCY § 1, is almost universally followed by the courts today. Note the essential elements of agency stated therein are (1) the agent acts on behalf of the principal, (2) the agent acts with the consent, express or implied, of the principal, and (3) the agent acts subject to the control, or right of control, of the principal. It is useful to keep these elements in mind in distinguishing the agency relationship from other, closely associated relationships. In *Cargill*, of course, the issue was whether a debtor-creditor or a principal-agent relationship existed. RESTATEMENT (SECOND) OF AGENCY §§ 14A through 14O list a number of other common business relationships which may have some, but not all, of the characteristics of agency.

2. The characterization of a relationship as one of principal and agent is significant, among other reasons, due to the liability which the principal bears for acts taken by the agent on behalf of the principal with her express or implied authorization. This is why Cargill is strenuously arguing here that its relationship is one of debtor-creditor rather than one of principal and agent. Is it fair to Cargill to characterize this relationship as agency when arguably all Cargill was trying to do was to safeguard its interests as a creditor of Warren? Does a decision such as this simply encourage a creditor to immediately resort to its legal remedies when the debtor defaults rather than work cooperatively with the debtor? Is it significant here that Cargill is one of the world's largest grain dealers and that the parties who stand to lose the most if Cargill is found not to be liable as principal are small Minnesota farmers? The issue of so-called "lender liability" where a creditor becomes liable to third parties for acts of its debtor has been a much litigated issue over the past decade. *See, e.g.* Hynes, *Lender Liability, The Dilemma of the Controlling Creditor*, 58 TENN. L. REV. 635 (1991).

## SHAHEEN v. YONTS
United States District Court for the Western District of Kentucky
2008 U.S. Dist. LEXIS 16020 (Mar. 3, 2008)

THOMAS B. RUSSELL, JUDGE.

This case concerns the death of Nadia Shaheen ("Shaheen"), the mother of the Plaintiff, Joseph Shaheen, who is the administrator of Shaheen's estate. It is alleged that in the early hours of November 11, 2005, Defendant Burgess Harrison Yonts's ("Yonts") car struck Shaheen, causing her death. Plaintiff contends that Yonts consumed alcohol at Nick's Family Sport's Pub and at the Lambda Chi Alpha Fraternity House on the campus of Murray State University prior to the accident, and that Yonts was legally intoxicated when his car struck Shaheen. The defendants in this matter were members of the Lambda Chi Alpha fraternity at the time of the accident. Yonts was also a member of the fraternity at that time.

\* \* \*

Plaintiff alleges that Yonts consumed alcohol while attending the Lambda Chi Alpha party. In support of this allegation, Plaintiff has submitted deposition testimony from a witness who observed Yonts at the party carrying a bottle of Mickey's malt liquor during most of the night, and a witness who saw Yont's drop a bottle of Mickey's. Another witness observed Yonts go to his parked car and either put something into, or take something out of his car, which Plaintiff argues was a commonplace method for fraternity members who did not live at the house to store their beer during parties.

Given this evidence, a reasonable jury could conclude that Yonts consumed alcohol while attending a party hosted by Lambda Chi Alpha. However, there is no evidence that would allow a jury to find that any Defendant provided Yonts with the alcohol he consumed. The issue before the Court is whether a social host may be liable for the injuries caused by the intoxication of an underage guest when the social host did not provide alcohol to the guest.

\* \* \*

By examining the statutory duties applicable to a social host who permits a minor to consume alcohol, the Court predicts that under Kentucky law, liability would only be imposed if the host in some way furnished the alcohol that the minor consumed. To arrive at this conclusion, the Court relied on the statutory assignment of proximate causation found in K.R.S. 413.241, which places culpability primarily on the intoxicated individual. *Estate of Vosnick v. RRJC, Inc.*, 225 F. Supp. 2d 737, 742 (E.D.K.Y. 2002). To determine if Kentucky courts would find the current case to be an exception to the general principle of limiting responsibility to the intoxicated individual, the Court attempted to apply the principles set by Kentucky courts' dram shop liability jurisprudence, which uses statutory standards to define the scope of common law duties. An examination of the relevant statutes leads the Court to conclude that Kentucky law would only recognize a cause of action by an injured third party if the social host served alcohol to a minor. As there is no evidence that Defendants furnished alcohol to Yonts the night of the accident, Defendants are entitled to judgment as a matter of law on Plaintiff's common law negligence claim. Merely hosting a party where attendees may bring alcohol is not enough to impose liability on a social host.

\* \* \*

In addition to Plaintiff's common law negligence claim, Plaintiff also alleges that Defendants were negligent per se. However, as stated above, there is no evidence that Defendants provided Yonts with alcohol, so they cannot be liable for violating K.R.S. 244.085(3) or K.R.S. 530.070(1).

The final statute that Plaintiff attempts to use as a basis to find Defendants negligent per se is K.R.S. 530.070(2), which states that "a person is guilty of unlawful transaction with a minor in the third degree when . . . he knowingly induces, assists, or causes a minor to engage in any other criminal activity." Plaintiff appears to argue that Defendants knowingly induced, assisted, or caused Yonts to violate K.R.S. 244.085(3), which forbids a minor from possessing alcohol for his own use. The only evidence before the Court is that Yonts consumed alcohol before he arrived at the party and he was seen possessing alcohol at the party. There is no evidence that any Defendant acted to induce, assist, or cause Yonts to engage in any forbidden conduct.

Finally, Plaintiff argues that Defendants negligently failed to control Yonts's consumption of alcohol while Yonts was attending the party on Defendants' property. This is a separate basis for liability than social host liability. In the case of social host responsibility, the social host is liable for the affirmative act of serving alcohol to a minor. Under this other theory of liability, however, the host is liable for his failure to perform the affirmative act of controlling the guest's dangerous conduct.

Generally, there is no affirmative duty to control another person's conduct to prevent him from harming third persons. *Grand Aerie Fraternal Order of Eagles v. Carneyhan*, 169 S.W.3d 840, 849 (Ky. 2005). "A duty can, however, arise to exercise reasonable care to prevent harm by controlling a third persons conduct where . . . A special relation exists between the actor and the third person which imposes a duty upon the actor to control the third person's conduct." *Id.* One such special relationship exists between an owner of land and the person using the land. *Id.* at 850 (citing *Restatement (Second) of Torts § 318* (1965)).

"There are two distinct types of claims based upon a defendant's special relationship with the person causing the harm," which can be classified as "negligent failure to warn" and "negligent failure to control." *Id.* at 850. In this case, Plaintiff argues that Defendants negligently failed to control Yonts's behavior.

In a negligent failure to control claim a defendant's "ability to control the person causing the harm assumes primary importance." *Id.* at 851. "[T]he defendant's ability to control the person who caused the harm must be real and not fictional and, if exercised, would meaningfully reduce the risk of the harm that actually occurred." *Id.* "A 'real' ability to control necessarily includes some sort of leverage, such as the threat of involuntary commitment, parole revocation, or loss of livelihood provided by an employment relationship." *Id.* at 853.

However, being the host of a party does not give the host sufficient control over a guest's conduct to be liable for a failure to control. In a case cited by the Kentucky Supreme Court, the Supreme Court of Texas "held that the social host had no duty to prevent their guest from consuming alcohol or later driving, in part because the hosts had no means of effective control over the guest." *Id.* (citing *Graff v. Beard*, 858 S.W.2d 918, 921–922 (Tex. 1993)).

The lack of effective means of control is demonstrated in the Texas Supreme Court's discussion of what actions by the host would be required to discharge the host's duty to prevent a guest from driving while intoxicated. *Graff*, 858 S.W.2d at 921. "Would a simple request not to drive suffice? Or is more required? Is the host required to physically restrain the guests, take their car keys, or disable their vehicles?" *Id.*

Therefore, Defendants did not have an affirmative duty to control Yonts the night of the party in their capacity as social hosts. The fact that Yonts was a member of Defendants' fraternity does not alter this analysis. Yonts's status as a member of Lambda Chi Alpha is not a special relationship that would trigger an independent duty for Defendants to control his behavior. Nor does the relationship give Defendants, through threat of expulsion from the fraternity, sufficient leverage to effectively control Yonts's conduct the night of the party.

For the above stated reasons, Defendants' Motions for Summary Judgment are GRANTED.

# NOTE

The *Shaheen* court emphasizes the "control" element of the agency relationship without addressing whether the fraternity member acts on behalf of and with consent of the fraternity. Isn't a fraternal organization a "special relationship"? Should the court have focused more on the other factors? Does this outcome seem fair in comparison to *Cargill*? Should courts impart greater liability on a prudent creditor, like Cargill, rather than a complacent and inattentive social host?

## BRUN v. CARUSO
### Superior Court of Massachusetts, Middlesex
### 2004 Mass. Super. LEXIS 547 (Nov. 5, 2004)

### MEMORANDUM OF DECISION AND ORDER UPON DEFENDANTS' MOTIONS FOR SUMMARY JUDGMENT

### INTRODUCTION

Plaintiff Robert F. Brun ("plaintiff"), as administrator of the estate of Sandra Berfield ("Berfield"), instituted this wrongful death action against defendants Steven Caruso ("Caruso"), Northeast Restaurant Corporation ("Northeast"), and Bickford's Family Restaurants, Inc. ("Bickford's"), arising out of Caruso's murder of Berfield, the plaintiff's decedent. The complaint alleges negligence claims against Northeast and Bickford's under the rubric "Failure to Provide a Secure Workplace."

### BACKGROUND

This case emanates from Caruso's stalking of Berfield over several years, culminating in his murder of her in 2000. From 1988 until her death, Berfield was employed by Northeast as a server at a restaurant in Medford, Massachusetts, known commonly as "Bickford's" ("Restaurant"). The Restaurant was owned and operated by Northeast pursuant to a licensing agreement with defendant Bickford's parent company, ELXSI, a California corporation. The agreement allowed Northeast to use certain Bickford's trademarks. Northeast, not Bickford's, operated the day-to-day activities of the Restaurant. Caruso was a regular patron of the Restaurant who had been visiting the establishment on a daily basis for approximately ten years, often coming in two or three times a day. Additionally, between early 1996 and October 8, 1998, he regularly was hired by Northeast as a "handyman" to perform repair and maintenance jobs at the Restaurant.

Prior to stalking and murdering Berfield, Caruso harassed other Restaurant servers despite their repeated complaints to Northeast's management. For example, starting in 1995 and continuing for almost a year, he began requesting the services of waitress Nellie Harrington ("Harrington") and would sit only in her station. It was not uncommon for him to wait over an hour to sit in Harrington's section even though there were other servers available. On one occasion, the hostess informed him that, because Harrington was too busy to wait on him, another waitress would take his order. He flew into a rage, threw his menus, and stormed out of the Restaurant.

Beginning in 1997, Caruso turned his unwanted attention towards Berfield by expressing a preference for being seated in her waitress section and sitting only there. On August 22, 1998, he showed up at the Restaurant while Berfield was working and washed her car in the parking lot without her permission. After doing so, he asked Berfield to go to the movies with him. When she declined his invitation, his behavior turned hostile. Berfield and other employees noticed that Caruso would stare menacingly at her for long periods of time. Soon after, Berfield told the Restaurant's manager, Alexander Dellagrotta ("Dellagrotta"), that she did not want to wait on Caruso anymore because his staring was scaring her and making her uncomfortable.

On August 24, 1998, Caruso arrived unannounced and uninvited at the home of Pamela Berfield ("Pamela"), Berfield's sister, while Berfield was there alone. When he knocked on the door, Berfield refused to open it. On or about August 25, 1998, he entered the Restaurant and asked to speak with Berfield, stating, "Her car isn't here," and then proceeded to the parking lot to look for her vehicle. During this visit, Caruso seated himself in Berfield's section. Soon thereafter, Dellagrotta told him that Berfield was no longer allowed to serve him and that he was not allowed to sit in her section.

In September of 1998, State Police Trooper Sean Sullivan ("Tpr. Sullivan"), a customer of the Restaurant, spoke with Caruso while they were both on the premises and told him to leave Berfield alone. Shortly after the conversation with the trooper, Caruso contacted Dellagrotta and threatened to file a lawsuit against the Restaurant. He claimed that Dellagrotta and the Restaurant discriminated against him when they told him that he could not sit in Berfield's section. Additionally, he asked Dellagrotta to arrange a meeting between himself and Berfield at a place other than the Restaurant. He also called Gerard Robertson ("Robertson"), the then vice president of operations for Northeast, and claimed that Tpr. Sullivan's discussion with him constituted an assault. He requested to meet with Robertson to discuss his "problem" with Berfield. During the meeting, Caruso told Robertson, "I want her terminated." Furthermore, he suggested to Robertson that Berfield was mentally unstable and even offered to pay for any psychiatric help that Berfield may require. As a result of the meeting, Robertson repeated to Caruso Dellagrotta's instruction that Berfield was no longer allowed to serve him and that he was not allowed to sit in her station.

From then on, Caruso sat in a different server section but still sat in the same room in which Berfield was working. While in Berfield's room, Caruso would stare continuously at her with an angry expression on his face. She complained to Robertson about the scowling and, as a result, Dellagrotta prohibited Caruso from sitting in the same room in which Berfield was working. As late as October 3, 1998, Dellagrotta reminded Caruso that he was not allowed to sit in Berfield's section and that he was not to stare at her.

On September 18, 1998, Pamela told Caruso that Berfield was attempting to get a restraining order against him. Two days later, on September 20, 1998, Berfield's tires were slashed. On September 29, 1998, Berfield heard a "popping noise" outside her apartment in Everett, Massachusetts, ran to the window, and saw Caruso standing by her car. Her tires again had been slashed. In response to this incident, she set up a video camera at her apartment on September 30, 1998, in an attempt to identify the individual responsible for the vandalism of her car. During the night of October 3, 1998, Berfield's video surveillance camera recorded the image of a white male wearing a black, hooded sweatshirt pouring something into her automobile's gas tank. The next morning, she discovered that battery acid had been poured into her car's fuel tank, rendering the vehicle inoperable.

On October 5, 1998, Berfield petitioned the Middlesex County Superior Court for a restraining order against Caruso due to his repeated stalking behavior. On October 8, 1998, the court issued a restraining order requiring Caruso to have no contact with Berfield and to stay at least 100 yards away from her and not to damage her car. After this restraining order was entered, Caruso never entered the Restaurant but did drive by it several times.

On October 25, 1998, Berfield saw Caruso pouring battery acid into her gas tank despite the restraining order. Her car again was disabled. Thereafter, on November 5, 1998, the Middlesex County Superior Court issued an amended order stating that Caruso must stay out of the Restaurant and 500 yards away from Berfield's apartment. On November 26, 1998, Caruso was arrested and charged with three counts of malicious destruction of Berfield's property. He was held without bail until January 8, 1999.

On March 30, 1999, Caruso drove back and forth in front of the Restaurant while Berfield was working there, thereby violating the restraining order. On April 23, 1999 his bail was revoked, and he was taken into custody to await trial on the malicious destruction of property charges. On May 13, 1999, Caruso was convicted of two counts of malicious destruction of property and sentenced to eighteen months in the house of correction. He was released on July 29, 1999. On December 25, 1999, he entered the Restaurant and cut the gas lines, allowing gas to fill the closed premises.

On January 20, 2000, Caruso left a package bomb outside of Berfield's apartment in Everett. * * * Berfield was killed instantly by the explosion when she opened the package bomb. Caruso was arrested and prosecuted for her murder. On August 15, 2003, he was convicted of first-degree murder.

* * *

II. Northeast

The plaintiff alleges that Northeast had a legal duty to protect Berfield from Caruso's violent actions because they were reasonably foreseeable. Northeast counters that it had no duty to protect Berfield from the criminal acts of a third party in these circumstances, especially in view of the passage of time between Caruso's last permissive entry into the Restaurant and Berfield's murder off the premises.

"As a general rule, there is no duty to protect another from the criminal acts of a third party." *Kavanagh v. Trustees of Boston University*, 440 Mass. 195, 201, 795 N.E.2d 1170 (2003). A duty may arise, however, where there is a "special relationship" between the defendant and the injured victim. *Id. See Mullins v. Pine Manor College*, 389 Mass. 47, 51–52, 449 N.E.2d 331 (1983); Restatement (Second) of Torts, § 314(A) (1965); Restatement (Second) of Agency, § 512(1) (1958). "A special relationship is based on the plaintiff's reasonable expectations and reliance that a defendant will anticipate harmful acts of a third person and take appropriate measures to protect the plaintiff from harm." *Kavanagh*, 440 Mass. at 201.

In the case at bar, evidence in the record creates a genuine issue of material fact as to whether Northeast and Berfield had a "special relationship" which was predicated on Berfield's reasonable expectations that Northeast would anticipate Caruso's predatory ways and take appropriate measures to protect her. Northeast owed a duty to its employees to provide a safe place to work, which included a duty to take reasonable precautions against exposing them to potentially dangerous individuals. Berfield was employed to have direct contact with the public, and Caruso, in addition to being a regular patron, frequently was hired by Northeast as a handyman, with access to all parts of the Restaurant. Thus, Northeast had an interest in keeping a troublesome, menacing employee and customer, such as Caruso, off the premises.

Furthermore, there is a clear issue as to whether the danger in Berfield's continued exposure to Caruso was reasonably foreseeable to Northeast. Caruso patronized the Restaurant for over a decade with unusual regularity and frequency. Northeast was on notice that he had harassed other waitresses before Berfield. It also was aware of his bizarre accusations and increasingly hostile, malicious behavior towards her, both on and off the premises. Then, on December 25, 1999, less than a month before Berfield's death, Caruso entered the Restaurant and cut the gas lines. Sadly, it is all too often within the range of human experience that obsessive behavior escalates into harassment and then into stalking, or worse. Therefore, in view of Northeast's knowledge of Caruso's campaign of vandalism and threatening behavior toward Berfield, an argument can be made that the danger he posed to Berfield was reasonably foreseeable.

Finally, there exists a true factual dispute as to whether Northeast breached its duty to Berfield in failing to protect her from the harm of Caruso's stalking, which culminated in her murder on January 20, 2000. Despite his obvious fixation upon Harrington and his alarming outburst when she could not serve him, Northeast did nothing to exclude Caruso as far back as 1995 and, indeed, even chose to hire him as a handyman, with unregulated access to the Restaurant. Despite Northeast's awareness of Caruso's escalating violence, it did nothing to keep him off the premises until the court interceded on October 8, 1998.

In this unusual case, a factfinder could determine that Northeast's inaction prior to October 8, 1998, increased the risk of harm to Berfield by exposing her to daily, direct contact with Caruso, who presented as a serial harasser. The plaintiff could argue that Northeast's failure to act tacitly encouraged and empowered Caruso to develop his obsessive attachment to Berfield, which led inexorably to her murder in January 2000. While it is true, as Northeast asserts, that Caruso did not enter the Restaurant permissibly during the fifteen months prior to Berfield's murder, it is for the factfinder to determine whether that lapse of time, during six months of which he was incarcerated, broke the chain of causation. See *Solimene v. Grauel & Co., K.G., 399 Mass. 790, 802, 507 N.E.2d 662 (1987)*. In addition, the fact that Berfield suffered a different kind of harm (murder) than that which was threatened by Northeast's negligence (stalking) does not relieve Northeast from liability. See *Restatement (Second) of Torts, § 281, Comment j* (1965); *Prosser on Torts, § 43*, at 259 (4th ed. 1971). For all these reasons, summary judgment for Northeast is not warranted.

## III. Bickford's

It is uncontroverted that neither Berfield nor Caruso were employees of Bickford's, and the plaintiff makes no claim of a special relationship between Berfield and Bickford's or any awareness on Bickford's part of any problems between Berfield and Caruso. Instead, the plaintiff contends that, nevertheless, Bickford's should be held vicariously liable for the alleged negligence of Northeast on account of the defendants' "License Agreement" ("Agreement"). The court disagrees.

Generally, a licensor cannot be held liable for the wrongful acts of the licensee absent extraordinary circumstances which give rise to an agency relationship. *Sherman v. Texas Co., 340 Mass. 606, 607–08, 165 N.E.2d 916 (1960)*. See also *McLaughlin v. McDonald's Corp. et al.*, Civil Action No. 98-40240-NG (2001) (Swartwood, J.) (interpreting Massachusetts law and finding that franchisor was not liable for franchisee's negligence because franchisor did not exercise sufficient control over franchisee as it did not participate in management of franchisee's business); *Wendy Hong Wu v. Dunkin' Donuts, Inc.*, 105 F. Supp. 2d 83, 87 (E.D.N.Y. 2000) (whether franchisor should be held vicariously liable for negligent conduct of its franchisee depends on whether "the franchisor controls the day-to-day operations of the franchisee, and more specifically whether the franchisor exercises a considerable degree of control over the instrumentality at issue in a given case"); No such extraordinary circumstances are present here.

In the instant action, there is no evidence that Bickford's managed the Restaurant or exerted "pervasive control" over its day-to-day operations or employees. *McLaughlin*, Civil Action No. 98-40240-NMG. Rather, Bickford's merely licensed its trademarks to Northeast pursuant to the Agreement. Specifically, that contract entitled Northeast to use Bickford's mark and name in the operation of the Restaurant in return for agreeing to adhere to Bickford's system, including matters such as building design and layout, menus, recipes, food preparation, and food and beverage specification. Additionally, Northeast agreed to indemnify and hold Bickford's harmless from all liability, damage, loss, and expense of whatever nature arising from the operation of the Restaurant. No agency relationship was implied in the Agreement.

There is nothing in the record to support the plaintiff's claim that Bickford's exerted proprietary control over the operation of its licensee, Northeast. Bickford's did not control the day-to-day activities, hiring or firing, or personnel decisions at the Restaurant; and it assumed no responsibility for any of the Restaurant's operational costs. Its involvement with the Restaurant was limited to providing some off-site accounting functions and issuing a product manual designed to maintain food quality and consistency. Thus, Bickford's did not exercise supervisory control over the Restaurant's operations sufficient to impute Northeast' negligence to it. As such, Bickford's is entitled to summary judgment.

For all the foregoing reasons, it is hereby *ORDERED* that Northeast's motion for summary judgment be *DENIED* and that Bickford's motion for summary judgment be *ALLOWED*.

# NOTES

1.  In allowing Bickford's motion for summary judgment, the court acknowledges day-to-day control versus generalized contractual control. Does such a distinction properly characterize the control exerted by a franchise agreement? The franchised business enterprise has become a ubiquitous fact of life in the past few decades. It is hard to imagine life without the multitude of franchised hotels, motels, fast food outlets, and other retail clothing and department stores which characterize our major shopping areas today. The goal of the franchise is to maintain uniformity among all of its franchisees and this necessarily means standardization and control over the products and methods of doing business. Should this fact alone lead to franchisor liability for the torts of its franchisees?

2.  Why should Bickford escape liability while Cargill was not so fortunate? Could corporate policy have prevented such a tragedy?

3.  Do authorities such as the police bear more responsibility? It is worth noting, Massachusetts recently enacted an anti-stalking measure in memory of the victim, Sandra Berfield, designed to prevent similar situations.

## ESTATE OF HAZELTON v. CAIN
Court of Appeals of Mississippi
950 So. 2d 231 (2007)

CHANDLER, J., for the Court:

Darlene Hester, Maggie Hazelton's representative, appeals from a summary judgment granted in favor of the defendants in a civil action for personal injuries and wrongful death allegedly resulting from negligent care and treatment rendered to the decedent, Hazelton, while she was a resident at Driftwood Nursing Center in Gulfport, Mississippi.

\*    \*    \*

The question before us is whether a genuine issue of fact exists to establish personal liability against Driftwood's licensee and administrator. We hold that summary judgment was proper because the record demonstrates insufficient evidence to withstand the motion.

In a negligence action, the plaintiff bears the burden of producing sufficient evidence to establish the existence of the conventional tort elements of duty, breach of duty, proximate causation, and injury. *Bailey v. Wheatley Estates Corp.*, 829 So.2d 1278, 1282 (P17) (Miss. Ct. App. 2002). Hester argues that a genuine issue of material fact exists as to whether Cain and Smith had a legal duty pursuant to the statutes and regulations for nursing homes, and also as to whether Cain and Smith breached that alleged duty. Hester maintains that Cain, as licensee for Driftwood, and Smith, as administrator, either knew or should have known of the alleged negligence against Hazelton, and that both men should have objected to the conduct or taken steps to prevent it. Cain and Smith argue that because they did not have direct involvement in any alleged tort, they are not liable.

## A. Duty

Hester asserts that Cain and Smith owed a legal duty to Hazelton under Mississippi Code Annotated Sections 43-11-1 to -13 (Rev. 2004) and the State's internal nursing home regulations. Section 43-11-13 authorizes the Mississippi State Department of Health to grant and revoke licenses for institutions assisting the aged and infirm. Miss. Code Ann. § 43-11-13. The rules, regulations and standards governing nursing homes are recorded in the Department of Health's Rules, Regulations and Minimum Standards for Institutions for the Aged or Infirm.

Hester argues that because a license is personal to a licensee, the licensee is therefore personally responsible for compliance with the rules and regulations and "shall be the person who [sic] the Department . . . will hold responsible for the operation of the home in compliance with these regulations." Likewise, the administrator must also hold a separate license which requires that he or she have the "authority and responsibility for the operation of the institution in all its administrative and professional functions."

Violation of a statute, regulation, or ordinance may support a cause of action for negligence per se where (1) the plaintiff is within the class protected, and (2) the harm sustained is the type sought to be prevented. *Palmer v. Anderson Infirmary Benevolent Ass'n.*, 656 So.2d 790, 795 (Miss. 1995) (citing *Boyer v. Tenn. Tom Constructors*, 702 F.2d 609, 611 (5th Cir. 1983)). Section H, Rule No. 408.1 of the Minimum Standards states that a patient "has a right of action for damages or other relief for deprivations of infringements of his right to adequate and proper treatment and care established by an applicable statute, rule, regulation or contract. . . . "

Although the statutes state that the purpose of section 43-11-1 is to establish standards to protect individuals in aged or infirm institutions, the record does not provide evidence to support the second prong required to find negligence per se. Hester merely makes general assertions that Hazelton suffered certain injuries, but no affidavit or substantive evidence is shown to either prove the alleged harm or to demonstrate a causal link between Cain and Smith to Hazelton. Likewise, no evidence was shown that Cain or Smith authorized or negligently failed to remedy alleged misconduct by subordinates.

Our supreme court held in *Moore v. Mem'l Hosp.*, 825 So.2d 658, 665 (P24) (Miss. 2002), that alleged violations of internal regulations do not give rise to an independent cause of action for damages and that although a violation of a regulation may serve as evidence of negligence, it does not, by itself, create a separate cause of action. While Moore focused on the State Board of Pharmacy's internal regulations, we find the holding to be applicable to the present case. In *Moore*, the mother of a child who was born with deformities as the result of medication taken by the mother during pregnancy sued the pharmacy which filled the prescription. The woman argued that the pharmacy was negligent by selling a drug which was contra indicated for pregnant women. She claimed that the state Board of Pharmacy's regulations created a legal duty for the pharmacy. Upon review of the state board's regulations, the court did not find any language which established a legal duty of care to be applied in a civil action. *Id.*

Similar to Moore, we find no language in the nursing homes statutes or regulations to expressly create a legal duty for licensees or administrators. As stated above, Sections 43-11-1 to -13 sets forth statutory requirements for nursing homes in Mississippi. No language is included which creates a specific legal duty for either a licensee or an administrator. According to the Minimum Standards, receiving a license for the nursing home makes the licensee "responsible for the operation of the home in compliance with these regulations," and gives an administrator, "authority and responsibility for the operation of the institution in all its administrative and professional functions." Minimum Standards, Rule 402.1 and 403.1.

Therefore, we must look at relevant case law to determine if a legal duty exists for a nursing home licensee or its administrator. It is well established that a nursing home or its owner may be held liable under general tort law principles for negligence regarding the care of a resident. However, we decline to extend this same duty to a licensee or administrator.

In *Turner v. Wilson*, 620 So.2d 545, 548 (Miss. 1993), our supreme court held that "Mississippi follows the general rule that individual liability of corporate officers or directors may not be predicated merely on their connection to the corporation but must have as their foundation individual wrongdoing." The officer or director must have some sort of direct participation, such as being the "guiding spirit behind the wrongful conduct or the central figure in the challenged corporate activity." *Id.* *Turner* further recognized:

> A director, officer, or agent is liable for the torts of the corporation or of other directors, officers, or agents when, and only when, he has participated in the tortious act, or has authorized or directed it, or has acted in his own behalf, or has had any knowledge of, or given any consent to, the act or transaction, or has acquiesced in it when he either knew or by the exercise of reasonable care should have known of it and should have objected and taken steps to prevent it.

*Id.* at 548–49 (citing 19 C.J.S. Corporations Section 544, p. 175 (1990)). Thus it follows that a corporate director is not personally liable to a third party merely by reason of his corporate status for the torts committed by other personnel. Some showing of direct personal involvement by the corporate officer in a decision or action which is causally related to the plaintiff's injury is required.

Hester fails to provide evidence to show that Cain or Smith directed or authorized any of the alleged conduct towards Hazelton. Cain stated that he was not active in the day to day management of the nursing home and did not directly supervise or control the activities of any employees. Smith also stated that he did not supervise or control the activities of any Driftwood employees or agents whom Hester claims to have harmed Hazelton. Hester did not offer any evidence or testimony to rebut these assertions. Therefore, we find Hester's argument to be without merit.

### B. Breach of Duty

Notwithstanding our finding that no separate legal duty exists for Cain or Smith, we will address Hester's assertion of breach of duty. Hester maintains that Cain, as licensee for Driftwood and Smith, as administrator, were negligent because they either knew or should have known of the alleged negligence against Hazelton, and should have objected to the conduct or taken steps to prevent it. Cain and Smith argue that because they did not have direct involvement in any alleged tort, they are not liable.

*            *            *

Cain testified that he conducted almost daily "walk-throughs" of the facility and regularly spoke with either Smith or the head of the nursing staff. Cain inquired about dietary concerns and patients who were reported to have pressure sores. No records indicate that Cain was ever made aware of Hazelton's specific condition or that any complaints were filed on Hazelton's behalf. Likewise, Smith asserted that he did not directly supervise or control the activities of any Driftwood employees whom Hester alleges caused Hazelton harm. Smith noted that he was the administrator of Driftwood for only a few months of Hazelton's residency. He resigned as administrator approximately two months before Hazelton passed away. Yet Hester asserts that a corporate officer or agent may be liable for the torts of the corporation or of other directors, officers or agents when he either knew or in the exercise of reasonable care should have known of the tortious conduct and should have taken steps to prevent it.

Hester relies on surveys and inspections conducted by the Mississippi Department of Health to prove that Cain and Smith should have been aware of the deficiencies, and that the existence of these reports created a sufficient issue of material fact as to Cain's and Smith's neglect of their legal duties. While these reports show that Driftwood was cited in July 1998 and April 1999 as needing to improve a variety of areas, the reports do not establish a causal connection between Cain and Smith and Hazelton's personal care, or that the men negligently handled their duties, or that any perceived problems were not readily corrected by the nursing home. While the surveys include the date on which the violations occurred, they do not include patients' or employees' names involved in the alleged violations.

Further, Hester does not offer any evidence linking the surveys to Hazelton. One of the surveys was conducted almost a year before Hazelton even became a resident of Driftwood. The second survey was conducted in the first few weeks of Hazelton's stay at Driftwood, but does not establish any connection to Hazelton's care. As we stated above, mere allegations of a breach of internal regulations do not establish a cause of action. Therefore, Hester's argument is without merit.

We find the evidence was insufficient to establish a genuine issue of material fact as to a licensee's or administrator's legal duty or that Cain and Smith breached any such duty. Therefore, we find it unnecessary to discuss the remaining elements of proximate cause and damages. Accordingly, we affirm the lower court's granting of the motion for summary judgment.

# NOTE

The issue of vicarious tort liability should be familiar to many students from the first-year Torts class. Issues of control, duty, and a "special relationship" become critical to imparting liability. The issue of whether an employee is a servant-agent or non-servant-agent (not subject to the control of the employer, often referred to as an independent contractor) is one of the most frequently litigated issues in agency law and is a constant concern for business organizations of all types. Why is the law willing to hold a principal liable in contract for acts of its agents, servant, and non-servant alike, yet is more hesitant to impose liability for torts?

## CHASE v. CONSOLIDATED FOODS CORP.
United States Court of Appeals, Seventh Circuit
744 F.2d 566 (1984)

POSNER, CIRCUIT JUDGE

David Chase brought this diversity suit against Consolidated Foods Corporation, claiming that Consolidated had broken its contract with Chase to sell him the Fuller Brush Company, a division of Consolidated. The jury gave judgment for Consolidated, and Chase appeals, claiming error in the instructions to the jury and in exclusion of evidence. The parties agree that Illinois law governs the substantive issues.

The alleged error in the instructions relates to the apparent authority of Newman, who was Consolidated's vice-president, secretary, and general counsel. Newman drafted an agreement for Chase to buy the Fuller Brush Company. Described as a letter of intent and signed by both parties (in June 1975), the agreement was expressly subject to the parties' negotiating a "definitive agreement" and to approval by Consolidated's board of directors. The agreement also allowed Chase to cancel it after studying the company — and in October he did cancel it. But negotiations resumed, and Newman prepared a new agreement in the form of a letter to Chase that began, "This is to confirm our understanding of the salient economic terms of your offer to acquire" Fuller Brush. The parties signed this agreement on November 17, 1975. It left a number of issues to subsequent negotiations-notably, determining the size of Fuller Brush's unfunded pension liability that the purchaser would assume-and did not specify a closing date for the sale.

Both agreements contain a formula for determining the purchase price of the Fuller Brush Company, although the record is not sufficient to enable us to compute an actual purchase price from the formula. What is clear, however, is that the November 17 agreement required Chase to put up $5 million in cash toward the total price. He wanted to borrow this money, and he thought that any lender would want to know whether Consolidated's board of directors had approved the sale. On November 26, at the request of Chase's associate, Calabro, Newman sent a telegram to Chase stating: "The Board of Directors of Consolidated Foods Corporation ratified the approval of the Executive Committee's agreement to sell the Fuller Brush Company to you based upon the terms outlined in the letter of November 17, 1975." But the board had not approved an agreement to sell; on November 26 it had approved the November 17 agreement only as a basis for further negotiations.

After November 26, relations between the parties went downhill. Consolidated says that Chase couldn't raise the $5 million; Chase says Consolidated decided to keep Fuller Brush Company because the company had started making money. The parties broke off negotiations in January, and later Chase brought this suit.

The main issue at trial was whether the November 17 agreement was a contract to sell Fuller Brush Company to Chase. The jury found it was not, and Chase has not appealed this finding. But he argues that the jury may have found as it did only because the judge did not instruct it correctly concerning Newman's apparent authority to bind Consolidated by his telegram of November 26, in which he said that the board of directors had approved the sale to Chase, though it had not. This was an important issue because Newman did not have actual authority to sell the Fuller Brush Company without getting the board's approval. The November 17 agreement became a binding contract of sale (on November 26) only if Newman's representation that the board had approved the sale was within the scope of his apparent authority to deal on Consolidated's behalf.

After making clear that only the board of directors had actual authority to sell Fuller Brush Company and that Chase had "the burden of proving the agent's authority to enter into the particular contract on which [Chase] rests his claim," the judge did give an instruction on apparent authority; only it is not a model of clarity. It states: "Apparent authority of an agent for its principal must be based on word and acts of his principal, and cannot be based on anything that the agent himself has said or done. The acts of an agent may be later ratified by a principal." The first sentence, which is the focus of Chase's objections, was taken verbatim from an instruction submitted by Consolidated; the second was added by the district judge.

Apart from the confusing change from neuter to masculine gender, and the singular "word" rather than "words," the problem with this instruction is that it is meant for a case where the principal is a human being rather than a corporation. Since a corporation can act only through agents, what does it mean to say that the agent's apparent authority must be based on the words and acts of the principal rather than the agent? Maybe it means that, for the corporation to be bound, the appearance of authority must be created by agents other than the agent whose authority is in question. He cannot just bootstrap himself into a position where he can bind his principal. He must be invested with apparent authority by the acts or statements or misleading omissions of other, and responsible, agents of his corporate principal. This interpretation would make the instruction a correct statement of Illinois agency law . . . but to assume that the jury so interpreted it would be unrealistic. Juries do not find it easy to understand the issues in commercial cases in the best of circumstances.

But we do not think the judge committed reversible error in giving this defective instruction and failing to give the instruction offered by Chase. That instruction was off the mark too. It states: "The actions of [various Consolidated officers including Newman] bind Consolidated if they acted within the powers Consolidated gave them or if Chase could reasonably have believed, based upon their titles, positions, actions, and the actions or inactions of Consolidated, that they were acting with Consolidated's authority." The problem is with the words, "or if Chase could reasonably have believed." The instruction nowhere requires that Chase have actually believed that Newman or the others were acting with Consolidated's authority. An appearance of authority that fools no one does not bind the principal.

The facts make this omission more than a technicality, for they strongly suggest that Chase knew perfectly well that Newman had no authority to bind the corporation to the sale of the Fuller Brush Company. Chase is a wealthy and experienced investor (he estimates his net worth to be $33 million). He must at least have suspected that the sale of an entire corporate division worth millions would (as it did) require the approval of the seller's board of directors (see American Law Institute, Principles of Corporate Governance: Analysis and Recommendations, Tent. Draft No. 2, § 3.02, comment f, at pp. 70–71 (April 13, 1984)), and that Consolidated's board would not approve the sale till the terms were fully worked out, which had not been done as of November 26. Nor would Consolidated be bound, under Illinois law, just by virtue of having given Newman some apparent authority to deal on its behalf by designating him as its secretary and general counsel. Even if it had given him the title of "president," this would not have invested him with apparent authority to "make a contract on its behalf which is unusual and extraordinary," that is, beyond the usual authority of a president, as a contract to sell a major corporate division would be.

As for the telegram of November 26, in which Newman stated that the board of directors had ratified the sale, not only had Calabro requested Newman to send the telegram but Calabro had dictated the critical statement in it-that the board had approved the agreement to sell Fuller Brush to Chase. The purpose of the telegram was to help Chase raise money for the deal by convincing lenders that the deal would go through. Then Chase would be able to pledge assets of Fuller Brush Company to whomever he borrowed money from to pay Consolidated-would, in other words, be able to arrange a leveraged buyout of the Fuller Brush Company and therefore not have to put up his own money after all. Given Calabro's role in the preparation of the telegram, we find it hard to see how Chase can argue that Newman misled him as to what Consolidated's board had done. But in any event the instruction offered by Chase would not have put before the jury the question whether Chase was actually misled.

The circumstances in which the telegram was sent also scotch Chase's alternative theory of apparent authority, which is that Consolidated, by holding out Newman to the world as Consolidated's corporate secretary, clothed him with apparent authority to represent truthfully what the board had done at its meeting of November 26. This is a perfectly valid theory but it has no application to the facts, since the representation was supplied by Calabro, Chase's agent, rather than Newman. In any event, if this theory was to be put to the jury, Chase was obliged to embody it in a clearer instruction than the one the judge quite properly refused to give.

With the circumstances so strongly suggestive of knowledge by Chase or Calabro that the board of directors had not approved the sale, that Newman had no authority to approve it on his own, and that he was not attempting to approve it in accommodating Calabro's request for help with Chase's efforts to finance the deal, Chase had (and failed) to come up with a better instruction on apparent authority: an instruction that would tell the jury that, to find for Chase, it had to find not only that he could reasonably have believed that Newman was authorized to (and attempted to) sell the Fuller Brush Company to Chase but also that he had actually believed these things.

\*     \*     \*

. . . [W]e find no reversible error. The judge did not give a plainly wrong instruction; he gave an unclear, an incomplete, at worst a misleading instruction. And the substitute offered by the plaintiff was not marred by a merely technical error; it missed an essential point bearing on the issue of apparent authority-the plaintiff's own knowledge that the board of directors had not approved the sale.

AFFIRMED.

# NOTE

Mr. Newman was the vice-president, secretary, and general counsel of Consolidated. Did he have actual authority to sell the Fuller Brush Company? What is a letter of intent? Why did the telegram not bind the corporation? If Mr. Chase had asked for a certified copy of a board resolution approving the transaction, and obtained one, would the resolution bind the corporation?

# Chapter 3

# SOLE PROPRIETORSHIPS AND PARTNERSHIPS

## A. THE SOLE PROPRIETORSHIP

### CREDIT ASSOCIATES OF MAUI, LTD. v. CARLBOM
Court of Appeals of Hawaii
50 P.3d 431 (2002)

Opinion of the Court by WATANABE, J.

In this assumpsit case, Plaintiff-Appellant Credit Associates of Maui, Ltd. (Credit Associates) challenges the September 26, 2000 judgment of the District Court of the Second Circuit (the district court), which awarded Credit Associates $3,077.79 against Aloha Screens, a sole proprietorship, but declined to hold Defendant-Appellee Cosco E. Carlbom, also known as Casco E. Carlbom (Carlbom), the sole proprietor of Aloha Screens, personally liable for the debts of Aloha Screens.

Because a sole proprietorship has no legal identity apart from its owner, we vacate the district court's judgment and remand with instructions that the district court enter a judgment holding Carlbom personally liable to Credit Associates for the debts of Aloha Screens.

On March 28, 2000, Credit Associates filed the underlying lawsuit against Carlbom, individually and doing business as Aloha Screens, seeking, in relevant part, to recover $3,077.79 for unpaid telephone and other services provided to Aloha Screens. The evidence adduced at trial revealed that Aloha Screens entered into an oral contract with GTE Hawaiian Telephone Company, now known as Verizon Hawaii (Verizon), for telephone services and "GTE Directory Advertising." Although Aloha Screens did make payments on some monthly bills invoiced by Verizon in 1997 and 1998, by May 21, 1998, Aloha Screens owed $3,077.79 in unpaid bills to Verizon. Verizon subsequently assigned its right to collect on this debt to Credit Associates.

Carlbom admitted at trial that he was the owner and sole proprietor of Aloha Screens, a sole proprietorship company that he formed in 1984. He also admitted that he was familiar with the four telephone numbers for which Aloha Screens owed Verizon $3,077.79 in unpaid bills, because "[t]hose were [Aloha Screens'] phone numbers." Based on these admissions, Credit Associates' attorney argued that Carlbom should be held personally liable for the debts of Aloha Screens.

\* \* \*

The district court specifically found that an "oral agreement was formed whereby 'Aloha Screens' promised to pay for telephone services provided by Verizon[.]" The district court also found that "Carlbom was the sole proprietor of Aloha Screens." Nevertheless, the district court concluded that "Carlbom is not personally liable for the debt incurred from services rendered by Verizon because Verizon did not have an agreement with [Carlbom] acknowledging personal liability of the debt. This is so because there was no evidence that [Carlbom] requested the above service in [sic] behalf of Aloha Screens, nor that he agreed to pay for it."

For the following reasons, and in light of the district court's findings, we hold that the district court was wrong when it concluded that Carlbom was not liable for the debt incurred from services rendered by Verizon to Aloha Screens.

## A.

First, a sole proprietorship has no legal identity apart from its owner. Black's Law Dictionary 1392 (6th ed.1990) defines "sole proprietorship" as

> "[a] form of business in which one person owns all the assets of the business in contrast to a partnership, trust or corporation. The sole proprietor is solely liable for all the debts of the business."

Similarly, one legal treatise has observed:

> "The basic disadvantages of the sole proprietorship arise from the complete identity of the business entity with the individual doing business. In contrast with the limited-liability characteristic of a corporation or limited partnership, the liabilities of the business venture are the personal liabilities of the individual proprietor. The financial risk of the sole proprietor is not limited to the amount invested in the business but encompasses all of his [or her] assets."

Z. Cavitch, Business Organizations § 1.04, at 1–22 (2002).

Although no Hawaii case has explicitly recognized the foregoing rule regarding the liability of a sole proprietor, other jurisdictions have. In *State v. ABC Towing*, 954 P.2d 575, 577–78 (Alaska Ct.App.1998), for example, the Alaska Court of Appeals held:

> "At common law, sole proprietorships are not "legal entities." Neither are partnerships . . . . Rather, sole proprietorships and partnerships are deemed to be merely the alter egos of the proprietor or the partners (as individuals). In a sole proprietorship, all of the proprietor's assets are completely at risk, and the sole proprietorship ceases to exist upon the proprietor's death. . . . "

\* \* \*

> "With regard to a sole proprietorship, Alaska law deems the "company" to be simply an alter ego of the proprietor, who is engaged in commerce under a nom d'affaires — an assumed name adopted for business purposes. *See Roeckl v. Federal Deposit Insurance Corp.*, 885 P.2d 1067 (Alaska 1994), which contains a lengthy discussion of an individual's legal ability to

conduct business or business transactions under an assumed name. *Roeckl* notes that, unless a person uses a fictitious business name in order to facilitate a fraud, it has always been legal for a person to transact business in the name of a fictitious entity that has no legal existence apart from the individual(s) running the business."

\* \* \*

In this case, the district court specifically found that Aloha Screens was indebted to Verizon pursuant to an "oral agreement" and that Carlbom "was the sole proprietor of Aloha Screens." Because a sole proprietorship cannot "conduct business" on its own and Aloha Screens was essentially a trade name under which Carlbom operated, Carlbom was, pursuant to the authority discussed above, personally liable for the $3,077.79 debt owed by Aloha Screens to Verizon. The district court incorrectly concluded otherwise.

## B.

At trial, the district court orally ruled that Verizon's failure to obtain Carlbom's signature on a written contract for telephone services provided to Aloha Screens was fatal to Credit Associates' attempt to recover from Carlbom any debt owed by Aloha Screens. For the following reasons, we conclude that the district court erred in so ruling.

First, it is well settled that "[a] contract need not be in writing unless a statute requires it. Conversely, an oral or parol contract is unenforceable where a statute requires it to be in writing."

\* \* \*

Second, the general rule is that

> [i]n the absence of a statute requiring a signature or an agreement that the contract shall not be binding until it is signed, *parties may become bound by the terms of a contract, even though they do not sign it,* where their assent is otherwise indicated, *such as by the acceptance of benefits under the contract, or the acceptance by one of the performance by the other.*

The Hawaii Supreme Court has expressed this rule as follows: "Performance or part performance of a contract required to be in writing will take the matter out of the statute of frauds, where the party seeking to enforce it has acted to his [or her] detriment in substantial reliance upon the oral agreement." *Shannon v. Waterhouse,* 58 Haw. 4, 5–6, 563 P.2d 391, 393 (1977).

In this case, Carlbom acknowledged that four telephone numbers listed on Verizon's invoices to Aloha Screens were for telephones furnished by Verizon for Aloha Screens' business. Since Aloha Screens accepted the benefits of the telephone and other services provided by Verizon in substantial reliance on Aloha Screens' oral agreement to pay for services executed, Aloha Screens and its sole proprietor, Carlbom, are liable for the cost of said services.

\* \* \*

For the foregoing reasons, we conclude that the district court was wrong when it held that Carlbom was not liable for the debts of Aloha Screens. Accordingly, we vacate the district court's judgment and remand this case with instructions that the district court enter a new judgment that holds Carlbom liable for the debts of Aloha Screens.

## NOTES

**1.** The Sole Proprietorship is the most common type of business entity in use in the United States. The individual proprietor may conduct business either in his or her own name or under a fictitious name, which usually must be registered under state law. However, as *Carlbom* indicates, the use of the name is irrelevant to the issue of liability since, regardless of the name chosen, the business and the individual are one and the same. This is a characteristic which the sole proprietorship and the general partnership generally have in common. However, the Revised Uniform Partnership Act (1997) has in some respects caused a partnership to be treated as a distinct entity.

**2.** One factor which may have led the trial court to err is that there was no evidence that the proprietor, Carlbom, had personally contacted the telephone company to contract for telephone service for Aloha Screens. After reading the materials in the preceding chapter, do you see why that is irrelevant to the result?

## CAMBRIDGE TOWNHOMES, LLC v. PACIFIC STAR, INC.
### Supreme Court of Washington
### 209 P.3d 863 (2009)

En Banc

Stephens, J. — Respondents Cambridge Townhomes, LLC, a developer, and Polygon Northwest Company (Polygon), a general contractor, were involved in a townhome condominium development project between 1997 and mid-2000. During construction, Polygon entered into a subcontract with intervenor Gerald Utley, who did business as P.J. Interprize during the time Polygon originally contracted with him. Utley subsequently incorporated P.J. Interprize, Inc. (P.J. Inc.) and signed a new contract with Polygon under the incorporated name. In early 2003, after the condominium project was substantially completed, the Cambridge Townhomes Homeowner's Association (Association) notified Polygon of several construction defects. Polygon settled with the Association and then in March 2004 filed suit for breach of contract and indemnification against various subcontractors, including P.J. Inc. Polygon did not file against Utley's sole proprietorship. Utley had filed for chapter 7 bankruptcy in February 2004. Polygon's claims against P.J. Inc. proceeded to a summary judgment hearing. After denying Polygon's motion to amend its complaint to include Utley, the trial court granted summary judgment in favor of P.J. Inc., dismissing Polygon's claims with prejudice. Polygon appealed, and the Court of Appeals reversed.

We affirm the Court of Appeals. We hold that P.J. Inc. may be liable for the sole proprietorship's construction defects under a theory of successor liability; that

Polygon's breach of contract claim against the sole proprietorship is not time-barred; that the trial court erred when it denied Polygon's motion to amend its complaint; and that Polygon's claim for indemnity from P.J. Inc. was within the scope of the parties' contractual indemnity clause.

## FACTS AND PROCEDURAL HISTORY

In approximately 1997, Cambridge and Polygon began work on a condominium development. The development was set to be constructed in three phases between 1997 and mid-2000, consisting of 40 multiunit buildings.

In August 1998, Polygon subcontracted with Gerald Utley, a sole proprietor doing business as P.J. Interprize, to install vinyl siding and trim on phase II of the project. In November 1998, the sole proprietorship's work on phase II was completed. On October 1, 1999, a temporary certificate of occupancy for phase II was issued.

Meanwhile, in January 1999, Utley incorporated his business as P.J. Inc. In April 1999, Polygon entered into a subcontract with P.J. Inc. for phase III of the project. This subcontract also included an indemnity agreement.

In early 2003, the Association notified Polygon of construction defects in the condominium development. In November 2003, Polygon and the Association agreed to settle conditioned upon funding.

In February 2004, Utley and his wife jointly filed for personal bankruptcy in the United States Bankruptcy Court for the Western District of Washington. In response to a request on the bankruptcy form to list all trade names used in the last six years, Utley listed P.J. Inc. Utley also listed the nature of his debts as business related. He named Cambridge as one of the numerous creditors to whom he owed money.

In March 2004, Polygon filed suit against the subcontractors involved in the condominium development, including P.J. Inc. Polygon asserted claims for breach of contract and indemnification. Polygon sued P.J. Inc. in its corporate capacity but did not list Utley or the sole proprietorship in its complaint.

In May 2004, Polygon filed a motion in the bankruptcy court to allow it to pursue claims against Utley in his capacity as a sole proprietor to the extent insurance assets were available. The court granted the motion, allowing Polygon to proceed in this action against Utley "for the purpose of pursuing any insurance proceeds that are the result of any insurance coverage the Debtor may possess."

In June 2004, the bankruptcy court issued a chapter 7 discharge order for Utley.

Meanwhile, the case against the subcontractors proceeded to summary judgment. In May 2005, the trial court dismissed the indemnity claims against all the subcontractors, including P.J. Inc., granting summary judgment in their favor. In October 2005, the trial court ruled that the bankruptcy discharge barred Polygon from pursuing claims against P.J. Inc. under a theory of successor liability for Utley's work as a sole proprietor. The court also denied Polygon's request to amend its complaint to add Utley as a defendant in his capacity as a sole proprietor. In

November 2005, Polygon filed a separate suit against the sole proprietorship. That same month, the court dismissed Polygon's breach of contract claims.

Polygon appealed. The Court of Appeals reversed, holding that P.J. Inc. could be held liable under a theory of successor liability for Utley's actions as a sole proprietor and that the bankruptcy discharge did not bar Polygon's claims against the sole proprietorship. *Cambridge Townhomes, LLC v. Pac. Star Roofing, Inc.*, No. 57328-4-I, 2007 WL 1666653, at *3–6, 2007 Wash. App. LEXIS 1487, at *10–15. The Court of Appeals also reversed the trial court's order denying Polygon's motion to amend its complaint to name Utley. P.J. Inc. petitioned this court for review, which we granted. We also granted Utley leave to intervene on behalf of the sole proprietorship.

## ANALYSIS

Summary judgment is appropriate only if there are no genuine issues of material fact and the moving party is entitled to judgment as a matter of law. * * *

Washington adheres to the general rule that a corporation purchasing the assets of another corporation does not become liable for the debts and liabilities of the selling corporation. *Hall v. Armstrong Cork, Inc.*, 103 Wn.2d 258, 261–62, 692 P.2d 787 (1984). An exception to this rule may exist, however, where (1) there is an express or implied agreement for the purchaser to assume liability; "(2) the purchase is a de facto merger or consolidation; (3) the purchaser is a mere continuation of the seller; or (4) the transfer of assets is for the fraudulent purpose of escaping liability."

The parties here focus on "mere continuation" as the relevant exception. Washington courts rely on several factors to determine whether a successor business is a mere continuation of a seller. *Cashar v. Redford*, 28 Wn. App. 394, 397, 624 P.2d 194 (1981). These include a common identity between the officers, directors, and stockholders of the selling and purchasing companies, and the sufficiency of the consideration running to the seller corporation in light of the assets being sold. *Id.* In considering these factors, the objective of the court is to discern whether the "purchaser represents 'merely a "new hat" for the seller.' " *Id.* (quoting *McKee v. Harris-Seybold Co.*, 109 N.J. Super. 555, 570, 264 A.2d 98 (1970)).

The Court of Appeals framed the issue here as one of first impression because instead of one corporation becoming a new corporation, we have a sole proprietorship becoming a corporation. *Cambridge*, 2007 WL 1666653, at *4, 2007 Wash. App. LEXIS 1487, at *12–13. But, as the Court of Appeals also noted, we have previously recognized in "reviewing the history of the mere continuation exception . . . that the exception was first expanded by a federal court when it found a corporation to be a mere continuation of a predecessor sole proprietorship." *Id.* (citing *Martin v. Abbot Labs.*, 102 Wn.2d 581, 611, 689 P.2d 368 (1984)). The particular form of the business entity should not be determinative.

The successor liability doctrine is a common law rule, and the principle it embraces is not linked to statutes or laws governing corporate entities. Though there is no continuation of officers, directors, or shareholders where a sole proprietorship is involved, we can consider the continuity of individuals in control of the business as satisfying this factor, which at any rate is not a rigid requirement for finding successor liability. Thus, we reject P.J. Inc.'s argument that as a matter of law, a corporation cannot be a mere continuation of a predecessor sole proprietorship.

Here, the undisputed facts show that P.J. Inc. is a mere continuation of the sole proprietorship. The business performed by P.J. Interprize and P.J. Inc. is the same. The same individual, Utley, was at the helm of both entities. The clients, at least in the case of Polygon, remained the same. There is no issue of sufficient consideration in this case because there was no sale of assets. Utley simply chose to incorporate his business. In sum, P.J. Inc. merely represented a new hat for the sole proprietorship. We therefore hold that P.J. Inc. assumed the sole proprietorship's liabilities under a theory of successor liability, subject to the limitations on recovery imposed by the bankruptcy court.

P.J. Inc. argues that Utley's bankruptcy discharge precluded P.J. Inc.'s liability as a successor to P.J. Interprize. We disagree. While the bankruptcy discharge may limit the assets available to Polygon for recovery pursuant to the terms imposed by the bankruptcy court, it does not prevent the imposition of liability under a successor liability theory. The Court of Appeals correctly observed that the effect of the bankruptcy court's ruling was to limit recovery to the sole proprietorship's insurance assets.

*  *  *

## CONCLUSION

We hold that P.J. Inc. is a mere continuation of the sole proprietorship and thus subject to successor liability. We affirm the Court of Appeals' holding that the trial court abused its discretion in denying Polygon's motion to amend its complaint and further hold that there is no statutory time bar under *RCW 4.16.326(1)(g)* to Polygon's ability to pursue a claim against the sole proprietorship. We also affirm the Court of Appeals' holding that the indemnification provision at issue is not limited to tort actions.

## B.  THE PARTNERSHIP

*Martin v. Peyton*, which follows, involves the definition of a partnership. Note that the persons arguing against partnership had never intended to be partners. In fact, the agreements signed expressly denied such intent. Should this factor be relevant?

The parties involved in this case were sophisticated and clearly intended to avoid the joint and several liability that is the inevitable consequence of partnership. At least that was true in 1927. Today, the Limited Liability Partnership (LLP) form of business organization could be used to limit liability, if not entirely, at least significantly.

This case was decided under the Uniform Partnership Act (UPA). Some states at present have adopted a model statute called the Revised Uniform Partnership Act

(RUPA). The partnership developed as a form of organization that did not require much knowledge of the law or formal filings of papers, or indeed even a written agreement. Thus, there are many cases decided under the UPA that involve unsophisticated parties that may have entered into a partnership, but never realized it at the time. It is not necessary to know that a partnership is a form of business organization in order to form one. Thus, the intent to form a partnership is not a pre-requisite for forming a partnership. What is necessary is the intent to do those things that constitute a partnership. This case is the other side of the coin. The parties here knew what a partnership was, but they wanted to avoid the liabilities. If the court had found this business transaction to be a true partnership, liability would have been imposed on the "partners" regardless of their intent.

## MARTIN v. PEYTON
### Court of Appeals of New York
### 158 N.E. 77 (1927)

ANDREWS, J.

Much ancient learning as to partnership is obsolete. Today only those who are partners between themselves may be charged for partnership debts by others. There is one exception. Now and then a recovery is allowed where in truth such relationship is absent. This is because the debtor may not deny the claim.

Partnership results from contract, express or implied. If denied, it may be proved by the production of some written instrument, by testimony as to some conversation, by circumstantial evidence. If nothing else appears, the receipt by the defendant of a share of the profits of the business is enough.

\* \* \*

An existing contract may be modified later by subsequent agreement, oral or written. A partnership may be so created where there was none before. And again, that the original agreement has been so modified may be proved by circumstantial evidence — by showing the conduct of the parties.

\* \* \*

"The plaintiff's position is not," we are told, "that the agreements of June 4, 1921, were a false expression or incomplete expression of the intention of the parties. We say that they express defendants' intention and that that intention was to create a relationship which as a matter of law constitutes a partnership." Nor may the claim of the plaintiff be rested on any question of estoppel. "The plaintiff's claim,' he stipulates, 'is a claim of actual partnership, not of partnership by estoppel, and liability is not sought to be predicated upon article 27 of the New York Partnership Law."

Remitted then, as we are, to the documents themselves, we refer to circumstances surrouding their execution only so far as is necessary to make them intelligible. And we are to remember that although the intention of the parties to avoid liability as partners is clear, although in language precise and definite they deny any design to then join the firm of K. N. & K.; although they say their interests in profits should be construed merely as a measure of compensation for loans, not an interest in profits as such; although they provide that they shall not be liable for any losses or treated as partners, the question still remains whether in fact they agree to so associate themselves with the firm as to 'carry on as co-owners a business for profit.'

In the spring of 1921 the firm of K. N. & K. found itself in financial difficulties. John R. Hall was one of the partners. He was a friend of Mr. Peyton. From him he obtained the loan of almost $500,000 of Liberty bonds, which K. N. & K. might use as collateral to secure bank advances. This, however, was not sufficient. The firm and its members had engaged in unwise speculations, and it was deeply involved. Mr. Hall was also intimately acquainted with George W. Perkins, Jr., and with Edward W. Freeman. He also knew Mrs. Peyton and Mrs. Perkins and Mrs. Freeman. All were anxious to help him. He therefore, representing K. N. & K., entered into negotiations with them. While they were pending a proposition was made that Mr. Peyton, Mr. Perkins, and Mr. Freeman, or some of them, should become partners. It met a decided refusal. Finally an agreement was reached. It is expressed in three documents, executed on the same day, all a part of the one transaction. They were drawn with care and are unambiguous. We shall refer to them as 'the agreement,' 'the indenture,' and 'the option.'

We have no doubt as to their general purpose. The respondents were to loan K. N. & K. $2,500,000 worth of liquid securities, which were to be returned to them on or before April 15, 1923. The firm might hypothecate them to secure loans totaling $2,000,000, using the proceeds as its business necessities required. To insure respondents against loss K. N. & K. were to turn over to them a large number of their own securities which may have been valuable, but which were of so speculative a nature that they could not be used as collateral for bank loans. In compensation for the loan the respondents were to receive 40 per cent of the profits of the firm until the return was made, not exceeding, however, $500,000, and not less than $100,000. Merely because the transaction involved the transfer of securities and not of cash does not prevent its being a loan, within the meaning of section 11. The respondents also were given an option to join the firm if they, or any of them, expressed a desire to do so before June 4, 1923.

\*     \*     \*

As representing the lenders, Mr. Peyton and Mr. Freeman are called "trustees." The loaned securities when used as collateral are not to be mingled with other securities of K. N. & K., and the trustees at all times are to be kept informed of all transactions affecting them. To them shall be paid all dividends and income accruing therefrom. They may also substitute for any of the securities loaned securities of equal value. With their consent the firm may sell any of its securities held by the respondents, the proceeds to go, however, to the trustees. In other similar ways the trustees may deal with these same securities, but the securities loaned shall always be sufficient in value to permit of their hypothecation for $2,000,000. If they rise in price, the excess may be withdrawn by the defendants. If they fall, they shall make good the deficiency.

So far, there is no hint that the transaction is not a loan of securities with a provision for compensation. Later a somewhat closer connection with the firm appears. Until the securities are returned, the directing management of the firm is to be in the hands of John R. Hall, and his life is to be insured for $1,000,000, and the policies are to be assigned as further collateral security to the trustees. These requirements are not unnatural. Hall was the one known and trusted by the defendants. Their acquaintance with the other members of the firm was of the slightest. These others had brought an old and established business to the verge of bankruptcy. As the respondents knew, they also had engaged in unsafe speculation. The respondents were about to loan $2,500,000 of good securities. As collateral they were to receive others of problematical value. What they required seems but ordinary caution. Nor does it imply an association in the business.

The trustees are to be kept advised as to the conduct of the business and consulted as to important matters. They may inspect the firm books and are entitled to any information they think important. Finally, they may veto any business they think highly speculative or injurious. Again we hold this but a proper precaution to safeguard the loan. The trustees may not initiate any transaction as a partner may do. They may not bind the firm by any action of their own. Under the circumstances the safety of the loan depended upon the business success of K. N. & K. This success was likely to be compromised by the inclination of its members to engage in speculation. No longer, if the respondents were to be protected, should it be allowed. The trustees therefore might prohibit it, and that their prohibition might be effective, information was to be furnished them. Not dissimilar agreements have been held proper to guard the interests of the lender.

As further security each member of K. N. & K. is to assign to the trustees their interest in the firm. No loan by the firm to any member is permitted and the amount each may draw is fixed. No other distribution of profits is to be made. So that realized profits may be calculated the existing capital is stated to be $700,000, and profits are to be realized promptly as good business practice will permit. In case the trustees think this is not done, the question is left to them and to Mr. Hall, and if they differ then to an arbitrator. There is no obligation that the firm shall continue the business. It may dissolve at any time. Again we conclude there is nothing here not properly adapted to secure the interest of the respondents as lenders. If their compensation is dependent on a percentage of the profits, still provision must be made to define what these profits shall be.

The "indenture" is substantially a mortgage of the collateral delivered by K. N. & K. to the trustees to secure the performance of the "agreement." It certainly does not strengthen the claim that the respondents were partners.

Finally we have the "option." It permits the respondents, or any of them, or their assignees or nominees to enter the firm at a later date if they desire to do so by buying 50 per cent or less of the interests therein of all or any of the members at a stated price. Or a corporation may, if the respondents and the members agree, be formed in place of the firm. Meanwhile, apparently with the design of protecting the firm business against improper or ill-judged action which might render the option valueless, each member of the firm is to place his resignation in hands of Mr. Hall. If at any time he and the trustees agree that such resignation should be accepted, that member shall then retire, receiving the value of his interest calculated as of the date of such retirement.

This last provision is somewhat unusual, yet it is not enough in itself to show that on June 4, 1921, a present partnership was created, nor taking these various papers as a whole do we reach such a result. It is quite true that even if one or two or three like provisions contained in such a contract do not require this conclusion, yet it is also true that when taken together a point may come where stipulations immaterial separately cover so wide a field that we should hold a partnership exists. As in other branches of the law, a question of degree is often the determining factor. Here that point has not been reached. * * *

The judgment appealed from should be affirmed, with costs.

# NOTE

RUPA makes some changes in sections 6 and 7 of the Uniform Partnership Act (UPA). RUPA combines sections 6 and 7 into section 202 of the RUPA. Section 7 of the UPA is really part of the definition of partnership, and no sensible reason exists for separating the two parts of the definition. Section 202 of RUPA states in part "the association of two or more person to carry on as co-owners of a business for profit creates a partnership, whether or not the persons intend to create a partnership." Does this definition confuse the existing state of the decisional law? Isn't intent a necessary part of the definition of partnership? Don't most of the decided cases construe intent as one of the elements of a partnership? Why does RUPA not define "association"? The Official Comment to the UPA suggests that "association" connotes intent. *See* Reuschlein & Gregory, Law of Agency & Partnership § 175 (2d ed.).

This case illustrates an attempt to get all the advantages of the partnership form without the disadvantage of joint and several liability. Is there anything wrong with that motive?

## MEINHARD v. SALMON
### Court of Appeals of New York
### 164 N.E. 545 (1928)

Cardozo, C.J.

On April 10, 1902, Louisa M. Gerry leased to the defendant Walter J. Salmon the premises known as the Hotel Bristol at the northwest corner of Forty-Second street and Fifth avenue in the city of New York. The lease was for a term of 20 years, commencing May 1, 1902, and ending April 30, 1922. The lessee undertook to change the hotel building for use as shops and offices at a cost of $200,000. Alterations and additions were to be accretions to the land.

Salmon, while in course of treaty with the lessor as to the execution of the lease, was in course of treaty with Meinhard, the plaintiff, for the necessary funds. The result was a joint venture with terms embodied in a writing. Meinhard was to pay to Salmon half of the moneys requisite to reconstruct, alter, manage, and operate the property. Salmon was to pay to Meinhard 40 per cent of the net profits for the first five years of the lease and 50 per cent for the years thereafter. If there were losses, each party was to bear them equally. Salmon, however, was to have sole power to 'manage, lease, underlet and operate' the building. There were to be certain pre-emptive rights for each in the contingency of death.

The two were coadventures, subject to fiduciary duties akin to those of partners. *King v. Barnes*, 109 N. Y. 267, 16 N. E. 332. As to this we are all agreed. The heavier weight of duty rested, however, upon Salmon. He was a coadventurer with Meinhard, but he was manager as well. During the early years of the enterprise, the building, reconstructed, was operated at a loss. If the relation had then ended, Meinhard as well as Salmon would have carried a heavy burden. Later the profits became large with the result that for each of the investors there came a rich return. For each the venture had its phases of fair weather and of foul. The two were in it jointly, for better or for worse.

When the lease was near its end, Elbridge T. Gerry had become the owner of the reversion. He owned much other property in the neighborhood, one lot adjoining the Bristol building on Fifth avenue and four lots on Forty-Second street. He had a plan to lease the entire tract for a long term to some one who would destroy the buildings then existing and put up another in their place. In the latter part of 1921, he submitted such a project to several capitalists and dealers. He was unable to carry it through with any of them. Then, in January, 1922, with less than four months of the lease to run, he approached the defendant Salmon. The result was a new lease to the Midpoint Realty Company, which is owned and controlled by Salmon, a lease covering the whole tract, and involving a huge outlay. The term is to be 20 years, but successive covenants for renewal will extend it to a maximum of 80 years at the will of either party. The existing buildings may remain unchanged for seven years. They are then to be torn down, and a new building to cost $3,000,000 is to be placed upon the site. The rental, which under the Bristol lease was only $55,000, is to be from $350,000 to $475,000 for the properties so combined. Salmon personally guaranteed the performance by the lessee of the covenants of the new lease until such time as the new building had been completed and fully paid for.

The lease between Gerry and the Midpoint Realty Company was signed and delivered on January 25, 1922. Salmon had not told Meinhard anything about it. Whatever his motive may have been, he had kept the negotiations to himself. Meinhard was not informed even of the bare existence of a project. The first that he knew of it was in February, when the lease was an accomplished fact. He then made demand on the defendants that the lease be held in trust as an asset of the venture, making offer upon the trial to share the personal obligations incidental to the guaranty. The demand was followed by refusal, and later by this suit. A referee gave judgment for the plaintiff, limiting the plaintiff's interest in the lease, however, to 25 per cent. The limitation was on the theory that the plaintiff's equity was to be restricted to one-half of so much of the value of the lease as was contributed or represented by the occupation of the Bristol site. Upon cross-appeals to the Appellate Division, the judgment was modified so as to enlarge the equitable interest to one-half of the whole lease. With this enlargement of plaintiff's interest, there went, of course, a corresponding enlargement of his attendant obligations. The case is now here on an appeal by the defendants.

Joint adventurers, like copartners, owe to one another, while the enterprise continues, the duty of the finest loyalty. Many forms of conduct permissible in a workaday world for those acting at arm's length, are forbidden to those bound by fiduciary ties. A trustee is held to something stricter than the morals of the market place. Not honesty alone, but the punctilio of an honor the most sensitive, is then the standard of behavior. As to this there has developed a tradition that is unbending and inveterate. Uncompromising rigidity has been the attitude of courts of equity when petitioned to undermine the rule of undivided loyalty by the "disintegrating erosion" of particular exceptions. * * * Only thus has the level of conduct for fiduciaries been kept at a level higher than that trodden by the crowd. It will not consciously be lowered by any judgment of this court.

The owner of the reversion, Mr. Gerry, had vainly striven to find a tenant who would favor his ambitious scheme of demolition and construction. Beffled in the search, he turned to the defendant Salmon in possession of the Bristol, the keystone of the project. He figured to himself beyond a doubt that the man in possession would prove a likely customer. To the eye of an observer, Salmon held the lease as owner in his own right, for himself and no one else. In fact he held it as a fiduciary, for himself and another, sharers in a common venture. If this fact had been proclaimed, if the lease by its terms had run in favor of a partnership, Mr. Gerry, we may fairly assume, would have laid before the partners, and not merely before one of them, his plan of reconstruction. The pre-emptive privilege, or, better, the pre-emptive opportunity, that was thus an incident of the enterprise, Salmon appropriate to himself in secrecy and silence. He might have warned Meinhard that the plan had been submitted, and that either would be free to compete for the award. If he had done this, we do not need to say whether he would have been under a duty, if successful in the competition, to hold the lease so acquired for the benefit of a venture than about to end, and thus prolong by indirection its responsibilities and duties. The trouble about his conduct is that he excluded his coadventurer from any chance to compete, from any chance to enjoy the opportunity for benefit that had come to him alone by virtue of his agency. This chance, if nothing more, he was under a duty to concede. The price of its denial is an extension of the trust at the option and for the benefit of the one whom he excluded.

No answer is it to say that the chance would have been of little value even if seasonably offered. Such a calculus of probabilities is beyond the science of the chancery. Salmon, the real estate operator, might have been preferred to Meinhard, the woolen merchant. On the other hand, Meinhard might have offered better terms, or reinforced his offer by alliance with the wealth of others. Perhaps he might even have persuaded the lessor to renew the Bristol lease alone, postponing for a time, in return for higher rentals, the improvement of adjoining lots. We know that even under the lease as made the time for the enlargement of the building was delayed for seven years. All these opportunities were cut away from him through another's intervention. He knew that Salmon was the manager. As the time drew near for the expiration of the lease, he would naturally assume from silence, if from nothing else, that the lessor was willing to extend it for a term of years, or at least to let it stand as a lease from year to year. Not impossibly the lessor would have done so, whatever his protestations of unwillingness, if Salmon had not given assent to a project more attractive. At all events, notice of termination, even if not necessary, might seem, not unreasonably, to be something to be looked for, if the business was over the another tenant was to enter. In the absence of such notice, the matter of an extension was one that would naturally be attended to by the manager of the enterprise, and not neglected altogether. At least, there was nothing in the situation to give warning to any one that while the lease was still in being, there had come to the manager an offer of extension which he had locked within his breast to be utilized by himself alone. The very fact that Salmon was in control with exclusive powers of direction charged him the more obviously with the duty of disclosure, since only through disclosure could opportunity be equalized. If he might cut off renewal by a purchase for his own benefit when four months were to pass before the lease would have an end, he might do so with equal right while there remained as many years. (cf. *Mitchell v. Read*, 61 N.Y. 123, 127). He might steal a march on his comrade under cover of the darkness, and then hold the captured ground. Loyalty and comradeship are not so easily abjured.

* * *

Certain it is also that there may be no abuse of special opportunities growing out of a special trust as manager of agent. * * *

A constructive trust is then the remedial device through which preference of self is made subordinate to loyalty to others. * * *

We have no thought to hold that Salmon was guilty of a conscious purpose to defraud. Very likely he assumed in all good faith that with the approaching end of the venture he might ignore his coadventurer and take the extension for himself. He had given to the enterprise time and labor as well as money. He had made it a success. Meinhard, who had given money, but neither time nor labor, had already been richly paid. There might seem to be something grasping in his insistence upon more. Such recriminations are not unusual when coadventurers fall out. They are not without their force if conduct is to be judged by the common standards of competitors. That is not to say that they have pertinency here. Salmon had put himself in a position in which thought of self was to be renounced, however hard the abnegation. He was much more than a coadventurer. He was a managing coadventurer. (*Clegg v. Edmondson*, 8 D. M. & G. 787, 807). For him and for those like him the rule of undivided loyalty is relentless and supreme. (*Wendt v. Fischer, supra, Munson v. Syracuse, etc., R. R. Co.*, 103 N.Y. 58, 74). A different question would be here if there were lacking any nexus of relation between the business conducted by the manager and the opportunity brought to him as an incident of management. (*Dean v. MacDowell*, 8 Ch. Div. 345, 354; *Aas v. Benham*, 1891 2 Ch. 244, 258; *Latta v. Kilbourn*, 150 U. S. 524). For this problem, as for most, there are distinctions of degree. If Salmon had received from Gerry a proposition to lease a building at a location far removed, he might have held for himself the privilege thus acquired, or so we shall assume. Here the subject-matter of the new lease was an extension and enlargement of the subject-matter of the old one. A managing coadventurer appropriating the benefit of such a lease without warning to his partner might fairly expect to be reproached with conduct that was underhand, or lacking, to say the least, in reasonable candor, if the partner were to surprise him in the act of signing the new instrument. Conduct subject to that reproach does not receive from equity a healing benediction.

A question remains as to the form and extent of the equitable interest to be allotted to the plaintiff. * * * An equal division of the shares might lead to other hardships. It might take away from Salmon the power of control and management which under the plan of the joint venture he was to have from first to last. The number of shares to be allotted to the plaintiff should, therefore, be reduced to such an extent as may be necessary to preserve to the defendant Salmon the expected measure of dominion. To that end an extra share should be added to his half.

The judgment * * * as so modified * * * should be affirmed with costs.

ANDREWS, J. (dissenting).

* * *

With this view of the law I am of the opinion that the issue here is simple. Was the transaction, in view of all the circumstances surrounding it, unfair and inequitable? I reach this conclusion for two reasons. There was no general partnership, merely a joint venture for a limited object, to end at a fixed time. The new lease, covering additional property, containing many new and unusual terms and conditions, with a possible duration of 80 years, was more nearly the purchase of the reversion than the ordinary renewal with which the authorities are concerned.

* * *

The referee finds that this arrangement did not create a partnership between Mr. Salmon and Mr. Meinhard. In this he is clearly right. He is equally right in holding that while no general partnership existed the two men had entered into a joint adventure and that while the legal title to the lease was in Mr. Salmon, Mr. Meinhard had some sort of an equitable interest therein. Mr. Salmon was to manage the property for their joint benefit. He was bound to use good faith. He could not willfully destroy the lease, the object of the adventure, to the detriment of Mr. Meinhard.

# NOTES

1. Justice Cardozo's discussion of the nature of fiduciary duty is a literary classic. The paragraph discussing the duty of the finest loyalty is frequently quoted by courts not only for joint venturers, but also for partners, and corporate officers and directors as well. The same standard has been applied to the case of shareholders in closely held corporations. The fiduciary standard in partnership law has developed from the law of agency. In agency law, the agent owes its principal a duty of loyalty (fiduciary duty) as well as many other duties. THE RESTATEMENT (SECOND) OF AGENCY contains an extensive list. Prior to the UPA, the courts reasoned that a partnership was not an entity but merely a reciprocal agency relationship. Each partner was simultaneously both an agent and a principal. It is very clear under the law of agency that an agent owes its principal a duty of loyalty, but the principal has no reciprocal duty (though the principal has some duties owed to its agent). The analytical problem with a partnership is that if each partner owes a duty of loyalty to the other partners, there is an inherent conflict. The principal case is a good example. If we regard the opportunity to develop the underlying real property after the expiration of the joint venture as an opportunity, which of the two

partners is entitled to it? It is logically impossible for both partners to put the other's interest first. A sensible resolution of the conflict is simply a duty of disclosure. If Salmon had told Meinhard, four months prior to the expiration of the joint venture, of his plans to deal with the owner of the property without including Meinhard, both joint venturers could have competed to obtain the new opportunity. Would such conduct violate a fiduciary duty? The case doesn't tell us the answer, but it should be clear that non-disclosure would always constitute a violation of fiduciary duty. A sensible way to interpret Cardozo's words is to require partners to disclose all material facts to their co-partners. Contract law has a concept called good faith. Some commentators argue that this is all that the fiduciary standard means. Certainly, a fiduciary standard includes good faith, but many courts have interpreted a fiduciary standard as more demanding.

**2.** A simpler way to explain this case is to limit its result to the actual fact situation. Meinhard was a woolen merchant while Salmon was the real estate expert and managing joint venturer. It certainly makes sense for the courts to protect the less sophisticated party, especially when the more sophisticated party is the one who will learn more about potential opportunities in the future.

## CRANDALL v. BABICH
Circuit Court of Nelson County, Virginia
81 Va. Cir. 486 (2008)

J. MICHAEL GAMBLE, JUDGE.

I am writing to furnish you with the decision of the court in these cases. In this regard, I find that Michael J. Crandall ("Crandall") is entitled to damages from Fulvio Babich ("Babich") and Summitt Builders, Inc. ("Summitt"). . . .

In 2005, Crandall, Babich, and Giunta reached an agreement to build modular homes in Nelson County, particularly in the Wintergreen area of Nelson County. This was an oral agreement never reduced to writing. Under the agreement each member of the joint venture would receive one-third of the profit. Babich, through Summitt (his company), would handle the administrative and financial aspects of the venture. Giunta would handle most of the painting and some of the carpentry and other hands-on aspects of the construction. Crandall would generally serve as a project manager of each job with duties to oversee the work and coordinate the tradesmen working on each house.

Under the evidence, the parties would generally divide the net proceeds after the payment of the expenses. As noted above, Babich would generally keep these records and make the distributions. He used Summitt to hold the money, make distributions, and enter into contracts. Thus, although the agreement was made by Babich, his corporation handled most of his duties in this respect.

\* \* \*

The joint venture seemed to function fairly well during the construction of the first five houses. However, the joint venture decided to build a model modular home on the property of [Norma Bradley]. Babich, Giunta, and Crandall agreed to build this house at cost for Bradley with the expectation that they would able to rent it at a favorable rate for three years. No portion of this proposal was put in writing. After the construction of the house, Bradley refused to execute a three-year lease on the terms sought by the joint venture. This, along with other issues, caused Babich and Giunta to terminate the joint venture relationship with Crandall. The other issues testified to by Babich and Giunta were the management fees charged by Crandall to Bradley, workmanship issues, and conflict of interest issues caused by Crandall working for a competing firm. As a result, in mid-2007 the joint venture was dissolved.

Crandall maintains that Babich and Summitt have not paid to him the money due from his share of the profits. Additionally, he maintains that he should be paid for his portion of the expenses that he paid in the Spec House and paid 15% of any profit from the Spec House.

The relationship of the parties in this case is a joint venture. A joint venture is established "where two or more parties enter into a special combination for the purpose of a specific business undertaking, jointly seeking a profit, gain, or other benefit, without any actual partnership or corporate designation." *PGI, Inc. v. Rathe Productions, Inc.*, 265 Va. 334, 340, 576 S.E. 2d 438, 441 (2003). In this case, Babich, Giunta, and Crandall clearly entered into a combination and business undertaking to build modular homes for a profit. This meets the definition of a joint venture.

The duties and liabilities of joint venturers are "substantially the same as those that govern partnerships." *Id.* at 342. Further, as noted in *PGI, Inc.*, a partner may maintain an action in law against a copartner on claims growing out of a single venture which has been completed with nothing remaining to be done except the payment of a partner's claims. Further, as noted in *PGI, Inc.*, an independent action for conversion may lie separate from the partnership duties.

Utilizing the above legal principles the court finds that Crandall has not been paid his full share under the joint venture, and Babich and Summitt have converted property that is rightfully Crandall's property. The damage reconciliation attached to this letter sets forth the computation of the damages. Under the gross damages to Crandall the . . . awards consist of profits not paid to Crandall. . . .

Additionally, Crandall is awarded $86.91 for the Crandall expenses not reimbursed. I find, however, that Crandall is responsible for one-third of the cost of the business. Therefore, the reimbursement should be for two-thirds of $2,200.00 rather than the full amount. This reduces to the net to $86.91.

I find that the joint venture had been terminated when the substantial work was done on the [subsequent] homes. A partnership, and by implication a joint venture, is dissolved when a partner withdraws. By the time that substantial work was performed on [the subsequent homes] Babich and Giunta had terminated the joint venture with Crandall. Crandall did not make any material contributions to either of these projects. Therefore, he is not entitled to recovery for these projects.

# NOTE

In contrast to the sophisticated parties in *Martin v. Peyton*, the parties in *Crandall* never reduced their arrangement to a formal written agreement. Nevertheless, the court rather easily finds the existence of a partnership among the parties. With equal ease, the *Crandall* court finds the partnership dissolved. Contrast *Meinhard v. Salmon*. Are these two cases consistent?

## P.I.M.L., INC. v. CHAIN LINK GRAPHIX, LLC
United States District Court, District of Minnesota
2006 U.S. Dist. LEXIS 88600 (Dec. 6, 2006)

OPINION BY: Donald D. Alsop

This action was before the Court and jury for trial on September 18, 2006. The case was tried in two phases. The jury returned its verdict in Phase I on September 25, 2006 and in Phase II on September 26, 2006.

The jury found that Defendants Edwin W. Davidson (Davidson), Christopher J. Hilburn (Hilburn), and John D. McKelvey (McKelvey) were pre-incorporation promoters of a business to be called Fashion Links. They also found that these Defendants engaged in a joint venture called Fashion Links. The jury found that at least one of these Defendants entered into a contract on behalf of Fashion Links with Plaintiff P.I.M.L. (PIML). The jury found that the contract was breached by nonpayment of commissions due Plaintiff on two separate accounts, namely Maurice's and Target.

\*    \*    \*

The Motion of Defendants McKelvey and Davidson is based upon the ground that there was no legally sufficient evidentiary basis to support any of the findings by the jury. They move in the alternative to have the monetary judgment amended to remove the statutory commission penalty of Minn. Stat. § 181.145.

The Motion of Defendants Chain Link Graphix, LLC 1 (Chain Link) and Christopher Hilburn pursuant to Rule 50(b) is based upon the following grounds:

1. As a matter of law, there was no legal basis to enter judgment against Hilburn personally for any alleged debt of Chain Link.

2. The jury's finding that PIML had a contractual relationship with Fashion Links for sales to Maurice's was contrary to the weight of the evidence.

3. The jury's findings with respect to Defendant Hilburn being a pre-incorporation promoter of Fashion Links or engaged in a joint venture called Fashion Links are not supported by the evidence as a matter of law.

The Court notes that the judgment ordered by the Court dismissed all claims of the Plaintiff against Chain Link Graphix, LLC.

Alternatively, the Defendants Chain Link and Hilburn move for an order granting a new trial or amending or altering the judgment entered against them.

## Renewed Motion for Judgment as a Matter of Law

The parties agree on the elements required to impose liability either as a pre-incorporation promoter or as a joint venturer. The essential dispute is whether or not the evidence at trial is legally sufficient to impose that type of liability upon the individual defendants.

\*    \*    \*

## Pre-Incorporation Promoter Liability

Each individual Defendant contends that no reasonable juror could have found that he was engaged as a pre-incorporation promoter of the business to be called Fashion Links. The Court does not agree.

During trial, evidence was presented that before Fashion Links was incorporated each Defendant had his own business card which contained his respective name and title in a company called Fashion Links. Moreover, Defendant Hilburn testified that he signed a document on behalf of Fashion Links and as a "partner" of Fashion Links. A copy of this document revealed Defendant Hilburn's signature and printed notation that he was a partner of Fashion Links at the time he signed the document. Defendant Davidson testified that he designed the Fashion Links business cards. There was evidence that Defendant McKelvey sent emails discussing business strategies for both the Target and Maurice's accounts. There was also testimony that Plaintiff met with the individual Defendants for an interview with a company called Fashion Links, even though Fashion Links had not been incorporated yet.

The Court instructed the jury that a promoter of a corporation is one who actually participates in taking preliminary steps in the organization of a new business or company and associates himself with others for the purpose of organizing the company and promoting its business. Viewing the evidence in the light most favorable to the non-moving Plaintiff, which the Court must do, the Court finds that reasonable jurors could differ as to whether the evidence showed that each of the individual Defendants was actively participating in the promotion of Fashion Links by taking preliminary steps in its formation prior to its incorporation. The Court is satisfied that the jury's findings as to each individual Defendant being a pre-incorporation promoter is amply supported by the evidence.

## Joint Venture Liability

Each individual Defendant also contends that no reasonable juror could have found that he was engaged in a joint venture of a business called Fashion Links.

There was evidence each Defendant referred to themselves as partners, had Fashion Links business cards and email addresses, and used these Fashion Links email accounts to discuss Target and Maurice's business with themselves and others. Moreover, there was evidence that Defendants McKelvey and Davidson each received payments from Fashion Links International following a letter of credit AMC/Target issued to Fashion Links International. Also, there was evidence that

Defendant Hilburn profited when he liquidated Chain Link.

Without objection, the Court instructed the jury that a person is engaged in a joint venture when that person contracts with another party to combine their money, property, time, or skill in business operation and share profits in some fixed proportion. The Court also instructed the jury that each person must have ownership of the property involved in the venture and the mutual right of control over that property.

Based on the evidence viewed in the light most favorable to Plaintiff, the Court finds that reasonable jurors could differ as to whether the Defendants had a contract to combine their money, property, time or skill in business operation and share profits in some fixed proportion.

As to the required element that each individual Defendant must have ownership of the property involved in the venture and the mutual right of control over that property, this is a closer question. However, assuming as true all facts which the prevailing party's evidence tended to prove, it would be reasonable to conclude that each individual Defendant had ownership over the property involved in the venture and the mutual right of control over that property.

The facts were in dispute as to whether each individual Defendant was engaged in the joint venture and it was for the jury to decide using the instructions the Court gave. Based on the evidence presented and viewed in the light most favorable to Plaintiff, the jury could have made an inference that each individual Defendant was engaged in a joint venture.

### Personal Liability of Hilburn

In addition to challenging the evidentiary basis for his personal liability as a promoter or joint venturer, Hilburn now asserts that the proper submission should have been whether Chain Link, the corporation, was the pre-incorporation promoter or joint venturer in Fashion Links. Hilburn argues that he can be individually liable only if PIML can "pierce the corporate veil" under the requisites of *Victoria Elevator Co. v. Meriden Grain Co.*, 283 N.W. 2d 509, 512 (Minn. 1979).

Hilburn's argument in this regard totally fails. Hilburn's individual liability under the theories of pre-incorporation promoter or joint venture liability does not require that the corporate veil be pierced. The jury found that Hilburn individually was a promoter and joint venturer separate and apart from Chain Link. The jury found that the contract at issue was between Plaintiff PIML and Fashion Links, not Chain Link.

At no time in extended pretrial proceedings, at the final pretrial, in proposed jury instructions, during final argument, or during oral motions under Rule 50 did the Defendant Hilburn even hint of an issue of piercing the corporate veil. This argument is of no merit and, in any event, it has been effectively waived.

\* \* \*

Renewed Motions for Judgment as a Matter of Law are DENIED.

## NOTE

One of the most advantageous characteristics of the corporate form is limited liability. Clearly, as evidenced by their later incorporation, the defendants sought to limit their personal liability. Should a business promoter receive less protection during the business' start-up period? Here, the court focuses upon the Defendants' representations as a partnership. While not part of the opinion, should the court have also focused on the plaintiff's reliance upon those representations? This concept will be revisited in Chapter 5.

## RNR INVESTMENTS LP v. PEOPLES FIRST COMMUNITY BANK
### Court of Appeals of Florida
### 812 So. 2d 561 (2002)

VAN NORTHWICK, J.

RNR Investments Limited Partnership (RNR) appeals a summary judgment of foreclosure granted in favor of appellee, Peoples First Community Bank (the Bank). RNR argues that the trial court erred in granting summary judgment because disputed issues of material fact remained with respect to one of RNR's affirmative defenses. In that affirmative defense, RNR alleged that the Bank was negligent in lending $960,000 to RNR without consent of the limited partners when, under RNR's Agreement of Limited Partnership, the authority of RNR's general partner was limited to obtaining financing up to $650,000. Under section 620.8301(1), Florida Statutes (2000), however, the Bank could rely upon the general partner's apparent authority to bind RNR, unless the Bank had actual knowledge or notice of his restricted authority. In opposing summary judgment, RNR produced no evidence showing that the Bank had actual knowledge or notice of restrictions imposed on the authority of RNR's general partner. Accordingly, no issues of material facts are in dispute and we affirm.

### Factual and Procedural History

RNR is a Florida limited partnership formed pursuant to chapter 620, Florida Statutes, to purchase vacant land in Destin, Florida, and to construct a house on the land for resale. Bernard Roeger was RNR's general partner and Heinz Rapp, Claus North, and S.E. Waltz, Inc., were limited partners. The agreement of limited partnership provides for various restrictions on the authority of the general partner. Paragraph 4.1 of the agreement required the general partner to prepare a budget covering the cost of acquisition and construction of the project (defined as the "Approved Budget") and further provided, in pertinent part, as follows:

> The Approved Budget for the Partnership is attached hereto as Exhibit "C" and is approved by evidence of the signatures of the Partners on the signature pages of this Agreement. . . . In no event, without Limited Partner Consent, shall the Approved Budget be exceeded by more than five percent (5%), nor shall any line item thereof be exceeded by more than ten percent (10%), . . .

Paragraph 4.3 restricted the general partner's ability to borrow, spend partnership funds and encumber partnership assets, if not specifically provided for in the Approved Budget. Finally, with respect to the development of the partnership project, paragraph 2.2(b) provided:

> The General Partner shall not incur debts, liabilities or obligations of the Partnership which will cause any line item in the Approved Budget to be exceeded by more than ten percent (10%) or which will cause the aggregate Approved Budget to be exceed by more than five percent (5%) unless the General Partner shall receive the prior written consent of the Limited Partner.

In June 1998, RNR, through its general partner, entered into a construction loan agreement, note and mortgage in the principal amount of $990,000. From June 25, 1998 through Mar. 13, 2000, the bank disbursed the aggregate sum of $952,699, by transfers into RNR's bank account. All draws were approved by an architect, who certified that the work had progressed as indicated and that the quality of the work was in accordance with the construction contract. No representative of RNR objected to any draw of funds or asserted that the amounts disbursed were not associated with the construction of the house.

RNR defaulted under the terms of the note and mortgage by failing to make payments due in July 2000 and all monthly payments due thereafter. The Bank filed a complaint seeking foreclosure. RNR filed an answer and affirmative defenses. In its first affirmative defense, RNR alleged that the Bank had failed to review the limitations on the general partner's authority in RNR's limited partnership agreement. RNR asserted that the Bank had negligently failed to investigate and to realize that the general partner had no authority to execute notes, a mortgage and a construction loan agreement and was estopped from foreclosing. The Bank filed a motion for summary judgment with supporting affidavits attesting to the amounts due and owing and the amount of disbursements under the loan.

In opposition to the summary judgment motion, RNR filed the affidavit of Stephen E. Waltz, the president one of RNR's limited partners, S.E. Waltz, Inc. In that affidavit, Mr. Waltz stated that the partners anticipated that RNR would need to finance the construction of the residence, but that paragraph 2.2(b) of the partnership agreement limited the amount of any loan the general partner could obtain on behalf of RNR to an amount that would not exceed by more than 10% the approved budget on any one line item or exceed the aggregate approved budget by more than 5%, unless the general partner received the prior written consent of the limited partners. Waltz alleged that the limited partners understood and orally agreed that the general partner would seek financing in the approximate amount of $650,000. Further, Waltz stated:

> Even though the limited partners had orally agreed to this amount, a written consent was never memorialized, and to my surprise, the [Bank], either through its employees or attorney, . . . never requested the same from any of the limited partners at any time prior to [or] after the closing on the loan from the [Bank] to RNR.

Waltz alleged that the partners learned in the spring of 2000 that, instead of obtaining a loan for $650,000, Roeger had obtained a loan for $990,000, which was secured by RNR's property. He stated that the limited partners did not consent to Roeger obtaining a loan from the Bank in the amount of $990,000 either orally or in writing and that the limited partners were never contacted by the Bank as to whether they had consented to a loan amount of $990,000.

RNR asserts that a copy of the limited partnership agreement was maintained at its offices. Nevertheless, the record contains no copy of an Approved Budget of the partnership or any evidence that would show that a copy of RNR's partnership agreement or any partnership budget was given to the Bank or that any notice of the general partner's restricted authority was provided to the Bank.

A hearing on the motion for summary judgment was held, however, a transcript of that hearing is not contained in the record. Thereafter, the trial court entered a summary final judgment of foreclosure in favor of the Bank. The foreclosure sale has been stayed pending the outcome of this appeal.

* * *

### Apparent Authority of the General Partner

Although the agency concept of apparent authority was applied to partnerships under the common law, *see, e.g., Taylor v. Cummer Lumber Co.*, 59 Fla. 638, 52 So. 614, 616 (1910), in Florida the extent to which the partnership is bound by the acts of a partner acting within the apparent authority is now governed by statute. Section 620.8301(1), Florida Statutes (2000)1, a part of the Florida Revised Uniform Partnership Act (FRUPA), provides:

> Each partner is an agent of the partnership for the purpose of its business. An act of a partner, including the execution of an instrument in the partnership name, for apparently carrying on in the ordinary scope of partnership business or business of the kind carried on by the partnership, in the geographic area in which the partnership operates, binds the partnership unless the partner had no authority to act for the partnership in the particular manner and the person with whom the partner was dealing knew or had received notification that the partner lacked authority.

Thus, even if a general partner's actual authority is restricted by the terms of the partnership agreement, the general partner possesses the apparent authority to bind the partnership in the ordinary course of partnership business or in the business of the kind carried on by the partnership, unless the third party "knew or had received a notification that the partner lacked authority." *Id.* "Knowledge" and "notice" under FRUPA are defined in section 620.8102. That section provides that "[a] person knows a fact if the person has actual knowledge of the fact." § 620.8102(1), Fla. Stat. (2000). Further, a third party has notice of a fact if that party "(a) [k]nows of the fact; (b) [h]as received notification of the fact; or (c) [h]as reason to know the fact exists from all other facts known to the person at the time in question." § 620.8102(2), Fla. Stat. (2000). Finally, under section 620.8303 a partnership may file a statement of partnership authority setting forth any restrictions in a general partner's authority.

Commentators have described the purpose of these knowledge and notice provisions, as follows:

> Under RUPA, the term knew is confined to actual knowledge, which is cognitive awareness. . . . Therefore, despite the similarity in language, RUPA provides greater protection [than the Uniform Partnership Act (UPA)] to third persons dealing with partners, who may rely on the partner's apparent authority absent actual knowledge or notification of a restriction in this regard. RUPA effects a slight reallocation of the risk of unauthorized agency power in favor of third parties. That is consistent with notions of the expanded liability of principals since the UPA was drafted.

> RUPA attempts to balance its shift toward greater protection of third parties by providing several new ways for partners to protect themselves against unauthorized actions by a rogue partner. First, the partnership may notify a third party of a partner's lack of authority. Such notification is effective upon receipt, whether or not the third party actually learns of it. More significantly, the partnership may file a statement of partnership authority restricting a partner's authority.

Donald J. Weidner & John W. Larson, *The Revised Uniform Partnership Act: The Reporters' Overview*, 49 BUS. LAW 1, 31–32 (1993) (footnotes omitted). "Absent actual knowledge, third parties have no duty to inspect the partnership agreement or inquire otherwise to ascertain the extent of a partner's actual authority in the ordinary course of business, . . . even if they have some reason to question it." *Id.* at 32 n. 200. The apparent authority provisions of section 620.8301(1), reflect a policy by the drafters that "the risk of loss from partner misconduct more appropriately belongs on the partnership than on third parties who do not knowingly participate in or take advantage of the misconduct . . . " J. Dennis Hayes, *Notice and Notification Under the Revised Uniform Partnership Act: Some Suggested Changes*, 2 J. SMALL & EMERGING BUS. L. 299, 308 (1998).

### Analysis

Under section 620.8301(1), the determination of whether a partner is acting with authority to bind the partnership involves a two-step analysis. The first step is to determine whether the partner purporting to bind the partnership apparently is carrying on the partnership business in the usual way or a business of the kind carried on by the partnership. An affirmative answer on this step ends the inquiry, unless it is shown that the person with whom the partner is dealing actually knew or had received a notification that the partner lacked authority. *See Kristerin Dev. Co. v. Granson Inv.*, 394 N.W.2d 325, 330 (Iowa 1986) (applying Iowa version of UPA). Here, it is undisputed that, in entering into the loan, the general partner was carrying on the business of RNR in the usual way. The dispositive question in this appeal is whether there are issues of material fact as to whether the Bank had actual knowledge or notice of restrictions on the general partner's authority.

RNR argues that, as a result of the restrictions on the general partner's authority in the partnership agreement, the Bank had constructive knowledge of the restrictions and was obligated to inquire as to the general partner's specific authority to bind RNR in the construction loan. We cannot agree. Under section 620.8301, the Bank could rely on the general partner's apparent authority, unless it had actual knowledge or notice of restrictions on that authority. While the RNR partners may have agreed upon restrictions that would limit the general partner to borrowing no more than $650,000 on behalf of the partnership, RNR does not contend and nothing before us would show that the Bank had actual knowledge or notice of any restrictions on the general partner's authority. Here, the partnership could have protected itself by filing a statement pursuant to section 620.8303 or by providing notice to the Bank of the specific restrictions on the authority of the general partner.

RNR relies on *Green River Assocs. v. Mark Twain Kansas City Bank*, 808 S.W.2d 894 (Mo. Ct. App. 1991), as authority for its argument that the Bank was negligent in providing financing in reliance upon the apparent authority of the general partner. RNR's reliance is misplaced. In *Green River*, the express language of the partnership agreement, known to the bank, required that the proceeds of the loan be deposited in the partnership bank account. The court found that, when the bank wired partnership money to an account of an entity other than the partnership, the bank knew that its actions were contrary to the partnership agreement. Therefore, the court reasoned, the bank could not argue that the general partner had apparent authority to direct the bank to disburse the funds to a non-partnership account. As a result, because the bank paid the loan proceeds to an entity other than the borrower, the court concluded that the partnership's note was void for lack of consideration. Interestingly, Green River rejected the partnership's claim based upon the bank's alleged negligence. Here, unlike Green River, all funds advanced by the Bank were paid into RNR's account. There is no basis for arguing a failure of consideration. Further, there is no fact in the record that would show that the Bank had actual knowledge or notice of restrictions on the general partner's authority.

Because there is no disputed issue of fact concerning whether the Bank had actual knowledge or notice of restrictions on the general partner's authority to borrow, summary judgment was proper.

AFFIRMED.

MINER AND WOLF, JJ., concur.

# NOTES

**1.** Consider how the apparent authority of a general partner differs from that of an agent in an ordinary principal-agent relationship. To state the question another way, would the court have found that Roeger, the general partner, had apparent authority if he had been acting on behalf of an individual and not a limited partnership?

**2.** As the court notes, a limited partnership is simply a sub-category of the general partnership and is governed by the provisions of the Florida Uniform Partnership Act, except to the extent that provisions of the Florida Uniform Limited Partnership Act are applicable. Thus, while limited partners have no management rights, general partners in a limited partnership have the same management rights as in a general partnership.

**3.** The court correctly determines that case is governed by section 303 of the Revised Uniform Partnership Act. This act, often referred to as RUPA, first became effective in 1997 and has currently been adopted by a majority of states. However, the original Uniform Partnership Act, drafted in 1914, remains in effect in a substantial minority of states. The corresponding provision in UPA (1914) is section 9(1) which provides:

> Every partner is an agent of the partnership for the purpose of its business, and the act of every partner, including the execution in the partnership name of any instrument, for apparently carrying on in the usual way the business of the partnership of which he is a member bind the partnership, unless the partner so acting has in fact no authority to act for the partnership in the particular matter, and the person with whom he is dealing has knowledge of the fact that he has no such authority.

Would this provision have changed the outcome of the *RNR* case?

## MOREN v. JAX RESTAURANT
### Court of Appeals of Minnesota
### 679 N.W.2d 165 (2004)

CRIPPEN, JUDGE.

Remington Moren, through his father, commenced a negligence action against appellant Jax Restaurant for injuries he sustained while on appellant's premises. The district court granted a summary judgment, dismissing appellant's third-party negligence complaint against respondent Nicole Moren, a partner in Jax Restaurant and the mother of Remington Moren. Because the court correctly determined that liability for Nicole Moren's negligence rested with the partnership, even if the partner's conduct partly served her personal interests, we affirm.

### FACTS

Jax Restaurant, the partnership, operates its business in Foley, Minnesota. One afternoon in October 2000, Nicole Moren, one of the Jax partners, completed her day shift at Jax at 4:00 p.m. and left to pick up her two-year-old son Remington from day care. At about 5:30, Moren returned to the restaurant with Remington after learning that her sister and partner, Amy Benedetti, needed help. Moren called her husband who told her that he would pick Remington up in about 20 minutes.

Because Nicole Moren did not want Remington running around the restaurant, she brought him into the kitchen with her, set him on top of the counter, and began rolling out pizza dough using the dough-pressing machine. As she was making pizzas, Remington reached his hand into the dough press. His hand was crushed, and he sustained permanent injuries.

Through his father, Remington commenced a negligence action against the partnership. The partnership served a third-party complaint on Nicole Moren, arguing that, in the event it was obligated to compensate Remington, the partnership was entitled to indemnity or contribution from Moren for her negligence. The district court's summary judgment was premised on a legal conclusion that Moren has no obligation to indemnify Jax Restaurant so long as the injury occurred while she was engaged in ordinary business conduct. The district court rejected the partnership's argument that its obligation to compensate Remington is diminished in proportion to the predominating negligence of Moren as a mother, although it is responsible for her conduct as a business owner. This appeal followed.

## ISSUE

Does Jax Restaurant have an indemnity right against Nicole Moren in the circumstances of this case?

## ANALYSIS

\*   \*   \*

Under Minnesota's Uniform Partnership Act of 1994 (UPA), a partnership is an entity distinct from its partners, and as such, a partnership may sue and be sued in the name of the partnership. Minn. Stat. §§ 323A.2-10, 323A.3-07 and 323A.12-01 (2002). "A partnership is liable for loss or injury caused to a person . . . as a result of a wrongful act or omission, or other actionable conduct, of a partner acting in the ordinary course of business of the partnership or with authority of the partnership." Minn. Stat. § 323A.3-05(a) (2002); see also *Bedow v. Watkins*, 552 N.W.2d 543, 546 (Minn.1996); *Shetka v. Kueppers, Kueppers, Von Feldt, & Salmen*, 454 N.W.2d 916, 919 (Minn.1990). Accordingly, a "partnership shall . . . indemnify a partner for liabilities incurred by the partner in the ordinary course of the business of the partnership. . . . " Minn. Stat. § 323A.4-01(c) (2002). Stated conversely, an "act of a partner which is not apparently for carrying on in the ordinary course the partnership business or business of the kind carried on by the partnership binds the partnership only if the act was authorized by the other partners." Minn. Stat. § 323A.3-01(2) (2002). Thus, under the plain language of the UPA, a partner has a right to indemnity from the partnership, but the partnership's claim of indemnity from a partner is not authorized or required.

The district court correctly concluded that Nicole Moren's conduct was in the ordinary course of business of the partnership and, as a result, indemnity by the partner to the partnership was inappropriate. It is undisputed that one of the cooks scheduled to work that evening did not come in, and that Moren's partner asked her to help in the kitchen. It also is undisputed that Moren was making pizzas for the partnership when her son was injured. Because her conduct at the time of the injury was in the ordinary course of business of the partnership, under the UPA, her conduct bound the partnership and it owes indemnity to her for her negligence. Minn. Stat. §§ 323A.3-05(a) and 323A.4-01(c).

Appellant heavily relies on one foreign case for the proposition that a partnership is entitled to a contribution or indemnity from a partner who is negligent. See *Flynn v. Reaves*, 135 Ga. App. 651, 218 S.E.2d 661 (1975). In *Flynn*, the Georgia

Court of Appeals held that "where a partner is sued individually by a plaintiff injured by the partner's sole negligence, the partner cannot seek contribution from his co-partners even though the negligent act occurred in the course of the partnership business."*Id.* at 663. But this case is inapplicable because the Georgia court applied common law partnership and agency principles and, like appellant, makes no mention of the UPA, which is the law in Minnesota.

Appellant also claims that because Nicole Moren's action of bringing Remington into the kitchen was partly motivated by personal reasons, her conduct was outside the ordinary course of business. Because it has not been previously addressed, there is no Minnesota authority regarding this issue. But there are two cases from outside of Minnesota that address the issue in a persuasive fashion. *Grotelueschen v. Am. Family Ins. Co.*, 171 Wis.2d 437, 492 N.W.2d 131, 137 (1992) (An "act can further part personal and part business purposes and still occur in the ordinary course of the partnership."); *Wolfe v. Harms*, 413 S.W.2d 204, 215 (Mo.1967) ("[E]ven if the predominant motive of the partner was to benefit himself or third persons, such does not prevent the concurrent business purpose from being within the scope of the partnership."). Adopting this rationale, we conclude that the conduct of Nicole Moren was no less in the ordinary course of business because it also served personal purposes. It is undisputed that Moren was acting for the benefit of the partnership by making pizzas when her son was injured, and even though she was simultaneously acting in her role as a mother, her conduct remained in the ordinary course of the partnership business.

The district court determined, and appellant strenuously disputes, that Amy Benedetti authorized Nicole's conduct, or at least that her conduct of bringing Remington into the kitchen was not prohibited by the rules of the partnership. Because under Minnesota law authorization from the other partners is merely an alternative basis for establishing partnership liability, we decline to address the issue of whether Nicole Moren's partner authorized her conduct.[1]

## DECISION

Because Minnesota law requires a partnership to indemnify its partners for the result of their negligence, the district court properly granted summary judgment to respondent Nicole Moren. In addition, we conclude that the conduct of a partner may be partly motivated by personal reasons and still occur in the ordinary course of business of the partnership.

Affirmed.

---

[1] [1] As stated earlier, under Minn. Stat. § 323A.3-05 a "partnership is liable for loss or injury caused to a person . . . as a result of a wrongful act . . . of a partner acting in the ordinary course of business of the partnership or with authority of the partnership." And under Minn. Stat. § 323A. 4-01(c) a partnership must indemnify a partner for liabilities incurred by the partner in the ordinary course of the business of the partnership.

# NOTE

Consider whether the rights of indemnification of a partnership against a partner are the same as those of a principal against an agent. For example, if A, who is running an errand at the request of her principal, negligently causes an automobile accident, she may be called upon to indemnify the principal. RESTATEMENT (SECOND) OF AGENCY § 401. However, if A is a partner and has the accident while pursuing partnership business, the *Moren* case indicates that the partnership may not obtain indemnification. Does this distinction make sense?

## BOHATCH v. BUTLER & BINION
Supreme Court of Texas
977 S.W.2d 543 (1998)

ENOCH, JUSTICE.

Partnerships exist by the agreement of the partners; partners have no duty to remain partners. The issue in this case is whether we should create an exception to this rule by holding that a partnership has a duty not to expel a partner for reporting suspected overbilling by another partner. The trial court rendered judgment for Colette Bohatch on her breach of fiduciary duty claim against Butler & Binion and several of its partners (collectively, "the firm"). The court of appeals held that there was no evidence that the firm breached a fiduciary duty and reversed the trial court's tort judgment; however, the court of appeals found evidence of a breach of the partnership agreement and rendered judgment for Bohatch on this ground. 905 S.W.2d 597. We affirm the court of appeals' judgment.

Bohatch became an associate in the Washington, D.C., office of Butler & Binion in 1986 after working for several years as Deputy Assistant General Counsel at the Federal Energy Regulatory Commission. John McDonald, the managing partner of the office, and Richard Powers, a partner, were the only other attorneys in the Washington office. The office did work for Pennzoil almost exclusively.

Bohatch was made partner in February 1990. She then began receiving internal firm reports showing the number of hours each attorney worked, billed, and collected. From her review of these reports, Bohatch became concerned that McDonald was overbilling Pennzoil and discussed the matter with Powers. Together they reviewed and copied portions of McDonald's time diary. Bohatch's review of McDonald's time entries increased her concern.

On July 15, 1990, Bohatch met with Louis Paine, the firm's managing partner, to report her concern that McDonald was overbilling Pennzoil. Paine said he would investigate. Later that day, Bohatch told Powers about her conversation with Paine.

The following day, McDonald met with Bohatch and informed her that Pennzoil was not satisfied with her work and wanted her work to be supervised. Bohatch testified that this was the first time she had ever heard criticism of her work for Pennzoil. The next day, Bohatch repeated her concerns to Paine and to R. Hayden Burns and Marion E. McDaniel, two other members of the firm's management committee, in a telephone conversation. Over the next month, Paine and Burns investigated Bohatch's complaint. They reviewed the Pennzoil bills and supporting computer print-outs for those bills. They then discussed the allegations with Pennzoil in-house counsel John Chapman, the firm's primary contact with Pennzoil. Chapman, who had a long-standing relationship with McDonald, responded that Pennzoil was satisfied that the bills were reasonable.

In August, Paine met with Bohatch and told her that the firm's investigation revealed no basis for her contentions. He added that she should begin looking for other employment, but that the firm would continue to provide her a monthly draw, insurance coverage, office space, and a secretary. After this meeting, Bohatch received no further work assignments from the firm.

In January 1991, the firm denied Bohatch a year-end partnership distribution for 1990 and reduced her tentative distribution share for 1991 to zero. In June, the firm paid Bohatch her monthly draw and told her that this draw would be her last. Finally, in August, the firm gave Bohatch until November to vacate her office.

By September, Bohatch had found new employment. She filed this suit on October 18, 1991, and the firm voted formally to expel her from the partnership three days later, October 21, 1991.

The trial court granted partial summary judgment for the firm on Bohatch's wrongful discharge claim, and also on her breach of fiduciary duty and breach of the duty of good faith and fair dealing claims for any conduct occurring after October 21, 1991 (the date Bohatch was formally expelled from the firm). The trial court denied the firm's summary judgment motion on Bohatch's breach of fiduciary duty and breach of the duty of good faith and fair dealing claims for conduct occurring before October 21, 1991. The breach of fiduciary duty claim and a breach of contract claim were tried to a jury. The jury found that the firm breached the partnership agreement and its fiduciary duty. It awarded Bohatch $57,000 for past lost wages, $250,000 for past mental anguish, $4,000,000 total in punitive damages (this amount was apportioned against several defendants), and attorney's fees. The trial court rendered judgment for Bohatch in the amounts found by the jury, except it disallowed attorney's fees because the judgment was based in tort. After suggesting remittitur, which Bohatch accepted, the trial court reduced the punitive damages to around $237,000.

All parties appealed. The court of appeals held that the firm's only duty to Bohatch was not to expel her in bad faith. The court of appeals stated that " 'bad faith' in this context means only that partners cannot expel another partner for self-gain." Id. Finding no evidence that the firm expelled Bohatch for self-gain, the court concluded that Bohatch could not recover for breach of fiduciary duty. However, the court concluded that the firm breached the partnership agreement when it reduced Bohatch's tentative partnership distribution for 1991 to zero without notice, and when it terminated her draw three months before she left. The court concluded that Bohatch was entitled to recover $35,000 in lost earnings for 1991 but none for 1990, and no mental anguish damages. Accordingly, the court rendered judgment for Bohatch for $35,000 plus $225,000 in attorney's fees.

We have long recognized as a matter of common law that "[t]he relationship between . . . partners . . . is fiduciary in character, and imposes upon all the participants the obligation of loyalty to the joint concern and of the utmost good faith, fairness, and honesty in their dealings with each other with respect to matters pertaining to the enterprise." *Fitz–Gerald v. Hull*, 150 Tex. 39, 237 S.W.2d 256, 264 (1951) (quotation omitted). Yet, partners have no obligation to remain partners; "at the heart of the partnership concept is the principle that partners may choose with whom they wish to be associated." *Gelder Med. Group v. Webber*, 41 N.Y.2d 680, 394 N.Y.S.2d 867, 870–71, 363 N.E.2d 573, 577 (1977). The issue presented, one of first impression, is whether the fiduciary relationship between and among partners creates an exception to the at-will nature of partnerships; that is, in this case, whether it gives rise to a duty not to expel a partner who reports suspected overbilling by another partner.

At the outset, we note that no party questions that the obligations of lawyers licensed to practice in the District of Columbia — including McDonald and Bohatch — were prescribed by the District of Columbia Code of Professional Responsibility in effect in 1990, and that in all other respects Texas law applies. Further, neither statutory nor contract law principles answer the question of whether the firm owed Bohatch a duty not to expel her. The Texas Uniform Partnership Act, Tex. Rev. Civ. Stat. Ann. art. 6701b, addresses expulsion of a partner only in the context of dissolution of the partnership. *See id.* §§ 31, 38. In this case, as provided by the partnership agreement, Bohatch's expulsion did not dissolve the partnership. Additionally, the new Texas Revised Partnership Act, Tex.Rev.Civ. Stat. Ann. art. 6701b–1.01 to –11.04, does not have retroactive effect and thus does not apply. *See id.* art. 6701b–11.03. Finally, the partnership agreement contemplates expulsion of a partner and prescribes procedures to be followed, but it does not specify or limit the grounds for expulsion. Thus, while Bohatch's claim that she was expelled in an improper way is governed by the partnership agreement, her claim that she was expelled for an improper reason is not. Therefore, we look to the common law to find the principles governing Bohatch's claim that the firm breached a duty when it expelled her.

*   *   *

The fiduciary duty that partners owe one another does not encompass a duty to remain partners or else answer in tort damages. Nonetheless, Bohatch and several distinguished legal scholars urge this Court to recognize that public policy requires a limited duty to remain partners — i.e., a partnership must retain a whistleblower partner. They argue that such an extension of a partner's fiduciary duty is necessary because permitting a law firm to retaliate against a partner who in good faith reports suspected overbilling would discourage compliance with rules of professional conduct and thereby hurt clients.

While this argument is not without some force, we must reject it. A partnership exists solely because the partners choose to place personal confidence and trust in one another. *See Holman*, 522 P.2d at 524 ("The foundation of a professional relationship is personal confidence and trust."). Just as a partner can be expelled, without a breach of any common law duty, over disagreements about firm policy or to resolve some other "fundamental schism," a partner can be expelled for accusing another partner of overbilling without subjecting the partnership to tort damages. Such charges, whether true or not, may have a profound effect on the personal confidence and trust essential to the partner relationship. Once such charges are made, partners may find it impossible to continue to work together to their mutual benefit and the benefit of their clients.

We are sensitive to the concern expressed by the dissenting Justices that "retaliation against a partner who tries in good faith to correct or report perceived misconduct virtually assures that others will not take these appropriate steps in the future." 977 S.W.2d at 561 (SPECTOR, J., dissenting). However, the dissenting Justices do not explain how the trust relationship necessary both for the firm's existence and for representing clients can survive such serious accusations by one partner against another. The threat of tort liability for expulsion would tend to force partners to remain in untenable circumstance — suspicious of and angry with each other — to their own detriment and that of their clients whose matters are neglected by lawyers distracted with intra-firm frictions.

Although concurring in the Court's judgment, Justice Hecht criticizes the Court for failing to "address amici's concerns that failing to impose liability will discourage attorneys from reporting unethical conduct." . . . To address the scholars' concerns, he proposes that a whistleblower be protected from expulsion, but only if the report, irrespective of being made in good faith, is proved to be correct. We fail to see how such an approach encourages compliance with ethical rules more than the approach we adopt today. Furthermore, the amici's position is that a reporting attorney must be in good faith, not that the attorney must be right. In short, Justice Hecht's approach ignores the question Bohatch presents, the amici write about, and the firm challenges — whether a partnership violates a fiduciary duty when it expels a partner who in good faith reports suspected ethical violations. The concerns of the amici are best addressed by a rule that clearly demarcates an attorney's ethical duties and the parameters of tort liability, rather than redefining "whistleblower."

We emphasize that our refusal to create an exception to the at-will nature of partnerships in no way obviates the ethical duties of lawyers. Such duties sometimes necessitate difficult decisions, as when a lawyer suspects overbilling by a colleague. The fact that the ethical duty to report may create an irreparable schism between partners neither excuses failure to report nor transforms expulsion as a means of resolving that schism into a tort.

We hold that the firm did not owe Bohatch a duty not to expel her for reporting suspected overbilling by another partner.

The court of appeals concluded that the firm breached the partnership agreement by reducing Bohatch's tentative distribution for 1991 to zero without the requisite notice. 905 S.W.2d at 606. The firm contests this finding on the ground that the management committee had the right to set tentative and year-end bonuses. However, the partnership agreement guarantees a monthly draw of $7,500 per month regardless of the tentative distribution. Moreover, the firm's right to reduce the bonus was contingent upon providing proper notice to Bohatch. The firm does not dispute that it did not give Bohatch notice that the firm was reducing her tentative distribution. Accordingly, the court of appeals did not err in finding the firm liable for breach of the partnership agreement. Moreover, because Bohatch's damages sound in contract, and because she sought attorney's fees at trial . . ., we affirm the court of appeals' award of Bohatch's attorney's fees.

\*   \*   \*

We affirm the court of appeals' judgment.

JUSTICE HECHT, concurring in the judgment.

The Court holds that partners in a law firm have no common-law liability for expelling one of their number for accusing another of unethical conduct. The dissent argues that partners in a law firm are liable for such conduct. Both views are unqualified; neither concedes or even considers whether "always" and "never" are separated by any distance. I think they must be. The Court's position is directly contrary to that of some of the leading scholars on the subject who have appeared here as amici curiae. The Court finds amici's arguments "not without some force", but rejects them completely. I do not believe amici's arguments can be rejected out of hand. The dissent, on the other hand, refuses even to acknowledge the serious impracticalities involved in maintaining the trust necessary between partners when one has accused another of unethical conduct. In the dissent's view, partners who would expel another for such accusations must simply either get over it or respond in damages. The dissent's view blinks reality.

The issue is not well developed; in fact, to our knowledge we are the first court to address it. It seems to me there must be some circumstances when expulsion for reporting an ethical violation is culpable and other circumstances when it is not. I have trouble justifying a 500-partner firm's expulsion of a partner for reporting overbilling of a client that saves the firm not only from ethical complaints but from liability to the client. But I cannot see how a five-partner firm can legitimately survive one partner's accusations that another is unethical. Between two such extreme examples I see a lot of ground.

This case does not force a choice between diametrically opposite views. Here, the report of unethical conduct, though made in good faith, was incorrect. That fact is significant to me because I think a law firm can always expel a partner for bad judgment, whether it relates to the representation of clients or the relationships with other partners, and whether it is in good faith. I would hold that Butler & Binion did not breach its fiduciary duty by expelling Colette Bohatch because she made a good-faith but nevertheless extremely serious charge against a senior partner that threatened the firm's relationship with an important client, her charge proved groundless, and her relationship with her partners was destroyed in the process. I cannot, however, extrapolate from this case, as the Court does, that no law firm can ever be liable for expelling a partner for reporting unethical conduct. Accordingly, I concur only in the Court's judgment.

\*   \*   \*

Scholars are divided over not only how but whether partners' common-law fiduciary duty to each other limit expulsion of a partner.

\*   \*   \*

But I am troubled by the arguments of the distinguished amici curiae that permitting a law firm to retaliate against a partner for reporting unethical behavior would discourage compliance with rules of conduct, hurt clients, and contravene public policy. Their arguments have force, but they do not explain how a relationship of trust necessary for both the existence of the firm and the representation of its clients can survive such serious accusations by one partner against another. The threat of liability for expulsion would tend to force partners to remain in untenable circumstances — suspicious of and angry with each other — to their own detriment and that of their clients whose matters are neglected by lawyers distracted with intra-firm frictions. If "at the heart of the partnership concept is the principle that partners may choose with whom they wish to be associated," . . . surely partners are not obliged to continue to associate with someone who has accused one of them of unethical conduct.

\*    \*    \*

Butler & Binion's expulsion of Bohatch did not discourage ethical conduct; it discouraged errors of judgment, which ought to be discouraged. Butler & Binion did not violate its fiduciary duty to Bohatch.

\*    \*    \*

I do not disagree with the Court's treatment of Bohatch's claim for breach of contract. Accordingly, I concur in the Court's judgment but not in its opinion.

JUSTICE SPECTOR, joined by CHIEF JUSTICE PHILLIPS, dissenting.

> What's the use you learning to do right when it's troublesome to do right and ain't no trouble to do wrong, and the wages is just the same?

> –*The Adventures of Huckleberry Finn*

The issue in this appeal is whether law partners violate a fiduciary duty by retaliating against one partner for questioning the billing practices of another partner. I would hold that partners violate their fiduciary duty to one another by punishing compliance with the Disciplinary Rules of Professional Conduct. Accordingly, I dissent.

\*    \*    \*

The majority views the partnership relationship among lawyers as strictly business. I disagree. The practice of law is a profession first, then a business. Moreover, it is a self-regulated profession subject to the Rules promulgated by this Court.

As attorneys, we take an oath to "honestly demean [ourselves] in the practice of law; and . . . discharge [our] duty to [our] client[s] to the best of [our] ability." TEX. GOV'T CODE § 82.037 (emphasis added). This oath of honesty and duty is not mere "self-adulatory bombast" but mandated by the Legislature. *See Schware v. Board of Bar Exam'rs*, 353 U.S. 232, 247, 77 S. Ct. 752, 760–761, 1 L. Ed. 2d 796 (FRANKFURTER, J. concurring) (noting that the rhetoric used to describe the esteemed role of the legal profession has real meaning). As attorneys, we bear responsibilities to our clients and the bar itself that transcend ordinary business relationships.

It is true that no high court has considered the issue of whether expulsion of a partner for complying with ethical rules violates law partners' fiduciary duty. The dearth of authority in this area does not, however, diminish the significance of this case. Instead, the scarcity of guiding case law only heightens the importance of this Court's decision.

\* \* \*

The duty to prevent overbilling and other misconduct exists for the protection of the client. Even if a report turns out to be mistaken or a client ultimately consents to the behavior in question, as in this case, retaliation against a partner who tries in good faith to correct or report perceived misconduct virtually assures that others will not take these appropriate steps in the future. Although I agree with the majority that partners have a right not to continue a partnership with someone against their will, they may still be liable for damages directly resulting from terminating that relationship.

\* \* \*

The Court's writing in this case sends an inappropriate signal to lawyers and to the public that the rules of professional responsibility are subordinate to a law firm's other interests. Under the majority opinion's vision for the legal profession, the wages would not even be the same for "doing right"; they diminish considerably and leave an attorney who acts ethically and in good faith without recourse. Accordingly, I respectfully dissent.

# NOTE

Justice Hecht points out that the law firm had 500 partners. Why is that fact relevant? Is it wise to have a rule that encourages partners to report unethical conduct to the firm, even if the report is incorrect?

## BANE v. FERGUESON
United States Court of Appeals, Seventh Circuit
890 F.2d 11 (1989)

POSNER, CIRCUIT JUDGE

The question presented by this appeal from the dismissal of the complaint (see 707 F. Supp. 988 (N.D. Ill. 1989)) is whether a retired partner in a law firm has either a common law or a statutory claim against the firm's managing council for acts of negligence that, by causing the firm to dissolve, terminate his retirement benefits. It is a diversity case governed by the law of Illinois, rather than a federal-question case governed by the Employee Retirement Income Security Act, 29 U.S.C. §§ 1001 et seq., because ERISA excludes partners from its protections.

Charles Bane practiced corporate and public utility law as a partner in the venerable Chicago law firm of Isham, Lincoln & Beale, founded more than a century ago by Abraham Lincoln's son Robert Todd Lincoln. In August 1985 the firm adopted a noncontributory retirement plan that entitled every retiring partner to a pension, the amount depending on his earnings from the firm on the eve of retirement. The plan instrument provided that the plan, and the payments under it, would end when and if the firm dissolved without a successor entity, and also that the amount paid out in pension benefits each year could not exceed five percent of the firm's net income in the preceding year. Four months after the plan was adopted, the plaintiff retired, moved to Florida with his wife, and began drawing his pension (to continue until his wife's death if he died first) of $27,483 a year. Bane was 72 years old when he retired. So far as appears, he had, apart from social security, no significant source of income other than the pension.

Several months after Bane's retirement, Isham, Lincoln & Beale merged with Reuben & Proctor, another large and successful Chicago firm. The merger proved to be a disaster, and the merged firm was dissolved in April 1988 without a successor-whereupon the payment of pension benefits to Bane ceased and he brought this suit. The suit alleges that the defendants were the members of the firm's managing council in the period leading up to the dissolution and that they acted unreasonably in deciding to merge the firm with Reuben & Procter, in purchasing computers and other office equipment, and in leaving the firm for greener pastures shortly before its dissolution. The suit does not allege that the defendants committed fraud, engaged in self-dealing, or deliberately sought to destroy or damage the law firm or harm the plaintiff; the charge is negligent mismanagement, not deliberate wrongdoing. The suit seeks damages, presumably the present value of the pension benefits to which the Banes would be entitled had the firm not dissolved.

\* \* \*

Bane has four theories of liability. The first is that the defendants, by committing acts of mismanagement that resulted in the dissolution of the firm, violated the Uniform Partnership Act, Ill.Rev.Stat. ch. 106 ½, ¶ 9(3)(c), which provides that "unless authorized by the other partners . . . one or more but less than all the partners have no authority to: Do any . . . act which would make it impossible to carry on the ordinary business of the partnership." This provision is inapplicable. Its purpose is not to make negligent partners liable to persons with whom the partnership transacts (such as Bane), but to limit the liability of the other partners for the unauthorized act of one partner. See *Hackney v. Johnson*, 601 S.W.2d 523, 525 (Tex. Civ. App. 1980). The purpose in other words is to protect partners. Bane ceased to be a partner when he retired in 1985.

Nor can Bane obtain legal relief on the theory that the defendants violated a fiduciary duty to him; they had none. A partner is a fiduciary of his partners, but not of his former partners, for the withdrawal of a partner terminates the partnership as to him. *Adams v. Jarvis*, 23 Wis. 2d 453, 458, 127 N.W.2d 400, 403 (1964). Bane must look elsewhere for the grounds of a fiduciary obligation running from his former partners to himself. The pension plan did not establish a trust, and even if, notwithstanding the absence of one, the plan's managers were fiduciaries of its beneficiaries (there are myriad sources of fiduciary duty besides a trust), the mismanagement was not of the plan but of the firm. There is no suggestion that the defendants failed to inform the plaintiff of his rights under the plan or miscalculated his benefits or mismanaged or misapplied funds set aside for the plan's beneficiaries; no funds were set aside for them. Even if the defendants were fiduciaries of the plaintiff, moreover, the business-judgment rule would shield them from liability for mere negligence in the operation of the firm, just as it would shield a corporation's directors and officers, who are fiduciaries of the shareholders. *See Cottle v. Hilton Hotels Corp.*, 635 F. Supp. 1094, 1099 (N.D. Ill. 1986).

That leaves for discussion Bane's claims of breach of contract and of tort. The plan instrument expressly decrees the death of the plan upon the dissolution of the firm, and nowhere is there expressed a commitment or even an undertaking to maintain the firm in existence, whether for the sake of the plan's beneficiaries or anyone else. Contracts have implicit as well as explicit terms, *see, e.g., Foster Enterprises, Inc. v. Germania Federal Savings & Loan Ass'n*, 97 Ill. App. 3d 22, 28, 52 Ill. Dec. 303, 308, 421 N.E.2d 1375, 1380 (1981); *Wood v. Duff-Gordon*, 222 N.Y. 88, 118 N.E. 214 (1917) (CARDOZO, J.), and one can imagine an argument that the plaintiff was induced to retire by an implied promise that the managing council would do everything possible to keep the firm going-that without such an implied promise he would not have retired, given his dependence on the firm's retirement plan for his income after he retired. But Bane does not make this argument and anyway it is hopeless. The plan required partners to retire by age 72, an age Bane had already reached when the plan was adopted. Were there no such requirement the question would be whether, by the creation of the retirement plan, the partnership impliedly undertook to insure the retired partners, out of the personal assets of the members of the managing council, against any cessation of retirement benefits that was due to mismanagement by the council which contributed to the demise of the firm. To state the question is to answer it. *See Cowles v. Morris & Co.*, 330 Ill. 11, 161 N.E. 150 (1928).

The last question, which is the most interesting because the most fundamental, is whether the defendants violated a duty of care to the plaintiff founded on general principles of tort law. What is the liability of the managers of a failed enterprise to persons harmed by the failure? When a large firm-whether a law firm, or a manufacturing enterprise, or a bank, or a railroad-fails, and shuts its doors, many persons besides the owners of the firm may be hurt in their pocketbooks-workers, suppliers, suppliers' workers, creditors (like Mr. Bane), and members of these persons' families. The collapse of Isham, Lincoln & Beale calls to mind Rosencrantz's metaphor of the "massy wheel/ Fixed on the summit of the highest mount,/ To whose huge spokes ten thousand lesser things/ Are mortised and adjoined, which when it falls/ Each small annexment, petty consequence,/ Attends the boisterous ruin." (Hamlet, Act III, sc. 3.) We can find no precedent in Illinois law or elsewhere for imposing tort liability on careless managers for the financial consequences of the collapse of the firm to all who are hurt by that collapse. "The act of dissolution of a corporation is not in itself sufficient foundation for [a] tort action even if it results in the breach of contracts. If the dissolution is motivated by good faith judgment for the benefit of the corporation rather than personal gain of the officers, directors or shareholders, no liability attaches to the dissolution." *Swager v. Couri*, 60 Ill. App. 3d 192, 196, 17 Ill. Dec. 457, 460, 376 N.E.2d 456, 459 (1978) (citations omitted). The competence, not the good faith, of the defendants is drawn in question by the complaint. And the principle of *Swager* is as applicable to a partnership as to a corporation.

There are a number of reasons for the principle. The dissolution of a firm is a loss to some but a gain to others-competitors and their employees, suppliers, and other dependents. Unless the gainers can be forced to disgorge their gains-and they cannot-full liability to the losers will result in overdeterrence. In addition, potential victims of a firm's dissolution can protect themselves through contract, and therefore do not need the protection of tort law; people should be encouraged to protect themselves through voluntary transactions rather than to look to tort law to repair the consequences of their improvidence. Finally, so massive and uncertain a contingent liability would be difficult to quantify, and hence difficult and costly to insure against, and as a result it might curtail risk-taking and entrepreneurship. Concretely, the threat of such liability in the present case might have deterred any partner from accepting election to the managing council of Isham, Lincoln & Beale and might have deterred the firm from establishing the retirement plan at all-the benefits of which were then so cruelly, but not maliciously, cut off.

We are sorry about the financial blow to the Banes but we agree with the district judge that there is no remedy under the law of Illinois.

Affirmed.

# NOTE

Isn't it obvious that the Illinois version of the UPA section 9(3)(c) is irrelevant to the facts of this case? Do the partners of a firm owe a fiduciary duty to retired partners? Judge Posner tells us that the business judgment rule shields partners from mere negligence. Where does it say that in the UPA? Do partners owe each other a duty of care? If so, is the standard more than ordinary negligence? Should partners have the business judgment rule to protect them if shareholders have it?

# FROST v. SPENCER
## Supreme Court of Alaska
### 218 P.3d 678 (2009)

PER CURIAM

Cathy Frost and John Spencer, friends since high school, started a business together in 1988 or 1989. That business, called Footloose Alaska, initially provided guided hunting expeditions and then expanded to offer catered events, including weddings. Frost and Spencer acquired real property in Girdwood, the Raven Glacier Lodge, as a location to house clients before flying them to remote areas for hunting trips and for use as the site of their catered events. That property was titled in Spencer's name because of residual financial complications from a prior business in which Frost had been a partner with her deceased husband, but the parties agree that they purchased the lodge together. Frost and Spencer also purchased Farewell Lake Lodge from Frost's parents. The two partners had different roles in running Footloose Alaska: Spencer "did all the flying and bush logistics and guiding, the carpentry, architectural work, landscaping, aircraft repair and maintenance," and Frost "did the marketing, the food service, [and] the public relations." The record does not indicate that they had a written partnership agreement.

Before and at the beginning of the business partnership, Frost and Spencer were "sporadically" romantically involved. There is no evidence in the record, nor does either party now assert, that they ever lived together.

By 2003 Frost and Spencer no longer had a functioning professional relationship. In February 2005 Spencer filed a complaint against Frost requesting a "dissolution of the parties' partnership interests" and a "division of their jointly acquired real and personal properties."

\*   \*   \*

Frost primarily argues in this appeal that the court's decision to resolve this case based on business partnership law, despite the parties' explicit agreement and expectation that the resolution would rest on domestic relations or domestic partnership law, violated her right to due process under the Alaska Constitution. She contends that the court's post-trial decision to apply a different body of substantive law than she anticipated meant that different evidence would be significant to the outcome of the case. She also argues that the superior court's refusal to extend her trial time or to grant a new trial violated due process because the strict time limits at trial, considered in light of the additional evidence made significant by the application of partnership law, prevented her from presenting relevant information to the court. Spencer responds that Frost was on notice that the court had before it the issue of what law applied. He also notes that he was subject to the same time limitations Frost faced at trial and argues that the court appropriately used its discretion in controlling the presentation of evidence.

\*   \*   \*

It is clear from the record that the parties had agreed to resolve the case under domestic relations or domestic partnership law. The superior court allowed for written responses precisely because "the parties have looked at this and applied the law of domestic cohabitants." Though the parties were permitted to and did submit written arguments before the court issued a final decision in the case, the court did not hold an additional evidentiary hearing after the court's announcement of its tentative ruling. Because basic fairness requires an opportunity to present relevant evidence, applying an unanticipated body of law could be an abuse of discretion if doing so were to make different outcome — determinative facts relevant. To assess Frost's abuse of discretion claim, then, we inquire whether the court's application of business partnership law would, if announced at the outset of the trial, have reasonably led Frost to present different evidence or to place more emphasis on some of the evidence that she did present.

The laws of domestic partnership and business partnership are distinct. We decided in *Tolan v. Kimball* that when a court oversees the separation of a nonmarried couple, "to the extent it is ascertainable, intent of the parties should control the distribution of property accumulated during the course of cohabitation." In *Tolan*, we held that it was not error for the superior court to determine that a former couple jointly owned the home they had shared, even though only one name was on the title, because both individuals had contributed to the down payment for and subsequent mortgage payments on the house, as well as to its physical upkeep. The evidence presented at trial in the suit between Frost and Spencer regarding the purchase and use of the real property and planes suggests that the parties anticipated the court would apply analogous logic here.

Different rules govern winding up the affairs of a business partnership. In Frost and Spencer's case, the superior court apparently applied the now-repealed version of the Alaska Uniform Partnership Act (AUPA) and neither party has argued to this court that failing to apply the current version was error. To be consistent with the proceedings below and because the changes in the code do not impact the result here, we too rely on the former statutory text. We note, however, that the superior court should use the current AUPA upon issuing a new ruling as required by this opinion. Winding up a partnership involves liquidating assets to repay the partnership's debts and then distributing remaining funds, if any, to the dissociating partners according to the capital contributions and share of profits or losses. Alaska Statute 32.05.330 described this process:

> When dissolution is caused in any way, except in contravention of the partnership agreement, each partner, as against the copartners and all persons claiming through them in respect of their interest in the partnership, unless otherwise agreed, may have the partnership property applied to discharge its liabilities, and the surplus applied to pay in cash the net amount owing to the respective partners.

The AUPA further commanded that liabilities were to be discharged in the following order: "(A) those owing to creditors other than partners; (B) those owing to partners other than for capital and profits; (C) those owing to partners in respect of capital; (D) those owing to partners in respect of profits."

These statements of law indicate that a court must find different facts to manage the termination of a partnership than it would to oversee the conclusion of a domestic relationship. In particular, in a business partnership dissolution the amount of each partner's capital contribution is critical because proceeds from the dissolution are applied to the return of capital on a dollar-for-dollar basis before profits may be distributed. Further, noncash contributions of personal services may qualify as capital contributions. By contrast, the precise amounts paid by each partner in a domestic partnership may be of little relevance. Loans made by a partner to a business partnership are likewise recovered on a dollar-for-dollar basis before profits are distributed and payments to a partner must be credited against distributions. Again, in the dissolution of a domestic partnership loans and payments may have little importance. In addition, if there are profits to distribute in a business partnership dissolution, the distribution of them must be according to the parties' agreement as to how profits should be shared. Thus, evidence as to the parties' agreement for sharing profits is critical in a business partnership dissolution. But when the entity being dissolved is a domestic partnership the court and the parties generally do not focus on profits or what the parties said as to how they would be shared. Finally, personal non-business items are seldom considered business partnership property, whereas they readily may be considered part of a domestic partnership.

In our view Frost has made a plausible showing that if she had known before the trial that the case was to be decided under business partnership law principles, her evidentiary presentation would have been different. We conclude that the court abused its discretion in refusing to grant her request for an additional evidentiary hearing following the court's announcement that the case would be decided under business partnership principles.

On remand a supplemental evidentiary hearing should be held. Both parties should be given sufficient time to present evidence relevant to a business partnership dissolution considering the size and value of the partnership and the duration of its existence.

Because Frost's request for an additional evidentiary hearing should have been granted, we Vacate the superior court's judgment, including its findings of fact, and Remand for further evidentiary proceedings.

## NOTE

Why is this case important? Both the plaintiff and defendant agreed that dissolution of their disputes would be resolved under domestic partnership law. Why then did the court choose to apply business partnership law over the explicit written agreement of the parties? The answer should become clear after reading the next case, *J&J Celcom v. AT&T*.

## PROBLEM 3.1

**1.** A, B, and C desire to form a partnership. Their contributions to capital of the partnership are as follows:

A 30

B 20

C 10

The ABC partnership continues for a period of time and then it is decided by all of the partners that it should be dissolved. The partners agree to pay all outside creditors off first, and then decide what to do with the funds left over. After all of the outside creditors are paid off, nothing is left. What happens now? Assume that the partnership agreement was oral. The Uniform Partnership Act (UPA) contains many default rules for the most part in section 18. Section 40 of the UPA is also relevant to the above problem. The judicial solution to the perceived inequity in the principal case is to treat services as capital. That seems like a sensible solution, but it has little support in the literal text of the statute. Did RUPA section 401 fix this problem or ignore it? *See Should the Uniform Partnership Act Be Revised?*, 43 Bus. Law. 121, 148 (1987).

**2.** Assume that D, E, and F form a corporation. They invest the following amounts in return for shares of common stock.

D 30 shares issued in return for 30

E 20 shares issued in return for 20

F 10 shares issued in return for 10

Assume the decision is made to dissolve the corporation. What happens then? Contrast the control structure of a partnership and a corporation. Which default rule is more likely to be in accordance with the wishes of the parties?

# J&J CELCOM v. AT&T WIRELESS SERVICES, INC.
### Supreme Court of Washington
### 169 P.3d 823 (2007)

EN BANC

C. JOHNSON, J. — This case involves a certified question from the United States Court of Appeals for the Ninth Circuit. We are asked to determine whether, under the Revised Uniform Partnership Act (RUPA), a controlling partner violates the duty of loyalty where the controlling partner causes the partnership to sell its assets to an affiliated party. We answer the certified question in the negative.

## FACTS AND PROCEDURAL HISTORY

While certain facts may remain disputed in the federal court proceedings, the Ninth Circuit provided the following description of the parties, their partnerships, and those facts we consider for our analysis. J&J Celcom and other former partners (minority partners) acquired their fractional interests in nine regional cellular telephone partnerships through a lottery. The key asset in each partnership included the right to own licenses for various cellular radio frequencies. At the time of the asset sales at issue in this case, the minority partners owned less than five percent of each partnership, and AT&T Wireless Services (AWS) owned the remainder. AWS provided wireless service to the customers and all technical and administrative services related to the partnerships.

To eliminate the expense of the administrative services related to the partnerships, AWS invoked its majority interest in each partnership and voted to buy out the minority partners. Initially, AWS offered to buy out the minority partners at a price slightly higher than the third party appraisal of four of the nine partnerships. AWS sent letters to the minority partners offering an opportunity to sell voluntarily. The letters stated that, if any minority partner declined the offer, AWS would vote to sell the assets of its partnership to an affiliated entity at the appraised value, dissolve the partnership, and pay the minority partners their pro rata share of the purchase price. Several minority partners accepted the offer but because some declined, AWS proceeded with the asset sales. The Ninth Circuit ruled that the asset sale transactions at issue were based on prices that were fair as a matter of law. *J&J Celcom v. AT&T Wireless Servs., Inc.*, 481 F.3d 1138 (9th Cir. 2007).

## CERTIFIED QUESTION

Does a controlling partner violate the duty of loyalty to the partnership or to dissenting minority partners where the controlling partner causes the partnership to sell all its assets to an affiliated party at a price determined by a third party appraisal, when the appraisal and the parties to the transaction are disclosed and the partnership agreement allows for sale of assets upon majority or supermajority vote, but the partnership agreement is silent on the subject of sale to a related party?

## SUMMARY OF CLAIMS DISMISSED

To put this question in the context of issues that have already been decided in the federal court proceedings, and to further narrow the answer we give in this case, we summarize those issues already resolved. The minority partners who opposed the asset sales filed suit in federal District Court for the Western District of Washington in Seattle. As the Ninth Circuit noted, these minority partners alleged:

(1)  Breach of Contract

(2)  Breach of Implied Covenant of Good Faith and Fair Dealing

(3)  Breach of Fiduciary Duties

(4)  Claims of Misrepresentation

(5)  Tortious Interference

(6)  Unjust Enrichment

After 15 months of discovery, AWS moved for summary judgment. The minority partners cross-moved for partial summary judgment on liability. The district court granted AWS's motion and denied the minority partners' motion.

The minority partners appealed. The Ninth Circuit affirmed the federal district court's grant of summary judgment for AWS on all but one of the issues. Further, the Ninth Circuit held that the asset sale transactions did not breach either the partnership agreements or the implied covenant of good faith and fair dealing. The sole remaining issue — a claim for breach of the duty of loyalty — is the subject of the certified question now before us.

\*     \*     \*

## ANALYSIS

The relevant portion of the Washington RUPA provides:

(1)  The only fiduciary duties a partner owes to the partnership and the other partners are the duty of loyalty and the duty of care set forth in subsections (2) and (3) of this section.

(2)  A partner's duty of loyalty to the partnership and the other partners is limited to the following:

   (a)  To account to the partnership and hold as trustee for it any property, profit, or benefit derived by the partner in the conduct and winding up of the partnership business or derived from a use by the partner of partnership property, including the appropriation of a partnership opportunity;

   (b)  To refrain from dealing with the partnership in the conduct or winding up of the partnership business as or on behalf of a party having an interest adverse to the partnership; and

     (c)   To refrain from competing with the partnership in the conduct of the partnership business before the dissolution of the partnership.

 (3)   A partner's duty of care to the partnership and the other partners in the conduct and winding up of the partnership business is limited to refraining from engaging in grossly negligent or reckless conduct, intentional misconduct, or a knowing violation of law.

 (4)   A partner shall discharge the duties to the partnership and the other partners under this chapter or under the partnership agreement and exercise any rights consistently with the obligation of good faith and fair dealing.

 (5)   A partner does not violate a duty or obligation under this chapter or under the partnership agreement merely because the partner's conduct furthers the partner's own interest.

Here, as the federal district court held, the partnership agreement expressly allows for sale of partnership assets by majority vote. The federal district court and Ninth Circuit ruled that when AWS sold the partnership assets, it disclosed material information, paid fair consideration, and acted in good faith as a matter of law. Also, the minority partners have offered no proof of damages as a result of AWS's sale of the partnership's assets. Therefore, we find nothing in Washington's RUPA, when applied to the present case, that indicates that AWS violated the duty of loyalty to the partnership.

In addition to Washington's RUPA, our finding is supported by Washington case law. We recognized in *Karle v. Seder*, 35 Wn.2d 542, 550, 214 P.2d 684 (1950) that a partner may lawfully purchase partnership assets from another partner, provided they act in good faith, pay fair consideration, and disclose material information. In *Bassan v. Investment Exchange Corp.*, 83 Wn.2d 922, 524 P.2d 233 (1974), we held that a partner has a duty to account for any benefit of profit held by the partner relating to any aspect of the partnership.

It is of interest to note that the Ninth Circuit perceived our holdings in *Karle* and *Bassan* as pointing "in different directions." *J&J Celcom*, 481 F.3d at 1142. However, we fail to see how the holdings conflict. The cases simply addressed different issues on completely different sets of facts.

*   *   *

In the context of the certified question, the holdings of *Karle* and *Bassan* do not conflict. In this case, the partnership agreement does not preclude the sale of the assets; the price paid was fair at the time as a matter of law and no bad faith exists as a matter of law.

CONCLUSION

Based on the narrow issue posed by the certified question and the procedural posture underlying our analysis, we answer the certified question no.

MADSEN, J. (concurring) — I agree with the majority that the question posed by the certified question from the Ninth Circuit Court of Appeals should be answered no. *However, the majority does not address the fact that Karle and Bassan were* decided under the UPA, not the Revised Uniform Partnership Act (RUPA), chapter 25.05 RCW, a point which the Ninth Circuit considered "critical."

* * *

RUPA represents a major overhaul in the nature of the fiduciary duties imposed on partners. There are two general views of the partnership relation: one emphasizes the fiduciary nature of the relationship and the other emphasizes the contractual nature of the relationship. The common law and the UPA are based on the fiduciary view, the fundamental principle of which is that partners must subordinate their own interests to the collective interest, absent consent of all the partners. Thus, under the common law and the UPA, the duty of loyalty prevented a partner from benefiting, directly or indirectly, from the partnership, more than any of the other partners. The broad approach from the *Restatement of Agency*, incorporated into partnership law, was that the duty of loyalty required a partner to act solely for the benefit of the partnership in all matters connected to the partnership. This required partners to disgorge any profits made without consent of the other partners.

* * *

RUPA represents a major shift away from the fiduciary view and toward the "libertarian" or "contractarian" view, by (a) expressly limiting fiduciary duties, (b) sanctioning a partner's pursuit of self-interest, and (c) allowing partners to waive most fiduciary duties by contract. RUPA was intended to bring the law of partnership into the "modern age," to make partnerships more rational, efficient, and stable business entities.

* * *

Our state legislature has adopted RUPA, and under its provisions, fiduciary duties are specifically set forth as explained below.

> First, a partner has a duty [t]o account to the partnership and hold as trustee for it any property, profit, or benefit derived by the partner in the conduct and winding up of the partnership business or derived from a use by the partner of partnership property, including the appropriation of a partnership opportunity, . . . [t]o refrain from dealing with the partnership in the conduct or winding up of the partnership business as or on behalf of a party having an interest adverse to the partnership, . . . [t]o refrain from competing with the partnership in the conduct of the partnership business before the dissolution of the partnership.

* * *

The drafter's comment to this provision provides that:

> [t]he duty not to compete applies only to the "conduct" of the partnership business; it does not extend to winding up the business, as do the other loyalty rules. Thus, a partner is free to compete immediately upon an event of dissolution under Section 801, unless the partnership agreement otherwise provides.

* * *

Upon dissolution, AT&T had the right to purchase the partnership assets for its own account, without violating the duty of loyalty. Thus, nothing prohibited AT&T from causing the partnership assets to be sold to an affiliated entity.

Because the certified question and the record indicate that AT&T acted in good faith, paid fair market value, and fully disclosed the nature of its self-dealing transaction, the transaction was not "manifestly unreasonable" within the meaning of RCW 25.05.015(2)(c). Thus, the majority correctly answers the question in the negative.

# NOTES

1.  Justice Madsen's concurrence provides a framework for analyzing the contrasting duties owed under the UPA and the RUPA. Under the RUPA, parties have the discretion to contractually limit fiduciary obligations. Historically, contract law predates the development of agency law. With that understanding, does the RUPA, as Justice Madsen asserts, truly reflect a more "modern" trend in business transactions?

2.  **The LLP and Other Limited Liability Entities.** In most states, a partnership can elect to become an LLP, or limited liability partnership. In general, the election is simple to make, requiring only a declaration that the partnership elects to become an LLP, coupled with the filing of a "statement of qualification" with the Secretary of State and the preparation of an annual report which must also be filed with the appropriate state agency. *See* UPA §§ 1001–1003 (1997). Under UPA section 306(c), a partner in an LLP is generally not personally liable for obligations of the partnership, whether contract or tort, "solely by reason of being partner." However, one recent case, *Megadyne Information Systems v. Rosner, Owens & Nunziato*, 2002 Cal. App. Unpub. LEXIS 8897 (Sept. 24, 2002) (opinion not certified for publication), indicates that it may not always be easy for a partner to escape liability for actions of his co-partners. In that case, the court, in denying defendants motion for summary judgment, stated:

> Pursuant to Corporations Code section 16306, subdivision (c), an individual partner of a registered limited liability partnership such as the Rosner firm has no vicarious liability for the tort(s) of another partner. Only the partnership and the individual partner are liable. (See Corp. Code, § 16306, subd. (e).) Consequently, Megadyne can only hold Nunziato and Rosner liable if they were involved in the handling of its matter. All three partners offered declarations averring Owens was "the sole attorney" who handled the Megadyne matter and that neither of the other two had "any involvement" in the case. To contradict that showing, Megadyne offered Owens's testimony that "there might have been discussions" with his two partners that Megadyne had a viable legal malpractice claim against Irell & Manella. This is sufficient to create a triable issue of fact as to whether the partners were personally involved in the firm's breach of fiduciary duties. If the partners had discussions that Megadyne could sue Irell & Manella for malpractice, it is reasonable to infer that they knew Mega-

dyne's claim against OCTA was time-barred and that they participated in the decision to not disclose this fact to Megadyne while the firm continued to represent it. In addition, the fact Nunziato's name was on the caption page of the claim filed with OCTA suggests his involvement in the case.

## Carol R. Goforth, *Limited Liability Partnerships: Does Arkansas Need Another Form of Business Enterprise?*
### 1995 ARK. L. NOTES 57[2]

Limited liability companies (LLCs), a form of business entity blending some of the most desirable attributes of partnerships and corporations, were unheard of in this country prior to 1977, when Wyoming enacted the first domestic LLC statute. Until quite recently, the Wyoming legislation was more of an aberration than anything else, but by the 1990's, LLCs had caught on in other jurisdictions. In fact, by the end of 1994, only three states had failed to enact legislation authorizing this new form of business entity. Arkansas authorized the formation of domestic LLCs in 1993, when the Small Business Entity Tax Pass Through Act was enacted into law, making Arkansas either the twenty-third or twenty-fourth state to permit organization of domestic LLCs.

Now statutes authorizing not one but two additional forms of business entity are sweeping across the nation, and Arkansas is only one of a number of states considering recognizing these new business entities. If you thought LLCs were interesting (or confusing), wait until you hear about limited liability partnerships (LLPs) and limited liability limited partnerships (LLLPs).

The first state to authorize LLPs and LLLPs was Texas, which enacted the original LLP/LLLP statute in 1991. As of the date of this writing, approximately half of all states had enacted LLP legislation, and some of these jurisdictions also recognize LLLPs. States with LLP legislation include Alabama, Arizona, Connecticut, Delaware, the District of Columbia, Georgia, Illinois, Iowa, Kansas, Kentucky, Louisiana, Maryland, Minnesota, Mississippi, Missouri, New Jersey, New Mexico, New York, North Carolina, Ohio, Pennsylvania, South Carolina, Texas, Utah, and Virginia. Of these states, Georgia, Mississippi and New Jersey only recognize foreign LLPs and do not authorize formation of domestic LLPs. In February of 1995, the Arkansas legislature began considering a bill which would allow LLPs and LLLPs to be formed in this state.

In order to answer the question of whether Arkansas really needs to authorize LLPs and LLLPs, this article will start out by examining the general structure of LLP legislation in other states and in the proposed Arkansas legislation. After LLPs have been considered, this article will explain the different considerations involved with LLLPs. Finally, it will examine the question of whether these new business entities should be recognized in Arkansas, and, if so, what form the enabling legislation in this state should take.

---

[2] Copyright © 1995. All rights reserved. Reprinted by permission.

## I. Understanding the LLP

Perhaps the best way of looking at LLPs is to understand that an LLP is basically a general partnership, with a few important modifications, all of which are spelled out in the applicable statutes. Because there is no model or uniform LLP Act, there is considerable variation in statutory language from state to state, although there is substantial similarity in general content for most of these statutes. This article uses the statutes from a handful of states to illustrate both the common themes and differences between various statutory models. For the most part, reference will be made to the LLP legislation in Delaware, Louisiana, Minnesota, New York and Texas, and to the version of Arkansas House Bill 2131 which was introduced by Representative Tom Courtway in April of 1995.

### A. Becoming an LLP — The Filing Requirements

The first step in becoming an LLP is for a general partnership to file an application with an appropriate state official, registering as an LLP. This filing requirement seems quite consistent with the general statutory approach taken with regard to other forms of business enterprise which offer owners protection from unlimited personal liability. One major difference between the filing for an LLP and the filing required for other limited liability entities is that in most states, in order to continue LLP status, a renewal application must be filed annually. In these states, if an LLP neglects to file its annual renewal, the liability protections offered to partners by LLP status terminate. Not all states, however, require an annual filing. The bill currently under consideration by the Arkansas legislature provides that a single filing will be sufficient to create a registered limited liability partnership.

Certain basic information is required in both the original application and every renewal. Typically, the original application must include such information as the name of the partnership (which generally must include some indication that the partnership in question is in fact an LLP or is seeking status as an LLP), the address of the partnership's principal office and/or registered office and service agent, and a brief statement of the business in which the partnership engages. Some states have additional requirements. For example, the Minnesota LLP legislation requires an express acknowledgment that the LLP's registration will expire in one year if it is not renewed.

In addition to these informational requirements, both types of documents must be accompanied by a fee. The amount of the required filing fee varies significantly from state to state. In some states, a flat fee is imposed. For example, a $100 fee is payable annually in Louisiana; a $135 annual fee is due in Minnesota; and a $200 fee must be paid in New York. In other states, the fee is tied to the number of partners in the LLP. In Delaware, an LLP must pay an annual fee of $100 for each partner, with a cap equal to the maximum annual corporate franchise tax (currently $150,000). In Texas, an LLP must pay an annual fee of $100 for each partner, with no cap. In other states, the filing fee may be based on different considerations, but these are the two most common approaches taken by LLP/LLLP legislation.

The Arkansas bill currently provides for a flat fee of $50.

## B. Insurance/Financial Responsibility Requirements

Filing appropriate documents and paying the required fee is not always enough to insure that a partnership will qualify as an LLP. In several states, achieving LLP status is conditioned upon maintaining certain required levels of insurance or being able to demonstrate a minimum level of financial responsibility. The type and amount of insurance or the minimum capitalization requirement depends on the jurisdiction. For example, Delaware requires an LLP to carry at least $1,000,000 of liability insurance of a kind that is designed to cover the kinds of negligence, wrongful acts, and misconduct for which liability is limited under the legislation. The Texas LLP statute imposes a requirement that the LLP carry at least $100,000 of liability insurance of a kind that is designed to cover the kinds of errors, omissions, negligence, incompetence, or malfeasance for which liability is limited under the Texas legislation. In both of these states, this insurance is not required if the LLP in question maintains the required amount of funds in a segregated account specifically designated for the satisfaction of judgments against the partnership or its partners based on the kinds of liability that is limited under the statute in question. It should be noted, however, that in some states, the insurance requirement is absolute, and may not be met simply by showing that the partnership has retained funds in a segregated account.

On the other hand, not all states have an insurance or financial responsibility requirement. For example, the Louisiana statute does not include any insurance or financial responsibility requirement. The statutes in these states more closely mirror the modern capitalization provisions governing corporations or LLCs. In other words, there is no minimum capital or specific amount of malpractice insurance required for LLPs in these states. The bill being considered by the Arkansas legislature adopts this model, and imposes no insurance or minimum capital requirements.

## C. Limited Liability for General Partners

The benefit of achieving LLP status is that partners in an LLP are protected from certain sorts of liability, whereas partners in an ordinary general partnership are liable for all debts of the partnership. Partners in an LLP are protected only from "certain sorts of liability" because the type of liability from which partners are insulated depends greatly on the jurisdiction * * *.

In essence, in any of these jurisdictions, and in most states with LLP legislation, a partner in an LLP is relieved of liability for the negligence, wrongful acts and misconduct of another partner and of employees, agents and representatives of the partnership, unless such other person was under the partner's direct supervision and control. In other words, partners in such an LLP would be liable only for their own conduct or the conduct of those under their supervision, at least in connection with claims founded on tortious conduct. Partners in these LLPs continue to be liable for contractual indebtedness of the partnership.

A very different approach has been taken by a few states. The Minnesota and New York legislation illustrate this alternative approach. In these jurisdictions, partners in an LLP are insulated from personal liability for any partnership debt, regardless of whether the obligation arose out of tortious misconduct or a contract.

\*     \*     \*

These statutes basically provide partners in an LLP with the same type of limited liability that shareholders of a corporation enjoy. Indications are that several states with liability provisions like those found in the Texas and Delaware statutes are considering amendments which would result in increased protection from personal liability for partners, more along the lines of the Minnesota and New York legislation.

\*     \*     \*

One other twist on the potential liability of general partners in an LLP or LLLP deserves special consideration. This is the issue of liability for the acts of others who are under the general partner's supervision.

In most states, the applicable statutory language provides that a partner will continue to be liable for the tortious misconduct of those under the partner's "direct supervision and control." The Texas LLP statute provides that the shield of limited liability does not extend to "errors, omissions, negligence, incompetence or malfeasance" committed by another who is "working under the supervision or direction" of the partner.

Unfortunately, most statutes offer little or no guidance as to the meaning of "supervision" or "direction" or "direct supervision and control." One commentator has suggested that the intent of such language is that the following individuals should not be denied protection: (i) managing partners or partners exercising supervisory authority for partnership affairs; and (ii) section heads or individuals acting in a general supervisory capacity. Of course, the ultimate interpretation of such language will be left to the courts.

\*     \*     \*

## II. Overview of LLLPs

LLLPs are very similar to LLPs. In fact, the only significant difference is that the new provisions relating to filing, insurance, and limited liability for general partners relate to limited partnerships rather than general partnerships. Obviously, the name of an LLP would be sightly different from the name of an LLP as well.

With regard to the effect of electing LLLP status, a limited partner in a limited partnership is already insulated against personal liability for debts of the partnership (unless the limited partner participates excessively in the control of the partnership), but a limited partnership must also have at least one general partner. The advantage of being an LLLP is therefore that the general partner(s) of the limited partnership will be insulated from personal liability, either arising out of the tortious misconduct of others or from any entity level debt, depending on the statutory language used. Other than that, an LLLP is much like an LLP, except that the basic structure is that of a limited partnership rather than a general partnership.

The only other fact worth emphasizing with regard to LLLPs is that far fewer states recognize the LLLP than the LLP. The proposed Arkansas bill would permit formation of domestic LLLPs.

### III. Should Arkansas Recognize LLPs and LLLPs?

\*    \*    \*

Moreover, a primary reason for authorizing LLCs in this state (that we should not place Arkansans and Arkansas businesses at a competitive disadvantage by restricting their choice of business entity options when persons in other states are not so limited), applies as strongly to adoption of LLPs and LLLPs. To the extent that the LLP and/or LLLP option better fits a particular business' needs, there seems to be little reason not to make that option available here since it is an option in at least half of the other American states, including our close and influential neighbor, Texas. In addition, since LLP and LLLP legislation is being so widely adopted in other jurisdictions, failure to enact such an Act in this state might well foster the impression that Arkansas is not receptive to businesses, certainly an undesirable image.

\*    \*    \*

There is also one other potential tax advantage to LLLPs as compared to LLCs, at least in certain circumstances. Where the entity is being chosen with estate planning objectives in mind, the LLLP may be the preferable choice because estate tax valuation rules may be more favorable for limited partnerships, including LLLPs, than for LLCs.

## NOTE

All states now permit LLPs and most, including Arkansas, permit LLLPs.

# Chapter 4

# THE LIMITED LIABILITY COMPANY

The Limited Liability Company (LLC) is a relatively recent invention that combines aspects of both corporations and partnerships. The first LLC statute was passed in Wyoming in 1977. At that time, there was a set of tax regulations in place known as the Kintner regulations that provided guidance on whether an entity would be treated as a corporation or a partnership for federal tax purposes. The Wyoming law carefully tracked those regulations to permit the creation of entities that qualified for conduit taxation as if they were partnerships, but it also provided that owners, called "members," were entitled to limited liability as if the LLCs were corporations. For several years, the jury was out as to whether such an entity would pass muster with the IRS, but finally, in 1988, the IRS ruled that an LLC satisfying the Kintner tests would be treated as a partnership for tax purposes even though it provided limited liability to its members. By that time, other states had passed LLC statutes, but when the IRS position became clear, the floodgates opened. Now all 50 states and the District of Columbia have LLC statutes.

The IRS created another seismic shift in 1997 when it conceded that, since it was possible to get both limited liability and conduit taxation within the same entity, there was really no reason to keep the Kintner regulations in place. Accordingly, it issued regulations permitting any entity except one formed as a corporation under state law to choose whether it will be taxed under the corporate or partnership provisions of the Internal Revenue Code. These regulations are known as the "check the box" regulations because, unless you check the box electing to be treated as a corporation, the IRS will assume that you prefer to be treated as a partnership. In response, states retrofitted their partnership statutes to provide avenues for partnerships and limited partnerships to provide limited liability to their partners. Most states now have Limited Liability Partnership (LLP) and Limited Liability Limited Partnership (LLLP) statutes, in addition to their LLC, corporation, and partnership statutes.

The Uniform Limited Liability Company Act was not approved until the early 1990s, after most states already had their LLC statutes in place. As a result, the laws may vary significantly from state to state, but they share many similar characteristics.

The great virtue of an LLC is its flexibility. It is seen as a creature of contract, and the members can basically write their own agreement about their rights and obligations. Although the statutory presumption is that, like partners in a partnership, all members have a right to participate in management and to bind the LLC to contracts, it is perfectly possible to structure an LLC with a board of managers much like a corporation's board of directors, and to limit the members' rights to participate in management. The default position is that, like partnership interests,

LLC interests are not freely transferable. Many statutes provide that, although fiduciary duties among members may not be completely eliminated, they may be defined in a way that may in fact limit their scope. Unlike a partnership, which requires at least two partners, most states permit LLCs to be formed and owned by a single member. This permits sole proprietors to use the LLC form to limit their liability for debts of the business.

An LLC is formed under state law by filing a document, the articles of organization, with an agency such as the secretary of state. This is generally a very simple document, with a more thorough contract among the members called the operating agreement specifying the owners' rights and duties. LLCs have become enormously popular as vehicles for operating small businesses, with LLC formations outpacing corporate formations in some states. Many practitioners initially hesitated to recommend LLCs to their clients because there was no case law to indicate how courts would interpret the statutes. However, the form has now been in use for long enough to have developed a reasonably robust body of authority, so there is no longer as much concern about what the statues mean or how they will be construed by the courts.

The following cases illustrate some of the issues that have arisen as the courts have attempted to deal with the statutory ambiguities of an entirely new form of business organization.

## PATMON v. HOBBS
Court of Appeals of Kentucky
280 S.W.3d 589 (2009)

CLAYTON, J.

Ann Patmon (Patmon) individually and on behalf of American Leasing and Management, LLC (American Leasing), appeals from the Jefferson Circuit Court September 24, 2007, judgment wherein the court found that damages could not be awarded for the value of the build-to-suit lease agreements that Lanier Hobbs (Hobbs) transferred from American Leasing to American Development and Leasing, LLC (American Development). The court determined that, because American Leasing would have been unable to perform the contracts, no corporate "opportunity," as defined under the common law of other states, could exist, thus barring any claim for damages for the build-to-suit leases. Patmon, however, contends that under Kentucky Revised Statutes (KRS) 275.170, certain fiduciary duties are owed by the manager-member to the company and its members, that Hobbs breached these duties, and therefore must compensate American Leasing and/or her for the value of the build-to-suit leases. We affirm in part and in so doing we adopt the doctrine of corporate opportunity, under which one entrusted with active corporate management, such as officer or director or manager-member, occupies fiduciary relationship and may not exploit this position by appropriating a business opportunity properly belonging to the corporation. But we vacate and remand the matter to the trial court for further proceedings consistent with this opinion and its adoption of the doctrine of corporate opportunity.

## FACTUAL BACKGROUND

American Leasing is a Kentucky limited liability company that is involved in construction and build-to-suit lease projects. Generally, American Leasing would purchase land in a predetermined location and then construct a building according to a client's specification. After the building is completed, the client then becomes a long-term tenant under a lease agreement. The build-to-suit leases produce a guaranteed long-term stream of rental income by allowing for the payment of the land purchase through rental income, which ultimately adds real estate assets to a company's (American Leasing's) balance sheet.

In early 2004, American Leasing was working on a $520,000 build-to-lease project for O'Reilly Auto Parts (O'Reilly) in Shively, Kentucky, and a $700,000 strip center construction project for Dr. Raley. Additionally, American Leasing and O'Reilly were in negotiations for three build-to-suit leases (Preston Highway in Louisville; Jeffersonville; and Clarksville, Indiana.) Initially, Hobbs was not an owner/member of American Leasing but worked as a contractor on the O'Reilly Auto Parts store. Hobb's company performed the excavating and concrete work. Through this interaction, he met Richard D. Pearson (Pearson), then the managing member of American Leasing, and began discussions about joining American Leasing. On February 9, 2004, Hobbs and Pearson entered into an Executive/ Partnership Agreement wherein Hobbs owned 51 percent, Pearson owned 44 percent, and Bruce Gray (Gray) owned 5 percent. Subsequently, around March 15, 2004, Hobbs and Pearson signed a "Consent Resolution and Agreement," which recognized that Hobbs was a 51-percent owner of American Leasing and the managing member of the Company.

At this time, Hobbs also learned that American Leasing was experiencing difficulty in paying the U.S. Bank loan for the O'Reilly project; therefore, he paid $5,823 to the bank to bring the loan into balance and later signed a personal guaranty on the loan. Following this transaction, Hobbs testified he discovered that American Leasing did not have the financial wherewithal to pursue the three additional O'Reilly projects. Specifically, Hobbs said that U.S. Bank indicated it would provide no additional financing to the company, the company had inadequate funding for other projects, and Hobbs himself did not have the funds to finance these projects.

Patmon's history in this action begins with her work with Hobbs in his excavation and concrete business. Further, in October 2003, Patmon loaned $30,415.16 to American Leasing and Pearson. When Pearson defaulted on the loan, Patmon obtained a default judgment against him on March 1, 2004. Later at a sheriff's sale held on May 5, 2004, Patmon purchased Pearson's membership certificate in American Leasing and became 44-percent owner of the company. Eventually, American Leasing paid Patmon in full for her loan to American Leasing and Pearson.

Meanwhile, Hobbs, on March 3, 2004, formed another company, American Development. He was the sole member of the company. After forming the company, he sent a letter to Ed Randall (Randall) at O'Reilly instructing that the pending Preston, Jeffersonville, and Clarksville leases be changed to reflect American Development as the proposed landlord rather than American Leasing.

In his deposition, Randall stated that, prior to Hobbs's letter, O'Reilly was prepared to enter into three agreements with American Leasing. In fact, Randall said he had never heard of American Development. Randall asked Hobbs to provide evidence to support this request. Hobbs provided the "Consent Resolution and Agreement" between Hobbs and Pearson that showed Hobbs as the managing member of American Leasing with authority to make such a change. The three leases were then transferred to American Development with no consideration paid to American Leasing by Hobbs or his new company. Subsequently, Hobbs and Steve Habeeb (Habeeb) formed another limited liability company which was eventually assigned these leases. The company was started so that Hobbs would provide the leases and Habeeb would obtain the financing for the projects. Habeeb had originally informed Hobbs that he would not be involved in any project with Pearson and was unwilling to finance any American Leasing projects.

Then, notwithstanding that Hobbs knew American Development would be landlord and construction manager for the three projects, he paid the deposits with American Leasing resources. On the same day that Hobbs formed American Development, March 4, 2004, American Leasing paid $2,000 for the Preston project, $100 for the Jeffersonville project, and $5,000 for the Clarksville project. Later, on April 28, 2004, American Leasing paid another $2,000 for the Preston project. In addition, on July 23, 2004, Hobbs used $1,527.46 in American Leasing funds to pay for signage for an American Development project. By the end of November 2004, Habeeb and Hobbs had secured financing for all three projects with American Development serving as the general contractor. This arrangement allowed Hobbs to profit from the construction phase as well as the leases themselves.

## PROCEDURAL BACKGROUND

On November 4, 2004, the first of two bench trials occurred in this case. The trial was held to resolve the membership of American Leasing. On March 31, 2005, the court held that Hobbs, Patmon and Gray were members of the company holding respectively 51 percent, 44 percent, and 5 percent ownership. Furthermore, the court deemed that Hobbs and Gray were owners as of February 9, 2004, denied Pearson's claim of ownership, and found that Patmon became a member on May 5, 2004, when she acquired Pearson's interest.

Following the court's first decision, Patmon, in her name and American Leasing's name, sued Hobbs because she had learned that American Leasing's three build-to-suit leases with O'Reilly had been diverted by Hobbs, without membership consent, to American Development. Following the second bench trial, on September 24, 2007, the court held that Hobbs must pay American Leasing $18,980.45, which included $9,100 in down payments to secure land for the build-to-suit leases later completed by American Development; $1,527.45 for signage for these projects; $7,500 for Hobbs's personal legal expenses; and $853 for his personal telephone bill.

The court, however, did not award damages for the value of the build-to-suit lease agreements. Patmon asserted at the trial that the value of these diverted leases is derived from the construction income, profits from the rental income, and value of the land purchased through the rental income. But as to the damages claimed for the statutory breach under KRS 275.170, the court held that because American Leasing was unable to perform the contracts, no "opportunity," as defined under the common law of other states, could exist, thus barring any claim for damages under KRS 275.170. Nonetheless, the court did note that it was unaware of any Kentucky cases specifically addressing diverted opportunity for fiduciary duty purposes.

## ANALYSIS

\* \* \*

### 2. Limited Liability Company

A limited liability company is a hybrid business entity having attributes of both a corporation and a partnership. Its owners are its members. Like corporations and limited partnerships, limited liability companies are creatures of statute. In Kentucky, there is relatively little caselaw regarding limited liability companies and no caselaw concerning fiduciary duties in the limited liability company context. Hence, the parties present this Court with an issue of first impression: whether under KRS 275.170 or by common law, Hobbs owed a fiduciary duty to American Leasing and Patmon.

While Kentucky courts have not directly addressed whether a member of a limited liability company owes a duty of loyalty to fellow members and the company, some jurisdictions have found such a duty. *See Credentials Plus, LLC v. Calderone*, 230 F. Supp. 2d 890, 899 (N.D. Ind. 2002).

### 3. Duty of loyalty

The Kentucky Supreme Court described the nature of a fiduciary duty:

> The [fiduciary] relation[ship] may exist under a variety of circumstances; it exists in all cases where there has been a special confidence reposed in one who in equity and good conscience is bound to act in good faith and with due regard to the interests of the one reposing confidence.

\* \* \*

Further, the Court held that even in the absence of a statutorily imposed duty, an officer or director of a company owes a fiduciary duty to the company. *Aero Drapery of Kentucky, Inc. v. Engdahl*, 507 S.W.2d 166, 168 (Ky. 1974). *Aero* goes further in describing the duty of loyalty:

> [w]henever a reasonably prudent fiduciary is aware of a conflict between his private interest and the corporate interest, he owes the duty of good faith and full disclosure of the circumstances to the corporation. \* \* \* Regarding partnership and the duty of loyalty, a "partner has a duty to share with the partnership those business opportunities clearly related to the subject

of its operations." * * * For the foregoing reasons, this Court finds that Kentucky limited liability companies, being similar to Kentucky partnerships and corporations, impose a common-law fiduciary duty on their officers and members in the absence of contrary provisions in the limited liability company operating agreement.

In sum, a breach-of-loyalty claim is based on the existence of a fiduciary duty between a principal and an agent. In general, members of a limited liability company are agents for the purpose of its business or affairs. KRS 275.135(1). But where the articles vest authority in a manager or managers, every manager is an agent of the limited liability company for the purpose of its business or affairs. KRS 275.135(2)(b). Consequently, as the managing member of American Leasing, Hobbs had a duty to act not only in the interests of American Leasing but also owed a basic duty of faithfulness and loyalty to the company.

As a result, one who acts as agent for another is not permitted to deal in the subject matter of the agency for his own benefit without the consent of the principal — the other members. Common sense as well as the law dictates that profits realized by an agent in the execution of his agency belong to the other members in the absence of an agreement to the contrary. The duty between principal and agent was discussed in *Stewart v. Kentucky Paving Co., Inc.*, 557 S.W. 2d 435 (Ky. App. 1977). The agent is bound to a high degree of good faith and is not entitled to avail himself of any advantage that his position may give him to profit at the employer's expense beyond the terms of the employment agreement. *Id* at 437. *Stewart* is particularly illustrative of the duty of loyalty and its breach. The parties therein misappropriated several leads, contract proposals, and contracts, resulting in the jobs being done by the parties' company, not the employer's company. Our Court found that the parties violated their fiduciary duty and upheld the trial court's measure of damages, which was the gross profit that the employer's company would have earned on the contracts. *Id.* at 436–39. Likewise, contrary to his fiduciary duty, Hobbs, who was the manager-partner of American Leasing, formed a competing business and transferred the build-to-suit leases from American Leasing to it. Hobbs's activity posits the question whether Hobbs acted in compliance with his duty of loyalty to the company. This duty is confirmed in the Executive/Partnership Agreement drafted and signed by Hobbs.

### 4. Liability of Members and Managers

The liability of members and managers of limited liability companies is outlined in KRS 275.170. It states that:

Unless otherwise provided in a written operating agreement:

(1) A member or manager shall not be liable, responsible, or accountable in damages or otherwise to the limited liability company or the members of the limited liability company for any action taken or failure to act on behalf of the limited liability company unless the act or omission constitutes wanton or reckless misconduct.

Further explanation is provided by the next subsection, which describes what a member/manager may not do unless more than one-half of the disinterested managers or a majority-in-interest of the members consent:

(2) Each member and manager shall account to the limited liability company and hold as trustee for it any profit or benefit derived by that person without the consent of more than one-half (1/2) by number of the disinterested managers, or a majority-in-interest of the members from:

   (a) Any transaction connected with the conduct or winding up of the limited liability company; or

   (b) Any use by the member or manager of its property, including, but not limited to, confidential or proprietary information of the limited liability company or other matters entrusted to the person as a result of his status as manager or member.

KRS 275.170(2)(a)-(b). To summarize, a member or manager must account to and hold as a trustee for a limited liability company any profit or benefit derived from the use of company property by that member or manager including, but not limited to, confidential, proprietary, or other matters entrusted to that person's status as manager or member. Hobbs concedes and the court found that he never obtained consent from any member of American Leasing to divert O'Reilly leases to American Development. These leases qualify as "confidential or proprietary information."

5. Diverted corporate opportunity

The next step in our analysis is to ascertain, in the absence of clear caselaw and statutory guidance, the duty of loyalty required by a managing member of a limited liability company. In the absence of a Kentucky case delineating the duty of loyalty in a limited liability company and based on the hybrid nature of a limited liability company, we look at an explanation of the duty of loyalty in the partnership context:

Under Kentucky law, partners owe the utmost good faith to each and every other partner. *See Axton v. Kentucky Bottlers Supply Co.*, 159 Ky. 51, 166 S.W. 776, 778 (1914). . . . Indeed, it has often been said, "there is no relation of trust or confidence known to law that requires of the parties a higher degree of good faith than that of a partnership." *Van Hooser v. Keenon*, 271 S.W.2d 270, 273 (Ky.1954).

Therefore, given that partners owe good faith to each other, we believe it follows logically and equitably that a managing member of a limited liability company also owes such a duty to other members (partners). Furthermore, this standard, in combination with KRS 275.170, leads us to the conclusion that Hobbs violated the duty of loyalty, and therefore, breached his fiduciary to his fellow members and to the company.

Indeed, in its finding of fact, conclusion of law, the trial court itself concluded:

Kentucky courts have not yet addressed the applicability of fiduciary duties in the limited liability company contest.

. . . KRS 275.170(2) creates a statutory duty of loyalty for self-interested transactions . . .

The Court finds that Hobbs violated the statutory standards in KRS 275.170[.]

But the court limited damages to the actual dollar amount of American Leasing's resources that Hobbs used for himself and for American Development. After awarding damages based only on this amount, the court, in essence, found no violation of KRS 275.170 when Hobbs took the three pending O'Reilly build-to-suit leases for his limited liability company, American Development. Rather than continuing with an analysis of fiduciary duty, the court, without any explanation, moved to a discussion of misappropriation of corporate opportunity. One theory of this doctrine holds that opportunity does not exist for a business if the business is financially unable to undertake the opportunity. Then, while observing that no Kentucky case details diverted opportunity as obviating fiduciary duty, the court cited cases from other jurisdictions explaining this rationale. . . .

In fact, Hobbs's entire rationale for disputing his liability for taking the leases from American Leasing to American Development is based on the doctrine of misappropriation of corporate opportunity and is based solely on three cases from other jurisdictions. But his analysis is limited. First, he does not discuss the *Miller* two-part test for establishing a *prima facie* case of usurpation of corporate opportunity, which states that the new business opportunity must be "so closely related to the existing or prospective activity of the corporation" that it constitutes a corporate opportunity. *Miller*, 222 N.W.2d at 81. Then Hobbs provides no discussion of whether he, by acquiring the opportunity, must have violated the duties of loyalty, good faith, and fair dealing toward the corporation. *Id.* Implicit in the use of this doctrine, however, is an acknowledgment that it was a business opportunity of American Leasing and that he violated his duties to the company. We would be remiss to not point out that the *Miller* case involves a discussion based on a corporation rather than a limited liability company. However, we see no difference between the fiduciary duties a director owes a corporation with shareholders or a member owes to a limited liability corporation.

In Kentucky, however, the focus is on the fiduciary's duty — not the lost opportunity. For instance, returning to *Aero*, we find the following cite:

There are numerous instances where a legitimate conflict of interest exists between a fiduciary and his corporation. Whenever a reasonably prudent fiduciary is aware of a conflict between his private interest and the corporate interest, he owes the duty of good faith and full disclosure of the circumstances to the corporation. "If dual interests are to be served, the disclosure to be effective must lay bare the truth, without ambiguity or reservation, in all of its stark significance." . . .

Further illustration of this principle is provided by *Urban J. Alexander Co. v. Trinkle*, 311 Ky. 635, 224 S.W.2d 923 (Ky. 1949), where the Court held the director was allowed to avail himself personally of an opportunity after making diligent efforts to pursue the opportunity for the company notwithstanding the fact that the company definitely could not have availed itself of the opportunity. *Id.* at 925–27. Hobbs shows no action in this regard other than his opinion that the company could not have completed the projects. More importantly, he never gives notice to any other member. Nonetheless, the court based its decision on a doctrine from another jurisdiction without explanation of Hobbs's fiduciary responsibility to his fellow members about the company's build-to-suit leases. Even though the court describes Hobbs's conduct as "dubious," it moves directly to the diverted corporate opportunity with no discussion of Hobbs's breach of the duty of loyalty or his actions in light of KRS 275.170.

Based on the court's use of the diversion of corporate opportunity as the basis for its decision, we shall examine Kentucky statutes that codify corporate conflict of interest for directors of a corporation. KRS 271B.8-310(1) states:

> A conflict of interest transaction shall be a transaction with the corporation in which a director of the corporation has a direct or indirect interest. A conflict of interest transaction shall not be voidable by the corporation solely because of the director's interest in the transaction if any one (1) of the following is true:

> > (a) The material facts of the transaction and the director's interest were disclosed or known to the board of directors or a committee of the board of directors and the board of directors or committee authorized, approved, or ratified the transaction;

> > (b) The material facts of the transaction and the director's interest were disclosed or known to the shareholders entitled to vote and they authorized, approved, or ratified the transaction; or

> > (c) The transaction was fair to the corporation.

Obviously, this statute is referring to directors of corporations rather than manager-members of limited liability, but we believe this statute is illustrative of Kentucky law regarding the primacy of fiduciary duty over misappropriation of corporate opportunity. But in order to concur with the trial court, we must determine not only that Hobbs's activities breached the statutory standards found in KRS 275.170 and KRS 271B.8-310(1), but we also must recognize the doctrine of diverted corporate opportunity. In light of the fact that Kentucky jurisprudence has never addressed this issue of lost opportunity and that this case is one of first impression, we adopt the business opportunity doctrine.

In doing so, however, we rely on the analysis found in *Miller:*

> [W]e believe a more helpful approach is to combine the 'line of business' test with the 'fairness' test and to adopt criteria involving a two-step process for determining the ultimate question of when liability for wrongful appropriation of a corporate opportunity should be imposed. The threshold question to be answered is whether a business opportunity presented is also a 'corporate' opportunity, i.e., whether the business opportunity is of sufficient importance and so closely related to an existing or prospective activity of the corporation as to warrant judicial sanctions against its personal acquisition by a managing officer or director of the corporation.

*Miller,* 222 N.W.2d at 81. Herein, the trial court has already determined that Hobbs's diversion of the O'Reilly build-to-suit lease projects was indeed a corporate opportunity of American Leasing that he diverted for his own use.

Having adopted the doctrine of corporate opportunity, we must next analyze whether American Leasing had the ability to undertake the O'Reilly project. During the bench trial, Hobbs argued that the three O'Reilly projects required completion by March 1, 2005. Moreover, he opined that American Leasing would have been unable to acquire the financing for the projects because U.S. Bank would not finance the projects and Habeeb refused to finance any project that involved Pearson. Hobbs posits that for these reasons, he had to form American Development so as not to lose the business prospect. This line of reasoning, however, is disingenuous. First, regardless of the company's ability to complete the projects, Hobbs could have and should have informed the other members. Moreover, notwithstanding the membership dispute, the record is clear that Hobbs knew the players — Pearson, Patmon, and Gray. The record shows no attempt by Hobbs to communicate his actions to the other members, explain his lack of communication to them, or to ask their assistance in obtaining financing for the projects. Further, a possibility exists that American Leasing could have sold its business opportunity to another venture and profited in that manner. At this juncture, it is pure speculation to assume that, even if Hobbs had exercised his duties of loyalty to American Leasing, it could not have completed or sold the leases.

Thus, we believe for the most part, that the court's legal analysis was correct. While it is true that transactions between a limited liability company and its managers are subject to fewer restrictions than are transactions between a corporation and its officers and directors, the transactions are still limited by the managers' obligation of good faith and fair dealing. Accordingly, the primary jurisprudence here is not whether the company could have completed the projects but whether Hobbs breached the statutory requisites found in KRS 275.170 and the common law as delineated in Kentucky. A member or manager must account to and hold as a trustee for the limited liability company any profit or benefit derived from transactions involving the use of a limited liability company's property by that member or manager without the consent of (i) one-half of the disinterested managers, (ii) one-half of the other persons (whether or not members) participating in management or (iii) a majority-in-interest of the members. *See* KRS 275.170(2). Hence, clearly the first prong of the business opportunity doctrine has been met: that is, Hobbs breached his fiduciary duty to American Leasing. After meeting the first prong of the doctrine of corporate opportunity, however, it is still necessary for Patmon to establish that American Leasing had the financial wherewithal to undertake the O'Reilly project. *Miller*, 222 N.W.2d at 71. While we are aware that Patmon opined during the course of the litigation that she did not know how American Leasing would have financed the project, she did so prior to the adoption of this doctrine. Thus, Patmon must now have the opportunity to address the burden of proof as to this issue.


6. Damages

Thus, we remand this case to the trial court to determine a remedy for Hobbs's common-law breach of fiduciary duty and failure to follow the statutory guidelines of KRS 275.170. Pursuant to KRS 275.170, at a minimum, Hobbs is required to hold in trust all benefits and profits derived by him as the result of his misuse of the build-to-suit leases. In so doing, the court shall determine the value of the build-to-suit leases that Hobbs diverted to American Development. We note that typically a breach of fiduciary duty in the partnership context results in an accounting (because profits, assets or opportunities have been diverted), or simply damages (again for the profits lost or losses incurred as a result of the breach.) *Bromberg and Ribstein on Partnership* P 16.07(i) (2005). For instance, the measure of damages in a similar case where company opportunity was misappropriated was the gross profit a company would have earned on the contracts. *See Kentucky Paving,* 557 S.W.2d at 436–39.

Further, pursuant to KRS 275.290 and KRS 275.300(1)(b), based on Hobbs's misconduct, the court is authorized to order the dissolution of American Leasing. The dissolution of the company will allow American Leasing to conclude its affairs, collect its assets and distribute the assets to its members. In light of Hobbs's misconduct, the court will need to decide, in the interest of justice, the percentage to be used in dividing the assets among the members.

Finally, Patmon will be able to present evidence as to whether American Leasing could have taken advantage of the business opportunity of the O'Reilly build-to-suit leases.

## CONCLUSION

Accordingly, we remand the September 24, 2007, judgment of the Jefferson Circuit Court for additional proceedings consistent with this opinion.

COMBS, CHIEF JUDGE CONCURRING:

I concur with the well-reasoned majority opinion in this unique and significant case. But I write separately in order to emphasize that this is indeed a case of first impression.

The trial court made numerous calls correctly. Its only error involved filling a hiatus in the law that often may only be decided in the course of an appeal. Short of clairvoyance, which is lacking in most humans, the trial court acted carefully and correctly within the only parameters of the precedent before it.

# HAGAN v. ADAMS PROPERTY ASSOCIATES, INC.
## Supreme Court of Virginia
### 482 S.E.2d 805 (1997)

ELIZABETH B. LACY, JUSTICE

In this appeal, we consider whether a transfer of real property from its owner to a limited liability company in which the owner is a member constitutes the sale of the property, entitling a real estate broker to a commission authorized by a listing agreement between the owner and broker.

Ralph E. and Maureen K. Hagan (collectively "Hagan") owned the Stuart Court Apartments (the property) in Richmond. On April 30, 1994, Hagan executed an agreement with Adams Property Associates, Inc. (Adams), giving Adams the exclusive right to sell the property for $1,600,000. The agreement provided that if the property was "sold or exchanged" within one year, with or without Adams' assistance, Hagan would pay Adams a fee of six percent of the "gross sales amount." Before the year expired, Hagan, Roy T. Tepper, and Lynn Parsons formed a limited liability company, Hagan, Parsons, & Tepper, L.L.C. (HPT). By deed dated April 23, 1995, Hagan transferred the property to HPT.

Adams filed a motion for judgment seeking recovery of a commission from Hagan pursuant to the April 1994 agreement. The trial court held that Adams was entitled to a commission because the transfer of the property to HPT constituted a sale of the property. Hagan appealed both the determination that a sale of the property occurred and the amount of the commission awarded.

Hagan first contends that transfer of legal title to the property to HPT represented his contribution to the capitalization of a new company, and capitalization of a new venture should not be classified as the sale of property, citing *Southpace Properties, Inc. v. Acquisition Group*, 5 F.3d 500, 504 (11th Cir.1993); Hagan also asserts that the transfer did not constitute a sale because he did not receive any present valuable consideration for his contribution. Hagan contends that, while his contribution determined what share of the ownership of the company he was entitled to receive, a new business such as HPT "involves an expectation of future profits and is always speculative." We disagree.

When Hagan transferred the property to HPT, he received more than an interest in the new company. Under the terms of the operating agreement executed in conjunction with the formation of HPT, HPT agreed to assume all liabilities existing on the property, which included the $1,028,000 unpaid balance on a first deed of trust note on the property. The record does not indicate whether the holder of the first deed of trust note released Hagan and substituted HPT as the obligor on the note. Even assuming such substitution did not occur, Hagan nevertheless received substantial relief from his debt obligation because, upon assuming all liabilities on the property, HPT became liable to Hagan for any amount Hagan would have had to pay the holder of the first deed of trust note. Also as part of the property transfer transaction, HPT executed a second deed of trust on the property securing a note payable to Hagan for $323,000. This note was due and payable when the property was subsequently sold, and it had priority over payments to anyone other than the beneficiary of the first deed of trust. Thus, in exchange for transfer of title to the property, Hagan received relief from his debt on the first deed of trust note as well as the benefit of a second deed of trust note and an interest in HPT. These benefits received by Hagan constituted valid consideration. *Brewer v. Bank of Danville*, 202 Va. 807, 815, 120 S.E.2d 273, 279 (1961).

Furthermore, the cases relied on by Hagan for the proposition that the contribution of property to a limited liability company is not a sale but the capitalization of a new company are inapposite. Those cases involved the capitalization of a partnership or entity governed by partnership law. As noted in those cases, a partnership is not an entity separate from the partners themselves; thus, in such circumstances, there is no transfer of property from one person to another, but only a change in the form of ownership. In this case, however, the new venture was a limited liability company, not a partnership.

Under the Virginia Limited Liability Company Act, Code §§ 13.1-1002 through 13.1-1073, a limited liability company is an unincorporated association with a registered agent and office. §§ 13.1-1002, –1015. It is an independent entity which can sue and be sued and its members are not personally liable for the debt or actions of the company. §§ 13.1-1009,–1019. In contrast to a partnership, a limited liability company in Virginia is an entity separate from its members and, thus, the transfer of property from a member to the limited liability company is more than a change in the form of ownership; it is a transfer from one entity or person to another. Accordingly, we agree with the trial court's conclusion that Hagan transferred the title of the property in exchange for valuable consideration and that this transfer was a sale of the property.

\* \* \*

Accordingly, we will affirm the judgment of the trial court holding that Hagan's transfer of title to the property to HPT was a sale of the property, that Adams was entitled to a commission on the gross sales amount, and that the gross sales amount is the debt relief plus the second deed of trust note Hagan received, $1,028,000 and $323,000, respectively, resulting in a commission of $81,060.

Affirmed.

# NOTES

**1.** This case illustrates one of the unintended pitfalls which may occur when individuals decide to change the form of legal ownership of their property. Is the court asking the right question when it decides the case based on the statutory recognition of the LLC as a legal entity separate and distinct from its members? Would a better way to approach the issue be to look at what the parties to the real estate listing agreement probably intended when they signed it or, in other words, did the parties to the listing agreement probably intend that the realtor's right to a commission would depend on the form of business entity to which the seller transferred the property?

**2.** In *Gebhart Family Inv., L.L.C. v. Nations Title Ins. of New York*, Inc., 752 A.2d 1222 (Md. Ct. Spec. App. 2000), plaintiffs, husband and wife, transferred ownership of real property to a family LLC formed for estate planning purposes. When an issue arose involving title to the property, defendant title insurance company denied coverage on the grounds that it had issued the policy to insure the named individuals, and not the LLC. Judgment in the trial court for defendants was affirmed by the Supreme Court, the court explaining that: "In contrast to a partnership, a limited liability company in Virginia is an entity separate from its members, and, thus, the transfer of property from a member to the limited liability company is more than a change in the form of ownership; it is a transfer from one entity to another." *Id.* at 764.

**3.** A similar case, involving the applicability of a title insurance policy to a partnership in which one of the original members had withdrawn and a new partner was admitted, is *Fairway Development v. Title Insurance Co.*, 621 F. Supp. 120 (N.D. Ohio 1985). That decision, decided under UPA (1914) was widely criticized.

However, in view of the fact that an LLC is expressly declared to be a legal entity, would you expect the *Gebhart* decision to be controversial?

## FRONTIER TRAYLOR SHEA, LLC v. METROPOLITAN AIRPORTS COMMISSION
### United States District Court, District of Minnesota
### 132 F. Supp. 2d 1193 (2000)

MONTGOMERY, DISTRICT JUDGE.

### I. INTRODUCTION

The above-entitled matter came on for hearing before the undersigned United States District Judge on November 3, 2000, pursuant to Plaintiff's Motion for Permanent Injunction [Doc. No. 8]. The dispute arises from the failure of Defendant Metropolitan Airports Commission to award Plaintiff Frontier Traylor Shea, LLC a contract to construct a light rail transit tunnel and station. For the reasons set forth below, Frontier Traylor Shea, LLC's motion is denied.

### II. BACKGROUND

#### A. Parties

Plaintiff in this action is Frontier Traylor Shea, LLC, a limited liability corporation ("Frontier LLC") created to submit a bid on the construction project at issue. The members of the LLC are Frontier-Kemper Constructors, Inc. ("Frontier"), Traylor Bros., Inc. ("Traylor"), and J.F. Shea Construction ("Shea"). J. Stip. § 2. Defendant is the Metropolitan Airports Commission ("MAC"), a public corporation organized under Minnesota law. * * *

#### B. Facts

The Hiawatha Light Rail Transit Project is developing a transportation corridor from the Mall of America in Bloomington, Minnesota to downtown Minneapolis. Part of the plan requires construction under the runway and through the Minneapolis/St. Paul International Airport terminal. As a result, the administrator of the airport, the MAC, the State of Minnesota, and the Metropolitan Council undertook the airport-related construction. These three groups entered into an agreement to serve as an outline of the rights and duties of the parties in respect to the project. J. Stip. Ex. B. The MAC was given the responsibility for finding a contractor for the job. Id. § 2.1. Because of the magnitude and time-sensitivity of the undertaking, the MAC implemented a pre-qualifications process to ensure that each bidder had the "experience and capabilities to complete the project prior to receiving the actual bids."

On February 23, 2000, the MAC sent out the "Request for Contractor's Pre-qualification Statement" to potential bidders. J. Stip. Ex. C. In response,

Frontier, Traylor and Shea submitted a statement listing the entity's "exact name" as the "Frontier / Traylor / Shea joint venture" ("Frontier JV"). In this document, the Frontier JV indicated that it was a "joint-and-several joint partnership." In response to the inquiry whether it was a corporation, the JV responded that it was "[n]ot applicable." Id. In addition to Frontier JV, five other bidders proffered a pre-qualification statement to the MAC, all were joint ventures. On June 30, 2000, the MAC requested bids on the project from entities that had pre-qualified. J. Stip. Ex. M. This document specified that only entities that pre-qualified with the MAC could tender a bid and enumerated those entities who were pre-qualified. "Frontier / Traylor / Shea, A Joint Venture" is listed as one of the entities.

On August 29, 2000, the MAC received a bid from Frontier LLC in the amount of $109,414,193. Id. Ex. N. It was the lowest bid received by the MAC, almost $500,000 less than the next lowest bid, tendered by the Obayashi Corp. / Johnson Brothers Corp., Joint Venture ("Obayashi"). Id. Ex. W, Ex. O. The MAC expressed concern that Frontier LLC was a limited liability company, as compared to the pre-qualified Frontier entity that identified itself as a joint venture partnership. The MAC sought legal advice on whether or not they could accept Frontier LLC's low bid. Id. Ex. U. The MAC's counsel advised on September 12, 2000, that the MAC's bidding specifications precluded an award to Frontier LLC as the low bidder because that entity was not pre-qualified. Id. Less than a week later, the MAC voted to reject Frontier LLC's bid on that basis and awarded the contract to Obayashi. Id. Ex. Y. Frontier LLC instituted this action soon thereafter.

## III. ANALYSIS

### A. Permanent Injunction Standard

Federal injunction procedures are laid out by Rule 65 of the Federal Rules of Civil Procedure. "In a preliminary injunction, a district court must balance four factors to determine whether injunctive relief is merited: 1) the threat of irreparable harm to the movant; 2) the balance between this harm and the harm to the nonmoving party should the injunction issue; 3) the likelihood of success on the merits; and 4) the public interest." * * *

### B. Analysis

In pursuing its permanent injunction, Frontier LLC must prove that it will prevail on the merits of its legal claim. Frontier LLC's alleges MAC cannot deny them the award of the construction contract because they submitted the low bid and complied with the bidding requirements. It is clear that "bids for municipal contracts must substantially comply with all the requirements relative thereto, as contained in statutes, charter provisions, ordinances, and advertisements." * * * The MAC made a determination that the Frontier LLC bid did not comply with the specification and bid solicitation document requirement that all bidders be pre-qualified. The pre-qualified entry was listed as Frontier / Traylor / Shea Joint Venture. Moreover, it further identified itself as a "joint-and-several joint partnership" and expressly disclaimed that it was a corporation. The MAC's listing of pre-qualified bidders able to participate in the bidding identified the entry as the "Frontier / Traylor / Shea Joint Venture." Conversely, the Frontier / Traylor / Shea entity that entered the eventual bid expressly labeled itself a Limited Liability Corporation.

Under Minnesota law, a joint venture is established "when two or more persons or entities combine their skill, time, property, and money in a business enterprise and agree to share the profits (and usually the losses) of the business." *Hansen International Sales Corp. v. KT's Kitchens, Inc.*, No. C5-96-2017, 1997 WL 147440, at *1 (Minn. Ct. App. 1997). * * * "The effect of a joint venture is to make individual defendants jointly liable due to their mutual undertaking." *Hansen*, 1997 WL 147440 at *1. * * * Although, the determination of whether an entity is a joint venture in "[e]ach case depends on its particular facts," four elements must exist: "(1) contribution, (2) joint proprietorship and mutual control, (3) sharing of profits, and (4) an express or implied contract." *Id.* Frontier LLC claims that a limited liability corporation is a joint venture. It claims that it meets the four required elements. The Minnesota Department of Administration defines a "joint venture" as simply "the temporary association of two or more businesses to secure and fulfill a procurement bid award." Minn. R. 1230.0150(11). Frontier LLC argues that it meets this definition. The treatise, Partnership & Joint Venture Agreements, states that "[j]oint ventures ordinarily take one of four basic forms: the corporate joint venture, the partnership joint venture, the limited liability company joint venture and the contractual joint venture." Richard D. Harroch, Partnership & Joint Venture Agreements, § 7.02(1) (2000). Frontier LLC cites to other courts that have referred to a limited liability company as a joint venture. *Cablevision of Boston, Inc. v. Public Improvement Commission*, 38 F. Supp. 2d 46, 51 (D. Mass. 1999) (referring to a limited liability company as a "joint venture" throughout the opinion), *aff'd* 184 F.3d 88 (1st Cir. 1999); *Elf Atochem N. Am., Inc. v. Jaffari*, 727 A.2d 286, 288 (Del. 1999) (the parties in the case "agreed to undertake a joint venture that was to be carried out using a limited liability company as the vehicle"). However, none of these cases construe Minnesota law or specifically analyze whether a limited liability corporation was a joint venture.

The MAC counters that a joint venture is like a partnership and cannot take the form of a limited liability company. The Eighth Circuit has commented that a "joint venture is a species of partnership." *Ringier America, Inc. v. Land O'Lakes, Inc.*, 106 F.3d 825, 828 (8th Cir. 1997). The court continued, commenting that "[u]nder Minnesota law, 'the rules and principles applicable to a partnership relation, with few if any material exceptions, govern and control the rights, duties, and obligations of the parties to a joint venture.' "*Id.* (citing *Rehnberg*, 52 N.W.2d at 457). Each entity making up the joint venture is individually jointly liable for the joint venture. *Hansen*, 1997 WL 147440 at *1 (citing *Curry v. McIntosh*, 389 N.W.2d 224, 228 (Minn. App. 1986)). The entity that pre-qualified, Frontier JV, identified itself as a joint venture partnership and the MAC avers that as such, each of the three entities in the joint venture would be individually liable for all the debts of the undertaking.

The MAC claims that Frontier LLC, which entered the low bid, has altered the structure of holding each member jointly liable for all the undertakings by its organization as a limited liability company. Frontier LLC was organized in Delaware, where the law states that the "debts, obligations and liabilities of a limited liability company . . . shall be solely the debts, obligations of the limited liability company, and no member or manager of a limited liability company shall be obligated personally for any such debt, obligation or liability of the limited liability company solely by reason of being a member or acting as a manager of the limited liability company." Del. Code Ann. tit. 6 § 18-303(a). The law also states that the members can "agree to be personally liable for any or all debts, obligations and liabilities of the limited liability company" if they wish. *Id.* at § 18-303(b).

Because Frontier LLC had not pre-qualified, it had not shown the MAC in its pre-qualification any agreement making each member jointly liable for all of the entity's obligations and liabilities. As a result, the MAC reasoned that the entity's bid on the contract is a material variance from the entity that pre-qualified because of the change from the joint venture partnership that applied for pre-qualification to the limited liability corporation that submitted the bid. As a result, the MAC, on advice of counsel, rejected the Frontier LLC bid because Frontier LLC had not pre-qualified, as was clearly required under the bid process' rules and specifications.

The MAC's decision to refuse the Frontier LLC bid is given a level of discretion under Minnesota law. *Bud Johnson Construction Co. v. Metropolitan Transit Commission*, 272 N.W.2d 31, 33 (Minn.1978) (quoting *Nielsen v. St. Paul*, 252 Minn. 12, 88 N.W.2d 853, 857 (1958)). Because the MAC's decision was based upon whether or not the requirements for bidding were fulfilled, this court must grant the MAC some latitude in respect to its decision and can only enjoin that determination if it is done "illegally, arbitrarily, capriciously, or unreasonably" Given the lack of clarity in the status of when a limited liability corporation is legally a joint venture and the conflicting documents presented to the MAC by Frontier JV and Frontier LLC, the decision that the Frontier LLC was not the same entity that pre-qualified cannot be said to be illegal, arbitrary, capricious or unreasonable. The specifications clearly state that all bidders must be pre-qualified to successfully bid on the project. Considering the magnitude and risk inherent in this project, it is certainly reasonable to require exacting compliance with bidding specifications to assure the public full protection. Distinctions over corporate form and their ramifications on issues of liability are of legitimate and serious concern given the project at issue.

Furthermore, there is no evidence that the MAC's decision was motivated by any other consideration than a good faith belief that Frontier LLC's bid did not comply with the established process. MAC's decision to not award the contract to Frontier LLC cannot be enjoined. Because the Supreme Court requires that a movant "must show actual success on the merits" to receive a permanent injunction, *Amoco Production Co. v. Village of Gambell*, 480 U.S. 531, 546 n. 12, 107 S. Ct. 1396, 94 L. Ed. 2d 542 (1987), Frontier LLC's failure to do so is dispositive of its motion. As a result, there is no need to discuss the other factors analyzing whether or not injunctive relief is merited. Frontier LLC's Motion for Permanent Injunction is denied.

# NOTES

1.   In *C&J Builders and Remodelers, LLC v. Geisenheimer*, 249 Conn. 415, 733 A.2d 193 (1999), the issue was whether an arbitration agreement entered into by a sole proprietorship, which subsequently converted into an LLC, was binding on the

parties. The court ruled for plaintiffs, holding that the arbitration clause was enforceable by the successor LLC, relying on Connecticut General Statutes sec. 34-200(a), governing the effect of the conversion of a partnership into an LLC, which provides that the LLC should be deemed to be the same entity that existed before the conversion and that all obligations of the converting partnership shall become obligations of the LLC. Although the statute was not expressly applicable to a sole proprietorship, the court saw no reason to distinguish between the conversion of a sole proprietorship into an LLC and of a partnership into an LLC and, for the sake of logical consistency, held that the same rule should apply to a sole proprietorship converting into an LLC.

2.   In *McConnell v. Hunt Sports Enterprises*, 725 N.E.2d 1193 (1999), the Court of Appeals of Ohio similarly borrowed from other business forms. In that case, the plaintiff filed for declaratory judgment against the defendant. At issue was whether the plaintiff had violated his fiduciary duties to his fellow LLC members when he negotiated personally with Nationwide Insurance to build a hockey arena for a proposed NHL franchise after negotiations between Nationwide and the LLC failed. In its holding, the court reasoned that it was not a breach of fiduciary duty for McConnell to obtain the franchise to the exclusion of the LLC. The court placed particular emphasis on the experience of the parties to the suit and specific language in the LLC's operating agreement that permitted the members to compete with it. Further, the court held, "in general terms, members of limited liability companies owe one another the duty of utmost trust and loyalty. However, such general duty in this case must be considered in the context of members' ability, pursuant to operating agreement, to compete with the company."

## UNITED STATES v. HAGERMAN
United States Court of Appeals, Seventh Circuit
545 F.3d 579 (2008)

POSNER, CIRCUIT JUDGE.

The defendants were convicted of criminal violations of the Clean Water Act, and Wabash was ordered to pay $250,000 in restitution to a federal Superfund account and was placed on probation (18 U.S.C. § 3563) for five years. Corporate probation has been called "a flexible vehicle for imposing a wide range of sanctions having the common feature of continued judicial control over aspects of corporate conduct." Richard Gruner, *To Let the Punishment Fit the Organization: Sanctioning Corporate Offenders Through Corporate Probation*, 16 AM. J. CRIM. L. 1, 3 (1988); *see also id.* at 4–6. The government, contending that Wabash had violated the conditions of probation by refusing to begin paying the restitution (and a $4,000 special assessment), that had been ordered, petitioned the district court for relief, as authorized by 18 U.S.C. § 3563(c). The court dismissed the petition after the government and Wabash resolved their differences by Wabash's agreeing to start paying restitution and to furnish specified information concerning the company's finances. Nevertheless, Wabash has filed an appeal to this court from the order of dismissal, as has its codefendant, Hagerman.

Hagerman's appeal must be dismissed because he was not a party to the probation-violation proceeding and no order naming him was entered. Wabash's appeal must also be dismissed, apart from doubts that Wabash was aggrieved by the dismissal of the probation-violation proceeding. Wabash has no lawyer in this court (it was represented in the district court by a lawyer who has since withdrawn). Hagerman, who is not a lawyer, claims the right to represent Wabash because he "is not only a major stockholder [presumably he means 'member,' since Wabash is an LLC, not a corporation] but is [also the] current President of [Wabash]." And it was Hagerman who filed this appeal on behalf of Wabash as well as himself. He complains about the deal that Wabash struck with the government, making this like an appeal by a party that agrees to a settlement but later thinks better of his decision and tries to get the appellate court to rescind it.

A corporation is not permitted to litigate in a federal court unless it is represented by a lawyer licensed to practice in that court. A limited liability company is not a corporation, but it is like one in being distinct from a natural person. "Limited liability companies are a 'relatively new business structure allowed by state statute,' having some features of corporations and some features of partnerships . . . For example, 'similar to a corporation, owners have limited personal liability for the debts and actions of the LLC'. . . 'Other features of LLCs are more like a partnership, providing management flexibility' . . . and in some cases affording 'the benefit of pass-through taxation." *McNamee v. Department of the Treasury*, 488 F.3d 100, 107 (2d Cir. 2007) (citations omitted).

We have not had occasion to rule on whether, like a corporation, an LLC can litigate only if represented by a lawyer. We can find only one appellate decision directly on point: *Lattanzio v. COMTA*, 481 F.3d 137 (2d Cir. 2007) (per curiam), held that an LLC can sue only if represented by a lawyer, even if as in that case (and possibly in this one, though when Wabash was created eight years ago it had two other members) the LLC has only one member. The same result, as noted in Lattanzio, has been reached in cases involving one-man corporations, not only our *Scandia Down* case but also *United States v. High Country Broadcasting Co.*, 3 F.3d 1244 (9th Cir. 1993) (per curiam), because it has no legal identity separate from the proprietor himself. But a partnership may not, * * * and as we said, an LLC is a cross between a corporation and a partnership.

An individual is permitted by 28 U.S.C. § 1654 to proceed pro se in a civil case in federal court because he might be unable to afford a lawyer, or a lawyer's fee might be too high relative to the stakes in the case to make litigation worthwhile other than on a pro se basis. *Timms v. Frank*, 953 F.2d 281, 285 (7th Cir. 1992) ("most litigants who sue without a lawyer do so because they cannot afford one"); Di Angelo v. Illinois Dep't of Public Aid, 891 F.2d 1260, 1264 (7th Cir. 1989) (concurring opinion) ("there will always be cases where the stakes are so low, the plaintiff so reprehensible, or the cause so unpopular that . . . the case will proceed without the participation of counsel"). There are many small corporations and corporation substitutes such as limited liability companies. But the right to conduct business in a form that confers privileges, such as the limited personal liability of the owners for tort or contract claims against the business, carries with it obligations one of which is to hire a lawyer if you want to sue or defend on behalf of the entity. Pro se litigation is a burden on the judiciary * * * and the burden is not to be borne when the litigant has chosen to do business in entity form. He must take the burdens with the benefits. *Lattanzio v. COMTA, supra*, 481 F.3d at 140. From that standpoint there is no difference between a corporation and a limited liability company, or indeed between either and a partnership, which although it does not provide its owners with limited liability confers other privileges, relating primarily to ease of formation and dissolution. That is why the privilege of pro se representation is, as we noted, denied to partnerships too.

The appeals are DISMISSED.

# NOTE

As a still relatively new statutory creation, the judicial limitations of the LLC form remain largely undefined. This phenomena is illustrated by the *Hagerman* case, which made it all the way to the United States Court of Appeals. Rather summarily, Judge Posner disposed of the issue and further clarified the limitations of the LLC form.

## ESTATE OF MARLENE R. COUNTRYMAN v. FARMERS COOPERATIVE ASSOCIATION
Supreme Court of Iowa
679 N.W.2d 598 (2004)

CADY, JUSTICE.

This appeal requires us to decide if a member and manager of an Iowa limited liability company can be liable for torts based on managerial conduct. The district court granted summary judgment for the limited liability company. On our review, we conclude we have jurisdiction of the appeal and that the record did not support summary judgment. We reverse and remand for further proceedings.

In the afternoon of September 6, 1999, an explosion leveled the home of Jerry Usovsky (Usovsky) in Richland, Iowa. Tragically, seven people who had gathered in the home to celebrate the Labor Day holiday died from the explosion. Six others were injured, some seriously. The likely cause of the explosion was stray propane gas. The survivors and executors of the estates of those who died eventually filed a lawsuit seeking monetary damages against a host of defendants. The legal theories of recovery included negligence, breach of warranty, and strict liability. The defendants included Iowa Double Circle, L.C. (Double Circle) and Farmers Cooperative Association of Keota (Keota).

Double Circle is an Iowa limited liability company. It is a supplier of propane, and delivered propane to Usovsky's home prior to the explosion. Keota is one of two members in Double Circle. It owns a ninety-five percent interest in the company. The other member is Farmland Industries, Inc. (Farmland Industries), a regional cooperative. Keota and Farmland Industries formed Double Circle in 1996 from an existing operation.

Keota is a farm cooperative that provides a variety of farm products and services to area farmers. It is a member of Farmland Industries and is managed by Dave Hopscheidt (Hopscheidt). The executive committee of Keota's board of directors serves as the board of directors of Double Circle, along with a representative of Farmland Industries. Keota provides managerial services to Double Circle, pursuant to a management agreement between Keota and Double Circle. Keota's duties under the agreement include "human resource and safety management." Hopscheidt oversees the daily operations of both Keota and Double Circle. However, Keota and Double Circle operate as separate entities and maintain separate finances.

Keota moved for summary judgment. It claimed the limited liability structure of Double Circle protected it from liability for any tortious acts of Double Circle based on its ownership interest and membership in Double Circle, or its management. It filed a supporting statement of undisputed facts with attached documents detailing the separate operations of Keota and Double Circle. The undisputed facts referred to an operating agreement providing that no member of the company would be liable for any tort solely by reason of being a member of the company. The attached documents also included a written agreement requiring Keota to provide management assistance and consulting services to Double Circle.

The plaintiffs resisted the motion by pointing to allegations in their petition indicating Keota participated in the claimed wrongdoing through the management decisions it made in consumer safety matters. For example, plaintiffs claimed Keota, through Hopscheidt, was negligent in failing to provide proper warnings to propane users, including the failure to warn users to install a gas detector, and to properly design the odorant added to the propane. Plaintiffs also sought to impose liability against Keota by piercing the corporate veil.

The district court granted summary judgment for Keota. It found plaintiffs failed to produce any facts to show that Keota engaged in conduct separate from its duties as director or manager of Double Circle. Consequently, it concluded Keota was protected as a matter of law from personal liability for claims of wrongful conduct attributable to Double Circle. It also concluded there was insufficient evidence as a matter of law to pierce the corporate veil.

*   *   *

The limited liability company, "LLC" as it is now known, is a hybrid business entity that is considered to have the attributes of a partnership for federal income tax purposes and the limited liability protections of a corporation. 5 Matthew G. Doré, Iowa Practice (Business Organizations) § 1.6, at 18–19 (2004) [hereinafter Doré]. As such, it provides for the operational advantages of a partnership by allowing the owners, called members, to participate in the management of the business. See id. § 1.6, at 20–21. Yet, the members and managers are protected from liability in the same manner shareholders, officers, and directors of a corporation are protected. Id. § 1.6, at 21.

The LLC first emerged as a business organization in 1977 and has now been adopted by statute in every state in the nation. Jerome P. Friedlander, II, The Limited Liability Company: With a State-By-State Review § 1:3 (1994 & Supp. 1997). Iowa joined the trend in 1992 with the passage of the Iowa Limited Liability Company Act (ILLCA). 1992 Iowa Acts ch. 1151 (codified at Iowa Code sections 490A.100-1601 (2003)). The ILLCA, among other features, permits the owners or members to centralize management in one or more managers or reserve all management powers to themselves. See Iowa Code § 490A.702; see also 5 Doré § 1.6, at 20–21.

Although the tax treatment of an LLC has been largely resolved, the contours of the limited liability of an LLC are less certain. See Karin Schwindt, Note, *Limited Liability Companies: Issues in Member Liability*, 44 UCLA L. REV. 1541, 1543–44 (1997). Only a few courts have specifically addressed the issue of tort liability. The ILLCA, however, describes the liability for members and managers of an LLC in four ways.

\* \* \*

The rules of liability derived from these statutes have been summarized as follows:

> Sections 490A.601 and 490A.603 of the Act generally provide that a member or manager of a limited liability company is not personally liable for acts or debts of the company solely by reason of being a member or manager, except in the following situations: (1) the ILLCA expressly provides for the person's liability; (2) the articles of organization provide for the person's liability; (3) the person has agreed in writing to be personally liable; (4) the person participates in tortious conduct; or (5) a shareholder of a corporation would be personally liable in the same situation, except that the failure to hold meetings and related formalities shall not be considered.

5 Doré § 13.12, at 287–88 (footnotes omitted).

This law frames our resolution of the summary judgment issue presented on appeal. While liability of members and managers is limited, the statute clearly imposes liability when they participate in tortious conduct. See Iowa Code § 490A.603(3). This approach is compatible with the longstanding approach to liability in corporate settings, where, under general agency principles, corporate officers and directors can be liable for their torts even when committed in their capacity as an officer. *Haupt v. Miller*, 514 N.W.2d 905, 907 (Iowa 1994); 3A Jennifer L. Berger et al., *Fletcher Cyclopedia of the Law of Private Corporations* § 1135, at 200–01 (perm. ed. rev. vol. 2002) [hereinafter *Fletcher*]. This approach has been explained as follows:

> Agency law generally, and Iowa law in particular, has long recognized that if a person commits a tort while acting for another person, the tortfeasor is personally liable for the tort, even if the person for whom he is acting is also vicariously liable for the same wrong. In other words, a person's status as an agent confers no immunity with respect to the person's own tort liability. Thus, if a member of a limited liability company injures another person while working in the course of the firm's business, the member is personally liable for that harm along with the company, just as the member would be if he worked for a firm organized as a corporation, a partnership, or any other business form.

5 Doré § 13.12, at 288 (footnotes omitted).

Keota suggests that liability of an LLC member or manager for tortious conduct is limited to conduct committed outside the member or manager role. Yet, this approach is contrary to the corporate model and agency principles upon which the liability of LLC members and managers is based, and cannot be found in the language of the statute. We acknowledge that the "participation in tortious conduct" standard would not impose tort liability on a manager for merely performing a general administrative duty. See *Haupt*, 514 N.W.2d at 909. There must be some participation. See 18B Am. Jur. 2d *Corporations* § 1877, at 724 (1985). The participation standard is consistent with the principle that members or managers are not liable based only on their status as members or managers. Instead, liability is derived from individual activities. Yet, a manager who takes part in the commission of a tort is liable even when the manager acts on behalf of a corporation. *See Haupt*, 514 N.W.2d at 909 (corporate officer liable for own tortious conduct where the officer acts under the corporate name or outside the corporate name). The ILLCA does not insulate a manager from liability for participation in tortious conduct merely because the conduct occurs within the scope and role as a manager. Keota argues this view of limited liability places section 490A.603(1) at odds with section 490A.603(3). We disagree. The limit on liability created for members and managers of LLCs in section 490A.603(1) means members and managers are not liable for company torts "solely by reason of being a member or manager" of an LLC. Iowa Code § 490A.603(1). The phrase "solely by reason of" refers to liability based upon membership or management status. It does not distinguish between conduct of a member or manager that may be separate and independent from the member or management role. Thus, it is not inconsistent to protect a member or manager from vicarious liability, while imposing liability when the member or manager participates in a tort. Liability of members of an LLC is limited, but not to the extent claimed by Keota.

Keota relies on *Curole v. Ochsner Clinic, L.L.C.*, 811 So. 2d 92, 96–97 (La. Ct. App. 2002), to support its position that owners and managers of an LLC are only liable for acts committed outside their capacity as a member or manager. While this was the conclusion reached in *Curole*, the case reveals that the Louisiana limited liability statute is substantially different from the Iowa statute. *Id.*; *see also* La. Rev. Stat. Ann. § 12:1320 (West 1994). The Louisiana statute does not contain the "solely by reason of" language of Iowa Code section 490A.603(1) and does not contain the "participation in tortious conduct" language of section 490A.603(3). *See* La. Rev. Stat. Ann. § 12.1320. Furthermore, other states that have discussed the topic of limited liability of LLC members and managers indicate that limited liability refers to liability based on the status of being a member or manager. *See Addy v. Myers*, 616 N.W.2d 359, 362 (N.D. 2000); Rebecca J. Huss, *Revamping Veil Piercing for all Limited Liability Entities: Forcing the Common Law Doctrine Into the Statutory Age*, 70 U. Cin. L. Rev. 95, 101–02 (2001).

It is also important to recognize that this case is not about holding an officer, director, or shareholder of Keota personally liable for participating in tortious conduct. Plaintiffs have not sued individual members of Keota. Instead, the lawsuit filed by the plaintiffs seeks to hold Keota liable for participating in certain torts as the designated manager of an LLC pursuant to the agreement under which it directed Hopscheidt to act for Keota in performing management services of Double Circle. While members and managers of an LLC are generally not personally liable for the acts of an LLC, Keota must also be viewed as a separate "legal" person. This approach means that corporate liability for the acts of corporate agents can result as a matter of agency law. 5 Doré § 15.3, at 378–79. In discussing the general rule of limited liability of directors, officers, and employees for acts of a corporation, one author explains:

> A similar result obtains under the doctrine of respondeat superior when corporate employees commit a tort. The corporation is the employer and principal of such persons. Thus, the corporation may be held vicariously liable for its employees' torts, but the corporation's directors, officers, and employees (other than those employees who committed the tort) will not face any exposure. In short, for liability purposes the corporation is distinct not only from its shareholders, but also from its directors, officers, employees, and other agents.

5 Doré § 15.3, at 379. *See generally* 3A *Fletcher* ch. 54 (discussing corporate liability for torts of officers and agents); *Meyer v. Holley*, 537 U.S. 280, 285–86, 123 S. Ct. 824, 829, 154 L. Ed. 2d 753, 761 (2003) (a corporation — not its owner or officer — is vicariously liable for torts of employees or agents). It is appropriate to apply this approach to cooperatives, such as Keota. See 18 Am. Jur. 2d *Cooperative Associations* § 12, at 281 (1985) (a cooperative is essentially a corporation). Thus, Keota can participate in torts through the conduct of those individuals acting on behalf of Keota.

We conclude that Keota is not protected from liability if it participated in tortious conduct in performing its duties as manager of Double Circle. Consequently, the district court improperly granted summary judgment based on the limited liability provisions of section 490A.603(1) and 490A.603(3). A trial is necessary to develop the facts relating to allegations of Keota's participation in the alleged torts.2

We reverse the summary judgment ruling of the district court on the issue of liability under chapter 490A, and remand for further proceedings. Plaintiffs did not appeal from that portion of the summary judgment ruling dismissing the claim for liability based on the theory of piercing the corporate veil, and that theory of recovery is not viable on remand.

REVERSED AND REMANDED.

All justices concur except CARTER, J., who takes no part.

# NOTES

**1.** The principal case represents the majority view with respect to personal liability of members of an LLC for tortious conduct. The same result would generally follow for corporate officers and directors.

**2.** Note that *Curole v. Oshner Clinic, supra,* cited by plaintiff in support of liability involved the Louisiana LLC Act, which contains different statutory language than the Iowa LLC Act involved in Countryman. The great variation in the language of LLC acts from state to state can serve as a trap for the careless attorney who fails to check the language of a particular act applicable in a given situation.

# BASTAN v. RJM & ASSOCIATES, LLC
## Superior Court of Connecticut
### 2001 Conn. Super. LEXIS 1605 (June 4, 2001)

BEACH, J.

This action seeks primarily to recover a deposit paid to a builder. The defendant Robert J. Moravek, Sr., allegedly was the sole member of RJM & Associates, LLC, the limited liability company which contracted with the plaintiff to build the house. The fourth count of the complaint seeks to impose personal liability upon Moravek individually; the count alleges that Moravek is the controlling member of the LLC, that he treated LLC funds as his own by paying virtually all of his personal expenses from the account of the LLC, thus draining the LLC's assets such that they are insufficient to meet its obligations, that by his conduct Moravek "caused the independence of said LLC to cease," and that adherence to the fiction of separate identity would defeat the interests of justice.

The defendant Moravek has moved to strike the fourth count. Although he expressly does not concede that the allegations would be sufficient to "pierce the veil" of corporate protection against individual liability, the thrust of his argument is that in the context of a member-operated limited liability company, there can be no piercing of the LLC veil. Recognizing that there is no binding Connecticut authority precisely on point, Moravek argues that the statutory scheme expressly allows the individual to manage the LLC; he also refers to several law review articles which note the difficulty with which the veil ought to be allowed to be pierced in the context of member-operated LLCs.

Having reviewed the authorities cited by both sides, I am not persuaded that the legislature intended the limitation on member liability to be absolute. HN1 Section 34-133(a) of the General Statutes provides that "(except as provided in (b)), a person who is a member or manager of a limited liability company is not liable, *solely* by reason of being a member or manager . . . for a debt, obligation or liability (of the LLC)." (Emphasis added.) HN2 Subsection (b) provides, *inter alia*, that the personal liability of a member "shall be no greater than that of a shareholder who is an employee of a corporation formed under Chapter 601." The legislature is deemed to have been aware of our HN3 deeply rooted common law remedy of imposing personal liability upon a shareholder of a corporation where the corporate shield has been used to promote injustice, and the legislature surely could have expressly created a blanket limitation of member liability had it so chosen. Not much imagination is required to hypothesize all sorts of pernicious uses of such a blanket limitation.

I hold, then, that HN4 the traditional notions of imposing boundaries on the limitation of individual liability apply to limited liability companies. * * * The defendant suggests that even if that is so, individual liability ought not be imposed on the so-called "identity" theory where the LLC is member-managed.

There have been at least two theories suggested as specific ways of piercing the corporate veil, the instrumentality rule and the identity rule. "The instrumentality rule requires, in any case but an express agency, proof of three elements: (1)

Control, not mere majority or complete stock control, but complete domination, not only of finances but of policy and business practice in respect to the transaction attacked so that the corporate entity as to this transaction had at the time no separate mind, will or existence of its own; (2) that such control must have been used by the defendant to commit fraud or wrong, to perpetrate the violation of a statutory or other positive legal duty, or a dishonest or unjust act in contravention of plaintiff's legal rights; and (3) that the aforesaid control and breach of duty must proximately cause the injury or unjust loss complained of." *Tomasso v. Armor Construction & Paving, Inc.*, 187 Conn. 544, 447 A.2d 406 (1982). Under the identity theory, the proponent must " 'show that there was such a unity of interest and ownership that the independence of the corporation had in effect ceased or had never begun, [such that] an adherence to the fiction of separate identity would serve only to defeat justice and equity by permitting the economic entity to escape liability arising out of an operation conducted by one corporation for the benefit of the whole enterprise.' *Saphir v. Neustad*, 177 Conn. 191,] 210[, 413 A.2d 843. The identity rule primarily applies to prevent injustice in the situation where two corporate entities are, in reality, controlled as one enterprise because of the existence of common owners, officers, directors or shareholders and because of the lack of observance of corporate formalities between the two entities. See *Zaist v. Olson*, 154 Conn. 563,] 575–76, 578, 227 A.2d 552 (and cases cited therein)." *Tomasso*, 187 Conn. at 559–60 (footnotes omitted).

*[handwritten margin note: identity theory]*

Although the narrowly defined identity theory would not appear to apply on the facts alleged in this case in any event, the narrow definitions may not be overwhelmingly significant. As stated by Justice Borden, the principle underlying the identity theory was applied to an individual in *Saphir*, and in any event:

> As a matter of policy I see no reason to permit recovery against a controlling individual under the instrumentality theory but to deny it under the identity theory. They are simply slightly different roads to the same destination. They both derive from the same principle: "Courts will . . . disregard the fiction of a separate legal entity to pierce the shield of immunity afforded by the corporate structure in a situation in which the corporate entity has been so controlled and dominated that justice requires liability to be imposed on the real actor." *Saphir v. Neustadt, supra*, 209. And they both require uniquely factual determinations by the trial court, in which "each case in which the issue is raised should be regarded as sui generis, to be decided in accordance with its own underlying facts." 1 Fletcher, op. cit., 41.3.

*Tomasso*, 187 Conn. at 577–78 (dissenting opinion) (footnotes omitted).

As stated by Judge Gill in *Litchfield Asset Management, supra*:

> The rationale behind the alter ego theory is that if the shareholders themselves, or the corporations themselves, disregard the legal separation, distinct properties, or proper formalities of the different corporate enterprises, then the law will likewise disregard them so far as is necessary to protect individual and corporate creditors." 1 W. Fletcher, Cyclopedia of the Law of Private Corporations (1990) § CT Page 13765 41.10, p. 614. The same theory applies in the case of a limited liability company. See, e.g., New

England National, LLC v. Kabro, 2000 Conn. Super. LEXIS 470, Superior Court, judicial district of New London. Docket No. 550014 (Feb. 16, 2000) (Martin, J.); see also M. Pruner, *supra*, §§ 3.1.1.4, 7.14, pp. 10, 106–07.

The defendant argues that because the statutory scheme allows members to manage LLCs; see § 34-140 of the General Statutes; there can be no equitable piercing of the veil because members are allowed to act as individuals. This argument overlooks the consideration that considerable structure is required in the formation and operation of LLCs; see, e.g., §§ 34-119 to 124 and indeed all of Chapter 613 of the General Statutes; and a person who ignores the intended separation between the individual and the company ought to be no better off than the sole shareholder who ignores corporate obligations.

The plaintiffs have alleged facts which, if true, can support a conclusion that the limitation contemplated in § 34-133 does not apply. The motion to strike, then, is denied.

## NOTES

1. As is the case generally with corporations, there are no statutory standards for when, if at all, it is appropriate to pierce the corporate veil in an LLC. The court's discussion in *Bastan* suggests that the standards developed by the courts in piercing the corporate veil, discussed in Chapter 6, *infra*, should generally apply to LLC's as well. Given the different structures of an LLC and a corporation, what differences, if any, should there be in the standards governing piercing the corporate veil?

2. Compare *Countryman*, which deals with liability for tortious conduct of a member of an LLC, with *Bastan* which is a contract case. Why does the court in *Countryman* refuse to hold that the defendant is immunized from liability by the LLC if he personally participated in the tortious conduct while the defendant in *Bastan* will only be liable if the more rigorous standards for piercing the veil can be established? Is the same tort versus contract distinction found if the business entity is a corporation rather than an LLC?

## ELF ATOCHEM NORTH AMERICA, INC. v. JAFFARI
### Supreme Court of Delaware
### 727 A.2d 286 (1999)

VEASEY, CHIEF JUSTICE:

This is a case of first impression before this Court involving the Delaware Limited Liability Company Act (the "Act"). The limited liability company ("LLC") is a relatively new entity that has emerged in recent years as an attractive vehicle to facilitate business relationships and transactions. The wording and architecture of the Act is somewhat complicated, but it is designed to achieve what is seemingly a simple concept-to permit persons or entities ("members") to join together in an environment of private ordering to form and operate the enterprise under an LLC agreement with tax benefits akin to a partnership and limited liability akin to the corporate form.

This is a purported derivative suit brought on behalf of a Delaware LLC calling into question whether: (1) the LLC, which did not itself execute the LLC agreement in this case ("the Agreement") defining its governance and operation, is nevertheless bound by the Agreement; and (2) contractual provisions directing that all disputes be resolved exclusively by arbitration or court proceedings in California are valid under the Act. Resolution of these issues requires us to examine the applicability and scope of certain provisions of the Act in light of the Agreement.

We hold that: (1) the Agreement is binding on the LLC as well as the members; and (2) since the Act does not prohibit the members of an LLC from vesting exclusive subject matter jurisdiction in arbitration proceedings (or court enforcement of arbitration) in California to resolve disputes, the contractual forum selection provisions must govern.

Accordingly, we affirm the judgment of the Court of Chancery dismissing the action brought in that court on the ground that the Agreement validly predetermined the for a in which disputes would be resolved, thus stripping the Court of Chancery of subject matter jurisdiction.

## Facts

Plaintiff below-appellant Elf Atochem North America, Inc., a Pennsylvania Corporation ("Elf"), manufactures and distributes solvent-based maskants to the aerospace and aviation industries throughout the world. Defendant below-appellee Cyrus A. Jaffari is the president of Malek, Inc., a California Corporation. Jaffari had developed an innovative, environmentally-friendly alternative to the solvent-based maskants that presently dominate the market.

For decades, the aerospace and aviation industries have used solvent-based maskants in the chemical milling process. Recently, however, the Environmental Protection Agency ("EPA") classified solvent-based maskants as hazardous chemicals and air contaminants. To avoid conflict with EPA regulations, Elf considered developing or distributing a maskant less harmful to the environment.

In the mid-nineties, Elf approached Jaffari and proposed investing in his product and assisting in its marketing. Jaffari found the proposal attractive since his company, Malek, Inc., possessed limited resources and little international sales expertise. Elf and Jaffari agreed to undertake a joint venture that was to be carried out using a limited liability company as the vehicle.

On October 29, 1996, Malek, Inc. caused to be filed a Certificate of Formation with the Delaware Secretary of State, thus forming Malek LLC, a Delaware limited liability company under the Act. The certificate of formation is a relatively brief and formal document that is the first statutory step in creating the LLC as a separate legal entity. The certificate does not contain a comprehensive agreement among the parties, and the statute contemplates that the certificate of formation is to be complemented by the terms of the Agreement.[1]

Next, Elf, Jaffari and Malek, Inc. entered into a series of agreements providing for the governance and operation of the joint venture. Of particular importance to this litigation, Elf, Malek, Inc., and Jaffari entered into the Agreement, a comprehensive and integrated document[2] of 38 single-spaced pages setting forth detailed provisions for the governance of Malek LLC, which is not itself a signatory to the Agreement. Elf and Malek LLC entered into an Exclusive Distributorship Agreement in which Elf would be the exclusive, worldwide distributor for Malek LLC. The Agreement provides that Jaffari will be the manager of Malek LLC. Jaffari and Malek LLC entered into an employment agreement providing for Jaffari's employment as chief executive officer of Malek LLC.

The Agreement is the operative document for purposes of this Opinion, however. Under the Agreement, Elf contributed $1 million in exchange for a 30 percent interest in Malek LLC. Malek, Inc. contributed its rights to the water-based maskant in exchange for a 70 percent interest in Malek LLC.

The Agreement contains an arbitration clause covering all disputes. The clause, Section 13.8, provides that "any controversy or dispute arising out of this Agreement, the interpretation of any of the provisions hereof, or the action or inaction of any Member or Manager hereunder shall be submitted to arbitration in San Francisco, California. . . . " Section 13.8 further provides: "No action . . . based upon any claim arising out of or related to this Agreement shall be instituted in any court by any Member except (a) an action to compel arbitration . . . or (b) an action to enforce an award obtained in an arbitration proceeding. . . . " The Agreement also contains a forum selection clause, Section 13.7, providing that all members consent to: "exclusive jurisdiction of the state and federal courts sitting in California in any action on a claim arising out of, under or in connection with this Agreement or the transactions contemplated by this Agreement, provided such claim is not required to be arbitrated pursuant to Section 13.8"; and personal jurisdiction in California. The Distribution Agreement contains no forum selection or arbitration clause.

## Elf's Suit in the Court of Chancery

On April 27, 1998, Elf sued Jaffari and Malek LLC, individually and derivatively on behalf of Malek LLC, in the Delaware Court of Chancery, seeking equitable remedies. Among other claims, Elf alleged that Jaffari breached his fiduciary duty to Malek LLC, pushed Malek LLC to the brink of insolvency by withdrawing funds for personal use, interfered with business opportunities, failed to make disclosures

---

[1] [5] *See* 6 Del. C. § 18-201(d) which provides:

> A limited liability company agreement may be entered into either before, after or at the time of the filing of a certificate of formation and, whether entered into before, after or at the time of such filing, may be made effective as of the formation of the limited liability company or at such other time or date as provided in the limited liability company agreement.

[2] [6] *See* the definition section of the statute, 6 Del.C. § 18-101(7), defining the term "limited liability company agreement" as "any agreement . . . of the . . . members as to the affairs of a limited liability company and the conduct of its business," and setting forth a nonexclusive list of what it may provide.

to Elf, and threatened to make poor quality maskant and to violate environmental regulations. Elf also alleged breach of contract, tortious interference with prospective business relations, and (solely as to Jaffari) fraud.

The Court of Chancery granted defendants' motion to dismiss based on lack of subject matter jurisdiction. The court held that Elf's claims arose under the Agreement, or the transactions contemplated by the agreement, and were directly related to Jaffari's actions as manager of Malek LLC. Therefore, the court found that the Agreement governed the question of jurisdiction and that only a court of law or arbitrator in California is empowered to decide these claims. Elf now appeals the order of the Court of Chancery dismissing the complaint.

### Contentions of the Parties

Elf claims that the Court of Chancery erred in holding that the arbitration and forum selection clauses in the Agreement governed, and thus deprived that court of jurisdiction to adjudicate all of Elf's claims, including its derivative claims made on behalf of Malek LLC. Elf contends that, since Malek LLC is not a party to the Agreement, it is not bound by the forum selection provisions. Elf also argues that the court erred in failing to classify its claim as derivative on behalf of Malek LLC against Jaffari as manager. Therefore, Elf claims that the Court of Chancery should have adjudicated the dispute. Finally, Elf argues that the dispute resolution clauses of the Agreement are invalid under Section 109(d) of the Act, which, it alleges, prohibits the parties from vesting exclusive jurisdiction in a forum outside of Delaware.[3]

Defendants claim that Elf contracted with Malek, Inc. and Jaffari that all disputes that arise out of, under, or in connection with the Agreement must be resolved exclusively in California by arbitration or court proceedings. Defendants allege that the characterization of Elf's claim as direct or derivative is irrelevant, as the Agreement provides that the members would not institute "any" action at law or equity except one to compel arbitration, and that any such action must be brought in California. Defendants also argue that, in reality, Elf's claims are direct, not derivative, claims against its fellow LLC members, Malek, Inc. and Jaffari.

With regard to the validity of Section 13.7, defendants argue that Section 18-109(d) of the Act is a permissive statute and does not prohibit the parties from vesting exclusive jurisdiction outside of Delaware. Thus, defendants assert that the Court of Chancery correctly held that the dispute resolution provisions of the Agreement are valid and apply to bar Elf from seeking relief in Delaware.

---

[3] [10] *See* 6 Del. C. § 18-109(d), which provides:

> In a written limited liability company agreement or other writing, a manager or member *may* consent to be subject to the nonexclusive jurisdiction of the courts of, or arbitration in, a specified jurisdiction, or the exclusive jurisdiction of the courts of the State of Delaware, or the exclusivity of arbitration in a specified jurisdiction or the State of Delaware. . . .

(Emphasis added.)

## General Summary of Background of the Act

The phenomenon of business arrangements using "alternative entities" has been developing rapidly over the past several years. Long gone are the days when business planners were confined to corporate or partnership structures.

\* \* \*

The Delaware [LLC] Act was adopted in October 1992. The Act is codified in Chapter 18 of Title 6 of the Delaware Code. To date, the Act has been amended six times with a view to modernization. The LLC is an attractive form of business entity because it combines corporate-type limited liability with partnership-type flexibility and tax advantages.[4] The Act can be characterized as a "flexible statute" because it generally permits members to engage in private ordering with substantial freedom of contract to govern their relationship, provided they do not contravene any mandatory provisions of the Act. Indeed, the LLC has been characterized as the "best of both worlds."

The Delaware Act has been modeled on the popular Delaware LP Act. In fact, its architecture and much of its wording is almost identical to that of the Delaware LP Act. Under the Act, a member of an LLC is treated much like a limited partner under the LP Act. The policy of freedom of contract underlies both the Act and the LP Act.

In August 1994, nearly two years after the enactment of the Delaware LLC Act, the Uniform Law Commissioners promulgated the Uniform Limited Liability Company Act (ULLCA).[5] To coordinate with later developments in federal tax guidelines regarding manager-managed LLCS, the Commissioners adopted minor changes in 1995. The Commissioners further amended the ULLCA in 1996. Despite its purpose to promote uniformity and consistency, the ULLCA has not been widely popular. In fact, only seven jurisdictions have adopted the ULLCA since its creation in 1994.[6] A notable commentator on LLCs has argued that legislatures should look to either the Delaware Act or the Prototype Act created by the ABA when drafting state statutes.[7]

\* \* \*

---

[4] [14] *See* 1 Larry E. Ribstein & Robert R. Keatinge, *Ribstein and Keatinge on Limited Liability Companies*, § 2.02, at 2 (1998); Martin I. Lubaroff & Paul M. Altman, *Delaware Limited Liability Companies, in Delaware Law of Corporations & Business Organizations*, § 20.1 (R. Franklin Balotti & Jesse A. Finkelstein eds., 1998).

[5] [21] Jennifer J. Johnson, *Limited Liability for Lawyers: General Partners Need Not Apply*, 51 Bus. Law. 85, n. 69 (1995). In addition to the ULLCA, a Prototype Limited Liability Company Act ("Prototype Act") was drafted by the Subcommittee on Limited Liability Companies of the ABA Section of Business Law. The Prototype Act was released in the Fall of 1993 and has formed the basis for several LLC statutes enacted since that time. *See id.*

[6] [23] To date, the seven jurisdictions that have adopted the ULLCA are Alabama, South Dakota, the U.S. Virgin Islands, Hawaii, South Carolina, Vermont, and West Virginia. *See* Uniform Limited Liability Company Act (1995), Table of Jurisdictions Wherein Act Has Been Adopted and additional information provided by the Uniform Law Commissioners (Mar. 17, 1999).

[7] [24] *See* Larry E. Ribstein, *A Critique of the Uniform Limited Liability Company Act*, 25 Stetson L. Rev. 311, 329 (1995).

### The Arbitration and Forum Selection Clauses in the Agreement are a Bar to Jurisdiction in the Court of Chancery

In vesting the Court of Chancery with jurisdiction, the Act accomplished at least three purposes: (1) it assured that the Court of Chancery has jurisdiction it might not otherwise have because it is a court of limited jurisdiction that requires traditional equitable relief or specific legislation to act; (2) it established the Court of Chancery as the default forum in the event the members did not provide another choice of forum or dispute resolution mechanism; and (3) it tends to center interpretive litigation in Delaware courts with the expectation of uniformity. Nevertheless, the arbitration provision of the Agreement in this case fosters the Delaware policy favoring alternate dispute resolution mechanisms, including arbitration. Such mechanisms are an important goal of Delaware legislation, court rules, and jurisprudence.

### Malek LLC's Failure to Sign the Agreement Does Not Affect the Members' Agreement Governing Dispute Resolution

Elf argues that because Malek LLC, on whose behalf Elf allegedly brings these claims, is not a party to the Agreement, the derivative claims it brought on behalf of Malek LLC are not governed by the arbitration and forum selection clauses of the Agreement.

Elf argues that Malek LLC came into existence on October 29, 1996, when the parties filed its Certificate of Formation with the Delaware Secretary of State. The parties did not sign the Agreement until November 4, 1996. Elf contends that Malek LLC existed as an LLC as of October 29, 1996, but never agreed to the Agreement because it did not sign it. Because Malek LLC never expressly assented to the arbitration and forum selection clauses within the Agreement, Elf argues it can sue derivatively on behalf of Malek LLC pursuant to 6 Del.C. § 18-1001.[8]

We are not persuaded by this argument. Section 18-101(7) defines the limited liability company agreement as "any agreement, written or oral, of the member or members as to the affairs of a limited liability company and the conduct of its business." Here, Malek, Inc. and Elf, the members of Malek LLC, executed the Agreement to carry out the affairs and business of Malek LLC and to provide for arbitration and forum selection.

Notwithstanding Malek LLC's failure to sign the Agreement, Elf's claims are subject to the arbitration and forum selection clauses of the Agreement. The Act is a statute designed to permit members maximum flexibility in entering into an agreement to govern their relationship. It is the members who are the real parties in interest. The LLC is simply their joint business vehicle. This is the contemplation of the statute in prescribing the outlines of a limited liability company agreement.

---

**8** [35] 6 Del.C. § 18-1001 provides: "Right to bring action. A member may . . . bring an action in the Court of Chancery in the right of a limited liability company to recover a judgment in its favor if managers or members with authority to do so have refused to bring the action or if an effort to cause those managers or members to bring the action is not likely to succeed."

Classification by Elf of its Claims as Derivative is Irrelevant

\* \* \*

[The court concludes that Delaware law allows for derivative suits against management of an LLC and that the LLC Agreement provides that members may not initiate such claims outside of California. The court then discussed, and rejects, the argument that the Delaware Court of Chancery has exclusive jurisdiction over their derivative claims.]

\* \* \*

### Conclusion

We affirm the judgment of the Court of Chancery dismissing Elf Atochem's amended complaint for lack of subject matter jurisdiction.

## NOTES

**1.** The Delaware LLC Act has proved to be popular with business lawyers, primarily due to the great flexibility which it gives to the members to modify its default rules through the Operating Agreement. Given Delaware's longstanding reputation as a business-friendly jurisdiction, this is not surprising.

**2.** As the court notes, the Uniform Limited Liability Company Act was adopted in 1994, relatively late in the game after a majority of all states had already adopted an LLC Act of their own. The unfortunate result is that there is little uniformity among the states, although differences seem to be narrowing due to frequent amendments. For example, the single member LLC, which was once allowed in only a handful of states, is now permitted in a majority of jurisdictions. The Uniform Law Commission of the National Conference of Commissioners on Uniform State Laws completed the Revised Uniform Limited Liability Company Act in 2006. As of this writing, it has been adopted by fewer than a dozen states.

## FIVE STAR CONCRETE, L.L.C. v. KLINK, INC.
### Court of Appeals of Indiana
### 693 N.E.2d 583 (1998)

STATON, JUDGE.

Five Star Concrete, L.L.C. ("Five Star") appeals the entry of summary judgment in favor of Klink, Inc. ("Klink"), a former member of Five Star, and also appeals the denial of its cross-motion for summary judgment. In regard to the granting of Klink's motion, Five Star raises the following consolidated and restated issue:

> I. Whether Klink, as a dissociating member of a limited liability company, has the legal right to receive a distribution equal to the net income allocated to it for taxation purposes.

Concerning the denial of its cross-motion for summary judgment, Five Star presents two restated issues:

II. Whether Klink affirmatively divested itself of all of its economic interest when it sold its membership units to Five Star.

III. Whether the method of valuing Klink's economic interest demonstrates that Klink was paid the current fair market value for its entire interest in Five Star.

We affirm in part, reverse in part and remand.

On June 14, 1994, Klink and four other corporations, all engaged in supplying ready-mix concrete, formed Five Star, a limited liability company ("LLC"), in order to furnish concrete to large construction projects. Klink contributed $38,500.00, 12.5% of the initial total capitalization, and was issued 12.5 ownership units.

In a letter dated October 13, 1995, Klink formally notified Five Star of its intent to withdraw from membership effective October 10, 1995. The remaining members decided to purchase Klink's ownership units and to continue the business. To accomplish this end, Five Star members met on October 23, 1995 and agreed that Klink would receive $61,047.22 for the value of its "units."

After Five Star's fiscal year ended December 31, 1995, Klink was allocated $31,889.02 of income, representing its share of the LLC's profits for the approximate ten-month period of 1995 when Klink was a member. The allocation did not result in a[9] monetary distribution to Klink. Instead, the allocation was made only for the purpose of properly determining Klink's tax liability. After receiving notification of the allocation, Klink filed a complaint against Five Star claiming that it was entitled to a distribution of cash in the sum of $31,889.02. Klink moved for summary judgment on its claim, and Five Star responded with its own motion for summary judgment, asserting that Klink had already been paid for its entire interest. Following a hearing, the trial court granted Klink's motion, finding that Klink had a legal right to receive a distribution of $31,889.02. The court also denied Five Star's cross-motion. Five Star appeals both rulings.

\* \* \*

Five Star first contends that the trial court improperly entered summary judgment in favor of Klink on the basis that Klink had the legal right to an actual distribution of $31,889.02, the amount allocated for taxation purposes. At the outset, we recognize that LLCs offer the same limited liability as the corporate form of business organization, but they are treated by federal and state taxing bodies in the same way as partnerships, that is, income "passes through" the entity and is taxed to the member, an owner of an interest in the company. PAUL J. GALANTI, 17 INDIANA PRACTICE, BUSINESS ORGANIZATIONS § 7A.1, at 38–39 (Supp. 1997). Limited liability companies are also governed by the Indiana Business Flexibility Act (the "Act"). *See* IND. CODE §§ 23-18-1-1 to 23-18-13-1 (1993). The Act empowers members to make

---

**9** [1] Unless a written operating agreement provides that a member may not withdraw by voluntary act, a member may withdraw from a limited liability company "at any time by giving thirty (30) days written notice to the other members . . . " IND. CODE § 23-18-6-6 (1993). Neither party addresses Klink's failure to give adequate notice, and we do not consider it in our analysis.

and amend operating agreements for managing the business and regulating the LLC's affairs, as long as these are not inconsistent with state law or the LLC's articles of organization. IND. CODE § 23-18-2-2(2) (1993).

Here, there is no dispute that the allocation, Klink's portion of Five Star's income, was proper. Five Star was being taxed as a "pass-through" entity, and the allocation was required by tax law as well as by the Operating Agreement. However, Klink insists that when there is an allocation to a dissociating member there is a corresponding obligation to make a cash distribution of income equal to the allocation. We do not agree.

Nowhere does the Act provide that allocation of income to members for income tax purposes creates an automatic legal right to receive a distribution in the amount of that income, even when a member is withdrawing from the LLC. Indeed, there are times that such a distribution would be unlawful. See IND. CODE § 23-18-5-6;[10] see also United States v. Basye, 410 U.S. 441, 453, 93 S. Ct. 1080, 1088, 35 L. Ed. 2d 412, 422 (1973) (each partner pays taxes on share of partnership's income without regard to whether that amount is actually distributed to partner).

The Operating Agreement is also silent regarding the timing and amount of distributions; thus, under the Act, these decisions are to be made by the majority of the members. See IND. CODE § 23-18-4-3(a) (1993). The evidence construed in favor of Five Star shows that Five Star made a distribution to all members in July of 1995; Klink's share was approximately $12,500.00. However, neither this distribution nor any other was made based upon the amount of income allocated to a member. Further, since that date no distributions were made to any members.

Conduit treatment under income tax law means that allocations occur regardless of the magnitude or timing of distributions. We conclude that the allocation of profits for tax reporting purposes did not provide Klink with a legal right under either the Act or the Operating Agreement to receive a distribution in the same amount. Summary judgment in favor of Klink was improvidently granted.

It does not follow, however, that Klink's interest in Five Star's profits for the ten-month period of 1995 should be ignored. Here, the member's share of Five Star's profits and losses is part of the total economic interest transferred in the buy-sell agreement. However, in this case, we cannot value that interest as a matter of law. This brings us to Five Star's next argument.

Divestment of Economic Interest

The minutes of the October 23, 1995 meeting memorializing the Five Star members' buy-sell agreement states that Klink would receive $61,047.22 for the

---

[10] [2] A distribution may not be made if after giving effect to the distribution:

   (1)   the limited liability company would not be able to pay its debts as the debts become due in the usual course of business; or

   (2)   the limited liability company's total assets would be less than the sum of its total liabilities plus, unless the operating agreement permits otherwise, the amount that would be needed if the affairs of the limited liability company were to be wound up at the time of the distribution to satisfy any preferential rights that are superior to the rights of members receiving the distribution.

value of its "units." Five Star contends that it is entitled to summary judgment because, when Klink sold its "units" to Five Star for $61,047.22, Klink divested itself of its entire economic interest, including its right to profits. Klink counters that the use of the term "units" proves that it sold less than all its interests for that amount.

Pursuant to the Operating Agreement, "unit" refers to "an interest in the Company representing a contribution to capital." This supports Klink's argument that it sold less than all of its economic rights in Five Star when it accepted the $61,047.22. However, as Five Star points out, under the same Operating Agreement, the members' interests are represented by the units held by each member. Thus, each unit generally entitled the members to one vote and to a proportionate share of the LLC's net income, gains, losses, deductions and credits. "Units," as used in the minutes, could reasonably denote either all or only part of Klink's economic interests in Five Star.

The minutes signed by all Five Star members purport to show agreement of the parties; however, mutual assent is necessary to the formation of every contract. The designated evidence supports an inference that the parties entered into the contract with materially different meanings attached to the word "unit." The trial court recognized the factual dispute and properly denied Five Star's motion for summary judgment.

## Valuation Method

In the "Facts" section of its brief, Five Star maintains that the valuation method chosen by the parties demonstrates that Klink actually received the fair market value of its entire interest. We analyze this as a separate argument.

Here, the parties determined fair market value by examining Five Star's September 30, 1995 balance sheet. Liabilities of $104,495.42 were subtracted from assets valued at $592,873.16, leaving $488,377.74. That amount was then multiplied by 12.5%, Klink's percentage of ownership, resulting in the agreed sum of $61,047.22. Five Star claims that, because it used an accrual basis of accounting, its September 30 balance sheets reflected the value of all accounts as of that date. It then maintains that, by using this valuation method, Klink received the amount upon which its complaint is based.

Valuing the interest of a member is a "complex task," more of a business matter than a legal one. There is no best method for valuation and much depends on the nature of the business. *Id.* The "book value" formula, used in this case, has the advantage of varying the value of the LLC as the balance sheet of the LLC changes; however, some assets are valued at their depreciated value rather than their actual fair market value. We do not agree with Five Star that resolution of this matter is appropriately decided as a matter of law. Five Star is not entitled to summary judgment on this ground.

In conclusion, Five Star has not shown that it was entitled to summary judgment, and we affirm the trial court's denial of its motion. Klink had no legal right to an actual distribution of $31,889.02, allotted for tax purposes; thus, we reverse the entry of summary judgment in Klink's favor and remand for proceedings consistent with this opinion.

Affirmed in part, reversed in part and remanded.

## NOTES

**1.** Would the problems which led to litigation here have arisen if an "S" corporation were involved instead of an LLC? Why didn't the parties here use an "S" corporation? (Hint: who can be shareholders in an "S" corporation?)

**2.** *Klink* illustrates the similarities in treatment between an LLC and a partnership when a member wishes to withdraw. It also illustrates the importance of drafting an operating agreement at the time the LLC is formed where variations from the statutory default rules would be desirable. Would it have been wiser for the parties to modify the default rule of section 23-18-6-6 of the Indiana Code to place restrictions on a member's right to withdraw? Could the parties have avoided this litigation if the LLC operating agreement specified the circumstances under which a withdrawing party is entitled to cash payment for his interest?

# Chapter 5

# FORMATION, PROMOTER'S LIABILITY, AND DEFECTIVE INCORPORATION

## A. ETHICAL PROBLEMS (AND MALPRACTICE) WITH THE MULTIPLE CLIENT

The first step in forming a corporation for your client is to determine who your client is. That is an easy task if your client is only one person. However, if two or more persons ask you to represent them, the applicable ethical rules and the potential for malpractice require that you proceed with great caution. Read Problem 5.1 before reading the following cases. As you read the cases in each section of this chapter, consider whether the questions of choice of law, issuance of stock, and identity of client would affect your advice to the client.

### PROBLEM 5.1

Able, Baker, and Carr meet with you for the first time. They have made an appointment with you to discuss their "business plans." In fact, you did not realize that you would be meeting all three of them. Your secretary made the appointment for Able, whom you represented in the past when you drafted his will. You remember that his will required that you research some matters in regard to estate-planning because he had substantial wealth. This was your only contact with Able and you have not seen him for a five-year period, even though you have sent him an annual reminder to make an appointment to review his will as well as his estate plan. Able introduces his younger brother Baker to you. Baker has just graduated from a prestigious business school with an MBA. He also introduces you to his brother-in-law Carr who also has an MBA but obtained it at least 10 years ago and has substantial business experience. Able is a well-respected physician who has a substantial income as well as assets.

They explain that they desire to form a corporation. Each would be an equal shareholder. Able would not work in the business, the others would. Baker and Carr desire to draw salaries. In fact, Carr would need a substantial salary because he would have to quit his existing job. The corporate entity would exploit certain patent rights which can be acquired for about $500,000. In addition, another $500,000 would be required during the start-up period which is estimated to be about two years. Able explains that when the corporation becomes profitable, he does not want any dividend income because his taxes are high enough as it is, but he does expect to be rewarded for his investment in some other way. He asks if you can offer any suggestions. Able and Carr indicate that they could invest substantial amounts, but Baker could only contribute his services. All three of the "clients" state that they do not want or need any outside investors to buy stock.

They then ask if you can represent them and ask how long it will to take to file the articles of incorporation for them. How would you advise them?

## B.   WHERE TO INCORPORATE

For most closely held corporations that will do business in only one state, the obvious choice is to incorporate where the business is located. If a corporation is incorporated in a state other than where it is located, additional complexity results. For example, if the corporation elects to be incorporated in Delaware and it is located in Florida, it must then file the appropriate documents to qualify as a foreign corporation in Florida. It now is subject to suit in two states and subject to taxation in two states. If the corporation ever desires to avail itself of the intrastate exemption under the Securities Act of 1933, it will not be able to do so, since section 3(a)(11) requires that the issuer of a corporation be incorporated within the jurisdiction where it does business.

For large corporations that will be publicly held and plan to do business in all states, Delaware incorporation is common. Some commentators suggest that Delaware's popularity is the result of a "race to the bottom," though others suggest that Delaware's large body of case law, precedent, and knowledgeable judiciary adequately explain the frequent choice of Delaware for incorporations.

## C.   CHOICE OF LAW

The cases in this section emphasize the importance of the state of incorporation for conflict of laws purposes. If there is a dispute between shareholders, or if a director is accused of breaching his fiduciary duty to a corporation, which state's law should apply to the matter?

In general, the law of the state of incorporation will be applied. SCOLES & HAY, CONFLICT OF LAWS § 23.1 *et seq.* (1982). This result is not immediately obvious, but it is the traditional choice of law rule and it has the obvious advantage of clarity as well as long usage. Applying the law of the jurisdiction of incorporation makes obvious sense because most corporations are small businesses that operate in only one state, and that state is the one in which the organizers are likely to incorporate. However, for larger corporations that operate in many state, or even nationwide, the law must supply an answer to the question as to what law applies. If we look at the corporate charter as a contract among the shareholders, a sensible rationale emerges. The traditional choice of law rule is simply the result of shareholder choice. When one buys corporate stock, one also chooses the law that applies. The following case illustrates the complexity which results when it is unclear which state's law governs.

# YATES v. BRIDGE TRADING CO.
## Court of Appeals of Missouri
### 844 S.W.2d 56 (1992)

PUDLOWSKI, J.

This case involves the issuance of stock for a promissory note by a Delaware corporation having its principal place of business in Missouri. Plaintiff-appellant, James M. Yates, appeals a court tried judgment by the Circuit Court for the City of St. Louis finding the contract arising from a stock purchase agreement void under Missouri law because the consideration exchanged for the stock was a promissory note.

On appeal, Yates argues that the trial court erred in entering judgment for respondent, Bridge Trading Company, on several grounds. First, appellant argues he had tendered full payment of a promissory note signed by appellant in exchange for shares curing any defect in the consideration paid for the shares. Next, appellant states the trial court erred in that he proved respondents had converted his shares. Appellant further argues that the trial court incorrectly applied section 351.160 of the General and Business Corporation Law of Missouri because the "internal affairs doctrine" bars the application of Missouri law to a stock issuance by a corporation organized under the laws of another state. § 351.160, RSMo 1986. Appellant urges, notwithstanding the choice of law stipulation contained in the disputed stock purchase agreement, that section 351.160 by its express and defined terms does not apply to stock issuances by foreign corporations.

Appellant also contends the trial court should have applied Delaware law to the stock issuance transaction based on the principles set out in the Restatement (Second) of the Conflict of Laws.

Appellant's next points of error assume that the court should have applied Delaware law and entered judgment for Yates based upon the application of that law. Appellant argues that under Delaware corporate law, stock issued in exchange for a promissory note is voidable (rather than void, as in Missouri), invoking the court's equitable jurisdiction, and balancing the equities entitles Yates to possession of the disputed shares of stock. Continuing on the assumption that the contract should be given effect in equity, appellant argues that respondents are barred by waiver, laches and estoppel from contesting the validity of the stock purchase agreement.

Appellant's final set of points centers on the effect of the dissolution and liquidation of Bridge Trading Company on its obligation under the stock purchase agreement to turn over the disputed shares to appellant.

We affirm.

## I. Facts

The instant case was tried without a jury entitling this court to review both findings of fact and conclusions of law made by the trial judge. . . . We are not firmly convinced that any finding was against the weight of the evidence and defer to the trial court's superior ability in evaluating the credibility of testifying witnesses.

In 1974, appellant Yates and defendants Charles A. Lebens, William C. Stafford, William P. Riley and Harry L. Franc, III, founded Bridge Holding Company (Holding), a Missouri corporation. Holding owned two subsidiary corporations, Bridge Trading Company (Old Trading) and Bridge Data Company (Data). Both subsidiaries were organized under the laws of Delaware and had their principal place of business in Missouri. Appellant served as the president of both Data and Holding until his removal from those positions in 1986.

The purpose of this corporate triangle was to develop and market a computer system — the "Bridge System" — to receive and process "real time, last sale" information from major security exchanges. The processed information was sold to institutional investors. Data and Old Trading were formed as separate corporations to comply with various New York Stock Exchange and SEC regulations. Data developed the computer system and received and processed the raw information. Old Trading sold the processed information to institutional customers. The two subsidiaries were closely related with each depending on the other for continuing viability.

In 1977, Holding sold 100% of its stock in Old Trading to Loewi & Co., a regional brokerage firm. After 1977, Old Trading was never again owned by Holding although the companies continued to be closely affiliated because of their symbiotic relationship. As part of the sale, Data entered into an exclusive marketing arrangement with Old Trading to sell the system's services to institutional customers. In 1978, Timothy Noble and others purchased Old Trading from Loewi. In 1981 or 1982, the board of directors at Old Trading decided to recapitalize Old Trading.

In April 1983, an agreement was reached in which certain individuals including appellant were offered the opportunity to purchase Old Trading stock. The stock purchase agreement, dated April 1, 1983, stipulated that the stock in Old Trading could be purchased for $3.56 per share. The stock purchase agreement expressly contemplated that the shares would be paid for with a promissory note. The note was secured by a pledge of the stock purchased from Old Trading. The promissory note, executed by the parties to the stock purchase agreement, was a demand note, and the trial court found that demand for payment was never made upon Yates before he tendered payment in 1987. The stock purchase agreement contained certain repurchase options and transfer restrictions. The agreement additionally provided: "This agreement and all restrictions on stock transfer created hereby shall terminate on the occurrence of . . . [t]he bankruptcy or dissolution of the company." The promissory note and the pledge agreement did not contain a similar restriction.

\* \* \*

Appellant did not participate in the negotiation or drafting of the stock purchase agreement. Appellant signed the stock purchase agreement and executed a promissory note for $64,080, secured by a pledge of the shares. In April 1983, each party listed in the table above, except James Schlueter, purchased the shares offered them in the stock purchase agreement by executing a promissory note. In November and December of 1983, all of the parties, except for appellant, who had purchased the stock paid the balance on their promissory notes. Seven of the nine parties to the stock purchase transaction received bonuses from Old Trading late in 1983 which they used to pay off the balance of their promissory notes and claim their pledged shares. Appellant did not receive a bonus and made no payment on the note at that time.

At no time did appellant receive a pay check from Old Trading nor was he formally an employee of Old Trading for tax purposes. Unlike defendants Lebens, Franc, Stafford, Riley and Hermanson who were paid by Old Trading, appellant received his pay from Data. He did not receive the late 1983 bonus from Old Trading as the employees of that company did. The trial court specifically found that appellant was never an employee of Old Trading in any sense of the word. Appellant was, however, an insider due to the close relationship between Data and Old Trading. His close working relationship with Old Trading was the reason behind his inclusion in the stock purchase plan.

After April 1983, appellant exercised his rights over the stock he had purchased with the promissory note. In 1986, a merger was proposed between Old Trading and Holding, the parent of Data. Appellant voted the 18,000 shares in opposition to that merger and, thereby, blocked its occurrence. In 1987, appellant again voted the 18,000 shares against another proposed merger. Appellant was listed in the proxy materials of Old Trading as the owner of 18,000 shares of Old Trading stock.

On June 30, 1987, Old Trading filed its articles of dissolution with the Secretary of State for the State of Delaware. In the process of dissolution, Old Trading transferred all of its assets to a subsidiary of Bridge Information Systems (Information) (f/k/a Holding). Information then distributed stock to the shareholders of moribund Old Trading at the rate of ten shares of Information stock for each share of Old Trading stock. During July 1987, appellant attempted to sell his shares of Old Trading to an outside company, TA Associates, for $75.00 per share but was unable to do so because defendants would not release his pledged stock certificate. Appellant was under the impression that his shares would be subject to certain transfer restrictions, and he informed TA Associates of those concerns.

On July 13, 1987, appellant dispatched a check to Old Trading for $90,000 as payment of his promissory note and accrued interest. In an August 14, 1987 letter, Old Trading refused to deliver the 18,000 shares to appellant and returned appellant's check. The trial court found that during this period the value of each share of Old Trading stock was $75.00 per share for a total value of $1,350,000.00 to appellant. During oral argument, appellant did not contest the valuation of the shares set by the trial court. At the ten to one exchange rate, appellant claims that he is entitled to 180,000 shares of Information stock which are being held in escrow pending the outcome of this litigation.

The trial court held that Missouri law controlled the issuance of stock and that the consideration paid for the stock was void under Missouri law. The court also held that the stock purchase agreement by its terms terminated when Old Trading filed its articles of dissolution, and appellant's tender of payment of the promissory note was, thereby, ineffective under both Missouri and Delaware law.

The principal issues on appeal are: (1) what law controls the transaction; (2) does that law validate the stock purchase agreement; and (3) what effect did the dissolution have on the stock purchase agreement.

## II. Choice of law

Old Trading was a Delaware corporation with its principal place of business in Missouri. This would normally mean that the corporate law of Delaware would control the stock issuance. Restatement (Second) of the Conflict of Laws § 302 comments e–g (1971). The stock purchase agreement at issue, however, contains a choice of law clause that selects the law of Missouri as governing the agreement.

Applying Missouri law to the instant case quite clearly renders the current stock purchase agreement void. Section 351.160(1) of the General and Business Corporation Law of Missouri provides, in part:

> No corporation shall issue shares . . . except for money paid, labor done, or property actually received; and all fictitious issues . . . shall be void . . . .

§ 351.160(1)[1], RSMo 1986. The Missouri Constitution, Art. XI, § 7, contains analogous language. The Missouri Supreme Court has held that a promissory note is not money or property and does not constitute valid consideration for stock.

In contrast to Missouri, Delaware treats the absence of valid consideration as rendering the stock issuance voidable rather than void. The court balances the equities to determine whether the corporation may cancel the shares or whether the party claiming entitlement to the shares may pay adequate consideration for the shares and cure the defect in consideration. *Blair v. F.H. Smith Co.*, 18 Del. Ch. 150, 156 A. 207, 213 (1931).

In support of his claim that Delaware law should have been applied to determine the validity of the stock issuance appellant advances three arguments.

## A. The Internal Affairs Doctrine

First, appellant urges that the internal affairs doctrine requires the application of Delaware law. The internal affairs doctrine provides that the law of the state of incorporation should be applied to settle disputes affecting the organic structure or internal administration of a corporation. The doctrine is recognized by statute in Missouri. See § 351.582(3), RSMo 1990. The state of incorporation is acknowledged as having a paramount interest in the internal administration of a corporation organized under its laws. *Pacific Intermountain Exp. Co. v. Best Truck L., Inc.*, 518 S.W.2d 469, 472 (Mo. App. 1974). The issuance of stock has been held to be one of the internal affairs of a corporation which requires the application of the laws of the

---

[1] [1] Interestingly, the Delaware Constitution provides for the same three types of consideration as in Missouri's Constitution — i.e. money paid, labor done, or personal or real property. Del. Const. Art. IX, § 3. Neither state considers promissory notes sufficiently tangible property to constitute valid consideration. Delaware, however, perhaps recognizing the more complex nature of modern transactions, does not close the door on parties without further inquiry.

state of incorporation. *Jackson*, 306 S.W.2d at 610; *Johanson*, 131 S.W.2d [509,] at 603.

We are confronted with a situation in which the parties have expressly chosen the law of Missouri in the stock purchase agreement. Appellant contends that the internal affairs doctrine bars the application of Missouri corporate law to the issuance of stock by a foreign corporation notwithstanding the choice of law provision. We disagree. This issue appears to be one of first impression in Missouri. Cases from other jurisdictions indicate that forum states having the most significant contacts with corporations organized under the laws of other states have cautiously applied the forum states' laws to the internal affairs of those corporations under limited circumstances. *See Wilson v. Louisiana–Pacific Resources, Inc.*, 138 Cal. App. 3d 216, 187 Cal. Rptr. 852 (1982). In the *Louisiana–Pacific case*, the California Court of Appeals justified applying California's mandatory cumulative voting provision to a Utah corporation on the rationale that sound public policy demands a legislature be vested with some control over "psuedo-foreign" [sic][2] corporations. *Id.* at 861.

Under this approach, if the corporation's sole contact with the state of incorporation is the naked fact of incorporation and all or most of its contacts lie within the forum state, the forum state can intervene in the internal affairs of the corporation so long as the shareholders of the corporation are not subjected to contradictory or inconsistent laws. *See Application of Dohring*, 142 Misc. 2d 429, 537 N.Y.S.2d 767 (N.Y. Supp. 1989). New York has applied its local common law right of dissolution to a Delaware corporation which was a psuedo-foreign [sic] corporation. *Id.* at 768–69. Other courts have used the Restatement (Second) of Conflict of Laws' most significant relationship approach to justify the application of local law to the internal affairs of psuedo-foreign [sic] corporations.

Old Trading was incorporated under the laws of Delaware, but had its principal place of business in Missouri and its stockholders lived, for the most part, in Missouri. One of the principal policy reasons for the internal affairs doctrine is to avoid the application of inconsistent or conflicting sets of laws to corporate affairs. Because the stock purchase agreement at issue applied to all Old Trading stock, the uniform application of Missouri law would not run afoul of this policy.[3] The cases discussed above indicate that courts and legislatures have increasingly regulated what was once rigidly designated as the internal affairs of a foreign corporation, especially if the foreign corporation has significant contacts with the forum. In light of the flexibility of the internal affairs doctrine as applied to psuedo-foreign [sic] corporations, and the low risk that stockholders would be subjected to inconsistent

---

[2] [2] Psuedo-foreign [sic] corporations are organized under the laws of a state other than the forum state, but have essentially all of their contacts with the forum state.

[3] [3] This factor prevents stockholders of Old Trading from being subjected to contradictory laws and is in accord with the SECOND RESTATEMENT OF CONFLICT'S position which provides in the comments to section 302.

> It is important that the validity of an entire share issue should be governed by a single law, because it would be impractical to have an entire issue held valid in some states and invalid in others. It is also important that a single law should govern all share issues of a corporation because only in this way can the shareholders be assured of uniformity of treatment.

laws in this case, we find that the internal affairs doctrine does not, in and of itself, bar the application of Missouri corporate law to the issuance of stock by a Delaware corporation. The parties were free to choose the law governing their stock issuance so long as there was a uniform law applied to all shareholders, and the parties and the corporation had substantial contacts with the state whose law was selected.

### B. Section 351.160

Appellant next argues that section 351.160(1) does not apply to foreign corporations by its express and defined terms. The section begins "*no corporation* shall issue shares . . . except for money paid, labor done, or property actually received . . . ." (Emphasis added). Appellant contends that the word "corporation" should be read as "domestic corporation." Section 351.015 provides definitions for chapter 351. That section contains the following definitions:

> (6) "Corporation" or "domestic corporation" includes corporations organized under this chapter or subject to some or all of the provisions of this chapter except a foreign corporation;

> (7) "Foreign Corporation" means a corporation for profit organized under laws other than the laws of this state . . . .

§ 351.015, RSMo 1986 (emphasis original). Appellant urges and we agree that section 351.160 should be read as the law applying to domestic corporations. However, we believe that the parties to the instant agreement could choose to have their agreement governed by the sections of the General and Business Corporation Law of Missouri by an express choice of law provision. In light of our discussion of the previous point, Old Tradings' close connection to this state, and the express choice by the parties to have Missouri law applied to the stock purchase agreement, we find nothing inherently improper with the application of provisions of Missouri corporate law to a corporation that would not normally be subject to those laws.

### C. Restatement (Second)

Appellant's third argument states that the choice of law rules in effect in Missouri prevent the application of Missouri law through a choice of law provision in the stock purchase agreement because parties may not choose a local law which makes an otherwise valid contract void. Missouri has adopted the Restatement (Second) of the Conflict of Laws in contract actions. *National Starch and Chemical Corp. v. Newman*, 577 S.W.2d 99, 102 (Mo. App. 1979). The Western District of this court has taken the position that when a choice of law provision renders a contract void, that choice of law provision will not be applied because it is presumed that parties enter contracts intending that they be valid. *State ex rel. St. Joseph Light & Power Co. v. Donelson*, 631 S.W.2d 887, 891–92 (Mo. App. 1982). In *Donelson*, the court relied on section 187 of the Second Restatement which applies when parties have an express choice of law provision in their agreement. Comment c to that section states, in part:

> [Parties to a contract] may incorporate into the contract by reference extrinsic material which may, among other things, be the provisions of some foreign law. In such instances, the forum will apply the applicable

provisions of the law of the designated state in order to effectuate the intentions of the parties. (Emphasis added).

In the instant case, we are faced with a situation in which the application of the local law of Missouri, expressly chosen by the parties, would render the stock purchase agreement void. Application of section 351.160 of our local corporate law fails to effectuate the presumed intent of the parties to enter a valid contract. Therefore, we decline to apply the local law of Missouri to the consideration issue in the stock purchase agreement based on the principles espoused by the Second Restatement and recognized by the Western District of Missouri. The law of Delaware will be applied on the issue of consideration exchanged for the shares.

## III. The Delaware Approach

Under Delaware law, the issuance of stock without consideration or for an insufficient consideration does not render the issuance void, but instead, renders it voidable. When a stock issuance is voidable, the relief adopted is that which is most in accord with the equities of a given case. Thus, appellant's contract was potentially valid pending a balancing of the equities. Normally, we would remand the case to the trial court for a balancing of the equities to determine whether equity would give effect to the contract despite the lack of consideration. In this case, we will proceed under the assumption that appellant's contract was potentially valid and that equity might have given it effect. We do so because we find that while up until the dissolution of Old Trading appellant may have held his stock validly under Delaware law, the dissolution of the corporation ended appellant's right to cure the defect in his consideration.

## IV. Effect of the Dissolution

On June 30, 1987, Old Trading filed its articles of dissolution and on July 13, 1987, appellant dispatched a check for $90,000 to Old Trading intended as full payment of his promissory note. Appellant argues that under the law of Delaware, the corporation had a three year winding up period to collect and pay its debts. Appellant contends that this statutory period allowed appellant time after the dissolution of the Old Trading in which to pay his note and redeem his shares.

Appellant's argument contains two flaws. First, the Second Restatement, discussed above, employs an issue by issue approach to the choice of law. *See, e.g.,* Restatement (Second) Conflict of Laws § 188 (1971). We declined to employ section 351.160 of the General and Business Corporations Law of Missouri to the stock purchase agreement because it did not give effect to the presumed intent of the parties. Our action does not mean that other provisions of Missouri corporate law do not apply to the agreement. It cannot be assumed that the issue of the fate of the stock purchase agreement upon dissolution can be decided in the same manner as the independent issue of consideration. Under the Second Restatement, these are separate determinations and could well be decided by the local law of different jurisdictions.

Second, irrespective of the local law applied to the issuance, the terms of the stock purchase agreement terminate that agreement upon dissolution of Old

Trading. Section 11.1 of the stock purchase agreement provides, in part: "[the] agreement and all restrictions on stock transfer created hereby shall terminate on the occurrence of any of the following events . . . [including] the bankruptcy or dissolution of the Corporation." Clearly, the parties intended for the agreement to terminate upon the dissolution of the corporation. This event is distinguishable from the choice of law provision which rendered the stock purchase agreement void ab initio.

At the date of dissolution, appellant had a voidable contract for the purchase of stock. Under neither the law of Missouri nor the law of Delaware is a promissory note adequate consideration for shares of stock. Appellant did not have an enforceable right in the shares until he paid adequate consideration. His right to cure ended, by the terms of the stock purchase agreement, upon dissolution of the corporation. Appellant's tender of payment of his promissory note after dissolution was not timely.

The judgment of the trial court is affirmed.

## NOTES

**1.** Why did the parties put a choice of law provision in the stock purchase agreement?

**2.** Should the court have held the choice of law provision to be invalid?

**3.** Should a corporation be permitted to issue stock in return for a mere promissory note?

**4.** Why did the court apply Delaware law to the first issue before it?

**5.** Could the parties to the stock purchase agreement have provided that the law of Florida should be applied? Assume that none of the shareholders or anyone connected with the transaction had a contact with Florida.

## D.  THE PROBLEM OF THE MULTIPLE CLIENT

### BRENNAN v. RUFFNER
Court of Appeal of Florida
640 So. 2d 143 (1994)

PARIENTE, J.

\*   \*   \*

We affirm a final summary judgment entered in favor of a lawyer and against a disgruntled minority shareholder of a closely held corporation. We find that an attorney/client relationship did not exist between the individual shareholder and the attorney representing the corporation. Consequently, there is no basis for a legal malpractice action. We further reject the other theories of liability asserted by appellant.

In 1976, appellant, Robert J. Brennan, M.D., (Dr. Brennan) along with a Dr. Martell, employed appellee, Charles L. Ruffner, Esq., (lawyer) to incorporate their medical practice as a professional association. In connection with the incorporation, the lawyer prepared a shareholder's agreement. In 1982, a third doctor, Dr. Mirmelli, joined the corporation, and each doctor became a one-third shareholder in the new firm. The lawyer, who was corporate counsel since 1976, was requested to draft a new shareholder's agreement. After approximately 8 months of negotiation, the shareholders executed a new shareholder's agreement. The new agreement included a provision for the involuntary termination of any shareholder by a majority vote of the two other shareholders. It is undisputed that Dr. Brennan was aware of this provision at the time he signed the documents and that he signed the agreement upon reassurances from Dr. Mirmelli that he would not join with Dr. Martell in using the provision against Dr. Brennan.

However, despite the assurances, in 1989 Dr. Martell and Dr. Mirmelli involuntarily terminated Dr. Brennan as a shareholder and employee of the corporation. Dr. Brennan instituted a lawsuit against Dr. Martell and Dr. Mirmelli claiming breach of contract and fraud in the inducement. The verified complaint in that lawsuit specifically alleged that Dr. Brennan was not represented by counsel in the negotiation of the shareholder's agreement. That lawsuit was settled. Dr. Brennan then filed this suit for legal malpractice, breach of contract, breach of fiduciary duty and breach of contract as a third party beneficiary. In contradiction to the sworn allegations of the first lawsuit, Dr. Brennan alleged in this complaint that the lawyer represented him individually, as well as the corporation, in the preparation and drafting of the agreement. The lawyer denied undertaking the representation of Dr. Brennan individually.

In a legal malpractice action, a plaintiff must prove three elements: the attorney's employment, the attorney's neglect of a reasonable duty and that such negligence resulted in and was the proximate cause of loss to the plaintiff. * * * Florida courts have uniformly limited attorney's liability for negligence in the performance of their professional duties to clients with whom they share privity of contract. *Angel, Cohen & Rogovin v. Oberon Inv.*, 512 So. 2d 192 (Fla. 1987); *Ginsberg v. Chastain*, 501 So. 2d 27 (Fla. 3d DCA 1986). "In a legal context, the term 'privity' is a word of art derived from the common law of contracts and used to describe the relationship of persons who are parties to a contract." * * * The only instances in Florida where the rule of privity has been relaxed is where the plaintiff is an intended third party beneficiary of the employment contract.

The material undisputed facts in this case support a legal conclusion that there was no privity of contract between Dr. Brennan and the corporation's lawyer. It is undisputed that the lawyer was representing the corporation. The issue raised by Dr. Brennan's complaint was whether the lawyer was also representing him individually. While Dr. Brennan made the initial contact with the lawyer, there is no evidence in the record to create a credible issue of fact that the lawyer ever represented Dr. Brennan individually. Dr. Brennan's sworn complaint against the other doctors, which preceded the legal malpractice action against the lawyer, states he was unrepresented by counsel in the negotiation of the shareholder's agreement.

Dr. Brennan argues that a separate duty to him as a shareholder arose by virtue of the lawyer's representation of the closely held corporation. Although never squarely decided in this state, we hold that where an attorney represents a closely held corporation, the attorney is not in privity with and therefore owes no separate duty of diligence and care to an individual shareholder absent special circumstances or an agreement to also represent the shareholder individually. While there is no specific ethical prohibition in Florida against dual representation of the corporation and the shareholder if the attorney is convinced that a conflict does not exist,[4] an attorney representing a corporation does not become the attorney for the individual stockholders merely because the attorney's actions on behalf of the corporation may also benefit the stockholders. The duty of an attorney for the corporation is first and foremost to the corporation, even though legal advice rendered to the corporation may affect the shareholders.

In addition, under the facts of this case, Dr. Brennan cannot claim that he was an intended third party beneficiary of the contract of representation with the corporation. Florida has extended the third party beneficiary exception to the privity requirement in legal malpractice actions to very limited instances, mainly in the area of will drafting, where it can be demonstrated that the intent of the client in engaging the services of the lawyer was to benefit a third party. In this case, there are no facts to support Dr. Brennan's assertion that the primary intent of the corporation in hiring the attorney to draft the shareholder's agreement was to directly benefit Dr. Brennan individually. Dr. Brennan admits that there was an inherent conflict of interest between the rights of the individual shareholder and the corporation. This alone expressly undercuts a third party beneficiary claim. A third party beneficiary theory of recovery has been rejected in other jurisdictions in similar circumstances on the basis that the individual shareholder cannot be an intended third party beneficiary of a shareholder's agreement because the interests of the corporation and the minority shareholder are potentially in opposition.

We also reject the notion that the lawyer in this case could be held liable to one of the minority shareholders for a breach of fiduciary duty. In any closely held corporation, there will be an inherent conflict between the potential rights of the minority shareholder and the rights of the corporation in a shareholder's agreement concerning termination. At the time this agreement was drafted, any one of the three shareholders could have ended up becoming the minority shareholder. While Dr. Brennan claimed in the complaint that the lawyer had a duty to advise him of

---

[4] [1] The Code of Professional Responsibility in effect in 1976 (the time the initial contractual relationship began) did not prohibit a lawyer from representing both a shareholder and the corporation. Although there was no Disciplinary Rule on the matter, Ethical Consideration 5-18 stated:

A lawyer employed or retained by a corporation or similar entity owes his allegiance to the entity and not to a stockholder, director, officer, employee, representative, or other person connected with the entity . . . . Occasionally a lawyer or other person connected with the entity to represent him in an individual capacity; in such case the lawyer may serve the individual only if the lawyer is convinced that differing interests are not present.

Even if 1988 is used as the date of employment, the rule in effect at that time permitted dual representation. Rule 4-1.13 of the rules regulating the Florida Bar allows a "lawyer representing an organization [to] also represent any of its directors, officers, employees, members, shareholders, or other constituents, subject to the provisions of rule 4-1.7 governs conflicts of interest.

a conflict of interest and never advised him of a potential conflict, the facts in the record do not support that contention. Dr. Brennan testified in deposition that he simply did not recall any conversations. However, the accountant for the corporation specifically remembered a conversation where the lawyer told the doctors collectively that he represented only the corporation in the drafting of the shareholder agreement. Absent some evidence that the corporation's lawyer conspired or acted with the two shareholders to insert provisions that would work to the detriment of the third shareholder; that the corporation's lawyer concealed his representation of another individual shareholder; or that the attorney agreed to the dual representation, there is no breach of fiduciary duty established in this case.

Finally, even assuming arguendo that a duty existed based on an attorney/client relationship, a third party beneficiary theory or a breach of fiduciary relationship, we simply do not find any factual dispute concerning the issue of proximate cause. It is undisputed that Dr. Brennan was aware of the provisions in the agreement and chose to take his chances upon being reassured by Dr. Mirmelli that he would never use the provisions against Dr. Brennan.

AFFIRMED.

# OPDYKE v. KENT LIQUOR MART, INC.
### Supreme Court of Delaware
### 181 A.2d 579 (1962)

SOUTHERLAND, CHIEF JUSTICE.

The principal issue in this case concerns the ownership of certain shares of stock of the defendant, Kent Liquor Mart, Inc.

In the summer of 1959 Milton R. Opdyke, the plaintiff, and George M. Smith, one of the defendants, discussed a possible venture into the liquor business. They learned of a vacant store in a shopping center near Dover. They interviewed Glenn A. Richter, one of the defendants. Richter was one of two members of Richter and Meyer, which owned the shopping center. He told them that the store would be available if he were made a co-owner of the business. They agreed.

Opdyke and Smith retained Herman C. Brown, Esq., an attorney practicing in Dover, to incorporate the business. The corporation was formed in September, 1959. The issued capital stock was 300 shares, of which each of the three men received 100. At the first incorporators and directors meetings all three men and Brown were present. There was some discussion of the desirability of restrictions on the sale of his stock by any stockholder. Brown explained to them the legal procedure required. Nothing ever came of this.

Application was made to the Alcoholic Beverage Control Commission for a liquor license. It was granted in June, 1960. The corporation borrowed $20,000 from the Bank of Delaware to provide funds for a stock of goods and working capital. All three stockholders and their wives joined in the note. The corporation also incurred a debt of $2600 to Richter & Meyer for the construction work.

The store was opened in August, 1960. It did not prosper as its owners had hoped.

At a meeting on October 9 Richter said he would be willing to get out of the business. At another meeting on October 20 Richter renewed his offer to withdraw. The terms of his offer are in dispute, but it is admitted that after discussing the matter Opdyke gave Richter a check for $415, on the face of which Opdyke endorsed: "For equity in the corporation." ($415 was the amount of the contribution of each stockholder.) Richter negotiated the check and retained the proceeds until after the bringing of this lawsuit. After October 20 Richter was not active in the business.

On November 19 Opdyke and Smith met. Smith was dissatisfied and wished to withdraw. They discussed a possible purchase by Opdyke, but the result is in dispute. On the following day Smith sold his shares to Richter for $415 and Richter's agreement to relieve Smith and his wife from the obligation at the Bank of Delaware. A new note was executed, joined in by Richter and Opdyke and their wives, and also by Robert Richter, Richter's nephew, and his wife.

Sometime later Richter transferred the 100 shares he had bought from Smith. He gave 60 to Robert Richter and 40 to Smith. Richter and Smith called on Brown and gave him instructions about the transfer of the shares. They were transferred on February 2, 1961. They also discussed the holding of a stockholders meeting. By that time Brown realized that the three men were not getting along.

Some days later Opdyke telephoned Brown that he (Opdyke) had bought Richter's shares. Brown asked him whether he (Opdyke) was not obligated to relieve Richter of Richter's liability to the bank. Opdyke said that he was not so obligated. Apparently Opdyke also went to see Brown about the matter prior to March 7.

Brown testified that he did not intend to be drawn into 'any fight among stockholders as to who owned what'; but as counsel for the corporation he thought he had some duty 'to try to straighten it out'. As above indicated, he had already gathered that some difficulty between them was building up. Brown accordingly suggested to Opdyke that a meeting be held.

On March 7 the meeting was held in Brown's office. At Brown's suggestion Mr. and Mrs. Opdyke came in first. Opdyke asserted that he had bought Richter's stock and showed Brown his cancelled check for $415 with the endorsement on its face. Brown indicated some doubt.

A half hour later Smith and Richter came in. A matter of renewing the lease on satisfactory terms was discussed and settled.

Brown then brought up the matter of Richter's stock. Because of the forthcoming stockholders' meeting he thought it desirable to attempt to adjust the difficulty. He said that Opdyke had a problem with respect to the ownership of some stock. He explained to them that he was not representing any of them individually, but was the attorney for the corporation. He suggested that they get their own attorneys. He also said that if they wished to discuss it, he would act as moderator.

He asked Opdyke to state his case. Opdyke did so. Richter replied that the stock had been sold with the understanding that Opdyke would relieve him (Richter) of his obligations; that Opdyke had not done so; and that Opdyke did not own the stock.

Apparently in an effort to settle the dispute, Opdyke asked Richter to let him have 60 of Richter's shares so that he would have control. Richter refused.

Brown then, also in an attempt to settle the dispute, asked Richter if he would still offer to transfer his original 100 shares to Opdyke if, in addition to the $415, Opdyke would arrange to relieve him of his obligations. Richter replied that he would do so. Brown asked Opdyke if he was satisfied to try this and Opdyke said: "Yes." Brown the asked Richter if Richter would agree to include the other 100 shares in the offer. Richter assented. Smith, the owner of 40 shares, also agreed. Opdyke seemed satisfied.

It was understood that Opdyke would have until March 13 to refinance the loan and the debt to Meyer and Richter. This time limit was extended. On March 24 Opdyke told Brown that he (Opdyke) was going to complete the deal. On the following Tuesday (March 28), Richter and Smith called to see Brown. Richter said that on that morning Opdyke had told him that the deal was off. Richter and Smith had a problem — a proposed sale of the corporation to a Mr. Behan for $30,000. To this Opdyke would not agree. After discussion Brown advised them to offer Behan two-thirds of the stock for $20,000. As they were leaving Brown said that he was sorry to see this happen, and that he would have some interest, on behalf of a client or of himself, in purchasing all or part of the corporation. They told him they were obligated to pursue the matter with Behan, but if he did not accept their offer they would be interested in talking to Brown about it.

Brown was then not in a position to buy the stock for himself because he already had an interest in another liquor store, and he thought that a regulation or ruling prohibited multiple holding of liquor licenses. However, on the afternoon of the 28th he unexpectedly effected a sale of that interest. He then called Richter at Richter's home, explained that he was now much more interested in the purchase of the stock of the Kent Liquor Mart, and asked whether, if Richter had a higher offer, Richter would be bound to go back to Behan. Richter said he would talk to Smith, but he, himself, would feel under no obligation to Behan if he had a higher offer. Brown then offered $21,000 for the two-thirds of the stock under the same conditions. Richter said he would consult Smith and advise Brown. Later Richter confirmed the sale. Brown went to Richter's home that evening and gave Richter a deposit of $1,000. Smith was present, and the method of payment of the contract price was agreed upon.

Before leaving Brown requested Richter and Smith not to tell Opdyke of the sale because he (Brown) wanted to tell Opdyke himself.

About nine o'clock the next morning, Brown went to the store and said:

> "Mickey, I have some news that is going to be a surprise for you, I am sure. I bought Mr. Richter and Mr. Smith and that group's stock last night, or agreed to buy it. I asked them not to tell you about it because I wanted to tell you about it myself."

Brown explained to Opdyke what the transaction was. He then told Opdyke that there were three ways in which their association could continue: (1) Brown would buy Opdyke's stock; or (2) Opdyke would retain his stock; or (3) they would not agree and "would have some kind of battle."

After more discussion Opdyke agreed (according to Brown) to continue as a "partner." The possibility that Opdyke's stock, because of his minor position, would 'become worth $10' was discussed. According to Brown's recollection, Opdyke first suggested it.

Opdyke said he was not angry at Brown, but he was angry at Richter and Smith, because he thought he had bought Richter's stock. Brown testified: 'He was angry and disappointed because I had told him that I had purchased Richter's stock'. His anger was directed at Richter, and several times he spoke of suing Richter because of this.

The matter of the new loan at the bank was discussed, and Opdyke agreed that he and his wife would sign the note. Later that day Brown arranged for the loan at the Farmers Bank. At six o'clock Opdyke came to Brown's office. Brown and two friends were there. Opdyke said he had nothing against Brown, but he was going to sue Richter. Opdyke again agreed to continue as a "partner".

About a week later the bank was about ready to close the matter. Brown went to the store to see Richter and Smith. In a little while Mr. and Mrs. Opdyke came in. Opdyke had just consulted another attorney. Brown started to explain about the closing, but noticed a stiffness in Opdyke's attitude with respect to consumating the transaction. Opdyke said he would have to call his attorney. He was advised to sign nothing and nothing was signed. The stock and Brown's note were placed in escrow.

The present suit in Chancery was thereafter instituted.

In the court below Opdyke sought various types of relief. Several questions were presented to the Vice Chancellor for decision. He decided them all in favor of the defendants and dismissed the bill.

Opdyke appeals. In this court he raises three of the questions raised below.

\*     \*     \*

Opdyke's third point raises a very serious question. He asserts that Brown, as a lawyer, owed him a fiduciary duty; and that when Brown acquired Richter's stock he violated that duty. He contends that Brown by the purchase acquired an interest adverse to his client, and also that Brown, even if his fiduciary relation had theretofore terminated, made use of information acquired in a confidential relationship in a way adverse to the interest of his former client.

Brown replies that his fiduciary duty was to the corporation only, and not to any of its stockholders. When the dispute between them arose he advised them that he was not representing any of them but only the corporation. Consequently, he argues, he was free to buy stock in the corporation from any stockholder.

The Vice Chancellor sustained this defense. He took the view that Brown's original employment was limited to the incorporation of the business and the obtaining of the liquor license; that the issuance, holding or transfer of shares was not within the terms of his employment; and that subsequent to incorporation he was attorney for the corporation and not for the stockholders. The Vice Chancellor therefore concluded that he was not precluded from buying the corporation's stock.

We observe at once that all of this reasoning is based upon the concept that the corporation has a separate existence from the individuals who are its stockholders. For purposes of corporation law this distinction is ordinarily sound, although even in that field the corporate fiction is on occasion disregarded.

But in determining the existence or nonexistence of the important relationship of attorney and client a broader approach is required. The question is, What in fact was the relationship between Brown and the three men? This is not a simple case, as defendants' counsel suggests, of an attorney for a corporation investing in its stock.

It is clear to us that Brown was, at the beginning of the venture, and also at its end, the attorney for the three men. The corporation was simply a form for the carrying on of a joint venture. For our present purpose Brown must be regarded as the attorney for three joint adventurers. When they fell out he undertook to resolve their differences. He very properly told them that he could not represent any one of them against another. This was so, not because of the corporate form of the enterprise, but because of the well-settled rule that if a lawyer is retained by two clients and they get into a dispute he cannot ordinarily represent either. Indeed, Brown's justifiable insistence on this neutrality was a recognition, conscious or not, of his fiduciary duty to all three men. That he was acting in his capacity as a lawyer admits of no doubt. Why were they discussing the matter in his office if not to obtain his help and counsel in their difficulty? In fact it was Brown who succeeded in evolving a possible settlement of the whole matter — a commendable effort.

Buy by these very acts he had emphasized his role of counselor to the three men. In suggesting the settlement he was discharging a characteristic function of the legal adviser. He could not escape the fiduciary obligations of this relationship by insisting that he was acting only for a corporation.

Upon the failure of his attempt to buy out the other stockholders, Opdyke was left with his claim against Richter for the original 100 shares. Brown knew that Opdyke had such a claim.

When Brown bought the Richter stock, he acquired an interest in the subject matter of the dispute between his clients. It was an interest necessarily adverse to that of one of them — Opdyke. Moreover, even if it be assumed, as the Vice Chancellor found, that the relationship of attorney and client had ceased with the failure of the settlement, yet he is still liable in this case because his knowledge that the stock was for sale was acquired directly from his role as counselor.

What was at stake here was the control of the business. On the face of the record, Richter and Smith had it; but Opdyke claimed it; and Brown, attorney for all three, acquired it without the consent or knowledge of Opdyke.

Possibly Brown may have relied on Richter's statement that the deal was off, indicating that Opdyke was abandoning all his claim. If so, he erred. He could relieve himself of his obligation to Opdyke only by the explicit consent of Opdyke, given after a full understanding of the position and of his legal rights.

Possibly Brown believed that Opdyke had no valid claim against Richter. If so, his belief was immaterial, and the subsequent determination that the claim was without merit is also immaterial.

It seems more likely, however, that he relied on the technical distinction between the corporation and the three men who composed it. But he must have had qualms about his position, for he made a special point of his desire to be the first to tell Opdyke what he had done.

It is said that after learning of Brown's purchase Opdyke voiced no objection and had no criticism of Brown. His failure to asset his legal rights is of no moment. He was not represented by separate counsel, and he naturally did not realize his legal position. It was Brown's duty to enlighten him, but this duty was not performed.

*   *   *

We regret that a member of our bar has succumbed to the temptation to put his own interest above that of his client. But that he did so we entertain no doubt.

The result must be that the Vice Chancellor's judgment dismissing the complaint must be reversed. This, of course, will mean the failure of any claim for damages on the injunction bond, over which he reserved jurisdiction.

A judgment should be entered embodying appropriate relief, inter alia, declaring Brown a constructive trustee for Opdyke in respect of the interest acquired by him under sales contract with Richter and the others.

*   *   *

The cause is remanded to the court below, with instructions to vacate the order of November 8, 1961, and for further proceedings not inconsistent with this opinion.

# NOTES

1.   The task of representing several shareholders with conflicting interests is always a difficult one. Frequently the shareholders will have different interests, either at the time of formation or subsequently. The Model Rules of Professional Conduct, adopted by the American Bar Association (ABA), prohibit representation of clients with adverse interests. However, "common representation is permissible where the clients are generally aligned in interest even though there is some difference of interest among them." MODEL RULES OF PROFESSIONAL CONDUCT RULE 1.7, cmt.

2.   Do the Model Rules make any sense for business transactions? Would it make sense to have a second set of ethical rules governing attorneys who negotiate and draft documents in business transactions?

3.   Note that the court states: "It is clear to us that Brown was . . . the attorney for the three men. The corporation was simply a form for the carrying on of a joint venture." Is this a rule of law, or a presumption for closely held corporations, or a finding of fact based upon this particular case? If the shareholders have an intractable dispute, can the attorney ever offer to resolve it by his purchase of stock

in the corporation? If you think he should be able to do this, are there any conditions that should be imposed?

## E.    FORMATION AND THE PROCESS OF INCORPORATION

First, the attorney should consult with the client about which jurisdiction in which to incorporate. Generally, that will be the state in which the corporation intends to have its principal operations, but there may be reasons to choose another jurisdiction in some circumstances. Most large corporations are incorporated in Delaware, for example.

The client should be instructed to avoid any business operations until the incorporation is completed, to avoid any possibility of being held personally liable for those activities.

The attorney should provide information and advice on a shareholders' agreement. To avoid future dissension and litigation, it is very important for business owners to adopt written agreements among themselves as to their rights with respect to such basic interests as rights or limitations with respect to selling their shares, rights to participate in the control of the corporation, and rights to receive financial returns from the corporation. In lieu of such an agreement, many states have statutory close corporation provisions that may be specifically opted into in the formation documents. These statutory provisions may provide a sort of "off the rack" agreement that may be appropriate for some businesses.

It is also important to caution the client against issuing any stock in the corporation without ensuring that the issuance is in compliance with both the state securities laws (generally called "Blue Sky Laws") and the federal securities laws. Any stock sales not in compliance with securities laws may have to be rescinded, which can result in a great deal of harm to the business.

### 1.    Drafting the Articles of Incorporation

To form a corporation, a document called the articles of incorporation (or, in Delaware, the certificate of incorporation) is drafted, signed by the incorporator(s), and filed with the Secretary of State, along with the required fees. Some jurisdictions may also require publication of a notice of incorporation. Many states now have websites that explain the incorporation process and even include form documents to make the filing process easier. It may also be possible to check online or by telephone to see whether the name your client has chosen is already in use by another corporation, in which case your client will not be permitted to use it.

Under MBCA section 2.02(a), the articles of incorporation must include only four items: the name of the corporation (which must comply with the requirements in section 4.01); the number of shares it is authorized to issue; the street address of the corporation's initial registered agent; and the name and address of each incorporator. Delaware has requirements similar to the Model Act, but section 102(a)(3) of the Delaware General Corporation Law also requires the certificate to state "[t]he nature of the business or purposes to be conducted or promoted." That requirement can be satisfied by a statement that the corporation's purpose is to engage in "any lawful act or activity." Under both Delaware law and the Model Act, the articles/certificate may include other matters beyond those required as a minimum.

MBCA section 4.01 requires the name to include some indication that the entity is in fact a corporation, so that persons dealing with the entity will be on notice that its owners are not liable for the debts of the business. Some jurisdictions have additional requirements, including maximum lengths, a name in letters and numbers (so that it can be indexed) rather than graphic representations, and no names that are obscene (in the judgment of the Secretary of State) or indicate an illegal purpose.

With respect to the number of authorized shares, unless the jurisdiction imposes a tax or fee based on the number of shares, it is generally good practice to authorize a large number. The corporation is not required to issue all of the shares that are authorized, but it is not permitted to issue more shares than are authorized. Adding to the number of authorized shares requires an amendment to the articles of incorporation, which requires a vote of the shareholders and a filing with the Secretary of State. That takes time and costs money, so better to set a high number at the outset. It is possible, but not necessary, to authorize more than one class of stock; for instance, the corporation may have both common and preferred stock. If multiple classes are authorized, either the special characteristics of each must be completely set out in the articles, or authority must be specifically delegated to the directors to designate those rights and preferences at a later date. *See* MBCA § 6.02.

Some states may still require a par value to be designated. If that is the case, current practice is to choose a very small amount, perhaps a penny or less per share. Shares may not legally be sold by the company for less than their par value, so a larger amount could impede a sale of the shares in the future. The articles of incorporation may also include provisions relating to cumulative voting and preemptive rights. *Cumulative voting* concerns voting for directors. Under "straight" voting, each share gets one vote for each directorial position. Under cumulative voting, each share gets a number of votes equal to the total number of directors being elected, and the shareholder may distribute those votes as she decides — all her votes for one director, if she so chooses. Cumulative voting permits shareholders to elect directors roughly in accordance with the number of shares they own. By contrast, with straight voting, whoever owns a majority of the stock has the power to elect all of the directors. *Preemptive rights* permit existing shareholders to purchase their proportional share of newly issued shares, so that their percentage ownership cannot be diluted without their acquiescence. The attorney should first check the statute to determine how the jurisdiction's default rule is worded. Under the MBCA, neither preemptive rights nor cumulative voting exists unless the articles of incorporation so provide.

## 2. The Process of Incorporation

Under MBCA section 2.03, the corporate existence begins when the articles are filed with the Secretary of State. However, section 2.05 provides that further steps must be taken to complete the organization. An organizational meeting must be held to accomplish these steps.

## 3.   Corporate Formalities

In general, the attorney must draft bylaws for the corporation as well as preparing the minutes of the organizational meeting. At this organizational stage, the initial directors are often named in the articles of incorporation. If they are not named, then the incorporators have the right to elect the first board of directors. At this first meeting of the directors, the bylaws are approved and the officers of the corporation are elected. The corporate seal is adopted, shares are issued in return for appropriate consideration. Further, the secretary of the corporation is directed to place a copy of the articles of incorporation in the minute book of corporation, and along with the President, instructed to cause to be issued stock certificates in those numbers and amounts that the Board has just approved. These corporate formalities are more than game playing. Without a paper trial to document the transaction, showing what the shareholders and officers intended, chaos will ensue later if there is a dispute. Further, failure to observe the corporate formalities is often reason for courts to ignore the entity status of the corporation. If the attorney stops at this point, the corporate entity will have a real existence but the clients will not be well served. Often the clients' interests demand some sort of shareholders' agreement. At the initial organization, agreements can be made easily without rancor. Arbitration clauses or buy-out agreements can be used to ensure harmony. Some clients may refuse this advice, but the careful attorney should give the advice anyway. Failure to advise the clients of reasonable ways of avoiding potential disasters may well constitute malpractice.

A very common illustration of malpractice is the attorney who files the articles of incorporation, prepares minutes of the organizational meeting, and then sends them out to his client(s). Nothing then happens for six months or more. The minutes are not signed by any of the appropriate officers, the unanimous consent forms are also unsigned, and the stock certificates are never issued. In the absence of the pre-incorporation agreement, it is difficult to prove who are the real shareholders. The careful attorney will protect the clients from this problem by a pre-incorporation agreement which specifies all important issues, such as consideration to be paid for the stock to be issued, as well as amount of shares to be issued to each shareholder. Frequently, each of the potential shareholders desire to assure future employment at fixed salaries. Matters such as these are generally covered by a pre-incorporation agreement.

## F.   SECURITIES LAW CONSIDERATIONS

Preparing the stock certificates is a simpler matter. However, issuing stock will create liability under state or federal law or both unless an exemption from registration exists. Most closely held corporations will qualify for the private offering exemption under section 4(a)(2) of the Securities Act of 1933 as well as some sort of small offering exemption under state law. However, a failure to think about this problem in advance may result in substantial liabilities both for the clients as well as the attorney. The case which follows is a good illustration.

# WARTZMAN v. HIGHTOWER PRODUCTIONS, LTD.
## Court of Special Appeals of Maryland
456 A.2d 82 (1983)

GETTY, J.

Woody Hightower did not succeed in breaking the Guinness World Record for flagpole sitting; his failure to accomplish this seemingly nebulous feat, however, did generate protracted litigation.

\* \* \*

Hightower Productions LTD. (appellees and cross-appellants) came into being in 1974 as a promotional venture conceived by Ira Adler, Frank Billitz and J. Daniel Quinn. The principals intended to employ a singer-entertainer who would live in a specially constructed mobile flagpole perch from April 1, 1975, until New Years Eve at which time he would descend in Times Square in New York before a nationwide television audience having established a new world record for flagpole sitting.

The young man selected to perform this feat was to be known as "Woody Hightower." The venture was to be publicized by radio and television exposure, by adopting a theme song and by having the uncrowned champion make appearances from his perch throughout the country at concerts, state fairs and shopping centers.

In November, 1974, the three principals approached Michael Kaminkow of the law firm of Wartzman, Rombro, Rudd and Omansky, P.A., for the specific purpose of incorporating their venture. Mr. Kaminkow, a trial attorney, referred them to his partner, Paul Wartzman.

The three principals met with Mr. Wartzman at his home and reviewed the promotional scheme with him. They indicated that they needed to sell stock to the public in order to raise the $250,000 necessary to finance the project. Shortly thereafter, the law firm prepared and filed the articles of incorporation and Hightower Productions Ltd. came into existence on November 6, 1974. The Articles of Incorporation authorized the issuance of one million shares of stock of the par value of 10¢ per share, or a total of $100,000.00.

Following incorporation, the three principals began developing the project. With an initial investment of $20,000, they opened a corporate account at Maryland National Bank and an office in the Pikesville Plaza Building. Then began the search for "Woody Hightower." After numerous interviews, twenty-three year old John Jordan emerged as "Woody Hightower."

After selecting the flagpole tenant, the corporation then sought and obtained a company to construct the premises to house him. This consisted of a seven foot wide perch that was to include a bed, toilet, water, refrigerator and heat. The accommodations were atop a hydraulic lift system mounted upon a flat bed tractor trailer.

Hightower employed two public relations specialists to coordinate press and public relations efforts and to obtain major corporate backers. "Woody" received a proclamation from the Mayor and City Council of Baltimore and after a press breakfast at the Hilton Hotel on "All Fools Day" ascended his home in the sky.

Within ten days, Hightower obtained a live appearance for "Woody" on the Mike Douglas Show, and a commitment for an appearance on the Wonderama television program. The principals anticipated a "snow-balling" effect from commercial enterprises as the project progressed with no substantial monetary commitments for approximately six months.

Hightower raised $43,000.00 by selling stock in the corporation. Within two weeks of "Woody's" ascension, another stockholders' meeting was scheduled, because the corporation was low on funds. At that time, Mr. Wartzman informed the principals that no further stock could be sold, because the corporation was "structured wrong", and it would be necessary to obtain the services of a securities attorney to correct the problem. Mr. Wartzman had acquired this information in a casual conversation with a friend who recommended that the corporation should consult with a securities specialist.

The problem was that the law firm had failed to prepare an offering memorandum and failed to assure that the corporation had made the required disclosures to prospective investors in accordance with the provisions of the Maryland Securities Act. Mr. Wartzman advised Hightower that the cost of the specialist would be between $10,000.00 and $15,000.00. Hightower asked the firm to pay for the required services and the request was rejected.

Hightower then employed substitute counsel and scheduled a shareholders' meeting on April 28, 1975. At that meeting, the stockholders were advised that Hightower was not in compliance with the securities laws; that $43,000.00, the amount investors had paid for issued stock, had to be covered by the promoters and placed in escrow; that the fee of a securities specialist would be $10,000.00 to $15,000.00 and that the additional work would require between six and eight weeks. In the interim, additional stock could not be sold, nor could "Woody" be exhibited across state lines. Faced with these problems, the shareholders decided to discontinue the entire project.

On October 8, 1975, Hightower filed suit alleging breach of contract and negligence for the law firm's failure to have created a corporation authorized to raise the capital necessary to fund the venture. At the trial, Hightower introduced into evidence its obligations and expenditures incurred in reliance on the defendant law firm's creation of a corporation authorized to raise the $250,000.00, necessary to fund the project. The development costs incurred included corporate obligations amounting to $155,339 including; initial investments by Adler and Billitz, $20,000; shareholders, excluding the three promoters, $43,010; outstanding liabilities exclusive of salaries, $58,929; liability to talent consultants, $25,000; and accrued salaries to employees, $8,400.

Individual liabilities to the three promoters, Adler, Billitz and Quinn, totaled $88,608, including loans to the corporation $44,692; repayment of corporate debt to Maryland National Bank, $8,016; and loss of salaries $36,000. The trial court disposed of the individual suit filed by the promoters, Adler, Billitz and Quinn and the cross complaint filed by the appellants. The only claim submitted for the jury's consideration was the claim of the corporation, Hightower, against the defendant law firm.

The jury returned a verdict in favor of Hightower in the amount of $170,508.43. Wartzman, Rombro, Rudd and Omansky, P.A., appealed to this Court. Hightower filed a cross appeal alleging that the jury should have been permitted to consider prejudgment interest.

\*     \*     \*

The appellants first contend that the jury verdict included all of Hightower's expenditures and obligations incurred during its existence resulting in the law firm being absolute surety for all costs incurred in a highly speculative venture. While they do not suggest the analogy, the appellants would no doubt equate the verdict as tantamount to holding the blacksmith liable for the value of the kingdom where the smith left out a nail in shoeing the king's horse, because of which the shoe was lost, the horse was lost, the king was lost and the kingdom was lost. Appellants contend that there is a lack of nexus or causation between the alleged failure of Mr. Wartzman to discharge his duties as an attorney and the loss claimed by Hightower. Stated differently, an unjust result will obtain where a person performing a collateral service for a new venture will, upon failure to fully perform the service, be liable as full guarantor for all costs incurred by the enterprise.

Ordinarily, profits lost due to a breach of contract are recoverable. Where anticipated profits are too speculative to be determined, monies spent in part performance, in preparation for or in reliance on the contract are recoverable.

\*     \*     \*

Recovery based upon reliance interest is not without limitation. If it can be shown that full performance would have resulted in a net loss, the plaintiff cannot escape the consequences of a bad bargain by falling back on his reliance interest. Where the breach has prevented an anticipated gain and made proof of loss difficult to ascertain, the injured party has a right to damages based upon his reliance interest, including expenditures made in preparation for performance, or in performance, less any loss that the party in breach can prove with reasonable certainty the injured party would have suffered had the contract been performed. Restatement, Second, Contracts, Sec. 349. \* \* \*

The appellants' contention that permitting the jury to consider reliance damages in this case rendered the appellants' insurers of the venture is without merit. Section 349 of the Restatement, cited above, expressly authorizes the breaching party to prove any loss that the injured party would have suffered had the contract been performed. Such proof would avoid making the breaching party a guarantor of the success of the venture.

As Judge Learned Hand stated \* \* \* :

> "It is often very hard to learn what the value of the performance would have been; and it is a common expedient, and a just one, in such situations to put the peril of the answer upon that party who by his wrong has made the issue relevant to the rights of the other. On principle therefore the proper solution would seem to be that the promisee may recover his outlay in preparation for the performance, subject to the privilege of the promisor to

reduce it by as much as he can show that the promisee would have lost if the contract had been performed."

In the present case the appellants knew, or should have known, that the success of the venture rested upon the ability of Hightower to sell stock and secure advertising as public interest in the adventure accelerated. Appellants' contention that their failure to properly incorporate Hightower was collateral and lacked the necessary nexus to permit consideration of reliance damages is not persuasive. The very life blood of the project depended on the corporation's ability to sell stock to fund the promotion. This is the reason for the employment of the appellants. In reliance thereon, Hightower sold stock and incurred substantial obligations. When it could no longer sell its stock, the entire project failed. No greater nexus need be established. Aside from questioning the expertise of the promoters based upon their previous employment, the appellants were unable to establish that the stunt was doomed to fail. The inability to establish that financial chaos was inevitable does not make the appellants insurers and does not preclude Hightower from recovering reliance damages. The issue was properly submitted to the jury.

*   *   *

Duty to Mitigate Damages

The evidence in this case establishes that Hightower did not have the $43,000.00 to place in escrow covering stock sold, did not have the $10,000.00 or $15,000.00 to employ a securities specialist and could not continue stock sales or exhibitions to obtain the necessary funds. Mr. Wartzman's offer to set up an appointment for Hightower with an expert in security transactions at Hightower's expense can hardly be construed as a mitigating device that Hightower was obligated to accept. The party who is in default may not mitigate his damages by showing that the other party could have reduced those damages by expending large amounts of money or incurring substantial obligations. * * *

The doctrine of avoidable consequences, moreover, does not apply where both parties have an equal opportunity to mitigate damages. Appellants had the same opportunity to employ and pay a securities specialist as they contend Hightower should have done. They refused. Having rejected Hightower's request to assume the costs of an additional attorney, they are estopped from asserting a failure by Hightower to reduce its loss.

There is no evidence in this case that the additional funds necessary to continue the operation pending a restructuring of the corporation were within the financial capabilities of Hightower. The Court properly declined to instruct the jury on the issue of mitigation.

JUDGMENT AFFIRMED.

# NOTES

1.  What acts of Mr. Wartzman or his firm constituted negligence? Why did the articles of incorporation authorize one million shares?

**2.** The court's opinion tells us that there was a breach of contract. What terms of the contract were breached by the law firm?

**3.** When the client told Mr. Wartzman that it was necessary to sell stock to the public, what advice or disclosure should he have given to the client?

**4.** Was any purpose served by filing the articles of incorporation that brought Hightower Productions, Ltd. into existence?

**5.** When Mr. Wartzman informed the principals that the corporation was "structured wrong" and that it would be necessary to obtain the services of a securities attorney, was his advice honest and complete? What should he have said?

**6.** If the principals sell stock without complying with the Maryland Securities Act, what potential liabilities would result?

**7.** Note that under the Securities Act of 1933 it would be a relatively simple task to sell $250,000 worth of stock to 35 or fewer investors. *See* Regulation D (Rules 501 through 508). Nonetheless, the promoters of Woody Hightower must comply with Maryland securities law. Most states exempt a small issuance from a registration requirement, but the transactional limit is frequently based on the number of offerees rather than buyers. In any event, it is often fewer than 35. Further, small issue exemptions are often conditioned on the absence of general solicitation. The Maryland Securities Act has a transactional exemption, Section 11-602(9), permitting the sale of securities to up to 35 persons within a 12-month period along with some other conditions. The significance of this for the attorney advising clients desiring to sell stock to more buyers than permitted by the exemption is that such conduct is considered a public offering under state law, and that a prospectus or offering memorandum must be prepared to comply with state law. The consequence for many small scale deals is that the legal costs are so high that the transaction may not go forward at all, unless dramatically restructured.

## G. DEFECTIVE INCORPORATION

At common law, failed attempts to incorporate often resulted in the individuals involved being held personally liable as partners. Because of the perceived injustice of such decisions and the resulting windfall given to a third party, who had never expected to look to the personal assets of the individuals involved, two similar but related judicial doctrines developed to ameliorate such harsh results. One is called "de facto corporation" and the other is "corporation by estoppel." The first attempt to deal with this problem was section 146 of the Model Business Corporation Act of 1969 (MBCA (1969)). Many courts interpreted section 146 to abolish the doctrine of de facto corporation but to retain the doctrine of corporation by estoppel. The distinction between the two doctrines is somewhat elusive. The drafters of the Model Business Corporation Act of 1984 (MBCA (1984)), discussed in *Sivers, infra*, appeared to be concerned by the windfall aspects of MBCA (1969). The result was MBCA (1984) section 2.04, which limits the liability of those who act for nonexistent corporations to those who "know" there was no incorporation. Unfortunately it does little to clarify whether the drafters intended the estoppel doctrine to survive. Because statutes based on both the 1969 and 1984 versions of the MBCA are in effect in various states, it is important to be aware of the significant differences in philosophy of the two approaches to pre-incorporation liability.

## LUCKY DAWG MOVERS, INC. v. WEE HAUL, INC.
### Court of Appeals of Texas
### 2011 Tex. App. LEXIS 8398 (Oct. 21, 2011)

LANG, J.

This is an appeal from a jury verdict in favor of Lucky Dawg Movers, Inc. f/k/a Wee Haul of Atlanta, Inc. d/b/a Apartment Movers against Wee Haul, Inc. d/b/a Apartment Movers ("Wee Haul"). The jury awarded Lucky Dawg $35,725.26 in damages after finding Wee Haul engaged in deceptive trade practices, that is, false, misleading, and deceptive acts or practices upon which Lucky Dawg relied. In a single issue, Lucky Dawg contends George B. Killick, president and director of Wee Haul, should be jointly and severally liable along with Wee Haul for the final judgment. Lucky Dawg raises two arguments in that regard. First, Lucky Dawg asserts that Killick should be jointly and severally liable . . . because at the time "the debt" was incurred, Wee Haul's corporate privileges and charter had been forfeited. See TEX.TAX CODE ANN. § 171.255 (West 2008) (corporate officers and directors personally liable for certain debt of corporation that has lost privileges). Second, Lucky Dawg asserts Killick should be jointly and severally liable with Wee Haul because Killick filed an assumed name certificate for "Wee Haul Inc.," he was allegedly doing business under the assumed name, and, . . . an individual doing business under an assumed name may be sued in the assumed name for purposes of enforcing against him a substantive right. We decide against Lucky Dawg on its sole issue and affirm the trial court's judgment.

The suit was brought by Lucky Dawg and Lucky Dawg's owner, Charles Manry. The jury found against Manry on his claims. Manry appealed the judgment along with Lucky Dawg, but raises no independent issues.

### I. Background

Wee Haul is a Texas corporation that provides residential moving services. It was founded in 1978 by Killick. In March 1996, Wee Haul lost its corporate privileges and forfeited its charter for failure to file a required franchise tax report. Wee Haul's privileges and charter were reinstated in August 2008 when the required reports were filed.

Lucky Dawg is a Georgia corporation, was purchased by Charles Manry in June 2006, and became a franchisee of Wee Haul pursuant to a "Master License Agreement" ("MLA") signed by both Manry and Killick. Killick signed in his capacity as Wee Haul's president. In April 2006, Killick filed an assumed name certificate for "Wee Haul Inc." and he testified at trial he "had been contemplating" changing Wee Haul's business form to a sole proprietorship.

The assumed name certificate in the record shows the assumed name of "Wee Haul Inc." There is no comma between "Haul" and "Inc." as there is in the corporate name on Wee Haul's corporate charter and as named in this suit.

Under the MLA, Lucky Dawg agreed, inter alia, to pay Wee Haul a monthly royalty equal to five percent of Lucky Dawg's gross revenues and Wee Haul agreed to assist Lucky Dawg with training, supply training manuals, and provide Lucky Dawg with a "pricing methodology" for calculating the price to charge customers for some of the services Lucky Dawg was to offer. Lucky Dawg filed suit against Wee Haul and Killick, individually, in August 2007 contending Wee Haul failed to comply with the provisions of the MLA.

\* \* \*

### B. Application of Law to Facts

Lucky Dawg alleges Killick "was doing business under the assumed name of Wee Haul, Inc." According to Lucky Dawg, because Killick "did business" under the assumed name, this suit against Wee Haul is also one against Killick. Therefore, "a judgment rendered against 'Wee Haul, Inc.' should also be a judgment rendered against Killick." Finally, Lucky Dawg argues the issue of Killick being sued under the assumed name was tried by consent. In response, Wee Haul and Killick argue Lucky Dawg sued Killick only in his individual capacity and no claim was ever made that he was liable based on the "assumed name" theory. According to Wee Haul and Killick, Lucky Dawg maintained that posture throughout trial. Therefore, they contend, Killick cannot be jointly and severally liable.

The record contains the assumed name certificate Killick signed for "Wee Haul Inc." that was filed and recorded in April 2006, two months before the MLA was signed. At the time the MLA was signed, Killick knew Wee Haul had lost its charter and corporate privileges in 1996. However, Killick did not tell Manry about that. Nevertheless, Killick signed the MLA in his capacity as Wee Haul's president. The record reflects Killick testified at trial that he "signed . . . [the] assumed name certificate" because he "had been contemplating changing it to a sole proprietorship to keep down bookkeeping efforts, requirements." (Emphasis added.) Further, Killick testified he did not tell Manry about his "contemplation" of changing Wee Haul to a sole proprietorship business form. However, Lucky Dawg has pointed to no evidence in the record, and we can find none, that shows that Killick was, in fact, "doing business" as Wee Haul Inc.

The record before us also contains an original petition filed in August 2007 and a fourth amended petition filed in January 2009. In the original petition, Lucky Dawg sued Killick in his individual capacity and asserted claims for fraud in the inducement and slander. No claim was stated based on an assumed name allegedly used by Killick. In the fourth amended petition, Lucky Dawg again sued Killick in his individual capacity for fraud in the inducement and slander, and added claims against him for tortious interference with business relationships, a declaratory judgment that Lucky Dawg had full right to use the name "Apartment Movers" in certain counties, violations of the DTPA, breach of good faith and fair dealing, and pursuant to section 171.255. Lucky Dawg did not, however, include in the amended petition a claim based upon Killick's use of an assumed name. Further, other than a reference to Wee Haul as "Killick's company" made at trial during questioning, Lucky Dawg offered no evidence supporting a claim against Killick under an assumed name and even consented to a jury charge that identified Killick separately from Wee Haul.

On the record before us, we conclude the trial court did not err in denying Lucky Dawg's motion to make the judgment against Wee Haul joint and several against Killick on this theory.

## V. Conclusion

Having concluded the judgment against Wee Haul should not be joint and several against Killick under either tax code section 171.255 or rule of civil procedure 28, we decide Lucky Dawg's sole issue against it and affirm the trial court's judgment.

## NOTES

1.  Compare the outcome in *P.I.M.L. v. Chain Link Graphix, LLC*, from Chapter 3, to *Lucky Dawg*. Why did the court find liability in the former and not in the latter? Did the plaintiff simply fail to litigate the matter properly, or is the court suggesting that liability for such actions doesn't exist? The court even notes that Killick was aware that Wee Haul had lost its charter and corporate privileges prior to executing the MLA.

2.  The comments to section 2.04 of the MBCA (1984) suggest that corporation by estoppel exists, but the text does not tell us in what form. The judicial treatment, such as that in *Lucky Dawg*, suggests that persons who act for a non-existent corporation will receive a sympathetic hearing. The comment to section 2.04 admits that "the section does not foreclose the possibility that [persons] may be estopped to impose personal liability . . . . This estoppel may be based on [perceived] inequity . . . ." The case above seems to suggest that acting on behalf of a defunct corporation doesn't automatically create such inequity.

3.  Another complication is that individual states provide for differing statutory treatment. For example, section 14-5-4 of the Official Code of Georgia Annotated provides, "the existence of a corporation claiming a charter under color of law cannot be collaterally attacked by persons who have dealt with it as a corporation. Such persons are estopped from denying its corporate existence." For a contrasting view, *see Fee Insurance Agency, Inc. v. Snyder*, 930 P.2d 1054 (Kan. 1997), where the Supreme Court of Kansas imposed personal liability on those acting on behalf of a corporation, even though the articles were properly filed with the appropriate state agency, but the corporation had failed to file with the county where business was located.

# SIVERS v. R & F CAPITAL CORP.
Court of Appeals of Oregon
858 P.2d 895 (1993)

WARREN, J.

In this breach of contract action, defendant Roy Rose appeals a final judgment entered after the trial court denied his motion for a directed verdict and the jury returned a verdict against him. We reverse.

Plaintiff and defendant are both experienced businessmen. Defendant is a shareholder and director of R & F Capital Corporation (R & F). In 1990, plaintiff and R & F entered into a commercial leasing agreement involving a warehouse space in Milwaukie, Oregon. Plaintiff signed the lease in his individual capacity, and defendant signed as "chairman" on behalf of R & F. The written agreement shows that the lease was "executed"[5] on January 12, 1990, and was to commence on January 17, 1990. The parties stipulated that R & F was incorporated on February 9, 1990.

In November, 1990, plaintiff sued R & F and defendant, alleging that R & F had breached the lease by failing to pay a number of rental installments for the warehouse space it occupied. The claim against defendant was that he was personally liable under ORS 60.054.2 During trial defendant moved for a directed verdict. Defendant assigns as error the trial court's denial of that motion.

In reviewing a denial of the motion for a directed verdict, we consider the evidence in the light most favorable to the party with the judgment . . . .

ORS 60.054 provides:

> "All persons purporting to act as or on behalf of a corporation, knowing there was no incorporation, are jointly and severally liable for liabilities created while so acting."

This provision was adopted in 1987 as part of SB 303, and is virtually identical to section 2.04 of the Revised Model Business Corporation Act (1984) (RMBCA).[6] Section 2.04 is a codification of the judicial exceptions to the general rule that those who prematurely act as, or on behalf of, a corporation are personally liable on all transactions entered into or liabilities incurred before incorporation. MBCA Annot. § 2.04, at 130. As written, section 2.04 "impose[s] liability only on persons who act as or on behalf of corporations 'knowing' that no corporation exists." MBCA Annot. § 2.04, at 133; see also *Micciche v. Billings*, 727 P.2d 367, 370 (Colo. 1986).

In proposing the adoption of section 2.04 of RMBCA in Oregon, the Task Force of the Oregon State Bar Business Law Section, which authored SB 303, wrote:

---

[5] [1] Plaintiff testified that the date of execution meant the date on which the lease was signed.

[6] [3] As of March 1, 1993, about 15 states have adopted provisions either identical to RMBCA section 2.04, or with minor modifications. See Model Business Corporation Act Annotated (MBCA Annot.) § 2.04, at 137 (3d. Ed. 1985).

"The Bill adopts RMBCA Section 2.04, deleting only the reference to incorporation under 'this Act,' as being too limiting. The Bill treats pre-incorporation liability in a manner consistent with the Model Act provision, although somewhat differently from [former] ORS § 57.793. It is those who purport to act on behalf of the corporation "knowing there was no incorporation" who are subject to liability under the Bill. Existing law subjects all those who 'assume to act as a corporation without the authority of a certificate of incorporation' to liability. *The Bill protects participants who act honestly but subject to the mistaken belief that the articles have been filed.* This section is consistent with the Revised Uniform Limited Partnership Act (1976), which provides that limited partners who contribute capital to a partnership with the mistaken belief that a limited partnership certificate has been filed are protected from liability. This appears to be consistent with Oregon case law concerning de facto corporations. See *Sherwood & Roberts v. Alexander*, 269 Or 389, [525 P.2d 135] (1974)." Oregon State Bar Business Law Section, Model Business Corporation Act Task Force, Report on Oregon Revised Model Business Corporation Act (March 24, 1987), § 18, p. 7. (Emphasis supplied.)

*See also* Comments on Oregon Revised Model Business Corporation Act (March 24, 1987), § 18, p. 6.

The wording of ORS 60.054 and the drafters' comments clearly indicate that the test for imposition of personal liability is one of actual knowledge. Further, it is plaintiff's burden to show that defendant has the requisite actual knowledge.

Plaintiff argues that there are facts from which the jury could find that defendant knew that R & F was not incorporated when he signed the lease. Under the circumstances of this case, we disagree. In his case-in-chief, plaintiff testified that he hired a commercial leasing agent in the negotiations of the lease in question. He personally had never met or spoken with defendant before. Plaintiff's employees prepared the lease, and typed in additional information on it. Plaintiff remembered that he signed the lease about January 12, 1990. At the time he signed, he understood that he was dealing with R & F, an Oregon corporation, not with defendant personally. He knew that R & F was a "start-up," but made no independent inquiries into its status, because he thought that R & F was then incorporated. It was not until May or June of 1990 when he first learned that R & F was not yet incorporated on January 12, 1990.

Plaintiff also called defendant as an adverse witness in his case-in-chief. Defendant testified that he was a businessman who created financing packages to buy companies. He had a controlling interest in two other companies. His highest net worth at one point was $56 million. He had been involved in setting up many corporations. However, he had no specific experience in incorporating, because his attorneys handled those aspects of his business. For example, he did not know when a corporation formally began its existence, although he understood that documents needed to be filed with the state and a copy would be returned upon incorporation.

With respect to R & F, defendant had no participation in its daily operation, other than attending board meetings and signing documents as "chairman." He entrusted Flaherty, an R & F director, with those daily duties. Defendant did not read the articles of incorporation of R & F until he was sued. He recalled that that document was given to him and was filed in December, 1989. He remembered that he signed the lease in late February or early March of 1990, although he had nothing to contradict the dates as shown on the lease.

After his motion for a directed verdict was denied, defendant and Alderman, another R & F director, testified in the defense. Their testimony was consistent with defendant's testimony in plaintiff's case-in-chief. Specifically, they testified that defendant signed the lease in late February or early March of 1990, after R & F had occupied the premises for some time, and that Flaherty was entrusted to incorporate R & F in December of 1989, but failed to do that. They both believed that R & F was incorporated in December of 1989. Defendant also testified that he started investing based on that belief, and that he would not have signed any document on behalf of a corporation if he had known that it was not incorporated.

Plaintiff does not argue that there is direct evidence that defendant knew that the corporation had not been formed when he signed the lease. To support his argument that there was circumstantial evidence, he points to defendant's vast experience as a businessman, his failure to read the articles of incorporation and his complete lack of responsibility for filing necessary corporate documents with the Secretary of State. His reliance on those facts is misplaced. At most, they show that defendant should have inquired into R & F's status and should have known that the corporation was not formed. They do not rise to the level of actual knowledge required under ORS 60.054. Plaintiff would have us construe ORS 60.054 as requiring a test of constructive knowledge. However, had the legislature intended to adopt such a test, it would not have used the unmodified term "knowing." * * *

A more fundamental argument plaintiff raises is that, although defendant testified that he believed that R & F was incorporated at the time he signed the lease, the jury could disbelieve him and affirmatively find that he had the requisite actual knowledge. That argument goes too far. Although a jury may disbelieve a witness based on demeanor, bias, motives, interest or inconsistent statements, there must be evidence, direct or circumstantial, from which the jury can reasonably find that a defendant possesses the requisite knowledge. In this case, defendant maintained throughout trial that he honestly believed that R & F was incorporated when he signed the lease. Plaintiff produced nothing to contradict that. The trial court should have granted defendant's motion for a directed verdict.

Reversed and remanded with instructions to enter judgment for defendant Rose.

## PLESE-GRAHAM, LLC v. LOSHBAUGH
### Court of Appeals of Washington
### 269 P.3d 1038 (2011)

Siddoway, J.

At issue in this case is the personal liability of Robert Loshbaugh, former president of a now defunct construction company, for obligations arising out of company business that were discussed and documented with a creditor during a period when the company had ceased operations and was administratively dissolved. The trial court granted summary judgment against Mr. Loshbaugh and his marital community on grounds that he agreed to answer personally for the company's obligation and, alternatively, that his promise that the company would pay could be enforced against him personally because it was made at a time when the corporation was de facto dissolved.

On appeal, Mr. Loshbaugh argues that because of an alleged failure to bring suit in the name of the real party in interest, neither the company's creditor nor its principals can enforce his alleged agreement, a position we reject. But we agree that questions of material fact as to Mr. Loshbaugh's personal liability made summary judgment inappropriate. We reverse the orders granting summary judgment and attorney fees and remand for trial.

## FACTS AND PROCEDURAL BACKGROUND

For several years up to and including 2008, Ed Loshbaugh & Sons, Inc., a licensed general contractor, per-formed construction work for Plese-Graham, LLC, a real estate developer. In 2008, Plese-Graham hired Loshbaugh & Sons to install the water and sewer system for its housing development known as Park Place Addition. In March 2009, after Loshbaugh & Sons underpaid one of its subcontractors, the subcontractor filed a lien against Plese-Graham's property. Failure to pay the subcontractor was symptomatic of Loshbaugh & Sons financial difficulties at the time. After several claims were made against its bond, the bond was cancelled on May 24, the company lost its contractor's license, and it ceased operations.

On June 24, Plese-Graham, which claims its principals were unaware of the extent of Loshbaugh & Sons' financial problems, paid the subcontractor $16,265.12 in exchange for release of its lien. Shortly thereafter, on June 30, Rod Plese, one of two members of Plese-Graham, secured the verbal agreement of Robert Loshbaugh — a Loshbaugh & Sons shareholder and director in addition to being its president — to sign a promissory note reimbursing Plese-Graham's payment to the subcontractor.

Mr. Plese and Mr. Loshbaugh disagree as to the capacity in which Mr. Loshbaugh was asked and agreed to sign. Mr. Plese drafted and sent a proposed promissory note identifying "Bob Loshbaugh" as the payor, which Mr. Loshbaugh rejected, asking that Mr. Plese modify it to substitute the company as payor. Clerk's Papers (CP) at 88. Mr. Plese complied and sent a second note, which, apart from the named payor, was identical to the first. Both notes were payable to "Rod V. Plese and Linda A. Plese, husband and wife." Following several e-mails sent by Mr. Plese in September and October asking whether Mr. Loshbaugh had signed and returned "the note," Mr. Loshbaugh indicated in e-mails on October 5 and 19 that he had. . . .

Loshbaugh & Sons' corporate license had expired without renewal on June 30, 2009 and the company was administratively dissolved by the Secretary of State on October 1, a few days before Mr. Loshbaugh's written assurances that a note had been signed and returned. Upon dissolution, the company had no assets with which to pay Plese-Graham and other creditors.

In December 2009, Plese-Graham filed a complaint against Loshbaugh & Sons and Robert Loshbaugh and his wife, among others. The complaint alleged that the defendants had been overpaid as a result of Plese-Graham's payment of the construction contract price and the additional cost of removing the lien.

Plese-Graham's claims were subject to mandatory arbitration. In July 2010, an arbitrator found Loshbaugh & Sons, Mr. Loshbaugh, and his marital community jointly and severally liable to Plese-Graham in the amount of $16,265.12, plus interest at 12 percent per annum from June 24, 2009.

Only Mr. Loshbaugh, individually, appealed the arbitrator's ruling to superior court. He, and thereafter Plese-Graham, moved the court for summary judgment. Both parties'motions addressed Mr. Loshbaugh's undisputed promise, although in a disputed capacity, to reimburse Plese-Graham's payment of the subcontractor and to formalize the agreement with a promissory note payable to Mr. and Mrs. Plese. Plese-Graham alleged two theories of recovery against Mr. Loshbaugh personally: (1) breach by Mr. Loshbaugh of a verbal promise to deliver a personal promissory note and (2) even if his promise was to deliver a corporate note, individual liability . . . or a theory of corporate disregard, where his promise was on behalf of a company that Plese-Graham argued was "de facto" dissolved.

Mr. Loshbaugh opposed Plese-Graham's motion with his affidavit disputing that he ever agreed, personally, to reimburse Plese-Graham's payment to the subcontractor. He also argued that enforcement of any such verbal promise, being a promise to answer for the debt of another, was barred by the statute of frauds. He disputed his alleged liability on alternative grounds that (1) Loshbaugh & Sons was not dissolved, de facto or otherwise, at the time he agreed to reimburse Plese-Graham's payment to the subcontractor and (2) in any event, any such agreement was a permitted "winding up" of the corporation's business under [the statute].

At the hearing on the cross motions for summary judgment, Mr. Loshbaugh's lawyer pointed out for the first time that Plese-Graham, the only named plaintiff, was not the payee named by the promissory notes — something he admitted having noticed only that morning. The trial court responded that "I will entertain a motion to join [the Pleses] as parties, if necessary" and the lawyer for Plese-Graham so moved; after hearing Mr. Loshbaugh's objection, the trial court granted the motion.

The trial court granted Plese-Graham's motion for summary judgment, denied Mr. Loshbaugh's cross motion, entered an order joining the Pleses as parties, and entered judgment . . . in favor of Plese-Graham. Mr. Loshbaugh moved for reconsideration and when that was denied, timely appealed. He assigns error to the trial court's (1) granting summary judgment to Rod and Linda Plese, who he argues were improperly joined; (2) granting summary judgment in favor of Plese-Graham, which was not the designated payee of the promise relied upon for the court's decision; (3) entering judgment against Mr. Loshbaugh individually absent a basis therefor; and (4) assessing fees and costs against Mr. Loshbaugh.

## ANALYSIS

We first address Mr. Loshbaugh's arguments that the trial court erred in recognizing either Plese-Graham or the Pleses as parties entitled to assert claims based on his agreement reached with Mr. Plese in the summer of 2009. He contends that the court's late joinder of the Pleses as plaintiffs prejudiced him, because he was prevented from developing discovery in support of a defense of lack of consideration. He assigns error to the trial court's entry of judgment in favor of Plese-Graham because it was not the payee identified by the promissory note relied upon by the court in entering judgment. We review a trial court's rulings on motions to amend a complaint and its application of civil rules for an abuse of discretion.

Having argued that the Pleses should have been plaintiffs, Mr. Loshbaugh cannot be heard to complain that they were joined. Their joinder accomplished the legitimate goal of a defendant objecting to the absence of a real party in interest: namely, to bind the real party to the result. Any goal of derailing resolution of a claim on the merits by seizing on a mistake in identifying the proper plaintiff is not one that finds support in the civil rules; it is the type of strategy CR 17(a) was adopted to avoid.

If the objection and joinder were late, it is a delay for which Mr. Loshbaugh bears responsibility. It cannot be said to have prejudiced him, where the lack of consideration defense he proposed to assert would have been unavailing. We find neither harm nor reversible error in the trial court's order joining the Pleses and recognizing claims by them as well as Plese-Graham.

\*     \*     \*

Mr. Loshbaugh next argues that the trial court erred when it granted summary judgment on the alternative rationale that he was jointly and severally liable for Loshbaugh & Sons' obligation to Plese-Graham by virtue of RCW 23B.02.040, which provides:

> All persons purporting to act as or on behalf of a corporation, knowing there was no incorporation under this title, are jointly and severally liable for liabilities created while so acting except for any liability to any person who also knew that there was no incorporation.

This provision of the Washington Business Corporation Act, Title 23B RCW, falls under the chapter entitled "Incorporation," is entitled "Liability for pre-incorporation transactions," and is most commonly applied to cases of promoters incurring liabilities before incorporation. Nonetheless, in *Equipto Division Aurora Equipment Co. v. Yarmouth*, 134 Wn.2d 356, 370, 950 P.2d 451 (1998), our Supreme Court carefully considered the legislative history of the provision, prior corporation acts and common law, and determined that the statute also applies to "post-dissolution transactions that violate the statutory restriction of winding up the corporate business." Summary judgment was appropriate, then, if Plese-Graham demonstrated that there was no genuine issue of material fact as to the statute's application to Mr. Loshbaugh.

As related in *Equipto*, a properly incorporated company has yearly responsibilities to maintain its corporate status, including paying license fees and filing annual reports. A failure to do so is grounds for administrative dissolution of the corporation by the Secretary of State. "Once dissolved, the corporation 'continues its corporate existence but may not carry on any business except that necessary to wind up and liquidate its business and affairs under RCW 23B.14.050 and notify claimants under RCW 23B.14.060.'" *Equipto*, 134 Wn.2d at 362 (quoting former RCW 23B.14.210(3) (1989)).

In analyzing RCW 23B.02.040, *Equipto* found the first element of a claim — that a defendant "purports to act as or on behalf of a corporation" — to be straightforward.134 Wn.2d at 364. The second — "knowing there was no incorporation under this title" — "present[ed] the greatest difficulty" because a corporation continues to exist during the period it is winding up and conditionally even longer, inasmuch as it can be reinstated nunc pro tunc. Despite this theoretical quandary over when there is no longer incorporation, the court found that case law and legislative history support using dissolution as the time when a risk of individual liability begins to attach. It held that "[a]ll knowing, unauthorized acts after dissolution potentially incur personal liability." As to the "knowledge" required, the court was persuaded by legislative history and decisions from other state courts that for a defendant to have joint and several liability, he or she must have had actual knowledge that the corporation was dissolved. Finally, the court recognized that the exception provided by the statute denies joint and several recovery to any plaintiff who itself knew, at the time of the transaction relied upon, that the corporation was dissolved.

Plese-Graham seeks to impose joint and several liability for Mr. Loshbaugh's actions on behalf of the company not only following its October 1 dissolution, but following its earlier "de facto dissolution," which Plese-Graham, relying on Black's Law Dictionary, defines as "[t]he termination and liquidation of a corporation's business." Yet in construing the meaning of "knowing there was no incorporation" for post-incorporation transactions in Equipto, the Supreme Court found the end of incorporation to arise at the earliest upon dissolution. Plese-Graham identifies no Washington case discussing the de facto dissolution of a corporation or authority from any other state that would support de facto dissolution as triggering individual liability. Imposing joint and several liability before administrative dissolution is irreconcilable with the language of RCW 23B.02.040 and its construction in Equipto.

With this understanding of RCW 23B.02.040 in mind, Mr. Loshbaugh demonstrated issues of material fact that were disputed or as to which Plese-Graham made no showing of the absence of an issue of material fact. First, the parties dispute whether Mr. Loshbaugh purported to act on behalf of Loshbaugh & Sons after its October 1 dissolution. Viewing the evidence in the light most favorable to Mr. Loshbaugh, his only act as or on behalf of Loshbaugh & Sons was an agreement made before October 1. While Plese-Graham and the court rely on the October communications, those communications can be construed to refer to acts on behalf of the corporation that had taken place at earlier times. Second, and assuming Mr. Loshbaugh is determined by the trier of fact to have acted on behalf of the company after October 1, the summary judgment submissions did not make a threshold showing that Mr. Loshbaugh had contemporaneous actual knowledge that Loshbaugh & Sons had been administratively dissolved. Perhaps Plese-Graham could have presented such evidence, but given its reliance on de facto dissolution as triggering individual liability it did not. The summary judgment burden is initially on the moving party to show the absence of any issue of material fact.

Third, if Mr. Plese was aware that Loshbaugh & Sons was dissolved at the time of the alleged post-dissolution action of Mr. Loshbaugh, then Plese-Graham is not entitled to enforce joint and several liability. Here again, because Plese-Graham's motion did not focus on events after October 1, it did not make a threshold showing that Plese-Graham's principals were unaware, themselves, of the dissolution. Fourth, if any post-October 1 action taken on behalf of the company by Mr. Loshbaugh was a "winding up" transaction as he contends, then joint and several liability does not arise. Only after the trier of fact determines whether Mr. Loshbaugh acted on behalf of the company following dissolution can it determine whether his actions constituted "business . . . appropriate to wind up and liquidate its business and affairs." Given these several disputed or unaddressed material facts, summary judgment was inappropriate.

As an alternative basis for summary judgment imposing personal liability for a company obligation, Plese-Graham argues that it demonstrated Mr. Loshbaugh's intentional use of the company to violate or evade a duty, giving rise to an action to pierce the corporate veil. *See, e.g., Morgan v. Burks*, 93 Wn.2d 580, 585, 611 P.2d 751 (1980). The trial court did not address this issue, but we may affirm summary judgment on any ground supported by the record.

The "duty owed" theory of corporate disregard has two components. First, the corporate form must have been intentionally used to violate or evade a duty; second, disregard must be "necessary and required to prevent unjustified loss to the injured party." The first element requires an abuse of the corporate form. Such abuse typically involves " 'fraud, misrepresentation, or some form of manipulation of the corporation to the stockholder's benefit and creditor's detriment.' " *Id.* at 410 (quoting *Truckweld Equip. Co. v. Olson*, 26 Wn. App. 638, 645, 618 P.2d 1017 (1980)). The wrongful corporate activities required as the second element must actually harm the party seeking relief so that disregard is necessary. Intentional misconduct must be the cause of the harm that is avoided by disregard.

Plese-Graham's evidence offered in support of its motion would not support summary judgment on this alternate ground. Its affidavits and exhibits do not clearly establish either the requisite wrongdoing or unjustified loss. The financial reverses and ultimate demise of Loshbaugh & Sons left Plese-Graham unpaid, but "harm alone does not create corporate misconduct." A corporate entity should not be disregarded solely because it cannot meet its obligations. As recognized . . . , "[t]he purpose of a corporation is to limit liability."

Since summary judgment against Mr. Loshbaugh was inappropriate under each of the theories advanced by Plese-Graham, the orders and judgment must be reversed and the case remanded for trial.

\* \* \*

We reverse the trial court's orders and judgment and remand for trial proceedings consistent with this opinion.

# NOTES

**1.** The court again hesitates to impose personal liability despite what seems like plain language of the statute. Why does the court hesitate? The court seems to focus upon the conduct of the parties, and absent corporate misconduct, seems reluctant to disregard the benefits of incorporation. What other practical implications may arise from dissolution of the corporate form?

2.   In addition to a voluntary dissolution, it is also possible for a corporation to, in effect, involuntarily dissolve by failing to renew the appropriate annual filings to remain in good corporate standing. The following article illustrates the embarrassing and costly practical implications which may result:

### Emily Heller, *Piedmont Hospital Has Its Name Snatched & Ransomed*

FULTON COUNTY DAILY REPORT, Jan. 23, 1998, at 1[7]

Piedmont Hospital in Buckhead, one of Atlanta's best-known corporations, has been forced to pay an entrepreneur $25,000 to get its name back.

On Wednesday the hospital wrote a check to a Jonesboro man who, through legal maneuverings, obtained the corporate name Piedmont Hospital Inc. from the Georgia secretary of state.

The hospital had relinquished its title through what its lawyers in papers in federal court called a clerical error.

State officials say the hospital allowed its corporate registration to lapse by failing to pay $15 in annual fees for 1996 and 1997. For failure to pay, the state administratively dissolved the company in July.

Such fate befalls about 1,000 companies a year, according to a spokeswoman in the Secretary of State's Office. She says most business owners easily fix the problem by paying up.

Unless, that is, someone snaps up the name, which happened to Piedmont Hospital.

The man who took it, James Michael Wallace, reserved the name in August and formally registered a corporation as Piedmont Hospital Inc. in November. His company is a consulting firm, doing business as The Wallace Group, which he said in a court paper intended to create employee training products and publish children's books.

### A Legal Lever

In an interview, Wallace said he hoped his ownership of the Piedmont name would give a bargaining chip with the hospital, with which he had two court fights going simultaneously.

Piedmont hospital had sued Wallace to collect the last $900 on his late wife's bill which totaled $50,000 to $100,000, Wallace says. Judy Wallace, who had lupus, sustained heart complications following Cesarean-section delivery of their third child and died five months later.

Wallace sued the hospital and a doctor, alleging that his wife's release three days after giving birth ultimately caused the complications and her death.

With both suits filed, Wallace says, he learned from his lawyer, general civil practitioner Matthew D. Gansereit, about the hospital's corporate dissolution.

Gansereit says he discovered it in July when he was talking to the Secretary of State's Office to determine who to serve.

Wallace, who has run two small businesses, says it didn't dawn on him right away that dissolution could help.

Gansereit says he and his client thought it might help with settlement negotiations to resolve the bill and the negligence suit.

Moreover, Wallace says, he wanted to get the hospital's attention and review his wife's care with the administrator.

"The name had value to Piedmont. Just how much value was debatable," Gansereit says.

Wallace refused two offers of $5,000 and the dropping of the collection suit. The hospital sued in federal court, claiming trademark violations, deceptive trade practices and unfair competition, among other things.

During the hearing last week, U.S. District Court Judge Orinda D. Evans ordered the hospital to pay Wallace $25,000, an amount a lawyer for the hospital proposed and ordered Wallace to relinquish the name by certain dates, according to court documents. The judge is expected to issue a written order soon. Piedmont Hospital and Health Services Inc. v. Wallace, No. 1:97-cv3857-ODE (N.D.Ga filed Dec. 30, 1997).

Throughout the fall, Gansereit talked about the dissolution with a string of the hospital's lawyers.

They offered, to no avail, to drop the collections case if Wallace would give back the name.

In the meantime, the hospital registered a new name — Piedmont Hospital & Health Services Inc. — with the Secretary of State's Office in October, records show.

In November Wallace formally registered his consulting company as Piedmont Hospital Inc., doing business as The Wallace Group. He says he had been contemplating doing so for months.

He also published a public notice of incorporation in the Decatur-Dekalb News/Era.

In late December the hospital sought a restraining order, claiming Wallace had misappropriated the hospital's name.

Moreover, the hospital's contracts with Medicare, Medicaid and insurers were at risk because they were in the name of Piedmont Hospital, according to Gansereit.

Evans issued a temporary restraining order and set the case for a hearing in January.

Wallace says he never intended to use the name Piedmont Hospital Inc. in public. He says he obtained a post office box in the name of The Wallace Group.

Gansereit says he told his client that the hospital had an "absolute right" under Georgia common law to use the trade name because it was first to use it. The hospital also had registered a federal service mark for the name.

But he says his client legally obtained the corporate name and had not infringed on the hospital's rights to the name because he hadn't done anything with it.

Nevertheless, Wallace was Piedmont Hospital Inc. in the eyes of the state. During his deposition, de declared to the hospital's lawyer, "I am the president of Piedmont Hospital Incorporated."

He says, however, that he knew it is "bittersweet." He lost the negligence suit against the hospital and doctor on summary judgment for failing to file a required expert affidavit.

"It's not exactly the ending we had hoped for, but it certainly turned out OK, all things considered, considering how outmatched we were," Wallace says.

### Clerical Mistake

\*   \*   \*

In a written statement responding to the Daily Report's questions, the hospital said the check for Piedmont Hospital Inc., one of seven corporations held by parent Piedmont Medical Center Inc., was "somehow misplaced by a clerk at the hospital" and not sent in with the other renewals in 1996.

When the hospital attempted to renew in 1997, the secretary of state said the amount due was $30 for both years.

"Before Piedmont could remedy the situation," the hospital was dissolved, the statement says.

The hospital says it regrets that the suit was necessary and that Wallace's registration had only "nuisance value."

Nevertheless, because the hospital had contracts in the name of Piedmont Hospital Inc., third parties "might have sought to renegotiate" had the name change been permanent, the statement says. "Any time someone steals your corporate name it is an important matter."

# H.   PROMOTERS LIABILITY

## COOPERS & LYBRAND v. FOX
Court of Appeals of Colorado
758 P.2d 683 (1988)

KELLY, C. J.

In an action based on breach of express and implied contracts, the plaintiff, Coopers & Lybrand (Coopers), appeals the judgment of the trial court in favor of the defendant, Garry J. Fox (Fox). Coopers contends that the trial court erred in ruling that Fox, a corporate promoter, could not be held liable on a pre-incorporation contract in the absence of an agreement that he would be so liable, and that Coopers had, and failed to sustain, the burden of proving any such agreement. We reverse.

On November 3, 1981, Fox met with a representative of Coopers, a national accounting firm, to request a tax opinion and other accounting services. Fox informed Coopers at this meeting that he was acting on behalf of a corporation he was in the process of forming, G. Fox and Partners, Inc. Coopers accepted the "engagement" with the knowledge that the corporation was not yet in existence.

G. Fox and Partners, Inc., was incorporated on December 4, 1981. Coopers completed its work by mid-December and billed "Mr. Garry R. [sic] Fox, Fox and Partners, Inc." in the amount of $10,827. When neither Fox nor G. Fox and Partners, Inc., paid the bill, Coopers sued Garry Fox, individually, for breach of express and implied contracts based on a theory of promoter liability.

Fox argued at trial that, although Coopers knew the corporation was not in existence when he engaged the firm's services, it either expressly or impliedly agreed to look solely to the corporation for payment. Coopers argued that its client was Garry Fox, not the corporation. The parties stipulated that Coopers had done the work, and Coopers presented uncontroverted testimony that the fee was fair and reasonable.

The trial court failed to make written findings of fact and conclusions of law. However, in its bench findings at the end of trial, the court found that there was no agreement, either express or implied, that would obligate Fox, individually, to pay Coopers' fee, in effect, because Coopers had failed to prove the existence of any such agreement. The court entered judgment in favor of Fox.

As a preliminary matter, we reject Fox's argument that he was acting only as an agent for the future corporation. One cannot act as the agent of a nonexistent principal. *Miser Gold Mining & Milling Co. v. Moody*, 37 Colo. 310, 86 P. 335 (1906).On the contrary, the uncontroverted facts place Fox squarely within the definition of a promoter. A promoter is one who, alone or with others, undertakes to form a corporation and to procure for it the rights, instrumentalities, and capital to enable it to conduct business.

When Fox first approached Coopers, he was in the process of forming G. Fox and Partners, Inc. He engaged Coopers' services for the future corporation's benefit. In addition, though not dispositive on the issue of his status as a promoter, Fox became the president, a director, and the principal shareholder of the corporation, which he funded, only nominally, with a $100 contribution. Under these circumstances, Fox cannot deny his role as a promoter.

Coopers asserts that the trial court erred in finding that Fox was under no obligation to pay Coopers' fee in the absence of an agreement that he would be personally liable. We agree.

As a general rule, promoters are personally liable for the contracts they make, though made on behalf of a corporation to be formed. *Quaker Hill, Inc. v. Parr*, 148 Colo. 45, 364 P.2d 1056 (1961). The well-recognized exception to the general rule of promoter liability is that if the contracting party knows the corporation is not in existence but nevertheless agrees to look solely to the corporation and not to the promoter for payment, then the promoter incurs no personal liability. *Quaker Hill, Inc. v. Parr, supra; Goodman v. Darden, supra.* In the absence of an express agreement, the existence of an agreement to release the promoter from liability may be shown by circumstances making it reasonably certain that the parties intended to and did enter into the agreement.

Here, the trial court found there was no agreement, either express or implied, regarding Fox's liability. Thus, in the absence of an agreement releasing him from liability, Fox is liable.

Coopers also contends that the trial court erred in ruling, in effect, that Coopers had the burden of proving any agreement regarding Fox's personal liability for payment of the fee. We agree.

Release of the promoter depends on the intent of the parties. As the proponent of an alleged agreement to release the promoter from liability, the promoter has the burden of proving the release agreement. *Goodman v. Darden, supra; see Quaker Hill, Inc. v. Parr, supra.*

Fox seeks to bring himself within the exception to the general rule of promoter liability. However, as the proponent of the exception, he must bear the burden of proving the existence of the alleged agreement releasing him from liability. The trial court found that there was no agreement regarding Fox's liability. Thus, Fox failed to sustain his burden of proof, and the trial court erred in granting judgment in his favor.

It is undisputed that the defendant, Garry J. Fox, engaged Coopers' services, that G. Fox and Partners, Inc., was not in existence at that time, that Coopers performed the work, and that the fee was reasonable. The only dispute, as the trial court found, is whether Garry Fox is liable for payment of the fee. We conclude that Fox is liable, as a matter of law, under the doctrine of promoter liability.

Accordingly, the judgment is reversed, and the cause is remanded with directions to enter judgment in favor of Coopers & Lybrand in the amount of $10,827, plus interest to be determined by the trial court . . . .

# NOTES

1.  What should Mr. Fox have done if he wished to avoid personal liability for the accounting services?

2.  Would the result of this case be different if Mr. Fox had formed the corporate entity prior to his hiring the accounting firm?

## ILLINOIS CONTROLS, INC. v. LANGHAM
### Supreme Court of Ohio
### 639 N.E.2d 771 (1994)

SWEENEY, J.

[Langham is the inventor of a device called the cross-slope monitor (CSM). The device is employed as an accessory for heavy-duty road graders to assure a consistent angle in the course of highway construction. He began to market the device through his unincorporated business, Langham Engineering. Illinois Controls, Inc. was formed to manufacture and market the CSM. Langham had sold about 100 of the CSM's for use on John Deere construction equipment, but desired to penetrate the larger market represented by Caterpillar Tractor Company (CAT).]

The present action requires us to determine the obligations created by the pre-incorporation agreement ("PIA"), whether such obligations have been breached and, if so, what parties are liable therefor. Appellees contend that the reference in the PIA to the marketing capabilities of Clark Balderson and BI was merely prefatory and therefore created no marketing obligation. The court of appeals agreed.

We are unable to concur in this conclusion. A review of the PIA reveals that the only "prefatory" language appears in the "whereas clause," which set forth the parties' desire to manufacture and sell CSMs. Significantly, Article II of the agreement, which recites Balderson's marketing obligations, is introduced by the following phrase: "NOW, THEREFORE, *pursuant to the mutual covenants herein contained, the parties hereto agree as follows.*" (Emphasis added.) The agreement leaves little doubt that marketing of the CSM was one of the "covenants" to which the parties "agreed" in the introductory sentence.

Even if it were not expressly set forth in the PIA, appellees would still have the obligation to exert reasonable efforts to market the CSM.

\* \* \*

Appellees further challenge the award of damages in favor of appellants Michael and Patricia Langham and against appellee Illinois Controls in the amount of $752,000, and the allocation of $454,000 of this sum to Clark Balderson and $298,000 to BI. The liability of Illinois Controls under the contract arises from the relationship between Clark Balderson and BI as corporate promoters and Illinois Controls as the resulting corporate entity.

The legal relationship between a promoter and the corporate enterprise he seeks to advance is analogous to that between an agent and his principal. Thus, legal principles governing the relationship are derived from the law of agency. *See* HENN & ALEXANDER, LAWS OF CORPORATIONS AND OTHER BUSINESS ENTERPRISES (3d ed. 1983), at 253, Section 111; 1 RESTATEMENT OF THE LAW 2D, AGENCY (1958) 216, Section 84, Comment d; 2 RESTATEMENT OF THE LAW 2D, AGENCY (1958) 78, Section 326, Comment b.

Where an agent purports to act for a principal without the latter's knowledge, the principal may nevertheless be liable on obligations arising from the transaction if the principal later adopts or ratifies the agreement arising from the transaction or receives benefits from the agreement with knowledge of its terms. *See* 1 RESTATEMENT OF THE LAW 2D, AGENCY (1958), Sections 82 and 98. This is true even where the principal lacked capacity at the time of the transaction giving rise to the obligation if, after obtaining such capacity, the principal manifests acceptance of the transaction. *See id.*, Sections 104 and 84, Comment d.

Likewise, a corporation, which is incapable of authorizing an agreement made on its behalf prior to its existence, may nevertheless adopt the agreement after its incorporation. Adoption may be manifested by the corporation's receipt of the contract's benefits with knowledge of its terms. *See City Bldg. Assn. No. 2 v. Zahner* (1881), 6 Ohio Dec. Rep. 1068; *Reif v. Williams Sportswear, Inc.* (1961), 9 N.Y.2d 387, 214 N.Y.S.2d 395, 174 N.E.2d 492; HENN & ALEXANDER, *supra*, at 253–254, Section 11, fn. 6.

A corporation is therefore liable for the breach of an agreement executed on its behalf by its promoters where the corporation expressly adopts the agreement or benefits from it with knowledge of its terms.

The record discloses substantial evidence of the benefits conferred upon Illinois Controls by Michael Langham pursuant to the PIA. These benefits include the exclusive use of the CSM patent and the manufacturing capabilities of the Spring Valley facility previously operated by Langham Engineering, the titles to two motor vehicles, and appellant's engineering and technical expertise, which enabled the corporation to produce its sole stock in trade, the CSM. It is therefore beyond dispute that the corporation knowingly derived benefits from the agreement executed on its behalf.

There was also sufficient evidence that Illinois Controls breached the PIA, resulting in damages to appellants. In exchange for Langham Engineering's assets, Illinois Controls was to assume its debts and the debt assumed by Michael Langham to facilitate the creation of the corporation. However, despite the transfer of certain assets, Michael Langham's offer to transfer the remaining assets, and Illinois Controls' exclusive use of Langham Engineering resources, the corporation never assumed the debt as promised, leaving Michael Langham responsible for personal debt amounting to approximately $784,000 (i.e., $185,000 in pre-existing debt and $599,000 worth of additional obligations). In addition to the unassumed debt, appellant was owed a minimum of $10,850 in unpaid royalties (i.e., seventy units x $3,100 x five percent). This evidence more than supports the jury award of $752,000 in favor of Michael and Patricia Langham against Illinois Controls. Moreover, the jury award of $110,000 in favor of Joseph and Catherine Flaherty against Illinois Controls is clearly supported by evidence of the corporation's failure to assume the debt owed them as required in the PIA and the accrued interest on the debt from the date of the breach.

Appellees Clark Balderson and BI additionally question the assessment of damages against them for breach of the agreement by Illinois Controls.

It is axiomatic that the promoters of a corporation are at least initially liable on any contracts they execute in furtherance of the corporate entity prior to its formation. See Henn & Alexander, supra, at 252, Section 111. The promoters are released from liability only where the contract provides that performance is to be the obligation of the corporation, *Mosier v. Parry* (1899), 60 Ohio St. 388, 404, 54 N.E. 364, 367; 1 SEAVER, OHIO CORPORATION LAW (1989) 25, Section 9(d)(i); the corporation is ultimately formed, HENN & ALEXANDER, *supra*, at 252, Section 111, fn. 1 and 2; and the corporation then formally adopts the contract, 1 Seaver, supra, at 26, Section 9(d)(ii).

It is generally recognized that where a pre-incorporation agreement merely indicates that it is undertaken on behalf of a corporation, the corporation will not be exclusively liable in the event of a breach. Under such circumstances the promoters of the corporation remain liable on the contract.

Formation of the corporation following execution of the contract is a prerequisite to any release of the promoters from liability arising from the pre-incorporation agreement. Inasmuch as the promoter-corporation relationship is based on agency principles, a promoter will not be released from liability if the corporation is never formed, because one may not be an agent for a nonexistent

Moreover, mere adoption of the contract by the corporation will not relieve promoters from liability in the absence of a subsequent novation. This view is founded upon "the well-settled principle of the law of contracts that a party to a contract cannot relieve himself from its obligations by the substitution of another person, without the consent of [the] other party." . . . Consequently, the promoters of a corporation who execute a contract on its behalf are personally liable for the breach thereof irrespective of the later adoption of the contract by the corporation unless the contract provides that performance thereunder is solely the responsibility of the corporation.

Applying these principles to the facts of the present case, we find that the promoters remain personally liable on the pre-incorporation agreement. While the corporation was subsequently formed as envisioned in the contract, the agreement does not state that the parties intended that the corporate entity was to be exclusively liable for any breach. Even if the agreement did so provide, there is no evidence that the corporation, once formed, formally adopted it.

Under the circumstances presented herein, both the promoters and the corporation are liable under the contract. See 1A Fletcher, supra, at 329, Section 190. The corporation is liable because it accepted benefits conferred by the PIA with knowledge of its terms. The promoters are liable because the corporation never formally adopted the PIA, and the PIA does not make the corporation solely responsible for the obligations arising thereunder.

Inasmuch as both the promoters of Illinois Controls and the corporation itself are liable, the nature of this shared liability remains to be determined. While our research has failed to discover an Ohio decision which has addressed this specific issue, resort to agency principles is, again, instructive. The relationship between a promoter and a corporation to be formed can be compared to the relationship between an agent and an undisclosed principal. Where a contract is made in furtherance of the interests of an undisclosed principal, both the principal and the agent are liable for breach of its underlying obligations. Under such circumstances, the agent and the undisclosed principal are jointly and severally liable for breach of the agreement. . . .

These holdings are consistent with the shared liability for a contractual obligation undertaken by a promoter on behalf of a yet-to-be-formed corporation.

[We therefore] conclude that where a corporation, with knowledge of the agreement's terms, benefits from a pre-incorporation agreement executed on its behalf by its promoters, the corporation and the promoters are jointly and severally liable for breach of the agreement unless the agreement provides that performance is solely the responsibility of the corporation or, subsequent to the formation of the corporate entity, a novation is executed whereby the corporation is substituted for the promoters as a party to the original agreement.

It is therefore unnecessary to consider the argument of appellees that there was insufficient evidence to support the conclusion that Clark Balderson and BI were the alter ego of Illinois Controls so as to permit the corporate veil of the latter entity to be pierced. Rather, Illinois Controls and the promoters thereof (Clark Balderson and BI) are jointly and severally liable to appellants for breach of the PIA.

Appellees further maintain that the judgment against them is precluded because appellants did not assert the promoter theory in their complaint.

Accordingly, it was sufficient that appellants set forth facts which, if proven, established their claim for relief. It was not incumbent upon them to plead the law which created the liability of each defendant for breach of contract or which rendered them jointly and severally liable under the PIA.

\* \* \*

The judgment of the court of appeals is therefore affirmed in part and reversed in part, and the cause is remanded to the trial court for reinstatement of judgment.

# NOTES

1.  This case is quite different from the de facto corporation cases in which individuals fail to incorporate or attempt to do so but fail. When individuals act prior to incorporation, the rules governing their conduct and liabilities come from the law of agency.

2.  The Restatement (Third) of Agency (2006) considers corporate promoters to be acting on behalf of a non-existent principal, and simply applies the general agency rule to this situation. Section 6.04 states:

Unless otherwise agreed, a person who, in dealing with another, purports to be acting on behalf of a non-existent or wholly incompetent, becomes a party to such a contract.

3.  Comment b to Section 326 is as follows:

The classic illustration of the rule stated in this section is the promoter.

When a promoter makes an agreement with another on behalf of a corporation to be formed, the following alternatives may represent the intent of the parties:

(1) They may understand that the other party is making a revocable offer to the nonexistent corporation which will result in a contract if the corporation is formed and accepts the offer prior to withdrawal. This is the normal understanding.

(2) They may understand that the other party is making an irrevocable offer for a limited time. Consideration to support the promise to keep the offer open can be found in an express or limited promise by the promoter to organize the corporation and use his best efforts to cause it to accept the offer.

(3) They may agree to a present contract by which the promoter is bound, but with an agreement that his liability terminates if the corporation is formed and manifests its willingness to become a party. There can be no ratification by the newly formed corporation, since it was not in existence when the agreement was made.

(4) They may agree to a present contract on which, even though the corporation becomes a party, the promoter remains liable either primarily or as surety for the performance of the corporation's obligations.

Which one of these possible alternatives or variants thereof, is intended as a matter of interpretation on the facts of the individual case?

# Chapter 6

# PIERCING THE CORPORATE VEIL

As discussed in Chapter 1, one of the distinguishing features of the business corporation is the limited liability which its shareholders generally enjoy. Shareholders, thus, may invest in a corporation secure in the knowledge that, if the business fails, their "downside risk" is limited to the purchase price which they paid for their stock. However, creditors finding a judgment-proof corporation are likely to seek other sources for satisfying an unpaid judgment against the corporation; the obvious sources for creditors are the owners of the corporation, particularly if they are also the officers and directors. Thus, it comes as no surprise to find that, for decades, piercing the corporate veil has been the most frequently litigated issue in corporate law.

There are two general categories of cases in which the shareholders of a corporation may be subjected to personal liability for claims against the corporation when the assets of the corporation are insufficient to fully satisfy the claims. One category of cases, which we have already discussed, may be characterized as the premature commencement of business or defective formation of the corporation cases. These cases do not occur frequently today, particularly in states which follow the Model Business Corporation Act (MBCA). MBCA section 2.03(b) establishes a bright line rule under which "the Secretary of State's filing of the Articles of Incorporation is conclusive proof the incorporators satisfied all conditions precedent to incorporation except in a proceeding by the state to cancel or revoke the incorporation or involuntarily dissolve the corporation." Thus, failure to comply with any of the statutory mandates in the incorporation process cannot be used by creditors to justify imposing personal liability on the incorporators or shareholders. MBCA section 2.04 provides that "All persons purporting to act on behalf of a corporation knowing that there was no incorporation under this Act are jointly and severally liable for all liabilities created by so acting." The requirement of knowledge of the non-existence of the corporation as a prerequisite to holding shareholders personally liable for pre-incorporation transactions eliminates all but a few cases involving liability for pre-incorporation transactions since it will be a rare occasion indeed where an individual will act on behalf of a corporation which he knows does not exist. Most of the cases imposing liability in this situation in the past involved individuals who mistakenly believed that the articles had been issued at the time the act in question occurred, yet under prior statutes the courts generally had held that good faith belief in the existence of the corporation was no defense.

The second category of cases which are the subject of this chapter involve situations where the legal existence of the corporation is not an issue. Rather, the plaintiff is seeking to hold the shareholders liable for obligations of the corporation based on general considerations of social policy and equity. This category of cases, commonly known as "piercing the corporate veil," is probably the most frequently litigated issue in corporate law yet, as you will soon see, the rule of law applied by the courts in these cases is difficult to articulate with any precision nor is it easy to predict the outcome of a given case in advance. Statutes generally provide no guidance; the doctrine is largely judicially created. As you go through the following cases, try and determine what the real issues at stake are and how the courts go about determining when a judicially made exception to the general precept of limited liability should be made.

## KING v. McHUGH
First Judicial District Court of Montana
2009 Mont. Dist. LEXIS 469 (Oct. 21, 2009)

MCCARTER, J.

Plaintiffs have moved for partial summary judgment. The motion has been submitted on the briefs.

### UNDISPUTED FACTUAL BACKGROUND

McHugh Mobile Home Park Partnership, LLP (the partnership), is in the business of leasing mobile home spaces and buying, reconditioning, and re-selling used mobile homes. Ed McHugh, with a 52 percent ownership interest, is the controlling general partner in the partnership. Peter Joseph McHugh III is the other partner, with a 48 percent ownership. McHugh Mobile Home Park, LLP, McHugh Mobile Home Park, and McHugh Properties operate as the same entity.

Cloverleaf Systems, Inc. (the corporation), was established in approximately 2000 by McHugh and his wife to buy and sell mobile homes. It held the same address as the partnership. The only transaction done by the corporation was the purchase of mobile home # 354 in 2001. Thereafter, all of McHugh's transactions were done through "McHugh Properties," which was wholly owned by the partnership.

The corporation consisted only of McHugh and his wife. McHugh was listed as the president, and his wife Jacqueline was listed as secretary. They had no other officers or employees. McHugh was the sole shareholder. The corporation did not hold annual meetings, did not maintain tax and business records, did not maintain its own checking account, or file corporation tax returns. The last annual report was filed with the Montana Secretary of State in 2002. On December 1, 2003, the Secretary of State dissolved the corporation for failure to file its annual report. McHughs took no action with respect to the dissolution of the corporation, nor did they make any distributions of its assets.

The mobile home at issue in this lawsuit is # 354 and was purchased by and titled in the name of the corporation. McHugh purchased it in the name of the corporation for his daughter Kathleen Kahla. Kahla later decided to sell the home and showed it to the Kings, who ultimately purchased it from "Clover Leaf Systems" on September 1, 2005. The Kings wrote two checks for the home — on September 2, 2005, Theresa King wrote a check to Ed McHugh for $10,000, and on that same day, the Kings drafted a cashier's check to Clover Leaf Systems for $44,900. At that time the corporation was defunct.

In their complaint, the Kings allege that Defendants misrepresented the condition of the trailer with respect to the presence of mold, water leaks, and other defects.

## DISCUSSION

\* \* \*

The Kings first assert that these Defendants are jointly and severally liable under the theory of piercing the corporate veil. The Montana Supreme Court has established a two-pronged test to determine whether the circumstances of the case are appropriate for piercing the corporate veil. First, the trier of fact must find that the defendant was the alter ego, an instrumentality or an agent of the corporation. Second, the trier of fact must find evidence that the corporation was used as a subterfuge to defeat public convenience, justify wrong, or perpetrate fraud. *Peschel Family Trust v. Colonna*, 317 Mont 127, 2003 MT 216, P24, 75 P.3d 793.

In their responsive brief, Defendants did not resist the assertion that McHugh, through himself and the partnership, was an alter ego of the corporation. The undisputed facts before the Court easily support that finding. Defendants do, however, assert that the second prong of the test is lacking for purposes of summary judgment.

The undisputed facts indicate that McHugh formed the corporation legitimately, but failed to administer the entity as a corporation, as described above. He used the corporation only once — to purchase the mobile home at issue. The corporation was no longer in existence when its name was used as the seller of the mobile home to the Kings. McHugh's undisputed testimony in his deposition, as well as the other facts presented in the attachments, indicate that the corporation's funds were at all times intermingled with the partnership. McHugh's knowing use of the non-existent corporation as the seller of the mobile home was a fraud upon the Kings. Nor is there any question that protecting McHugh from the Kings in this lawsuit would result in inequity to the Kings who would have no recourse against a non-existent corporation. Failure to pierce the corporate veil in this instance would lead to manifest injustice.

The Court concludes that there are no material facts in dispute with respect to the issue of piercing the corporate veil. Summary judgment is GRANTED to the Kings with respect to this issue.

The Kings next assert that McHugh and his partnership are jointly and severally liable under section 35-1-119, MCA. That statute provides:

> Liability of and to ostensible corporations. All persons who assume to act as
> a corporation without authority so to do shall be jointly and severally liable
> for all debts and liabilities incurred or arising as a result thereof.

McHugh is clearly liable under this statute, since he represented himself to be the president of the non-existent corporation in the sale of the mobile home to the Kings. The record also indicates, without dispute, that the partnership was the actual entity involved in the sale of the mobile home to the Kings.

Defendants did not respond to this statutory issue in their briefs, and the Court finds merit in the Kings' argument. Partial summary judgment is therefore GRANTED to the Kings with respect to this issue.

# NOTES

**1.**    The two part test utilized in Montana is typical of the approach followed by many courts, although the precise articulation of it tends to vary considerably from one jurisdiction to another. What are the factors that a court would find persuasive in finding an "alter ego"?

**2.**    Does the court adequately identify the factors which enable it to decide whether piercing the corporate veil will prevent injustice? Does this phrase mean anything more than that the court will pierce the veil if it believes that the result will be equitable?

## FRIGIDAIRE SALES CORP. v. UNION PROPERTIES, INC.
### Supreme Court of Washington
### 562 P.2d 244 (1977)

HAMILTON, J.

Petitioner, Frigidaire Sales Corporation, sought review of a Court of Appeals decision which held that limited partners do not incur general liability for the limited partnership's obligations simply because they are officers, directors, or shareholders of the corporate general partner. . . . We granted review, and now affirm the decision of the Court of Appeals.

. . . Petitioner entered into a contract with Commercial Investors (Commercial), a limited partnership. Respondents, Leonard Mannon and Raleigh Baxter, were limited partners of Commercial. Respondents were also officers, directors, and shareholders of Union Properties, Inc., the only general partner of Commercial. Respondents controlled Union Properties, and through their control of Union Properties they exercised the day-to-day control and management of Commercial. Commercial breached the contract, and petitioner brought suit against Union Properties and respondents. The trial court concluded that respondents did not incur general liability for Commercial's obligations by reason of their control of Commercial, and the Court of Appeals affirmed.

We first note that petitioner does not contend that respondents acted improperly by setting up the limited partnership with a corporation as the sole general partner. Limited partnerships are a statutory form of business organization, and parties creating a limited partnership must follow the statutory requirements. In Washington, parties may form a limited partnership with a corporation as the sole general partner. . . .

Petitioner's sole contention is that respondents should incur general liability for the limited partnership's obligations [under the Uniform Limited Partnership Act provision that removes the limitation of limited liability of a limited partner who "takes part in the control of the business"][1] because they exercised the day-to-day control and management of Commercial. Respondents, on the other hand, argue that Commercial was controlled by Union Properties, a separate legal entity, and not by respondents in their individual capacities.

\* \* \*

However, we agree with our Court of Appeals analysis that this concern with minimum capitalization is not peculiar to limited partnerships with corporate general partners, but may arise anytime a creditor deals with a corporation . . . . Because our limited partnership statutes permit parties to form a limited partnership with a corporation as the sole general partner, this concern about minimal capitalization, standing by itself, does not justify a finding that the limited partners incur general liability for their control of the corporate general partner. . . . If a corporate general partner is inadequately capitalized, the rights of a creditor are adequately protected under the "piercing-the-corporate-veil" doctrine of corporation law. . . .

Furthermore, petitioner was never led to believe that respondents were acting in any capacity other than in their corporate capacities. The parties stipulated at the trial that respondents never acted in any direct, personal capacity. When the shareholders of a corporation, who are also the corporation's officers and directors, conscientiously keep the affairs of the corporation separate from their personal affairs, and no fraud or manifest injustice is perpetrated upon third persons who

---

[1] [1] At the time the parties entered into the contract, RCW 25.08.070 read as follows:

A limited partner shall not become liable as a general partner unless, in addition to the exercise of his rights and powers as limited partner, he takes part in the control of the business.

Laws of 1955, ch. 15, s 25.08.070, p. 140.

In 1972, the legislature amended RCW 25.08.070 by adding two additional sections. Laws of 1972, 1st Ex. Sess., ch. 113, s 2, p. 253. RCW 25.08.070 presently reads:

(1) A limited partner shall not become liable as a general partner unless, in addition to the exercise of his rights and powers as limited partner, he takes part in the control of the business.

(2) A limited partner shall not be deemed to take part in the control of the business by virtue of his possessing or exercising a power, specified in the certificate, to vote upon matters affecting the basic structure of the partnership, including the following matters or others of a similar nature:

    (a) Election, removal, or substitution of general partners, including, but not limited to, transfer of a majority of the voting stock of a corporate general partner.

    (b) Termination of the partnership.

    (c) Amendment of the partnership agreement.

    (d) Sale of all or substantially all of the assets of the partnership.

(3) The statement of powers set forth in subsection (2) of this section shall not be construed as exclusive or as indication that any other powers possessed or exercised by a limited partner shall be sufficient to cause such limited partner to be deemed to take part in the control of the business within the meaning of subsection (1) of this section.

deal with the corporation, the corporation's separate entity should be respected. . . .

For us to find that respondents incurred general liability for the limited partnership's obligations . . . would require us to . . . totally ignore the corporate entity of Union Properties, when petitioner knew it was dealing with that corporate entity. There can be no doubt that respondents, in fact, controlled the corporation. However, they did so only in their capacities as agents for their principal, the corporate general partner. Although the corporation was a separate entity, it could act only through its board of directors, officers, and agents. . . . Petitioner entered into the contract with Commercial. Respondents signed the contract in their capacities as president and secretary-treasurer of Union Properties, the general partner of Commercial. In the eyes of the law it was Union Properties, as a separate corporate entity, which entered into the contract with petitioner and controlled the limited partnership.

Further, because respondents scrupulously separated their actions on behalf of the corporation from their personal actions, petitioner never mistakenly assumed that respondents were general partners with general liability. . . . Petitioner knew Union Properties was the sole general partner and did not rely on respondents' control by assuming that they were also general partners. If petitioner had not wished to rely on the solvency of Union Properties as the only general partner, it could have insisted that respondents personally guarantee contractual performance. Because petitioner entered into the contract knowing that Union Properties was the only party with general liability, and because in the eyes of the law it was Union Properties, a separate entity, which controlled the limited partnership, there is no reason for us to find that respondents incurred general liability for their acts done as officers of the corporate general partner.

The decision of the Court of Appeals is affirmed.

## NOTES

**1.** At first blush, the decision to create a limited partnership with a corporate general partner might seem strange. In fact, this piggy-backing of one form of business entity on top of another has been quite common, particularly in real estate development businesses where it is anticipated that the business will generate substantial losses which the parties want to pass through to the individual investors in the business to offset earned income from other sources. The use of the limited partnership alone would allow this. However, since section 303 of the Revised Uniform Limited Partnership Act (RULPA) provides that limited partners forfeit their limited liability if they participate in the control of the business, a pure limited partnership will not be attractive to someone who actively manages the properties owned by the business. The answer, then, has been to create a corporation to serve as the general partner of the limited partnership and have the limited partners serve as officers and directors of the corporation. Although it was unclear under many corporate codes whether a corporation had the power to be a general partner of a partnership, this ambiguity has been expressly resolved in favor of recognizing this power in MBCA (1984) section 3.02(9).

**2.** Are there not dangers that third parties dealing with a limited partnership with a corporate general partner will mistakenly believe that the individuals with whom they are dealing are general partners? Does MBCA section 3.02(9) mean that plaintiffs must show that actual confusion, not merely the possibility of confusion, resulted in order to pierce the veil?

**3.** The court discusses whether the adequacy of the capitalization of the corporation serving as a general partner in a limited partnership should be treated any differently in this context than in other categories of piercing the corporate veil cases and concludes that it should not. Do you agree?

# IN RE SILICONE GEL BREAST IMPLANTS PRODUCTS LIABILITY LITIGATION
### United States District Court, District of Alabama
### 887 F. Supp. 1447 (1995)

POINTER, CHIEF JUDGE.

Under submission after appropriate discovery, extensive briefing, and oral argument is the motion for summary judgment filed by defendant Bristol-Myers Squibb Co. Bristol is the sole shareholder of Medical Engineering Corporation, a major supplier of breast implants, but has never itself manufactured or distributed breast implants. Bristol asserts that the evidence is insufficient for the plaintiffs' claims to proceed against it, whether through piercing the corporate veil or under a theory of direct liability. The parties agree that, with discovery substantially complete, this motion is ripe for decision. For the reasons stated below, the court concludes that Bristol is not entitled to summary judgment.

\* \* \*

## II. CHOICE OF LAW

In federal multidistrict proceedings, the transferee court applies the substantive law of the transferor courts. . . . The transferor courts in diversity cases would be bound to apply the law of the forum state, including its choice of law rules. . . .

This MDL proceeding involves diversity-jurisdiction cases filed in, or removed to, federal courts in 90 of the 94 districts, located in virtually every state, the District of Columbia, Puerto Rico, and the Virgin Islands. This court must therefore look to the laws of the several states to determine whether Bristol's motion should be granted. Many states would call for this court, when addressing "alter ego" and other "veil piercing" issues, to apply the law of Delaware, where Bristol and MEC are incorporated. But, under choice-of-law rules in other jurisdictions, this court may be obliged to apply the laws of many different states. Because of variations in applicable state law, summary judgment could be proper in some cases while not warranted in others.

## III. FACTS

For purposes of Bristol's summary judgment motion, the court treats the following facts as established, either because they are not in genuine dispute or because they are supported by evidence viewed in the light most favorable to the plaintiffs.

MEC was incorporated in Wisconsin in 1969, with its principal place of business in Racine. It was an independent, privately-held corporation manufacturing a variety of medical and plastic surgery devices, including breast implants. In 1982, after an extensive due diligence review that included information regarding capsular contracture, rupture, and gel bleed, Bristol, a Delaware corporation, purchased MEC's stock for $28 million through a series of mergers and corporate reorganizations. [After a series of formalistic transactions, MEC became, in 1982, a Delaware corporation, wholly owned by Bristol.]

In 1988 Bristol expanded its breast implant business by purchasing from the Cooper Companies two other breast-implant manufacturers, Natural Y Surgical Specialties, Inc. and Aesthetech Corporation. Though executed in the name of MEC and the Cooper Companies, the purchase was negotiated between Bristol and the Cooper Companies, and the purchase price of $8.7 million was paid from a Bristol account (though charged to MEC). The due diligence review, which indicated potential hazards and possible liability relating to polyurethane-coated breast implants, was conducted jointly by MEC and Bristol.

Documents reflect that MEC has had, at least in form, a board of three directors, generally consisting of the Bristol Vice President then serving as President of Bristol's Health Care Group, another Bristol executive, and MEC's president. Bristol's Health Care Group President, who reported to Bristol's president or chairman, could not be outvoted by the other two MEC board members. Several of the former MEC presidents did not recall that MEC had a board, let alone that they were members; and one of these stated that he did not attend, call, or receive notice of board meetings in his five years of service because he had a designated Bristol officer to contact. The few resolutions that were adopted by MEC's board were apparently prepared by Bristol officials.

MEC prepared "significant event" reports for Bristol's Corporate Policy Committee. These reports included information on breast implant production, such as publicity, testing, expenses, lawsuit settlements, and backorders caused by sterilization difficulties. Neither Bristol managers nor MEC Presidents recall any orders or recommendations being issued by Bristol as a result of these reviews. Bristol also required MEC to prepare and submit a five-year plan for its review.

MEC submitted budgets for approval by Bristol's senior management. For this submission, MEC filled out a series of standard Bristol forms that included information on projected sales, profits and losses, cash flow, balance sheets, and capital requirements. Bristol had the authority to modify this budget, though it rarely, if ever, actually did so. Cash received by MEC was transferred to an account maintained by Bristol. This money was credited to MEC, but the interest earned was credited to Bristol. Bristol was MEC's banker, providing such loans as it determined MEC needed. Bristol required MEC to obtain its approval for capital appropriations, though most, if not all, of these requests were approved.

Bristol set the employment policies and wage scales that applied to MEC's employees. Before hiring a top executive or negotiating the salary, MEC was required to seek Bristol's approval. Before hiring a vice president of MEC, MEC's president and his superior at Bristol interviewed the candidate. Key executive employees were rated on the Bristol schedule. Bristol set a target for salary increases below the key executive level and approved those for employees above that level. Key executives of MEC received stock options for Bristol stock. MEC employees could participate in Bristol's pension and savings plans.

Bristol provided various services to MEC. Zimmer International, another Bristol subsidiary, distributed MEC breast implants but did not receive any benefit for doing so. Bristol's corporate development group assisted MEC in seeking out new product lines. Bristol's scientific experts researched the hazards of breast implants and polyurethane foam. Bristol provided funds for MEC to conduct sales contests. Bristol funded tests on breast implants. Another Bristol subsidiary, ConvaTec, assisted MEC in developing its premarket approval application (PMAA) regarding breast implants for the FDA. In addition to this assistance, Bristol hired an outside laboratory to verify ConvaTec's analysis. Bristol also conducted post-market surveillance at the request of the FDA. Some of Bristol's in-house counsel acted as MEC attorneys. These attorneys advised MEC on virtually every aspect of its business including budgets, price increases, new product development, package inserts, liability, compliance with FDA regulations, and negotiated settlements with individuals claiming damages from breast implants. They also developed the system for handling complaints about MEC products. They reviewed all breast implant promotional materials and responses to allegations of harm and liability.

Bristol's Technical Evaluation and Service Department ("TESD") performed auditing and review functions for MEC once or twice a year. They performed all Good Manufacturing Practices (GMP) audits at MEC. These audits were designed to ensure consistent quality of MEC's products. Bristol expected MEC to comply with any manufacturing deficiencies TESD found. A number of the conditions listed as needing corrective action regarded breast implants. TESD also audited MEC's sterilization and lab companies.

Bristol's public relations department issued statements regarding the allegations of TDA production and cancer in rats implanted with polyurethane implants. Bristol's corporate communication department prepared question and answer scripts for MEC employees for use in responding to questions about breast implant safety. Bristol's public affairs department developed a strategic plan to address concerns about the MEME implant and to respond to questions and concerns about the safety of breast implants in general. Bristol's press releases consistently represented that Bristol was researching breast implant safety. For example, in a release dated July 9, 1991, Bristol stated that tests underway would "confirm the well-established safety profile of polyurethane coated breast implants" and that Bristol completed testing which showed that earlier findings concerning the production of TDA from the breakdown of polyurethane were the result of inappropriate testing conditions. In a statement dated July 24, 1991, Bristol represented that numerous other studies were being undertaken to assure the public and the FDA of the safety of polyurethane coated breast implants.

Bristol's name and logo were contained in the package inserts and promotional products regarding breast implants, apparently as a marketing tool to increase confidence in the product. Bristol's name was used in all sales and promotional communications with physicians.

MEC posted a profit every year between 1983 and 1990. Total sales increased from approximately $14 million in 1983 to $65 million in 1990. Bristol never received dividends from MEC. Bristol prepared consolidated federal income tax returns but MEC prepared its own Wisconsin tax forms. Bristol also purchased insurance for MEC under its policy. This insurance has a face value of over $2 billion.

Bristol's executive vice president suspended MEC's sales of polyurethane coated breast implants on April 17, 1991, and determined not to submit a PMAA for the implants to the FDA. MEC ceased its breast implant business in 1991 and later that year MEC ceased all operations by selling its urology division. This sale could not have occurred without Bristol's approval, and proceeds from the sale were turned over to Bristol, which then executed a low-interest demand note for $57,518,888 payable to MEC. MEC's only assets at this time are this demand note and its indemnity insurance.

## IV. ANALYSIS

The various theories of recovery made by plaintiffs against Bristol can be generally divided between those involving "corporate control" and those asserting direct liability. The corporate control claims deal with piercing the corporate veil to abrogate limited liability and hold Bristol responsible for actions of MEC. The direct liability theories include strict products liability, negligence, negligent failure to warn, negligence per se for not complying with FDA regulations, misrepresentation, fraud, and participation.

### A. "Corporate Control" Claims

The potential for abuse of the corporate form is greatest when, as here, the corporation is owned by a single shareholder. The evaluation of corporate control claims cannot, however, disregard the fact that, no different from other stockholders, a parent corporation is expected — indeed, required — to exert some control over its subsidiary. Limited liability is the rule, not the exception. . . . However, when a corporation is so controlled as to be the alter ego or mere instrumentality of its stockholder, the corporate form may be disregarded in the interests of justice. So far as this court has been able to determine, some variation of this theory of liability is recognized in all jurisdictions.

An initial question is whether veil-piercing may ever be resolved by summary judgment. Ordinarily the fact-intensive nature of the issue will require that it be resolved only through a trial. Summary judgment, however, can be proper if, as occurred earlier in this litigation with respect to claims against Dow Chemical and Corning, the evidence presented could lead to but one result. Because the court concludes that a jury (or in some jurisdictions, the judge acting in equity) could —

and, under the laws of many states, probably should — find that MEC was but the alter ego of Bristol, summary judgment must be denied.

The totality of circumstances must be evaluated in determining whether a subsidiary may be found to be the alter ego or mere instrumentality of the parent corporation. Although the standards are not identical in each state, all jurisdictions require a showing of substantial domination. Among the factors to be considered are whether:

- the parent and the subsidiary have common directors or officers
- the parent and the subsidiary have common business departments
- the parent and the subsidiary file consolidated financial statements and tax returns
- the parent finances the subsidiary
- the parent caused the incorporation of the subsidiary
- the subsidiary operates with grossly inadequate capital
- the parent pays the salaries and other expenses of the subsidiary
- the subsidiary receives no business except that given to it by the parent
- the parent uses the subsidiary's property as its own
- the daily operations of the two corporations are not kept separate
- the subsidiary does not observe the basic corporate formalities, such as keeping separate books and records and holding shareholder and board meetings.

*   *   *

The fact-finder at a trial could find that the evidence supports the conclusion that many of these factors have been proven: two of MEC's three directors were Bristol directors; MEC was part of Bristol's Health Care group and used Bristol's legal, auditing, and communications departments; MEC and Bristol filed consolidated federal tax returns and Bristol prepared consolidated financial reports; Bristol operated as MEC's finance company, providing loans for the purchase of Aesthetech and Natural Y, receiving interest on MEC's funds, and requiring MEC to make requests for capital appropriations; Bristol effectively used MEC's resources as its own by obtaining interest on MEC's money and requiring MEC to make requests for capital appropriations to obtain its own funds; some members of MEC's board were not aware that MEC had a board of directors, let alone that they were members; and the senior Bristol member of MEC's board could not be out-voted by the other two directors. These facts, even apart from evidence that might establish some of the other factors listed above, would provide significant support for a finding at trial that MEC is Bristol's alter ego.

Bristol contends that a finding of fraud or like misconduct is necessary to pierce the corporate veil. Despite Bristol's contentions to the contrary, Delaware courts — to which Bristol would have this court look — do not necessarily require a showing of fraud if a subsidiary is found to be the mere instrumentality or alter ego of its sole stockholder. . . . In addition, many jurisdictions that require a showing of fraud, injustice, or inequity in a contract case do not in a tort situation. . . . A rational distinction can be drawn between tort and contract cases. In actions based on contract, "the creditor has willingly transacted business with the subsidiary" although it could have insisted on assurances that would make the parent also responsible. [*United States v. Jon-T Chems., Inc.*, 768 F.2d 686, 693 (5th Cir. 1985), *cert. denied*, 475 U.S. 1014 (1986).] In a tort situation, however, the injured party had no such choice; the limitations on corporate liability were, from its standpoint, fortuitous and non-consensual.

There is, however, evidence precluding summary judgment even in jurisdictions that require a finding of fraud, inequity, or injustice. This conclusion is not based merely on the evidence that, even accepting Bristol's contentions regarding the amount of insurance available to MEC, MEC may have insufficient funds to satisfy the potential risks of responding to, and defending against, the numerous existing and potential claims of the plaintiffs. Equally significant is the fact that Bristol permitted its name to appear on breast implant advertisements, packages, and product inserts to improve sales by giving the product additional credibility. Combined with the evidence of potentially insufficient assets, this fact would support a finding that it would be inequitable and unjust to allow Bristol now to avoid liability to those induced to believe Bristol was vouching for this product.

Because the evidence available at a trial could support — if not, under some state laws, perhaps mandate — a finding that the corporate veil should be pierced, Bristol is not entitled through summary judgment to dismissal of the claims against it.

## B. Direct Liability Claims

There is an additional reason why Bristol is not entitled to summary judgment. Under the law in most jurisdictions, it may also be subject to liability under at least one of the direct liability claims made by plaintiffs; namely, the theory of negligent undertaking pursuant to Restatement (Second) of Torts § 324A. That section provides:

> One who undertakes, gratuitously or for consideration, to render services to another which he should recognize as necessary for the protection of a third person or his things, is subject to liability to the third person for physical harm resulting from his failure to exercise reasonable care to [perform] his undertakings, if
>
> (a)  his failure to exercise reasonable care increases the risk of harm, or
>
> (b)  he has undertaken to perform a duty owed by the other to the third person, or
>
> (c)  the harm is suffered because of a reliance of the other or the third person upon the undertaking.

Under this theory, frequently applied in connection with safety inspections by insurers or with third-party repairs to equipment or premises, a duty that would not otherwise have existed can arise when an individual or company nevertheless undertakes to perform some action. . . . The potential liability for failure to use reasonable care in such circumstances extends to persons who may reasonably be expected to suffer harm from that negligence. Doctrinally, a cause of action under § 324A does not involve an assertion of derivative liability but one of direct liability, since it is based on the actions of defendant itself. The existence of a parent-subsidiary relationship, while not required, is obviously no defense to such a claim.

\* \* \*

By allowing its name to be placed on breast implant packages and product inserts, Bristol held itself out as supporting the product, apparently to increase confidence in the product and to increase sales. Bristol also issued press releases stating that polyurethane-coated breast implants were safe. Having engaged in this type of marketing, it cannot now deny its potential responsibility under § 324A.

\* \* \*

Plaintiffs have asserted various other direct liability claims against Bristol in addition to those under § 324A. Having concluded that, because of genuine disputes relating to corporate control issues and relating to potential liability under § 324A, Bristol is not entitled to summary judgment, the court declines to address such alternative causes of action.

## V. CONCLUSION

By separate order, Bristol's motion for summary judgment will be denied. As with other orders denying summary judgment, this decision is interlocutory and does not constitute a holding that Bristol is liable to the plaintiffs.

## NOTES

1. This case illustrates the court's approach to piercing the corporate veil in a parent-subsidiary corporation context, i.e., where the shareholder of the corporation whose veil is sought to be pierced is another corporation. Should the court's approach be different in such a case than where an individual shareholder is involved?

2. The court's opinion contains language which indicates that a more sympathetic approach is appropriate in a tort than in a contract case on the ground that a contract creditor usually deals on a voluntary basis with the corporation and is in a position to investigate its finances and, if appropriate, demand a personal guarantee while a tort victim almost always is not able to choose its tortfeasor. While this might lead to the conclusion that it is easier to pierce the corporate veil in a tort case than in a contract case, a study by Professor Robert Thompson does not substantiate this hypothesis. In a sample of cases, the veil was successfully pierced in 42 percent of the contracts cases but in only 31 percent of the tort cases. Thompson, *Piercing the Corporate Veil: An Empirical Study*, 76 CORNELL L. REV. 1036 (1991). What factors might lead to this result?

3. This case illustrates the application of the "unitary test" applied in determining whether to pierce the corporate veil which is followed in many jurisdictions in contrast to the two part test in *King*. Is there any substantial difference between

the two or is the distinction more one of form than of substance?

# WALKOVSZKY v. CARLTON
## Court of Appeals of New York
### 223 N.E.2d 6 (1966)

Fuld, J.

This case involves what appears to be a rather common practice in the taxicab industry of vesting the ownership of a taxi fleet in many corporations, each owning only one or two cabs.

The complaint alleges that the plaintiff was severely injured four years ago in New York City when he was run down by a taxicab owned by the defendant Seon Cab Corporation and negligently operated at the time by the defendant Marchese. The individual defendant, Carlton, is claimed to be a stockholder of 10 corporations, including Seon, each of which has but two cabs registered in its name, and it is implied that only the minimum automobile liability insurance required by law (in the amount of $10,000) is carried on any one cab. Although seemingly independent of one another, these corporations are alleged to be "operated . . . as a single entity, unit and enterprise" with regard to financing, supplies, repairs, employees and garaging, and all are named as defendants.[2] The plaintiff asserts that he is also entitled to hold their stockholders personally liable for the damages sought because the multiple corporate structure constitutes an unlawful attempt 'to defraud members of the general public' who might be injured by the cabs.

The defendant Carlton has moved . . . to dismiss the complaint on the ground that as to him it "fails to state a cause of action". The court at Special Term granted the motion but the Appellate Division, by a divided vote, reversed. . . .

The law permits the incorporation of a business for the very purpose of enabling its proprietors to escape personal liability . . . but . . . the courts will disregard the corporate form, or, to use accepted terminology, "pierce the corporate veil", whenever necessary "to prevent fraud or to achieve equity." . . . In determining whether liability should be extended to reach assets beyond those belonging to the corporation, we are guided, as Judge Cardozo noted, by "general rules of agency". (*Berkey v. Third Ave. Ry. Co.*, 244 N.Y. 84, 95, 155 N.E. 58, 61, 50 A.L.R. 599.) In other words, whenever anyone uses control of the corporation to further his own rather than the corporation's business, he will be liable for the corporation's acts "upon the principle of Respondeat superior applicable even where the agent is a natural person."

In [*Mangan v. Terminal Transp. System,*] (247 App. Div. 853, 286 N.Y.S. 666), the plaintiff was injured as a result of the negligent operation of a cab owned and operated by one of four corporations affiliated with the defendant Terminal. Although the defendant was not a stockholder of any of the operating companies, both the defendant and the operating companies were owned, for the most part, by the same parties. The defendant's name (Terminal) was conspicuously displayed on

---

[2] [1] The corporate owner of a garage is also included as a defendant.

the sides of all of the taxis used in the enterprise and, in point of fact, the defendant actually serviced, inspected, repaired and dispatched them. These facts were deemed to provide sufficient cause for piercing the corporate veil of the operating company — the nominal owner of the cab which injured the plaintiff — and holding the defendant liable. The operating companies were simply instrumentalities for carrying on the business of the defendant without imposing upon it financial and other liabilities incident to the actual ownership and operation of the cabs. . . .

In the case before us, the plaintiff has explicitly alleged that none of the corporations 'had a separate existence of their own' and, as indicated above, all are named as defendants. However, it is one thing to assert that a corporation is a fragment of a larger corporate combine which actually conducts the business. (*See* Berle, *The Theory of Enterprise Entity*, 47 COL. L. REV. 343, 348–350.) It is quite another to claim that the corporation is a "dummy" for its individual stockholders who are in reality carrying on the business in their personal capacities for purely personal rather than corporate ends. . . . Either circumstance would justify treating the corporation as an agent and piercing the corporate veil to reach the principal but a different result would follow in each case. In the first, only a larger *corporate* entity would be held financially responsible (*see, e.g., Mangan v. Terminal Transp. System . . .*) while, in the other, the stockholder would be personally liable. . . . Either the stockholder is conducting the business in his individual capacity or he is not. If he is, he will be liable; if he is not, then it does not matter — insofar as his personal liability is concerned — that the enterprise is actually being carried on by a larger "enterprise entity." . . .

\* \* \*

The individual defendant is charged with having "organized, managed, dominated and controlled" a fragmented corporate entity but there are no allegations that he was conducting business in his individual capacity. Had the taxicab fleet been owned by a single corporation, it would be readily apparent that the plaintiff would face formidable barriers in attempting to establish personal liability on the part of the corporation's stockholders. The fact that the fleet ownership has been deliberately split up among many corporations does not ease the plaintiff's burden in that respect. The corporate form may not be disregarded merely because the assets of the corporation, together with the mandatory insurance coverage of the vehicle which struck the plaintiff, are insufficient to assure him the recovery sought. If Carlton were to be held individually liable on those facts alone, the decision would apply equally to the thousands of cabs which are owned by their individual drivers who conduct their businesses through corporations . . . and carry the minimum insurance required by subdivision 1 (par. (a)) of section 370 of the Vehicle and Traffic Law, Consol. Laws, c. 71. These taxi owner-operators are entitled to form such corporations . . . and we agree with the court at Special Term that, if the insurance coverage required by statute "is inadequate for the protection of the public, the remedy lies not with the courts but with the Legislature." It may very well be sound policy to require that certain corporations must take out liability insurance which will afford adequate compensation to their potential tort victims. However, the responsibility for imposing conditions on the privilege of incorporation has been committed by the Constitution to the Legislature (N.Y. Const., art. X, § 1) and it may not be fairly implied, from any statute, that the Legislature intended, without the slightest discussion or debate, to require of taxi corporations that they carry automobile liability insurance over and above that mandated by the Vehicle and Traffic Law.[3]

This is not to say that it is impossible for the plaintiff to state a valid cause of action against the defendant Carlton. However, the simple fact is that the plaintiff has just not done so here. While the complaint alleges that the separate corporations were undercapitalized and that their assets have been intermingled, it is barren of any "sufficiently particular(ized) statements" . . . that the defendant Carlton and his associates are actually doing business in their individual capacities, shuttling their personal funds in and out of the corporations "without regard to formality and to suit their immediate convenience." . . . Nothing of the sort has in fact been charged, and it cannot reasonably or logically be inferred from the happenstance that the business of Seon Cab Corporation may actually be carried on by a larger corporate entity composed of many corporations which, under general principles of agency, would be liable to each other's creditors in contract and in tort.[4]

In point of fact, the principle relied upon in the complaint to sustain the imposition of personal liability is not agency but fraud. Such a cause of action cannot withstand analysis. If it is not fraudulent for the owner-operator of a single cab corporation to take out only the minimum required liability insurance, the enterprise does not become either illicit or fraudulent merely because it consists of many such corporations. The plaintiff's injuries are the same regardless of whether the cab which strikes him is owned by a single corporation or part of a fleet with ownership fragmented among many corporations. Whatever rights he may be able to assert against parties other than the registered owner of the vehicle come into being not because he has been defrauded but because, under the principle of Respondeat superior, he is entitled to hold the whole enterprise responsible for the acts of its agents.

*     *     *

The order of the Appellate Division should be reversed. . . .

KEATING, J. (dissenting).

The defendant Carlton, the shareholder here sought to be held for the negligence of the driver of a taxicab, was a principal shareholder and organizer of the

---

[3] [2] There is no merit to the contention that the ownership and operation of the taxi fleet 'constituted a breach of hack owners regulations as promulgated by (the) Police Department of the City of New York.' Those regulations are clearly applicable to individual owner-operators and fleet owners alike. They were not intended to prevent either incorporation of a single-vehicle taxi business or multiple incorporation of a taxi fleet.

[4] [3] In his affidavit in opposition to the motion to dismiss, the plaintiff's counsel claimed that corporate assets had been 'milked out' of, and 'siphoned off' from the enterprise. Quite apart from the fact that these allegations are far too vague and conclusory, the charge is premature. If the plaintiff succeeds in his action and becomes a judgment creditor of the corporation, he may then sue and attempt to hold the individual defendants accountable for any dividends and property that were wrongfully distributed (Business Corporation Law, ss 510, 719, 720).

defendant corporation which owned the taxicab. The corporation was one of 10 organized by the defendant, each containing two cabs and each cab having the 'minimum liability' insurance coverage mandated by section 370 of the Vehicle and Traffic Law. The sole assets of these operating corporations are the vehicles themselves and they are apparently subject to mortgages.[5]

From their inception these corporations were intentionally undercapitalized for the purpose of avoiding responsibility for acts which were bound to arise as a result of the operation of a large taxi fleet having cars out on the street 24 hours a day and engaged in public transportation. And during the course of the corporations' existence all income was continually drained out of the corporations for the same purpose.

The issue presented by this action is whether the policy of this State, which affords those desiring to engage in a business enterprise the privilege of limited liability through the use of the corporate device, is so strong that it will permit that privilege to continue no matter how much it is abused, no matter how irresponsibly the corporation is operated, no matter what the cost to the public. I do not believe that it is.

Under the circumstances of this case the shareholders should all be held individually liable to this plaintiff for the injuries he suffered. . . . At least, the matter should not be disposed of on the pleadings by a dismissal of the complaint. "If a corporation is organized and carries on business without substantial capital in such a way that the corporation is likely to have no sufficient assets available to meet its debts, it is inequitable that shareholders should set up such a flimsy organization to escape personal liability. The attempt to do corporate business without providing any sufficient basis of financial responsibility to creditors is an abuse of the separate entity and will be ineffectual to exempt the shareholders from corporate debts. It is coming to be recognized as the policy of law that shareholders should in good faith put at the risk of the business unincumbered capital reasonably adequate for its prospective liabilities. If capital is illusory or trifling compared with the business to be done and the risks of loss, this is a ground for denying the separate entity privilege." (BALLANTINE, CORPORATIONS (rev. ed., 1946), § 129, pp. 302–303.)

In *Minton v. Cavaney*, 56 Cal. 2d 576, 15 Cal. Rptr. 641, 364 P.2d 473, the Supreme Court of California had occasion to discuss this problem in a negligence case. The corporation of which the defendant was an organizer, director and officer operated a public swimming pool. One afternoon the plaintiffs' daughter drowned in the pool as a result of the alleged negligence of the corporation.

Justice ROGER TRAYNOR, speaking for the court, outlined the applicable law in this area. "[Shareholders will be personally liable] *when they provide inadequate capitalization and actively participate in the conduct of corporate affairs*". (56 Cal. 2d, p. 579; italics supplied.)

Examining the facts of the case in light of the legal principles just enumerated, he found that "[it was] undisputed that there was no attempt to provide adequate

---

[5] [*] It appears that the medallions, which are of considerable value, are judgment proof. (Administrative Code of City of New York, s 436–2.0.)

capitalization. (The corporation) never had any substantial assets. It leased the pool that it operated, and the lease was forfeited for failure to pay the rent. Its capital was 'trifling compared with the business to be done and the risks of loss.' "

It seems obvious that one of 'the risks of loss' referred to was the possibility of drownings due to the negligence of the corporation. And the defendant's failure to provide such assets or any fund for recovery resulted in his being held personally liable.

\* \* \*

The defendant Carlton claims that, because the minimum amount of insurance required by the statute was obtained, the corporate veil cannot and should not be pierced despite the fact that the assets of the corporation which owned the cab were 'trifling compared with the business to be done and the risks of loss' which were certain to be encountered. I do not agree.

The Legislature in requiring minimum liability insurance of $10,000, no doubt, intended to provide at least some small fund for recovery against those individuals and corporations who just did not have and were not able to raise or accumulate assets sufficient to satisfy the claims of those who were injured as a result of their negligence. It certainly could not have intended to shield those individuals who organized corporations, with the specific intent of avoiding responsibility to the public, where the operation of the corporate enterprise yielded profits sufficient to purchase additional insurance. Moreover, it is reasonable to assume that the Legislature believed that those individuals and corporations having substantial assets would take out insurance far in excess of the minimum in order to protect those assets from depletion. Given the costs of hospital care and treatment and the nature of injuries sustained in auto collisions, it would be unreasonable to assume that the Legislature believed that the minimum provided in the statute would in and of itself be sufficient to recompense 'innocent victims of motor vehicle accidents . . . for the injury and financial loss inflicted upon them'.

The defendant, however, argues that the failure of the Legislature to increase the minimum insurance requirements indicates legislative acquiescence in this scheme to avoid liability and responsibility to the public. In the absence of a clear legislative statement, approval of a scheme having such serious consequences is not to be so lightly inferred.

The defendant contends that the court will be encroaching upon the legislative domain by ignoring the corporate veil and holding the individual shareholder. This argument was answered by Mr. Justice Douglas in *Anderson v. Abbott*, [321 U.S.] 366–367, where he wrote that: ". . . *Judicial interference to cripple or defeat a legislative policy is one thing; judicial interference with the plans of those whose corporate or other devices would circumvent that policy is quite another. Once the purpose or effect of the scheme is clear, once the legislative policy is plain, we would indeed forsake a great tradition to say we were helpless to fashion the instruments for appropriate relief." (Emphasis added.)

The defendant contends that a decision holding him personally liable would discourage people from engaging in corporate enterprise.

What I would merely hold is that a participating shareholder of a corporation vested with a public interest, organized with capital insufficient to meet liabilities which are certain to arise in the ordinary course of the corporation's business, may be held personally responsible for such liabilities. Where corporate income is not sufficient to cover the cost of insurance premiums above the statutory minimum or where initially adequate finances dwindle under the pressure of competition, bad times or extraordinary and unexpected liability, obviously the shareholder will not be held liable (HENN, CORPORATIONS, p. 208, n.7).

The only types of corporate enterprises that will be discouraged as a result of a decision allowing the individual shareholder to be sued will be those such as the one in question, designed solely to abuse the corporate privilege at the expense of the public interest.

For these reasons I would vote to affirm the order of the Appellate Division. [Plaintiff's amended complaint, with new allegations that the defendant and his associates were "conducting the business of taxicab fleet in their individual capacities," was held to state a cause of action. 29 A.D.2d 763, 287 N.Y.2d 714, 244 N.E.2d 55, 296 N.Y.S.2d 362 (1968).]

## KINNEY SHOE CORP. v. POLAN
United States Court of Appeals, Fourth Circuit
939 F.2d 209 (1991)

CHAPMAN, JUDGE:

Plaintiff-appellant Kinney Shoe Corporation ("Kinney") brought this action in the United States District Court for the Southern District of West Virginia against Lincoln M. Polan ("Polan") seeking to recover money owed on a sublease between Kinney and Industrial Realty Company ("Industrial"). Polan is the sole shareholder of Industrial. The district court found that Polan was not personally liable on the lease between Kinney and Industrial. Kinney appeals asserting that the corporate veil should be pierced, and we agree.

### I.

The district court based its order on facts which were stipulated by the parties. In 1984 Polan formed two corporations, Industrial and Polan Industries, Inc., for the purpose of re-establishing an industrial manufacturing business. The certificate of incorporation for Polan Industries, Inc. was issued by the West Virginia Secretary of State in November 1984. The following month the certificate of incorporation for Industrial was issued. Polan was the owner of both corporations. Although certificates of incorporation were issued, no organizational meetings were held, and no officers were elected.

In November 1984 Polan and Kinney began negotiating the sublease of a building in which Kinney held a leasehold interest. The building was owned by the Cabell County Commission and financed by industrial revenue bonds issued in 1968 to induce Kinney to locate a manufacturing plant in Huntington, West Virginia. Under the terms of the lease, Kinney was legally obligated to make payments on the bonds on a semi-annual basis through January 1, 1993, at which time it had the right to purchase the property. Kinney had ceased using the building as a manufacturing plant in June 1983.

The term of the sublease from Kinney to Industrial commenced in December 1984, even though the written lease was not signed by the parties until April 5, 1985. On April 15, 1985, Industrial subleased part of the building to Polan Industries for fifty percent of the rental amount due Kinney. Polan signed both subleases on behalf of the respective companies.

Other than the sublease with Kinney, Industrial had no assets, no income and no bank account. Industrial issued no stock certificates because nothing was ever paid in to this corporation. Industrial's only income was from its sublease to Polan Industries, Inc. The first rental payment to Kinney was made out of Polan's personal funds, and no further payments were made by Polan or by Polan Industries, Inc. to either Industrial or to Kinney.

Kinney filed suit against Industrial for unpaid rent and obtained a judgment in the amount of $166,400.00 on June 19, 1987. A writ of possession was issued, but because Polan Industries, Inc. had filed for bankruptcy, Kinney did not gain possession for six months. Kinney leased the building until it was sold on September 1, 1988. Kinney then filed this action against Polan individually to collect the amount owed by Industrial to Kinney. Since the amount to which Kinney is entitled is undisputed, the only issue is whether Kinney can pierce the corporate veil and hold Polan personally liable.

The district court held that Kinney had assumed the risk of Industrial's undercapitalization and was not entitled to pierce the corporate veil. Kinney appeals, and we reverse.

## II.

We have long recognized that a corporation is an entity, separate and distinct from its officers and stockholders, and the individual stockholders are not responsible for the debts of the corporation. *See, e.g., DeWitt Truck Brokers, Inc. v. W. Ray Flemming Fruit Co.*, 540 F.2d 681, 683 (4th Cir. 1976). This concept, however, is a fiction of the law " 'and it is now well settled, as a general principle, that the fiction should be disregarded when it is urged with an intent not within its reason and purpose, and in such a way that its retention would produce injustices or inequitable consequences.' " *Laya v. Erin Homes*, Inc., 352 S.E.2d 93, 97–98 (W. Va. 1986) (quoting *Sanders v. Roselawn Memorial Gardens, Inc.*, 152 W.Va. 91, 159 S.E.2d 784, 786 (1968).

Piercing the corporate veil is an equitable remedy, and the burden rests with the party asserting such claim. *DeWitt Truck Brokers*, 540 F.2d at 683. A totality of the circumstances test is used in determining whether to pierce the corporate veil, and each case must be decided on its own facts. The district court's findings of facts may be overturned only if clearly erroneous. *Id.*

Kinney seeks to pierce the corporate veil of Industrial so as to hold Polan personally liable on the sublease debt. The Supreme Court of Appeals of West Virginia has set forth a two prong test to be used in determining whether to pierce a corporate veil in a breach of contract case. This test raises two issues: first, is the unity of interest and ownership such that the separate personalities of the corporation and the individual shareholder no longer exist; and second, would an equitable result occur if the acts are treated as those of the corporation alone. *Laya*, 352 S.E.2d at 99. Numerous factors have been identified as relevant in making this determination. . . .[6]

It is undisputed that Industrial was not adequately capitalized. Actually, it had no paid in capital. Polan had put nothing into this corporation, and it did not observe any corporate formalities. As the West Virginia court stated in Laya, " 'individuals who wish to enjoy limited personal liability for business activities under a corporate umbrella should be expected to adhere to the relatively simple formalities of creating and maintaining a corporate entity.' " *Laya*, 352 S.E.2d at 100 n.6 (quoting

---

[6] [*] The following factors were identified in *Laya*:

(1) commingling of funds and other assets of the corporation with those of the individual shareholders;

(2) diversion of the corporation's funds or assets to noncorporate uses (to the personal uses of the corporation's shareholders);

(3) failure to maintain the corporate formalities necessary for the issuance of or subscription to the corporation's stock, such as formal approval of the stock issue by the board of directors;

(4) an individual shareholder representing to persons outside the corporation that he or she is personally liable for the debts or other obligations of the corporation;

(5) failure to maintain corporate minutes or adequate corporate records;

(6) identical equitable ownership in two entities;

(7) identity of the directors and officers of two entities who are responsible for supervision and management (a partnership or sole proprietorship and a corporation owned and managed by the same parties);

(8) failure to adequately capitalize a corporation for the reasonable risks of the corporate undertaking;

(9) absence of separately held corporate assets;

(10) use of a corporation as a mere shell or conduit to operate a single venture or some particular aspect of the business of an individual or another corporation;

(11) sole ownership of all the stock by one individual or members of a single family;

(12) use of the same office or business location by the corporation and its individual shareholder(s);

(13) employment of the same employees or attorney by the corporation and its shareholder(s);

(14) concealment or misrepresentation of the identity of the ownership, management or financial interests in the corporation, and concealment of personal business activities of the shareholders (sole shareholders do not reveal the association with a corporation, which makes loans to them without adequate security);

(15) disregard of legal formalities and failure to maintain proper arm's length relationships among related entities;

(16) use of a corporate entity as a conduit to procure labor, services or merchandise for another person or entity;

(17) diversion of corporate assets from the corporation by or to a stockholder or other person or entity to the detriment of creditors, or the manipulation of assets and liabilities between entities to concentrate the assets in one and the liabilities in another;

(18) contracting by the corporation with another person with the intent to avoid risk of nonperformance by use of the corporate entity; or the use of a corporation as a subterfuge for illegal transactions;

(19) the formation and use of the corporation to assume the existing liabilities of another person or entity. *Laya*, 352 S.E.2d at 98–99 (footnote omitted).

*Labadie Coal Co. v. Black*, 672 F.2d 92, 96–97 (D.C. Cir.1982)). This, the court stated, is " 'a relatively small price to pay for limited liability.' " *Id.* Another important factor is adequate capitalization. "Grossly inadequate capitalization combined with disregard of corporate formalities, causing basic unfairness, are sufficient to pierce the corporate veil in order to hold the shareholder(s) actively participating in the operation of the business personally liable for a breach of contract to the party who entered into the contract with the corporation." *Laya*, 352 S.E.2d at 101–02.

In this case, Polan bought no stock, made no capital contribution, kept no minutes, and elected no officers for Industrial. In addition, Polan attempted to protect his assets by placing them in Polan Industries, Inc. and interposing Industrial between Polan Industries, Inc. and Kinney so as to prevent Kinney from going against the corporation with assets. Polan gave no explanation or justification for the existence of Industrial as the intermediary between Polan Industries, Inc. and Kinney. Polan was obviously trying to limit his liability and the liability of Polan Industries, Inc. by setting up a paper curtain constructed of nothing more than Industrial's certificate of incorporation. These facts present the classic scenario for an action to pierce the corporate veil so as to reach the responsible party and produce an equitable result. Accordingly, we hold that the district court correctly found that the two prong test in *Laya* had been satisfied.

In *Laya*, the court also noted that when determining whether to pierce a corporate veil a third prong may apply in certain cases. The court stated:

> When, under the circumstances, it would be reasonable for that particular type of a party [those contract creditors capable of protecting themselves] entering into a contract with the corporation, for example, a bank or other lending institution, to conduct an investigation of the credit of the corporation prior to entering into the contract, such party will be charged with the knowledge that a reasonable credit investigation would disclose. If such an investigation would disclose that the corporation is grossly undercapitalized, based upon the nature and the magnitude of the corporate undertaking, such party will be deemed to have assumed the risk of the gross undercapitalization and will not be permitted to pierce the corporate veil.

*Laya*, 352 S.E.2d at 100. The district court applied this third prong and concluded that Kinney "assumed the risk of Industrial's defaulting" and that "the application of the doctrine of 'piercing the corporate veil' ought not and does not [apply]." While we agree that the two prong test of *Laya* was satisfied, we hold that the district court's conclusion that Kinney had assumed the risk is clearly erroneous.

Without deciding whether the third prong should be extended beyond the context of the financial institution lender mentioned in *Laya*, we hold that, even if it applies to creditors such as Kinney, it does not prevent Kinney from piercing the corporate veil in this case. The third prong is permissive and not mandatory. This is not a factual situation that calls for the third prong, if we are to seek an equitable result. Polan set up Industrial to limit his liability and the liability of Polan Industries, Inc. in their dealings with Kinney. A stockholder's liability is limited to the amount he has invested in the corporation, but Polan invested nothing in

Industrial. This corporation was no more than a shell — a transparent shell. When nothing is invested in the corporation, the corporation provides no protection to its owner; nothing in, nothing out, no protection. If Polan wishes the protection of a corporation to limit his liability, he must follow the simple formalities of maintaining the corporation. This he failed to do, and he may not relieve his circumstances by saying Kinney should have known better.

## III.

For the foregoing reasons, we hold that Polan is personally liable for the debt of Industrial, and the decision of the district court is reversed and this case is remanded with instructions to enter judgment for the plaintiff.

Reversed and remanded with instructions.

# NOTES

**1.** The *Walkovszky* and *Kinney Shoe* opinions raise the issue of undercapitalization as a factor in piercing the corporate veil. Precisely what is meant by undercapitalization? In a sense, any case in which piercing the corporate veil is asserted involves a corporation which is undercapitalized in the sense of being unable to satisfy the judgment creditor's claim, yet clearly this alone is insufficient to justify a pierce. The limited liability which shareholders enjoy would be essentially meaningless if it were not honored merely because the corporation was unable to honor its obligations, whether contractual or tort. The real issue is how much more than "mere" undercapitalization should be required. In reading *Walkovszky* and other cases in this chapter, try and determine what other factors were present which may have influenced the court in reaching its decision.

**2.** In *Walkovszky*, do you find convincing the majority's argument that the New York legislature has, in effect, said that a corporation complying with the statutorily mandated minimum amount of liability insurance is not undercapitalized? How does Judge Keating's dissent answer this?

**3.** If you are troubled by defendant Carlton's deliberate splitting of his business of operating a fleet of taxicabs into several different corporations each owning two cabs, consider whether, from the standpoint of protecting the public, this defendant is any different than, e.g., an individual of modest means who is able to scrape up just enough capital to purchase a taxicab medallion and lease a taxicab but has no other assets to satisfy a judgment so that an individual tort victim, as a practical matter, must look solely to the liability insurance carried by the individual. Stated somewhat differently, is it an abuse of the corporate form of doing business for an affluent individual to split up her business operations among different corporations so as to limit her monetary exposure to a modest amount or is this one of the legitimate advantages which limited liability is supposed to provide?

**4.** In *Kinney*, what factors lead the court to conclude that undercapitalization should justify a pierce? Are there significant differences in defendant's conduct of and operation of the corporation in *Kinney* which go beyond "mere undercapitalization"?

**5.** Professor Thompson's study, *supra*, found that undercapitalization was a factor identified by the courts in cases where the veil was successfully pierced in 19% of the contracts cases but in only 13% of the torts cases. What factors might explain this discrepancy?

## UNITED STATES v. BESTFOODS
Supreme Court of the United States
524 U.S. 51 (1998)

SOUTER, J. , delivered the opinion for a unanimous Court.

The United States brought this action for the costs of cleaning up industrial waste generated by a chemical plant. The issue before us, under the Comprehensive Environmental Response, Compensation, and Liability Act of 1980 (CERCLA), 94 Stat. 2767, as amended, 42 U.S.C. § 9601 *et seq.*, is whether a parent corporation that actively participated in, and exercised control over, the operations of a subsidiary may, without more, be held liable as an operator of a polluting facility owned or operated by the subsidiary. We answer no, unless the corporate veil may be pierced. But a corporate parent that actively participated in, and exercised control over, the operations of the facility itself may be held directly liable in its own right as an operator of the facility.

I

In 1980, CERCLA was enacted in response to the serious environmental and health risks posed by industrial pollution. See *Exxon Corp. v. Hunt*, 475 U.S. 355, 358–359, 106 S. Ct. 1103, 1107–1108, 89 L. Ed. 2d 364 (1986)."As its name implies, CERCLA is a comprehensive statute that grants the President broad power to command government agencies and private parties to clean up hazardous waste sites." *Key Tronic Corp. v. United States*, 511 U.S. 809, 814, 114 S. Ct. 1960, 1964, 128 L. Ed. 2d 797 (1994). If it satisfies certain statutory conditions, the United States may, for instance, use the "Hazardous Substance Superfund" to finance cleanup efforts, *see* 42 U.S.C. §§ 9601(11), 9604; 26 U.S.C. § 9507, which it may then replenish by suits brought under § 107 of the Act against, among others, "any person who at the time of disposal of any hazardous substance owned or operated any facility." 42 U.S.C. § 9607(a)(2). So, those actually "responsible for any damage, environmental harm, or injury from chemical poisons [may be tagged with] the cost of their actions," S. Rep. No. 96-848, pp. 13 (1980).[7] The term "person" is defined in CERCLA to include corporations and other business organizations, see 42 U.S.C. § 9601(21), and the term "facility" enjoys a broad and detailed definition as well, see § 9601(9).[8] The phrase "owner or operator" is defined only by tautology, however, as

---

[7] [1] "CERCLA . . . imposes the costs of the cleanup on those responsible for the contamination." Pennsylvania v. Union Gas Co., 491 U.S. 1, 7, 109 S. Ct. 2273, 2277, 105 L. Ed. 2d 1 (1989). "The remedy that Congress felt it needed in CERCLA is sweeping: everyone who is potentially responsible for hazardous-waste contamination may be forced to contribute to the costs of cleanup." Id., at 21, 109 S. Ct., at 2285 (plurality opinion of Brennan, J.).

[8] "The term 'facility' means (A) any building, structure, installation, equipment, pipe or pipeline

"any person owning or operating" a facility, § 9601(20)(A)(ii), and it is this bit of circularity that prompts our review. Cf. *Exxon Corp. v. Hunt*, supra, at 363, 106 S. Ct., at 1109 (CERCLA, "unfortunately, is not a model of legislative draftsmanship").

## II

In 1957, Ott Chemical Co. (Ott I) began manufacturing chemicals at a plant near Muskegon, Michigan, and its intentional and unintentional dumping of hazardous substances significantly polluted the soil and ground water at the site. In 1965, respondent CPC International Inc.[9] incorporated a wholly owned subsidiary to buy Ott I's assets in exchange for CPC stock. The new company, also dubbed Ott Chemical Co. (Ott II), continued chemical manufacturing at the site, and continued to pollute its surroundings. CPC kept the managers of Ott I, including its founder, president, and principal shareholder, Arnold Ott, on board as officers of Ott II. Arnold Ott and several other Ott II officers and directors were also given positions at CPC, and they performed duties for both corporations.

In 1972, CPC sold Ott II to Story Chemical Company, which operated the Muskegon plant until its bankruptcy in 1977. Shortly thereafter, when respondent Michigan Department of Natural Resources (MDNR)[10] examined the site for environmental damage, it found the land littered with thousands of leaking and even exploding drums of waste, and the soil and water saturated with noxious chemicals. MDNR sought a buyer for the property who would be willing to contribute toward its cleanup, and after extensive negotiations, respondent Aerojet–General Corp. arranged for transfer of the site from the Story bankruptcy trustee in 1977. Aerojet created a wholly owned California subsidiary, Cordova Chemical Company (Cordova/California), to purchase the property, and Cordova/California in turn created a wholly owned Michigan subsidiary, Cordova Chemical Company of Michigan (Cordova/Michigan), which manufactured chemicals at the site until 1986.[11]

By 1981, the federal Environmental Protection Agency had undertaken to see the site cleaned up, and its long-term remedial plan called for expenditures well into the tens of millions of dollars. To recover some of that money, the United States filed this action under § 107 in 1989, naming five defendants as responsible parties: CPC,

---

(including any pipe into a sewer or publicly owned treatment works), well, pit, pond, lagoon, impoundment, ditch, landfill, storage container, motor vehicle, rolling stock, or aircraft, or (B) any site or area where a hazardous substance has been deposited, stored, disposed of, or placed, or otherwise come to be located; but does not include any consumer product in consumer use or any vessel."

   [9]   [3] CPC has recently changed its name to Bestfoods. Consistently with the briefs and the opinions below, we use the name CPC herein.

   [10]   [4] The powers and responsibilities of MDNR have since been transferred to the Michigan Department of Environmental Quality.

   [11]   [5] Cordova/California and MDNR entered into a contract under which Cordova/California agreed to undertake certain cleanup actions, and MDNR agreed to share in the funding of those actions and to indemnify Cordova/California for various expenses. The Michigan Court of Appeals has held that this agreement requires MDNR to indemnify Aerojet and its Cordova subsidiaries for any CERCLA liability that they may incur in connection with their activities at the Muskegon facility. *See Cordova Chemical Co. v. Dept. of Natural Resources*, 212 Mich. App. 144, 536 N.W.2d 860 (1995), leave to appeal denied, 453 Mich. 901, 554 N.W.2d 319 (1996).

Aerojet, Cordova/California, Cordova/Michigan, and Arnold Ott. * * * After the parties (and MDNR) had launched a flurry of contribution claims, counterclaims, and cross-claims, the District Court consolidated the cases for trial in three phases: liability, remedy, and insurance coverage. So far, only the first phase has been completed; in 1991, the District Court held a 15-day bench trial on the issue of liability. Because the parties stipulated that the Muskegon plant was a "facility" within the meaning of 42 U.S.C. § 9601(9), that hazardous substances had been released at the facility, and that the United States had incurred reimbursable response costs to clean up the site, the trial focused on the issues of whether CPC and Aerojet, as the parent corporations of Ott II and the Cordova companies, had "owned or operated" the facility within the meaning of § 107(a)(2).

The District Court said that operator liability may attach to a parent corporation both directly, when the parent itself operates the facility, and indirectly, when the corporate veil can be pierced under state law. *See CPC Int'l, Inc. v. Aerojet-General Corp.*, 777 F. Supp. 549, 572 (W.D. Mich. 1991). The court explained that, while CERCLA imposes direct liability in situations in which the corporate veil cannot be pierced under traditional concepts of corporate law, "the statute and its legislative history do not suggest that CERCLA rejects entirely the crucial limits to liability that are inherent to corporate law." *Id.*, at 573. As the District Court put it:

> "a parent corporation is directly liable under section 107(a)(2) as an operator only when it has exerted power or influence over its subsidiary by actively participating in and exercising control over the subsidiary's business during a period of disposal of hazardous waste. A parent's actual participation in and control over a subsidiary's functions and decision-making creates 'operator' liability under CERCLA; a parent's mere oversight of a subsidiary's business in a manner appropriate and consistent with the investment relationship between a parent and its wholly owned subsidiary does not." *Ibid.*

Applying that test to the facts of this case, the District Court held both CPC and Aerojet liable under § 107(a)(2) as operators. As to CPC, the court found it particularly telling that CPC selected Ott II's board of directors and populated its executive ranks with CPC officials, and that a CPC official, G.R.D. Williams, played a significant role in shaping Ott II's environmental compliance policy.

After a divided panel of the Court of Appeals for the Sixth Circuit reversed in part, *United States v. Cordova/Michigan*, 59 F.3d 584, that court granted rehearing en banc and vacated the panel decision, 67 F.3d 586 (1995) This time, 7 judges to 6, the court again reversed the District Court in part. 113 F.3d 572 (1997). The majority remarked on the possibility that a parent company might be held directly liable as an operator of a facility owned by its subsidiary: "At least conceivably, a parent might independently operate the facility in the stead of its subsidiary; or, as a sort of joint venturer, actually operate the facility alongside its subsidiary." *Id.*, at 579. But the court refused to go any further and rejected the District Court's analysis with the explanation:

> "[that] where a parent corporation is sought to be held liable as an operator pursuant to 42 U.S.C. § 9607(a)(2) based upon the extent of its control of its subsidiary which owns the facility, the parent will be liable only when the

> requirements necessary to pierce the corporate veil [under state law] are
> met. In other words, . . . whether the parent will be liable as an operator
> depends upon whether the degree to which it controls its subsidiary and the
> extent and manner of its involvement with the facility, amount to the abuse
> of the corporate form that will warrant piercing the corporate veil and
> disregarding the separate corporate entities of the parent and subsidiary."
> *Id.*, at 580.

Applying Michigan veil-piercing law, the Court of Appeals decided that neither CPC nor Aerojet was liable for controlling the actions of its subsidiaries, since the parent and subsidiary corporations maintained separate personalities and the parents did not utilize the subsidiary corporate form to perpetrate fraud or subvert justice.

We granted certiorari, . . . to resolve a conflict among the Circuits over the extent to which parent corporations may be held liable under CERCLA for operating facilities ostensibly under the control of their subsidiaries. We now vacate and remand.

## III

It is a general principle of corporate law deeply "ingrained in our economic and legal systems" that a parent corporation (so-called because of control through ownership of another corporation's stock) is not liable for the acts of its subsidiaries. Douglas [& Shanks, *Insulation from Liability Through Subsidiary Corporations*, 39 YALE L.J. 193 (1929), at] 196 (footnotes omitted). . . . Although this respect for corporate distinctions when the subsidiary is a polluter has been severely criticized in the literature, *see, e.g., Note, Liability of Parent Corporations for Hazardous Waste Cleanup and Damages*, 99 HARV. L. REV. 986 (1986), nothing in CERCLA purports to reject this bedrock principle, and against this venerable common-law backdrop, the congressional silence is audible. *Cf. Edmonds v. Compagnie Generale Transatlantique*, 443 U.S. 256, 266–267, 99 S. Ct. 2753, 2759, 61 L. Ed. 2d 521 (1979) ("silence is most eloquent, for such reticence while contemplating an important and controversial change in existing law is unlikely"). The Government has indeed made no claim that a corporate parent is liable as an owner or an operator under § 107 simply because its subsidiary is subject to liability for owning or operating a polluting facility.

But there is an equally fundamental principle of corporate law, applicable to the parent-subsidiary relationship as well as generally, that the corporate veil may be pierced and the shareholder held liable for the corporation's conduct when, inter alia, the corporate form would otherwise be misused to accomplish certain wrongful purposes, most notably fraud, on the shareholder's behalf. . . . Nothing in CERCLA purports to rewrite this well-settled rule, either. CERCLA is thus like many another congressional enactment in giving no indication that "the entire corpus of state corporation law is to be replaced simply because a plaintiff's cause of action is based upon a federal statute," *Burks v. Lasker*, 441 U.S. 471, 478, 99 S. Ct. 1831, 1837, 60 L. Ed. 2d 404 (1979), and the failure of the statute to speak to a matter as fundamental as the liability implications of corporate ownership demands application of the rule that "[i]n order to abrogate a common-law principle, the statute must speak directly to the question addressed by the common law," *United*

*States v. Texas*, 507 U.S. 529, 534, 113 S. Ct. 1631, 1634, 123 L. Ed. 2d 245 (1993) (internal quotation marks omitted). The Court of Appeals was accordingly correct in holding that when (but only when) the corporate veil may be pierced[12], may a parent corporation be charged with derivative CERCLA liability for its subsidiary's actions.[13]

## IV

### A

If the Act rested liability entirely on ownership of a polluting facility, this opinion might end here; but CERCLA liability may turn on operation as well as ownership, and nothing in the statute's terms bars a parent corporation from direct liability for its own actions in operating a facility owned by its subsidiary. As Justice (then-Professor) Douglas noted almost 70 years ago, derivative liability cases are to be distinguished from those in which "the alleged wrong can seemingly be traced to the parent through the conduit of its own personnel and management" and "the parent is directly a participant in the wrong complained of." Douglas 207, 208. . . . In such instances, the parent is directly liable for its own actions. See H. Henn & J. Alexander, Laws of Corporations 347 (3d ed. 1983) (hereinafter Henn & Alexander) ("Apart from corporation law principles, a shareholder, whether a natural person or a corporation, may be liable on the ground that such shareholder's activity resulted in the liability"). The fact that a corporate subsidiary happens to own a polluting facility operated by its parent does nothing, then, to displace the rule that the parent "corporation is [itself] responsible for the wrongs committed by its agents in the course of its business," *Mine Workers v. Coronado Coal Co.*, 259 U.S. 344, 395, 42 S. Ct. 570, 577, 66 L. Ed. 975 (1922), and whereas the rules of veil piercing limit derivative liability for the actions of another corporation, CERCLA's "operator" provision is concerned primarily with direct liability for one's own actions. *See, e.g., Sidney S. Arst Co. v. Pipefitters Welfare Ed. Fund*, 25 F.3d 417, 420 (C.A.7 1994) ("the direct, personal liability provided by CERCLA is distinct from the derivative liability that results from piercing the corporate veil" (internal quotation marks omitted). It is this direct liability that is properly seen as being at issue here.

Under the plain language of the statute, any person who operates a polluting facility is directly liable for the costs of cleaning up the pollution. *See* 42 U.S.C. § 9607(a)(2). This is so regardless of whether that person is the facility's owner, the owner's parent corporation or business partner, or even a saboteur who sneaks into

---

[12] [9] There is significant disagreement among courts and commentators over whether, in enforcing CERCLA's indirect liability, courts should borrow state law, or instead apply a federal common law of veil piercing. . . .

[13] [10] Some courts and commentators have suggested that this indirect, veil-piercing approach can subject a parent corporation to liability only as an owner, and not as an operator. *See, e.g., Lansford-Coaldale Joint Water Auth. v. Tonolli Corp.*, supra, at 1220; Oswald, *Bifurcation of the Owner and Operator Analysis under CERCLA*, 72 WASH. U.L.Q. 223, 281–282 (1994) (hereinafter Oswald). We think it is otherwise, however. If a subsidiary that operates, but does not own, a facility is so pervasively controlled by its parent for a sufficiently improper purpose to warrant veil piercing, the parent may be held derivatively liable for the subsidiary's acts as an operator.

the facility at night to discharge its poisons out of malice. If any such act of operating a corporate subsidiary's facility is done on behalf of a parent corporation, the existence of the parent-subsidiary relationship under state corporate law is simply irrelevant to the issue of direct liability. See *Riverside Market Dev. Corp. v. International Bldg. Prods.*, Inc., 931 F.2d 327, 330 (C.A.5) ("CERCLA prevents individuals from hiding behind the corporate shield when, as 'operators,' they themselves actually participate in the wrongful conduct prohibited by the Act"), *cert. denied*, 502 U.S. 1004, 112 S. Ct. 636, 116 L. Ed. 2d 654 (1991); *United States v. Kayser-Roth Corp.*, 910 F.2d 24, 26 (C.A.1 1990) ("[A] person who is an operator of a facility is not protected from liability by the legal structure of ownership").[14]

This much is easy to say: the difficulty comes in defining actions sufficient to constitute direct parental "operation." Here of course we may again rue the uselessness of CERCLA's definition of a facility's "operator" as "any person . . . operating" the facility, 42 U.S.C. § 9601(20)(A)(ii), which leaves us to do the best we can to give the term its "ordinary or natural meaning." *Bailey v. United States*, 516 U.S. 137, 145, 116 S. Ct. 501, 506, 133 L. Ed. 2d 472 (1995) (internal quotation marks omitted). In a mechanical sense, to "operate" ordinarily means "to control the functioning of; run: operate a sewing machine." AMERICAN HERITAGE DICTIONARY 1268 (3d ed. 1992); *see also* WEBSTER'S NEW INTERNATIONAL DICTIONARY 1707 (2d ed. 1958) ("to work; as, to operate a machine"). And in the organizational sense more obviously intended by CERCLA, the word ordinarily means "[t]o conduct the affairs of; manage: operate a business." AMERICAN HERITAGE DICTIONARY, *supra*, at 1268; *see also* WEBSTER'S NEW INTERNATIONAL DICTIONARY, *supra*, at 1707 ("to manage"). So, under CERCLA, an operator is simply someone who directs the workings of, manages, or conducts the affairs of a facility. To sharpen the definition for purposes of CERCLA's concern with environmental contamination, an operator must manage, direct, or conduct operations specifically related to pollution, that is, operations having to do with the leakage or disposal of hazardous waste, or decisions about compliance with environmental regulations.


B


With this understanding, we are satisfied that the Court of Appeals correctly rejected the District Court's analysis of direct liability. But we also think that the appeals court erred in limiting direct liability under the statute to a parent's sole or joint venture operation, so as to eliminate any possible finding that CPC is liable as an operator on the facts of this case.

---

[14] [12] See Oswald [, *Bifurcation of the Owner and Operator Analysis Under* CERCLA, 72 WASH. U.L.Q. 223 (1994), at] 257 ("There are . . . instances . . . in which the parent has not sufficiently overstepped the bounds of corporate separateness to warrant piercing, yet is involved enough in the facility's activities that it should be held liable as an operator. Imagine, for example, a parent who strictly observed corporate formalities, avoided intertwining officers and directors, and adequately capitalized its subsidiary, yet provided active, daily supervision and control over hazardous waste disposal activities of the subsidiary. Such a parent should not escape liability just because its activities do not justify a piercing of the subsidiary's veil").

1

By emphasizing that "CPC is directly liable under section 107(a)(2) as an operator because CPC actively participated in and exerted significant control over Ott II's business and decision-making," 777 F. Supp., at 574, the District Court applied the "actual control" test of whether the parent "actually operated the business of its subsidiary," *id.*, at 573, as several Circuits have employed it, *see, e.g., United States v. Kayser-Roth Corp., supra*, at 27 (operator liability "requires active involvement in the affairs of the subsidiary"); *Jacksonville Elec. Auth. v. Bernuth Corp.*, 996 F.2d 1107, 1110 (C.A.11 1993) (parent is liable if it "actually exercised control over, or was otherwise intimately involved in the operations of, the [subsidiary] corporation immediately responsible for the operation of the facility" (internal quotation marks omitted)).

The well-taken objection to the actual control test, however, is its fusion of direct and indirect liability; the test is administered by asking a question about the relationship between the two corporations (an issue going to indirect liability) instead of a question about the parent's interaction with the subsidiary's facility (the source of any direct liability). If, however, direct liability for the parent's operation of the facility is to be kept distinct from derivative liability for the subsidiary's own operation, the focus of the enquiry must necessarily be different under the two tests. "The question is not whether the parent operates the subsidiary, but rather whether it operates the facility, and that operation is evidenced by participation in the activities of the facility, not the subsidiary. Control of the subsidiary, if extensive enough, gives rise to indirect liability under piercing doctrine, not direct liability under the statutory language." Oswald 269; *see also Schiavone v. Pearce*, 79 F.3d 248, 254 (C.A.2 1996) ("Any liabilities [the parent] may have as an operator, then, stem directly from its control over the plant"). The District Court was therefore mistaken to rest its analysis on CPC's relationship with Ott II, premising liability on little more than "CPC's 100-percent ownership of Ott II" and "CPC's active participation in, and at times majority control over, Ott II's board of directors." 777 F. Supp., at 575. The analysis should instead have rested on the relationship between CPC and the Muskegon facility itself.

In addition to (and perhaps as a reflection of) the erroneous focus on the relationship between CPC and Ott II, even those findings of the District Court that might be taken to speak to the extent of CPC's activity at the facility itself are flawed, for the District Court wrongly assumed that the actions of the joint officers and directors are necessarily attributable to CPC. The District Court emphasized the facts that CPC placed its own high-level officials on Ott II's board of directors and in key management positions at Ott II, and that those individuals made major policy decisions and conducted day-to-day operations at the facility: "Although Ott II corporate officers set the day-to-day operating policies for the company without any need to obtain formal approval from CPC, CPC actively participated in this decision-making because high-ranking CPC officers served in Ott II management positions." *Id.*, at 559; *see also id.*, at 575 (relying on "CPC's involvement in major decision-making and day-to-day operations through CPC officials who served within Ott II management, including the positions of president and chief executive officer," and on "the conduct of CPC officials with respect to Ott II affairs, particularly Arnold Ott"); *id.*, at 558 ("CPC actively participated in, and at times controlled, the policy-making decisions of its subsidiary through its representation on the Ott II board of directors"); *id.*, at 559 ("CPC also actively participated in and exerted control over day-to-day decision-making at Ott II through representation in the highest levels of the subsidiary's management").

In imposing direct liability on these grounds, the District Court failed to recognize that "it is entirely appropriate for directors of a parent corporation to serve as directors of its subsidiary, and that fact alone may not serve to expose the parent corporation to liability for its subsidiary's acts." *American Protein Corp. v. AB Volvo*, 844 F.2d 56, 57(C.A.2), *cert. denied*, 488 U.S. 852, 109 S. Ct. 136, 102 L. Ed. 2d 109 (1988); *see also Kingston Dry Dock Co. v. Lake Champlain Transp. Co.*, 31 F.2d 265, 267 (C.A.2 1929) (L. HAND, J.) ("Control through the ownership of shares does not fuse the corporations, even when the directors are common to each"); Henn & Alexander[, LAWS OF CORPORATIONS (3d. ed. 1983), at 355] (noting that it is "normal" for a parent and subsidiary to "have identical directors and officers").

This recognition that the corporate personalities remain distinct has its corollary in the "well established principle [of corporate law] that directors and officers holding positions with a parent and its subsidiary can and do 'change hats' to represent the two corporations separately, despite their common ownership." *Lusk v. Foxmeyer Health Corp.*, 129 F.3d 773, 779 (C.A.5 1997); *see also Fisser v. International Bank*, 282 F.2d 231, 238 (C.A.2 1960). Since courts generally presume "that the directors are wearing their 'subsidiary hats' and not their 'parent hats' when acting for the subsidiary," P. Blumberg, LAW OF CORPORATE GROUPS: PROCEDURAL PROBLEMS IN THE LAW OF PARENT AND SUBSIDIARY CORPORATIONS § 1.02.1, p. 12 (1983); *see, e.g., United States v. Jon-T Chemicals, Inc.*, 768 F.2d 686, 691 (C.A.5 1985), *cert. denied*, 475 U.S. 1014, 106 S. Ct. 1194, 89 L. Ed. 2d 309 (1986), it cannot be enough to establish liability here that dual officers and directors made policy decisions and supervised activities at the facility. The Government would have to show that, despite the general presumption to the contrary, the officers and directors were acting in their capacities as CPC officers and directors, and not as Ott II officers and directors, when they committed those acts. The District Court made no such enquiry here, however, disregarding entirely this time-honored common-law rule.

In sum, the District Court's focus on the relationship between parent and subsidiary (rather than parent and facility), combined with its automatic attribution of the actions of dual officers and directors to the corporate parent, erroneously, even if unintentionally, treated CERCLA as though it displaced or fundamentally altered common-law standards of limited liability. Indeed, if the evidence of common corporate personnel acting at management and directorial levels were enough to support a finding of a parent corporation's direct operator liability under CERCLA, then the possibility of resort to veil piercing to establish indirect, derivative liability for the subsidiary's violations would be academic. There would in essence be a relaxed, CERCLA-specific rule of derivative liability that would banish traditional standards and expectations from the law of CERCLA liability. But, as we have said, such a rule does not arise from congressional silence, and CERCLA's silence is dispositive.

2

We accordingly agree with the Court of Appeals that a participation-and-control test looking to the parent's supervision over the subsidiary, especially one that assumes that dual officers always act on behalf of the parent, cannot be used to identify operation of a facility resulting in direct parental liability. Nonetheless, a return to the ordinary meaning of the word "operate" in the organizational sense will indicate why we think that the Sixth Circuit stopped short when it confined its examples of direct parental operation to exclusive or joint ventures, and declined to find at least the possibility of direct operation by CPC in this case.

In our enquiry into the meaning Congress presumably had in mind when it used the verb "to operate," we recognized that the statute obviously meant something more than mere mechanical activation of pumps and valves, and must be read to contemplate "operation" as including the exercise of direction over the facility's activities. *See* [AMERICAN HERITAGE DICTIONARY 1268] *supra*, at 13. The Court of Appeals recognized this by indicating that a parent can be held directly liable when the parent operates the facility in the stead of its subsidiary or alongside the subsidiary in some sort of a joint venture. *See* 113 F.3d, at 579. We anticipated a further possibility above, however, when we observed that a dual officer or director might depart so far from the norms of parental influence exercised through dual officeholding as to serve the parent, even when ostensibly acting on behalf of the subsidiary in operating the facility. *See* n. 13, *supra*. Yet another possibility, suggested by the facts of this case, is that an agent of the parent with no hat to wear but the parent's hat might manage or direct activities at the facility.

Identifying such an occurrence calls for line-drawing yet again, since the acts of direct operation that give rise to parental liability must necessarily be distinguished from the interference that stems from the normal relationship between parent and subsidiary. Again norms of corporate behavior (undisturbed by any CERCLA provision) are crucial reference points. Just as we may look to such norms in identifying the limits of the presumption that a dual officeholder acts in his ostensible capacity, so here we may refer to them in distinguishing a parental officer's oversight of a subsidiary from such an officer's control over the operation of the subsidiary's facility. "Activities that involve the facility but which are consistent with the parent's investor status, such as monitoring of the subsidiary's performance, supervision of the subsidiary's finance and capital budget decisions, and articulation of general policies and procedures, should not give rise to direct liability." Oswald [*supra* note 10, at] 282. The critical question is whether, in degree and detail, actions directed to the facility by an agent of the parent alone are eccentric under accepted norms of parental oversight of a subsidiary's facility.

There is, in fact, some evidence that CPC engaged in just this type and degree of activity at the Muskegon plant. The District Court's opinion speaks of an agent of CPC alone who played a conspicuous part in dealing with the toxic risks emanating from the operation of the plant. G.R.D. Williams worked only for CPC; he was not an employee, officer, or director of Ott II, *see* Tr. of Oral Arg. 7, and thus, his actions were of necessity taken only on behalf of CPC. The District Court found that "CPC became directly involved in environmental and regulatory matters through the work of . . . Williams, CPC's governmental and environmental affairs

director. Williams . . . became heavily involved in environmental issues at Ott II."
777 F. Supp., at 561. He "actively participated in and exerted control over a variety
of Ott II environmental matters," *ibid.*, and he "issued directives regarding Ott II's
responses to regulatory inquiries," *id.*, at 575.

We think that these findings are enough to raise an issue of CPC's operation of
the facility through Williams's actions, though we would draw no ultimate conclusion
from these findings at this point. Not only would we be deciding in the first instance
an issue on which the trial and appellate courts did not focus, but the very fact that
the District Court did not see the case as we do suggests that there may be still
more to be known about Williams's activities. Indeed, even as the factual findings
stand, the trial court offered little in the way of concrete detail for its conclusions
about Williams's role in Ott II's environmental affairs, and the parties vigorously
dispute the extent of Williams's involvement. Prudence thus counsels us to remand,
on the theory of direct operation set out here, for reevaluation of Williams's role, and
of the role of any other CPC agent who might be said to have had a part in operating
the Muskegon facility.

## V

The judgment of the Court of Appeals for the Sixth Circuit is vacated, and the
case is remanded with instructions to return it to the District Court for further
proceedings consistent with this opinion.

## NOTES

1. When the Supreme Court accepted *certiorari* in *Bestfoods*, many environmental lawyers anticipated that the decision would be of considerable assistance in
clarifying the degree to which CERCLA's imposition of liability on "owners" and
"operators" of hazardous waste facilities departed from common law standards
utilized in analyzing parent-subsidiary piercing the corporate veil cases. Was the
Supreme Court successful in its attempts to clarify the law?

2. If Congress intended to expand the scope of parent corporation liability
beyond common law standards, shouldn't it have included more elaborate definitions
of "owner" and "operator" in the statute? If Congress did not so intend, wouldn't it
have been better to say nothing at all?

3. After *Bestfoods*, is it likely that parent corporation liability will be found very
often under the standard articulated by the Court? How often will a parent
corporation likely be found to be heavily involved in the operation of subsidiary's
individual plant where it is not also heavily involved in managing the subsidiary's
affairs generally and thus open to liability under conventional piercing the corporate
veil doctrine?

# HILL v. BEVERLY ENTERPRISES-MISSISSIPPI, INC.
## United States District Court, Southern District of Mississippi
### 305 F. Supp. 2d 644 (2003)

LEE, J.

This cause is before the court on the motion of plaintiff Lawrence Hill, by and through Letha Kincaid and Eugene Hill, to remand pursuant to 28 U.S.C. § 1447. Defendants Beverly Enterprises-Mississippi, Inc. and Beverly Health and Rehabilitation (collectively, Beverly), along with James C. Landers and David Devereaux, have responded in opposition to the motion and the court, having considered the memoranda of authorities, together with attachments submitted by the parties, concludes that plaintiff's motion is well taken and should be granted.

\* \* \*

In their complaint, plaintiffs allege that defendants Lindsay, Landers and Devereaux were responsible for the management and supervision of the facility, that they failed to properly hire, supervise and train nursing personnel, and they failed to ensure that adequate records were prepared and maintained. In their notice of removal and response to plaintiff's motion to remand, defendants submit that Lindsay, the nursing home administrator, and Landers and Dereveaux, as licensees of the nursing home, can have no personal liability to plaintiff because there is no allegation or proof by plaintiff that these defendants had any direct or personal participation in Lawrence Hill's care and because plaintiff's allegations do not attempt to link their alleged negligence in management and supervision to Mr. Hill's injuries.

Obviously, "liability cannot attach where a defendant does not, as a legal matter, owe a duty of care to the one allegedly injured," *Box v. Beverly Health and Rehabilitation Servs., Inc. et al.*, Civil Action No. 3:03CV22-SAA, slip op. at 5 (N.D. Miss. May 30, 2003), and thus, the first question that presents itself is whether it can be said that a reasonable possibility exists under Mississippi law that the nursing home administrator or licensees owed a duty of care to Lawrence Hill. Assuming the answer is yes, the questions that follow relate to the nature of the duty owed, whether the duty was breached and if any such breach proximately caused the injuries of which plaintiffs complain.

As the court recognized in *Box*, there is no Mississippi statute or case law specific to the question of whether a nursing home administrator owes a legal duty of care to the residents under his supervision. *Box*, No. 3:03CV22-SAA, slip op. at 6. However, in the court's opinion, applying general principles of agency law to the allegations of plaintiff's complaint, this issue must be resolved in favor of finding that such a duty does exist.

It is well settled under Mississippi law that an employee, officer or director of a corporate entity incurs liability only when he "directly participates in or authorizes the commission of a tort." *Hart v. Bayer Corp.*, 199 F.3d 239, 247 (5th Cir. 2000). Defendants here argue that since plaintiffs do not allege that the defendant administrator or licensees directly participated in the care provided to Lawrence

Hill, or that they personally directed or authorized the commission of the torts alleged to have been committed by employees of the facility, it follows that they cannot be held personally liable. Defendants' myopic view of "direct participation," however, does not withstand scrutiny.

Although Magistrate Judge Allen Alexander, in the Northern District of Mississippi, denied the plaintiff's motion to remand in *Box, supra*, she did so because the plaintiff, in response to evidence from the defendants, had failed to present his own evidence that his decedent's death was connected to any breach of duty, i.e. "faulty, tortious management," by the nursing home administrator. Notably, however, Judge Alexander recognized that under Mississippi law, particularly where the employee or agent of an employee charged with tort liability holds a managerial or administrative position, "direct participation" does not necessarily mean "hands-on participation" in the tortious act itself, so the fact that a nursing home administrator may not have participated in the day-to-day care of a resident is not determinative of the question of the administrator's potential liability.

\* \* \*

The reasoning of these cases is sound. Mississippi law, both common law and statutory, places certain duties squarely on the nursing home administrator, and to the extent that such duties are not performed, or are performed negligently, with resulting harm to any resident of the nursing home facility, it may rightly be said that the administrator personally and directly participated in the tort which caused the harm. There is no requirement of personal *contact* but rather of personal *participation* in the tort; and a breach by the administrator of her own duties constitutes direct, personal participation.

\* \* \*

[Plaintiff's motion to remand for trial was granted.]

# NOTES

**1.** Is this a form of piercing the corporate veil case? If so, why doesn't the court approach it with the type of analysis typically used in piercing the veil situations?

**2.** Compare *Hill* with *Walkovszky v. Carlton, supra*, another tort case involving personal injury. Do you see why the court's analysis in *Hill* differs from *Walkovsky?*

# Chapter 7

# SPECIAL PROBLEMS OF THE CLOSELY HELD CORPORATION

In this casebook the authors will use the phrase closely held corporation quite frequently. What we mean by the term is a corporation whose shares are not traded in a securities market. Large publicly held corporations are generally owned by thousands of shareholders and shares of such companies are generally traded on the New York Stock Exchange (N.Y.S.E.), American Stock Exchange or on Nasdaq. The distinguishing feature of a closely held corporation from a publicly held corporation is that the shareholders of the former have no public market for their shares. It is the lack of a market place that makes closely held corporations unique. If you own shares of a corporation that is listed on an exchange, and you think that the officers are paid excessive compensation, or that dividends are not high enough, or if you simply want the fair market value of your shares for whatever reason, you have a simple remedy by selling your shares at market value. In fact, even if you desire to try to persuade the incumbent management or the other shareholders that the corporation should change its policies, that is almost always a foolish course. The cost of communicating with the other shareholders is likely to be so high as to make the attempt to do so prohibitive.

In contrast, closely held corporations are normally formed by small groups of people who plan to start a new business. Most of the investors will want to work in the business, and will expect their financial reward to come from salary or dividends. The normal expectation is that no shares will be sold to outsiders. The fear is that outsiders will fail to understand the business or else have private agendas of their own. Thus, the tranquil relationships of the initial founders might well be disturbed if outsiders are permitted to enter merely by purchasing shares from the initial investors. The most common strategy is to place restrictions on the sale of shares so that no transfers will occur unless the corporation or its existing shareholders have a right of first refusal. This mechanism works well enough if the corporation has the ability to purchase the shares, but the greatest difficulty for the shareholders of closely held corporations is the lack of ready market for their shares. Those shares often pay no dividends. In judging the value of the shares of a closely held corporation, failure to pay dividends is quite critical. The shares will not attract buyers looking for a steady income. Nor will anyone buy shares in such a corporation hoping for a capital gain on resale. It will be impossible to find a buyer that foolish.

In contrast, large publicly held corporations quite frequently pay no dividends without suffering these consequences. They generally desire to reinvest the profits of the enterprise so as to bring about expansion and growth in the future. However, this policy presents no problem for their shareholders. These corporations have a market for their shares. Shareholders can sell their shares and receive the fair market value.

## PROBLEM 7.1

The typical scenario for the closely held corporation is the freeze out. (Some authorities prefer the phrase "squeeze out.") Let's assume that the corporation has 2 shareholders, A and B. Each has invested $50,000 in the corporation, and there is a board of directors of 3 persons. A and B are both directors, as is their attorney, C. At the organizational meeting of the Board of Directors, A was elected President at a salary of $50,000 per year, and B was elected Vice President at a salary of $50,000 per year. Each officer was granted an employment contract of one year, and the corporation adopted a policy of paying no dividends at the present time. Each shareholder held 50,000 shares of stock. A and B got along quite well for the first few months, but eventually their relationship deteriorated. Nonetheless, the business prospered. One year later, at the board meeting to elect new officers, A and B deadlocked on every proposal. C was silent. After a short private conference, C moved that A be elected President at a salary of $75,000 per year. The motion carried 2 to 1. A then moved that C be retained as Vice President and General Counsel at a salary of $25,000 a year, with the understanding that this position was part time in nature. B was then told by A that he must leave the premises immediately since there was no need for his services. B asked what would be done with the $10 million of retained earnings. A's reply was that further study was necessary, and that a management consulting firm would be retained to advise the corporation. The management consulting firm later advised that all of the corporation's earnings would be necessary for expansion of the corporation's facilities and that no dividends would be paid in the foreseeable future.

Consider the dilemma of B. He has lost his job. He has invested $50,000 which he can't get back out. He has stock with little or no market value. In the typical freeze out, A will generously offer to buy B's stock for a small fraction of its value. The cases that follow in this chapter will consider how the careful attorney can prevent problems of this nature from occurring, or at least minimizing the consequences. As you read the cases, consider this scenario and ask what the attorney might have done to avoid the problem in the first place.

## A.  THE CORPORATE NORMS

The older, and by now generally regarded as anachronistic, view was that the corporate form had only one scheme of governance and standard rules that applied to all corporate entities regardless of size or existence of a market for shares. Typical of this view is *Jackson v. Hooper*, 75 A. 568 (N.J. Super. Ct. App. Div. 1910). "[T]he law never contemplated that persons engaged in business as partners may incorporate, with the intent to obtain the advantages and immunities of a corporate form, and then, Proteus-like, become at will a co-partnership or a corporation, as the exigencies or purposes . . . may from time to time require. . . . They cannot be partners inter sese and a corporation to the rest of the world." The modern view is quite different. The leading case was *Galler v. Galler*, 203 N.E.2d 577 (Ill. 1964). The *Galler* decision was quite influential in bringing about judicial and legislative changes in the treatment of closely held corporations. *Galler* evinced a judicial attitude that was sympathetic to the needs and desires of the shareholders of closely held corporations. The court approved a shareholders' agreement that deviated in many ways from the traditional rules of corporate law. One example was the traditional corporate law rule that the business and affairs of the corporation are to be managed by its board of directors. One consequence of this view is that agreements by the shareholders could be held invalid because they interfered with the full authority of the board to run corporate affairs. The *Galler* court approved the shareholder's agreement allocating dividend income between two groups of shareholders. Another deviation from the corporate norms was the right of each group of shareholders to designate a representative to sit on the board of directors. The corporate norm would require an election by the shareholders.

## B.  FIDUCIARY DUTIES OF SHAREHOLDERS IN CLOSELY HELD CORPORATIONS

### DIMAGGIO v. ROSARIO
Court of Appeals of Indiana
950 N.E.2d 1272 (2011)

KIRSCH, J.

Victor J. DiMaggio III ("DiMaggio") appeals the trial court's order dismissing his complaint for usurpation of a corporate opportunity against Liberty Lake Estates, LLC ("LLE"), Mark Nebel ("Nebel"), and William C. Haak ("Haak") (collectively "the Appellees") and Elias Rosario ("Rosario"). DiMaggio raises the following restated issue for our review: whether the trial court erred when it dismissed his complaint for failure to state a claim upon which relief can be granted on the grounds that Indiana does not recognize a cause of action against a third-party non-fiduciary for usurpation of a corporate opportunity of a closely held corporation.

We affirm.

### FACTS AND PROCEDURAL HISTORY

DiMaggio and Rosario are shareholders in Galleria Realty Corporation ("Galleria"), which was an Indiana corporation with its principal place of business in Lake County, Indiana and involved in the business of real estate development. Galleria was formed on December 19, 1997, and DiMaggio and Rosario have been the shareholders of the corporation since its inception. LLE is an Indiana limited liability company with its principal place of business in Porter County, Indiana. LLE was formed on June 23, 2003 to pursue real estate development in Porter County. Rosario, Nebel, and Haak are all members of LLE.

On March 26, 2008, DiMaggio filed a complaint against Rosario and the Appellees, alleging, among other things, that the Appellees usurped a corporate opportunity from Galleria, which caused damages to DiMaggio. DiMaggio specifically stated that Nebel and Haak actively participated with Rosario, who owed a fiduciary duty to DiMaggio, his fellow shareholder in Galleria, in usurping Galleria's corporate opportunity; he further alleged that, because Galleria's business was real estate development, Rosario should have presented Galleria with the opportunity to develop real estate in Porter County prior to his formation of LLE with Nebel and Haak. On June 16, 2008, the Appellees filed a motion to dismiss DiMaggio's complaint on the basis that it failed to state a claim upon which relief can be granted. The trial court granted the Appellees' motion and dismissed the complaint against the Appellees without prejudice. DiMaggio now appeals.

* * *

DiMaggio argues that the trial court erred when it granted the Appellees' motion to dismiss for failure to state a claim upon which relief can be granted. He contends that, when the facts of the case are considered, "a cognizable claim was asserted against the dismissed defendants and the trial court's dismissal of the claim was improper." Although there are no Indiana cases that directly state that non-fiduciaries can be held liable for usurping a corporate opportunity as a corporate fiduciary can be, *see McLinden v. Coco*, 765 N.E.2d 606, 615 (Ind. Ct. App. 2002) ("A share-holder's fiduciary duty requires that he 'not appropriate to his own use a business opportunity that in equity and fairness belongs to the corporation.' "), DiMaggio initially claims that "it can be inferred that such a cause of action is supported by Indiana law" based upon *Dreyer & Reinbold, Inc. v. AutoXchange-.com, Inc.*, 771 N.E.2d 764 (Ind. Ct. App. 2002), trans. denied. We disagree.

Indiana courts have characterized closely-held corporations as incorporated partnerships and, as such, have imposed a fiduciary duty upon shareholding partners to deal fairly not only with the corporation but with fellow shareholders as well. . . . Consequently, shareholders in a close corporation stand in a fiduciary relationship to each other, and as such, must deal fairly, honestly, and openly with the corporation and with their fellow shareholders. . . . Moreover, shareholders may not act out of avarice, expediency, or self-interest in derogation of their duty of loyalty to the other stockholders and to the corporation. *Id.* A shareholder's fiduciary duty requires that he not appropriate to his own use a business opportunity that in equity and fairness belongs to the corporation.

In *Dreyer & Reinbold*, AutoXchange brought a suit against Dreyer, alleging, among other things, that Dreyer had conspired with a shareholder of AutoXchange to usurp AutoXchange's corporate opportunity. *Id.* at 766. Dreyer filed a Trial Rule 12(B)(6) motion to dismiss for failure to state a claim upon which relief can be granted, which was denied by the trial court. No appeal was taken from the denial of Dreyer's motion to dismiss, and the case ultimately came to this court on appeal for issues unrelated to the motion to dismiss. DiMaggio asserts that, even though there was no specific finding that Indiana law allowed a claim to proceed against a non-fiduciary for usurping a corporate opportunity, this court's silence regarding the trial court's denial of the motion to dismiss supports an inference that we "tacitly agreed that such a cause of action exists in Indiana."

*Dreyer & Reinbold* does not stand for such a proposition. Although the trial court denied Dreyer's motion to dismiss AutoXchange's complaint, which included an allegation of third-party liability for usurping a corporate opportunity, this court's decision on appeal did not expressly or tacitly recognize such a cause of action existed. The denial of the motion to dismiss was not an issue before this court; we did not reach the merits of such issue, and we decline to find that the *Dreyer & Reinbold* case stands for the proposition that Indiana recognizes a claim that non-fiduciaries can be held liable for usurping a corporate opportunity.

DiMaggio next argues that, even if Indiana has not yet decided that non-fiduciaries can be liable for usurping a corporate opportunity, this court should look to other jurisdictions for guidance and should so hold.

*       *       *

DiMaggio asserts that Indiana should adopt the holdings of other jurisdictions that a person who knowingly joins with or aids and abets a fiduciary in an enterprise constituting a breach of the fiduciary relationship becomes jointly and severally liable with the fiduciary for any damages accruing from such breach. *See Steelvest, Inc. v. Scansteel Serv. Ctr.*, 807 S.W.2d 476, 485 (Ky. 1991) ("[A] person who knowingly joins with or aids and abets a fiduciary in an enterprise constituting a breach of the fiduciary relationship becomes jointly and severally liable with the fiduciary for any profits that may accrue."); *BBF, Inc. v. Germanium Power Devices Corp.*, 13 Mass. App. Ct. 166, 430 N.E.2d 1221, 1224 (Mass. App. Ct. 1982) (finding trial court was justified in concluding that third-party defendant who did not owe fiduciary duty to company could still be jointly and severally liable when non-fiduciary knowingly participated with fiduciary in appropriating corporate opportunity of company); *Raines v. Toney*, 228 Ark. 1170, 313 S.W.2d 802, 810 (Ark. 1958) ("[O]ne who knowingly aids, encourages, or cooperates with a fiduciary in the breach of his duty becomes equally liable with such fiduciary."); *L.A. Young Spring & Wire Corp. v. Falls*, 307 Mich. 69, 11 N.W.2d 329, 343 (Mich. 1943) ("One who knowingly joins a fiduciary in an enterprise where the personal interest of the latter is or may be antagonistic to his trust becomes jointly and severally liable with him for the profits of the enterprise."). Therefore, the cause of action that DiMaggio asserts this court should adopt requires that, in order to be held jointly and severally liable with a fiduciary of a corporation, a non-fiduciary must act knowingly when he or she joins with or aids and abets the fiduciary in an endeavor constituting a breach of the fiduciary relationship.

Without deciding at this time whether Indiana should adopt DiMaggio's proposed cause of action, we conclude that, even if we were to recognize the cause of action existed in Indiana, DiMaggio's complaint did not state a claim upon which relief can be granted against the Appellees. In his complaint, DiMaggio alleges only that "Nebel and Haak actively participated with Rosario in usurping Galleria's corporate opportunity thereby causing damages to DiMaggio." Nowhere in his complaint does he allege that the Appellees acted knowingly or intentionally in usurping the corporate opportunity. All of the cases from other jurisdictions cited by DiMaggio require that the non-fiduciary must act knowingly when he or she joins a fiduciary in an enterprise constituting a breach of fiduciary duty. Here, DiMaggio has not alleged any knowing conduct on the part of the Appellees. Therefore, while we save for another day the decision as to whether Indiana should adopt such a cause of action, we conclude that, even if such a cause of action were to be recognized in Indiana, his complaint fails to state a claim upon which relief can be granted. The trial court did not err when it granted the Appellees' motion to dismiss.

Affirmed.

# NOTE

The corporate opportunity doctrine is the legal principle providing that directors, officers, and controlling shareholders of a corporation must not take for themselves any business opportunity that could benefit the corporation, but the court in *Dimaggio* suggests that the corporate opportunity doctrine may be applicable to third parties. The court while dismissing the case on technical grounds, acknowledges that such duties may be extended to non-parties who knowingly aid and abet a fiduciary's breach of duty. Courts consistently treat close corporations with heightened fiduciary duties. Why?

## HOLLAND v. BURKE
Superior Court of Massachusetts, Barnstable
24 Mass. L. Rep. 551 (2008)

CONNON, J.

Plaintiff Richard C. Holland ("Holland") filed this suit against the other shareholders of a limited liability company and two close corporations seeking equitable relief and damages for alleged breaches of fiduciary duty in terminating his employment and misappropriating corporate funds. During a jury-waived trial conducted between January 16 and January 23, 2008, Holland stipulated that he would seek damages for only the years 2005 and 2006. This Court took the matter under advisement and now issues the following findings of fact, rulings of law, and order for judgment.

### FINDINGS OF FACT

Holland has a degree in hotel and restaurant management and worked briefly in that industry before working in finance with several companies including Paine Webber and State Street Global Advisors. In 1999, Holland was employed by Mitchell Hutchins in New York City, where he was making a million dollar salary. Holland decided that he was financially comfortable and retired to Provincetown for a more relaxed lifestyle. Holland obtained a real estate license and worked as a real estate broker in Provincetown.

In 2001, defendants Sean F. Burke ("Burke") and Phillip E. Mossy ("Mossy") came to Provincetown to search for space in which to own and operate a restaurant. Mossy had lived in the San Diego area and was part owner/operator of several successful restaurants there. Burke's background was in the liquor distribution business, and he and Mossy together were part owners/operators of the Bayou Bar and Grill in San Diego. Mossy and Burke learned that the Red Inn on Commercial Street in Provincetown, a dilapidated inn no longer in operation, was for sale.

Defendant David L. Silva ("Silva"), a Provincetown native, was well-known around town and owned and operated Silva's Seafood Connection, a Provincetown restaurant. Holland, Burke, Mossy, and Silva socialized with the same group of friends in Provincetown. Mossy and Burke decided to place a bid on the Red Inn, and asked Holland whether he would become an investor. Holland asked Silva questions about running a restaurant in Provincetown and told Silva about the availability of the Red Inn. Silva expressed interest in joining the venture, and the four men decided to purchase and renovate the Red Inn together.

Holland worked closely with Lester Murphy, a corporate attorney in Dennis, to create the necessary corporate documents. On December 6, 2001, the four men formed the Red Inn, LLC ("the LLC") . . . to own the Red Inn. Holland, Burke, Mossy, and Silva each own a 25% beneficial interest in the LLC. Holland and Silva were the Managers of the LLC.

On December 6, 2001, Holland, Burke, Mossy, and Silva signed an "Operating Agreement" for the LLC. All four men carefully reviewed the Operating Agreement before executing it. Article II, section 2.2 of the Operating Agreement states:

> [T]he Manager of the LLC shall serve as such until resignation, death or a judicial adjudication of incompetence, or until seventy percent (70%) of the Members elect a new Manager or Managers at a meeting called by the Members or Manager for such a purpose.

Article III, section 3.2 states that except as otherwise provided in the Operating Agreement, no member shall have the right:

> \* \* \*
>
> (b) To have his capital contribution repaid except to the extent provided in this Agreement.
>
> (c) To require partition of the Company's property or to compel any sale or appraisal of the Company's assets.
>
> (d) To sell or assign his interest in the Company or to constitute the vendee or assignee thereunder, except as provided in this Agreement.
>
> (e) To voluntarily withdraw as a Member from the Company.

Article III, section 3.6 further provides:

> No Member may terminate his membership in the Company or have any right to distributions respecting his membership interest (upon withdrawal or resignation from the Company or otherwise) except as expressly set forth herein. No Member shall have the right to demand or receive property other than cash in return for such Member's contribution.

Article V, section 5.1(b) provides:

> Except as otherwise provided in this Section 5, no Member shall be obligated or permitted to contribute any additional capital to the Company. No interest shall accrue on any contributions to the capital of the Company, and no Member shall have the right to withdraw or to be repaid any capital contributed by it or to receive any other payment in respect of its interest

in the Company, including without limitation as a result of the withdrawal or resignation of such Member from the Company, except as specifically provided in this Agreement.

Article V, section 5.2 of the Operating Agreement provides:

The contribution of each Member is to be returned to such member only upon the termination and liquidation of the Company, but contributions may be returned prior to such time if agreed upon by all Members.

Article VII, section 7.1 provides in relevant part:

No Member may sell, assign, give, pledge, hypothecate, encumber or transfer . . . such Member's interest in the Company or any part thereof, unless said Member delivers an offer of sale of interest to the Company at least sixty (60) days prior to said Member's prospective disposition of his interest in the Company for liquidation by it at the then fair value of said Member's contribution of property or service to the Company (the "Offer"). The Offer shall state the name and address of the proposed transferee and the price or consideration, if any to be paid by such transferee . . .

Section 7.1 gives the LLC the right, within 20 days after notice of the Offer, to elect to purchase the member's interest at a purchase price set forth in section 7.2:

the lesser of (a) the price therefor that the Member has been offered or has offered, or (b) the amount of cash and/or the value of the property and/or services contributed by the Member to the Company as reflected in said Member's capital contribution of Exhibit A hereto.

Section 7.3 states that if the parties cannot agree on a purchase price under Section 7.2, the Company shall elect and pay an independent business appraiser to appraise the value of the Member's capital contribution, and that appraisal will be binding. Under Section 7.5, if the Company does not elect to purchase the Member's interest, the Member may transfer it to the individual named in the Offer, but that individual cannot become a Member of the LLC unless 70% of the other Members consent.

The LLC purchased the Red Inn on December 20, 2001. The purchase price was $2.4 million because of its prime waterfront location. Holland, Burke, Mossy, and Silva each contributed $185,000 to acquire the Red Inn, with $15,000.00 from each party set aside for renovations. The remainder of the financing came from Seaman's Bank, with personal guarantees from each of the four men.

The parties formed the Red Inn of Provincetown, Inc. under Chapter 156B to operate the Red Inn and the Red Inn Restaurant. Each of the four men is a 25% stockholder in that corporation. Holland was named the President and Treasurer, while Silva was named the Clerk. Holland, Burke, Mossy, and Silva are each directors of the corporation. The Red Inn of Provincetown, Inc. is a tenant of the LLC and pays rent.

The parties worked hard to prepare the Red Inn for opening in the spring of 2002. All of the parties had something to offer by way of their talents and background. Burke set up the dining room, worked as a chef, and created a business model. Holland engaged a contractor for the renovations and was responsible for advertising, marketing, and public relations. Little to no compensation was paid during this period of renovations. After substantial effort by all, the Red Inn opened in April of 2002, with a grand kickoff on May 2, 2002.

It was understood and agreed that all four men would work at the Red Inn full time in different capacities. Mossy was the executive chef, in charge of the kitchen, Burke was in charge of the bar, Silva helped out in the kitchen, and Holland managed the finances. None of the four had employment contracts and all were employees-at-will. The first year in operation was better than expected and toward the end of the season each party took a weekly salary of $250. The Inn was closed for the winter season and during the first three months of 2003, the parties made additional renovations to the premises. Also during the winter of 2003, Holland, Burke, Mossy, and Silva traveled together to Puerto Vallarta, Mexico for a month. Holland wrote the deposit check for the trip from the LLC's account. During this retreat, Mossy explored local restaurants to obtain ideas to improve the Red Inn's kitchen.

The Red Inn re-opened in the spring of 2003 and once again the business exceeded expectations and the parties were able to take out $500 per week. While working at the Red Inn, all four owners provided free meals and drinks to their friends. Toward the end of the 2003 season, the parties became aware that the Anchor Inn, also located in Provincetown, was up for sale. During the winter of 2004, Holland, Burke, Mossy, and Silva again traveled to Puerto Vallarta, Mexico, and Holland prepared and signed the deposit check for this trip from corporate funds. While in Mexico, the four discussed the possible purchase of the Anchor Inn. On May 19, 2004, the LLC purchased the Anchor Inn for $4.5 million, with $1.5 million financed by the Cape Cod Cooperative Bank, $2.5 million from the seller, $50,000 cash from Mossy, $50,000 cash from Burke, and $150,000.00 from Burke's mother. All four men signed personal guarantees for the loans. The parties formed a new corporation, 175 Commercial Street, Inc., to operate the Anchor Inn. Holland, Burke, Mossy, and Silva each owned 25% of the stock of this new corporation, and each was a director. Holland was the President and Treasurer of this corporation. 175 Commercial Street, Inc. is a tenant of the LLC and pays rent.

The Anchor Inn was in good condition and required no renovations. In the spring of 2004, Holland became the manager of the Anchor Inn and had primary responsibility for its operation.

The other shareholders, save Silva, worked primarily at the Red Inn but also worked shifts at the Anchor Inn. None of them took a salary from the Anchor Inn, although from May through November, the Anchor Inn was financially successful. The four men decided to travel to Mexico for the upcoming winter, and Holland submitted a deposit check on behalf of the LLC.

During the summer of 2004, Holland complained to various individuals that he was increasingly unhappy working in the businesses. Holland was becoming dissatisfied with his relationship with the remaining stockholders. Employees were complaining to him that the other shareholders were taking food and liquor from the Red Inn, guests were being treated rudely, and Burke, Mossy, and Silva were not working their assigned hours. Holland was an articulate and principled individual who had a different philosophy on how a business should be run. He was at odds with the other shareholders with respect to company sponsored trips to Mexico, inattention and accountability issues, and a general overall distaste for the others' collective approach to running a business.

As a result of this dissatisfaction, on October 1, 2004, Holland presented to Burke, Mossy, and Silva a document prepared by him entitled, "Departure and Future Strategies" which contained four alternative proposals. One proposal was that the other shareholders would purchase Holland's interests. In addition to some calculations on values less liabilities, Holland proposed that he would surrender all of his shares for a total price of $750,000. He suggested that this amount could be obtained from a new member or $250,000 each from Burke, Mossy, and Silva. The second proposal was that the Red Inn and the Anchor Inn would be valued, split, and owned separately. The third proposal was that Holland would purchase the other shareholders' interests. The final proposal was that the LLC (parent of both the Red Inn and the Anchor Inn) would continue to own both companies with member percentages intact and unchanged, but definitive operating agreements would be created for each individual company and include specific enforceable duties and responsibilities for each of the four shareholders. In addition, a predetermined percentage of operating revenues would be paid to the LLC with failure to meet predetermined revenue triggering enforceable financial and managerial penalties.

Burke, Mossy, and Silva did not agree to any of the four proposals, which they believed did not comply with the Operating Agreement. In addition, they did not have enough capital to purchase Holland's shares and did not want to split the two businesses up. In response to this impasse, Holland cancelled the LLC's credit cards, which the LLC used to purchase goods and services. Holland also wrote himself a check from LLC funds in the amount of one-quarter of the cost of the upcoming Mexico trip. Burke, Mossy, and Silva contacted Attorney Lester Murphy about the proper way to end Holland's employment and day-to-day responsibilities. Attorney Murphy stated that he could no longer represent the corporations because Holland had already contacted him about LLC issues. The three men then contacted another attorney, Robin Reid, for assistance.

Silva as clerk called special meetings of the LLC and of the shareholders and directors of the two corporations for November 4, 2004. The meetings began at 4:15 p.m. and lasted only approximately 40 minutes. At these meetings, which Holland attended, the other shareholders voted to remove Holland as a Director, Manager and President and Treasurer of the operating corporations. Holland, of course, dissented from these votes. Holland was asked to turn over his keys to the Red Inn and the Anchor Inn and to stay away from the properties. Holland continued to receive $500 per week until the end of the year, and his health insurance was continued until March of 2006.

Holland still retains his 25% interest in the LLC and the operating corporations. None of the entities has ever declared dividends.

\* \* \*

Despite the disagreements among the four shareholders, the businesses prospered.

\*    \*    \*

Holland filed this action against his fellow shareholders on March 4, 2005. Although the Amended Complaint asserts seven counts, Holland withdrew Counts II, III, and IV prior to opening statements. Count I of the Amended Complaint seeks declaratory relief that Holland was unlawfully removed as President, Director, Manager and Treasurer of the LLC and as an officer and director of the Red Inn of Provincetown, Inc. and 175 Commercial Street, Inc. Count V alleges that the defendants breached their fiduciary duty to Holland by the defalcation of funds and the misuse of corporate credit cards. The next Count alleges that the defendants improperly removed Holland from participation in and management of the businesses. Count VI seeks equitable relief to permit Holland to participate in the business of the Red Inn and Anchor Inn. Finally, Count VII seeks an accounting of the gross receipts, expenses, liabilities, and distribution of earnings of the two corporations and LLC.

Count II sought the dissolution of the Red Inn; Count III sought the dissolution of The Red Inn of Provincetown, Inc. and Count IV sought the dissolution of 175 Commercial Street, Inc.

\*    \*    \*

## RULINGS OF LAW

It is undisputed that Red Inn of Provincetown, Inc. and 175 Commercial Street, Inc. are close corporations under Massachusetts law. A close corporation is defined as one which has a small number of stockholders, no ready market for its stock, and substantial majority stockholder participation in the management, direction, and operations of the corporation. Shareholders in a close corporation owe one another a fiduciary duty of utmost good faith and fair dealing in the operation of the enterprise. Despite the existence of this duty, the controlling group in a close corporation must have some room to maneuver in establishing the business policy of the corporation. The determination of whether the majority has breached its fiduciary duty to the minority is a matter of law for the court, as is the appropriate remedy for any breach.

### Removal of Holland as Officer and Director

Count I of the Amended Complaint seeks declaratory relief that Holland was unlawfully removed as President, Director, Manager and Treasurer of the LLC and as an officer and director of the Red Inn of Provincetown, Inc. and 175 Commercial Street, Inc. The second Count V alleges that the defendants breached their fiduciary duty to Holland by improperly removing him from these positions. Count VII seeks equitable relief to allow him to participate in the business operations of the two inns. In essence, Holland alleges that Burke, Mossy, and Silva have frozen him out of the LLC and operating corporations.

The majority interests in a close corporation must have a large measure of discretion with respect to corporate governance, including the declaration or withholding of dividends, establishing the salaries of corporate officers, dismissing directors with or without cause, and hiring and firing corporate employees. Nonetheless, the majority's discretion to make corporate decisions is restrained by the fiduciary duty of utmost good faith and loyalty owed by all stockholders in a close corporation to one another, and the majority cannot employ oppressive devices to "freeze out" the minority by frustrating the minority's reasonable expectation of benefit from their ownership of shares.

Where a corporation uses employee salaries as the primary method of distributing the available corporate earnings, a freeze out may be accomplished by depriving minority stockholders of corporate offices and employment by the company. *Brodie v. Jordan*, 447 Mass. at 869. Whether there is a freeze out in this situation depends on the shareholders' reasonable expectations of benefit. *Id.* at 869–70. Here, Holland has not established that he had a reasonable expectation of continued employment with the Red Inn and Anchor Inn, that a guaranty of employment was a major reason for his investment of capital, or that he was relying on employment by the LLC and two corporations for his livelihood. . . . In contrast to his co-venturers, Holland lacked significant experience in the restaurant and hospitality industry, and was financially secure enough to have retired from his career in finance. The evidence at trial did not demonstrate that Holland was relying on a salary as manager and officer as the principal return on his investment, and the salaries taken by the parties were minimal. . . . Rather, the credible evidence established that Holland's primary motivation in joining the enterprise was to invest in the land and the two businesses, an interest which Holland retains by virtue of his stock ownership. Moreover, Holland had repeatedly expressed dissatisfaction with working long hours at low wages in the day-to-day operation of the inns. Accordingly, Holland has not proven an improper freeze out based on his termination as a manager and officer.

Holland also complains that the majority improperly froze him out by terminating him as a director of the operating companies. A freeze out may occur when the majority injures a minority shareholder's non-economic interests in management of the enterprise and corporate decision-making by removing him as officer or director. *Id.* at 870; *Wilkes v. Springside Nursing Home, Inc.*, 370 Mass 842 (1976). However, it is not sufficient for a party challenging a corporate action to merely label it a "freeze out." Freeze-outs, by definition, are coercive and manifestly inequitable. Courts must ensure that application of the strict fiduciary duty standard does not impose limitations on legitimate action by the controlling group which will unduly hamper its effectiveness in managing the corporation. *Id.* at 850. The majority has certain rights to selfish ownership of a close corporation which must be balanced against their fiduciary duty to the minority. *Id.* at 851. Thus, when a minority shareholder alleges a breach of fiduciary duty by the controlling majority, the court must examine whether the controlling group can demonstrate a legitimate business purpose for their actions. Once the majority advances such a purpose, the complaining shareholder must establish that the same legitimate objective could have been achieved through an alternative course of action less harmful to the minority's interests. The court should then weigh the legitimate business purpose against the practicability of a less harmful alternative.

*[margin handwritten note: Freeze out by firing]*

*[margin handwritten note: Freeze out by removing him as director]*

Here, Holland invested his capital and time in the LLC and operating corporations with the expectation that he would continue to participate in corporate decisions. Nonetheless, there was a legitimate business purpose for removing Holland as a director and officer: to preserve and continue the successful operation of the Red Inn and Anchor Inn. The credible evidence established a breakdown over time of the relationship between Holland on the one hand and the other three shareholders with respect to the day-to-day operations of the two inns and the long-term goal of the venture. Holland proposed to resolve this problem by essentially dividing and selling the businesses in order to recapture his investment, whereas Burke, Mossy, and Silva were dedicated to the continued operation of the inns. Thus, there was a legitimate business purpose for removing Holland. Holland has not demonstrated that the same objective practicably could have been achieved through an alternative course of action less harmful to his interests. The majority shareholders were not required to accept any of the four alternative proposals contained in Holland's "Departure and Future Strategies." It is clear that they could not afford to purchase Holland's interests, nor did they wish to have Holland buy them out of the businesses they had created and built, or split the two inns into separate ownership.

Further, the defendants' vote to terminate Holland as a manager, director, and officer was in accordance with the terms of the Operating Agreement and the operating documents of the two corporations. In contrast, Holland's proposals for his departure conflicted with the terms of the Operating Agreement, which gives members very limited rights to transfer their interests or withdraw their capital from the venture.

Finally, Holland's termination does not appear to have been motivated by a desire on the part of Burke, Mossy, and Silva to gain financially at Holland's expense. . . . Nor was the majority's primary motive to prevent Holland from continuing to receive money from the corporations. *Id.* at 847. There is no evidence that the majority's management of the enterprise is such as to place Holland at risk on his personal loan guaranties. Thus, Holland has not demonstrated that the majority's conduct was coercive and manifestly inequitable so as to deprive him of his interest in the corporations or frustrate his purpose in entering into the corporate venture. *Cf. Bodio v. Ellis*, 401 Mass. 1, 9–10, 513 N.E.2d 684 (1987) (shareholder/director's acquisition of additional stock in order to force another shareholder/director to retire was a freeze out which breached fiduciary duty and warranted equitable relief, where the two shareholders at all times had expectation of equal control); *Donahue v. Rodd Electrotype Co. of New England, Inc.*, 367 Mass. at 598–600 (improper "freeze out" occurred where majority deprived the minority of equal opportunity to have its stock repurchased by the corporation); *Crowley v. Communications for Hosp.*, Inc., 30 Mass. App. Ct. 751 (1991) (majority froze out minority stockholder by paying themselves excessive compensation, refusing to declare dividends, failing to redeem minority shares on same basis as was available to the majority, and attempting to purchase minority shares at bargain price).

For all these reasons, Holland has not established that his termination as manager, director, officer, and/or employee of the LLC and the operating corporations constituted a breach of fiduciary duty. The defendants are thus entitled to judgment in their favor on Count I, the second Count V, and Count VI of the Amended Complaint.

## Misappropriation of Corporate Sums

The first Count V alleges that the defendants breached their fiduciary duty to Holland by diverting large amounts of money from the corporation, making improper use of corporate credit cards, and failing to make distributions to him. The directors, officers, and controlling shareholders of a close corporation are charged with a paramount duty of loyalty. They are bound to act with absolute fidelity and may not act out of avarice, expediency, or self-interest in derogation of their duty of loyalty to the corporation and to the other shareholders. . . . They must subordinate their personal pecuniary interests to their fiduciary duty, and must refrain from promoting their own interests in a manner injurious to the corporation.

The diversion of corporate funds for personal use is a breach of the fiduciary duty of loyalty. *Allied Freightways, Inc. v. Cholfin*, 325 Mass. 630, 631 (1950). Holland alleges in the Amended Complaint that Burke, Mossy, and Silva have misappropriated huge sums of money from the operation of the inns, hoarded cash in a safe rather than depositing it in the LLC's account, and distributed the cash amongst themselves without making any distribution to him. These allegations in essence assert a claim of conversion of corporate funds. Conversion is an intentional and wrongful exercise of ownership, control, or dominion over personal property to which one has no right of possession, in a manner inconsistent with the rights of one who has a present entitlement to possession. Holland has failed to prove by a preponderance of the credible evidence any misappropriation or conversion of corporate funds.

Holland further alleges in the Amended Complaint that Burke, Mossy, and Silva have improperly used business credits cards for personal vacation, travel, and expense purposes and have not properly accounted for this use. However, Holland simply failed to introduce at trial any credible evidence of misuse of corporate credit cards or funds. To the extent that Holland challenges the trips to Mexico, the credible evidence established that such trips were largely in the nature of business retreats, and Holland himself wrote the checks for and was a willing participant in these annual trips until his relations with the others soured. Holland has not established by the preponderance of the credible evidence any breach of fiduciary duty from the misuse of corporate credit cards or funds. Accordingly, the defendants are entitled to judgment on Count V alleging a breach of fiduciary duty based on the misappropriation or misuse of corporate funds.

## Accounting

Finally, in Count VII of the Amended Complaint, Holland demands an accounting of all gross receipts, money paid for expenses and liabilities, and distribution of earnings for the LLC, the Red Inn of Provincetown, Inc., and 175 Commercial Street, Inc. Equitable relief in the nature of an accounting is available where there is a fiduciary relationship between the parties and damages are due one of the parties following a fiduciary breach or fraud. Here, Holland failed to prove any breach of fiduciary duty by the defendants which would entitle him to the remedy of an equitable accounting. In any event, Article II, section 2.4(c) of the Operating Agreement of the LLC allows any member to obtain an audit or review of the LLC's books by a certified public accountant of his choice at his own expense. To the extent that Holland has concerns about the LLC's finances, he can avail himself of that contractual remedy.

## ORDER FOR JUDGMENT

For the foregoing reasons, it is hereby ORDERED that judgment enter in favor of defendants. . . .

## RAMOS v. ESTRADA
### Court of Appeals of California
### 8 Cal. App. 4th 1070 (1992)

GILBERT, J.

Defendants Tila and Angel Estrada appeal a judgment which states they breached a written corporate shareholder voting agreement. We hold that a corporate shareholders' voting agreement may be valid even though the corporation is not technically a close corporation. We affirm.

## FACTS

Plaintiffs Leopoldo Ramos et al. formed Broadcast Corporation for the purpose of obtaining a Federal Communications Commission (FCC) construction permit to build a Spanish language television station in Ventura County.

Ramos and his wife held 50 percent of Broadcast Corp. stock. The remaining 50 percent was issued in equal amounts to five other couples. The Estradas were one of the couples who purchased a 10 percent interest in Broadcast Corp. Tila Estrada became president of Broadcast Corp., sometimes known as the "Broadcast Group."

In 1986, Broadcast Corp. merged with a competing applicant group, Ventura 41 Television Associates (Ventura 41), to form Costa del Oro Television, Inc. (Television Inc.). The merger agreement authorized the issuance of 10,002 shares of Television Inc. voting stock.

Initially, Television Inc. was to issue 5,000 shares to Broadcast Corp. and 5,000 to Ventura 41. Each group would have the right to elect half of an eight member board of directors. The two remaining outstanding shares were to be issued to Broadcast Corp. after the television station had operated at full power for six months. Television Inc.'s board would then increase to nine members, five of whom would be elected by Broadcast Corp.

The merger agreement contained restrictions on the transfer of stock and required each group to adopt internal shareholder agreements to carry out the merger agreement. With FCC approval, Broadcast Corp. and Ventura 41 modified their agreement to permit stock in Television Inc. to be issued directly to the respective owners of the merged entities instead of to the entities themselves. Ventura 41 sought this change so that Television Inc. would be treated as a Subchapter S corporation for tax purposes. In part, Broadcast Group agreed to this change in exchange for approval by Ventura 41 of the agreement at issue here, which is known as the June Broadcast Agreement. Among other things, the June Broadcast Agreement provides for block voting for directors by the Broadcast Group shareholders according to their ownership.

In January 1987, Broadcast Group executed a written shareholder agreement, known as the January Broadcast Agreement, to govern the voting and transfer of Broadcast Corp. shares in Television Inc. stock. At a later date, Broadcast Group drafted a written schedule showing the valuation of shares transferred pursuant to the January Broadcast Agreement. It set the price for purchase and sale of shares as their investment cost plus 8 percent per annum.

In June 1987, the shareholders of Broadcast Group executed a Master Share-holder Agreement. This agreement was designed to implement the Merger Agreement. It permits direct shareholder ownership of stock and governs various voting and transfer provisions. It requires that shareholder votes be made in the manner voted by the majority of the shareholders.

Members of Broadcast Group subscribed for shares of Television Inc. in their respective proportion of ownership pursuant to written subscription agreements attached to the Master Shareholder Agreement. The Ventura 41 group acted similarly.

Television Inc. issued stock to these subscribers in December 1987, and they elected an eight-member board. They also elected Leopoldo Ramos president, and Tila Estrada as one of the directors.

At a special directors' meeting held on October 8, 1988, Tila Estrada voted with the Ventura 41 group block to remove Ramos as president and to replace him with Walter Ulloa, a member of Ventura 41. She also joined Ventura 41 in voting to remove Romualdo Ochoa, a Broadcast Group member, as secretary and to replace him with herself.

Under the June Broadcast Agreement and the Merger Agreement, each of the groups were required to vote for the directors upon whom a majority of each respective group had agreed. The terms of that agreement expressly state that failure to adhere to the agreement constitutes an election by the shareholder to sell his or her shares pursuant to buy/sell provisions of the agreement. The agreement also calls for specific enforcement of such buy/sell provisions.

On October 15, 1988, the Broadcast Group noticed another meeting to decide how its members would vote their shares for directors at the annual meeting. All members attended except the Estradas. The group agreed to nominate another slate of directors which did not include either of the Estradas. [The Estradas were notified of the results of this meeting.]

The Estradas unilaterally declared the June Broadcast Agreement null and void as of October 15, 1988, in a letter dictated for them by Paul Zevnik, the attorney for Ventura 41. Tila Estrada refused to recognize the October 15 vote of the majority of the Broadcast Group to replace her as a director of Television Inc. Ramos et al. sued the Estradas for breach of the June Broadcast Agreement, among other things.

The court ruled that the Estradas materially breached the valid June Broadcast Agreement, and it ordered their shares sold in accordance with the specific enforcement provisions of the June Broadcast Agreement. The court restrained the Estradas from voting their shares other than as provided in the June Broadcast Agreement.

## DISCUSSION

The Estradas contend that the June Broadcast Agreement is void because it constitutes an expired proxy which the Estradas validly revoked.

\* \* \*

Corporations Code section 178 defines a proxy to be "a written authorization signed . . . by a shareholder . . . *giving another person or persons* power to vote with respect to the shares of such shareholder."

Section 7.1 of the June Broadcast Agreement details the voting arrangement among the shareholders. It states, in pertinent part:

> "The Stockholders agree that they shall consult with each other prior to voting their shares in the Company. They shall attempt in good faith to reach a consensus as to the outcome of any such vote. In the case of a vote for directors, they agree that no director shall be selected who is not acceptable to at least one member (i.e., spousal unit) of each of Group A and Group B. (See ¶ 1.2(b)(1) above [which states that: 'The Stockholders shall be divided into two groups, Group "A" being composed of Leopoldo Ramos and Cecilia Morris, and Group "B" being composed of all the other Stockholders.'].) In the case of all *votes of Stockholders* they agree that, following consultation and compliance with the other provisions of this paragraph, *they will all vote their stock in the manner voted by a majority* of the Stockholders." (Second italics in original.)

No proxies are created by this agreement. The agreement has the characteristics of a shareholders' voting agreement expressly authorized by section 706, subdivision (a) for close corporations. (See also Legis. Com. com. to § 186, West's Ann. Corp. Code (1990) p. 52, [Deering's Ann. Corp. Code § 186 (1977) pp. 49–50], regarding proxies.) Although the articles of incorporation do not contain the talismanic statement that "This corporation is a close corporation," the arrangements of this corporation, and in particular this voting agreement, are strikingly similar to ones authorized by the Code for close corporations.

Section 706, subdivision (a) states, in pertinent part: "an agreement between two or more shareholders of a close corporation, if in writing and signed by the parties thereto, may provide that in exercising any voting rights the shares held by them shall be voted as provided by the agreement, or as the parties may agree or as determined in accordance with a procedure agreed upon by them. . . . "

Here, the members of this corporation executed a written agreement providing that they shall try to reach a consensus on all votes and that they shall consult with one another and vote their own stock in accordance with the majority of the stockholders. They entered into this agreement because they "mutually desire[d]" to limit the transferability of their stock to ensure "the Company does not pass into the control of persons whose interests might be incompatible with the interests of the Company and of the Stockholders, establishing their mutual rights and obligations in the event of death, and establishing a mechanism for determining how the Stockholders' voting rights in the Company shall be exercised . . . ."

Even though this corporation does not qualify as a close corporation, this agreement is valid and binding on the Estradas. Section 706, subdivision (d) states: "This section shall not invalidate any voting or other agreement among shareholders . . . which agreement . . . is not otherwise illegal."

The Legislative Committee comment regarding section 706, subdivision (d) states that "[t]his subdivision is intended to preserve any agreements which would be upheld under court decisions *even though they do not comply with one or more of the requirements of this section, including voting agreements of corporations other than close corporations*." (West's Ann.Corp.Code, § 706 (1990) p. 330, italics added.) The California Practice Guide indicates that such "pooling" agreements are valid not only for close corporations, but also "among any number of shareholders of other corporations as well." (FRIEDMAN, CAL. PRACTICE GUIDE CORPORATIONS (The Rutter Group 1992) ¶ 3:159.2, p. 3–31.)

The Estradas cite *Dulin v. Pacific Wood and Coal Co.* (1894) 103 Cal. 357, 35 P. 1045, and *Smith v. S.F. & N.P. Ry. Co.* (1897) 115 Cal. 584, 47 P. 582, as support for their argument that the agreement is an expired proxy which they revoked. Their reliance on these cases is misplaced.

In *Dulin*, defendant Clugston claimed there was an oral agreement among the shareholders that he would be president of defendant corporation and receive a salary in exchange for various loans and a mortgage to the corporation. At a later election, certain stockholders cumulated their votes and plaintiff Dulin was elected president. Clugston charged a conspiracy to defeat him.

The Supreme Court found that the alleged verbal agreement was void and that there had never been an express agreement to elect Clugston. (*Dulin v. Pacific Wood and Coal Co., supra*, 103 Cal. at p. 363, 35 P. 1045.) No proxy had been given to vote the stock of the others involved, "nor was any required by the agreement to be given." In short, there was no voting agreement whatsoever, oral or written which could be enforced.

The *Dulin* court never considered whether the objects of the alleged oral agreement were lawful or proper. As Marsh on California Corporation Law explains, "[t]his case would seem to hold nothing more than that the alleged agreement was unenforceable because it was oral." (3 MARSH, CAL. CORPORATION LAW (3d ed. 1991 supp.) § 22.10, p. 1857.)

In *Smith, supra*, three individuals purchased a majority share of stock in a corporation. To keep control of the corporation, they entered into a written agreement to pool their votes so as to vote in a block for a five-year period. Although two of the three agreed on a slate for an election, the third attempted to repudiate the agreement. The two presented the vote of all the stock held by the trio in accordance with their agreement; the third attempted to vote his own stock in the manner he desired.

The court held that the express, written agreement validly called for the trio to vote their shares as a block. (*Smith v. S.F. & N.P. Ry. Co., supra*, 115 Cal. at p. 598, 47 P. 582.) The court viewed the agreement as a power (to vote) coupled with an interest (in purchasing stock) which was supported by consideration. (*Id.*, at p. 600, 47 P. 582.) The court construed the agreement as an agency; a proxy which could not be repudiated. (*Id.*, at pp. 598–599, 47 P. 582.)

There is *dicta* in *Smith* suggesting that the agreement in that case constituted an irrevocable proxy. Said the court: "It is not in violation of any rule or principle of law for stockholders, who own a majority of the stock in a corporation, to cause its affairs to be managed in such way as they may think best calculated to further the ends of the corporation, and, for this purpose, *to appoint one or more proxies who shall vote in such a way as will carry out their plan. Nor is it against public policy for two or more stockholders to agree . . . upon the officers whom they will elect, and they may do this either by themselves, or through their proxies . . . ."* (*Smith v. S.F. & N.P. Ry. Co., supra*, 115 Cal. at pp. 600–601, 47 P. 582, italics added.)

The *Smith* court also held that "[a]ny plan of procedure they [stockholders] may agree upon implies a previous comparison of views, and there is nothing illegal in an agreement to be bound by the will of the majority as to the means by which the result shall be reached. If they are in accord as to the ultimate purpose, it is but reasonable that the will of the majority should prevail as to the mode by which it may be accomplished."(*Smith v. S.F. & N.P. Ry. Co., supra*, 115 Cal. at p. 601, 47 P. 582.)

In the instant case, the only difference from *Smith* is that the shareholders here chose to vote their stocks themselves, and not by proxy. What the *Smith* court held, however, is that voting agreements, like the one here, are valid. If the shareholders are unable to reach a consensus, then each shareholder must vote his or her shares according to the will of the majority.

The instant agreement is valid, enforceable and supported by consideration. It states, in pertinent part, that the stockholders entered into the agreement for the purposes of "limiting the transferability of . . . stock in the Company, ensuring that the Company does not pass into the control of persons whose interests might be incompatible with the interests of the Company and of the Stockholders, establishing their mutual rights and obligations in the event of death, and establishing a mechanism for determining how the Stockholders' voting rights . . . shall be exercised . . . ."

Section 7.2 of the agreement states that "[t]he Stockholders understand and acknowledge that the purpose of the foregoing arrangement is to preserve their relative voting power in the Company . . . . Accordingly, in the event that a Stockholder fails to abide by this arrangement for whatever reason, that failure shall constitute on [sic] irrevocable election by the Stockholder to sell his stock in the Company, triggering the same rights of purchase provided in Article IV above."

The agreement calls for enforcement by specific performance of its terms because the stock is not readily marketable. Section 709, subdivision (c) expressly permits enforcement of shareholder voting agreements by such equitable remedies. It states, in pertinent part: "The court may determine the person entitled to the office of director or may order a new election to be held or appointment to be made, may determine the validity, effectiveness and construction of voting agreements . . . and the right of persons to vote and may direct such other relief as may be just and proper."

The Estradas contend that the forced sale provision is unconscionable and oppressive. They portray themselves as naive, small-town business people who were forced to sign an adhesion agreement without reviewing its contents.

Substantial evidence supports the findings that Tila Estrada has been a licensed real estate broker. She is an astute businesswoman experienced with contracts concerning real property. The consent and signatures of the Estradas to the agreement were not procured by fraud, duress or other wrongful conduct of Ramos. The Estradas read and discussed with other members of Broadcast Group, and with their own counsel, the voting, buy/sell and other provisions of the agreement and the January Broadcast Agreement, as well as various drafts of these documents, and they freely signed these agreements.

On direct examination, under Evidence Code section 776, Tila Estrada admitted she owns and operates a real estate brokerage business; she regularly reviews a broad variety of real estate documents; she and her husband own and manage investment property; and she has considered herself "to be an astute business woman" since 1985. Tila Estrada also has been a participant and owner in another application before the FCC, for an FM radio station, before the instant suit was filed.

Ms. Estrada stated she got copies "of all the drafts and all the Shareholders Agreements." She discussed these agreements with other members of Broadcast Group and with its counsel, Mr. Howard Weiss.

The June Broadcast Agreement, including its voting and buy/sell provisions, was unanimously executed after the Estradas had a full and fair opportunity to consider it in its entirety. As the trial court found, the buy-out provisions at issue here are valid, favored by courts and enforceable by specific performance. (*And see* 3 MARSH, *supra*, at § 22.14, p. 1867; *see generally Vannucci v. Pedrini* (1932) 217 Cal. 138, 144–145, 17 P.2d 706, on the right of those who are the original incorporators to enter into a corporate agreement requiring limitations on shareholder actions so as to preserve control of the corporation as set forth in their executed agreements.)

The Estradas breached the agreement by their written repudiation of it. Their breach constituted an election to sell their Television Inc. shares in accordance with the terms of the buy/sell provisions in the agreement. This election does not constitute a forfeiture — they violated the agreement voluntarily, aware of the consequences of their acts and they are provided full compensation, per their agreement.

The judgment is affirmed. Costs to Ramos.

# NOTES

1.   This case deals with a voting agreement rather than a voting trust. Voting trusts are discussed at Section D, *infra*. This type of agreement is sometimes called a pooling agreement. Voting agreements can often be used to accomplish the same purposes as voting trusts. This entire area of corporate law illustrates the difficulties brought about by adherence to formalism. If we characterize the agreement here as a voting trust, it is likely illegal and void for failure to comply with the statutory or case law requirements for a voting trust. If we characterize it as a proxy, it may be invalid or simply unenforceable. Using proxies as part of a shareholder agreement is often quite sensible, but the danger to note is that at common law proxies were considered simply to be agency relationships, and a principal could always revoke. The common law test for irrevocable agencies is very complex. The *Smith* case cited by the court suggested that the voting agreement there would be an irrevocable proxy coupled with an interest. The *Smith* case in reality broadened the common law agency test for what constituted an irrevocable agency. Statutory reforms since that time have eased the requirements and permit many types of proxies to be irrevocable. Note that in this case, the argument presented was to the court that the voting agreement was an expired proxy which the Estradas validly revoked. Why did the court reject that argument? What is the difference between a proxy and a voting agreement?

2.   In contrast to the *Ramos* court, Delaware has espoused a stricter adherence to corporate law for closely held corporations that have not chosen to opt in to the close corporation statute. In *Nixon v. Blackwell*, 626 A.2d 1366 (1993), the court noted that minority shareholders in close corporations could easily be taken advantage of by the majority. Instead of providing special consideration for such a shareholder, however, the court suggested that he should either think twice about buying the stock in the first place, or alternatively make sure that he was protected by contract from the majority's overreaching.

3.   A famous case, *Ringling Bros. Barnum & Bailey Combined Shows v. Ringling*, 53 A.2d 441 (Del. 1947), involved an intrafamily squabble over control of the circus's management. Two of the three shareholders had entered into an agreement requiring them to pool their votes, which would permit them to elect five of the company's seven directors. The two had a falling out, and one refused to vote in the manner required by the agreement. The court found that the agreement was valid, but that it had no enforcement mechanism, so it merely invalidated the votes of the breaching shareholder. By contrast, the *Ramos* contract provided for specific enforcement, allowing the court to force the sale of Ms. Estrada's shares.

4.   If all of the parties to voting agreement understand it and agree to it, is there any reason not to enforce it?

5.   The Estradas contend that the forced sale provision was unconscionable and oppressive. Should such agreements be enforced against the naïve and unsophisticated? Does valuation at investment cost plus 8% annum sound unfair?

## C.  DEVIATIONS FROM THE CORPORATE NORMS

### SOMERS v. AAA TEMPORARY SERVICES, INC.
Appellate Court of Illinois
284 N.E.2d 462 (1972)

Lorenz, J.

This case involves an action brought to declare invalid the action by the two sole shareholders of a corporation amending the corporate by-laws to reduce the number of directors from three to two. The plaintiff, Wesley Somers, was not a shareholder but was the third director whose position was eliminated by the change in the by-laws. The trial court entered judgment on the pleadings in favor of plaintiff. From that judgment the defendant corporation and Lillian Raimer, one of the Shareholders, now appeal. Defendant Michaelene Kay, the other shareholder, did not file an appearance in the trial court nor is she prosecuting this appeal.

Defendant corporation, AAA Temporary Services, Inc., (hereinafter referred to as the "corporation") was incorporated under the laws of the State of Illinois on April 29, 1967, for the purpose of furnishing and supplying temporary stenographers, clerical, industrial and other forms of male and female help and assistance. Its issued and outstanding capital stock at the time plaintiff filed his action consisted of 50 shares of common stock. Twenty-five of these shares were owned by defendant Lillian Raimer, who was the president of the corporation; the remaining twenty-five shares were owned by defendant Michaelene Kay, who was the secretary and treasurer of the corporation. Plaintiff did not own any shares at the time he filed his action, nor had he ever owned any of the capital stock of the corporation.

The corporation's articles of incorporation provided that 'The number of directors to be elected at the first meeting of the shareholders is three.' It is undisputed that the first meeting of shareholders was held on May 2, 1967. The three directors elected at that meeting were Lillian Raimer, Michaelene Kay and Wesley Somers. The by-laws were adopted shortly after incorporation and provided in pertinent part that "Each director shall hold office until the annual meeting of shareholders, or until his successor shall have been elected and qualified." The by-laws also called for an annual meeting of the shareholders to be held on the second Monday of each year. The by-laws further provided that a regular meeting of the board of directors would be held " . . . immediately after, and at the same place as the annual meeting of shareholders."

No annual meeting was held on the second Monday in 1968 nor at any time during 1968. The second Monday in 1969 was on January 13, 1969. On that date, defendant Lillian Raimer contends that she and Michaelene Kay, the sole shareholders of the corporation, signed a waiver of notice of the annual shareholders meeting. The meeting was then allegedly conducted for the purpose of, among other things, amending the by-laws of the corporation to reduce the number of directors from three to two. Thereupon, the by-laws were purportedly amended to provide that the "number of directors shall be two." The two shareholders then elected themselves as the two directors, signed a waiver of notice for the annual directors' meeting and conducted the directors' meeting.

Plaintiff denies that the annual shareholders' and directors' meetings for 1969 were actually convened or held on January 13, 1969. He further contends that the actions allegedly taken at the meetings by the two shareholders were not discussed until the last several days of January, 1969. Even if it is conceded that such meetings were held, it is appellee's contention that the resolutions adopted by the shareholders were unlawful and not within the power and authority of the shareholders. Accordingly, plaintiff brought an action to declare invalid the action by the shareholders reducing the number of directors from three to two. Upon his motion for judgment on the pleadings, the trial court declared the reduction of directors by the two shareholders to be illegal and void, found the correct number of directors of the corporation to be three not two and held that Wesley Somers is still a director of the corporation. Defendants Lillian Raimer and the corporation appeal from the trial court's judgment on the pleadings.

Appellants urge that the principal question presented on appeal is simply whether the two sole shareholders of a close corporation may validly agree that the by-laws of the corporation be amended to reduce the number of directors from three to two and thereupon elect themselves as the two sole directors. We feel that this statement of the issue is somewhat misleading in view of the facts in this case. The question is not whether such an agreement can be made. At issue is whether the shareholders have the power to amend the by-laws where, as here, such power has not been reserved to the shareholders by the Articles of Incorporation.

The Illinois Business Corporation Act provides that the number directors may be increased or decreased by amendment to the by-laws. (Ill. Rev. Stat. 1969, ch. 32, par. 157.34.) The Act further states that the power to amend the by-laws is "vested in the board of directors, unless reserved to the shareholders by the articles of incorporation."(Ill. Rev. Stat. 1969, ch. 32, par. 157.25.)

The power to amend the by-laws of AAA Temporary Services, Inc. was not reserved to the shareholders by its Articles of Incorporation. Therefore, this power would rest with the directors. It is clear that the action of the shareholders, amending the by-laws to provide for two instead of three directors, was not in compliance with Section 25 of the Illinois Business Corporation Act. Since only the directors of a corporation have the statutory right to amend the by-laws, where such power has not been reserved to the shareholders, we sustain the trial court's holding that the amendment to the by-laws of the corporation at the January 13, 1969, meeting was a nullity. (In this regard, note that we accept the trial court's ruling to the effect that a meeting of shareholders was in fact convened and held on January 13, 1969.)

In spite of the language of Section 25 of the Illinois Business Corporation Act, appellants strongly urge that the action by the shareholders of the corporation should be allowed to stand because the corporation is a close one. As a matter of fact, appellants have constructed almost their entire argument around the framework of the Illinois Supreme Court's decision in the case of *Galler v. Galler*, (1964), 32 Ill. 2d 16, 203 N.E.2d 577. The principal thrust of the *Galler* decision is that, in the context of a particular fact situation, there is no reason for preventing those in control of a close corporation from reaching any agreements concerning the management of the corporation which are agreeable to all, though such agreements are not within the letter of the Business Corporation Act.

It is important to note, however, that the Supreme Court in *Galler* imposed limitations on the operation and use of this general rule for close corporations. First, the Court indicated that such agreements should be permitted only where no fraud or apparent injury would be worked upon the public, minority interests or creditors. Then, more directly in point to the instant case, the Court went on to caution that shareholder agreements which violate statutory language are not permitted. The Court said in its opinion:

> "There is no reason why mature men should not be able to adapt the statutory form to the structure they want, so long as they do not endanger other stockholders, creditors, or the public, or violate a clearly mandatory provision of the corporation laws."

The Galler Court did not say that the Illinois Business Corporation Act may be disregarded in the case of a close corporation. Slight deviations from corporate norms may be permitted. However, action by the shareholders which is in direct contravention of the statute cannot be allowed. Appellant's contention that there is no conceivable way in which *Galler* can be distinguished from the instant case must, therefore, be rejected. The language of Section 25 of the Business Corporation Act is clearly mandatory regarding the amendment of the corporate by-laws. Accordingly, it is obvious to us that the holding in the *Galler* case gives no sanction to appellants to disregard the clear and unambiguous language of that section of the Act.

Finally, defendant Raimer in her answer questions the motives of plaintiff in bringing this action by alleging a conspiracy between Somers and defendant Kay. Raimer alleges that plaintiff is a close friend and business adviser of Kay. It is Raimer's contention that, in this capacity, Somers conspired with Kay to oust Raimer from her office as president and a director of the corporation by filing the instant complaint. Although plaintiff in his reply admitted that he was a close friend and adviser of Kay and worked part-time for her in a separate business venture, he denied any bad motives in instituting this suit. An examination of Illinois law on the question as to whether an alleged bad motive constitutes a valid legal defense reveals that our courts have consistently held that it does not. It is generally accepted that where the plaintiff asserts a valid cause of action, his motive in bringing the action is immaterial. A plaintiff's right of recovery is in no way barred by the motive which prompts him to bring the action. (*See Mexican Asphalt Co. v. Mexican Asphalt Paving Co.* (1895), 61 Ill. App. 354; *People v. Ittner* (1911), 165 Ill. App. 360.) Since plaintiff had a valid cause of action in this case, we find his motives in bringing the action to be immaterial.

The judgment of the trial court is affirmed.

## NOTES

1.   This case is a good illustration of the problems that can occur when two persons form a corporation without a competently drafted shareholders' agreement. Note that we have only two shareholders. If both shareholders contribute equally to

the capital of the corporation, and both plan to be active in the business, it is likely that both desire an equal voice in running the business.

**2.** Why were articles of incorporation prepared that provided for a board of directors with three members? Why were bylaws prepared which cut the size of the board to two?

**3.** The court tells us that slight deviations from corporate norms may be permitted. However, action in direct contravention of the statute cannot be allowed. Is this a helpful legal standard?

## D. ALLOCATION OF VOTING POWER: MULTIPLE CLASSES OF STOCK, VOTING TRUSTS AND SHAREHOLDER AGREEMENTS

### LEHRMAN v. COHEN
Supreme Court of Delaware
222 A.2d 800 (1966)

HERRMANN, J.

The primary problem presented on this appeal involves the applicability of the Delaware Voting Trust Statute.[1] Other questions involve the legality of stock having voting power but no dividend or liquidation rights except repayment of par value, and an alleged unlawful delegation of directorial duties and powers.

These are the material facts:

Giant Food Inc. (hereinafter the "Company") was incorporated in Delaware in 1935 by the defendant N. M. Cohen and Samuel Lehrman, deceased father of the plaintiff Jacob Lehrman. From its inception, the Company was controlled by the

---

[1]  [1] 8 Del.C. s 218 provides in part as follows:

"§ 218. Voting trusts

'(a) One or more stockholders may by agreement in writing deposit capital stock of an original issue with or transfer capital stock to any person or persons, or corporation or corporations authorized to act as trustee, for the purpose of vesting in such person or persons, corporation or corporations, who may be designated voting trustee or voting trustees, the right to vote thereon for any period of time determined by such agreement, not exceeding ten years, upon the terms and conditions stated in such agreement. Such agreement may contain any other lawful provisions not inconsistent with said purpose. After the filing of a copy of such agreement in the principal office of the corporation in the State of Delaware, which copy shall be open to the inspection of any stockholder of the corporation or any beneficiary of the trust under said agreement daily during business hours, certificates of stock shall be issued to the voting trustees to represent any stock of an original issue so deposited with them, and any certificates of stock so transferred to the voting trustees shall be surrendered and cancelled and new certificates therefor shall be issued to the voting trustees, and in the certificates so issued it shall appear that they are issued pursuant to such agreement, and in the entry of such voting trustees as owners of such stock in the proper books of the issuing corporation that fact shall also be noted. The voting trustees may vote upon the stock so issued or transferred during the period in such agreement specified. . . .' "

Cohen and Lehrman families, each of which owned equal quantities of the voting stock, designated Class AC (held by the Cohen family) and Class AL (held by the Lehrman family) common stock. The two classes of stock have cumulative voting rights and each is entitled to elect two members of the Company's four-member board of directors.

Over the years, as may have been expected, there were differences of opinion between the Cohen and Lehrman families as to operating policies of the Company. Samuel Lehrman died in 1949; each of his children inherited part of his stock in the Company; but a dispute arose among the children regarding an Inter vivos gift of certain shares made to the plaintiff by his father shortly before his death. To eliminate the Lerhman family dispute and its possible disruption of the affairs of the Company, an arrangement was made which settled the dispute and permitted the plaintiff to acquire all of the outstanding Class AL stock, thereby vesting in him voting power equal to that held by the Cohen family. The arrangement involved repurchase by the Company of the stock held by the plaintiff's brothers and sister, their relinquishment of any claim to the stock gift, and an equalizing surrender of certain stock by the Cohens to the Company for retirement. An essential part of the arrangement, upon the insistence of the Cohens, was the establishment of a fifth directorship to obviate the risk of deadlock which would have continued if the equal division of voting power between AL and AC stock were continued.

To implement the arrangement, on December 31, 1949, the Company's certificate of incorporation was amended, Inter alia, to create a third class of voting stock, designated Class AD common stock, entitled to elect the fifth director. Article Fourth of the amendment to the certificate of incorporation provided for the issuance of one share of Class AD stock, having a par value of $10. and the following rights and powers:

> "The holder of Class AD common stock shall be entitled to all of the rights and privileges pertaining to common stock without any limitations, prohibitions restrictions or qualifications except that the holder of said Class AD stock shall not be entitled to receive any dividends declared and paid by the corporation, shall not be entitled to share in the distribution of assets of the corporation upon liquidation or dissolution either partial or final, except to the extent of the par value of said Class AD common stock, and in the election of Directors shall have the right to vote for and elect one of the five Directors hereinafter provided for."

> "The corporation shall have the right, at any time, to redeem and call in the Class AD stock by paying to the holder thereof the par value of said stock, provided however, that such redemption or call shall be authorized and directed by the affirmative vote of four of the five Directors hereinafter provided for."

By resolution of the board of directors, the share of Class AD stock was issued forthwith to the defendant Joseph B. Danzansky, who had served as counsel to the Company since 1944. All corporate action regarding the creation and the issuance of the Class AD stock was accomplished by the unanimous vote of the AC and AL stockholders and of the board of directors. In April 1950, pursuant to the arrangement, Danzansky voted his share of AD stock to elect himself as the

Company's fifth director; and he served as such until the institution of this action in 1964. During that entire period, the AC and AL stock have been voted to elect two directors each. From 1950 through 1964, Danzansky regularly attended board meetings, raised and discussed general items of business, and voted on all issues as they came before the board. He was not obliged to break any deadlock among the directors prior to October 1, 1964 because no such deadlock arose before that date.

Beginning in December 1959, 200,000 shares of non-voting common stock of the Company were sold in a public issue for over $3,000,000. Each prospectus published in connection with the public issue contained the following statement:

> "Common Stock AD is not a participating stock, and the only purpose for the provision and issuance of such stock is to prevent a deadlock in case the Directors elected by the Common Stock AC and the Directors elected by the Common Stock AL cannot teach an agreement."

\*     \*     \*

From the outset and until October 1, 1964, the defendant N. M. Cohen was president of the Company. On that date, a resolution was adopted at the Company's annual stockholders' meeting to give Danzansky a fifteen year executive employment contract at an annual salary of $67,600., and options for 25,000 shares of the non-voting common stock of the Company. The AC and AD stock were voted in favor and the AL stock was voted against the resolution. At a directors meeting held the same day, Danzansky was elected president of the Company by a 3-2 vote, the two AL directors voting in opposition. On December 11, 1964, Danzansky resigned as director and voted his share of AD stock to elect as the fifth director. Millard F. West, Jr., a former AL director and investment banker whose firm was one of the underwriters of the public issue of the Company's stock. The newly constituted board ratified the election of Danzansky as president; and, on January 27, 1965, after the commencement of this action and after a review and report by a committee consisting of the new AD director and one AL director, Danzansky's employment contract was approved and adopted with certain modifications.

The plaintiff brought this action on December 11, 1964, basing it upon two claims: The First Claim charges that the creation, issuance, and voting of the one share of Class AD stock resulted in an arrangement illegal under the law of this State for the reasons hereinafter set forth. The Second Claim, addressed to the events of October 1, 1964, charges that the election of Danzansky as president of the Company and his employment contract violated the terms of the 1959 deadlock-breaking arrangement, as made between the holders of the AC and AL stock, and constituted breaches of contract and fiduciary duty. The plaintiff and the defendants filed cross-motions for summary judgment as to the First Claim. The Court of Chancery, after considering the contentions now before us and discussed Infra, granted summary judgment in favor of the defendants and denied the plaintiff's motion for summary judgment. The plaintiff appeals.

## I.

The plaintiff's primary contention is that the Class AD stock arrangement is, in substance and effect, a voting trust; that, as such, it is illegal because not limited to a ten year period as required by the Voting Trust Statute. The defendants deny that the AD stock arrangement constitutes a disguised voting trust; but they concede that if it is, the arrangement is illegal for violation of the Statute. Thus, issue is clearly joined on the point.

The criteria of a voting trust under our decisions have been summarized by this Court in *Abercrombie v. Davies*, 36 Del. Ch. 371, 130 A.2d 338 (1957). The tests there set forth, accepted by both sides of this cause as being applicable, are as follows: (1) the voting rights of the stock are separated from the other attributes of ownership; (2) the voting rights granted are intended to be irrevocable for a definite period of time; and (3) the principal purpose 4 of the grant of voting rights is to acquire voting control of the corporation.

Adopting and applying these tests, the plaintiff says, as to the first element, that the AD arrangement provides for a divorcement of voting rights from beneficial ownership of the AC and AL stock; that the creation and issuance of the share of AD stock is tantamount to a pooling by the AC and AL stockholders of a portion of their voting stock and giving it to a trustee, in the person of the AD stockholder, to vote for the election of the fifth director; that after the creation of the AD stock, the AC and AL stockholders each hold but 40% Of the voting power, and the AD stockholder holds the controlling balance of 20%; that the AD stock has no property rights except the right to a return of the $10 paid as the par value; and that, therefore, there has been a transfer of the voting rights devoid of any participating property rights. So runs the argument of the plaintiff in support of his contention that the first of the Abercrombie criteria for a voting trust is met.

The contention is unacceptable. The AD arrangement did not separate the voting rights of the AC or the AL stock from the other attributes of ownership of those classes of stock. Each AC and AL stockholder retains complete control over the voting of his stock; each can vote his stock directly; no AL or AC stockholder is divested of his right to vote his stock as he sees fit; no AL or AC stock can be voted against the shareholder's wishes; and the AL and AC stock continue to elect two directors each.

The AD stock arrangement, as we view it, became a part of the capitalization of the Company. The fact that there is but a single share, or that the par value is nominal, is of no legal significance; the one share and the $10 par value might have been multiplied many times over, with the same consequence. It is true that the creation of the separate class of AD stock may have diluted the voting Power which had previously existed in the AC and AL stock-the usual consequence when additional voting stock is created-but the creation of the new class did not divest and separate the voting Rights which remain vested in each AC and AL shareholder, together with the other attributes of the ownership of that stock. The fallacy of the plaintiff's position lies in his premise that since the voting power of the AC and AL stock was reduced by the creation of the AD stock, the percentage of reduction became the Res of a voting trust. In any recapitalization involving the creation of additional voting stock, the voting power of the previously existing stock is diminished; but a voting trust is not necessarily the result.

Since the holders of the Class AC and Class AL stock of the Company did not separate the voting rights from the other attributes of ownership of those classes when they created the Class AD stock, the first *Abercrombie* test of a voting trust is not met.

This conclusion disposes of the second and third *Abercrombie* tests, i.e., that the voting rights granted are irrevocable for a definite period of time, and that the principal object of the grant of voting rights is voting control of the corporation. Having held that the AC and AL stockholders have not divested themselves of their voting rights, although they may have diluted their voting powers, we do not reach the remaining *Abercrombie* tests, both of which assume the divestiture of voting rights.

In the final analysis, the essence of the question raised by the plaintiff in this connection is this: Is the substance and purpose of the AD stock arrangement sufficiently close to the substance and purpose of § 218 to warrant its being subjected to the restrictions and conditions imposed by that Statute? The answer is negative not only for the reasons above stated, but also because § 218 regulates trusts and pooling agreements amounting to trusts, not other and different types of arrangements and undertakings possible among stockholders. The AD Stock arrangement is neither a trust nor a pooling agreement.

We hold, therefore, that the Class AD stock arrangement is not controlled by the Voting Trust Statute.


II.

The plaintiff's second point is that even if the Class AD stock arrangement is not a voting trust in substance and effect, the AD stock is illegal, nevertheless, because the creation of a class of stock having voting rights only, and lacking any substantial participating proprietary interest in the corporation, violates the public policy of this State as declared in § 218.

The fallacy of this argument is twofold: First, it is more accurate to say that what the law has disfavored, and what the public policy underlying the Voting Trust Statute means to contol, is the separation of the vote from the stock-not from the stock ownership. 5 FLETCHER CYCLOPEDIA CORPORATIONS, § 2080, pp. 363–369; compare *Abercrombie v. Davies, supra.* Clearly, the AD stock arrangement is not violative of that public policy. Secondly, there is nothing in § 218, either expressed or implied, which requires that all stock of a Delaware corporation must have both voting rights and proprietary interests. Indeed, public policy to the contrary seems clearly expressed by 8 Del. C. § 151(a)5 which authorizes, in very broad terms, such voting powers and participating rights as may be stated in the certificate of incorporation. Non-voting stock is specifically authorized by s 151(a); and in the light thereof, consistency does not permit the conclusion, urged by the plaintiff, that the present public policy of this State condemns the separation of voting rights from beneficial stock ownership.

We conclude that the plaintiff's contention in this regard cannot withstand the force and effect of § 151(a). In our view, that Statute permits the creation of stock having voting rights only, as well as stock having property rights only. The voting powers and the participating rights of the Class AD stock being specified in the

Company's certificate of incorporation, we are of the opinion that the Class AD stock is legal by virtue of § 151(a).

\* \* \*

We are told that if the AD stock arrangement is allowed thus to stand, our Voting Trust Statute will become a "dead letter" because it will be possible to evade and circumvent its purpose simply by issuing a class of non-participating voting stock, as was done here. We have three negative reactions to this argument:

First, it presupposes a divestiture of the voting rights of the AC and AL stock-an untenable supposition as has been stated. Secondly, it fails to take into account the main purpose of a Voting Trust Statute: to avoid secret, uncontrolled combinations of stockholders formed to acquire voting control of the corporation to the possible detriment of non-participating shareholders. . . . It may not be said that the AD stock arrangement contravenes that purpose. Finally on this point, if we misconceive the legislative intent, and if the AD stock arrangement in this case reveals a loophole in § 218 which should be plugged, it is for the General Assembly to accomplish-not for us to attempt by interstitial judicial legislation.

## III.

The plaintiff advances yet another reason for invalidating the AD stock. The essence of this argument is that the only function of that class of stock is to break directorial deadlocks; that the issuance of the AD stock is merely a technical divice to permit that result; that, as such, it is illegal because it permits the AC and AL directors of the Company to delegate their statutory duties to the AD director as an arbitrator.

We see nothing inherently wrong or contrary to the public policy of this State, as plaintiff seems to suggest, about a device, otherwise lawful, designed by the stockholders of a corporation to break deadlocks of directors. The plaintiff says in this connection, that if public policy sanctioned such device, our General Corporation Law would provide for it. The fallacy of this argument lies in the assumption that legislative silence is a dependable indicator of public policy. . . . We know of no reason, either under our statutes or our decisions, which would prevent the stockholders of a Delaware corporation from protecting themselves and their corporation, by a plan otherwise lawful, against the paralyzing and often fatal consequences of a stalemate in the directorate of the corporation. We hold, therefore, that the AD stock arrangement had a proper purpose.

As to the means adopted for the accomplishment of that purpose, we find the AD stock arrangement valid by virtue of § 141(a) of the Delaware Corporation Law which provides:

> "The business of every corporation organized under the provisions of this
> chapter shall be managed by a board of directors, except as hereinafter or
> in its certificate of incorporation otherwise provided."

The AD stock arrangement was created by the unanimous action of the stockholders of the Company by amendment to the certificate of incorporation. The stockholders thereby provided how the business of the corporation is to be managed, as is their privilege and right under § 141(a). It was this stockholder action which delegated to the AD director whatever powers and duties he possesses; they were not delegated to him by his fellow directors, either out of their own powers and duties, or otherwise.

It is settled, of course, as a general principle, that directors may not delegate their duty to manage the corporate enterprise. But there is no conflict with that principle where, as here, the delegation of duty, if any, is made not by the directors but by stockholder action under § 141(a), via the certificate of incorporation.

In our judgment, therefore, the AD stock arrangement is not invalid on the ground that it permits the AC and AL directors of the Company to delegate their statutory duties to the AD director.

On this point, the plaintiff relies mainly upon the Chancery Court decision in *Abercrombie v. Davies*, 35 Del. Ch. 599, 611, 123 A.2d 893 (1956). There, in considering an agreement requiring all eight directors to submit a disputed question to an arbitrator if seven were unable to agree, the Chancery Court stated that legal sanction may not be accorded to an agreement, at least when made by less than all the stockholders, which takes from the board of directors the power of determining substantial management policy. The plaintiff's reliance is misplaced, because, Inter alia, the *Abercrombie* arrangement was not created by the certificate of incorporation, within the authority of § 141(a).

\*   \*   \*

Our conclusions upon these questions make it unnecessary to discuss the defendants' contentions that the plaintiff's action is barred by the principles of estoppel, laches, acquiescence and ratification.

Finding no error in the judgment below, it is affirmed.

## NOTES

**1.** Note that this case deals with a corporation that has publicly held stock. Nonetheless the arrangement used suggests a simple mechanism to avoid deadlock in closely held corporations. Very likely few investors would have found the chance to invest in the non-voting common stock attractive if a deadlock could have occurred. The Cohens and the Lehrmans evidently found it to mutual advantage to insure continuity of management in the event that they failed to agree in the future. Consider why the parties did not use a voting trust or pooling agreement. The answer is that based on the Delaware cases of the time either method would yield unpredictable results. This mechanism, which truly illustrates magnificent lawyering, accomplished nearly the result of a pooling agreement or a voting trust but in a manner that was far more likely to be upheld by the Delaware courts. Note also that the three classes of stock (actually four if we count the non-voting stock) permit the Cohens and the Lehrmans to reassert control if they ever agree. One way to look at this arrangement is to consider it as a substitute for arbitration, or as a substitute for the appointment of a provisional director to break deadlocks.

2.   Note that the court considered and rejected the argument that this device constituted an illegal voting trust. Voting trusts are used most frequently in reorganizing publicly held corporations that are insolvent, or nearly so. The creditors of such corporations may be willing to take a chance on long term profitability if they are assured of competent management by officers who do not have to fear being voted out of office by a new board of directors. A voting trust is often a good solution, especially if the trustees are persons trusted by both creditors and shareholders.

3.   Generally voting trusts are subject to strict statutory controls. See MBCA section 7.30, requiring a written agreement in which the shares are deposited with the voting trustee who becomes the record owner of those shares. A voting trust may not be valid for more than 10 years but that time period may be extended by unanimous agreement. A copy of the agreement must be deposited with the corporate secretary and made available for inspection by all shareholders. Secret trusts are assumed to be evil. Presumably, secrecy will not exist if a copy of the trust agreement is on file in the registered office of the corporation. Why is secrecy considered to be an evil? Consider the case of a closely held corporation with 10 shareholders, each owning 10% of the shares. If six of the shareholders agree to vote their shares so as to control the corporation, is such an agreement illegal and void? Let the same six shareholders set up a secret trust, and the agreement will be struck down as an illegal voting trust. Why? For a closely held corporation, is 10 years long enough to tie up control? Is 10 years long enough, if you get two years notice that the trust will not be renewed?

4.   In contrast to the strict controls on voting trusts, the modern tendency is to allow shareholders to enter into simple contractual agreements governing how they will vote their shares. *See* MBCA § 7.31(a) (2004). The only statutory requirement is that the agreement be contained in a signed writing. Also, section 7.31(b) provides that it is specifically enforceable. In general, a simple contractual voting agreement will be preferable to a voting trust in the close corporation due to its flexibility and informality.

## E.   DISSOLUTION AND DEADLOCK

### IN RE RADOM & NEIDORFF
Court of Appeals of New York
119 N.E.2d 563 (1954)

DESMOND, J.

Radom & Neidorff, Inc., the proposed dissolution of which is before us here, is a domestic corporation which has for many years, conducted, with great success, the business of lithographing or printing musical compositions. For some thirty years prior to February 18, 1950, Henry Neidorff, now deceased, husband of respondent Anna Neidorff, and David Radom, brother-in-law of Neidorff and brother of Mrs. Neidorff, were the sole stockholders, each holding eighty shares. Henry Neidorff's will made his wife his executrix and bequeathed her the stock, so that, ever since his death, petitioner-appellant David Radom and Anna Neidorff, brother and sister, have been the sole and equal stockholders. Although brother and sister, they were unfriendly before Neidorff's death and their estrangement continues. On July 17, 1950, five months after Neidorff's death, Radom brought this proceeding, praying that the corporation be dissolved under section 103 of the [New York] General Corporation Law, Consol. Laws, c. 23, the applicable part of which is as follows:

§ 103. Petition in case of deadlock

"Unless otherwise provided in the certificate of incorporation, if a corporation has an even number of directors who are equally divided respecting the management of its affairs, or if the votes of its stockholders are so divided that they cannot elect a board of directors, the holders of one-half of the stock entitled to vote at an election of directors may present a verified petition for dissolution of the corporation as prescribed in this article."

That statute, like others in article 9 of the General Corporation Law, describes the situations in which dissolution may be petitioned for, but, as we shall show later, it does not mandate the granting of the relief in every such case.

The petition here stated to the court that the corporation is solvent and its operations successful, but that, since Henry Neidorff's death, his widow (respondent here) has refused to co-operate with petitioner as president, and that she refuses to sign his salary checks, leaving him without salary, although he has the sole burden of running the business. It was alleged, too, that, because of 'unresolved disagreements' between petitioner and respondent, election of any directors, at a stockholders' meeting held for that purpose in June, 1950, had proved impossible. A schedule attached to the petition showed corporate assets consisting of machinery and supplies worth about $9,500, cash about $82,000, and no indebtedness except about $17,000 owed to petitioner (plus his salary claim). Mrs Neidorff's answering papers alleged that, while her husband was alive, the two owners had each drawn about $25,000 per year from the corporation, that, shortly after her husband's death, petitioner had asked her to allow him alone to sign all checks, which request she refused, that he had then offered her $75,000 for her stock, and, on her rejection thereof, had threatened to have the corporation dissolved and to buy it in at a low price or, if she should be the purchaser, that he would start a competing business. She further alleged that she has not, since her husband's death, interfered with Radom's conduct of the business and has signed all corporate checks sent her by him except checks for his own salary which, she says, she declined to sign because of a stockholder's derivative suit brought by her against Radom, and still pending, charging him with enriching himself at this corporation's expense.

Because of other litigation now concluded (see *Matter of Radom's Estate*, 305 N.Y. 679) to which Mrs. Neidorff was not a party, but which had to do with a contest as to the ownership of the Radom stock, respondent's answering papers in this dissolution proceeding were not filed until three years after the petition was entered. From the answering papers it appears, without dispute, that for those three years, the corporation's profits before taxes had totaled about $242,000, or an annual average of about $71,000, on a gross annual business of about $250,000, and that the corporation had, in 1953, about $300,000 on deposit in banks. There are many other accusations and counter accusations in these wordy papers, but the only material facts are undisputed: first, that these two equal stockholders dislike and distrust each other; second, that, despite the feuding and backbiting, there is no stalemate or impasse as to corporate policies; third, that the corporation is not sick but flourishing; fourth, that dissolution is not necessary for the corporation or for either stockholder; and, fifth, that petitioner, though he is in an uncomfortable and disagreeable situation for which he may or may not be at fault, has no grievance cognizable by a court except as to the nonpayment of his salary, hardly a ground for dissolving the corporation.

Special Term held that these papers showed a basic and irreconcilable conflict between the two stockholders requiring dissolution, for the protection of both of them, if the petition's allegations should be proven. An order for a reference was, accordingly, made, but respondent appealed therefrom, and no hearings were held by the Referee. The Appellate Division reversed the order and dismissed the petition, pointing out, among other things, that not only have the corporation's activities not been paralyzed but that its profits have increased and its assets trebled during the pendency of this proceeding, that the failure of petitioner to receive his salary did not frustrate the corporate business and was remediable by means other than dissolution. The dismissal of the proceeding was "without prejudice, however, to the bringing of another proceeding should deadlock in fact arise in the selection of a board of directors, at a meeting of stockholders to be duly called, or if other deadlock should occur threatening impairment or in fact impairing the economic operations of the corporation." (282 App. Div. 854.) Petitioner then appealed to this court.

It is worthy of passing mention, at least, that respondent has, in her papers, formally offered, and repeated the offer on the argument of the appeal before us, "to have the third director named by the American Arbitration Association, any Bar Association or any recognized and respected public body."

Clearly, the dismissal of this petition was within the discretion of the Appellate Division. . . . Even when majority stockholders file a petition because of internal corporate conflicts, the order is granted only when the competing interests "are so discordant as to prevent efficient management" and the "object of its corporate existence cannot be attained." . . . The prime inquiry is, always, as to necessity for dissolution, that is, whether judicially imposed death "will be beneficial to the stockholders or members and not injurious to the public." . . .

The order should be affirmed, with costs.

FULD, J. (dissenting).

Section 103 of the General Corporation Law, insofar as here relevant, permits a petition for dissolution of a corporation by the holders of one half of the shares of stock entitled to vote for directors "if the votes of its stockholders are so divided that they cannot elect a board of directors." That is the precise situation in the case before us, for the petition explicitly recites that petitioner Radom and respondent Neidorff "are hopelessly deadlocked with respect to the management and operation of the corporation" and that serious disputes have developed between them with the result that "the votes of the two stockholders are so divided that they cannot elect a Board of Directors."

The court is given discretion, by section 106 of the General Corporation Law, to "entertain or dismiss the application" for dissolution.

* * *

I would not, however, rest decision on that ground alone. Even if, however, the Appellate Division possessed the power to dismiss the petition without a hearing, its decision in this case constitutes a gross abuse of discretion. Whether petitioner will be able to sustain his claims, I do not know, but it seems exceeding plain that he has alleged more than enough to entitle him to a hearing and to an opportunity to present his proofs.

* * *

For upwards of thirty years, petitioner Radom and Henry Neidorff, respondent's husband, shared equally in the ownership and management of Radom & Neidorff, Inc. Through all that time, their relationship was harmonious as well as profitable. Neidorff died in 1950, at which time respondent, through inheritance, acquired her present 50% stock interest in the business. Since then, all has been discord and conflict. The parties, brother and sister, are at complete loggerheads; they have been unable to elect a board of directors; dividends have neither been declared nor distributed, although the corporation has earned profits; debts of the corporation have gone unpaid, although the corporation is solvent; petitioner, who since Neidorff's death has been the sole manager of the business, has not received a penny of his salary — amounting to $25,000 a year because — respondent has refused to sign any corporate check to his order. More, petitioner's business judgment and integrity, never before questioned, have been directly attacked in the stockholder's derivative suit, instituted by respondent, charging that he has falsified the corporation's records, converted its assets and otherwise enriched himself at its expense. Negotiations looking to the purchase by one stockholder of the other's interest were begun — in an effort to end the impasse — but they, too, have failed.

In very truth, as petitioner states in his papers, "a corporation of this type, with only two stockholders in it cannot continue to operate with incessant litigation and feuding between the two stockholders, and with differences as fundamental and wholly irreconcilable as are those of Mrs. Neidorff and myself. . . . [S]ettlement of these differences cannot be effected, while continuance on the present basis is impossible, so that there is no alternative to judicial dissolution." Indeed, petitioner avers, in view of the unceasing discord and the fact that he has had to work without salary and advance his own money to the corporation, he does not, whether or no dissolution be granted, "propose to continue to labor in and operate this business."

It is, then, undisputed and indisputable that the stockholders are not able to elect a board of directors. In addition, it is manifest, on the facts alleged, that the Supreme Court could find that the stockholders are hopelessly deadlocked vis-a-vis the management of the corporation; that the corporation cannot long continue to function effectively or profitably under such conditions; that petitioner's resignation as president and manager — which he contemplates — will be highly detrimental to the interests of both corporation and stockholders and cannot help but result in substantial loss; and that petitioner is not responsible for the deadlock that exists. In such circumstances, the requisite statutory hearing may well establish that dissolution is indispensable, the only remedy available. As the high court of New Jersey recently declared in applying to somewhat comparable facts a statute similar to section 103 of our General Corporation Law (*Matter of Collins-Doan Co.*, 3 N.J. 382, 396), "In the case at hand, *there is a want of that community of interest essential to corporate operation.* Dissolution will serve the interests of the shareholders as well as public policy. . . . And, if the statutory authority be deemed discretionary in essence, there is no ground for withholding its affirmative exercise here, *for there is no alternative corrective remedy.* . . . The dissention is such as to defeat the end for which the corporation was organized." (Emphasis supplied.)

Here, too, the asserted dissension, the court could find, permits of no real or effective remedy but a section 103 dissolution. And that is confirmed by a consideration of the alternatives seemingly open to petitioner. He could remain as president and manager of the corporation, without compensation, completely at odds with his embittered sister certainly neither a natural nor a satisfying way in which to conduct a business. Or he could carry out his present plan to quit the enterprise and thereby risk a loss, to corporation and stockholders, far greater than that involved in terminating the business. Or he could, without quitting, set up a competing enterprise and thereby expose himself to suit for breach of fiduciary duty to the corporation. (*Cf. Duane Jones Co. v. Burke*, 306 N.Y. 172)It is difficult to believe that the legislature could have intended to put one in petitioner's position to such a choice. Reason plainly indicates, and the law allows, the reasonable course of orderly dissolution pursuant to section 103.

Respondent, however, suggests that, in view of the fact that petitioner is managing the business profitably, he should continue to do so, defend against the stockholder's suit which she brought attacking his honor and integrity and himself start an action for the compensation denied him for more than three years. But, it seems self-evident, more and further litigation would only aggravate, not cure, the underlying deadlock of which petitioner complains. (*See Saltz v. Saltz Bros.*, 84 F.2d 246, certiorari denied 299 U.S. 567.) And, if he were to bring the suggested suit for salary due him, the question arises, whom should he sue, and who is to defend?[2] The mere proposal that petitioner embark on a series of actions against the corporation, of which he is president and half owner, indicates the extent of the present impasse, as well as the futility of perpetuating it. The same is true of the other alternative suggested by respondent, namely, that the third of the three directors, required by section 5 of the Stock Corporation Law, Consol. Laws, be appointed by an impartial party. The deadlock of which petitioner complains is between the stockholders, not the directors, and, when stockholders are deadlocked, section 103 calls for dissolution, not arbitration. Beyond that, and even if the offer to elect an impartial director were relevant, it would still be necessary to inquire when it was made and under what circumstances. It does not justify, alone or in conjunction with the other facts, a summary dismissal of the proceeding without a hearing.

---

[2] [1] In this connection, it is, perhaps, of some moment that, according to petitioner, he is the sole officer and director of the corporation, cf. Civ. Practice Act, s 228.

Although respondent relies on the fact that the corporation is now solvent and operating at a profit, it is manifest that, if petitioner carries out his plan to resign as president and quits the business, there may be irreparable loss, not alone to him and respondent, as the owners of the corporation, but also to the corporation's creditors. Quite apart from that, however, the sole issue under section 103 is whether there is a deadlock as to the management of the corporation, not whether business is being conducted at a profit or loss. . . . Whether the petition should or should not be entertained surely cannot be made to turn on proof that the corporation is on the verge of ruin or insolvency.

Insolvency may be a predicate for dissolution, but not under section 103. By virtue of other provisions of Article 9 of the General Corporation Law sections 101 and 102 directors and stockholders may seek dissolution, when the corporation is insolvent, in order to prevent further loss to the owners and creditors. Section 103, however which bears the title, "Petition in case of deadlock" was designed to serve a far different purpose. As amended in 1944, upon the recommendation of the Law Revision Commission, that section provides for dissolution "if the votes of its stockholders are so divided that they cannot elect a board of directors". Nothing in the statute itself or in its legislative history suggests that a "Petition in case of deadlock" must wait until the corporation's profits have dried up and financial reverses set in. Had the commission or the legislature intended to incorporate such a qualification into section 103, it could readily have done so. The only test envisaged by the commission, however, was that which the legislature enacted, see 1944 Report of N. Y. Law Revision Commission, N.Y. Legis. Doc., 1944, No. 65(K), pp. 5–7, and a court may not import any other.

Nor does section 117 require or suggest any contrary conclusion. That section provides that if *after a hearing*, (§ 116), it shall appear "that a dissolution will be beneficial to the stockholders . . . and not injurious to the public, the court must make a final order dissolving the corporation." It would certainly be "beneficial" to dissolve the corporation if the court were to find that there is a continuing, irreparable stalemate in the corporate management, for which petitioner is not primarily at fault. Indeed, . . . this court did not even impose those limitations, when it declared that "The Legislature has decided that a vote of a majority of the shares or half of them in case of a deadlock, is sufficient to *force a dissolution*." (Emphasis supplied.) Be that as is may, though, the issue here is, not the propriety of dissolution, but petitioner's right to be heard on that question. . . . In advance of that hearing and in the light of the plain language of section 103, we may not say that dissolution could, under no conceivable set of circumstances, be "beneficial to the stockholders", unless it also appears that it would enable the corporation to avoid pecuniary loss.

Until there has been a hearing, it is impossible to decide that "dissolution is not necessary" or that "there is no stalemate or impasse as to corporate policies." . . . In point of fact, petitioner expressly denies both of these allegations; and, despite respondent's protestations, it is significant that she has not pointed to even one matter on which she and petitioner have agreed. Nor may we take at face value respondent's claim that she is willing to defer to petitioner's business judgment in the future. It is, to say the least, highly implausible that she is willing and even anxious to have her affairs managed by a person whom she has charged with deliberate fraud, conversion and mismanagement. As the court said in *Matter of Yenidje Tobacco Co., Ltd.*[, 1916, 2 Ch. 426] . . . which also involved the dissolution of a deadlocked two-man corporation "when one of the two partners has commenced, and has not discontinued, an action charging his co-partner with fraud . . . is it likely, is it reasonable, is it common sense, to suppose those two partners can work together in the manner in which they ought to work in the conduct of the . . . business?" And, even if it is 'likely' that these two persons, petitioner and respondent, can work together, the issue should not, and may not, be resolved before it has even been heard.

The court's decision seems to compel petitioner to abandon the management of the enterprise as a condition to his seeking dissolution. I find no basis in the statute or elsewhere for requiring that irreparable injury must occur before resort may be had to the remedy designed to avert it.

The order of the Appellate Division should be reversed and that at Special Term affirmed.

## NOTES

**1.** Is the mere fact that you find it difficult to get along with the other shareholder enough for the court to grant dissolution as a remedy?

**2.** Was Mrs. Neidorff being reasonable when she offered to have a third director named by an impartial body?

**3.** Was Mr. Radom's buy-out offer fair?

**4.** Would dissolution here be a fair solution to the problem?

**5.** Why didn't Mr. Radom simply quit and start a competing business?

**6.** Let's assume that Mr. Radom and Mr. Neidorff had formed a partnership for their business rather than a corporation. Would the survivor, Mr. Radom, be better off?

**7.** Let's assume that they had formed an LLC (if they had existed back then). What result?

---

Question 6 and 7 are designed to raise the questions of fragility of form. Corporations endure forever. Their existence is perpetual. That may not be an advantage, as Mr. Radom found out. However, partnerships are much more easily dissolved, and this feature of easy dissolution has both advantages and disadvantages. The basic problem this case presents is that of a disaster that occurred as a result of a lack of planning. Whatever solution might be considered fair could have been placed in an enforceable shareholders' agreement. That is a slight overstatement as of 1954, but certainly at the present date, there are no real obstacles to an enforceable shareholders' agreement. What may have lulled the shareholders into a false sense of security is the 30 years of harmonious relationship between them. It's easy to believe such profitable and harmonious conditions will endure forever. But death strikes down shareholders without notice. Corporations endure, but the perpetual existence granted to the corporate entity is a cruel illusion. The entity continues but not the reasons for having created it.

## F.  STOCK TRANSFER RESTRICTIONS

### RAINMAKER INTERNATIONAL, INC. v. SEAVIEW MEZZANINE FUND, L.P.

United States District Court, Southern District of Georgia
2011 U.S. Dist. LEXIS 22348 (Mar. 2, 2011)

Moore, J.

The pertinent facts of this case are not in dispute. In June 2006, Defendant Studio One entered into an Advisory Agreement with Great Eastern Securities ("GES"). The contract, dated June 2, 2006, provided that GES would supply investment advisory services to Studio One for one year in exchange for 100,000 shares of Studio One stock. The stock certificate provided by Studio One included the following restrictive legend:

> THE SHARES REPRESENTED HEREBY HAVE NOT BEEN REG-ISTERED UNDER THE SECURITIES ACT OF 1933, AS AMENDED, AND MAY NOT BE SOLD, TRANSFERRED, ASSIGNED, PLEDGED, HYPOTHECATED OR OTHERWISE DISPOSED OF UNLESS AND UNTIL REGISTERED UNDER SUCH ACT, OR UNLESS THE COM-PANY HAS RECEIVED AN OPINION OF COUNSEL OR OTHER EVIDENCE, SATISFACTORY TO THE COMPANY AND ITS COUN-SEL, THAT SUCH REGISTRATION IS NOT REQUIRED.

Despite the language of the contract stating that GES would provide these services for one year, Seaview disputes that the agreement was for one year.

Meanwhile in August of 2006, Great Eastern Holdings ("GEH"), of which GES was a wholly owned subsidiary, pledged the Studio One stock to Seaview as collateral for a $1,200,000 loan. As early as December of 2006, GEH was in default on the loan. As a result, Seaview sought to liquidate the Studio One stock to recoup its losses. Seaview delivered the Studio One stock certificate to Rainmaker, which was to assist Seaview in liquidating the stock.

Upon receiving the stock certificate, Rainmaker requested that Studio One remove the restrictive legend to facilitate the liquidation. In response, Studio One informed Rainmaker that GES failed to comply with the restrictive legend when it pledged the stock as collateral, and requested that Rainmaker return the stock to Studio One. Faced with competing claims to the stock certificate, Rainmaker instituted this action in interpleader, naming Seaview and Studio One as Defendants.

In its Motion for Summary Judgment, Seaview argues that it has a perfected security interest in the stock certificate and was without notice of any adverse claim. In its motion, Studio One argues that both GES and Seaview failed to obtain an opinion of counsel that the shares were not required to be registered upon transfer, as required by the restrictive legend. Studio One reasons that this failure invalidates any transfer from GES to Seaview and requires the stock certificate to be returned to Studio One.

## I. CHOICE OF LAW

\* \* \*

A federal court exercising its diversity jurisdiction must apply the choice of law rules applicable to the forum state in which it sits. Under Georgia law, "[t]he rights and duties of the issuer with respect to registration of transfer" are governed by the laws in place within a company's state of incorporation. O.C.G.A. § 11-8-110(a)(2). However, Georgia law also provides that "[t]he local law of the jurisdiction in which a security certificate is located at the time of delivery governs whether an adverse claim can be asserted against a person to whom the security certificate is delivered."

The Georgia statute is taken from the Section 8-110 of the Uniform Commercial Code. The commentary to U.C.C. § 8-110 makes clear that the purpose of the provision is to provide parties a single body of law on matters pertaining to the transfer of a security. Absent this unitary rule, the rights or duties of any party with respect to transfer may depend on an unpredictable and ever shifting set of state laws. This would deprive a corporation the ability to regulate the transfer of its shares by precluding the corporation from selecting a jurisdiction whose laws will allow it to achieve the corporation's desired result. Therefore, § 8-110 makes the law of the issuer's jurisdiction applicable to disputes concerning the rights and duties of parties involved in the transfer of a security.

In this case, both parties are, in part, correct. The Court has identified two primary issues in this case. First, whether Defendant Seaview failed to comply with the restrictive legend on the stock certificate when it accepted the certificate as security for a loan. This issue relates to the rights of an issuer of a security with respect to the security's transfer. Therefore, the Court must apply Delaware law when resolving this issue because the stock was issued by a Delaware corporation-Defendant Studio One.

\* \* \*

For the purposes of ruling on Defendant Studio One's motion, the Court will assume that the legend is an attempted restriction on transferability rather than a Rule 144 legend under 17 C.F.R. § 230.144.

The second issue is whether any failure to abide by the restrictive legend prevented Defendant Seaview from obtaining a valid security interest in the stock free from any adverse claim by Defendant Studio One. This question does not specifically involve the rights of an issuer with respect to the transfer of a security. Rather, this question involves "whether an adverse claim can be asserted against a person to whom the security certificate is delivered." O.C.G.A. § 11-8-110. In resolving this question, the Court must look to New York law because the law of the jurisdiction where the security was delivered governs the ability of a party to assert an adverse claim against the security.

## II. DEFENDANT STUDIO ONE'S MOTION
## FOR SUMMARY JUDGMENT

In its motion for summary judgment, Defendant Studio One argues that Defendant Seaview could not have obtained an interest in the stock because it failed to comply with the restrictive legend. Defendant Studio One reasons that the legend was a contractual restriction on transfer and that, under Delaware law, Defendant Seaview's failure to comply with the legend renders the purported transfer of stock void. In response, Defendant Seaview contends that the legend is required pursuant to 17 C.F.R. § 230.144 and was inapplicable to the transaction between it and GES.

When assessing the merits of Defendant Studio One's motion, the Court, despite having doubts, will accept Defendant Studio One's characterization of the legend as a contractual restriction on the stock certificate's transferability. However, in its attempt to change what appears to the Court to be a regulatory restriction on the transfer of unregistered securities, see 17 C.F.R. § 230.144, into a contractual one, Defendant Studio One overlooked one critical requirement: under Delaware law, a company must be authorized by its articles of incorporation or bylaws to restrict the transfer of its securities. The Delaware code does allow restrictions on the transfer of a corporation's securities, but those restrictions must "be imposed by the certificate of incorporation or by the bylaws" of the company. Furthermore, any restriction imposed by a corporation on the transfer of its stock must be "reasonably necessary to advance the corporation's welfare or attain the objectives set forth in the corporation's charter."

In this case, the Court directed Defendant Studio One to supplement the record with a copy of its articles of incorporation and bylaws in effect at the time the stock was transferred to GES. After conducting a review of those documents, the Court concludes that the purported restriction on transferability is invalid. While the bylaws do state that "[n]o transfer of shares shall be made on the books of this Corporation if such transfer is in violation of a lawful restriction noted conspicuously on the certificate," the bylaws do not specifically provide for the imposition of any particular restriction on transfer. That is, the bylaws fail to define what type of restriction the corporation may place on the stock certificate, only that a transfer in violation of any lawful restriction is void. This type of broad language, which fails to note either the scope or purpose of the restriction, is inoperative as a grant of authority for the corporation to restrict the transferability of its shares. . . . As a result, this argument does not provide a basis to award Defendant Studio One summary judgment.

In actuality, neither the articles of incorporation nor the bylaws contain any restriction at all. Instead, only the bylaws contain a statement that invalidates transfers violative of some other lawfully imposed restriction. However, no specific restrictions are authorized in either the articles or the bylaws.

The problem with Defendant Studio One's argument is that it wants to treat the legend as a contractual restriction on transfer instead of a regulatory restriction under 17 C.F.R. § 230.144. When discussing the legend, Defendant Studio One even cites Del. Code Ann. tit. 8, § 202(a), which grants corporations the power to place restrictions on the transfer of its securities. However, Defendant Studio One turns a blind eye to § 202(b), which requires that the company's articles of incorporation or bylaws grant it the power to impose the specific restriction. Ironically, the bylaws would not have to provide for the imposition of a regulatory restriction on the stock certificate. However, Defendant Studio One presented the legend as a contractual restriction, which the Court has accepted for the purposes of ruling on its motion. As discussed above, the end result is that Defendant Studio One failed to establish its entitlement to summary judgment on this issue. Accordingly, Defendant Studio One's Motion for Summary Judgment is DENIED.

## III. DEFENDANT SEAVIEW'S MOTION FOR SUMMARY JUDGMENT

In its motion, Defendant Seaview argues that it acquired a perfected security interest in the stock certificate prior to any notice that Defendant Studio One may have an adverse claim. In response, Defendant Studio One argues that Defendant Seaview cannot be a bona fide purchaser because it failed to comply with the restrictive legend printed on the stock certificate. In addition to arguing that the transfer was invalid due to Defendant Seaview's failure to comply with the restrictive legend, which the Court has disposed of above, Defendant Studio One also argues that Defendant Seaview would have received notice of the adverse claim if it had complied with the legend. More specifically, Defendant Studio One's contention is that if Defendant Seaview attempted to comply with the legend by providing satisfactory evidence that registration of the transfer was not required, Defendant Studio One would have immediately informed Defendant Seaview of the adverse claim.

In New York, a party may perfect its security interest in a stock certificate by taking delivery of the certificated security. Delivery of a certificated security occurs when a party acquires possession of the certificate. N.Y. U.C.C. § 8-301(a)(1); see id. § 9-313 ("A secured party may perfect a security interest in certificated securities by taking delivery of the certificated securities under Section 8-301."). Should a party enforce its security interest, it becomes a "purchaser" of the certificated security. See N.Y. U.C.C. § 1-201(32) to (33). When a party becomes a purchaser of the stock certificate, it is protected from adverse claims if the following three conditions have been met: (1) the purchaser gave value; (2) the purchaser obtained control of the certificated security; and (3) the purchaser had no notice of the adverse claim. Id. § 8-303.

There are two scenarios in which a purchaser obtains knowledge of an adverse claim. The purchaser obtains actual knowledge of the adverse claim. Absent actual knowledge, the purchaser could be "aware of facts sufficient to indicate that there is a significant probability that the adverse claim exists and deliberately avoids information that would establish the existence of the adverse claim," otherwise known as willful blindness. Under the willful blindness test, a party has notice of an adverse claim if it is "aware of facts sufficient to indicate that there is a significant probability that an adverse claim exists and deliberately avoids information that might establish the existence of the adverse claim."

In this case, the dispute concerns whether Defendant Seaview had notice of Defendant Studio One's adverse claim to the stock certificate. Both sides agree that Defendant Seaview did not have actual knowledge of any adverse claim. Therefore, the penultimate issue is whether Defendant Seaview was "aware of facts sufficient to indicate that there is a significant probability that an adverse claim exists and deliberately avoids information that might establish the existence of the adverse claim." In its response to Defendant Seaview's motion, Defendant Studio One contends that "[t]he conspicuous restrictive legend on the face of the stock certificate is surely enough to arouse suspicion."

After considering Defendant Studio One's argument, the Court does not agree and holds that, as a matter of law, the restrictive legend on the stock certificate did not give Defendant Seaview notice of any adverse claim. Unlike a true restriction on transferability, the legend in this case only requires the transferee to either obtain an opinion of counsel or provide information satisfactory to Defendant Studio One that the stock is not required to be registered under the Securities Act of 1933. It is difficult for this Court to comprehend how a legend regarding registration would give Defendant Seaview notice of any adverse claim to the stock, much less that there was a significant probability that GES failed to fulfill its contract with Defendant Studio One.

The Court is willing to accept Defendant Studio One's notion that if Defendant Seaview had contacted it about the inapplicability of registration, Defendant Studio One would have informed Defendant Seaview of its potential claim to the stock in question. However, this is not the proper focal point for testing willful blindness. For Defendant Seaview to be found willfully blind, it must have been "aware of facts sufficient to indicate that there [was] a significant probability that an adverse claim exist[ed] and deliberately avoid[ed] information that might establish [its] existence." It is not enough that there existed circumstances that, in and of themselves, would have inevitably led a party to discover an adverse claim. Rather, the test requires that the circumstances themselves would make a party aware that there exists a significant probability that someone may have an adverse claim over the stock. A legend regarding regis-tration requirements, standing alone, fails to rise to that level. Because the Court finds that there are no disputes of material fact, Defendant Seaview's Motion for Summary Judgment is GRANTED.

The Court pauses at this point to note that there is no evidence in the record that Defendant Studio One ever asserted this adverse claim against anyone other than Defendant Seaview. Importantly, the record makes no mention that Defendant Studio One either requested return of the stock from or filed a breach of contract action against GES, which was in bankruptcy. Taking this into account, the Court cannot help but observe that this case appears to be a clever attempt by Defendant Studio One to avoid the roadblocks to recovery presented by GES's bankruptcy, as evinced by the many questions that a ruling in its favor would present. For example, if the transfer restriction was breached, why would the remedy be the return of the stock to Defendant Studio One rather than GES? Also, is the correct remedy for GES's alleged breach the return of the stock or money damages? In any event, the Court has ruled on these motions according to its understanding of the law, despite its disapprobation concerning Defendant Studio One's apparent end run around GES's bankruptcy.

The cases Defendant Studio One uses to support its position are unavailing. Plaintiff relies on *Carr v. Marietta Corp.*, 211 F.3d 724 (2d Cir. 2000), for the proposition that a restrictive legend on a stock certificate denotes suspicious circumstances, requiring the party seeking to acquire the certificate to diligently investigate the possibility of adverse claims to the stock. In *Carr*, the plaintiff's brother had received stock from the defendant, a prior employer, as part of a stock purchase agreement. The stock certificate contained a two part restrictive legend that permitted the shares to be reacquired by the defendant, and prohibited transfer unless it is registered under the Securities Act of 1933 or exempt from registration. However, the plaintiff's brother never paid the full consideration called for in the agreement. Yet, the brother pledged the stock as collateral for a loan obtained from a third party, on which he later defaulted . . . . The lender attempted to tender the shares to the defendant pursuant to a stock buyback program. The defendant, however, refused to repurchase the shares because the defendant never fully paid for them. Eventually, the plaintiff purchased the lender's rights against her brother and brought suit against the defendant to force it to repurchase the shares. Id. In rejecting the plaintiff's argument that she took possession of the stock without notice of any adverse claim, the court concluded that she had been willfully ignorant of several facts indicating the presence of an adverse claim.

*Carr*, however, will not support the great weight Defendant Studio One places on it. While the court did note that the plaintiff "admitted that she read the restrictive legend appearing on the face of the share certificate and was aware that it constituted a restriction on the transferability of the shares," it also cited five other reasons why the plaintiff should have been aware of the defendant's adverse claim, including "obtain[ing] the shares with full knowledge that the transfer agent had refused to repurchase the shares . . . on a prior occasion," the knowledge that her brother was indebted to the defendant, and the fact that she purchased a total of $132,633.62 in judgments for $27,500. In short, the court in *Carr* identified much more than just a restrictive legend that, when viewed in the totality, indicated that the plaintiff "engaged in a purposeful effort to avoid knowing that her brother failed to pay for the stock. In this case, Defendant Studio One relies solely on the restrictive legend when arguing that Defendant Seaview was willfully blind to the adverse claim. This fact alone easily distinguishes *Carr* from this case.

Defendant Studio One points out that GES was fined by the National Association of Securities Dealers ("NASD"). In addition, Defendant Studio One states that the representative of GES assigned to advise Defendant Studio One under the contract was suspended by the NASD. Importantly, Defendant Studio One only alleges that these events occurred, not that Defendant Seaview knew about them. Further, the Court does not find it unreasonable that Defendant Seaview would forego a thorough investigation of each GES employee's status with professional associations and GES's past contractual agreements. Absent knowledge of these circumstances by Defendant Seaview, the fact that they exist is woefully insufficient to establish that Defendant Seaview was willfully blind to any default by GES.

Similarly, Defendant Studio One's reliance on *Drexel Burnham Lambert Group, Inc. v. Galadari*, 1987 U.S. Dist. LEXIS 5030, 1987 WL 6164 (S.D.N.Y. Jan. 29, 1987), is also misplaced. In *Drexel*, the court determined that a restrictive legend on a stock certificate, which prohibited any transfer of the stock absent approval by the corporation's board of directors, would give notice of a potential adverse claim. But again, in *Drexel* the restrictive legend was one of several factors the court highlighted in determining whether the plaintiff had notice of an adverse claim. The court also pointed out that the stock transfer lacked a proper endorsement, and that there was a discrepancy between the signature on the stock registration and other documents. Indeed, the court noted that the plaintiff did not qualify as a protected purchaser in light "of the existence of several indications of adverse claims." In this case, the restrictive legend is not a strict prohibition on transfer absent board approval. Also, there are not several indications of an adverse claim in this case. As discussed above, the Court finds that, as a matter of law, the restrictive legend by itself did not place Defendant Seaview on notice of a significant probability of adverse claims.

*   *   *

For the foregoing reasons, Defendant Seaview's Motion for Summary Judgment is GRANTED and Defendant Studio One's Motion for Summary Judgment is DENIED. The Clerk of Court is DIRECTED to release the 100,000 shares of Studio One stock held in this Court's registry to defendant Seaview and to close this case.

## FRANDSEN v. JENSEN-SUNDQUIST AGENCY, INC.
### United States Court of Appeals, Seventh Circuit
### 802 F.2d 941 (1986)

POSNER, J.

The appeals in this diversity suit require us to consider issues of Wisconsin contract and tort law in the setting of a dispute over the rights of a minority shareholder in a closely held corporation. The facts are as follows. In 1975 Walter Jensen owned all the stock of Jensen-Sundquist Agency, Inc., a holding company whose principal asset was a majority of the stock of the First Bank of Grantsburg; Jensen-Sundquist also owned a small insurance company. That year Jensen sold 52 percent of his stock in the holding company to members of his family — the "majority bloc," as we shall call them and the interest they acquired; 8 percent to Dennis Frandsen, a substantial businessman who was not a member of Jensen's family and who paid Jensen $97,000 for the stock; and the rest, in smaller chunks, to other non-family members. By a stockholder agreement drafted by Jensen and a lawyer representing the bank and Jensen's family, the majority bloc agreed "that should they at any time offer to sell their stock in Jensen-Sundquist, Inc., . . . they will first offer their stock to [Frandsen and six other minority shareholders who had negotiated for this provision] at the same price as may be offered to [the majority bloc] . . . and . . . they will not sell their stock to any other person, firm, or organization without first offering said stock" to these minority shareholders "at the same price and upon the same terms." The majority bloc also agreed not to "sell any of their shares to anyone without at the same time offering to purchase all the shares of" these minority shareholders "at the same price." Thus if the majority bloc offered to sell its shares it had to give Frandsen a right to buy the shares at the offer price. If Frandsen declined, the second protective provision came into play: the majority bloc had to offer to buy his shares at the same price at which it sold its own shares.

In 1984 the president of Jensen-Sundquist began discussions with First Wisconsin Corporation, Wisconsin's largest bank holding company, looking to the acquisition by First Wisconsin of First Bank of Grantsburg, Jensen-Sundquist's principal property. A price of $88 per share of stock in the First Bank of Grantsburg was agreed to in principle. The acquisition was to be effected (we simplify slightly) by First Wisconsin's buying Jensen-Sundquist for cash, followed by a merger of First Bank of Grantsburg into a bank subsidiary of First Wisconsin. Each stockholder of Jensen-Sundquist would receive $62 per share, which would translate into $88 per share of the bank. (The reasons that the share values were not the same were that there were more holding company shares than bank shares and that the holding company had another asset besides the bank — the insurance company.) Jensen-Sundquist asked each of the minority shareholders to sign a waiver of any rights he "may have" in the transaction, rights arising from the stockholder agreement, but advised each shareholder that in counsel's opinion the shareholder had no rights other than to receive $62 per share.

Each of the minority shareholders except Frandsen signed or was expected to sign the waiver. Frandsen not only refused to sign but announced that he was exercising his right of first refusal and would buy the majority bloc's shares at $62 a share. (He also offered to buy out the other minority shareholders.) The majority did not want to sell its shares to him — Frandsen says because the president of Jensen-Sundquist, who was also the chairman of the board of First Bank of Grantsburg and a member of the majority bloc, was afraid he would lose his job if Frandsen took over. The deal was restructured. Jensen-Sundquist agreed to sell its shares in First Bank of Grantsburg to First Wisconsin at $88 a share and then liquidate, so that in the end all the stockholders would end up with cash plus the insurance company and First Wisconsin would end up with the bank, which was all it had ever wanted out of the deal. All this was done over Frandsen's protest. He then brought this suit against the majority bloc, charging breach of the stockholder agreement, and against First Wisconsin, charging tortious interference with his contract rights. The district judge granted summary judgment for the defendants and Frandsen appeals.

The interpretation of an unambiguous contract is a question of law. . . . When, however, the meaning of a contract is inscrutable without oral evidence — evidence for example on the meaning of terms that the contract does not use in their ordinary dictionary senses — there must be a trial, and the issue of interpretation gets resolved by the jury. . . . Frandsen was therefore entitled to a trial on his breach of contract claim if but only if the stockholder agreement was not clear enough for the judge to be able to decide, on the basis of the agreement itself and the undisputed background facts, whether Frandsen's right of first refusal had been violated.

The case would be easy if the transaction had been structured from the start as a simple acquisition by First Wisconsin of First Bank of Grantsburg from Jensen-Sundquist. Nothing in the stockholder agreement suggests that any minority shareholder has the right to block the sale by Jensen-Sundquist of any of its assets, including its principal asset, a controlling interest in First Bank of Grantsburg. The right of first refusal is a right to buy the shares of the majority bloc in Jensen-Sundquist if they are offered for sale, and there would be no offer of sale if Jensen-Sundquist simply sold some or for that matter all of its assets and became an investment company instead of a bank holding company. Nor did the contract entitle Frandsen to insist that the deal be configured so as to trigger his right of first refusal. . . .

The case is a little harder because the transaction was originally configured as a purchase of the holding company rather than just of the bank, an asset of the holding company. . . . And Frandsen points out that under the stockholder agreement his right of first refusal was triggered by an offer, so that the fact the offer was later withdrawn would not affect his right of first refusal if he had already tried to exercise it — and he had tried, before the defendants reconfigured the transaction. But the point is academic, because we agree with the district judge that there never was an offer within the scope of the agreement. The part of the agreement that grants a right of first refusal refers to an offer to sell "their stock," and to a sale of "their stock," and the "their" refers to the majority shareholders. They never offered to sell their stock to First Wisconsin. First Wisconsin was not interested in becoming a majority shareholder of Jensen-Sundquist, in owning an insurance company, and in dealing with Frandsen and the other minority shareholders. It just wanted the bank.

What is more, a sale of stock was never contemplated, again for the reason that First Wisconsin was not interested in becoming a shareholder of Jensen-Sundquist. The transaction originally contemplated was a merger of Jensen-Sundquist into First Wisconsin. In a merger, as the word implies, the acquired firm disappears as a distinct legal entity. . . . In effect, the shareholders of the merged firm yield up all of the assets of the firm, receiving either cash or securities in exchange, and the firm dissolves. In this case the shareholders would have received cash. Their shares would have disappeared but not by sale, for in a merger the shares of the acquired firm are not bought, they are extinguished. There would have been no Jensen-Sundquist after the merger, and no shareholders in Jensen-Sundquist.

The distinction between a sale of shares and a merger is such a familiar one in the business world that it is unbelievable that so experienced a businessman as Frandsen would have overlooked it. It is true that he was not represented by a lawyer in connection with the stockholder agreement, but when an experienced businessman deliberately eschews legal assistance in making a contract he cannot by doing so obtain a legal advantage over a represented party should a dispute arise.

Nor are we persuaded by Frandsen's argument that if interpreted literally the stockholder agreement gave him no right of first refusal worthy of the name. It is true that under that interpretation if as happened the majority bloc did not want to sell out to him, all it had to do was find a merger partner. But these alternatives are not identical in all but form, as he argues. The majority bloc was only 52 percent. If the majority wanted to sell its stock to someone who wanted a controlling interest in the company rather than the company itself or an asset of the company such as the First Bank of Grantsburg, it had to offer its shares to Frandsen first (and to the other six minority shareholders who had a right of first refusal — what would have happened if all had exercised their right we need not speculate about). If it wanted to bypass Frandsen it had to find someone willing to buy not just its shares, but the company.

Most important, Frandsen may have been concerned not with a sale of the company itself at a price agreeable to a majority and therefore likely to be attractive to him as well, but with a sale of the majority bloc that would leave him a minority shareholder in a company owned by strangers. The lot of a minority shareholder in a closely held company is not an enviable one, even in the best of circumstances. A majority coalition may gang up on him. And he may not have the usual recourse of a victimized minority shareholder — to sell out. For there may be no market for his shares, except the very people who have ganged up on him. . . . William A. Gregory, *Stock Transfer Restrictions in Close Corporations*, 1978 So. Ill. U.L.J. 477. Frandsen may just have wanted to protect himself against being put at the mercy of a new and perhaps hostile majority bloc. The right of first refusal was one protection against this danger.

Against this Frandsen argues that the right of first refusal must have had an additional purpose, for otherwise it would merely have duplicated the second protective provision in the stockholder agreement, which guaranteed that the majority bloc if it sold its shares would offer to buy his shares at the same price. It is true that this provision protected Frandsen against finding himself a minority shareholder in a company controlled by persons other than the members of the original majority bloc, but it did so at the price of forcing him to leave the company. The right of first refusal enabled him to remain in the company by buying out the majority bloc at the same price that the bloc was willing to sell its shares to others. It thus gave him additional protection. It did not give him protection against a sale of the company itself but this does not make the agreement incoherent or unclear, for his only concern may have been with the possibility of finding himself confronted with a new majority bloc, and that is the only possibility he may have thought it important to negotiate with reference to.

We note in this connection that Frandsen himself had once taken over a bank by paying a premium to a majority of shareholders and then, after he acquired control in this way, buying out the minority shareholders at a lower price. Evidently he wanted to make sure that no one did this to him in Jensen-Sundquist by buying the majority bloc and then making life uncomfortable for him and the other minority shareholders so that they would sell their shares on the cheap. The stockholder agreement that he negotiated with Jensen was well designed to protect him against a maneuver that he had practiced himself. The defendants' efforts to get Frandsen to sign a waiver do not as he argues establish a practical construction of the stockholder agreement as entitling him to exercise his right of first refusal in the event of a proposed merger. A waiver is like a quitclaim deed: the signer waives whatever rights he may have, but does not warrant that he has any rights to waive.

Frandsen's principal argument is that the word "sell" is sufficiently ambiguous to embrace a disposition that has the same practical effect as a sale of the majority bloc's shares. This may be; *Wilson v. Whinery*, 37 Wash. App. 24, 28–29, 678 P.2d 354, 357 (1984), held that a transfer of all beneficial use of parcel B, "thereby granting [the transferee] substantial control over parcel B," was a sale of B for purposes of a right of first refusal triggered by such a sale. But our main point has been that a sale of the majority bloc's shares is not the same thing as a sale of either all or some of the holding company's assets. The sale of assets does not result in substituting a new majority bloc, and that is the possibility at which the protective provisions are aimed. This appears with sufficient clarity, moreover, to justify the district judge's refusal to go outside the text of the contract to find its meaning.

Any lingering doubts of the propriety of this course are dispelled by the rule that rights of first refusal are to be interpreted narrowly. . . . This may seem to be one of those fusty "canons of construction" that invite ridicule because they have no basis and contradict each other and are advanced simply as rhetorical flourishes to embellish decisions reached on other, more practical grounds. *See, e.g.*, Llewellyn, *The Common Law Tradition: Deciding Appeals 521–35 (1960); Note, Intent, Clear Statements and the Common Law: Statutory Interpretation in the Supreme Court*, 95 HARV. L. REV. 892 (1982). But actually it makes some sense. The effect of a right of first refusal is to add a party to a transaction, for the right is triggered by an offer of sale, and the effect is therefore to inject the holder of the right into the sale transaction. Adding a party to a transaction increases the costs of transacting exponentially; the formula for the number of links required to connect up all the members of an n-member set is $n(n-1)/2$, meaning that, for example, increasing the number of parties to a transaction from three to four increases the number of required linkages from three to six. Certainly the claim of a right of first refusal complicated the transaction here! If all the costs of the more complicated transaction were borne by the parties, it would hardly be a matter of social concern. But some of the costs are borne by the taxpayers who support the court system, and the courts are not enthusiastic about this, and have decided not to be hospitable to such rights. The right is enforceable but only if the contract clearly confers it.

In any event this rule of interpretation is well established in Wisconsin and hence beyond our power to question in this diversity case; and it reinforces the conclusion that Frandsen's right of first refusal was not triggered by a proposal to merge Jensen-Sundquist into First Wisconsin, and even more clearly not by the actual transaction, whereby First Wisconsin bought Jensen-Sundquist's bank and Jensen-Sundquist then liquidated. Although we find no Wisconsin case on point (thus necessitating this extended analysis), a number of cases from other jurisdictions hold that a sale of the corporation's assets does not trigger a right of first refusal applicable to the corporation's stock.

One case gives us pause. *McCarthy v. Osborn*, 65 So.2d 776, 223 La. 305 (1953), held that a sale of a corporation violated the plaintiff's right of first refusal (a right conditioned as in this case on a sale of the corporation's shares, not assets), since the effect of the sale was to convey the stock as well as assets of the corporation. What happened here was the sale by the corporation (Jensen-Sundquist) of its asset, the First Bank of Grantsburg, a sale that left Jensen-Sundquist, and Frandsen's stock in Jensen-Sundquist, intact, followed by Jensen-Sundquist's liquidating, which left Frandsen with cash, thus in a sense accomplishing in two steps what the defendants in *McCarthy v. Osborn* had accomplished in one. But nothing in Frandsen's right of first refusal was intended to protect him against liquidation. As we have stressed, the danger against which the right protected him was that the majority bloc might be sold to a new majority, leaving him a minority shareholder confronted by persons whom he might distrust. Liquidation eliminated that danger. If the distinction seems somewhat formalistic, this is an area of law where formalitites are important, as they are the method by which sophisticated businessmen make their contractual rights definite and limit the authority of the courts to redo their deal.

\*    \*    \*

If as we believe no contractual right of Frandsen's was violated by the transaction, it is more than difficult to see how First Wisconsin could have been guilty of a tortious interference with his contractual rights.

\*    \*    \*

In cases where no breach of contract results from the interference, the tort is really a branch of the law of unfair competition, and it is necessary for liability that the alleged tortfeasor have gone beyond the accepted norms of fair competition. For First Wisconsin to want to acquire First Bank of Grantsburg from Jensen-Sundquist and to make suggestions for how the sale could be carried out in a way that would violate nobody's legal rights would not violate the norms of fair competition; it would exemplify them.

The district judge correctly dismissed all of Frandsen's claims.

AFFIRMED.

# NOTE

Frandsen and six other minority shareholders had negotiated for a right of first refusal. The majority in effect agreed that before they sold their stock to any other person they would first offer it to Frandsen and the others at the same price and terms. The court concluded that the contract right did not cover the merger transaction even if the merger had practically the identical economic effect. Do you agree with the court's decision? The court states that rights of first refusal are narrowly construed. Is that a sensible rule of law? Restrictions on the rights to sell stock derive from the basic property rule that limits restraints on alienation. Does that doctrine, developed in the area of real property, make sense with personal property?

## G. SPECIAL PROBLEMS OF LITIGATION (DIRECT OR DERIVATIVE)

When a minority shareholder in a closely held corporation is the victim of a freeze out or other form of oppression, judicial formalism is an obstacle to obtaining a remedy. Some courts apply the business judgment rule, and deny any remedy to the oppressed shareholder. Another obstacle is the form of the lawsuit. Although most derivative lawsuits involve publicly held corporations, some courts reason that the derivative suit with all of its procedural obstacles is the only remedy for the oppressed shareholder. The two most common ways to avoid this result are first, to find that the injury done to the shareholder was a direct injury, and therefore, the shareholder's lawsuit can proceed, or second, that even if the suit is considered to be derivative in nature, that an exception exists to permit some flexibility in the rules that might ordinarily apply in derivative litigation. The following case provides a good discussion of the issues involved in this type of controversy.

## LANDSTROM v. SHAVER
### Supreme Court of South Dakota
### 561 N.W.2d 1 (1997)

GILBERTSON, J.

This case involves both legal and equitable claims asserted by Jo Landstrom [hereinafter Landstrom], a minority shareholder, in Black Hills Jewelry Manufacturing Company [hereinafter BHJMC]. Her suit is against the remaining shareholders in BHJMC, Milt Shaver [hereinafter Shaver], Jack Devereaux [hereinafter Devereaux], and Constance Drew [hereinafter Drew]. The case was tried on an equitable claim of shareholder oppression and legal claims of breach of fiduciary duty, tortious interference with prospective economic advantage, negligent misrepresentation and negligence. The equitable and legal claims were tried simultaneously with a jury rendering a verdict for Landstrom on the legal claims and an advisory verdict in favor of Landstrom on the equitable claim. Thereafter the trial court entered findings of fact and conclusions of law in favor of Landstrom on the equitable claim consistent with the advisory verdict of the jury.

The jury found Shaver, Devereaux and Drew intentionally interfered with Landstrom's business relations and expectancies by failure to either sell the stock of all the shareholders or allow Landstrom to sell her stock. Damages were determined to be $10 million apportioned by the jury to be paid 40% by Shaver and 30% each by Devereaux and Drew. The jury found that Shaver breached his fiduciary duty by failing to disclose a veto provision in a 1987 buy-sell agreement. It awarded damages of $4 million. The jury also found that Shaver, Devereaux and Drew breached their fiduciary duty to Landstrom by refusing to properly direct BHJMC. It awarded $4 million in damages, apportioned 40% against Shaver, 30% against Devereaux, and 30% against Drew. The jury further found Shaver negligently misrepresented to Landstrom the 1987 revisions in the buy-sell agreement and awarded damages at $3 million. However this award was later determined by the trial court to be duplicative with the award of breach of fiduciary duty by Shaver and therefore was remitted. The jury found that Shaver, Devereaux and Drew were negligent by "failing to properly direct the company" but determined that no additional damages had been proved. Thus, after the post-trial proceedings, damages were awarded at $18 million on the legal claims.

The trial court further entered a judgment that appropriate relief on the equitable claim would be for Devereaux and Drew to purchase Landstrom's minority interest in BHJMC for $8.4 million. We affirm in part and reverse in part.

\*    \*    \*

We conclude that under either the reasonable expectations test or the burdensome, harsh and wrongful conduct test, as a matter of law, Landstrom has failed to establish oppression. All she has established is that she was outvoted and subjectively disappointed with corporate management. There are none of the traditional hallmarks of action by majority shareholders which have been held to constitute oppression. We are unwilling to elevate subjective minority shareholder dissatisfaction to constitute oppression.

3. Did the trial court err in allowing Landstrom to proceed directly against the individual shareholders rather than requiring a derivative action?

The majority rule is that an action to redress injuries to a corporation cannot be maintained by a shareholder on an individual basis but must be brought derivatively. . . . The generally recognized rule for determining whether a cause of action belongs to the corporation, rather than to an individual shareholder, is to ascertain whether "the injury to each stockholder is of the same character." *Arent v. Distribution Sciences, Inc.* 975 F.2d 1370, 1372 (8th Cir. 1992).[3] In other words, under the general rule, for a shareholder to maintain an individual action, the shareholder must establish a "special injury" which is separate and distinct from that of other shareholders. *Cowin v. Bresler*, 741 F.2d 410, 415 (D.C. Cir. 1984); *Engstrand [v. West Des Moines State Bank]*, 516 N.W.2d [797 (Iowa 1994)] at 799; *Myerson [v. Coopers & Lybrand]*, 448 N.W.2d [129 (1989)] at 133. Diminution in the value of stock is a loss that is sustained by all shareholders and thus subject to the derivative action requirement.

This Court has followed this general rule on two occasions. In *Glover v. Manila Gold Mine & Mill. Co.*, 19 S.D. 559, 104 N.W. 261 (S.D. 1905), we held the plaintiff's claim of an individual judgment was not appropriate as the plaintiff had alleged the damages accrued to the corporation and not individually to himself:

The right of stockholders to bring such an action is clearly sustained by the decision of this court in the case of *Loftus v. Farmers' Shipping Ass'n*, 8 S.D. 201, 65 N.W. 1076, in which this court held that stockholders of a corporation may bring an action on behalf of the corporation against its directors, who by their fraudulent management and conduct of the business of the corporation are fraudulently and intentionally so conducting the business of the same as to depreciate the value of the stockholders' interest therein, and in effect to deprive them of their property.

\* \* \*

In *Jepsen v. Peterson*, 69 S.D. 388, 10 N.W.2d 749, 750 (S.D. 1943), we again recognized the derivative rule with a limited exception. This exception provides that "if a corporation refuses to prosecute an action in its favor, equity to prevent a failure of justice disregards the corporate entity and permits suit to be brought and maintained by a stockholder to protect rights beneficially belonging to him. The right exists because of special injury to him." The burden of proof would fall upon

---

[3] [13] In *Thomas v. Dickson*, 250 Ga. 772, 301 S.E.2d 49, 51 (1983) the court stated there were four reasons to justify this general rule: (1) it prevents a multiplicity of lawsuits by shareholders; (2) it protects corporate creditors by putting the proceeds of the recovery back in the corporation; (3) it protects the interests of all shareholders by increasing the value of their shares, instead of allowing a recovery by one shareholder to prejudice the rights of others not a party to the suit; and (4) it adequately compensates the injured shareholder by increasing the value of the shareholder's shares.

the shareholder to establish that such "special injury" did indeed exist.

\* \* \*

A minority of courts now permit that when a minority shareholder in a close corporation brings claims alleging wrongdoing by the majority shareholders, the claims are not automatically held to be brought derivatively.

\* \* \*

> The derivative-direct distinction makes little sense when the only interested parties are two individuals or sets of shareholders, one who is in control and the other who is not. In this context, the debate over derivative status can become 'purely technical.' There is no practical need to insist on derivative suits when there is little likelihood of a multiplicity of suits or harm to creditors. Any recovery in a derivative suit would return funds to the control of the defendant, rather than to the injured party. In some of these traditional derivative claims brought as direct actions, courts focus on the disproportionate impact of the challenged corporate actions. For example, when assets are alleged to be sold to insiders at inadequate prices, only the minority shareholders bear the loss and the majority receives any benefits in their capacity as purchasers.

O'Neal & Thompson, O'NEAL'S CLOSE CORPORATIONS, § 8.16 at 103 (3d ed. 1994).

The trial court followed Barth's adoption of the American Law Institute's proposed rule for determining when a shareholder in a closely-held corporation may proceed by direct, rather than derivative action.

> In the case of a closely-held corporation, the court in its discretion may treat an action raising derivative claims as a direct action, exempt it from those restrictions and defenses applicable only to derivative actions, and order an individual recovery, if it finds that to do so will not (i) unfairly expose the corporation or the defendants to a multiplicity of actions, (ii) materially prejudice the interests of creditors of the corporation, or (iii) interfere with a fair distribution of the recovery among all interested persons.

*Barth* [*v. Barth*], 659 N.E.2d [559 (Ind. 1995)] at 562 (quoting ALI, Principles of Corporate Governance § 701(d)).

Applying the above criteria to the facts in this case, the trial court found: (1) that requiring a derivative action might result in a distribution to BHJMC and the shareholders which was inequitable as Landstrom is suing the only other shareholders who would then participate in the majority of the relief should Landstrom prevail; (2) that allowing a direct action against the Defendant shareholders would not expose BHJMC to multiple suits, but would rather tend to reduce the potential for multiple litigation; and (3) that there was no indication that a direct action would materially prejudice any interests of any creditors or inhibit BHJMC's ability to continue doing business. An additional consideration recognized by the trial court was that there would be an equitable cause of action by Landstrom in her personal capacity against the Defendants for oppression.

Defendants attack the ALI minority rule as posing great potential for abuse of a corporation and its majority shareholders by a disgruntled minority shareholder. Their point is not without merit. A minority shareholder in a close corporation may have different goals than a majority. A dispute over maximization of short-term profits as against the long-term financial health and growth of the corporation is an obvious example.[4] Here, there was evidence presented in the record of this case that BHJMC has suffered financially because of the effect this litigation has had upon it. Thus, we must weigh the interests of the corporation and its majority and minority shareholders, creditors and its employees in determining what is an appropriate balance of each parties' rights.

We have given careful consideration to the case law cited by both Landstrom and the Defendants in support of their opposing positions on this issue. We conclude that given our case law and that of other jurisdictions, it is the better course to continue to follow the majority rule and not adopt the ALI proposed rule. The basis for this rationale is well set forth by *Bagdon v. Bridgestone/Firestone, Inc.*, 916 F.2d 379, 384 (7th Cir. 1990) *cert. denied*, 500 U.S. 952, 111 S.Ct. 2257, 114 L.Ed.2d 710 (1991), where the court criticized the concept behind the ALI rule finding the rule was an ill-advised attempt at removing the distinctions of the structure of a close corporation and that of a partnership:

> The premise of this extension may be questioned. Corporations are not partnerships. Whether to incorporate entails a choice of many formalities. Commercial rules should be predictable; this objective is best served by treating corporations as what they are, allowing the investors and other participants to vary the rule by contract if they think deviations are warranted. So it is understandable that not all states have joined the [ALI] parade. (emphasis original).

Landstrom seeks the best of both business entities: limited liability provided by a corporate structure and direct compensation for corporate losses. "That cushy position is not one the law affords. Investors who created the corporate form cannot rend the veil they wove." *Kagan v. Edison Bros. Stores, Inc.*, 907 F.2d 690, 693 (7th Cir. 1990). Recovery by the corporation ensures that all of the corporate participants-stockholders, trade creditors, employees and others will recover according to their contractual and statutory obligations. *Kagan*, 907 F.2d at 692. We have consistently held that a corporation is an entity separate and distinct from its shareholders.

The ALI rule does not include all relevant considerations concerning the type of dispute now before us. A significant defect is that it fails to address whether a derivative suit can suffice to adequately compensate the injured shareholder. Daniel S. Kleinberger and Imanta Bergmanis, *Direct vs. Derivative, or What's a Lawsuit Between Friends in an "Incorporated Partnership?"* 22 Wm Mitchell L Rev 1203,

---

[4] [16] South Dakota is a state that contains substantial numbers of small corporations given the number of independently owned businesses and farms. Those who operate and manage these farms and businesses, often the majority shareholders, should not be subject to the demands of minority shareholders whose concern may be solely that of dividends and not the farm or business itself. Many of these small corporations and their management are ill-prepared to invest the time and money required to fend off a minority shareholder suit and are therefore influenced by the mere threat of such litigation.

1265 n.315 (1996). Since that is the ultimate goal should the plaintiff prevail on the evidentiary burden, this flaw seriously weakens the benefit from an adoption of the rule.

Beyond the policy considerations, which do not support an adoption of the ALI rule in South Dakota, when one applies the ALI criteria to the facts of this case, it is also found wanting. The first criterion to supposedly guide the trial court's discretion is whether invocation of the rule will unfairly expose the corporation or the defendants to a multiplicity of actions. In reality, this provided no guidance to the trial court in this action as all shareholders and the corporation were already parties to the suit. This apparently is a common occurrence in ALI cases.

The second criterion is whether adoption of the rule will materially prejudice the interests of creditors of the corporation. Given BHJMC's recent financial tailspin, the confidence of the creditors in BHJMC to survive this condition and meet its financial obligations in the future would be best served by paying the millions awarded as damages, to BHJMC rather than individually to Landstrom, if there were a basis to award damages in the first place.

Finally, there is the question of whether requiring a derivative action might result in an unfair distribution of the recovery among all interested persons. A key reason the trial court permitted Landstrom to pursue an individual action was:

> that requiring a derivative action might result in a distribution to BHJMC and the shareholders which was inequitable as Landstrom is suing the only other shareholders who would then participate in the majority of the relief should Landstrom prevail.

This reasoning is flawed. In a derivative suit, the defendants pay to the corporation the total damages occasioned by their wrongful conduct. The value of a plaintiff's shares are increased according to the percentage of stock owned. This provides no windfall to the defendants as they are paying the total amount of damages. When defendants pay the total amount of damages out of one pocket to restore the corporation to its original value, the fact that the value of their own stock is also returned to the predamage level does not put the same amount of money in the individual defendant's other pocket.[5]

The diminution in value of a stockholder's investment is a concommitant of the corporate injuries resulting in lost profits. A fortiori, any redress obtained by the corporations would run to the benefit of their stockholders, and to permit the latter to proceed with those claims would permit a double recovery.

The end result of the ALI rule may be what occurred here, the majority shareholders are forced by litigation (or even in some cases, the threat of it) to buy out the minority shareholders' shares "which corporate law rarely if ever requires."

---

[5] [17] As an example, assume total damages to a corporation are $100,000. The defendants pay $100,000 out of one pocket to the corporation. Assuming also that there are three equal shareholders one who is the plaintiff and the other two the defendants, the value of the plaintiff's stock is restored to its predamage value by adding $33,333.33. The fact that the value of the defendants' stock is also returned to its predamage level by adding $66,666.66 does not put $100,000 in defendants' other pocket, nor detract from the plaintiff's full recovery of the original value of plaintiff's stock.

*Frank v. Hadesman & Frank, Inc.*, 83 F.3d 158, 162 (7th Cir. 1996) (criticizing the proposed ALI rule). For all of the above reasons we decline to adopt the ALI rule.[6]

An alternate basis for upholding the individual verdict for Landstrom would be to show she sustained a special injury. This special injury must be separate and distinct from the injury suffered by other shareholders, not injury separate and distinct from an injury suffered by the corporation. With the evidentiary failure to establish her individual causes of action, her claim for special injury must fail. As such, it was error for the trial court to allow Landstrom individual recovery rather than to pursue a derivative claim against the defendants for failure to properly direct BHJMC. Thus, the verdict for $4 million against the defendants for failure to properly direct the corporation must be reversed.

*       *       *

5. Did Shaver breach a fiduciary duty to Landstrom by failing to disclose the veto power provision in the 1987 revision to the 1977 buy-sell agreement?

Shaver appeals the jury's award to Landstrom of $4 million against him for finding that he breached a fiduciary duty to Landstrom by failing to disclose to her the insertion of the veto provision in the 1987 amendments to the 1977 buy-sell agreement.

The existence of a fiduciary duty and the scope of that duty are questions of law for the trial court. *Garrett v. BankWest, Inc.*, 459 N.W.2d 833, 839 (S.D. 1990). In *Case [v. Murdock*, 488 N.W.2d (S.D. 1992),] at 890, we held that directors of a corporation occupy a fiduciary position in respect to the corporation and its shareholders, and as such are required to exercise the utmost good faith in all transactions pertaining to a director's duty.

We are persuaded by the trial court's findings of fact that Shaver had the 1987 veto provision created for his own self-interest and failed in his fiduciary duty to fellow Director Landstrom to tell her of its existence. We held in *Schurr* that a director of a corporation has a duty to make a full and frank disclosure of the circumstances in a deal affecting the corporation and was not to undertake such dealing without sanction of the corporation.

However, Shaver passed away on November 22, 1992. With his death also died any veto power under the agreement.

Shaver argues that Landstrom sustained no damages and thus the jury's verdict of $4 million is insupportable. The rule against uncertain damages applies to damages that are not definite or certain results of the wrong. "Uncertainty as to the fact is fatal to recovery, but uncertainty as to the measure or extent of the damages does not bar recovery."

Landstrom points to no damages other than the arguments she has already presented under her intentional interference with business relations and expectancy cause of action. She candidly admitted this fact at trial.

---

[6] [18] It would appear that those courts which have adopted the ALI rule have done so when faced with claims of fraud or freeze-outs, neither of which were alleged or proven here. * * *

\*     \*     \*

As she had no identifiable third party purchaser or valid objective expectancy of one, she sustained no damage by the veto provision or the improper manner it came to be. While we do not condone the actions of Shaver, we must hold that they were not the cause of any damage sustained by Landstrom. The trial court should have granted the Defendants' motion for a directed verdict or judgment notwithstanding the verdict on this issue. As such the jury's verdict on this cause of action must be reversed.

\*     \*     \*

We have held that duplication of damages of the same nature and purpose are not appropriate. Mash v. Cutler, 488 N.W.2d 642, 646 (S.D. 1992). Here, however, with the fiduciary verdict now overturned against Shaver, the basis for the trial court's ruling no longer exists.

\*     \*     \*

We affirm on issues one and six and reverse the remaining issues. The case is remanded to the trial court for further proceedings consistent with a derivative action should Landstrom elect to pursue it.

## NOTE

The distinction between direct and derivative lawsuits is far from clear. For example, should a suit to enjoin a merger be considered direct or derivative? *See Eisenberg v. Flying Tiger Line, Inc.*, 451 F.2d 267 (2d Cir. 1971). The district court considered the action to be derivative, but the appellate court considered it to be direct, and thus not required to post security. For large publicly held corporations, direct actions might well bring about chaos if every shareholder could sue in his own name. But for closely held corporations, the American Law Institute (ALI) proposed rule seems quite sensible. Even without adopting the provisions of the ALI, there is sufficient case authority for the courts to modify existing rules. Normally, a money judgment in a derivative suit goes to the corporation, but courts have made exceptions to give the money to those injured rather than the wrongdoers.

The business judgment rule makes sense when there is a majority of independent directors (as in a publicly held corporation) but when all of the directors have conflicting economic interests, the rule is not very helpful. Occasionally, attorneys for minority shareholders will argue that the plaintiff is entitled to attorney's fees if he wins, since the cause of action is derivative.

## H.  SPECIAL PROBLEMS WITH ARBITRATION

Although shareholder agreements can prevent many potential problems for shareholders in closely held corporations, it is prudent to consider using an arbitration clause to prevent needless litigation. If major decisions require unanimous approval, or an 80% majority, arbitration may be a sensible method of resolving disagreements. Arbitration clauses should be drafted in the broadest possible terms to avoid litigation over whether the matter in question is arbitrable at all.

## BOSWORTH v. EHRENREICH
United States District Court, District of New Jersey
823 F. Supp. 1175 (1993)

BASSLER, J.

\* \* \*

### I. BACKGROUND

This case involves a closely held corporation with three co-owners who recently have found it difficult to agree on how to run their business. Bosworth, Scalice and the defendant, Melvin Ehrenreich, each hold a one-third ownership of Hi-Pro Marketing, Inc., an Illinois corporation which manufactures "sculptured" sports cards. Under a Shareholders Agreement signed on May 1, 1991, Scalice was to serve as President, Bosworth as Vice-President and Ehrenreich as Secretary-Treasurer. For the past four months, however, these co-owners have engaged in various disputes. The alliances among them have continually shifted, in a corporate game of "musical directors' chairs."

The problems apparently began seriously to affect Hi-Pro's corporate structure on February 10, 1993, when Bosworth and Ehrenreich asked Scalice to resign as an officer and director of the corporation. All three men that day signed a hand-written document entitled "Terms of Buyout," under which Scalice would purportedly "sell back all stock in Hi-Pro, Inc." (See Affidavit of Edward F. Clark, Esq., Exhibit B). Scalice, however, denies that he ever agreed to resign or sell back his shares, though he acknowledges that he did not participate directly in the daily activities of the corporation for nearly four months after the February 10, 1993 meeting. (Deposition of John Scalice, at 41).

\* \* \*

Despite his pursuit of legal remedies against Bosworth, Scalice nevertheless acknowledges that he was also attempting to work out an agreement with Bosworth, to the exclusion of Ehrenreich. Scalice and Bosworth would "[u]ltimately buy [Ehrenreich] out, . . . or Mr. Ehrenreich would have been fired as an employee, kept on as a director and stockholder and just allowed to sit there."(Deposition of John Scalice, at 50). Scalice states that he and Bosworth called a director's meeting for May 11, 1993, later rescheduled for May 21, 1993, in which they planned, in Scalice's words, "to get rid of Mel."

By May 21, 1993, the corporate alliances among the three co-owners had shifted again. Scalice had now worked out his disagreements with Ehrenreich. Bosworth was now the odd man out. Scalice and Ehrenreich voted that day to terminate Bosworth as an officer of Hi-Pro. This vote represented an abrupt change in position for Ehrenreich. In fact, as recently as May 13, 1993, Ehrenreich had informed Bosworth that he objected to notice of the directors meeting being given to Scalice, "who is no longer a director of this corporation, and is not entitled to attend."

\* \* \*

In any event, the parties agree that Scalice then contacted Ehrenreich by phone and the two men conducted a "director's meeting." At that meeting, the two men voted to terminate Bosworth's employment with Hi-Pro, to elect Scalice as Chief Executive Officer and Steven Merker, the brother of William Merker, as Chief Financial Officer and Vice-President.

On that same day, Ehrenreich alleges, Bosworth sent a fax to Midwest Bank, "withdrawing all funds in the operating account and applying these funds to pay down a line of credit which had expired on April 2, 1993." Bosworth allegedly knew that three checks had been drawn on the funds in the operating account, including a $300,000 check payable to the National Football League. Ehrenreich states that, to prevent the checks from being dishonored, he worked out an emergency agreement with the bank and an unnamed outside investor, "who invested $381,000 of his personal funds."

\* \* \*

After a discovery dispute arose among the parties, United States Magistrate Judge Dennis M. Cavanaugh on May 28, 1993 ordered that Ehrenreich make himself available for a deposition in Illinois on Memorial Day, May 31, 1993. Ehrenreich, however, did not comply with Judge Cavanaugh's order and has not yet been deposed. The Court has warned Ehrenreich and the other parties that it will not condone further disregard of such an order.

Bosworth now applies for immediate injunctive relief. He alleges that the actions of the defendants at the May 21, 1993 meeting, at which he was purportedly terminated as a Hi–Pro employee, were "oppressive" under Illinois law. He seeks either a provisional director, appointed by the Court to resolve the deadlock on the board of directors, or, alternatively, to have his stock purchased at fair value by the defendants.

Ehrenreich has filed a signed declaration in opposition to Bosworth's request for injunctive relief. Scalice has filed a brief and an affidavit of Edward F. Clark, Esq., in opposition. Scalice has also filed a motion to stay this action pending arbitration. He asserts that the disputes raised in Boswort's verified complaint must be arbitrated in accordance with Article 13 of the Shareholders' Agreement.

The parties also disagree on Scalice's status with the corporation. Bosworth argues that Scalice should not longer act as a director, as he resigned February 10, 1993. According to both Scalice and Ehrenreich, however, Scalice did not resign and continues to hold a director's position.

## II. DISCUSSION

For the reasons discussed below, the Court agrees with Scalice that Bosworth's complaint is arbitrable and concerns issues which must be resolved by a New York arbitrator. This Court, however, does not have the power to compel arbitration outside the District of New Jersey. Under the Federal Arbitration Act, . . . any petition to compel arbitration or confirm an arbitration award must be filed in the Southern District of New York. The Court, therefore, transfers venue in this action . . . to the Southern District of New York.

The Court, however, is extremely concerned about irreparable harm to the corporation Hi–Pro, and indirectly, to the three co-owners, Bosworth, Scalice and Ehrenreich, which will result unless the present state of corporate chaos is brought under some semblance of control. Therefore, the Court will appoint a provisional director, with two votes, to help stabilize the corporate operations pending arbitration.

The Court, furthermore:

(1)  permits Scalice to serve as a director and to serve as President;

(2)  permits Bosworth and Ehrenreich to continue as voting members of the board of directors;

(3)  orders that the board of directors make only routine business decisions pending the arbitration, unless the corporation's financial stability requires emergent action; and

(4)  restrains the parties from implementing the resolutions and/or agreements of Scalice and Ehrenreich, as reflected in the minutes of the May 21, 1993 "directors' meeting."

## A. Federal Arbitration Act

Congress has enacted the Federal Arbitration Act, 9 U.S.C. § 1 et seq., "to reverse the longstanding judicial hostility to arbitration agreements that had existed at English common law and had been adopted by American courts, and to place arbitration agreements upon the same footing as other contracts."

\* \* \*

The parties do not dispute that the Shareholders Agreement for Hi-Pro Marketing, a closed corporation which distributes products nationally, is a transaction involving interstate commerce. Therefore, the Court must look to the Federal Arbitration Act to determine the effect of the arbitration clause in Article 13. . . .

Having reviewed the verified complaint, the Court concludes that all three counts are arbitrable under the broad language in Article 13 of the Shareholders Agreement. Article 13 provides, in part:

> Any controversy arising out of or relating to this Agreement or any modification, extension or termination thereof, including any claim for damages and/or rescission, shall be resolved by arbitration in New York, New York in accordance with the Rules then obtaining of the American Arbitration Association. The parties consent to the jurisdiction of the Court of the State of New York, County of New York, and of the Federal District Court of the Southern District of New York, for all purposes in connection with such arbitration . . .

Section 4 of the Act allows a litigant to petition a federal district court to enforce an arbitration agreement. . . . A district court, before compelling an unwilling party to arbitrate, "must engage in a limited review to ensure that the dispute is arbitrable — i.e., that a valid agreement to arbitrate exists between the parties and that the specific dispute falls within the substantive scope of that agreement." If the court finds that the dispute falls within the scope of the arbitration agreement, it may not consider the merits, but must refer the matter to arbitration.

The Court operates under "a presumption of arbitrability in the sense that 'an order to arbitrate the particular grievance should not be denied unless it may be said with positive assurance that the arbitration clause is not susceptible of an interpretation that covers the asserted dispute.' " . . .

The Court finds that the Article 13 arbitration clause is broadly worded. It refers to "[a]ny controversy arising out of or relating to this Agreement or any modification, extension or termination thereof." Compare *Goodwin v. Elkins & Co.*, 730 F.2d 99, 109–110 (3d Cir.), *cert. denied*, 469 U.S. 831 (1984) (clause which stated "[a]ny controversy arising hereunder" considered broad in sweep). . . .

Bosworth has acknowledged at page 15 of his brief that Count III, which asks the Court to restrain the defendants from terminating his employment, is arbitrable. He argues, however, that the provisions of the Shareholders Agreement are "not relevant" to Counts I and II.

\*     \*     \*

In Count I of the complaint, Bosworth seeks a Court-ordered purchase of his stock by the defendants, alleging that the purported termination of Bosworth on May 21, 1993 was illegal and oppressive. In Count Two, he seeks the appointment of a provisional director, alleging that he and Ehrenreich are hopelessly deadlocked in trying to operate the corporation.

\*     \*     \*

Having concluded that all three counts of Bosworth's complaint fall within the Article 13 arbitration clause, the Court must now consider Scalice's motion to stay the action pending arbitration. As a threshold matter, the Court concludes that Scalice is also moving to compel arbitration. Although his motion does not specifically request this relief, his brief at pages 13–14 strongly imply that he seeks this relief.

The Court is faced with a dilemma: Article 13 provides for arbitration in New York City. However section 4 of the Arbitration Act provides that arbitration must take place "within the district in which the petition for an order directing such arbitration is filed." 9 U.S.C. § 4. Therefore, only the federal district court for the Southern District of New York could compel arbitration in that district.

\*     \*     \*

Therefore, the Court may not compel arbitration in New York and will not, even if it could, compel arbitration in New Jersey. The Court, therefore, will transfer venue to the Southern District of New York under 28 U.S.C. § 1406(a), to further the intent of the parties as expressed in Article 13 of the Shareholders Agreement.

\* \* \*

Under Section 12.55 of the Illinois Business Corporation Act, a trial court may, in lieu of dismissing the action or ordering dissolution of the corporation, appoint a provisional director. 805 Ill. Ann. Stat. ch. 5, para. 12.55(a)(1) (Smith-Hurd 1993). The trial court has the discretion to appoint a provisional director "if it appears that such action by the court will remedy the grounds alleged by the complaining shareholder to support the jurisdiction of the court under Section 12.50." Ill. Ann. Stat. ch. 5, para. 12.55(b).

Section 12.50 sets for the grounds for judicial dissolution of a corporation. Subsection (b) of that section provides that, to establish grounds for dissolution, a shareholder must show either:

(1)  The directors are deadlocked, whether because of even division in the number thereof or because of greater than majority voting requirements in the articles of incorporation or the by-laws, in the management of the corporate affairs; the shareholders are unable to break the deadlock; and either irreparable injury to the corporation is thereby caused or threatened or the business of the corporation can no longer be conducted to the general advantage of the shareholders; or

(2)  The directors or those in control of the corporation have acted, or will act in a manner that is illegal, oppressive or fraudulent; or

(3)  The corporate assets are being misapplied or wasted.

Based upon the facts available, the Court concludes that Section 12.50(b) applies here. The actions of all three directors — Bosworth, Ehrenreich and Scalice — have created a deadlock on the board. Even though the Shareholders Agreement provides for three votes on the board of directors, the events of February 10, 1993, in which Scalice purportedly resigned as a director, leave the constitution of the board in doubt.

Furthermore, given the ever-shifting allegiances among the three board co-owners over the past four months, it is quite possible that one or more of them in the near future will act in a manner that is oppressive toward one or more of the others. In fact, the Court finds that the actions of Scalice and Ehrenreich, in voting to terminate Bosworth's employment on May 21, 1993, was oppressive.

Such action by the defendants demonstrates the kind of arbitrary, overbearing and heavy-handed course of conduct that the Illinois courts have held to be "oppressive." See *Hager-Freeman v. Spircoff*, 229 Ill. App. 3d 262, 171 Ill. Dec. 1, 10, 593 N.E.2d 821, 830, *appeal denied*, 146 Ill. 2d 627, 176 Ill. Dec. 797, 602 N.E.2d 451 (1992). The fact that Ehrenreich completely changed his position, repudiating his earlier acceptance of Scalice's resignation of February 10, 1993, gives further credence to Bosworth's claims of oppression and director deadlock.

\* \* \*

Under Illinois law, the court should appoint a provisional director after considering the best interests of the corporation, not those of the various factions in the litigation. Abreu v. Unica Industrial Sales, Inc., 224 Ill. App. 3d 439, 166 Ill. Dec. 703, 707, 586 N.E.2d 661, 665 (1991). The appointment serves as a less drastic alternative to dissolving the corporation and is meant "to help guide the company through a crisis towards the goal of stabilization and prosperity." . . . Therefore, the Court will follow Bosworth's suggestion that the provisional director be allowed to cast two votes. This avoids the possibility of a 2–2 split among the four directors' votes.

The Court believes that the presence of a provisional director on the board, especially one with no ties to the three other directors, is likely to have a stabilizing effect on the corporation which it badly needs. Without such a provisional director, the Court fears for the corporation's survival, even in the near term, given the inability of the other three directors to work out their differences.

*     *     *

The public interest here is formalized in the Illinois corporate statutes, which specifically provide for the appointment of a provisional director to help guide a troubled corporation through a crisis and toward stabilization. *See Abreu*, 586 N.E.2d at 665. The Court, therefore, finds that this factor weighs in favor of the requested injunctive relief.

*     *     *

Bosworth has made two, alternative requests: (1) He wishes the Court to order Scalice and Ehrenreich to sell him back his shares in the corporation; or (2) to appoint a provisional director with two votes on the board. For the following reasons, the Court will take the second suggested course of action.

In light of the arbitration clause in the Shareholders Agreement, the Court finds it would be inappropriate to enforce a buyout for Bosworth pending arbitration. Bosworth can be adequately compensated, if necessary, after the arbitration has run its course.

The Court will, however, continue in force parts (a), (b) and (c) of the preliminary restraints it imposed May 24, 1993. These restraints, in part, allow Bosworth to continue as an employee of Hi–Pro, receive a salary, and use the Fort Lee, N.J. offices. The Court will also continue the $5,000 bond Bosworth has already posted.

On the other hand, the Court will modify parts (d) and (e) of those restraints, which now apply only to the defendants. The Court will enjoin any party to this litigation from: (d) engaging in any transaction regarding the issuance, sale, transfer, pledge or other commitment of stock of Hi–Pro; and (e) selling or disposing of any of Hi–Pro's assets other than in the ordinary course of business.

The Court has reviewed the suggestions by the plaintiff and the defendants for the office of provisional director. However, the Court has decided that the best interests of the corporation, and the public, are served by appointing a provisional director not affiliated in any way with either side.

The Court, therefore, appoints Robert J. Chalfin, Esq., as provisional director for Hi–Pro. His primary purpose will be to attempt to provide a unifying influence on the warring factions in the corporation. He will be able to cast two votes at meetings of the board. Except as provided by this Court, he will act according to the by-laws and the Shareholders Agreement. In accordance with Section 12.55(d) of the Illinois

Act, the provisional director shall report to the Court in the Southern District, whenever appropriate, concerning the status of the corporation's business.

As provided in Section 12.55(e), the Court will allow reasonable compensation to be paid to the provisional director for services rendered and reimbursement of reasonable costs and expenses, which amounts shall be paid by the corporation. The Court orders that the corporation pay the provisional director at the rate of $225 per hour, plus costs.

\* \* \*

In light of the Court's conclusions that this matter is arbitrable and that arbitration should take place in New York, N.Y., the Court dismisses as moot Scalice's motions to compel arbitration and to stay the action pending arbitration. Scalice, if he wishes, may re-file these motions in the Southern District of New York.

## III. CONCLUSION

For the reasons discussed above, the Court grants in part and denies in part Bosworth's application for a preliminary injunction. The Court also transfers venue under 28 U.S.C. § 1406(a) to the Southern District of New York and dismisses as moot Scalice's motion to compel arbitration and for a stay of this action pending arbitration. An appropriate order follows.

## NOTE

This case illustrates a contemporary judicial approach to arbitration. The broadly drafted arbitration clause in part led to the sensible result. Many courts will construe arbitration clauses narrowly, and if the party resisting arbitration contends that the contract is not clear as to what must be arbitrated, delay and expense will result. An arbitration clause that specifically included the question of arbitrability might well remove that ambiguity.

Although this case involved arbitration, for many closely held corporations, arbitration should be the second step, not the first. A shareholder agreement might well specify that mediation be attempted first before arbitration. If sensitive matters such as salary and dividends could be considered by impartial arbiters, the parties might be likely to accept those decisions.

Arbitration should be considered mandatory if the shareholder agreement requires unanimity or a high vote. If the shareholders or directors deadlock, some courts may consider that conduct to be a breach of fiduciary duty. An arbitration clause could avoid the possibility of dissolution.

## I.  FAMILY LAW ISSUES

Often owners of stock in closely held corporations are forced to deal with the problems of dividing ownership interests as a result of divorce. The better solution is normally to give most of the closely held stock to the spouse with the most business experience with the corporation, but that solution may not be viable unless other more liquid assets exist. The following case shows an innovative judicial response to the problem.

## RETZER v. RETZER
Supreme Court of Mississippi
578 So. 2d 580 (1990)

HAWKINS, J.

Michael L. Retzer was granted a divorce from Nancy B. Retzer in the chancery court of Washington County on the ground of adultery. He has appealed the chancery court award unto his wife of a cash award of $275,000, periodic alimony in the amount of $88,000 per year and custody of their children. We reverse and render on the lump sum award, and affirm on the award of custody. We affirm the annual award of $88,000 per year, not as alimony, however, but as a fair return on Mrs. Retzer's ownership of 1,600 shares in Retzer and Retzer, Inc., a close corporation in which Mr. Retzer is the majority shareholder.

### FACTS

\* \* \*

According to Mr. Retzer, McDonald's corporation required more than an investor for a local franchise. The corporation wanted to assure itself the applicant could successfully operate one of its restaurants. He was required to work free for a thousand hours in McDonald's places of business and attend several training schools.

Mr. Retzer filed a financial statement with Sunburst Bank (formerly Grenada Bank) dated July 1, 1972, in support of a requested loan. It lists $44,200 cash assets. He testified approximately $25,000 of this sum were his savings, and another $20,000 a loan from his parents. This statement shows annual salaries of Mr. and Mrs. Retzer to be, respectively, $13,200 and $7,100. The Retzers secured a $65,000 loan from the First National Bank of Greenville in January, 1973, with both signing the note.

A McDonald's franchise, called a "License Agreement," runs for a 20-year term. The agreement also provides that during the last three years of the term, McDonald's may decide whether to extend the franchise for another 20-year period. On November 22, 1972, a License Agreement was executed by the licensor corporation, and "Michael L. Retzer and Nancy B. Retzer" as licensees.

At trial there was a disagreement as to Mrs. Retzer's initial investment. According to her, all of her teacher's salary went into a joint savings account and was part of the cash assets used to invest in the business. If so, it would have amounted to somewhere between $10,000 and $14,000. Mrs. Retzer brought no cash into the marriage. Mr. Retzer, on the other hand, testified Mrs. Retzer always spent beyond their means, and none of her funds went into the business. The 1972 financial statement contains no entry showing assets in a savings account. However, the $44,200 cash assets listed could have included a savings account.

When the business opened in 1972, Mr. Retzer was the manager, with two assistant managers, and testified he worked eighteen hours a day. Mrs. Retzer helped for several weeks, but returned to her teaching. She later did advise as to the interior decoration and employees' uniforms. Also, at one time she attempted to help settle a strike. Except for what has been noted, the entire management and operation of the business was by Mr. Retzer.

The business was quite successful.

\* \* \*

## OBLIGATION OF MR. RETZER TO MRS. RETZER

Mr. Retzer does have substantial financial obligations to Mrs. Retzer, however, arising from her ownership of almost half of the shares of Retzer and Retzer, Inc.

Courts look quite differently upon the respective duties existing between majority and minority shareholders in publicly held and close corporations. F. O'Neal, OPPRESSION OF MINORITY SHAREHOLDERS, § 3.06 at 78 (1975); Comment, *The Strict Good Faith Standard-Fiduciary Duties to Minority Shareholders in Close Corporations*, 33 MERCER LAW REVIEW 595 (1982); *Donahue v. Rodd Electrotype Co. of New England, Inc.*, 367 Mass. 578, 328 N.E.2d 505 (1975); *Smith v. Atlantic Properties, Inc.*, 12 Mass. App. 201, 422 N.E.2d 798 (1981) (holding minority shareholders also have fiduciary duties to majority shareholders). Retzer and Retzer, Inc., is a very close close corporation, which has existed solely for the financial benefit of two people, the Retzers. This corporation has no other purpose except through legal ownership of five McDonald's restaurants to create wealth for and furnish income to Mr. Retzer and Mrs. Retzer. For almost two decades, and through Mr. Retzer's management, the corporation has indeed furnished them both with large incomes.

Now, through ownership of ten more shares than she, Mr. Retzer has control of the management of Retzer and Retzer. As such, under well settled principles he has a fiduciary obligation to Mrs. Retzer in the management of her property, and imposed with a trustee's duty to preserve, protect and produce income from her corporate shares. *See, Donahue, . . .*; *Matter of Kemp & Beatley, Inc.*, 473 N.E.2d 1173, 1177 (1984); O'Neal's OPPRESSION OF MINORITY SHAREHOLDERS, § 7.17 (1985); Comment, supra, p. 27, at 593; 18 C.J.S. Corporations, § 327; 18A Am. Jur. 2d § 764, p. 633. In fact, it has been held that he holds the same duty as a managing partner owes the other partner in the management of partnership affairs. . . . Any relaxation of this solemn obligation will be at his peril.[7]

He must manage the corporation prudently, and after paying necessary and reasonable expenses, and setting aside whatever is reasonably necessary for corporate reserves and equipment and facilities, pay her 49.8% of the net remaining. He will not be acting at arm's length, but as trustee over her shares. He must keep her currently, fully and accurately informed and abreast of his

---

[7] [5] One outstanding fact from this record is that throughout their turbulent marriage, both Mr. and Mrs. Retzer have had able legal counsel. Mr. Retzer will be well advised of his trust responsibility, and Mrs. Retzer of her ample avenues of relief in event of any deviation by him.

management, and under regular periodic accounting. While their interest as husband and wife was essentially identical, now they are adverse to each other. This will make his conduct as trustee that much more subject to close scrutiny by a chancery court.

Just as it has authority to require a husband to pay his wife periodic and lump sum alimony from his property and estate, the chancery court clearly has authority to require a divorced husband to pay his wife whatever is due her in his management of her property. There was no manifest error in the chancellor's ordering Mr. Retzer to see that she received an income of $7,333.33 per month from Retzer and Retzer. This is neither a floor nor a ceiling, but from the present financial information an amount the chancellor considered reasonable. We find no occasion to reverse this amount. It will, of course, be subject to change, depending upon the economic welfare of the corporation.

With the hostility existing between them, it would no doubt be preferable if somehow the property of Mr. and Mrs. Retzer were entirely separate, with neither depending on the other. Indeed, having imposed upon him the obligation of a trustee, the greater burden in this continued economic joinder may very well fall upon Mr. Retzer. The fact remains that at present they are siamese twins in Retzer and Retzer. If the burden becomes unduly oppressive for either, the chancery court is not without power to give relief, even to appointing a receivership for the corporation or dissolving it.

\*     \*     \*

We therefore affirm the amount of monthly income Mrs. Retzer is to receive, but amend the judgment to reflect this as an obligation of Mr. Retzer to see that she receives this sum from his management of the corporation.

The error of the chancellor, as above noted, was in decreeing that Mr. Retzer pay Mrs. Retzer $88,000 per year, or $7,333.33 per month, as alimony. The chancellor, of course, recognized the difficulty of this holding, because in the same decree he held that any sum received by Mrs. Retzer from the corporation would correspondingly reduce his alimony obligation.

Our holding should also be preferable to Mrs. Retzer as there will be no financial impediment to her remarrying.

\*     \*     \*

The decree of the chancery court is accordingly reversed and rendered on the $275,000 lump sum award to Mrs. Retzer, and affirmed on the award of custody of the children. The $88,000 annual award to her is affirmed, but modified as a fiduciary obligation of Mr. Retzer to Mrs. Retzer to see that she gets that return from her ownership of 1,600 corporate shares in Retzer and Retzer.

AFFIRMED in part; REVERSED and RENDERED in part.

PRATHER, J. DISSENTING:

\*     \*     \*

The court is of the opinion that in light of the financial obligations that are involved with their various assets and with the fact that his management is essential to the success of a substantial portion of the assets, it is not appropriate that the assets themselves be transferred, but that he be directed to transfer cash in lieu of assets to her. In order to avoid undue financial strain on him, the court determines that this $275,000.00 should be paid to her in the following manner: $100,000.00 to be paid November 1, 1988; $75,000.00 to be paid May 1, 1989; and $100,000.00 to be paid May 1, 1990. He is further to pay to her interest at the rate of 8% per annum compounded annually on all sums due after November 1, 1988, with said interest to be computed from November 1, 1988.

The court is further of the opinion that this payment alone will not assure an equitable division of the assets of the parties in light of the fact that the principal asset which Mrs. Retzer now has and which she will have after these payments will continue to be her stock in Retzer and Retzer. Since Mr. Retzer owns approximately 51% of the stock in the corporation, he is in the position to control the corporation and to have all its earnings paid out in salaries to himself or in the position to inequitably erode her asset. The court determines that it must in some manner address this if it is to achieve a fair and reasonable equitable division of the assets. This Court recognizes that Retzer and Retzer is not a party to this lawsuit and that it has no authority over the corporation. The court on the other hand recognizes that it has determined that Mrs. Retzer's interest in the corporation is worth approximately $1,100,000.00, and that she must have some reasonable return on this sum if an equitable division is to be achieved. In light of his being in a position to control the operation of the corporation this court concludes that it must take some action to see that Mr. Retzer handles this matter fairly. This is a unique factual situation insofar as this court can determine from the case law in this state and this court following the mandates of existing case law that it achieve an equitable division of the assets determines that this court of equity must frame some appropriate remedy for this situation. The court concludes that the way to do so is to require him to pay periodic alimony to her if Retzer and Retzer does not provide her with revenue. In seeking to frame this solution the court has attempted to leave him with options available to him to minimize his tax liabilities. The court, therefore, concludes that a fair return on her asset would be 8% and if he uses this asset he should have to pay her such return on it. The court thus finds that he should be required to pay her $88,000.00 per year alimony, less any sums she receives from Retzer and Retzer in the form of compensation, dividends, bonuses, or other benefits. This alimony should be paid to her monthly at the rate of $7,333.33, which will be due on the first day of each month beginning October 1, 1988. Thus, if she receives $2,000.00 per month from the corporation he would have to pay only $5,333.33 per month alimony. If the corporation makes any payments to her in substantial sums, they may serve to reduce his alimony obligations for the ensuing months in an amount equivalent to the amount paid by the corporation. For example, if on January 1, the corporation pays her a $25,000.000 bonus, then for the next three months no alimony would be due and for the next month only $3,000.01

would be due. Thus, she is assured of income for her support. If she receives it from her asset then he would not have to pay her alimony. If her asset does not produce the income, then he would be required to provide it for her in the form of alimony.

This requirement to pay this sum to her shall terminate if she sells her interest in Retzer and Retzer, for then she would have the proceeds of the sale of this substantial asset with which she would be able to fully support herself, and when she has those sums the court determines further alimony would not be required. This alimony requirement should also terminate if she remarries, for at that point this court concludes it would be inappropriate for alimony to be paid or for the court to mandate payment which might be used to support a new husband. If remarriage occurs, she will have to proceed as any other minority stockholder to protect her position in the corporation. . . .

This decision satisfied neither Mike nor Nancy. Both appealed, but Nancy subsequently decided to withdraw her petition and seek an affirmance of the chancellor's award.

\* \* \*

The chancellor's reasoning upon which the alimony award was based is persuasive and fair.

## NOTES

1.  According to the facts of the case, Mrs. Retzer is entitled to slightly less than half (49.8%) of the corporation's stock. Is 8% a reasonable rate of return on her stock valued by the court at $1.1 million? Should this payment of $88,000 per year terminate on remarriage? What remedies will Mrs. Retzer have then, if she wants some income from her locked in investment?

If Mr. and Mrs. Retzer had contemplated the possibility of divorce, would they have bargained for the deal that the courts imposed on them?

2.  Why didn't the court simply give Mrs. Retzer preferred stock with a mandatory dividend of 8%? The preferred could have been given voting control if any dividend was not paid on a timely basis. Would that be a better solution than the one the court came up with? If there is any chance that the common stock will appreciate substantially over a period of time, the court could have made the preferred stock convertible into common at the option of the holder.

3.  This case illustrates a common problem in dividing marital property. Placing an accurate value on stock is very difficult if it is not traded on an exchange. Even a good faith effort to value the stock may deprive one spouse of her fair share of the marital property if future appreciation is likely but hard to ascertain. The solution that this case discusses seems a reasonable solution to the problem.

# Chapter 8

# CAPITALIZING THE CORPORATION

## A. THE FINANCIAL STRUCTURE OF THE CORPORATION: DEBT AND EQUITY SECURITIES

This section discusses the financial structure of the corporation. One of the basic decisions which the founders of a new corporation must make is in determining the "capital structure" of the corporation. By capital structure we mean the various sources of financing which will enable the corporation to commence its ordinary business activities. In this regard, the fundamental distinction is between debt and equity. Equity securities, common stock, and preferred stock represent ownership in the corporation. Debt, on the other hand, represents a contractual promise to pay to third parties who may or may not also be owners of the corporation. A detailed discussion of the financing of the corporation and the various types of characteristics of various debt and equity instrument is beyond the scope of an introductory course in corporations and is covered in a course in Corporate Finance at many schools. The following brief overview, however, is intended to acquaint you with the fundamental characteristics of debt and equity and the major legal issues surrounding their use.

### 1. Equity

Equity represents the ownership interest in the corporation. Section 6.01 of the Model Business Corporation Act (MBCA) gives the incorporators broad authority to determine the structure of the equity interests in the corporation. Section 6.01(b) provides that "the articles of incorporation must authorize one or more classes of shares with unlimited voting rights and that have the right to receive the net assets of the corporation upon dissolution." Beyond that, the statute gives the drafters *carte blanche* to create various classes of equity securities with widely varying characteristics in areas such as (1) the right to vote for the board of directors, (2) the right to receive dividends, (3) the right to convert from one class of shares into another, and (4) the right to preference in receipt of dividends or distributions of capital if the corporation is liquidated. Significantly, section 6.01 departs from traditional terminology in refusing to use the phrase "preferred stock" to refer to classes of securities which have preferential rights to the receipt of dividends or other characteristics. However, because the terms remain in common use by practitioners and courts, we will use them here to distinguish the basic characteristics of different types of equity.

**Common Stock:**

The basic characteristics of common stock are as follows:

1. *Risk of loss of investment*: High. Because common stock represents the residual ownership interest in the corporation, common shareholders are entitled to whatever is left over after all creditors, and holders of preferred stock, are paid off. In bankruptcy proceedings, common shareholders typically receive little or nothing.

2. *Right of control*: High. There must be at least one class of voting common stockholders which has the right to elect the board of directors and, thus, indirectly, determine the course of events of the corporation.

3. *Right to receive the profits of the corporation*: Common shareholders have the right to receive dividends in the amount declared by the board of directors which is limited only by the financial resources of the corporation and the relatively lenient statutory test applicable.

4. *Right to return of capital*: None. The basic voting common stock of the corporation must remain in existence for the duration of the corporation's existence. Thus, a common shareholder's only means to compel the return of his investment is if he can persuade the board of directors to vote to liquidate the corporation. Of course, he is generally free to sell his shares of stock to a third party but, in the case of a closely held corporation that is usually not a viable alternative since there is no market for its shares.

**Preferred stock:**

The MBCA no longer uses the term "preferred stock," instead choosing simply to state in section 6.02(c) that the board may create additional classes of shares beyond the one class required by 6.02(b) with whatever rights and privileges it chooses. Nonetheless, because the term "preferred stock" remains in general use, we use it here. One advantage of the MBCA approach in section 6.02(c) is to emphasize that preferred stock is essentially a matter of contract. The drafters of the articles of incorporation may create additional classes of stock with whatever permutations and combinations of rights and privileges they wish. Generally, however, preferred stock will possess some or all of the following characteristics:

1. *Right to preferential distribution of assets*: The distribution is at a stated amount per share upon liquidation of the corporation.

2. *Limited voting rights*: Preferred stock is typically non-voting, although often there are provisions for voting rights which may be triggered if the corporation fails to pay a specified dividend on the preferred shares.

3. *Right to a fixed dividend*: Preferred stock typically carries the right to receive a fixed annual dividend which must be paid before the common shareholders may be paid any dividend at all. Most preferred stock is "cumulative" meaning that if the board fails to pay a dividend on a specified date, it must make up those past dividends at a future date before a common dividend can be declared.

4. *Right of redemption*: The corporation may reserve the right to "call" or redeem preferred stock at specified intervals in the future if it finds it no

longer needs the capital raised by its issuance.

5. *Right to convert into common shares*: Preferred stock may contain a conversion right giving the holder the right to convert each preferred share into a specified number of common shares at a stated price.

**Warrants and options:**

A warrant or option is not itself an equity security. Rather it represents the contractual right of the holder to require the issuer to sell her a specified number of shares of the security, usually common stock, at a specified price for a specific period of time. For example, a warrant might give the holder the right to buy 100 shares of XYZ Corp. at a price of $50 per share at any time up to December 31, 2013. If, at any time the warrant was issued, the corporation's stock was trading at $45, the warrant would have no intrinsic value, since someone could buy XYZ Corp. stock in the open market for a price less than the exercise price of the warrant. However, if the corporation's stock rises to, *e.g.*, $60 per share, the warrant has an intrinsic value of $10 per share since, by exercising the warrant and purchasing the stock from the corporation for $50 per share, the holder has saved $10 per share as compared with the price of purchasing the same stock on the market.

Warrants or options, thus, give the holder the right to profit from appreciation in the corporation's stock without actually owning that stock. On the other hand, if the price of a corporation's stock does not rise above the exercise price before the warrant's expiration date, it becomes worthless at expiration; the investor, thus, loses all the money he paid for the warrant. Warrants are often issued in conjunction with the sale of debt securities as a "sweetener" to induce prospective purchasers to purchase debt securities by giving them the potential to profit from appreciation in the corporation's stock. Options are often issued by corporations as part of an incentive compensation package to attract and retain desirable officer, directors and other key employees. Also, a large public market in speculative options which are issued not by the corporation but by private individuals has developed: such options are traded on the Chicago Board Options Exchange and several exchanges as well.

# NOTE: SECURITIES LAW CONSIDERATIONS

Most law schools offer a separate course covering federal and state laws governing the regulation of securities. Thus, the topic will not be treated in detail here. However, because many students with only an occasional corporate practice may run afoul of such legislation in connection with the formation of a close corporation, it is important that they possess some knowledge of the federal statutes in this area, the Securities Act of 1933, 15 U.S.C. §§ 77a–7aa, and the Securities Exchange Act of 1934, 15 U.S.C. § 78a *et. seq*. In addition, most states have passed legislation known as "Blue Sky Laws" governing the issuance of securities. The Securities Exchange Act of 1934 will be discussed later in connection with the chapters dealing with the solicitation of proxies, insider trading, takeover bids, and leverage buyouts. Here, our concern is primarily with the Securities Act of 1933, which governs the issuance of securities by a newly formed corporation, or issuance of additional securities by an existing corporation.

In the wake of the stock market crash of 1929 and the massive losses suffered by many investors, Congress passed the Securities Act of 1933 to regulate the issuance of securities by corporations engaged in interstate commerce. The act has two major thrusts. First, it requires a corporation to prepare a "registration statement" which must be approved by and filed with the Securities Exchange Commission (SEC), a federal administrative agency established by the Act, before securities subject to it may be issued. This document contains detailed financial disclosures concerning the proposed business of the corporation and its principal founders. A "prospectus," which is essentially a summary of the principal disclosures in the registration statement, must be distributed to prospective investors who are solicited to purchase shares in the new corporation. The preparation of the registration statement is an expensive and time consuming proposition, involving the services of accountants and lawyers skilled in the intricacies of the securities laws. The cost of such services can be quite prohibitive for a newly formed close corporation and thus must be avoided, if possible. Fortunately, there are a number of quite broad exemptions from the registration requirements of the 1933 Act which cover most closely held corporations of modest size and capitalization. The three exemptions most commonly used are the following.

1. *The intra-state offering exemption under section 3(a)(11), 15 U.S.C. § 77c(a)(11). Securities issued and sold solely to persons who are residents within the state in which the corporation is incorporated are exempt from registration.* While this exemption might seem rather straightforward, the SEC has interpreted its requirements strictly so that many securities lawyers prefer not to rely upon it. For example, if securities of a Florida corporation are mistakenly and in good faith sold to an individual who is not a bona fide resident of the state, such as a seasonal resident of Florida with his primary home in Michigan, the exemption is destroyed and the entire issue of securities is considered unlawfully issued, even though all of the other residents are bona fide residents of Florida. This exposes the incorporators and the lawyers for the corporation to substantial criminal penalties provided for the sale of unregistered securities. The SEC has issued Rule 147, 17 C.F.R. §§ 230.147 *et. seq.*, which provides a "safe harbor" for securities issued under the intrastate offering exemption, provided that the provisions of the rule are fulfilled.

2. *The small issue exemption under section 3(b), 15 U.S.C. § 77c(b), and 4(a)(6), 15 U.S.C. § 77d(a)(6), of the 1933 Act.* This is a frequently utilized exemption for small business corporations. Generally, it exempts from registration the issuance of up to $5 million worth of securities offered to the public, provided that the SEC finds that compliance with the act is not necessary to protect the public. The SEC has promulgated Regulation D, 17 C.F.R. § 230.501 *et seq.* which sets forth detailed criteria indicating the circumstances under which the SEC will consider small issues to be exempt from registration.

3. *Another frequently utilized exemption is the exemption under section 4(a)(2) of the 1933 Act, 15 U.S.C. § 77d(a)(2), for "transactions by the issuer not involving any public offering."* This exemption is usually referred to simply as the "private offering" exemption. The scope of this exemption is not defined by statute. The leading case interpreting this exemption is *SEC v. Ralston Purina Co.*, 346 U.S. 119 (1953), in which the Supreme Court adopted a functional test, stating that "the applicability of [section 4(2)] should turn on whether the particular class of persons

affected needs the protection of the Act. An offering to those who are shown to be able to fend for themselves is a transaction 'not involving any public offering.' " *Id.* at 125. Because the boundaries of this exemption are not clearly defined, most practitioners today rely on Regulation D if the value of the securities to be issued falls below the stated limits.

The attorney for an existing or contemplated small business corporation must also be aware of state "Blue Sky Laws" governing the issuance of securities. Indeed, the closely held corporation is more likely to fall within the jurisdiction of state securities legislation than federal. Because of the lack of uniformity of such legislation, it is difficult to generalize about it here. The lawyer contemplating an issuance of securities must be careful to check such state legislation not only in the state of incorporation but also in every state in which the securities may be offered for sale. Compliance with such legislation when offerings are to be made in several states can prove to be a major headache for the promoter and her attorney. *See Wartzman v. Hightower Prods.*, 456 A.2d 82 (Md. Ct. Spec. App. 1983), Ch. 5, Section F, *supra*, which illustrates the substantial liabilities which may result from the sale of unregistered securities. In addition, the sale of unregistered securities is a felony under the 1933 Act, thereby exposing the defendants to fines and even the possibility of imprisonment.

# NOTE: PREEMPTIVE RIGHTS

An important issue which corporate counsel and her clients must consider while drafting the articles of incorporation is whether or not to provide for preemptive rights for shares issued. Shares issued with preemptive rights are given the right to subscribe on a pro rata basis to any new issue of shares of the same class by the corporation at a subsequent time. For example, suppose shareholder, Jones, holds 100 shares of common stock in a corporation with 1000 shares outstanding. If the corporation subsequently issues another 500 shares of stock, Jones must be offered the right to purchase 10% of the newly issued shares, or 50 shares. If he does so, Jones will retain a 10% ownership interest in the corporation (150 shares out of 1500 outstanding).

Preemptive rights have two benefits. First, they enable a shareholder to retain her proportionate voting interest in the corporation. This is most important in the closely held corporation, where the exercise of preemptive rights may be essential to maintain a shareholder's control of the corporation, or in the case of a minority shareholder, the right to elect one or more directors if the corporation has cumulative voting. Secondly, they enable the shareholder to retain a proportionate interest in the equity of the corporation. If new shares are issued below book value, a shareholder who does not exercise preemptive rights will suffer a dilution of her equity in the corporation, in effect a portion of her interest in the corporation will be transferred to the new investor who purchases shares at what amounts to a bargain price.

Preemptive rights have been held to exist at common law in states where they are not provided for in the corporate code. *Stokes v. Continental Trust Co.*, 78 N.E. 1090 (N.Y. App. Div. 1903). Today the issue is almost universally dealt with by statute. The statutes generally take one of three approaches: (1) preemptive rights are provided as a matter of right for all corporations and may not be abolished by the articles of incorporation; (2) preemptive rights exist unless eliminated by the articles of incorporation; or (3) preemptive rights do not exist unless expressly granted by the articles of incorporation. Section 6.30 of the 1984 MBCA takes the third approach, the so-called "opt-in" approach, in effect reversing the common law default rule granting preemptive rights. This reverses the position taken in the 1969 MBCA which followed the common law approach and provided for the "opt-out rule."

The reason for the change in the default rule of the 1969 MBCA probably reflects the influence on the latest revision of the act of those whose primary interest is in the large publicly traded corporation. Preemptive rights are generally not necessary in such corporations and may be nuisance when new issues of stock are made. In the large corporation, preservation of a shareholder's voting interest is of little value when even the largest shareholder holds, at best, a very small percentage of the total shares outstanding. Thus, preserving control rights for the shareholder is not an important consideration. Furthermore, the presence of preemptive rights may complicate and delay a public offering of new shares, since the corporation must make a mass mailing to thousands of shareholders and wait several weeks to determine how many wish to exercise their rights.

Because preemptive rights may be of critical importance to shareholders in a close corporation, it is an important issue which the attorney should raise with her client(s) when the articles of incorporation are being drafted. This is especially true in states with "opt-in" statutes, since affirmative action is required in order to establish preemptive rights, something which most clients will probably find desirable.

Preemptive rights do not fully protect the shareholder's interest in the close corporation from dilution. First, if the shareholder does not have the financing available to purchase the shares offered him, the bare existence of preemptive rights are of no value to him; in a public corporation these rights may have value and at least can be sold, this will almost never be true in the close corporation. This difficulty is compounded if the majority shareholder is aware of the inability of the minority to finance the exercise of preemptive rights and deliberately issue the new shares below book value. In that case, the shareholder suffers a dilution in the value of his existing shares as well as a loss of voting power. In *Katzowitz v. Sidler*, 249 N.E.2d 359 (N.Y. App. Div. 1969), the court held that where the controlling shareholders issue new shares "markedly below book value . . . and when the remaining share-holder-directors benefit from the issuance, a case for judicial relief has been established." *Id.* at 364. Thus, a court of equity may provide some relief to the minority shareholder but such relief will probably be available only in extreme situations, because valuation of the shares of a closely held corporation is something which is difficult to establish with any degree of certainty.

## 2.  Debt Securities

A corporation may or may not issue debt securities upon its formation, *i.e.*, there is no statutory requirement that a corporation issue debt, yet as a practical matter virtually all new business will find it necessary to carry some debt of either a short or long term nature. The basic distinguishing characteristics of debt are as follows:

1. *Risk of loss*: Lower than common stock. Holders of debt securities are creditors who are entitled to be repaid their claims in full upon the liquidation or bankruptcy of the corporation, before common or preferred shareholders receive anything. This does not mean, of course, that debt security holders are guaranteed to receive repayment in full. The assets of a financially troubled corporation are frequently insufficient to pay the claims of all creditors, let alone of equity security holders.

2. *Right of control*: None. Debt holders are not the owners of the corporation, they are creditors, and thus do not have the right to vote for the board of directors or otherwise control the affairs of the corporation. However, the terms of bank loan agreements or bond indentures often contain elaborate limitations upon the otherwise unfettered right of the board of directors to determine the course of the business (*e.g.*, the right of the board to issue additional indebtedness or to undertake risky business ventures), which amounts to an indirect right to control the business.

3. *Participation in profits*: None. The debt holder is entitled to the payment of interest at a rate and at the time specified in the debt instrument, but generally no more. Even if the corporation becomes spectacularly profitable, the debt holder is not entitled to share in the corporation's good fortunes.

4. *Right to return of capital at time certain*: Yes. The holder of a debt instrument has a contractual right to the return of the principal sum on the date specified. If it is not paid he can commence bankruptcy proceedings to force the corporation to pay. As with preferred stock, the previous statements are generalizations based on common usage and are subject to variation. Because a debt obligation is essentially a matter of contract between the corporation and the holder, there are few statutory limitations upon the terms of its creation.

## OBRE v. ALBAN TRACTOR CO.
Court of Appeals of Maryland
179 A.2d 861 (1962)

SYBERT, J.

The single question raised by this appeal is whether the Chancellor erred in his finding that a note of a corporation to its principal stockholder represented a risk capital investment in the corporation and not a bona fide debt entitling the stockholder to share as a general creditor in distribution of the corporation's assets due to insolvency.

The Annel Corporation began its existence in January, 1959, when the appellant, Henry Obre, and F. Stevens Nelson pooled certain equipment and cash for the purpose of forming the corporation to engage in the dirt moving and road building business. As his share, Obre transferred to the corporation equipment independently appraised at $63,874.86, plus $1,673.24 cash, for a total of $65,548.10. Nelson's contribution was equipment valued at $8,495.00 and $1,505.00 in cash, totaling

$10,000.00.

In return, Obre received $20,000.00 par value non-voting preferred stock and $10,000.00 par value voting common stock. In addition, he received the corporation's unsecured note for $35,548.10, dated January 2, 1959, which was the date of the incorporation. The note, which is the subject of this appeal, was made payable five years after date and carried interest at the rate of five per cent per annum, though no interest was ever actually paid. Nelson received for his contribution voting common stock of $10,000.00 par value.

The corporation, with Obre as president and Nelson as vice-president, experienced financial difficulty very soon after beginning its operations, requiring Obre to pay certain creditors and meet a payroll in March, 1959, by use of his own funds. For the same reason he discontinued taking his salary of $75.00 a week in May, 1959. In April, 1959, the corporation borrowed $27,079.20 from a bank, securing the loan with a chattel mortgage. During its period of operation the corporation prepared monthly financial reports in which Obre's note was listed as a debt of the corporation. In 1959 the corporation showed an operating loss of $14,324.67. Its continued lack of success led to the execution of a deed of trust for the benefit of creditors on October 19, 1960, and the Circuit Court for Baltimore County, sitting in equity, assumed jurisdiction of the trust.

Obre filed four separate claims in the case which were excepted to by Alban Tractor Co. and certain other trade creditors (appellees here). The Chancellor, after hearing, issued a decree sustaining the exceptions to Obre's claim on the note in question, on the ground that the note represented a contribution to the capital of the corporation and not a bona fide debt owed to Obre upon which he could share as a general creditor. The Chancellor based his decision on his finding that the corporation could not have carried on its operations without the equipment contributed by Obre. He felt that the fact that the note was given on the same day the corporation was formed, and that it was a five year note, indicated that the transaction was not a loan but was really a risk capital contribution. He held that, in view of these factors, equity required that the claim be subordinated to the claims of the general creditors. Under the circumstances of this case we are unable to agree with the conclusion of the Chancellor.

*     *     *

It is significant in this case that no element of fraud, misrepresentation or estoppel was alleged in regard to the execution of the note, or the fact that it was held out as being a loan and not a capital investment. This factor distinguishes the case at bar from two Maryland cases in this area, *Cantor v. Balto. Overall Mfg. Co.*, 121 Md. 65, 87 A. 1115 (1913), and *Dollar Cleansers v. Mcgregor, supra*, [161 A. 159 (1932),] where claims by a stockholder-creditor were subordinated because of substantial fraud or misrepresentation. However, appellees contend that they have shown a "subordinating equity" in that the corporation, in which Obre was a dominant stockholder, was an undercapitalized venture, and that where such a situation exists, fraud or mismanagement need not be present in order to subordinate the claims of the principal stockholders. The test in such a case, it is argued, is whether the transaction can be justified within the bounds of reason and fairness. There is, principally in bankruptcy cases, some authority indicating support for this argument. See, for example, *Costello v. Fazio*, 256 F.2d 903 (9th Cir. 1958); *L & M Realty Corporation v. Leo*, 249 F.2d 668 (4th Cir. 1957). However, even if we assume, without deciding, that there may be situations in which the doctrine of subordination would be applied in a case short of fraud or estoppel, on general equitable principles, we do not believe that the facts present such a case here.

It is noted that in drawing up their corporate plan Obre and Nelson were assisted by a well-known and reputable firm of certified public accountants. Because of the expressed desire of Obre and Nelson that their control of the corporation be equal from the outset, and their ownership eventually equal, the corporate structure had to be planned carefully. Since Obre's contribution in the way of equipment was substantially greater than that of Nelson, the stock was issued so that each received an equal amount of common voting stock, but additional preferred stock was issued to Obre with the condition that it should have voting power if and when it became necessary to pass the dividend on the preferred stock. The remaining excess of assets brought in by Obre, over and above the stock issued to him, was not to be considered a capital investment since this would have made the desired end of eventual equal ownership that much more difficult. Hence the note in question was executed for the excess of $35,548.10. The result of this planning was that a permanent equity capital of $40,000 would be invested, which, as was noted in a memorandum of the firm planning the corporate structure, "all parties consider is entirely adequate for the foreseeable needs of the corporation." The note was made payable in five years, instead of in equal annual installments, for the explicit purpose of gaining tax advantage.

\* \* \*

. . . There is no showing that $40,000 was inadequate capitalization for an enterprise of this size, particularly in view of the careful planning that went into determining its capital structure. What may appear hazardous by hindsight may not have been unreasonable at the outset. It is not unusual in corporate financing to have approximately one-half of contributions put in as risk capital and the balance as loan capital. There can be no question but that, if a third party had advanced the money represented by Obre's note, he would validly be considered a creditor of the corporation.

Our view in no way compromises the position of the corporate creditor. As this Court stated in *Dollar Cleansers & Dyers v. McGregor, supra*, (at 109 of 163 Md.):

> "So long as the corporate plan is adopted and pursued in good faith and in accordance with the registration and other laws of the state, those dealing with the corporation have only themselves to blame if they suffer from neglect to seek information obtainable from public records and other available sources."

It is obvious that the creditors in this case could have determined (if they actually did not do so) the financial status of the corporation by simply inspecting the stock issuance certificate filed with the State Tax Commission, or by requesting financial reports, or by obtaining credit ratings from the sources available. . . .

In our opinion there is no basis in fact or law to justify the subordinating of appellant's claim under the note, and the decree must therefore be reversed.

# NOTES

1.   What is the basis for the subordinating claim being made by plaintiff? Would plaintiff have been more likely to succeed if he had attempted to pierce the corporate veil on the grounds that the corporation was inadequately capitalized?

2.   Why do you suppose defendants included the $20,000 of preferred stock in the capitalization of the corporation rather than simply issuing themselves a promissory note for $55,348.10 ($20,000 more than the actual note) and using no preferred stock at all? If they had done so, how might that have affected the likelihood of plaintiff's success?

## IN RE FETT ROOFING AND SHEET METAL CO.
United States District Court, Eastern District of Virginia
438 F. Supp. 726 (1977)

CLARKE, DISTRICT JUDGE

This matter comes before the Court on the appeal by plaintiff from an order of United States Bankruptcy Judge Hal J. Bonney, Jr., which dismissed plaintiffs' complaint, subordinated the note claims of the plaintiff to the claims of all other creditors and set aside deeds of trust which purported to secure the note claims. Appellant contends that the Bankruptcy Judge's findings of fact and conclusions of law were completely erroneous and that appellant's claims against the bankrupt should be reinstated. Jurisdiction of this Court is based on 28 U.S.C. § 1334; Bankruptcy Act §§ 38, 39(c), 11 U.S.C. §§ 66, 67(c); and Bankruptcy Rule 801.

### The Facts

The record below discloses that the bankrupt, Fett Roofing and Sheet Metal Co., Inc., was owned and run prior to 1965 by plaintiff herein, Donald M. Fett, Sr., as a sole proprietorship. During 1965, Mr. Fett incorporated his business, transferring to the new corporation assets worth $4,914.85 for which he received 25 shares of stock. The stated capital of the corporation was never increased during the course of the corporation's existence. Mr. Fett was the sole stockholder and also the president of the corporation. The roofing business continued to be run completely by Mr. Fett much as it had been prior to its incorporation. In short, Fett Roofing was a classic "one-man" corporation. Over the years, plaintiff advanced money to his business as the need arose. Three of these transactions made in 1974, 1975 and 1976 involved the transfer to the corporation of $7,500, $40,000 and $30,000, respectively. In each instance plaintiff borrowed from the American National Bank, made the funds available to his business and took back demand promissory notes. On April 6, 1976, at a time his business had become insolvent, plaintiff recorded three deeds of trust intended to secure these notes with the realty, inventory, equipment and receivables of Fett Roofing and Sheet Metal Co., Inc. The deeds were backdated to indicate the dates on which the money had actually been borrowed. On November 8, 1976, an involuntary petition in bankruptcy was filed.

After a trial in which both sides presented considerable evidence and the plaintiff personally testified regarding his claim, Judge Bonney made the following findings of fact.

1. The bankrupt was undercapitalized at its inception in 1965, and remained undercapitalized throughout its existence. The capital necessary for the operation and continuation of its business was provided by the complainant in the form of so-called loans on an "as-needed" basis. Promissory notes, including the three involved herein, were given to the complainant in the course of such transactions.

2. The three deeds of trust which purport to secure the said notes were all back-dated to create the impression that they were executed contemporaneously with the advance of funds and the giving of the notes; all three were in fact executed and recorded during the first week of April 1976, when the notes were, by their terms, past due.

3. The purpose of the deeds of trust was to delay, hinder, and defraud the creditors of the bankrupt, and to give the complainant a preference over them, in the event a liquidation of assets became necessary.

4. Complainant was in sole control of the affairs of the bankrupt, and was its sole stockholder. His interests were at all times identical to and indistinguishable from that of the bankrupt; he was the alter ego of the bankrupt.

5. At the time these three deeds of trust were executed and recorded, the bankrupt was, and for several months had been, unable to meet its obligations as they came due in the ordinary course of business. Many of the debts listed in the schedules filed by the bankrupt were incurred and delinquent prior to April 1976.

6. Complainant knew that his corporation was insolvent no later than February 1976.

Based on these findings, Judge Bonney concluded that the advances made by plaintiff to his corporation were actually contributions to capital, not loans, and that claims based on them therefore should be subordinated to those of all the other creditors of the bankrupt. The Judge further found that even if the transfers had been bona fide loans, the deeds of trust intended to secure them would have been null and void as having been given with actual intent to delay, hinder and defraud creditors in violation of § 67d(2)(d) of the Bankruptcy Act, 11 U.S.C. § 107(d)(2)(d). In addition, Judge Bonney determined that such loans were given in fraud of creditors under state law and therefore were voidable under § 70(e) of the Bankruptcy Act, 11 U.S.C. § 110(e).

Because we have concluded that the Bankruptcy Judge was correct in his determination that the plaintiff's transfers of money to his corporation were capital contributions and not loans we do not consider the soundness of the last two legal findings.

## The Law

\*    \*    \*

A director, officer, majority shareholder, relatives thereof or any other person in a fiduciary relation with a corporation can lawfully make a secured loan to the corporate beneficiary. *Faucette v. Van Dolson*, 397 F.2d 287 (4th Cir.), *cert. denied*, 393 U.S. 938, 89 S. Ct. 301, 21 L. Ed. 2d 274 (1968). However, when challenged in court a fiduciary's transaction with the corporation will be subjected to "rigorous scrutiny" and the burden will be on him " . . . not only to prove the good faith of the transaction but also to show its inherent fairness from the viewpoint of the corporation and those interested therein." *Pepper v. Litton*, 308 U.S. 295, 60 S. Ct. 238, 84 L. Ed. 281 (1939); *Geddes v. Anaconda Copper Mining Co.*, 254 U.S. 590, 599, 41 S. Ct. 209, 65 L. Ed. 425 (1921). *See also, Twin-Lick Oil Co. v. Marbury*, 91 U.S. 587, 23 L. Ed. 328 (1875).

Where a director or majority shareholder asserts a claim against his own corporation, a bankruptcy court, sitting as a court of equity, will disregard the outward appearances of the transaction and determine its actual character and effect.

> Similar results have properly been reached in ordinary bankruptcy pro-ceedings. Thus, salary claims of officers, directors and stockholders in the bankruptcy of "one-man" or family corporations have been disallowed or subordinated where the courts have been satisfied that allowance of the claims would not be fair or equitable to other creditors. And that result may be reached . . . where on the facts the bankrupt has been used merely as a corporate pocket of the dominant stockholder, who, with disregard of the substance or form of corporate management, has treated its affairs as his own. And so-called loans or advances by the dominant or controlling stockholder will be subordinated to claims of other creditors and thus treated in effect as capital contributions by the stockholder not only in the foregoing types of situations but also where the paid-in capital is purely nominal, the capital necessary for the scope and magnitude of the operation of the company being furnished by the stockholder as a loan.

*Pepper v. Litton, supra* 308 U.S. at 308–310, 60 S. Ct. at 246.

The record on this appeal reveals the bankrupt to have been a large construction contractor requiring ample amounts of capital. As indicated above, the corporation was capitalized at slightly under $5,000 when it was created in 1965. No increment to this initial amount was ever formally made. According to the schedule filed with the Bankruptcy Judge, the bankrupt's debt to secured creditors alone stood at $413,000. This is a debt-to-equity ratio of over 80 to 1. While this fact by itself will not serve to convert what is otherwise a bona fide loan into a contribution to capital, it does cast serious doubt on the advances by a person in plaintiff's special situation being considered debt rather than equity. The fact that no evidence was adduced by plaintiff to show that the "borrowings" in question were formally authorized by the corporation or that interest was ever paid on them, coupled with the undisputed day-in-and-day-out control over corporate affairs wielded by plaintiff, as president and sole stockholder leave little doubt that plaintiff, ignoring corporate formalities, was infusing new capital into his business and avoiding such necessities as charter amendment or the issuance of new stock. The record discloses that the funds transferred to the corporations were used to finance the acquisition of equipment and material necessary to the functioning of the business. Although one of the advances was used to pay a bona fide tax liability, this does not affect its character as a capital contribution under the particular circumstances of this case. *In re Trimble Co.*, 479 F.2d 103, 115 (3d Cir. 1973). The fact that plaintiff at various times characterized these advances as "re-capitalization" can only reinforce a conclusion which consideration of the entire record makes inevitable. The Courts of this circuit have had no reluctance to pierce through surface appearances in these matters and distinguish contributions to capital from genuine loans. In *Braddy v. Randolph*, 352 F.2d 80 (4th Cir. 1965), a case with some striking similarities to the present dispute, the plaintiff, president, director and a principal stockholder of a bankrupt corporation, filed four claims based on four notes secured by deeds of trust. In affirming the rejection of these claims, the Court of Appeals stated:

> To finance this volume and to keep the business going even though operating at a loss, the Bankrupt borrowed heavily and constantly from the four officers and the North Carolina National Bank (hereinafter Bank). The money which officers, Braddy, Zeliff, Craft and Foster, "loaned" the Bankrupt was normally acquired from the Bank by use of their personal credit and personal assets. Based on the volume of business and the fact that the Bankrupt began borrowing from the officers and the Bank at the outset of operations, we think the referee and court could reasonably conclude that these "loans" were necessitated by the initial insufficiency of the Bankrupt's equity capital and that the "loans" made by the officers were, in effect, contributions to capital. Securities & Exchange Com'n v. Liberty Baking Corp., 240 F.2d 511, 515 (2 Cir. 1957). Rather than invest more capital the officers and stockholders, by the use of the borrowed funds, substantially shifted and evaded the ordinary financial risks connected with this type of business enterprise and, at the same time, permitted the corporation to remain in a constant state of or in imminent danger of insolvency.

*   *   *

Although the advances contested here were made well after the corporation was created, there is evidence in the record that plaintiff had "loaned" the bankrupt money over the years and that the transfers here in issue were only the latest in a series of contributions made necessary by the corporation's grossly inadequate capitalization. Since these three transactions were "part of a plan of permanent personal financing," the fact that they did not occur at the outset of corporate existence is not crucial and the claims based on them are properly subordinated to those of other creditors. *Boyum v. Johnson*, 127 F.2d 491, 494 (8th Cir. 1942); *Duberstein v. Werner*, 256 F. Supp. 515 (E.D.N.Y. 1966).

Since the transfers made by plaintiff to the bankrupt were, in contemplation of law, capital contributions the deeds of trust purporting to secure these advances were properly set aside since there was in fact "no debt to be secured." *Arnold v. Phillips*, 117 F.2d 497, 501 (5th Cir. 1941).

As the cases make clear, no one fact will result in the determination that putative loans are actually contributions to capital. The Court is guided by equitable principles that look to the result of the transaction as well as to the formal indicia of its character. A person in the special position of the plaintiff " . . . cannot by the use of the corporate device avail himself of the privileges normally permitted outsiders in a race of creditors."*Pepper v. Litton, supra*, 308 U.S. at 311, 60 S. Ct. at 247. It is not necessary that fraud, deceit or calculated breach of trust be shown. Where, as here, a corporate insider, indeed the corporate alter ego has so arranged his dealings with his corporate principal that he achieves an unfair advantage over outside creditors dealing at arms length, the Court will subordinate his claim to theirs. *Pepper v. Litton, supra; In re Trimble Co., supra; Costello v. Fazio*, 256 F.2d 903 (9th Cir. 1958); *Goldie v. Cox*, 130 F.2d 695 (8th Cir. 1942); *Boyum v. Johnson, supra; Arnold v. Phillips, supra; In re Dean and Jean Fashions, Inc.*, 329 F. Supp. 663 (W.D. Okl.1971); *In re Regency*, 96 F. Supp. 535 (D.N.J.1951); 3A COLLIER ON BANKRUPTCY § 63.06 at 1797 (14th ed. 1975).

* * *

For the foregoing reasons, the Order appealed from is AFFIRMED.

## NOTES

1.   Plaintiff's arguments in *Obre* and *Fett Roofing* that the debt held by a major shareholder should be treated as if it were equity so that the shareholder's right to recover it should be subordinated to the claims of other creditors is known as the "Deep Rock" doctrine in federal bankruptcy proceedings. *Cf. Taylor v. Standard Gas & Elec. Co.*, 306 U.S. 307 (1939).

2.   Is the test applied by the bankruptcy court in *Fett Roofing* more favorable to the plaintiff seeking to subordinate debt held by a principle shareholder than the rule applied in *Obre*, or are there other reasons for the different result in the two cases?

## NOTE: TREATMENT OF DEBT AS EQUITY
## FOR TAX PURPOSES

The issue of whether debt should be taken at face value or should be treated as equity for federal income tax purposes is a frequently litigated issue. Because interest payments are deductible in calculating the net corporate income, whereas dividend payments are not, there is a temptation to "over leverage" a corporation to maximize the favorable tax treatment accorded interest. However, the IRS has long taken a dim view of what it considers to be excessive debt, particularly in the closely held corporation, and will often argue that the deduction claimed for interest payments should be denied because what is nominally debt should be treated as equity for federal income tax purposes. In *Estate of Mixon v. United States*, 464 F.2d 394 (5th Cir. 1972), the court announced over a dozen factors which should be considered in determining whether debt should be treated as "constructive equity" for tax purposes. The "*Mixon* factors" have been widely followed by other Circuits as well, because the IRS has never promulgated regulations dealing with this area. (At one point a set of proposed regulations was issued and subsequently withdrawn due to difficulty in forming a consensus as to the factors which should bear on this determination.) Thus, the totality of the facts test from *Mixon* remains the controlling authority, albeit a hazy one, for practitioners seeking to advise clients concerning the proper ratio of debt to equity.

# METROPOLITAN LIFE INS. CO. v.
# RJR NABISCO, INC.

United States District Court, Southern District of New York
716 F. Supp. 1504 (1989)

Jon M. Walker, United States District Judge.

## I. INTRODUCTION

The corporate parties to this action are among the country's most sophisticated financial institutions, as familiar with the Wall Street investment community and the securities market as American consumers are with the Oreo cookies and Winston cigarettes made by defendant RJR Nabisco, Inc. (sometimes "the company" or "RJR Nabisco"). The present action traces its origins to October 20, 1988, when F. Ross Johnson, then the Chief Executive Officer of RJR Nabisco, proposed a $17 billion leveraged buy-out ("LBO") of the company's shareholders, at $75 per share.[1] Within a few days, a bidding war developed among the investment group led by Johnson and the investment firm of Kohlberg Kravis Roberts & Co. ("KKR"), and others. On December 1, 1988, a special committee of RJR Nabisco directors, established by the company specifically to consider the competing proposals, recommended that the company accept the KKR proposal, a $24 billion LBO that called for the purchase of the company's outstanding stock at roughly $109 per share.

\*    \*    \*

Plaintiffs now allege, in short, that RJR Nabisco's actions have drastically impaired the value of bonds previously issued to plaintiffs by, in effect, misappropriating the value of those bonds to help finance the LBO and to distribute an enormous windfall to the company's shareholders. As a result, plaintiffs argue, they have unfairly suffered a multimillion dollar loss in the value of their bonds.[2]

\*    \*    \*

The motions and cross-motions are based on plaintiffs' Amended Complaint,

---

[1] [1] A leveraged buy-out occurs when a group of investors, usually including members of a company's management team, buy the company under financial arrangements that include little equity and significant new debt. The necessary debt financing typically includes mortgages or high risk/high yield bonds, popularly known as "junk bonds." Additionally, a portion of this debt is generally secured by the company's assets. Some of the acquired company's assets are usually sold after the transaction is completed in order to reduce the debt incurred in the acquisition.

[2] [4] Agencies like Standard & Poor's and Moody's generally rate bonds in two broad categories: investment grade and speculative grade. Standard & Poor's rates investment grade bonds from "AAA" to "BBB." Moody's rates those bonds from "AAA" to "Baa3." Speculative grade bonds are rated either "BB" and lower, or "Ba1" and lower, by Standard & Poor's and Moody's, respectively. See, e.g., Standard and Poor's Debt Rating Criteria at 10–11. No one disputes that, subsequent to the announcement of the LBO, the RJR Nabisco bonds lost their "A" ratings.

which sets forth nine counts.[3] Plaintiffs move for summary judgment pursuant to Fed.R.Civ.P. 56 against the company on Count I, which alleges a "Breach of Implied Covenant of Good Faith and Fair Dealing," and against both defendants on Count V, which is labeled simply "In Equity."

\* \* \*

Although the numbers involved in this case are large, and the financing necessary to complete the LBO unprecedented[4], the legal principles nonetheless remain discrete and familiar. Yet while the instant motions thus primarily require the Court to evaluate and apply traditional rules of equity and contract interpretation, plaintiffs do raise issues of first impression in the context of an LBO. At the heart of the present motions lies plaintiffs' claim that RJR Nabisco violated a restrictive covenant-not an explicit covenant found within the four corners of the relevant bond indentures, but rather an implied covenant of good faith and fair dealing-not to incur the debt necessary to facilitate the LBO and thereby betray what plaintiffs claim was the fundamental basis of their bargain with the company. The company, plaintiffs assert, consistently reassured its bondholders that it had a "mandate" from its Board of Directors to maintain RJR Nabisco's preferred credit rating. Plaintiffs ask this Court first to imply a covenant of good faith and fair dealing that would prevent the recent transaction, then to hold that this covenant has been breached, and finally to require RJR Nabisco to redeem their bonds.

RJR Nabisco defends the LBO by pointing to express provisions in the bond indentures that, inter alia, permit mergers and the assumption of additional debt. These provisions, as well as others that could have been included but were not, were known to the market and to plaintiffs, sophisticated investors who freely bought the bonds and were equally free to sell them at any time. Any attempt by this Court to create contractual terms post hoc, defendants contend, not only finds no basis in the controlling law and undisputed facts of this case, but also would constitute an impermissible invasion into the free and open operation of the marketplace.

For the reasons set forth below, this Court agrees with defendants. There being no express covenant between the parties that would restrict the incurrence of new debt, and no perceived direction to that end from covenants that are express, this Court will not imply a covenant to prevent the recent LBO and thereby create an

---

[3] [6] Count I alleges a breach of an implied covenant of good faith and fair dealing (against defendant RJR Nabisco); Count II alleges fraud (against both defendants); Count III alleges violations of Section 10(b) of the Securities Exchange Act of 1934 (against both defendants); Count IV alleges violations of Section 11 of the 1933 Act (on behalf of plaintiff Jefferson-Pilot Life Insurance Company against both defendants); Count V is labeled "In Equity," and is asserted against both defendants; Count VI alleges breach of duties (against defendant Johnson); Count VII alleges tortious interference with property (against Johnson); Count VIII alleges tortious interference with contract (against Johnson); and Count IX alleges a violation of the fraudulent conveyance laws (against RJR Nabisco).

[4] [8] On February 9, 1989, KKR completed its tender offer for roughly 74 percent of RJR Nabisco's common stock (of which approximately 97% of the outstanding shares were tendered) and all of its Series B Cumulative Preferred Stock (of which approximately 95% of the outstanding shares were tendered). Approximately $18 billion in cash was paid out to these stockholders. KKR acquired the remaining stock in the late April merger through the issuance of roughly $4.1 billion of pay-in-kind exchangeable preferred stock and roughly $1.8 billion in face amount of convertible debentures. *See* Bradley Reply Aff. para 2.

indenture term that, while bargained for in other contexts, was not bargained for here and was not even within the mutual contemplation of the parties.

## II. BACKGROUND

### A. The Parties:

Metropolitan Life Insurance Co. ("MetLife"), incorporated in New York, is a life insurance company that provides pension benefits for 42 million individuals. According to its most recent annual report, MetLife's assets exceed $88 billion and its debt securities holdings exceed $49 billion. . . . MetLife alleges that it owns $340,542,000 in principal amount of six separate RJR Nabisco debt issues, bonds allegedly purchased between July 1975 and July 1988. Some bonds become due as early as this year; others will not become due until 2017. The bonds bear interest rates of anywhere from 8 to 10.25 percent. MetLife also owned 186,000 shares of RJR Nabisco common stock at the time this suit was filed.

Jefferson-Pilot Life Insurance Co. ("Jefferson-Pilot") is a North Carolina company that has more than $3 billion in total assets, $1.5 billion of which are invested in debt securities. Jefferson-Pilot alleges that it owns $9.34 million in principal amount of three separate RJR Nabisco debt issues, allegedly purchased between June 1978 and June 1988. Those bonds, bearing interest rates of anywhere from 8.45 to 10.75 percent, become due in 1993 and 1998.

RJR Nabisco, a Delaware corporation, is a consumer products holding company that owns some of the country's best known product lines, including LifeSavers candy, Oreo cookies, and Winston cigarettes. The company was formed in 1985, when R.J. Reynolds Industries, Inc. ("R.J. Reynolds") merged with Nabisco Brands, Inc. ("Nabisco Brands"). In 1979, and thus before the R.J. Reynolds-Nabisco Brands merger, R.J. Reynolds acquired the Del Monte Corporation ("Del Monte"), which distributes canned fruits and vegetables. From January 1987 until February 1989, co-defendant Johnson served as the company's CEO. KKR, a private investment firm, organizes funds through which investors provide pools of equity to finance LBOs.

### B. The Indentures:

The bonds[5] implicated by this suit are governed by long, detailed indentures, which in turn are governed by New York contract law.[6] No one disputes that the holders of public bond issues, like plaintiffs here, often enter the market after the indentures have been negotiated and memorialized. Thus, those indentures are

---

[5] [9] For the purposes of this Opinion, the terms "bonds," "debentures," and "notes" will be used interchangeably. Any distinctions among these terms are not relevant to the present motions.

[6] [10] Both sides agree that New York law controls this Court's interpretation of the indentures, which contain explicit designations to that effect. See, e.g., P.Mem. at 26; D. Mem at 15 n.23. The indentures themselves provide that they "shall be deemed to be a contract under the laws of the State of New York, and for all purposes shall be construed in accordance with the laws of said State, except as may otherwise be required by mandatory provisions of law." Bradley Aff., Exh. L, § 12.8.

often not the product of face-to-face negotiations between the ultimate holders and the issuing company. What remains equally true, however, is that underwriters ordinarily negotiate the terms of the indentures with the issuers. Since the underwriters must then sell or place the bonds, they necessarily negotiate in part with the interests of the buyers in mind. Moreover, these indentures were not secret agreements foisted upon unwitting participants in the bond market. No successive holder is required to accept or to continue to hold the bonds, governed by their accompanying indentures; indeed, plaintiffs readily admit that they could have sold their bonds right up until the announcement of the LBO. Instead, sophisticated investors like plaintiffs are well aware of the indenture terms and, presumably, review them carefully before lending hundreds of millions of dollars to any company.

Indeed, the prospectuses for the indentures contain a statement relevant to this action:

> The Indenture contains no restrictions on the creation of unsecured short-term debt by [RJR Nabisco] or its subsidiaries, no restriction on the creation of unsecured Funded Debt by [RJR Nabisco] or its subsidiaries which are not Restricted Subsidiaries, and no restriction on the payment of dividends by [RJR Nabisco].

Further, as plaintiffs themselves note, the contracts at issue "[do] not impose debt limits, since debt is assumed to be used for productive purposes."

### 1. The relevant Articles:

A typical RJR Nabisco indenture contains thirteen Articles. At least four of them are relevant to the present motions and thus merit a brief review.

Article Three delineates the covenants of the issuer. Most important, it first provides for payment of principal and interest. It then addresses various mechanical provisions regarding such matters as payment terms and trustee vacancies. The Article also contains "negative pledge" and related provisions, which restrict mortgages or other liens on the assets of RJR Nabisco or its subsidiaries and seek to protect the bondholders from being subordinated to other debt.

Article Five describes various procedures to remedy defaults and the responsibilities of the Trustee. This Article includes the distinction in the indentures noted above. . . . In seven of the nine securities at issue, a provision in Article Five prohibits bondholders from suing for any remedy based on rights in the indentures unless 25 percent of the holders have requested in writing that the indenture trustee seek such relief, and, after 60 days, the trustee has not sued. Defendants argue that this provision precludes plaintiffs from suing on these seven securities. Given its holdings today, see infra, the Court need not address this issue.

Article Nine governs the adoption of supplemental indentures. . . .

Article Ten addresses a potential "Consolidation, Merger, Sale or Conveyance," and explicitly sets forth the conditions under which the company can consolidate or merge into or with any other corporation. It provides explicitly that RJR Nabisco "may consolidate with, or sell or convey, all or substantially all of its assets to, or merge into or with any other corporation," so long as the new entity is a United States corporation, and so long as it assumes RJR Nabisco's debt. The Article also requires that any such transaction not result in the company's default under any indenture provision.

### 2. The elimination of restrictive covenants:

In its Amended Complaint, MetLife lists the six debt issues on which it bases its claims. Indentures for two of those issues-the 10.25 percent Notes due in 1990, of which MetLife continues to hold $10 million, and the 8.9 percent Debentures due in 1996, of which MetLife continues to hold $50 million-once contained express covenants that, among other things, restricted the company's ability to incur precisely the sort of debt involved in the recent LBO. In order to eliminate those restrictions, the parties to this action renegotiated the terms of those indentures, first in 1983 and then again in 1985.

*    *    *

### 3. The recognition and effect of the LBO trend:

Other internal MetLife documents help frame the background to this action, for they accurately describe the changing securities markets and the responses those changes engendered from sophisticated market participants, such as MetLife and Jefferson-Pilot. At least as early as 1982, MetLife recognized an LBO's effect on bond values.[7] In the spring of that year, MetLife participated in the financing of an LBO of a company called Reeves Brothers ("Reeves"). At the time of that LBO, MetLife also held bonds in that company. Subsequent to the LBO, as a MetLife memorandum explained, the "Debentures of Reeves were downgraded by Standard & Poor's from BBB to B and by Moody's from Baal to Ba3, thereby lowering the value of the Notes and Debentures held by [MetLife]." MetLife Memorandum, dated August 20, 1982.

MetLife further recognized its "inability to force any type of payout of the [Reeves'] Notes or the Debentures as a result of the buy-out [which] was somewhat disturbing at the time we considered a participation in the new financing. However," the memorandum continued,

> [O]ur concern was tempered since, as a stockholder in [the holding company used to facilitate the transaction], we would benefit from the increased net income attributable to the continued presence of the low coupon indebtedness. The recent downgrading of the Reeves Debentures and the consequent "loss" in value has again raised questions regarding our ability to have forced a payout. *Questions have also been raised about our*

---

[7] [14] MetLife itself began investing in LBOs as early as 1980. See MetLife Special Projects Memorandum, dated June 17, 1989, attached as Bradley Aff.Exh. V, at 1 ("[MetLife's] history of investing in leveraged buyout transactions dates back to 1980; and through 1984, [MetLife] reviewed a large number of LBO investment opportunities presented to us by various investment banking firms and LBO specialists. Over this five-year period, [MetLife] invested, on a direct basis, approximately $430 million to purchase debt and equity securities in 10 such transactions . . . ").

*ability to force payouts in similar future situations, particularly when we
would not be participating in the buy-out financing.*

*Id.* (emphasis added). In the memorandum, MetLife sought to answer those very
"questions" about how it might force payouts in "similar future situations."

> *A method of closing this apparent "loophole," thereby forcing a payout of
> [MetLife's] holdings, would be through a covenant dealing with a change
> in ownership.* Such a covenant is fairly standard in financings with
> privately-held companies . . . It provides the lender with an option to end
> a particular borrowing relationship via some type of special redemption
> . . .

*Id.,* at 2 (emphasis added).

A more comprehensive memorandum, prepared in late 1985, evaluated and
explained several aspects of the corporate world's increasing use of mergers,
takeovers and other debt-financed transactions. That memorandum first reviewed
the available protection for lenders such as MetLife:

> Covenants are incorporated into loan documents to ensure that after a
> lender makes a loan, the creditworthiness of the borrower and the lender's
> ability to reach the borrower's assets do not deteriorate substantially.
> Restrictions on the incurrence of debt, sale of assets, mergers, dividends,
> restricted payments and loans and advances to affiliates are some of the
> traditional negative covenants that can help protect lenders in the event
> their obligors become involved in undesirable merger/takeover situations.

MetLife Northeastern Office Memorandum, dated November 27, 1985. The memorandum then surveyed market realities:

> Because almost any industrial company is apt to engineer a takeover or be
> taken over itself, Business Week says that investors are beginning to view
> debt securities of high grade industrial corporations as Wall Street's
> riskiest investments. In addition, because public bondholders do not enjoy
> the protection of any restrictive covenants, owners of high grade corporates
> face substantial losses from takeover situations, if not immediately, then
> when the bond market finally adjusts. . . . [T]here have been 10–15
> merger/takeover/LBO situations where, due to the lack of covenant pro-
> tection, [MetLife] has had no choice but to remain a lender to a less
> creditworthy obligor. . . . The fact that the quality of our investment
> portfolio is greater than the other large insurance companies . . . may
> indicate that we have negotiated better covenant protection than other
> institutions, thus generally being able to require prepayment when situa-
> tions become too risky . . . [However,] a problem exists. And because the
> current merger craze is not likely to decelerate and because there exist
> vehicles to circumvent traditional covenants, the problem will probably
> continue. Therefore, perhaps it is time to institute appropriate language
> designed to protect Metropolitan from the negative implications of mergers
> and takeovers.

*Id.* at 2-4 (emphasis added).[8]

Indeed, MetLife does not dispute that, as a member of a bondholders' association, it received and discussed a proposed model indenture, which included a "comprehensive covenant" entitled "Limitations on Shareholders' Payments."[9] As becomes clear from reading the proposed-but never adopted-provision, it was "intend[ed] to provide protection against all of the types of situations in which shareholders profit at the expense of bondholders." *Id.* The provision dictated that the "[c]orporation will not, and will not permit any [s]ubsidiary to, directly or indirectly, make any [s]hareholder [p]ayment unless . . . (1) the aggregate amount of all [s]hareholder payments during the period [at issue] . . . shall not exceed [figure left blank]." The term "shareholder payments" is defined to include "restructuring distributions, stock repurchases, debt incurred or guaranteed to finance merger payments to shareholders, etc."

Apparently, that provision-or provisions with similar intentions-never went beyond the discussion stage at MetLife. That fact is easily understood; indeed, MetLife's own documents articulate several reasonable, undisputed explanations:

> While it would be possible to broaden the change in ownership covenant to cover any acquisition-oriented transaction, *we might well encounter significant resistance in implementation with larger public companies . . .* With respect to implementation, we would be faced with the task of imposing a non-standard limitation on potential borrowers, *which could be a difficult task in today's highly competitive marketplace. Competitive pressures notwithstanding, it would seem that management of larger public companies would be particularly opposed to such a covenant since its effect would be to increase the cost of an acquisition* (due to an assumed debt repayment), a factor that could well lower the price of any tender offer (thereby impacting shareholders).

Bradley Reply Aff.Exh. D, at 3 (emphasis added). The November 1985 memorandum explained that

> " . . . obviously, our ability to implement methods of takeover protection will vary between the public and private market. In that public securities do not contain any meaningful covenants, it would be very difficult for

---

[8] [15] During discovery, MetLife produced from its files an article that appeared in The New York Times on January 7, 1986. The article, like the memoranda discussed above, reviewed the position of bondholders like MetLife and Jefferson-Pilot:

> "Debt-financed acquisitions, as well as those defensive actions to thwart takeovers, have generally resulted in lower bond ratings . . . Of course, a major problem for debtholders is that, compared with shareholders, they have relatively little power over management decisions. Their rights are essentially confined to the covenants restricting, say, the level of debt a company can accrue."

Bradley Reply Aff.Exh. H (emphasis added).

[9] [16] *See* Bradley Resp.Aff.Exh. F. That exhibit is an August 5, 1988 letter from the New York law firm of Kaye, Scholer, Fierman, Hays & Handler. A partner at that firm sent the letter to "Indenture Group Members," including MetLife, who participated in the Institutional Bondholders' Rights Association ("the IBRA"). The "Limitations on Shareholders' Payments" provision appears in a draft IBRA model indenture. *See* Bradley Resp.Aff. paras. 3, 7.

[MetLife] to demand takeover protection in public bonds. Such a requirement would effectively take us out of the public industrial market. A recent Business Week article does suggest, however, that there is increasing talk among lending institutions about requiring blue chip companies to compensate them for the growing risk of downgradings. *This talk, regarding such protection as restrictions on future debt financings, is met with skepticism by the investment banking community which feels that CFO's are not about to give up the option of adding debt and do not really care if their companies' credit ratings drop a notch or two."*

Bradley Resp.Aff.Exh. A, at 8 (emphasis added).

The Court quotes these documents at such length not because they represent an "admission" or "waiver" from MetLife, or an "assumption of risk" in any tort sense, or its "consent" to any particular course of conduct-all terms discussed at even greater length in the parties' submissions. *See, e.g.*, P. Opp. at 31–36; P. Reply at 16-17; D. Reply at 15–16. Rather, the documents set forth the background to the present action, and highlight the risks inherent in the market itself, for any investor. Investors as sophisticated as MetLife and Jefferson-Pilot would be hard-pressed to plead ignorance of these market risks. Indeed, MetLife has not disputed the facts asserted in its own internal documents. Nor has Jefferson-Pilot-presumably an institution no less sophisticated than MetLife-offered any reason to believe that its understanding of the securities market differed in any material respect from the description and analysis set forth in the MetLife documents. Those documents, after all, were not born in a vacuum. They are descriptions of, and responses to, the market in which investors like MetLife and Jefferson-Pilot knowingly participated.

These documents must be read in conjunction with plaintiffs' Amended Complaint. That document asserts that the LBO "undermines the foundation of the investment grade debt market . . . "; that, although "the indentures do not purport to limit dividends or debt . . . such covenants were believed unnecessary with blue chip companies . . . "; that "the transaction contradicts the premise of the investment grade market . . . "; and, finally, that "this buy-out was not contemplated at the time the debt was issued, contradicts the premise of the investment grade ratings that RJR Nabisco actively solicited and received, and is inconsistent with the understandings of the market . . . which plaintiffs relied upon."

Solely for the purposes of these motions, the Court accepts various factual assertions advanced by plaintiffs: first, that RJR Nabisco actively solicited "investment grade" ratings for its debt; second, that it relied on descriptions of its strong capital structure and earnings record which included prominent display of its ability to pay the interest obligations on its long-term debt several times over; and third, that the company made express or implied representations not contained in the relevant indentures concerning its future creditworthiness. In support of those allegations, plaintiffs have marshaled a number of speeches made by co-defendant Johnson and other executives of RJR Nabisco.[10]

---

[10] [18] *See, e.g.*, Address by F. Ross Johnson, November 12, 1987, P.Exh. 8, at 5 ("Our strong balance sheet is a cornerstone of our strategies. It gives us the resources to modernize facilities, develop new technologies, bring on new products, and support our leading brands around the world."); Remarks of

## III. DISCUSSION

At the outset, the Court notes that nothing in its evaluation is substantively altered by the speeches given or remarks made by RJR Nabisco executives, or the opinions of various individuals-what, for instance, former RJR Nabisco Treasurer Dowdle personally did or did not "firmly believe" the indentures meant. *See supra, and generally* Chappell, Dowdle and Howard Affidavits. The parol evidence rule bars plaintiffs from arguing that the speeches made by company executives prove defendants agreed or acquiesced to a term that does not appear in the indentures. *See West, Weir & Bartel, Inc. v. Mary Carter Paint Co.*, 25 N.Y.2d 535, 540, 307 N.Y.S.2d 449, 452, 255 N.E.2d 709, 712 (1969) ("The rule in this State is well settled that the construction of a plain and unambiguous contract is for the Court to pass on, and that circumstances extrinsic to the agreement will not be considered when the intention of the parties can be gathered from the instrument itself.") In interpreting these contracts, this Court must be concerned with what the parties intended, but only to the extent that what they intended is evidenced by what is written in the indentures. *See, e.g., Rodolitz v. Neptune Paper Products, Inc.*, 22 N.Y.2d 383, 386-7, 292 N.Y.S.2d 878, 881, 239 N.E.2d 628, 630 (1968); *Raleigh Associates v. Henry*, 302 N.Y. 467, 473, 99 N.E.2d 289 (1951).

The indentures at issue clearly address the eventuality of a merger. They impose certain related restrictions not at issue in this suit, but no restriction that would prevent the recent RJR Nabisco merger transaction. . . .

Under certain circumstances, however, courts will, as plaintiffs note, consider extrinsic evidence to evaluate the scope of an implied covenant of good faith. *See Valley National Bank v. Babylon Chrysler-Plymouth, Inc.*, 53 Misc.2d 1029, 1031–32, 280 N.Y.S.2d 786, 788–89 (Sup.Ct. Nassau), *aff'd*, 28 A.D.2d 1092, 284 N.Y.S.2d 849 (2d Dep't 1967) (Relying on custom and usage because "[w]hen a contract fails to establish the time for performance, the law implies that the act shall be done within a reasonable time . . . ").[11] However, the Second Circuit has established a different rule for customary, or boilerplate, provisions of detailed indentures used and relied upon throughout the securities market, such as those at issue. [*See*] *Sharon Steel Corporation v. Chase Manhattan Bank, N.A.*, 691 F.2d 1039 (2d Cir.1982). . . . Ignoring these principles, plaintiffs would have this Court vary what they themselves have admitted is "indenture boilerplate," of "standard" agreements to comport with collateral representations and their subjective under-

---

Edward J. Robinson, Executive Vice President and Chief Financial Officer, February 15, 1988, P.Exh. 6, at 1 ("RJR Nabisco's financial strategy is . . . to enhance the strength of the balance sheet by reducing the level of debt as well as lowering the cost of existing debt."); Remarks by Dr. Robert J. Carbonell, Vice Chairman of RJR Nabisco, June 3, 1987, P.Exh. 10, at 5 ("We will not sacrifice our longer-term health for the sake of short term heroics.").

[11] [19] In support of this proposition, plaintiffs also rely on *Reback v. Story Productions, Inc.*, 15 Misc.2d 681, 181 N.Y.S.2d 980 , modified and aff'd, 9 A.D.2d 880, 193 N.Y.S.2d 520 (1st Dep't 1959). The court in that case, however, was presented with an ambiguous written agreement. See 181 N.Y.S.2d at 983. Plaintiffs similarly rely on *Van Gemert v. Boeing Co.*, 520 F.2d 1373 (2d Cir.), cert. denied, 423 U.S. 947, 96 S. Ct. 364, 46 L. Ed. 2d 282 (1975) ("*Van Gemert I*"). In that case, however, the right asserted was addressed by an express provision which provided a framework for determining the scope and effect of the implied covenant. *See infra.*

standings.[12]

## A. Plaintiffs' Case Against the RJR Nabisco LBO:

### 1. Count One: The implied covenant:

In their first count, plaintiffs assert that defendant RJR Nabisco owes a continuing duty of good faith and fair dealing in connection with the contract [i.e., the indentures] through which it borrowed money from MetLife, Jefferson-Pilot and other holders of its debt, including a duty not to frustrate the purpose of the contracts to the debt holders or to deprive the debt holders of the intended object of the contracts-purchase of investment-grade securities.

In the "buy-out," the company breaches the duty [or implied covenant] of good faith and fair dealing by, inter alia, destroying the investment grade quality of the debt and transferring that value to the "buy-out" proponents and to the shareholders. . . .

A plaintiff always can allege a violation of an express covenant. If there has been such a violation, of course, the court need not reach the question of whether or not an implied covenant has been violated. . . .

In contracts like bond indentures, "an implied covenant . . . derives its substance directly from the language of the Indenture, and "cannot give the holders of Debentures any rights inconsistent with those set out in the Indenture." [*Where*] *plaintiffs' contractual rights [have not been] violated, there can have been no breach of an implied covenant." Gardner & Florence Call Cowles Foundation v. Empire*

---

[12] [20] To a certain extent, this discussion is academic. Even if the Court did consider the extrinsic evidence offered by plaintiffs, its ultimate decision would be no different. Based on that extrinsic evidence, plaintiffs attempt to establish that an implied covenant of good faith is necessary to protect the benefits of their agreements. That inquiry necessarily asks the Court to determine whether the existing contractual terms should be construed to preclude defendants from engaging in an LBO along the lines of the recently completed transaction. However, even evaluating all facts-such as the public statements made by company executives — in the light most favorable to plaintiffs, these plaintiffs fail as a matter of law to establish that the purported "fundamental basis" of their bargain with defendants created a contractual obligation on the part of the defendants not to engage in an LBO. It is first worth noting that plaintiffs have quoted selectively from certain speeches and remarks made by RJR Nabisco executives; in some respects, those public statements are more equivocal than plaintiffs would have this Court believe. *See, e.g.,* P.Exh. 3 at 25 ("[W]e believe our strong balance sheet and our debt capacity . . . provide us with the flexibility to pursue any conceivable strategy or financial option we choose.") More important, those representations are improperly raised under the rubric of an implied covenant of good faith when they cannot properly or reasonably be construed as evidencing a binding agreement or acquiescence by defendants to substantive restrictive covenants. Moreover, nothing like the mutual understanding plaintiffs now advance has been shown; in fact, as far as these parties are concerned, quite the opposite is true. *See infra* at 39–40. Thus, as a matter of law, and accepting all extrinsic evidence offered, the "implied covenant of good faith" does not serve these plaintiffs in the way they represent. As explained more fully below, by relying on extrinsic evidence and the familiar implied covenant of good faith, plaintiffs do not seek to protect an existing contractual right; they seek to create a new one, and thus to obtain a better bargain than originally agreed upon. Therefore, even if the parol evidence rule did not block plaintiffs' path, their course would not be followed.

The parol evidence rule of course does not bar descriptions of either the background of this suit or market realities consistent with the contracts at issue.

*Inc.*, 589 F.Supp. 669, 673 (S.D.N.Y.1984), vacated on procedural grounds, 754 F.2d 478 (2d Cir.1985) (quoting *Broad v. Rockwell*, 642 F.2d 929, 957 (5th Cir.) (en banc), *cert. denied*, 454 U.S. 965 (1981)) (emphasis added).

\* \* \*

The appropriate analysis, then, is first to examine the indentures to determine "the fruits of the agreement" between the parties, and then to decide whether those "fruits" have been spoiled—which is to say, whether plaintiffs' contractual rights have been violated by defendants.

The *American Bar Foundation's Commentaries on Indentures* ("the Commentaries "), relied upon and respected by both plaintiffs and defendants, describes the rights and risks generally found in bond indentures like those at issue:

> The most obvious and important characteristic of long-term debt financing is that the holder ordinarily has not bargained for and does not expect any substantial gain in the value of the security to compensate for the risk of loss . . . The significant fact, *which accounts in part for the detailed protective provisions of the typical long-term debt financing instrument, is that the lender (the purchaser of the debt security) can expect only interest at the prescribed rate plus the eventual return of the principal.* Except for possible increases in the market value of the debt security because of changes in interest rates, the debt security will seldom be worth more than the lender paid for it . . . It may, of course, become worth much less. Accordingly, the typical investor in a long-term debt security is primarily interested in every reasonable assurance that the principal and interest will be paid when due. . . . Short of bankruptcy, *the debt security holder can do nothing to protect himself against actions of the borrower which jeopardize its ability to pay the debt unless he . . . establishes his rights through contractual provisions set forth in the debt agreement or indenture.*

*Id.* at 1-2 (1971) (emphasis added).

A review of the parties' submissions and the indentures themselves satisfies the Court that the substantive "fruits" guaranteed by those contracts and relevant to the present motions include the periodic and regular payment of interest and the eventual repayment of principal. *See, e.g.,* Bradley Aff.Exh. L, § 3.1 ("The Issuer covenants . . . that it will duly and punctually pay . . . the principal of, and interest on, each of the Securities . . . at the respective times and in the manner provided in such Securities . . . "). According to a typical indenture, a default shall occur if the company either (1) fails to pay principal when due; (2) fails to make a timely sinking fund payment; (3) fails to pay within 30 days of the due date thereof any interest on the date; or (4) fails duly to observe or perform any of the express covenants or agreements set forth in the agreement. *See, e.g.,* Brad.Aff.Exh.L, § 5.1.23 Plaintiffs' Amended Complaint nowhere alleges that RJR Nabisco has breached these contractual obligations; interest payments continue and there is no reason to believe that the principal will not be paid when due.[13]

---

[13] [24] The Court here incorporates by reference its earlier discussion not only of plaintiffs' failure to demonstrate sufficiently a risk of irreparable harm on their motion for a preliminary injunction, but also

It is not necessary to decide that indentures like those at issue could never support a finding of additional benefits, under different circumstances with different parties. Rather, for present purposes, it is sufficient to conclude what obligation is not covered, either explicitly or implicitly, by these contracts held by these plaintiffs. Accordingly, this Court holds that the "fruits" of these indentures do not include an implied restrictive covenant that would prevent the incurrence of new debt to facilitate the recent LBO. To hold otherwise would permit these plaintiffs to straightjacket the company in order to guarantee their investment. These plaintiffs do not invoke an implied covenant of good faith to protect a legitimate, mutually contemplated benefit of the indentures; rather, they seek to have this Court create an additional benefit for which they did not bargain.[14]

\* \* \*

The sort of unbounded and one-sided elasticity urged by plaintiffs would interfere with and destabilize the market. And this Court, like the parties to these contracts, cannot ignore or disavow the marketplace in which the contract is performed. Nor can it ignore the expectations of that market-expectations, for instance, that the terms of an indenture will be upheld, and that a court will not, sua sponte, add new substantive terms to that indenture as it sees fit.[15] The Court has no reason to believe that the market, in evaluating bonds such as those at issue here, did not discount for the possibility that any company, even one the size of RJR

---

defendants' proof concerning the financing of the LBO and the company's current equity base. *See supra* at 4–5. Consequently, the Court rejects plaintiffs' general assertion that the LBO "subjects existing debtholders to dramatically greater risk of non-payment, and the Company to a significant risk of insolvency." Am.Comp. para. 26. In brief, there is no implied covenant restricting any action that might subject plaintiffs' investment to greater risk of non-payment. What plaintiffs have failed to allege is that an interest or principal payment due them has not been paid, or that any other explicit contractual right has not been honored.

[14] [25] The cases relied on by plaintiffs are not to the contrary. They invoke an implied covenant where it proves necessary to fulfill the explicit terms of an agreement, or to give meaning to ambiguous terms. *See, e.g., Grad v. Roberts*, 14 N.Y.2d 70, 248 N.Y.S.2d 633, 636, 198 N.E.2d 26, 28 (1964) (court relied on implied covenant to effect "performance of [an] option agreement according to its terms"); *Zilg v. Prentice-Hall, Inc.*, 717 F.2d 671 (2d Cir.1983), *cert. denied*, 466 U.S. 938, 104 S. Ct. 1911, 80 L. Ed. 2d 460 (1984). In *Zilg*, the Second Circuit first described a contract which, on its face, established the publisher's obligation to publish, advertise and publicize the book at issue. The court then determined that "the contract in question establishes a relationship between the publisher and author which implies an obligation upon the former to make certain [good faith] efforts in publishing a book it has accepted notwithstanding the clause which leaves the number of volumes to be printed and the advertising budget to the publisher's discretion." 717 F.2d at 679. In other words, the court there sought to ensure a meaningful fulfillment of the contract's express terms. *See also Van Gemert I, supra; Pittsburgh Terminal, supra*. In the latter two cases, the courts sought to protect the bondholders' express, bargained-for rights.

[15] [26] *Cf. Broad v. Rockwell*, 642 F.2d at 943 ("Not least among the parties 'who must comply with or refer to the indenture' are the members of the investing public and their investment advisors. A large degree of uniformity in the language of debenture indentures is essential to the effective functioning of the financial markets: uniformity of the indentures that govern competing debenture issues is what makes it possible meaningfully to compare one debenture issue with another, focusing only on the business provisions of the issue . . . ") (citation omitted); *Sharon Steel Corporation v. Chase Manhattan Bank, N.A.*, 691 F.2d. 1039, 1048 (2d Cir.1982) (Winter, J.) ("[U]niformity in interpretation is important to the efficiency of capital markets . . . [T]he creation of enduring uncertainties as to the meaning of boilerplate provisions would decrease the value of all debenture issues and greatly impair the efficient working of capital markets.").

Nabisco, might engage in an LBO heavily financed by debt. That the bonds did not lose any of their value until the October 20, 1988 announcement of a possible RJR Nabisco LBO only suggests that the market had theretofore evaluated the risks of such a transaction as slight.

*   *   *

Ultimately, plaintiffs cannot escape the inherent illogic of their argument. On the one hand, it is undisputed that investors like plaintiffs recognized that companies like RJR Nabisco strenuously opposed additional restrictive covenants that might limit the incurrence of new debt or the company's ability to engage in a merger. Furthermore, plaintiffs argue that they had no choice other than to accept the indentures as written, without additional restrictive covenants, or to "abandon" the market.

Yet on the other hand, plaintiffs ask this Court to imply a covenant that would have just that restrictive effect because, they contend, it reflects precisely the fundamental assumption of the market and the fundamental basis of their bargain with defendants. If that truly were the case here, it is difficult to imagine why an insistence on that term would have forced the plaintiffs to abandon the market. The Second Circuit has offered a better explanation: "[a] promise by the defendant should be implied only if the court may rightfully assume that the parties would have included it in their written agreement had their attention been called to it . . . *Any such assumption in this case would be completely unwarranted." Neuman v. Pike*, 591 F.2d 191, 195 (2d Cir. 1979) (emphasis added, citations omitted).

In the final analysis, plaintiffs offer no objective or reasonable standard for a court to use in its effort to define the sort of actions their "implied covenant" would permit a corporation to take, and those it would not.[16]

*   *   *

### 2. Count Five: In Equity:

Count Five substantially restates and re-alleges the contract claims advanced in Count I. . . . For present purposes, it makes no difference how plaintiffs characterize their arguments.[17] Their equity claims cannot survive defendants' motion for

---

[16] [28] Under plaintiffs' theory, bondholders might ask a court to prohibit a company like RJR Nabisco not only from engaging in an LBO, but also from entering a new line of business-with the attendant costs of building new physical plants and hiring new workers-or from acquiring new businesses such as RJR Nabisco did when it acquired Del Monte.

[17] [31] For much the same reason, the Court rejects defendants' reliance on cases *like In re Kemp & Beatley, Inc.*, 64 N.Y.2d 63, 70, 484 N.Y.S.2d 799, 803, 473 N.E.2d 1173, 1177 (1984), for "the ancient principle that equity jurisdiction will not lie when there exists a remedy at law." *See, e.g.*, D.Mem. at 26. That case contemplated a classic equitable remedy — the dissolution of a corporation. And in that respect, it accurately set forth a rule of law; no court will, for instance, enter an injunction or order specific performance or dissolution if an adequate legal remedy remains available. The Court has already denied plaintiffs' request for an injunction. To the extent that Count V does in fact merely restate plaintiffs' prayer for injunctive relief — "it would be unconscionable to allow the 'buy-out' to proceed until defendants make restitution to the debtholders," Am.Comp. para. 53 — it is of course inappropriate. As far as the Court can determine, however, and reading plaintiffs' "In Equity" Count as charitably as

summary judgment.

In their papers, plaintiffs variously attempt to justify Count V as being based on unjust enrichment, frustration of purpose, an alleged breach of something approaching a fiduciary duty, or a general claim of unconscionability. Each claim fails. . . .

## B. Defendants' Remaining Motions:

\*     \*     \*

### 1. Rule 10b-5:

Defendants move to dismiss pursuant to Fed.R.Civ.P. 12(c) Count III, the Rule 10b-5 counts, as to those six debt issues purchased by plaintiffs prior to September 1987, which is when plaintiffs allege in their complaint that defendants first began to develop an LBO plan. Plaintiffs admit that Rule 10b-5 is limited to purchases or sales during the period of non-disclosure or misrepresentation. . . . The rule does not afford relief to those who forgo a purchase or sale and instead merely hold in reliance of a nondisclosure or misrepresentation. . . . The first, second, third, fifth, seventh and eighth securities listed in the Amended Complaint fail to satisfy this requirement, at least on the facts as presently pleaded.[18] Accordingly, the Court grants defendants' motion on Count III as to those issues. Plaintiffs correctly note, however, that the disclosure-related common law fraud claims are not restricted to purchases and sales. . . . Thus, the Court denies defendants' motion to dismiss Count II on this basis.

\*     \*     \*

## III. CONCLUSION

For the reasons set forth above, the Court grants defendants summary judgment on Counts I and V, judgment on the pleadings for certain of the securities at issue in Count III, and dismisses for want of requisite particularity Counts II, III, and IX. All remaining motions made by the parties are denied in all respects. Plaintiffs shall have twenty days to re-plead.

So Ordered.

## NOTES

1. "Leveraged buyouts" (LBOs), as described by the court in footnote 1, occurred with great frequency in the mid to late 1980's. The RJR LBO was, at the

---

possible, the claims advanced by plaintiffs in Count V do not necessarily seek such an exclusive remedy. In general, remedies based on claims of unjust enrichment or frustration of purpose are certainly quantifiable and subject to money damages, and would thus support a legal remedy.

[18] [35] It remains unclear how the fourth security listed in the Amended Complaint fares under the controlling law. If plaintiffs purchased portions of that issue prior to September 1987, then, of course, the Court's above holding applies equally here.

time, the largest ever. A leveraged buyout results not just in a change of the ownership of the corporation but also in a drastic change in the corporation's capital structure by greatly increasing the ratio of debt to equity.

This conversion of RJR Nabisco into a "highly leveraged" corporation is why plaintiff bondholders were concerned enough to bring an action, even though the bonds which they had purchased were not in default the leverage buyout of RJR Nabisco, resulted, in effect, in the substitution of billions of dollars of additional debt securities for the common stock which was repurchased this increased the total annual interest payments which RJR was contractually obligated to make by an astronomical sum and substantially increased the likelihood that at some future time, RJR would not have sufficient income to make these interest payments. The decline in the market value of the plaintiff's bonds and downgrading of the credit rating of the bonds was a reflection of this increase in default risk. While an LBO significantly increases the risk that he corporation may default on the interest payments due its bondholders, it greatly increases the potential rewards to the few remaining shareholders because the earnings of the corporation will be split among far fewer shareholders after the LBO than was the case before.

2.   The opinion contains an elaborate discussion of the RJR bond indentures. An indenture is a contract between the issuing corporation and the bondholders which as the opinion indicates, contains elaborate covenants designed to prevent the corporation from taking action which would increase the risk of the corporation defaulting on the bonds in the future. An indenture is required by the Federal Trust Indenture Act of 1939 for the bonds of certain publicly traded corporations. A third party, the indenture trustee, who is typically a large bank or other financial institution, is charged with supervising the compliance of the bondholders in the event the corporation fails to comply with any provisions or defaults on the payment of principal or interest due on the bonds. The reason why the bondholders are plaintiffs in this suit, rather than the indenture trustees, is simply that the bonds are not in default and no provision of the indenture has been violated.

3.   As the opinion indicates, even sophisticated financial institutions such as MetLife may find that a bond indenture does not provide them with all the protection which they require to safeguard their investments. Given this fact, why is the court in *MetLife* so reluctant to find that bondholders are owed a fiduciary duty as are stockholders? The court's treatment of the relation between the corporation and bondholders as being almost exclusively governed by contract is in accordance with the overwhelming majority of courts which have considered the issue and illustrates a fundamental distinction between debt and equity.

4.   Plaintiff argued both that defendants breached a fiduciary duty to bondholders and that defendants breached an implied covenant of good faith which is part of the bond indenture. Which of these arguments appears to be stronger? Are they simply different ways of saying the same thing?

5.   Not all commentators would agree with the court in *MetLife* that no fiduciary duty should be owed to bondholders. For an argument in favor of such duty, see McDaniel, *Bondholders and Stockholders*, 13 J. CORP. L. 205 (1988). For an article applauding the courts' reluctance to find a fiduciary duty, see Hurst and McGuiness, *the Corporation, The Bondholder and Fiduciary Duties*, 10 J.L. & COM. 187 (1991).

**6.** There are a few opinions where the courts have been willing to provide protection for bondholders by way of finding an implied covenant of good faith or a fiduciary duty requiring certain acts by the debtor beyond those spelled out in the bond indenture. Generally, these cases involve rights which might be considered procedural rather than substantive. *See, e.g., Pittsburgh Terminal Corp v. The Baltimore & O.R.R. Co.*, 680 F.2d 933 (3rd Cir.) *cert. denied*, 459 U.S. 1056 (1982); *Van Gemert v. Boeing Co.*, 520 F.2d 1373 (2d. Cir.), *cert. denied*, 423 U.S. 947 (1975).

## B. THE SHAREHOLDER'S OBLIGATION TO PAY AND PAR VALUE

### HANEWALD v. BRYAN'S INC.
Supreme Court of North Dakota
429 N.W.2d 414 (1988)

MESCHKE, J.

Harold E. Hanewald appealed from that part of his judgment for $38,600 plus interest against Bryan's, Inc. which refused to impose personal liability upon Keith, Joan, and George Bryan for that insolvent corporation's debt. We reverse the ruling that Keith and Joan Bryan were not personally liable.

On July 19, 1984, Keith and Joan Bryan incorporated Bryan's, Inc. to "engage in and operate a general retail clothing, and related items, store. . . . " The Certificate of Incorporation was issued by the Secretary of State on July 25, 1984. The first meeting of the board of directors elected Keith Bryan as president and Joan Bryan as secretary-treasurer of Bryan's, Inc. George Bryan was elected vice-president, appointed registered agent, and designated manager of the prospective business. The Articles of Incorporation authorized the corporation to issue "100 shares of common stock with a par value of $1,000 per share" with "total authorized capitalization [of] $100,000.00." Bryan's, Inc. issued 50 shares of stock to Keith Bryan and 50 shares of stock to Joan Bryan. The trial court found that "Bryan's, Inc. did not receive any payment, either in labor, services, money, or property, for the stock which was issued."

On August 30, 1984, Hanewald sold his dry goods store in Hazen to Bryan's, Inc. Bryan's, Inc. bought the inventory, furniture, and fixtures of the business for $60,000, and leased the building for $600 per month for a period of five years. Bryan's, Inc. paid Hanewald $55,000 in cash and gave him a promissory note for $5,000, due August 30, 1985, for the remainder of the purchase price. The $55,000 payment to Hanewald was made from a loan by the Union State Bank of Hazen to the corporation, personally guaranteed by Keith and Joan Bryan.

Bryan's, Inc. began operating the retail clothing store on September 1, 1984. The business, however, lasted only four months with an operating loss of $4,840. In late December 1984, Keith and Joan Bryan decided to close the Hazen store. Thereafter, George Bryan, with the assistance of a brother and local employees, packed and removed the remaining inventory and delivered it for resale to other stores in Montana operated by the Bryan family. Bryan's, Inc. sent a "Notice of Rescission" to Hanewald on January 3, 1985, in an attempt to avoid the lease. The corporation was involuntarily dissolved by operation of law on August 1, 1986, for failure to file its annual report with the Secretary of State.

Bryan's, Inc. did not pay the $5,000 promissory note to Hanewald but paid off the rest of its creditors. Debts paid included the $55,000 loan from Union State Bank and a $10,000 loan from Keith and Joan Bryan. The Bryan loan had been, according to the trial court, "intended to be used for operating costs and expenses."

Hanewald sued the corporation and the Bryans for breach of the lease agreement and the promissory note, seeking to hold the Bryans personally liable. The defendants counterclaimed, alleging that Hanewald had fraudulently misrepresented the business's profitability in negotiating its sale. After a trial without a jury, the trial court entered judgment against Bryan's, Inc. for $38,600 plus interest on Hanewald's claims and ruled against the defendants on their counterclaim. The defendants have not cross appealed these rulings.

The trial court, however, refused to hold the individual defendants personally liable for the judgment against Bryan's, Inc., stating:

> "Bryan's, Inc. was formed in a classic manner, the $10,000.00 loan by Keith Bryan being more than sufficient operating capital. Bryan's Inc. paid all obligations except the obligation to Hanewald in a timely fashion, and since there was no evidence of bad faith by the Bryans, the corporate shield of Bryan's Inc. should not be pierced."

Hanewald appealed from the refusal to hold the individual defendants personally liable.

Insofar as the judgment fails to impose personal liability upon Keith and Joan Bryan, the corporation's sole shareholders, we agree with Hanewald that the trial court erred. We base our decision on the Bryans' statutory duty to pay for shares that were issued to them by Bryan's, Inc.

Organizing a corporation to avoid personal liability is legitimate. Indeed, it is one of the primary advantages of doing business in the corporate form. *See generally* 1 W. FLETCHER, CYCLOPEDIA OF THE LAW OF PRIVATE CORPORATIONS § 14 (1983); J. Gillespie, *The Thin Corporate Line: Loss of Limited Liability Protection*, 45 N.D. L. Rev. 363 (1969). However, the limited personal liability of shareholders does not come free. As this court said in *Bryan v. Northwest Beverages*, 69 N.D. 274, 285 N.W. 689, 694 (1939), "the mere formation of a corporation, fixing the amount of its capital stock, and receiving a certificate of incorporation, do not create anything of value upon which the company can do business." It is the shareholders' initial capital investments which protects their personal assets from further liability in the corporate enterprise. See *Cross v. Farmers' Elevator Co. of Dawson*, 31 N.D. 116, 153 N.W. 279, 282 (1915); *Jablonsky v. Klemm*, 377 N.W.2d 560, 566 (N.D.1985) (quoting *Briggs Transp. Co. v. Starr Sales Co.*, 262 N.W.2d 805, 810 (Iowa 1978)) ["shareholders should in good faith put at the risk of the business unencumbered capital reasonably adequate for its prospective liabilities."]; and J. Gillespie, *supra*, 45 N.D. L. Rev. at 388 ["Proper capitalization might be envisioned as the principal prerequisite for the insulation of limited liability."]. Thus, generally, shareholders are not liable for corporate debts beyond the capital they have contributed to the corporation. *See* 1 F. O'NEAL AND R. THOMPSON, O'NEAL'S CLOSE CORPORATIONS § 1.09 (3rd ed. 1987).

This protection for corporate shareholders was codified in the statute in effect when Bryan's, Inc. was incorporated and when this action was commenced, former § 10-19-22, N.D.C.C. [North Dakota Century Code]:

> "Liability of subscribers and shareholders. — A holder of or subscriber to shares of a corporation shall be under no obligation to the corporation or its creditors with respect to such shares other than the obligation to pay to the corporation the full consideration for which such shares were issued or to be issued."

This statute obligated shareholders to pay for their shares as a prerequisite for their limited personal liability.

The kinds of consideration paid for corporate shares may vary. Article XII, § 9 of the state constitution says that "no corporation shall issue stock or bonds except for money, labor done, or money or property actually received; and all fictitious increase of stock or indebtedness shall be void." Section 10-19-16, N.D.C.C., allowed "the consideration for the issuance of shares [to] be paid, in whole or in part, in money, in other property, tangible or intangible, or in labor or services actually performed for the corporation. . . . [But] neither promissory notes nor future services shall constitute payment or part payment for shares of a corporation." And only "when payment of the consideration . . . shall have been received by the corporation, [can] such shares . . . be considered fully paid and nonassessable." *Id.* The purpose of these constitutional and statutory provisions is "to protect the public and those dealing with the corporation. . . . " *Bryan v. Northwest Beverages, supra,* 285 N.W. at 694.

In this case, Bryan's, Inc. was authorized to issue 100 shares of stock each having a par value of $1,000. Keith Bryan and Joan Bryan, two of the original incorporators and members of the board of directors, were each issued 50 shares. The trial court determined that "Bryan's Inc. did not receive any payment, either in labor, services, money, or property, for the stock which was issued." Bryans have not challenged this finding of fact on this appeal. We hold that Bryans' failure to pay for their shares in the corporation makes them personally liable under § 10-19-22, N.D.C.C., for the corporation's debt to Hanewald.

Drafters' comments to § 25 of the Model Business Corporation Act, upon which § 10-19-22 was based, sketched the principles:

> "The liability of a subscriber for the unpaid portion of his subscription and the liability of a shareholder for the unpaid balance of the full consideration for which his shares were issued are based upon contract principles. The liability of a shareholder to whom shares are issued for overvalued property or services is a breach of contract. These liabilities have not been considered to be exceptions to the absolute limited liability concept. Where statutes have been silent, courts have differed as to whether the cause of action on the liabilities of shareholders for unpaid consideration for shares issued or to be issued may be asserted by a creditor directly, by the corporation itself or its receiver, or by a creditor on behalf of the

corporation. The Model Act is also silent on the subject for the reason that it can be better treated elsewhere." 1 Model Business Corporation Act Annotated 2d, Comment to § 25, at pp. 509-510 (1971).

This court, in *Marshall-Wells Hardware Co. v. New Era Coal Co.*, 13 N.D. 396, 100 N.W. 1084 (1904), held that creditors could directly enforce shareholders' liabilities to pay for shares held by them under statutes analogous to § 10-19-22. We believe that the shareholder liability created by § 10-19-22 may likewise be enforced in a direct action by a creditor of the corporation.

Our conclusion comports with the generally recognized rule, derived from common law, that "a shareholder is liable to corporate creditors to the extent his stock has not been paid for." 18A Am. Jur. 2d Corporations § 863, at p. 739 (1985). *See also, Id.* at §§ 906 and 907. One commentator has observed:

> "For a corporation to issue its stock as a gratuity violates the rights of existing stockholders who do not consent, and is a fraud upon subsequent subscribers, and upon subsequent creditors who deal with it on the faith of its capital stock. The former may sue to enjoin the issue of the stock, or to cancel it if it has been issued, and has not reached the hands of a bona fide purchaser; and the latter, according to the weight of authority, may compel payment by the person to whom it was issued, to such extent as may be necessary for the payment of their claims." 11 W. Fletcher, Cyclopedia of the Law of Private Corporations § 5202, at p. 450 (1986).

The shareholder "is liable to the extent of the difference between the par value and the amount actually paid," and "to such an extent only as may be necessary for the satisfaction of" the creditor's claim. 11 W. Fletcher, *supra*, § 5241, at pp. 550, 551.

The defendants asserted, and the trial court ruled, that the $10,000 loan from Keith and Joan Bryan to the corporation was nevertheless "more than sufficient operating capital" to run the business. However, a shareholder's loan is a debt, not an asset, of the corporation. Where, as here, a loan was repaid by the corporation to the shareholders before its operations were abandoned, the loan cannot be considered a capital contribution.

We conclude that the trial court, having found that Keith and Joan Bryan had not paid for their stock, erred as a matter of law in refusing to hold them personally liable for the corporation's debt to Hanewald. The debt to Hanewald does not exceed the difference between the par value of their stock and the amount they actually paid. Therefore, we reverse in part to remand for entry of judgment holding Keith and Joan Bryan jointly and severally liable for the entire corporate debt to Hanewald. The judgment is otherwise affirmed.

## NOTES: OBLIGATION OF SHAREHOLDER TO PAY FOR SHARES: THE DEMISE OF PAR VALUE AND WATERED STOCK

1.   MBCA section 6.22(a) is substantially similar to the language of the North Dakota statute quoted in the court's opinion. The statute provides the authority for the limited liability of shareholders, provided that the full consideration for the

shares issued has actually been paid, and also provides that, notwithstanding the language of subsection (a), a shareholder "may become personally liable by reason of his acts or conduct." This provision, in effect, leaves the door open to personal liability of shareholders under, inter alia, the doctrine of piercing the corporate veil as well as under state fraudulent conveyance statutes and federal bankruptcy laws.

**2.** The court's opinion, citing both the North Dakota Constitution and section 10-19-16 of the North Dakota Century Code, indicates that payment for shares consisting of promissory notes or promises to render future services do not constitute valid consideration for the issuance of shares. N.D. CENT. CODE § 10-19-16. This provision was eliminated from the 1984 MBCA. Section 6.21(b) now provides that "[t]he board of directors may authorize shares to be issued for consideration consisting of any tangible or intangible property or benefit to the corporation, including cash, promissory notes, services performed, contracts for services to be performed, or other securities of the corporation." And subsection (c) provides that the judgment of the board of directors concerning the adequacy of the consideration received for shares is "conclusive." These sweeping changes have the effect of making it very difficult for creditors or other shareholders to argue that the consideration received for shares of stock is less than the stated value of the stock. Cases brought challenging the issuance of such "watered stock" used to be commonplace. Were these changes wise or do they invite fraud?

**3.** The opinion notes that the shares of Bryan's Inc. which were issued to Keith and Joan Bryan had a "par value" of $1000 per share which, the opinion assumes, was the price at which the shares were to be issued. Under MBCA (1969), and under many state corporate codes still in effect today, shares of stock were required to have a "par value" which was the minimum price at which such stock legally could be sold. The theory was that having a par value protected creditors by assuring them that at least a minimum amount of capital, consisting of the par value times the number of shares issued, had been paid into the corporate treasury. However such protection was more illusory than real since, once the corporation was functioning as a going concern, it might quickly exhaust the capital paid for the shares. Furthermore, promoters seized on the device of fixing a nominal par value ranging from a few cents to a dollar a share for the stock but actually selling that stock at a much higher price. The use of "low par" stock made it difficult for creditors to argue that consideration paid for stock was inadequate (so-called "watered stock") since the statutes of the time commonly provided that the only obligation on the corporation was to issue stock for a consideration equal or greater than its par value. Thus, the total par value of the stock issued was a relatively trifling sum and provided no real protection to creditors, even at the outset.

Growing realization that the concept of par value provided no real protection to creditors or shareholders led to its abandonment in the MBCA (1984) in favor of the language of section 6.22(a), quoted *supra*. In fact, probably the most dramatic changes in the latest version of the MBCA relate to the abandonment of the concept of par value in section 6.22 together with the sweeping discretion given to the board of directors to determine the type and adequacy of consideration received for shares in section 6.21. These provisions effectively do away with the concepts of "watered stock" and "par value."

4. Would Keith and Joan Bryan have been any better off if, instead of simply not paying for the shares issued to themselves, they had given the corporation their promissory notes in payment for the stock? How might that have changed the legal strategy of Harold Hanewold in seeking to collect on his judgment?

## C.  DIVIDENDS

### DODGE v. FORD MOTOR CO.
Supreme Court of Michigan
170 N.W. 668 (1919)

[Ford Motor Company was extremely prosperous in the early decades of the 20th Century. Beginning in 1908 and thereafter, the company paid a regular dividend totaling 60% of its net profits and, in 1911 through 1915 it paid special dividends of over $40 million. Henry Ford, the majority shareholder with 58% of the outstanding stock who dominated the board of directors, then stated that no more special dividends would be paid and that the profits would be reinvested in the business. Plaintiffs, holders of 10% of the company's stock sued to compel the payment of a dividend of at least 75% of the corporation's surplus. The lower court, ruling for plaintiff's, ordered payment of a dividend of $19,275,000.]

OSTRANDER, J.

\*    \*    \*

When plaintiffs made their complaint and demand for further dividends, the Ford Motor Company had concluded its most prosperous year of business. The demand for its cars at the price of the preceding year continued. It could make and could market in the year beginning August 1, 1916, more than 500,000 cars. Sales of parts and repairs would necessarily increase. The cost of materials was likely to advance, and perhaps the price of labor; but it reasonably might have expected a profit for the year of upwards of $60,000,000. It had assets of more than $132,000,000, a surplus of almost $112,000,000, and its cash on hand and municipal bonds were nearly $54,000,000. Its total liabilities, including capital stock, was a little over $20,000,000. It had declared no special dividend during the business year except the October, 1915, dividend. It had been the practice, under similar circumstances, to declare larger dividends. Considering only these facts, a refusal to declare and pay further dividends appears to be not an exercise of discretion on the part of the directors, but an arbitrary refusal to do what the circumstances required to be done. These facts and others call upon the directors to justify their action, or failure or refusal to act. In justification, the defendants have offered testimony tending to prove, and which does prove, the following facts: It had been the policy of the corporation for a considerable time to annually reduce the selling price of cars, while keeping up, or improving, their quality. As early as in June, 1915, a general plan for the expansion of the productive capacity of the concern by a practical duplication of its plant had been talked over by the executive officers and directors and agreed upon; not all of the details having been settled, and no formal action of directors having been taken. The erection of a smelter was considered, and engineering and other data in connection therewith secured. * * *

The plan, as affecting the profits of the business for the year beginning August 1, 1916, and thereafter, calls for a reduction in the selling price of the cars. It is true that this price might be at any time increased, but the plan called for the reduction in price of $80 a car. The capacity of the plant, without the additions thereto voted to be made (without a part of them at least), would produce more than 600,000 cars annually. This number, and more, could have been sold for $440 instead of $360, a difference in the return for capital, labor, and materials employed of at least $48,000,000. In short, the plan does not call for and is not intended to produce immediately a more profitable business, but a less profitable one; not only less profitable than formerly, but less profitable than it is admitted it might be made. The apparent immediate effect will be to diminish the value of shares and the returns to shareholders.

It is the contention of plaintiffs that the apparent effect of the plan is intended to be the continued and continuing effect of it, and that it is deliberately proposed, not of record and not by official corporate declaration, but nevertheless proposed, to continue the corporation henceforth as a semi-eleemosynary institution and not as a business institution. In support of this contention, they point to the attitude and to the expressions of Mr. Henry Ford.

*     *     *

"My ambition," said Mr. Ford, "is to employ still more men, to spread the benefits of this industrial system to the greatest possible number, to help them build up their lives and their homes. To do this we are putting the greatest share of our profits back in the business."

"With regard to dividends, the company paid sixty percent on its capitalization of two million dollars, or $1,200,000, leaving $58,000,000 to reinvest for the growth of the company. This is Mr. Ford's policy at present, and it is understood that the other stockholders cheerfully accede to this plan."

He had made up his mind in the summer of 1916 that no dividends other than the regular dividends should be paid, "for the present."

*     *     *

The record, and especially the testimony of Mr. Ford, convinces that he has to some extent the attitude towards shareholders of one who has dispensed and distributed to them large gains and that they should be content to take what he chooses to give. His testimony creates the impression, also, that he thinks the Ford Motor Company has made too much money, has had too large profits, and that, although large profits might be still earned, a sharing of them with the public, by reducing the price of the output of the company, ought to be undertaken. We have no doubt that certain sentiments, philanthropic and altruistic, creditable to Mr. Ford, had large influence in determining the policy to be pursued by the Ford Motor Company — the policy which has been herein referred to.

It is said by his counsel that —

"Although a manufacturing corporation cannot engage in humanitarian works as its principal business, the fact that it is organized for profit does not prevent the existence of implied powers to carry on with humanitarian motives such charitable works as are incidental to the main business of the corporation."

\*   \*   \*

In discussing this proposition, counsel have referred to decisions such as *Hawes v. Oakland*, 104 U. S. 450,; *Taunton v. Royal Ins. Co.*, 2 Hem. & Miller, 135; *Henderson v. Bank of Australia*, L. R. 40 Ch. Div. 170; *Steinway v. Steinway & Sons*, 40 N. Y. Supp. 718; People v. Hotchkiss, 136 App. Div. 150. These cases, after all, like all others in which the subject is treated, turn finally upon the point, the question, whether it appears that the directors were not acting for the best interests of the corporation. . . . There should be no confusion (of which there is evidence) of the duties which Mr. Ford conceives that he and the stockholders owe to the general public and the duties which in law he and his co-directors owe to protesting, minority stockholders. A business corporation is organized and carried on primarily for the profit of the stockholders. The powers of the directors are to be employed for that end. The discretion of directors is to be exercised in the choice of means to attain that end, and does not extend to a change in the end itself, to the reduction of profits, or to the non-distribution of profits among stockholders in order to devote them to other purposes.

. . . As we have pointed out, and the proposition does not require argument to sustain it, it is not within the lawful powers of a board of directors to shape and conduct the affairs of a corporation for the merely incidental benefit of shareholders and for the primary purpose of benefiting others, and no one will contend that, if the avowed purpose of the defendant directors was to sacrifice the interests of shareholders, it would not be the duty of the courts to interfere.

We are not, however, persuaded that we should interfere with the proposed expansion of the business of the Ford Motor Company. In view of the fact that the selling price of products may be increased at any time, the ultimate results of the larger business cannot be certainly estimated. The judges are not business experts. . . . We are not satisfied that the alleged motives of the directors, in so far as they are reflected in the conduct of the business, menace the interests of shareholders. It is enough to say, perhaps, that the court of equity is at all times open to complaining shareholders having a just grievance.

Assuming the general plan and policy of expansion and the details of it to have been sufficiently, formally, approved at the October and November, 1917, meetings of directors, and assuming further that the plan and policy and the details agreed upon were for the best ultimate interest of the company and therefore of its shareholders, what does it amount to in justification of a refusal to declare and pay a special dividend or dividends? The Ford Motor Company was able to estimate with nicety its income and profit. It could sell more cars than it could make. Having ascertained what it would cost to produce a car and to sell it, the profit upon each car depended upon the selling price. That being fixed, the yearly income and profit was determinable, and, within slight variations, was certain.

. . . The company was continuing business, at a profit — a cash business. If the total cost of proposed expenditures had been immediately withdrawn in cash from the cash surplus (money and bonds) on hand August 1, 1916, there would have remained nearly $30,000,000.

Defendants say, and it is true, that a considerable cash balance must be at all times carried by such a concern. But, as has been stated, there was a large daily, weekly, monthly, receipt of cash. The output was practically continuous and was continuously, and within a few days, turned into cash. Moreover, the contemplated expenditures were not to be immediately made. The large sum appropriated for the smelter plant was payable over a considerable period of time. So that, without going further, it would appear that, accepting and approving the plan of the directors, it was their duty to distribute on or near the 1st of August, 1916, a very large sum of money to stockholders.

. . . It is obvious that an annual dividend of 60 percent upon $2,000,000, or $1,200,000, is the equivalent of a very small dividend upon $100,000,000, or more.

The decree of the court below fixing and determining the specific amount to be distributed to stockholders is affirmed. . . .

STEERE, FELLOWS, STONE, and BROOKE, JJ., concurred with OSTRANDER, J. MOORE, J. (concurring):

I agree with what is said by JUSTICE OSTRANDER upon the subject of capitalization. I agree with what he says as to the smelting enterprise on the River Rouge. I do not agree with all that is said by him in his discussion of the question of dividends. I do agree with him in his conclusion that the accumulation of so large a surplus establishes the fact that there has been an arbitrary refusal to distribute funds that ought to have been distributed to the stockholders as dividends. I therefore agree with the conclusion reached by him upon that phase of the case.

BIRD, C. J., and KUHN, J., concurred with MOORE, J.

# NOTES

1. *Dodge v. Ford Motor Co.* is one of only a few cases in which the directors' decision regarding the amount of a dividend has been successfully challenged. Plaintiffs in the case were the Dodge brothers, founders of the Dodge Motor Car Company, now a part of Chrysler Corporation. Other than their own immediate monetary gain, why might they have been anxious to force Ford to declare a larger dividend?

2. To the extent that Henry Ford thought it proper to operate the corporation for the benefit of groups other than his fellow shareholders, he was ahead of his time. Today, there is widespread acceptance of the legitimacy of operating the corporation for the benefit of groups other than the shareholders. The legitimacy of corporate charitable giving, although challenged in the past, is now explicitly authorized in MBCA section 3.02(13). More broadly, many states have adopted so-called "constituency" statutes which generally allow the directors, in determin-

ing what course of action is in the best interest of the corporation, to consider the interests of employees, suppliers, customers, and the communities in which they operate. These statutes were adopted primarily to give directors more discretion in opposing unwanted third party take-over bids which, due to the premium price would almost always be in the interest of the shareholders. However, the ABA Committee on Corporate Laws has rejected proposed amendments of MBCA section 8.30 to include such "constituency" language, primarily because of concern that such language essentially removes any ascertainable standard of conduct against which directors actions can be judged. *See* ABA Committee on Corporate Laws, Other Constituency Statutes: Potential for Confusion.

## KONSTAND v. PRIME GROUP REALTY TRUST
Appellate Court of Illinois, First District
2011 Ill. App. Unpub. LEXIS 2356 (Sept. 29, 2011)

STERBA, J.

PGRT was organized in 1997 as a Maryland real estate investment trust with primary real estate holdings located primarily in the Chicago area. Two classes of shares in PGRT were issued, common shares and series B preferred shares. Under PGRT's Articles of Incorporation (Articles), its Board is granted "full, exclusive and absolute power, control and authority" over the property and business of PGRT. The Articles further provide that PGRT's preferred shareholders are entitled to fixed quarterly dividends, a liquidation preference of $25 per share, and the right to elect two board members in the event that preferred dividends are not paid for six consecutive quarters. The preferred share dividends are cumulative, so that even if the Board exercises its discretion and opts not to pay the dividends in a given quarter, the dividends continue to accrue. The Articles prohibit the payment of common share dividends unless PGRT is current on all preferred dividend payments. Konstand has owned preferred shares since October 2004. He currently owns 3,507.895 preferred shares in PGRT.

Common shares of PGRT were traded on the New York Stock Exchange from November 12, 1997 until July 1, 2005, at which time Prime Office acquired all of PGRT's common shares in a merger transaction. Prime Office is a wholly owned subsidiary of Lightstone, which is owned by Lichtenstein. Following the acquisition, PGRT's Board consisted of: Lichtenstein, Chairman and Principal of Lightstone; Patterson, PGRT's President and Chief Executive Officer; Schurer, Chief Financial Officer of Lightstone; de Vinck, Senior Vice President of Lightstone; and three independent members, Whittemore, Sabin and Tominus. In 2007, Owen, President and Chief Operating Officer of Lightstone, replaced Schurer on the Board.

Between 2005 and mid-2008, the Board declared three common dividend distributions to Prime Office, the sole common shareholder. The first dividend of $30 million was paid in July 2005, a second dividend of $76 million was paid in February 2006, and a third dividend of $15 million was paid in May 2008. At the time of the first dividend, PGRT had a cash balance of $70 million. In January 2006, just prior to the declaration of the second dividend, PGRT obtained loans totaling $113 million, secured by real estate owned by PGRT.

On October 20, 2009, Konstand filed a shareholder derivative action alleging that the July 2005 and February 2006 dividend distributions constituted a breach of fiduciary duty. Konstand stated that he filed the action on behalf of himself and all preferred shareholders similarly situated for the benefit of PGRT. Konstand alleged that Lightstone and Lichtenstein used their control of PGRT to engage in a scheme of corporate waste and looting. Konstand further stated that the dividend distributions and the obtained loans were not based upon any legitimate business purpose and were not made in the best interest of PGRT. The complaint alleged that the Board owed a fiduciary duty to the preferred shareholders and to the company itself, and that it breached that duty when it distributed the two dividend payments. The circuit court found that all of the allegations regarding breach of fiduciary duty were conclusory and that more facts were necessary. The court further found that there were no allegations in the complaint that the contract governing the preferred shareholders' entitlement to dividends was breached, or that the Maryland statute governing the distribution of dividends was violated. Finally, the court found that the allegations regarding demand futility were conclusory. The complaint was therefore dismissed without prejudice.

On October 2, 2010, Konstand filed an amended complaint in which he extended his breach of fiduciary duty claims to include the May 2008 dividend distribution. The amended complaint also included direct quotes from U.S. Securities and Exchange Commission (SEC) filings relating to the control of PGRT and the fact that the majority of the Board members were not independent. The complaint included additional quotes from SEC filings related to PGRT's operating losses and insufficient cash resources. The breach of fiduciary duty counts were amended to include allegations that the Board violated the standard of care required under the Maryland business judgment rule. On January 5, 2011, the circuit court dismissed the amended complaint with prejudice, finding that the complaint failed to allege facts to support the proposition that the dividend payments caused insolvency in violation of Maryland law. Konstand timely filed this appeal.

\* \* \*

Konstand argues that the circuit court erred in dismissing his complaint because he adequately pled breaches of fiduciary duty where he alleged that the 3 dividend distributions in question contributed to PGRT's cash flow problems that eventually required the attempted sale of the company. Konstand also argues that he adequately pled that demand on the Board was futile, as required for a shareholder to bring a derivative action without first making a demand on the Board to pursue the claim on behalf of the company. Finally, Konstand contends that the circuit court erred in dismissing his complaint on the grounds that he did not plead that the payment of the dividends rendered PGRT insolvent because a breach of fiduciary duty can still occur even if the dividend payments complied with the applicable statute.

\* \* \*

Section 2-311 of the Maryland Code provides:

"(a) (1) No distribution may be made if, after giving effect to the distribution:

(i) The corporation would not be able to pay indebtedness of the corporation as the indebtedness becomes due in the usual course of business; or

(ii) . . . the corporation's total assets would be less than the sum of the corporation's total liabilities plus, unless the charter permits otherwise, the amount that would be needed, if the corporation were to be dissolved at the time of the distribution, to satisfy the preferential rights upon dissolution of stockholders whose preferential rights on dissolution are superior to those receiving the distribution."

Md. Code Ann., Corps. & Ass'ns § 2-311(a)(1) (2008).

Although this statute, referred to by the circuit court and the parties as the "dividend statute," was relied on by the circuit court in its finding that Konstand failed to state a cause of action upon which relief may be granted, Konstand dismisses this statute as "irrelevant" in his briefs. He first claims that the dividend statute "simply limits dividend distributions for insolvent or soon to be insolvent companies." In his reply brief, Konstand asserts that the dividend statute "simply confers the right to issue dividends." He does not cite to any case law for either of these assertions, and we decline to read these interpretations into the purpose of this statute. The title of section 2-311 is "Limitations on distributions." The statute clearly details the circumstances under which dividend distributions are prohibited for all companies.

In arguing that the dividend distributions constituted a breach of fiduciary duty, Konstand never suggests that the Board violated Maryland's dividend statute. Rather, he contends that the Board can still breach its fiduciary duty even if it complies with the dividend statute, relying on *Sinclair Oil Corp. v. Levien*, 280 A.2d 717, 721 (Del. 1971), in which the court stated that even when a company complies with the applicable statute, a court can still interfere with dividend payments if the plaintiff can prove that a particular dividend was not grounded on any reasonable business objective. In his reply brief, Konstand further relies on a footnote in *Renbaum v. Custom Holding, Inc.*, 386 Md. 28, 54 n.22, 871 A.2d 554 (2005), in which the court stated that "the decision to distribute dividends is a discretionary act by the board of directors in most cases and may be subject to review under the business judgment rule."

However, we note that although Konstand cites the Maryland business judgment rule statute (Md. Code Ann., Corps. & Ass'ns § 2-405(1)(a) (West 2008)) in his reply brief, he never provides the text of this statute and does not cite any cases in which the statute was determined to have been violated. Indeed, he does not even argue that the Board violated this statute. Similarly, Konstand does not argue that he met his burden as stated in *Sinclair Oil* of proving that any of the dividend payments he challenges were not grounded on any reasonable business objective. Instead, Konstand merely states that the Board breached its fiduciary duty by wasting PGRT's assets through the payment of excessive dividends in bad faith, relying on quotes from various SEC filings related to cash flow problems. Konstand cites no case law to support his claims of corporate waste and bad faith. . . . Therefore, this court will address Konstand's arguments only to the extent that he has developed those arguments in his briefs. Konstand devotes the bulk of his argument section to the three dividend payments and the additional loans taken out by PGRT to fund the second dividend payment, but his argument consists primarily of conclusory statements about corporate waste and looting.

Moreover, the cases Konstand relies on do not support his arguments. In *Sinclair Oil*, the parent company owned about 97% of its subsidiary's stock and nominated all members of its board of directors. *Sinclair Oil*, 280 A.2d at 719. Over a 6 year period, the board of directors authorized the payment of $108,000,000 in dividends, which exceeded the subsidiary's earnings in that period by $38,000,000. Although the payments were still made in compliance with a Delaware statute authorizing payment of dividends out of surplus or net profits, the plaintiff in Sinclair Oil argued that the decision to pay the dividends was based on an improper motive.

The court in *Sinclair Oil* noted that because the dividends complied with the Delaware statute, "the alleged excessiveness of the payments alone would not state a cause of action." *Id.* at 721. The court went on to state:

> "Nevertheless, compliance with the applicable statute may not, under all circumstances, justify all dividend payments. If a plaintiff can meet his burden of proving that a dividend cannot be grounded on any reasonable business objective, then the courts can and will interfere with the board's decision to pay the dividend." *Id.*

However, the court concluded that the plaintiff in *Sinclair Oil* had not met this burden where he simply argued that the dividend payments drained the subsidiary of cash to the extent that it was unable to expand. Instead of bolstering Konstand's argument, this case does the opposite. Alleged excessiveness of the payments alone is not sufficient grounds for stating a cause of action. Even if this case does stand for the proposition that mere compliance with the applicable statute may not be enough to justify all dividend payments, Konstand has not shown that any of the three dividend payments were not grounded on any reasonable business objective. Instead, he simply concludes that certain negative or cautionary statements, in various SEC filings and letters spanning 6 years, demonstrate that the three dividend payments constituted corporate waste and looting.

Similarly, Konstand's reliance on Renbaum is misplaced. Konstand focuses on the language in *Renbaum* that the distribution of dividends may be subject to the business judgment rule, and appears to ignore the language that the distribution of dividends is a discretionary act. *See Renbaum*, 386 Md. at 54 n.22. Moreover, Konstand does not even describe what the business judgment rule is, nor does he suggest that the Board failed to comply with this statute in any way.

Although Konstand's complaint alleges that the Board breached its fiduciary duty to both the preferred shareholders and PGRT, the appellees correctly note that, in general, the only duties owed to preferred shareholders are contractual. . . . Konstand appears to concede this point, stating in his reply brief that he merely seeks to vindicate PGRT's rights. Thus, Konstand's argument on appeal is that the Board breached its fiduciary duty to PGRT through corporate waste and bad faith in spite of the fact that the Board did not violate Maryland's dividend statute.

In *Sinclair Oil,* the court stated that under the business judgment rule, "a court will not interfere with the judgment of a board of directors unless there is a showing of gross and palpable overreaching." *Sinclair Oil,* 280 A.2d at 720. Even if we were to agree with Konstand that mere compliance with the dividend statute was insufficient, Konstand has not shown that the three dividend payments constituted "gross and palpable overreaching." It is well settled that the payment of dividends rests in the discretion of the board of directors and that courts will not interfere with the judgment of the board unless fraud or gross abuse of discretion have been shown.

Konstand asks this court to rule that compliance with the Maryland dividend statute alone does not absolve the Board of liability for breach of fiduciary duty through corporate waste and bad faith, yet he does not phrase his arguments in the language of the cases he relies upon for this proposition. Rather than arguing that the dividend payments were not based on any reasonable business objective or that the Board violated the business judgment rule, Konstand simply contends that the dividend payments were made in bad faith and constituted corporate waste. However, he has cited no case law discussing what constitutes corporate waste or bad faith.

Bad faith on the part of a board "will be inferred where 'the decision is so beyond the bounds of reasonable judgment that it seems essentially inexplicable on any [other] ground.' " *In re Rexene Corp. Shareholders Litigation,* Nos. 10, 897, 11,300, 1991 Del. Ch. LEXIS 81, 1991 WL 77529 at *4 (quoting *In re J.P. Stevens & Co. Shareholders Litigation,* 542 A.2d 770, 780 (Del. Ch. 1988)). Thus, the test for bad faith is just as stringent, if not more so, than the test in Sinclair Oil. A transaction constitutes corporate waste if "what the corporation has received is so inadequate in value that no person of ordinary, sound business judgment would deem it worth what the corporation has paid." *Id.* Where the transaction in question is a dividend payment, the size of the dividend cannot be compared to any amount received by the corporation, so the test for waste is the same as the test for bad faith.

A Maryland court in another suit involving the same defendants and the same dividend distributions dealt with the issue of bad faith in an unpublished opinion in *Jolly Roger Fund, LP v. Prime Group Realty Trust,* No. 24-C-06-010433, 2007 Md. Cir. Ct. LEXIS 10 (Aug. 16, 2007). Although the court in *Jolly Roger* was addressing the issue of the contractual rights of the preferred shareholders, its determination on the issue of good faith and fair dealing is relevant here. After noting that the Board had extensive authority to conduct PGRT's affairs, the court concluded:

> "None of the transactions, sales, or other related events as presented to this Court demonstrate that PGRT acted in bad faith, or otherwise rendered PGRT an empty shell of a company. PGRT unquestionably remains a going concern."

Konstand provides selective financial data relating to cash on hand at the time of the first dividend payment, and makes references to outstanding debt, but provides no additional financial information about PGRT's overall condition at any specific time. He quotes from a letter sent to the preferred shareholders in 2011, nearly 6 years after the first dividend distribution, in which PGRT urges the shareholders to approve a possible merger because without the merger, PGRT would be unable to generate sufficient cash flow to sustain its operations. However, this does not constitute evidence that PGRT's situation in 2011 was a direct result of the dividend payments, nor that the Board authorized the payments in bad faith.

Moreover, Konstand has provided no evidence that the decision to authorize the three dividend payments in question was so beyond the bounds of reasonable judgment as to seem inexplicable or that the dividend payments were not grounded on any reasonable business objective, and he has made no showing of gross-overreaching, self-dealing or unconscionable conduct. The Maryland dividend statute provides clear guidelines for what constitutes excessive dividend payments. In the absence of pleading facts that would show that PGRT violated this statute, the only way Konstand can survive a motion to dismiss is by showing that one of the other tests he relies on were met, or by showing that, in spite of compliance with the statute, the dividend payments were made in bad faith.

Because the dividend payments did not violate Maryland law and Konstand has shown no evidence of bad faith or corporate waste despite the Board's compliance with the statute, we conclude that the circuit court correctly dismissed Konstand's complaint for failure to state a cause of action upon which relief may be granted. Because we are affirming the dismissal of his complaint, we decline to address Konstand's arguments related to demand futility.

AFFIRMED.

## GIACOPELLI v. GUIDUCCI

Supreme Court of New York, Queens County

2007 N.Y. Misc. LEXIS 3859 (Apr. 17, 2007)

LANE, J.

### A. Procedural Background

Plaintiffs brought this action individually and derivatively against defendants seeking monetary damages and equitable relief alleging three causes of action in the Complaint: (1) for breach of fiduciary duty, misappropriation of corporate assets and self-dealing, (2) for an accounting, and (3) to compel the distribution of retained earnings.

### B. Factual Background

Plaintiffs James J. Giacopelli and Doris J. Giacopelli, his wife, and defendant Dino Guiducci ("Guiducci") are stockholders of Madison Plaza Homes, Inc. ("MPH"). MPH is a closely held domestic real estate corporation organized on December 12, 1978 for the express purposes, among others things, of acquiring, developing, constructing and leasing real properties, and which owns income producing rental properties in Queens County, New York. Guiducci owns 75 percent of the stock and plaintiffs, as joint tenants with right of survivorship, own 25 percent of the stock. The corporation has only two directors. Dino Guiducci is a director and president, while James J. Giacopelli is a director and secretary. The Bylaws provide that corporate action requires unanimous consent of the two (2) directors, so that neither, director has voting control. Up until December 31, 2005, MPH had accumulated earnings of $1,886,115.00. For the period of January 1997 through June 2003, MPH made regular distributions to plaintiffs totaling $315,000.00. MPH has not declared a dividend or made a distribution to the stockholders since 2001. Since in or about December, 2001, plaintiffs have demanded that Guiducci distribute to them 25 percent of the accumulated corporate earnings, but MPH has declined to do so. By letter dated May 16, 2003, Dino Guiducci as director and president of MPH, notified Giacopelli "that there are no planned shareholder distributions at this time." Although plaintiffs have not received a distribution of the corporate profits, plaintiffs have paid personal income taxes on such corporate profits based upon their proportionate ownership of the outstanding shares of stock. Defendant Guiducci contends that he is seeking to retain and accumulate the earnings for the purpose of creating a capital fund to use to finance the purchase of prospective investment real estate property and that they, the plaintiffs, have nothing to do with the making of policy concerning declaration and distribution of dividends in the corporate defendant. The issue between plaintiffs and the defendant Guiducci concerns his objection to the distribution of the corporate earnings to the plaintiffs. This action was commenced on June 17, 2005.

*    *    *

## D. Summary of Corporation Law

The third cause of action in the Complaint upon which this motion is based is essentially a claim by the stockholders and director Giacopelli to compel the declaration of a dividend upon all of the outstanding stock. (The court notes that it appears that plaintiffs apparently are seeking a declaration of a dividend solely upon their 25 percent share of the out-standing stock and not upon all of the outstanding stock).

### 1. Stockholder

Generally, a stockholder has no individual cause of action to recover dividends that have not been declared. All that a stockholder can do is to sue in equity to cause the court to perform a corporate function which the directors would have executed except for bad faith (*Gordon v. Elliman*, 306 NY 456, 119 N.E.2d 331 [1954]). Unlike an action at law by stockholders to recover dividends that have been declared, a suit in equity to compel the declaration of dividends is, in theory against recalcitrant directors to cause them to perform their duty as officials of the corporation.

The management of a corporation is vested in its board of directors. It is a part of the function of the directors to determine: whether or not dividends should be paid, the amount of such dividends, and when they should be paid. The stockholders cannot substitute their judgment for that of the directors (*Liebman v. Auto Strop Co.*, 241 NY 427, 150 N.E. 505 [1926] [The court held that where the directors, in their discretion, have failed to declare a dividend, the court will not interfere with such discretion unless such failure was the result of bad faith or a clear abuse of discretion on the part of the directors, unless it is shown that the directors have acted or are about to act in bad faith and for a dishonest purpose. However, in a proper case, of course, a court of equity will interfere, but Facts must be presented from which the court can find that such action has underlying it a fraudulent purpose and corrupt intent].

## 2. Corporate Directors

It is well settled that "whether or not dividends shall be paid, and the amount of the dividend at any time, is primarily to be determined by the directors, and there must be bad faith or a clear abuse of discretion on their part to justify a court of equity in interfering; accordingly, unless fraud, bad faith or dishonesty on the part of directors can be shown, their judgment in withholding a dividend from the stockholders will be regarded as conclusive" (*Gordon v. Elliman*, 306 NY 456, 459, [1954], citing: 11 FLETCHER'S CYCLOPEDIA CORPORATIONS [Perm. ed.], § 5325). The New York cases, amply sustain the necessity to establish bad faith on the directors' part (*City Bank Farmers' Trust Co v. Hewitt Realty Co.*, 257 N.Y. 62 [1931]; Courts will not ordinarily make determinations as to whether a corporation shall declare dividends, as internal management of corporation rests within sound discretion of board of directors and only in instances where it is shown that refusal to declare dividends is harmful to corporation and stockholders generally, will court depart from general rule.

*    *    *

The management of a corporation is vested in its board of directors. It is a part of the function of the directors to determine whether or not dividends should be paid, the amount of such dividends, and when they should be paid. It is the prerogative of the board of directors to declare a dividend which, in the absence of fraud, bad faith or dishonesty, is conclusive. Question of whether or not dividend is to be declared or distribution of some kind should be made is exclusively a matter of business judgment for corporation's board of directors.

Plaintiffs do not contend, and have proffered no evidence to show that there exists any internal dissension with respect to the daily operation of the defendant corporation's business activities. For purposes of this motion for partial summary judgment, plaintiffs' interests are solely driven by their desire to get cash out of the corporation, especially in light of the fact that they have already paid personal income taxes based on MPH's accumulated earnings and profits.

Plaintiffs in their capacities as stockholders and director contend that defendant Guiducci has refused to agree to a distribution of corporate earnings. One director, plaintiff Giacopelli has elected that the corporation declare a dividend, and the other director, defendant Guiducci has opposed any distribution or dividend. The internal dissension does not arise from the day-to-day operation of the corporation, but rather, it principally derives from a business disagreement between two 50 percent voting directors concerning the business decision with respect to whether the corporation should retain earnings for future purchases of real estate or whether the earnings should be distributed to the stockholders.

Other than the bald conclusory allegation by plaintiffs that defendant Guiducci's refusal to distribute MPH's accumulated earnings is an act of bad faith and dishonesty and is abuse of discretion, plaintiffs have failed to proffer any evidence to support such conclusion. Plaintiffs fail to allege any conduct that constitutes dishonesty, or bad faith on the part of defendant other than defendant's refusal to agree with plaintiffs' demand to declare a distribution of corporate earnings.

Plaintiffs contend that defendant Guiducci's reason for retaining the corporate earnings for the purpose of accumulating capital to finance future purchases of investment real estate is an exercise of unsound business judgment, bad faith, or at best a pretext. Although plaintiffs submitted evidence showing that as of 2005, MPH had cash on hand in excess of $1,886,115.00, and from 2000 has operated at a profit, such evidence is insufficient to show that there is no triable issue of fact that the decision of defendant Guiducci to not declare or pay dividends was in bad faith or abuse of discretion, or unsound business judgment as a matter of law.

Plaintiffs failed to submit any evidence to show that the dispute between the parties is no more than a deadlock between the two 50 percent voting directors of a corporation over a decision to declare and distribute dividends. On the record plaintiffs have presented to this court, plaintiffs have failed to demonstrate that there is no triable issue of fact as to whether there was no valid business reason to withhold distribution of accumulated earnings. Plaintiffs have failed to make a prima facie showing that the inability of the two 50 percent voting directors to agree on whether corporate earnings should be distributed as dividends constitutes grounds for a court in equity to interfere with the internal management and operation of the corporation absent factual proof of fraud, bad faith or dishonesty.

On the other hand, defendant has submitted evidence to establish a triable issue of fact as to whether the decision to retain and accumulate earnings to provide capital for MPH to purchase additional investment property indicates sound judgment and business management. Sound business management must look, not only to the present requirements of the business, but it must closely consider the requirements of the future as well. Defendant established a triable issue of fact as to whether it is sound business management judgment to not distribute any or part of the accumulated earnings in dividends for the reason of accumulating capital to finance future purchases of real estate.

*   *   *

Whether it is considered a failure of plaintiffs to establish a prima facie case or defendants raising triable issues, the record on this motion does not permit a conclusion that as a matter of law the defendant's decision to accumulate earnings for the purpose of making future purchases of real estate was an act or conduct that constitutes bad faith or dishonesty on the part of the defendant Guiducci.

Accordingly, plaintiffs' motion for partial summary judgment is denied.

## NOTES

**1.** The two previous cases illustrate the deference courts afford to directors regarding the payment of dividends. As the cases indicate, the courts usually side with controlling shareholder as long as there are plausible business reasons to support the decision regarding dividends, even if undeniable harm results.

**2.** After studying the policies underlying the business judgment rule in the Duty of Care chapter, you may better understand the reasons why the courts are reluctant to second guess decisions regarding the payment of dividends.

## NOTE: STATUTORY CONTROLS GOVERNING THE PAYMENT OF DIVIDENDS

The previous cases have dealt with common law standards applicable to the board of director's decisions regarding the payment of dividends. A detailed examination of this area of the law is customarily left to an advanced course in Corporate Finance. However, lest the student leave with the misimpression that there is no statutory authority in point, a brief discussion of relevant statutory authority is included here.

In past decades, states have utilized a variety of statutory controls over the payment of dividends. The most common of these were: (1) an "earned surplus" test which restricted the payment of dividends to the corporation's unrestricted earned surplus, *i.e.*, its accumulated, undistributed net income; (2) a "balance sheet surplus test" which allowed dividends to be paid to the point where, after payment, asset were at least equal to liabilities plus "capital stock" (the total par value of all stock outstanding); an "insolvency test" which allowed the payment of dividends as long as the ability of the corporation to pay its debts as they became due was not impaired and (4) a "nimble dividend" test which allowed the corporation to pay its dividends out of the current year's net earnings, even though the accumulated earned surplus of the corporation was a deficit. Many statutes combine two or more of these tests. The 1969 version of the MBCA, which was widely adopted, combined the earned surplus test with the balance sheet surplus and equity insolvency tests. *See* § 45. Each of these tests suffered from a number of defects; they were difficult and confusing to apply and the outcome depended on what set of accounting principles were employed. For an excellent account of these mechanics and the shortcomings of each of these tests, see B. Manning, Legal Capital (Foundation Press, 2d ed. 1991). Furthermore, because they were easily evaded, they provided little or no real protection to the creditors and others who they were intended to protect.

One of the major innovations of the 1984 version of the Model Business Corporation Act was its substantial simplification of the statutory treatment of dividends. These innovations, some of which seemed at the time to be revolutionary, are as follows:

(1)   MBCA section 6.40 (1984) defines all distributions of cash by the corporation, whether in the form of cash dividends, redemption of shares or repurchase of shares, as "distributions" and all are treated in a similar manner. The MBCA (1969) and many state statutes based upon it utilized different tests for each, even though the effect on the corporation's creditors of cash flowing out of the corporation was the same.

(2)   The basic test adopted for distributions under section 6.40(c) requires that, after distribution, assets must at least be equal to liabilities plus liquidation preferences, if any, on preferred stock and that the corporation be able to pay its

debts as they become due. The test is more lenient than that contained in MBCA (1969). First, an equity cushion of "legal capital" is no longer required (indeed the concepts of par value and "stated capital" discussed earlier in this chapter have been abandoned). Second, there is no requirement that dividends be paid out of earned surplus. Third, the MBCA (1984) does not require that the directors employ Generally Accepted Accounting Principles but allows them to use any accounting principles or method of valuation "that is reasonable under the circumstances."

In adopting a relatively lenient standard, the Drafters of the MBCA (1984) implicitly recognized the reality so well stated by Manning, *supra*, that statutory dividend tests rarely provided any real protection for shareholders and served mainly as a trap for the unwary, particularly unsophisticated individuals in small family corporations. The real protections for creditors are most often contractual in nature rather than statutory. Publicly traded bonds are required by the Federal Trust Indenture Act, 15 U.S.C. § 77aaa *et seq.*, to be issued under a trust indenture, an elaborate document containing a wealth of protections limiting the freedom of the corporation to incur additional indebtedness or pay imprudent cash dividends and requiring it to maintain a conservative balance sheet, among other things. Furthermore, an indenture trustee must be appointed to supervise compliance with terms of the indenture and, if necessary, bring suit on behalf of bondholders against the corporation to enforce its provisions. *See, e.g., Metropolitan Life Insurance Co. v. RJR Nabisco, supra*, for examples of bond covenants. Even in close corporations not subject to the Trust Indenture Act, banks and other lenders typically include protective covenants in loan agreements or require personal guarantees from shareholders and do not rely on statutory protections to safeguard their interests.

In conclusion, it is necessary to be aware of statutory provisions regulating dividends because violations expose the individuals involved to potentially serious consequences. Most state statutes make directors voting to declare an unlawful dividend personally liable to creditors for losses suffered as a result, *e.g.*, MBCA (1984) § 8.33. However, an attorney representing an actual or potential creditor needs to realize that he or she must rely primarily on individually negotiated contractual provisions to provide meaningful protection to the creditor against imprudent action by the corporation.

## NOTE: STOCK DIVIDENDS AND STOCK SPLITS

In addition to cash dividends, a corporation may also declare a stock dividend to its shareholders payable in shares of stock of the corporation. A corporation may also declare a stock split in which existing shares of stock are split into additional shares of stock of the corporation. The transactions differ essentially in accounting treatment rather than in substance; both stock dividends and stock splits have the effect of increasing the number of shares of stock outstanding. A corporation which declares a 100% stock dividend and one which declares a two for one stock split have both doubled the number of shares held by each its shareholders.

It is important to emphasize that, in both cases the real wealth of the shareholder remains unchanged by the transaction. This is due to the fact that the total number of shares of the corporation has increased in direct proportion to the number of new shares issued so the shareholders' percentage ownership of the corporation remains unchanged. Thus, if a corporation with 1000 shares outstanding declares a two for one stock split, a shareholder holding 100 shares before the split, or 10% of the number of shares outstanding, will hold 200 shares after the split. However, because the total number of shares issued by the corporation has increased from 1000 to 2000, the shareholder's percentage ownership in the corporation remains unchanged at 10%. Occasionally confusion results from incorrect use of terminology in the press. One might read a story stating that the board of directors of XYZ Corp. declared a "stock dividend" of 50 cents per share. This is not technically a stock dividend but rather a cash dividend of 50 cents per share of stock.

If there is no real effect on the shareholder's wealth, why then do corporations declare stock splits and stock dividends? First, in public corporations, the primary reason may be to decrease the market price per share, thereby increasing the marketability of the corporation's stock. A two for one split, for example, should cause the market price of a corporation whose stock is trading at $50 per share to decrease to around $25 per share. Since most investors prefer to deal in "round lots" of multiples of 100 shares of stock, this means that after the split $2500 will purchase 100 shares versus $5000 before the split. Also a closely held corporation preparing to make a public offering of its securities may find that, if it has comparatively few shares outstanding with a book value in the thousands of dollars, it needs to split its stock by a large amount, e.g., 100 for one or 1000 for one, both to reduce the price per share and to create a larger number of shares to offer to the public. Second, many economists believe that a stock split or dividend has a "signaling effect" to investors, indicating that the board of directors has confidence in the corporation's future prosperity. Many stock splits or large stock dividends do in fact come at a time when the price per share of the corporation has increased due to steadily increased earnings, a situation which the board may attempt to publicize by declaring the split or dividend thereby hoping to further increase investor interest in the stock.

Third, a corporation wishing to conserve cash yet send a positive signal to shareholders may declare a stock dividend of a few percent, thereby giving shareholders a few new shares of stock while avoiding a distribution of cash from the corporation's treasury. Thus a corporation might choose to declare a two percent stock dividend in lieu of a $1.00 per share cash dividend. A shareholder holding 100 shares who desires to realize some additional cash may then sell off the two shares of stock received in the stock dividend while preserving his initial round lot of 100 shares. A small stock dividend has the further advantage over a cash dividend in that the stock dividend, per se, is not a taxable event to the shareholder. It is only when the shareholder sells the shares received that he is subject to a capital gains tax liability on the proceeds.

Ordinarily, all that is required to effectuate a stock dividend or stock split is a resolution passed by the board of directors authorizing the transaction and setting forth its terms. The board must, however, be careful that the larger number of shares which will be outstanding after the transaction does not exceed the number of shares authorized in the articles of incorporation. If it would, then an amendment must first be authorized by the board and submitted to the shareholders for approval. There are also accounting consequences to such a transaction which may be troublesome, particularly in jurisdictions with older "par value" legal capital statutes along the lines of those in MBCA (1969). In such jurisdictions, either the par value per share must be reduced in proportion to the number of new shares of stock issued, or funds equal to the par value of the newly issued shares, must be transferred from capital stock to the stated capital account. Increasing the stated capital account is undesirable from the board's point of view because it reduces the earned surplus or capital surplus available from which dividends may be declared. Thus, the board usually prefers to reduce the par value per share before declaring a sizable stock dividend or stock split.

# Chapter 9

# CORPORATE GOVERNANCE AND THE ROLES OF OFFICERS, DIRECTORS, AND SHAREHOLDERS

## A.  THE ROLES OF SHAREHOLDERS VS. DIRECTORS

### AUER v. DRESSEL
Court of Appeals of New York
118 N.E.2d 590 (1954)

DESMOND, J.

This article 78 of the Civil Practice Act proceeding was brought by class A stockholders of appellant R. Hoe & Co., Inc., for an order in the nature of mandamus to compel the president of Hoe to comply with a positive duty imposed on him by the corporation's by-laws. Section 2 of article I of those by-laws says that 'It shall be the duty of President to call a special meeting whenever requested in writing so to do, by stockholders owning a majority of the capital stock entitled to vote at such meeting'. On October 16, 1953, petitioners submitted to the president written requests for a special meeting of class A stockholders, which writings were signed in the of the holders of record of slightly more than 55% of the class A stock. The president failed to call the meeting and, after waiting a week, the petitioners brought the present proceeding. The answer of the corporation and its president was not forthcoming until October 28, 1953, and it contained, in response to the petition's allegation that the demand was by more than a majority of class A stockholders, only a denial that the corporation and the president had any knowledge or information sufficient to form a belief as to the stockholding of those who has signed the requests. Since the president, when he filed that answer has had before him for at least ten days the signed requests themselves, his denial that he had any information sufficient for a belief as to the adequacy of the number of signatures was obviously perfunctory and raised no issue whatever (see *People ex rel. Kelly v. Common Council of The City of Brooklyn*, 77 N.Y. 503, 511; *People ex rel. Joseph Fallert Brewing Co. v. Lyman*, 53 App. Div. 470, 474, *aff'd.* 168 N.Y. 669; *Matter of Guess*, 16 Misc. 306, 307). There was no discretion in this corporate officer as to whether or not to call a meeting when a demand therefor was put before him by owners of the required number of shares. The important right of stockholders to have such meetings called will be of little practical value if corporate management can ignore the requests, force the stockholders to commence legal proceedings, and then, by purely formal denials, put the stockholders to lengthy and expensive litigation, to establish facts as to stockholdings which are peculiarly within the knowledge of the corporate officers. In such a situation, Special Term did the correct thing in disposing of the matter summarily, as commanded by section 1295 of the Civil Practice Act (see Third Annual Report of N.Y. Judicial Council, 1937, pp. 186–188; *Ackerman v. Kern*, 256 App. Div. 626, 629, 630, *aff'd.* 281 N.Y. 87).

The petition was opposed on the further alleged ground that none of the four purposes for which petitioners wished the meeting called was a proper one for such a class A stockholders' meeting. Those four stated purposes were these: (A) to vote, upon a resolution indorsing the administration of petitioner Joseph L. Auer, who had been removed as president by the directors, and demanding that he be reinstated as such president; (B) voting upon a proposal to amend the charter and by-laws to provide that vacancies on the board of directors, arising from the removal of a director by stockholders or by resignation of a director against whom charges have been preferred, may be filled, for the unexpired term, by the stockholders only of the class theretofore represented by the director so removed or so resigned; (C) voting upon a proposal that the stockholders hear certain charges preferred, in the requests, against four of the directors, determine whether the conduct of such directors or any of them was inimical to the corporation and, if so, to vote upon their removal and vote for the election of their successors; and (D) voting upon a proposal to amend the by-laws so as to provide that half of the total number of directors in office and, in any event, not less than one third of the whole authorized number of directors constitute a quorum of the directors.

The Hoe certificate of incorporation provides for eleven directors, of whom the class A stockholders, more than a majority of whom join in this petition, elect nine and the common stockholders elect two. The obvious purpose of the meeting here sought to be called (aside from the endorsement and reinstatement of former president Auer) is to hear charges against four of the class A directors, to remove them if the charges be proven, to amend the by-laws so that the successor directors be elected by the class A stockholders, and further to amend the by-laws so that an effective quorum of directors will be made up of no fewer than half of the directors in office and no fewer than one third of the whole authorized number of directors. No reason appears why the class A stockholders should not be allowed to vote on any or all of those proposals.

The stockholders, by expressing their approval of Mr. Auer's conduct as president and their demand that he be put back in that office, will not be able, directly, to effect that change in officers, but there is nothing invalid in their so expressing themselves and thus putting on notice the directors who will stand for election at the annual meeting. As to purpose (B), that is, amending the charter and by-laws to authorize the stockholders to fill vacancies as to class A directors who have been removed on charges or who have resigned, it seems to be settled law that the stockholders who are empowered to elect directors have the inherent power to remove them for cause (*In re Koch*, 257 N.Y. 318, 321, 322; *Abberger v. Kulp*, 156 Misc. 210, 212; 1 *White on New York Corporations*, pp. 558–559; 2 *Fletcher's Cyclopedia Corporations* [Perm.Ed.], §§ 351, 356. Of course, as the *Koch* case points out, there must be the service of specific charges, adequate notice and full opportunity of meeting the accusations, but there is no present showing of any lack of any of those in this instance. Since these particular stockholders have the right to elect nine directors and to remove them on proven charges, it is not inappropriate that they should use their further power to amend the by-laws to elect the successors of such directors as shall be removed after hearing, or who shall resign pending hearing. Quite pertinent at this point is *Rogers v. Hill* (289 U.S. 582, 589) which made light of an argument that stockholders, by giving power to the directors to make by-laws, had lost their own power to make them; quoting a New Jersey case, the United States Supreme Court said: "It would be preposterous to leave the real owners of the corporate property at the mercy of their agents, and the law has not done so." Such a change in the by-laws, dealing with class A directors only, has no effect on the voting rights of the common stockholders, which rights have to do with the selection of the remaining two directors only. True, the certificate of incorporation authorizes the board of directors to remove any director on charges, but we do not consider that provision as an abdication by the stockholders of their own traditional, inherent power to remove their own directors. Rather, it provides an additional method. Were that not so, the stockholders might find themselves without effective remedy in a case where a majority of the directors were accused of wrongdoing and, obviously, would be unwilling to remove themselves from office.

We fail to see, in the proposal to allow class A stockholders to fill vacancies as to class A directors, any impairment or any violation of paragraph (h) of article Third of the certificate of incorporation, which says that class A stock has exclusive voting rights with respect to all matters "other than the election of directors." That negative language should not be taken to mean that class A stockholders, who have an absolute right to elect nine of these eleven directors, cannot amend their by-laws to guarantee a similar right, in the class A stockholders and to the exclusion of common stockholders, to fill vacancies in the class A group of directors.

There is urged upon us the impracticability and unfairness of constituting the numerous stockholders a tribunal to hear charges made by themselves, and the incongruity of letting the stockholders hear and pass on those charges by proxy. Such questions are really not before us at all on this appeal. The charges here are not, on their face, frivolous or inconsequential, and all that we are holding as to the charges is that a meeting may be held to deal with them. Any director illegally removed can have his remedy in the courts.

The order should be affirmed, with costs, and the Special Term directed forthwith to make an order in the same form as the Appellate Division order with appropriate changes of dates.

Van Voorhis, J. (dissenting).

*      *      *

An examination of the request for a special meeting by these stockholders indicates that none of the proposals could be voted upon legally at the projected meeting. The purposes of the meeting are listed as A, B, C and D. Purpose A is described as "Voting upon a resolution endorsing the administration of Joseph L. Auer, as President of the corporation, and demanding his immediate reinstatement as President." For the stockholders to vote on this proposition would be an idle gesture, since it is provided by section 27 of the General Corporation Law, Consol. Laws, that "The business of a corporation shall be managed by its board of directors." The directors of Hoe have been elected by the stockholders for stated terms which have not expired, and it is their function and not that of the stockholders to appoint the officers of the corporation.

Purpose B of the special meeting is to vote upon a proposal to amend the certificate and the by-laws so as to provide "that vacancies on the Board of Directors arising from the removal of a director by stockholders or by resignation of a director against whom charges have been preferred may be filled, for the unexpired term, only by the stockholders of the class theretofore represented by the director so removed." This proposal is interwoven with the next one (C), which is about to be discussed, which is to remove four directors from office before the expiration of their terms in order to alter the control of the corporation. Proposal B must be read in the context that the certificate of incorporation provides for eleven directors, of whom the class A stockholders elect nine and the common stockholders two. So long as any class A shares are outstanding, the voting rights with respect to all matters "other than the election of directors" are vested exclusively in the holders of class A stock, with one exception now irrelevant. This means that the common stockholders are entitled to participate directly in the election of two directors, who, in turn, are authorized by the certificate to vote to fill vacancies occurring among the directors elected by the class A shareholders. This proposed amendment would deprive the directors elected by the common stockholders of the power to participate in filling the vacancies which petitioners hope to create among the class A directors, four of whom they seek to remove by proposal C which is about to be discussed. Such an alteration would impair the existing right of the common stockholders to participate in filling vacancies upon the board of directors and could not be legally adopted at this meeting demanded by petitioners from which the common stockholders are excluded. The effect would be to reclassify voting powers of the common stockholders within the meaning of subdivision 3 of section 35 of the Stock Corporation Law, which is something that section 51 prohibits without the vote of "the holders of all shares of any class or classes that will be adversely affected," and this is ordained even "regardless of any provision to the contrary in the certificate of incorporation."

Purpose C of the special meeting is to vote "upon a proposal that the Stockholders (1) hear the charges preferred against Harry K. Barr, William L. Canady, Neil P. Cullom and Edwin L. Munzert, and their answers thereto; (2) determine whether such conduct on their part or on the part of any of them was inimical to the best interest of R. Hoe & Co., Inc., and if so (3) vote upon the removal of said persons or any of them as directors of R. Hoe & Co., Inc., for such conduct, and (4) vote for the election of directors to fill any vacancies on the Board of Directors which the Stockholders may be authorized to fill." By means of this proposal, it is sought to change the control of the corporation and to accomplish what A could not achieve, viz., remove the existing president and reappoint Mr. Joseph L. Auer as president of the corporation. Neither the language nor the policy of the corporation law subjects directors to recall by the stockholders before their terms of office have expired, merely for the reason that the stockholders wish to change the policy of the corporation. [T]his court said that "It would be somewhat startling to the business world if we definitely announced that the directors of a corporation were mere employees and that the stockholders of the corporation have the power to convene from time to time and remove at will any or all of the directors, although their respective terms of office have not expired." Fraud or breach of fiduciary duty must be shown. . . . In that event, directors may be removed from office before expiration of term by an action brought under subdivision 4 of section 60 of the General Corporation Law. In addition to such procedure, paragraph Fourteenth of the certificate of incorporation states: "Any director of the corporation may at any time be removed for cause as such director by resolution adopted by a majority of the whole number of directors then in office, provided that such director, prior to his removal, shall have received a copy of the charges against him and shall have had an opportunity to be heard thereon by the board. The By-Laws may provide the manner of presentation of the charges and of the hearing thereon."

Petitioners have instituted this proceeding on the theory that although no power is conferred upon the stockholders by the certificate or the by-laws to remove directors before the expiration of their terms, with or without cause, power to do so for cause is inherent in them as the body authorized to elect the directors . . .. Petitioners have argued that the grant of this power to the board of directors to remove some of their number for cause after trial, does not eliminate what is asserted to be the inherent right of the stockholders to do likewise. No cases are cited in support of the latter proposition.

* * *

The petition fails to state facts on account of which the remaining directors would be disqualified to hear and decide whatever charges may be presented against the four directors above named, nor has any reason been shown why the delegation of this power to the directors in the corporate charter does not preclude the exercise of the same power by the stockholders. If petitioners' position be correct, separate trials on the same charges might be conducted by both the board of directors and by the stockholders, with conflicting results.

Such cases as have been cited in support of a power in the stockholders to remove directors for cause are clear in holding that such action can be taken only subject to the rule that "specific charges must be served, adequate notice must be given, and full opportunity of meeting the accusations must be afforded." . . .

Although the demand by these petitioners for a special meeting contains no specification of charges against these four directors, the proxy statement, circulated by their protective committee, does describe certain charges. No point appears to be made of the circumstance that they are not contained in the demand for the meeting. Nevertheless, although this proxy statement enumerates these charges and announces that a resolution will be introduced at the special meeting to hear them, to determine whether sufficient cause exists for the removal of said persons as directors, and, if so, to remove them and to fill the resulting vacancies, the stockholders thus solicited are requested to sign proxies running to persons nominated by petitioners' protective committee. Inasmuch as this committee, with which petitioners are affiliated, has already charged in the most forceful terms that at least one of these directors has been guilty of misconduct and that "his clique of directors have removed Joseph L. Auer as President," it is reasonable to assume that the case of the accused directors has already been prejudged by those who will vote the proxies alleged to represent 255,658 shares of class A stock, and that the 1,200 shareholders who are claimed to have signed proxies have (whether they know it or not) voted, in effect, to remove these directors before they have been tried. The consequence is that these directors are to be adjudged guilty of fraud or breach of faith in absentia by shareholders who have neither heard nor ever will hear the evidence against them or in their behalf. Such a procedure does not conform to the requirements [the law].

*     *     *

It is not for the courts to determine which of these warring factions is pursuing the wiser policy for the corporation. If these petitioners consider that the stockholders made a mistake in the election of the present directors, they should not be permitted to correct it by recalling them before the expiration of their terms on charges of fraud or breach of fiduciary duty without a full and fair trial, which, if not conducted in court under section 60 of the General Corporation Law, is required to be held before the remaining directors under paragraph Fourteenth of the certificate of incorporation. The difficulty inherent in conducting such a trial by proxy may well have been the reason on account of which the incorporators delegated that function to the board of directors under paragraph Fourteenth of the certificate of incorporation. If it were to develop (the papers before the court do not contain evidence of such a fact) that enough of the other directors would be disqualified so that it would be impossible to obtain a quorum for the purpose, it may well be doubted that these directors could be tried before so large a number of stockholders sitting in person (if it were possible to assemble them in one place) or that they could sit in judgment by proxy. In ancient Athens evidence is said to have been heard and judgment pronounced in court by as many as 500 jurors known as dicasts, but in this instance, if petitioners be correct in their figures, there are 1,200 class A stockholders who have signed requests or proxies, and these are alleged to hold only somewhat more than half of the outstanding shares. Since it would be impossible for so large a number to conduct a trial in person, they could only do so by proxy. Voting by proxy is the accepted procedure to express the will of large numbers of stockholders on questions of corporate policy within their province to determine, and it would be suitable in this instance if the certificate of incorporation had reserved to stockholders the power to recall directors without cause before expiration of term, as in *Abberger v. Kulp* (156 Misc. 210) but it is altogether unsuited to the performance of duties which partake of the nature of the judicial function, involving, as this would need to do if the accused directors are to be removed before the expiration of their terms, a decision after trial that they have been guilty of faithlessness or fraud. Section 60 of the General Corporation Law is always available for that purpose if the occasion requires.

The final proposal to be voted on at this special meeting (D) relates simply to an amendment to the by-laws so as to provide that a quorum shall consist of not less than one half of the number of directors holding office and in no event less than one third of the authorized number of directors. Section 8 of article II of the by-laws already provides that one half of the total number of directors shall constitute a quorum; the modification that a quorum shall in no event be less than one third of the authorized number of directors was proposed in the event of the removal of the four defendant directors whom petitioners seek to eliminate.

In as much as we consider that for the foregoing reasons none of the business for which the special meeting is proposed to be called could legally be transacted, this proceeding should be dismissed. It is not necessary to analyze whether under other circumstances an order would lie in the nature of an alternative rather than a peremptory mandamus.

The petition should be dismissed, with costs in all courts.

## CENTAUR PARTNERS, IV v. NATIONAL INTERGROUP, INC.
Supreme Court of Delaware
582 A.2d 923 (1990)

WALSH, J.

This is an appeal by Centaur Partners, IV ("Centaur") from a decision of the Court of Chancery which determined that the classified Board of Directors of National Intergroup, Inc. ("National") could not be enlarged without an 80% supermajority stockholder vote. The Chancery litigation was a result of Centaur's efforts to increase the size of National's board of directors through the use of written consents to amend the by-laws in order to permit a majority of the board to be elected at the 1990 annual stockholders meeting.

We conclude that the Court of Chancery correctly determined that Article Eighth of National's charter was clear and unambiguous in requiring that an 80% supermajority would be needed to amend the by-laws of National, thereby overcoming the presumption of majority rule. Accordingly, we affirm the decision of the Court of Chancery.

Centaur is an investment partnership created to purchase, acquire, and effect transactions with respect to the securities of corporations listed on the New York Stock Exchange. At the time this action was filed, Centaur and the other members of its group (the "Centaur Group") owned 3,595,500 shares of National's common stock, which represented 16.53% of the shares outstanding. National is a Delaware corporation with its principal place of business in Pittsburgh, Pennsylvania. It is engaged in the wholesale distribution of pharmaceuticals, with significant operations and investments in the metals business.

On January 29, 1990, the Centaur Group filed a Schedule 13D with the Securities and Exchange Commission. In this filing, the Centaur Group stated that it believed the common stock of National to be undervalued and that stockholders could best realize value through the sale of all or a substantial part of the assets of National. The Centaur Group asserted that this could only be accomplished through the installation of a new slate of directors, to be elected at the 1990 annual stockholders meeting. This slate would be selected by Centaur and be committed to the sale of National or a substantial portion of its assets. In an effort to attain their objective, the Centaur Group sought to amend National's by-laws to provide for the enlargement of the board of directors from 9 to 15 members. This amendment would permit the Centaur Group to achieve the election of 8 directors at the 1990 annual meeting, thus giving the Centaur Group a majority of the directors on the board.

The Centaur Group stated in its 13D filing that in order to amend the by-laws, it required the written consent of a majority of the outstanding shares of common stock entitled to vote. The Centaur Group also claimed that it anticipates that National will argue that an 80% supermajority is needed to enlarge the board of directors. In order to resolve this dispute, Centaur brought a declaratory action in the Court of Chancery.

The present controversy has its genesis in a previous modification of National's certificate of incorporation and by-laws. On May 17, 1984, National held its 1984 annual stockholders meeting. Prior to this meeting, management proxies were issued which contained amendments to both the certificate of incorporation and the by-laws. In its original form, Article Eighth of the certificate of incorporation provided that the number of directors shall be set in the by-laws; the number of directors, however, could not be less than three. At the 1984 annual meeting, the stockholders approved the amendment of Article Eighth. The amended version of Article Eighth maintained its predecessor's requirement that the number of directors be fixed as provided in the by-laws and that the number not be less than three. The amended Article Eighth added two additional requirements. The first requirement was that of a classified board. The board was to be divided into three classes, with each class to serve a term of three years, and a new class to be elected each year. Second, the amended version of Article Eighth required that the affirmative vote of the holders of 80% or more of the voting power of the shares outstanding be required to amend this provision "or any similar provision" in the by-laws of the Corporation.

Section 16 of the original by-laws of National provided that the number of directors shall be fixed by the board of directors and that number shall not be less than three. At the 1984 annual meeting, the stockholders voted to amend the by-laws. The amended version of Section 16 states that the board of directors shall set the number of directors and that it shall not be less than three. The amended version of Section 16 also provides for the creation of a classified board and for the affirmative vote of 80% or more of the holders of the stock outstanding in order "to amend or repeal, or adopt any provision inconsistent with, this Section 16 or Section 139 of these By-Laws."

Centaur's declaratory judgment action sought a determination that the consents of only 50.1% of the outstanding shares would be required to amend the by-laws. Upon cross motions for summary judgment, the Court of Chancery held that National's charter and by-laws unambiguously require the affirmative approval of 80% of National's outstanding shares to amend or repeal, or adopt any provision inconsistent with, the classified board provision or the provision authorizing the board of directors to set the size of the board. The court rejected Centaur's contention that the "or any similar provision" language of Article Eighth was ambiguous and in the face of such ambiguity majority vote must control. This appeal followed.

The Court of Chancery ruled as a matter of law, upon cross motions for summary judgment, that National's charter and by-laws required a supermajority vote to change the composition of its board of directors. The construction or interpretation of a corporate certificate or by-law is a question of law subject to de novo review by this Court.

The Delaware General Corporation Law does not specify the percentage of votes necessary for the election of directors. *See* 8 Del. C. § 216. In the event the certificate of incorporation or by-laws fail to fix a percentage, a plurality of the votes present or represented by proxy at the stockholders meeting is required. 8 Del. C. § 216(3). Therefore, in the absence of a charter or by-law provision to the contrary, the rule in corporate elections is that the affirmative vote of a plurality of the shareholders is sufficient to elect directors.

In order to abrogate the rule of plurality control, charter and by-law provisions purporting to have that effect must be clear and unambiguous. . . . Such provisions do not achieve ambiguity simply because the parties disagree concerning their meaning. It is only if the disputed language, read in proper context, is reasonably susceptible of different interpretations that ambiguity may be found to exist.

In *Standard Power* [*& Light Corp. v. Investment Associates, Inc.*, 51 A.2d 572 (Del. Sup. 1947)], this Court held that the rules of corporate democracy are based in large part upon the principle that a majority of the votes cast at a stockholders meeting is sufficient to elect directors. 51 A.2d at 576. Although by statute a simple plurality provision now suffices, the result is the same: a charter or bylaw provision which purports to alter this principle must be "positive, explicit, clear and readily understandable . . . ." *Id.* This presumption is overcome only by a clear, unambiguous and unequivocal statement, in the charter or by-laws of a corporation, expressing the stockholders' desire that a specific percentage of votes be required.

The Delaware General Corporation Law affords considerable flexibility in the construction of mechanisms for corporate governance and control. One example of such a device is the supermajority vote provision. *Cf. Berlin v. Emerald Partners*, Del. Supr., 552 A.2d 482, 489 n.8 (1988) ("Supermajority vote provisions were originally formulated as antitakeover devices. By requiring a greater percentage of stockholders to approve a proposed action, stockholders are given more power to defeat actions adverse to their interests."). Thus, a high vote requirement may protect a minority shareholder against squeeze-out techniques employed by insurgents able to command a bare majority of votes. F. O'Neal & R. Thompson, *O'Neal's Oppression of Minority Shareholders* § 9:08, at 19 (2d ed. 1985). However, supermajority provisions give minority shareholders the power to veto the will of the majority, effectively disenfranchising the majority.

There exists in Delaware "a general policy against disenfranchisement." *Blasius Indus. v. Atlas Corp.*, Del. Ch., 564 A.2d 651, 669 (1988). This policy is based upon the belief that "the shareholder franchise is the ideological underpinning upon which the legitimacy of directorial power rests." Therefore, high vote requirements which purport to protect minority shareholders by disenfranchising the majority, must be clear and unambiguous. There must be no doubt that the shareholders intended that a supermajority would be required. When a provision which seeks to require the approval of a supermajority is unclear or ambiguous, the fundamental principle of majority rule will be held to apply.

In the present case, the charter and by-law provisions are not unclear or ambiguous. Article Eighth of National's charter provides that an 80% supermajority vote shall be required to amend or repeal that portion of the charter which requires three equal classes of directors, with one third to be elected annually, "or any similar provision contained in the By-Laws of the corporation." Section 16 of the by-laws states that the board of directors shall fix the number of directors and that it shall not be less than three. Section 16 also provides that an 80% vote shall be required to adopt a provision inconsistent with Section 16 or Section 13.

These provisions are clearly similar. They are similar because they address the same subject and impose the same requirement. The subject addressed by these provisions is amendments to the charter or by-laws which affect the size and election of the board of directors. The requirement imposed by these provisions is an 80% supermajority to amend the by-laws in order to enlarge the board of directors. Thus, the affirmative vote of 80% of the stockholders is required to amend the by-laws and enlarge the board of directors of National.

Centaur argues that the articles of incorporation do not explicitly require an 80% supermajority vote for the repeal of the entirety of Section 16. Centaur claims that the requirement only applies to those provisions which are similar and that the only similar provisions are the provisions which state that the directors shall be divided as equally as possible among the three classes. Thus, it is argued, the 80% requirement should not apply because Centaur does not wish to amend this provision. We disagree.

Corporate charters and by-laws are contracts among the shareholders of a corporation and the general rules of contract interpretation are held to apply. In the interpretation of charter and by-law provisions, "courts must give effect to the intent of the parties as revealed by the language of the certificate and the circumstances surrounding its creation and adoption." *Waggoner v. Laster*, Del. Supr., 581 A.2d 1127, 1134 (1990). Therefore, the intent of the stockholders in enacting particular charter or by-law amendments is instructive in determining whether any ambiguity exists.

In the present case, the context in which the amendments to the certificate of incorporation and accompanying by-laws were approved by the shareholders indicate that they were adopted in tandem and intended to be complementary. The relevant amendments to the certificate of incorporation and the accompanying by-law provision were adopted at the 1984 annual stockholders meeting. The changes were contained in the proxy materials which were distributed to the stockholders prior to the 1984 annual meeting. In a section entitled "Election of Directors by Class," the proxy materials state:

> [T]he Board of Directors has unanimously adopted resolutions recommending that the stockholders amend the Corporation's Certificate of Incorporation and the Corporation's By-Laws to provide for the division of the Corporation's directors into three classes, the directors in each class to serve for a term of three years . . . . The proposed amendments also contain a provision, which, if adopted, shall provide that the affirmative vote of the holders of 80% or more of the outstanding stock of the Corporation be required to amend or repeal these new provisions in the Certificate of Incorporation and the By-Laws.

This explanation illustrates the intended result of the proposed combined change in the charter and by-laws that the board be classified and that a supermajority vote of 80% or more be required to amend any portion of these two provisions.

The classification of the board and the 80% supermajority vote are designed to insure continuity in the board of directors and avoid hostile attempts to takeover the corporation. As the proxy materials recite:

> [a] further purpose of the proposed change is to discourage unfriendly takeovers of the Corporation. The attempts to seize control of public companies through the accumulation of substantial stock positions followed by a tender offer and squeeze out merger are well known today. These transactions are often followed by a substantial restructuring of the company, a significant disposition of assets or other extraordinary corporate action.

Given the clear language of the proxy materials, the conclusion is inescapable that the stockholders, in adopting these two provisions, evidenced an intent to classify the board and impose an 80% supermajority requirement on amendments to these sections in order to thwart attempts to seize control of National.

The Vice Chancellor determined that both the charter and by-law provisions deal with the number of directors, the classified nature of the board and the vote required to amend these provisions. We agree and find that Centaur's reading of Section 16 completely abrogates the intention of the stockholders who adopted these provisions at the 1984 annual meeting. Article Eighth clearly and unequivocally establishes a classified board with no more than a third of the board subject to replacement (other than death or resignation) in any one year. Moreover, both the charter provisions and the by-law provisions confer solely on the directors the power to fix the number of directors on the board "from time to time." Centaur's argument for a 50% threshold is contrary to the clear purpose reflected in the language of the amended certificate of incorporation. The proxy materials issued prior to the 1984 annual meeting indicate the intent of the stockholders in adopting the amendments was to impose an 80% supermajority requirement on attempts to amend these provisions.

Finally, in the event Centaur's by-law amendment were to be adopted it would be void. The Delaware General Corporation Law provides: "the bylaws may contain any provision, *not inconsistent* with law or with the certificate of incorporation . . . ." 8 Del.C. § 109(b) (emphasis added). Where a by-law provision is in conflict with a provision of the charter, the by-law provision is a "nullity." *Burr v. Burr Corp.*, Del. Ch., 291 A.2d 409, 410 (1972); see *Prickett v. American Steel and Pump Corp.*, Del. Ch., 253 A.2d 86, 88 (1969).

Centaur's proposed amendment to Section 16 of the by-laws states: "the number of Directors of the Corporation shall be fixed at fifteen (15) commencing as of the election of directors at the 1990 Annual Meeting of Stockholders. The foregoing sentence is not subject to amendment, alteration or repeal by the Board of Directors." Article Eighth of the articles of incorporation provides: "[t]he number of directors of the Corporation shall be fixed by and may from time to time be altered as provided in the By-Laws . . . ." To the extent that the directors have general authority to adopt or amend corporate by-laws, these two provisions are in obvious conflict. The by-law amendment proposed by Centaur fixes the number of directors at fifteen. Article Eight grants the board broad authority to fix the number of directors, which power may be exercised from time to time through the adoption of by-laws. Because the proposed provision is clearly "inconsistent with" the directors' power to enlarge the board without limit, it would be a nullity if adopted.

\*     \*     \*

AFFIRMED.

## John C. Coffee, Jr., *The Bylaw Battlefield: Can Institutions Change the Outcome of Corporate Control Contests?*
### 51 U. MIAMI L. REV. 605 (1997)[1]

What, if anything, can institutional investors do to influence the course and outcome of corporate control contests? The traditional answer was relatively little. To be sure, institutions could tender their shares in a tender offer or vote in a proxy contest to oust the incumbent board, but such a role was essentially reactive and contingent. It required that an offer actually be made before institutions could respond on an after-the-fact basis. Similarly, institutions have occasionally conducted precatory proxy campaigns calling upon the board to redeem its poison pill, but management was free to ignore these requests (and has done so).

Thus, the practical question is whether institutional investors can take some form of mandatory action in advance of a corporate control contest that effectively constrains management from resisting it. This year, institutions are trying. On several occasions this year, institutional shareholders have taken the initiative and conducted proxy solicitations to adopt a bylaw amendment that, under defined circumstances, would require the corporation's board of directors to redeem its poison pill in the face of a "fair" and fully financed tender offer for all the corporation's shares. If this can be done, the viability of the poison pill as the critical linchpin in management's defense strategy can be substantially undercut. Today, the poison pill can be overcome in most jurisdictions only by a proxy contest that unseats the incumbent directors; however, the target corporation has an effective defense to this technique: namely, the use of a staggered board, which typically stretches out the proxy fight for two elections and often the better part of two years (during which time the target may find other suitors to outbid the original bidder).

Thus, the prospect of a shareholder mandated redemption of the poison pill would significantly shift the balance of the advantage between bidder and target by telescoping the time it takes the bidder to achieve control. Even the more modest prospect that bylaw amendments might provide that poison pills could not be renewed or modified in the future without shareholder approval would have significant impact, because most shareholder rights plans were adopted in the mid to late 1980s and are now coming up for renewal. Thus, the advent of shareholder-passed bylaw amendments restricting defensive techniques could mark a significant new chapter in the continuing saga of the takeover wars.

---

\*    \*    \*

In 1992, Robert Monks, a leading shareholder activist, sought to include a proposal in Exxon's proxy statement to amend Exxon's bylaws in order to establish a three person shareholder advisory committee ("SAC") that would review Exxon's management and advise the board of shareholder views. This shareholder-elected SAC would have had the power to retain outside advisors, prepare reports and an annual evaluation that would be included in the corporation's proxy statement; its total budget could have run up to $12 million per year. Despite this arguable encroachment upon the board's authority, the SEC refused to let Exxon exclude the proposal under Rule 14a-8(c)(1).

\*    \*    \*

Ambiguous as the Exxon no action letter was, it was overshadowed later that year when CalPERS submitted a similar proposal to create an SAC to Pennzoil Corporation for inclusion in its proxy statement. This proposed bylaw had one additional important feature: it could not be amended or repealed without the approval of shareholders. In early 1993, the SEC staff granted Pennzoil's requested no action letter, thereby permitting the CalPERS proposal to be excluded. The staff seems to have been primarily troubled by a feature that was also present in the Exxon proposal: namely, a shareholder authorization of corporate funds without board approval. In response, CalPERS immediately revised its proposal, making it entirely precatory. Again, the SEC staff permitted the revised proposal to be excluded. This time, the rationale was that the ability of shareholders to adopt a bylaw that could not be amended by the directors raised "a substantial question under Delaware law." Given the "questionable validity of such bylaw amendment" in the SEC staff's view, the proposal could be excluded under Rule 14a8(c)(1).

\*    \*    \*

*See* Pennzoil Corp., SEC No-Action Letter, 1993 SEC No-Act. LEXIS 50 (Mar. 22, 1993). *See also* Henry Lesser & Ashley G. Gable, *Bylaw Amendment Proposals Since Exxon*, THE CORPORATE GOVERNANCE ADVISOR 12–13 (May/June 1996). While Exxon was a New Jersey corporation, Pennzoil was a Delaware corporation. Although this difference could justify a difference in outcome if the statutory provisions were different, nothing in the SEC's analysis in these two "no action" letters suggests that their differing outcomes were based on statutory differences.

\*    \*    \*

It would be the equivalent of reviewing Hamlet without noting who played the Prince of Denmark to discuss the new proliferation of shareholder-proposed bylaw amendments without focusing on the pivotal role of labor unions in these contests. Not only did the Teamsters bring the *Fleming* case [*International Brotherhood of Teamsters General Fund v. Fleming Cos.*, 1997 U.S. Dist. LEXIS 2980 (W.D. Okla. Jan. 24, 1997) — Eds.], but several other unions — among the Hotel Employees & Restaurant Employees International Union ("HERE") and the United Food and Commercial Workers Union ("UFCW") — have this year proposed a variety of bylaw amendments at other companies, which seek to redeem the poison pill, eliminate staggered boards, or establish confidential voting policies.

Some of these proposals have been advanced by unions, such as the Teamsters, that are substantial equity holders and have no discernable conflict of interest, but others have been proposed by unions (such as the UFCW) that hold only a token number of shares and view their activism as an extension of the collective-bargaining process. Understandably, managements tend to regard at least the latter form of activism as simple harassment; in effect, the union is attacking the poison pill not to profit as a shareholder, but to create a nuisance value that will enable it to negotiate higher worker benefits or salaries. For example, HERE has proposed a mandatory bylaw amendment that would require Harrah's Entertainment Inc. to not adopt or maintain any poison pill. . . .

## B.   CUMULATIVE VOTING

### ALLEN v. PARK NATIONAL BANK
United States Court of Appeals, Seventh Circuit
116 F.3d 284 (1997)

POSNER, CHIEF JUDGE.

This suit arises out of a struggle between Raymond Allen and Sanford Takiff for control of a national bank. It was filed by Allen, initially against the bank and its president, complaining that the bank's action in adjourning the shareholders' meeting at which the board of directors was to be elected in 1996, and in subsequently seating a board dominated by Takiff, violated provisions of the National Bank Act, 12 U.S.C. §§ 61, 71, regarding the orderly governance of national banks. Allen asked for an injunction commanding the bank to seat a board in accordance with the ballots that he had cast at the meeting. Takiff was allowed to intervene in the suit under Fed. R. Civ. P. 24(a) as a defendant and file a counterclaim against Allen under the ancillary jurisdiction of the federal courts (now a part of their supplemental jurisdiction, 28 U.S.C. § 1367(a)), claiming that Allen was entitled to no relief because he had cast votes for directors in such a way as to violate an agreement between the two men, and seeking an injunction commanding Allen to comply with the agreement as Takiff interpreted it. (The parties do not make clear what state's law governs the interpretation of the agreement, but it appears to be Illinois law, and we shall so assume.) The district judge conducted a bench trial. Although testimony and other evidence going beyond the text of the agreement were introduced, the judge concluded that he didn't have to resolve any evidentiary disputes because the agreement was unambiguous after all. He agreed with Takiff's interpretation and ordered Allen to cast votes in future elections for directors in accordance with that interpretation.

Allen and Takiff are equal owners of a holding company that owns the bulk of the shares in the bank. But Allen is the president of the company and under its bylaws votes the shares in elections for the bank's directors. Takiff, and Takiff family trusts that he appears to control although he is not the trustee, own additional shares in the bank; we shall call these Takiffss "directly owned" shares. The bank's board of directors has fourteen members, and Takiff claims that Allen agreed to cast an equal number of the holding company's bank votes for seven board candidates nominated by Allen and seven nominated by Takiff. If Takiff is right, then by concentrating the votes of his directly owned shares on two additional candidates he can elect nine directors, leaving Allen with only five. Allen claims the right to concentrate the holding company's votes on his seven nominees so that he can defeat the two additional Takiff candidates.

The holding company, P.N.B. Financial Corporation, had been formed by Allen and Takiff in 1978 to acquire the bank. Allen was made president of P.N.B. with power as we noted to vote its shares, and Takiff vice-president. P.N.B. owns 84 percent of the common stock of the bank, Takiff and his family 13 percent, Allen only .2 percent, and other shareholders the balance of less than 3 percent. Eventually the partners fell out, and in 1991 Takiff brought a suit in state court under section 12.50(b) of the Illinois Business Corporation Act, 805 ILCS 5/12.50(b), against Allen and the holding company to dissolve the holding company and distribute its shares in the bank to Allen and Takiff, which would give Takiff 55 percent of the bank's common stock. The suit was settled the following year. The holding company was not dissolved, but the settlement agreement provides that "P.N.B. will nominate (to the extent not nominated by others), and all its shares in the Bank will be voted for, election of seven directors nominated by Allen . . . and seven directors nominated by Takiff."

The National Bank Act ordains cumulative voting for directors. 12 U.S.C. § 61. That is, each shareholder is entitled to cast votes equal to the number of his shares times the number of directors to be elected and he can distribute his votes among the candidates as he wishes — he can cast all his votes for one candidate, or spread them evenly over all his candidates, or do anything in between. If the holding company spread its votes evenly among the seven nominees of Allen and the seven of Takiff, each of the fourteen would get 86,000 votes. This would enable Takiff to knock off two of Allen's nominees with two additional nominees of his own, because the bank shares directly owned by Takiff have 188,000 votes, enabling him to cast 94,000 votes for each of two nominees. Takiff saw this possibility and caused two additional candidates to be nominated in order to break the deadlock with Allen and seize control of the board. To defeat Takiff's maneuver, Allen cast 95,000 votes for each of his seven nominees and only 76,000 for each of Takiff's original seven and none for the additional nominees. By doing this, he defeated-or would have, had the meeting not been interrupted — not Takiff's additional nominees, who had more votes than any of Takiff's original ones, but two of the original ones, each of whom received only 78,000 votes (76,000 votes cast by the holding company at Allen's direction and 2,000 from other shareholders). The district court held that Allen's maneuver violated the settlement agreement.

The briefs range widely over the evidence introduced at trial — for remember that the district judge did conduct a trial, even though he concluded that the agreement was unambiguous and therefore the evidence that had been presented at trial was irrelevant. The district judge thought it clear that the agreement required Allen to distribute P.N.B.'s shares equally across seven Allen and seven Takiff nominees rather than to maneuver so as to prevent Takiff from using the bank shares that he owned directly to elect a majority of the board. The judge was probably right in his interpretation (the qualification is critical), if only because Allen's interpretation makes the agreement ambiguous and thus invites litigation.

Allen claims the right to decide, subject no doubt to judicial review, that candidates not nominated by Takiff are really Takiff nominees, entitling Allen to withhold crucial votes from the official Takiff nominees, that is, the nominees submitted by Takiff to Allen in the latter's capacity as president of and vote-caster for the holding company. Suppose Takiff sold the shares he directly owns, as of course he might. The purchaser would have 188,000 votes to cast for his own candidates, and suppose he cast 94,000 for each of two. Under Allen's view of the settlement agreement with Takiff, Allen could, if he deemed the purchaser an ally of Takiff, distribute the holding company's votes in such a way that all Allen's nominees were elected but that two of Takiff's official nominees, having only 76,000 votes, were defeated by the new shareholder — who might be (or become) not an ally of Takiff's but an ally of Allen's, giving Allen a nine to five margin over Takiff in the bank's board of directors. This prospect would make Takiff very reluctant to sell his directly owned shares; yet under Allen's interpretation of the settlement agreement, these shares though controlled by Takiff give him no increment in voting power, for although Takiff (including his family trusts) owns directly or indirectly 55 percent of the bank and Allen only 42 percent, Allen claims the right to deadlock the board of directors. A court asked to evaluate the consistency of Allen's action with the agreement would not be obligated to accept Allen's view of who was an ally of whom — but how likely is it that Takiff agreed in the settlement agreement to make the identification of alliances a litigable issue? Not very, especially with the danger of corporate paralysis that is implicit in an agreement that creates a deadlocked board of directors.

But to be certain that Allen's interpretation is wrong, we would have to know more about the likely outcome of the suit for dissolution. If Allen was likely to have won it, this would have given him the leverage to obtain the deadlock. For unless the holding company was dissolved, Allen would continue to enjoy the right to cast all the votes of the holding company in favor of the candidates of his choice, giving him control over the board of directors of the bank because the holding company owns 84 percent of the bank's common stock. If instead the suit to dissolve the holding company and distribute its holdings of bank stock to Allen and Takiff was quite likely to succeed, giving Takiff control of the bank, then Takiff, whose lawyer drafted the settlement agreement, would surely not have agreed to give Allen the room to maneuver that he claims, had the issue arisen in the negotiations. The record contains no evidence concerning the likely outcome of the dissolution suit. But it is germane to note the uncontradicted evidence that had the holding company been dissolved, Allen and Takiff would each have faced a $2 million tax liability, and this is a reason to believe that Takiff brought the suit to induce a settlement with Allen rather than to dissolve the holding company and take over the bank; so this would be a bit of evidence in support of Allen's interpretation.

All this argumentative to and froing would be of no moment if the agreement were crystal clear, or if the extrinsic evidence interpreted as favorably to Allen as the record permits showed that the judge would have committed a clear error had he accepted Allen's interpretation. Neither condition is satisfied. The agreement does not say that Allen is to cast the same number of votes for each of the fourteen nominees, and, although the implication is that he is to do that, it may conceivably be overborne if the effect would be to defeat the even division of the board that the agreement seems also to contemplate. The evidence that might disambiguate the agreement is either disputed or simply missing. In retrospect, since the district judge conducted a trial it would have been a good idea, in order to avoid a succession of appeals, for him to have decided the case not only on the assumption that the agreement was clear on its face but also on the alternative assumption that it was not. He did not do so, so we must remand for further proceedings consistent with this opinion.

Vacated and remanded.

# NOTE

There are two types of voting, straight and cumulative. With straight voting, each shareholder is entitled to one vote for each director. With straight voting, a 51% shareholder will always be able to elect all of the directors. Cumulative voting gives each shareholder votes equal to the number of directors being elected times the number of shares. For example, if a shareholder has 100 shares and 5 directors are being elected, the shareholder will have 500 votes. She can vote all 500 shares for one director, or split the votes among candidates. The purpose of cumulative voting is to maximize the voting power of minority shareholders. Cumulative voting is rarely a good idea for closely held corporations because it is confusing. Making mistakes in voting shares can easily lead to a loss of control. Closely held corporations provide minority shareholders with representation on the board by shareholder agreement. That is a simpler and better device.

Publicly held corporations prefer straight voting because it leads to more stability of management. Letting dissident groups elect a director or two only leads to a proxy fight down the road. However, some states require cumulative voting. The mechanics of cumulative voting are simple to understand. The formula to elect a given number of directors is as follows:

$$X = \frac{S \times d}{D + 1} + 1$$

X = number of shares necessary to elect directors
S = number of shares at the annual meeting of shareholders
d = number of directors you want to elect
D = total number of directors to be elected

Assume that the corporation has 9 directors. You wish to elect 1. How many shares to you need? Assume that 1000 shares will vote at the annual meeting. The formula results in the answer of 101 shares. You don't really need 101 shares. 100 and 1/32 shares will work just as well, but most corporations don't have fractional shares.

# NOTE: CLASSIFIED BOARDS OF DIRECTORS

It is common for state business corporation codes to permit classification of boards. The U.S. Senate is an example of classification. Instead of electing all the members at the same time, the terms are staggered and 1/3 of the membership is elected for six year terms. Most states set some limits on how long the terms can be. Three year terms and three classes of directors are common limits on length of term and number of shares. Classified boards are a common technique to make a corporation less attractive to take over. Unless state law permits a majority of the shareholders to remove the directors without cause, a classified board will delay effective control. Classified boards also dilute the effect of cumulative voting.

## C. CORPORATE FORMALITIES AND AUTHORITY OF OFFICERS

In this section we focus on the complexities brought about by the complex governance scheme mandated by corporate law. Corporations are entities, i.e. artificial persons. They can act only through agents. The board of directors of the corporation makes its decisions. The decisions of the board are implemented by officers and employees. For large publicly held corporations, this management structure makes sense. For small, informally run, close corporations, it makes little sense, if any. Contrast the partnership. Partners can make decisions any way they prefer. They don't need to have formal meetings with notice. They don't need to adopt bylaws or elect officers. Third parties don't need to worry about whether the partnership is bound, because partnership law provides for a broad grant of apparent authority to each partner. Corporate formalities are not a problem for the large publicly held corporation. It would be impractical to consult all of the shareholders or even any number of them. In contrast, most shareholders of closely held corporations regard corporate formalities as a nuisance at best.

The first problem is the concept that the decisions of the corporate entity must be made by its board of directors, and second, that the decisions must be made "as a board." The older cases would invalidate decisions made by the five members of the board of directors unless they met as a group. For example, if director *A* prepares a resolution and signs it to indicate his consent and approval, and then sends it to director *B* for signature with instructions to send it to directors *C* and so forth, then the resolution signed by all five directors does not bind the corporation because the decision was not made "as a board." The reasoning of the older cases is that using the corporate form was a privilege granted by the state and that as a condition, the state demanded that the particular scheme of governance must be used. The scheme of governance chosen by the state was actual, in-person meetings where debate and discussion could take place. Presumably, decisions rendered as a result of such mandatory scheme would be better than those made informally. Modern courts and legislatures are far more concerned with validating the decision made by the owner of the business. Several mechanisms alleviate this problem. Most states permit the board to act by unanimous written consent. Thus, if the five directors each sign an identical board resolution, the corporate entity is bound. Further, the decisions use basic agency concepts, such as ratification, to protect third parties.

Because corporations are artificial persons, they can only act through agents. The traditional practice was for the state corporate code to require that each corporation have at least two officers, generally a president and a secretary. Common practice was for the board of directors to elect a vice president and a treasurer as well. The Model Business Corporation Act (MBCA) no longer requires that the officers have specific names. Thus, corporations are free to innovate. Although the corporation's officers could bind the corporate entity using the agency doctrines of implied or apparent authority, most third parties, especially lenders, would insist on nothing less than a resolution duly adopted by the board of directors. Such resolutions were normally certified by the secretary of the corporation, and the authenticity of the resolution was attested to by the secretary as well. These procedures protected third parties who relied in good faith on the documentation furnished. The following cases illustrate the importance of complying with the corporate formalities. Failure to do so merely encourages attempts at invalidating the transactions by third parties who seek a windfall.

The agency doctrines of apparent authority and ratification will normally protect third parties who deal with corporations. It is important to distinguish the agency doctrine of implied authority from that of apparent authority. Apparent authority is often described as estoppel. It requires the third party to reasonably believe that the agent (president, vice-president, etc.) is authorized to bind the corporation. For the doctrine to apply, the corporation must have created that misleading appearance (called "holding out"). In contrast, the implied authority of an agent is resolved by looking at the relationship between the principal (corporation) and the agent (officer). In general, courts have found little implied authority for corporate officers, though many modern courts go further than the earlier cases. In addition, for closely held corporations, courts have developed the doctrine of informal action. If the shareholders permit the officers to bind the corporation without insisting on directors' meetings and the like, many courts will say that this conduct is acquiescence to an informal method of decision making and will thus bind the entity.

## STEWART CAPITAL CORP. v. ANDRUS
United States District Court, Southern District of New York
468 F. Supp. 1261 (1979)

POLLACK, J.

This is a suit for a declaratory judgment and an injunction against the Secretary of Interior by the highest bidder for an off-shore oil and gas lease which was awarded to the lower bidders because of a presumed defect of the higher bid submitted, in that an attestation by an Assistant-Secretary was allegedly required by the corporation's own resolutions (not by the Secretary of Interior) but not supplied with the plaintiff's bid.

\* \* \*

The Notice required all bids to be submitted in accordance with applicable regulations. It prescribed the form of bid, which form included a specific requirement of signature by the bidder on each bid. Bidders were required to submit with each bid one-fifth of the amount of the bid, either in cash or by check payable to the order of the BLM.

Plaintiff submitted a bid on Tract 49-125 in the amount of $213,000 and enclosed a certified check of the corporation signed by its Assistant-Secretary, Irene Rose Robinson, for $42,600 in accordance with the Notice of Sale. The bid was signed by the plaintiff's president. The defendants Murphy and Ocean also submitted a joint bid on Tract 49-125 in the amount of $212,000.

The bids were opened and read on February 28, 1979. The check signed by the Assistant-Secretary submitted with the bid signed by the president of the plaintiff in the amount of $42,600 was deposited for collection in a bank with the endorsement of the BLM for credit to the Treasurer of the United States.

On March 29, 1979, the defendant Andrus announced a decision to award the lease on Tract 49-125 to defendants Murphy and Ocean and plaintiff was notified by the Secretary of the Interior that its bid contained a technical deficiency, namely that the signature of the plaintiff's president on its bid was not attested by its Assistant-Secretary. Because of this supposed defect the defendant Andrus characterized the bid as "deficient" and "legally unacceptable" in reliance on an analysis submitted to him by the Solicitor of the Department. . . .

[The Department of the Interior required each bid to contain items, one of which was:]

> (4) a copy either of the minutes of the Board of Directors' meeting or of the by-laws indicating the person signing the bid has the authority to do so, or, in lieu of the foregoing, a certificate of the bidder's corporate secretary or assistant secretary to that effect, over the corporate seal, or appropriate reference to the Bureau of Land Management records in which such documents previously have been submitted. . . .

Plaintiff's bid submission consisted of the following documents:

> [a certified check in the required amount and] . . . a notarized certificate of the Assistant-Secretary of plaintiff as to resolutions of the plaintiff's Board of Directors. . . .

The plaintiff's documents completely satisfied the requirements of 43 C.F.R. § 3302.4. However, the BLM's memorandum to the defendant Andrus concluded plaintiff's bid was "deficient" and "legally unacceptable." . . .

The plaintiff's Assistant-Secretary submitted several certificates to the documents which accompanied the bid as well as the certified check which she signed for the required deposit to be made by the corporation. She certified that the following resolutions as well as the facts expressed therein were duly adopted at a meeting of the Board of Directors of the plaintiff held on February 27, 1979:

> RESOLVED, that Alexander Stewart Bowers, the President of the Company be and hereby is authorized and directed to execute all documents required for bidding for federal leases at Mid-Atlantic Outer Continental

Shelf Oil and Gas Lease Sale No. 49,[2] and further RESOLVED, that Irene Rose Robinson, the Asst. Secretary of the Company is hereby authorized and directed to execute and attest to all such documents and to execute a certificate attesting to the fact that the resolutions have been duly adopted and are in full force and effect.

\*    \*    \*

The evidence at the trial established that there are no requirements of the Department of Interior as to who should sign bids; that each bidder establishes its own formalities in expressing the bid; that the Department of Interior does not require an attestation to the bid or to the signature thereon.

The omission of a formal attestation by the Assistant-Secretary to the bid form does not detract from the legal validity and binding effect of the bid. Defendants' assertion that plaintiff's bid is "deficient" and "invalid" is premised on the erroneous legal proposition that attestation is a substantive requisite to the bid's binding effect. In reality, absent explicit statutory provision to the contrary, attestation is a mere formality of bearing witness to, or affirming the genuineness of, the execution of a document.

> [A]n acknowledgment is necessary merely . . . to authorize (the) introduction (of corporate instruments) in evidence without other proof of execution; and if the acknowledgment is insufficient on its face, . . . the instrument is not entitled to be introduced in evidence without proof of its execution.

> Acknowledgment is not necessary to make the instrument valid as between the parties, unless the statute so provides; and it follows that a defective acknowledgment does not invalidate the instrument in the absence of a statute to the contrary.

In 7 C.J.S. "Attestation" is defined as

> meaning an act by which one certifies the truth of a fact; an act of authentication; a signature; . . . the act of witnessing the signature of an instrument . . . ; the authentication of an instrument by the requisite number of witnesses. (*Id.* at 692–93).

The effect of attestation upon the authority of a corporate officer to make an offer which binds the corporation depends upon state law, and as plaintiff is incorporated in Delaware, the law of that state is controlling in this controversy.

The Delaware General Corporation Law does not, in any instance, require attestation of a business document as a requisite to the validity of that document as a corporate act. It specifies attestation as one means of affirming the authenticity of

---

[2] [*] N.B. The facts contained therein were attested as such by the Assistant-Secretary by her signature:

"IN WITNESS WHEREOF, I have executed the foregoing certificate this 27th day of February, 1979"

"Irene Rose Robinson, Assistant-Secretary."

a document only in the case of organic corporate instruments, which are required to be filed with the Secretary of State.

In this case, no statute or regulation requires attestation and it is conceded that counter-signature of plaintiff's bid was not contemplated by Interior Department regulations. The presence or absence of attestation has no effect whatsoever on the validity of plaintiff's bid as a binding offer.

\*     \*     \*

The Court concludes that the signature of plaintiff's president on the bid form was in all respects genuine; that plaintiff's bid was legally binding on the plaintiff if accepted by the defendant Andrus; that the omission of a further formal attestation did not make the bid insufficient or unsigned; and that the submission by the Assistant-Secretary of the certified documents and certified check with the bid package, all signed by her, was sufficient attestation if any were needed. The check sufficiently witnessed and authenticated the bid and ratified it as the authorized act of the corporation.

The plaintiff is the "highest responsible qualified bidder" on the tract in question and under the regulations is the "successful bidder."

\*     \*     \*

Judgment should be entered accordingly.

## NOTE

As the principal case indicates, the board of directors is normally authorized to exercise "all corporate powers" and "the business and affairs of the corporation" are managed by or under the direction of the board. MBCA § 801(b). The board is empowered to act, by a regular or special meeting, MBCA § 8.20, or by unanimous consent resolution signed by all directors without a meeting. MBCA § 8.21. The MBCA does not require that the corporation have any specific officers. Cf. MBCA § 8.40. However, it is customary to have a corporate secretary to empower her to certify the authenticity of any resolutions passed by the board. In the principal case, the Board specifically authorized the Secretary to certify that all corporate formalities needed to bind the Stewart Capital Corporation to its bid had been complied with. The court says that this is sufficient and that a formal attestation by the Secretary is not required since it was not necessary to bind the corporation under Delaware law.

### FRADKIN v. ERNST
United States District Court, Northern District of Ohio
571 F. Supp. 829 (1983)

Dowd, J.

This case involves a challenge to the implementation of the 1983 stock option plan (Plan) for the senior executives of Mohawk Rubber Company (Mohawk). The Plan was approved by Mohawk's Directors on January 4, 1983, and presented to and allegedly approved by the shareholders at Mohawk's Annual Meeting. Plaintiff contends that a proxy statement issued to shareholders describing the Plan prior to the Annual Meeting violated the federal securities laws. Plaintiff also argues that the Plan constitutes corporate waste and that the Plan was not approved by the requisite number of shareholders at Mohawk's annual shareholder's meeting.

## I. PROCEDURAL HISTORY

Plaintiff filed the complaint in this case on March 25, 1983. An amended complaint, raising class action and derivative claims, was filed on April 18, 1983 and is now the subject of this law suit. Count I of the amended complaint alleges violations of § 14(a) of the Securities Exchange Act of 1934 and SEC Rule 14a-9. Count II alleges a cause of action in common law corporate waste. Count III of the amended complaint seeks a declaratory judgment that the Plan was not approved pursuant to the terms of the Plan. Finally, Count IV of the Amended Complaint seeks a declaratory judgment that the Plan was not approved pursuant to Mohawk's code of regulations.

The Court laid out the early procedural history of this case in its order denying the defendant's motion to dismiss and granting plaintiff's motion for class certification.

This case was tried to the Court from June 9, 1983 through June 13, 1983. At the close of the testimony, a briefing schedule was agreed to by the parties. Defendants further agreed to take no further action toward implementing the Plan pending the Court's resolution of this lawsuit. Based upon the trial testimony and the exhibits introduced into evidence, the Court makes the following findings of fact and conclusions of law:

\* \* \*

Mohawk Rubber Company is an Ohio corporation with its principal offices in Hudson, Ohio. Mohawk's principal business is the manufacture of tires sold in the replacement market for passenger cars and trucks. Mohawk also operates other diverse enterprises related to the rubber industry. During the last five years, Mohawk has experienced substantial financial success, in contrast to the losses being experienced by many of the larger tire companies. In 1982, Mohawk had net earnings of $8.8 million on net sales of over $214 million.

Mohawk's stock is traded on the New York Stock Exchange. As of the record date for the 1983 annual meeting, there were 2,163,565 shares of Mohawk common stock outstanding divided among approximately 2600 shareholders. During 1982, Mohawk's shares traded at prices ranging from $15 1/4 to $25 1/8 per share. During the second quarter of 1983, the market price of Mohawk's stock rose as high as $32 3/4 per share.

Because of Mohawk's success and the relatively small portion of stock controlled by management, the investment community has viewed Mohawk as an ideal takeover candidate.

\*     \*     \*

Defendants Henry F. Fawcett and William T. Ernst are the principal executives of Mohawk. Fawcett has been an employee of Mohawk since 1946 and has held a variety of positions over the course of that career. Currently 63 years of age, Fawcett has been Chairman of the Board and chief executive officer of Mohawk since 1979 and owns approximately 2% of Mohawk's outstanding common stock. William Ernst has also been employed by Mohawk since 1946. He has held various positions in the corporation and has been Mohawk's president and chief operating officer since 1979. Currently 63 years of age, Ernst owns approximately .5% of Mohawk's outstanding stock.

Mohawk's Board of Directors, in addition to Fawcett and Ernst, includes five outside directors. Those directors are Charles W. Enyart, a director of the company since 1935; C. Blake McDowell, Jr., a partner in a law firm which does a substantial amount of Mohawk's legal work; Dr. Charles A. Sanders, the executive vice president of E.R. Squibb and Sons; Ralph T. Shipley, Fawcett's brother-in-law and a former vice president of The Timken Company; and William B. Saxbe, a former United States Senator and Attorney General of the United States. As a group, the outside directors have significant personal and business ties to the corporation. In recent years, the Board assumed a relatively passive role in supervising the corporation's conduct and frequently conducted its meetings informally.

The plaintiff in this case, Albert Fradkin, owns 1000 shares of Mohawk common stock. Fradkin's capacity to prosecute this lawsuit was the subject of a motion to dismiss filed by defendants.

B. Executive Compensation for Fawcett and Ernst

During 1981, Fawcett and Ernst entered into lucrative long term employment agreements with Mohawk. The principal components of their compensation are a salary and a bonus based upon Mohawks earnings. Historically, Ernst has received an annual bonus representing approximately 3% of Mohawk's earnings. Fawcett's bonus represents approximately 5% of Mohawk's earnings. For the year 1982, Fawcett and Ernst earned $607,125 and $444,608 respectively in salary and bonus. These employment agreements remain in effect, absent a termination for cause, for three years after notice of termination is given.

Fawcett and Ernst are covered by both Mohawk's Pension Plan for Salaried Employees and Mohawk's Supplemental Retirement Income Plan. Under the terms of the Pension Plan, Fawcett is entitled to receive a lifetime annuity (ten years certain) in the amount of $189,469.00 annually. Ernst would receive the same annuity in the amount of $131,269.00 annually. Fawcett and Ernst will also receive benefits under Mohawk's Supplemental Retirement Income Plan. These additional benefits are keyed to their salary and bonus during the five years preceding retirement and the consumer price index. If Fawcett and Ernst were to elect to receive these payments as life-time annuities (ten years certain) beginning at age 65, the annual annuity to Fawcett would be $198,280.00 and to Ernst $142,552.00.

Since 1978, Fawcett and Ernst's compensation has also included a stock option plan. Fawcett earned profits of $132,132.00, and Ernst $89,942.00 upon the surrender and cancellation of stock appreciation rights (SARs)[3] relating to stock options granted them between 1978 and 1982. A stock option plan approved by Mohawk's Board of Directors in 1982 provided for an additional grant of stock options to Fawcett and Ernst, but limited the grant to stock valued at $100,000.00 per individual per calendar year. The Board terminated the 1982 Plan at the time it adopted the 1983 Plan.

## C. Development of 1983 Stock Option Plan

Mohawk's Board of Directors discussed the adequacy of the compensation available to Fawcett and Ernst under the 1982 stock option plan at the October 1982 Board meeting. At that time, the directors, particularly Dr. Sanders, expressed the view that the 1982 Plan provided inadequate benefits to Fawcett and Ernst. No official action was taken, but Ernst was directed to give this subject further consideration. Dr. Sanders reiterated his views in a December 1982 letter to McDowell.

\* \* \*

## D. Terms of the 1983 Stock Option Plan

The Plan provided for grants to Fawcett and Ernst of both options and SARs in tandem with options on 200,000 shares of Mohawk common stock with Fawcett to receive options on 120,000 shares and Ernst to receive options on 80,000 shares. In total, these proposed grants represent 9.25% of Mohawk's then outstanding common stock. Absent a change in control, and subject to the provisions of Exchange Act § 16(b) dealing with insider trading, this arrangement would allow Fawcett and Ernst to receive $200,000.00 for each dollar per share increase in the value of Mohawk's common stock above the exercise price of the options.

Under the terms of the Plan, the exercise price of the options was keyed to the market price on the day of the grant. The value of the options, therefore, was tied to the market price of Mohawk's shares on the day of the grant. As a result an increase in the market price of Mohawk shares prior to the grant would diminish the value of the options to Fawcett and Ernst.

\* \* \*

Under the terms of the Plan, any options granted would be invalidated if the Plan failed to receive approval by the holders of the majority of the common stock present or represented and entitled to vote at the 1983 annual meeting. This approval requirement, which tracks the language of Exchange Act Rule 16b-3, apparently was designed to qualify the Plan for the exemption to the short swing

---

[3] [6] SARs are a recent development in executive compensation. They serve as a substitute for the grant and exercise of stock option rights. An executive exercising option rights to gain the benefit of an appreciation in the market price of the stock must borrow the money needed to exercise the options and purchase the stock. The executive must then sell the stock on the open market in order to receive any profit. SARs, on the other hand, short circuit this process by allowing a single payment by the corporation of the amount of appreciation on the stock to the grantee. There is no purchase or sale of stock, yet the grantee receives the value of the appreciation in the stock.

profit rules of § 16(b) of the Exchange Act.

E. Events of January 4, 1983

On December 17, 1982, certain large shareholders of Mohawk filed an amended Schedule 13D indicating their intent to seek out other investors who might be interested in acquiring Mohawk. During the weeks that followed, the value of Mohawk's stock rose steadily.

\* \* \*

On January 4, 1983, sixteen days before the regularly scheduled Board of Directors meeting at which the Plan was to be presented, Ernst telephoned the Directors individually to obtain approval for the Plan. No prior written notice was given to the Directors, and the Plan was not before them in written form prior to the telephone calls. Throughout the day, Ernst called each Director individually and explained the Plan. At no time were all of the Directors on the phone at the same time, and only one call was placed to each Director.

During each conversation, Ernst explained the provisions of the Plan. The complete details of the Plan were not explained with all of the Directors. Ernst did not tell all of the Directors the number of options to be granted. Further, Shipley and Saxbe did not learn that there were SARs attached to the options. Also, Saxbe did not learn of the multiplier provision of the Plan until months later.

Each Director orally approved the Plan as described to him. However, the Plan that was ultimately presented to the shareholders was not in final form at the time of the January 4, 1983 phone calls. Most significantly, the capped provision to the calculations in the event of a reorganization transaction was not included in the draft of the Plan discussed on January 4, 1983.

During the phone calls, Saxbe, McDowell, and Sanders agreed to serve on the Option Committee. Their appointment to the Option Committee, however, was not discussed with the other Directors. The members of the Option Committee did not meet or speak with each other on January 4, 1983, nor did they take any action to grant options to Fawcett and Ernst on January 4, 1983.[4]

Sometime after January 4, 1983, minutes of the "Board of Directors Meeting" and "Option Committee Meeting" were prepared. Those minutes outline the events of January 4, 1983, as if they had taken place in formal meetings. The minutes describe motions being made and seconded and debate taking place. While the minutes may describe the intent of the directors, they constitute a fictionalization of what might have happened had actual meetings taken place. The events of January 4, 1983, contained none of the procedures of a regular, formal meeting. To the extent, therefore, that the minutes suggest that a meeting took place in which regular procedures were followed, the minutes are inaccurate.

---

**4** [15] OHIO REV. CODE § 1701.63(A), the provision authorizing the appointment of committees of the Board of Directors, provides for the creation of committees by action of the Directors. In this case, the appointment was not discussed by the other Directors. The option committee, therefore, was never properly appointed under Ohio law.

## F. Signing of the Option Agreements

Pursuant to the Plan, option agreements were prepared between Fawcett and Ernst and Mohawk. Those agreements state that they were signed by Fawcett, Ernst, and the members of the Option Committee on January 4, 1983. In fact, those agreements were signed at the January 20, 1983, regular meeting of the Mohawk Board of Directors. The Plan was not discussed at the January 20, 1983 Board meeting.

## G. Proxy statement

On March 7, 1983, Mohawk sent its shareholders a notice and proxy statement for the Annual Meeting of Shareholders scheduled for April 12, 1983. The proxy statement indicated that the two principal items of business scheduled to come before the meeting were a proposal to re-elect Ernst, McDowell and Saxbe as Directors and a proposal to adopt the Plan. In a letter to Mohawk's shareholders which accompanied the proxy statement, Fawcett and Ernst urged the shareholders to give prompt attention to the proxy and indicated that the Board of Directors unanimously recommended a vote for the Plan.

The proxy statement also contained a lengthy description of the Plan [as well as the full text as an Exhibit].

\* \* \*

On March 17, 1983, representatives of Independence met with Fawcett and Ernst to discuss the Plan and the proxy statement, along with Independence's efforts to obtain a seat on Mohawk's Board of Directors. At that meeting, Independence's representatives advised Fawcett and Ernst that they viewed the proxy statement as misleading because of its failure to fully disclose all of the benefits payable to Fawcett and Ernst. On March 22, 1983, Independence filed an amendment to its Schedule 13D which stated that Independence did not intend to support the adoption of the Plan because the benefits payable under the Plan were "excessive." Independence further stated that it believed the Plan was not in the best interests of the corporation.

Subsequently, on March 25, 1983, this action was commenced. Plaintiff filed a verified complaint in this Court seeking, among other things, a preliminary and permanent injunction barring the submission of the Plan to a shareholders' vote at Mohawk's annual meeting. On March 30, 1983, Judge John Manos of this Court entered an Order allowing the vote to go forward, but enjoining Mohawk from taking any steps toward implementing the Plan pending a trial on the merits.

\* \* \*

## K. Events following the annual meeting

At the May, 1983, meeting of the Board of Directors, Fawcett and Ernst presented a document entitled "Approval of Directors of the Mohawk Rubber Company to Action Without a Meeting" to the Directors. The document, which was designed to cure the Board's failure to have a formal meeting on January 4, 1983, was signed by all of the pre-annual meeting directors, including Saxbe. The new Director, F. Peter Zoch, III, did not sign the document. A similar document entitled "Approval of Option Committee of the Directors of the Mohawk Rubber Company to Action Without a Meeting" was also signed by Sanders, McDowell and Saxbe on or about May 19, 1983. That document was designed to cure the failure of the Option Committee to hold a formal meeting on January 4, 1983.

Jurisdiction in this case is not in dispute. Federal district courts have exclusive jurisdiction for violations of the securities laws. Exchange Act § 27. The private right of action for violations of § 14(a) of the Securities Act was recognized by the Supreme Court in *J.I. Case Company v. Borak*, 377 U.S. 426, 84 S. Ct. 1555, 12 L. Ed. 2d 423 (1964). The remaining state law claims are properly before the Court under this Court's pendant jurisdiction because they arise out of the same nucleus of operative facts as the federal securities action. Personal jurisdiction and venue are proper in this Court because Mohawk has its principal place of business within the Northern District of Ohio.

This action is properly maintainable as a shareholder's derivative action and as a class action. Fradkin was a Mohawk shareholder at the time all of the relevant events in this litigation took place. The action was not brought collusively to confer jurisdiction upon the Court. Although plaintiff made no demand on Mohawk's Board to commence this action, such a demand would have been futile.

## A. Approval of the plan

As a threshold matter, the Court must consider whether the Plan was approved by the shareholders' vote at the annual meeting. The parties do not dispute the final vote totals from the meeting. The parties dispute, however, the applicable standard for determining whether such a vote represents approval of the Plan.

[The court concluded that the Plan was not approved by the shareholders.]

## B. Violations of Exchange Act § 14(a) and Exchange Act Rule 14a-9

[The court summarizes the legal standard under the federal proxy rules.]

> An omitted fact is material if there is a substantial likelihood that a reasonable investor would consider it important in deciding how to vote . . . it does not require proof of the substantial likelihood that disclosure of the omitted fact would have caused a reasonable investor to change his vote. What the standard does contemplate is the showing of a substantial likelihood that, under all the circumstances, the omitted fact would have assumed actual significance in the deliberations of the reasonable shareholder. Put another way, there must be substantial likelihood that the disclosure of the omitted fact would have been viewed by the reasonable investors having significantly altered the "total mix" of information made available.

[TSC Industries, Inc. v. Northway, Inc., 426 U.S. 438 (1976)] at 449. . . .

\* \* \*

The issue of materiality may be characterized as a mixed question of law and fact . . . the determination requires delicate assessments of the inference a "reasonable shareholder" would draw from a given set of facts and the significance of those inferences to him, and these assessments are peculiarly one for the trier of fact.

\* \* \*

In light of these standards, the Court will now individually analyze the materiality of the alleged misstatements or omissions in the proxy statement.

### The January 4, 1983 Board Meeting

In relevant part, the proxy statement states that:

> The Board of Directors, at its meeting of January 4, 1983, adopted, and directed to be submitted to the shareholders of the Company for their approval, the 1983 Non-Qualified Stock Option Plan . . . .

Plaintiff contends that this disclosure is materially false or misleading. Defendants have presented a two-tiered defense. Defendants argue that the disclosure, while not precisely accurate, accurately represents the effect of what happened on January 4, 1983. Alternatively, defendants argue that to the extent the proxy statement is inaccurate, that inaccuracy does not meet the standard for materiality under Rule 14a-9.

Defendants do not argue that the Board of Directors met in a typical formal meeting on January 4, 1983. Nor do defendants argue that the events of January 4, 1983, represent a telephonic meeting of the Board of Directors pursuant to OHIO REV. CODE § 1701.61 (B–C). Defendants argue, however, that the gravity of any procedural irregularities is reduced because the Board's activities of January 4, 1983, constituted valid corporate action and the individual directors' unanimously approved the Plan.[5]

Upon review, the Court finds defendants have cited two cases in which Ohio Courts have refused to invalidate corporate action because of procedural irregularities. *See In re B-F Building Corp.*, 284 F.2d 679 (6th Cir. 1960); *Piening v. Titus, Inc.*, 113 Ohio App. 532, 179 N.E.2d 374 (1960). Both of these cases, however, are factually distinguishable from this case. In both of these prior cases, the Court's rulings were limited to a statement that a corporation could not invalidate its own agreements with third parties because of a failure on the part of the corporation to follow appropriate procedures. As such, the cases stand for the proposition that a corporation is estopped from invalidating its actions because of procedural defects where an outside party has relied on the appearance of proper corporate action. In this case, the roles are reversed. The parties who rely on the procedurally defective corporate action are corporate insiders and the party seeking to invalidate the

---

[5] Although Ohio will recognize a telephonic Board of Directors' meeting pursuant to OHIO REV. CODE § 1701.61(B), the events of January 4, 1983, do not constitute such a meeting. The statute requires that "all persons participating can hear each other" if the meeting is conducted by telephone. Further, written notice of the time and place of the meeting was not supplied to the Directors as required by OHIO REV. CODE§ 1701.61(C). Neither of these requirements are met by the events of January 4, 1983.

corporate action is an outside party. The Court, therefore, concludes that this case is distinguishable from B-F Building and Piening and that the events of January 4, 1983, do not qualify as valid corporate action in the context of this litigation.

The Court also finds defendant's argument that the unanimous approval of the Directors of the Plan cures any procedural defect that took place not well taken.

> It is fundamental that officers of boards can act as a board only when assembled as a board, and by deliberate and concerted action dispose of the issue under consideration [and] that they cannot act in an individual capacity outside of a formal meeting . . . .

2 W. FLETCHER, ENCYCLOPEDIA OF CORPORATIONS § 392 (1982). Procedural regularities and interaction among board members, therefore, are critical in determining the legitimacy of board of directors' actions. Absent such procedural regularities, a board may not act on behalf of a corporation. Where, as here, the Board has not met and acted as a board, the individual assent of the Board members will not serve as a substitute for these procedural regularities.

Having concluded that the events of January 4, 1983 did not constitute valid action of the Board of Directors under Ohio law and that the Director's unanimous approval of the Plan did not cure this procedural defect, the Court must now consider the accuracy of the disclosure made in the proxy statement. The proxy statement gives every indication that the Board took valid, formal action on January 4, 1983. As such, the proxy statement is false and misleading to the extent that it suggests that valid formal action took place. The only issue remaining before the Court, therefore, is whether the false and misleading disclosure in the proxy statement is sufficiently material to constitute a 14a-9 violation.

The materiality of a false or misleading disclosure regarding the actions of a corporate board or committee was considered in *SEC v. Falstaff Brewing Corp.*, 629 F.2d 62 (D.C. Cir. 1980); *cert. denied sub nom. Kalmanovitz v. SEC*, 449 U.S. 1012, 101 S. Ct. 569 (1980). That case involved a proxy statement which referred to an audit committee. In fact, the audit committee never met or functioned. The District Court concluded that the mention of the audit committee in the proxy statement "created the false impression that the board of directors was exercising careful oversight of the company's finances." *Id.* at 75. The Court of Appeals affirmed, stating:

> The existence of a committee implies a structured investigation and analysis of a company's fiscal welfare. Informal procedures may be adequate, but formal entities such as committees create at least the impression of great care and precision through detailed review and oversight. Stating that an audit committee, with its implication of careful oversight, existed when it did not thus is misleading . . . .

The Court, therefore, concluded that this disclosure in the proxy statement was false and misleading in violation of Rule 14a-9.

Upon review, the Court finds the Falstaff Court's reasoning persuasive. In this case, the disclosures warrant a reasonable investor to believe that the Board of Directors had taken formal action and given deliberate consideration of the Plan. To the contrary, there was very little oversight and no discussion of the Plan by the Board of Directors. Given the public prominence of the Directors, a reasonable investor would consider the approval of the Board important in determining how to vote on the Plan. The Court, therefore, finds that the disclosures regarding the Board of Director's actions are materially false and misleading.

\* \* \*

[The court concluded that the Plan was not approved by the shareholders, and that the proxy statement was materially false and misleading with respect to the actions of the board of directors and the option committee. The court granted relief by declaring the options and related SARs to be null and void. The Plan was also declared to be of no further force or effect.]

## NOTES

1.   This case illustrates the consequences of failing to follow corporate formalities. If Ohio law permitted a telephonic meeting by the directors, why was that procedure not used? Does this case represent merely an obsession with legal technicalities or is there an important policy at stake?

2.   Was the attorney who prepared the proxy statement careless? Should he have insisted on an accurate description of the details of adoption of the Plan?

3.   An older case, *Baldwin v. Canfield*, 1 N.W. 261 (Minn. 1879), states the common law rule that directors can make decisions for the corporation only when assembled as a board. In that case, the transaction involved a conveyance. Each of the directors signed the deed seriatim, and it was contended that since unanimous consent was obtained, the transaction bound the corporation. The court invalidated the transaction.

4.   Is it ever proper to prepare minutes and backdate them so that they describe "a fictionalization of what might have happened had actual meetings taken place"?

## VILLAGE OF BROWN DEER v. CITY OF MILWAUKEE
### Supreme Court of Wisconsin
### 114 N.W.2d 493 (1962)

GORDON, J.

\* \* \*

There are four principal issues raised upon the challenge to this annexation:

1. Whether the signature on the petition made on behalf of the Evert Container Corporation was properly authorized.

\* \* \*

We conclude that the assessed valuation of the Evert Container Corporation, in the sum of $231,375, was improperly included in the computation of the total assessed value for which owners had signed on the annexation petition.

* * *

The Evert Container Corporation has an eleven member board of directors. Charles Evert is president of the corporation, the majority stockholder and a member of the board of directors. Although he discussed the question of his signing the petition with a majority of the members of the board of directors before he actually signed, the evidence is clear that Mr. Evert purported to sign on behalf of the corporation without obtaining either formal authorization from the board of directors or informal authorization as permitted under sec. 180.91, Stats.

Brown Deer contends that Milwaukee has no standing to challenge the authority of the president, Mr. Evert, to sign the petition on behalf of the corporation. As a general rule, if a corporation does not raise the objection that an officer lacked authority to do an act on behalf of the corporation, such objection may not be raised by a third person.

However, we believe that when a corporation purports to perform a political act, as opposed to a business act, other interested parties may be heard to challenge the validity thereof. . . .

We conclude that an interested municipality may raise the question of the lack of authority of a person purporting to sign an annexation petition on behalf of a corporation. Certainly Milwaukee could challenge the legal title of a person who signed an annexation petition as an owner of real estate. We see no difference in principle.

Sec. 180.30, Stats.1955, provides:

"The business and affairs of a corporation shall be managed by a board of directors. . . ."

Sec. 180.91, Stats.1955, provides as follows:

"Any action required by the articles of incorporation or by-laws of any corporation or any provision of law to be taken at a meeting or any other action which may be taken at a meeting, may be taken without a meeting if a consent in writing setting forth the action so taken shall be signed by all of the shareholders, subscribers, directors or members of a committee thereof entitled to vote with respect to the subject matter thereof. Such consent shall have the same force and effect as a unanimous vote, and may be stated as such in any articles or document filed with the secretary of state under this chapter."

Sec. 180.91 was adopted in order to permit informal action by the board of directors. Corporations owe their existence to the statutes. Those who would enjoy the benefits that attend the corporate form of operation are obliged to conduct their affairs in accordance with the laws which authorized them. In 2 FLETCHER, CYCLOPEDIA CORPORATIONS, sec. 392, p. 227, it is stated:

"By the overwhelming weight of authority, when the power to do particular acts, or general authority to manage the affairs of the corporation, is vested in the directors or trustees, it is vested in them, not individually, but as a board, and, as a general rule, they can act so as to bind the corporation only when they act as a board and at a legal meeting."

The legislature having specified the means whereby corporations could function informally, it becomes incumbent upon the courts to enforce such legislative pronouncements. The legislature has said that the corporation could act informally, without a meeting, by obtaining the consent in writing of all of the Directors. In our opinion, this pronouncement has preempted the field and prohibits corporations from acting informally without complying with sec. 180.91, Stats.

One of those who helped draft the Wisconsin Business Corporation Law, Dean George Young, has discussed this section in 1952 Wis. L. Rev. 5, and he says, at p. 19:

> "In addition, informal action may be taken without any meeting under section 180.91 by either directors or shareholders upon the unanimous written consent of all entitled to vote upon the subject of the action taken. Permitting corporate action based solely upon written assent, of course, sacrifices whatever wisdom there may be in requiring that decisions be made only after face to face discussion, but the advantage of flexibility probably outweighs any disadvantage. In any event, we all know that in fact many corporate meetings are held without the requisite formalities and the waivers and minutes are later prepared ex post facto to show compliance with the law. Such subterfuges should no longer be excusable under the new provision."

The presence of apparent authority and estoppel which might prevent the application of this rule in matters which flow in the normal course of business cannot apply where the action of the directors relates to a political determination and is outside of the ordinary course of normal business operations.

*   *   *

[W]e believe it is clear that the corporation may not validly act in an informal manner unless it be in compliance with the statutes.

There can be no doubt as to the rule in Wisconsin in view of the enactment of sec. 180.91 by the Wisconsin legislature. Fletcher also makes the following statement in his treatise at sec. 396 with respect to the effect of a statute permitting informal corporate action:

> "Of course, a statute may authorize particular acts to be done by the directors acting otherwise than as a board and at a formal meeting. But where it is claimed that the statutes of the state permit the corporation to dispense with this eminently wise and just rule, the construction will be strictly against any such contention."

The fact (1) that Mr. Evert owned 51 per cent of the stock of the corporation, or (2) that he may have been accustomed to resolving the problems of the corporation as a sole owner, or (3) that the board of directors met infrequently, or (4) that the corporation subsequently ratified his act do not derogate from the clear mandate of the statute. . . . Accordingly, ratification is of no avail.

\* \* \*

CURRIE, J. (dissenting in part).

I respectfully dissent from the holding of the majority that a third party may question the binding effect upon a corporation of a written instrument executed by its president in the corporate name, be it a contract, or a petition addressed to some public body. Furthermore, as applied to the facts relating to the signing of the annexation petitions by the two corporations in question, Evert Container Corporation and Good Hope Investment Company, I deem the result of this holding to be a serious miscarriage of justice.

Charles Evert, who subscribed the Corrigan tract annexation petition in behalf of the Evert Container Corporation, is the president and majority stockholder of the corporation. Some fo the directors resided outside of Wisconsin and the board of directors and stockholders customarily held only an annual meeting. At this annual meeting of stockholders, they customarily ratified all acts of the officers and directors. Hence, it is clear that Evert Container Corporation established a pattern of conduct which, at least by implication, delegated broad power to the president and clothed him with the apparent authority to represent and bind the corporation in all of its affairs and transactions between annual meetings. There was no evidence that the directors or stockholders ever refused to ratify any act performed by Evert as president during the yearly intervals between meetings.

\* \* \*

From these facts it is apparent that each corporation desired to join in the annexation petitions. The general rule is clearly established that a third person may not raise the objection that a corporate officer lacked authority to do an act on behalf of the corporation, and thus void the corporate act, if no objection to the act was raised by the corporation. The apparent theory behind this rule is that the failure of the corporation to object to an unauthorized act done in its behalf constitutes a tacit ratification, and that the policy of the law favors an interpretation which permits parties to rely on acts taken in behalf of corporations.

Traditionally, the title of a corporation to property may be challenged by one without the corporate structure, while only the corporation, or one acting in its behalf, has the right to challenge the authority of a managing officer to act for the corporation.

Statutory requirements that a corporation must follow a certain specified procedure, in authorizing action by its president, are made for the protection of the corporation and its shareholders, not as a sword to be used by a third party such as the city of Milwaukee in this action.

The majority concludes that the only way informal corporate action may legally be taken is by strict adherence to the provisions of sec. 180.91, Stats.

\* \* \*

The basic decision really boils down to a policy determination. The majority decided in favor of a policy permitting interested third parties to attack the authority of corporate officers who have acted on behalf of their corporation, where the action has not been attacked by the corporation. It also decided that the only way such action can be taken is by strict adherence to the statutory formalities. The result of this decision is to impugn the ability of both third parties and members of a corporation to rely on acts of corporate officers. The social utility of definiteness of corporation action outweighs the utility of letting a city utilize every insignificant flaw to avoid an annexation. As technical as annexation proceedings now are, it would seem better to look to substance rather than strictly to form.

The better rule would be that an annexation petition, signed in behalf of a corporation landowner by its chief executive officer, is binding on the corporation, unless attacked by the corporation or its shareholders prior to the expiration of the 90 day limitation period provided by sec. 62.07(3), Stats., 1955. Therefore, I would hold that the city of Milwaukee has no right in this action to challenge the signatures to the petitions of Evert Container Corporation and Good Hope Investment Company. This would require that the trial court's judgment upholding the Johnson tract annexation be affirmed, and that the validity of the Corrigan tract annexation be determined on the other issues mentioned but not passed upon by the majority opinion.

## NOTE

The majority holds that unanimous written consent statutes are the exclusive method of informal action, and thus pre-empt the many cases that permit informal action. An example of a case finding that the corporation was bound under the "informal action doctrine" is *Mickshaw v. Coca Cola Bottling Co.*, 70 A.2d 467 (Pa. Super. Ct. 1950). However, most, if not all, cases recognizing informal action by the directors as binding on the corporation arose prior to the widespread adoption of director unanimous consent statutes. Do you agree with the Wisconsin Supreme Court that such statutes should pre-empt application of the informal action doctrine or are there some situations where it should still be applied?

## DELJOO v. SUNTRUST MORTGAGE, INC.
### Court of Appeals of Georgia
### 671 S.E.2d 234 (2008)

RUFFIN, J.

SunTrust Mortgage, Inc. financed Doris Milton's purchase of a residence in the Villas at Hidden Hills subdivision. Shakrookh, a/k/a Daniel, Deljoo holds a security deed on the property; SunTrust and Milton were unaware of the security deed at the time Milton purchased the property. SunTrust sued Deljoo, seeking to cancel the security deed or otherwise quiet title in the property as to Deljoo's security deed. Deljoo filed a motion for summary judgment, as did SunTrust and Milton. The trial court granted SunTrust and Milton's motion for summary judgment and denied Deljoo's motion. Deljoo appeals and, for reasons that follow, we affirm in part and reverse in part.

\*    \*    \*

The record reflects that Vanguard Builders and Developers, LLC purchased the lot at issue from S & F Construction in August 2001; the purchase agreement referenced only an outstanding loan from Tucker Federal Bank. In June 2005 Milton purchased from Vanguard the following property:

> [a]ll that tract or parcel of land lying and being in Land Lot 28 of the 16th District, DeKalb County, Georgia, being Lot 16, Villas at Hidden Hills Subdivision, as per plat thereof recorded in Plat Book 109, page 40, DeKalb County, Georgia Records, which recorded plat is incorporated herein by reference and made a part of this description.

When Milton purchased the property, Vanguard executed an owner's affidavit stating that "there are no encumbrances or liens of any nature against said property that are not being paid in full and satisfied by affiant as a result of the transaction wherein this affidavit is given nor is there any other person or entity claiming any interest therein, EXCEPT: [n]one."

Deljoo's security deed from S & F Construction, Inc., executed in December 2000 (the "Deljoo deed"), referred to Lots 15 and 16 of the Villas at Hidden Hills, but mistakenly described them as "being in Land Lot 18 of the 16th District, DeKalb County, Georgia." The title examination performed for Milton did not reveal the Deljoo deed. No pay-off to Deljoo was made at Milton's closing. The trial court concluded that the incorrect land lot number in the legal description of the Deljoo deed took it outside the chain of title and that Milton and SunTrust were therefore bona fide purchasers without notice of the Deljoo deed and entitled to summary judgment.

Deljoo argues that the trial court erred in finding that the incorrect land lot number in the legal description of his security deed takes the deed outside the chain of title. We rejected Deljoo's argument and affirmed, in *Deljoo v. SunTrust Mtg.*, that the trial court had not erred in so finding. The Supreme Court reversed, and we therefore vacate our earlier opinion, adopt the opinion of the Supreme Court as our own, and herein consider Deljoo's remaining enumerations of error.

In its order on the cross-motions for summary judgment, the trial court found that a genuine issue of material fact existed as to whether the Deljoo deed was properly executed, because: (1) the deed was signed only by the president of S & F Construction, Sohrab Moghadam, who signed "above the signature line for S & F Construction, without there being any indication of the office he held or his authority or intent to bind the corporation"; and (2) the corporate seal of S & F Construction affixed below Moghadam's signature was not legible on the documents provided to the trial court. Deljoo contends that this finding was in error and that he is entitled to summary judgment.

We agree with the trial court that a genuine issue of material fact remains as to the validity of the deed. OCGA § 14-5-7 (a) provides that

> [I]nstruments executed by a corporation conveying an interest in real property, when signed by the president or vice-president and attested or countersigned by the secretary or an assistant secretary or the cashier or

assistant cashier of the corporation, shall be conclusive evidence that the president or vice-president of the corporation executing the document does in fact occupy the official position indicated; that the signature of such officer subscribed thereto is genuine; and that the execution of the document on behalf of the corporation has been duly authorized.

And even if the deed was not signed by two corporate officers, "the presence of an attested corporate seal indicates authority to execute the document on behalf of the corporation." Here, however, because the deed was signed only by Moghadam, with no reference to his title, the corporate seal was illegible to the trial court, and SunTrust and Milton have pointed to some evidence that S & F's corporate practice in documents signed on its behalf by Moghadam was to include his title, we affirm the trial court's denial of summary judgment on this basis.

# NOTE

While corporate formalities might seem rather mundane, they can have tremendous real world implications. Why is a corporate seal so important? Recall that under Agency Law, authority can be actual, implied, or apparent. What other factors would be relevant? *See Schmidt v. Farm Credit Services*, 977 F.2d 511 (10th Cir. 1992).

# D.  QUORUM REQUIREMENTS

## SCHOEN v. CONSUMERS UNITED GROUP, INC.
United States District Court, District of Columbia
670 F. Supp. 367 (1986)

PRATT, J.

On February 4, 1985, Richard D. Schoen was formally demoted from his position as Chief Financial Officer of Consumers United Group, Inc. (CUG) to temporary Senior Accountant of Consumers United Insurance Company (CUIC), a subsidiary of CUG. His salary dropped correspondingly, from approximately $49,000 to $31,000. Schoen has brought a diversity action against both CUG and CUIC for age discrimination, breach of contract and other unlawful acts. Before the court are the parties' cross-motions for summary judgment.

In January 1971, Richard Schoen was hired by International Group Plans (IGP), the corporate predecessor of defendant CUG, as Vice President for Accounting and Data Processing. He was then forty-two years old. Schoen did not sign or receive a formal employment contract. Rather, the President of IGP, James Gibbons, sent him "just a very conventional letter" confirming Gibbons' earlier, oral offer of the job at a starting salary of $30,000 per year.

Schoen rose to the position of Chief Financial Officer (CFO) of CUG in 1975. His duties as CFO are stated to include preparation and implementation of the annual financial plan, overall cash management of the company, negotiation of bank loans, real estate transactions, legal coordination with outside counsel, management of

CUG's investment program, and negotiation with insurance carriers.

The evaluations of Schoen's performanance during this period include mixed reviews.

\* \* \*

In the meantime CUG was suffering from a severe financial crisis. . . . Faced with the problem of being overstaffed as a result of heavy operating losses, CUG leaders developed an "action plan" to trim the number of company personnel. . . .

Yet in November 1983, two of the three members of the Team, Gibbons and Delbert Clark, met with Schoen. Gibbons told Schoen that reorganization of the company left no place for him. Gibbons offered Schoen the choice of either resigning immediately and providing accounting services to CUG on a contract basis or remaining at the company, temporarily, at full pay, while looking for another job. He did not offer Schoen the option of remaining at CUG permanently. Schoen chose to stay temporarily and look for a job outside the company.

. . . Hopkins directed Schoen either to resign from CUG or to assume a position as temporary Senior Accountant for CUIC. When Schoen did not suggest a third option, he was placed at the Senior Accountant position at a salary of $31,000. Although Hopkins' memo indicated that this was a "temporary" job and would last three to six months, Schoen continues to hold that position today.

On February 20, 1985 Schoen filed the present action in this court against CUG and CUIC. His complaint alleged . . . breach of an alleged contract guaranteeing lifetime employment without reduction in salary.

\* \* \*

### Lifetime Employment Without Salary Reduction

The only issue here is whether defendants were obligated by contract to maintain Schoen's salary. Schoen has never left defendants' service. Thus, his claim that defendants breached a promise to provide lifetime employment fails to state a claim upon which relief can be granted.

The record further reveals no evidence of a contract prohibiting defendants from reducing Schoen's salary. In general we must assume that the parties intended an ordinary business contract, unless the parties express a contrary intent. Schoen admits that he had no written contract of employment but was hired into an ordinary at-will relationship. The only written statement by defendants on the issue of salary reductions not only fails to proscribe but even permits such action.

Plaintiff's reliance on the resolution adopted by the CUG Board is misplaced. On November 4, 1983, four members of the Board passed a resolution to maintain the salaries of CUG employees who are removed. However, this Board meeting lacked a quorum. Since CUG is a Delaware corporation, a majority of the total number of directors makes up a quorum. Del. Corp. Law Ann. § 141(b) (1984); CUG By-Laws, Def. Ex. 19, at 8. On November 4, 1983, there were twelve authorized directors of CUG, Hopkins Dep. at 103, of whom only five were present at the meeting. This lack of a quorum renders the resolution that was passed void and of no force and effect.[6]

Plaintiff has not shown that the November 4, 1983 resolution, although itself void, was merely confirming a policy that already existed. Plaintiff emphasizes the October 24, 1983 report of Charmaine Carter that "long standing CUG policy" guaranteed salary maintenance. This memorandum, which cites no written statement but reflects Carter's personal opinion, hardly demonstrates CUG policy.

\*   \*   \*

We do not doubt that defendants' actions have caused Schoen hurt, embarrassment and financial loss. Our role, however, is to award relief only where such injuries derive from unlawful conduct. With the exception of the second part of the retaliation claim, defendants have demonstrated the absence of any liability. We therefore grant summary judgment for defendants on all but that aspect of the retaliation count involving Schoen's removal as Secretary of the Board

## WHITE v. THATCHER FINANCIAL GROUP, INC.
Court of Appeals of Colorado
940 P.2d 1034 (1996)

JONES, J.

Defendant, Thatcher Financial Group, Inc. (TFG), appeals the judgment entered on a jury verdict in favor of plaintiff, William M. White, on his claims for breach of contract. We affirm.

White inherited a controlling ownership interest in First National Bank of Salida in 1983. Some time in late 1987, Salida Bank was converted from a commercial bank to a federal savings bank and its assets were transferred to the new federal savings bank known as Thatcher Bank. White and the other shareholders exchanged their stock in Salida Bank for stock in TFG, which was the holding company created to hold ownership interest in Thatcher Bank.

Following the conversion, White became the controlling shareholder of TFG, and there were approximately ten minority shareholders. Prior to November 1987, TFG had four directors on its board. In November 1987, two of those directors resigned and a new director was appointed to the board in December 1987. That director then resigned in early 1988 and the vacancy remained unfilled. During the pertinent period here, White was chairman of the board of directors and TFG's chief executive officer.

In 1990, TFG's other director resigned and White appointed Kelsey Kennedy as the second director. At no time did White or the shareholders appoint a third director. During the next two years of TFG's existence, White was the chief executive officer of TFG but received no salary from TFG. In addition, in an attempt to develop business and raise money for TFG, White made cash advances to TFG that enabled it to transact business and develop certain projects.

---

[6] [8] The fact that the CUG Board has often transacted business without a quorum present, Pl. Opp. at 33–34, does not invalidate this resolution when challenged.

In July 1992, Pitkin County Bank became the controlling shareholder of TFG. Shortly thereafter, White and Kennedy resigned as directors of TFG. White then filed this action against TFG to collect past salary unpaid from January 1991 through July 1992, and other amounts he had advanced to TFG in order for it to operate during the previous years.

The jury returned a verdict in favor of White for reimbursement for payments made in connection with costs and expenses for the preparation of a private placement memorandum, for past salary, and for the repayment of miscellaneous advances. In addition, the jury found in favor of White on TFG's counterclaim for breach of fiduciary duty. The jury found in favor of TFG on White's claim for reimbursement of payments made in connection with a real estate development project. This appeal followed.

TFG first contends that any agreement between it and White to reimburse White for costs and expenses advanced to TFG or for a salary is not valid and binding on TFG since, during the time in which the alleged agreements were reached, TFG had only two directors on its board and, therefore, was in violation of the law. We disagree.

At all relevant times hereto, Colo. Sess. Laws 1983, ch. 68, § 7-5-102 at 398 provided that the number of directors of a corporation shall not be fewer than three if there are three or more shareholders of the corporation. In addition, § 7-5-102 provided that, at each annual meeting of the shareholders, the shareholders shall elect directors to hold office until the next succeeding annual meeting. TFG argues that this statute was violated by the maintenance of a board of only two directors and that, therefore, any actions taken, or agreements entered into, by the board were invalid and not binding on the corporation.

Colo. Sess. Laws 1963, ch. 84, § 31-31-4, also applicable at the time in question, provided that any vacancy occurring in a board of directors may be filled by the affirmative vote of a majority of the remaining directors. TFG's bylaws also so provided.

In addition, prior to its repeal, Colo. Sess. Laws 1977, ch. 68, § 7-5-106 at 375 provided that a majority of the number of directors determined pursuant to § 7-5-102 shall constitute a quorum for the transaction of business. That section further provided that an act of the majority of the directors present at a meeting at which a quorum was present shall be the act of the board of directors. Again, TFG's bylaws were in accord with that statute.

It is under these now repealed, but applicable, statutes that we must determine whether, under the circumstances here, a board's actions are binding on a corporation when the board consists of fewer than three directors as required by § 7-5-102. We conclude that they are.

When TFG was first formed, the board of directors consisted of four people. Thereafter, two resigned and a third member was elected to the board. Thus, the board was properly constituted under the applicable statute.

Thereafter, one of the board members resigned and the vacancy remained unfilled. Approximately one year later another director of the board resigned and was replaced. However, the vacancy left by the third director's resignation still remained unfilled.

Although § 7-5-104 provided that a vacancy on the board of directors may be filled by the affirmative vote of a majority of the remaining directors, the section did not mandate when such vacancy must be filled. In addition, § 7-5-106 clearly provided that a majority of directors shall constitute a quorum for the transaction of business by a corporation and that the act of a majority of the directors present at a meeting in which the quorum was present shall be the act of the board of directors.

Here, when the TFG board of directors approved any alleged agreements to reimburse White for costs and expenses in connection with the private placement memorandum, miscellaneous expenses, and to pay him a salary, such approval, if taken by a majority of a quorum of directors in attendance, was binding on the corporation. Further, at all relevant times in which the alleged agreements between TFG and White occurred, it is undisputed that two of the three directors required by § 7-5-102 were present at all board meetings and both voted in favor of all actions taken by the board.

Since the General Assembly in § 7-5-102 did not specifically provide that any actions taken by a board of directors with fewer than three directors on the board shall be invalid and not binding on a corporation, and other applicable statutes suggest otherwise, we refuse to place such a burdensome interpretation on that section.

Specifically, § 7-5-106 provides that, when a quorum of the board of directors is present at a meeting, the act of a majority of directors shall be the act of the board. *See Peoples Bank v. Banking Board*, 164 Colo. 564, 436 P.2d 681 (1968) (where only 5 of 7 bank board members were available, and vote was 3 to 2 to approve charter, court interpreted similar language found in the banking code as meaning that a quorum of the banking board in attendance could act for the board); *Gumaer v. Cripple Creek Tunnel, Transportation & Mining Co.*, 40 Colo. 1, 90 P. 81 (1907) (if a quorum of the board of directors is present, a majority of the quorum can legally do any act that the entire board is authorized to do). *See also O'Gorman v. Industrial Claim Appeals Office*, 826 P.2d 390 (Colo. App. 1991) (increase in number of panel members did not change procedure whereby 2 panel members who agree can resolve cases); *Jacobson v. Moskowitz*, 27 N.Y.2d 67, 313 N.Y.S.2d 684, 261 N.E.2d 613 (1970) (where quorum of board is 75% of directors but resignations made 75% attendance impossible for several years, vitality of the corporation was to be preserved and paralysis of its functions and its dissolution were to be avoided by the practical procedure of allowing a majority of directors in office to act for corporation and to fill vacancies on board); *Bahar v. Schwartzreich*, 204 A.D.2d 441, 611 N.Y.S.2d 619 (1994).

We recognize that, generally, if a corporation has fewer directors than the minimum required by statute, the issue arises whether the directors may act as a board. However, there are exceptions to the general rule that they may not act. These exceptions may include internal affairs of the corporation which must be carried on from necessity, and matters in which third parties reasonably believe a duly constituted board has acted on the corporation's behalf.

\* \* \*

We find further support for our conclusion in the cases and comments concerning the modern practice of closely held corporations.

As to closely held corporations, in particular, action taken informally can be valid even though corporate formalities are not followed. Thus, corporations with few shareholders, and in which directors personally and directly conduct the business, act with little formality.

Furthermore, allowing a corporation to escape liability for actions or agreements by its board that involve third parties would place an excessive burden on parties dealing with a corporation to ensure that the corporation's board was properly constituted pursuant to § 7-5-102. To allow a corporation to avoid such obligations, based upon the technical requirement provided for in § 7-5-102, would slow the corporate business world significantly. While we recognize that White was not a third party who was unaware of TFG's technical non-compliance with § 7-5-102, the jury's finding that White had not breached his fiduciary duties to the corporation also supports the conclusion that TFG should not be able to avoid liability for the actions of a quorum of its board.

Here, the record reflects that TFG had approximately ten minority shareholders and a small board of directors, members of which actually, directly, and personally conducted the business of the corporation. Clearly, the custom and practice of the corporation was to operate with fewer than the required number of directors, but still with a quorum of the board, and the jury here apparently so found.

Therefore, we conclude that any actions taken by TFG's board of directors when it consisted of only two directors were binding on TFG.

Accordingly, the judgment of the trial court is affirmed.

## NOTES

**1.** The MBCA does not specify a minimum number of directors. Thus the problem discussed in *White* would not arise in an MBCA state. However, a minority of states still requires a minimum of three directors, so the attorney dealing with a foreign corporation needs to check the statutes of an unfamiliar jurisdiction to determine its requirements.

**2.** MBCA section 8.24 deals with quorum and voting requirements. Generally a majority of directors constitutes a quorum but it may be reduced to as low as one-third by the articles of incorporation. Unless a supermajority vote is required by the articles or by-laws the affirmative vote of majority of directors present will be sufficient to bind the corporation.

## E.   AUTHORITY OF OFFICERS

The following cases discuss the authority of various officers to bind the corporation. The cases are very fact-specific, and rely heavily on agency principles, especially the doctrine of apparent authority.

## 1.  Chairman of the Board

## AMERICAN EXPRESS CO. v. LOPEZ
Civil Court of the City of New York
72 Misc. 2d 648 (1973)

LANE, J.

This matter has been submitted to me upon an agreed statement of facts presenting a single issue of law. Does the chairman of the Board of Directors of a corporation, who is not the Chief Executive Officer, have implied or apparent authority to pledge the credit of the corporation by virtue of obtaining the issuance to himself of an American Express credit card in the name of the corporation?

Broadly stated the rule is that general officer of a corporation has apparent authority to act in accordance with the normal practices of his corporation and of the business in which the corporation is engaged (*Traitel Marble Co. v. Brown Brothers, Inc.*, 159 App. Div. 485, 486; *Lyon v. West Side Transfer Co.*, 132 App. Div. 777, 779; *Goldenberg v. Bartell Broadcasting Corp.*, 47 Misc. 2d 105, 109). To state the rule, however, does not answer the question posed by this action, nor, to the knowledge of the Court and counsel, has any recorded case in this area of the law concerned itself with a chairman of the board of directors.

A chairman is not one of the usual officers designated in Section 715 of the Business Corporation Law of New York. Yet the statute does recognize the existence of such an office and accepts it for certain purposes as an alternative to the presidency; Sections 104 and 508. It is an office in evolution assuming different roles in different corporations. In some it is held by a chief executive officer who has relinquished day by day operations to a younger man while still holding the reins of power; in others it is held by a retired chief executive officer whose counsel and advice are still valued; in still others it provides a formula for dividing up between two relatively equal principals the control of the corporation.

The specific role of the office in Uniworld Group, Inc., the corporate defendant before me is not revealed in the agreed upon statement of facts. But whatever the specific role of the office, its holder in any corporation would be one of the corporation's senior citizens who would be accepted freely as speaking for the corporation by the vendors of the relatively narrow spectrum of goods and services covered by an American Express card and by American Express itself. Certainly he would be expected to have the right to commit the corporation for tickets, hotel rooms and other transportation expenses, for office furnishings, for meals and other entertainment expenses, equipment and other supplies, etc. Why shouldn't he and his corporation also have the advantage of the assurance of credit and record keeping made available by American Express?

Defendant's position is that, by the very title, a chairman of the board's apparent authority is limited to presiding at directors' meetings. On that theory a secretary's apparent authority would be limited to keeping minutes and sending out notices. The Court of Appeals has long ago rejected any such strait jacket for the law (*Hastings v. Brooklyn Life Ins. Co.*, 138 N.Y. 473, 479).

My conclusion is that in today's business world, Mr. Lopez as Chairman of the Board (like any other senior officer of a corporation) had apparent authority to get himself a credit card and charge the corporation with responsibility for it. The issue of whether the particular goods or services for which he used the card would put the vendors and/or American Express on notice of lack of corporate purpose has not been presented to me.

Plaintiff may have judgment as prayed for in the complaint together with the costs and disbursements of this action.

## 2. President

### INDIAN ACRES CLUB OF THORNBURG, INC. v. ESTATE OF GLOVER
Circuit Court of Spotsylvania County, Virginia
37 Va. Cir. 478 (1996)

LEDBETTER, J.

In this declaratory judgment action, the court is asked to determine the validity of a lease assignment.

\*    \*    \*

On July 26, 1986, The Club's board of directors adopted a resolution specifically barring its officers and employees from binding the Club to any contract that purports to lease or permit exclusive use of real estate owned or controlled by the Club without approval of the board. Further, the resolution prohibits officers and employees of the Club from entering into any other contract or agreement for a term exceeding three years without approval of the board. The resolution was readopted on October 25, 1986, and "three years" was changed to "one year". The resolution, as modified, went through second reading and was officially adopted on November 22, 1986.

Crowe was a member of the board when these resolutions were discussed and adopted. In fact, she seconded the motion for passage of the resolution on second reading and voted in favor of it.

The keeper of the corporate records testified without contradiction that the resolution has not been modified or repealed since its adoption in 1986. She also testified that the lease addendum removing the non-assignability clause from Glover's lease was never approved by the board; in fact, the board was unaware of it until this controversy arose.

\*    \*    \*

As for the 1988 addendum removing the non-assignability clause, it is clear from the evidence that Ritter, acting as president of the Club, had no authority to sign it. In fact, he acted contrary to the express directives of the board of directors of the corporation in signing the addendum.

Notwithstanding Ritter's lack of actual authority to change a material provision of the lease, it is suggested that Ritter, as president of the corporation, had implied powers to make the addendum. A corporate president does have certain implied powers to act on behalf of the corporation. However, the implied authority of a corporate president is limited to acts within the ordinary course of the corporation's business. *Mosell Realty Corp. v. Schofield*, 183 Va. 782 (1945). Authority to bind the corporation to a multi-year lease, or to change a material term of such a lease, cannot be imputed or implied in this case. The Club is not in the business of leasing real estate. It is a property owners' association, and the terms of a long-term lease of its store premises and fixtures are not in the usual course of the corporation's operations. Such a transaction under these circumstances was an extraordinary transaction that the president had no implied power to negotiate and carry out. *See* 4B M.J., Corporations § 173; 1A M.J., Agency § 24 et. seq. Further, no agent, including a corporate president, can possess an implied power to do an action that is specifically prohibited by his principal.

In addition to actual and implied powers, corporate presidents and other agents can be clothed with a degree of "apparent authority." Under some circumstances, apparent authority even when in conflict with actual authority can bind the principal. *See* 1A M.J., Agency '25.

Crowe cannot rest her case on the apparent authority of Ritter because she knew that he had no authority whatever to negotiate and sign a lease or a lease addendum without approval of the board. As explained above, the evidence shows that she was present at the board meetings when the resolution that precluded Ritter from binding the Club to such agreements was discussed and adopted. She seconded the motion for its adoption. She voted for it.

\* \* \*

Because Ritter flagrantly disregarded specific board instructions when he executed the lease addendum removing the non-assignability clause, and Crowe knew he had no authority to do that, the lease addendum is ultra vires and void. Because the addendum is void, Glover's attempt to assign the lease to Crowe in contravention of the terms of the original lease is ineffectual.

\* \* \*

For the reasons explained, the court will declare that the purported lease assignment is invalid and Crowe must vacate the premises without delay.

## 3. Vice President

### KAVANOS v. HANCOCK BANK AND TRUST CO.
Appeals Court of Massachusetts
439 N.E.2d 311 (1982)

KASS, J.

At the close of the plaintiff's evidence, the defendant moved for a directed verdict, which the trial judge allowed. The judge's reason for so doing was that the plaintiff, in his contract action, failed to introduce sufficient evidence tending to prove that the bank officer who made the agreement with which the plaintiff sought to charge the bank had any authority to make it. Upon review of the record we are of opinion that there was evidence which, if believed, warranted a finding that the bank officer had the requisite authority or that the bank officer had apparent authority to make the agreement in controversy. We, therefore, reverse the judgment.

\* \* \*

Among the exhibits introduced was a document which Brown identified as his job description. In broad terms he was to manage the commercial and consumer loan division. In furtherance of a duty to develop and maintain "a profitable loan portfolio," he, "personally, or through subordinates," was to "direct the resolution of particularly complex and/or unusual credit, lending or collection problems related to important customers." He was also to "[m]aintain a continuous review of the loan portfolio and oversee the resolution of significant delinquent and workout loans." That language sketches an authority to alter a subsidiary aspect of a loan or workout agreement. Restatement (Second) of Agency § 33 (1957) ("An agent is authorized to do, and to do only, what it is reasonable for him to infer that the principal desires him to do in the light of the principal's manifestations and the facts as he knows or should know them at the time he acts"). See also §§ 34 and 35 relating to circumstances considered in interpreting authority and when incidental authority is inferred. The jury could have believed that the sale of stock with repurchase option was a furtherance of a workout arrangement and Brown's job description would have supported a jury finding that he had authority to amend the repurchase option in a manner that did not fundamentally alter the agreement, that is, to substitute for the price certain in the agreement, as amended, a right of last refusal or a cash payment should the property be sold to someone else. It was a revision which afforded the Bank a chance to realize more money from the 1025, Inc. stock; it did not commit the Bank to a loan in excess of Brown's lending authority, to a sale or purchase of property of the Bank, or any step which, in the business context, was so major or unusual that a businessman in Brown's position would reasonably expect to require a vote of the board of directors.

\* \* \*

Whether Brown's job description impliedly authorized the right of last refusal or cash payment modification is a question of how, in the circumstances, a person in

Brown's position could reasonably interpret his authority. Whether Brown had apparent authority to make the July 16, 1976, modification is a question of how, in the circumstances, a third person, e.g., a customer of the Bank such as Kanavos, would reasonably interpret Brown's authority in light of the manifestations of his principal, the Bank.

Titles of office generally do not establish apparent authority. *James F. Monaghan Inc. v. M. Lowenstein & Sons*, 290 Mass. 331, 330, 195 N.E. 101 (1935) (vice-president had no apparent authority to authorize preparation of plans for a finishing mill). *Kelly v. Citizens Fin. Co. of Lowell, Inc.*, 306 Mass. 531, 532–533 (1940) (president did not, by virtue of the office alone [i.e., in the absence of evidence as to general authority, implied or apparent], have apparent authority to hire a lawyer for his company). Brown's status as executive vice-president was not, therefore, a badge of apparent authority to modify agreements to which the Bank was a party.

Trappings of office, e.g., office and furnishings, private secretary, while they may have some tendency to suggest executive responsibility, do not without other evidence provide a basis for finding apparent authority. Apparent authority is drawn from a variety of circumstances. Thus . . . it was held apparent authority could be found because an officer who was a director, vice-president and treasurer took an active part in directing the affairs of the bank in question and was seen by third parties talking with customers and negotiating with them.

In the instant case there was evidence of the following variety of circumstances: Brown's title of executive vice-president; the location of his office opposite the president; his frequent communications with the president; the long course of dealing and negotiations; the encouragement of Kanavos by the president to deal with Brown; the earlier amendment of the agreement by Brown on behalf of the Bank on material points, namely the price to be paid by the Bank for the shares and the repurchase price; the size of the Bank (fourteen or fifteen branches in addition to the main office); the secondary, rather than fundamental, nature of the change in the terms of the agreement now repudiated by the Bank, measured against the context of the overall transaction; and Brown's broad operating authority over the Executive House — all these added together would support a finding of apparent authority. When a corporate officer, as here, is allowed to exercise general executive responsibilities, the "public expectation is that the corporation should be bound to engagements made on its behalf by those who presume to have, and convincingly appear to have, the power to agree." Kempin, *The Corporate Officer and the Law of Agency*, 44 Va. L. Rev. 1273, 1280 (1958). This principle does not apply, of course, where in the business context, the requirement of specific authority is presumed, e.g., the sale of a major asset by a corporation or a transaction which by its nature commits the corporation to an obligation outside the scope of its usual activity. *See Bloomberg v. Greylock Bdcst. Co.*, 342 Mass. 542, 548 (1961). The modification agreement signed by Brown and dated July 16, 1976, should have been admitted in evidence, and a verdict should not have been directed.

Judgment reversed.

## 4.  Certificate of Secretary

# CONTEL CREDIT CORP. v. CENTRAL CHEVROLET, INC.
Appeals Court of Massachusetts
557 N.E.2d 77 (1990)

PERRETTA, J.

Contel Credit Corporation (Contel) financed the lease of a telephone system to Hallman Chevrolet, Inc. (Hallman). Payment of the lease was guaranteed by Central Chevrolet, Inc. (Central). Central's guaranty was signed by one Joseph Pugia, who claimed to be Central's vice president and chief operations officer. The guaranty was supported by a certificate of the secretary of Central, certifying that Central's board of directors had authorized Pugia to execute and deliver the guaranty on Hallman's debt. Hallman went bankrupt, and Contel brought this action against Central to recover on the guaranty. The judge found that Pugia was neither an officer nor director of either Hallman or Central and that Pugia had obtained the certificate of the secretary by trickery. He concluded that Contel should have verified Pugia's representations, and dismissed the complaint. On Contel's appeal, we conclude that, on the facts found by the judge, there was no basis for denying Contel the right to rely upon the certificate of the secretary of Central. We reverse the judgment.

We relate the facts found by the judge as they are warranted by the evidence. Maynard Hallman was the original owner of both Central and Hallman. Central did business in West Springfield, and Hallman was located in Salem. Maynard Hallman's son was in charge of the Salem dealership. Floyd Volk was the president of Central, and, since 1981, its sole stockholder. Pugia worked for Central as a general manager from November 1, 1981, until December 31, 1982.

With these facts as background, we turn to the spring of 1982. By that time, it had become apparent that Maynard Hallman's son should not have been put in charge of Hallman. As described by the judge, the Salem dealership was in a "mess." The son was removed. In the late spring of 1982, Volk and Pugia travelled to Salem to try to correct the problems at Hallman which the son had caused. During that time, Volk entertained thoughts about buying the Salem dealership from Maynard Hallman. He could not do so, however, because of his interest in the West Springfield dealership, Central.Pugia then decided to purchase the Salem agency. Volk had no objection to his general manager's leaving Central and buying Hallman, as the two businesses were noncompeting. Indeed, Volk assisted Pugia. He wrote to the "Chevrolet Zone Office" on November 9, 1982, and gave his "permission for . . . [his] General Manager/Vice President," Pugia, to become the dealer principal of Hallman.

It was no later than September that Volk made his last business trip to Salem. Pugia, however, since deciding to buy Hallman, had been travelling to Salem with greater frequency for some months. In August, without Volk's knowledge, Pugia obtained from Contel a corporate guaranty form which he signed, describing himself as Central's "V.P.C.O.O." (vice president chief operations officer). Next, he "persuaded" the secretary and treasurer of Central to sign the "Certificate of the Secretary on the reverse side of the form, assuring her that she was signing as a witness." The form which Pugia gave to her, however, was blank. She testified that Pugia wanted her "to witness his signature but there was no signature on it."

There is no need to speculate as to whom the judge believed or why:

> "I find it difficult to believe that an experienced business woman [the secretary] would do such a stupid thing but having observed Pugia as a witness, I find him completely without scruple and undoubtedly a persuasive con man. In effect, he tricked . . . [the secretary] into signing the Certificate of the Secretary certifying to corporate resolutions which had never been presented to or voted on by the Central Chevrolet directors." In addition to this deception, the judge found (based upon the inference that he drew from the face of the guaranty) that Pugia "secretly, without telling anyone and certainly without authorization, obtained a corporate stamp and placed the corporate seal in three places on the Corporate Guaranty."

Recovery on the guaranty was denied Contel because the judge found that Contel "never checked Pugia's credentials" with Volk and that although there was, "at one time," common ownership of Central and Hallman, they were separate and distinct corporations. Contel "was completely unjustified in assuming there was any legitimate basis" for Central to guarantee Hallman's debt, and it had an "obligation to verify in some way the statements of Pugia." For these reasons, the judge concluded that Central was not "estopped from denying an obligation under the fraudulent and spurious" corporate guaranty. On the facts found, this conclusion is erroneous.

Unless disallowed by self-imposed restrictions, a corporation is authorized "to . . . give guarantees." Notwithstanding this statutory authorization and even if Pugia had been the vice president of Central, a corporate guaranty of the debt of an unrelated corporation is not a routine business decision within the delegable managerial functions of a corporate officer. *See Kelly v. Citizens Fin. Co.*, 306 Mass. 531, 532–533 (1940); *Boston Athletic Assn. v. International Marathons, Inc.*, 392 Mass. 356, 365 (1984); *Kanavos v. Hancock Bank & Trust Co.*, 14 Mass. App. Ct. 326, 332 (1982). As stated in *Williams v. Dugan*, 217 Mass. 526, 527 (1914); "The power to borrow money or to execute and deliver promissory notes is one of the most important which a principal can confer upon an agent. It is fraught with great possibilities of financial calamity. It is not lightly to be implied. It either must be granted by express terms or flow as a necessary and inevitable consequence from the nature of the agency actually created."

Contel's argument is not based upon a claim that Central cloaked Pugia with the apparent authority to give its guaranty for Hallman's debt. *See Kanavos v. Hancock Bank & Trust Co.*, 14 Mass. App. Ct. at 333, noting that the doctrine of apparent authority "does not apply, of course, where in the business context, the requirement of specific authority is presumed." Rather, it is Contel's position that the certificate of the secretary provided it with the requisite verification, that is, Central's granting of specific or express authority to Pugia to execute and deliver its corporate guaranty.

There is record support for all the judge's findings concerning Pugia's trickery and deceit in respect to Central and Hallman. But there is nothing in the record to show that Contel knew or should have known of Pugia's dishonesty, and, therefore, there was no basis for denying Contel the right to rely upon the certificate of the secretary certifying to Pugia's express authority to bind Central as Hallman's guarantor.

It follows from what we have said that the judgment is reversed. As Central's liability on the guarantee has been established, the matter is remanded to the Superior Court for further proceedings on the sole issue of damages.

So ordered.

## 5. Treasurer

### IDEAL FOODS, INC. v. ACTION LEASING CORP.
Court of Appeal of Florida
413 So. 2d 416 (1982)

COBB, J.

The issue in this case is whether Richard Maru, the secretary-treasurer and minority shareholder of the appellant-defendant, Ideal Foods, Inc. (Ideal), had the authority to bind Ideal in certain leases with the plaintiff-appellee, Action Leasing Corporation (ALCO). Because Maru had no such authority, we reverse.

ALCO sued to recover on leases signed by Maru. Ideal defended on the ground that Maru lacked authority to bind it. In order to bind Ideal in this case, Maru must have had either (1) inherent authority, i.e., authority by virtue of his position in the company, or (2) apparent authority, i.e., the authority the principal knowingly permits his agent to assume or which the principal by his actions or words holds out the agent as possessing. Neither as shareholder nor as secretary-treasurer did Maru have the inherent authority to bind Ideal. The secretary of a corporation, merely as such, is a ministerial officer, without authority to transact the business of the corporation upon his volition and judgment. *People v. International Steel Corp.*, 102 Cal. App. 2d Supp. 935, 226 P.2d 587 (1951). Similarly, a treasurer has no authority to bind a corporation in dealings with third persons unless expressly or impliedly authorized to do so. 19 C.J.S. Corporations § 1001 (1940).[7]

Maru had no inherent authority to bind Ideal; any liability must have been predicated upon principles of apparent authority.

Maru had no such apparent authority. Apparent authority is grounded in estoppel. *Stiles v. Gordon Land Co.*, 44 So. 2d 417 (Fla. 1950). Its three primary elements are: (1) representation by the principal, (2) reliance upon that represen-

---

[7] [1] Like every other corporate agent, a secretary-treasurer may have more extensive functions then those ordinarily incident to the office. See Van Denburgh v. Tungsten Reef Mines Co., 67 P.2d 360 (1937). While Maru had at one time been Ideal's general manager, he had left Ideal to work at its wholly-owned subsidiary approximately six months before entering into the leases upon which his motion was based.

tation by a third person, and (3) a change of position by the third person in reliance upon such representation. In the present case, Maru had been working solely at Ideal's subsidiary for approximately six months before he signed the contracts with ALCO. Additionally, ALCO's representative knew that Maru no longer ran Ideal. The proof, therefore, does not support a finding of apparent authority.

Because Maru lacked both inherent and apparent authority to bind Ideal contractually, the trial court erred by finding in favor of ALCO. We therefore reverse for entry of judgment in favor of Ideal.

Reversed and remanded with instructions.

## F.  CORPORATE SOCIAL RESPONSIBILITY

In this section we will consider broader questions of social policy. Related to the question of whether directors may consider objectives other than maximizing profits for the shareholders are such matters as constituency statutes, as well as the issue of considering the interests of creditors.

### A.P. SMITH MANUFACTURING CO. v. BARLOW
#### Supreme Court of New Jersey
#### 98 A.2d 581 (1953)

Jacobs, J.

The Chancery Division, in a well-reasoned opinion by Judge Stein, determined that a donation by the plaintiff The A. P. Smith Manufacturing Company to Princeton University was Intra vires. . . .

The company was incorporated in 1896 and is engaged in the manufacture and sale of valves, fire hydrants and special equipment, mainly for water and gas industries. Its plant is located in East Orange and Bloomfield and it has approximately 300 employees. Over the years the company has contributed regularly to the local community chest and on occasions to Upsala College in East Orange and Newark University, now part of Rutgers, the State University. On July 24, 1951 the board of directors adopted a resolution which set forth that it was in the corporation's best interests to join with others in the 1951 Annual Giving to Princeton University, and appropriated the sum of $1,500 to be transferred by the corporation's treasurer to the university as a contribution towards its maintenance. When this action was questioned by stockholders the corporation instituted a declaratory judgment action in the Chancery Division and trial was had in due course.

Mr. Hubert F. O'Brien, the president of the company, testified that he considered the contribution to be a sound investment, that the public expects corporations to aid philanthropic and benevolent institutions, that they obtain good will in the community by so doing, and that their charitable donations create favorable environment for their business operations. In addition, he expressed the thought that in contributing to liberal arts institutions, corporations were furthering their self-interest in assuring the free flow of properly trained personnel for administrative and other corporate employment. Mr. Frank W. Abrams, chairman of the board of the Standard Oil Company of New Jersey, testified that corporations are expected to acknowledge their public responsibilities in support of the essential elements of our free enterprise system. He indicated that it was not "good business" to disappoint "this reasonable and justified public expectation," nor was it good business for corporations "to take substantial benefits from their membership in the economic community while avoiding the normally accepted obligations of citizenship in the social community." Mr. Irving S. Olds, former chairman of the board of the United States Steel Corporation, pointed out that corporations have a self-interest in the maintenance of liberal education as the bulwark of good government. He stated that 'Capitalism and free enterprise owe their survival in no small degree to the existence of our private, independent universities' and that if American business does not aid in their maintenance it is not "properly protecting the long-range interest of its stockholders, its employees and its customers." Similarly, Dr. Harold W. Dodds, President of Princeton University, suggested that if private institutions of higher learning were replaced by governmental institutions our society would be vastly different and private enterprise in other fields would fade out rather promptly. Further on he stated that "democratic society will not long endure if it does not nourish within itself strong centers of non-governmental fountains of knowledge, opinions of all sorts not governmentally or politically originated. If the time comes when all these centers are absorbed into government, then freedom as we know it, I submit, is at an end."

The objecting stockholders have not disputed any of the foregoing testimony nor the showing of great need by Princeton and other private institutions of higher learning and the important public service being rendered by them for democratic government and industry alike. Similarly, they have acknowledged that for over two decades there has been state legislation on our books which expresses a strong public policy in favor of corporate contributions such as that being questioned by them. Nevertheless, they have taken the position that (1) the plaintiff's certificate of incorporation does not expressly authorize the contribution and under common-law principles the company does not possess any implied or incidental power to make it, and (2) the New Jersey statutes which expressly authorize the contribution may not constitutionally be applied to the plaintiff, a corporation created long before their enactment.

In his discussion of the early history of business corporations Professor Williston refers to a 1702 publication where the author stated flatly that "The general intent and end of all civil incorporations is for better government." And he points out that the early corporate charters, particularly their recitals, furnish additional support for the notion that the corporate object was the public one of managing and ordering the trade as well as the private one of profit for the members. *See* 3 Select Essays on Anglo-American Legal History 201 (1909); 1 Fletcher, Corporations (rev. ed. 1931), 6. *See also Currie's Administrators v. Mutual Assurance Society*, 4 Hen. & M. 315, 347 (Va. Sup. Ct. App. 1809), where Judge Roane referred to the English corporate charters and expressed the view that acts of incorporation ought never to be passed "but in consideration of services to be rendered to the public." However, with later economic and social developments and the free availability of the corporate device for all trades, the end of private profit became generally accepted as the controlling one in all businesses other than those classed broadly as public utilities. *Cf.* Dodd, *For Whom Are Corporate Managers Trustees?*, 45 Harv. L. Rev. 1145, 1148 (1932). As a concomitant the common-law rule developed that those who managed the corporation could not disburse any corporate funds for philanthropic or other worthy public cause unless the expenditure would benefit the corporation. *Hutton v. West Cork Railway Company*, 23 Ch.D. 654 (1883); *Dodge v. Ford Motor Co.*, 204 Mich. 459, 170 N.W. 668, 3 A.L.R. 413 (Sup. Ct. 1919).

\* \* \*

"It was also considered, in making the subscriptions or donations, that the company would receive advertisement of substantial value, including the good will of many influential citizens and of its patrons, who were interested in the success of the development of these branches of education, and, on the other hand, suffer a loss of prestige if the contributions were not made, in view of the fact that business competitors had donated and shown a commendable public spirit in that relation. In the circumstances the rule of law that may fairly be applied is that the action of the officers of the company was not ultra vires, but was in fact within their corporate powers, since it tended to promote the welfare of the business in which the corporation was engaged."

"But it is equally well established that corporations are permitted to make substantial contributions to have the outward form of gifts where the activity being promoted by the so-called gift tends reasonably to promote the good-will of the business of the contributing corporation. Courts recognize in such cases that although there is no dollar and cent supporting consideration, yet there is often substantial indirect benefit accruing to the corporation which supports such action. So-called contributions by corporations to churches, schools, hospitals, and civic improvement funds, and the establishment of bonus and pension plans with the payment of large sums flowing therefrom have been upheld many times as reasonable business expenditures rather than being classified as charitable gifts."

The foregoing authorities illustrate how courts, while adhering to the terms of the common-law rule, have applied it very broadly to enable worthy corporate donations with indirect benefits to the corporations.

"Next is the question of dues, donations, and philanthropies of the Company. It is a matter for the discretion of corporate management in making donations and paying dues. In that respect a corporation does not occupy a status far different from an individual. An individual determines the propriety of joining organizations, and contributing to their support by paying dues, and all contribution to public charities, etc., according to his means. He does not make such contributions above his means with the hope that his employer will increase his compensation accordingly. A corporation likewise should not do so. Its ultimate purpose, from its own standpoint, is to earn and pay dividends. If, as a matter of judgment, it desires to take part of its earnings, just as would an individual, and contribute them to a worthy public cause, it may do so; but we do not feel that it should be allowed to increase its earnings to take care thereof."

\*    \*    \*

When the wealth of the nation was primarily in the hands of individuals they discharged their responsibilities as citizens by donating freely for charitable purposes. With the transfer of most of the wealth to corporate hands and the imposition of heavy burdens of individual taxation, they have been unable to keep pace with increased philanthropic needs. They have therefore, with justification, turned to corporations to assume the modern obligations of good citizenship in the same manner as humans do. Congress and state legislatures have enacted laws which encourage corporate contributions, and much has recently been written to indicate the crying need and adequate legal basis therefor.

\*    \*    \*

In 1950 a more comprehensive statute was enacted. In this enactment the Legislature declared that it shall be the public policy of our State and in furtherance of the public interest and welfare that encouragement be given to the creation and maintenance of institutions engaged in community fund, hospital, charitable, philanthropic, educational, scientific or benevolent activities or patriotic or civic activities conducive to the betterment of social and economic conditions; and it expressly empowered corporations acting singly or with others to contribute reasonable sums to such institutions, provided, however, that the contribution shall not be permissible if the donee institution owns more than 10% of the voting stock of the donor and provided, further, that the contribution shall not exceed 1% of capital and surplus unless the excess is authorized by the stockholders at a regular or special meeting. To insure that the grant of express power in the 1950 statute would not displace pre-existing power at common law or otherwise, the Legislature provided that the "act shall not be construed as directly or indirectly minimizing or interpreting the rights and powers of corporations, as heretofore existing, with reference to appropriations, expenditures or contributions of the nature above specified." N.J.S.A. 14:3-13.3. It may be noted that statutes relating to charitable contributions by corporations have now been passed in 29 states.

\*    \*    \*

In the light of all of the foregoing we have no hesitancy in sustaining the validity of the donation by the plaintiff. There is no suggestion that it was made indiscriminately or to a pet charity of the corporate directors in furtherance of personal rather than corporate ends. On the contrary, it was made to a preeminent institution of higher learning, was modest in amount and well within the limitations imposed by the statutory enactments, and was voluntarily made in the reasonable belief that it would aid the public welfare and advance the interests of the plaintiff as a private corporation and as part of the community in which it operates. We find that it was a lawful exercise of the corporation's implied and incidental powers under common-law principles and that it came within the express authority of the pertinent state legislation. As has been indicated, there is now widespread belief throughout the nation that free and vigorous non-governmental institutions of learning are vital to our democracy and the system of free enterprise and that withdrawal of corporate authority to make such contributions within reasonable limits would seriously threaten their continuance. Corporations have come to recognize this and with their enlightenment have sought in varying measures, as has the plaintiff by its contribution, to insure and strengthen the society which gives them existence and the means of aiding themselves and their fellow citizens. Clearly then, the appellants, as individual stockholders whose private interests rest entirely upon the well-being of the plaintiff corporation, ought not be permitted to close their eyes to present-day realities and thwart the long-visioned corporate action in recognizing and voluntarily discharging its high obligations as a constituent of our modern social structure.

The judgment entered in the Chancery Division is in all respects Affirmed.

## NOTE

The following case appears in two places in the casebook. It appears, supra, where the relevant issue is the power of the board of directors to pay or withhold the payment of dividends. It appears here to illustrate the power of the board of directors to make decisions as to charitable donations or as to wages. Mr. Ford believed in a policy of high wages and low prices.

## DODGE v. FORD MOTOR CO.
### Supreme Court of Michigan
### 170 N.W. 668 (1919)

OSTRANDER, J.

It is the contention of plaintiffs that the apparent effect of the plan is intended to be the continued and continuing effect of it, and that it is deliberately proposed, not of record and not by official corporate declaration, but nevertheless proposed, to continue the corporation henceforth as a semi-eleemosynary institution and not as a business institution. In support of this contention, they point to the attitude and to the expressions of Mr. Henry Ford.

Mr. Henry Ford is the dominant force in the business of the Ford Motor Company. No plan of operations could be adopted unless he consented, and no board of directors can be elected whom he does not favor. One of the directors of the company has no stock. One share was assigned to him to qualify him for the position, but it is not claimed that he owns it. A business, one of the largest in the world, and one of the most profitable, has been built up. It employs many men, at good pay.

"My ambition," said Mr. Ford, "is to employ still more men, to spread the benefits of this industrial system to the greatest possible number, to help them build up their lives and their homes. To do this we are putting the greatest share of our profits back in the business."

"With regard to dividends, the company paid sixty percent on its capitalization of two million dollars, or $1,200,000, leaving $58,000,000 to reinvest for the growth of the company. This is Mr. Ford's policy at present, and it is understood that the other stockholders cheerfully accede to this plan."

He had made up his mind in the summer of 1916 that no dividends other than the regular dividends should be paid, "for the present."

*    *    *

The record, and especially the testimony of Mr. Ford, convinces that he has to some extent the attitude towards shareholders of one who has dispensed and distributed to them large gains and that they should be content to take what he chooses to give. His testimony creates the impression, also, that he thinks the Ford Motor Company has made too much money, has had too large profits, and that, although large profits might be still earned, a sharing of them with the public, by reducing the price of the output of the company, ought to be undertaken. We have no doubt that certain sentiments, philanthropic and altruistic, creditable to Mr. Ford, had large influence in determining the policy to be pursued by the Ford Motor Company — the policy which has been herein referred to.

It is said by his counsel that —

"Although a manufacturing corporation cannot engage in humanitarian works as its principal business, the fact that it is organized for profit does not prevent the existence of implied powers to carry on with humanitarian motives such charitable works as are incidental to the main business of the corporation."

And again:

"As the expenditures complained of are being made in an expansion of the business which the company is organized to carry on, and for purposes within the powers of the corporation as hereinbefore shown, the question is as to whether such expenditures are rendered illegal because influenced to some extent by humanitarian motives and purposes on the part of the members of the board of directors."

*    *    *

These cases, after all, like all others in which the subject is treated, turn finally upon the point, the question, whether it appears that the directors were not acting for the best interests of the corporation. We do not draw in question, nor do counsel for the plaintiffs do so, the validity of the general proposition stated by counsel nor the soundness of the opinions delivered in the cases cited. The case presented here is not like any of them. The difference between an incidental humanitarian expenditure of corporate funds for the benefit of the employees, like the building of a hospital for their use and the employment of agencies for the betterment of their condition, and a general purpose and plan to benefit mankind at the expense of others, is obvious. There should be no confusion (of which there is evidence) of the duties which Mr. Ford conceives that he and the stockholders owe to the general public and the duties which in law he and his co-directors owe to protesting, minority stockholders. A business corporation is organized and carried on primarily for the profit of the stockholders. The powers of the directors are to be employed for that end. The discretion of directors is to be exercised in the choice of means to attain that end, and does not extend to a change in the end itself, to the reduction of profits, or to the non-distribution of profits among stockholders in order to devote them to other purposes.

There is committed to the discretion of directors, a discretion to be exercised in good faith, the infinite details of business, including the wages which shall be paid to employees, the number of hours they shall work, the conditions under which labor shall be carried on, and the price for which products shall be offered to the public. It is said by appellants that the motives of the board members are not material and will not be inquired into by the court so long as their acts are within their lawful powers. As we have pointed out, and the proposition does not require argument to sustain it, it is not within the lawful powers of a board of directors to shape and conduct the affairs of a corporation for the merely incidental benefit of shareholders and for the primary purpose of benefiting others, and no one will contend that, if the avowed purpose of the defendant directors was to sacrifice the interests of shareholders, it would not be the duty of the courts to interfere.

We are not, however, persuaded that we should interfere with the proposed expansion of the business of the Ford Motor Company. In view of the fact that the selling price of products may be increased at any time, the ultimate results of the larger business cannot be certainly estimated. The judges are not business experts. It is recognized that plans must often be made for a long future, for expected competition, for a continuing as well as an immediately profitable venture.

# NOTE

The principal case discusses the power of corporations to make gifts. Most corporate codes permit donations for charitable purposes. Closely held corporations rarely make donations, but it is common practice for large corporations. The argument is often made that it would be better for the corporation to distribute larger dividends to the shareholders and let them decide which charities, if any, deserve the donations.

This case also raises the general issue of what limits exist on the powers of corporations. Every corporations code has a long list of the powers of corporations. One of the basic powers of a corporation is the power to sue and be sued in the corporate name. Unincorporated associations lack this power unless there is a civil procedure statute generally called a common name statute that permits those associations to sue or be sued. Most codes also specifically permit a corporation to be a partner in a partnership or a joint venturer in a joint venture. This is simply to clarify the law since several older cases held that corporations could not be partners in a partnership on the ground that the directors were delegating away their duty to manage the business and affairs of the corporation.

Some lawyers will list all of the powers that state law grants to the corporation in the articles of incorporation. Why do you think they do that?

The *Dodge* case was cited in the principal case. The major issue in the case was whether the trial court's decision to compel a dividend was proper. However, the case contains some interesting analysis as to the proper objectives of a business corporation. Was Mr. Ford's policy of reducing the price of cars altruistic?

## KAHN v. SULLIVAN
Supreme Court of Delaware
594 A.2d 48 (1991)

Holland, J.

This is an appeal from the approval of the settlement of one of three civil actions brought in the Court of Chancery by certain shareholders of Occidental Petroleum Corporation ("Occidental"). Each civil action challenged a decision by Occidental's board of directors (the "Board"), through a special committee of Occidental's outside directors ("the Special Committee"), to make a charitable donation. The purpose of the charitable donation was to construct and fund an art museum.

The shareholder plaintiffs in this litigation, Joseph Sullivan and Alan Brody, agreed to a settlement of their class and derivative actions subject to the approval of the Court of Chancery. The settlement was authorized, on behalf of Occidental, by the Special Committee. The shareholder plaintiffs in the other two civil actions, Alan R. Kahn ("Kahn") and Barnett Stepak ("Stepak"), appeared in the Sullivan action and objected to the proposed settlement. California Public Employees Retirement System ("CalPERS") was permitted to intervene as a shareholder plaintiff in the Kahn action and also appeared in opposition to the proposed settlement in the Sullivan action.

\* \* \*

The Objectors contend that the Court of Chancery abused its discretion in approving the settlement in the Sullivan action. The Objectors' first contention is that the Court of Chancery erred in holding that it was "highly probable" that the protection of the business judgment rule would successfully apply to the actions taken by the directors of Occidental who had been named as defendants. The Objectors' second contention is that the Court of Chancery abused its discretion in finding that the shareholder plaintiffs' claims of corporate waste were weak. Finally, the Objectors contend that the Court of Chancery abused its discretion in approving the settlement because the consideration for the settlement was inadequate in view of the strength of the claims which were being compromised.

The applicable standard of appellate review requires this Court to examine the record for an abuse of discretion by the Court of Chancery in approving the settlement. We have carefully reviewed the record and considered the Objectors' contentions. We have concluded that the decision of the Court of Chancery must be affirmed.

Occidental is a Delaware corporation. According to the parties, Occidental has about 290 million shares of stock outstanding which are held by approximately 495 thousand shareholders. For the year ending December 31, 1988, Occidental had assets of approximately twenty billion dollars, operating revenues of twenty billion dollars and pre-tax earnings of $574 million. Its corporate headquarters are located in Los Angeles, California.

At the time of his death on December 10, 1990, Dr. Hammer was Occidental's chief executive officer and the chairman of its board of directors. Since the early

1920's, Dr. Hammer had been a serious art collector. When Dr. Hammer died, he personally and The Armand Hammer Foundation (the "Foundation"), owned three major collections of art (referred to in their entirety as "the Art Collection"). The Art Collection, valued at $300–$400 million included: "Five Centuries of Art," more than 100 works by artists such as Rembrandt, Rubens, Renoir and Van Gogh; the Codex Hammer, a rare manuscript by Leonardo da Vinci; and the world's most extensive private collection of paintings, lithographs and bronzes by the French satirist Honore Daumier. . . .

For many years, the Board has determined that it is in the best interest of Occidental to support and promote the acquisition and exhibition of the Art Collection. Through Occidental's financial support and sponsorship, the Art Collection has been viewed by more than six million people in more than twenty-five American cities and at least eighteen foreign countries. The majority of those exhibitions have been in areas where Occidental has operations or was negotiating business contracts. Occidental's Annual Reports to its shareholders have described the benefits and good will which it attributes to the financial support that Occidental has provided for the Art Collection.

Dr. Hammer enjoyed an ongoing relationship with the Los Angeles County Museum of Art ("LACMA") for several decades. In 1968, Dr. Hammer agreed to donate a number of paintings to LACMA, as well as funds to purchase additional art. For approximately twenty years thereafter, Dr. Hammer both publicly and privately expressed his intention to donate the Art Collection to LACMA. However, Dr. Hammer and LACMA had never entered into a binding agreement to that effect. Nevertheless, LACMA named one of its buildings the Frances and Armand Hammer Wing in recognition of Dr. Hammer's gifts.

Occidental approved of Dr. Hammer's decision to permanently display the Art Collection at LACMA. In fact, it made substantial financial contributions to facilitate that display. In 1982, for example, Occidental paid two million dollars to expand and refurbish the Hammer Wing at LACMA.

In 1987, Dr. Hammer presented Daniel N. Belin, Esquire ("Belin"), the president of LACMA's Board of Trustees, with a thirty-nine page proposed agreement which set forth the terms upon which Dr. Hammer would permanently locate the Art Collection at LACMA. LACMA and Dr. Hammer tried, but were unable to reach a binding agreement. Consequently, Dr. Hammer concluded that he would make arrangements for the permanent display of the Art Collection at a location other than at LACMA. On January 8, 1988, Dr. Hammer wrote a letter to Belin which stated that he had "decided to create my own museum to house" the Art Collection.

On January 19, 1988, at a meeting of the executive committee of Occidental's board of directors ("the Executive Committee"), Dr. Hammer proposed that Occidental, in conjunction with the Foundation, construct a museum for the Art Collection. After discussing Occidental's history of identification with the Art Collection, the Executive Committee decided that it was in Occidental's best interest to accept Dr. Hammer's proposal. The Executive Committee approved the negotiation of arrangements for the preliminary design and construction of an art museum. It would be located adjacent to Occidental's headquarters, on the site of an existing parking garage used by Occidental for its employees. The Executive

Committee also decided that once the art museum project was substantially defined, a final proposal would be presented to the Board or the Executive Committee for approval and authorization.

The art museum concept was announced publicly on January 21, 1988. On February 11, 1988, the Board approved the Executive Committee's prior actions. Occidental informed its shareholders of the preliminary plan to construct The Armand Hammer Museum and Cultural Center of Art ("the Museum") in its 1987 Annual Report. In accordance with the January 19, 1988 resolutions passed by the Executive Committee, construction of a new parking garage for Occidental began in the fall of 1988. The Board approved a construction bond on November 10, 1988.

On December 15, 1988, the Board was presented with a detailed plan for the Museum proposal. The Board approved the concept and authorized a complete study of the proposal. Following the December 15th Board meeting, the law firm of Dilworth, Paxson, Kalish & Kauffman ("Dilworth") was retained by the Board to examine the Museum proposal and to prepare a memorandum addressing the issues relevant to the Board's consideration of the proposal. The law firm of Skadden, Arps, Slate, Meagher & Flom ("Skadden Arps") was retained to represent the new legal entity which would be necessitated by the Museum proposal. Occidental's public accountants, Arthur Andersen & Co. ("Arthur Andersen"), were also asked to examine the Museum proposal.

On or about February 6, 1989, ten days prior to the Board's prescheduled February 16 meeting, Dilworth provided each member of the Board with a ninety-six page memorandum. It contained a definition of the Museum proposal and the anticipated magnitude of the proposed charitable donation by Occidental. It reviewed the authority of the Board to approve such a donation and the reasonableness of the proposed donation. The Dilworth memorandum included an analysis of the donation's effect on Occidental's financial condition, the potential for good will and other benefits to Occidental, and a comparison of the proposed charitable contribution by Occidental to the charitable contributions of other corporations.

The advance distribution of the Dilworth memorandum was supplemented on February 10, 1989 by a tax opinion letter from Skadden Arps. That same day, the Board also received a consulting report from the Duncan Appraisal Corporation. The latter document addressed the option price for the Museum's purchase of Occidental's headquarters building, museum facility and parking garage in thirty years as contemplated by the Museum proposal.

\* \* \*

[T]he Board resolved to appoint the Special Committee, comprised of its eight independent and disinterested outside directors, to further review and to act upon the Museum proposal:

\* \* \*

FURTHER RESOLVED, that the Special Committee shall consist of the following directors of the Corporation: Senator Gore, Mr. Kluge, Mr. Krim, Mr. Nizer, Mr. Nolley, Dr. Piper, Mr. Syriani and Miss Tomich.

FURTHER RESOLVED, that the Special Committee shall have and is hereby granted full authority to consider, act on, approve and authorize the Proposal and the Special Committee's action respecting the Proposal shall be deemed the action of the Board of Directors of the Corporation and shall bind the Corporation to the same extent as an action of the full Board of Directors.

\* \* \*

On February 16, 1989, the Special Committee unanimously approved the Museum proposal, subject to certain conditions. The proposal approved by the Special Committee included the following provisions:

(1) Occidental would construct a new museum building, renovate portions of four floors of its adjacent headquarters for use by the Museum, and construct a parking garage beneath the museum for its own use for a total cost of approximately $50 million.

(2) Occidental would lease the Museum building and the four floors of its headquarters to the Museum rent-free for a term of thirty years. Occidental would continue to pay the property taxes, and the Museum would pay the utilities and maintenance expenses;

(3) Occidental would purchase a thirty-year annuity at an estimated cost of $35.6 million to provide for the funding of the Museum's operations during its initial years;

(4) Occidental would grant the Museum an irrevocable option to purchase the Museum building, the parking garage, and the Occidental headquarters building in thirty years for $55 million;

(5) Dr. Hammer and the Foundation would transfer the Art Collection entirely to the Museum;

(6) The Museum would be named for Dr. Hammer — The Armand Hammer Museum of Art and Cultural Center.

(7) Occidental would have representation on the board of directors of the Museum;

(8) Occidental would receive public recognition for its role in establishing the Museum, for example, by the naming of the courtyard, library, or auditorium for Occidental and Occidental would have the right to use the Museum, and be entitled to "corporate sponsor" rights.

The Special Committee's unanimous approval of the proposal was subject to the following conditions:

(1) The incorporation of the Museum as a non-profit corporation under Delaware law;

(2) The determination by the Internal Revenue Service that the Museum would be a tax-exempt entity under the Internal Revenue Code;

(3) The receipt of supplementation of the February opinion letters to reflect tax issues discussed at the meeting, including the question of self-dealing; and

(4)  The execution of the necessary documents relating to (a) the lease of the Museum facilities, (b) the Museum's option to purchase Occidental's headquarters, (c) Occidental's lease-back rights if the option was exercised, and (d) an agreement for the transfer of the Collection from the Foundation and Dr. Hammer to the Museum, including a full inventory of the art.

\* \* \*

Settlement negotiations were entered into almost immediately between Occidental and the attorneys for the plaintiffs in the Sullivan action. The attorney for the plaintiffs in the Kahn action was invited to attend the settlement negotiations. After the parties to the Sullivan action were in substantial agreement, the attorney for the plaintiffs in the Kahn action said it was up to his clients whether to accept the settlement, but that he was not going to recommend it.

On June 3, 1989, the parties to the Sullivan action signed a Memorandum of Understanding that set forth a proposed settlement in general terms. The proposed settlement was subject to the right of the plaintiffs to engage in additional discovery to confirm the fairness and adequacy of the proposed settlement.

On June 9, 1989, the plaintiffs in the Kahn action moved for a preliminary injunction to enjoin the proposed settlement in the Sullivan action and also for expedited discovery. An order granting limited expedited discovery on the motion was entered over the defendants' objection. The motion for a preliminary injunction was denied by the Court of Chancery on July 19, 1989.

In denying the motion for injunctive relief, the Court of Chancery found that Kahn would suffer no irreparable harm if a proposed settlement in Sullivan was subsequently finalized and submitted for approval since Kahn, as a stockholder of Occidental, would have the opportunity to appear and object to the settlement. The Court of Chancery also identified six issues to be addressed at any future settlement hearing:

(1) the failure of the Special Committee appointed by the directors of Occidental to hire its own counsel and advisors or even to formally approve the challenged acts; (2) the now worthlessness of a prior donation by Occidental to the Los Angeles County Museum; (3) the huge attorney fees which the parties have apparently decided to seek or not oppose; (4) the egocentric nature of some of Armand Hammer's objections to the Los Angeles County Museum being the recipient of his donation; (5) the issue of who really owns the art; and (6) the lack of any direct substantial benefit to the stockholders.

On July 20, 1989, the Special Committee met to discuss the Museum proposal. At that time, the Special Committee was in receipt of a number of documents required as a result of the conditions precedent it had imposed on February 16, 1989 before it would finally approve the Museum proposal. Those documents included: the Certificate of Incorporation of The Armand Hammer Museum of Art and Cultural Center, Inc.; Internal Revenue Service correspondence; opinion letters in draft form from Skadden Arps and Dilworth (later supplemented); a draft lease and option agreement; the Memorandum of Understanding in the Sullivan action; a list of the art works being transferred; and a proposed agreement for the transfer of the Collection to the Museum ("Transfer Agreement"). After reviewing the afore-mentioned documents and revising the Transfer Agreement, the Special Committee unanimously resolved that the conditions for approval, which it had imposed at their February 16, 1989 meeting, had been satisfied. The Special Committee then authorized Occidental to enter into the lease agreement with the Museum and "to purchase a thirty-nine million dollar annuity, or other financial arrangement, for the benefit of the Museum, as contemplated by the proposal."

The parties to the Sullivan action presented the Court of Chancery with a fully executed Stipulation of Compromise, Settlement and Release agreement ("the Settlement") on January 24, 1990. This agreement was only slightly changed from the June 3, 1989 Memorandum of Understanding. The Settlement, inter alia, provided:

(1) The Museum building shall be named the "Occidental Petroleum Cultural Center Building" with the name displayed appropriately on the building.

(2) Occidental shall be treated as a corporate sponsor by the Museum for as long as the Museum occupies the building.

(3) Occidental's contribution of the building shall be recognized by the Museum in public references to the facility.

(4) Three of Occidental's directors shall serve on the Museum's Board (or no less than one-third of the total Museum Board) with Occidental having the option to designate a fourth director.

(5) There shall be an immediate loan of substantially all of the art collections of Dr. Hammer to the Museum and there shall be an actual transfer of ownership of the collections upon Dr. Hammer's death or the commencement of operation of the Museum — whichever later occurs.

(6) All future charitable contributions by Occidental to any Hammer-affiliated charities shall be limited by the size of the dividends paid to Occidental's common stockholders. At current dividend levels, Occidental's annual contributions to Hammer-affiliated charities pursuant to this limitation could not exceed approximately three cents per share.

(7) Any amounts Occidental pays for construction of the Museum in excess of $50 million and any amounts paid to the Foundation upon Dr. Hammer's death must be charged against the agreed ceiling on limitations to Hammer-affiliated charities.

(8) Occidental's expenditures for the Museum construction shall not exceed $50 million, except that an additional $10 million may be expended through December 31, 1990 but only if such additional expenditures do not enlarge the scope of construction and if such expenditures are approved by the Special Committee. Amounts in excess of $50 million must be charged against the limitation on donations to Hammer-affiliated charities.

(9) Occidental shall be entitled to receive 50% of any consideration received in excess of a $55 million option price for the Museum property or 50% of any consideration the Museum receives from the assignment or transfer of its option or lease to a third party.

(10)   Plaintiffs' attorneys' fees in the Sullivan action shall not exceed $1.4 million.

\* \* \*

On April 4, 1990, the settlement hearing in the Sullivan action was held. A number of shareholders appeared or wrote letters objecting to the Settlement. The Objectors argued that the decision of the Special Committee on February 16 to approve the charitable donation to fund the Museum proposal was neither informed nor deliberate and was not cured by any subsequent conduct. Therefore, the Objectors argued that the actions by the Special Committee were not entitled to the protection of the business judgment rule. The Objectors also argued that the charitable donation to the Museum proposal constituted a waste of Occidental's corporate assets. Consequently, in view of the merits of the claims being compromised, the Objectors submitted that the benefits of the proposed Settlement in the Sullivan action were inadequate.

\* \* \*

On August 7, 1990, the Court of Chancery found the Settlement to be reasonable under all of the circumstances. The Court of Chancery concluded that the claims asserted by the shareholder plaintiffs would likely be dismissed before or after trial. While noting its own displeasure with the Settlement, the Court of Chancery explained that its role in reviewing the proposed Settlement was restricted to determining in its own business judgment whether, on balance, the Settlement was reasonable. The Court opined that although the benefit to be received from the Settlement was meager, it was adequate considering all the facts and circumstances.

Despite this Court's expressed displeasure with the settlement efforts, as set forth in its July 19, 1989 opinion in Kahn, the settlement now before the Court is only slightly changed from the June 3, 1989 Memorandum of Understanding.

\* \* \*

[Therefore] the settlement in the Court's opinion leaves much to be desired.

The Court's role in reviewing the proposed Settlement, however, is quite restricted. If the Court was a stockholder of Occidental it might for new directors, if it was on the Board it might vote for new management and if it was a member of the Special Committee it might vote against the Museum project. But its options are limited in reviewing a proposed settlement to applying Delaware law to the facts adduced in the record and then determining in its business judgment whether, on balance, the settlement is reasonable.

\* \* \*

The Objectors argue that the Court of Chancery erroneously concluded that the Settlement was fair, reasonable and adequate to protect the interests of the shareholders of Occidental. "In analyzing such arguments, this Court has always been assiduous in distinguishing between the function and legal obligations imposed upon the Court of Chancery in initially reviewing a proposed settlement and the appropriate appellate standards by which this Court must subsequently examine such a decision."

*   *   *

In determining the fairness of a settlement, the Court of Chancery is not required to afford the parties an opportunity to have a trial on the merits of the issues presented. Id. Nevertheless, the approval of a class action settlement by the Court of Chancery does require more than a cursory scrutiny of the issues presented. The balance between these two extremes has been described as follows:

> . . . the [Court of Chancery's] function is to consider the nature of the [plaintiff's] claim, the possible defenses thereto, the legal and factual circumstances of the case, and then to apply its own business judgment in deciding whether the settlement is reasonable in light of these factors.

*   *   *

Consequently, for this Court to set aside a settlement which has been found by the Court of Chancery to be fair and reasonable, the evidence in the record must be so strongly to the contrary that the approval of the settlement constituted an abuse of discretion.

The Objectors' third argument in the Court of Chancery, challenging the viability of the business judgment rule as a successful defense, was based upon Van Gorkom and contended that the Special Committee and other directors were grossly negligent in failing to inform themselves of all material information reasonably available to them.[8] Thus, the Objectors argued that even if, arguendo, the Special Committee was itself independent and formally approved the Museum proposal after its retention of independent legal counsel, such approval would not have cured the Special Committee's prior failure to exercise due care. The Court of Chancery found the record showed that the Special Committee had given due consideration to the Museum proposal and rejected the Objectors' argument to the contrary. *See generally Smith v. Van Gorkom*, Del. Supr., 488 A.2d 858 (1985).

The Court of Chancery carefully considered each of the Objectors' arguments in response to the merits of the suggested business judgment rule defense. It concluded that if the Sullivan action proceeded, it was highly probable in deciding a motion to dismiss, a motion for summary judgment, or a post-trial motion, the actions of "the Special Committee would be protected by the presumption of propriety afforded by the business judgment rule." Specifically, the Court of Chancery concluded that it would have been decided that the Special Committee, comprised of Occidental's outside directors, was independent and made an informed decision to approve the charitable donation to the Museum proposal.

Following its analysis and conclusion that the business judgment rule would have been applicable to any judicial examination of the Special Committee's actions, the Court of Chancery considered the shareholder plaintiffs' claim that the Board and the Special Committee's approval of the charitable donation to the Museum proposal constituted a waste of Occidental's corporate assets. In doing so, it

---

[8] [25] The Objectors submit that, inter alia, the Special Committee was apparently uninformed as to potential tax consequences of the charitable donation, the value of the Art Collection, how much of the Art Collection had been purchased with donations from Occidental, and what the cost for the Museum's rent-free use of the property would be to Occidental.

recognized that charitable donations by Delaware corporations are expressly authorized by 8 Del. C. § 122(9). It also recognized that although § 122(9) places no limitations on the size of a charitable corporate gift, that section has been construed "to authorize any reasonable corporate gift of a charitable or educational nature." *Theodora Holding Corp. v. Henderson*, Del. Ch., 257 A.2d 398, 405 (1969). Thus, the Court of Chancery concluded that the test to be applied in examining the merits of a claim alleging corporate waste "is that of reasonableness, a test in which the provisions of the Internal Revenue Code pertaining to charitable gifts by corporations furnish a helpful guide." *Id.* We agree with that conclusion.

The Objectors argued that Occidental's charitable contribution to the Museum proposal was unreasonable and a waste of corporate assets because it was excessive.[9] The Court of Chancery recognized that not every charitable gift constitutes a valid corporate action. Nevertheless, the Court of Chancery concluded, given the net worth of Occidental, its annual net income before taxes, and the tax benefits to Occidental, that the gift to the Museum was within the range of reasonableness established in *Theodora Holding Corp. v. Henderson*, Del. Ch., 257 A.2d 398, 405 (1969). Therefore, the Court of Chancery found that it was "reasonably probable" that plaintiffs would fail on their claim of waste. That finding is supported by the record and is the product of an orderly and logical deductive process.

*        *        *

[A]fter considering the legal and factual circumstances of the case sub judice, the Court of Chancery examined the value of the Settlement. The proponents of the Settlement argued that the monetary value of having the Museum building called the "Occidental Petroleum Cultural Center Building" was approximately ten million dollars. The Court of Chancery noted that, in support of their valuation arguments, the proponents also argued that the Settlement: (1) reinforced and assured Occidental's identification with and meaningful participation in the affairs of the Museum; (2) reinforced and protected the charitable nature and consequences of Occidental's gifts by securing the prompt delivery and irrevocable transfer of the Art Collection to the Museum; (3) imposed meaningful controls upon the total construction costs that Occidental will pay, which had already forced the reduction of the construction budget by $19.4 million; (4) placed meaningful restrictions upon Occidental's future charitable donations to "Hammer" affiliated entities and avoided increases in posthumous payments to the Foundation or any other designated recipient after Dr. Hammer's death; (5) restored to Occidental an equitable portion of any appreciation of the properties in the event the Museum exercised its option and disposed of the properties or transferred its option for value; and (6) guaranteed that the Art Collection would continue to be located in the Los Angeles

---

[9] [26] The Objectors also argued that the Museum project duplicated facilities previously funded by Occidental; served no social need; was designed primarily to enhance the personal reputation of Dr. Hammer; and resulted in damage (not good will) to Occidental. The Court of Chancery concluded that these concerns were ones about which reasonable minds could differ. That conclusion is also supported by the record and is the product of an orderly deductive process. *Levitt v. Bouvier*, 287 A.2d at 673. Therefore, we find no abuse of discretion by the Court of Chancery with respect to its assessment of these claims.

area and remain available for the enjoyment of the American public rather than dissipated into private collections or sold abroad.

The Court of Chancery characterized the proponents' efforts to quantify the monetary value of most of the Settlement benefits as "speculative." The Court of Chancery also viewed the estimate that naming the building for Occidental would have a ten million dollar value to Occidental with "a good deal of skepticism." Nevertheless, the Court of Chancery found that Occidental would, in fact, receive an economic benefit in the form of good will from the charitable donation to the Museum proposal. It also found that Occidental would derive an economic benefit from being able to utilize the Museum, adjacent to its corporate headquarters, in the promotion of its business.

*    *    *

The strength of claims raised in a class action lawsuit helps to determine whether the consideration received for their settlement is adequate and whether dismissal with prejudice is appropriate. Thus, if the [Court of Chancery] were to find that the plaintiff class was being asked to sacrifice a facially credible claim for a small consideration, he would be justified in rejecting a settlement as unfair. Conversely, where the [Court of Chancery] finds that the plaintiff's potential challenges have little chance of success, he has good reason to approve the proposed settlement.

The Court of Chancery found that "the benefit [of the Settlement] to the stockholders of Occidental is sufficient to support the Settlement and is adequate, if only barely so, when compared to the weakness of the plaintiffs' claims." The Court of Chancery concluded that "although the Settlement is meager, it is adequate considering all the facts and circumstances."

### Conclusion

The reasonableness of a particular class action settlement is addressed to the discretion of the Court of Chancery, on a case by case basis, in light of all of the relevant circumstances.

Therefore, the decision of the Court of Chancery is AFFIRMED.

# NOTE

Does this look like a pet charity? This case also provides an illustration of the scrutiny courts give to the settlement of class actions. Is the standard very demanding?

## GAS SERVICE CO. v. STATE CORPORATION COMMISSION OF KANSAS
Court of Appeals of Kansas
662 P.2d 264 (1983)

ABBOTT, J.

This is a review of two orders of the State Corporation Commission of Kansas arising from a rate hearing, pursuant to K.S.A. 66-118d. Both orders appealed from resulted from an application by The Gas Service Company (Gas Service) for a rate increase of $20,310,464 (Docket No. 132,996-U).

\* \* \*

[The] Gas Service requested a review in which it raises four issues as follows:

\* \* \*

2. The Commission erred in disallowing Gas Service expenses for dues, donations and charitable contributions;

\* \* \*

In *Midwest Gas Users Ass'n v. Kansas Corporation Commission*, 5 Kan. App. 2d 653, Syl. para. 3, 623 P.2d 924, rev. denied 229 Kan. 670 (1981), it was held: "The matter of rate design involves a policy decision which is legislative in nature, and the Commission's orders in that regard demand utmost deference from the judicial branch."

With our basic scope of review in mind, we turn to the issues in this case.

\* \* \*

Gas Service also argues the Commission erred in disallowing as operating expenses the dues and charitable donations made during the test year. The Commission disallowed all of the contributions and dues and devoted some three pages of its order to explaining why it was doing so. The Commission basically determined ratepayers should not be required to involuntarily pay dues and charitable donations made by a utility. It further determined there was a lack of evidence by Gas Service to show the reasonableness of any of the dues and charitable donations. We deem the latter argument to be of no real significance. For at least twenty years, utilities have been allowed to include in operating expenses the dues and charitable donations they pay, subject only to a reasonableness standard. Most of the $105,041 disallowed here (about 25 cents a year per user) was given to legitimate, recognized charitable organizations such as United Way, Heart Association, Menninger's, and to educational institutions. In addition, Gas Service paid dues such as those to Chamber of Commerce, and to Rotary Club and Kiwanis Club for its key employees. Staff counsel conceded at oral argument that the Commission is now disallowing charitable donations and dues as a matter of policy, and we deem that to be the issue before us. The list of charitable donations and dues paid by Gas Service is such that it would be unreasonable to disallow them in toto, for at least a substantial number of them are reasonable on their face without further evidence as to their reasonableness. Thus, the issue before us is not their reasonableness but whether the Commission can, as a matter of policy, disallow all dues and charitable contributions as operating expenses.

The Supreme Court in *Southwestern Bell Tel. Co. v. State Corporation Commission*, 192 Kan. 39, Syl. para. 8, 386 P.2d 515 (1963), stated:

> "The reasonable cost of meeting civic responsibilities such as Chamber of Commerce dues and charitable donations should be allowed as an operating expense in a public utility rate investigation, but they are subject to close scrutiny as to reasonableness."

In the absence of some indication that the Supreme Court will no longer follow its earlier decision, we are duty-bound to follow its prior case law. Although only one member of the court that wrote Southwestern Bell Tel. Co. is still a member of the Supreme Court, we have no indication the Court would change its position. We are aware of the considerable authority existing to support the argument that whether to allow dues and charitable donations as operating expenses is a political issue to be decided by the legislature and not a legal issue. However, the Supreme Court has spoken, and since we are of the opinion that Southwestern Bell Tel. Co. controls the proceeding before us, we are duty-bound to follow it. In the future, if the Commission on remand truly believes any charitable donations or dues are unreasonable, it should state specifically which it finds to be unreasonable and its reasons for so finding.

Those parts of the Commission's order in docket No. 132,996-U that refuse to adjust the test year to recognize the loss of sales to Phillips Petroleum refinery and disallow as operating expenses in toto the dues and charitable donations made by Gas Service during the test year are unreasonable and are hereby vacated.

Affirmed in part, reversed in part and remanded to the State Corporation Commission for further proceedings.

# NOTE

This case raises the same issue as corporate donations, but in a different context. In public utility rate-making the issue is whether the cost of charitable donations should be allocated to the ratepayer. Under corporate law, if the donations are reasonable in amount and serve some incidental purpose, they would be allowed. In the rate-making cases, the question is whether the shareholders or the ratepayers should bear the cost. What is the purpose of these donations? Are they necessary in order to provide gas service? Do they benefit the ratepayer?

## CREDIT LYONNAIS BANK NEDERLAND, NV v. PATHE COMMUNICATIONS CORP.

Court of Chancery of Delaware
1991 Del. Ch. LEXIS 215 (Dec. 30, 1991)

*no longer good law*

In these circumstances where the company was in bankruptcy until May 28 and even thereafter the directors labored in the shadow of that prospect, Mr. Ladd and his associates were appropriately mindful of the potential differing interests between the corporation and its 98% shareholder. At least where a corporation is operating in the vicinity of insolvency, a board of directors is not merely the agent of the residue risk bearers, but owes its duty to the corporate enterprise.[10]

Thus, the best evaluation is that the current value of the equity is $3.55 million ($15.55 million expected value of judgment on appeal, $12 million liability to bondholders). Now assume an offer to settle at $12.5 million (also consider one at $17.5 million). By what standard do the directors of the company evaluate the fairness of these offers? The creditors of this solvent company would be in favor of accepting either a $12.5 million offer or a $17.5 million offer. In either event they will avoid the 75% risk of insolvency and default. The stockholders, however, will plainly be opposed to acceptance of a $12.5 million settlement (under which they get practically nothing). More importantly, they very well may be opposed to acceptance of the $17.5 million offer under which the residual value of the corporation would increase from $3.5 to $5.5 million. This is so because the litigation alternative, with its 25% probability of $39 million outcome to them ($51 million — $12 million) has an expected valued to the residual risk bearer of $9.75 million ($39 million x 25% chance of affirmance), substantially greater than the $5.5 million available to them in the settlement. While in fact the stockholders' preference would reflect their appetite for risk, it is possible (and with diversified shareholders likely) that shareholders would prefer rejection of both settlement offers.

But if we consider the community of interests that the corporation represents it seems apparent that one should in this hypothetical accept the best settlement offer available providing it is greater than $15.55 million, and one below that amount should be rejected. But that result will not be reached by a director who thinks he owes duties directly to shareholders only. It will be reached by directors who are capable of conceiving of the corporation as a legal and economic entity. Such directors will recognize that in managing the business affairs of a solvent corporation in the vicinity of insolvency, circumstances may arise when the right (both the efficient and the fair) course to follow for the corporation may diverge from the choice that he stockholders (or the creditors, or the employees, or any single group interested in the corporation) would make if given the opportunity to act.

---

[10] [55] The possibility of insolvency can do curious things to incentives, exposing creditors to risks of opportunistic behavior and creating complexities for directors. Consider, for example, a solvent corporation having a single asset, a judgment for $51 million against a solvent debtor. The judgment is on appeal and thus subject to modification or reversal. Assume that the only liabilities of the company are to bondholders in the amount of $12 million. Assume that the array of probable outcomes of the appeal is as follows.

|  | Expected Value |
| --- | --- |
| 25% chance of affirmance ($51mm) | $12.75 |
| 70% chance of affirmance ($4mm) | $2.80 |
| 5% chance of reversal ($0) | $0 |
| Expected Value of Judgment on Appeal | $15.55 |

## NOTE

The above excerpt from Chancellor Allen's opinion illustrates a situation in which it is appropriate to consider the interests of groups other than the shareholders. In general the board of directors owes a fiduciary duty to the shareholders alone. Why do the directors owe a duty to creditors when a corporation is in the vicinity of insolvency? What does Chancellor Allen mean by "vicinity of insolvency"?

## G.  CONSTITUENCY STATUTES

The Delaware Supreme Court in analyzing defensive measures to a tender offer stated:

> If a defensive measure is to come within the ambit of the business judgment rule, it must be reasonable in relation to the threat posed. This entails an analysis by the directors of the nature of the takeover bid and its effect on the corporate enterprise. Examples of such concerns may include: inadequacy of the price offered, nature and timing of the offer, questions of illegality, the impact on "constituencies other than shareholders (i.e., creditors, customers, employees, and perhaps even the community generally)" . . ..

*Unocal Corp. v. Mesa Petroleum Co.*, 493 A.2d 946 (Del. 1985). At least 28 states have enacted statutes permitting directors to consider the effect of a takeover on constituencies other than shareholders.

### Ronald M. Green, *Shareholders as Stakeholders: Changing Metaphors of Corporate Governance*
### 50 WASH. & LEE L. REV. 1409 (1993)[11]

Recently, the argument that corporate management should consider the interests of many constituencies appears to have attained some hearing within the world of corporate law. A handful of Delaware court decisions have modestly expanded the business judgment rule to allow corporate directors to take into account the impact of their decision making on other corporate "stakeholder" groups, especially employees and local communities. These decisions, however, require that measures taken on behalf of other constituencies produce "some rationally related benefit accruing to the shareholders." Over the past two decades, twenty-eight states have passed "other constituency" statutes permitting, though usually not requiring, senior managers and corporate directors to consider the interests of other stakeholders. Charles Hansen notes that these statutes are "remarkably consistent" with one another.[12] Generally, they permit directors, while acting in the best interests of the corporation, to take into account a variety of constituencies other than shareholders, including employees, communities, customers, and suppliers. Because these statutes, with few exceptions, specify that the impact on other

---

[11] Copyright © 1993. All rights reserved. Reprinted by permission of the author and *Washington and Lee Law Review*.

[12] [10] [Charles, Hansen, *Other Constituency Statutes: A Search for Perspective*, 466 BUS. LAW. 1355 (1991).]

constituencies must have a relationship to the best interests of the corporation, understood in terms of shareholder gain, they represent little more than codifications of the business judgment rule as it has recently been interpreted by the Delaware courts. As a result, it seems fair to say that these legal developments do not really challenge the dominant principal-agent, fiduciary metaphor and, in some respects, they even reinforce it. Court decisions have widened the latitude of fiduciary decision making, but they have not altered its ultimate priorities. In every case, the claims and welfare of other corporate stakeholders must also serve the long-term interests of shareholders, a strict requirement. If we consider that "other constituency" statutes often were passed in reaction to the takeover battles of the 1980s and that these statutes moderate directors' duties to shareholders only in the context of mergers or acquisitions, the claim that these statutes represent a fundamental change in corporate legal perspectives is weakened further. By and large, these statutes aim to strengthen the hand of management in its efforts to ward off "third party" hostile raiders, or upstart managers, whose conduct threatens more traditional lines of corporate control and obligation.

*   *   *

The Minnesota statute is typical in this regard. It reads:

> In discharging the duties of the position of director, a director may in considering the best interests of the corporation, consider the interests of the corporation's employees, customers, suppliers, and creditors, the economy of the state and nation, community and societal considerations, and the long-term as well as short-term interests of the corporation and its shareholders including the possibility that these interests may be best served by the continued independence of the corporation.

Minn. Stat. Ann. 302A.251(5) (West Supp. 1993).

Hansen singles out the statutes of Connecticut, Iowa, Indiana, and Pennsylvania (especially the latter's 1990 amendments) as the only ones among the 28 that permit or require directors to place other constituencies on a footing with stockholders. Hansen, *supra.* note 9, at 1370, 1375. The Committee on Corporate Laws of the American Bar Association places Georgia's statute in this category.

# Chapter 10

# MANAGEMENT'S DUTIES TO THE CORPORATION

## A.  DIRECTORS' DUTY OF CARE

### JORDAN v. THE EARTHGRAINS COMPANIES, INC.
Court of Appeals of North Carolina
576 S.E.2d 336 (2003)

TIMMONS-GOODSON, J.

Mary Jordan, et al (hereinafter referred to collectively as "plaintiffs") appeal from an order of the trial court granting summary judgment in favor of The Earthgrains Company, Anheuser–Busch, Inc., and Campbell Taggart Company (hereinafter collectively, "defendants"). For reasons stated herein, we affirm the trial court's decision.

An examination of the pleadings, exhibits, and depositions filed in response to defendants' summary judgment motion, considered in the light most favorable to plaintiff, tends to show the following: The Earthgrains Company ("Earthgrains") is a national baking company operating several plants nationwide, including a plant located in Charlotte, North Carolina. Earthgrains is owned by Campbell Taggart Baking Companies, Inc. ("Campbell"), which in turn is a wholly-owned subsidiary of Anheuser–Busch Companies ("Anheuser").

In 1993, Barry Beracha ("Beracha") was hired as Chief Executive Officer of Campbell. In 1995, Anheuser decided to "spin-off" Campbell's common stock by distributing it to Anheuser shareholders. This plan would allow Campbell to become an independent publicly-owned company. On 1 August 1995, Beracha traveled to the Charlotte plant to conduct a meeting regarding the status of the Charlotte plant ("the August 1995 meeting"). At that time, plaintiffs were employed at the Charlotte plant operated by Earthgrains. The August 1995 meeting and the events following the meeting are the basis for three lawsuits filed by plaintiffs.

During the August 1995 meeting, plaintiffs questioned Beracha about job security and the economic status of the Charlotte plant. According to plaintiffs, Beracha reported that the Charlotte plant was profitable and that their jobs were secure. However, according to defendants, Beracha was asked if any jobs would be lost as a result of the spin-off of common stock to defendants' shareholders. Defendants contend that Beracha reported that the Charlotte plant would not close and plaintiffs would not lose their jobs as a result of the spin-off procedure.

On 6 December 1995, plaintiffs were notified that the Charlotte plant would close in February 1996. Plaintiffs filed a class action lawsuit on 24 February 1997 in federal court alleging Title VII violations and contending that statements made by Beracha in the August 1995 meeting constituted fraudulent misrepresentation. Defendants were granted summary judgment, a decision which was eventually affirmed by the United States Court of Appeals for the Fourth Circuit. On 9 February 1999, plaintiffs filed a second lawsuit in federal court, but later dismissed the action.

On 3 May 2000, plaintiffs filed a lawsuit in Mecklenburg County Superior Court alleging negligent misrepresentation. In the complaint, plaintiffs contended that the statements made by Beracha in the August 1995 meeting led them to believe that the Charlotte plant was profitable and that plaintiffs' jobs were secure. Plaintiffs further allege that at the time of the August 1995 meeting, Beracha knew that the operating costs of the Charlotte plant far exceeded its revenue, but that Beracha failed to inform them of this fact.

Defendants thereafter filed a motion for summary judgment which came before the trial court on 19 June 2001. Upon review of the evidence and argument by counsel, the trial court granted defendants' motion for summary judgment on 10 July 2001. Plaintiffs appeal.

Plaintiffs argue that the trial court erred in granting summary judgment in favor of defendants when (1) there are genuine issues of material fact for a claim of negligent misrepresentation, (2) their claim for negligent misrepresentation was not barred by collateral estoppel or res judicata, and (3) plaintiffs were not subject to a collective bargaining agreement. For the reasons stated herein, we disagree.

Plaintiffs argue that genuine issues of material fact exist concerning their claim for negligent misrepresentation. It is well established that "the tort of negligent misrepresentation occurs when (1) a party justifiably relies (2) to his detriment (3) on information prepared without reasonable care (4) by one who owed the relying party a duty of care." *Raritan River Steel Co. v. Cherry, Bekaert & Holland*, 322 N.C. 200, 206, 367 S.E.2d 609, 612 (1988), *reversed on other grounds*, 329 N.C. 646, 407 S.E.2d 178 (1991). Generally, directors of a corporation owe a fiduciary duty to the corporation. *Keener Lumber Co. v. Perry*, 149 N.C. App. 19, 26, 560 S.E.2d 817, 822, disc. review denied, 356 N.C. 164, 568 S.E.2d 196 356 N.C. 164, 568 S.E.2d 196 (2002). When there are allegations that a director of a corporation has breached a fiduciary duty, the action is properly maintained by the corporation. *Id.*

Therefore, in order to show error, plaintiffs in the instant case must be able to show that Beracha owed plaintiffs a duty of care, which was breached, and that they justifiably relied on the alleged misrepresentations made by Beracha. Viewing the evidence in the light most favorable to plaintiffs, there are no genuine issues of material fact concerning the essential elements of duty of care, breach of duty and justifiable reliance, and defendants are entitled to judgment as a matter of law. Thus, plaintiffs' claims could not withstand a summary judgment motion.

In the instant case, plaintiffs fail to show that Beracha owed a duty to report accurate information about the Charlotte plan's financial status. The evidence tends to show that Beracha is the president and chief executive officer of Campbell. In his position as the director of a corporation, Beracha only owed a duty of care to the corporation and not to individual employees. Therefore, plaintiffs fail to show that Beracha owed them a duty of care, which is an essential element of negligent misrepresentation.

Plaintiffs further argue that even if Beracha was "under no duty to speak, when he did speak he was under a duty to give competent information and plaintiffs were justified in relying on Beracha's statements." We disagree.

In *Simms v. Prudential Life Ins. Co. of Am.*, 140 N.C. App. 529, 537 S.E.2d 237 (2000), disc. review denied, 353 N.C. 381, 547 S.E.2d 18 (2001), a corporation's president and chief operating officer informed potential stock buyers that the corporation could emerge from bankruptcy reorganization as a revitalized entity, and that an investment in the corporation could be valuable and profitable. This Court held that the buyers of stock in the corporation could not recover on a theory of negligent misrepresentation after their stock lost its value because neither the president nor the corporation was in the business of giving financial advice, and the president did not obtain a pecuniary gain from the investment. *Id.* at 534, 537 S.E.2d at 241. The *Sims* Court defined a breach of duty owed in negligent misrepresentation as:

> " . . . One who, in the course of his business, profession or employment, or in any other transaction in which he has a pecuniary interest, supplies false information for the guidance of others in their business transactions, [and thus] is subject to liability for pecuniary loss caused to them by their justifiable reliance upon the information, if he fails to exercise reasonable care or competence in obtaining or communicating the information."

*Id.* (quoting *Marcus Bros. Textiles Inc.*, 350 N.C. at 218, 513 S.E.2d at 323–24).

In the case at bar, plaintiffs fail to show that (1) Beracha was offering them guidance in a business transaction; (2) that the alleged information was false; (3) that defendants had a pecuniary interest in inducing plaintiffs to continue employment; or (4) that plaintiffs were justified in relying on the alleged information. The evidence tends to show that plaintiffs and defendants were not engaged in a business transaction; however, Beracha's visit to the Charlotte plant was shortly after the public announcement of the spin-off of stock by defendants, and plaintiffs were concerned with how the spin-off would affect the Charlotte plant. During the meeting, plaintiffs and Beracha discussed the spin-off and Beracha informed plaintiffs that the spin-off did not affect the Charlotte plant. Plaintiffs offer no evidence to the contrary, but merely contend that Beracha reported to them that the Charlotte plant was profitable. The record further reveals that after a study commission reviewed the operation of the Charlotte plant, the committee recommended that the Charlotte plant be closed. Beracha approved the committee's recommendation on 16 November 1995, which was approximately four months after the August 1995 meeting. Therefore, Beracha could not provide false information regarding the Charlotte plant's closure and thus could not breach any alleged duty owed to plaintiffs.

Assuming, *arguendo*, that plaintiffs' claims are true, they fail to show that defendants had a pecuniary interest by allegedly informing plaintiffs that the Charlotte plant was profitable. Plaintiffs fail to claim that Beracha's alleged representations were calculated or made with the intent to deceive plaintiffs. A further review of the record reveals that consistent with obligations under the National Labor Relations Act, defendants, represented by the International Brotherhood of Teamsters Local Union 71, negotiated with the union concerning the terms and arrangements for the Charlotte plant's closure. The agreement contained a special bonus package not mandated by the collective bargaining agreement. Assuming, as argued by plaintiffs, that Beracha knew the Charlotte plant was not profitable, defendants would obviously lose money by advising plaintiffs to continue employment, close the plant, and then negotiate a bonus package for plaintiffs. The union agreement is inconsistent with plaintiff's argument that defendants obtained a pecuniary interest by inducing plaintiffs to continue employment with defendants. Without the essential element that defendants breached an alleged duty of care, plaintiffs' claim for negligent misrepresentation must fail.

Additionally, plaintiffs fail to show justifiable reliance. Plaintiffs contend that it was "reasonable" for them to conclude that Beracha conducted "all necessary investigations regarding the profitability" of the Charlotte plant in preparation of the August 1995 meeting. Plaintiffs offer no further evidence to establish that they relied on the representations made by Beracha to their detriment.

"Justifiable reliance is an element of negligent misrepresentation in North Carolina." *APAC–Carolina, Inc. v. Greensboro–High Point Airport Authority*, 110 N.C.App. 664, 680, 431 S.E.2d 508, 517 (1993). The evidence tends to show that plaintiffs offer no evidence that they relied on Beracha's statements or that such reliance was justified. Therefore, we conclude that any reliance by plaintiffs was not justified for several reasons. First, plaintiffs failed to inspect financial information posted inside the Charlotte plant. Second, plaintiffs failed to show that they declined any job offers in order to remain with defendants based on comments made at the August 1995 meeting. Third, Beracha did not know in the August 1995 meeting that the commission study would recommend the closure of the Charlotte plant.

Since essential elements of negligent misrepresentation are absent in this case, we conclude the trial court did not err in granting summary judgment in favor of defendants.

In light of the foregoing, we decline to address plaintiffs' remaining assignments of error.

Affirmed.

# NOTES

1.   This case clearly states the law. A corporate officer owes his duty of care only to the corporation, not to the employees. Corporate officers frequently make statements to the effect that the employees are very important to the corporation and that the officers and the corporation value their employees highly. Nonetheless, the officers owe their duties of care and loyalty only to the corporation.

2.   Was it a prudent decision of Mr. Beracha to speak about the job security and economic status of the Charlotte plant?

**3.** Many states have laws that permit the board of directors to consider the interests of the employees and other groups when making decisions about a takeover bid. Also, Credit Lyonnais suggests that the board of directors must consider the interests of the creditors when the corporation is in the "vicinity of insolvency."

# SHLENKSY v. WRIGLEY
## Appellate Court of Illinois
## 237 N.E.2d 776 (1968)

SULLIVAN, J.

This is an appeal from a dismissal of plaintiff's amended complaint on motion of the defendants. The action was a stockholders' derivative suit against the directors for negligence and mismanagement. The corporation was also made a defendant. Plaintiff sought damages and an order that defendants cause the installation of lights in Wrigley Field and the scheduling of night baseball games.

Plaintiff is a minority stockholder of defendant corporation, Chicago National League Ball Club (Inc.), a Delaware corporation with its principal place of business in Chicago, Illinois. Defendant corporation owns and operates the major league professional baseball team known as the Chicago Cubs. The corporation also engages in the operation of Wrigley Field, the Cubs' home park, the concessionaire sales during Cubs' home games, television and radio broadcasts of Cubs' home games, the leasing of the field for football games and other events and receives its share, as visiting team, of admission moneys from games played in other National League stadia. The individual defendants are directors of the Cubs and have served for varying periods of years. Defendant Philip K. Wrigley is also president of the corporation and owner of approximately 80% of the stock therein.

Plaintiff alleges that since night baseball was first played in 1935 nineteen of the twenty major league teams have scheduled night games. In 1966, out of a total of 1620 games in the major leagues, 932 were played at night. Plaintiff alleges that every member of the major leagues, other than the Cubs, scheduled substantially all of its home games in 1966 at night, exclusive of opening days, Saturdays, Sundays, holidays and days prohibited by league rules. Allegedly this has been done for the specific purpose of maximizing attendance and thereby maximizing revenue and income.

The Cubs, in the years 1961-65, sustained operating losses from its direct baseball operations. Plaintiff attributes those losses to inadequate attendance at Cubs' home games. He concludes that if the directors continue to refuse to install lights at Wrigley Field and schedule night baseball games, the Cubs will continue to sustain comparable losses and its financial condition will continue to deteriorate.

Plaintiff alleges that, except for the year 1963, attendance at Cubs' home games has been substantially below that at their road games, many of which were played at night.

Plaintiff compares attendance at Cubs' games with that of the Chicago White

Sox, an American League club, whose weekday games were generally played at night. The weekend attendance figures for the two teams was similar; however, the White Sox week-night games drew many more patrons than did the Cubs' weekday games.

Plaintiff alleges that the funds for the installation of lights can be readily obtained through financing and the cost of installation would be far more than offset and recaptured by increased revenues and incomes resulting from the increased attendance.

Plaintiff further alleges that defendant Wrigley has refused to install lights, not because of interest in the welfare of the corporation but because of his personal opinions "that baseball is a 'daytime sport' and that the installation of lights and night baseball games will have a deteriorating effect upon the surrounding neighborhood." It is alleged that he has admitted that he is not interested in whether the Cubs would benefit financially from such action because of his concern for the neighborhood, and that he would be willing for the team to play night games if a new stadium were built in Chicago.

Plaintiff alleges that the other defendant directors, with full knowledge of the foregoing matters, have acquiesced in the policy laid down by Wrigley and have permitted him to dominate the board of directors in matters involving the installation of lights and scheduling of night games, even though they knew he was not motivated by a good faith concern as to the best interests of defendant corporation, but solely by his personal views set forth above. It is charged that the directors are acting for a reason or reasons contrary and wholly unrelated to the business interests of the corporation; that such arbitrary and capricious acts constitute mismanagement and waste of corporate assets, and that the directors have been negligent in failing to exercise reasonable care and prudence in the management of the corporate affairs.

The question on appeal is whether plaintiff's amended complaint states a cause of action. It is plaintiff's position that fraud, illegality and conflict of interest are not the only bases for a stockholder's derivative action against the directors. Contrari-wise, defendants argue that the courts will not step in and interfere with honest business judgment of the directors unless there is a showing of fraud, illegality or conflict of interest.

The cases in this area are numerous and each differs from the others on a factual basis. However, the courts have pronounced certain ground rules which appear in all cases and which are then applied to the given factual situation. The court in *Wheeler v. Pullman Iron and Steel Company*, 143 Ill. 197, 207, 32 N.E. 420, 423, said:

> "It is, however, fundamental in the law of corporations, that the majority of its stockholders shall control the policy of the corporation, and regulate and govern the lawful exercise of its franchise and business. * * * Every one purchasing or subscribing for stock in a corporation impliedly agrees that he will be bound by the acts and proceedings done or sanctioned by a majority of the shareholders, or by the agents of the corporation duly chosen by such majority, within the scope of the powers conferred by the

charter, and courts of equity will not undertake to control the policy or business methods of a corporation, although it may be seen that a wiser policy might be adopted and the business more successful if other methods were pursued. The majority of shares of its stock, or the agents by the holders thereof lawfully chosen, must be permitted to control the business of the corporation in their discretion, when not in violation of its charter or some public law, or corruptly and fraudulently subversive of the rights and interests of the corporation or of a shareholder."

The standards set in Delaware are also clearly stated in the cases. In *Davis v. Louisville Gas & Electric Co.*, 16 Del. Ch. 157, 142 A. 654, a minority shareholder sought to have the directors enjoined from amending the certificate of incorporation. The court said on page 659:

> "We have then a conflict in view between the responsible managers of a corporation and an overwhelming majority of its stockholders on the one hand and a dissenting minority on the other — a conflict touching matters of business policy, such as has occasioned innumerable applications to courts to intervene and determine which of the two conflicting views should prevail. The response which courts make to such applications is that it is not their function to resolve for corporations questions of policy and business management. The directors are chosen to pass upon such questions and their judgment unless shown to be tainted with fraud is accepted as final. The judgment of the directors of corporations enjoys the benefit of a presumption that it was formed in good faith and was designed to promote the best interests of the corporation they serve." (Emphasis supplied).

*       *       *

Plaintiff argues that the allegations of his amended complaint are sufficient to set forth a cause of action under the principles set out in *Dodge v. Ford Motor Co.*, 204 Mich. 459, 170 N.W. 668. In that case plaintiff, owner of about 10% of the outstanding stock, brought suit against the directors seeking payment of additional dividends and the enjoining of further business expansion. In ruling on the request for dividends the court indicated that the motives of Ford in keeping so much money in the corporation for expansion and security were to benefit the public generally and spread the profits out by means of more jobs, etc. The court felt that these were not only far from related to the good of the stockholders, but amounted to a change in the ends of the corporation and that this was not a purpose contemplated or allowed by the corporate charter. The court relied on language found in *Hunter v. Roberts, Throp & Co.*, 83 Mich. 63, 47 N.W. 131, 134, wherein it was said:

> "Courts of equity will not interfere in the management of the directors unless it is clearly made to appear that they are guilty of fraud or misappropriation of the corporate funds, or refuse to declare a dividend when the corporation has a surplus of net profits which it can, without detriment to its business, divide among its stockholders, and when a refusal to do so would amount to such an abuse of discretion as would constitute a fraud or breach of that good faith which they are bound to exercise toward the stockholders."

From the authority relied upon in that case it is clear that the court felt that there must be fraud or a breach of that good faith which directors are bound to exercise toward the stockholders in order to justify the courts entering into the internal affairs of corporations. This is made clear when the court refused to interfere with the directors' decision to expand the business. The following appears on page 684 of 170 N.W.:

> "We are not, however, persuaded that we should interfere with the proposed expansion of the business of the Ford Motor Company. In view of the fact that the selling price of products may be increased at any time, the ultimate results of the larger business cannot be certainly estimated. The judges are not business experts. It is recognized that plans must often be made for a long future, for expected competition, for a continuing as well as an immediately profitable venture. . . . We are not satisfied that the alleged motives of the directors, in so far as they are reflected in the conduct of business, menace the interests of the shareholders." (Emphasis supplied).

Plaintiff in the instant case argues that the directors are acting for reasons unrelated to the financial interest and welfare of the Cubs. However, we are not satisfied that the motives assigned to Philip K. Wrigley, and through him to the other directors, are contrary to the best interests of the corporation and the stockholders. For example, it appears to us that the effect on the surrounding neighborhood might well be considered by a director who was considering the patrons who would or would not attend the games if the park were in a poor neighborhood. Furthermore, the long run interest of the corporation in its property value at Wrigley Field might demand all efforts to keep the neighborhood from deteriorating. By these thoughts we do not mean to say that we have decided that the decision of the directors was a correct one. That is beyond our jurisdiction and ability. We are merely saying that the decision is one properly before directors and the motives alleged in the amended complaint showed no fraud, illegality or conflict of interest in their making of that decision.

While all the courts do not insist that one or more of the three elements must be present for a stockholder's derivative action to lie, nevertheless we feel that unless the conduct of the defendants at least borders on one of the elements, the courts should not interfere. The trial court in the instant case acted properly in dismissing plaintiff's amended complaint.

We feel that plaintiff's amended complaint was also defective in failing to allege damage to the corporation. . . .

There is no allegation that the night games played by the other nineteen teams enhanced their financial position or that the profits, if any, of those teams were directly related to the number of night games scheduled. There is an allegation that the installation of lights and scheduling of night games in Wrigley Field would have resulted in large amounts of additional revenues and incomes from increased attendance and related sources of income. Further, the cost of installation of lights, funds for which are allegedly readily available by financing, would be more than offset and recaptured by increased revenues. However, no allegation is made that there will be a net benefit to the corporation from such action, considering all increased costs.

Plaintiff claims that the losses of defendant corporation are due to poor attendance at home games. However, it appears from the amended complaint, taken as a whole, that factors other than attendance affect the net earnings or losses. For example, in 1962, attendance at home and road games decreased appreciably as compared with 1961, and yet the loss from direct baseball operation and of the whole corporation was considerably less.

The record shows that plaintiff did not feel he could allege that the increased revenues would be sufficient to cure the corporate deficit. The only cost plaintiff was at all concerned with was that of installation of lights. No mention was made of operation and maintenance of the lights or other possible increases in operating costs of night games and we cannot speculate as to what other factors might influence the increase or decrease of profits if the Cubs were to play night home games.

*   *   *

Finally, we do not agree with plaintiff's contention that failure to follow the example of the other major league clubs in scheduling night games constituted negligence. Plaintiff made no allegation that these teams' night schedules were profitable or that the purpose for which night baseball had been undertaken was fulfilled. Furthermore, it cannot be said that directors, even those of corporations that are losing money, must follow the lead of the other corporations in the field. Directors are elected for their business capabilities and judgment and the courts cannot require them to forego their judgment because of the decisions of directors of other companies. Courts may not decide these questions in the absence of a clear showing of dereliction of duty on the part of the specific directors and mere failure to "follow the crowd" is not such a dereliction.

# NOTES

**1.** The attitude of the court in *Shlensky v. Wrigley* is typical of that of courts in duty of care cases, and indicates why it is so difficult for plaintiffs to prevail. Should not the court at least have allowed the case to go the jury given factors such as (1) the consistent losses suffered by the Chicago Cubs over the years, and (2) that the Cubs were the only team in Major League Baseball to play no home night games? Does the court suggest that in at least part of the problem was with the adequacy of plaintiff's complaint?

**2.** Reconsider *Dodge v. Ford*, Chapter 8, Section C, *supra*. *Ford* and *Wrigley* exhibit many similarities in that both involved public corporations with a wealthy controlling shareholder who seemed to have other primary objectives than the profitability of the corporation. Why didn't the court in *Wrigley* hold the defendant's conduct invalid based on the rationale employed in *Ford*?

# SMITH v. VAN GORKOM
Supreme Court of Delaware
488 A.2d 858 (1984)

HORSEY, J.

This appeal from the Court of Chancery involves a class action brought by shareholders of the defendant Trans Union Corporation ("Trans Union" or "the Company"), originally seeking rescission of a cash-out merger of Trans Union into the defendant New T Company ("New T"), a wholly-owned subsidiary of the defendant, Marmon Group, Inc. ("Marmon"). Alternate relief in the form of damages is sought against the defendant members of the Board of Directors of Trans Union, New T, and Jay A. Pritzker and Robert A. Pritzker, owners of Marmon.

Following trial, the former Chancellor granted judgment for the defendant directors by unreported letter opinion dated July 6, 1982. Judgment was based on two findings: (1) that the Board of Directors had acted in an informed manner so as to be entitled to protection of the business judgment rule in approving the cash-out merger; and (2) that the shareholder vote approving the merger should not be set aside because the stockholders had been "fairly informed" by the Board of Directors before voting thereon. The plaintiffs appeal.

Speaking for the majority of the Court, we conclude that both rulings of the Court of Chancery are clearly erroneous. Therefore, we reverse and direct that judgment be entered in favor of the plaintiffs and against the defendant directors for the fair value of the plaintiffs' stockholdings in Trans Union, in accordance with *Weinberger v. UOP, Inc.*, Del. Supr., 457 A.2d 701 (1983).

We hold: (1) that the Board's decision, reached September 20, 1980, to approve the proposed cash-out merger was not the product of an informed business judgment; (2) that the Board's subsequent efforts to amend the Merger Agreement and take other curative action were ineffectual, both legally and factually; and (3) that the Board did not deal with complete candor with the stockholders by failing to disclose all material facts, which they knew or should have known, before securing the stockholders' approval of the merger.

## I.

The nature of this case requires a detailed factual statement. The following facts are essentially uncontradicted:

## –A–

Trans Union was a publicly-traded, diversified holding company, the principal earnings of which were generated by its railcar leasing business. During the period here involved, the Company had a cash flow of hundreds of millions of dollars annually. However, the Company had difficulty in generating sufficient taxable income to offset increasingly large investment tax credits (ITCs). Accelerated depreciation deductions had decreased available taxable income against which to offset accumulating ITCs. The Company took these deductions, despite their effect on usable ITCs, because the rental price in the railcar leasing market had already impounded the purported tax savings.

In the late 1970's, together with other capital-intensive firms, Trans Union lobbied in Congress to have ITCs refundable in cash to firms which could not fully utilize the credit. During the summer of 1980, defendant Jerome W. Van Gorkom, Trans Union's Chairman and Chief Executive Officer, testified and lobbied in Congress for refundability of ITCs and against further accelerated depreciation. By the end of August, Van Gorkom was convinced that Congress would neither accept the refundability concept nor curtail further accelerated depreciation.

Beginning in the late 1960's, and continuing through the 1970's, Trans Union pursued a program of acquiring small companies in order to increase available taxable income. In July 1980, Trans Union Management prepared the annual revision of the Company's Five Year Forecast. This report was presented to the Board of Directors at its July, 1980 meeting. The report projected an annual income growth of about 20%. The report also concluded that Trans Union would have about $195 million in spare cash between 1980 and 1985, "with the surplus growing rapidly from 1982 onward." The report referred to the ITC situation as a "nagging problem" and, given that problem, the leasing company "would still appear to be constrained to a tax breakeven." The report then listed four alternative uses of the projected 1982–1985 equity surplus: (1) stock repurchase; (2) dividend increases; (3) a major acquisition program; and (4) combinations of the above. The sale of Trans Union was not among the alternatives. The report emphasized that, despite the overall surplus, the operation of the Company would consume all available equity for the next several years, and concluded: "As a result, we have sufficient time to fully develop our course of action."

–B–

On August 27, 1980, Van Gorkom met with Senior Management of Trans Union. Van Gorkom reported on his lobbying efforts in Washington and his desire to find a solution to the tax credit problem more permanent than a continued program of acquisitions. Various alternatives were suggested and discussed preliminarily, including the sale of Trans Union to a company with a large amount of taxable income.

Donald Romans, Chief Financial Officer of Trans Union, stated that his department had done a "very brief bit of work on the possibility of a leveraged buy-out." This work had been prompted by a media article which Romans had seen regarding a leveraged buy-out by management. The work consisted of a "preliminary study" of the cash which could be generated by the Company if it participated in a leveraged buy-out. As Romans stated, this analysis "was very first and rough cut at seeing whether a cash flow would support what might be considered a high price for this type of transaction."

On September 5, at another Senior Management meeting which Van Gorkom attended, Romans again brought up the idea of a leveraged buy-out as a "possible strategic alternative" to the Company's acquisition program. Romans and Bruce S. Chelberg, President and Chief Operating Officer of Trans Union, had been working on the matter in preparation for the meeting. According to Romans: They did not "come up" with a price for the Company. They merely "ran the numbers" at $50 a share and at $60 a share with the "rough form" of their cash figures at the time. Their "figures indicated that $50 would be very easy to do but $60 would be very difficult to do under those figures." This work did not purport to establish a fair price for either the Company or 100% of the stock. It was intended to determine the cash flow needed to service the debt that would "probably" be incurred in a leveraged buy-out, based on "rough calculations" without "any benefit of experts to identify what the limits were to that, and so forth." These computations were not considered extensive and no conclusion was reached.

At this meeting, Van Gorkom stated that he would be willing to take $55 per share for his own 75,000 shares. He vetoed the suggestion of a leveraged buy-out by Management, however, as involving a potential conflict of interest for Management. Van Gorkom, a certified public accountant and lawyer, had been an officer of Trans Union for 24 years, its Chief Executive Officer for more than 17 years, and Chairman of its Board for 2 years. It is noteworthy in this connection that he was then approaching 65 years of age and mandatory retirement.

For several days following the September 5 meeting, Van Gorkom pondered the idea of a sale. He had participated in many acquisitions as a manager and director of Trans Union and as a director of other companies. He was familiar with acquisition procedures, valuation methods, and negotiations; and he privately considered the pros and cons of whether Trans Union should seek a privately or publicly-held purchaser.

Van Gorkom decided to meet with Jay A. Pritzker, a well-known corporate takeover specialist and a social acquaintance. However, rather than approaching Pritzker simply to determine his interest in acquiring Trans Union, Van Gorkom assembled a proposed per share price for sale of the Company and a financing structure by which to accomplish the sale. Van Gorkom did so without consulting either his Board or any members of Senior Management except one: Carl Peterson, Trans Union's Controller. Telling Peterson that he wanted no other person on his staff to know what he was doing, but without telling him why, Van Gorkom directed Peterson to calculate the feasibility of a leveraged buy-out at an assumed price per share of $55. Apart from the Company's historic stock market price[1], and Van Gorkom's long association with Trans Union, the record is devoid of any competent evidence that $55 represented the per share intrinsic value of the Company.

Having thus chosen the $55 figure, based solely on the availability of a leveraged buy-out, Van Gorkom multiplied the price per share by the number of shares outstanding to reach a total value of the Company of $690 million. Van Gorkom told Peterson to use this $690 million figure and to assume a $200 million equity contribution by the buyer. Based on these assumptions, Van Gorkom directed

---

[1] [5] The common stock of Trans Union was traded on the New York Stock Exchange. Over the five year period from 1975 through 1979, Trans Union's stock had traded within a range of a high of $39 1/2 and a low of $24 1/4. Its high and low range for 1980 through September 19 (the last trading day before announcement of the merger) was $38 1/4–$29 1/2.

Peterson to determine whether the debt portion of the purchase price could be paid off in five years or less if financed by Trans Union's cash flow as projected in the Five Year Forecast, and by the sale of certain weaker divisions identified in a study done for Trans Union by the Boston Consulting Group ("BCG study"). Peterson reported that, of the purchase price, approximately $50–80 million would remain outstanding after five years. Van Gorkom was disappointed, but decided to meet with Pritzker nevertheless.

Van Gorkom arranged a meeting with Pritzker at the latter's home on Saturday, September 13, 1980. Van Gorkom prefaced his presentation by stating to Pritzker: "Now as far as you are concerned, I can, I think, show how you can pay a substantial premium over the present stock price and pay off most of the loan in the first five years. . . . If you could pay $55 for this Company, here is a way in which I think it can be financed."

Van Gorkom then reviewed with Pritzker his calculations based upon his proposed price of $55 per share. Although Pritzker mentioned $50 as a more attractive figure, no other price was mentioned. However, Van Gorkom stated that to be sure that $55 was the best price obtainable, Trans Union should be free to accept any better offer. Pritzker demurred, stating that his organization would serve as a "stalking horse" for an "auction contest" only if Trans Union would permit Pritzker to buy 1,750,000 shares of Trans Union stock at market price which Pritzker could then sell to any higher bidder. After further discussion on this point, Pritzker told Van Gorkom that he would give him a more definite reaction soon.

On Monday, September 15, Pritzker advised Van Gorkom that he was interested in the $55 cash-out merger proposal and requested more information on Trans Union. Van Gorkom agreed to meet privately with Pritzker, accompanied by Peterson, Chelberg, and Michael Carpenter, Trans Union's consultant from the Boston Consulting Group. The meetings took place on September 16 and 17. Van Gorkom was "astounded that events were moving with such amazing rapidity."

On Thursday, September 18, Van Gorkom met again with Pritzker. At that time, Van Gorkom knew that Pritzker intended to make a cash-out merger offer at Van Gorkom's proposed $55 per share. Pritzker instructed his attorney, a merger and acquisition specialist, to begin drafting merger documents. There was no further discussion of the $55 price. However, the number of shares of Trans Union's treasury stock to be offered to Pritzker was negotiated down to one million shares; the price was set at $38–75 cents above the per share price at the close of the market on September 19. At this point, Pritzker insisted that the Trans Union Board act on his merger proposal within the next three days, stating to Van Gorkom: "We have to have a decision by no later than Sunday [evening, September 21] before the opening of the English stock exchange on Monday morning." Pritzker's lawyer was then instructed to draft the merger documents, to be reviewed by Van Gorkom's lawyer, "sometimes with discussion and sometimes not, in the haste to get it finished."

On Friday, September 19, Van Gorkom, Chelberg, and Pritzker consulted with Trans Union's lead bank regarding the financing of Pritzker's purchase of Trans Union. The bank indicated that it could form a syndicate of banks that would finance the transaction. On the same day, Van Gorkom retained James Brennan, Esquire, to advise Trans Union on the legal aspects of the merger. Van Gorkom did not consult with William Browder, a Vice-President and director of Trans Union and former head of its legal department, or with William Moore, then the head of Trans Union's legal staff.

On Friday, September 19, Van Gorkom called a special meeting of the Trans Union Board for noon the following day. He also called a meeting of the Company's Senior Management to convene at 11:00 a.m., prior to the meeting of the Board. No one, except Chelberg and Peterson, was told the purpose of the meetings. Van Gorkom did not invite Trans Union's investment banker, Salomon Brothers or its Chicago-based partner, to attend.

Of those present at the Senior Management meeting on September 20, only Chelberg and Peterson had prior knowledge of Pritzker's offer. Van Gorkom disclosed the offer and described its terms, but he furnished no copies of the proposed Merger Agreement. Romans announced that his department had done a second study which showed that, for a leveraged buy-out, the price range for Trans Union stock was between $55 and $65 per share. Van Gorkom neither saw the study nor asked Romans to make it available for the Board meeting.

Senior Management's reaction to the Pritzker proposal was completely negative. No member of Management, except Chelberg and Peterson, supported the proposal. Romans objected to the price as being too low; he was critical of the timing and suggested that consideration should be given to the adverse tax consequences of an all-cash deal for low-basis shareholders; and he took the position that the agreement to sell Pritzker one million newly-issued shares at market price would inhibit other offers, as would the prohibitions against soliciting bids and furnishing inside information to other bidders. Romans argued that the Pritzker proposal was a "lock up" and amounted to "an agreed merger as opposed to an offer." Nevertheless, Van Gorkom proceeded to the Board meeting as scheduled without further delay.

Ten directors served on the Trans Union Board, five inside (defendants Bonser, O'Boyle, Browder, Chelberg, and Van Gorkom) and five outside (defendants Wallis, Johnson, Lanterman, Morgan and Reneker). All directors were present at the meeting, except O'Boyle who was ill. Of the outside directors, four were corporate chief executive officers and one was the former Dean of the University of Chicago Business School. None was an investment banker or trained financial analyst. All members of the Board were well informed about the Company and its operations as a going concern. They were familiar with the current financial condition of the Company, as well as operating and earnings projections reported in the recent Five Year Forecast. The Board generally received regular and detailed reports and was kept abreast of the accumulated investment tax credit and accelerated depreciation problem.

Van Gorkom began the Special Meeting of the Board with a twenty-minute oral presentation. Copies of the proposed Merger Agreement were delivered too late for study before or during the meeting.[2] He reviewed the Company's ITC and depreciation problems and the efforts theretofore made to solve them. He discussed

---

[2] [7] The record is not clear as to the terms of the Merger Agreement. The Agreement, as originally

his initial meeting with Pritzker and his motivation in arranging that meeting. Van Gorkom did not disclose to the Board, however, the methodology by which he alone had arrived at the $55 figure, or the fact that he first proposed the $55 price in his negotiations with Pritzker.

Van Gorkom outlined the terms of the Pritzker offer as follows: Pritzker would pay $55 in cash for all outstanding shares of Trans Union stock upon completion of which Trans Union would be merged into New T Company, a subsidiary wholly-owned by Pritzker and formed to implement the merger; for a period of 90 days, Trans Union could receive, but could not actively solicit, competing offers; the offer had to be acted on by the next evening, Sunday, September 21; Trans Union could only furnish to competing bidders published information, and not proprietary information; the offer was subject to Pritzker obtaining the necessary financing by October 10, 1980; if the financing contingency were met or waived by Pritzker, Trans Union was required to sell to Pritzker one million newly-issued shares of Trans Union at $38 per share.

Van Gorkom took the position that putting Trans Union "up for auction" through a 90-day market test would validate a decision by the Board that $55 was a fair price. He told the Board that the "free market will have an opportunity to judge whether $55 is a fair price." Van Gorkom framed the decision before the Board not as whether $55 per share was the highest price that could be obtained, but as whether the $55 price was a fair price that the stockholders should be given the opportunity to accept or reject.

Attorney Brennan advised the members of the Board that they might be sued if they failed to accept the offer and that a fairness opinion was not required as a matter of law.

Romans attended the meeting as chief financial officer of the Company. He told the Board that he had not been involved in the negotiations with Pritzker and knew nothing about the merger proposal until the morning of the meeting; that his studies did not indicate either a fair price for the stock or a valuation of the Company; that he did not see his role as directly addressing the fairness issue; and that he and his people "were trying to search for ways to justify a price in connection with such a [leveraged buy-out] transaction, rather than to say what the shares are worth." Romans testified:

> I told the Board that the study ran the numbers at 50 and 60, and then the subsequent study at 55 and 65, and that was not the same thing as saying that I have a valuation of the company at X dollars. But it was a way — a first step towards reaching that conclusion.

Romans told the Board that, in his opinion, $55 was "in the range of a fair price," but "at the beginning of the range."

Chelberg, Trans Union's President, supported Van Gorkom's presentation and

---

presented to the Board on September 20, was never produced by defendants despite demands by the plaintiffs. Nor is it clear that the directors were given an opportunity to study the Merger Agreement before voting on it. All that can be said is that Brennan had the Agreement before him during the meeting.

representations. He testified that he "participated to make sure that the Board members collectively were clear on the details of the agreement or offer from Pritzker;" that he "participated in the discussion with Mr. Brennan, inquiring of him about the necessity for valuation opinions in spite of the way in which this particular offer was couched;" and that he was otherwise actively involved in supporting the positions being taken by Van Gorkom before the Board about "the necessity to act immediately on this offer," and about "the adequacy of the $55 and the question of how that would be tested."

The Board meeting of September 20 lasted about two hours. Based solely upon Van Gorkom's oral presentation, Chelberg's supporting representations, Romans' oral statement, Brennan's legal advice, and their knowledge of the market history of the Company's stock[3], the directors approved the proposed Merger Agreement. However, the Board later claimed to have attached two conditions to its acceptance: (1) that Trans Union reserved the right to accept any better offer that was made during the market test period; and (2) that Trans Union could share its proprietary information with any other potential bidders. While the Board now claims to have reserved the right to accept any better offer received after the announcement of the Pritzker agreement (even though the minutes of the meeting do not reflect this), it is undisputed that the Board did not reserve the right to actively solicit alternate offers.

The Merger Agreement was executed by Van Gorkom during the evening of September 20 at a formal social event that he hosted for the opening of the Chicago Lyric Opera. Neither he nor any other director read the agreement prior to its signing and delivery to Pritzker.

\* \* \*

On Monday, September 22, the Company issued a press release announcing that Trans Union had entered into a "definitive" Merger Agreement with an affiliate of the Marmon Group, Inc., a Pritzker holding company. Within 10 days of the public announcement, dissent among Senior Management over the merger had become widespread. Faced with threatened resignations of key officers, Van Gorkom met with Pritzker who agreed to several modifications of the Agreement. Pritzker was willing to do so provided that Van Gorkom could persuade the dissidents to remain on the Company payroll for at least six months after consummation of the merger.

Van Gorkom reconvened the Board on October 8 and secured the directors' approval of the proposed amendments — sight unseen. The Board also authorized the employment of Salomon Brothers, its investment banker, to solicit other offers for Trans Union during the proposed "market test" period.

The next day, October 9, Trans Union issued a press release announcing: (1) that

---

[3] [9] The Trial Court stated the premium relationship of the $55 price to the market history of the Company's stock as follows:

> . . . the merger price offered to the stockholders of Trans Union represented a premium of 62% over the average of the high and low prices at which Trans Union stock had traded in 1980, a premium of 48% over the last closing price, and a premium of 39% over the highest price at which the stock of Trans Union had traded any time during the prior six years.

Pritzker had obtained "the financing commitments necessary to consummate" the merger with Trans Union; (2) that Pritzker had acquired one million shares of Trans Union common stock at $38 per share; (3) that Trans Union was now permitted to actively seek other offers and had retained Salomon Brothers for that purpose; and (4) that if a more favorable offer were not received before February 1, 1981, Trans Union's shareholders would thereafter meet to vote on the Pritzker proposal.

It was not until the following day, October 10, that the actual amendments to the Merger Agreement were prepared by Pritzker and delivered to Van Gorkom for execution. As will be seen, the amendments were considerably at variance with Van Gorkom's representations of the amendments to the Board on October 8; and the amendments placed serious constraints on Trans Union's ability to negotiate a better deal and withdraw from the Pritzker agreement. Nevertheless, Van Gorkom proceeded to execute what became the October 10 amendments to the Merger Agreement without conferring further with the Board members and apparently without comprehending the actual implications of the amendments. . . .

Salomon Brothers' efforts to over a three-month period from October 21 to January 21 produced only one serious suitor for Trans Union — General Electric Credit Corporation ("GE Credit"), a subsidiary of the General Electric Company. However, GE Credit was unwilling to make an offer for Trans Union unless Trans Union first rescinded its Merger Agreement with Pritzker. When Pritzker refused, GE Credit terminated further discussions with Trans Union in early January.

In the meantime, in early December, the investment firm of Kohlberg, Kravis, Roberts & Co. ("KKR"), the only other concern to make a firm offer for Trans Union, withdrew its offer under circumstances hereinafter detailed. . . .

[A later portion of the opinion gives the following additional information about the KKR and G.E. Credit overtures:]

> The KKR proposal was the first and only offer received subsequent to the Pritzker Merger Agreement. The offer resulted primarily from the efforts of Romans and other senior officers to propose an alternative to Pritzkerss acquisition of Trans Union. In late September, Romans' group contacted KKR about the possibility of a leveraged buy-out by all members of Management, except Van Gorkom. By early October, Henry R. Kravis of KKR gave Romans written notice of KKR's "interest in making an offer to purchase 100%" of Trans Union's common stock.

Thereafter, and until early December, Romans' group worked with KKR to develop a proposal. It did so with Van Gorkom's knowledge and apparently grudging consent. On December 2, Kravis and Romans hand-delivered to Van Gorkom a formal letter-offer to purchase all of Trans Union's assets and to assume all of its liabilities for an aggregate cash consideration equivalent to $60 per share. The offer was contingent upon completing equity and bank financing of $650 million, which Kravis represented as 80% complete. The KKR letter made reference to discussions with major banks regarding the loan portion of the buy-out cost and stated that KKR was "confident that commitments for the bank financing . . . can be obtained within two or three weeks." The purchasing group was to include certain named key members of Trans Union's Senior Management, excluding Van Gorkom, and a major

Canadian company. Kravis stated that they were willing to enter into a "definitive agreement" under terms and conditions "substantially the same" as those contained in Trans Union's agreement with Pritzker. The offer was addressed to Trans Union's Board of Directors and a meeting with the Board, scheduled for that afternoon, was requested.

Van Gorkom's reaction to the KKR proposal was completely negative; he did not view the offer as being firm because of its financing condition. It was pointed out, to no avail, that Pritzker's offer had not only been similarly conditioned, but accepted on an expedited basis. Van Gorkom refused Kravis' request that Trans Union issue a press release announcing KKR's offer, on the ground that it might "chill" any other offer. Romans and Kravis left with the understanding that their proposal would be presented to Trans Union's Board that afternoon.

Within a matter of hours and shortly before the scheduled Board meeting, Kravis withdrew his letter-offer. He gave as his reason a sudden decision by the Chief Officer of Trans Union's rail car leasing operation to withdraw from the KKR purchasing group. Van Gorkom had spoken to that officer about his participation in the KKR proposal immediately after his meeting with Romans and Kravis. However, Van Gorkom denied any responsibility for the officer's change of mind.

At the Board meeting later that afternoon, Van Gorkom did not inform the directors of the KKR proposal because he considered it "dead." Van Gorkom did not contact KKR again until January 20, when faced with the realities of this lawsuit, he then attempted to reopen negotiations. KKR declined due to the imminence of the February 10 stockholder meeting.

GE Credit Corporation's interest in Trans Union did not develop until November; and it made no written proposal until mid-January. Even then, its proposal was not in the form of an offer. Had there been time to do so, GE Credit was prepared to offer between $2 and $5 per share above the $55 per share price which Pritzker offered. But GE Credit needed an additional 60 to 90 days; and it was unwilling to make a formal offer without a concession from Pritzker extending the February 10 "deadline" for Trans Union's stockholder meeting. As previously stated, Pritzker refused to grant such extension; and on January 21, GE Credit terminated further negotiations with Trans Union. Its stated reasons, among others, were its "unwillingness to become involved in a bidding contest with Pritzker in the absence of the willingness of [the Pritzker interests] to terminate the proposed $55 cash merger."

\*   \*   \*

On December 19, this litigation was commenced and, within four weeks, the plaintiffs had deposed eight of the ten directors of Trans Union, including Van Gorkom, Chelberg and Romans, its Chief Financial Officer. On January 21, Management's Proxy Statement for the February 10 shareholder meeting was mailed to Trans Union's stockholders. On January 26, Trans Union's Board met and, after a lengthy meeting, voted to proceed with the Pritzker merger. The Board also approved for mailing, "on or about January 27," a Supplement to its Proxy Statement. The Supplement purportedly set forth all information relevant to the Pritzker Merger Agreement, which had not been divulged in the first Proxy Statement.

On February 10, the stockholders of Trans Union approved the Pritzker merger proposal. Of the outstanding shares, 69.9% were voted in favor of the merger; 7.25% were voted against the merger; and 22.85% were not voted.

## II.

We turn to the issue of the application of the business judgment rule to the September 20 meeting of the Board.

The Court of Chancery concluded from the evidence that the Board of Directors' approval of the Pritzker merger proposal fell within the protection of the business judgment rule. The Court found that the Board had given sufficient time and attention to the transaction, since the directors had considered the Pritzker proposal on three different occasions, on September 20, and on October 8, 1980 and finally on January 26, 1981. On that basis, the Court reasoned that the Board had acquired, over the four-month period, sufficient information to reach an informed business judgment on the cash-out merger proposal. The Court ruled:

> . . . that given the market value of Trans Union's stock, the business acumen of the members of the board of Trans Union, the substantial premium over market offered by the Pritzkers and the ultimate effect on the merger price provided by the prospect of other bids for the stock in question, that the board of directors of Trans Union did not act recklessly or improvidently in determining on a course of action which they believed to be in the best interest of the stockholders of Trans Union.

The Court of Chancery made but one finding; i.e., that the Board's conduct over the entire period from September 20 through January 26, 1981 was not reckless or improvident, but informed. This ultimate conclusion was premised upon three subordinate findings, one explicit and two implied. The Court's explicit finding was that Trans Union's Board was "free to turn down the Pritzker proposal" not only on September 20 but also on October 8, 1980 and on January 26, 1981. The Court's implied, subordinate findings were: (1) that no legally binding agreement was reached by the parties until January 26; and (2) that if a higher offer were to be forthcoming, the market test would have produced it, and Trans Union would have been contractually free to accept such higher offer. However, the Court offered no factual basis or legal support for any of these findings; and the record compels contrary conclusions.

\*    \*    \*

[W]e conclude that the Court's ultimate finding that the Board's conduct was not "reckless or imprudent" is contrary to the record and not the product of a logical and deductive reasoning process.

The plaintiffs contend that the Court of Chancery erred as a matter of law by exonerating the defendant directors under the business judgment rule without first determining whether the rule's threshold condition of "due care and prudence" was satisfied. The plaintiffs assert that the Trial Court found the defendant directors to have reached an informed business judgment on the basis of "extraneous considerations and events that occurred after September 20, 1980." The defendants deny that the Trial Court committed legal error in relying upon post-September 20, 1980 events and the directors' later acquired knowledge. The defendants further submit that their decision to accept $55 per share was informed because: (1) they were "highly qualified;" (2) they were "well-informed;" and (3) they deliberated over the "proposal" not once but three times. On essentially this evidence and under our standard of review, the defendants assert that affirmance is required. We must disagree.

Under Delaware law, the business judgment rule is the offspring of the fundamental principle, codified in 8 Del. C. § 141(a), that the business and affairs of a Delaware corporation are managed by or under its board of directors. *Pogostin v. Rice*, Del. Supr., 480 A.2d 619, 624 (1984); *Aronson v. Lewis*, Del. Supr., 473 A.2d 805, 811 (1984); *Zapata Corp. v. Maldonado*, Del. Supr., 430 A.2d 779, 782 (1981). In carrying out their managerial roles, directors are charged with an unyielding fiduciary duty to the corporation and its shareholders. *Loft, Inc. v. Guth*, Del. Ch., 2 A.2d 225 (1938), *aff'd*, Del. Supr., 5 A.2d 503 (1939). The business judgment rule exists to protect and promote the full and free exercise of the managerial power granted to Delaware directors. *Zapata Corp. v. Maldonado, supra* at 782. The rule itself "is a presumption that in making a business decision, the directors of a corporation acted on an informed basis, in good faith and in the honest belief that the action taken was in the best interests of the company." *Aronson, supra* at 812. Thus, the party attacking a board decision as uninformed must rebut the presumption that its business judgment was an informed one. *Id.*

The determination of whether a business judgment is an informed one turns on whether the directors have informed themselves "prior to making a business decision, of all material information reasonably available to them." *Id.*

Under the business judgment rule there is no protection for directors who have made "an unintelligent or unadvised judgment." *Mitchell v. Highland-Western Glass*, Del. Ch., 167 A. 831, 833 (1933). A director's duty to inform himself in preparation for a decision derives from the fiduciary capacity in which he serves the corporation and its stockholders. *Lutz v. Boas*, Del. Ch., 171 A.2d 381 (1961). *See Weinberger v. UOP, Inc., supra; Guth v. Loft, supra.* Since a director is vested with the responsibility for the management of the affairs of the corporation, he must execute that duty with the recognition that he acts on behalf of others. Such obligation does not tolerate faithlessness or self-dealing. But fulfillment of the fiduciary function requires more than the mere absence of bad faith or fraud. Representation of the financial interests of others imposes on a director an affirmative duty to protect those interests and to proceed with a critical eye in assessing information of the type and under the circumstances present here. *See Lutz v. Boas, supra; Guth v. Loft, supra* at 510.

Thus, a director's duty to exercise an informed business judgment is in the nature of a duty of care, as distinguished from a duty of loyalty. Here, there were no allegations of fraud, bad faith, or self-dealing, or proof thereof. Hence, it is presumed that the directors reached their business judgment in good faith, *Allaun v. Consolidated Oil Co.*, Del. Ch., 147 A. 257 (1929), and considerations of motive are irrelevant to the issue before us.

The standard of care applicable to a director's duty of care has also been recently restated by this Court. In *Aronson, supra*, we stated:

> While the Delaware cases use a variety of terms to describe the applicable standard of care, our analysis satisfies us that under the business judgment rule director liability is predicated upon concepts of gross negligence. (footnote omitted)

473 A.2d at 812.

We again confirm that view. We think the concept of gross negligence is also the proper standard for determining whether a business judgment reached by a board of directors was an informed one.

In the specific context of a proposed merger of domestic corporations, a director has a duty under 8 Del. C. § 251(b), along with his fellow directors, to act in an informed and deliberate manner in determining whether to approve an agreement of merger before submitting the proposal to the stockholders. Certainly in the merger context, a director may not abdicate that duty by leaving to the shareholders alone the decision to approve or disapprove the agreement. *See Beard v. Elster*, Del. Supr., 160 A.2d 731, 737 (1960). Only an agreement of merger satisfying the requirements of 8 Del. C. § 251(b) may be submitted to the shareholders under § 251(c). *See generally Aronson v. Lewis*, supra at 811–13; *see also Pogostin v. Rice*, *supra*.

It is against those standards that the conduct of the directors of Trans Union must be tested, as a matter of law and as a matter of fact, regarding their exercise of an informed business judgment in voting to approve the Pritzker merger proposal.

## III.

The defendants argue that the determination of whether their decision to accept $55 per share for Trans Union represented an informed business judgment requires consideration, not only of that which they knew and learned on September 20, but also of that which they subsequently learned and did over the following four month period before the shareholders met to vote on the proposal in February, 1981. The defendants thereby seek to reduce the significance of their action on September 20 and to widen the time frame for determining whether their decision to accept the Pritzker proposal was an informed one. Thus, the defendants contend that what the directors did and learned subsequent to September 20 and through January 26, 1981, was properly taken into account by the Trial Court in determining whether the Board's judgment was an informed one. We disagree with this post hoc approach.

The issue of whether the directors reached an informed decision to "sell" the Company on September 20, 1980 must be determined only upon the basis of the information then reasonably available to the directors and relevant to their decision to accept the Pritzker merger proposal. This is not to say that the directors were precluded from altering their original plan of action, had they done so in an informed manner. What we do say is that the question of whether the directors reached an informed business judgment in agreeing to sell the Company, pursuant to the terms of the September 20 Agreement presents, in reality, two questions: (A) whether the directors reached an informed business judgment on September 20, 1980; and (B) if they did not, whether the directors' actions taken subsequent to September 20 were adequate to cure any infirmity in their action taken on September 20. We first consider the directors' September 20 action in terms of their reaching an informed business judgment.

–A–

On the record before us, we must conclude that the Board of Directors did not reach an informed business judgment on September 20, 1980 in voting to "sell" the Company for $55 per share pursuant to the Pritzker cash-out merger proposal. Our reasons, in summary, are as follows:

The directors (1) did not adequately inform themselves as to Van Gorkom's role in forcing the "sale" of the Company and in establishing the per share purchase price; (2) were uninformed as to the intrinsic value of the Company; and (3) given these circumstances, at a minimum, were grossly negligent in approving the "sale" of the Company upon two hours' consideration, without prior notice, and without the exigency of a crisis or emergency.

As has been noted, the Board based its September 20 decision to approve the cash-out merger primarily on Van Gorkom's representations. None of the directors, other than Van Gorkom and Chelberg, had any prior knowledge that the purpose of the meeting was to propose a cash-out merger of Trans Union. No members of Senior Management were present, other than Chelberg, Romans and Peterson; and the latter two had only learned of the proposed sale an hour earlier. Both general counsel Moore and former general counsel Browder attended the meeting, but were equally uninformed as to the purpose of the meeting and the documents to be acted upon.

Without any documents before them concerning the proposed transaction, the members of the Board were required to rely entirely upon Van Gorkom's 20-minute oral presentation of the proposal. No written summary of the terms of the merger was presented; the directors were given no documentation to support the adequacy of $55 price per share for sale of the Company; and the Board had before it nothing more than Van Gorkom's statement of his understanding of the substance of an agreement which he admittedly had never read, nor which any member of the Board had ever seen. . . .[4]

The defendants rely on the following factors to sustain the Trial Court's finding that the Board's decision was an informed one: (1) the magnitude of the premium or spread between the $55 Pritzker offering price and Trans Union's current market price of $38 per share; (2) the amendment of the Agreement as submitted on

---

[4] [15] Section 141(e) provides in pertinent part:

A member of the board of directors . . . shall, in the performance of his duties, be fully protected in relying in good faith upon the books of accounts or reports made to the corporation by any of its officers, or by an independent certified public accountant, or by an appraiser selected with reasonable care by the board of directors . . . , or in relying in good faith upon other records of the corporation.

September 20 to permit the Board to accept any better offer during the "market test" period; (3) the collective experience and expertise of the Board's "inside" and "outside" directors; and (4) their reliance on Brennan's legal advice that the directors might be sued if they rejected the Pritzker proposal. We discuss each of these grounds *seriatim*:

### (1)

A substantial premium may provide one reason to recommend a merger, but in the absence of other sound valuation information, the fact of a premium alone does not provide an adequate basis upon which to assess the fairness of an offering price. Here, the judgment reached as to the adequacy of the premium was based on a comparison between the historically depressed Trans Union market price and the amount of the Pritzker offer. Using market price as a basis for concluding that the premium adequately reflected the true value of the Company was a clearly faulty, indeed fallacious, premise, as the defendants' own evidence demonstrates.

\* \* \*

The parties do not dispute that a publicly-traded stock price is solely a measure of the value of a minority position and, thus, market price represents only the value of a single share. Nevertheless, on September 20, the Board assessed the adequacy of the premium over market, offered by Pritzker, solely by comparing it with Trans Union's current and historical stock price.

Indeed, as of September 20, the Board had no other information on which to base a determination of the intrinsic value of Trans Union as a going concern. As of September 20, the Board had made no evaluation of the Company designed to value the entire enterprise, nor had the Board ever previously considered selling the Company or consenting to a buy-out merger. Thus, the adequacy of a premium is indeterminate unless it is assessed in terms of other competent and sound valuation information that reflects the value of the particular business.

Despite the foregoing facts and circumstances, there was no call by the Board, either on September 20 or thereafter, for any valuation study or documentation of the $55 price per share as a measure of the fair value of the Company in a cash-out context. It is undisputed that the major asset of Trans Union was its cash flow. Yet, at no time did the Board call for a valuation study taking into account that highly significant element of the Company's assets.

We do not imply that an outside valuation study is essential to support an informed business judgment; nor do we state that fairness opinions by independent investment bankers are required as a matter of law. Often insiders familiar with the business of a going concern are in a better position than are outsiders to gather relevant information; and under appropriate circumstances, such directors may be fully protected in relying in good faith upon the valuation reports of their management. *See* 8 Del. C. § 141(e). *See also Cheff v. Mathes*, [Del. Supr., 41 Del. Ch. 494 (1964)].

Here, the record establishes that the Board did not request its Chief Financial Officer, Romans, to make any valuation study or review of the proposal to determine the adequacy of $55 per share for sale of the Company. On the record before us: The Board rested on Romans' elicited response that the $55 figure was within a "fair price range" within the context of a leveraged buy-out. No director sought any further information from Romans. No director asked him why he put $55 at the bottom of his range. No director asked Romans for any details as to his study, the reason why it had been undertaken or its depth. No director asked to see the study; and no director asked Romans whether Trans Union's finance department could do a fairness study within the remaining 36-hour[5] period available under the Pritzker offer.

Had the Board, or any member, made an inquiry of Romans, he presumably would have responded as he testified: that his calculations were rough and preliminary; and, that the study was not designed to determine the fair value of the Company, but rather to assess the feasibility of a leveraged buy-out financed by the Company's projected cash flow, making certain assumptions as to the purchaser's borrowing needs. Romans would have presumably also informed the Board of his view, and the widespread view of Senior Management, that the timing of the offer was wrong and the offer inadequate.

The record also establishes that the Board accepted without scrutiny Van Gorkom's representation as to the fairness of the $55 price per share for sale of the Company — a subject that the Board had never previously considered. The Board thereby failed to discover that Van Gorkom had suggested the $55 price to Pritzker and, most crucially, that Van Gorkom had arrived at the $55 figure based on calculations designed solely to determine the feasibility of a leveraged buy-out.[6] No questions were raised either as to the tax implications of a cash-out merger or how the price for the one million share option granted Pritzker was calculated.

We do not say that the Board of Directors was not entitled to give some credence to Van Gorkom's representation that $55 was an adequate or fair price. Under § 141(e), the directors were entitled to rely upon their chairman's opinion of value and adequacy, provided that such opinion was reached on a sound basis. Here, the issue is whether the directors informed themselves as to all information that was reasonably available to them. Had they done so, they would have learned of the source and derivation of the $55 price and could not reasonably have relied thereupon in good faith.

None of the directors, Management or outside, were investment bankers or

---

[5] [18] Romans' department study was not made available to the Board until circulation of Trans Union's Supplementary Proxy Statement and the Board's meeting of January 26, 1981, on the eve of the shareholder meeting; and, as has been noted, the study has never been produced for inclusion in the record in this case.

[6] [19] As of September 20 the directors did not know: that Van Gorkom had arrived at the $55 figure alone, and subjectively, as the figure to be used by Controller Peterson in creating a feasible structure for a leveraged buy-out by a prospective purchaser; that Van Gorkom had not sought advice, information or assistance from either inside or outside Trans Union directors as to the value of the Company as an entity or the fair price per share for 100% of its stock; that Van Gorkom had not consulted with the Company's investment bankers or other financial analysts; that Van Gorkom had not consulted with or confided in any officer or director of the Company except Chelberg; and that Van Gorkom had deliberately chosen to ignore the advice and opinion of the members of his Senior Management group regarding the adequacy of the $55 price.

financial analysts. Yet the Board did not consider recessing the meeting until a later hour that day (or requesting an extension of Pritzker's Sunday evening deadline) to give it time to elicit more information as to the sufficiency of the offer, either from inside Management (in particular Romans) or from Trans Union's own investment banker, Salomon Brothers, whose Chicago specialist in merger and acquisitions was known to the Board and familiar with Trans Union's affairs.

Thus, the record compels the conclusion that on September 20 the Board lacked valuation information adequate to reach an informed business judgment as to the fairness of $55 per share for sale of the Company.

### (2)

[The court then determined that there was not a sufficient "post September 20 market test" of the $55 price which could support the reasonableness of the board's decision.]

### (3)

The directors' unfounded reliance on both the premium and the market test as the basis for accepting the Pritzker proposal undermines the defendants' remaining contention that the Board's collective experience and sophistication was a sufficient basis for finding that it reached its September 20 decision with informed, reasonable deliberation.[7] Compare *Gimbel v. Signal Companies, Inc.*, Del. Ch., 316 A.2d 599 (1974), *aff'd per curiam*, Del. Supr., 316 A.2d 619 (1974). There, the Court of Chancery preliminary enjoined a board's sale of stock of its wholly-owned subsidiary for an alleged grossly inadequate price. It did so based on a finding that the business judgment rule had been pierced for failure of management to give its board "the opportunity to make a reasonable and reasoned decision." 316 A.2d at 615. The Court there reached this result notwithstanding the board's sophistication and experience; the company's need of immediate cash; and the board's need to act promptly due to the impact of an energy crisis on the value of the underlying assets being sold — all of its subsidiary's oil and gas interests. The Court found those factors denoting competence to be outweighed by evidence of gross negligence; that management in effect sprang the deal on the board by negotiating the asset sale without informing the board; that the buyer intended to "force a quick decision" by the board; that the board meeting was called on only one-and-a-half days' notice; that its outside directors were not notified of the meeting's purpose; that during a meeting spanning "a couple of hours" a sale of assets worth $480 million was approved; and that the Board failed to obtain a current appraisal of its oil and gas

---

[7] [21] Trans Union's five "inside" directors had backgrounds in law and accounting, 116 years of collective employment by the Company and 68 years of combined experience on its Board. Trans Union's five "outside" directors included four chief executives of major corporations and an economist who was a former dean of a major school of business and chancellor of a university. The "outside" directors had 78 years of combined experience as chief executive officers of major corporations and 50 years of cumulative experience as directors of Trans Union. Thus, defendants argue that the Board was eminently qualified to reach an informed judgment on the proposed "sale" of Trans Union notwithstanding their lack of any advance notice of the proposal, the shortness of their deliberation, and their determination not to consult with their investment banker or to obtain a fairness opinion.

interests. The analogy of *Signal* to the case at bar is significant.

(4)

Part of the defense is based on a claim that the directors relied on legal advice rendered at the September 20 meeting by James Brennan, Esquire, who was present at Van Gorkom's request. Unfortunately, Brennan did not appear and testify at trial even though his firm participated in the defense of this action. There is no contemporaneous evidence of the advice given by Brennan on September 20, only the later deposition and trial testimony of certain directors as to their recollections or understanding of what was said at the meeting. Since counsel did not testify, and the advice attributed to Brennan is hearsay received by the Trial Court over the plaintiffs' objections, we consider it only in the context of the directors' present claims. In fairness to counsel, we make no findings that the advice attributed to him was in fact given. We focus solely on the efficacy of the defendants' claims, made months and years later, in an effort to extricate themselves from liability.

Several defendants testified that Brennan advised them that Delaware law did not require a fairness opinion or an outside valuation of the Company before the Board could act on the Pritzker proposal. If given, the advice was correct. However, that did not end the matter. Unless the directors had before them adequate information regarding the intrinsic value of the Company, upon which a proper exercise of business judgment could be made, mere advice of this type is meaningless; and, given this record of the defendants' failures, it constitutes no defense here.[8]

We conclude that Trans Union's Board was grossly negligent in that it failed to act with informed reasonable deliberation in agreeing to the Pritzker merger proposal on September 20; and we further conclude that the Trial Court erred as a matter of law in failing to address that question before determining whether the directors' later conduct was sufficient to cure its initial error.

A second claim is that counsel advised the Board it would be subject to lawsuits if it rejected the $55 per share offer. It is, of course, a fact of corporate life that today when faced with difficult or sensitive issues, directors often are subject to suit, irrespective of the decisions they make. However, counsel's mere acknowledgement of this circumstance cannot be rationally translated into a justification for a board permitting itself to be stampeded into a patently unadvised act. While suit might result from the rejection of a merger or tender offer, Delaware law makes clear that a board acting within the ambit of the business judgment rule faces no ultimate liability. *Pogostin v. Rice, supra.* Thus, we cannot conclude that the mere threat of litigation, acknowledged by counsel, constitutes either legal advice or any valid basis upon which to pursue an uninformed course.

Since we conclude that Brennan's purported advice is of no consequence to the

---

[8] [22] Nonetheless, we are satisfied that in an appropriate factual context a proper exercise of business judgment may include, as one of its aspects, reasonable reliance upon the advice of counsel. This is wholly outside the statutory protections of 8 Del. C. § 141(e) involving reliance upon reports of officers, certain experts and books and records of the company.

defense of this case, it is unnecessary for us to invoke the adverse inferences which may be attributable to one failing to appear at trial and testify.

–B–

[The court then concluded and rejected defendants' contention that the board's actions on October 9, 1980 and January 16, 1981 cured its failures committed earlier.]

IV.

Whether the directors of Trans Union should be treated as one or individually in terms of invoking the protection of the business judgment rule and the applicability of 8 Del. C. § 141(c) are questions which were not originally addressed by the parties in their briefing of this case. This resulted in a supplemental briefing and a second rehearing en banc on two basic questions: (a) whether one or more of the directors were deprived of the protection of the business judgment rule by evidence of an absence of good faith; and (b) whether one or more of the outside directors were entitled to invoke the protection of 8 Del. C. § 141(e) by evidence of a reasonable, good faith reliance on "reports," including legal advice, rendered the Board by certain inside directors and the Board's special counsel, Brennan.

The parties' response, including reargument, has led the majority of the Court to conclude: (1) that since all of the defendant directors, outside as well as inside, take a unified position, we are required to treat all of the directors as one as to whether they are entitled to the protection of the business judgment rule; and (2) that considerations of good faith, including the presumption that the directors acted in good faith, are irrelevant in determining the threshold issue of whether the directors as a Board exercised an informed business judgment. For the same reason, we must reject defense counsel's ad hominem argument for affirmance: that reversal may result in a multi-million dollar class award against the defendants for having made an allegedly uninformed business judgment in a transaction not involving any personal gain, self-dealing or claim of bad faith.

In their brief, the defendants similarly mistake the business judgment rule's application to this case by erroneously invoking presumptions of good faith and "wide discretion":

> This is a case in which plaintiff challenged the exercise of business judgment by an independent Board of Directors. There were no allegations and no proof of fraud, bad faith, or self-dealing by the directors. . . .

The business judgment rule, which was properly applied by the Chancellor, allows directors wide discretion in the matter of valuation and affords room for honest differences of opinion. In order to prevail, plaintiffs had the heavy burden of proving that the merger price was so grossly inadequate as to display itself as a badge of fraud. That is a burden which plaintiffs have not met.

However, plaintiffs have not claimed, nor did the Trial Court decide, that $55 was a grossly inadequate price per share for sale of the Company. That being so, the presumption that a board's judgment as to adequacy of price represents an honest exercise of business judgment (absent proof that the sale price was grossly inadequate) is irrelevant to the threshold question of whether an informed judgment was reached. Compare *Sinclair Oil Corp. v. Levien*, Del. Supr., 280 A.2d 717 (1971); *Kelly v. Bell*, Del. Supr., 266 A.2d 878, 879 (1970); *Cole v. National Cash Credit Association*, Del. Ch., 156 A. 183 (1931); *Allaun v. Consolidated Oil Co., supra*; *Allen Chemical & Dye Corp. v. Steel & Tube Co. of America*, Del. Ch., 120 A. 486 (1923).

## V.

The defendants ultimately rely on the stockholder vote of February 10 for exoneration. The defendants contend that the stockholders' "overwhelming" vote approving the Pritzker Merger Agreement had the legal effect of curing any failure of the Board to reach an informed business judgment in its approval of the merger.

The parties tacitly agree that a discovered failure of the Board to reach an informed business judgment in approving the merger constitutes a voidable, rather than a void, act. Hence, the merger can be sustained, notwithstanding the infirmity of the Board's action, if its approval by majority vote of the shareholders is found to have been based on an informed electorate. *Cf. Michelson v. Duncan*, Del. Supr., 407 A.2d 211 (1979), *aff'g in part and rev'g in part*, Del. Ch., 386 A.2d 1144 (1978). The disagreement between the parties arises over: (1) the Board's burden of disclosing to the shareholders all relevant and material information; and (2) the sufficiency of the evidence as to whether the Board satisfied that burden.

[The court concluded that the shareholders were not fully informed of all material and "germane" facts when the transaction was approved on February 10, 1981.]

We hold, therefore, that the Trial Court committed reversible error in applying the business judgment rule in favor of the director defendants in this case.

On remand, the Court of Chancery shall conduct an evidentiary hearing to determine the fair value of the shares represented by the plaintiffs' class, based on the intrinsic value of Trans Union on September 20, 1980. Such valuation shall be made in accordance with *Weinberger v. UOP, Inc., supra* at 712–715. Thereafter, an award of damages may be entered to the extent that the fair value of Trans Union exceeds $55 per share. . . .

REVERSED and REMANDED for proceedings consistent herewith.

McNEILLY, JUSTICE, dissenting:

The majority opinion reads like an advocate's closing address to a hostile jury. And I say that not lightly. Throughout the opinion great emphasis is directed only to the negative, with nothing more than lip service granted the positive aspects of this case. In my opinion Chancellor Marvel (retired) should have been affirmed. The Chancellor's opinion was the product of well reasoned conclusions, based upon a sound deductive process, clearly supported by the evidence and entitled to deference in this appeal. Because of my diametrical opposition to all evidentiary conclusions of the majority, I respectfully dissent.

It would serve no useful purpose, particularly at this late date, for me to dissent at great length. I restrain myself from doing so, but feel compelled to at least point out what I consider to be the most glaring deficiencies in the majority opinion. The majority has spoken and has effectively said that Trans Union's Directors have been the victims of a "fast shuffle" by Van Gorkom and Pritzker. That is the beginning of the majority's comedy of errors. The first and most important error made is the majority's assessment of the directors' knowledge of the affairs of Trans Union and their combined ability to act in this situation under the protection of the business judgment rule.

Trans Union's Board of Directors consisted of ten men, five of whom were "inside" directors and five of whom were "outside" directors. The "inside" directors were Van Gorkom, Chelberg, Bonser, William B. Browder, Senior Vice-President-Law, and Thomas P. O'Boyle, Senior Vice-President-Administration. At the time the merger was proposed the inside five directors had collectively been employed by the Company for 116 years and had 68 years of combined experience as directors. The "outside" directors were A.W. Wallis, William B. Johnson, Joseph B. Lanterman, Graham J. Morgan and Robert W. Reneker. With the exception of Wallis, these were all chief executive officers of Chicago based corporations that were at least as large as Trans Union. The five "outside" directors had 78 years of combined experience as chief executive officers, and 53 years cumulative service as Trans Union directors.

The inside directors wear their badge of expertise in the corporate affairs of Trans Union on their sleeves. But what about the outsiders? Dr. Wallis is or was an economist and math statistician, a professor of economics at Yale University, dean of the graduate school of business at the University of Chicago, and Chancellor of the University of Rochester. Dr. Wallis had been on the Board of Trans Union since 1962. He also was on the Board of Bausch & Lomb, Kodak, Metropolitan Life Insurance Company, Standard Oil and others.

William B. Johnson is a University of Pennsylvania law graduate, President of Railway Express until 1966, Chairman and Chief Executive of I.C. Industries Holding Company, and member of Trans Union's Board since 1968.

Joseph Lanterman, a Certified Public Accountant, is or was President and Chief Executive of American Steel, on the Board of International Harvester, Peoples Energy, Illinois Bell Telephone, Harris Bank and Trust Company, Kemper Insurance Company and a director of Trans Union for four years.

Graham Morgan is a chemist, was Chairman and Chief Executive Officer of U.S. Gypsum, and in the 17 and 18 years prior to the Trans Union transaction had been involved in 31 or 32 corporate takeovers.

Robert Reneker attended University of Chicago and Harvard Business Schools. He was President and Chief Executive of Swift and Company, director of Trans Union since 1971, and member of the Boards of seven other corporations including U.S. Gypsum and the Chicago Tribune.

Directors of this caliber are not ordinarily taken in by a "fast shuffle". I submit they were not taken into this multi-million dollar corporate transaction without being fully informed and aware of the state of the art as it pertained to the entire corporate panoroma of Trans Union. True, even directors such as these, with their business acumen, interest and expertise, can go astray. I do not believe that to be the case here. These men knew Trans Union like the back of their hands and were more than well qualified to make on the spot informed business judgments concerning the affairs of Trans Union including a 100% sale of the corporation. Lest we forget, the corporate world of then and now operates on what is so aptly referred to as "the fast track." These men were at the time an integral part of that world, all professional business men, not intellectual figureheads.

The majority of this Court holds that the Board's decision, reached on September 20, 1980, to approve the merger was not the product of an informed business judgment, that the Board's subsequent efforts to amend the Merger Agreement and take other curative action were legally and factually ineffectual, and that the Board did not deal with complete candor with the stockholders by failing to disclose all material facts, which they knew or should have known, before securing the stockholders' approval of the merger. I disagree.

*   *   *

[JUSTICE CHRISTIE also wrote a dissenting opinion.]

# NOTES

**1.** Taking into consideration what the opinion tells us concerning the background and knowledge of the various members of the board of directors, is it (a) fair or (b) desirable to hold all directors to the same standard of care?

**2.** Shortly after it was decided, *Smith v. Van Gorkom* was widely believed to have tightened significantly the conditions under which the business judgment rule will exonerate directors' conduct under the duty of care as compared to cases such as, *e.g. Shlensky v. Wrigley.* Is this really true or could *Van Gorkom* more accurately be explained as a case involving an extreme set of facts in which directors behaved in a remarkably casual manner in approving a multi-million dollar transaction?

**3.** The relationship between a director's duty of care and the business judgment rule is not easy to articulate. The business judgment rule is not articulated in section 8.30(a) of the Model Business Corporation Act (MBCA), which holds a director to the standard of care which "an ordinarily prudent person would exercise under similar circumstances." MBCA § 8.30(a). However, this language is misleading to the extent that it implies that ordinary negligence constitutes a breach of a director's duty of care. In fact cases such as *Van Gorkom* and *Shlensky* consistently use language such as "bad faith" or "gross negligence" to indicate that somewhat more leniency is given to directors than the statutory language would imply. Although the business judgment rule is not codified in the MBCA, the American Law Institute Corporate Governance Project has attempted to do so in section 401(c) which provides:

> A director or officer who makes a business judgment in good faith fulfills the duty [of care] under this Section if the director or officer:
>
> (1) is not interested in the subject of the business judgment; (2) is informed with respect to the subject of the business judgment to the

extent the director or officer reasonably believes to be appropriate under the circumstances; and (3) rationally believes that the business judgment is in the best interest of the corporation.

4.   *Van Gorkom's* standard of due deliberation based on a careful analysis of the record as a whole is more of procedure than of substance. It has been criticized on the grounds that it may simply result in directors "going through the motions" while they, in fact, will continue to rely on the subjective recommendations of the key executive officers and inside directors in deciding on the merits of the transaction. Is this criticism valid or are there some real benefits to effectively forcing the creation of a detailed paper record before a transaction is approved?

5.   One concrete result in *Van Gorkom* was that many states amended their corporation codes in various ways, which had the effect of making it difficult or impossible to recover monetary damages from directors even when they had been found to have violated their duty of care. The most popular form of statute is the so-called "charter option statute" which allows corporations to include in the articles of incorporation a provision severely limiting directors' personal liability for monetary damages, except in cases involving a breach of the director's duty of loyalty, intentional misconduct, or bad faith knowing the violations of the law. *E.g.* Del. Gen Corp. Law § 102(b)(7). Other states have adopted statutes amending the duty of care across the board and setting a cap on monetary damages.

6.   These excerpts are from the Powers Report, prepared in 2002 by a Special Investigative Committee of the Board of Directors of Enron Corp. Does the Powers Report suggest that the directors violated their duty of care?

> **The Board of Directors**. With respect to the issues that are the subject of this investigation, the Board of Directors failed, in our judgment, in its oversight duties. This had serious consequences for Enron, its employees, and its shareholders. The Board of Directors approved the arrangements that allowed the Company's CFO to serve as general partner in partnerships that participated in significant financial transactions with Enron. As noted earlier, the two members of the Special Investigative Committee who have participated in this review of the Board's actions believe this decision was fundamentally flawed. The Board substantially underestimated the severity of the conflict and overestimated the degree to which management controls and procedures could contain the problem.
>
> After having authorized a conflict of interest creating as much risk as this one, the Board had an obligation to give careful attention to the transactions that followed. It failed to do this. It cannot be faulted for the various instances in which it was apparently denied important information concerning certain of the transactions in question. However, it can and should be faulted for failing to demand more information, and for failing to probe and understand the information that did come to it. The Board authorized the Rhythms transaction and three of the Raptor transactions. It appears that many of its members did not understand those transactions — the economic rationale, the consequences, and the risks. Nor does it appear that they reacted to warning signs in those transactions as they were presented, including the statement to the Finance Committee in May

2000 that the proposed Raptor transaction raised a risk of "accounting scrutiny." We do note, however, that the Committee was told that Andersen was "comfortable" with the transaction. As complex as the transactions were, the existence of Fastow's conflict of interest demanded that the Board gain a better understanding of the LJM transactions that came before it, and ensure (whether through one of its Committees or through use of outside consultants) that they were fair to Enron.

The Audit and Compliance Committee, and later the Finance Committee, took on a specific role in the control structure by carrying out periodic reviews of the LJM transactions. This was an opportunity to probe the transactions thoroughly, and to seek outside advice as to any issues outside the Board members' expertise. Instead, these reviews appear to have been too brief, too limited in scope, and too superficial to serve their intended function. The Compensation Committee was given the role of reviewing Fastow's compensation from the LJM entities, and did not carry out this review. This remained the case even after the Committees were on notice that the LJM transactions were contributing very large percentages of Enron's earnings. In sum, the Board did not effectively meet its obligation with respect to the LJM transactions.

The Board, and in particular the Audit and Compliance Committee, has the duty of ultimate oversight over the Company's financial reporting. While the primary responsibility for the financial reporting abuses discussed in the Report lies with Management, the participating members of this Committee believe those abuses could and should have been prevented or detected at an earlier time had the Board been more aggressive and vigilant.

**Outside Professional Advisors.** The evidence available to us suggests that Andersen did not fulfill its professional responsibilities in connection with its audits of Enron's financial statements, or its obligation to bring to the attention of Enron's Board (or the Audit and Compliance Committee) concerns about Enron's internal controls over the related-party transactions. Andersen has admitted that it erred in concluding that the Rhythms transaction was structured properly under the SPE non-consolidation rules. Enron was required to restate its financial results for 1999 and 2000 as a result. Andersen participated in the structuring and accounting treatment of the Raptor transactions, and charged over $1 million for its services, yet it apparently failed to provide the objective accounting judgment that should have prevented these transactions from going forward. According to Enron's internal accountants (though this apparently has been disputed by Andersen), Andersen also reviewed and approved the recording of additional equity in March 2001 in connection with this restructuring. In September 2001, Andersen required Enron to reverse this accounting treatment, leading to the $1.2 billion reduction of equity. Andersen apparently failed to note or take action with respect to the deficiencies in Enron's public disclosure documents.

# FRANCIS v. UNITED JERSEY BANK
### Supreme Court of New Jersey
### 432 A.2d 814 (1981)

POLLOCK, J.

The primary issue on this appeal is whether a corporate director is personally liable in negligence for the failure to prevent the misappropriation of trust funds by other directors who were also officers and shareholders of the corporation.

Plaintiffs are trustees in bankruptcy of Pritchard & Baird Intermediaries Corp. (Pritchard & Baird), a reinsurance broker or intermediary. Defendant Lillian P. Overcash is the daughter of Lillian G. Pritchard and the executrix of her estate. At the time of her death, Mrs. Pritchard was a director and the largest single shareholder of Pritchard & Baird. Because Mrs. Pritchard died after the institution of suit but before trial, her executrix was substituted as a defendant. United Jersey Bank is joined as the administrator of the estate of Charles Pritchard, Sr., who had been president, director and majority shareholder of Pritchard & Baird.

This litigation focuses on payments made by Pritchard & Baird to Charles Pritchard, Jr. and William Pritchard, who were sons of Mr. and Mrs. Charles Pritchard, Sr., as well as officers, directors and shareholders of the corporation. Claims against Charles, Jr. and William are being pursued in bankruptcy proceedings against them.

\* \* \*

. . . [T]he initial question is whether Mrs. Pritchard was negligent in not noticing and trying to prevent the misappropriation of funds held by the corporation in an implied trust. A further question is whether her negligence was the proximate cause of the plaintiffs' losses. Both lower courts found that she was liable in negligence for the losses caused by the wrongdoing of Charles, Jr. and William. We affirm.

## I

The matrix for our decision is the customs and practices of the reinsurance industry and the role of Pritchard & Baird as a reinsurance broker. Reinsurance involves a contract under which one insurer agrees to indemnify another for loss sustained under the latter's policy of insurance. Insurance companies that insure against losses arising out of fire or other casualty seek at times to minimize their exposure by sharing risks with other insurance companies. Thus, when the face amount of a policy is comparatively large, the company may enlist one or more insurers to participate in that risk. Similarly, an insurance company's loss potential and overall exposure may be reduced by reinsuring a part of an entire class of policies (e.g., 25% of all of its fire insurance policies). The selling insurance company is known as a ceding company. The entity that assumes the obligation is designated as the reinsurer.

The reinsurance broker arranges the contract between the ceding company and the reinsurer. . . . In most instances, the ceding company and the reinsurer do not communicate with each other, but rely upon the reinsurance broker. The ceding company pays premiums due a reinsurer to the broker. * * *

* * *

* * * When incorporated under the laws of the State of New York in 1959, Pritchard & Baird had five directors: Charles Pritchard, Sr., his wife Lillian Pritchard, their son Charles Pritchard, Jr., George Baird and his wife Marjorie. William Pritchard, another son, became director in 1960. . . . The corporation issued 200 shares of common stock. Charles Pritchard, Sr. acquired 120 shares, his sons Charles Pritchard, Jr., 15 and William, 15; Mr. and Mrs. Baird owned the remaining 50. In June 1964, Baird and his wife resigned as directors and sold their stock to the corporation. From that time on the corporation operated as a close family corporation with Mr. and Mrs. Pritchard and their two sons as the only directors. After the death of Charles, Sr. in 1973, only the remaining three directors continued to operate as the board. Lillian Pritchard inherited 72 of her husband's 120 shares in Pritchard & Baird, thereby becoming the largest shareholder in the corporation with 48% of the stock.

The corporate minute books reflect only perfunctory activities by the directors, related almost exclusively to the election of officers and adoption of banking resolutions and a retirement plan. None of the minutes for any of the meetings contain a discussion of the loans to Charles, Jr. and William or of the financial condition of the corporation. Moreover, upon instructions of Charles, Jr. that financial statements were not to be circulated to anyone else, the company's statements for the fiscal years beginning February 1, 1970, were delivered only to him.

Charles Pritchard, Sr. was the chief executive and controlled the business in the years following Baird's withdrawal. Beginning in 1966, he gradually relinquished control over the operations of the corporation. In 1968, Charles, Jr. became president and William became executive vice president. Charles, Sr. apparently became ill in 1971 and during the last year and a half of his life was not involved in the affairs of the business. He continued, however, to serve as a director until his death on December 10, 1973. Notwithstanding the presence of Charles, Sr. on the board until his death in 1973, Charles, Jr. dominated the management of the corporation and the board from 1968 until the bankruptcy in 1975.

Contrary to the industry custom of segregating funds, Pritchard & Baird commingled the funds of reinsurers and ceding companies with its own funds. All monies (including commissions, premiums and loss monies) were deposited in a single account. Charles, Sr. began the practice of withdrawing funds from the commingled account in transactions identified on the corporate books as "loans." As long as Charles, Sr. controlled the corporation, the "loans" correlated with corporate profits and were repaid at the end of each year. Starting in 1970, however, Charles, Jr. and William begin to siphon ever-increasing sums from the corporation under the guise of loans. As of January 31, 1970, the "loans" to Charles, Jr. were $230,932 and to William were $207,329. At least by January 31, 1973, the annual increase in the loans exceeded annual corporate revenues. By October 1975, the year of bankruptcy, the "shareholders' loans" had metastasized to a total of $12,333,514.47.

The trial court rejected the characterization of the payments as "loans." 162 N.J. Super. at 365, 392 A.2d 1233. No corporate resolution authorized the "loans," and no note or other instrument evidenced the debt. Charles, Jr. and William paid no interest on the amounts received. The "loans" were not repaid or reduced from one year to the next; rather, they increased annually.

\*     \*     \*

The "loans" were reflected on financial statements that were prepared annually as of January 31, the end of the corporate fiscal year. Although an outside certified public accountant prepared the 1970 financial statement, the corporation prepared only internal financial statements from 1971-1975. In all instances, the statements were simple documents, consisting of three or four 81/2 X 11 inch sheets.

The statements of financial condition from 1970 forward demonstrated:

### WORKING CAPITAL SHAREHOLDERS' NET BROKERAGE

|  | DEFICIT | LOANS | INCOME |
|---|---|---|---|
| 1970 | $389,022 | $509,941 | $807,229 |
| 1971 | not available | not available | not available |
| 1972 | $1,684,289 | $1,825,911 | $1,546,263 |
| 1973 | $3,506,460 | $3,700,542 | $1,736,349 |
| 1974 | $6,939,007 | $7,080,629 | $876,182 |
| 1975 | $10,176,419 | $10,298,039 | $551,598. |

Those financial statements showed working capital deficits increasing annually in tandem with the amounts that Charles, Jr. and William withdrew as "shareholders' loans." In the last complete year of business (January 31, 1974, to January 31, 1975), "shareholders' loans" and the correlative working capital deficit increased by approximately $3,200,000.

\*     \*     \*

The pattern that emerges from these figures is the substantial increase in the monies appropriated by Charles Pritchard, Jr. and William Pritchard after their father's withdrawal from the business and the sharp decline in the profitability of the operation after his death. This led ultimately to the filing in December, 1975, of an involuntary petition in bankruptcy and the appointments of the plaintiffs as trustees in bankruptcy of Pritchard & Baird.

Mrs. Pritchard was not active in the business of Pritchard & Baird and knew virtually nothing of its corporate affairs. She briefly visited the corporate offices in Morristown on only one occasion, and she never read or obtained the annual financial statements. She was unfamiliar with the rudiments of reinsurance and made no effort to assure that the policies and practices of the corporation, particularly pertaining to the withdrawal of funds, complied with industry custom or relevant law. Although her husband had warned her that Charles, Jr. would "take the shirt off my back," Mrs. Pritchard did not pay any attention to her duties as a director or to the affairs of the corporation. 162 N.J. Super. at 370, 392 A.2d 1233.

After her husband died in December 1973, Mrs. Pritchard became incapacitated and was bedridden for a six-month period. She became listless at this time and started to drink rather heavily. Her physical condition deteriorated, and in 1978 she died. The trial court rejected testimony seeking to exonerate her because she "was old, was grief-stricken at the loss of her husband, sometimes consumed too much alcohol and was psychologically overborne by her sons." 162 N.J. Super. at 371, 392 A.2d 1233. That court found that she was competent to act and that the reason Mrs. Pritchard never knew what her sons "were doing was because she never made the slightest effort to discharge any of her responsibilities as a director of Pritchard & Baird." 162 N.J. Super. at 372, 392 A.2d 1233.

\* \* \*

## III

Individual liability of a corporate director for acts of the corporation is a prickly problem. Generally directors are accorded broad immunity and are not insurers of corporate activities. The problem is particularly nettlesome when a third party asserts that a director, because of nonfeasance, is liable for losses caused by acts of insiders, who in this case were officers, directors and shareholders. Determination of the liability of Mrs. Pritchard requires findings that she had a duty to the clients of Pritchard & Baird, that she breached that duty and that her breach was a proximate cause of their losses.

The New Jersey Business Corporation Act, which took effect on January 1, 1969, was a comprehensive revision of the statutes relating to business corporations. One section, N.J.S.A. 14A:6-14, concerning a director's general obligation makes it incumbent upon directors to

> discharge their duties in good faith and with that degree of diligence, care and skill which ordinarily prudent men would exercise under similar circumstances in like positions. (N.J.S.A. 14A:6-14)

This provision was based primarily on section 43 of the Model Business Corporation Act and is derived also from section 717 of the New York Business Corporation Law (L.1961, c.855, effective September 1, 1963). . . .

\* \* \*

. . . In addition to requiring that directors act honestly and in good faith, the New York courts recognized that the nature and extent of reasonable care depended upon the type of corporation, its size and financial resources. Thus, a bank director was held to stricter accountability than the director of an ordinary business.[9] *Hun v. Cary, supra*, 82 N.Y. at 71; *Litwin v. Allen*, 25 N.Y.S. 2d 667, 678 (Sup. Ct. 1940).

---

[9] [1] The obligations of directors of banks involve some additional consideration because of their relationship to the public generally and depositors in particular. Statutes impose certain requirements on bank directors. For example, directors of national banks must take an oath that they will diligently and honestly administer the affairs of the bank and will not permit violation of the banking laws. Moreover, they must satisfy certain requirements such as residence, citizenship, stockholdings and not

* * *

As a general rule, a director should acquire at least a rudimentary understanding of the business of the corporation. Accordingly, a director should become familiar with the fundamentals of the business in which the corporation is engaged. Campbell, supra, 62 N.J.Eq. at 416, 50 A. 120 Because directors are bound to exercise ordinary care, they cannot set up as a defense lack of the knowledge needed to exercise the requisite degree of care. If one "feels that he has not had sufficient business experience to qualify him to perform the duties of a director, he should either acquire the knowledge by inquiry, or refuse to act." Ibid.

Directors are under a continuing obligation to keep informed about the activities of the corporation. Otherwise, they may not be able to participate in the overall management of corporate affairs. Barnes v. Andrews, 298 F. 614 (S.D.N.Y. 1924) (director guilty of misprision of office for not keeping himself informed about the details of corporate business); Atherton v. Anderson 99 F.2d 883, 889–890 (6 Cir. 1938) (ignorance no defense to director liability because of director's "duty to know the facts"); Campbell, supra, 62 N.J. Eq. at 409, 50 A. 120 (directors "bound to acquaint themselves with . . . extent . . . of supervision exercised by officers"); Williams v. McKay, 46 N.J. Eq. 25, 36, 18 A. 824 (Ch. 1889) (director under duty to supervise managers and practices to determine whether business methods were safe and proper). Directors may not shut their eyes to corporate misconduct and then claim that because they did not see the misconduct, they did not have a duty to look. The sentinel asleep at his post contributes nothing to the enterprise he is charged to protect. Wilkinson v. Dodd, 42 N.J. Eq. 234, 245, 7 A. 327 (Ch. 1886), aff'd 42 N.J. Eq. 647, 9 A. 685 (E. & A. 1887).

Directorial management does not require a detailed inspection of day-to-day activities, but rather a general monitoring of corporate affairs and policies. Williams v. McKay, supra, at 37, 18 A. 824. Accordingly, a director is well advised to attend board meetings regularly. Indeed, a director who is absent from a board meeting is presumed to concur in action taken on a corporate matter, unless he files a "dissent with the secretary of the corporation within a reasonable time after learning of such action." N.J.S.A. 14A:6-13 (Supp. 1981–1982). Regular attendance does not mean that directors must attend every meeting, but that directors should attend meetings as a matter of practice. A director of a publicly held corporation might be expected to attend regular monthly meetings, but a director of a small, family corporation might be asked to attend only an annual meeting. The point is that one of the responsibilities of a director is to attend meetings of the board of which he or she is a member. * * *

While directors are not required to audit corporate books, they should maintain familiarity with the financial status of the corporation by a regular review of financial statements. Campbell, supra, 62 N.J. Eq. at 415, 50 A. 120; Williams, supra, 46 N.J. Eq. at 38–39, 18 A. 824; see Section of Corporation, Banking and Business Law, American Bar Association, "Corporate Director's Guidebook," 33 Bus.Law. 1595, 1608 (1978) (Guidebook); N. Lattin, THE LAW OF CORPORATIONS 280 (2 ed. 1971). In some circumstances, directors may be charged with assuring that

---

serving as an investment banker. 12 U.S.C.A. §§ 77–78. See generally R. BARNETT, RESPONSIBILITIES & LIABILITIES OF BANK DIRECTORS (1980).

bookkeeping methods conform to industry custom and usage. *Lippitt v. Ashley*, 89 Conn. 451, 464, 94 A. 995, 1000 (Sup. Ct. 1915). The extent of review, as well as the nature and frequency of financial statements, depends not only on the customs of the industry, but also on the nature of the corporation and the business in which it is engaged. Financial statements of some small corporations may be prepared internally and only on an annual basis; in a large publicly held corporation, the statements may be produced monthly or at some other regular interval. Adequate financial review normally would be more informal in a private corporation than in a publicly held corporation.

*   *   *

. . . Sometimes the duty of a director may require more than consulting with outside counsel. A director may have a duty to take reasonable means to prevent illegal conduct by co-directors; in any appropriate case, this may include threat of suit. *See Selheimer v. Manganese Corp.*, 423 Pa. 563, 572, 584, 224 A.2d 634, 640, 646 (Sup. Ct. 1966) (director exonerated when he objected, resigned, organized shareholder action group, and threatened suit).

A director is not an ornament, but an essential component of corporate governance. Consequently, a director cannot protect himself behind a paper shield bearing the motto, "dummy director." The New Jersey Business Corporation Act, in imposing a standard of ordinary care on all directors, confirms that dummy, figurehead and accommodation directors are anachronisms with no place in New Jersey law. . . . Thus, all directors are responsible for managing the business and affairs of the corporation.

The factors that impel expanded responsibility in the large, publicly held corporation may not be present in a small, close corporation.[10] Nonetheless, a close

---

[10] [3] Our decision is based on directorial responsibilities arising under state statutory and common law as distinguished from the Securities Act of 1933, 15 U.S.C. §§ 77a *et seq.*, and the Securities Exchange Act of 1934, 15 U.S.C. § 78a *et seq.* Nonetheless, we recognize significant developments in directorial liability under both Acts and related rules and regulations of the Securities and Exchange Commission. For example, an outside director may be liable in negligence under section 11 of the 1933 Act for the failure to make a reasonable investigation before signing a registration statement. *Escott v. Barchris Constr. Corp.*, 283 F. Supp. 643, 687–689 (S.D.N.Y. 1968); *see also Feit v. Leasco Data Processing Equip. Corp.*, 332 F. Supp. 544, 575–576 (E.D.N.Y.1971) (outside director who was partner in law firm for corporation considered an insider). The Securities and Exchange Commission has made it clear that outside directors should become knowledgeable about a company's business and accounting practices so that they may make "an informed judgment of its more important affairs of the abilities and integrity of the officers." Securities Exchange Act of 1934, Release No. 11,516 (July 2, 1975). With respect to actions under section 10 of the 1934 Act and Rule 10b5, which prohibit false statements in the purchase or sale of securities, liability is not imposed for mere negligence, but only if one acts with scienter, i.e., the intent to deceive, manipulate or defraud. *Ernst & Ernst v. Hochfelder*, 425 U.S. 185, 96 S. Ct. 1375, 47 L. Ed. 2d 668 (1976) outside accountant not liable in negligence for failure to conduct a proper audit).

Recently the United States Supreme Court described the Federal Securities Acts in the area of director liability as "regulatory and prohibitory in nature it often limits the exercise of directorial power, but only rarely creates it." *Burks v. Lasker*, 441 U.S. 471, 99 S. Ct. 1831, 1837, 60 L. Ed. 2d 404 (1979). In *Burks*, the Court described corporations as creatures of state law and declared "it is state law which is the font of corporate directors' powers." *Ibid. See generally* Goldstein & Shepherd, "Director Duties and Liabilities under the Securities Acts and Corporation Laws," 36 *Wash. & Lee L. Rev.* 759, 763–773 (1979).

corporation may, because of the nature of its business, be affected with a public interest. For example, the stock of a bank may be closely held, but because of the nature of banking the directors would be subject to greater liability than those of another close corporation. Even in a small corporation, a director is held to the standard of that degree of care that an ordinarily prudent director would use under the circumstances.

A director's duty of care does not exist in the abstract, but must be considered in relation to specific obligees. In general, the relationship of a corporate director to the corporation and its stockholders is that of a fiduciary. *Whitfield v. Kern*, 122 N.J. Eq. 332, 341, 192 A. 48 (E. & A. 1937). Shareholders have a right to expect that directors will exercise reasonable supervision and control over the policies and practices of a corporation. The institutional integrity of a corporation depends upon the proper discharge by directors of those duties.

While directors may owe a fiduciary duty to creditors also, that obligation generally has not been recognized in the absence of insolvency. *Whitfield, supra,* 122 N.J. Eq. at 342, 345, 192 A. 48. With certain corporations, however, directors are seemed to owe a duty to creditors and other third parties even when the corporation is solvent. Although depositors of a bank are considered in some respects to be creditors, courts have recognized that directors may owe them a fiduciary duty. *See Campbell,* supra, 62 N.J. Eq. at 406–407, 50 A. 120. Directors of nonbanking corporations may owe a similar duty when the corporation holds funds of others in trust. *Cf. McGlynn v. Schultz,* 90 N.J. Super. 505, 218 A. 408 (Ch. Div. 1966), aff'd 95 N.J. Super. 412, 231 A.2d 386 (App. Div.) certif. den. 50 N.J. 409, 235 A.2d 901 (1967) (directors who did not insist on segregating trust funds held by corporation liable to the cestuis que trust).

*     *     *

As a reinsurance broker, Pritchard & Baird received annually as a fiduciary millions of dollars of clients' money which it was under a duty to segregate.[4] To this extent, it resembled a bank rather than a small family business. Accordingly, Mrs. Pritchard's relationship to the clientele of Pritchard & Baird was akin to that of a director of a bank to its depositors. . . .

As a director of a substantial reinsurance brokerage corporation, she should have known that it received annually millions of dollars of loss and premium funds which it held in trust for ceding and reinsurance companies. Mrs. Pritchard should have obtained and read the annual statements of financial condition of Pritchard & Baird. Although she had a right to rely upon financial statements prepared in accordance with N.J.S.A. 14A:6-14, such reliance would not excuse her conduct. The reason is that those statements disclosed on their face the misappropriation of trust funds.

From those statements, she should have realized that, as of January 31, 1970, her sons were withdrawing substantial trust funds under the guise of "Shareholders' Loans." The financial statements for each fiscal year commencing with that of January 31, 1970, disclosed that the working capital deficits and the "loans" were escalating in tandem. Detecting a misappropriation of funds would not have required special expertise or extraordinary diligence; a cursory reading of the financial statements would have revealed the pillage. Thus, if Mrs. Pritchard had read the financial statements, she would have known that her sons were converting trust funds. When financial statements demonstrate that insiders are bleeding a corporation to death, a director should notice and try to stanch the flow of blood.

In summary, Mrs. Pritchard was charged with the obligation of basic knowledge and supervision of the business of Pritchard & Baird. Under the circumstances, this obligation included reading and understanding financial statements, and making reasonable attempts at detection and prevention of the illegal conduct of other officers and directors. She had a duty to protect the clients of Pritchard & Baird against policies and practices that would result in the misappropriation of money they had entrusted to the corporation. She breached that duty.

## IV

Nonetheless, the negligence of Mrs. Pritchard does not result in liability unless it is a proximate cause of the loss. Analysis of proximate cause requires an initial determination of cause-in-fact. Causation-in-fact calls for a finding that the defendant's act or omission was a necessary antecedent of the loss, i.e.., that if the defendant had observed his or her duty of care, the loss would not have occurred. Further, the plaintiff has the burden of establishing the amount of the loss or damages caused by the negligence of the defendant. Thus, the plaintiff must establish not only a breach of duty, "but in addition that the performance by the director of his duty would have avoided loss, and the amount of the resulting loss." [1 HORNSTEIN, CORPORATION LAW AND PRACTICE, § 446 at 566.]

Cases involving nonfeasance present a much more difficult causation question than those in which the director has committed an affirmative act of negligence leading to the loss. Analysis in cases of negligent omissions calls for determination of the reasonable steps a director should have taken and whether that course of action would have averted the loss.

*     *     *

In this case, the scope of Mrs. Pritchard's duties was determined by the precarious financial condition of Pritchard & Baird, its fiduciary relationship to its clients and the implied trust in which it held their funds. Thus viewed, the scope of her duties encompassed all reasonable action to stop the continuing conversion. Her duties extended beyond mere objection and resignation to reasonable attempts to prevent the misappropriation of the trust funds.

A leading case discussing causation where the director's liability is predicated upon a negligent failure to act is Barnes v. Andrews, 298 F. 614 (S.D.N.Y. 1924). In that case the court exonerated a figurehead director who served for eight months on a board that held one meeting after his election, a meeting he was forced to miss because of the death of his mother. Writing for the court, Judge Learned Hand distinguished a director who fails to prevent general mismanagement from one such as Mrs. Pritchard who failed to stop an illegal "loan":

> When the corporate funds have been illegally lent, it is a fair inference that a protest would have stopped the loan, and that the director's neglect caused the loss. But when a business fails from general mismanagement,

business incapacity, or bad judgment, how is it possible to say that a single director could have made the company successful, or how much in dollars he could have saved? [*Id.* at 616–617.]

Pointing out the absence of proof of proximate cause between defendant's negligence and the company's insolvency, Judge Hand also wrote:

The plaintiff must, however, go further than to show that (the director) should have been more active in his duties. This cause of action rests upon a tort, as much though it be a tort of omission as though it had rested upon a positive act. The plaintiff must accept the burden of showing that the performance of the defendant's duties would have avoided loss, and what loss it would have avoided. [*Id.* at 616.]

\*     \*     \*

In assessing whether Mrs. Pritchard's conduct was a legal or proximate cause of the conversion, "(l)egal responsibility must be limited to those causes which are so closely connected with the result and of such significance that the law is justified in imposing liability." [W. Prosser, Law of Torts, § 41 at 237 (4th ed. 1971).] Such a judicial determination involves not only considerations of causation-in-fact and matters of policy, but also common sense and logic. *Caputzal v. The Lindsay Co.*, 48 N.J. 69, 77–78, (1966). The act or the failure to act must be a substantial factor in producing the harm.

Within Pritchard & Baird, several factors contributed to the loss of the funds: comingling of corporate and client monies, conversion of funds by Charles, Jr. and William and dereliction of her duties by Mrs. Pritchard. The wrongdoing of her sons, although the immediate cause of the loss, should not excuse Mrs. Pritchard from her negligence which also was a substantial factor contributing to the loss. Her sons knew that she, the only other director, was not reviewing their conduct; they spawned their fraud in the backwater of her neglect. Her neglect of duty contributed to the climate of corruption; her failure to act contributed to the continuation of that corruption. Consequently, her conduct was a substantial factor contributing to the loss.

Analysis of proximate cause is especially difficult in a corporate context where the allegation is that nonfeasance of a director is a proximate cause of damage to a third party. Where a case involves nonfeasance, no one can say "with absolute certainty what would have occurred if the defendant had acted otherwise." Prosser, *supra*, § 41 at 242. Nonetheless, where it is reasonable to conclude that the failure to act would produce a particular result and that result has followed, causation may be inferred. *Ibid.* We conclude that even if Mrs. Pritchard's mere objection had not stopped the depredations of her sons, her consultation with an attorney and the threat of suit would have deterred them. That conclusion flows as a matter of common sense and logic from the record. Whether in other situations a director has a duty to do more than protest and resign is best left to case-by-case determinations. In this case, we are satisfied that there was a duty to do more than object and resign. Consequently, we find that Mrs. Pritchard's negligence was a proximate cause of the misappropriations.

\* \* \*

The judgment of the Appellate Division is affirmed.

## NOTES

1.  Is it fair to impose liability on a "passive director" such as Pritchard in a closely held family corporation for mere failure to act? If Mrs. Pritchard had simply resigned from the board before the illegal actions took place, isn't it unlikely that her sons would have taken action to fill the vacancy with someone who might have discovered their fraudulent conduct? Thus, her resignation would probably have had no effect as far as protecting innocent third parties.

2.  Nonetheless, *Francis* illustrates the general tendency of the courts to hold directors to a unitary standard of care regardless of their state of health, degree of involvement in the affairs of the corporation, or whether they may be a mere "accommodation director." Attorneys are often asked by clients to serve on the boards of closely held corporations which they have formed, although they are not expected to participate actively in the management of the corporation's business affairs. However, cases such as *Francis* indicate that an attorney who takes a seat on the board does so at her own peril if she fails to at least actively monitor the affairs of the corporation. For a case holding an attorney liable despite a plea that he was merely accommodation director, *see Minton v. Cavaney*, 364 P.2d 473 (Cal. 1961).

3.  The court mentions that directors of banks are often held to a higher standard of care than are directors of non-financial corporations. Does that distinction make sense?

## MILLER v. AMERICAN TELEPHONE AND TELEGRAPH CO.
### United States Court of Appeals, Third Circuit
### 507 F.2d 759 (1974)

SEITZ, CHIEF JUDGE.

Plaintiffs, stockholders in American Telephone and Telegraph Company ("AT&T"), brought a stockholders' derivative action in the Eastern District of Pennsylvania against AT&T and all but one of its directors. The suit centered upon the failure of AT&T to collect an outstanding debt of some $1.5 million owed to the company by the Democratic National Committee ('DNC') for communications services provided by AT&T during the 1968 Democratic national convention. Federal diversity jurisdiction was invoked under 28 U.S.C. § 1332.

Plaintiffs' complaint alleged that "neither the officers or directors of AT&T have taken any action to recover the amount owed' from on or about August 20, 1968, when the debt was incurred, until May 31, 1972, the date plaintiffs' amended complaint was filed. The failure to collect was alleged to have involved a breach of the defendant directors' duty to exercise diligence in handling the affairs of the corporation, to have resulted in affording a preference to the DNC in collection procedures in violation of § 202(a) of the Communications Act of 1934, 47 U.S.C. § 202(a) (1970), and to have amounted to AT&T's making a "contribution" to the DNC in violation of a federal prohibition on corporate campaign spending, 18 U.S.C. § 610 (1970).

Plaintiffs sought permanent relief in the form of an injunction requiring AT&T to collect the debt, an injunction against providing further services to the DNC until the debt was paid in full, and a surcharge for the benefit of the corporation against the defendant directors in the amount of the debt plus interest from the due date. A request for a preliminary injunction against the provision of services to the 1972 Democratic convention was denied by the district court after an evidentiary hearing.

On motion of the defendants, the district court dismissed the complaint for failure to state a claim upon which relief could be granted. 364 F. Supp. 648 (E.D. Pa. 1973). The court stated that collection procedures were properly within the discretion of the directors whose determination would not be overturned by the court in the absence of an allegation that the conduct of the directors was "plainly illegal, unreasonable, or in breach of a fiduciary duty . . . " *Id.* at 651. Plaintiffs appeal from dismissal of their complaint.

In viewing the motion to dismiss, we must consider all facts alleged in the complaint and every inference fairly deductible therefrom in the light most favorable to the plaintiffs. A complaint should not be dismissed unless it appears that the plaintiffs would not be entitled to relief under any facts which they might prove in support of their claim. Judging plaintiffs' complaint by these standards, we feel that it does state a claim upon which relief can be granted for breach of fiduciary duty arising from the alleged violation of 18 U.S.C. § 610.

## I.

The pertinent law on the question of the defendant directors' fiduciary duties in this diversity action is that of New York, the state of AT & T's incorporation. The sound business judgment rule, the basis of the district court's dismissal of plaintiffs' complaint, expresses the unanimous decision of American courts to eschew intervention in corporate decision-making if the judgment of directors and officers in uninfluenced by personal considerations and is exercised in good faith. Underlying the rule is the assumption that reasonable diligence has been used in reaching the decision which the rule is invoked to justify.

Had plaintiffs' complaint alleged only failure to pursue a corporate claim, application of the sound business judgment rule would support the district court's ruling that a shareholder could not attack the directors' decision. Where, however, the decision not to collect a debt owed the corporation is itself alleged to have been an illegal act, different rules apply. When New York law regarding such acts by directors is considered in conjunction with the underlying purposes of the particular statute involved here, we are convinced that the business judgment rule cannot insulate the defendant directors from liability if they did in fact breach 18 U.S.C. § 610, as plaintiffs have charged.

*Roth v. Robertson*, 64 Misc. 343, 118 N.Y.S. 351 (Sup. Ct. 1909), illustrates the proposition that even though committed to benefit the corporation, illegal acts may amount to a breach of fiduciary duty in New York. In *Roth*, the managing director of an amusement park company had allegedly used corporate funds to purchase the silence of persons who threatened to complain about unlawful Sunday operation of the park. Recovery from the defendant director was sustained on the ground that the money was an illegal payment:

> For reasons of public policy, we are clearly of the opinion that payments of corporate funds for such purposes as those disclosed in this case must be condemned, and officers of a corporation making them held to a strict accountability, and be compelled to refund the amounts so wasted for the benefit of stockholders . . . To hold any other rule would be establishing a dangerous precedent, tacitly countenancing the wasting of corporate funds for purposes of corrupting public morals. *Id.* at 346, 118 N.Y.S. at 353.

The plaintiffs' complaint in the instant case alleges a similar "waste" of $1.5 million through an illegal campaign contribution.

*Abrams v. Allen*, 297 N.Y. 52, 74 N.E.2d 305 (1947), reflects an affirmation by the New York Court of Appeals of the principle of Roth that directors must be restrained from engaging in activities which are against public policy. In Abrams the court held that a cause of action was stated by an allegation in a derivative complaint that the directors of Remington Rand, Inc., had relocated corporate plants and curtailed production solely for the purpose of intimidating and punishing employees for their involvement in a labor dispute. The Court of Appeals acknowledged that, "depending on the circumstances," proof of the allegations in the complaint might sustain recovery, inter alia, under the rule that directors are liable for corporate loss caused by the commission of an "unlawful or immoral act." *Id.* at 55, 74 N.E.2d at 306. In support of its holding, the court noted that the closing of factories for the purpose alleged was opposed to the public policy of the state and nation as embodied in the New York Labor Law and the National Labor Relations Act. *Id.* at 56, 74 N.E.2d at 307.3

The alleged violation of the federal prohibition against corporate political contributions not only involves the corporation in criminal activity but similarly contravenes a policy of Congress clearly enunciated in 18 U.S.C. § 610.[11] That statute and its predecessor reflect congressional efforts: (1) to destroy the influence of corporations over elections through financial contributions and (2) to check the practice of using corporate funds to benefit political parties without the consent of the stockholders. *United States v. CIO*, 335 U.S. 106, 113, 68 S. Ct. 1349, 92 L. Ed. 1849 (1948).

The fact that shareholders are within the class for whose protection the statute was enacted gives force to the argument that the alleged breach of that statute

---

[11] [4] We note that prior to June 1, 1974, corporate political contributions made "directly or indirectly" violated New York law. Law of July 20, 1965, ch. 1031, § 43, (1965) N.Y. Laws 1783 (repealed 1974). Furthermore, apart from the statutory prohibition, political donations by corporations were apparently ultra vires acts in New York. *See People ex rel. Perkins v. Moss*, 187 N.Y. 410, 80 N.E. 383 (1907). Corporations or organizations financially supported by corporations doing business in the state are now permitted to make contributions up to $5,000 per year. N.Y. Election Law § 480 (McKinney's Consol.Laws, c. 17, Supp. 1974).

should give rise to cause of action in those shareholders to force the return to the corporation of illegally contributed funds. Since political contributions by corporations can be checked and shareholder control over the political use of general corporate funds effectuated only if directors are restrained from causing the corporation to violate the statute, such a violation seems a particularly appropriate basis for finding breach of the defendant directors' fiduciary duty to the corporation. Under such circumstances, the directors cannot be insulated from liability on the ground that the contribution was made in the exercise of sound business judgment.

Since plaintiffs have alleged actual damage to the corporation from the transaction in the form of the loss of a $1.5 million increment to AT&T's treasury, we conclude that the complaint does state a claim upon which relief can be granted sufficient to withstand a motion to dismiss.

## II.

We have accepted plaintiffs' allegation of a violation of 18 U.S.C. § 610 as a shorthand designation of the elements necessary to establish a breach of that statute. This is consonant with the federal practice of notice pleading. *See Conley v. Gibson*, 355 U.S. 41, 47–48, 78 S. Ct. 99, 2 L. Ed. 2d 80 (1957); Fed. R. Civ.P. 8(f). That such a designation is sufficient for pleading purposes does not, however, relieve plaintiffs of their ultimate obligation to prove the elements of the statutory violation as part of their proof of breach of fiduciary duty. At the appropriate time, plaintiffs will be required to produce evidence sufficient to establish three distinct elements comprising a violation of 18 U.S.C. § 610: that AT&T (1) made a contribution of money or anything of value to the DNC (2) in connection with a federal election (3) for the purpose of influencing the outcome of that election. *See United States v. Boyle*, 482 F.2d 755, 157 U.S. App. D.C. 166, *cert. denied*, 414 U.S. 1076, 94 S. Ct. 593, 38 L. Ed. 2d 483 (1973); *United States v. Lewis Food Co., Inc.*, 366 F.2d 710 (9th Cir. 1966). The first two of these elements are obvious from the face of the statute; the third was supplied by legislative history prior to being made explicit by 1972 amendments to definitions applicable to § 610.

## A "Contribution" to the DNC

In proving a contribution to the DNC, plaintiffs will be required to establish that AT&T did in fact make a gift to the DNC of the value of the communications services provided to the 1968 Democratic convention. Such a gift could be shown, for example, by demonstrating that the services were provided with no intention to collect for them. Likewise, plaintiffs could meet their burden in this respect by proving that although a valid debt was created at the time the services were rendered, that debt was discharged formally or informally by the defendants or is no longer legally collectible as a result of the defendants' failure to sue upon it within the appropriate period of limitation. In any event, as a threshold matter, plaintiffs will be required to show that actions of the defendants have resulted in the surrender of a valid claim of $1.5 million for services rendered to the DNC.

## In Connection With a Federal Election

Plaintiffs must also establish that the contribution was in connection with a federal election. Obviously, the communications services were provided in connection with the 1968 election. If, however, a valid debt was created at that time and the alleged gift was made at some later time when the debt was forgiven or became legally uncollectible, the contribution may have been made in connection with a subsequent federal election. Plaintiffs did not allege the date of the contribution in their complaint, but their burden on remand will include establishing a nexus between the alleged gift and a federal election.

## For the Purpose of Influencing an Election

Finally, plaintiffs must also convince the fact finder that the gift, whenever made, was made for the purpose of aiding one candidate or party in a federal election. Proof of non-collection of a debt owed by the DNC will be insufficient to establish the statutory violation upon which the defendants' breach of fiduciary duty is predicated; plaintiffs must shoulder the burden of proving an impermissible motivation underlying the alleged inaction. In the absence of direct proof of a partisan purpose on the part of the defendants, plaintiffs may produce evidence sufficient to justify the inference that the only discernible reason for the failure to pursue the debtor was a desire to assist the Democratic Party in achieving success in a federal election. At a minimum, plaintiffs must establish that legitimate business justifications did not underlie the alleged inaction of the defendant directors. The possibility of the existence of such reasonable business motives illustrates the need for proof of more than mere non-collection even of the debt of a political party in order to establish a breach of 18 U.S.C. § 610.[12]

## III.

In addition to advancing claims of breach of fiduciary duty by the defendants, plaintiffs have urged in this court that we "imply" a direct federal cause of action in their favor against the defendant directors for the alleged violations of 18 U.S.C. § 610 and 47 U.S.C. § 202(a). A federal law count was nowhere included in the plaintiffs' complaint and there is no indication in the record that this question was ever presented to the district court. After remand of this case, plaintiffs will have an opportunity to move to amend their complaint pursuant to Rule 15, Fed. R. Civ. P., and the district court will act upon any such motion within the discretion afforded under that rule.

The order of the district court will be reversed and the case remanded for further proceedings consistent with this opinion.

---

[12] [9] Compiling an unsecured debt of this magnitude is no longer possible under new regulations of the Federal Communications Commission adopted May 5, 1972. The FCC regulations, 47 C.F.R. § 64.801–804 (1973), permit the granting of unsecured credit to political candidates but require termination of services if charges remain unpaid for 15 days and the debtor does not pay within 7 days after notice given 'forthwith' upon expiration of the 15 day period. Common carriers are explicitly required to act to collect the unpaid balance prior to the running of the one year statute of limitations found in 47 U.S.C. § 415(a) (1970).

## NOTE

The problem of policing corporate participation in the political process has been a troublesome one. In *Gall v. Exxon*, 418 F. Supp. 508 (S.D.N.Y. 1976), a shareholders' derivative suit challenged the alleged payment by Exxon of millions of dollars in political contributions to Italian political parties and failure to disclose such payments in violation of the Securities and Exchange Commission (SEC) proxy rules. The Board appointed a special committee of independent directors to investigate the matter and, while concluding that the acts in fact did take place, it found that it would not be in the best interest of the corporation to pursue an action for damages against the parties responsible for the contributions. The District Court sustained the Committee's decision to dismiss the derivative suit against a challenge that the decision not to pursue the action violated the business judgment rule. Is this case significantly different from *Miller v. AT&T*?

## GRAHAM v. ALLIS-CHALMERS MANUFACTURING CO.
### Supreme Court of Delaware
### 188 A.2d 125 (1963)

WOLCOTT, J.

This is a derivative action on behalf of Allis-Chalmers against its directors and four of its non-director employees. The complaint is based upon indictments of Allis-Chalmers and the four non-director employees named as defendants herein who, with the corporation, entered pleas of guilty to the indictments. The indictments, eight in number, charged violations of the Federal anti-trust laws. The suit seeks to recover damages which Allis-Chalmers is claimed to have suffered by reason of these violations.

\*     \*     \*

The complaint alleges actual knowledge on the part of the director defendants of the anti-trust conduct upon which the indictments were based or, in the alternative, knowledge of facts which should have put them on notice of such conduct.

However, the hearing and depositions produced no evidence that any director had any actual knowledge of the anti-trust activity, or had actual knowledge of any facts which should have put them on notice that anti-trust activity was being carried on by some of their company's employees. The plaintiffs, appellants here, thereupon shifted the theory of the case to the proposition that the directors are liable as a matter of law by reason of their failure to take action designed to learn of and prevent anti-trust activity on the part of any employees of Allis-Chalmers.

By this appeal the plaintiffs seek to have us reverse the Vice Chancellor's ruling of non-liability of the defendant directors upon this theory . . ..

Allis-Chalmers is a manufacturer of a variety of electrical equipment. It employs in excess of 31,000 people, has a total of 24 plants, 145 sales offices, 5000 dealers and distributors, and its sales volume is in excess of $500,000,000 annually. The operations of the company are conducted by two groups, each of which is under the direction of a senior vice president. One of these groups is the Industries Group under the direction of Singleton, director defendant. This group is divided into five divisions. One of these, the Power Equipment Division, produced the products, the sale of which involved the anti-trust activities referred to in the indictments. The Power Equipment Division, presided over by McMullen, non-director defendant, contains ten departments, each of which is presided over by a manager or general manager.

The operating policy of Allis-Chalmers is to decentralize by the delegation of authority to the lowest possible management level capable of fulfilling the delegated responsibility. Thus, prices of products are ordinarily set by the particular department manager, except that if the product being priced is large and special, the department manager might confer with the general manager of the division. Products of a standard character involving repetitive manufacturing processes are sold out of a price list which is established by a price leader for the electrical equipment industry as a whole.

Annually, the Board of Directors reviews group and departmental profit goal budgets. On occasion, the Board considers general questions concerning price levels, but because of the complexity of the company's operations the Board does not participate in decisions fixing the prices of specific products.

The Board of Directors of fourteen members, four of whom are officers, meets once a month, October excepted, and considers a previously prepared agenda for the meeting. Supplied to the Directors at the meetings are financial and operating data relating to all phases of the company's activities. The Board meetings are customarily of several hours duration in which all the Directors participate actively. Apparently, the Board considers and decides matters concerning the general business policy of the company. By reason of the extent and complexity of the company's operations, it is not practicable for the Board to consider in detail specific problems of the various divisions.

The indictments to which Allis-Chalmers and the four non-director defendants pled guilty charge that the company and individual non-director defendants, commencing in 1956, conspired with other manufacturers and their employees to fix prices and to rig bids to private electric utilities and governmental agencies in violation of the anti-trust laws of the United States. None of the director defendants in this cause were named as defendants in the indictments. Indeed, the Federal Government acknowledged that it had uncovered no probative evidence which could lead to the conviction of the defendant directors.

The first actual knowledge the directors had of anti-trust violations by some of the company's employees was in the summer of 1959 from newspaper stories that TVA proposed an investigation of identical bids. Singleton, in charge of the Industries Group of the company, investigated but unearthed nothing. Thereafter, in November of 1959, some of the company's employees were subpoenaed before the Grand Jury. Further investigation by the company's Legal Division gave reason to suspect the illegal activity and all of the subpoenaed employees were instructed to tell the whole truth.

Thereafter, on February 8, 1960, at the direction of the Board, a policy statement relating to anti-trust problems was issued, and the Legal Division commenced a series of meetings with all employees of the company in possible areas of anti-trust activity. The purpose and effect of these steps was to eliminate any possibility of further and future violations of the antitrust laws.

As we have pointed out, there is no evidence in the record that the defendant directors had actual knowledge of the illegal anti-trust actions of the company's employees. Plaintiffs, however, point to two FTC decrees of 1937 as warning to the directors that anti-trust activity by the company's employees had taken place in the past. It is argued that they were thus put on notice of their duty to ferret out such activity and to take active steps to insure that it would not be repeated.

The decrees in question were consent decrees entered in 1937 against Allis-Chalmers and nine others enjoining agreements to fix uniform prices on condensors and turbine generators. The decrees recited that they were consented to for the sole purpose of avoiding the trouble and expense of the proceeding.

None of the director defendants were directors or officers of Allis-Chalmers in 1937. The director defendants and now officers of the company either were employed in very subordinate capacities or had no connection with the company in 1937. At the time, copies of the decrees were circulated to the heads of concerned departments and were explained to the Managers Committee.

In 1943, Singleton, officer and director defendant, first learned of the decrees upon becoming Assistant Manager of the Steam Turbine Department, and consulted the company's General Counsel as to them. He investigated his department and learned the decrees were being complied with and, in any event, he concluded that the company had not in the first place been guilty of the practice enjoined.

Stevenson, officer and director defendant, first learned of the decrees in 1951 in a conversation with Singleton about their respective areas of the company's operations. He satisfied himself that the company was not then and in fact had not been guilty of quoting uniform prices and had consented to the decrees in order to avoid the expense and vexation of the proceeding.

Scholl, officer and director defendant, learned of the decrees in 1956 in a discussion with Singleton on matters affecting the Industries Group. He was informed that no similar problem was then in existence in the company.

Plaintiffs argue that because of the 1937 consent decrees, the directors were put on notice that they should take steps to ensure that no employee of Allis-Chalmers would violate the anti-trust laws. The difficulty the argument has is that only three of the present directors knew of the decrees, and all three of them satisfied themselves that Allis-Chalmers had not engaged in the practice enjoined and had consented to the decrees merely to avoid expense and the necessity of defending the company's position. Under the circumstances, we think knowledge by three of the directors that in 1937 the company had consented to the entry of decrees enjoining it from doing something they had satisfied themselves it had never done, did not put the Board on notice of the possibility of future illegal price fixing.

Plaintiffs have wholly failed to establish either actual notice or imputed notice to the Board of Directors of facts which should have put them on guard, and have caused them to take steps to prevent the future possibility of illegal price fixing and bid rigging. Plaintiffs say that as a minimum in this respect the Board should have taken the steps it took in 1960 when knowledge of the facts first actually came to their attention as a result of the Grand Jury investigation. Whatever duty, however, there was upon the Board to take such steps, the fact of the 1937 decrees has no bearing upon the question, for under the circumstances they were notice of nothing.

Plaintiffs are thus forced to rely solely upon the legal proposition advanced by them that directors of a corporation, as a matter of law, are liable for losses suffered by their corporations by reason of their gross inattention to the common law duty of actively supervising and managing the corporate affairs. Plaintiffs rely mainly upon *Briggs v. Spaulding*, 141 U.S. 132, 11 S. Ct. 924, 35 L.Ed. 662.

From the *Briggs* case and others cited by plaintiffs, *e g., Bowerman v. Hamner*, 250 U.S. 504, 39 S. Ct. 549, 63 L. Ed. 1113; *Gamble v. Brown*, 4 Cir., 29 F.2d 366, and *Atherton v. Anderson*, 6 Cir., 99 F.2d 883, it appears that directors of a corporation in managing the corporate affairs are bound to use that amount of care which ordinarily careful and prudent men would use in similar circumstances. Their duties are those of control, and whether or not by neglect they have made themselves liable for failure to exercise proper control depends on the circumstances and facts of the particular case.

The precise charge made against these director defendants is that, even though they had no knowledge of any suspicion of wrongdoing on the part of the company's employees, they still should have put into effect a system of watchfulness which would have brought such misconduct to their attention in ample time to have brought it to an end. However, the *Briggs* case expressly rejects such an idea. On the contrary, it appears that directors are entitled to rely on the honesty and integrity of their subordinates until something occurs to put them on suspicion that something is wrong. If such occurs and goes unheeded, then liability of the directors might well follow, but absent cause for suspicion there is no duty upon the directors to install and operate a corporate system of espionage to ferret out wrongdoing which they have no reason to suspect exists.

The duties of the Allis-Chalmers Directors were fixed by the nature of the enterprise which employed in excess of 30,000 persons, and extended over a large geographical area. By force of necessity, the company's Directors could not know personally all the company's employees. The very magnitude of the enterprise required them to confine their control to the broad policy decisions. That they did this is clear from the record. At the meetings of the Board in which all Directors participated, these questions were considered and decided on the basis of summaries, reports and corporate records. These they were entitled to rely on, not only, we think, under general principles of the common law, but by reason of 8 Del. C. § 141(f) as well, which in terms fully protects a director who relies on such in the performance of his duties.

In the last analysis, the question of whether a corporate director has become liable for losses to the corporation through neglect of duty is determined by the circumstances. If he has recklessly reposed confidence in an obviously untrustworthy employee, has refused or neglected cavalierly to perform his duty as a director, or has ignored either willfully or through inattention obvious danger signs of employee wrongdoing, the law will cast the burden of liability upon him. This is not the case at bar, however, for as soon as it became evident that there were grounds for suspicion, the Board acted promptly to end it and prevent its recurrence.

Plaintiffs say these steps should have been taken long before, even in the absence of suspicion, but we think not, for we know of no rule of law which requires a corporate director to assume, with no justification whatsoever, that all corporate employees are incipient law violators who, but for a tight checkrein, will give free vent to their unlawful propensities.

We therefore affirm the Vice Chancellor's ruling that the individual director defendants are not liable as a matter of law merely because, unknown to them, some employees of Allis-Chalmers violated the anti-trust laws thus subjecting the corporation to loss.

*   *   *

The judgment of the court below is affirmed.

# NOTES

**1.** The principal case is typical of the reasoning by the courts in cases where defendant directors are, in effect, pleading ignorance as a defense. Unless there is evidence that the directors either know or have reason to know of an employee's wrongdoing, the directors typically will be exonerated. An example of a case where liability has been found is *Bates v. Dresser*, 251 U.S. 524 (1920), where defendant, the bank's president and a director, was held liable for losses resulting from embezzlement by an employee. Justice Holmes emphasized that the president had knowledge that the employee was living well beyond the means of an ordinary bank teller and thus had a duty to investigate further to determine the source of the employee's income. Since an examination of bank records under the employee's control would have led to earlier discovery of the embezzlement and thus mitigate the losses, the president was held liable.

**2.** The continued validity of the decision in *Graham v. Allis-Chalmers* was recently brought into question by Chancellor Allen in his 1996 opinion in *In re Caremark, Inc. Derivative Litigation*, 698 A.2d 959 (Del. Ch. 1996), in which he indicated that the board may, consistent with the business judgment rule, be held to have an affirmative obligation to establish procedures to detect corporate wrongdoing. In his opinion, the Chancellor said:

> The complaint charges the director defendants with breach of their duty of attention or care in connection with the on-going operation of the corporation's business. The claim is that the directors allowed a situation to develop and continue which exposed the corporation to enormous legal liability and that in so doing they violated a duty to be active monitors of corporate performance. The complaint thus does not charge either director self-dealing or the more difficult loyalty-type problems arising from cases of suspect director motivation, such as entrenchment or sale of control contexts. The theory here advanced is possibly the most difficult theory in corporation law upon which a plaintiff might hope to win a judgment. The

good policy reasons why it is so difficult to charge directors with responsibility for corporate losses for an alleged breach of care, where there is no conflict of interest or no facts suggesting suspect motivation involved, were recently described in *Gagliardi v. TriFoods Int'l, Inc.*, Del. Ch., 683 A.2d 1049, 1051 (1996) (1996 Del. Ch. LEXIS 87 at p. 20).

1. Potential liability for directorial decisions: Director liability for a breach of the duty to exercise appropriate attention may, in theory, arise in two distinct contexts. First, such liability may be said to follow from a board decision that results in a loss because that decision was ill advised or "negligent". Second, liability to the corporation for a loss may be said to arise from an unconsidered failure of the board to act in circumstances in which due attention would, arguably, have prevented the loss. *See generally Veasey & Seitz, The Business Judgment Rule in the Revised Model Act* . . . 63 Texas L. Rev. 1483 (1985). The first class of cases will typically be subject to review under the director-protective business judgment rule, assuming the decision made was the product of a process that was either deliberately considered in good faith or was otherwise rational. . . .

The second class of cases in which director liability for inattention is theoretically possible entail circumstances in which a loss eventuates not from a decision but, from unconsidered inaction. Most of the decisions that a corporation, acting through its human agents, makes are, of course, not the subject of director attention. Legally, the board itself will be required only to authorize the most significant corporate acts or transactions: mergers, changes in capital structure, fundamental changes in business, appointment and compensation of the CEO, etc. As the facts of this case graphically demonstrate, ordinary business decisions that are made by officers and employees deeper in the interior of the organization can, however, vitally affect the welfare of the corporation and its ability to achieve its various strategic and financial goals. If this case did not prove the point itself, recent business history would. . . .

In 1963, the Delaware Supreme Court in *Graham v. Allis-Chalmers Mfg. Co.*, addressed the question of potential liability of board members for losses experienced by the corporation as a result of the corporation having violated the anti-trust laws of the United States. There was no claim in that case that the directors knew about the behavior of subordinate employees of the corporation that had resulted in the liability. Rather, as in this case, the claim asserted was that the directors ought to have known of it and if they had known they would have been under a duty to bring the corporation into compliance with the law and thus save the corporation from the loss. The Delaware Supreme Court concluded that, under the facts as they appeared, there was no basis to find that the directors had breached a duty to be informed of the ongoing operations of the firm. In notably colorful terms, the court stated that "absent cause for suspicion there is no duty upon the directors to install and operate a corporate system of espionage to ferret out wrongdoing which they have no reason to suspect exists." The Court found that there were no grounds for suspicion in that case and, thus, concluded that the directors were blamelessly unaware of the conduct leading to the corporate liability.

How does one generalize this holding today? Can it be said today that, absent some ground giving rise to suspicion of violation of law, that corporate directors have no duty to assure that a corporate information gathering and reporting systems exists which represents a good faith attempt to provide senior management and the Board with information respecting material acts, events or conditions within the corporation, including compliance with applicable statutes and regulations? I certainly do not believe so. I doubt that such a broad generalization of the Graham holding would have been accepted by the Supreme Court in 1963. The case can be more narrowly interpreted as standing for the proposition that, absent grounds to suspect deception, neither corporate boards nor senior officers can be charged with wrongdoing simply for assuming the integrity of employees and the honesty of their dealings on the company's behalf. *See* 188 A.2d at 130–31.

A broader interpretation of *Graham v. Allis-Chalmers*-that it means that a corporate board has no responsibility to assure that appropriate information and reporting systems are established by management-would not, in any event, be accepted by the Delaware Supreme Court in 1996, in my opinion. In stating the basis for this view, I start with the recognition that in recent years the Delaware Supreme Court has made it clear-especially in its jurisprudence concerning takeovers, from *Smith v. Van Gorkom* through *Paramount Communications v. QVC* [637 A.2d 34 (1993)] — the seriousness with which the corporation law views the role of the corporate board. Secondly, I note the elementary fact that relevant and timely *information* is an essential predicate for satisfaction of the board's supervisory and monitoring role under Section 141 of the Delaware General Corporation Law. Thirdly, I note the potential impact of the federal organizational sentencing guidelines on any business organization. Any rational person attempting in good faith to meet an organizational gover-nance responsibility would be bound to take into account this development and the enhanced penalties and the opportunities for reduced sanctions that it offers.

In light of these developments, it would, in my opinion, be a mistake to conclude that our Supreme Court's statement in *Graham* concerning "espionage" means that corporate boards may satisfy their obligation to be reasonably informed concerning the corporation, without assuring them-selves that information and reporting systems exist in the organization that are reasonably designed to provide to senior management and to the board itself timely, accurate information sufficient to allow management and the board, each within its scope, to reach informed judgments concerning both the corporation's compliance with law and its business performance.

Obviously the level of detail that is appropriate for such an information system is a question of business judgment. And obviously too, no rationally designed information and reporting system will remove the possibility that the corporation will violate laws or regulations, or that senior officers or directors may nevertheless sometimes be misled or otherwise fail reasonably to detect acts material to the corporation's compliance with the law. But it is important that the board exercise a good faith judgment that the corporation's information and reporting system is in concept and design adequate to assure the board that appropriate information will come to its attention in a timely manner as a matter of ordinary operations, so that it may satisfy its responsibility.

Thus, I am of the view that a director's obligation includes a duty to attempt in good faith to assure that a corporate information and reporting system, which the board concludes is adequate, exists, and that failure to do so under some circumstances may, in theory at least, render a director liable for losses caused by non-compliance with applicable legal standards.

. . .

698 A.2d at 967–70.

## B.  DUTY OF LOYALTY — CONFLICTS OF INTEREST

### 1.  General Principles

Think back to *Meinhard v. Salmon, supra* Ch. 3, Sec. B. Justice Cardozo spoke of the duty owed by Salmon to Meinhard in language that conjures up thoughts of chivalry and knights in shining armor. This duty of loyalty is owed by agents to their principals. Since partners are deemed to be agents of their partnerships and the other partners, it is owed by partners to their firms and each other. The duty of loyalty is also owed by both officers and directors to the corporation and its shareholders, even though directors do not fit neatly within the normal conception of agents. Remember that an agent is one who acts on behalf of, and subject to the control of, a principal. Although directors do run the corporation on behalf of its shareholders, they are not subject to shareholder control. Instead, state statutes grant control and decision making authority to the board of directors. The shareholders have the right to elect the directors, but not to tell them how to do their jobs. Nonetheless, directors are fiduciaries, and as such, they have a duty of loyalty. They are obliged to act for the benefit of the corporation rather than for their own personal benefit in all matters connected with their status.

Consider the following:

Corporate officers and directors are not permitted to use their position of trust and confidence to further their private interests. While technically not trustees, they stand in a fiduciary relation to the corporation and its stockholders. A public policy, existing through the years, and derived from a profound knowledge of human characteristics and motives, has established a rule that demands of a corporate officer or director, peremptorily and inexorably, the most scrupulous observance of his duty, not only affirmatively to protect the interests of the corporation committed to his charge, but also to refrain from doing anything that would work injury to the corporation, or to deprive it of profit or advantage which his skill and ability might properly bring to it, or to enable it to make in the reasonable and lawful exercise of its powers. The rule that requires an undivided and unselfish loyalty to the corporation demands that there shall be no conflict between duty and self-interest. The occasions for the determination of honesty, good faith and loyal conduct are many and varied, and no hard and fast rule can be formulated. The standard of loyalty is measured by no fixed scale.

*Guth v. Loft*, 5 A.2d 503, 510 (Del. 1939).

# PFEIFFER v. TOLL
## Court of Chancery of Delaware
### 989 A.2d 683 (2010)

LASTER, VICE CHANCELLOR.

Plaintiff Milton Pfeiffer is a stockholder of nominal defendant Toll Brothers, Inc. ("Toll Brothers" or the "Company"). He brought this action to recover damages suffered by Toll Brothers resulting from alleged insider trading by the defendants. The defendants have moved to dismiss his Verified Amended Shareholder Derivative Complaint (the "Complaint"). I deny the motion.

## I. FACTUAL BACKGROUND

I assume the following facts to be true for purposes of the motion to dismiss. . . .

### A. The Individual Defendants

The individual defendants account for eight of the eleven members of the board of directors of Toll Brothers (the "Board") at the time this action was filed. The eight individual defendants all sold significant amounts of stock during the period from December 2004 through September 2005. The Complaint alleges they did so while in possession of material, non-public information about Toll Brothers' future prospects.

Defendant Robert I. Toll ("R. Toll") and his brother, defendant Bruce E. Toll ("B. Toll"), co-founded the Company's predecessor in 1967. The current entity was incorporated in May 1986 in preparation for an initial public offering in June 1986. R. Toll has served since 1986 as the Company's Chairman and Chief Executive Officer. B. Toll served from 1986 until 1998 as the Company's President and Chief Operating Officer. B. Toll continues to serve as a director and as a paid consultant to the Company.

Defendants Zvi Barzilay and Joel H. Rassman are senior officers of the Company. Barzilay joined Toll Brothers' predecessor in 1980 and has been the Company's Chief Operating Officer since 1998. He has been a director since 1994. Rassman joined Toll Brothers' predecessor in 1984 and has been the Company's Executive Vice President, Treasurer, and Chief Financial Officer since 2002. He has been a director since 1996. I refer to R. Toll, Barzilay, and Rassman as the "Officer

Defendants."

Defendants Robert S. Blank, Richard Braemer, Carl Marbach, and Paul E. Shapiro are outside directors of Toll Brothers. I refer to them as the "Outside Director Defendants." B. Toll is *sui generis*. He is not currently an officer of the Company; nor is he an independent, outside director.

## B. Toll Brothers

Nominal defendant Toll Brothers is a Delaware corporation with its headquarters in Horsham, Pennsylvania. The Company designs, builds, markets, and arranges financing for single-family homes in luxury residential communities throughout the United States. Its shares trade publicly on the New York Stock Exchange under the symbol "TOL."

Toll Brothers' business model turns on developing residential communities, and a key operating metric is the number of communities where Toll Brothers is actively selling homes. Relatedly, a key driver of the Company's future performance is the number of communities where Toll Brothers has received regulatory approval to build homes. Toll Brothers can then start taking orders for homes, which in turn generate the Company's earnings three to four quarters later, when the sales close.

Toll Brothers' senior management closely monitors a range of metrics relating to the Company's core business. The Complaint quotes from Toll Brothers' 2004 annual report, which describes a process by which the entire senior management team reviews in detail three times per year the progress of each community owned or controlled by Toll Brothers. The Complaint alleges that on earnings calls R. Toll referred to written reports comparing community traffic by year and by month, stated that senior management closely monitored the Company's backlog on a weekly basis, and noted that senior management received weekly sales reports from each selling community. In addition to these Company statements, the Complaint quotes an article from the April 8, 2005 issue of *Fortune* that further describes the Company's internal monitoring of core business metrics.

## C. Toll Brothers' Projections Of 20% Net Income Growth

In 2003 and 2004, the luxury residential market experienced booming growth. Toll Brothers rode the wave to record financial performance. Revenues in 2003 increased by 19% over 2002, then increased again in 2004 by another 40% over 2003. Closings in 2003 were up 11% over 2002, then up another 35% in 2004. Backlog in 2003 was up 39% over 2002, then grew by another 44% in 2004. Toll Brothers announced record earnings per share for the fourth quarter of 2004, up 87% over fourth quarter 2003.

Against the backdrop of this parabolic trend, Toll Brothers predicted greater things to come. In the letter to stockholders in the Company's 2004 annual report, Toll Brothers projected "at least 20%" growth in net income for 2006. This projection was based on the Company adding 20 new communities by the end of 2005, thereby increasing its total communities from 220 to 240. The letter to stockholders rejected the notion that there was a "housing bubble" that was about to pop. Signed by R. Toll, B. Toll, and Barzilay, the letter stated: "We strongly disagree: we believe demand is being driven by fundamental demographics and home prices are rising due to the imbalance between supply and demand." The letter explained that Toll Brothers' "luxury brand" was "less affected by rising mortgage rates" and stated that "it should be a long time before rates make a difference to our luxury home buyers."

Throughout the first eleven months of 2005, Toll Brothers reiterated its projection of 20% net income growth in 2006 and again in 2007. The Complaint describes Toll Brothers' public filings and quotes relevant statements. Even as Toll Brothers' operating results continued their parabolic trend, Toll Brothers stood by the projections of 20% net income growth in both 2006 and 2007.

The Complaint describes in detail the Officer Defendants' efforts to buttress the projections against market concern. As the markets became worried about a housing bubble during mid-2005 and began to question the ability of homebuilders to maintain their red-hot performance, the Officer Defendants expressed all the more confidence in Toll Brothers' projections. They asserted that they did not perceive any downturn in the housing market, and they represented that the Company was uniquely positioned to weather any problems that might occur. According to the Officer Defendants, Toll Brothers catered to a niche market of luxury home buyers who were not affected by rising interest rates. They discounted indications that traffic in the Company's communities was slowing and that the rate at which new contracts were signed was declining. They downplayed regulatory delays that were hampering Toll Brothers' efforts to open new communities.

\*    \*    \*

[The court details repeated instances of public statements by Toll officers during 2005 about the company's bright prospects.]

On October 3, 2005, *USA Today* published an article on Toll Brothers. R. Toll was quoted as saying: "We expect 2005 to be 80% up over '04, and we expect an approximately 20% increase for '06 [and in] '07 . . . we expect[] a 20% increase over '06. So that's pretty good moving and grooving." On October 16, *The New York Times* published an article on Toll Brothers. R. Toll was cited as expecting Toll Brothers to "grow by 20 percent for the next two years and then will strive for 15 percent annually after that."

## D. The Downward Revisions In December 2005

On November 8, 2005, Toll Brothers announced its preliminary fourth quarter results for 2005. Although the Company again reported record net income, management's tone was tempered. R. Toll was quoted as saying that despite the Company's record performance for the quarter, "we believe a shortage of selling communities, coupled with some softening of demand in a number of markets, negatively impacted our contract results." He blamed "an increasingly complex regulatory process" for delays in opening new communities and announced that the Company had reached only 230 selling communities by October 31, short of the 237 communities he had projected on August 25. He added that the Company would stay at 230 selling communities through the end of the first quarter of 2006. During management's conference call to discuss the numbers, they cited "softening" demand that was being seen "pretty much across the board." R. Toll stated that foot traffic — people visiting the Company's selling communities — had been "down for about a year."

On December 8, 2005, Toll Brothers reported its 2005 results. The release explained that despite "record fiscal year and fourth-quarter results for earnings, revenues, backlog and contracts," the housing market was "not as robust today as it was throughout 2004." Management lowered its annual growth projections for 2006 to just 0.5% and reiterated that Toll Brothers would stay at 230 selling communities through the first quarter of 2006. This was the first time Toll Brothers modified its projection of 20% net income growth in 2006, and the number fell off a cliff to 0.5%.

The reaction from the media and analysts was profoundly negative. Susquehanna Financial Group issued a report titled, "TOL Creates an Unforgettable Day in the Homebuilder Universe." Susquehanna noted that order growth and selling-communities growth had "disappear[ed]" and that the negative results were "completely unexpected." The *Dallas Morning News* reported that "toxic words crossed the wires: 'softening demand.'"

The Complaint explains that Toll Brothers' actual results for 2006 and 2007 were even more disappointing than the downwardly revised projections anticipated. I do not dwell on the actual results in 2006 and 2007 because the claims in this action must rise or fall based on what the defendants knew in 2005, not whether they accurately foresaw what would happen in 2006 and 2007.

E. The Defendants' Knowledge Prior to December 2005

The Complaint alleges that from December 2004 on, the defendants knew their representations about 2006 and 2007 had no reasonable basis in fact. The defendants admitted in December 2005 that foot traffic was down for "about a year" and fewer prospective customers were visiting Toll Brothers' communities. They also knew that the rate at which new contracts were signed was trending lower throughout 2005, although they attempted to explain it away and even claimed that Toll Brothers caused the trend by "ration[ing] supply to maximize profit." They also knew that the regulatory approval process was becoming increasingly complex and time consuming, such that their projections about the number of selling communities that could be opened were no longer accurate. Without new communities, Toll Brothers could not make sales or achieve projected earnings growth. Because the community approval process takes months, the defendants knew those trends well before they reduced their projections.

F. The Performance of Toll Brothers' Stock Price

During the period of time when Toll Brothers' management was projecting 20% growth in net income for 2006 and 2007, Toll Brothers' common stock significantly outperformed the S&P Homebuilders Index, a peer index of large, national homebuilders. Prior to late 2004, when Toll Brothers began to make its 20% projections, Toll Brothers traded in line with the index. During the time that Toll

Brothers was projecting 20% growth in net income for 2006 and 2007, the trading price of Toll Brothers' stock more than doubled, from $28.50 in December 2004 to over $58.00 in July 2005.

During this same period, and particularly during the summer and fall of 2005, the defendants sold shares. The eight defendants collectively sold 14 million shares for proceeds of over $615 million. Barzilay sold 92% of his shares. Blank sold 93% of his shares. Shapiro sold 84% of his shares. Marbach sold 82% of his shares. Rassman sold 68% of his shares. Braemer sold 52% of his shares. B. Toll and R. Toll, who during their long tenures as co-founders of the Company had not previously sold significant amounts of stock, respectively sold 37% and 29% of their shares. These trades were inconsistent with the past trading patterns and are suspicious in timing and amount.

## II. LEGAL ANALYSIS

The Complaint sets forth two counts. Count I asserts a claim for breach of fiduciary duty under *Brophy v. Cities Service Co.*, 31 Del. Ch. 241, 70 A.2d 5 (Del. Ch. 1949), which recognized the right of a Delaware corporation to recover from its fiduciaries for harm caused by insider trading. Count II asserts a generalized claim for contribution and indemnification. The defendants (including Toll Brothers as nominal defendant) have moved to dismiss these claims. First, all defendants contend that the Complaint fails to plead demand futility for purposes of Court of Chancery Rule 23.1. Second, all defendants contend that the statute of limitations bars any claims based on the individual defendants' stock sales. Third, the Outside Director Defendants argue that a claim for breach of fiduciary duty has not been pled as to them. Finally, and most boldly, the defendants argue that Delaware should abandon its traditional role of policing against breaches of the duty of loyalty by fiduciaries of Delaware corporations, at least where the underlying wrong involves insider trading, and that *Brophy* is an outdated precedent that should be rejected.

A. The Complaint Adequately Pleads Demand Futility.

[The court concludes that demand is futile in this case. The majority of the directors were also named defendants in a federal insider trading case involving the same facts. Therefore, a decision to proceed with this suit would conflict with their ability to defend themselves against federal liability.]

\* \* \*

B. The Complaint Adequately Pleads A Basis For Tolling The Statute Of Limitations.

. . . Absent a basis for tolling, this action was not timely filed.

I am satisfied for pleadings purposes that a basis for tolling exists. This Court has stated:

Under the theory of equitable tolling, the statute of limitations is tolled for claims of wrongful self-dealing, even in the absence of actual fraudulent concealment, where a plaintiff reasonably relies on the competence and good faith of a fiduciary. Underlying this doctrine is the idea that even an attentive and diligent investor may rely, in complete propriety, upon the good faith of fiduciaries.

*Weiss v. Swanson*, 948 A.2d 433, 451 (Del. Ch. 2008). Moreover, in a well-known decision issued last year, Vice Chancellor Strine held:

The obvious purpose of the equitable tolling doctrine is to ensure that fiduciaries cannot use their own success at concealing their misconduct as a method of immunizing themselves from accountability for their wrong-doing.

\* \* \*

Many of the worst acts of fiduciary misconduct have involved frauds that personally benefited insiders as an indirect effect of directly inflating the corporation's stock price by the artificial means of cooking the books. To allow fiduciaries who engaged in illegal conduct to wield a limitations defense against stockholders who relied in good faith on those fiduciaries when their disclosures provided no fair inquiry notice of claims would be inequitable.

*In re Am. Int'l Group Inc.*, 965 A.2d 763, 813 (Del. Ch. 2009) (hereinafter *"A/G"*).

In discussing Toll Brothers' prospects from December 2004 until December 2005, senior management remained positive and consistently reaffirmed their growth projections. . . .

It was not until December 8, 2005, that management officially abandoned the projection of 20% growth that forms the centerpiece of the Complaint. I hold that the statute was equitably tolled until December 8, 2005. This action was thus timely filed.

C. The Complaint Adequately Pleads That The Defendants Engaged In Insider Trading.

The Outside Director Defendants argue that the Complaint fails to state a claim against them for breach of the duty of loyalty based on insider trading. I disagree.

"[A] plaintiff seeking to prevail on a *Brophy* claim ultimately must show that: 1) the corporate fiduciary possessed material, nonpublic company information; and 2) the corporate fiduciary used that information improperly by making trades because she was motivated, in whole or in part, by the substance of that information." *In re Oracle Corp.*, 867 A.2d 904, 934 (Del. Ch. 2004) (hereinafter *"Oracle"*), aff'd, 872 A.2d 960 (Del. 2005). . . .

\* \* \*

When a plaintiff alleges that insiders traded on internal information inconsistent with projections previously provided to the market, the complaint must allege that the defendants possessed information about the company's performance that created a substantial likelihood of an extreme departure from projected results. *Oracle*, 867 A.2d at 939–40. . . .

\* \* \*

The Outside Director Defendants argue that the Complaint does not plead facts showing that they "actually had knowledge of the purported material non-public information." Def. Op. Br. at 23. Even when Rule 9(b) applies — and here it does not —" knowledge or other condition of mind of a person can be averred generally." Ct. Ch. R. 9(b). Outside of the procedural context of Rule 23.1, a complaint need only plead a reasonable basis from which knowledge can be inferred.

The Complaint alleges that beginning in October 2004, Toll Brothers consistently and repeatedly projected 20% growth in net income during 2006 and 2007. The Complaint credibly alleges that based on Toll Brothers' own statements about the limits of the Company's visibility into its future prospects, and based on internal and closely monitored metrics, the defendants knew Toll Brothers could not meet those projections. The Complaint alleges that in November and December 2005 the Officer Defendants finally came clean to the public markets and admitted that throughout 2005 their internal metrics had been trending down.

The Complaint further alleges that to mollify market concern, the Officer Defendants expressed all the more confidence in their projections, engaging in behavior that more closely resembled unabashed and unrestrained cheerleading. The Complaint describes statements by R. Toll to the effect that rising interest rates did not concern him, because the Company had continued to "blast and rock and roll" in other periods of interest rate hikes. At another point, when asked about substantial short-selling of Toll Brothers' stock, R. Toll responded: "The shorts are going to get crushed. You ain't seen nothing yet." R. Toll described the stock as a "fabulous" and "tremendous" buy at the same time he was unloading large blocks of his shares. He dismissed "bubble mania" and described Toll Brothers' business as "a match made in heaven."

A senior executive can be bullish about his company without sounding like he is auditioning to replace Jim Cramer on *Mad Money*. Juxtaposed against the allegations about the underlying trends in Toll Brothers' business, these statements are striking. Coupled with massive sales of securities, they amount to a red flag. They are sufficient to plead a claim for breach of fiduciary duty both under *Oracle* and *Malone*.

I recognize the need to distinguish between the Officer Defendants (along with B. Toll who signed on to the 2004 annual letter to stockholders) and the Outside Director Defendants. Several factors combine to convince me that knowledge and use of inside information is adequately pled under the plaintiff-friendly Rule 12(b)(6) standard. Principal among these factors is the nature of the information in question. The Complaint does not contend that outside directors should have uncovered financial fraud, second-guessed technical accounting judgments, or known about concerns expressed by low-level employees within the organization. The Complaint turns on information about the core operations of the Company and the basis for projections that it consistently provided to the markets for over a year.

The projections were issued in preliminary earnings releases, final earnings releases, Form 10-Qs, and the 2004 Form 10-K. Senior management discussed the projections on earnings calls, during media appearances, and in interviews. The Complaint alleges that the projections were false for reasons that likewise relate to the core operations of the Company. Toll Brothers itself has described its focus on key metrics — like traffic through its communities, signed contracts, and the number of selling communities. Two of the Outside Director Defendants served on the audit committee, which had specific responsibility under its charter for earnings releases and earnings guidance.

Under Section 141(a) of the General Corporation Law, directors have the statutory power *and responsibility* to direct and oversee the business and affairs of the corporation. 8 *Del. C.* § 141(a). It would afford an ostrich-like immunity to directors not to grant the plaintiff a Rule 12(b)(6) inference that the Outside Director Defendants knew about core information of this type.

\*     \*     \*

I also regard the trades made by the Outside Director Defendants as sufficiently unusual in timing and amount to support a pleading-stage inference that the sellers took advantage of confidential corporate information not yet available to the public to unload significant blocks of shares before the market's view of Toll Brothers' prospects dramatically changed. I thus find that the Complaint supports an inference that all of the individual defendants, including the Outside Director Defendants, made trades that were motivated, in whole or in part, by their knowledge of Toll Brothers' prospects. *Oracle*, 867 A.2d at 934; *accord AIG*, 965 A.2d at 800.

I reject the Outside Director Defendants' contention that inside information about Toll Brothers' true prospects was not material. . . .

I also reject the Outside Director Defendants' suggestion that they could have done a better job at insider trading. They point out that they sold their shares at a weighted-average price more than 20% below Toll Brothers' peak, arguing that if they were seeking to exploit inside information, "they presumably would have timed their sales to maximize their profits." Def. Op. Br. at 30. The fact that a defendant could have misused inside information more effectively does not defeat an otherwise valid inference of insider trading. *AIG*, 965 A.2d at 801. . . .

I therefore hold that the Complaint states a claim under *Brophy* against all of the defendants, including the Outside Director Defendants. This does not mean, of course, that the plaintiff will succeed on his claim. The Rule 12(b)(6) inference that I have granted will not aid the plaintiff at later stages of this litigation. He must ultimately prove his case, and the defendants (and particularly the Outside Director Defendants) will likely have strong defenses. *See, e.g.*, 8 *Del. C.* § 141(e).

D. *Brophy* Remains Good Law.

Having rejected the defendants' other arguments for dismissal, I must confront their assertion that *Brophy* is no longer good law. The defendants characterize *Brophy* as a persistent anachronism from a time before the current federal insider trading regime, when this Court felt compelled to address insider trading because of the absence of any other remedy. The defendants thus view *Brophy* as a well-meaning stretch that is no longer needed and, worse, conflicts with federal policies and enforcement mechanisms. These are views I do not share.

*Brophy* was not a one-off decision. Ten years before *Brophy*, the Delaware Supreme Court issued its iconic warning to fiduciaries who selfishly misappropriate corporate assets, including confidential corporate information, for personal gain. *Guth v. Loft, Inc.*, 23 Del. Ch. 255, 5 A.2d 503 (Del. 1939). The *Guth* Court stated:

> Corporate officers and directors are not permitted to use their position of trust and confidence to further their private interests. While technically not trustees, they stand in a fiduciary relation to the corporation and its stockholders. A public policy, existing through the years, and derived from a profound knowledge of human characteristics and motives, has established a rule that demands of a corporate officer or director, peremptorily and inexorably, the most scrupulous observance of his duty, not only affirmatively to protect the interests of the corporation committed to his charge, but also to refrain from doing anything that would work injury to the corporation, or to deprive it of profit or advantage which his skill and ability might properly bring to it, or to enable it to make in the reasonable and lawful exercise of its powers. The rule that requires an undivided and unselfish loyalty to the corporation demands that there shall be no conflict between duty and self-interest. The occasions for the determination of honesty, good faith and loyal conduct are many and varied, and no hard and fast rule can be formulated. The standard of loyalty is measured by no fixed scale.

> If an officer or director of a corporation, in violation of his duty as such, acquires gain or advantage for himself, the law charges the interest so acquired with a trust for the benefit of the corporation, at its election, while it denies to the betrayer all benefit and profit. The rule, inveterate and uncompromising in its rigidity, does not rest upon the narrow ground of injury or damage to the corporation resulting from a betrayal of confidence, but upon a broader foundation of a wise public policy that, for the purpose of removing all temptation, extinguishes all possibility of profit flowing from a breach of the confidence imposed by the fiduciary relation. Given the relation between the parties, a certain result follows; and a constructive trust is the remedial device through which precedence of self is compelled to give way to the stern demands of loyalty.

*Id.* at 510. Over seventy years later, *Guth v. Loft* remains the seminal Delaware decision addressing the duty of loyalty.

In *Brophy*, Chancellor Harrington relied on these foundational principles in declining to dismiss a derivative claim brought against the executive secretary of one of the directors of Cities Service Company. 70 A.2d at 7–8. The secretary allegedly knew that Cities Service planned to make open-market purchases that would likely boost its stock price. The secretary purchased shares for his personal account in advance of the corporate repurchase and later sold the shares for a profit after the market price rose. *Id.* at 7. Chancellor Harrington recognized that "in the absence of special circumstances, corporate officers and directors may purchase and sell its capital stock at will, and without any liability to the corporation." *Id.* at 8. He nevertheless held that because the secretary acquired knowledge about the corporation's plans in the course of his employment, *i.e.* it was confidential corporate information, "the application of general principles would seem to require the conclusion that he cannot use that information for his own personal gain." *Id.* In broad language, Chancellor Harrington rejected the argument that the corporation suffered no harm as a result of the secretary's activities. He explained: "In equity, when the breach of a confidential relation by an employee is relied on and an accounting for any resulting profits is sought, loss to the corporation need not be charged in the complaint." *Id.* He continued: "Public policy will not permit an employee occupying a position of trust and confidence toward[s] his employer to abuse that relation to his own profit, regardless of whether his employer suffers a loss." *Id.*

In the ensuing decades, the Delaware Supreme Court has cited *Brophy* approvingly when discussing how the duty of loyalty governs the misuse of confidential corporate information by fiduciaries.[13] This Court has repeatedly cited and applied it.[14]

---

[13] [4] *See Oberly v. Kirby*, 592 A.2d 445, 463 (Del. 1991) ("[T]he absence of specific damage to a beneficiary is not the sole test for determining disloyalty by one occupying a fiduciary position. It is an act of disloyalty for a fiduciary to profit personally from the use of information secured in a confidential relationship, even if such profit or advantage is not gained at the expense of the fiduciary. The result is nonetheless one of unjust enrichment which will not be countenanced by a Court of Equity.") (citing *Brophy*); *Mills Acquisition Co. v. Macmillan, Inc.*, 559 A.2d 1261, 1283 (Del. 1989) (citing *Brophy* as supporting duty of fair dealing by "those who are privy to material information obtained in the course of representing corporate interests" and holding that "[a]t a minimum, this rule dictates that fiduciaries, corporate or otherwise, may not use superior information or knowledge to mislead others in the performance of their own fiduciary obligations"); *Weinberger v. UOP, Inc.*, 457 A.2d 701, 711 (Del. 1983) ("[O]ne possessing superior knowledge may not mislead any stockholder by use of corporate information to which the latter is not privy. Delaware has long imposed this duty even upon persons who are not corporate officers or directors, but who nonetheless are privy to matters of interest or significance to their company.") (citing *Brophy*); *Singer v. Magnavox Co.*, 380 A.2d 969, 977 (Del. 1977) (citing *Brophy* as one of many precedents enforcing the "fiduciary obligation of honesty, loyalty, good faith and fairness"), *overruled on other grounds by Weinberger*, 457 A.2d at 715; *see also Adams v. Jankouskas*, 452 A.2d 148, 152 (Del. 1982) (citing *Brophy* as authority for imposing constructive trust "when a defendant's fraudulent, unfair or unconscionable conduct causes him to be unjustly enriched at the expense of another to whom he owed some duty").

[14] [5] *See, e.g., AIG*, 965 A.2d at 800 ("A breach of fiduciary duty claim premised on insider trading, also known as a *Brophy* claim, arises where 1) the corporate fiduciary possessed material, nonpublic company information; and 2) the corporate fiduciary used that information improperly by making trades because she was motivated, in whole or in part, by the substance of that information.") (internal quotations and citations omitted); *Latesco, L.P. v. Wayport, Inc.*, 2009 Del. Ch. LEXIS 145, 2009 WL 2246793, at *6 (Del. Ch. July 24, 2009) ("A *Brophy* claim is fundamentally derivative in nature, because it arises out of the misuse of corporate property — that is, confidential information — by a fiduciary of the corporation, for the benefit of the fiduciary and to the detriment of the corporation.") (citing *Brophy*); *Guttman*, 823 A.2d at 505 ("Delaware law has long held . . . that directors who misuse company information to profit at the expense of innocent buyers of their stock should disgorge their profits.") (citing *Brophy*); *Rattner*, 2003 Del. Ch. LEXIS 103, 2003 WL 22284323, at *10–11 ("Delaware has recognized a cause of action against directors who abuse their knowledge of a corporation's private information at the expense of unwitting purchasers of their stock. . . . [C]ritically, it must be shown that each sale by each individual defendant was entered into and completed on the basis of, and because of, adverse material non-public information.") (internal quotations omitted) (citing *Brophy*); *Rosenberg v.*

*   *   *

4. *Brophy* Serves Important Delaware Public Policies And Is Aligned With Federal Law.

The duty of loyalty has paramount importance under Delaware law. Delaware's consistent corporate philosophy has been to grant deference to boards in exercising their authority to direct and oversee the business and affairs of the corporation, balanced by assiduous protection of the stockholders' right to elect new directors and meaningful enforcement of fiduciary duties, with particular emphasis on the duty of loyalty. Section 102(b)(7) embodies this policy by precluding a certificate of incorporation from purporting to eliminate or limit the personal liability of a director "[f]or any breach of the director's duty of loyalty to the corporation or its stockholders," "for acts or omissions not in good faith or which involve intentional misconduct or a knowing violation of law," or "for any transaction from which the director derived an improper personal benefit." 8 *Del C.* § 102(b)(7). Indemnification is similarly barred unless the individual "acted in good faith and in a manner the person reasonably believed to be in or not opposed to the best interests of the corporation." *Id.* at §§ 145(a) & (b). Our case law has consistently stressed the importance of the duty of loyalty.[15]

Maintaining *Brophy* as a cause of action fulfills Delaware's strong public policy of policing against loyalty violations by fiduciaries. It serves to protect the corporation's interest in its confidential information and to ensure that the information is not misused for private gain. *Latesco*, 2009 Del. Ch. LEXIS 145, 2009 WL 2246793, at *6 . . . . Eliminating the remedy would be equivalent to transferring ownership of information from the corporation to its fiduciaries, which is contrary to Delaware law.

---

*Oolie*, 1989 Del. Ch. LEXIS 152, 1989 WL 122084, at *3 (Del. Ch. Oct. 16, 1989) ("The principle, as announced in *Brophy*, is that, if a person in a confidential or fiduciary position, in breach of his duty, uses his knowledge to make a profit for himself, he is accountable for such profit.") (internal quotations omitted) (citing *Brophy*); *Stepak v. Ross*, 1985 Del. Ch. LEXIS 508, 1985 WL 21137, at *5 (Del. Ch. Sept. 5, 1985) ("It is, of course, clear that Warner is entitled to recover all insider profits made by the individual defendants if the individual defendants breached their fiduciary duties to Warner.") (citing *Brophy*); *see also Deloitte LLP v. Flanagan*, 2009 Del. Ch. LEXIS 220, 2009 WL 5200657, at *7-8 (Del. Ch. Dec. 29, 2009) (applying *Brophy*-like reasoning in partnership context); *Zimmerman*, 2005 Del. Ch. LEXIS 135, 2005 WL 2266566, at *5, *7-8 (applying *Brophy*-like reasoning for insider-trading claims against directors).

[15] [11] *See, e.g., Stone v. Ritter*, 911 A.2d 362, 370 (Del. 2006) (describing the directors' duty of loyalty as an onerous one); *Venhill Ltd. ex rel. Stallkamp v. Hillman*, 2008 Del. Ch. LEXIS 67, 2008 WL 2270488, at *30 n.104 (Del. Ch. June 3, 2008) (noting that the duty of loyalty rests "upon a broader foundation of a wise public policy that, for purposes of removing all temptation, extinguishes all possibility of profit flowing from the breach of confidence imposed by the fiduciary relation"); *In re Primedia Inc. Deriv. Litig.*, 910 A.2d 248, 262 (Del. Ch. 2006) ("Concerns of equity and deterrence justify loosening normally stringent requirements of causation and damages when a breach of the duty of loyalty is shown.") (internal citations omitted); *Technicorp Int'l II, Inc. v. Johnston*, 2000 Del. Ch. LEXIS 81, 2000 WL 713750, at *5 (Del. Ch. May 31, 2000) ("[T]he duty of loyalty of a director [imposes] a special obligation upon a director in any of his relationships with the corporation."); *Boyer v. Wilmington Materials, Inc.*, 754 A.2d 881, 906 (Del. Ch. 1999) (discussing the "strict imposition of penalties under Delaware law . . . designed to discourage disloyalty").

Delaware is of course mindful of the fact that our national and state governments share jurisdiction over corporations. . . .

Contrary to the defendants' assertions, the standards applied under *Brophy* do not conflict with the federal securities laws. "Delaware case law makes the same policy judgment as federal law does, which is that insider trading claims depend importantly on proof that the selling defendants acted with *scienter*." *Guttman*, 823 A.2d at 505. The elements of a *Brophy* claim similarly "more or less track the key requirements to recover against an insider under federal law." *Oracle*, 867 A.2d at 934. I thus conclude that the "reasoned application" of *Brophy* that was articulated in *AIG, Oracle*, and *Guttman* is "not out of step with federal law." *Oracle*, 867 A.2d at 929, 932. I decline the defendants' invitation to reject *Brophy*.

**E. The Contribution And Indemnification Claim Can Proceed.**

\* \* \*

**F. The Parties Will Confer Regarding Further Proceedings.**

Although I have denied the defendants' motion to dismiss, I do not believe that this case should proceed with full-blown merits discovery, and certainly not in a manner that is duplicative of the Federal Securities Action. It would be counter-intuitive if an action such as this one, which exists to recover for harm imposed on the corporation, was permitted to proceed in a way that increased the burden on the corporation. At a minimum, sensible coordination with the Federal Securities Action is warranted. A stay of this action pending the litigation of the Federal Securities Action also could make sense. Rather than deciding this issue without input from the parties, I direct that they confer on how to approach this case prudently in light of its purpose. If the parties cannot agree on a fitting solution, the defendants should take the lead in seeking my assistance by filing an appropriate motion, to which the plaintiff may respond.

## III. CONCLUSION

For the foregoing reasons, I deny the defendants' motions to dismiss. IT IS SO ORDERED.

## 2.  The Corporate Opportunity Doctrine

One frequent context in which the duty of loyalty is litigated is when corporate officers and directors engage in business activities outside of their corporate jobs. Although officers and directors must avoid conflicts of interest in carrying out their responsibilities to their corporations, courts have acknowledged that these individuals do have the right to engage in separate business activities. What limits are there on the extent to which officers and directors may pursue business opportunities?

# BROZ v. CELLULAR INFORMATION SYSTEMS, INC.
Supreme Court of Delaware
673 A.2d 148 (1996)

VEASEY, CHIEF JUSTICE:

In this appeal, we consider the application of the doctrine of corporate opportunity. The Court of Chancery decided that the defendant, a corporate director, breached his fiduciary duty by not formally presenting to the corporation an opportunity which had come to the director individually and independent of the director's relationship with the corporation. Here the opportunity was not one in which the corporation in its current mode had an interest or which it had the financial ability to acquire, but, under the unique circumstances here, that mode was subject to change by virtue of the impending acquisition of the corporation by another entity.

We conclude that, although a corporate director may be shielded from liability by offering to the corporation an opportunity which has come to the director independently and individually, the failure of the director to present the opportunity does not necessarily result in the improper usurpation of a corporate opportunity. We further conclude that, if the corporation is a target or potential target of an acquisition by another company which has an interest and ability to entertain the opportunity, the director of the target company does not have a fiduciary duty to present the opportunity to the target company. Accordingly, the judgment of the Court of Chancery is *Reversed.*

## I. *The Contentions of the Parties and the Decision Below*

Robert F. Broz ("Broz") is the President and sole stockholder of RFB Cellular, Inc.("RFBC"), a Delaware corporation engaged in the business of providing cellular telephone service in the Midwestern United States. At the time of the conduct at issue in this appeal, Broz was also a member of the board of directors of plaintiff below-appellee, Cellular Information Systems, Inc. ("CIS"). CIS is a publicly held Delaware corporation and a competitor of RFBC.

The conduct before the Court involves the purchase by Broz of a cellular telephone service license for the benefit of RFBC. The license in question, known as the Michigan-2 Rural Service Area Cellular License ("Michigan-2"), is issued by the Federal Communications Commission ("FCC") and entitles its holder to provide cellular telephone service to a portion of northern Michigan. CIS brought an action against Broz and RFBC for equitable relief, contending that the purchase of this license by Broz constituted a usurpation of a corporate opportunity properly belonging to CIS, irrespective of whether or not CIS was interested in the Michigan-2 opportunity at the time it was offered to Broz.

The principal basis for the contention of CIS is that PriCellular, Inc. ("PriCellular"), another cellular communications company which was contemporaneously engaged in an acquisition of CIS, was interested in the Michigan-2 opportunity. CIS contends that, in determining whether the Michigan-2 opportunity rightfully belonged to CIS, Broz was required to consider the interests of PriCellular insofar as those interests would come into alignment with those of CIS as a result of PriCellular's acquisition plans.

\* \* \*

## II. *Facts*

Broz has been the President and sole stockholder of RFBC since 1992. RFBC owns and operates an FCC license area, known as the Michigan-4 Rural Service Area Cellular License ("Michigan-4"). The license entitles RFBC to provide cellular telephone service to a portion of rural Michigan. Although Broz' efforts have been devoted primarily to the business operations of RFBC, he also served as an outside director of CIS at the time of the events at issue in this case. CIS was at all times fully aware of Broz' relationship with RFBC and the obligations incumbent upon him by virtue of that relationship.

In April of 1994, Mackinac Cellular Corp. ("Mackinac") sought to divest itself of Michigan-2 the license area immediately adjacent to Michigan-4. To this end, Mackinac contacted Daniels & Associates ("Daniels") and arranged for the broker- age firm to seek potential purchasers for Michigan-2. In compiling a list of prospects, Daniels included RFBC as a likely candidate. In May of 1994, David Rhodes, a representative of Daniels, contacted Broz and broached the subject of RFBC's possible acquisition of Michigan-2. Broz later signed a confidentiality agreement at the request of Mackinac, and received the offering materials pertaining to Michigan-2.

Michigan-2 was not, however, offered to CIS. Apparently, Daniels did not consider CIS to be a viable purchaser for Michigan-2 in light of CIS' recent financial difficulties. The record shows that, at the time Michigan-2 was offered to Broz, CIS had recently emerged from lengthy and contentious Chapter 11 proceedings. Pursuant to the Chapter 11 Plan of Reorganization, CIS entered into a loan agreement that substantially impaired the company's ability to undertake new acquisitions or to incur new debt. In fact, CIS would have been unable to purchase Michigan-2 without the approval of its creditors.

The CIS reorganization resulted from the failure of CIS' rather ambitious plans for expansion. From 1989 onward, CIS had embarked on a series of cellular license acquisitions. In 1992, however, CIS' financing failed, necessitating the liquidation of the company's holdings and reduction of the company's total indebtedness. During the period from early 1992 until the time of CIS' emergence from bankruptcy in 1994, CIS divested itself of some fifteen separate cellular license systems. CIS contracted to sell four additional license areas on May 27, 1994, leaving CIS with only five remaining license areas, all of which were outside of the Midwest.

On June 13, 1994, following a meeting of the CIS board, Broz spoke with CIS' Chief Executive Officer, Richard Treibick ("Treibick"), concerning his interest in acquiring Michigan-2. Treibick communicated to Broz that CIS was not interested in Michigan-2. Treibick further stated that he had been made aware of the Michigan-2 opportunity prior to the conversation with Broz, and that any offer to acquire Michigan-2 was rejected. After the commencement of the PriCellular tender offer, in August of 1994, Broz contacted another CIS director, Peter Schiff ("Schiff"), to discuss the possible acquisition of Michigan-2 by RFBC. Schiff, like Treibick, indicated that CIS had neither the wherewithal nor the inclination to purchase Michigan-2. In late September of 1994, Broz also contacted Stanley Bloch ("Bloch"), a director and counsel for CIS, to request that Bloch represent RFBC in its dealings with Mackinac. Bloch agreed to represent RFBC, and, like Schiff and Treibick, expressed his belief that CIS was not at all interested in the transaction. Ultimately, all the CIS directors testified at trial that, had Broz inquired at that time, they each would have expressed the opinion that CIS was not interested in Michigan-2.

On June 28, 1994, following various overtures from PriCellular concerning an acquisition of CIS six CIS directors entered into agreements with PriCellular to sell their shares in CIS at a price of $2.00 per share. These agreements were contingent upon, *inter alia*, the consummation of a PriCellular tender offer for all CIS shares at the same price. Pursuant to their agreements with PriCellular, the CIS directors also entered into a "standstill" agreement which prevented the directors from engaging in any transaction outside the regular course of CIS' business or incurring any new liabilities until the close of the PriCellular tender offer. On August 2, 1994, PriCellular commenced a tender offer for all outstanding shares of CIS at $2.00 per share. The PriCellular tender offer mirrored the standstill agreements entered into by the CIS directors.

PriCellular's tender offer was originally scheduled to close on September 16, 1994. At the time the tender offer was launched, however, the source of the $106,000,000 in financing required to consummate the transaction was still in doubt. PriCellular originally planned to structure the transaction around bank loans. When this financing fell through, PriCellular resorted to a junk bond offering. PriCellular's financing difficulties generated a great deal of concern among the CIS insiders whether the tender offer was, in fact, viable. Financing difficulties ultimately caused PriCellular to delay the closing date of the tender offer from September 16, 1994 until October 14, 1994 and then again until November 9, 1994.

On August 6, September 6 and September 21, 1994, Broz submitted written offers to Mackinac for the purchase of Michigan-2. During this time period, PriCellular also began negotiations with Mackinac to arrange an option for the purchase of Michigan-2. PriCellular's interest in Michigan-2 was fully disclosed to CIS' chief executive, Treibick, who did not express any interest in Michigan-2, and was actually incredulous that PriCellular would want to acquire the license. Nevertheless, CIS was fully aware that PriCellular and Broz were bidding for Michigan-2 and did not interpose CIS in this bidding war.

In late September of 1994, PriCellular reached agreement with Mackinac on an option to purchase Michigan-2. The exercise price of the option agreement was set at $6.7 million, with the option remaining in force until December 15, 1994. Pursuant to the agreement, the right to exercise the option was not transferrable to any party other than a subsidiary of PriCellular. Therefore, it could not have been transferred to CIS. The agreement further provided that Mackinac was free to sell Michigan-2 to any party who was willing to exceed the exercise price of the Mackinac-PriCellular option contract by at least $500,000. On November 14, 1994, Broz agreed to pay Mackinac $7.2 million for the Michigan-2 license, thereby meeting the terms of the option agreement. An asset purchase agreement was thereafter executed by Mackinac and RFBC.

Nine days later, on November 23, 1994, PriCellular completed its financing and closed its tender offer for CIS. Prior to that point, PriCellular owned no equity interest in CIS. Subsequent to the consummation of the PriCellular tender offer for CIS, members of the CIS board of directors, including Broz, were discharged and replaced with a slate of PriCellular nominees. On March 2, 1995, this action was commenced by CIS in the Court of Chancery.

*   *   *

### IV. *Application of the Corporate Opportunity Doctrine*

The doctrine of corporate opportunity represents but one species of the broad fiduciary duties assumed by a corporate director or officer. A corporate fiduciary agrees to place the interests of the corporation before his or her own in appropriate circumstances. In light of the diverse and often competing obligations faced by directors and officers, however, the corporate opportunity doctrine arose as a means of defining the parameters of fiduciary duty in instances of potential conflict. The classic statement of the doctrine is derived from the venerable case of *Guth v. Loft, Inc.*, 5 A.2d 503 (Del. 1939). In *Guth*, this Court held that:

> if there is presented to a corporate officer or director a business opportunity which the corporation is financially able to undertake, is, from its nature, in the line of the corporation's business and is of practical advantage to it, is one in which the corporation has an interest or a reasonable expectancy, and, by embracing the opportunity, the self-interest of the officer or director will be brought into conflict with that of the corporation, the law will not permit him to seize the opportunity for himself.

*Guth*, 5 A.2d at 510–11.

The corporate opportunity doctrine, as delineated by *Guth* and its progeny, holds that a corporate officer or director may not take a business opportunity for his own if:(1) the corporation is financially able to exploit the opportunity; (2) the opportunity is within the corporation's line of business; (3) the corporation has an interest or expectancy in the opportunity; and (4) by taking the opportunity for his own, the corporate fiduciary will thereby be placed in a position inimical to his duties to the corporation. The Court in *Guth* also derived a corollary which states that a director or officer may take a corporate opportunity if: (1) the opportunity is presented to the director or officer in his individual and not his corporate capacity; (2) the opportunity is not essential to the corporation; (3) the corporation holds no interest or expectancy in the opportunity; and (4) the director or officer has not wrongfully employed the resources of the corporation in pursuing or exploiting the opportunity. *Guth*, 5 A.2d at 509.

Thus, the contours of this doctrine are well established. It is important to note, however, that the tests enunciated in *Guth* and subsequent cases provide guidelines to be considered by a reviewing court in balancing the equities of an individual case.

No one factor is dispositive and all factors must be taken into account insofar as they are applicable. Cases involving a claim of usurpation of a corporate opportunity range over a multitude of factual settings. Hard and fast rules are not easily crafted to deal with such an array of complex situations. As this Court noted in *Johnston v. Greene*, Del. Supr., 35 Del. Ch. 479, 121 A.2d 919 (1956), the determination of "[w]hether or not [a]director has appropriated for himself something that in fairness should belong to [the]corporation is 'a factual question to be decided by reasonable inference from objective facts.' " *Id.* at 923 (quoting *Guth*, 5 A.2d at 513*).* In the instant case, we find that the facts do not support the conclusion that Broz misappropriated a corporate opportunity.

We note at the outset that Broz became aware of the Michigan-2 opportunity in his individual and not his corporate capacity. As the Court of Chancery found, "Broz did not misuse proprietary information that came to him in a corporate capacity nor did he otherwise use any power he might have over the governance of the corporation to advance his own interests." 663 A.2d at 1185. This fact is not the subject of serious dispute. In fact, it is clear from the record that Mackinac did not consider CIS a viable candidate for the acquisition of Michigan-2. Accordingly, Mackinac did not offer the property to CIS. In this factual posture, many of the fundamental concerns undergirding the law of corporate opportunity are not present (e.g., misappropriation of the corporation's proprietary information). The burden imposed upon Broz to show adherence to his fiduciary duties to CIS is thus lessened to some extent. *See Science Accessories Corporation.*, 425 A.2d at 964 (holding that because opportunity to purchase new technology was "an 'outside' opportunity not available to SAC, defendants' failure to disclose the concept to SAC and their taking it [for] themselves for purposes of competing with SAC cannot be found to be in breach of any agency fiduciary duty"). Nevertheless, this fact is not dispositive. The determination of whether a particular fiduciary has usurped a corporate opportunity necessitates a careful examination of the circumstances, giving due credence to the factors enunciated in *Guth* and subsequent cases.

We turn now to an analysis of the factors relied on by the trial court. First, we find that CIS was not financially capable of exploiting the Michigan-2 opportunity. Although the Court of Chancery concluded otherwise, we hold that this finding was not supported by the evidence. *Levitt*, 287 A.2d at 673. The record shows that CIS was in a precarious financial position at the time Mackinac presented the Michigan-2 opportunity to Broz. Having recently emerged from lengthy and contentious bankruptcy proceedings, CIS was not in a position to commit capital to the acquisition of new assets. Further, the loan agreement entered into by CIS and its creditors severely limited the discretion of CIS as to the acquisition of new assets and substantially restricted the ability of CIS to incur new debt.

The Court of Chancery based its contrary finding on the fact that PriCellular had purchased an option to acquire CIS' bank debt. Thus, the court reasoned, PriCellular was in a position to exercise that option and then waive any unfavorable restrictions that would stand in the way of a CIS acquisition of Michigan-2. The trial court, however, disregarded the fact that PriCellular's own financial situation was not particularly stable. PriCellular was unable to finance the acquisition of CIS through conventional bank loans and was forced to use the more risky mechanism of a junk bond offering to raise the required capital. Thus, the court's statement that

"PriCellular had other sources of financing to permit the funding of that purchase" is clearly not free from dispute. Moreover, as discussed *infra*, the fact that PriCellular had available sources of financing is immaterial to the analysis. At the time that Broz was required to decide whether to accept the Michigan-2 opportunity, PriCellular had not yet acquired CIS, and any plans to do so were wholly speculative. Thus, contrary to the Court of Chancery's finding, Broz was not obligated to consider the contingency of a PriCellular acquisition of CIS and the related contingency of PriCellular thereafter waiving restrictions on the CIS bank debt. Broz was required to consider the facts only as they existed at the time he determined to accept the Mackinac offer and embark on his efforts to bring the transaction to fruition. *Guth*, 5 A.2d at 513.

Second, while it may be said with some certainty that the Michigan-2 opportunity was within CIS' line of business, it is not equally clear that CIS had a cognizable interest or expectancy in the license.[16] Under the third factor laid down by this Court in *Guth*, for an opportunity to be deemed to belong to the fiduciary's corporation, the corporation must have an interest or expectancy in that opportunity. As this Court stated in *Johnston*, 121 A.2d at 924, "[f]or the corporation to have an actual or expectant interest in any specific property, there must be some tie between that property and the nature of the corporate business." Despite the fact that the nature of the Michigan-2 opportunity was historically close to the core operations of CIS, changes were in process. At the time the opportunity was presented, CIS was actively engaged in the process of divesting its cellular license holdings. CIS' articulated business plan did not involve any new acquisitions. Further, as indicated by the testimony of the entire CIS board, the Michigan- 2 license would not have been of interest to CIS even absent CIS' financial difficulties and CIS' then current desire to liquidate its cellular license holdings. Thus, CIS had no interest or expectancy in the Michigan-2 opportunity. *Cf. Guth*, 5 A.2d at 514 (holding that Loft had an interest or expectancy in the Pepsi opportunity by virtue of its need for cola syrup for use in its retail stores).

Finally, the corporate opportunity doctrine is implicated only in cases where the fiduciary's seizure of an opportunity results in a conflict between the fiduciary's duties to the corporation and the self-interest of the director as actualized by the exploitation of the opportunity. In the instant case, Broz' interest in acquiring and profiting from Michigan-2 created no duties that were inimical to his obligations to CIS. Broz, at all times relevant to the instant appeal, was the sole party in interest

---

**16** [7] The language in the *Guth* opinion relating to "line of business" is less than clear:

> Where a corporation is engaged in a certain business, and an opportunity is presented to it embracing an activity as to which it has fundamental knowledge, practical experience and ability to pursue, which, logically and naturally, *is adaptable to its business having regard for its financial position*, and is consonant with its reasonable needs and aspirations for expansion, it may properly be said that the opportunity is within the corporation's line of business.

*Guth*, 5 A.2d at 514 (emphasis supplied). This formulation of the definition of the term "line of business" suggests that the business strategy and financial well-being of the corporation are also relevant to a determination of whether the opportunity is within the corporation's line of business. Since we find that these considerations are decisive under the other factors enunciated by the Court in *Guth*, we do not reach the question of whether they are here relevant to a determination of the corporation's line of business.

in RFBC, a competitor of CIS. CIS was fully aware of Broz' potentially conflicting duties. Broz, however, comported himself in a manner that was wholly in accord with his obligations to CIS. Broz took care not to usurp any opportunity which CIS was willing and able to pursue. Broz sought only to compete with an outside entity, PriCellular, for acquisition of an opportunity which both sought to possess. Broz was not obligated to refrain from competition with PriCellular. Therefore, the totality of the circumstances indicates that Broz did not usurp an opportunity that properly belonged to CIS.

## A. *Presentation to the Board*

In concluding that Broz had usurped a corporate opportunity, the Court of Chancery placed great emphasis on the fact that Broz had not formally presented the matter to the CIS board. The court held that "in such circumstances as existed at the latest after October 14, 1994 (date of PriCellular's option contract on Michigan 2 RSA) it was the obligation of Mr. Broz as a director of CIS to take the transaction to the CIS board for its formal action . . . ." 663 A.2d at 1185. In so holding, the trial court erroneously grafted a new requirement onto the law of corporate opportunity, viz., the requirement of formal presentation under circumstances where the corporation does not have an interest, expectancy or financial ability.

The teaching of *Guth* and its progeny is that the director or officer must analyze the situation ex ante to determine whether the opportunity is one rightfully belonging to the corporation. If the director or officer believes, based on one of the factors articulated above, that the corporation is not entitled to the opportunity, then he may take it for himself. Of course, presenting the opportunity to the board creates a kind of "safe harbor" for the director, which removes the specter of a post hoc judicial determination that the director or officer has improperly usurped a corporate opportunity. Thus, presentation avoids the possibility that an error in the fiduciary's assessment of the situation will create future liability for breach of fiduciary duty. It is not the law of Delaware that presentation to the board is a necessary prerequisite to a finding that a corporate opportunity has not been usurped.

\* \* \*

## B. *Alignment of Interests Between CIS and PriCellular:*

\* \* \*

. . . Broz was under no duty to consider the interests of PriCellular when he chose to purchase Michigan-2. As stated in *Guth*, a director's right to "appropriate [an] . . . opportunity depends [on] the circumstances existing at the time it presented itself to him without regard to subsequent events." *Guth*, 5 A.2d at 513. At the time Broz purchased Michigan-2, PriCellular had not yet acquired CIS. Any plans to do so would still have been wholly speculative. Accordingly, Broz was not required to consider the contingent and uncertain plans of PriCellular in reaching his determination of how to proceed.

Whether or not the CIS board would, at some time, have chosen to acquire Michigan-2 in order to make CIS a more attractive acquisition target for PriCellular or to enhance the synergy of any combined enterprise, is speculative. The trial court found this to be a plausible scenario and therefore found that, pursuant to the factors laid down in *Guth*, CIS had a valid interest or expectancy in the license. This speculative finding cuts against the statements made by CIS' Chief Executive and the entire CIS board of directors and ignores the fact that CIS still lacked the wherewithal to acquire Michigan-2, even if one takes into account the possible availability of PriCellular's financing. Thus, the fact of PriCellular's plans to acquire CIS is immaterial and does not change the analysis.

In reaching our conclusion on this point, we note that certainty and predictability are values to be promoted in our corporation law. *See Williams v. Geier*, 671 A.2d 1368, n.36 (Del. Supr. 1996). Broz, as an active participant in the cellular telephone industry, was entitled to proceed in his own economic interest in the absence of any countervailing duty. The right of a director or officer to engage in business affairs outside of his or her fiduciary capacity would be illusory if these individuals were required to consider every potential, future occurrence in determining whether a particular business strategy would implicate fiduciary duty concerns. In order for a director to engage meaningfully in business unrelated to his or her corporate role, the director must be allowed to make decisions based on the situation as it exists at the time a given opportunity is presented. Absent such a rule, the corporate fiduciary would be constrained to refrain from exploiting any opportunity for fear of liability based on the occurrence of subsequent events. This state of affairs would unduly restrict officers and directors and would be antithetical to certainty in corporation law.

### V. *Conclusion*

The corporate opportunity doctrine represents a judicially crafted effort to harmonize the competing demands placed on corporate fiduciaries in a modern business environment. The doctrine seeks to reduce the possibility of conflict between a director's duties to the corporation and interests unrelated to that role. In the instant case, Broz adhered to his obligations to CIS. We hold that the Court of Chancery erred as a matter of law in concluding that Broz had a duty formally to present the Michigan-2 opportunity to the CIS board. We also hold that the trial court erred in its application of the corporate opportunity doctrine under the unusual facts of this case, where CIS had no interest or financial ability to acquire the opportunity, but the impending acquisition of CIS by PriCellular would or could have caused a change in those circumstances.

Therefore, we hold that Broz did not breach his fiduciary duties to CIS. Accordingly, we *Reverse* the judgment of the Court of Chancery holding that Broz diverted a corporate opportunity properly belonging to CIS and imposing a constructive trust.

# KLINICKI v. LUNDGREN
Supreme Court of Oregon
695 P.2d 906 (1985)

In Banc. Jones, J.

The factual and legal background of this complicated litigation was succinctly set forth by Chief Judge Joseph in the Court of Appeals opinion as follows:

"In January, 1977, plaintiff Klinicki conceived the idea of engaging in the air transportation business in Berlin, West Germany. He discussed the idea with his friend, defendant Lundgren. At that time, both men were furloughed Pan American pilots stationed in West Germany. They decided to enter the air transportation business, planning to begin operations with an air taxi service and later to expand into other service, such as regularly scheduled flights or charter flights. In April, 1977, they incorporated Berlinair, Inc., as a closely held Oregon corporation. Plaintiff was a vice-president and a director. Lundgren was the corporation's president and a director. Each man owned 33 percent of the company stock. Lelco, Inc., a corporation owned by Lundgren and members of his family, owned 33 percent of the stock. The corporation's attorney owned the remaining one percent of the stock. Berlinair obtained the necessary governmental licenses, purchased an aircraft and in November, 1977, began passenger service.

"As president, Lundgren was responsible, in part, for developing and promoting Berlinair's transportation business. Plaintiff was in charge of operations and maintenance. In November, 1977, plaintiff and Lundgren, as representatives of Berlinair, met with representatives of the Berliner Flug Ring (BFR), a consortium of Berlin travel agents that contracts for charter flights to take sallow German tourists to sunnier climes. The BFR contract was considered a lucrative business opportunity by those familiar with the air transportation business, and plaintiff and defendant had contemplated pursuing the contract when they formed Berlinair. After the initial meeting, all subsequent contacts with BFR were made by Lundgren or other Berlinair employees acting under his directions.

"During the early stages of negotiations, Lundgren believed that Berlinair could not obtain the contract because BFR was then satisfied with its carrier. In early June, 1978, however, Lundgren learned that there was a good chance that the BFR contract might be available. He informed a BFR representative that he would make a proposal on behalf of a new company. On July 7, 1978, he incorporated Air Berlin Charter Company (ABC) and was its sole owner. On August 20, 1978, ABC presented BFR with a contract proposal, and after a series of discussions it was awarded the contract on September 1, 1978. Lundgren effectively concealed from plaintiff his negotiations with BFR and his diversion of the BFR contract to ABC, even though he used Berlinair working time, staff, money and facilities.

"Plaintiff, as a minority stockholder in Berlinair, brought a derivative action against ABC for usurping a corporate opportunity of Berlinair. He also brought an individual claim against Lundgren for compensatory and punitive damages based on breach of fiduciary duty.

"The trial court found that ABC, acting through Lundgren, had wrongfully diverted the BFR contract, which was a corporate opportunity of Berlinair. The court imposed a constructive trust on ABC in favor of Berlinair, ordered an accounting by ABC and enjoined ABC from transferring its assets. The trial court also found that Lundgren, as an officer and director of Berlinair, had breached his fiduciary duties of good faith, fair dealing and full disclosure owed to plaintiff individually and to Berlinair. . . ."

ABC appealed to the Court of Appeals contending that it did not usurp a corporate opportunity of Berlinair. Plaintiff cross-appealed from the trial court's dismissal of the punitive damages claim and from the entry of judgment in favor of Lundgren notwithstanding the verdict on that issue. The Court of Appeals affirmed the trial court on all issues.

## I. THE APPEAL BY AIR BERLIN CHARTER CO. (ABC)

ABC petitions for review to this court contending that the concealment and diversion of the BFR contract was not a usurpation of a corporate opportunity, because Berlinair did not have the financial ability to undertake that contract. ABC argues that proof of financial ability is a necessary part of a corporate opportunity case and that plaintiff had the burden of proof on that issue and did not carry that burden.

There is no dispute that the corporate opportunity doctrine precludes corporate fiduciaries from diverting to themselves business opportunities in which the corporation has an expectancy, property interest or right, or which in fairness should otherwise belong to the corporation. *See* Henn & Alexander, Laws of Corporations 632–37, § 237 (3rd ed 1983). The doctrine follows from a corporate fiduciary's duty of undivided loyalty to the corporation. ABC agrees that, unless Berlinair's financial inability to undertake the contract makes a difference, the BFR contract was a corporate opportunity of Berlinair.

We first address the issue, resolved by the Court of Appeals in Berlinair's favor, of the relevance of a corporation's financial ability to undertake a business opportunity to proving a diversion of corporate opportunity claim. This is an issue of first impression in Oregon.

\* \* \*

Before proceeding further our initial task must be to define what is meant by "corporate opportunity," and to determine when, if ever, a corporate fiduciary may take personal advantage of such an opportunity. Our resolution of this case will be limited to announcing a rule to be applied when allegations of usurpation of a corporate opportunity are made against a director of a close corporation. The determination of a rule to apply to similar situations arising between a director and a publicly held corporation presents problems and concepts which may not necessarily require us to apply an identical rule in that similar but distinguishable context.

As we mentioned at the outset, this issue is a matter of first impression in this state. While courts universally stress the high standard of fiduciary duty owed by directors and officers to their corporation, there are distinct schools of thought on the circumstances in which business opportunities may be taken for personal advantage. One group of jurisdictions severely restricts the corporate official's freedom to take advantage of opportunities by saying that the ability to undertake the opportunity is irrelevant and usurpation is essentially prohibited; other jurisdictions use a test which gives relatively wide latitude to the corporate official on the theory that financial ability to undertake a corporate opportunity is a prerequisite to the existence of a corporate opportunity.

[The court then discusses a number of cases and articles illustrating these schools of thought.]

\*   \*   \*

On April 13, 1984, the American Law Institute published its "Tentative Draft No. 3" concerning "Principles of Corporate Governance: Analysis and Recommendations." The draft, of course, does not represent the position of the ALI, but it does contain definitions and rules which we find helpful in resolving the main issue in this case. Section 5.12 of the draft, which contains the proposed general rule and definition, reads as follows:

"(a)  *General Rule:*

"A director or principal senior executive may not take a corporate opportunity for himself or an associate unless:

"(1)  The corporate opportunity has first been offered to the corporation, and disclosure has been made to the corporate decisionmaker of all material facts known to the director or principal senior executive concerning his conflict of interest and the corporate opportunity (unless the corporate decisionmaker is otherwise aware of such material facts); and

"(2)  The corporate opportunity has been rejected by the corporation in a manner that meets one of the following standards:

"(A)  In the case of a rejection of a corporate opportunity that was authorized by disinterested directors following such disclosure, the directors who authorized the rejection acted in a manner that meets the standards of the business judgment rule set forth in § 4.01(d);[17]

---

[17] [8] Section 4.01 provides in pertinent part:

"A director has a duty to his corporation to perform his functions in good faith, in a manner that he reasonably believes to be in the best interests of the corporation . . . and with the care that an ordinarily prudent person would reasonably be expected to exercise in a like profession and under similar circumstances."

"(B) In the case of a rejection that was authorized or ratified by disinterested shareholders following such disclosure, the rejection was not equivalent to a waste of corporate assets; and

"(C) In the case of a rejection that was not authorized or ratified in the manner contemplated in § 5.12(a)(2)(A) or (B) or permitted by the terms of a [validly adopted] standard of the corporation . . ., the taking of the opportunity was fair to the corporation.

"(b) *Definition of a Corporate Opportunity:*

"A corporate opportunity means any opportunity to engage in a business activity (including acquisition or use of any contract right or other tangible or intangible property) that:

"(1) In the case of a principal senior executive or any director, is an opportunity that is communicated or otherwise made available to him either:

"(A) in connection with the performance of his obligations as a principal senior executive or director or under circumstances that should reasonably lead him to believe that the person offering the opportunity expects him to offer it to the corporation, or

"(B) through the use of corporate information or property, if the resulting opportunity is one that the principal senior executive or director should reasonably be expected to believe would be of interest to the corporation; or

"(2) In the case of a principal senior executive or a director who is a full-time employee of the corporation, is an opportunity that he knows or reasonably should know is closely related to the business in which the corporation is engaged or may reasonably be expected to engage." (Bracketed section references omitted.)

Section 5.12 presents an approach very similar to that suggested by Chief Judge Joseph in the Court of Appeals decision rendered in this case. Section 5.12 generally would require an opportunity that could be advantageous to the corporation to be offered to the corporation by a director or principal senior executive before he takes it for himself. Section 5.12 declines to adopt the rigid rule expressed in *Irving Trust Co. v. Deutsch* [73 F.2d 121 (2d Cir. 1934)], which precludes a person subject to the duty of loyalty from pursuing a rejected opportunity. The proposed rule permits a director or principal senior executive to deal with his corporation so long as he deals fairly with full disclosure and bears the burden of proving fairness unless the corporate opportunity was rejected by disinterested directors or shareholders.

\* \* \*

Where a director or principal senior executive of a close corporation wishes to take personal advantage of a "corporate opportunity," as defined by the proposed rule, the director or principal senior executive must comply strictly with the following procedure:

---

*See, Devlin v. Moore,* 64 Or 433, 462, 130 P 35, 45 (1913).

(1)  the director or principal senior executive must promptly offer the opportunity and disclose all material facts known regarding the opportunity to the disinterested directors or, if there is no disinterested director, to the disinterested shareholders. If the director or principal senior executive learns of other material facts after such disclosure, the director or principal senior executive must disclose these additional facts in a like manner before personally taking the opportunity.

(2)  The director or principal senior executive may take advantage of the corporate opportunity only after full disclosure and only if the opportunity is rejected by a majority of the disinterested directors or, if there are no disinterested directors, by a majority of the disinterested shareholders. If, after full disclosure, the disinterested directors or shareholders unreasonably fail to reject the offer, the interested director or principal senior executive may proceed to take the opportunity if he can prove the taking was otherwise "fair" to the corporation. Full disclosure to the appropriate corporate body is, however, an absolute condition precedent to the validity of any forthcoming rejection as well as to the availability to the director or principal senior executive of the defense of fairness.

(3)  An appropriation of a corporate opportunity may be ratified by rejection of the opportunity by a majority of disinterested directors or a majority of disinterested shareholders, after full disclosure subject to the same rules as set out above for prior offer, disclosure and rejection. Where a director or principal senior executive of a close corporation appropriates a corporate opportunity without first fully disclosing the opportunity and offering it to the corporation, absent ratification, that director or principal senior executive holds the opportunity in trust for the corporation.

Applying these rules to the facts in this case, we conclude:

(1)  Lundgren, as director and principal executive officer of Berlinair, owed a fiduciary duty to Berlinair.

(2)  The BFR contract was a "corporate opportunity" of Berlinair.

(3)  Lundgren formed ABC for the purpose of usurping the opportunity presented to Berlinair by the BFR contract.

(4)  Lundgren did not offer Berlinair the BFR contract.

(5)  Lundgren did not attempt to obtain the consent of Berlinair to his taking of the BFR corporate opportunity.

(6)  Lundgren did not fully disclose to Berlinair his intent to appropriate the opportunity for himself and ABC.

(7)  Berlinair never rejected the opportunity presented by the BFR contract.

(8)  Berlinair never ratified the appropriation of the BFR contract.

(9)  Lundgren, acting for ABC, misappropriated the BFR contract.

Because of the above, the defendant may not now contend that Berlinair did not have the financial ability to successfully pursue the BFR contract. As stated in proposed Section 5.12(c) of the Principles of Corporate Governance, *supra*, "If the challenging party satisfies the burden of proving that a corporate opportunity was taken without being offered to the corporation, the challenging party will prevail."

This specific conclusion is also backed by what some might call a legal platitude and others might call a legal classic. When placing special burdens on those in positions of trust, it is worthwhile to recall the well-known admonition of Chief Justice Cardozo speaking for the New York Court of Appeals:

> "Joint adventurers, like copartners, owe to one another, while the enterprise continues, the duty of the finest loyalty. Many forms of conduct permissible in a workaday world for those acting at arm's length, are forbidden to those bound by fiduciary ties. A trustee is held to something stricter than the morals of the market place. Not honesty alone, but the punctilio of an honor the most sensitive, is then the standard of behavior. As to this there has developed a tradition that is unbending and inveterate. Uncompromising rigidity has been the attitude of courts of equity when petitioned to undermine the rule of undivided loyalty by the 'disintegrating erosion' of particular exceptions . . . . Only thus has the level of conduct for fiduciaries been kept at a level higher than that trodden by the crowd. It will not consciously be lowered by any judgment of this court."

*Meinhard v. Salmon*, 249 NY 458, 463–64, 164 NE 545, 546 (1928).

\* \* \*

The Court of Appeals is affirmed.

## IN RE EBAY, INC. SHAREHOLDERS LITIGATION
Court of Chancery of Delaware
2004 Del. Ch. LEXIS 4 (Feb. 11, 2004)

CHANDLER, CHANCELLOR

Shareholders of eBay, Inc. filed these consolidated derivative actions against certain eBay directors and officers for usurping corporate opportunities. Plaintiffs allege that eBay's investment banking advisor, Goldman Sachs Group, engaged in "spinning," a practice that involves allocating shares of lucrative initial public offerings of stock to favored clients. In effect, the plaintiff shareholders allege that Goldman Sachs bribed certain eBay insiders, using the currency of highly profitable investment opportunities-opportunities that should have been offered to, or provided for the benefit of, eBay rather than the favored insiders. Plaintiffs accuse Goldman Sachs of aiding and abetting the corporate insiders breach of their fiduciary duty of loyalty to eBay.

The individual eBay defendants, as well as Goldman Sachs, have moved to dismiss these consolidated actions for failure to state a claim and for failure to make a pre-suit demand on eBay's board of directors as required under Chancery Court Rule 23.1. For reasons I briefly discuss below, I deny all of the defendants' motions to dismiss.

## I. BACKGROUND FACTS

The facts, as alleged in the complaint, are straightforward. In 1995, defendants Pierre M. Omidyar and Jeffrey Skoll founded nominal defendant eBay, a Delaware corporation, as a sole proprietorship. eBay is a pioneer in online trading platforms, providing a virtual auction community for buyers and sellers to list items for sale and to bid on items of interest. In 1998, eBay retained Goldman Sachs and other investment banks to underwrite an initial public offering of common stock. Goldman Sachs was the lead underwriter. The stock was priced at $18 per share. Goldman Sachs purchased about 1.2 million shares. Shares of eBay stock became immensely valuable during 1998 and 1999, rising to $175 per share in early April 1999. Around that time, eBay made a secondary offering, issuing 6.5 million shares of common stock at $170 per share for a total of $1.1 billion. Goldman Sachs again served as lead underwriter. Goldman Sachs was asked in 2001 to serve as eBay's financial advisor in connection with an acquisition by eBay of PayPal, Inc. For these services, eBay has paid Goldman Sachs over $8 million.

During this same time period, Goldman Sachs "rewarded" the individual defendants by allocating to them thousands of IPO shares, managed by Goldman Sachs, at the initial offering price. Because the IPO market during this particular period of time was extremely active, prices of initial stock offerings often doubled or tripled in a single day. Investors who were well connected, either to Goldman Sachs or to similarly situated investment banks serving as IPO underwriters, were able to flip these investments into instant profit by selling the equities in a few days or even in a few hours after they were initially purchased.

The essential allegation of the complaint is that Goldman Sachs provided these IPO share allocations to the individual defendants to show appreciation for eBay's business and to enhance Goldman Sachs' chances of obtaining future eBay business. In addition to co-founding eBay, defendant Omidyar has been eBay's CEO, CFO and President. He is eBay's largest stockholder, owning more than 23% of the company's equity. Goldman Sachs allocated Omidyar shares in at least forty IPOs at the initial offering price. Omidyar resold these securities in the public market for millions of dollars in profit. Defendant Whitman owns 3.3% of eBay stock and has been President, CEO and a director since early 1998. Whitman also has been a director of Goldman Sachs since 2001. Goldman Sachs allocated Whitman shares in over a 100 IPOs at the initial offering price. Whitman sold these equities in the open market and reaped millions of dollars in profit. Defendant Skoll, in addition to co-founding eBay, has served in various positions at the company, including Vice-President of Strategic Planning and Analysis and President. He served as an eBay director from December 1996 to March 1998. Skoll is eBay's second largest stockholder, owning about 13% of the company. Goldman Sachs has allocated Skoll shares in at least 75 IPOs at the initial offering price, which Skoll promptly resold on the open market, allowing him to realize millions of dollars in profit. Finally, defendant Robert C. Kagle has served as an eBay director since June 1997. Goldman Sachs allocated Kagle shares in at least 25 IPOs at the initial offering price. Kagle promptly resold these equities, and recorded millions of dollars in profit.

## II. ANALYSIS

### A. Demand Futility

[This portion of the case is included *infra* in the materials on derivative lawsuits.]

### B. Corporate Opportunity

Plaintiffs have stated a claim that defendants usurped a corporate opportunity of eBay. Defendants insist that Goldman Sachs' IPO allocations to eBay's insider directors were "collateral investments opportunities" that arose by virtue of the inside directors status as wealthy individuals. They argue that this is not a corporate opportunity within the corporation's line of business or an opportunity in which the corporation had an interest or expectancy.[18] These arguments are unavailing.

First, no one disputes that eBay financially was able to exploit the opportunities in question. Second, eBay was in the business of investing in securities. The complaint alleges that eBay "consistently invested a portion of its cash on hand in marketable securities." According to eBay's 1999 10-K, for example, eBay had more than $550 million invested in equity and debt securities. eBay invested more than $181 million in "short-term investments" and $373 million in "long-term investments." Thus, investing was "a line of business" of eBay. Third, the facts alleged in the complaint suggest that investing was integral to eBay's cash management strategies and a significant part of its business. Finally, it is no answer to say, as do defendants, that IPOs are risky investments. It is undisputed that eBay was never given an opportunity to turn down the IPO allocations as too risky.

Defendants also argue that to view the IPO allocations in question as corporate opportunities will mean that every advantageous investment opportunity that comes to an officer or director will be considered a corporate opportunity. On the contrary, the allegations in the complaint in this case indicate that unique, below-market price investment opportunities were offered by Goldman Sachs to the insider defendants as financial inducements to maintain and secure corporate business. This was not an instance where a broker offered advice to a director about an investment in a marketable security. The conduct challenged here involved a large investment bank that regularly did business with a company steering highly lucrative IPO allocations to select insider directors and officers at that company, allegedly both to reward them for past business and to induce them to direct future business to that investment bank. This is a far cry from the defendants' characterization of the conduct in question as merely "a broker's investment recommendations" to a wealthy client.

Nor can one seriously argue that this conduct did not place the insider defendants in a position of conflict with their duties to the corporation. One can realistically characterize these IPO allocations as a form of commercial discount or

---

**18** [3] *See Broz v. Cellular Info. Sys. Inc.*, 673 A.2d 148, 155 (Del. 1996) (listing factors to find corporate opportunity).

rebate for past or future investment banking services. Viewed pragmatically, it is easy to understand how steering such commercial rebates to certain insider directors places those directors in an obvious conflict between their self-interest and the corporation's interest. . . .

Finally, even if one assumes that IPO allocations like those in question here do not constitute a corporate opportunity, a cognizable claim is nevertheless stated on the common law ground that an agent is under a duty to account for profits obtained personally in connection with transactions related to his or her company. The complaint gives rise to a reasonable inference that the insider directors accepted a commission or gratuity that rightfully belonged to eBay but that was improperly diverted to them. Even if this conduct does not run afoul of the corporate opportunity doctrine, it may still constitute a breach of the fiduciary duty of loyalty.[19] Thus, even if one does not consider Goldman Sachs' IPO allocations to these corporate insiders-allocations that generated millions of dollars in profit-to be a corporate opportunity, the defendant directors were nevertheless not free to accept this consideration from a company, Goldman Sachs, that was doing significant business with eBay and that arguably intended the consideration as an inducement to maintaining the business relationship in the future.[20]

## C. Aiding and Abetting Claim

Plaintiffs' complaint adequately alleges the existence of a fiduciary relationship, that the individual defendants breached their fiduciary duty and that plaintiffs have been damaged because of the concerted actions of the individual defendants and Goldman Sachs. Goldman Sachs, however, disputes whether it "knowingly participated" in the eBay insiders' alleged breach of fiduciary duty.[21] The allegation, however, is that Goldman Sachs had provided underwriting and investment advisory services to eBay for years and that it knew that each of the individual defendants owed a fiduciary duty to eBay not to profit personally at eBay's expense and to devote their undivided loyalty to the interests of eBay. Goldman Sachs also knew or had reason to know of eBay's investment of excess cash in marketable securities and debt. Goldman Sachs was aware (or charged with a duty to know) of earlier SEC interpretations that prohibited steering "hot issue" securities to persons in a position to direct future business to the broker-dealer. Taken together, these allegations allege a claim for aiding and abetting sufficient to withstand a motion to dismiss.

## III. CONCLUSION

For all of the above reasons, I deny the defendants' motions to dismiss the complaint in this consolidated action.

---

[19] [7] *Gibralt Capital Corp. v. Smith*, 2001 Del. Ch. LEXIS 68, 2001 WL 647837, at *9 . . . (Del. Ch. May 8, 2001); *Thorpe v. CERBCO, Inc.*, 676 A.2d 436, 444 (Del. 1996).

[20] [8] RESTATEMENT (SECOND) OF AGENCY § 388 (1957).

[21] [9] Knowing participation obviously is the fourth element of the claim for aiding and abetting. *See generally Jackson Nat'l Life Ins. Co. v. Kennedy*, 741 A.2d 377, 381 (Del. Ch. 1999).

IT IS SO ORDERED.

## 3.   Cleansing Conflicts of Interest

### FLIEGLER v. LAWRENCE
Supreme Court of Delaware
361 A.2d 218 (1976)

OPINION BY: McNEILLY

In this shareholder derivative action brought on behalf of Agau Mines, Inc., a Delaware corporation, (Agau) against its officers and directors and United States Antimony Corporation, a Montana corporation (USAC), we are asked to decide whether the individual defendants, in their capacity as directors and officers of both corporations, wrongfully usurped a corporate opportunity belonging to Agau, and whether all defendants wrongfully profited by causing Agau to exercise an option to purchase that opportunity. The Court of Chancery found in favor of the defendants on both issues. (1974). Reference is made to that opinion for a full statement of the facts; what follows here is but a brief resume of the events giving rise to this litigation.

I

In November, 1969, defendant, John C. Lawrence (then president of Agau, a publicly held corporation engaged in a dualphased gold and silver exploratory venture) in his individual capacity, acquired certain antimony properties under a lease option for $60,000. Lawrence offered to transfer the properties, which were then "a raw prospect", to Agau, but after consulting with other members of Agau's board of directors, he and they agreed that the corporation's legal and financial position would not permit acquisition and development of the properties at that time. Thus, it was decided to transfer the properties to USAC, (a closely held corporation formed just for this purpose and a majority of whose stock was owned by the individual defendants) where capital necessary for development of the properties could be raised without risk to Agau through the sale of USAC stock; it was also decided to grant Agau a long-term option to acquire USAC if the properties proved to be of commercial value.

In January, 1970, the option agreement was executed by Agau and USAC. Upon its exercise and approval by Agau shareholders, Agau was to deliver 800,000 shares of its restricted investment stock for all authorized and issued shares of USAC. The exchange was calculated on the basis of reimbursement to USAC and its shareholders for their costs in developing the properties to a point where it could be ascertained if they had commercial value. Such costs were anticipated to range from $250,000 to $500,000. At the time the plan was conceived, Agau shares traded over-the-counter, bid at $5/8 to $3/4 and asked at $1 to $1 1/4. Applying to these quotations a 50% discount for the investment restrictions, the parties agreed that 800,000 Agau shares would reflect the range of anticipated costs in developing USAC and, accordingly, that figure was adopted.

In July, 1970, the Agau board resolved to exercise the option, an action which was approved by majority vote of the shareholders in October, 1970. Subsequently, plaintiff instituted this suit on behalf of Agau to recover the 800,000 shares and for an accounting.

## II

The Vice-Chancellor determined that the chance to acquire the antimony claims was a corporate opportunity which should have been (and was) offered to Agau, but because the corporation was not in a position, either financially or legally, to accept the opportunity at that time, the individual defendants were entitled to acquire it for themselves after Agau rejected it.

We agree with these conclusions for the reasons stated by the Vice-Chancellor, which are based on settled Delaware law. *Equity Corp. v. Milton*, Del. Supr., 43 Del. Ch. 160, 221 A.2d 494 (1966); *Guth v. Loft, Inc.*, Del. Supr., 23 Del. Ch. 255, 5 A.2d 503 (1939); also see *Wolfensohn v. Madison Fund, Inc.*, Del. Supr., 253 A.2d 72 (1969). Accordingly, Agau was not entitled to the properties without consideration.

## III

Plaintiff contends that because the individual defendants personally profited through the use of Agau's resources, *viz.*, personnel (primarily Lawrence) to develop the USAC properties and stock purchase warrants to secure a $300,000. indebtedness (incurred by USAC because it could not raise sufficient capital through sale of stock), they must be compelled to account to Agau for that profit. This argument pre-supposes that defendants did in fact so misuse corporate assets; however, the record reveals substantial evidence to support the Vice-Chancellor's conclusion that there was no misuse of either Agau personnel or warrants. Issuance of the warrants in fact enhanced the value of Agau's option at a time when there was reason to believe that USAC's antimony properties had a "considerable potential", and plaintiff did not prove that alleged use of Agau's personnel and equipment was detrimental to the corporation.

Nevertheless, our inquiry cannot stop here, for it is clear that the individual defendants stood on both sides of the transaction in implementing and fixing the terms of the option agreement. Accordingly, the burden is upon them to demonstrate its intrinsic fairness *Johnston v. Greene*, Del. Supr., 35 Del. Ch. 479, 121 A.2d 919 (1956); *Sterling v. Mayflower Hotel Corp.*, Del. Supr., 33 Del. Ch. 293, 93 A.2d 107 (1952); *Gottlieb v. Heyden Chemical Corp.*, Del. Supr., 33 Del. Ch. 82, 90 A.2d 660 (1952); *David J. Greene & Co., v. Dunhill International, Inc.*, Del. Ch., 249 A.2d 427 (1968). We agree with the Vice-Chancellor that the record reveals no bad faith on the part of the individual defendants. But that is not determinative. The issue is where the 800,000 restricted investment shares of Agau stock, objectively, was a fair price for Agau to pay for USAC as a wholly-owned subsidiary.

## A.

Preliminarily, defendants argue that they have been relieved of the burden of proving fairness by reason of shareholder ratification of the Board's decision to exercise the option. They rely on 8 Del. C. § 144(a)(2) and *Gottlieb v. Heyden Chemical Corp.*, Del. Supr., 33 Del. Ch. 177, 91 A.2d 57 (1952).

In *Gottlieb*, this Court stated that shareholder ratification of an "interested transaction", although less than unanimous, shifts the burden of proof to an objecting shareholder to demonstrate that the terms are so unequal as to amount to a gift or waste of corporate assets. Also see *Saxe v. Brady*, 40 Del. Ch. 474, 184 A.2d 602 (1962). The Court explained: "[The] entire atmosphere is freshened and a new set of rules invoked where formal approval has been given by a majority of independent, fully informed [shareholders]." 91 A.2d at 59.

The purported ratification by the Agau shareholders would not affect the burden of proof in this case because the majority of shares voted in favor of exercising the option were cast by defendants in their capacity as Agau shareholders. Only about one-third of the "disinterested" shareholders voted, and we cannot assume that such non-voting shareholders either approved or disapproved. Under these circumstances, we cannot say that "the entire atmosphere has been freshened" and that departure from the objective fairness test is permissible. Compare *Schiff v. R.K.O. Pictures Corp.*, 34 Del. Ch. 329, 104 A.2d 267 (1954), with *David J. Greene & Co. v. Dunhill International, Inc.*, *supra*, and *Abelow v. Symonds*, 40 Del. Ch. 462, 184 A.2d 173 (1962). In short, defendants have not established factually a basis for applying *Gottlieb*.

Nor do we believe the Legislature intended a contrary policy and rule to prevail by enacting 8 Del. C. § 144, which provides, in part:

(a) No contract or transaction between a corporation and 1 or more of its directors or officers, or between a corporation and any other corporation, partnership, association, or other organization in which 1 or more of its directors or officers, are directors or officers, or have a financial interest, shall be void or voidable solely for this reason, or solely because the director or officer is present at or participates in the meeting of the board or committee which authorizes the contract or transaction, or solely because his or their votes are counted for such purpose, if:

(1) The material facts as to his relationship or interest and as to the contract or transaction are disclosed or are known to the board of directors or the committee, and the board of committee in good faith authorizes the contract or transaction by the affirmative votes of a majority of the disinterested directors, even though the disinterested directors be less than a quorum; or

(2) The material facts as his relationship or interest and as to the contract or transaction are disclosed or are known to the shareholders entitled to vote thereon, and the contract or transaction is specifically approved in good faith by vote of the shareholders; or

(3) The contract or transaction is fair as to the corporation as of the time it is authorized, approved or ratified, by the board of directors, a committee, or the shareholders.

Defendants argue that the transaction here in question is protected by § 144(a)(2)which, they contend, does not require that ratifying shareholders be "disinterested" or "independent"; nor, they argue, is there warrant for reading such a requirement into the statute. See Folk, *The Delaware General Corporation Law — A Commentary and Analysis* (1972), pp. 85–86. We do not read the statute as providing the broad immunity for which defendants contend. It merely removes an "interested director" cloud when its terms are met and provides against invalidation of an agreement "solely" because such a director or officer is involved. Nothing in the statute sanctions unfairness to Agau or removes the transaction from judicial scrutiny.

## B.

Turning to the transaction itself, we note at the outset that from the time the option arrangement was conceived until the time it was implemented, there occurred marked changes in several of the factors which formed the basis for the terms of the exchange. . . .

. . . [W]e conclude that defendants have proven the intrinsic fairness of the transaction. Agau received properties which by themselves were clearly of substantial value. But more importantly, it received a promising, potentially self-financing and profit generating enterprise with proven markets and commercial capability which could well be expected to provide Agau at the very least with the cash it sorely needed to undertake further exploration and development of its own properties if not to stay in existence. For those reasons, we believe that the interest given to the USAC shareholders was a fair price to pay. Accordingly, we have no doubt but that this transaction was one which at that time would have commended itself to an independent corporation in Agau's position.

Affirmed.

# IN RE WHEELABRATOR TECHNOLOGIES, INC. SHAREHOLDERS LITIGATION
Court of Chancery of Delaware
663 A.2d 1194 (1995)

JACOBS, VICE CHANCELLOR

The question of whether or not shareholder ratification should operate to extinguish a duty of loyalty claim cannot be decided in a vacuum, divorced from the broader issue of what generally are the legal consequences of a fully-informed shareholder approval of a challenged transaction. The Delaware case law addressing that broader topic is not reducible to a single clear rule or unifying principle. Indeed, the law in that area might be thought to lack coherence because the decisions addressing the effect of shareholder "ratification" have fragmented that subject into three distinct compartments, only one of which involves "claim extinguishment."

The basic structure of stockholder ratification law is, at first glance, deceptively simple. Delaware law distinguishes between acts of directors (or management) that are "void" and acts that are "voidable." As the Supreme Court stated in *Michelson v. Duncan*, 407 A.2d 211, 218–19 (1979):

> The essential distinction between voidable and void acts is that the former are those which may be found to have been performed in the interest of the corporation but beyond the authority of management, as distinguished from acts which are *ultra vires*, fraudulent, or waste of corporate assets. The practical distinction, for our purposes, is that voidable acts are susceptible to cure by shareholder approval while void acts are not. (citations omitted).

One possible reading of *Michelson* is that all "voidable" acts are "susceptible to cure by shareholder approval." Under that reading, shareholder ratification might be thought to constitute a "full defense" (407 A.2d at 219) that would automatically extinguish all claims challenging such acts as a breach of fiduciary duty. Any such reading, however, would be overbroad, because the case law governing the consequences of ratification does not support that view and, in fact, is far more complex.

The Delaware Supreme Court has found shareholder ratification of "voidable" director conduct to result in claim-extinguishment in only two circumstances. The first is where the directors act in good faith, but exceed the board's *de jure* authority. In that circumstance, *Michelson* holds that "a validly accomplished shareholder ratification relates back to cure otherwise unauthorized acts of officers and directors." 407 A.2d at 219. The second circumstance is where the directors fail "to reach an informed business judgment" in approving a transaction. *Van Gorkom*, 488 A.2d at 889.

Except for these two situations, no party has identified any type of board action that the Delaware Supreme Court has deemed "voidable" for claim extinguishment purposes. More specifically, no Supreme Court case has held that shareholder ratification operates automatically to extinguish a duty of loyalty claim. To the contrary, the ratification cases involving duty of loyalty claims have uniformly held that the effect of shareholder ratification is to alter the standard of review, or to shift the burden of proof, or both. Those cases further frustrate any effort to describe the "ratification" landscape in terms of a simple rule.

The ratification decisions that involve duty of loyalty claims are of two kinds: (a) "interested" transaction cases between a corporation and its directors (or between the corporation and an entity in which the corporation's directors are also directors or have a financial interest), and (b) cases involving a transaction between the corporation and its controlling shareholder.

Regarding the first category, 8 *Del.* C. § 144(a)(2) pertinently provides that an "interested" transaction of this kind will not be voidable if it is approved in good faith by a majority of disinterested stockholders. Approval by fully informed, disinterested shareholders pursuant to § 144(a)(2) invokes "the business judgment rule and limits judicial review to issues of gift or waste with the burden of proof upon the party attacking the transaction." *Marciano v. Nakash*, Del. Supr., 535 A.2d 400, 405 n.3 (1987). The result is the same in "interested" transaction cases not decided under § 144:

> Where there has been independent shareholder ratification of interested director actions, the objecting stockholder has the burden of showing that no person of ordinary sound business judgment would say that the consideration received for the options was a fair exchange for the options granted.

*Michelson*, 407 A.2d at 224 (quoting *Kaufman v. Shoenberg*, Del. Ch., 33 Del. Ch. 211, 91 A.2d 786, 791 (1952), at 791); *see also Gottlieb v. Heyden Chem. Corp.*, Del. Supr., 33 Del. Ch. 177, 91 A.2d 57, 59 (1952); and *Citron v. E.I. DuPont de Nemours & Co.*, 584 A.2d 490, 501 (citing authorities reaching the same result in mergers involving fiduciaries that were not controlling stockholders).

The second category concerns duty of loyalty cases arising out of transactions between the corporation and its controlling stockholder. Those cases involve primarily parent-subsidiary mergers that were conditioned upon receiving "majority of the minority" stockholder approval. In a parent-subsidiary merger, the standard of review is ordinarily entire fairness, with the directors having the burden of proving that the merger was entirely fair. *Weinberger v. UOP, Inc.*, 457 A.2d 701, 703. But where the merger is conditioned upon approval by a "majority of the minority" stockholder vote, and such approval is granted, the standard of review remains entire fairness, but the burden of demonstrating that the merger was unfair shifts to the plaintiff. *Kahn v. Lynch Communication Sys.*, Del. Supr., 638 A.2d 1110 (1994); *Rosenblatt v. Getty Oil Co.*, 493 A.2d 929, 937-38 (1985); *Weinberger*, at 710; *Citron*, at 502. . . .

\*     \*     \*

To repeat: in only two circumstances has the Delaware Supreme Court held that a fully-informed shareholder vote operates to extinguish a claim: (1) where the board of directors takes action that, although not alleged to constitute *ultra vires*, fraud, or waste, is claimed to exceed the board's authority; and (2) where it is claimed that the directors failed to exercise due care to adequately inform themselves before committing the corporation to a transaction. In no case has the Supreme Court held that stockholder ratification automatically extinguishes a claim for breach of the directors' duty of loyalty. Rather, the operative effect of shareholder ratification in duty of loyalty cases has been either to change the standard of review to the business judgment rule, with the burden of proof resting upon the plaintiff, or to leave "entire fairness" as the review standard, but shift the burden of proof to the plaintiff. Thus, the Supreme Court ratification decisions do not support the defendants' position.

That being the present state of the law, the question then becomes whether there exists a policy or doctrinal basis that would justify extending the claim-extinguishing effect of shareholder ratification to cases involving duty of loyalty claims. *Van Gorkom* does not articulate a basis, and the parties have suggested none. . . .

## 4.  Parent-Subsidiary Dealings

### SINCLAIR OIL CORP. v. LEVIEN
Supreme Court of Delaware
280 A.2d 717 (1971)

Wolcott, C.J.

This is an appeal by the defendant, Sinclair Oil Corporation (hereafter Sinclair), from an order of the Court of Chancery, 261 A.2d 911 in a derivative action requiring Sinclair to account for damages sustained by its subsidiary, Sinclair Venezuelan Oil Company (hereafter Sinven), organized by Sinclair for the purpose of operating in Venezuela, as a result of dividends paid by Sinven, the denial to Sinven of industrial development, and a breach of contract between Sinclair's wholly-owned subsidiary, Sinclair International Oil Company, and Sinven.

Sinclair, operating primarily as a holding company, is in the business of exploring for oil and of producing and marketing crude oil and oil products. At all times relevant to this litigation, it owned about 97% of Sinven's stock. The plaintiff owns about 3000 of 120,000 publicly held shares of Sinven. Sinven, incorporated in 1922, has been engaged in petroleum operations primarily in Venezuela and since 1959 has operated exclusively in Venezuela.

Sinclair nominates all members of Sinven's board of directors. The Chancellor found as a fact that the directors were not independent of Sinclair. Almost without exception, they were officers, directors, or employees of corporations in the Sinclair complex. By reason of Sinclair's domination, it is clear that Sinclair owed Sinven a fiduciary duty. *Getty Oil Company v. Skelly Oil Co.*, 267 A.2d 883 (Del. Supr. 1970); *Cottrell v. Pawcatuck Co.*, 35 Del. Ch. 309, 116 A.2d 787 (1955). Sinclair concedes this.

The Chancellor held that because of Sinclair's fiduciary duty and its control over Sinven, its relationship with Sinven must meet the test of intrinsic fairness. The standard of intrinsic fairness involves both a high degree of fairness and a shift in the burden of proof. Under this standard the burden is on Sinclair to prove, subject to careful judicial scrutiny, that its transactions with Sinven were objectively fair. *Guth v. Loft, Inc.*, 23 Del. Ch. 255, 5 A.2d 503 (1939); *Sterling v. Mayflower Hotel Corp.*, 33 Del. Ch. 293, 93 A.2d 107, 38 A.L.R.2d 425 (Del. Supr. 1952); *Getty Oil Co. v. Skelly Oil Co., supra.*

Sinclair argues that the transactions between it and Sinven should be tested, not by the test of intrinsic fairness with the accompanying shift of the burden of proof, but by the business judgment rule under which a court will not interfere with the judgment of a board of directors unless there is a showing of gross and palpable overreaching. *Meyerson v. El Paso Natural Gas Co.*, 246 A.2d 789 (Del. Ch. 1967). A board of directors enjoys a presumption of sound business judgment, and its decisions will not be disturbed if they can be attributed to any rational business purpose. A court under such circumstances will not substitute its own notions of what is or is not sound business judgment.

We think, however, that Sinclair's argument in this respect is misconceived. When the situation involves a parent and a subsidiary, with the parent controlling the transaction and fixing the terms, the test of intrinsic fairness, with its resulting shifting of the burden of proof, is applied. *Sterling v. Mayflower Hotel Corp., supra; David J. Greene & Co. v. Dunhill International, Inc.*, 249 A.2d 427 (Del. Ch. 1968); *Bastian v. Bourns, Inc.*, 256 A.2d 680 (Del. Ch. 1969) *aff'd. per curiam* (unreported) (Del. Supr. 1970). The basic situation for the application of the rule is the one in which the parent has received a benefit to the exclusion and at the expense of the subsidiary.

Recently, this court dealt with the question of fairness in parent-subsidiary dealings in *Getty Oil Co. v. Skelly Oil Co., supra*. In that case, both parent and subsidiary were in the business of refining and marketing crude oil and crude oil products. The Oil Import Board ruled that the subsidiary, because it was controlled by the parent, was no longer entitled to a separate allocation of imported crude oil. The subsidiary then contended that it had a right to share the quota of crude oil allotted to the parent. We ruled that the business judgment standard should be applied to determine this contention. Although the subsidiary suffered a loss through the administration of the oil import quotas, the parent gained nothing. The parent's quota was derived solely from its own past use. The past use of the subsidiary did not cause an increase in the parent's quota, nor did the parent usurp a quota of the subsidiary. Since the parent received nothing from the subsidiary to the exclusion of the minority stockholders of the subsidiary, there was no self-dealing. Therefore, the business judgment standard was properly applied.

A parent does indeed owe a fiduciary duty to its subsidiary when there are parent subsidiary dealings. However, this alone will not evoke the intrinsic fairness standard. This standard will be applied only when the fiduciary duty is accompanied by self-dealing — the situation when a parent is on both sides of a transaction with its subsidiary. Self-dealing occurs when the parent, by virtue of its domination of the subsidiary, causes the subsidiary to act in such a way that the parent receives something from the subsidiary to the exclusion of, and detriment to, the minority stockholders of the subsidiary.

We turn now to the facts. The plaintiff argues that, from 1960 through 1966, Sinclair caused Sinven to pay out such excessive dividends that the industrial development of Sinven was effectively prevented, and it became in reality a corporation in dissolution.

From 1960 through 1966, Sinven paid out $108,000,000 in dividends ($38,000,000 in excess of Sinven's earnings during the same period). The Chancellor held that Sinclair caused these dividends to be paid during a period when it had a need for large amounts of cash. Although the dividends paid exceeded earnings, the plaintiff concedes that the payments were made in compliance with [Delaware General Corporation Law,] 8 Del. C. § 170, authorizing payment of dividends out of surplus or net profits. However, the plaintiff attacks these dividends on the ground that they resulted from an improper motive — Sinclair's need for cash. The Chancellor, applying the intrinsic fairness standard, held that Sinclair did not sustain its burden of proving that its transactions were intrinsically fair to the minority stockholders of Sinven.

Since it is admitted that the dividends were paid in strict compliance with 8 Del. C. § 170, the alleged excessiveness of the payments alone would not state a cause of action. Nevertheless, compliance with the applicable statute may not, under all circumstances, justify all dividend payments. If a plaintiff can meet his burden of proving that a dividend cannot be grounded on any reasonable business objective, then the courts can and will interfere with the board's decision to pay the dividend.

Sinclair contends that it is improper to apply the intrinsic fairness standard to dividend payments even when the board which voted for the dividends is completely dominated. In support of this contention, Sinclair relies heavily on *American District Telegraph Co. [ADT] v. Grinnell Corp.*, (N.Y. Sup. Ct. 1969) *aff'd.*, 33 A.D.2d 769, 306 N.Y.S.2d 209 (1969). Plaintiffs were minority stockholders of ADT, a subsidiary of Grinnell. The plaintiffs alleged that Grinnell, realizing that it would soon have to sell its ADT stock because of a pending anti-trust action, caused ADT to pay excessive dividends. Because the dividend payments conformed with applicable statutory law, and the plaintiffs could not prove an abuse of discretion, the court ruled that the complaint did not state a cause of action. Other decisions seem to support Sinclair's contention. In *Metropolitan Casualty Ins. Co. v. First State Bank of Temple*, 54 S.W.2d 358 (Tex. Civ. App. 1932), *rev'd on other grounds*, 79 S.W.2d 835 (Sup. Ct. 1935), the court held that a majority of interested directors does not void a declaration of dividends because all directors, by necessity, are interested in and benefited by a dividend declaration. *See, also, Schwartz v. Kahn*, 183 Misc. 252, 50 N.Y.S.2d 931 (1944); *Weinberger v. Quinn*, 264 A.D. 405, 35 N.Y.S.2d 567 (1942).

We do not accept the argument that the intrinsic fairness test can never be applied to a dividend declaration by a dominated board, although a dividend declaration by a dominated board will not inevitably demand the application of the intrinsic fairness standard. *Moskowitz v. Bantrell*, 41 Del. Ch. 177, 190 A.2d 749 (Del. Supr. 1963). If such a dividend is in essence self-dealing by the parent, then the intrinsic fairness standard is the proper standard. For example, suppose a parent dominates a subsidiary and its board of directors. The subsidiary has outstanding two classes of stock, X and Y. Class X is owned by the parent and Class Y is owned by minority stockholders of the subsidiary. If the subsidiary, at the direction of the parent, declares a dividend on its Class X stock only, this might well be self-dealing by the parent. It would be receiving something from the subsidiary to the exclusion of and detrimental to its minority stockholders. This self-dealing, coupled with the parents' fiduciary duty, would make intrinsic fairness the proper standard by which to evaluate the dividend payments.

Consequently it must be determined whether the dividend payments by Sinven were, in essence, self-dealing by Sinclair. The dividends resulted in great sums of money being transferred from Sinven to Sinclair. However, a proportionate share of this money was received by the minority shareholders of Sinven. Sinclair received nothing from Sinven to the exclusion of its minority stockholders. As such, these dividends were not self-dealing. We hold therefore that the Chancellor erred in applying the intrinsic fairness test as to these dividend payments. The business judgment standard should have been applied.

We conclude that the facts demonstrate that the dividend payments complied with the business judgment standard and with 8 Del. C. § 170. The motives for causing the declaration of dividends are immaterial unless the plaintiff can show that the dividend payments resulted from improper motives and amounted to waste. The plaintiff contends only that the dividend payments drained Sinven of cash to such an extent that it was prevented from expanding.

The plaintiff proved no business opportunities which came to Sinven independently and which Sinclair either took to itself or denied to Sinven. As a matter of fact, with two minor exceptions which resulted in losses, all of Sinven's operations have been conducted in Venezuela, and Sinclair had a policy of exploiting its oil properties located in different countries by subsidiaries located in the particular countries.

From 1960 to 1966 Sinclair purchased or developed oil fields in Alaska, Canada, Paraguay, and other places around the world. The plaintiff contends that these were all opportunities which could have been taken by Sinven. The Chancellor concluded that Sinclair had not proved that its denial of expansion opportunities to Sinven was intrinsically fair. He based this conclusion on the following findings of fact. Sinclair made no real effort to expand Sinven. The excessive dividends paid by Sinven resulted in so great a cash drain as to effectively deny to Sinven any ability to expand. During this same period Sinclair actively pursued a company-wide policy of developing through its subsidiaries new sources of revenue, but Sinven was not permitted to participate and was confined in its activities to Venezuela.

However, the plaintiff could point to no opportunities which came to Sinven. Therefore, Sinclair usurped no business opportunity belonging to Sinven. Since Sinclair received nothing from Sinven to the exclusion of and detriment to Sinven's minority stockholders, there was no self-dealing. Therefore, business judgment is the proper standard by which to evaluate Sinclair's expansion policies.

Since there is no proof of self-dealing on the part of Sinclair, it follows that the expansion policy of Sinclair and the methods used to achieve the desired result must, as far as Sinclair's treatment of Sinven is concerned, be tested by the standards of the business judgment rule. Accordingly, Sinclair's decision, absent fraud or gross overreaching, to achieve expansion through the medium of its subsidiaries, other than Sinven, must be upheld.

Even if Sinclair was wrong in developing these opportunities as it did, the question arises, with which subsidiaries should these opportunities have been shared? No evidence indicates a unique need or ability of Sinven to develop these opportunities. The decision of which subsidiaries would be used to implement Sinclair's expansion policy was one of business judgment with which a court will not interfere absent a showing of gross and palpable overreaching. *Meyerson v. El Paso Natural Gas Co.*, 246 A.2d 789 (Del. Ch. 1967). No such showing has been made here.

Next, Sinclair argues that the Chancellor committed error when he held it liable to Sinven for breach of contract.

In 1961 Sinclair created Sinclair International Oil Company (hereafter International), a wholly owned subsidiary used for the purpose of coordinating all of Sinclair's foreign operations. All crude purchases by Sinclair were made thereafter through International.

On September 28, 1961, Sinclair caused Sinven to contract with International whereby Sinven agreed to sell all of its crude oil and refined products to International at specified prices. The contract provided for minimum and maximum quantities and prices. The plaintiff contends that Sinclair caused this contract to be breached in two respects. Although the contract called for payment on receipt, International's payments lagged as much as 30 days after receipt. Also, the contract required International to purchase at least a fixed minimum amount of crude and refined products from Sinven. International did not comply with this requirement.

Clearly, Sinclair's act of contracting with its dominated subsidiary was self-dealing. Under the contract Sinclair received the products produced by Sinven, and of course the minority shareholders of Sinven were not able to share in the receipt of these products. If the contract was breached, then Sinclair received these products to the detriment of Sinven's minority shareholders. We agree with the Chancellor's finding that the contract was breached by Sinclair, both as to the time of payments and the amounts purchased.

Although a parent need not bind itself by a contract with its dominated subsidiary, Sinclair chose to operate in this manner. As Sinclair has received the benefits of this contract, so must it comply with the contractual duties.

Under the intrinsic fairness standard, Sinclair must prove that its causing Sinven not to enforce the contract was intrinsically fair to the minority shareholders of Sinven. Sinclair has failed to meet this burden. Late payments were clearly breaches for which Sinven should have sought and received adequate damages. As to the quantities purchased, Sinclair argues that it purchased all the products produced by Sinven. This, however, does not satisfy the standard of intrinsic fairness. Sinclair has failed to prove that Sinven could not possibly have produced or someway have obtained the contract minimums. As such, Sinclair must account on this claim.

Finally, Sinclair argues that the Chancellor committed error in refusing to allow it a credit or setoff of all benefits provided by it to Sinven with respect to all the alleged damages. The Chancellor held that setoff should be allowed on specific transactions, e.g., benefits to Sinven under the contract with International, but denied an over all setoff against all damages claimed. We agree with the Chancellor, although the point may well be moot in view of our holding that Sinclair is not required to account for the alleged excessiveness of the dividend payments.

We will therefore reverse that part of the Chancellor's order that requires Sinclair to account to Sinven for damages sustained as a result of dividends paid between 1960 and 1966, and by reason of the denial to Sinven of expansion during that period. We will affirm the remaining portion of that order and remand the cause for further proceedings.

# NOTES

**1.** *Sinclair* illustrates the types of problems which can arise when the interests of minority shareholders of a partially owned subsidiary conflict, or appear to conflict, with those of the parent. Does the court's definition of "self-dealing," which is limited to situations where the parent corporation receives something to the exclusion of the minority shareholders, provide adequate protection to the minority shareholders? If not, do you see why the court may have felt that the test it adopted was the lesser of two evils in dealing with a situation fraught with difficulties?

**2.** Because a situation involving a partially owned subsidiary invites litigation by the minority shareholders, one solution is for the parent to seek to eliminate them by merging the subsidiary into the parent and giving the minority shareholders cash or bonds in exchange for their equity interest. However, as the next case indicates, such a transaction, itself, invites litigation if it is not carefully structured.

## WEINBERGER v. UOP, INC.
### Supreme Court of Delaware
### 457 A.2d 701 (1983)

Moore, J.

This post-trial appeal was reheard en banc from a decision of the Court of Chancery. It was brought by the class action plaintiff below, a former shareholder of UOP, Inc., who challenged the elimination of UOP's minority shareholders by a cashout merger between UOP and its majority owner, The Signal Companies, Inc. Originally, the defendants in this action were Signal, UOP, certain officers and directors of those companies, and UOP's investment banker, Lehman Brothers Kuhn Loeb, Inc. The present Chancellor held that the terms of the merger were fair to the plaintiff and the other minority shareholders of UOP. Accordingly, he entered judgment in favor of the defendants.

Numerous points were raised by the parties, but we address only the following questions presented by the trial court's opinion:

> 1) The plaintiff's duty to plead sufficient facts demonstrating the unfairness of the challenged merger; 2) The burden of proof upon the parties where the merger has been approved by the purportedly informed vote of a majority of the minority shareholders; 3) The fairness of the merger in terms of adequacy of the defendants' disclosures to the minority shareholders; 4) The fairness of the merger in terms of adequacy of the price paid for the minority shares and the remedy appropriate to that issue; and 5) The continued force and effect of *Singer v. Magnavox Co.*, Del. Supr., 380 A.2d 969, 980 (1977), and its progeny.

In ruling for the defendants, the Chancellor re-stated his earlier conclusion that the plaintiff in a suit challenging a cash-out merger must allege specific acts of fraud, misrepresentation, or other items of misconduct to demonstrate the unfairness of the merger terms to the minority. We approve this rule and affirm it.

The Chancellor also held that even though the ultimate burden of proof is on the majority shareholder to show by a preponderance of the evidence that the transaction is fair, it is first the burden of the plaintiff attacking the merger to demonstrate some basis for invoking the fairness obligation. We agree with that principle. However, where corporate action has been approved by an informed vote of a majority of the minority shareholders, we conclude that the burden entirely shifts to the plaintiff to show that the transaction was unfair to the minority. *See, e.g., Michelson v. Duncan*, Del. Supr., 407 A.2d 211, 224 (1979). But in all this, the burden clearly remains on those relying on the vote to show that they completely disclosed all material facts relevant to the transaction.

Here, the record does not support a conclusion that the minority stockholder vote was an informed one. Material information, necessary to acquaint those shareholders with the bargaining positions of Signal and UOP, was withheld under circumstances amounting to a breach of fiduciary duty. We therefore conclude that this merger does not meet the test of fairness, at least as we address that concept, and no burden thus shifted to the plaintiff by reason of the minority shareholder vote. Accordingly, we reverse and remand for further proceedings consistent herewith.

In considering the nature of the remedy available under our law to minority shareholders in a cash-out merger, we believe that it is, and hereafter should be, an appraisal under 8 Del. C. § 262 as hereinafter construed. We therefore overrule *Lynch v. Vickers Energy Corp.*, Del. Supr., 429 A.2d 497 (1981) (*Lynch II*) to the extent that it purports to limit a stockholder's monetary relief to a specific damage formula. *See Lynch II*, 429 A.2d at 507–08 (McNeilly & Quillen, JJ., dissenting). But to give full effect to section 262 within the framework of the General Corporation Law we adopt a more liberal, less rigid and stylized, approach to the valuation process than has heretofore been permitted by our courts. While the present state of these proceedings does not admit the plaintiff to the appraisal remedy per se, the practical effect of the remedy we do grant him will be co-extensive with the liberalized valuation and appraisal methods we herein approve for cases coming after this decision.

Our treatment of these matters has necessarily led us to a reconsideration of the business purpose rule announced in the trilogy of *Singer v. Magnavox Co., supra; Tanzer v. International General Industries, Inc.*, Del. Supr., 379 A.2d 1121 (1977); and *Roland International Corp. v. Najjar*, Del. Supr., 407 A.2d 1032 (1979). For the reasons hereafter set forth we consider that the business purpose requirement of these cases is no longer the law of Delaware.

## I.

The facts found by the trial court, pertinent to the issues before us, are supported by the record, and we draw from them as set out in the Chancellor's opinion.

Signal is a diversified, technically based company operating through various subsidiaries. Its stock is publicly traded on the New York, Philadelphia and Pacific Stock Exchanges. UOP, formerly known as Universal Oil Products Company, was a diversified industrial company engaged in various lines of business, including petroleum and petrochemical services and related products, construction, fabricated metal products, transportation, equipment products, chemicals and plastics, and other products and services including land development, lumber products and waste disposal. Its stock was publicly held and listed on the New York Stock Exchange.

In 1974 Signal sold one of its wholly-owned subsidiaries for $420,000,000 in cash. *See Gimbel v. Signal Companies, Inc.*, Del. Ch., 316 A.2d 599, *aff'd*, Del. Supr., 316 A.2d 619 (1974). While looking to invest this cash surplus, Signal became interested in UOP as a possible acquisition. Friendly negotiations ensued, and Signal proposed to acquire a controlling interest in UOP at a price of $19 per share. UOP's representatives sought $25 per share. In the arm's length bargaining that followed, an understanding was reached whereby Signal agreed to purchase from UOP 1,500,000 shares of UOP's authorized but unissued stock at $21 per share.

This purchase was contingent upon Signal making a successful cash tender offer for 4,300,000 publicly held shares of UOP, also at a price of $21 per share. This combined method of acquisition permitted Signal to acquire 5,800,000 shares of stock, representing 50.5% of UOP's outstanding shares. The UOP board of directors advised the company's shareholders that it had no objection to Signal's tender offer at that price. Immediately before the announcement of the tender offer, UOP's common stock had been trading on the New York Stock Exchange at a fraction under $14 per share.

The negotiations between Signal and UOP occurred during April 1975, and the resulting tender offer was greatly oversubscribed. However, Signal limited its total purchase of the tendered shares so that, when coupled with the stock bought from UOP, it had achieved its goal of becoming a 50.5% shareholder of UOP.

Although UOP's board consisted of thirteen directors, Signal nominated and elected only six. Of these, five were either directors or employees of Signal. The sixth, a partner in the banking firm of Lazard Freres & Co., had been one of Signal's representatives in the negotiations and bargaining with UOP concerning the tender offer and purchase price of the UOP shares.

However, the president and chief executive officer of UOP retired during 1975, and Signal caused him to be replaced by James V. Crawford, a long-time employee and senior executive vice president of one of Signal's wholly-owned subsidiaries. Crawford succeeded his predecessor on UOP's board of directors and also was made a director of Signal.

By the end of 1977 Signal basically was unsuccessful in finding other suitable investment candidates for its excess cash, and by February 1978 considered that it had no other realistic acquisitions available to it on a friendly basis. Once again its attention turned to UOP.

The trial court found that at the instigation of certain Signal management personnel, including William W. Walkup, its board chairman, and Forrest N. Shumway, its president, a feasibility study was made concerning the possible acquisition of the balance of UOP's outstanding shares. This study was performed by two Signal officers, Charles S. Arledge, vice president (director of planning), and Andrew J. Chitiea, senior vice president (chief financial officer). Messrs. Walkup,

Shumway, Arledge and Chitiea were all directors of UOP in addition to their membership on the Signal board.

Arledge and Chitiea concluded that it would be a good investment for Signal to acquire the remaining 49.5% of UOP shares at any price up to $24 each. Their report was discussed between Walkup and Shumway who, along with Arledge, Chitiea and Brewster L. Arms, internal counsel for Signal, constituted Signal's senior management. In particular, they talked about the proper price to be paid if the acquisition was pursued, purportedly keeping in mind that as UOP's majority shareholder, Signal owed a fiduciary responsibility to both its own stockholders as well as to UOP's minority. It was ultimately agreed that a meeting of Signal's Executive Committee would be called to propose that Signal acquire the remaining outstanding stock of UOP through a cash-out merger in the range of $20 to $21 per share.

The Executive Committee meeting was set for February 28, 1978. As a courtesy, UOP's president, Crawford, was invited to attend, although he was not a member of Signal's executive committee. On his arrival, and prior to the meeting, Crawford was asked to meet privately with Walkup and Shumway. He was then told of Signal's plan to acquire full ownership of UOP and was asked for his reaction to the proposed price range of $20 to $21 per share. Crawford said he thought such a price would be "generous," and that it was certainly one which should be submitted to UOP's minority shareholders for their ultimate consideration. He stated, however, that Signal's 100% ownership could cause internal problems at UOP. He believed that employees would have to be given some assurance of their future place in a fully-owned Signal subsidiary. Otherwise, he feared the departure of essential personnel. Also, many of UOP's key employees had stock option incentive programs which would be wiped out by a merger. Crawford therefore urged that some adjustment would have to be made, such as providing a comparable incentive in Signal's shares, if after the merger he was to maintain his quality of personnel and efficiency at UOP.

Thus, Crawford voiced no objection to the $20 to $21 price range, nor did he suggest that Signal should consider paying more than $21 per share for the minority interests. Later, at the Executive Committee meeting the same factors were discussed, with Crawford repeating the position he earlier took with Walkup and Shumway. Also considered was the 1975 tender offer and the fact that it had been greatly oversubscribed at $21 per share. For many reasons, Signal's management concluded that the acquisition of UOP's minority shares provided the solution to a number of its business problems.

Thus, it was the consensus that a price of $20 to $21 per share would be fair to both Signal and the minority shareholders of UOP. Signal's executive committee authorized its management "to negotiate" with UOP "for a cash acquisition of the minority ownership in UOP, Inc., with the intention of presenting a proposal to [Signal's] board of directors . . . on March 6, 1978." Immediately after this February 28, 1978 meeting, Signal issued a press release stating:

> The Signal Companies, Inc. and UOP, Inc. are conducting negotiations for the acquisition for cash by Signal of the 49.5 per cent of UOP which it does

not presently own, announced Forrest N. Shumway, president and chief executive officer of Signal, and James V. Crawford, UOP president.

Price and other terms of the proposed transaction have not yet been finalized and would be subject to approval of the boards of directors of Signal and UOP, scheduled to meet early next week, the stockholders of UOP and certain federal agencies.

The announcement also referred to the fact that the closing price of UOP's common stock on that day was $14.50 per share.

Two days later, on March 2, 1978, Signal issued a second press release stating that its management would recommend a price in the range of $20 to $21 per share for UOP's 49.5% minority interest. This announcement referred to Signal's earlier statement that "negotiations" were being conducted for the acquisition of the minority shares.

Between Tuesday, February 28, 1978 and Monday, March 6, 1978, a total of four business days, Crawford spoke by telephone with all of UOP's non-Signal, i.e., outside, directors. Also during that period, Crawford retained Lehman Brothers to render a fairness opinion as to the price offered the minority for its stock. He gave two reasons for this choice. First, the time schedule between the announcement and the board meetings was short (by then only three business days) and since Lehman Brothers had been acting as UOP's investment banker for many years, Crawford felt that it would be in the best position to respond on such brief notice. Second, James W. Glanville, a long-time director of UOP and a partner in Lehman Brothers, had acted as a financial advisor to UOP for many years. Crawford believed that Glanville's familiarity with UOP, as a member of its board, would also be of assistance in enabling Lehman Brothers to render a fairness opinion within the existing time constraints.

Crawford telephoned Glanville, who gave his assurance that Lehman Brothers had no conflicts that would prevent it from accepting the task. Glanville's immediate personal reaction was that a price of $20 to $21 would certainly be fair, since it represented almost a 50% premium over UOP's market price. Glanville sought a $250,000 fee for Lehman Brothers' services, but Crawford thought this too much. After further discussions Glanville finally agreed that Lehman Brothers would render its fairness opinion for $150,000.

During this period Crawford also had several telephone contacts with Signal officials. In only one of them, however, was the price of the shares discussed. In a conversation with Walkup, Crawford advised that as a result of his communications with UOP's non-Signal directors, it was his feeling that the price would have to be the top of the proposed range, or $21 per share, if the approval of UOP's outside directors was to be obtained. But again, he did not seek any price higher than $21.

Glanville assembled a three-man Lehman Brothers team to do the work on the fairness opinion. These persons examined relevant documents and information concerning UOP, including its annual reports and its Securities and Exchange Commission filings from 1973 through 1976, as well as its audited financial statements for 1977, its interim reports to shareholders, and its recent and historical market prices and trading volumes. In addition, on Friday, March 3, 1978, two members of the Lehman Brothers team flew to UOP's headquarters in Des Plaines, Illinois, to perform a "due diligence" visit, during the course of which they interviewed Crawford as well as UOP's general counsel, its chief financial officer, and other key executives and personnel.

As a result, the Lehman Brothers team concluded that "the price of either $20 or $21 would be a fair price for the remaining shares of UOP." They telephoned this impression to Glanville, who was spending the weekend in Vermont.

On Monday morning, March 6, 1978, Glanville and the senior member of the Lehman Brothers team flew to Des Plaines to attend the scheduled UOP directors meeting. Glanville looked over the assembled information during the flight. The two had with them the draft of a "fairness opinion letter" in which the price had been left blank. Either during or immediately prior to the directors' meeting, the two-page "fairness opinion letter" was typed in final form and the price of $21 per share was inserted.

On March 6, 1978, both the Signal and UOP boards were convened to consider the proposed merger. Telephone communications were maintained between the two meetings. Walkup, Signal's board chairman, and also a UOP director, attended UOP's meeting with Crawford in order to present Signal's position and answer any questions that UOP's non-Signal directors might have. Arledge and Chitiea, along with Signal's other designees on UOP's board, participated by conference telephone. All of UOP's outside directors attended the meeting either in person or by conference telephone.

First, Signal's board unanimously adopted a resolution authorizing Signal to propose to UOP a cash merger of $21 per share as outlined in a certain merger agreement and other supporting documents. This proposal required that the merger be approved by a majority of UOP's outstanding minority shares voting at the stockholders meeting at which the merger would be considered, and that the minority shares voting in favor of the merger, when coupled with Signal's 50.5% interest would have to comprise at least two-thirds of all UOP shares. Otherwise the proposed merger would be deemed disapproved.

UOP's board then considered the proposal. Copies of the agreement were delivered to the directors in attendance, and other copies had been forwarded earlier to the directors participating by telephone. They also had before them UOP financial data for 1974–1977, UOP's most recent financial statements, market price information, and budget projections for 1978. In addition they had Lehman Brothers' hurriedly prepared fairness opinion letter finding the price of $21 to be fair. Glanville, the Lehman Brothers partner, and UOP director, commented on the information that had gone into preparation of the letter.

Signal also suggests that the Arledge-Chitiea feasibility study, indicating that a price of up to $24 per share would be a "good investment" for Signal, was discussed at the UOP directors' meeting. The Chancellor made no such finding, and our independent review of the record, detailed *infra*, satisfies us by a preponderance of the evidence that there was no discussion of this document at UOP's board meeting. Furthermore, it is clear beyond peradventure that nothing in that report was ever disclosed to UOP's minority shareholders prior to their approval of the merger.

After consideration of Signal's proposal, Walkup and Crawford left the meeting to permit a free and uninhibited exchange between UOP's non-Signal directors. Upon their return a resolution to accept Signal's offer was then proposed and adopted. While Signal's men on UOP's board participated in various aspects of the meeting, they abstained from voting. However, the minutes show that each of them "if voting would have voted yes."

On March 7, 1978, UOP sent a letter to its shareholders advising them of the action taken by UOP's board with respect to Signal's offer. This document pointed out, among other things, that on February 28, 1978 "both companies had announced negotiations were being conducted."

Despite the swift board action of the two companies, the merger was not submitted to UOP's shareholders until their annual meeting on May 26, 1978. In the notice of that meeting and proxy statement sent to shareholders in May, UOP's management and board urged that the merger be approved. The proxy statement also advised:

> The price was determined after *discussions* between James V. Crawford, a director of Signal and Chief Executive Officer of UOP, and officers of Signal which took place during meetings on February 28, 1978, and in the course of several subsequent telephone conversations. (Emphasis added.)

In the original draft of the proxy statement the word "negotiations" had been used rather than "discussions." However, when the Securities and Exchange Commission sought details of the "negotiations" as part of its review of these materials, the term was deleted and the word "discussions" was substituted. The proxy statement indicated that the vote of UOP's board in approving the merger had been unanimous. It also advised the shareholders that Lehman Brothers had given its opinion that the merger price of $21 per share was fair to UOP's minority. However, it did not disclose the hurried method by which this conclusion was reached.

As of the record date of UOP's annual meeting, there were 11,488,302 shares of UOP common stock outstanding, 5,688,302 of which were owned by the minority. At the meeting only 56%, or 3,208,652, of the minority shares were voted. Of these, 2,953,812, or 51.9% of the total minority, voted for the merger, and 254,840 voted against it. When Signal's stock was added to the minority shares voting in favor, a total of 76.2% of UOP's outstanding shares approved the merger while only 2.2% opposed it.

By its terms the merger became effective on May 26, 1978, and each share of UOP's stock held by the minority was automatically converted into a right to receive $21 cash.

## II.

### A.

A primary issue mandating reversal is the preparation by two UOP directors, Arledge and Chitiea, of their feasibility study for the exclusive use and benefit of

Signal. This document was of obvious significance to both Signal and UOP. Using UOP data, it described the advantages to Signal of ousting the minority at a price range of $21–$24 per share. Mr. Arledge, one of the authors, outlined the benefits to Signal:

*Purpose of the Merger*

1) Provides an outstanding investment opportunity for Signal — (Better than any recent acquisition we have seen.)

2) Increases Signal's earnings.

3) Facilitates the flow of resources between Signal and its subsidiaries — (Big factor — works both ways.)

4) Provides cost savings potential for Signal and UOP.

5) Improves the percentage of Signal's 'operating earnings' as opposed to 'holding company earnings'.

6) Simplifies the understanding of Signal.

7) Facilitates technological exchange among Signal's subsidiaries.

8) Eliminates potential conflicts of interest.

Having written those words, solely for the use of Signal, it is clear from the record that neither Arledge nor Chitiea shared this report with their fellow directors of UOP. We are satisfied that no one else did either. This conduct hardly meets the fiduciary standards applicable to such a transaction. . . .

The Arledge-Chitiea report speaks for itself in supporting the Chancellor's finding that a price of up to $24 was a "good investment" for Signal. It shows that a return on the investment at $21 would be 15.7% versus 15.5% at $24 per share. This was a difference of only two-tenths of one percent, while it meant over $17,000,000 to the minority. Under such circumstances, paying UOP's minority shareholders $24 would have had relatively little long-term effect on Signal, and the Chancellor's findings concerning the benefit to Signal, even at a price of $24, were obviously correct. *Levitt v. Bouvier*, Del. Supr., 287 A.2d 671, 673 (1972).

Certainly, this was a matter of material significance to UOP and its shareholders. Since the study was prepared by two UOP directors, using UOP information for the exclusive benefit of Signal, and nothing whatever was done to disclose it to the outside UOP directors or the minority shareholders, a question of breach of fiduciary duty arises. This problem occurs because there were common Signal-UOP directors participating, at least to some extent, in the UOP board's decision-making processes without full disclosure of the conflicts they faced.

Although perfection is not possible, or expected, the result here could have been entirely different if UOP had appointed an independent negotiating committee of its outside directors to deal with Signal at arm's length. *See, e.g., Harriman v. E.I. duPont de Nemours & Co.*, 411 F. Supp. 133 (D. Del. 1975). Since fairness in this context can be equated to conduct by a theoretical, wholly independent, board of directors acting upon the matter before them, it is unfortunate that this course apparently was neither considered nor pursued. *Johnston v. Greene*, Del. Supr., 35

Del. Ch. 479, 121 A.2d 919, 925 (1956). Particularly in a parent-subsidiary context, a showing that the action taken was as though each of the contending parties had in fact exerted its bargaining power against the other at arm's length is strong evidence that the transaction meets the test of fairness. *Getty Oil Co. v. Skelly Oil Co.*, Del. Supr., 267 A.2d 883, 886 (1970); *Puma v. Marriott*, Del. Ch., 283 A.2d 693, 696 (1971).

### B.

In assessing this situation, the Court of Chancery was required to:

> examine what information defendants had and to measure it against what they gave to the minority stockholders, in a context in which 'complete candor'is required. In other words, the limited function of the Court was to determine whether defendants had disclosed all information in their possession germane to the transaction in issue. And by 'germane' we mean, for present purposes, information such as a reasonable shareholder would consider important in deciding whether to sell or retain stock.

> \* \* \*

> . . . Completeness, not adequacy, is both the norm and the mandate under present circumstances.

*Lynch v. Vickers Energy Corp.*, Del. Supr., 383 A.2d 278, 281 (1977) (*Lynch I*). This is merely stating in another way the long-existing principle of Delaware law that these Signal designated directors on UOP's board still owed UOP and its shareholders an uncompromising duty of loyalty. The classic language of *Guth v. Loft, Inc.*, Del. Supr., 23 Del. Ch. 255, 5 A.2d 503, 510 (1939), requires no embellishment:

> A public policy, existing through the years, and derived from a profound knowledge of human characteristics and motives, has established a rule that demands of a corporate officer or director, peremptorily and inexorably, the most scrupulous observance of his duty, not only affirmatively to protect the interests of the corporation committed to his charge, but also to refrain from doing anything that would work injury to the corporation, or to deprive it of profit or advantage which his skill and ability might properly bring to it, or to enable it to make in the reasonable and lawful exercise of its powers. The rule that requires an undivided and unselfish loyalty to the corporation demands that there shall be no conflict between duty and self-interest.

Given the absence of any attempt to structure this transaction on an arm's length basis, Signal cannot escape the effects of the conflicts it faced, particularly when its designees on UOP's board did not totally abstain from participation in the matter. There is no "safe harbor" for such divided loyalties in Delaware. When directors of a Delaware corporation are on both sides of a transaction, they are required to demonstrate their utmost good faith and the most scrupulous inherent fairness of the bargain. *Gottlieb v. Heyden Chemical Corp.*, Del. Supr., 33 Del. Ch. 177, 91 A.2d 57, 57–58 (1952). The requirement of fairness is unflinching in its demand that where one stands on both sides of a transaction, he has the burden of establishing its entire fairness, sufficient to pass the test of careful scrutiny by the courts. *Sterling v. Mayflower Hotel Corp.*, Del. Supr., 33 Del. Ch. 293, 93 A.2d 107, 110 (1952); *Bastian v. Bourns, Inc.*, Del. Ch., 256 A.2d 680, 681 (1969), *aff'd*, Del. Supr., 278 A.2d 467 (1970); *David J. Greene & Co. v. Dunhill International Inc.*, Del. Ch., 249 A.2d 427, 431 (1968).

There is no dilution of this obligation where one holds dual or multiple directorships, as in a parent-subsidiary context. *Levien v. Sinclair Oil Corp.*, Del. Ch., 261 A.2d 911, 915 (1969). Thus, individuals who act in a dual capacity as directors of two corporations, one of whom is parent and the other subsidiary, owe the same duty of good management to both corporations, and in the absence of an independent negotiating structure (see note 7, *supra*), or the directors' total abstention from any participation in the matter, this duty is to be exercised in light of what is best for both companies.*Warshaw v. Calhoun*, Del. Supr., 43 Del. Ch. 148, 221 A.2d 487, 492 (1966). The record demonstrates that Signal has not met this obligation.

### C.

The concept of fairness has two basic aspects: fair dealing and fair price. The former embraces questions of when the transaction was timed, how it was initiated, structured, negotiated, disclosed to the directors, and how the approvals of the directors and the stockholders were obtained. The latter aspect of fairness relates to the economic and financial considerations of the proposed merger, including all relevant factors:assets, market value, earnings, future prospects, and any other elements that affect the intrinsic or inherent value of a company's stock. Moore, *The "Interested" Director or Officer Transaction*, 4 Del. J. Corp. L. 674, 676 (1979); Nathan & Shapiro, *Legal Standard of Fairness of Merger Terms Under Delaware Law*, 2 Del. J. Corp. L. 44, 46–47 (1977). *See Tri-Continental Corp. v. Battye*, Del. Supr., 31 Del. Ch. 523, 74 A.2d 71,72 (1950); 8 Del. C. § 262(h). However, the test for fairness is not a bifurcated one as between fair dealing and price. All aspects of the issue must be examined as a whole since the question is one of entire fairness. However, in a non-fraudulent transaction we recognize that price may be the preponderant consideration outweighing other features of the merger. Here, we address the two basic aspects of fairness separately because we find reversible error as to both.

### D.

Part of fair dealing is the obvious duty of candor required by *Lynch I, supra*. Moreover, one possessing superior knowledge may not mislead any stockholder by use of corporate information to which the latter is not privy. *Lank v. Steiner*, Del. Supr., 43 Del. Ch. 262, 224 A.2d 242, 244 (1966). Delaware has long imposed this duty even upon persons who are not corporate officers or directors, but who nonetheless are privy to matters of interest or significance to their company. *Brophy v. Cities Service Co.*, Del. Ch., 31 Del. Ch. 241, 70 A.2d 5, 7 (1949). With the well-established Delaware law on the subject, and the Court of Chancery's findings of fact here, it is inevitable that the obvious conflicts posed by Arledge and Chitiea's preparation of their "feasibility study," derived from UOP information, for the sole use and benefit of Signal, cannot pass muster.

The Arledge-Chitiea report is but one aspect of the element of fair dealing. How did this merger evolve? It is clear that it was entirely initiated by Signal. The serious time constraints under which the principals acted were all set by Signal. It had not found a suitable outlet for its excess cash and considered UOP a desirable investment, particularly since it was now in a position to acquire the whole company for itself. For whatever reasons, and they were only Signal's, the entire transaction was presented to and approved by UOP's board within four business days. Standing alone, this is not necessarily indicative of any lack of fairness by a majority shareholder. It was what occurred, or more properly, what did not occur, during this brief period that makes the time constraints imposed by Signal relevant to the issue of fairness.

The structure of the transaction, again, was Signal's doing. So far as negotiations were concerned, it is clear that they were modest at best. Crawford, Signal's man at UOP, never really talked price with Signal, except to accede to its management's statements on the subject, and to convey to Signal the UOP outside directors' view that as between the $20–$21 range under consideration, it would have to be $21. The latter is not a surprising outcome, but hardly arm's length negotiations. Only the protection of benefits for UOP's key employees and the issue of Lehman Brothers' fee approached any concept of bargaining.

As we have noted, the matter of disclosure to the UOP directors was wholly flawed by the conflicts of interest raised by the Arledge-Chitiea report. All of those conflicts were resolved by Signal in its own favor without divulging any aspect of them to UOP.

This cannot but undermine a conclusion that this merger meets any reasonable test of fairness. The outside UOP directors lacked one material piece of information generated by two of their colleagues, but shared only with Signal. True, the UOP board had the Lehman Brothers' fairness opinion, but that firm has been blamed by the plaintiff for the hurried task it performed, when more properly the responsibility for this lies with Signal. There was no disclosure of the circumstances surrounding the rather cursory preparation of the Lehman Brothers' fairness opinion. Instead, the impression was given UOP's minority that a careful study had been made, when in fact speed was the hallmark, and Mr. Glanville, Lehman's partner in charge of the matter, and also a UOP director, having spent the weekend in Vermont, brought a draft of the "fairness opinion letter" to the UOP directors' meeting on March 6, 1978 with the price left blank. We can only conclude from the record that the rush imposed on Lehman Brothers by Signal's timetable contributed to the difficulties under which this investment banking firm attempted to perform its responsibilities. Yet, none of this was disclosed to UOP's minority.

Finally, the minority stockholders were denied the critical information that Signal considered a price of $24 to be a good investment. Since this would have meant over $17,000,000 more to the minority, we cannot conclude that the shareholder vote was an informed one. Under the circumstances, an approval by a majority of the minority was meaningless. *Lynch I*, 383 A.2d at 279, 281; *Cahall v. Lofland*, Del. Ch., 12 Del. Ch. 299, 114 A. 224 (1921).

Given these particulars and the Delaware law on the subject, the record does not establish that this transaction satisfies any reasonable concept of fair dealing, and the Chancellor's findings in that regard must be reversed.

### E.

Turning to the matter of price, plaintiff also challenges its fairness. His evidence was that on the date the merger was approved the stock was worth at least $26 per share. In support, he offered the testimony of a chartered investment analyst who used two basic approaches to valuation: a comparative analysis of the premium paid over market in ten other tender offer-merger combinations, and a discounted cash flow analysis.

In this breach of fiduciary duty case, the Chancellor perceived that the approach to valuation was the same as that in an appraisal proceeding. Consistent with precedent, he rejected plaintiff's method of proof and accepted defendants' evidence of value as being in accord with practice under prior case law. This means that the so-called "Delaware block" or weighted average method was employed wherein the elements of value, i.e., assets, market price, earnings, etc., were assigned a particular weight and the resulting amounts added to determine the value per share. This procedure has been in use for decades. *See In re General Realty & Utilities Corp.*, Del. Ch., 29 Del. Ch. 480, 52 A.2d 6, 14–15 (1947). However, to the extent it excludes other generally accepted techniques used in the financial community and the courts, it is now clearly outmoded. It is time we recognize this in appraisal and other stock valuation proceedings and bring our law current on the subject.

While the Chancellor rejected plaintiff's discounted cash flow method of valuing UOP's stock, as not corresponding with "either logic or the existing law" (426 A.2d at 1360), it is significant that this was essentially the focus, i.e., earnings potential of UOP, of Messrs. Arledge and Chitiea in their evaluation of the merger. Accordingly, the standard "Delaware block" or weighted average method of valuation, formerly employed in appraisal and other stock valuation cases, shall no longer exclusively control such proceedings. We believe that a more liberal approach must include proof of value by any techniques or methods which are generally considered acceptable in the financial community and otherwise admissible in court, subject only to our interpretation of 8 Del. C. § 262(h), *infra. See also* D.R.E. 702–05. This will obviate the very structured and mechanistic procedure that has heretofore governed such matters. *See Jacques Coe & Co. v. Minneapolis-Moline Co.*, Del. Ch., 31 Del. Ch. 368, 75 A.2d 244, 247 (1950); *Tri-Continental Corp. v. Battye*, Del. Ch., 31 Del. Ch. 101, 66 A.2d 910, 917–18 (1949); *In re General Realty and Utilities Corp., supra.*

Fair price obviously requires consideration of all relevant factors involving the value of a company. This has long been the law of Delaware as stated in *Tri-Continental Corp. v. Battye*, [Del. Supr.,] 74 A.2d [71 (1950)]:

> The basic concept of value under the appraisal statute is that the stockholder is entitled to be paid for that which has been taken from him, viz., his proportionate interest in a going concern. By value of the

> stockholder's proportionate interest in the corporate enterprise is meant the true or intrinsic value of his stock which has been taken by the merger. In determining what figure represents this true or intrinsic value, the appraiser and the courts must take into consideration all factors and elements which reasonably might enter into the fixing of value. Thus, market value, asset value, dividends, earning prospects, the nature of the enterprise and any other facts which were known or which could be ascertained as of the date of merger and which throw any light on *future prospects* of the merged corporation are not only pertinent to an inquiry as to the value of the dissenting stockholders' interest, but *must be considered* by the agency fixing the value. (Emphasis added.)

This is not only in accord with the realities of present day affairs, but it is thoroughly consonant with the purpose and intent of our statutory law. Under 8 Del. C. § 262(h), the Court of Chancery:

> shall appraise the shares, determining their *fair* value exclusive of any element of value arising from the accomplishment or expectation of the merger, together with a fair rate of interest, if any, to be paid upon the amount determined to be the *fair* value. In determining such *fair* value, the Court shall take into account *all relevant factors* . . . (Emphasis added)

*See also Bell v. Kirby Lumber Corp.*, Del. Supr., 413 A.2d 137, 150–51 (1980) (Quillen, J., concurring).

It is significant that section 262 now mandates the determination of "fair" value based upon "all relevant factors." Only the speculative elements of value that may arise from the accomplishment or expectation" of the merger are excluded. We take this to be a very narrow exception to the appraisal process, designed to eliminate use of *pro forma* data and projections of a speculative variety relating to the completion of a merger. But elements of future value, including the nature of the enterprise, which are known or susceptible of proof as of the date of the merger and not the product of speculation, may be considered. When the trial court deems it appropriate, fair value also includes any damages, resulting from the taking, which the stockholders sustain as a class. If that was not the case, then the obligation to consider "all relevant factors" in the valuation process would be eroded. We are supported in this view not only by *Tri-Continental Corp.*, 74 A.2d at 72, but also by the evolutionary amendments to section 262.

Prior to an amendment in 1976, the earlier relevant provision of section 262 stated:

> (f) The appraiser shall determine the value of the stock of the stockholders . . . The Court shall by its decree determine the value of the stock of the stockholders entitled to payment therefor . . .

The first references to "fair" value occurred in a 1976 amendment to section 262(f), which provided:

> (f) . . . the Court shall appraise the shares, determining their fair value exclusively of any element of value arising from the accomplishment or expectation of the merger. . . .

It was not until the 1981 amendment to section 262 that the reference to "fair value" was repeatedly emphasized and the statutory mandate that the Court "take into account all relevant factors" appeared [section 262(h)]. Clearly, there is a legislative intent to fully compensate shareholders for whatever their loss may be, subject only to the narrow limitation that one can not take speculative effects of the merger into account.

Although the Chancellor received the plaintiff's evidence, his opinion indicates that the use of it was precluded because of past Delaware practice. While we do not suggest a monetary result one way or the other, we do think the plaintiff's evidence should be part of the factual mix and weighed as such. Until the $21 price is measured on remand by the valuation standards mandated by Delaware law, there can be no finding at the present stage of these proceedings that the price is fair. Given the lack of any candid disclosure of the material facts surrounding establishment of the $21 price, the majority of the minority vote, approving the merger, is meaningless.

The plaintiff has not sought an appraisal, but rescissory damages of the type contemplated by *Lynch v. Vickers Energy Corp.*, Del. Supr., 429 A.2d 497, 505–06 (1981) (*Lynch II*). In view of the approach to valuation that we announce today, we see no basis in our law for *Lynch II*'s exclusive monetary formula for relief. On remand the plaintiff will be permitted to test the fairness of the $21 price by the standards we herein establish, in conformity with the principle applicable to an appraisal — that fair value be determined by taking "into account all relevant factors" [*see* 8 Del. C. § 262(h), *supra*]. In our view this includes the elements of rescissory damages if the Chancellor considers them susceptible of proof and a remedy appropriate to all the issues of fairness before him. To the extent that *Lynch II*, 429 A.2d at 505–06, purports to limit the Chancellor's discretion to a single remedial formula for monetary damages in a cash-out merger, it is overruled.

While a plaintiff's monetary remedy ordinarily should be confined to the more liberalized appraisal proceeding herein established, we do not intend any limitation on the historic powers of the Chancellor to grant such other relief as the facts of a particular case may dictate. The appraisal remedy we approve may not be adequate in certain cases, particularly where fraud, misrepresentation, self-dealing, deliberate waste of corporate assets, or gross and palpable overreaching are involved. *Cole v. National Cash Credit Association*, Del. Ch., 18 Del. Ch. 47, 156 A. 183, 187 (1931). Under such circumstances, the Chancellor's powers are complete to fashion any form of equitable and monetary relief as may be appropriate, including rescissory damages. Since it is apparent that this long completed transaction is too involved to undo, and in view of the Chancellor's discretion, the award, if any, should be in the form of monetary damages based upon entire fairness standards, i.e., fair dealing and fair price.

Obviously, there are other litigants, like the plaintiff, who abjured an appraisal and whose rights to challenge the element of fair value must be preserved.[22] Accordingly, the quasi-appraisal remedy we grant the plaintiff here will apply only

---

22 [8] Under 8 Del. C. § 262(a), (d) & (e), a stockholder is required to act within certain time periods to perfect the right to an appraisal.

to: (1) this case; (2) any case now pending on appeal to this Court; (3) any case now pending in the Court of Chancery which has not yet been appealed but which may be eligible for direct appeal to this Court; (4) any case challenging a cash-out merger, the effective date of which is on or before February 1, 1983; and (5) any proposed merger to be presented at a shareholders' meeting, the notification of which is mailed to the stockholders on or before February 23, 1983. Thereafter, the provisions of 8 Del. C. § 262, as herein construed, respecting the scope of an appraisal and the means for perfecting the same, shall govern the financial remedy available to minority shareholders in a cash-out merger. Thus, we return to the well established principles of *Stauffer v. Standard Brands, Inc.*, Del. Supr., 41 Del. Ch. 7, 187 A.2d 78 (1962) and *David J. Greene & Co.v. Schenley Industries, Inc.*, Del. Ch., 281 A.2d 30 (1971), mandating a stockholder's recourse to the basic remedy of an appraisal.

### III.

Finally, we address the matter of business purpose. The defendants contend that the purpose of this merger was not a proper subject of inquiry by the trial court. The plaintiff says that no valid purpose existed — the entire transaction was a mere subterfuge designed to eliminate the minority. The Chancellor ruled otherwise, but in so doing he clearly circumscribed the thrust and effect of *Singer. Weinberger v. UOP*, 426 A.2d at 1342–43, 1348–50. This has led to the thoroughly sound observation that the business purpose test "may be . . . virtually interpreted out of existence, as it was in *Weinberger.*"

The requirement of a business purpose is new to our law of mergers and was a departure from prior case law. *See Stauffer v. Standard Brands, Inc., supra; David J. Greene & Co. v. Schenley Industries, Inc., supra.*

In view of the fairness test which has long been applicable to parent-subsidiary mergers, *Sterling v. Mayflower Hotel Corp.*, Del. Supr., 33 Del. Ch. 293, 93 A.2d 107,109–10 (1952), the expanded appraisal remedy now available to shareholders, and the broad discretion of the Chancellor to fashion such relief as the facts of a given case may dictate, we do not believe that any additional meaningful protection is afforded minority shareholders by the business purpose requirement of the trilogy of *Singer, Tanzer, Najjar,* and their progeny. Accordingly, such requirement shall no longer be of any force or effect.

The judgment of the Court of Chancery, finding both the circumstances of the merger and the price paid the minority shareholders to be fair, is reversed. The matter is remanded for further proceedings consistent herewith. Upon remand the plaintiff's post-trial motion to enlarge the class should be granted.

## NOTES

1. Most statutory tests dealing with contracts involving interested directors, such as Section 144 of the Delaware General Corporation Law, discussed in *Fliegler v. Lawrence, supra,* provide a variety of means, some procedural and some substantive, which may be utilized to validate such a contract. The decision in *Weinberger,* by contrast, imposes an even more stringent test on transactions

between a corporation and its partially owned subsidiary, which requires that the parent bear the burden of proving of both procedural ("fair dealing") and substantive ("fair price") fairness for the transaction to stand. This reflects the court's view that minority shareholders of a partially owned subsidiary are particularly subject to exploitation by the parent corporation and that especially stringent protections are needed. Do you agree?

2.   As the court noted, one way in which a parent might avoid the need to bear the burden of proving entire fairness would be to appoint an independent negotiating committee to handle negotiations on behalf of the subsidiary. In *Kahn v. Lynch Communication Systems*, 638 A.2d 1110 (Del. 1994), the court had occasion to put this dictum to the test. The case involved an acquisition of Lynch Communication Systems, Inc. (the subsidiary) by Alcatel U.S.A. Corporation (the parent.) Lynch had established an independent committee to handle the negotiations with Alcatel. After lengthy negotiations, the Committee approved a cash out merger of Lynch into Alcatel. Plaintiff, a minority shareholder of Lynch, sued claiming breach of fiduciary duty in approving the merger at an inadequate price. The Supreme Court, reversing the Chancellor, held that the use of an Independent Committee here did not cause the transaction to resemble a true arm's length bargain so as to shift the burden of proving unfairness to the plaintiff minority shareholder. The Court stated:

> "A condition precedent to finding that the burden of proving entire fairness has shifted in an interested merger transaction is a careful judicial analysis of the factual circumstances of each case. Particular consideration must be given to evidence of whether the special committee was truly independent, fully informed and had the freedom to negotiate at arms length . . . ."

Although perfection is not possible, "unless the controlling or dominating shareholder can demonstrate that it has not only formed an independent committee but also replicated a process" as though each of the contending parties had in fact exerted its bargaining power at arm's length, "the burden of proving entire fairness will not shift. *Weinberger v. UOP, Inc.*, 457 A.2d at 709–10 n.7." 638 A.2d at 1130.

On remand, the Chancellor found that, applying the standard specified by the Supreme Court, the parent had met its burden of proof that the transaction was fair to the minority shareholders. On appeal this ruling was upheld in *Kahn v. Lynch Communication Systems*, 669 A.2d 79 (Del. 1995).

## 5.   Sarbanes-Oxley

In July 2002, in response to the Enron and Worldcom scandals, Congress passed the Sarbanes-Oxley Act, P.L. 107–124. The Act was intended to promote investor confidence in the securities markets and to impose new duties on officers, directors, attorneys, and auditors of publicly traded companies. Most of the law applies only to large, public companies which are required to file Forms 10-K with the SEC. It primarily amends existing provisions of the Securities Exchange Act of 1934 or the Federal Criminal Code. The following briefly summarizes the high points of this important statute.

Title I of the Act establishes the Public Company Accounting Oversight Board. The Board is charged with overseeing the audit of public companies, establishing standards for audit reports, investigating registered public accounting firms, and enforcing compliance with professional standards. The Act directs the Board to establish auditing standards and ethical standards for registered public accounting firms who prepare audit reports on public companies. It also mandates periodic inspections of accounting firms conducting audits of corporations subject to the Act. The *audit report* is a financial summary in which the public accounting firm audits the issuer for compliance with securities laws and makes a conclusion regarding the audited financial statement, report, or other document. In the audit report, the public accounting firm can also "assert that no such opinion can be expressed." The public accounting firm is responsible for undertaking an objective evaluation of the company's internal financial controls and adherence to its own financial reporting procedures.

Title II addresses auditor independence. It prohibits auditors from rendering consulting or other non-auditing services to a client contemporaneously with an audit. In addition, it prohibits an audit partner from being the lead auditor for a particular company for more than five consecutive years. There is a one-year freeze on an auditor performing audit services if a company's senior executives have been employed by that auditor or participated in an audit during the prior year.

Title III addresses corporate responsibility. It requires each member of the audit committee to be a member of the board of directors but be otherwise independent, not receiving any other fees or compensation from the company. Furthermore, the SEC is required to issue rules requiring the CEO and CFO of companies to certify personally that the financial reports do not contain any untrue statements or material omissions and fairly present the financial condition of the company. The officers are also charged with establishing internal controls to ensure that they receive all material information concerning the company's finances. The Act makes it unlawful for corporate officers to exert improper influence on auditors in an attempt to make the audit materially misleading. Also, the CEO and CFO must surrender bonuses and other incentive compensation received if the company is required by its auditors to restate its earnings due to materially misleading statements. The Act amends the Securities and Exchange Act of 1934 to prohibit a violator from serving as an officer or director if his or her individual conduct demonstrates that he or she is "unfit" to serve. With respect to attorneys, the Act charges them with reporting violations of the securities laws and breaches of fiduciary duty by the company's officers to the company's chief legal counsel or the CEO of the company. Finally, the Act allows civil penalties to be imposed which are placed in a "disgorgement fund" for the benefit of victims of securities violations.

Title IV of the Act deals with financial disclosures. It requires that financial reports filed with the SEC reflect all material correcting adjustments which have been identified, and requires disclosure of all material, off-balance sheet transactions, which may have a material effect on the financial status of the issuer.

Title V addresses conflicts of interest in the investment banking community. It contains provisions designed to ensure that research analysts are not subject to the supervision of, or unduly influenced by, persons involved in investment banking activities. It also establishes "blackout periods" for brokers and dealers involve in a public offering of securities, prohibiting them from distributing research reports during a public offering. Title VI authorizes increased appropriations for the SEC to enable it to step up enforcement activities of both new and existing provisions of the Securities Exchange Act of 1934 and other statutes.

Title VII authorizes studies of the securities markets and major participants in it to determine if further legislation or administrative regulation is required.

Title VIII imposes criminal penalties for knowingly destroying or falsifying documents in an attempt to interfere with a federal investigation. It extends the statute of limitations for private rights of action under the securities laws to up to two years after the discovery of a cause of action or five years after the date of violation. Finally, it provides protection to whistleblowers by prohibiting retaliation against any employee for assisting in an investigation of fraud or other unlawful conduct by the employer.

Title IX of the Act provides for increased penalties for mail and wire fraud from five years to up to 20 years, increases fines for violations of ERISA to $500,000 and 10 years imprisonment, and establishes criminal liability for the failure of corporate officers to file and certify financial reports required under the Act, including penalties of up to 10 years for knowingly filing a report that does not comply with the Act or twenty years for willfully certifying a statement that the officer knows does not comply with the Act.

Title X encourages, but does not require, the company's CEO to sign the federal tax return. Title XI amends federal criminal law to provide for sentences of up to 20 years for tampering with records or otherwise interfering with a federal investigation. It also authorizes the SEC to obtain injunctive relief to freeze extraordinary payments to designated persons who are under investigation for suspected violations of the Act. Furthermore, it authorizes the SEC to prohibit violators of rules from serving as an officer or director of a publicly traded company if it deems them "unfit" to serve. Finally, the Act increases penalties for violations of the Securities Exchange Act of 1934 to up to $25 million dollars and up to 20 years imprisonment.

Three sections of Sarbanes-Oxley are responsible for most of the reporting and certification rules imposed on public accounting companies and corporate officers. Section 302 requires the SEC to adopt rules requiring the principal executive and financial officers to certify the annual and quarterly reports. Section 404(a) requires the SEC to adopt rules requiring reporting companies to annually include "an internal control report." Annual reports must include statements related to the establishment and maintenance of internal control structures and procedures for financial reporting, as well as indicate the "effectiveness of the internal control structure and procedures of the issuer. . . . " And Section 404(b) requires registered public accounting firms to analyze the internal control report.

These three provisions in Sarbanes-Oxley resulted in numerous new duties applicable to public companies. For instance, principal executive officers of public companies are required to certify the company's periodic reports. Public companies must maintain disclosure controls and procedures, maintain internal control over financial reporting, and annually assess the effectiveness of the company's internal control over financial reporting. Public accountants must audit annually and report on the company's internal control over financial reporting, attest to the public company management's assessment of the effectiveness of the company's internal control over financial reporting and review management's quarterly evaluation of changes in the company's internal control over financial reporting. Finally, the company's management must annually evaluate any changes in the company's internal control over financial reporting that materially affected or is likely to affect the company's internal control over financial reporting and disclose the results and evaluate periodically the effectiveness of the company's disclosure controls and procedures and disclose the results.

## C.   DUTY OF GOOD FAITH

### 1.   General Principles

Corporate directors are generally protected by the business judgment rule, a presumption that they have acted in conformity with their fiduciary duties. The Delaware court has noted that "a shareholder plaintiff challenging a board decision has the burden at the outset to rebut the rule's presumption. To rebut the rule, a shareholder plaintiff assumes the burden of providing evidence that directors, in reaching their challenged decision, breached *any one of the triads of their fiduciary duty — good faith, loyalty or due care.*" Cede & Co. v. Technicolor, 634 A.2d 345, 361 (Del. 1991) (emphasis added). We have examined the duty of care and the duty of loyalty; we now turn to the duty of good faith.

Think back once again to *Meinhard v. Salmon, supra* Ch. 3, Sec. B. Justice Cardozo focused on Salmon's obligation to *disclose* the opportunity to continue and expand the lease more than on whether Salmon was actually required to share the business going forward. Breach of the duty of good faith has rarely been used as a stand-alone cause of action in the way that breach of the duty of care or loyalty has, so there is less commentary about the scope of the duty. It has been described as a duty of candor and full disclosure, or as an honest and genuine attempt to do right by the shareholders. There have been several recent decisions in Delaware, however, in which the courts have attempted to define this duty more fully. Rather than conceiving of it as an equal member of the triad, the courts now speak in terms of the duty of faith as being an aspect of the duty of loyalty.

## BREHM v. EISNER
## (IN RE WALT DISNEY CO.
## DERIVATIVE LITIGATION)
Supreme Court of Delaware
906 A.2d 27 (2006)

JACOBS, JUSTICE:

In August 1995, Michael Ovitz ("Ovitz") and The Walt Disney Company ("Disney" or the "Company") entered into an employment agreement under which Ovitz would serve as President of Disney for five years. In December 1996, only fourteen months after he commenced employment, Ovitz was terminated without cause, resulting in a severance payout to Ovitz valued at approximately $130 million.

In January 1997, several Disney shareholders brought derivative actions in the Court of Chancery, on behalf of Disney, against Ovitz and the directors of Disney who served at the time of the events complained of (the "Disney defendants"). The plaintiffs claimed that the $130 million severance payout was the product of fiduciary duty and contractual breaches by Ovitz, and breaches of fiduciary duty by the Disney defendants, and a waste of assets. . . . The Court entered judgment in favor of all defendants on all claims alleged in the amended complaint.

The plaintiffs have appealed from that judgment . . . .

### I. *THE FACTS*

\* \* \*

In 1994 Disney lost in a tragic helicopter crash its President and Chief Operating Officer, Frank Wells, who together with Michael Eisner, Disney's Chairman and Chief Executive Officer, had enjoyed remarkable success at the Company's helm. Eisner temporarily assumed Disney's presidency, but only three months later, heart disease required Eisner to undergo quadruple bypass surgery. Those two events persuaded Eisner and Disney's board of directors that the time had come to identify a successor to Eisner.

Eisner's prime candidate for the position was Michael Ovitz, who was the leading partner and one of the founders of Creative Artists Agency ("CAA"), the premier talent agency whose business model had reshaped the entire industry. By 1995, CAA had 550 employees and a roster of about 1400 of Hollywood's top actors, directors, writers, and musicians. That roster generated about $150 million in annual revenues and an annual income of over $20 million for Ovitz, who was regarded as one of the most powerful figures in Hollywood.

Eisner and Ovitz had enjoyed a social and professional relationship that spanned nearly 25 years. Although in the past the two men had casually discussed possibly working together, in 1995, when Ovitz began negotiations to leave CAA and join Music Corporation of America ("MCA"), Eisner became seriously interested in recruiting Ovitz to join Disney. Eisner shared that desire with Disney's board members on an individual basis. . . .

[Disney director Irwin] Russell assumed the lead in negotiating the financial terms of the Ovitz employment contract. In the course of negotiations, Russell learned from Ovitz's attorney, Bob Goldman, that Ovitz owned 55% of CAA and earned approximately $20 to $25 million a year from that company. From the beginning Ovitz made it clear that he would not give up his 55% interest in CAA without "downside protection." Considerable negotiation then ensued over downside protection issues. During the summer of 1995, the parties agreed to a draft version of Ovitz's employment agreement (the "OEA") modeled after Eisner's and the late Mr. Wells' employment contracts. As described by the Chancellor, the draft agreement included the following terms:

> Under the proposed OEA, Ovitz would receive a five-year contract with two tranches of options. The first tranche consisted of three million options vesting in equal parts in the third, fourth, and fifth years, and if the value of those options at the end of the five years had not appreciated to $50 million, Disney would make up the difference. The second tranche consisted of two million options that would vest immediately if Disney and Ovitz opted to renew the contract.

> The proposed OEA sought to protect both parties in the event that Ovitz's employment ended prematurely, and provided that absent defined causes, neither party could terminate the agreement without penalty. If Ovitz, for example, walked away, for any reason other than those permitted under the OEA, he would forfeit any benefits remaining under the OEA and could be enjoined from working for a competitor. Likewise, if Disney fired Ovitz for any reason other than gross negligence or malfeasance, Ovitz would be entitled to a non-fault payment (Non-Fault Termination or "NFT"), which consisted of his remaining salary, $7.5 million a year for unaccrued bonuses, the immediate vesting of his first tranche of options and a $10 million cash out payment for the second tranche of options. * * *

Ovitz's tenure as President of the Walt Disney Company officially began on October 1, 1995, the date that the OEA was executed. When Ovitz took office, the initial reaction was optimistic, and Ovitz did make some positive contributions while serving as President of the Company. By the fall of 1996, however, it had become clear that Ovitz was "a poor fit with his fellow executives." By then the Disney directors were discussing that the disconnect between Ovitz and the Company was likely irreparable and that Ovitz would have to be terminated. . . .

A December 27, 1996 letter from [Disney Director, Executive Vice President, and General Counsel Sanford] Litvack to Ovitz, which Ovitz signed, memorialized the termination, accelerated Ovitz's departure date from January 31, 1997 to December 31, 1996, and informed Ovitz that he would receive roughly $38 million in cash and that the first tranche of three million options would vest immediately. By the terms of that letter agreement, Ovitz's tenure as an executive and a director of Disney officially ended on December 27, 1996. Shortly thereafter, Disney paid Ovitz what was owed under the OEA for an NFT, minus a holdback of $1 million pending final settlement of Ovitz's accounts. One month after Disney paid Ovitz, the plaintiffs filed this action. . . .

The appellants' claims of error are most easily analyzed in two separate groupings: (1) the claims against the Disney defendants and (2) the claims against Ovitz. The first category encompasses the claims that the Disney defendants breached their fiduciary duties to act with due care and in good faith by (1) approving the OEA, and specifically, its NFT provisions; and (2) approving the NFT severance payment to Ovitz upon his termination-a payment that is also claimed to constitute corporate waste. It is notable that the appellants do *not* contend that the Disney defendants are directly liable as a consequence of those fiduciary duty breaches. Rather, appellants' core argument is indirect, *i.e.*, that those breaches of fiduciary duty deprive the Disney defendants of the protection of business judgment review, and require them to shoulder the burden of establishing that their acts were entirely fair to Disney. That burden, the appellants contend, the Disney defendants failed to carry. The appellants claim that by ruling that the Disney defendants did not breach their fiduciary duty to act with due care or in good faith, the Court of Chancery committed reversible error in numerous respects. Alternatively, the appellants claim that even if the business judgment presumptions apply, the Disney defendants are nonetheless liable, because the NFT payout constituted corporate waste and the Court of Chancery erred in concluding otherwise. . . .

A. *Claims Arising From The Approval Of The OEA And Ovitz's Election As President*

As earlier noted, the appellants' core argument in the trial court was that the Disney defendants' approval of the OEA and election of Ovitz as President were not entitled to business judgment rule protection, because those actions were either grossly negligent or not performed in good faith. The Court of Chancery rejected these arguments, and held that the appellants had failed to prove that the Disney defendants had breached any fiduciary duty.

For clarity of presentation we address the claimed errors relating to the fiduciary duty of care rulings separately from those that relate to the directors' fiduciary duty to act in good faith.

\* \* \*

. . . Our law presumes that "in making a business decision the directors of a corporation acted on an informed basis, in good faith, and in the honest belief that the action taken was in the best interests of the company." Aronson v. Lewis, 473 A.2d 805, 812 (Del. 1984). Those presumptions can be rebutted if the plaintiff shows that the directors breached their fiduciary duty of care or of loyalty or acted in bad faith. If that is shown, the burden then shifts to the director defendants to demonstrate that the challenged act or transaction was entirely fair to the corporation and its shareholders. *Emerald Partners v. Berlin*, 787 A.2d 85, 91 (Del. 2001), *Brehm v. Eisner*, 746 A.2d 244, 264 n.66 (Del. 2000).

Because no duty of loyalty claim was asserted against the Disney defendants, the only way to rebut the business judgment rule presumptions would be to show that the Disney defendants had either breached their duty of care or had not acted in good faith. At trial, the plaintiff-appellants attempted to establish both grounds, but the Chancellor determined that the plaintiffs had failed to prove either.

[Duty of care discussion omitted.]

* * *

## 2. *The Good Faith Determinations*

The Court of Chancery held that the business judgment rule presumptions protected the decisions of the compensation committee and the remaining Disney directors, not only because they had acted with due care but also because they had not acted in bad faith. That latter ruling, the appellants claim, was reversible error because the Chancellor formulated and then applied an incorrect definition of bad faith.

In its Opinion the Court of Chancery defined bad faith as follows:

> Upon long and careful consideration, I am of the opinion that the concept of *intentional dereliction of duty*, a *conscious disregard for one's responsibilities*, is an appropriate (although not the only) standard for determining whether fiduciaries have acted in good faith. Deliberate indifference and inaction *in the face of a duty to act* is, in my mind, conduct that is clearly disloyal to the corporation. It is the epitome of faithless conduct.

2005 Del. Ch. LEXIS 113, [Post-trial Op.] at *36 (italics in original, footnotes omitted).

The appellants contend that definition is erroneous for two reasons. First they claim that the trial court had adopted a different definition in its 2003 decision denying the motion to dismiss the complaint, and the Court's post-trial (2005) definition materially altered the 2003 definition to appellants' prejudice. . . .

Second, the appellants claim that the Chancellor's post-trial definition of bad faith is erroneous substantively. . . .

The appellants' first argument-that there is a real, significant difference between the Chancellor's pre-trial and post-trial definitions of bad faith-is plainly wrong. We perceive no substantive difference between the Court of Chancery's 2003 definition of bad faith-a "conscious[] and intentional[] disregard[] [of] responsibilities, adopting a we don't care about the risks' attitude . . ." — and its 2005 post-trial definition — an "intentional dereliction of duty, a conscious disregard for one's responsibilities." Both formulations express the same concept, although in slightly different language.

* * *

For that reason, our analysis of the appellants' bad faith claim could end at this point. In other circumstances it would. This case, however, is one in which the duty to act in good faith has played a prominent role, yet to date is not a well-developed area of our corporate fiduciary law. The Chancellor observed, after surveying the sparse case law on the subject, that both the meaning and the contours of the duty to act in good faith were "shrouded in the fog of . . . hazy jurisprudence. 2005 Del. Ch. LEXIS 113, [Post-trial Op.] at *35. Although the good faith concept has recently been the subject of considerable scholarly writing,[23] which includes articles focused

---

[23] [99] See, e.g., Hillary A. Sale, Delaware's Good Faith, 89 Cornell L. Rev. 456 (2004); Matthew R.

on this specific case,[24] the duty to act in good faith is, up to this point relatively uncharted. Because of the increased recognition of the importance of good faith, some conceptual guidance to the corporate community may be helpful. For that reason we proceed to address the merits of the appellants' second argument.

The precise question is whether the Chancellor's articulated standard for bad faith corporate fiduciary conduct-intentional dereliction of duty, a conscious disregard for one's responsibilities-is legally correct. In approaching that question, we note that the Chancellor characterized that definition as "*an* appropriate (*although not the only*) standard for determining whether fiduciaries have acted in good faith." 2005 Del. Ch. LEXIS 113, [Post-trial Op.] at *36 (italics added, italics in original omitted). That observation is accurate and helpful, because as a matter of simple logic, at least three different categories of fiduciary behavior are candidates for the "bad faith" pejorative label.

The first category involves so-called "subjective bad faith," that is, fiduciary conduct motivated by an actual intent to do harm. That such conduct constitutes classic, quintessential bad faith is a proposition so well accepted in the liturgy of fiduciary law that it borders on axiomatic.[25] We need not dwell further on this category, because no such conduct is claimed to have occurred, or did occur, in this case.

The second category of conduct, which is at the opposite end of the spectrum, involves lack of due care-that is, fiduciary action taken solely by reason of gross negligence and without any malevolent intent. In this case, appellants assert claims of gross negligence to establish breaches not only of director due care but also of the directors' duty to act in good faith. Although the Chancellor found, and we agree, that the appellants failed to establish gross negligence, to afford guidance we

---

Berry, Does Delaware's Section 102(b)(7) Protect Reckless Directors From Personal Liability? Only if Delaware Courts Act in Good Faith, 79 Wash. L. Rev. 1125 (2004); John L. Reed and Matt Neiderman, Good Faith and the Ability of Directors to Assert § 102(b)(7) of the Delaware Corporation Law as a Defense to Claims Alleging Abdication, Lack of Oversight, and Similar Breaches of Fiduciary Duty, 29 Del. J. Corp. L. 111 (2004); David Rosenberg, Making Sense of Good Faith in Delaware Corporate Fiduciary Law: A Contractarian Approach, 29 Del. J. Corp. L. 491 (2004); Sean J. Griffith, Good Faith Business Judgment: A Theory of Rhetoric in Corporate Law Jurisprudence, 55 Duke L. J. 1 (2005) ("Griffith"); Melvin A. Eisenberg, The Duty of Good Faith in Corporate Law, 31 Del. J. Corp. L. 1 (2005); Filippo Rossi, Making Sense of the Delaware Supreme Court's Triad of Fiduciary Duties (June 22, 2005), available at http://ssrn.com/abstract=755784; Christopher M. Bruner, "Good Faith," State of Mind, and the Outer Boundaries of Director Liability in Corporate Law (Boston Univ. Sch. of Law Working Paper No. 05-19), available at http://ssrn.com/abstract=832944; Sean J. Griffith & Myron T. Steele, On Corporate Law Federalism Threatening the Thaumatrope, 61 Bus. Law. 1 (2005)

[24] [100] *See, e.g.,* Robert Baker, *In Re Walt Disney: What It Means To The Definition Of Good Faith, Exculpatory Clauses, and the Nature of Executive Compensation,* 4 Fla. St. U. Bus. Rev. 261 (2004–2005); Tara L. Dunn, *The Developing Theory of Good Faith In Director Conduct: Are Delaware Courts Ready To Force Corporate Directors To Go Out-Of-Pocket After Disney IV?,* 83 Denv. U. L. Rev. 531 (2005).

[25] [102] The Chancellor so recognized. 2005 Del. Ch. LEXIS 113, [Post-trial Op.] at *35 ("An action taken with the intent to harm the corporation is a disloyal act in bad faith."). *See McGowan v. Ferro,* 859 A.2d 1012, 1036 (Del. Ch. 2004) ("Bad faith is not simply bad judgment or negligence,' but rather implies the conscious doing of a wrong because of dishonest purpose or moral obliquity . . . it contemplates a state of mind affirmatively operating with furtive design or ill will.' ") (quoting *Desert Equities, Inc. v. Morgan Stanley Leveraged Equity Fund, II, L.P.,* 624 A.2d 1199, 1208, n.16 (Del. 1993)).

address the issue of whether gross negligence (including a failure to inform one's self of available material facts), without more, can also constitute bad faith. The answer is clearly no.

From a broad philosophical standpoint, that question is more complex than would appear . . . . But, in the pragmatic, conduct-regulating legal realm which calls for more precise conceptual line drawing, the answer is that grossly negligent conduct, without more, does not and cannot constitute a breach of the fiduciary duty to act in good faith. The conduct that is the subject of due care may overlap with the conduct that comes within the rubric of good faith in a psychological sense, but from a legal standpoint those duties are and must remain quite distinct. Both our legislative history and our common law jurisprudence distinguish sharply between the duties to exercise due care and to act in good faith, and highly significant consequences flow from that distinction.

The Delaware General Assembly has addressed the distinction between bad faith and a failure to exercise due care (*i.e.*, gross negligence) in two separate contexts. The first is Section 102(b)(7) of the DGCL, which authorizes Delaware corporations, by a provision in the certificate of incorporation, to exculpate their directors from monetary damage liability for a breach of the duty of care. That exculpatory provision affords significant protection to directors of Delaware corporations. The statute carves out several exceptions, however, including most relevantly, "for acts or omissions not in good faith. . . . " Thus, a corporation can exculpate its directors from monetary liability for a breach of the duty of care, but not for conduct that is not in good faith. To adopt a definition of bad faith that would cause a violation of the duty of care automatically to become an act or omission "not in good faith," would eviscerate the protections accorded to directors by the General Assembly's adoption of Section 102(b)(7).

A second legislative recognition of the distinction between fiduciary conduct that is grossly negligent and conduct that is not in good faith, is Delaware's indemnification statute, found at 8 *Del. C.* § 145. To oversimplify, subsections (a) and (b) of that statute permit a corporation to indemnify (*inter alia*) any person who is or was a director, officer, employee or agent of the corporation against expenses (including attorneys' fees), judgments, fines and amounts paid in settlement of specified actions, suits or proceedings, where (among other things): (i) that person is, was, or is threatened to be made a party to that action, suit or proceeding, and (ii) that person "acted in good faith and in a manner the person reasonably believed to be in or not opposed to the best interests of the corporation. . . . " Thus, under Delaware statutory law a director or officer of a corporation can be indemnified for liability (and litigation expenses) incurred by reason of a violation of the duty of care, but not for a violation of the duty to act in good faith.

Section 145, like Section 102(b)(7), evidences the intent of the Delaware General Assembly to afford significant protections to directors (and, in the case of Section 145, other fiduciaries) of Delaware corporations. To adopt a definition that conflates the duty of care with the duty to act in good faith by making a violation of the former an automatic violation of the latter, would nullify those legislative protections and defeat the General Assembly's intent. There is no basis in policy, precedent or common sense that would justify dismantling the distinction between gross negligence and bad faith.

That leaves the third category of fiduciary conduct, which falls in between the first two categories of (1) conduct motivated by subjective bad intent and (2) conduct resulting from gross negligence. This third category is what the Chancellor's definition of bad faith-intentional dereliction of duty, a conscious disregard for one's responsibilities-is intended to capture. The question is whether such misconduct is properly treated as a non-exculpable, non-indemnifiable violation of the fiduciary duty to act in good faith. In our view it must be, for at least two reasons.

First, the universe of fiduciary misconduct is not limited to either disloyalty in the classic sense (*i.e.*, preferring the adverse self-interest of the fiduciary or of a related person to the interest of the corporation) or gross negligence. Cases have arisen where corporate directors have no conflicting self-interest in a decision, yet engage in misconduct that is more culpable than simple inattention or failure to be informed of all facts material to the decision. To protect the interests of the corporation and its shareholders, fiduciary conduct of this kind, which does not involve disloyalty (as traditionally defined) but is qualitatively more culpable than gross negligence, should be proscribed. A vehicle is needed to address such violations doctrinally, and that doctrinal vehicle is the duty to act in good faith. The Chancellor implicitly so recognized in his Opinion, where he identified different examples of bad faith as follows:

> The good faith required of a corporate fiduciary includes not simply the duties of care and loyalty, in the narrow sense that I have discussed them above, but all actions required by a true faithfulness and devotion to the interests of the corporation and its shareholders. A failure to act in good faith may be shown, for instance, where the fiduciary intentionally acts with a purpose other than that of advancing the best interests of the corporation, where the fiduciary acts with the intent to violate applicable positive law, or where the fiduciary intentionally fails to act in the face of a known duty to act, demonstrating a conscious disregard for his duties. There may be other examples of bad faith yet to be proven or alleged, but these three are the most salient.

2005 Del. Ch. LEXIS 113, [Post-trial Op.] at *36 (footnotes omitted).

Those articulated examples of bad faith are not new to our jurisprudence. Indeed, they echo pronouncements our courts have made throughout the decades.[26]

---

**26** [111] *See, e.g., Allaun v. Consol. Oil Co.*, 16 Del. Ch. 318, 147 A. 257, 261 (Del. Ch. 1929) (further judicial scrutiny is warranted if the transaction results from the directors'"reckless indifference to or a deliberate disregard of the interests of the whole body of stockholders"); *Gimbel v. Signal Cos., Inc.*, 316 A.2d 599, 604 (Del. Ch. 1974), *aff'd*, 316 A.2d 619 (Del. 1974) (injunction denied because, *inter alia*, there was "nothing in the record [that] would justify a finding . . . that the directors acted for any personal advantage or out of improper motive or intentional disregard of shareholder interests"); *In re Caremark Int'l Derivative Litig.*, 698 A.2d 959, 971 (Del. Ch. 1996) ("only a sustained or systematic failure of the board to exercise oversight-such as an utter failure to attempt to assure a reasonable information and reporting system exists — will establish the lack of good faith that is a necessary condition to liability."); *Nagy v. Bistricer*, 770 A.2d 43, 48, n.2 (Del. Ch. 2000) (observing that the utility of the duty of good faith "may rest in its constant reminder . . . that, regardless of his motive, a director who consciously

Second, the legislature has also recognized this intermediate category of fiduciary misconduct, which ranks between conduct involving subjective bad faith and gross negligence. Section 102(b)(7)(ii) of the DGCL expressly denies money damage exculpation for "acts or omissions not in good faith or which involve intentional misconduct or a knowing violation of law." By its very terms that provision distinguishes between "intentional misconduct" and a "knowing violation of law" (both examples of subjective bad faith) on the one hand, and "acts . . . not in good faith," on the other. Because the statute exculpates directors only for conduct amounting to gross negligence, the statutory denial of exculpation for "acts . . . not in good faith" must encompass the intermediate category of misconduct captured by the Chancellor's definition of bad faith.

For these reasons, we uphold the Court of Chancery's definition as a legally appropriate, although not the exclusive, definition of fiduciary bad faith. We need go no further. To engage in an effort to craft (in the Court's words) "a definitive and categorical definition of the universe of acts that would constitute bad faith" would be unwise and is unnecessary to dispose of the issues presented on this appeal. 2005 Del. Ch. LEXIS 113, [Post-trial Op.] at *36. For the same reason, we do not reach or otherwise address the issue of whether the fiduciary duty to act in good faith is a duty that, like the duties of care and loyalty, can serve as an independent basis for imposing liability upon corporate officers and directors. That issue is not before us on this appeal.

Having sustained the Chancellor's finding that the Disney directors acted in good faith when approving the OEA and electing Ovitz as President, we next address the claims arising out of the decision to pay Ovitz the amount called for by the NFT provisions of the OEA.

B. *Claims Arising From The Payment Of The NFT Severance Payout To Ovitz*

*   *   *

2. *In Concluding That Ovitz Could Not Be Terminated For Cause, Did Litvack or Eisner Breach Any Fiduciary Duty?*

It is undisputed that Litvack and Eisner (based on Litvack's advice) both concluded that if Ovitz was to be terminated, it could only be without cause, because no basis existed to terminate Ovitz for cause. The appellants argued in the Court of Chancery that the business judgment presumptions do not protect that conclusion, because by permitting Ovitz to be terminated without cause, Litvack and Eisner acted in bad faith and without exercising due care. Rejecting that claim, the Chancellor determined independently, as a matter of fact and law, that (1) Ovitz had not engaged in any conduct as President that constituted gross negligence or malfeasance-the standard for an NFT under the OEA; and (2) in arriving at that same conclusion in 1996, Litvack and Eisner did not breach their fiduciary duty of care or their duty to act in good faith.

---

disregards his duties to the corporation and its stockholders may suffer a personal judgment for monetary damages for any harm he causes," even if for a reason "other than personal pecuniary interest").

The appellants now urge that those rulings constitute reversible error. To the extent the trial court's rulings are legal, we review them *de novo*, to the extent they involve factual findings based upon determinations of witness credibility, we will uphold them, *Hudak*, 806 A.2d at 151, n.28; and to the extent a factual finding is based on an expert opinion, it "may be overturned only if arbitrary or lacking any evidentiary support." *Cavalier Oil Corp. v. Harnett*, 564 A.2d 1137, 1146 (Del. 1989). Measured by these standards of review, the appellants have failed to establish error of any kind.

\*    \*    \*

At the trial level, the appellants attempted to show, as a factual matter, that Ovitz's conduct as President met the standard for a termination for cause, because (i) Ovitz intentionally failed to follow Eisner's directives and was insubordinate, (ii) Ovitz was a habitual liar, and (iii) Ovitz violated Company policies relating to expenses and to reporting gifts he gave while President of Disney. The Court found the facts contrary to appellants' position. As to the first accusation, the Court found that many of Ovitz's efforts failed to produce results "often because his efforts reflected an opposite philosophy than that held by Eisner, Iger, and Roth. This does not mean that Ovitz intentionally failed to follow Eisner's directives or that he was insubordinate." 2005 Del. Ch. LEXIS 113, [Post-trial Op.] at \*14. As to the second, the Court found that:

> In the absence of any concrete evidence that Ovitz told a material falsehood during his tenure at Disney, plaintiffs fall back on alleging that Ovitz's disclosures regarding his earn-out with, and past income from, CAA, were false or materially misleading. As a neutral fact-finder, I find that the evidence simply does not support either of those assertions.

*Id.* at \*15.

And, as to the third accusation, the Court found "that Ovitz was not in violation of The Walt Disney Company's policies relating to expenses or giving and receiving gifts." *Id.* at \*16. Accordingly, the appellants' claim that the Chancellor incorrectly determined that Ovitz could not legally be terminated for cause lacks any factual foundation.

Despite their inability to show factual or legal error in the Chancellor's determination that Ovitz could not be terminated for cause, appellants contend that Litvack and Eisner breached their fiduciary duty to exercise due care and to act in good faith in reaching that same conclusion. The Court of Chancery scrutinized the record to determine independently whether, in reaching their conclusion, Litvack and Eisner had separately exercised due care and acted in good faith. The Court determined that they had properly discharged both duties. Appellants' attack upon that determination lacks merit, because it is also without basis in the factual record.

After considering the OEA and Ovitz's conduct, Litvack concluded, and advised Eisner, that Disney had no basis to terminate Ovitz for cause and that Disney should comply with its contractual obligations. Even though Litvack personally did not want to grant a NFT to Ovitz, he concluded that for Disney to assert falsely that there was cause would be both unethical and harmful to Disney's reputation. As to Litvack, the Court of Chancery held:

I do not intend to imply by these conclusions that Litvack was an infallible source of legal knowledge. Nevertheless, Litvack's less astute moments as a legal counsel do not impugn his good faith or preparedness in reaching his conclusions with respect to whether Ovitz could have been terminated for cause. . . .

\*    \*    \*

In conclusion, Litvack gave the proper advice and came to the proper conclusions when it was necessary. He was adequately informed in his decisions, and he acted in good faith for what he believed were the best interests of the Company. *Id.* at \*50.

With respect to Eisner, the Chancellor found that faced with a situation where he was unable to work well with Ovitz, who required close and constant supervision, Eisner had three options: 1) keep Ovitz as President and continue trying to make things work; 2) keep Ovitz at Disney, but in a role other than as President; or 3) terminate Ovitz. The first option was unacceptable, and the second would have entitled Ovitz to the NFT, or at the very least would have resulted in a costly lawsuit to determine whether Ovitz was so entitled. After an unsuccessful effort to "trade" Ovitz to Sony, that left only the third option, which was to terminate Ovitz and pay the NFT. The Chancellor found that in choosing this alternative, Eisner had breached no duty and had exercised his business judgment:

> . . . I conclude that Eisner's actions in connection with the termination are, for the most part, consistent with what is expected of a faithful fiduciary. Eisner unexpectedly found himself confronted with a situation that did not have an easy solution. He weighed the alternatives, received advice from counsel and then exercised his business judgment in the manner he thought best for the corporation. Eisner knew all the material information reasonably available when making the decision, he did not neglect an affirmative duty to act (or fail to cause the board to act) and he acted in what he believed were the best interests of the Company, taking into account the cost to the Company of the decision and the potential alternatives. Eisner was not personally interested in the transaction in any way that would make him incapable of exercising business judgment, and I conclude that the plaintiffs have not demonstrated by a preponderance of the evidence that Eisner breached his fiduciary duties or acted in bad faith in connection with Ovitz's termination and receipt of the NFT. *Id.* at \*51.

These determinations rest squarely on factual findings that, in turn, are based upon the Chancellor's assessment of the credibility of Eisner and other witnesses. Even though the Chancellor found much to criticize in Eisner's "imperial CEO" style of governance, nothing has been shown to overturn the factual basis for the Court's conclusion that, in the end, Eisner's conduct satisfied the standards required of him as a fiduciary.

*3. Were The Remaining Directors Entitled To Rely Upon Eisner's And Litvack's Advice That Ovitz Could Not Be Fired For Cause?*

The appellants' third claim of error challenges the Chancellor's conclusion that the remaining new board members could rely upon Litvack's and Eisner's advice that Ovitz could be terminated only without cause. The short answer to that challenge is that, for the reasons previously discussed, the advice the remaining directors received and relied upon was accurate. Moreover, the directors' reliance on that advice was found to be in good faith. Although formal board action was not necessary, the remaining directors all supported the decision to terminate Ovitz based on the information given by Eisner and Litvack. The Chancellor found credible the directors' testimony that they believed that Disney would be better off without Ovitz, and the appellants offer no basis to overturn that finding.

\* \* \*

To summarize, the Court of Chancery correctly determined that the decisions of the Disney defendants to approve the OEA, to hire Ovitz as President, and then to terminate him on an NFT basis, were protected business judgments, made without any violations of fiduciary duty. Having so concluded, it is unnecessary for the Court to reach the appellants' contention that the Disney defendants were required to prove that the payment of the NFT severance to Ovitz was entirely fair.

## V. *THE WASTE CLAIM*

The appellants' final claim is that even if the approval of the OEA was protected by the business judgment rule presumptions, the payment of the severance amount to Ovitz constituted waste. This claim is rooted in the doctrine that a plaintiff who fails to rebut the business judgment rule presumptions is not entitled to any remedy unless the transaction constitutes waste. *In re J.P. Stevens & Co., Inc. S'holders Litig.*, 542 A.2d 770, 780 (Del. Ch. 1988). The Court of Chancery rejected the appellants' waste claim, and the appellants claim that in so doing the Court committed error.

To recover on a claim of corporate waste, the plaintiffs must shoulder the burden of proving that the exchange was "so one sided that no business person of ordinary, sound judgment could conclude that the corporation has received adequate consideration." *Brehm*, 746 A.2d at 263. A claim of waste will arise only in the rare, "unconscionable case where directors irrationally squander or give away corporate assets." *Id.* This onerous standard for waste is a corollary of the proposition that where business judgment presumptions are applicable, the board's decision will be upheld unless it cannot be "attributed to any rational business purpose." *Sinclair Oil Corp. v. Levien*, 280 A.2d 717, 720 (Del. 1971); *see also Unocal Corp. v. Mesa Petroleum Co.*, 493 A.2d 946, 954 (Del. 1995).

The claim that the payment of the NFT amount to Ovitz, without more, constituted waste is meritless on its face, because at the time the NFT amounts were paid, Disney was contractually obligated to pay them. The payment of a contractually obligated amount cannot constitute waste, unless the contractual obligation is itself wasteful. Accordingly, the proper focus of a waste analysis must be whether the amounts required to be paid in the event of an NFT were wasteful *ex ante*.

Appellants claim that the NFT provisions of the OEA were wasteful because they incentivized Ovitz to perform poorly in order to obtain payment of the NFT provisions. The Chancellor found that the record did not support that contention:

> Terminating Ovitz and paying the NFT did not constitute waste because he could not be terminated for cause and because many of the defendants gave credible testimony that the Company would be better off without Ovitz, meaning that would be impossible for me to conclude that the termination and receipt of NFT benefits result in "an exchange that is so one sided that no business person of ordinary, sound judgment could conclude that the corporation has received adequate consideration," or a situation where the defendants have "irrationally squandered or given away corporate assets." In other words, defendants did not commit waste.

2005 Del. Ch. LEXIS 113, [Post-trial Op.] at *39.

That ruling is erroneous, the appellants argue, because the NFT provisions of the OEA were wasteful in their very design. Specifically, the OEA gave Ovitz every incentive to leave the Company before serving out the full term of his contract. The appellants urge that although the OEA may have induced Ovitz to join Disney as President, no contractual safeguards were in place to retain him in that position. In essence, appellants claim that the NFT provisions of the OEA created an irrational incentive for Ovitz to get himself fired.

That claim does not come close to satisfying the high hurdle required to establish waste. The approval of the NFT provisions in the OEA had a rational business purpose: to induce Ovitz to leave CAA, at what would otherwise be a considerable cost to him, in order to join Disney. The Chancellor found that the evidence does not support any notion that the OEA irrationally incentivized Ovitz to get himself fired. Indeed, all the credible evidence supports the Chancellor's conclusion that Ovitz resisted, at every turn, all suggestions, communicated directly or indirectly by Eisner, that Ovitz leave Disney. Ovitz had no control over whether or not he would be fired, either with or without cause. To suggest that at the time he entered into the OEA Ovitz would engineer an early departure at the cost of his extraordinary reputation in the entertainment industry and his historical friendship with Eisner, is not only fanciful but also without proof in the record. Indeed, the Chancellor found that it was "patently unreasonable to assume that Ovitz intended to perform just poorly enough to be fired quickly, but not so poorly that he could be terminated for cause." *Id.* at *38.

We agree. Because the appellants have failed to show that the approval of the NFT terms of the OEA was not a rational business decision, their waste claim must fail.

# STONE v. RITTER

Supreme Court of Delaware

911 A.2d 362 (2006)

HOLLAND, JUSTICE:

This is an appeal from a final judgment of the Court of Chancery dismissing a derivative complaint against fifteen present and former directors of AmSouth Bancorporation ("AmSouth"), a Delaware corporation. The plaintiffs-appellants, William and Sandra Stone, are AmSouth shareholders and filed their derivative complaint without making a pre-suit demand on AmSouth's board of directors (the "Board"). The Court of Chancery held that the plaintiffs had failed to adequately plead that such a demand would have been futile. The Court, therefore, dismissed the derivative complaint under Court of Chancery Rule 23.1.

The Court of Chancery characterized the allegations in the derivative complaint as a "classic *Caremark* claim," a claim that derives its name from *In re Caremark Int'l Deriv. Litig.*, 698 A.2d 959 (Del. Ch. 1996). In *Caremark*, the Court of Chancery recognized that: "[g]enerally where a claim of directorial liability for corporate loss is predicated upon ignorance of liability creating activities within the corporation . . . only a sustained or systematic failure of the board to exercise oversight — such as an utter failure to attempt to assure a reasonable information and reporting system exists — will establish the lack of good faith that is a necessary condition to liability." *Id.* at 971.

In this appeal, the plaintiffs acknowledge that the directors neither "knew [n]or should have known that violations of law were occurring," *i.e.*, that there were no "red flags" before the directors. Nevertheless, the plaintiffs argue that the Court of Chancery erred by dismissing the derivative complaint which alleged that "the defendants had utterly failed to implement any sort of statutorily required monitoring, reporting or information controls that would have enabled them to learn of problems requiring their attention." The defendants argue that the plaintiffs' assertions are contradicted by the derivative complaint itself and by the documents incorporated therein by reference.

Consistent with our opinion in *In re Walt Disney Co. Deriv. Litig*, 906 A.2d 27 (Del. 2006), we hold that *Caremark* articulates the necessary conditions for assessing director oversight liability. We also conclude that the *Caremark* standard was properly applied to evaluate the derivative complaint in this case. Accordingly, the judgment of the Court of Chancery must be affirmed.

*Facts*

This derivative action is brought on AmSouth's behalf by William and Sandra Stone, who allege that they owned AmSouth common stock "at all relevant times." The nominal defendant, AmSouth, is a Delaware corporation with its principal executive offices in Birmingham, Alabama. During the relevant period, AmSouth's wholly-owned subsidiary, AmSouth Bank, operated about 600 commercial banking branches in six states throughout the southeastern United States and employed more than 11,600 people.

In 2004, AmSouth and Amsouth Bank paid $40 million in fines and $10 million in civil penalties to resolve government and regulatory investigations pertaining principally to the failure by bank employees to file "Suspicious Activity Reports" ("SARs"), as required by the federal Bank Secrecy Act ("BSA") and various anti-money-laundering ("AML") regulations. Those investigations were conducted by the United States Attorney's Office for the Southern District of Mississippi ("USAO"), the Federal Reserve, FinCEN and the Alabama Banking Department. No fines or penalties were imposed on AmSouth's directors, and no other regulatory action was taken against them. . . .

On October 12, 2004, the Federal Reserve and the Alabama Banking Department concurrently issued a Cease and Desist Order against AmSouth, requiring it, for the first time, to improve its BSA/AML program. That Cease and Desist Order required AmSouth to (among other things) engage an independent consultant "to conduct a comprehensive review of the Bank's AML Compliance program and make recommendations, as appropriate, for new policies and procedures to be implemented by the Bank." KPMG Forensic Services ("KPMG") performed the role of independent consultant and issued its report on December 10, 2004 (the "KPMG Report").

Also on October 12, 2004, FinCEN and the Federal Reserve jointly assessed a $10 million civil penalty against AmSouth for operating an inadequate anti-money-laundering program and for failing to file SARs. In connection with that assessment, FinCEN issued a written Assessment of Civil Money Penalty (the "Assessment"), which included detailed "determinations" regarding AmSouth's BSA compliance procedures. FinCEN found that "AmSouth violated the suspicious activity reporting requirements of the Bank Secrecy Act," and that "[s]ince April 24, 2002, AmSouth has been in violation of the anti-money-laundering program requirements of the Bank Secrecy Act." Among FinCEN's specific determinations were its conclusions that "AmSouth's [AML compliance] program lacked adequate board and management oversight," and that "reporting to management for the purposes of monitoring and oversight of compliance activities was materially deficient." AmSouth neither admitted nor denied FinCEN's determinations in this or any other forum.

### Demand Futility and Director Independence

It is a fundamental principle of the Delaware General Corporation Law that "[t]he business and affairs of every corporation organized under this chapter shall be managed by or under the direction of a board of directors . . . ." 8 Del. C. § 141(a)(2006). Thus, "by its very nature [a] derivative action impinges on the managerial freedom of directors." *Pogostin v. Rice*, 480 A.2d 619, 624 (Del. 1984). Therefore, the right of a stockholder to prosecute a derivative suit is limited to situations where either the stockholder has demanded the directors pursue a corporate claim and the directors have wrongfully refused to do so, or where demand is excused because the directors are incapable of making an impartial decision regarding whether to institute such litigation. Court of Chancery Rule 23.1, accordingly, requires that the complaint in a derivative action "allege with particularity the efforts, if any, made by the plaintiff to obtain the action the plaintiff desires from the directors [or] the reasons for the plaintiff's failure to obtain the action or for not making the effort."

In this appeal, the plaintiffs concede that "[t]he standards for determining demand futility in the absence of a business decision" are set forth in *Rales v. Blasband*, 634 A.2d 927 (Del. 1993). To excuse demand under *Rales*, "a court must determine whether or not the particularized factual allegations of a derivative stockholder complaint create a reasonable doubt that, as of the time the complaint is filed, the board of directors could have properly exercised its independent and disinterested business judgment in responding to a demand." *Id.* at 934. The plaintiffs attempt to satisfy the *Rales* test in this proceeding by asserting that the incumbent defendant directors "face a substantial likelihood of liability" that renders them "personally interested in the outcome of the decision on whether to pursue the claims asserted in the complaint," and are therefore not disinterested or independent.

Critical to this demand excused argument is the fact that the directors' potential personal liability depends upon whether or not their conduct can be exculpated by the section 102(b)(7) provision contained in the AmSouth certificate of incorporation. Such a provision can exculpate directors from monetary liability for a breach of the duty of care, but not for conduct that is not in good faith or a breach of the duty of loyalty. The standard for assessing a director's potential personal liability for failing to act in good faith in discharging his or her oversight responsibilities has evolved beginning with our decision in *Graham v. Allis-Chalmers Manufacturing Company*, 188 A.2d 125 (Del. 1963), through the Court of Chancery's *Caremark* decision to our most recent decision in *Disney*. A brief discussion of that evolution will help illuminate the standard that we adopt in this case.

### Graham and Caremark

*Graham* was a derivative action brought against the directors of Allis-Chalmers for failure to prevent violations of federal anti-trust laws by Allis-Chalmers employees. There was no claim that the Allis-Chalmers directors knew of the employees' conduct that resulted in the corporation's liability. Rather, the plaintiffs claimed that the Allis-Chalmers directors *should have known* of the illegal conduct by the corporation's employees. In *Graham*, this Court held that "*absent cause for suspicion* there is no duty upon the directors to install and operate a corporate system of espionage to ferret out wrongdoing which they have no reason to suspect exists." 188 A.2d at 130 (emphasis added).

In *Caremark*, the Court of Chancery reassessed the applicability of our holding in *Graham* when called upon to approve a settlement of a derivative lawsuit brought against the directors of Caremark International, Inc. The plaintiffs claimed that the Caremark directors should have known that certain officers and employees of Caremark were involved in violations of the federal Anti-Referral Payments Law. That law prohibits health care providers from paying any form of remuneration to induce the referral of Medicare or Medicaid patients. The plaintiffs claimed that the *Caremark* directors breached their fiduciary duty for having "allowed a situation to develop and continue which exposed the corporation to enormous legal liability and that in so doing they violated a duty to be active monitors of corporate performance." 698 A.2d at 967.

In evaluating whether to approve the proposed settlement agreement in *Caremark*, the Court of Chancery narrowly construed our holding in *Graham* "as standing for the proposition that, absent grounds to suspect deception, neither corporate boards nor senior officers can be charged with wrongdoing simply for assuming the integrity of employees and the honesty of their dealings on the company's behalf." *Id.* at 969. The *Caremark* Court opined it would be a "mistake" to interpret this Court's decision in *Graham* to mean that:

> corporate boards may satisfy their obligation to be reasonably informed concerning the corporation, without assuring themselves that information and reporting systems exist in the organization that are reasonably designed to provide to senior management and to the board itself timely, accurate information sufficient to allow management and the board, each within its scope, to reach informed judgments concerning both the corporation's compliance with law and its business performance.

*Id.* at 970.

To the contrary, the *Caremark* Court stated, "it is important that the board exercise a good faith judgment that the corporation's information and reporting system is in concept and design adequate to assure the board that appropriate information will come to its attention in a timely manner as a matter of ordinary operations, so that it may satisfy its responsibility."[27] The *Caremark* Court recognized, however, that "the duty to act in good faith to be informed cannot be thought to require directors to possess detailed information about all aspects of the operation of the enterprise." *Id.* at 971. The Court of Chancery then formulated the following standard for assessing the liability of directors where the directors are unaware of employee misconduct that results in the corporation being held liable:

> Generally where a claim of directorial liability for corporate loss is predicated upon ignorance of liability creating activities within the corporation, as in *Graham* or in this case, . . . only a sustained or systematic failure of the board to exercise oversight — such as an utter failure to attempt to assure a reasonable information and reporting system exists — will establish the lack of good faith that is a necessary condition to liability.

### Caremark Standard Approved

As evidenced by the language quoted above, the *Caremark* standard for so-called "oversight" liability draws heavily upon the concept of director failure to act in good faith. That is consistent with the definition(s) of bad faith recently approved by this Court in its recent *Disney* decision, where we held that a failure to act in good faith requires conduct that is qualitatively different from, and more culpable than, the conduct giving rise to a violation of the fiduciary duty of care (i.e., gross negligence). In *Disney*, we identified the following examples of conduct that would establish a failure to act in good faith:

---

[27] [21] [*In re Caremark Int'l Inc. Deriv. Litig.*, 698 A.2d 959, 970 (Del. Ch. 1996).]

A failure to act in good faith may be shown, for instance, where the fiduciary intentionally acts with a purpose other than that of advancing the best interests of the corporation, where the fiduciary acts with the intent to violate applicable positive law, or where the fiduciary intentionally fails to act in the face of a known duty to act, demonstrating a conscious disregard for his duties. There may be other examples of bad faith yet to be proven or alleged, but these three are the most salient.

906 A.2d at 67.

The third of these examples describes, and is fully consistent with, the lack of good faith conduct that the *Caremark* court held was a "necessary condition" for director oversight liability, i.e., "a sustained or systematic failure of the board to exercise oversight — such as an utter failure to attempt to assure a reasonable information and reporting system exists . . . ." *Caremark*, 698 A.2d at 971.

Indeed, our opinion in *Disney* cited *Caremark* with approval for that proposition. *Disney*, 906 A.2d at 67 n.111. Accordingly, the Court of Chancery applied the correct standard in assessing whether demand was excused in this case where failure to exercise oversight was the basis or theory of the plaintiffs' claim for relief.

It is important, in this context, to clarify a doctrinal issue that is critical to understanding fiduciary liability under *Caremark* as we construe that case. The phraseology used in *Caremark* and that we employ here — describing the lack of good faith as a "necessary condition to liability" — is deliberate. The purpose of that formulation is to communicate that a failure to act in good faith is not conduct that results, *ipso facto*, in the direct imposition of fiduciary liability. The failure to act in good faith may result in liability because the requirement to act in good faith "is a subsidiary element[,]" i.e., a condition, "of the fundamental duty of loyalty." *Guttman v. Huang*, 823 A.2d 492, 506 n.34 (Del. Ch. 2003). It follows that because a showing of bad faith conduct, in the sense described in *Disney* and *Caremark*, is essential to establish director oversight liability, the fiduciary duty violated by that conduct is the duty of loyalty.

This view of a failure to act in good faith results in two additional doctrinal consequences. First, although good faith may be described colloquially as part of a "triad" of fiduciary duties that includes the duties of care and loyalty, the obligation to act in good faith does not establish an independent fiduciary duty that stands on the same footing as the duties of care and loyalty. Only the latter two duties, where violated, may directly result in liability, whereas a failure to act in good faith may do so, but indirectly. The second doctrinal consequence is that the fiduciary duty of loyalty is not limited to cases involving a financial or other cognizable fiduciary conflict of interest. It also encompasses cases where the fiduciary fails to act in good faith. As the Court of Chancery aptly put it in *Guttman*, "[a] director cannot act loyally towards the corporation unless she acts in the good faith belief that her actions are in the corporation's best interest." 823 A.2d at 506 n.34.

We hold that *Caremark* articulates the necessary conditions predicate for director oversight liability: (a) the directors utterly failed to implement any reporting or information system or controls; *or* (b) having implemented such a system or controls, consciously failed to monitor or oversee its operations thus disabling themselves from being informed of risks or problems requiring their attention. In either case, imposition of liability requires a showing that the directors knew that they were not discharging their fiduciary obligations. Where directors fail to act in the face of a known duty to act, thereby demonstrating a conscious disregard for their responsibilities, they breach their duty of loyalty by failing to discharge that fiduciary obligation in good faith.

### Chancery Court Decision

The plaintiffs contend that demand is excused under Rule 23.1 because AmSouth's directors breached their oversight duty and, as a result, face a "substantial likelihood of liability" as a result of their "utter failure" to act in good faith to put into place policies and procedures to ensure compliance with BSA and AML obligations. The Court of Chancery found that the plaintiffs did not plead the existence of "red flags" — "facts showing that the board ever was aware that AmSouth's internal controls were inadequate, that these inadequacies would result in illegal activity, and that the board chose to do nothing about problems it allegedly knew existed." In dismissing the derivative complaint in this action, the Court of Chancery concluded:

> This case is not about a board's failure to carefully consider a material corporate decision that was presented to the board. This is a case where information was not reaching the board because of ineffective internal controls. . . . With the benefit of hindsight, it is beyond question that AmSouth's internal controls with respect to the Bank Secrecy Act and anti-money laundering regulations compliance were inadequate. Neither party disputes that the lack of internal controls resulted in a huge fine — $50 million, alleged to be the largest ever of its kind. The fact of those losses, however, is not alone enough for a court to conclude that a majority of the corporation's board of directors is disqualified from considering demand that AmSouth bring suit against those responsible.

*Stone v. Ritter*, 2006 Del. Ch. LEXIS 20, C.A. No. 1570-N (Del. Ch. 2006) (Letter Opinion).

This Court reviews *de novo* a Court of Chancery's decision to dismiss a derivative suit under Rule 23.1. *Beam ex rel. Martha Stewart Living Omnimedia Inc. v. Stewart*, 845 A.2d 1040, 1048 (Del. 2004).

### Reasonable Reporting System Existed

The KPMG Report evaluated the various components of AmSouth's longstanding BSA/AML compliance program. The KPMG Report reflects that AmSouth's Board dedicated considerable resources to the BSA/AML compliance program and put into place numerous procedures and systems to attempt to ensure compliance. According to KPMG, the program's various components exhibited between a low and high degree of compliance with applicable laws and regulations.

The KPMG Report describes the numerous AmSouth employees, departments and committees established by the Board to oversee AmSouth's compliance with the

BSA and to report violations to management and the Board[.] . . .

The KPMG Report reflects that the directors not only discharged their oversight responsibility to establish an information and reporting system, but also proved that the system was designed to permit the directors to periodically monitor AmSouth's compliance with BSA and AML regulations. For example, as KPMG noted in 2004, AmSouth's designated BSA Officer "has made annual high-level presentations to the Board of Directors in each of the last five years." Further, the Board's Audit and Community Responsibility Committee (the "Audit Committee") oversaw AmSouth's BSA/AML compliance program on a quarterly basis. The KPMG Report states that "the BSA Officer presents BSA/AML training to the Board of Directors annually," and the "Corporate Security training is also presented to the Board of Directors."

The KPMG Report shows that AmSouth's Board at various times enacted written policies and procedures designed to ensure compliance with the BSA and AML regulations. For example, the Board adopted an amended bank-wide "BSA/AML Policy" on July 17, 2003 — four months before AmSouth became aware that it was the target of a government investigation. That policy was produced to plaintiffs in response to their demand to inspect AmSouth's books and records pursuant to 8 Del. C. 220 (2006) and is included in plaintiffs' appendix. Among other things, the July 17, 2003, BSA/AML Policy directs all AmSouth employees to immediately report suspicious transactions or activity to the BSA/AML Compliance Department or Corporate Security.

### Complaint Properly Dismissed

In this case, the adequacy of the plaintiffs' assertion that demand is excused depends on whether the complaint alleges facts sufficient to show that the defendant *directors* are potentially personally liable for the failure of non-director bank *employees* to file SARs. Delaware courts have recognized that "[m]ost of the decisions that a corporation, acting through its human agents, makes are, of course, not the subject of director attention." *Caremark*, 698 A.2d at 968.

Consequently, a claim that directors are subject to personal liability for employee failures is "possibly the most difficult theory in corporation law upon which a plaintiff might hope to win a judgment." *Id.* at 967.

For the plaintiffs' derivative complaint to withstand a motion to dismiss, "only a sustained or systematic failure of the board to exercise oversight-such as an utter failure to attempt to assure a reasonable information and reporting system exists — will establish the lack of good faith that is a necessary condition to liability." *Id.* at 971. As the *Caremark* decision noted:

> Such a test of liability — lack of good faith as evidenced by sustained or systematic failure of a director to exercise reasonable oversight — is quite high. But, a demanding test of liability in the oversight context is probably beneficial to corporate shareholders as a class, as it is in the board decision context, since it makes board service by qualified persons more likely, while continuing to act as a stimulus to *good faith performance of duty* by such directors.

*Id.* (emphasis in original).

The KPMG Report — which the plaintiffs explicitly incorporated by reference into their derivative complaint — refutes the assertion that the directors "never took the necessary steps . . . to ensure that a reasonable BSA compliance and reporting system existed." KPMG's findings reflect that the Board received and approved relevant policies and procedures, delegated to certain employees and departments the responsibility for filing SARs and monitoring compliance, and exercised oversight by relying on periodic reports from them. Although there ultimately may have been failures by employees to report deficiencies to the Board, there is no basis for an oversight claim seeking to hold the directors personally liable for such failures by the employees.

With the benefit of hindsight, the plaintiffs' complaint seeks to equate a bad outcome with bad faith. The lacuna in the plaintiffs' argument is a failure to recognize that the directors' good faith exercise of oversight responsibility may not invariably prevent employees from violating criminal laws, or from causing the corporation to incur significant financial liability, or both, as occurred in *Graham, Caremark* and this very case. In the absence of red flags, good faith in the context of oversight must be measured by the directors' actions "to assure a reasonable information and reporting system exists" and not by second-guessing after the occurrence of employee conduct that results in an unintended adverse outcome. Accordingly, we hold that the Court of Chancery properly applied *Caremark* and dismissed the plaintiffs' derivative complaint for failure to excuse demand by alleging particularized facts that created reason to doubt whether the directors had acted in good faith in exercising their oversight responsibilities.

## 2. Exculpation and Good Faith

As mentioned in n.5 following *Smith v. van Gorkom, supra* Sec. A, many states amended their corporate codes to permit corporations in their charters to exculpate directors from personal liability. One such statute is section 102(b)(7) of the Delaware General Corporation Law, 8 Del. C. § 102(b)(7). The language permits a corporation's certificate of incorporation to include:

> (7) A provision eliminating or limiting the personal liability of a director to the corporation or its stockholders for monetary damages for breach of fiduciary duty as a director, provided that such provision shall not eliminate or limit the liability of a director: (i) For any breach of the director's duty of loyalty to the corporation or its stockholders; (ii) for acts or omissions not in good faith or which involve intentional misconduct or a knowing violation of law; (iii) under § 174 of this title; or (iv) for any transaction from which the director derived an improper personal benefit.

8 Del. C. § 102(b)(7) (2011).

Many corporations have taken advantage of the availability this and similar statutes in other states to try to protect their directors from personal liability. If the plaintiff's claim alleges only that directors breached their duty of care (gross negligence), the charter provision will shield directors from money damages, and the case may be dismissed. Note, however, that the provision specifically prohibits exculpation if the director's conduct was not in good faith. *See, e.g., Emerald Partners v. Berlin*, 787 A.2d 85 (Del. 2001). Note also that the language only limits the directors' liability for money damages, not for equitable relief. An exculpatory provision in the corporation's charter will not protect directors against an injunction, for example. And there is one more important limit: exculpation is available only to directors, not to officers. *See McPadden v. Sidhu*, 964 A.2d 1262 (Del. Ch. 2008). "Though an officer owes to the corporation identical fiduciary duties of care and loyalty as owed by directors, an officer does not benefit from the protections of a *Section 102(b)(7)* exculpatory provision, which are only available to directors. [Therefore], so long as plaintiff has alleged a violation of care or loyalty, the complaint proceeds against [an officer]." *Id.* at 1275–76 (footnotes omitted).

## D.  EXECUTIVE COMPENSATION

### 1.  Dodd-Frank

Congress passed the Dodd-Frank Wall Street Reform and Consumer Protection Act on July 15, 2010, and President Obama signed it into law on July 21. The Dodd-Frank Act is a comprehensive attempt to overhaul the financial industry by ending "too big to fail" financial institutions and implementing consumer and investor protections. Called the biggest financial reform since the Great Depression, the Dodd-Frank Act is divided into 16 titles, which touch nearly every individual, institution, and aspect of the financial industry. The Act outlines ambitious goals to increase transparency and secure the financial industry.

The Act carries significant ramifications for executive compensation and corporate governance.

Section 951 of the Act amends the Securities Exchange Act of 1934 to add Section 14A, requiring public companies to periodically include a shareholder resolution in their proxy materials to approve executive compensation. However, this "say on pay" is not binding on the company.

Section 952 requires that all members of the board's compensation committee be independent directors. The SEC is directed to pass rules defining independence, taking into account factors including source of compensation and affiliation with the company, a subsidiary, or an affiliate of a subsidiary. The compensation committee may retain a compensation consultant to assist it, but if they do so, they must disclose that they did. They must also disclose whether the consultant's work raised any conflict of interest, and if so, how it was dealt with. (The New York Stock Exchange already requires this for the companies it lists, and also requires that all members of the nominating/corporate governance committee be independent. *See* NYSE Listed Company Manual Section 303A. Section 301 of the Sarbanes Oxley Act of 2002 requires that all members of a company's audit committee be independent.)

Section 953 requires the company to disclose "information that shows the relationship between executive compensation actually paid and the financial performance of the issuer. . . . " The company must also disclose the median compensation of its employees (excluding the CEO), the annual total compensation of the CEO, and the ratio between them.

Section 954 is a "clawback" provision, providing that if the company is required to restate its financial statements because they did not comply with the securities laws, the company must require current and former executives who received incentive compensation, including stock options, to return any excess compensation they received, based on the corrected numbers.

Section 971 authorizes the SEC to require companies to include in their proxy materials shareholder nominees to the board of directors. In response, the SEC adopted Rule 14a-11, giving shareholders or shareholder groups owning at least 3% of the company's voting securities for at least three years the power to nominate candidates for the board. However, the rule was almost immediately struck down in a decision finding that the SEC acted without sufficient consideration of the rule's relative costs and benefits. *See Business Roundtable v. Securities and Exchange Commission*, 647 F.3d 1144 (D.C. Cir. 2011). The court noted that "the Commission has a unique obligation to consider the effect of a new rule upon 'efficiency, competition, and capital formation,' 15 U.S.C. §§ 78c(f), 78w(a)(2), 80a-2(c), and its failure to 'apprise itself — and hence the public and the Congress — of the economic consequences of a proposed regulation' makes promulgation of the rule arbitrary and capricious and not in accordance with law." *Id.* at 1148 (citations omitted).

Section 972 amends the 1934 Act to add Section 14B, requiring the company to explain why its CEO and Chair of the Board of Directors either are or are not the same person. There has been increasing consensus that it is a bad idea to have the same person serve in both positions, based on the built-in conflicts in trying to play both roles.

A recent study indicates that CEO compensation in large companies is nearly 350 times that of the average worker. *See Trends in CEO Pay*, accessed September 21, 2011 at http://www.aflcio.org/corporatewatch/paywatch/ceopay.cfm. Do you think the say-on-pay provision will have any effect on executive compensation? Are large companies likely to accede to non-binding votes by shareholders? Should they?

Similarly ambitious goals to reform corporate governance were enacted in the Sarbanes-Oxley Act of 2002. Do you think the Dodd-Frank Act can reform Wall Street culture? How does imposing greater regulatory hurdles and reporting costs on corporations actually affect the way companies operate? *See* Stephen M. Bainbridge, *Dodd Frank: Quack Federal Corporate Governance Round II*, 95 MINN. L. REV. 1779 (2011).

## 2.  Disclosure and Waste

### LEWIS v. VOGELSTEIN
Court of Chancery of Delaware
699 A.2d 327 (1997)

ALLEN, CHANCELLOR

This shareholders' suit challenges a stock option compensation plan for the directors of Mattel, Inc., which was approved or ratified by the shareholders of the company at its 1996 Annual Meeting of Shareholders. Two claims are asserted.

First, and most interestingly, plaintiff asserts that the proxy statement that solicited shareholder proxies to vote in favor of the adoption of the 1996 Mattel Stock Option Plan ("1996 Plan" or "Plan") was materially incomplete and misleading, because it did not include an estimated present value of the stock option grants to which directors might become entitled under the Plan. Thus, the first claim asserts that the corporate directors had, in the circumstances presented, a duty to disclose the present value of future options as estimated by some option-pricing formula, such as the Black-Scholes option-pricing model.

Second, it is asserted that the grants of options actually made under the 1996 Plan did not offer reasonable assurance to the corporation that it would receive adequate value in exchange for such grants, and that such grants represent excessively large compensation for the directors in relation to the value of their service to Mattel. For these reasons, the granting of the option is said to constitute a breach of fiduciary duty.

On this motion, this substantive liability theory is also pressed as an "entire fairness" claim. Plaintiff maintains that because the Plan constitutes a self-interested transaction by the incumbent directors, all of whom qualify for grants under the 1996 Plan, they must justify it as entirely fair in order to avoid liability for breach of loyalty, which it is said they cannot do. As shown below, this approach does not constitute a different claim than that stated above.

Pending is defendants' motion to dismiss the complaint for failure to state a claim upon which relief may be granted. A motion of this type may be granted only when it appears reasonably certain that plaintiff would not be entitled to the relief requested, even if all the facts as stated in the complaint are true and all inferences fairly inferable from those allegations are drawn in plaintiff's favor. *Rabkin v. Philip A. Hunt Chem. Corp.*, Del. Supr., 498 A.2d 1099 (1985).

For the reasons set forth below I conclude that there is no legal obligation for corporate directors who seek shareholder ratification of a plan of officer or director option grants, to make and disclose an estimate of present value of future options under a plan of the type described in the complaint. There is, therefore, no basis to conclude that failure to set forth such estimate constitutes a violation of any board obligation to set forth all material facts in connection with a ratification vote. Second, I conclude that the allegations of the complaint are not necessarily inconsistent with a conclusion that the 1996 Plan constitutes a waste of corporate assets. Thus, the complaint may not be dismissed as failing to state a claim.

## I.

The facts as they appear in the pleading are as follows. The Plan was adopted in 1996 and ratified by the company's shareholders at the 1996 annual meeting. It contemplates two forms of stock option grants to the company's directors: a one-time grant of options on a block of stock and subsequent, smaller annual grants of further options.

With respect to the one-time grant, the Plan provides that each outside director will qualify for a grant of options on 15,000 shares of Mattel common stock at the market price on the day such options are granted (the "one-time options"). The one-time options are alleged to be exercisable immediately upon being granted although they will achieve economic value, if ever, only with the passage of time. It is alleged that if not exercised, they remain valid for ten years.[28]

With respect to the second type of option grant, the Plan qualifies each director for a grant of options upon his or her re-election to the board each year (the "Annual Options"). The maximum number of options grantable to a director pursuant to the annual options provision depends on the number of years the director has served on the Mattel board. Those outside directors with five or fewer years of service will qualify to receive options on no more than 5,000 shares, while those with more than five years service will qualify for options to purchase up to 10,000 shares. Once granted, these options vest over a four year period, at a rate of 25% per year. When exercisable, they entitle the holder to buy stock at the market price on the day of the grant. According to the complaint, options granted pursuant to the annual options provision also expire ten years from their grant date, whether or not the holder has remained on the board.

When the shareholders were asked to ratify the adoption of the Plan, as is typically true, no estimated present value of options that were authorized to be granted under the Plan was stated in the proxy solicitation materials.

## II.

As the presence of valid shareholder ratification of executive or director compensation plans importantly affects the form of judicial review of such grants, it is logical to begin an analysis of the legal sufficiency of the complaint by analyzing the sufficiency of the attack on the disclosures made in connection with the ratification vote.

---

[28] [2] As to the term of the one-time options there exists a material dispute of relevant fact. The complaint alleges those options are valid for ten years. Defendants assert however that a reading of the Plan itself certainly establishes that in fact the options expire sixty days after an outside director ceases to be a member of Mattel's board or in ten years whichever occurs first. Thus, according to defendants, the value of the options only continues while the grantee is serving on the board and is, presumably, affected by their motivational effect. This fact if true would render these options very difficult to value under option pricing theory. The procedural setting of the motion requires me to assume that plaintiff's allegation is correct.

A. Disclosure Obligation:

I first note a preliminary point: The complaint's assertion is not simply that the ratification of the 1996 Plan by the Mattel shareholders was ineffective because it was defective. If that were the whole of plaintiff's theory, the effect of any defect in disclosure under it would be only to deny to the board the benefits that ratification bestows in such a case. See *In re Wheelabrator Tech., Inc. Shareholders Litig.*, Del. Ch., 663 A.2d 1194 (1995). The thrust of the allegation, however, is that in seeking ratification and in, allegedly, failing fully to disclose material facts, the board has committed an independent wrong. Despite the fact that shareholder approval was not required for the authorization of this transaction and was sought only for its effect on the standard of judicial review, there is language in Delaware cases dealing with "fair process", suggesting that a misdisclosure may make available a remedy, even if the shareholder vote was not required to authorize the transaction and the transaction can substantively satisfy a fairness test. *Cf. In re Tri-Star Pictures, Inc., Litig.*, 634 A.2d 319, 333 (1993) (nominal damages available for misdisclosure in all events).

In all events, in this instance, the theory advanced is that the alleged non-disclosure itself breaches a duty of candor and gives rise to a remedy. The defect alleged is that *the shareholders were not told the present value of the compensation to the outside directors that the Plan contemplated i.e.*, the present value of the options that were authorized. It is alleged that the present value of the one-time options was as much as $180,000 per director and that that "fact" would be material to a Mattel shareholder in voting whether or not to ratify the board's action in adopting the 1996 Plan. According to plaintiff, the shareholders needed to have a specific dollar valuation of the options in order to decide whether to ratify the 1996 Plan. Such a valuation could, plaintiff suggests, be determined by application of formulas such as the widely-used option-pricing model first devised by Professors Fischer Black and Myron Scholes. Plaintiff urges that this court should hold that because no such valuation was provided to the shareholders, the proxy statement failed to disclose material matter and was, therefore, defective.

B. Disclosure of Estimated Present Value of Options to be Granted:

Estimates of option values are a species of "soft information" that would be derived from sources such as the specific terms of a plan (including when and for how long options are exercisable), historical information concerning the volatility of the securities that will be authorized to be optioned, and debatable assumptions about the future. Permissible and mandated disclosure of "soft information" — valuation opinions and projections most commonly — are problematic for federal and state disclosure law. Such estimates are inherently more easily subject to intentional manipulation or innocent error than data concerning historical facts. Such estimates raise threats to the quality and effectiveness of disclosure not raised by disclosure of historical data.

As the terms of the options granted under the 1996 Plan demonstrate, option-pricing models, when applied to executive or director stock options, are subject to special problems. Significant doubt exists whether the Black-Scholes option-pricing formula, or other, similar option-pricing models, provide a sufficiently reliable estimate of the value of options with terms such as those granted to the outside directors of Mattel.[29]

First, the Black-Scholes formula assumes that the options being valued are issued and publicly traded. Publicly-traded options have certain common characteristics that are important in assessing their value. Steven Huddart & Mark Lang, *Employee Stock Exercises: An Empirical Analysis*, 21 J. Acct. & Econ. 1, 9 (1996). The options granted to the Mattel directors under the Plan include restrictive terms that are different from those of typical, publicly-traded options and which may affect their value. Importantly, for instance, the directors' options are not assignable.

Second, the Black-Scholes model overstates the value of options that can be exercised at any time during their term because it does not take into account the cost-reducing effect of early exercise. Huddart & Lang at 18. The Mattel directors' one-time options are not options that are exercisable on a set date. They can be exercised at any time after the grant for a period, according to plaintiff, of up to ten years.

Third, the value of publicly-traded options and restricted options responds very differently to increased volatility of the price of the underlying stock. The volatility of the stock price is one of the important variables in the Black-Scholes formula. Ross, et al., Corporate Finance 629–31 (3d ed. 1993). Publicly-traded options increase in value as the price volatility of the underlying stock increases. The value of options of the type granted to the Mattel directors, on the other hand, arguably decreases with increased volatility, because the holders are more likely to exercise the options early since they cannot be traded. Nalin Kulatilaka & Alan J. Marcus, *Valuing Employee Stock Options*, Fin. Analysts J. Nov.–Dec. 1994, at 46, 51.

Plaintiff argues that option pricing techniques are sufficiently developed so that the Financial Accounting Standards Board ("FASB") requires that financial statements state a value of options granted to directors according to a stock-option pricing model. Thus, they assert, the same information should be given to shareholders by directors seeking ratification. There are salient differences, however, between financial statement disclosure of an estimated value of stock options under a plan and disclosure for the purpose of shareholder ratification of adoption of the plan. For instance, financial statements are compiled at the end of the fiscal year, *when the value of the options granted can be assessed with greater certainty*, than is possible at the time the option plan is authorized or ratified since the market price at time of issue is known at that later point.

More broadly, it may be the case that good public policy recommends the disclosure to shareholders of estimates of present value (determined by one

---

[29] [8] For example, the term of such an option — a critical variable in estimating present value — is uncertain because it *expires when exercised, at any time during its life*, rather than at a fixed period at its maturity. *See also* footnote 2, regarding the dispute in this case concerning whether options terminate sixty days after any director to be employed by Mattel. Such a provision would also make calculation of a present value of the option grant difficult since the probability of a directors' termination at any (or every) point during the ten year term is impossible to know and very hard to responsibly estimate. Thus, one of the vital components of an option-pricing formula, the life of the option, appears quite problematic in instances of this sort.

technique or another) of options that may be granted as compensation to senior officers and directors, when feasible techniques produce reliable estimates. But while it is unquestionably the case that corporation law plays an important part in the development of public policy in the area of directors' legal relations to corporations and shareholders, including disclosure law, it does not follow that the fiduciary duty of corporate directors is the appropriate instrument to determine and implement sound public policy with respect to this technical issue.

What makes good sense — good policy — in terms of *mandated corporate disclosure* concerning prospective option grants involves not simply the moral intuition that directors should be candid with shareholders with respect to relevant facts, but inescapably involves technical judgments concerning what is feasible and helpful in varying circumstances. Judgments concerning what disclosure, if any, of estimated present values of options should be mandated are best made at this stage of the science, not by a court under a very general materiality standard, but by an agency with finance expertise. An administrative agency — the Securities and Exchange Commission — has a technical staff, is able to hold public hearings, and can, thus, receive wide and expert input, and can specify forms of disclosure, if appropriate. It can propose rules for comment and can easily amend rules that do not work well in practice. As just one example, any option-pricing formula premised on the assumptions that underlie Professors Black and Scholes's model would be concerned with the expected volatility of the stock over the term of option. How that volatility is itself estimated would be a significant factor in any standardized disclosure regime. But this certainly is not the type of inquiry that the judicial process is designed optimally to address. Clearly, determining whether disclosure of estimates of the present value of options ought to be mandated, and how those values ought to be calculated, is not a subject that lends itself to the blunt instrument of duty of loyalty analysis.

In all events, for these reasons, I conclude that, given the tools currently used in financial analysis, a careful board or compensation committee may customarily be expected to consider whether expert estimates of the present value of option grants will be informative and reliable to itself or to shareholders. And if such estimates are deemed by the board, acting in good faith, to be reliable and helpful, the board may elect to disclose them to the shareholders, if it seeks ratification of its actions. But, such "soft information" estimates may be highly problematic and not helpful at all, as for example would likely be the case here, if the options terminate two months after the holder leaves Mattel's board, instead of continuing for ten years, as defendants assert. *See supra* note 2.

While generally the materiality of "facts" omitted from a proxy statement is a question of fact unsuitable for determination on a motion to dismiss, nevertheless, I conclude that the allegations of failure to disclose estimated present value calculations fails to state a claim upon which relief may be granted. Where shareholder ratification of a plan of option compensation is involved, the duty of disclosure is satisfied by the disclosure or fair summary of all of the relevant terms and conditions of the proposed plan of compensation, together with any material extrinsic fact within the board's knowledge bearing on the issue. The directors' fiduciary duty of disclosure does not mandate that the board disclose one or more estimates of present value of options that may be granted under the plan. Such estimates may be an appropriate subject of disclosure where they are generated competently, and disclosed in a good faith effort to inform shareholder action, but no case is cited in which disclosure of such estimates has been mandated in order to satisfy the directors' fiduciary duty and I lack sufficient confidence to break that fresh ground. *Absent allegations of intentional manipulation,* where shareholder ratification of a plan of stock option compensation is sought, what may constitute appropriate disclosure respecting estimated present (or other) values of such options grantable under the plan is a subject better left to the judgment of the Securities and Exchange Commission and, subject to that regulatory regime, the judgment of the board seeking such approval.

## III.

Thus, concluding that the complaint does not state a claim for breach of any duty to fully disclose material facts to shareholders in connection with the board's request that the shareholders ratify the board's act of creating a directors' stock option plan, I turn to the motion to dismiss the complaint's allegation to the effect that the Plan, or grants under it, constitute a breach of the directors' fiduciary duty of loyalty. As the Plan contemplates grants to the directors that approved the Plan and who recommended it to the shareholders, we start by observing that it constitutes self-dealing that would ordinarily require that the directors prove that the grants involved were, in the circumstances, entirely fair to the corporation. *Weinberger v. U. O. P., Inc., Del. Supr.*, 457 A.2d 701 (1983). However, it is the case that the shareholders have ratified the directors' action. That ratification is attacked only on the ground just treated. Thus, for these purposes I assume that the ratification was effective. The question then becomes what is the effect of informed shareholder ratification on a transaction of this type (*i.e.*, officer or director pay).

### A. Shareholder Ratification Under Delaware Law:

What is the effect under Delaware corporation law of shareholder ratification of an interested transaction? The answer to this apparently simple question appears less clear than one would hope or indeed expect. Four possible effects of shareholder ratification appear logically available: First, one might conclude that an effective shareholder ratification acts as a complete defense to any charge of breach of duty. Second, one might conclude that the effect of such ratification is to shift the substantive test on judicial review of the act from one of fairness that would otherwise be obtained (because the transaction is an interested one) to one of waste. Third, one might conclude that the ratification shifts the burden of proof of unfairness to plaintiff, but leaves that shareholder-protective test in place. Fourth, one might conclude (perhaps because of great respect for the collective action disabilities that attend shareholder action in public corporations) that shareholder ratification offers no assurance of assent of a character that deserves judicial recognition. Thus, under this approach, ratification on full information would be afforded no effect. Excepting the fourth of these effects, there are cases in this jurisdiction that reflect each of these approaches to the effect of shareholder voting to approve a transaction.[30]

In order to state my own understanding I first note that by shareholder ratification I do not refer to every instance in which shareholders vote affirmatively with respect to a question placed before them. I exclude from the question those instances in which shareholder votes are a necessary step in authorizing a transaction. Thus the law of ratification as here discussed has no direct bearing on shareholder action to amend a certificate of incorporation or bylaws. *Cf. Williams v. Geier*, Del. Supr., 671 A.2d 1368 (1996); nor does that law bear on shareholder votes necessary to authorize a merger, a sale of substantially all the corporation's assets, or to dissolve the enterprise. For analytical purposes one can set such cases aside.

### 1. *Ratification generally*:

I start with principles broader than those of corporation law. Ratification is a concept deriving from the law of agency which contemplates the *ex post* conferring upon or confirming of the legal authority of an agent in circumstances in which the agent had no authority or arguably had no authority. Restatement (Second) of Agency § 82 (1958). To be effective, of course, the agent must fully disclose all relevant circumstances with respect to the transaction to the principal prior to the ratification. *See, e.g., Breen v. Air Freight Ltd. v. Air Cargo, Inc., et al.*, 470 F.2d 767, 773 (2d Cir. 1972); Restatement (Second) of Agency § 91 (1958). Beyond that, since the relationship between a principal and agent is fiduciary in character, the agent in seeking ratification must act not only with candor, but with loyalty. Thus an attempt to coerce the principal's consent improperly will invalidate the effectiveness of the ratification.[31] RESTATEMENT (SECOND) OF AGENCY § 100 (1958).

Assuming that a ratification by an agent is validly obtained, what is its effect? One way of conceptualizing that effect is that it provides, after the fact, the grant of authority that may have been wanting at the time of the agent's act. Another might be to view the ratification as consent or as an estoppel by the principal to deny a lack of authority. *See* Restatement (Second) of Agency § 103 (1958). In either event the effect of informed ratification is to validate or affirm the act of the agent as the act of the principal. *Id.* § 182.

Application of these general ratification principles to shareholder ratification is complicated by three other factors. First, most generally, in the case of shareholder

---

[30] [10] *See, e.g., In re Wheelabrator Technologies, Inc. Shareholders Litig.*, Del. Ch., 663 A.2d 1194 (1995) (effect one: effective ratification eliminates any claim for breach of duty of care but only breach of care); *Michelson v. Duncan*, Del. Supr., 407 A.2d 211, 224 (1979) (effect two: effective ratification of director interested transaction triggers waste standard); *Citron v. E.I. DuPont de Nemours & Co.*, Del. Ch., 584 A.2d 490, 500–502 (1990), *quoted with approval in Kahn v. Lynch Communication*, Del. Supr. 638 A.2d 1110 (1994) (effect three: effective ratification shifts burden of fairness to plaintiff).

[31] [11] What constitutes an improper attempt to coerce consent and what constitutes fair conditions set by the agent would, like most fiduciary duty questions, be difficult to generalize about *ex ante*. For example a statement by an agent seeking ratification that unless this transaction is ratified the agent will exercise a legal power to terminate his agency would seem ordinarily within his power and not improper, but if he has arranged things so that the principal's interests are particularly vulnerable at that moment, he is arguably exploiting the relationship and improperly coercing consent.

ratification there is of course no single individual acting as principal, but rather a class or group of divergent individuals — the class of shareholders. This aggregate quality of the principal means that decisions to affirm or ratify an act will be subject to collective action disabilities; that some portion of the body doing the ratifying may in fact have conflicting interests in the transaction; and some dissenting members of the class may be able to assert more or less convincingly that the "will" of the principal is wrong, or even corrupt and ought not to be binding on the class. In the case of individual ratification these issues won't arise, assuming that the principal does not suffer from multiple personality disorder. Thus the collective nature of shareholder ratification makes it more likely that following a claimed shareholder ratification, nevertheless, there is a litigated claim on behalf of the principal that the agent lacked authority or breached its duty. The second, mildly complicating factor present in shareholder ratification is the fact that in corporation law the "ratification" that shareholders provide will often not be directed to lack of legal authority of an agent but will relate to the consistency of some authorized director action with the equitable duty of loyalty. Thus shareholder ratification sometimes acts not to confer legal authority — but as in this case — to affirm that action taken is consistent with shareholder interests. Third, when what is "ratified" is a director conflict transaction, the statutory law — in Delaware Section 144 of the Delaware General Corporation Law — may bear on the effect.[32]

### 2. *Shareholder ratification*:

These differences between shareholder ratification of director action and classic ratification by a single principal, do lead to a difference in the effect of a valid ratification in the shareholder context. The principal novelty added to ratification law generally by the shareholder context, is the idea — no doubt analogously present in other contexts in which common interests are held — that, in addition to a claim that ratification was defective because of incomplete information or coercion, shareholder ratification is subject to a claim by a member of the class that the ratification is ineffectual (1) because a majority of those affirming the transaction had a conflicting interest with respect to it or (2) because the transaction that is ratified constituted a corporate waste. As to the second of these, it has long been held that shareholders may not ratify a waste except by a unanimous vote. *Saxe v. Brady*, Del. Ch., 40 Del. Ch. 474, 184 A.2d 602, 605 (1962). The idea behind this rule

---

[32] [12] Most jurisdictions have enacted statutes that appear to offer a procedural technique for removing courts from a fairness evaluation of the terms of director conflict transactions. Generally courts have given them a very narrow interpretation, however. In Delaware that statute enacted in 1967 — Act of July 3, 1967, Ch. 50, 56 Del. Laws 151, 170 (1967) amended in 1969 — is Section 144 of the DGCL. Early on it was narrowly held that compliance with that section simply removed the automatic taint of a director conflict transaction, but nevertheless left the transaction subject to substantive judicial review for fairness. *See Fliegler v. Lawrence*, Del. Supr., 361 A.2d 218, 222 (1976) (involving claimed independent board action, not ratification by shareholders). This interpretation tended to be the general judicial response to these "safe-harbor" statutes. *See Cookies Food Prod., Inc. v. Lakes Warehouse Distrib., Inc.*, 430 N.W.2d 447, 452–453 (Iowa 1988) (requiring directors who engage in self-dealing to prove that they have acted in good faith). *See also Cohen v. Ayers*, 596 F.2d 733, 740 (7th Cir. 1979) (stating that under New York statutory law, in an unratified transaction involving interested directors the burden is on the directors to establish the fairness of the transaction, but where shareholder or disinterested-director ratification has occurred, the burden shifts to the challenger).

is apparently that a transaction that satisfies the high standard of waste constitutes a gift of corporate property and no one should be forced against their will to make a gift of their property. In all events, informed, uncoerced, disinterested shareholder ratification of a transaction in which corporate directors have a material conflict of interest has the effect of protecting the transaction from judicial review except on the basis of waste. *Keenan v. Eshleman*, Del. Supr., 23 Del. Ch. 234, 2 A.2d 904 (1938); *Gottlieb v. Heyden Chem. Corp.*, Del. Supr., 33 Del. Ch. 177, 91 A.2d 57, 58 (1952); *Steiner v. Meyerson*, Fed. Sec. L. Rep. (CCH) P98, 857, Allen, C. (July 18, 1995).[33]

### B. The Waste Standard:

The judicial standard for determination of corporate waste is well developed. Roughly, a waste entails an exchange of corporate assets for consideration so disproportionately small as to lie beyond the range at which any reasonable person might be willing to trade. *See Saxe v. Brady*, 40 Del. Ch. 474, 184 A.2d 602, 610; *Grobow v. Perot*, Del. Supr., 539 A.2d 180, 189 (1988). Most often the claim is associated with a transfer of corporate assets that serves no corporate purpose; or for which no consideration at all is received. Such a transfer is in effect a gift. If, however, there is *any substantial* consideration received by the corporation, and if there is a *good faith judgment* that in the circumstances the transaction is worthwhile, there should be no finding of waste, even if the fact finder would conclude a post that the transaction was unreasonably risky. Any other rule would deter corporate boards from the optimal rational acceptance of risk, for reasons explained elsewhere. *See Gagliardi v. TriFoods Intern., Inc.*, Del. Ch., 683 A.2d 1049 (1996). Courts are ill-fitted to attempt to weigh the "adequacy" of consideration under the waste standard or, *ex post*, to judge appropriate degrees of business risk.

### C. Ratification of Officer or Director Option Grants:

Let me turn now to the history of the Delaware law treating shareholder ratification of corporate plans that authorize the granting of stock options to corporate officers and directors. What is interesting about this law is that while it is consistent with the foregoing general treatment of shareholder ratification — *i.e.*, it appears to hold that informed, non coerced ratification validates any such plan or grant, unless the plan is wasteful[34] — in its earlier expressions, the waste standard used by the courts in fact was not a waste standard at all, but was a form of "reasonableness" or proportionality review.

---

[33] [13] Claims of breach of a duty of care seem difficult to relate to analysis under the waste standard. Duty of care analysis in this or other settings relate to deviations from ordinary care in the circumstances. Probably for this reason, it has been held, on authority, that ratification of a transaction that is thereafter made the subject of a breach of care claim is effective to defeat such a claim completely. *See In re Wheelabrator Tech., Inc. Shareholders Litig.*, Del. Ch., 663 A.2d 1194, 1200 (1995).

[34] [14] See *Michelson v. Duncan*, Del. Supr., 407 A.2d 211 (1979); *Beard v. Elster*, Del. Supr., 39 Del. Ch. 153, 160 A.2d 731 (1960).

1. *Development of Delaware law of option compensation:*

It is fair to say I think that Delaware law took a skeptical or suspicious stance towards the innovation of stock option compensation as it developed in a major way following World War II. *See, e.g., Kerbs, et al. v. California Eastern Airways*, Inc., Del. Supr., 33 Del. Ch. 69, 90 A.2d 652 (1952); *Gottlieb v. Heyden Chem. Corp.*, Del. Supr., 33 Del. Ch. 177, 91 A.2d 57 (1952); *Id.*, 90 A.2d 660 (1952); *Id.*, Del. Ch., 34 Del. Ch. 84, 99 A.2d 507 (1953). Such skepticism is a fairly natural consequence of the common law of director compensation[35] and of the experience that corporate law judges had over the decades with schemes to water stock or to divert investors funds into the hands of promoters or management.[36]

The early Delaware cases on option compensation established that, even in the presence of informed ratification, in order for stock option grants to be valid a two-part test had to be satisfied. First it was seen as necessary that the court conclude that the grant contemplates that the corporation will receive "sufficient consideration." E.g., *Kerbs*, at 90 A.2d 652, 656 (1952). "Sufficient consideration" as employed in the early cases does not seem like a waste standard: "Sufficient consideration to the corporation may be, *inter alia*, the retention of the services of an employee, or the gaining of the services of a new employee, *provided there is a reasonable relationship between the value of the services . . . and the value of the options . . .*". *Kerbs* at 656 (emphasis added).

Secondly it was held early on that, in addition, the plan or the circumstances of the grant must include "conditions or the existence of circumstances *which may be expected to insure* that the contemplated consideration will in fact pass to the corporation." *Kerbs* at 656 (emphasis added). Elsewhere the Supreme Court spoke of "circumstances which may reasonably be regarded as *sufficient to insure* that the corporation will receive that which it desires . . .". *Id.* at 657 (emphasis added).

This (1) weighing of the reasonableness of the relationship between the value of the consideration flowing both ways and (2) evaluating the sufficiency of the circumstances to insure receipt of the benefit sought, seem rather distant from the substance of a waste standard of judicial review. Indeed these tests seem to be a form of heightened scrutiny that is now sometimes referred to as an intermediate or proportionality review. *Cf. Unocal Corp. v. Mesa Petroleum, Co.*, Del. Supr., 493 A.2d 946 (1985); *Paramount Communications v. QVC Network*, Del. Supr., 637 A.2d 34 (1993).

In all events, these tests were in fact operationally very problematic. Valuing an option grant (as part of a reasonable relationship test) is quite difficult, even under today's more highly developed techniques of financial analysis. This would be especially true where, as this case exemplifies, the options are tied to and conditioned upon a continued status as an officer or director. Even more problematic is valuing — or judicially reviewing a judgment of equivalency of value of — the

---

[35] [15] *See, e.g., Cahall v. Lofland*, Del. Ch., 12 Del. Ch. 299, 114 A. 224, *aff'd*, 13 Del. Ch. 384, 118 A. 1 (1922) (directors serve without compensation unless it is explicitly authorized by its charter or by shareholders; director compensation where authorized is "scrutinized closely"; directors may not evaluate the value of their labor when it provides consideration for issuance of stock).

[36] [16] *See, e.g., Scully v. Automobile Financing Co.*, Del. Ch., 12 Del. Ch. 174, 109 A. 49 (1920).

future benefits that the corporation hopes to obtain from the option grant. There is no objective metric to gauge *ex ante* incentive effects of owning options by officers or directors.[37] Beyond this operational problem, the approach of these early option cases may be thought to raise the question, why was it necessary for the court reviewing a stock option grant to conclude that the circumstances insure that the corporation will receive the benefits it seeks to achieve.[38] In other contexts, even where interested transactions are involved, a fair (*i.e.*, valid and enforceable) contract might contemplate payment in exchange for a probability of corporation benefit. A corporation, for example, certainly could acquire from an officer or director at a fair price a property interest that had only prospective commercial value.

In *Beard v. Elster*, Del. Supr., 39 Del. Ch. 153, 160 A.2d 731 (1960), the Delaware Supreme Court relaxed slightly the general formulation of *Kerbs et al.*,[39] and rejected the reading of *Kerbs* to the effect that the corporation had to have (or insure receipt of) legally *cognizable* consideration in order to make an option grant valid. The court also emphasized the effect that approval by an independent board or committee might have. It held that what was necessary to validate an officer or director stock option grant was a finding that a reasonable board could conclude from the circumstances that the corporation may reasonably expect to receive a proportionate benefit. A good faith determination by a disinterested board or committee to that effect, at least when ratified by a disinterested shareholder vote, entitled such a grant to business judgment protection (*i.e.*, classic waste standard). *See generally* David A. Drexler, et al., Delaware Corporation Law & Practice § 14.03[2] (1997). After *Beard*, judicial review of officer and director option grants sensibly focused in practice less on attempting independently to assess whether the corporation in fact would receive proportionate value, and more on the procedures used to authorize and ratify such grants. But *Beard* addressed only a situation in which an independent committee of the board functioned on the question.

### 2. *Current law on ratification effect on option grants*:

A substantive question that remains however is whether in practice the waste standard that is utilized where informed shareholders ratify a grant of options adopted and recommended by a self-interested board is the classical waste test (*i.e.*, no consideration; gift; no person of ordinary prudence could possibly agree, etc.) or whether, in fact, it *is a species of intermediate review* in which the court assesses reasonableness in relationship to perceived benefits.

The Supreme Court has not expressly deviated from the "proportionality"

---

[37] [17] The benefits that Mattel contemplates receiving from the grant of options, according to its Proxy Statement, is to "attract, retain and reward . . . directors" and "to strengthen the mutuality of interests between [the option-recipients] and . . . stockholders." Proxy Statement at 12.

[38] [18] *But see supra* note 15.

[39] [19] "All stock option plans must . . . contain conditions, or [the] surrounding circumstances [must be] such, that the corporation *may reasonably expect* to receive the contemplated benefit from the grant of options [, and] (2) there must be a reasonable relationship between the value of the benefit passing to the corporation and the value of the options granted." *Beard v. Elster*, 160 A.2d at 737 (1960). (emphasis added)

approach to waste of its earlier decision, although in recent decades it has had few occasions to address the subject. In *Michelson v. Duncan*, Del. Supr., 407 A.2d 211 (1979), a stock option case in which ratification had occurred, however, the court repeatedly referred to the relevant test where ratification had occurred as that of "gift or waste" and plainly meant by waste, the absence of *any consideration* (". . . when there are issues of fact as to the existence of consideration, a full hearing is required regardless of shareholder ratification." 407 A.2d at 223). Issues of "sufficiency" of consideration or adequacy of assurance that a benefit or proportionate benefit would be achieved were not referenced.

The Court of Chancery has interpreted the waste standard in the ratified option context as invoking not a proportionality or reasonableness test a la *Kerbs* but the traditional waste standard referred to in *Michelson*. See, e.g., *Steiner v. Meyerson*, Fed. Sec. L. Rep. (CCH) P98,857, Allen, C. (July 18, 1995); *Zupnick v. Goizueta*, Del. Ch., 698 A.2d 384 (1997) (both granting motions to dismiss shareholder claims that options grants constituted actionable waste).

In according substantial effect to shareholder ratification these more recent cases are not unmindful of the collective action problem faced by shareholders in public corporations. These problems do render the assent that ratification can afford very different in character from the assent that a single individual may give. In this age in which institutional shareholders have grown strong and can more easily communicate,[40] however, that assent, is, I think, a more rational means to monitor compensation than judicial determinations of the "fairness," or sufficiency of consideration, which seems a useful technique principally, I suppose, to those unfamiliar with the limitations of courts and their litigation processes. In all events, the classic waste standard does afford some protection against egregious cases or "constructive fraud."

\*     \*     \*

Before ruling on the pending motion to dismiss the substantive claim of breach of fiduciary duty, under a waste standard, I should make one other observation. The standard for determination of motions to dismiss is of course well established and understood. Where under any state of facts consistent with the factual allegations of the complaint the plaintiff would be entitled to a judgment, the complaint may not be dismissed as legally defective. See, e.g., *Rabkin v. Philip A. Hunt Chem. Corp.*, *supra*. It is also the case that in some instances "mere conclusions" may be held to be insufficient to withstand an otherwise well made motion. Since what is a "well pleaded" fact and what is a "mere conclusion" is not always clear, there is often and inevitably some small room for the exercise of informed judgment by courts in determining motions to dismiss under the appropriate test. Consider for example allegations that an arm's-length corporate transaction constitutes a waste of assets. Such an allegation is inherently factual and not easily amenable to determination on a motion to dismiss and indeed often not on a motion for summary judgment. See, e.g., *Michelson v. Duncan*, Del. Supr., 407 A.2d 211 (1979). Yet it cannot be the case that allegations of the facts of any (or every) transaction coupled with a statement that the transaction constitutes a waste of assets, necessarily states a claim upon

---

[40] [20] *See* SEC Rule 14(a)(8), 17 CFR 240.14a-9 (1996).

which discovery may be had; such a rule would, in this area, constitute an undue encouragement to strike suits. Certainly some set of facts, if true, may be said as a matter of law not to constitute waste. For example, a claim that the grant of options on stock with a market price of say $5,000 to a corporate director, exercisable at a future time, if the optionee is still an officer or director of the issuer, constitutes a corporate waste, would in my opinion be subject to dismissal on motion, despite the contextual nature of judgments concerning waste. *See Steiner v. Meyerson*, Fed. Sec. L. Rep. (CCH) P98, 857, Allen, C. (July 18, 1995); *Zupnick v. Goizueta*, 698 A.2d 384, Del. Ch., (1997). In some instances the facts alleged, if true, will be so far from satisfying the waste standard that dismissal is appropriate.

This is not such a case in my opinion. Giving the pleader the presumptions to which he is entitled on this motion, I cannot conclude that no set of facts could be shown that would permit the court to conclude that the grant of these options, particularly focusing upon the one-time options, constituted an exchange to which no reasonable person not acting under compulsion and in good faith could agree. In so concluding, I do not mean to suggest a view that these grants are suspect, only that one time option grants to directors of this size seem at this point sufficiently unusual to require the court to refer to evidence before making an adjudication of their validity and consistency with fiduciary duty. Thus, for that reason the motion to dismiss will be denied. It is so Ordered.

### 3. Unjust Enrichment and Equitable Fraud

## IN RE HEALTHSOUTH CORP. SHAREHOLDERS LITIGATION
### Court of Chancery of Delaware
### 845 A.2d 1096 (2003)

STRINE, VICE CHANCELLOR.

In this opinion, I address a motion for summary judgment in this derivative action filed by stockholders of HealthSouth, Inc. The plaintiffs' motion seeks relief for a transaction in which defendant Richard M. Scrushy, HealthSouth's former Chairman and Chief Executive Officer, extinguished a loan of over $25 million that he owed to the company. In that transaction, Scrushy gave the company shares valued in the stock market at the dollar amount of the principal balance then needed to pay off the loan in full. The premise of the transaction, suggested, understood and communicated by Scrushy, was that the stock market price was a reliable indicator of the value of his stock, having been set in large measure in reliance upon the company's certified financial statements and other public releases regarding its financial health and prospects. As CEO of HealthSouth, Scrushy was charged with the responsibility of ensuring the proper preparation of these documents by his management team.

Shortly after he transferred some of his shares to HealthSouth in order to retire his debt, the first public revelations of financial problems at HealthSouth were revealed. Those and later revelations indicated that the financial information upon which the market was relying when HealthSouth accepted Scrushy's shares to retire his debt was materially misleading. On this record, that fact is undisputed and the extent of the material problems in HealthSouth's financial statements exceeds $2 billion. The result of the discovery of these problems was and remains a sharp decline in the price of HealthSouth's stock from the level used by the company in retiring Scrushy's debt.

Because Scrushy represented to HealthSouth that the market price was a reliable way to price his shares fairly, he was necessarily also representing that the company's financial releases were materially accurate. That representation was false, regardless of whether Scrushy knew it was. As a result of that inaccurate representation, HealthSouth received shares worth less than the value of the loan Scrushy was retiring.

For purposes of pressing this motion, the plaintiffs have accepted the notion that Scrushy, although responsible for ensuring the preparation of accurate financial information, was not aware that the company's financial statements and public releases were materially inaccurate. They have proceeded on this basis (although they believe that Scrushy was aware) because they contend that his actual knowledge of the material inaccuracy of these documents is irrelevant to their claims of unjust enrichment and equitable fraud, neither of which require that Scrushy have possessed an illicit state of mind.

I agree.

On the basis of undisputed facts, I find in this opinion that Scrushy is liable to HealthSouth under theories of unjust enrichment and equitable fraud, as neither theory is dependent on Scrushy's actual knowledge of the inaccuracy of Health-South's financial information. The HealthSouth board was entitled to and did rely upon Scrushy's assurance of the fairness of the market price as a transactional pricing mechanism. After all, as the company's CEO, he was in a better position than the rest of the board to assess the reliability of the company's financial statements and press releases, given that it was his job to assure that management prepared those documents with care and accuracy. To its detriment and Scrushy's unjust benefit, HealthSouth took back shares worth far less than Scrushy represented they were worth. To remedy the injury to HealthSouth, rescission is a fitting and practicable remedy, coupled with pre-judgment interest.

## I. Factual Background

In May 1999, HealthSouth's shareholders approved an Executive Equity Loan Plan (the "Loan Plan" or "Plan"). Under that Plan, HealthSouth could make loans to executive officers in order to help them purchase HealthSouth common stock. Later that year, Scrushy, who was then HealthSouth's Chairman and CEO, borrowed $25,218,114.87 under the Plan (the "Loan"). With the Loan proceeds, Scrushy bought 4,362,297 shares of HealthSouth stock at approximately $5.78 per share.

At the end of June 2002, Scrushy informed HealthSouth that he was willing to repay the Loan in advance of its maturity date. The reasons for this are unclear and not material to the disposition of this motion.[41] Scrushy wanted to repay the Loan with HealthSouth stock.

The Compensation Committee of HealthSouth's board of directors met twice to consider that issue. At its second meeting, the Compensation Committee approved a transaction whereby it would take back shares of HealthSouth stock from Scrushy in order to cancel the principal balance of the loan. The Compensation Committee agreed that it would value Scrushy's stock based on the average between the high and low trading prices for HealthSouth stock on July 31, 2002. On August 1, 2002, Scrushy transferred sufficient shares, valued at the average July 31, 2002 trading price of $10.06 per share, to satisfy the principal balance of the Loan. HealthSouth then cancelled the Loan. Hereafter, I refer to this transaction as the "Buyback."

Less than a month after the Buyback, HealthSouth issued a press release containing several important pieces of information. First, the press release announced a proposal whereby HealthSouth would spin off its surgery centers into a separate business. Second, the press release announced that Scrushy would step down as HealthSouth's CEO, turning that position over to the company's President and Chief Operating Officer, William T. Owens. Scrushy was to remain as Chairman of both HealthSouth and the spun-off surgery centers business. Finally, and most relevantly, the press release announced that HealthSouth was reducing its projected earnings before interest, taxes, depreciation and amortization by approximately $175 million annually from what had previously been publicly announced. As important, HealthSouth indicated that its "initial assessment" of projected EBITDA might prove "incorrect" and the company was therefore "discontinuing earnings guidance for the remainder of 2002 and 2003."

HealthSouth attributed this sharp deviation from its previous guidance to changes in the policy of the Centers for Medicare and Medicaid Services ("CMS") regarding reimbursement for outpatient therapy services (the "CMS Reimbursement Policy"). In the press release, HealthSouth contended that it had sought guidance regarding the effect of this Policy in July and August and received confusing feedback, but decided to implement new practices reflecting a conservative interpretation of the CMS Reimbursement Policy. Scrushy provided an extensive quote in the press release, in which he attributed the spin-off of the surgery business in part to the CMS Reimbursement Policy, arguing that the surgery centers business would be valued more highly if it were separated from those aspects of HealthSouth affected by the CMS Reimbursement Policy. As of the date of this press release, HealthSouth had not made any prior public disclosure of the possible effect of the CMS Reimbursement Policy, which was announced in a directive on May 17, 2002 — over two months before the Buyback.

As a result of the press release in August 2002, the price of HealthSouth shares fell dramatically. But even worse news was yet to come.

---

[41] [1] By this time, the Sarbanes-Oxley Act prohibited loans to corporate executives on a prospective basis, providing one plausibly legitimate reason for the transaction. *See also infra* note 27 (discussing purported business rationales for repayment of the Loan with HealthSouth stock). The plaintiffs, more cynically, might infer that Scrushy wished to eliminate his obligation to repay the Loan in cash using overvalued stock before evidence of material misstatements in HealthSouth's financial filings became public.

As 2002 proceeded, HealthSouth backtracked on the proposed spin-off of the surgery centers. Scrushy also returned to his post as CEO. Then, on March 3, 2003, HealthSouth announced financial results for the first quarter of 2003 and the year ending December 31, 2002. Scrushy was quoted in the announcement, which included material adjustments to HealthSouth's financial statements, such as:

- A write-down of $445 million in the fourth quarter of HealthSouth's 2002 fiscal year, which ended December 31, 2002;

- "Other unusual charges" of $194.8 million, $175.8 million of which were cash charges and $65.8 million of which related primarily to fiscal years 2001 and earlier.

The release makes clear that a good deal of the other cash charges related to periods before the Buyback, because they, among other things, reflected adjustments to the accounting treatment of older accounts receivable.

In the press release, Scrushy is quoted as predicting that HealthSouth had hit "a bottom from which" it expected to "see growth in 2003." Unlike Nostrodamus, Scrushy did not have to wait long to have his prediction proven wrong.

Soon after the March 3, 2003 announcement, the integrity of HealthSouth's financial statements became the subject of further publicity. On March 19, 2003, the Securities and Exchange Commission filed a complaint against HealthSouth and Scrushy alleging violations of the federal securities laws. That same day, the United States Attorney for the Northern District of Alabama announced that Weston Smith — Health South's former Chief Financial Officer who held that position during 2002 — had pled guilty to charges, including conspiring to falsify the financial statements of HealthSouth in a period beginning in 1997 and continuing to that time.

Scrushy was also placed on administrative leave that day.

A crisis then ensued at HealthSouth, as the price of its shares plummeted and the NYSE suspended their trading. On March 24, 2003, HealthSouth announced that it had retained Price Waterhouse Coopers to conduct a forensic audit of its financial statements. In view of the various confidence-shaking events that had transpired, the company informed the public that its previous financial statements could no longer be relied upon. The company further announced its retention of a turn-around specialist to help the company stabilize its affairs, which were in financial free-fall. On March 25, 2003, HealthSouth announced that the NYSE had given a formal notice of its proposal to delist the company's shares.

Then, on March 31, 2003, Scrushy was formally fired as CEO. Independent board member Robert May replaced him as interim CEO. Scrushy insisted on remaining as a director of HealthSouth.

In April 2003, HealthSouth was unable to make interest payments to certain of its noteholders, thus falling into default on its obligations. Thereafter, HealthSouth ceased making interest and principal payments on its outstanding obligations. Throughout that period and continuing forward, the company has been attempting to stabilize its affairs and avoid bankruptcy.

To that end, in May 2003, HealthSouth engaged PriceWaterhouseCoopers as its new accountants, replacing Ernst & Young. On July 7, 2003, the company announced a preliminary business plan update, which contained certain heavily caveated projections of the company's performance for the coming year. In that same announcement, the company reiterated the unreliability of its previous financial statements, noted that its former auditors Ernst & Young had withdrawn their audit reports on all previous filings, and indicated that it had not yet determined the "the extent of any required restatement of our prior financial reports." The company did, however, provide this summary of the status of PwC's work:

\*    \*    \*

As of this date of this opinion, fifteen HealthSouth executives have pled guilty to crimes centering on the intentional falsification of HealthSouth's financial statements. Among those pleading guilty were William T. Owens, Scrushy's top subordinate in 2002 and his successor as CEO for a brief period; the previously mentioned Weston Smith, who was HealthSouth's CFO in 2002; and every Health-South CFO who had served under Scrushy during HealthSouth's time as a public company. Both the executives who pled guilty and the federal government have alleged that Scrushy was integral to the alleged conspiracy at HealthSouth and he remains the ultimate target of the federal government's investigative and prosecutorial efforts, having recently been indicted.

Remaining on the HealthSouth website to this date is the following disclaimer:

> In light of recent investigations into HealthSouth's financial reporting and related activity, the financial statements currently found on this website should no longer be relied upon. Additional information will be provided as it becomes available.

This statement is markedly less confidence-inspiring than were HealthSouth's financial statements as of the time of the Buyback. At that time, HealthSouth's full year results for FY 2001 showed revenues of $4.4 billion and net earnings of $202 million, or $0.52 per share. For the first quarter of FY 2002, ending on March 31, 2002, HealthSouth reported revenues of $1.13 billion and earnings of $0.27 per share, an improvement of $0.08 per share over the comparable quarter in FY 2001. Put simply, the stable, profitable company portrayed by the financial statements that the market relied upon in material part to set the trading price of HealthSouth on July 31, 2002 was in fact quite different than the actual HealthSouth that existed as of that date.

As of the date of this opinion, HealthSouth has managed to avoid falling into bankruptcy and some measure of stability has been restored to the company's operations, after new management and outside advisors worked out arrangements with creditors and began servicing the company's debt. Although this has restored some value to HealthSouth's common stock, that stock continues to trade at prices well below the price accorded to Scrushy in the Buyback.

## II. The Plaintiffs' Motion For Summary Judgment

The plaintiffs move for summary judgment on two counts of their amended complaint. The factual premise of each count is similar: Scrushy, HealthSouth's Chairman, CEO, and director retired an outstanding debt to HealthSouth by tendering to it stock, which was valued on the basis of the prevailing market price on July 31, 2002. Fundamental to that Buyback transaction from HealthSouth's perspective was the reliability of the market price as an accurate and fair basis by which to value the shares Scrushy tendered in order to retire his debt to HealthSouth.

The plaintiffs now argue that the Buyback should be rescinded under two theories. First, the plaintiffs contend that Scrushy was unjustly enriched by the Buyback because he was able to retire a debt on the cheap based on a market price set in reliance upon materially misleading financial statements that Scrushy himself had signed. Therefore, Scrushy should be required to make restitution. Second, the plaintiffs argue that Scrushy is liable to HealthSouth for making an innocent misrepresentation of fact. Having premised the Buyback on the notion that HealthSouth's market price was a fair proxy for value, Scrushy also impliedly represented that the financial statements that he had signed and that were influential to that market price were materially accurate. Because HealthSouth reasonably relied upon the market price and those financial statements in valuing the stock Scrushy provided the company in the Buyback, it is eligible to receive rescissory relief from Scrushy.

## III. The Procedural Standard

On this motion, the plaintiffs bear the burden to demonstrate that there is no genuine issue of material fact regarding the dispute and that they are entitled to judgment as a matter of law. When, as here, the plaintiffs have supported their position on a question of fact with admissible evidence and pointed to the absence of proof bolstering the non-moving party's claims, Scrushy, as the non-moving party, must come forward with admissible evidence creating a triable issue of fact or suffer an adverse judgment.

## IV. Scrushy's Posture

Scrushy faces criminal charges. For that and other tactical reasons, he has responded to the plaintiffs' motion for summary judgment without filing either a substantive affidavit or an affidavit seeking discovery under Rule 56(f). Rather, he has advanced several legal arguments and two major factual arguments in order to defeat the motion.

The first factual argument is that Scrushy is the innocent victim of a massive conspiracy to commit fraud executed by fifteen of his managerial subordinates without his participation or knowledge. This argument is unsupported by admissible evidence but it flavors his entire answering brief. Most of that document heaps blame on Scrushy's subordinates and on HealthSouth as an entity for its accounting problems. Scrushy's argument that he did not commit conscious wrongdoing in connection with HealthSouth's financial statements is not, for the most part, relevant to the pending motion because the plaintiffs have not premised their motion on the proposition that Scrushy had actual knowledge of the falsity (or put less pejoratively, the material inaccuracy) of HealthSouth's financial statements as of the time of the Buyback.

The more relevant factual argument Scrushy makes is that the plaintiffs have not produced sufficient evidence to show that HealthSouth's financial statements were materially misleading as of the time of the Buyback. This argument is not based on Scrushy's submission of his own evidence showing that HealthSouth's financial statements were in fact materially accurate as of the Buyback. *He has produced no evidence of that kind.* Rather, the argument rests primarily on the notion that because PwC has not finished its work, any inference drawn from its work to date would be unreliable.

As a prelude to addressing the motion, I address this factual argument and find it lacking in merit. At the summary judgment stage, the evidence submitted by the plaintiffs is adequate to show that the financial statements and other public guidance of HealthSouth were materially misleading as of the date of the Buyback. This evidence includes:

- the press release Scrushy caused HealthSouth to issue in August 2002 indicating that HealthSouth's public earning projections as of the time of the Buyback were optimistic by over $175 million in EBITDA annually and that no reliable earnings guidance could be given;

- the company's own announcements indicating that the financial statements existing as of the Buyback cannot be relied upon;

- the PwC public estimate of restatements of over $2.5 billion with the possibility of additional material restatements in excess of that number; and

- the March 3, 2003 press release put out under Scrushy's supervision reflecting material adjustments to HealthSouth's financials for periods pre-dating the Buyback and relevant to the July 31, 2002 trading price of HealthSouth's shares.

I need not consider, as the plaintiffs ask me to do, the guilty pleas of Scrushy's subordinates to reach the conclusion that HealthSouth's financial statements were materially deficient as of the Buyback. In the face of the extensive evidence I have cited — all of which would be admissible directly or through witness testimony as to its substance — Scrushy has stood mute. Nothing in his papers gives any hint that he actually believes that HealthSouth's financial statements were accurate as of that date. Indeed, to the contrary, Scrushy's brief suggests that he believes that HealthSouth's statements were not materially accurate. He just disclaims personal responsibility for their inaccuracy, attributing it to misconduct by his subordinates of which he was then unaware.

I therefore find that there is no material dispute of fact that HealthSouth's financial statements were materially misleading as of the date of the Buyback and decide the motion before me on that basis.

### V. The Plaintiffs Have Made Out The Elements Of Each Of Their Claims

#### A. Unjust Enrichment

The Delaware Supreme Court recently defined unjust enrichment as the unjust retention of a benefit to the loss of another, or the retention of money or property of another against the fundamental principles of justice or equity and good conscience. To obtain restitution, the plaintiffs were required to show that the defendants were unjustly enriched, that the defendants secured a benefit, and that it would be unconscionable to allow them to retain that benefit. Restitution is permitted even when the defendant retaining the benefit is not a wrongdoer. Restitution serves to deprive the defendant of benefits that in equity and good conscience he ought not to keep, *even though he may have received those benefits honestly in the first instance*, and even though the plaintiff may have suffered no demonstrable losses.

Schock v. Nash, 732 A.2d 217, 232–233 (Del. 1999) (internal quotation marks and footnotes omitted, emphasis added).

It seems obvious that the plaintiffs have proven that the Buyback unjustly enriched Scrushy. As CEO of HealthSouth, Scrushy was charged with managerial responsibility for overseeing the preparation of accurate and reliable financial statements. In the Buyback, HealthSouth relied upon the integrity of the market price for its stock in order to establish the value of Scrushy's shares fairly.

As between HealthSouth and its stockholders, on the one hand, and Scrushy, on the other, there is no question that Scrushy is the party with superior access to information and the primary duty to ensure the accuracy of the financial statements. As CEO of HealthSouth, Scrushy was the key executive at the company and was responsible to HealthSouth's board for the accurate preparation of financial statements. HealthSouth's board was entitled to rely upon Scrushy's reports and recommendations, including his implicit representation — as a HealthSouth fiduciary — that HealthSouth's market price was a reliable indicator of the value of the shares he was transmitting to HealthSouth in the Buyback.

Through conscious wrongdoing, negligent oversight of his subordinates, or innocent failure to catch the misdeeds or inaccuracies of his underlings, Scrushy signed financial statements for HealthSouth that were materially inaccurate. These financial statements formed the most important information on which the market price of HealthSouth's stock was based on July 31, 2002. The market price was what was used to guarantee the fairness of the Buyback to Healthsouth. Whether or not Scrushy breached any cognizable duty in signing those statements, he was undoubtedly unjustly enriched when the company of which he was a fiduciary bought back shares from him at a price inflated by false financial statements he had signed. After all, it was his managerial responsibility to ensure the filing of accurate statements and he should not, as a fiduciary, benefit at the expense of the object of his trust when his efforts were insufficient.

### B. Innocent Misrepresentation

To make out their claim of innocent misrepresentation, the plaintiffs must show: 1) a false statement by Scrushy; 2) made with the intent to induce HealthSouth to act; 3) upon which HealthSouth justifiably relied in acting; and 4) injury. Equity "provide[s] a remedy for negligent or innocent misrepresentations: the defendant did not have to know or believe that his statement was false or to have proceeded in reckless disregard of the truth."

On the undisputed facts, the plaintiffs have made the required showing.

First, Scrushy represented to HealthSouth that the market price was a reliable way to value his shares, thereby vouching again for the integrity of the financial statements he had signed (and earnings projections he had caused the company to make).

Second, this representation was false as the market price was not a reliable indicator of value because that price was materially distorted by HealthSouth's release of inaccurate information.

Third, Scrushy intended for HealthSouth to rely on the accuracy of the stock market price as a fair way to value his shares in the Buyback. In other words, he intended HealthSouth to conclude that the market price was reliable in large measure because the company's financial statements and press releases regarding its prospects were materially accurate and not misleading.

Fourth, HealthSouth's board could justifiably rely upon Scrushy's assurance that a market price set on the basis of financial statements and other information he signed or authorized for release as HealthSouth's CEO was a fair pricing mechanism.

Finally, the evidence is clear that a true picture of HealthSouth as of the date of the Buyback was far less appealing to the eye than the one permitted by its financial statements, leading Scrushy to receive unduly excessive value for his shares in the Buyback.

## VI. Scrushy's *In Pari Delicto* And Unclean Hands Defenses Are Meritless

Scrushy's major argument to avoid summary judgment is that HealthSouth is equally culpable with him regarding the inaccuracy of its financial statements and that the legal doctrine of *in pari delicto*, and its equitable counterpart, the doctrine of unclean hands, respectively, bar the plaintiffs' unjust enrichment and innocent misrepresentation claims. For rather obvious reasons, this argument lacks logical force.

The CEO of a major corporation like HealthSouth possesses an enormous amount of authority and therefore owes the corporation a corresponding degree of responsibility. HealthSouth's board of directors was entitled to rely upon Scrushy and his management team, particularly in the preparation of the company's financial statements, an area in which management has traditionally been preeminent. In the process of preparing and signing financial statements, Scrushy necessarily represented to the company's board, audit committee, outside auditors, and its public stockholders that the financial statements his management team had prepared were materially accurate in all respects. As the auditor's report for HealthSouth's FY 2001 10-K stated: "These financial statements and schedule are the responsibility of the Company's management."

Scrushy seeks to turn this relationship around and portray HealthSouth as an *entity* that is equally culpable with him for any falsity in the financial statements. If Scrushy's subordinates were the cause of the falsity, says Scrushy, then HealthSouth as an entity is equally to blame with him for failing to catch this subordinate-level fraud. This is transparently silly.

If Scrushy's subordinates blew one — or several seasons' full of pitches — past him, that still does not absolve him or render him on equal status with HealthSouth as an entity. It was Scrushy's duty to ensure the filing of accurate financial statements. Having failed to do so (for whatever reason) and having materially benefited from that failure in the Buyback, Scrushy cannot wield the doctrine of *in pari delicto* to escape liability. It is because corporations must act through living fiduciaries such as Scrushy that the application of the *in pari delicto* doctrine has been rejected in situations when corporate fiduciaries seek to avoid responsibility for their own conduct vis-a-vis their corporations.[42] Stated simply, HealthSouth is not at "equal fault" with Scrushy for the material deficiencies in HealthSouth's financial statements because it was Scrushy who was the ultimate manager responsible for ensuring the integrity of those statements.[43] The reality that HealthSouth itself might be liable to third-parties due to the failure of its managers (under Scrushy's supervision) to prepare materially accurate financial statements does not mean that HealthSouth has no right to seek recompense from those managers for the harm they caused it.[44] To hold otherwise would be to leave the constituencies of corporate entities — including public stockholders and creditors — with no recourse when their corporation is injured by its managers.[45] Like its

---

[42] [20] *In re Walnut Leasing Co.*, 1999 U.S. Dist. LEXIS 14517, 1999 WL 729267, at *5 (E.D. Pa. Sept. 8, 1999) ("Vis-a-vis their corporations, insiders cannot avoid the consequences of their own handiwork."); *In re Granite Partners, L.P.*, 194 B.R. 318, 332 (Bankr.S.D.N.Y. 1996) ("*In pari delicto* bars claims against third parties, but does not apply to corporate insiders or partners.").

[43] [21] *Cf. Tarasi v. Pittsburgh Nat'l Bank*, 555 F.2d 1152, 1156 (3d Cir. 1977) ("*In pari delicto*, which literally means 'of equal fault,' is one of the common law doctrines fashioned to assure that transgressors will not be allowed to profit from their own wrongdoing.").

[44] [22] For similar reasons, Scrushy's attempt to impute to HealthSouth knowledge that its insiders possessed of the inaccuracy of the company's financial statements is futile. When corporate fiduciaries — such as HealthSouth managers — have a self-interest in concealing information — such as the falsity of the financial statements that they had helped prepare — their knowledge cannot be imputed to the corporation. *See* 18B Am. Jur. 2d *Corporations* § 1680 (2003) ("An exception to the general rule that the knowledge of an officer or agent will be imputed to the corporation arises when an officer . . . is acting in a transaction in which he is personally or adversely interested or is engaged in the perpetration of an independent fraudulent transaction, where the knowledge relates to such transaction and it would be to his interest to conceal it."). *See also Am. Standard Credit, Inc. v. Nat'l Cement Co.*, 643 F.2d 248, 271 (5th Cir. 1981) (quoting 3 William Meade Fletcher, Fletcher Cyclopedia of the Law of Private Corporations § 819 (perm. ed., rev. vol. 1975) and articulating same rule). Logically, this exception to imputation applies with even more force in an action between an insider and the corporation. Here, imputation would be totally illogical. According to Scrushy, he — as CEO — had no knowledge of any improper accounting practices by his managerial subordinates. These subordinates performed their accounting-related duties for reasons wholly unconnected with the Buyback and, if they committed wrongdoing, had a motive to conceal that wrongdoing from the HealthSouth board. Given this reality, if Scrushy himself claims ignorance of wrongdoing by those who directly report to him, on what logical basis should HealthSouth be imputed to have knowledge of that wrongdoing in an action between itself and Scrushy?

[45] [23] *Cf. Ruckle v. Roto Am. Corp.*, 339 F.2d 24, 29 (2d Cir. 1964) ("There can be no more effective way to emasculate the policies of the federal securities laws than to deny relief [in a derivative action] solely because a fraud was committed by a director rather than by an outsider.").

equitable counterpart the unclean hands doctrine, the *in pari delicto* defense will not be applied when its acceptance would contravene an important public policy.[46]

Given this discussion, it is rather obvious that Scrushy's attempt to wield the unclean hands defense as a shield also cannot succeed. The reasons why this is so are several. But I will state only two. First, as between Scrushy and HealthSouth, HealthSouth has engaged in no inequitable conduct in connection with the Buyback. All it did was rely upon a market price premised upon financial statements prepared by Scrushy's management team and represented by him to be accurate to the best of his knowledge. Second, and most important, the unclean hands doctrine is primarily a matter of public policy. Here, it would work an injustice to permit Scrushy to shield himself from responsibility to HealthSouth for its reliance upon financial statements prepared under his own direction.

## VIII. The Correct Remedy Is Rescission

In his answering brief, Scrushy raises a myriad of other insubstantial arguments designed to avoid summary judgment. They do not merit extended discussion. Instead, I pause only to address Scrushy's argument that it is premature for this court to determine a remedy because there are complicated factual questions that preclude the imposition of an immediate remedy.

The reality is that it just isn't so. This is a situation in which rescission is a warranted and fitting remedy, whether considered as restitution for the unjust enrichment count or as an equitable remedy for the misrepresentation count. The plaintiffs asserted their claims regarding the Buyback very promptly, putting Scrushy on notice early after he caused HealthSouth to issue the August 2002 press release regarding the effect of the changes in the CMS Reimbursement Policy, an announcement that caused a plunge in HealthSouth's stock price. The economic premise on which HealthSouth based the Buyback was unsound, and unfair to it, and correspondingly too generous to Scrushy. HealthSouth is entitled to rescissory relief. The mechanism for granting that relief is simple: HealthSouth shall return to Scrushy the shares it received from him in the Buyback. In return, Scrushy's Loan will be treated as reinstated as of the date of the Buyback. Scrushy shall then pay to HealthSouth the amount of principal and interest that would have been owing to HealthSouth on the date that the Loan would have become payable in full absent the Buyback — 30 days from Scrushy's March 31, 2003 termination. In addition to that sum, Scrushy shall pay pre-judgment interest on the prior sum, running at the contract Loan rate from that date until the date that judgment is entered. With the assistance of counsel for HealthSouth and with notice as to form from Scrushy's counsel, the plaintiffs' counsel should prepare a judgment incorporating that concept. Plaintiffs' counsel shall also confer with counsel for HealthSouth and see if agreement can be reached on an appropriate fee award and, if not, shall establish a schedule for the prompt presentation of a request for fees.

---

[46] [24] *Seacord v. Seacord*, 33 Del. 458, 33 Del. 485, 139 A. 80, 81, 3 W.W. Harr. 485 (Del. Super. 1927) ("[*In pari delicto* and unclean hands] have always been regarded by courts of equity as without controlling force in all cases in which public policy is considered as advanced by allowing either party to sue for relief against the transaction.").

## IX. Conclusion

For the foregoing reasons, the plaintiffs' motion for summary judgment is granted as to the counts of the amended complaint against defendant Scrushy for unjust enrichment and equitable fraud. . . .

# Chapter 11

# SECURITIES FRAUD AND INSIDER TRADING

## A. SECURITIES EXCHANGE ACT OF 1934: SECTION 10(b) AND RULE 10b-5

### 1. Text of the Statute and Rule

After the market crash of 1929, people were afraid to invest money in the securities markets because they believed that they would be taken advantage of by market professionals and corporate insiders. Congress attempted to deal with those concerns by requiring companies to provide full and truthful information to the public, by regulating brokers and dealers, by establishing the Securities and Exchange Commission, and by prohibiting deceptive conduct in connection with securities transactions. Section 10(b) of the Securities Exchange Act of 1934 prohibits fraud in connection with the purchase or sale of securities. It reads in part as follows:

15 U.S.C. § 78j. Manipulative and deceptive devices

It shall be unlawful for any person, directly or indirectly, by the use of any means or instrumentality of interstate commerce or of the mails, or of any facility of any national securities exchange—

\* \* \*

(b) To use or employ, in connection with the purchase or sale of any security registered on a national securities exchange or any security not so registered, or any securities-based swap agreement, any manipulative or deceptive device or contrivance in contravention of such rules and regulations as the Commission may prescribe as necessary or appropriate in the public interest or for the protection of investors.

Section 10(b) does not contain language to make it enforceable until the SEC promulgates rules under it, so Rule 10b-5 was adopted in 1942.

17 C.F.R. § 240.10b-5 Employment of manipulative and deceptive devices.

It shall be unlawful for any person, directly or indirectly, by the use of any means or instrumentality of interstate commerce, or of the mails or of any facility of any national securities exchange,

(a) To employ any device, scheme, or artifice to defraud,

(b) To make any untrue statement of a material fact or to omit to state a material fact necessary in order to make the statements made, in the light of the circumstances under which they were made, not misleading, or

(c) To engage in any act, practice, or course of business which operates or would operate as a fraud or deceit upon any person,

in connection with the purchase or sale of any security.

## 2. The Prima Facie Case

The Securities Exchange Act of 1934 primarily regulates large public companies and their securities. However, although Rule 10b-5 was promulgated under section 10(b) of the 1934 Act, its application is not limited to publicly traded securities. It can apply to transactions in the securities of small, closely held businesses as well.

Neither Section 10(b) nor Rule 10b-5 provides for an express private right of action. Nevertheless, courts have permitted individual plaintiffs to sue for violation of Rule 10b-5 since early in the Rule's history. *See Kardon v. National Gypsum Co.*, 69 F. Supp. 512 (E.D. Pa. 1946). Therefore, violations of Rule 10b-5 may be litigated by individual plaintiffs, by the Securities and Exchange Commission, or even in criminal actions by the Justice Department.

To establish a Rule 10b-5 claim, the government must prove that the defendant:

1. either made a misstatement or omitted something when there was a duty to disclose it,

2. the misstatement or omission was material,

3. the defendant had scienter, and

4. the misstatement or omission was in connection with the purchase or sale of securities.

If the case is brought by a private plaintiff, the plaintiff must also prove reliance, causation, and damages.

We will examine cases that flesh out several of these elements.

## 3. Misrepresentation

### RISSMAN v. RISSMAN
United States Court of Appeals, Seventh Circuit
213 F.3d 381 (2000)

EASTERBROOK, CIRCUIT JUDGE.

Gerald Rissman formed Tiger Electronics to make toys and games. In 1979 Gerald gave his sons Arnold, Randall, and Samuel large blocks of stock in the firm: Gerald kept 400 shares and gave Randall 400, Arnold 100, and Samuel 100. In 1986 both Gerald and Samuel withdrew from the venture. Tiger bought Gerald's stock, and Arnold bought Samuel's, leaving Randall with 2/3 of the shares and Arnold with the rest. Randall managed the business while Arnold served as a salesman. Arnold did not elect himself to the board of directors, though Tiger employed cumulative voting, which would have enabled him to do so. When the brothers had a falling out, Arnold sold his shares to Randall for $17 million. Thirteen months later, Tiger sold its assets (including its name and trademarks) for $335 million to Hasbro, another toy maker, and was renamed Lion Holdings. Arnold contends in this suit under the federal securities laws (with state-law claims under the supplemental jurisdiction) that he would not have sold for as little as $17 million, and perhaps would not have sold at all, had Randall not deceived him into thinking that Randall would never take Tiger public or sell it to a third party. Arnold says that these statements convinced him that his stock would remain illiquid and not pay dividends, so he sold for whatever Randall was willing to pay. Arnold now wants the extra $95 million he would have received had he retained his stock until the sale to Hasbro. Because the district judge granted summary judgment to the defendants, see 1999 U.S. Dist. LEXIS 10611 (N.D. Ill.), we must assume that Randall told Arnold that he was determined to keep Tiger a family firm. Likewise we must assume that Randall secretly planned to sell after acquiring Arnold's shares. But we need *not* assume that Arnold relied on Randall's statements (equivalently, that the statements were material to and caused Arnold's decision), and without reliance Arnold has no claim under sec. 10(b) or Rule 10b-5. See 15 U.S.C. sec. 78j(b); 17 C.F.R. sec. 240.10b-5; *Basic, Inc. v. Levinson*, 485 U.S. 224, 243, 99 L. Ed. 2d 194, 108 S. Ct. 978 (1988). Arnold asked Randall to put in writing, as part of the agreement, a representation that Randall would never sell Tiger. Randall refused to make such a representation. Instead he warranted (accurately) that he was not aware of any offers to purchase Tiger and was not engaged in negotiations for its sale. Contrast *Jordan v. Duff & Phelps, Inc.*, 815 F.2d 429 (7th Cir. 1987). The parties also agreed that if Tiger were sold before Arnold had received all installments of the purchase price, then payment of the principal and interest would be accelerated. Having sought broader assurances, and having been refused, Arnold could not persuade a reasonable trier of fact that he relied on Randall's oral statements. See *Karazanos v. Madison Two Associates*, 147 F.3d 624, 628–31 (7th Cir. 1998). Having signed an agreement providing for acceleration as a consequence of sale, Arnold is in no position to contend that he relied on the impossibility of sale.

Indeed, Arnold represented as part of the transaction that he had *not* relied on any prior oral statement:

> The parties further declare that they have not relied upon any representation of any party hereby released [Randall] or of their attorneys [Glick], agents, or other representatives concerning the nature or extent of their respective injuries or damages.

That is pretty clear, but to foreclose quibbling Arnold made these warranties to Randall:

> (a) no promise or inducement for this Agreement has been made to him except as set forth herein; (b) this Agreement is executed by [Arnold] freely and voluntarily, and without reliance upon any statement or representation by Purchaser, the Company, any of the Affiliates or O.R. Rissman or any of their attorneys or agents except as set forth herein; (c) he has read and

fully understands this Agreement and the meaning of its provisions; (d) he is legally competent to enter into this Agreement and to accept full responsibility therefor; and (e) he has been advised to consult with counsel before entering into this Agreement and has had the opportunity to do so.

Arnold does not contend that any representation in the stock purchase agreement is untrue or misleading; his entire case rests on Randall's oral statements. Yet Arnold assured Randall that he had not relied on these statements. Securities law does not permit a party to a stock transaction to disavow such representations — to say, in effect, "I lied when I told you I wasn't relying on your prior statements" and then to seek damages for their contents. Stock transactions would be impossibly uncertain if federal law precluded parties from agreeing to rely on the written word alone. "Without such a principle, sellers would have no protection against plausible liars and gullible jurors." *Carr v. CIGNA Securities, Inc.*, 95 F.3d 544, 547 (7th Cir. 1996).

Two courts of appeals have held that non-reliance clauses in written stock-purchase agreements preclude any possibility of damages under the federal securities laws for prior oral statements. *Jackvony v. RIHT Financial Corp.*, 873 F.2d 411 (1st Cir. 1989) (Breyer, J.); *One-O-One Enterprises, Inc. v. Caruso*, 270 U.S. App. D.C. 251, 848 F.2d 1283 (D.C. Cir. 1988) (R.B. Ginsburg, J.). Several of this circuit's opinions intimate agreement with these decisions, though we have yet to encounter a situation squarely covered by them. See *SEC v. Jakubowski*, 150 F.3d 675, 681 (7th Cir. 1998); *Pommer v. Medtest Corp.*, 961 F.2d 620, 625 (7th Cir. 1992); *Astor Chauffeured Limousine Co. v. Runnfeldt Investment Corp.*, 910 F.2d 1540, 1545–46 (7th Cir. 1990). Jackvony and One-O-One fit Arnold's claim like a glove, and we now follow those cases by holding that a written anti-reliance clause precludes any claim of deceit by prior representations. The principle is functionally the same as a doctrine long accepted in this circuit: that a person who has received written disclosure of the truth may not claim to rely on contrary oral falsehoods. . . . A non-reliance clause is not identical to a truthful disclosure, but it has a similar function: it ensures that both the transaction and any subsequent litigation proceed on the basis of the parties' writings, which are less subject to the vagaries of memory and the risks of fabrication.

Memory plays tricks. Acting in the best of faith, people may "remember" things that never occurred but now serve their interests. Or they may remember events with a change of emphasis or nuance that makes a substantial difference to meaning. Express or implied qualifications may be lost in the folds of time. A statement such as "I won't sell at current prices" may be recalled years later as "I won't sell." Prudent people protect themselves against the limitations of memory (and the temptation to shade the truth) by limiting their dealings to those memorialized in writing, and promoting the primacy of the written word is a principal function of the federal securities laws.

Failure to enforce agreements such as the one between Arnold and Randall could not make sellers of securities better off in the long run. Faced with an unavoidable risk of claims based on oral statements, persons transacting in securities would reduce the price they pay, setting aside the difference as a reserve for risk. If, as Arnold says, Randall was willing to pay $17 million and not a penny more, then a legal rule entitling Arnold to an extra $95 million if Tiger should be sold in the future would have scotched the deal (the option value of the deferred payment exceeds), leaving Arnold with no cash and the full risk of the venture. Arnold can't have both $17 million with certainty and a continuing right to 1/3 of any premium Randall negotiates for the firm, while bearing no risk of loss from the fickle toy business; that would make him better off than if he had held his shares throughout.

Negotiation could have avoided this litigation. Instead of taking the maximum Randall was willing to pay unconditionally, Arnold could have sought a lower guaranteed payment (say, $10 million) plus a kicker if Tiger were sold or taken public. Because random events (or Randall's efforts) would dominate Tiger's prosperity over the long run, the kicker would fall with time. Perhaps Arnold could have asked for 25% of any proceeds on a sale within a year, diminishing 1% every other month after that (so that Randall would keep all proceeds of a sale more than 62 months after the transaction with Arnold). Many variations on this formula were possible; all would have put Randall to the test, for if he really planned not to sell, the approach would have been attractive to him because it reduced his total payment. Likewise it would have been attractive to Arnold if he believed that Randall wanted to sell as soon as he could receive more than 2/3 of the gains. Yet Arnold never proposed a payment formula that would share the risk (and rewards) between the brothers, and the one he proposes after the fact in this litigation — $17 million with certainty and a perpetual right to 1/3 of any later premium — is just about the only formula that could not conceivably have been the outcome of bargaining.

Arnold calls the no-reliance clauses "boilerplate," and they were; transactions lawyers have language of this sort stored up for reuse. But the fact that language has been used before does not make it less binding when used again. Phrases become boilerplate when many parties find that the language serves their ends. That's a reason to enforce the promises, not to disregard them. People negotiate about the presence of boilerplate clauses. The sort of no-reliance clauses that appeared in the Rissmans' agreement were missing from other transactions, such as the ones in *Astor Chauffeured Limousine and Acme Propane, Inc. v. Tenexco, Inc.*, 844 F.2d 1317 (7th Cir. 1988). Still other transactions, such as the one discussed in *LHLC Corp. v. Cluett, Peabody & Co.*, 842 F.2d 928 (7th Cir. 1988), include "strict reliance" clauses, entitling one party to rely on every representation ever made by the other. Arnold could have negotiated for the elimination of the no-reliance clauses, or the inclusion of a strict-reliance clause, but in exchange he would have had to accept a price lower than $17 million. Judges need not speculate about the reason a clause appears or is omitted, however; what matters when litigation breaks out is what the parties actually signed.

Contractual language serves its functions only if enforced consistently. This is one of the advantages of boilerplate, which usually has a record of predictable interpretation and application. If as Arnold says the extent of his reliance is a jury question even after he warranted his non-reliance, then the clause has been nullified, and people in Arnold's position will be worse off tomorrow for reasons we have explained. *Rowe v. Maremont Corp.*, 850 F.2d 1226 (7th Cir. 1988), on which Arnold principally relies, does not assist him. Maremont contended that as a matter of law no oral representations survive a written contract; we rejected that conclusion in *Rowe*, 850 F.2d at 1234, and again in *Astor Chauffeured Limousine*, but in neither *Rowe* nor *Astor Chauffeured Limousine* had the parties included a no-reliance warranty in their written agreement. Arnold, by giving Randall such a warranty, put himself in a different position.

## NOTE

With respect to the requirement that plaintiff prove misrepresentation, also consider *Santa Fe v. Green*, 430 U.S. 462 (1977), in which the Court held that plaintiff must allege misrepresentation or deception; breach of fiduciary duty or financial unfairness alone is not enough to make out a claim under Rule 10b-5. Breach of fiduciary duty alone remains primarily a claim under state law rather than federal law. As we will see in the insider trading cases, though, breach of fiduciary duty is relevant in determining liability under Rule 10b-5.

## 4.   Materiality, Reliance, and Causation

### BASIC, INC. v. LEVINSON
Supreme Court of the United States
485 U.S. 224 (1988)

JUSTICE BLACKMUN delivered the Opinion of the Court.

This case requires us to apply the materiality requirement of § 10(b) of the Securities Exchange Act of 1934, 48 Stat. 881, as amended, 15 U.S.C. § 78a *et seq.* (1934 Act), and the Securities and Exchange Commissions Rule 10b-5, promulgated there under, *see* 17 CFR § 240.10b-5 (1987), in the content of preliminary corporate merger discussions. We must also determine whether a person who traded a corporation's shares on a securities exchange after the issuance of a materially misleading statement by the corporation may invoke a rebuttable presumption that, in trading, he relied on the integrity of the price set by the market.

I

Prior to December 20, 1978, Basic Incorporated was a publicly traded company primarily engaged in the business of manufacturing chemical refractories for the steel industry. As early as 1965 or 1966, Combustion Engineering, Inc., a company producing mostly alumina-based refractories, expressed some interest in acquiring Basic, but was deterred from pursuing this inclination seriously because of antitrust concerns it then entertained. *See* App. 81–83. In 1976, however, regulatory action opened the way to a renewal of Combustion's interest. The "Strategic Plan," dated October 25, 1976, for Combustion's Industrial Products Group included the objective: "Acquire Basic Inc. $30 million." App. 337.

Beginning in September 1976, Combustion representatives had meetings and telephone conversations with Basic officers and directors, including petitioners here, concerning the possibility of a merger. During 1977 and 1978, Basic made three public statements denying that it was engaged in merger negotiations. On

December 18, 1978, Basic asked the New York Stock Exchange to suspend trading in its shares and issued a release stating that it had been "approached" by another company concerning a merger. *Id.*, at 413. On December 19, Basic's board endorsed Combustion's offer of $46 per share for its common stock, *id.*, at 335, 414–416, and on the following day publicly announced its approval of Combustion's tender offer for all outstanding shares.

Respondents are former Basic shareholders who sold their stock after Basic's first public statement of October 21, 1977, and before the suspension of trading in December 1978. Respondents brought a class action against Basic and its directors, asserting that the defendants issued three false or misleading public statements and thereby were in violation of § 10(b) of the 1934 Act and of Rule 10b-5. Respondents alleged that they were injured by selling Basic shares at artificially depressed prices in a market affected by petitioners' misleading statements and in reliance thereon.

The District Court adopted a presumption of reliance by members of the plaintiff class upon petitioners' public statements that enabled the court to conclude that common questions of fact or law predominated over particular questions pertaining to individual plaintiffs. *See* Fed. Rule Civ. Proc. 23(b)(3). The District Court therefore certified respondents' class. On the merits, however, the District Court granted summary judgment for the defendants. It held that, as a matter of law, any misstatements were immaterial: there were no negotiations ongoing at the time of the first statement, and although negotiations were taking place when the second and third statements were issued, those negotiations were not "destined, with reasonable certainty, to become a merger agreement in principle." App. to Pet. for Cert. 103a.

The United States Court of Appeals for the Sixth Circuit affirmed the class certification, but reversed the District Court's summary judgment, and remanded the case. 786 F.2d 741 (1986). The court reasoned that while petitioners were under no general duty to disclose their discussions with Combustion, any statement the company voluntarily released could not be " 'so incomplete as to mislead.' " *Id.*, at 746, quoting *SEC v. Texas Gulf Sulphur Co.* 401 F.2d 833, 862 (2d Cir. 1968) (en banc), *cert. denied sub nom. Coats v. SEC*, 394 U.S. 976 (1969). In the Court of Appeals' view, Basic's statements that no negotiations were taking place, and that it knew of no corporate developments to account for the heavy trading activity, were misleading. With respect to materiality, the court rejected the argument that preliminary merger discussions are immaterial as a matter of law, and held that "once a statement is made denying the existence of any discussions, even discussions that might not have been material in absence of the denial are material because they make the statement made untrue." 786 F.2d, at 749. The Court of Appeals joined a number of other circuits in accepting the "fraud-on-the-market theory" to create a rebuttable presumption that respondents relied on petitioners' material misrepresentations, noting that without the presumption it would be impractical to certify a class under Fed. Rule Civ. Proc. 23(b)(3). *See* 786 F.2d, at 750–751.

We granted certiorari, 484 U.S. 1083 (1987), to resolve the split, see Part III, *infra*, among the Courts of Appeals as to the standard of materiality applicable to preliminary merger discussions, and to determine whether the courts below properly applied a presumption of reliance in certifying the class, rather than requiring each class member to show direct reliance on Basic's statements.

## II

The 1934 Act was designed to protect investors against manipulation of stock prices. *See* S. Rep. No. 792, 73d Cong., 2d Sess., 1–5 (1934). Underlying the adoption of extensive disclosure requirements was a legislative philosophy: "There cannot be honest markets without honest publicity. Manipulation and dishonest practices of the market place thrive upon mystery and secrecy." H.R. Rep. No. 1383, 73d Cong., 2d Sess., 11 (1934). This Court "repeatedly has described the 'fundamental purpose' of the Act as implementing a 'philosophy of full disclosure.'" *Santa Fe Industries, Inc. v. Green,* 430 U.S. 462, 477–478 (1977), quoting *SEC v. Capital Gains Research Bureau, Inc.,* 375 U.S. 180, 186 (1963).

Pursuant to its authority under § 10(b) of the 1934 Act, 15 U.S.C. § 78j, the Securities and Exchange Commission promulgated Rule 10b-5. Judicial interpretation and application, legislative acquiescence, and the passage of time have removed any doubt that a private cause of action exists for a violation of § 10(b) and Rule 10b-5, and constitutes an essential tool for enforcement of the 1934 Act's requirements. *See, e.g., Ernst & Ernst v. Hochfelder,* 425 U.S. 185, 196 (1976); *Blue Chip Stamps v. Manor Drug Stores,* 421 U.S. 723, 730 (1975).

The Court previously has addressed various positive and common-law requirements for a violation of § 10(b) or of Rule 10b-5. *See, e.g., Santa Fe Industries, Inc. v. Green, supra* ("manipulative or deceptive" requirement of the statute); *Blue Chip Stamps v. Manor Drug Stores, supra* ("in connection with the purchase or sale" requirement of the Rule); *Dirks v. SEC,* 463 U.S. 646 (1983) (duty to disclose); *Chiarella v. United* States, 445 U.S. 222 (1980) (same); *Ernst & Ernst v. Hochfelder, supra* (scienter). *See also Carpenter v. United States,* 484 U.S. 19 (1987) (confidentiality). The Court also explicitly has defined a standard of materiality under the securities laws, *see TSC Industries, Inc. v. Northway, Inc.,* 426 U.S. 438 (1976), concluding in the proxy solicitation context that "an omitted fact is material if there is a substantial likelihood that a reasonable shareholder would consider it important in deciding how to vote." *Id.,* at 449. Acknowledging that certain information concerning corporate developments could well be of "dubious significance," *id.,* at 448, the Court was careful not to set too low a standard of materiality; it was concerned that a minimal standard might bring an overabundance of information within its reach, and lead management "simply to bury the shareholders in an avalanche of trivial information — a result that is hardly conducive to informed decisionmaking." *Id.,* at 448–449. It further explained that to fulfill the materiality requirement "there must be a substantial likelihood that the disclosure of the omitted fact would have been viewed by the reasonable investor as having significantly altered the 'total mix' of information made available." *Id.,* at 449. We now expressly adopt the *TSC Industries* standard of materiality for the § 10(b) and Rule 10b-5 context.

## III

The application of this materiality standard to preliminary merger discussions is not self-evident. Where the impact of the corporate development on the target's fortune is certain and clear, the *TSC Industries* materiality definition admits straightforward application. Where, on the other hand, the event is contingent or speculative in nature, it is difficult to ascertain whether the "reasonable investor" would have considered the omitted information significant at the time. Merger negotiations, because of the ever present possibility that the contemplated transaction will not be effectuated, fall into the latter category.

## A

Petitioners urge upon us a Third Circuit test for resolving this difficulty. *See* Brief for Petitioners 20–22. Under this approach, preliminary merger discussions do not become material until "agreement-in-principle" as to the price and structure of the transaction has been reached between the would-be merger partners. *See Greenfield v. Heublein, Inc.*, 74 F.2d 751, 757 (3d Cir. 1984), *cert. denied*, 469 U.S. 1215 (1985). By definition, then, information concerning any negotiations not yet at the agreement-in-principle stage could be withheld or even misrepresented without a violation of Rule 10b-5.

Three rationales have been offered in support of the "agreement-in-principle" test. The first derives from the concern expressed in *TSC Industries* that an investor not be overwhelmed by excessively detailed and trivial information, and focuses on the substantial risk that preliminary merger discussions may collapse: because such discussions are inherently tentative, disclosure of their existence itself could mislead investors and foster false optimism. *See Greenfield v. Heublein, Inc.*, 742 F.2d, at 756; *Reiss v. Pan American World Airways, Inc.*, 711 F.2d 11, 14 (2d Cir. 1983). The other two justifications for the agreement-in-principle standard are based on management concerns: because the requirement of "agreement-in-principle" limits the scope of disclosure obligations, it helps preserve the confidentiality of merger discussions where earlier disclosure might prejudice the negotiations; and the test also provides a usable, bright-line rule for determining when disclosure must be made. *See Greenfield v. Heublein, Inc.*, 742 F.2d, at 757; *Flamm v. Eberstadt*, 814 F. 2d 1169, 1176–1178 (7th Cir.), *cert. denied*, 484 U.S. 853 (1987).

None of these policy-based rationales, however, purports to explain why drawing the line at agreement-in-principle reflects the significance of the information upon the investor's decision. The first rationale, and the only one connected to the concerns expressed in *TSC Industries*, stands soundly rejected, even by a Court of Appeals that otherwise has accepted the wisdom of the agreement-in-principle test. "It assumes that investors are nitwits, unable to appreciate — even when told — that mergers are risky propositions up until the closing." *Flamm v. Eberstadt*, 814 F.2d, at 1175. Disclosure, and not paternalistic withholding of accurate information, is the policy chosen and expressed by Congress. We have recognized time and again, a "fundamental purpose" of the various securities acts, "was to substitute a philosophy of full disclosure for the philosophy of caveat emptor and thus to achieve a high standard of business ethics in the securities industry." *SEC v. Capital Gains Research Bureau, Inc.*, 375 U.S. 180, 186 (1963). *Accord, Affiliated Ute Citizens v.*

*United States*, 406 U.S. 128, 151 (1972); *Santa Fe Industries, Inc. v. Green*, 430 U.S. 462, 477 (1977). The role of the materiality requirement is not to "attribute to investors a child-like simplicity, an inability to grasp the probabilistic significance of negotiations," *Flamm v. Eberstadt*, 814 F.2d, at 1175, but to filter out essentially useless information that a reasonable investor would not consider significant, even as part of a larger "mix" of factors to consider in making his investment decision. *TSC Industries, Inc. v. Northway, Inc.*, 426 U.S., at 448–449.

The second rationale, the importance of secrecy during the early stages of merger discussions, also seems irrelevant to an assessment whether their existence is significant to the trading decision of a reasonable investor. To avoid a "bidding war" over its target, an acquiring firm often will insist that negotiations remain confidential, see, e.g., *In re Carnation Co.*, Exchange Act Release No. 22214, 33 SEC Docket 1025 (1985), and at least one Court of Appeals has stated that "silence pending settlement of the price and structure of a deal is beneficial to most investors, most of the time." *Flamm v. Eberstadt*, 814 F.2d, at 1177.

We need not ascertain, however, whether secrecy necessarily maximizes shareholder wealth — although we note that the proposition is at least disputed as a matter of theory and empirical research — for this case does not concern the timing of a disclosure; it concerns only its accuracy and completeness. We face here the narrow question whether information concerning the existence and status of preliminary merger discussions is significant to the reasonable investor's trading decision. Arguments based on the premise that some disclosure would be "premature" in a sense are more properly considered under the rubric of an issuer's duty to disclose. The "secrecy" rationale is simply inapposite to the definition of materiality.

The final justification offered in support of the agreement-in-principle test seems to be directed solely at the comfort of corporate managers. A bright-line rule indeed is easier to follow than a standard that requires the exercise of judgment in the light of all the circumstances. But ease of application alone is not an excuse for ignoring the purposes of the securities acts and Congress' policy decisions. Any approach that designates a single fact or occurrence as always determinative of an inherently fact-specific finding such as materiality, must necessarily be over- or underinclusive. In *TSC Industries* this Court explained: "The determination [of materiality] requires delicate assessments of the inferences a 'reasonable shareholder' would draw from a given set of facts and the significance of those inferences to him. . . . " 426 U.S., at 450. After much study, the Advisory Committee on Corporate Disclosure cautioned the SEC against administratively confining materiality to a rigid formula. Courts also would do well to heed this advice.

We therefore find no valid justification for artificially excluding from the definition of materiality information concerning merger discussions, which would otherwise be considered significant to the trading decision of a reasonable investor, merely because agreement-in-principle as to price and structure has not yet been reached by the parties or their representatives.

## B

The Sixth Circuit explicitly rejected the agreement-in-principle test, as we do today, but in its place adopted a rule that, if taken literally, would be equally insensitive, in our view, to the distinction between materiality and the other elements of an action under Rule 10b-5:

> "When a company whose stock is publicly traded makes a statement, as Basic did, that 'no negotiations' are underway, and that the corporation knows of 'no reason for the stock's activity,' and that 'management is unaware of any present or pending corporate development that would result in the abnormally heavy trading activity,' information concerning ongoing acquisition discussions becomes material *by virtue of the statement denying their existence.* . . .

* * *

> " . . . In analyzing whether information regarding merger discussions is material such that it must be affirmatively disclosed to avoid a violation of Rule 10b-5, the discussions and their progress are the primary considerations. However, once a statement is made denying the existence of any discussions, even discussions that might not have been material in absence of the denial are material because they make the statement made untrue." 786 F.2d, at 748–749 (emphasis in original).

This approach, however, fails to recognize that, in order to prevail on a Rule 10b-5 claim, a plaintiff must show that the statements were *misleading* as to a *material* fact. It is not enough that a statement is false or incomplete, if the misrepresented fact is otherwise insignificant.

## C

Even before this Court's decision in *TSC Industries*, the Second Circuit had explained the role of the materiality requirement of Rule 10b-5, with respect to contingent or speculative information or events, in a manner that gave that term meaning that is independent of the other provisions of the Rule. Under such circumstances, materiality "will depend at any given time upon a balancing of both the indicated probability that the event will occur and the anticipated magnitude of the event in light of the totality of the company activity." *SEC v. Texas Gulf Sulphur Co.*, 401 F.2d, at 849. Interestingly, neither the Third Circuit decision adopting the agreement-in-principle test nor petitioners here take issue with this general standard. Rather, they suggest that with respect to preliminary merger discussions, there are good reasons to draw a line at agreement on price and structure.

In a subsequent decision, the late Judge Friendly, writing for a Second Circuit panel, applied the *Texas Gulf Sulphur* probability/magnitude approach in the specific context of preliminary merger negotiations. After acknowledging that materiality is something to be determined on the basis of the particular facts of each case, he stated:

"Since a merger in which it is bought out is the most important event that can occur in a small corporation's life, to wit, its death, we think that inside information, as regards a merger of this sort, can become material at an earlier stage than would be the case as regards lesser transactions — and this even though the mortality rate of mergers in such formative stages is doubtless high."

*SEC v. Geon Industries, Inc.*, 531 F.2d 39, 47–48 (2d Cir. 1976).

We agree with that analysis.

Whether merger discussions in any particular case are material therefore depends on the facts. Generally, in order to assess the probability that the event will occur, a factfinder will need to look to indicia of interest in the transaction at the highest corporate levels. Without attempting to catalog all such possible factors, we note by way of example that board resolutions, instructions to investment bankers, and actual negotiations between principals or their intermediaries may serve as indicia of interest. To assess the magnitude of the transaction to the issuer of the securities allegedly manipulated, a factfinder will need to consider such facts as the size of the two corporate entities and of the potential premiums over market value. No particular event or factor short of closing the transaction need be either necessary or sufficient by itself to render merger discussions material.[1]

As we clarify today, materiality depends on the significance the reasonable investor would place on the withheld or misrepresented information. The fact-specific inquiry we endorse here is consistent with the approach a number of courts have taken in assessing the materiality of merger negotiations. Because the standard of materiality we have adopted differs from that used by both courts below, we remand the case for reconsideration of the question whether a grant of summary judgment is appropriate on this record.

---

[1] [17] To be actionable, of course, a statement must also be misleading. Silence, absent a duty to disclose, is not misleading under Rule 10b-5. "No comment" statements are generally the functional equivalent of silence. *See In re Carnation Co., supra. See also* New York Stock Exchange Listed Company Manual § 202.01, reprinted in 3CCH Fed. Sec. L. Rep. para. 23,515 (premature public announcement may properly be delayed for valid business purpose and where adequate security can be maintained); American Stock Exchange Company Guide §§ 401–405, reprinted in 3 CCH Fed. Sec. L. Rep. paras. 23,124A–23,124E (similar provisions).

It has been suggested that given current market practices, a "no comment" statement is tantamount to an admission that merger discussions are underway. *See Flamm v. Eberstadt*, 814 F.2d, at 1178. That may well hold true to the extent that issuers adopt a policy of truthfully denying merger rumors when no discussions are underway, and of issuing "no comment" statements when they are in the midst of negotiations. There are, of course, other statement policies firms could adopt; we need not now advise issuers as to what kind of practice to follow, within the range permitted by law. Perhaps more importantly, we think that creating an exception to a regulatory scheme founded on a prodisclosure legislative philosophy, because complying with the regulation might be "bad for business," is a role for Congress, not this Court. *See also id.*, at 1182 (opinion concurring in the judgment and concurring in part).

## IV

### A

We turn to the question of reliance and the fraud-on-the-market theory. Succinctly put:

> "The fraud on the market theory is based on the hypothesis that, in an open and developed securities market, the price of a company's stock is determined by the available material information regarding the company and its business. . . . Misleading statements will therefore defraud purchasers of stock even if the purchasers do not directly rely on the misstatements. . . . The causal connection between the defendants' fraud and the plaintiffs' purchase of stock in such a case is no less significant than in a case of direct reliance on misrepresentations." *Peil v. Speiser*, 806 F.2d 1154, 1160–1161 (3d Cir. 1986).

Our task, of course, is not to assess the general validity of the theory, but to consider whether it was proper for the courts below to apply a rebuttable presumption of reliance, supported in part by the fraud-on-the-market theory. Cf. the comments of the dissent, *post*, [part C of the dissent].

This case required resolution of several common questions of law and fact concerning the falsity or misleading nature of the three public statements made by Basic, the presence or absence of scienter, and the materiality of the misrepresentations, if any. In their amended complaint, the named plaintiffs alleged that in reliance on Basic's statements they sold their shares of Basic stock in the depressed market created by petitioners. *See* Amended Complaint in No. C79-1220 (ND Ohio) paras. 27, 29, 35, 40; *see also id.*, at para. 33 (alleging effect on market price of Basic's statements). Requiring proof of individualized reliance from each member of the proposed plaintiff class effectively would have prevented respondents from proceeding with a class action, since individual issues then would have overwhelmed the common ones. The District Court found that the presumption of reliance created by the fraud-on-the-market theory provided "a practical resolution to the problem of balancing the substantive requirement of proof of reliance in securities cases against the procedural requisites of [Fed. Rule Civ. Proc.] 23." The District Court thus concluded that with reference to each public statement and its impact upon the open market for Basic shares, common questions predominated over individual questions, as required by Fed. Rule Civ. Proc. 23(a)(2) and (b)(3).

Petitioners and their amici complain that the fraud-on-the-market theory effectively eliminates the requirement that a plaintiff asserting a claim under Rule 10b-5 prove reliance. They note that reliance is and long has been an element of common-law fraud, *see e.g., Restatement (Second) of Torts* § 525 (1977); *Prosser and Keeton on The Law of Torts* § 108 (5th ed. 1984), and argue that because the analogous express right of action includes a reliance requirement, *see, e.g.,* § 18(a) of the 1934 Act, as amended,15 U.S.C. § 78r(a), so too must an action implied under § 10(b).

We agree that reliance is an element of a Rule 10b-5 cause of action. *See Ernst & Ernst v. Hochfelder*, 425 U.S., at 206 (quoting Senate Report). Reliance provides the requisite causal connection between a defendant's misrepresentation and a plaintiff's injury. *See, e.g., Wilson v. Comtech Telecommunications Corp.*, 648 F.2d 88, 92 (2d Cir. 1981); *List v. Fashion Park, Inc.*, 340 F.2d 457, 462 (2d Cir.), *cert. denied sub nom. List v. Lerner*, 382 U.S. 811 (1965). There is, however, more than one way to demonstrate the causal connection. Indeed, we previously have dispensed with a requirement of positive proof of reliance, where a duty to disclose material information had been breached, concluding that the necessary nexus between the plaintiffs' injury and the defendant's wrongful conduct had been established. *See Affiliated Ute Citizens v. United States*, 406 U.S., at 153–154. Similarly, we did not require proof that material omissions or misstatements in a proxy statement decisively affected voting, because the proxy solicitation itself, rather than the defect in the solicitation materials, served as an essential link in the transaction. *See Mills v. Electric Auto-Lite Co.*, 396 U.S. 375, 384–385 (1970). The modern securities markets, literally involving millions of shares changing hands daily, differ from the face-to-face transactions contemplated by early fraud cases, and our understanding of Rule 10b-5's reliance requirement must encompass these differences.

> "In face-to-face transactions, the inquiry into an investor's reliance upon information is into the subjective pricing of that information by that investor. With the presence of a market, the market is interposed between seller and buyer and, ideally, transmits information to the investor in the processed form of a market price. Thus the market is performing a substantial part of the valuation process performed by the investor in a face-to-face transaction. The market is acting as the unpaid agent of the investor, informing him that given all the information available to it, the value of the stock is worth the market price." *In re LTV Securities* Litigation, 88 F.R.D. 134, 143 (ND Tex. 1980).

*Accord, e.g., Peil v. Speiser*, 806 F.2d, at 1161 ("In an open and developed market, the dissemination of material misrepresentations or withholding of material information typically affects the price of the stock, and purchasers generally rely on the price of the stock as a reflection of its value"); *Blackie v. Barrack*, 524 F.2d 891, 908 (9th Cir. 1975) ("the same causal nexus can be adequately established indirectly, by proof of materiality coupled with the common sense that a stock purchaser does not ordinarily seek to purchase a loss in the form of artificially inflated stock"), *cert. denied*, 429 U.S. 816 (1976).

### B

Presumptions typically serve to assist courts in managing circumstances in which direct proof, for one reason or another, is rendered difficult. *See, e.g.*, D. Louisell & C. Mueller, *Federal Evidence* 541–542 (1977). The courts below accepted a presumption, created by the fraud-on-the-market theory and subject to rebuttal by petitioners, that persons who had traded Basic shares had done so in reliance on the integrity of the price set by the market, but because of petitioners' material misrepresentations that price had been fraudulently depressed. Requiring a plaintiff to show a speculative state of facts, i.e., how he would have acted if omitted material information had been disclosed, *see Affiliated Ute Citizens v. United*

*States*, 406 U. S., at 153–154, or if the misrepresentation had not been made, *see Sharp v. Coopers & Lybrand*, 649 F.2d 175, 188 (3d Cir. 1981), *cert. denied*, 455 U.S. 938 (1982), would place an unnecessarily unrealistic evidentiary burden on the Rule 10b-5 plaintiff who has traded on an impersonal market. *Cf. Mills v. Electric Auto-Lite Co.*, 396 U.S., at 385.

Arising out of considerations of fairness, public policy, and probability, as well as judicial economy, presumptions are also useful devices for allocating the burdens of proof between parties. *See* E. Cleary, *McCormick on Evidence* 968–969 (3rd ed. 1984); *see also* Fed. Rule Evid. 301 and notes. The presumption of reliance employed in this case is consistent with, and, by facilitating Rule 10b-5 litigation, supports, the congressional policy embodied in the 1934 Act. In drafting that Act, Congress expressly relied on the premise that securities markets are affected by information, and enacted legislation to facilitate an investor's reliance on the integrity of those markets:

> "No investor, no speculator, can safely buy and sell securities upon the exchanges without having an intelligent basis for forming his judgment as to the value of the securities he buys or sells. The idea of a free and open public market is built upon the theory that competing judgments of buyers and sellers as to the fair price of a security brings [sic] about a situation where the market price reflects as nearly as possible a just price. Just as artificial manipulation tends to upset the true function of an open market, so the hiding and secreting of important information obstructs the operation of the markets as indices of real value." H.R. Rep. No. 1383 at 11.

\*     \*     \*

The presumption is also supported by common sense and probability. Recent empirical studies have tended to confirm Congress' premise that the market price of shares traded on well-developed markets reflects all publicly available information, and, hence, any material misrepresentations. We need not determine by adjudication what economists and social scientists have debated through the use of sophisticated statistical analysis and the application of economic theory. For purposes of accepting the presumption of reliance in this case, we need only believe that market professionals generally consider most publicly announced material statements about companies, thereby affecting stock market prices. It has been noted that "it is hard to imagine that there ever is a buyer or seller who does not rely on market integrity. Who would knowingly roll the dice in a crooked crap game?" *Schlanger v. Four-Phase Systems Inc.*, 555 F. Supp. 535, 538 (SDNY 1982). Indeed, nearly every court that has considered the proposition has concluded that where materially misleading statements have been disseminated into an impersonal, well-developed market for securities, the reliance of individual plaintiffs on the integrity of the market price may be presumed. Commentators generally have applauded the adoption of one variation or another of the fraud-on-the-market theory. An investor who buys or sells stock at the price set by the market does so in reliance on the integrity of that price. Because most publicly available information is reflected in market price, an investor's reliance on any public material misrepresentations, therefore, may be presumed for purposes of a Rule 10b-5 action.

C

The Court of Appeals found that petitioners "made public material misrepresentations and [respondents] sold Basic stock in an impersonal, efficient market. Thus the class, as defined by the district court, has established the threshold facts for proving their loss." 786 F.2d, at 751. The court acknowledged that petitioners may rebut proof of the elements giving rise to the presumption, or show that the misrepresentation in fact did not lead to a distortion of price or that an individual plaintiff traded or would have traded despite his knowing the statement was false. *Id.*, at 750 n.6.

Any showing that severs the link between the alleged misrepresentation and either the price received (or paid) by the plaintiff, or his decision to trade at a fair market price, will be sufficient to rebut the presumption of reliance. For example, if petitioners could show that the "market makers" were privy to the truth about the merger discussions here with Combustion, and thus that the market price would not have been affected by their misrepresentations, the causal connection could be broken: the basis for finding that the fraud had been transmitted through market price would be gone. Similarly, if, despite petitioners' allegedly fraudulent attempt to manipulate market price, news of the merger discussions credibly entered the market and dissipated the effects of the misstatements, those who traded Basic shares after the corrective statements would have no direct or indirect connection with the fraud. Petitioners also could rebut the presumption of reliance as to plaintiffs who would have divested themselves of their Basic shares without relying on the integrity of the market. For example, a plaintiff who believed that Basic's statements were false and that Basic was indeed engaged in merger discussions, and who consequently believed that Basic stock was artificially underpriced, but sold his shares nevertheless because of other unrelated concerns, e.g., potential antitrust problems, or political pressures to divest from shares of certain businesses, could not be said to have relied on the integrity of a price he knew had been manipulated.

V

In summary:

1. We specifically adopt, for the § 10(b) and Rule 10b-5 context, the standard of materiality set forth in *TSC Industries, Inc. v. Northway, Inc.*, 426 U.S., at 449.

2. We reject "agreement-in-principle as to price and structure" as the bright-line rule for materiality.

3. We also reject the proposition that "information becomes material by virtue of a public statement denying it."

4. Materiality in the merger context depends on the probability that the transaction will be consummated, and its significance to the issuer of the securities. Materiality depends on the facts and thus is to be determined on a case-by-case basis.

5. It is not inappropriate to apply a presumption of reliance supported by the fraud-on-the-market theory.

6. That presumption, however, is rebuttable.

7. The District Court's certification of the class here was appropriate when made but is subject on remand to such adjustment, if any, as developing circumstances demand.

The judgment of the Court of Appeals is vacated and the case is remanded to that court for further proceedings consistent with this opinion.

It is so ordered.

THE CHIEF JUSTICE, JUSTICE SCALIA, and JUSTICE KENNEDY took no part in the consideration or decision of this case.

JUSTICE WHITE, with whom JUSTICE O'CONNOR joins, concurring in part and dissenting in part.

I join Parts I–III of the Court's opinion, as I agree that the standard of materiality we set forth in *TSC Industries, Inc. v. Northway, Inc.*, 426 U.S. 438, 449 (1976), should be applied to actions under § 10(b) and Rule 10b-5. But I dissent from the remainder of the Court's holding because I do not agree that the "fraud-on-the-market" theory should be applied in this case. * * *

* * *

C

At the bottom of the Court's conclusion that the fraud-on-the-market theory sustains a presumption of reliance is the assumption that individuals rely "on the integrity of the market price" when buying or selling stock in "impersonal, well-developed market[s] for securities." *Ante*, at [part IV A of the Court's opinion]. Even if I was prepared to accept (as a matter of common sense or general understanding) the assumption that most persons buying or selling stock do so in response to the market price, the fraud-on-the-market theory goes further. For in adopting a "presumption of reliance," the Court also assumes that buyers and sellers rely — not just on the market price — but on the "integrity" of that price. It is this aspect of the fraud-on-the-market hypothesis which most mystifies me.

To define the term "integrity of the market price," the majority quotes approvingly from cases which suggest that investors are entitled to " 'rely on the price of a stock as a reflection of its value.' " *Ante*, at [part IV A of the Court's opinion] (quoting *Pell v. Speiser*, 806 F.2d 1154, 1161 (3d Cir. 1986)). But the meaning of this phrase eludes me, for it implicitly suggests that stocks have some "true value" that is measurable by a standard other than their market price. While the Scholastics of Medieval times professed a means to make such a valuation of a commodity's "worth," I doubt that the federal courts of our day are similarly equipped.

Even if securities had some "value" — knowable and distinct from the market price of a stock — investors do not always share the Court's presumption that a stock's price is a "reflection of [this] value." Indeed, "many investors purchase or sell stock because they believe the price *inaccurately* reflects the corporation's worth." *See* Black, *Fraud on the Market: A Criticism of Dispensing with Reliance Requirements in Certain Open Market Transactions,* 62 N.C. L. REV. 435, 455 (1984) (emphasis added). If investors really believed that stock prices reflected a stock's "value," many sellers would never sell, and many buyers never buy (given the time and cost associated with executing a stock transaction). As we recognized just a few years ago: "Investors act on inevitably incomplete or inaccurate information, [consequently] there are always winners and losers; but those who have 'lost' have not necessarily been defrauded." *Dirks v. SEC,* 463 U.S. 646, 667, n.27 (1983). Yet today, the Court allows investors to recover who can show little more than that they sold stock at a lower price than what might have been. . . .

\* \* \*

## IV

In sum, I think the court's embracement of the fraud-on-the-market theory represents a departure in securities law that we are ill-suited to commence — and even less equipped to control as it proceeds. As a result, I must respectfully dissent.

## NOTES

1.   From the defendant's perspective, the fraud on the market theory improperly shifts the burden of proof on reliance from the plaintiff to the defendant. However, without the fraud on the market theory, it would be practically impossible to certify a class for purposes of a Rule 10b-5 action. In many situations, the fraudulent conduct complained of has caused relatively small losses to a large number of investors. No single investor may have sufficient loss to justify the expense of bringing a lawsuit against a defendant with both the incentive and a deep enough pocket to delay and drive up the cost of litigation. Therefore, in the absence of some way to certify a class, defendants might have less incentive to obey the law. The *Halliburton* case that follows is a more recent attempt by a defendant to prevent class certification.

2.   The holding in *Basic* that a "totality of the facts" test would determine whether an impending take-over was material under Rule 10b-5 disappointed many in the securities industry who were hoping that the "agreement in principle" test would be adopted instead. Do the benefits of certainty provided by the agreement in principle approach outweigh the deficiencies of this test discussed in the opinion?

3.   The *TSC Industries, Inc. v. Northway, Inc.* decision, from which the materiality test in *Basic* is derived, was a case arising under the SEC proxy rules. However, its test has now been applied in determining the materiality issue under a variety of anti-fraud provisions of the 1934 Act, and it is even cited by state courts confronted with issues of materiality.

4.   The fraud on the market theory has been the subject of some controversy among scholars. For a discussion of the theory, *compare* Langevoort, *Theories,*

*Assumptions and Securities Regulation: Market Efficiency Revisited*, 140 U. Pa. L. Rev. 851 (1992), with Carney, *The Limits of the Fraud on the Market Doctrine*, 44 Bus. Law. 1259 (1989).

## ERICA P. JOHN FUND, INC. v. HALLIBURTON CO.
### Supreme Court of the United States
### 131 S. Ct. 2179 (2011)

JUDGES: Roberts, C. J., delivered the opinion for a unanimous Court.

To prevail on the merits in a private securities fraud action, investors must demonstrate that the defendant's deceptive conduct caused their claimed economic loss. This requirement is commonly referred to as "loss causation." The question presented in this case is whether securities fraud plaintiffs must also prove loss causation in order to obtain class certification. We hold that they need not.

### I

Petitioner Erica P. John Fund, Inc. (EPJ Fund), is the lead plaintiff in a putative securities fraud class action filed against Halliburton Co. and one of its executives (collectively Halliburton). The suit was brought on behalf of all investors who purchased Halliburton common stock between June 3, 1999, and December 7, 2001.

EPJ Fund alleges that Halliburton made various misrepresentations designed to inflate its stock price, in violation of § 10(b) of the Securities Exchange Act of 1934 and Securities and Exchange Commission Rule 10b-5. See 48 Stat. 891, 15 U.S.C. § 78j(b); 17 CFR § 240.10b-5 (2010). The complaint asserts that Halliburton deliberately made false statements about (1) the scope of its potential liability in asbestos litigation, (2) its expected revenue from certain construction contracts, and (3) the benefits of its merger with another company. EPJ Fund contends that Halliburton later made a number of corrective disclosures that caused its stock price to drop and, consequently, investors to lose money.

After defeating a motion to dismiss, EPJ Fund sought to have its proposed class certified pursuant to Federal Rule of Civil Procedure 23. The parties agreed, and the District Court held, that EPJ Fund satisfied the general requirements for class actions set out in Rule 23(a): The class was sufficiently numerous, there were common questions of law or fact, the claims of the representative parties were typical, and the representative parties would fairly and adequately protect the interests of the class.

The District Court also found that the action could proceed as a class action under Rule 23(b)(3), but for one problem: Circuit precedent required securities fraud plaintiffs to prove "loss causation" in order to obtain class certification. *Id.*, at 4a, and n.2 (citing *Oscar Private Equity Invs. v. Allegiance Telecom, Inc.*, 487 F.3d 261, 269 (CA5 2007)). As the District Court explained, loss causation is the " 'causal connection between the material misrepresentation and the [economic] loss' " suffered by investors. App. to Pet. for Cert. 5a, and n.3 (quoting *Dura Pharms., Inc. v. Broudo*, 544 U.S. 336, 342, 125 S. Ct. 1627, 161 L. Ed. 2d 577 (2005)). After reviewing the alleged misrepresentations and corrective disclosures, the District Court concluded that it could not certify the class in this case because EPJ Fund had "failed to establish loss causation with respect to any" of its claims. The court made clear, however, that absent "this stringent loss causation requirement," it would have granted the Fund's certification request.

The Court of Appeals affirmed the denial of class certification. . . .

We granted the Fund's petition for certiorari, 562 U.S. ___, 131 S. Ct. 856, 178 L. Ed. 2d 622 (2011), to resolve a conflict among the Circuits as to whether securities fraud plaintiffs must prove loss causation in order to obtain class certification. Compare 597 F.3d at 334 (case below), with *In re Salomon Analyst Metromedia Litigation*, 544 F.3d 474, 483 (CA2 2008) (not requiring investors to prove loss causation at class certification stage); *Schleicher v. Wendt*, 618 F.3d 679, 687 (CA7 2010) (same); *In re DVI, Inc. Secs. Litig.*, 639 F.3d 623, 2011 U.S. App. LEXIS 6302, No. 08-8033 etc., 2011 WL 1125926, *7 (CA3, Mar. 29, 2011) (same; decided after certiorari was granted).

## II

EPJ Fund contends that the Court of Appeals erred by requiring proof of loss causation for class certification. We agree.

## A

As noted, the sole dispute here is whether EPJ Fund satisfied the prerequisites of Rule 23(b)(3). In order to certify a class under that Rule, a court must find "that the questions of law or fact common to class members predominate over any questions affecting only individual members, and that a class action is superior to other available methods for fairly and efficiently adjudicating the controversy."Fed. Rule Civ. Proc. 23(b)(3). Considering whether "questions of law or fact common to class members predominate" begins, of course, with the elements of the underlying cause of action. The elements of a private securities fraud claim based on violations of § 10(b) and Rule 10b-5 are: " '(1) a material misrepresentation or omission by the defendant; (2) scienter; (3) a connection between the misrepresentation or omission and the purchase or sale of a security; (4) reliance upon the misrepresentation or omission; (5) economic loss; and (6) loss causation.' " *Matrixx Initiatives, Inc. v. Siracusano*, 563 U.S. ___, ___, 131 S. Ct. 1309, 179 L. Ed. 2d 398, 409 (2011) (quoting *Stoneridge Investment Partners, LLC v. Scientific-Atlanta, Inc.*, 552 U.S. 148, 157, 128 S. Ct. 761, 169 L. Ed. 2d 627 (2008)).

Whether common questions of law or fact predominate in a securities fraud action often turns on the element of reliance. The courts below determined that EPJ Fund had to prove the separate element of loss causation in order to establish that reliance was capable of resolution on a common, classwide basis.

"Reliance by the plaintiff upon the defendant's deceptive acts is an essential element of the § 10(b) private cause of action." *Stoneridge, supra*, at 159, 128 S. Ct. 761, 169 L. Ed. 2d 627. This is because proof of reliance ensures that there is a proper "connection between a defendant's misrepresentation and a plaintiff's injury." *Basic Inc. v. Levinson*, 485 U.S. 224, 243, 108 S. Ct. 978, 99 L. Ed. 2d 194 (1988). The traditional (and most direct) way a plaintiff can demonstrate reliance is by showing that he was aware of a company's statement and engaged in a relevant transaction — *e.g.*, purchasing common stock — based on that specific misrepresentation. In that situation, the plaintiff plainly would have relied on the company's deceptive conduct. A plaintiff unaware of the relevant statement, on the other hand, could not establish reliance on that basis.

We recognized in *Basic*, however, that limiting proof of reliance in such a way "would place an unnecessarily unrealistic evidentiary burden on the Rule 10b-5 plaintiff who has traded on an impersonal market." *Id.*, at 245, 108 S. Ct. 978, 99 L. Ed. 2d 194. We also observed that "[r]equiring proof of individualized reliance from each member of the proposed plaintiff class effectively would" prevent such plaintiffs "from proceeding with a class action, since individual issues" would "overwhelm[ ] the common ones." *Id.*, at 242, 108 S. Ct. 978, 99 L. Ed. 2d 194.

The Court in *Basic* sought to alleviate those related concerns by permitting plaintiffs to invoke a rebuttable presumption of reliance based on what is known as the "fraud-on-the-market" theory. According to that theory, "the market price of shares traded on well-developed markets reflects all publicly available information, and, hence, any material misrepresentations." *Id.*, at 246, 108 S. Ct. 978, 99 L. Ed. 2d 194. Because the market "transmits information to the investor in the processed form of a market price," we can assume, the Court explained, that an investor relies on public misstatements whenever he "buys or sells stock at the price set by the market." *Id.*, at 244, 247, 108 S. Ct. 978, 99 L. Ed. 2d 194 (internal quotation marks omitted); see also *Stoneridge, supra*, at 159, 128 S. Ct. 761, 169 L. Ed. 2d 627; *Dura Pharmaceuticals*, 544 U.S., at 341–342, 125 S. Ct. 1627, 161 L. Ed. 2d 577. The Court also made clear that the presumption was just that, and could be rebutted by appropriate evidence. See *Basic, supra*, at 248, 108 S. Ct. 978, 99 L. Ed. 2d 194.

B

It is undisputed that securities fraud plaintiffs must prove certain things in order to invoke *Basic*'s rebuttable presumption of reliance. It is common ground, for example, that plaintiffs must demonstrate that the alleged misrepresentations were publicly known (else how would the market take them into account?), that the stock traded in an efficient market, and that the relevant transaction took place "between the time the misrepresentations were made and the time the truth was revealed." *Basic*, 485 U.S., at 248, n.27, 108 S. Ct. 978, 99 L. Ed. 2d 194; *id.*, at 241–247, 108 S. Ct. 978, 99 L. Ed. 2d 194; see also *Stoneridge, supra*, at 159, 128 S. Ct. 761, 169 L. Ed. 2d 627.

According to the Court of Appeals, EPJ Fund also had to establish loss causation at the certification stage to "trigger the fraud-on-the-market presumption." 597 F.3d at 335 (internal quotation marks omitted); see *ibid.* (EPJ Fund must "establish a causal link between the alleged falsehoods and its losses in order to invoke the fraud-on-the-market presumption"). The court determined that, in order to invoke a rebuttable presumption of reliance, EPJ Fund needed to prove that the decline in Halliburton's stock was "because of the correction to a prior misleading statement" and "that the subsequent loss could not otherwise be explained by some additional factors revealed then to the market." *Id.*, at 336 (emphasis deleted). This is the loss causation requirement as we have described it. See *Dura Pharmaceuticals, supra*, at 342, 125 S. Ct. 1627, 161 L. Ed. 2d 577; see also 15 U.S.C. § 78u-4(b)(4).

The Court of Appeals' requirement is not justified by *Basic* or its logic. To begin, we have never before mentioned loss causation as a precondition for invoking *Basic*'s rebuttable presumption of reliance. The term "loss causation" does not even appear in our *Basic* opinion. And for good reason: Loss causation addresses a matter different from whether an investor relied on a misrepresentation, presumptively or otherwise, when buying or selling a stock.

We have referred to the element of reliance in a private Rule 10b-5 action as "transaction causation," not loss causation. *Dura Pharmaceuticals, supra*, at 341–342, 125 S. Ct. 1627, 161 L. Ed. 2d 577 (citing *Basic, supra*, at 248–249, 108 S. Ct. 978, 99 L. Ed. 2d 194). Consistent with that description, when considering whether a plaintiff has relied on a misrepresentation, we have typically focused on facts surrounding the investor's decision to engage in the transaction. See *Dura Pharmaceuticals, supra*, at 342, 125 S. Ct. 1627, 161 L. Ed. 2d 577. Under *Basic*'s fraud-on-the-market doctrine, an investor presumptively relies on a defendant's misrepresentation if that "information is reflected in [the] market price" of the stock at the time of the relevant transaction. See *Basic*, 485 U.S., at 247, 108 S. Ct. 978, 99 L. Ed. 2d 194.

Loss causation, by contrast, requires a plaintiff to show that a misrepresentation that affected the integrity of the market price *also* caused a subsequent economic loss. As we made clear in *Dura Pharmaceuticals*, the fact that a stock's "price on the date of purchase was inflated because of [a] misrepresentation" does not necessarily mean that the misstatement is the cause of a later decline in value. 544 U.S., at 342, 125 S. Ct. 1627, 161 L. Ed. 2d 577 (emphasis deleted; internal quotation marks omitted). We observed that the drop could instead be the result of other intervening causes, such as "changed economic circumstances, changed investor expectations, new industry-specific or firm-specific facts, conditions, or other events." *Id.*, at 342–343, 125 S. Ct. 1627, 161 L. Ed. 2d 577. If one of those factors were responsible for the loss or part of it, a plaintiff would not be able to prove loss causation to that extent. This is true even if the investor purchased the stock at a distorted price, and thereby presumptively relied on the misrepresentation reflected in that price.

According to the Court of Appeals, however, an inability to prove loss causation would prevent a plaintiff from invoking the rebuttable presumption of reliance. Such a rule contravenes *Basic*'s fundamental premise — that an investor presumptively relies on a misrepresentation so long as it was reflected in the market price at the time of his transaction. The fact that a subsequent loss may have been caused by factors other than the revelation of a misrepresentation has nothing to do with whether an investor relied on the misrepresentation in the first place, either directly or presumptively through the fraud-on-the-market theory. Loss causation has no logical connection to the facts necessary to establish the efficient market predicate to the fraud-on-the-market theory.

\* \* \*

Because we conclude the Court of Appeals erred by requiring EPJ Fund to prove loss causation at the certification stage, we need not, and do not, address any other question about *Basic*, its presumption, or how and when it may be rebutted. To the extent Halliburton has preserved any further arguments against class certification, they may be addressed in the first instance by the Court of Appeals on remand.

The judgment of the Court of Appeals is vacated, and the case is remanded for further proceedings consistent with this opinion.

*It is so ordered.*

---

This case went back to the appellate court, back to the district court, was appealed, and made its way back to the Supreme Court in March 2014. As of this writing, there is no decision.

## B.  INSIDER TRADING

### NOTES: STATUTORY MODIFICATIONS

1.  In 1984, Congress enacted the Insider Trading Sanctions Act of 1984, Pub. L. No. 98-376. The Act expressly granted the SEC the power to impose civil penalties on violators, in addition to the disgorgement of the profit gained by the illegal activity. The penalty imposed may be up to three times the amount of the profit gained, or loss avoided, by the illegal transaction. This statute substantially increased the leverage of the SEC in negotiating settlements of insider trading cases.

2.  Four years later, Congress passed the Insider Trading and Securities Fraud Enforcement Act of 1988, Pub. L. No. 100-704, which increased substantially the criminal penalties for willful violations of the Securities Acts from $100,000 and 5-year imprisonment to $1,000,000 and 10-year imprisonment for individuals and a fine of up to $2,500,000 when the defendant is other than a natural person. Also, Congress has amended section 20A of the Securities Exchange Act of 1934 to provide expressly that defendants guilty of unlawful insider trading are liable to all persons who contemporaneously traded in the market at the time defendant was engaged in unlawful trading. Prior to its enactment, the Circuits were split on whether such private actions should be allowed in the absence of privity with defendants.

3.  The Private Securities Litigation Reform Act of 1995, Pub. L. No. 104-67, was not passed to deal with insider trading actions, but with other actions brought under Rule 10b-5 which were generally felt to be brought primarily for their settlement value. A common scenario would be where a company had issued an earnings forecast which subsequently proved to be overly optimistic so that, when actual earnings were announced, the share price would plunge. Shortly thereafter, plaintiff, often at the instigation of a professional class action attorney, would bring an action against corporate management under Rule 10b-5 for issuing a misleading earnings forecast. Because such suits can be difficult and time-consuming to defend,

they would often be settled even where the case on the merits was dubious. Congress attempted to deal with this problem primarily by imposing procedural obstacles to class actions including (1) requiring the facts constituting the cause of action to be pleaded with particularity at the outset, thus attempting to avoid discovery "fishing expeditions"; (2) provisions delaying discovery until after defendant had a chance to dismiss the action; (3) strengthening Rule 11 sanctions against attorneys bringing frivolous actions; (4) imposing proportionate liability against defendants, in lieu of joint and several liability; (5) imposing new heightened duties on corporate auditors to identify and report suspected illegal conduct; (6) defining new more clear cut measures of damages; and (7) establishing a "safe harbor" for management earnings projections which would, if followed, make management immune from suits for allegedly misleading earnings forecasts.

**4.** In November 1998, President Clinton signed the Securities Litigation Uniform Standards Act. The Act was passed in response to concerns that the 1995 Securities Litigation Reform Act might simply have the effect of moving securities fraud actions barred by that statute to the state courts for remedies under state law. The Act effectively requires that securities fraud class actions involving nationally traded securities be brought solely in federal court under federal law, thus effectively preempting state law in the cases to which it applies.

**5.** Although many changes have been made by statute, equally significant are changes which have been considered but not made. Most notable is that Congress and the SEC have repeatedly refused to define specifically the term "insider trading." Also, the fraud on the market theory has yet to be dealt with by Congress, although many questions remain as to its scope after the *Basic* decision. Furthermore, the precise scope of private, as opposed to SEC, causes of action remains unclear, as does the issue of "tippee" liability. Finally, the precise state of mind required of a defendant remains uncertain.

## 1.  Traditional Rule

### GOODWIN v. AGASSIZ
Supreme Judicial Court of Massachusetts
186 N.E. 659 (1933)

RUGG, CHIEF JUSTICE

A stockholder in a corporation seeks in this suit relief for losses suffered by him in selling shares of stock in Cliff Mining Company by way of accounting, rescission of sales, or redelivery of shares. The named defendants are MacNaughton, a resident of Michigan not served or appearing, and Agassiz, a resident of this Commonwealth, the active party defendant.

The trial judge made findings of fact, rulings, and an order dismissing the bill. There is no report of the evidence. The case must be considered on the footing that the findings are true. The facts thus displayed are these: The defendants, in May, 1926, purchased through brokers on the Boston stock exchange seven hundred shares of stock of the Cliff Mining Company which up to that time the plaintiff had owned. Agassiz was president and director and MacNaughton a director and general manager of the company. They had certain knowledge, material as to the value of the stock, which the plaintiff did not have. The plaintiff contends that such purchase in all the circumstances without disclosure to him of that knowledge was a wrong against him. That knowledge was that an experienced geologist had formulated in writing in March, 1926, a theory as to the possible existence of copper deposits under conditions prevailing in the region where the property of the company was located. That region was known as the mineral belt in northern Michigan, where are located mines of several copper mining companies. Another such company, of which the defendants were officers, had made extensive geological surveys of its lands. In consequence of recommendations resulting from that survey, exploration was started on property of the Cliff Mining Company in 1925. That exploration was ended in May, 1926, because completed unsuccessfully, and the equipment was removed. The defendants discussed the geologist's theory shortly after it was formulated. Both felt that the theory had value and should be tested, but they agreed that, before starting to test it, options should be obtained by another copper company of which they were officers on land adjacent to or nearby in the copper belt, that if the geologist's theory were known to the owners of such other land there might be difficulty in securing options, and that that theory should not be communicated to any one unless it became absolutely necessary. Thereafter, options were secured which, if taken up, would involve a large expenditure by the other company. The defendants both thought, also, that, if there was any merit in the geologist's theory, the price of Cliff Mining Company stock in the market would go up. Its stock was quoted and bought and sold on the Boston stock exchange. Pursuant to agreement, they bought many shares of that stock through agents on joint account. The plaintiff first learned of the closing of exploratory operations on property of the Cliff Mining Company from an article in a paper on May 15, 1926, and immediately sold his shares of stock through brokers. It does not appear that the defendants were in any way responsible for the publication of that article. The plaintiff did not know that the purchase was made for the defendants and they did not know that his stock was being bought for them. There was no communication between them touching the subject. The plaintiff would not have sold his stock if he had known of the geologist's theory. The finding is express that the defendants were not guilty of fraud, that they committed no breach of duty owed by them to the Cliff Mining Company, and that that company was not harmed by the nondisclosure of the geologist's theory, or by their purchases of its stock, or by shutting down the exploratory operations.

The contention of the plaintiff is that the purchase of his stock in the company by the defendants without disclosing to him as a stockholder their knowledge of the geologist's theory, their belief that the theory had value, the keeping secret the existence of the theory, discontinuance by the defendants of exploratory operations begun in 1925 on property of the Cliff Mining Company and their plan ultimately to test the value of the theory, constitute actionable wrong for which he as stockholder can recover.

The trial judge ruled that conditions may exist which would make it the duty of an officer of a corporation purchasing its stock from a stockholder to inform him as to knowledge possessed by the buyer and not by the seller, but found, on all the circumstances developed by the trial and set out at some length by him in his decision, that there was no fiduciary relation requiring such disclosure by the defendants to the plaintiff before buying his stock in the manner in which they did.

The question presented is whether the decree dismissing the bill rightly was entered on the facts found.

The directors of a commercial corporation stand in a relation of trust to the corporation and are bound to exercise the strictest good faith in respect to its property and business. The contention that directors also occupy the position of trustee toward individual stockholders in the corporation is plainly contrary to repeated decisions of this court and cannot be supported. In *Smith v. Hurd*, 12 Met. 371, 384, it was said by Chief Justice Shaw: "There is no legal privity, relation, or immediate connexion, between the holders of shares in a bank, in their individual capacity, on the one side, and the directors of the bank on the other. The directors are not the bailees, the factors, agents or trustees of such individual stockholders." . . . In *Blabon v. Hay*, 169 N.E. 268, occurs this language with reference to sale of stock in a corporation by a stockholder to two of its directors: "The fact that the defendants were directors created no fiduciary relation between them and the plaintiff in the matter of the sale of his stock."

The principle thus established is supported by an imposing weight of authority in other jurisdictions. . . . A rule holding that directors are trustees for individual stockholders with respect to their stock prevails in comparatively few States; but in view of our own adjudications it is not necessary to review decisions to that effect. . . .

While the general principle is as stated, circumstances may exist requiring that transactions between a director and a stockholder as to stock in the corporation be set aside. The knowledge naturally in the possession of a director as to the condition of a corporation places upon him a peculiar obligation to observe every requirement of fair dealing when directly buying or selling its stock. Mere silence does not usually amount to a breach of duty, but parties may stand in such relation to each other that an equitable responsibility arises to communicate facts. Purchases and sales of stock dealt in on the stock exchange are commonly impersonal affairs. An honest director would be in a difficult situation if he could neither buy nor sell on the stock exchange shares of stock in his corporation without first seeking out the other actual ultimate party to the transaction and disclosing to him everything which a court or jury might later find that he then knew affecting the real or speculative value of such shares. Business of that nature is a matter to be governed by practical rules. Fiduciary obligations of directors ought not to be made so onerous that men of experience and ability will be deterred from accepting such office. Law in its sanctions is not coextensive with morality. It cannot undertake to put all parties to every contract on an equality as to knowledge, experience, skill and shrewdness. It cannot undertake to relieve against hard bargains made between competent parties without fraud. On the other hand, directors cannot rightly be allowed to indulge with impunity in practices which do violence to prevailing standards of upright business men. Therefore, where a director personally seeks a stockholder for the purpose of buying his shares without making disclosure of material facts within his peculiar knowledge and not within reach of the stockholder, the transaction will be closely scrutinized and relief may be granted in appropriate instances. The applicable legal principles "have almost always been the fundamental ethical rules of right and wrong." . . .

The precise question to be decided in the case at bar is whether on the facts found the defendants as directors had a right to buy stock of the plaintiff, a stockholder. Every element of actual fraud or misdoing by the defendants is negatived by the findings. Fraud cannot be presumed; it must be proved. The facts found afford no ground for inferring fraud or conspiracy. The only knowledge possessed by the defendants not open to the plaintiff was the existence of a theory formulated in a thesis by a geologist as to the possible existence of copper deposits where certain geological conditions existed common to the property of the Cliff Mining Company and that of other mining companies in its neighborhood. This thesis did not express an opinion that copper deposits would be found at any particular spot or on property of any specified owner. Whether that theory was sound or fallacious, no one knew, and so far as appears has never been demonstrated. The defendants made no representations to anybody about the theory. No facts found placed upon them any obligation to disclose the theory. A few days after the thesis expounding the theory was brought to the attention of the defendants, the annual report by the directors of the Cliff Mining Company for the calendar year 1925, signed by Agassiz for the directors, was issued. It did not cover the time when the theory was formulated. The report described the status of the operations under the exploration which had been begun in 1925. At the annual meeting of the stockholders of the company held early in April, 1926, no reference was made to the theory. It was then at most a hope, possibly an expectation. It had not passed the nebulous stage. No disclosure was made of it. The Cliff Mining Company was not harmed by the nondisclosure. There would have been no advantage to it, so far as appears, from a disclosure. The disclosure would have been detrimental to the interests of another mining corporation in which the defendants were directors. In the circumstances there was no duty on the part of the defendants to set forth to the stockholders at the annual meeting their faith, aspirations and plans for the future. Events as they developed might render advisable radical changes in such views. Disclosure of the theory, if it ultimately was proved to be erroneous or without foundation in fact, might involve the defendants in litigation with those who might act on the hypothesis that it was correct. The stock of the Cliff Mining Company was bought and sold on the stock exchange. The identity of buyers and seller of the stock in question in fact was not known to the parties and perhaps could not readily have been ascertained. The defendants caused the shares to be bought through brokers on the stock exchange. They said nothing to anybody as to the reasons actuating them. The plaintiff was no novice. He was a member of the Boston stock exchange and had kept a record of sales of Cliff Mining Company stock. He acted upon his own judgment in selling his stock. He made no inquiries of the defendants or of other officers of the company. The result is that the plaintiff cannot prevail.

Decree dismissing bill affirmed with costs.

# NOTES

1. In insider trading cases, the plaintiff frequently is complaining of an omission, or failure to speak, rather than an affirmative misrepresentation. Therefore, the plaintiff must prove not only that the defendant failed to communicate material information to the plaintiff, but also that the defendant had a duty to communicate. Although Rule 10b-5 is a federal regulation, this duty is frequently established by looking to state law concepts of fiduciary duty. In *Goodwin*, the plaintiff's theory was that directors and officers of the company owed stockholders like plaintiff a fiduciary duty, and that these insiders could not act on nonpublic information in a way to benefit themselves without disclosing the information to stockholders. However, the case was brought in state court under state common law principles, not under Rule 10b-5. Why do you think that is so? *Goodwin* illustrates the obstacles facing a plaintiff in bringing an insider trading case at common law. Because the action required proof of something close to common law fraud, such actions were virtually impossible to bring when cases involved anonymous, impersonal dealing on the stock exchanges.

2. Even at common law, many courts recognized that under "special circumstances" an action might be brought against an insider for trading on the basis of confidential, inside information. The best known example is *Strong v. Repide*, 213 U.S. 419 (1909). There, a majority shareholder and director were conducting negotiations to sell certain valuable real estate owned by the corporation. While negotiations were pending, defendant purchased plaintiff's stock without disclosing the negotiations and the likely future sale of the real estate. After the real estate was sold, the shares of the corporation were worth about 10 times what defendant paid for them. The court ruled for plaintiff, pointing to, among other things, the fact that defendant took pains to conceal his identity from plaintiff, presumably knowing that plaintiff would become suspicious if he purchased the shares directly from him. Under the circumstances, the court concluded that defendant had a duty to disclose the impending sale of the real estate and had breached his fiduciary duty owed to plaintiff by not doing so.

## SEC v. TEXAS GULF SULPHUR CO.
United States Court of Appeals, Second Circuit
401 F.2d 833 (1968)

WATERMAN, CIRCUIT JUDGE:

This action derives from the exploratory activities of TGS begun in 1957 on the Canadian Shield in eastern Canada. In March of 1959, aerial geophysical surveys were conducted over more than 15,000 square miles of this area by a group led by defendant Mollison, a mining engineer and a Vice President of TGS. The group included defendant Holyk, TGS's chief geologist, defendant Clayton, an electrical engineer and geophysicist, and defendant Darke, a geologist. These operations resulted in the detection of numerous anomalies, i.e., extraordinary variations in the conductivity of rocks, one of which was on the Kidd 55 segment of land located near Timmins, Ontario.

On October 29 and 30, 1963, Clayton conducted a ground geophysical survey on the northeast portion of the Kidd 55 segment which confirmed the presence of an anomaly and indicated the necessity of diamond core drilling for further evaluation. Drilling of the initial hole, K-55-1, at the strongest part of the anomaly was commenced on November 8 and terminated on November 12 at a depth of 655 feet. Visual estimates by Holyk of the core of K-55-1 indicated an average copper content of 1.15% and an average zinc content of 8.64% over a length of 599 feet. This visual estimate convinced TGS that it was desirable to acquire the remainder of the Kidd 55 segment, and in order to facilitate this acquisition TGS President Stephens instructed the exploration group to keep the results of K-55-1 confidential and undisclosed even as to other officers, directors, and employees of TGS. The hole was concealed and a barren core was intentionally drilled off the anomaly. Meanwhile, the core of K-55-1 had been shipped to Utah for chemical assay which, when received in early December, revealed an average mineral content of 1.18% copper, 8.26% zinc, and 3.94% ounces of silver per ton over a length of 602 feet. These results were so remarkable that neither Clayton, an experienced geophysicist, nor four other TGS expert witnesses, had ever seen or heard of a comparable initial exploratory drill hole in a base metal deposit. So, the trial court concluded, "There is no doubt that the drill core of K-55-1 was unusually good and that it excited the interest and speculation of those who knew about it." 258 F. Supp 262, 282 (S.D.N.Y. 1966). By March 27, 1964, TGS decided that the land acquisition program had advanced to such a point that the company might well resume drilling, and drilling was resumed on March 31.

During this period, from November 12, 1963 when K-55-1 was completed, to March 31, 1964 when drilling was resumed, certain of the individual defendants . . . purchased TGS stock or calls thereon. A "call" is a negotiable option contract by which the bearer has the right to buy from the writer of the contract a certain number of shares of a particular stock at a fixed price on or before a certain agreed-upon date. Prior to these transactions these persons had owned 1135 shares of TGS stock and possessed no calls; thereafter they owned a total of 8235 shares and possessed 12,300 calls.

*   *   *

[Drilling operations between March 31 and April 10 provided further evidence of a commercially valuable discovery.]

Meanwhile, rumors that a major ore strike was in the making had been circulating throughout Canada. On the morning of Saturday, April 11, Stephens at his home in Greenwich, Conn. read in the New York Herald Tribune and in the New York Times unauthorized reports of the TGS drilling which seemed to infer a rich strike from the fact that the drill cores had been flown to the United States for chemical assay. Stephens immediately contacted Fogarty at his home in Rye, N.Y., who in turn telephoned and later that day visited Mollison at Mollison's home in Greenwich to obtain a current report and evaluation of the drilling progress. The following morning, Sunday, Fogarty again telephoned Mollison, inquiring whether Mollison had any further information and told him to return to Timmins with Holyk, the TGS Chief Geologist, as soon as possible "to move things along." With the aid of one Carroll, a public relations consultant, Fogarty drafted a press release designed to quell the rumors, which release, after having been channeled through Stephens and Huntington, a TGS attorney, was issued at 3:00 P.M. on Sunday, April 12, and which appeared in the morning newspapers of general circulation on Monday, April 13. It read in pertinent part as follows:

NEW YORK, April 12 — The following statement was made today by Dr. Charles F. Fogarty, executive vice president of Texas Gulf Sulphur Company, in regard to the company's drilling operations near Timmins, Ontario, Canada. Dr. Fogarty said:

"During the past few days, the exploration activities of Texas Gulf Sulphur in the area of Timmins, Ontario, have been widely reported in the press, coupled with rumors of a substantial copper discovery there. These reports exaggerate the scale of operations, and mention plans and statistics of size and grade of ore that are without factual basis and have evidently originated by speculation of people not connected with TGS.

"The facts are as follows. TGS has been exploring in the Timmins area for six years as part of its overall search in Canada and elsewhere for various minerals — lead, copper, zinc, etc. During the course of this work, in Timmins as well as in Eastern Canada, TGS has conducted exploration entirely on its own, without the participation by others. Numerous prospects have been investigated by geophysical means and a large number of selected ones have been core-drilled. These cores are sent to the United States for assay and detailed examination as a matter of routine and on advice of expert Canadian legal counsel. No inferences as to grade can be drawn from this procedure.

"Most of the areas drilled in Eastern Canada have revealed either barren pyrite or graphite without value; a few have resulted in discoveries of small or marginal sulphide ore bodies.

"Recent drilling on one property near Timmins has led to preliminary indications that more drilling would be required for proper evaluation of this prospect. The drilling done to date has not been conclusive, but the statements made by many outside quarters are unreliable and include information and figures that are not available to TGS.

"The work done to date has not been sufficient to reach definite conclusions and any statement as to size and grade of ore would be premature and possibly misleading. When we have progressed to the point where reasonable and logical conclusions can be made, TGS will issue a definite statement to its stockholders and to the public in order to clarify the Timmins project."

The release purported to give the Timmins drilling results as of the release date, April 12. From Mollison Fogarty had been told of the developments through 7:00 P.M. on April 10, and of the remarkable discoveries made up to that time, detailed supra, which discoveries, according to the calculations of the experts who testified for the SEC at the hearing, demonstrated that TGS had already discovered 6.2 to 8.3 million tons of proven ore having gross assay values from $26 to $29 per ton. TGS experts, on the other hand, denied at the hearing that proven or probable ore could have been calculated on April 11 or 12 because there was then no assurance of continuity in the mineralized zone.

The evidence as to the effect of this release on the investing public was equivocal and less than abundant. On April 13 the New York Herald Tribune in an article head-noted "Copper Rumor Deflated" quoted from the TGS release of April 12 and backtracked from its original April 11 report of a major strike but nevertheless inferred from the TGS release that "recent mineral exploratory activity near Timmins, Ontario, has provided preliminary favorable results, sufficient at least to require a step-up in drilling operations." Some witnesses who testified at the hearing stated that they found the release encouraging. On the other hand, a Canadian mining security specialist, Roche, stated that "earlier in the week [before April 16] we had a Dow Jones saying that they [TGS] didn't have anything basically" and a TGS stock specialist for the Midwest Stock Exchange became concerned about his long position in the stock after reading the release. The trial court stated only that "While, in retrospect, the press release may appear gloomy or incomplete, this does not make it misleading or deceptive on the basis of the facts then known." Id. at 296.

\*     \*     \*

While drilling activity ensued to completion, TGC officials were taking steps toward ultimate disclosure of the discovery. On April 13, a previously-invited reporter for The Northern Miner, a Canadian mining industry journal, visited the drillsite, interviewed Mollison, Holyk and Darke, and prepared an article which confirmed a 10 million ton ore strike. This report, after having been submitted to Mollison and returned to the reporter unamended on April 15, was published in the April 16 issue. A statement relative to the extent of the discovery, in substantial part drafted by Mollison, was given to the Ontario Minister of Mines for release to the Canadian media. Mollison and Holyk expected it to be released over the airways at 11 P.M. on April 15th, but, for undisclosed reasons, it was not released until 9:40 A.M. on the 16th. An official detailed statement, announcing a strike of at least 25 million tons of ore, based on the drilling data set forth above, was read to representatives of American financial media from 10:00 A.M. to 10:10 or 10:15 A.M. on April 16, and appeared over Merrill Lynch's private wire at 10:29 A.M. and, somewhat later than expected, over the Dow Jones ticker tape at 10:54 A.M.

Between the time the first press release was issued on April 12 and the dissemination of the TGS official announcement on the morning of April 16, the only defendants before us on appeal who engaged in market activity were Clayton and Crawford and TGS director Coates. Clayton ordered 200 shares of TGS stock through his Canadian broker on April 15 and the order was executed that day over the Midwest Stock Exchange. Crawford ordered 300 shares at midnight on the 15th and another 300 shares at 8:30 A.M. the next day, and these orders were executed over the Midwest Exchange in Chicago at its opening on April 16. Coates left the TGS press conference and called his broker son-in-law Haemisegger shortly before 10:20 A.M. on the 16th and ordered 2,000 shares of TGS for family trust accounts of which Coates was a trustee but not a beneficiary; Haemisegger executed this order over the New York and Midwest Exchanges, and he and his customers purchased 1500 additional shares.

During the period of drilling in Timmins, the market price of TGS stock fluctuated but steadily gained overall. On Friday, November 8, when the drilling began, the stock closed at 17 3/8; on Friday, November 15, after K-55-1 had been completed, it closed at 18. After a slight decline to 16 3/8 by Friday, November 22, the price rose to 20 7/8 by December 13, when the chemical assay results of K-55-1 were received, and closed at a high of 24 1/8 on February 21, the day after the stock options had been issued. It had reached a price of 26 by March 31, after the land acquisition program had been completed and drilling had been resumed, and continued to ascend to 30 1/8 by the close of trading on April 10, at which time the drilling progress up to then was evaluated for the April 12th press release. On April 13, the day on which the April 12 release was disseminated, TGS opened at 30 1/8, rose immediately to a high of 32 and gradually tapered off to close at 30 7/8. It closed at 30 1/4 the next day, and at 29 3/8 on April 15. On April 16, the day of the official announcement of the Timmins discovery, the price climbed to a high of 37 and closed at 36 3/8. By May 15, TGS stock was selling at 58 1/4.

\*   \*   \*

Rule 10b-5 was promulgated pursuant to the grant of authority given the SEC by Congress in Section 10(b) of the Securities Exchange Act of 1934 (15 U.S.C. § 78j(b)). By that Act Congress purposed to prevent inequitable and unfair practices and to insure fairness in securities transactions generally, whether conducted face-to-face, over the counter, or on exchanges. . . . The essence of the Rule is that anyone who, trading for his own account in the securities of a corporation has "access, directly or indirectly, to information intended to be available only for a corporate purpose and not for the personal benefit of anyone" may not take "advantage of such information knowing it is unavailable to those with whom he is dealing," i.e., the investing public. Matter of Cady, Roberts & Co., 40 SEC 907, 912 (1961). Insiders, as directors or management officers are, of course, by this Rule, precluded from so unfairly dealing, but the Rule is also applicable to one possessing the information who may not be strictly termed an "insider" within the meaning of Sec. 16(b) of the Act. Cady, Roberts, supra. Thus, anyone in possession of material inside information must either disclose it to the investing public, or, if he is disabled from disclosing it in order to protect a corporate confidence, or he chooses not to do so, must abstain from trading in or recommending the securities concerned while such inside information remains undisclosed. So, it is here no justification for insider activity that disclosure was forbidden by the legitimate corporate objective of acquiring options to purchase the land surrounding the exploration site; if the information was, as the SEC contends, material, its possessors should have kept out of the market until disclosure was accomplished. Cady, Roberts, supra at 911.

B. *Material Inside Information*

\*   \*   \*

. . . As we stated in List v. Fashion Park, Inc., 340 F.2d 457, 462, "The basic test of materiality . . . is whether a *reasonable* man would attach importance . . . in determining his choice of action in the transaction in question. Restatement, Torts § 538(2) (a); accord Prosser, Torts 554–55; I Harper & James, Torts 565–66."

(Emphasis supplied.) * * *

* * * [W]hether facts are material within Rule 10b-5 when the facts relate to a particular event and are undisclosed by those persons who are knowledgeable thereof will depend at any given time upon a balancing of both the indicated probability that the event will occur and the anticipated magnitude of the event in light of the totality of the company activity. Here, notwithstanding the trial court's conclusion that the results of the first drill core, K-55-1, were "too 'remote' * * * to have had any significant impact on the market, i.e., to be deemed material," 258 F. Supp. at 283, knowledge of the possibility, which surely was more than marginal, of the existence of a mine of the vast magnitude indicated by the remarkably rich drill core located rather close to the surface (suggesting mineability by the less expensive openpit method) within the confines of a large anomaly (suggesting an extensive region of mineralization) might well have affected the price of TGS stock and would certainly have been an important fact to a reasonable, if speculative, investor in deciding whether he should buy, sell, or hold. After all, this first drill core was "unusually good and * * * excited the interest and speculation of those who knew about it." 258 F. Supp. at 282.

. . . Our survey of the facts found below conclusively establishes that knowledge of the results of the discovery hole, K-55-1, would have been important to a reasonable investor and might have affected the price of the stock. We do not suggest that material facts must be disclosed immediately; the timing of disclosure is a matter for the business judgment of the corporate officers entrusted with the management of the corporation within the affirmative disclosure requirements promulgated by the exchanges and by the SEC. Here, a valuable corporate purpose was served by delaying the publication of the K-55-1 discovery. We do intend to convey, however, that where a corporate purpose is thus served by withholding the news of a material fact, those persons who are thus quite properly true to their corporate trust must not during the period of non-disclosure deal personally in the corporation's securities or give to outsiders confidential information not generally available to all the corporations' stockholders and to the public at large. On April 16, The Northern Miner, a trade publication in wide circulation among mining stock specialists, called K-55-1, the discovery hole, "one of the most impressive drill holes completed in modern times." Roche, a Canadian broker whose firm specialized in mining securities, characterized the importance to investors of the results of K-55-1. He stated that the completion of "the first drill hole" with "a 600 foot drill core is very very significant . . . anything over 200 feet is considered very significant and 600 feet is just beyond your wildest imagination." . . .

Finally, a major factor in determining whether the K-55-1 discovery was a material fact is the importance attached to the drilling results by those who knew about it. In view of other unrelated recent developments favorably affecting TGS, participation by an informed person in a regular stock-purchase program, or even sporadic trading by an informed person, might lend only nominal support to the inference of the materiality of the K-55-1 discovery; nevertheless, the timing by those who knew of it of their stock purchases and their purchases of *short-term* calls — purchases in some cases by individuals who had never before purchased calls or even TGS stock — virtually compels the inference that the insiders were influenced by the drilling results. . . .

\*   \*   \*

The core of Rule 10b-5 is the implementation of the Congressional purpose that all investors should have equal access to the rewards of participation in securities transactions. It was the intent of Congress that all members of the investing public should be subject to identical market risks, — which market risks include, of course the risk that one's evaluative capacity or one's capital available to put at risk may exceed another's capacity or capital. The insiders here were not trading on an equal footing with the outside investors. They alone were in a position to evaluate the probability and magnitude of what seemed from the outset to be a major ore strike; they alone could invest safely, secure in the expectation that the price of TGS stock would rise substantially in the event such a major strike should materialize, but would decline little, if at all, in the event of failure, for the public, ignorant at the outset of the favorable probabilities would likewise be unaware of the unproductive exploration, and the additional exploration costs would not significantly affect TGS market prices. Such inequities based upon unequal access to knowledge should not be shrugged off as inevitable in our way of life, or, in view of the congressional concern in the area, remain uncorrected.

We hold, therefore, that all transactions in TGS stock or calls by individuals apprised of the drilling results of K-55-1 were made in violation of Rule 10b-5. . . .

\*   \*   \*

## C. *When May Insiders Act?*

Appellant Crawford, who ordered the purchase of TGS stock shortly before the TGS April 16 official announcement, and defendant Coates, who placed orders with and communicated the news to his broker immediately after the official announcement was read at the TGS-called press conference, concede that they were in possession of material information. They contend, however, that their purchases were not proscribed purchases for the news had already been effectively disclosed. We disagree.

Crawford telephoned his orders to his Chicago broker about midnight on April 15 and again at 8:30 in the morning of the 16th, with instructions to buy at the opening of the Midwest Stock Exchange that morning. The trial court's finding that "he sought to, and did, 'beat the news,' " 258 F. Supp. at 287, is well documented by the record. The rumors of a major ore strike which had been circulated in Canada and, to a lesser extent, in New York, had been disclaimed by the TGS press release of April 12, which significantly promised the public an official detailed announcement when possibilities had ripened into actualities. The abbreviated announcement to the Canadian press at 9:40 A.M. on the 16th by the Ontario Minister of Mines and the report carried by The Northern Miner, parts of which had sporadically reached New York on the morning of the 16th through reports from Canadian affiliates to a few New York investment firms, are assuredly not the equivalent of the official 10–15 minute announcement which was not released to the American financial press until after 10:00 A.M. Crawford's orders had been placed before that. Before insiders may act upon material information, such information must have been effectively disclosed in a manner sufficient to insure its availability to the investing public.

Particularly here, where a formal announcement to the entire financial news media had been promised in a prior official release known to the media, all insider activity must await dissemination of the promised official announcement.

Coates was absolved by the court below because his telephone order was placed shortly before 10:20 A.M. on April 16, which was after the announcement had been made even though the news could not be considered already a matter of public information. 258 F. Supp. at 288. This result seems to have been predicated upon a misinterpretation of dicta in *Cady, Roberts*, where the SEC instructed insiders to "keep out of the market until the established procedures for public release of the information are *carried out* instead of hastening to execute transactions in advance of, and in frustration of, the objectives of the release," 40 SEC at 915 (emphasis supplied). The reading of a news release, which prompted Coates into action, is merely the first step in the process of dissemination required for compliance with the regulatory objective of providing all investors with an equal opportunity to make informed investment judgments. Assuming that the contents of the official release could instantaneously be acted upon, at the minimum Coates should have waited until the news could reasonably have been expected to appear over the media of widest circulation, the Dow Jones broad tape, rather than hastening to insure an advantage to himself and his broker son-in-law.

\* \* \*

## II. THE CORPORATE DEFENDANT

### [A.] *Introductory*

At 3:00 P.M. on April 12, 1964, evidently believing it desirable to comment upon the rumors concerning the Timmins project, TGS issued the press release quoted . . . supra. The SEC argued below and maintains on this appeal that this release painted a misleading and deceptive picture of the drilling progress at the time of its issuance, and hence violated Rule 10b-5(2). TGS relies on the holding of the court below that "[t]he issuance of the release produced no unusual market action" and "[i]n the absence of a showing that the purpose of the April 12 press release was to affect the market price of TGS stock to the advantage of TGS or its insiders, the issuance of the press release did not constitute a violation of Section 10(b) or Rule 10b-5 since it was not issued 'in connection with the purchase or sale of any security'" and, alternatively, "even if it had been established that the April 12 release was issued in connection with the purchase or sale of any security, the Commission has failed to demonstrate that it was false, misleading or deceptive." 258 F. Supp. at 294.

\* \* \*

### B. *The "In Connection With . . . " Requirement.*

In adjudicating upon the relationship of this phrase to the case before us it would appear that the court below used a standard that does not reflect the congressional purpose that prompted the passage of the Securities Exchange Act of 1934.

The dominant congressional purposes underlying the Securities Exchange Act of 1934 were to promote free and open public securities markets and to protect the investing public from suffering inequities in trading, including, specifically, inequities that follow from trading that has been stimulated by the publication of false or misleading corporate information releases. . . .

\*     \*     \*

Therefore it seems clear from the legislative purpose Congress expressed in the Act, and the legislative history of Section 10(b) that Congress when it used the phrase "in connection with the purchase or sale of any security" intended only that the device employed, whatever it might be, be of a sort that would cause reasonable investors to rely thereon, and, in connection therewith, so relying, cause them to purchase or sell a corporation's securities. There is no indication that Congress intended that the corporations or persons responsible for the issuance of a misleading statement would not violate the section unless they engaged in related securities transactions or otherwise acted with wrongful motives; indeed, the obvious purposes of the Act to protect the investing public and to secure fair dealing in the securities markets would be seriously undermined by applying such a gloss onto the legislative language. . . . We do not believe that Congress intended that the proscriptions of the Act would not be violated unless the makers of a misleading statement also participated in pertinent securities transactions in connection therewith, or unless it could be shown that the issuance of the statement was motivated by a plan to benefit the corporation or themselves at the expense of a duped investing public.

\*     \*     \*

As was pointed out by the trial court, 258 F. Supp. at 293, the intent of the Securities Exchange Act of 1934 is the protection of investors against fraud. Therefore, it would seem elementary that the Commission has a duty to police management so as to prevent corporate practices which are reasonably likely fraudulently to injure investors. And, of course, as we have already emphasized, a corporation's misleading material statement may injure an investor irrespective of whether the corporation itself, or those individuals managing it, are contemporaneously buying or selling the stock of the corporation. . . .

More important, however, is the realization which we must again underscore at the risk of repetition, that the investing public is hurt by exposure to false or deceptive statements irrespective of the purpose underlying their issuance. It does not appear to be unfair to impose upon corporate management a duty to ascertain the truth of any statements the corporation releases to its shareholders or to the investing public at large. Accordingly, we hold that Rule 10b-5 is violated whenever assertions are made, as here, in a manner reasonably calculated to influence the investing public, e.g., by means of the financial media, Fleischer, supra, 51 Va. L. REV. at 1294–95, if such assertions are false or misleading or are so incomplete as to mislead irrespective of whether the issuance of the release was motivated by corporate officials for ulterior purposes. It seems clear, however, that if corporate management demonstrates that it was diligent in ascertaining that the information it published was the whole truth and that such diligently obtained information was disseminated in good faith, Rule 10b-5 would not have been violated.

## C. *Did the Issuance of the April 12 Release Violate Rule 10b-5?*

Turning first to the question of whether the release was misleading, i.e., whether it conveyed to the public a false impression of the drilling situation at the time of its issuance, we note initially that the trial court did not actually decide this question. . . . While we certainly agree with the trial court that "in retrospect, the press release may appear gloomy or incomplete," 258 F. Supp. at 296, we cannot, from the present record, by applying the standard Congress intended, definitively conclude that it was deceptive or misleading to the reasonable investor, or that he would have been misled by it. Certain newspaper accounts of the release viewed the release as confirming the existence of preliminary favorable developments, and this optimistic view was held by some brokers, so it could be that the reasonable investor would have read between the lines of what appears to us to be an inconclusive and negative statement and would have envisioned the actual situation at the Kidd segment on April 12. On the other hand, in view of the decline of the market price of TGS stock from a high of 32 on the morning of April 13 when the release was disseminated to 29 3/8 by the close of trading on April 15, and the reaction to the release by other brokers, it is far from certain that the release was generally interpreted as a highly encouraging report or even encouraging at all. Accordingly, we remand this issue to the district court that took testimony and heard and saw the witnesses for a determination of the character of the release in the light of the facts existing at the time of the release, by applying the standard of whether the reasonable investor, in the exercise of due care, would have been misled by it.

*      *      *

We conclude, then, that, having established that the release was issued in a manner reasonably calculated to affect the market price of TGS stock and to influence the investing public, we must remand to the district court to decide whether the release was misleading to the reasonable investor and if found to be misleading, whether the court in its discretion should issue the injunction the SEC seeks.

*      *      *

[Concurrence omitted.]

[Dissent omitted.]

# NOTES

1.   *Texas Gulf Sulfur* is the seminal case in the modern era of the regulation of insider trading under Rule 10b-5. Although the case was decided over 50 years ago, its discussions of materiality and when insiders are free to trade remain as timely as ever. Would the *TGS* court have ruled in favor of plaintiff in *Goodwin v. Agassiz* or are there factors in that case which would make it a difficult case to win even under Rule 10b-5?

2.   The court in *TGS* speaks only of a "duty to disclose or abstain from trading" thereby indicating that Rule 10b-5 imposes no affirmative duty on an insider to disclose developments as long as he or she does not trade. However, disclosure obligations may arise from other sources. Publicly held companies must comply with a regime of periodic disclosure, including annual, quarterly, and special reports specified in the 1934 Act. More generally, the SEC has stated that corporations have an affirmative duty to report publicly material corporate developments promptly. *See* Rel. 34-8995, 35 Fed. Reg. 16733 (1970). And, for companies whose securities are listed on stock exchanges, there may be contractual duties to disclose. For example, Section 202.05 of the New York Stock Exchange Listed Company Manual provides, "A listed company is expected to release quickly to the public any news or information which might reasonably be expected to materially affect the market for its securities." Section 202.03 is even broader:

> The market activity of a company's securities should be closely watched at a time when consideration is being given to significant corporate matters. If rumors or unusual market activity indicate that information on impending developments has leaked out, a frank and explicit announcement is clearly required. If rumors are in fact false or inaccurate, they should be promptly denied or clarified. A statement to the effect that the company knows of no corporate developments to account for the unusual market activity can have a salutary effect. It is obvious that if such a public statement is contemplated, management should be checked prior to any public comment so as to avoid any embarrassment or potential criticism. If rumors are correct or there are developments, an immediate candid statement to the public as to the state of negotiations or of development of corporate plans in the rumored area must be made directly and openly. Such statements are essential despite the business inconvenience which may be caused and even though the matter may not as yet have been presented to the company's Board of Directors for consideration.

3.   Notice that, although TGS itself did not trade, it was still a viable defendant because of its allegedly misleading press release. The court concluded that the release could be considered to be "in connection with" the purchase or sale of securities even though the defendant did not buy or sell. Compare that conclusion with the Court's holding in *Blue Chip Stamps*, discussed in the note *infra*.

4.   A lively debate has taken place in academia concerning whether it is desirable to prohibit insider trading at all. The classic defense of insider trading is found in MANNE, INSIDER TRADING AND THE STOCKMARKET (1966). *See also* Carlton and Fischel, *The Regulation of Insider Trading*, 35 STAN. L. REV. 857 (1983). Generally those favoring insider trading argue as follows: (1) No demonstrable harm occurs to anyone through insider trading, at least where buyers and sellers are dealing in the anonymous public markets; (2) insider trading may be desirable as a form of incentive compensation for officers and directors, which therefore indirectly benefits outsider shareholders as well as insiders; and (3) insider trading promotes efficient pricing of securities by fully reflecting all available information in the price of securities. On the other side, those opposed to insider trading generally argue (1) it is unfair, and (2) it diminishes public confidence in the integrity of the securities markets. *See, e.g.*, Klock, *Mainstream Economics and the Case for Prohibiting*

*Insider Trading*, 10 GA. ST. U. L. REV. 297 (1994); Wang, *Trading on Material Nonpublic Information on Impersonal Stock Markets: Who is Harmed and Who Can Sue Whom Under SEC Rule 10b-5?*, 54 S. CAL. L. REV. 1217 (1981).

# NOTES: CASES LIMITING RULE 10b-5 ACTIONS

In the three year period from 1975–77, the Supreme Court decided three cases that had the effect of substantially limiting the scope of actions which could be brought under Rule 10b-5.

**1.** In *Blue Chip Stamps v. Manor Drug Stores*, 421 U.S. 723 (1975), plaintiff brought a Rule 10b-5 action claiming that he was offered an opportunity to purchase securities but failed to do so due to misleadingly pessimistic statements in the prospectus. However, the Court, following the widely-cited Second Circuit decision in *Birnbaum v. Newport Steel Corp.*, 193 F.2d 461 (2d Cir. 1952), held that only an actual purchaser, not a potential purchaser, has standing to sue under Rule 10b-5. The Court relied first on the actual language of the rule, which requires that the fraudulent misstatement be "in connection with the purchase or sale" of a security. Second, the Court expressed concern that it would open the floodgates to too many potential plaintiffs if everyone who was offered, but refused the opportunity to purchase a security which subsequently appreciated, had standing to pursue a Rule 10b-5 action.

**2.** In *Ernst and Ernst v. Hochfelder*, 425 U.S. 185 (1976), the plaintiffs had invested in a fraudulent securities scheme. Since the perpetrator of the fraud had committed suicide, leaving no assets to satisfy their claims, the plaintiffs sued the brokerage firm's accountants, claiming that they were negligent in conducting an audit and thus failed to uncover the fraud. There was no claim that defendant profited from or participated in the fraud, but plaintiff argued that defendant's negligence was enough to subject it to an action under Rule 10b-5. The Court rejected plaintiff's claim, holding that in order to maintain an action under Rule 10b-5, plaintiff must prove that defendant possessed "scienter," an intent to manipulate, deceive or defraud. Negligence alone was not enough. The Court relied primarily on the statutory language which speaks of "manipulative or deceptive devices" as connoting a congressional intent to confine actions to defendants guilty of knowing or intentional misconduct. In 1980, in *Aaron v. SEC*, 446 U.S. 680 (1980), the Court extended the scienter requirement to enforcement actions brought by the SEC seeking injunctive relief.

Subsequent decisions in several Circuits, however, have to some extent mitigated the "scienter" requirement by holding that gross negligence or reckless misconduct can satisfy the scienter requirement. *See, e.g., First Interstate Bank of Denver, N.A. v. Pring*, 969 F.2d 891 (10th Cir. 1992).

**3.** In *Sante Fe Industries Inc. v. Green*, 430 U.S. 462 (1977), plaintiffs were minority shareholders in Kirby Lumber Corp., a 92% subsidiary of Santa Fe Industries. Santa Fe arranged to merge Kirby into itself under Delaware's short form merger statute and eliminate the minority shareholders by paying them cash for their shares. Plaintiffs sued under Rule 10b-5. They did not allege either misrepresentation or non-disclosure of material facts but argued that the price offered was inadequate and constituted a breach of the majority's fiduciary duty to the minority in violation of Rule 10b-5. The Supreme Court, holding for the defendant, held that Rule 10b-5 does not reach cases of financial unfairness where no fraud, misrepresentation, or deception is alleged. It relied on the language of the statute and the rule, arguing that a transaction cannot be either "deceptive or manipulative" if full disclosure of all material facts has been made. The Court also noted that actions amounting to breach of fiduciary duty have traditionally been relegated to state law and, in the interests of comity and federalism, it would be reluctant to interpret Rule 10b-5 so broadly as to infringe on areas traditionally left to state law, absent a clear indication by Congress that it intended to do so.

4.   In a later case, *Central Bank of Denver, N.A. v. First Interstate Bank of Denver, N.A.*, 511 U.S. 164 (1994), the Supreme Court decided that plaintiffs could not bring actions for aiding and abetting violations of Rule 10b-5, but only for direct violations.

> As in earlier cases considering conduct prohibited by § 10(b), we again conclude that the statute prohibits only the making of a material misstatement (or omission) or the commission of a manipulative act. See *Santa Fe Industries*, 430 U.S. at 473 ("language of § 10(b) gives no indication that Congress meant to prohibit any conduct not involving manipulation or deception"); *Ernst & Ernst*, 425 U.S. at 214 ("When a statute speaks so specifically in terms of manipulation and deception . . . , we are quite unwilling to extend the scope of the statute"). The proscription does not include giving aid to a person who commits a manipulative or deceptive act. We cannot amend the statute to create liability for acts that are not themselves manipulative or deceptive within the meaning of the statute.

*Central Bank of Denver*, 511 U.S. at 177–78.

Congress responded to this holding by providing, in section 104 of the Private Securities Litigation Reform Act of 1995, that aiding and abetting liability under Rule 10b-5 is available in actions brought by the SEC, although it is not available in private actions. *See* 15 U.S.C. § 78t(e).

## 2.   Liability of Tippees

### DIRKS v. SEC

Supreme Court of the United States

463 U.S. 646 (1983)

JUSTICE POWELL delivered the opinion of the Court.

Petitioner Raymond Dirks received material nonpublic information from "insiders" of a corporation with which he had no connection. He disclosed this information to investors who relied on it in trading in the shares of the corporation. The question is whether Dirks violated the antifraud provisions of the federal securities laws by this disclosure.

# I

In 1973, Dirks was an officer of a New York broker-dealer firm who specialized in providing investment analysis of insurance company securities to institutional investors. On March 6, Dirks received information from Ronald Secrist, a former officer of Equity Funding of America. Secrist alleged that the assets of Equity Funding, a diversified corporation primarily engaged in selling life insurance and mutual funds, were vastly overstated as the result of fraudulent corporate practices. Secrist also stated that various regulatory agencies had failed to act on similar charges made by Equity Funding employees. He urged Dirks to verify the fraud and disclose it publicly.

Dirks decided to investigate the allegations. He visited Equity Funding's headquarters in Los Angeles and interviewed several officers and employees of the corporation. The senior management denied any wrongdoing, but certain corporation employees corroborated the charges of fraud. Neither Dirks nor his firm owned or traded any Equity Funding stock, but throughout his investigation he openly discussed the information he had obtained with a number of clients and investors. Some of these persons sold their holdings of Equity Funding securities, including five investment advisers who liquidated holdings of more than $16 million.

While Dirks was in Los Angeles, he was in touch regularly with William Blundell, the Wall Street Journal's Los Angeles bureau chief. Dirks urged Blundell to write a story on the fraud allegations. Blundell did not believe, however, that such a massive fraud could go undetected and declined to write the story. He feared that publishing such damaging hearsay might be libelous.

During the 2-week period in which Dirks pursued his investigation and spread word of Secrist's charges, the price of Equity Funding stock fell from $26 per share to less than $15 per share. This led the New York Stock Exchange to halt trading on March 27. Shortly thereafter California insurance authorities impounded Equity Funding's records and uncovered evidence of the fraud. Only then did the Securities and Exchange Commission (SEC) file a complaint against Equity Funding and only then, on April 2, did the Wall Street Journal publish a front-page story based largely on information assembled by Dirks. Equity Funding immediately went into receivership.

The SEC began an investigation into Dirks' role in the exposure of the fraud. After a hearing by an Administrative Law Judge, the SEC found that Dirks had aided and abetted violations of § 17(a) of the Securities Act of 1933, 48 Stat. 84, as amended, 15 U.S.C. § 77q(a), § 10(b) of the Securities Exchange Act of 1934, 48 Stat. 891, 15 U.S.C. § 78j(b), and SEC Rule 10b-5, 17 CFR § 240.10b-5 (1983), by repeating the allegations of fraud to members of the investment community who later sold their Equity Funding stock. The SEC concluded: "Where 'tippees' — regardless of their motivation or occupation — come into possession of material 'corporate information that they know is confidential and know or should know came from a corporate insider,' they must either publicly disclose that information or refrain from trading." 21 S.E.C. Docket 1401, 1407 (1981) (footnote omitted) (quoting *Chiarella v. United States*, 445 U.S. 222, 230, n.12 (1980)). Recognizing, however, that Dirks "played an important role in bringing [Equity Funding's] massive fraud to light," 21 S.E.C. Docket, at 1412, the SEC only censured him.

Dirks sought review in the Court of Appeals for the District of Columbia Circuit. The court entered judgment against Dirks . . . .

In view of the importance to the SEC and to the securities industry of the question presented by this case, we granted a writ of certiorari. 459 U.S. 1014 (1982). We now reverse.

## II

In the seminal case of *In re Cady, Roberts & Co.*, 40 S.E.C. 907 (1961), the SEC recognized that the common law in some jurisdictions imposes on "corporate 'insiders,' particularly officers, directors, or controlling stockholders" an "affirmative duty of disclosure . . . when dealing in securities." *Id.*, at 911, and n.13. The SEC found that not only did breach of this common-law duty also establish the elements of a Rule 10b-5 violation, but that individuals other than corporate insiders could be obligated either to disclose material nonpublic information before trading or to abstain from trading altogether. *Id.*, at 912. In *Chiarella*, we accepted the two elements set out in *Cady, Roberts* for establishing a Rule 10b-5 violation: "(i) the existence of a relationship affording access to inside information intended to be available only for a corporate purpose, and (ii) the unfairness of allowing a corporate insider to take advantage of that information by trading without disclosure." 445 U.S., at 227. In examining whether *Chiarella* had an obligation to disclose or abstain, the Court found that there is no general duty to disclose before trading on material nonpublic information, and held that "a duty to disclose under § 10(b) does not arise from the mere possession of nonpublic market information." *Id.*, at 235. Such a duty arises rather from the existence of a fiduciary relationship. *See id.*, at 227–235.

Not "all breaches of fiduciary duty in connection with a securities transaction," however, come within the ambit of Rule 10b-5. *Santa Fe Industries, Inc. v. Green*, 430 U.S. 462, 472 (1977). There must also be "manipulation or deception." *Id.*, at 473. In an inside-trading case this fraud derives from the "inherent unfairness involved where one takes advantage" of "information intended to be available only for a corporate purpose and not for the personal benefit of anyone." *In re Merrill Lynch, Pierce, Fenner & Smith, Inc.*, 43 S.E.C. 933, 936 (1968). Thus, an insider will be liable under Rule 10b-5 for inside trading only where he fails to disclose material nonpublic information before trading on it and thus makes "secret profits." *Cady, Roberts, supra*, at 916, n.31.

## III

We were explicit in *Chiarella* in saying that there can be no duty to disclose where the person who has traded on inside information "was not [the corporation's] agent, . . . was not a fiduciary, [or] was not a person in whom the sellers [of the securities] had placed their trust and confidence." 445 U.S., at 232. Not to require such a fiduciary relationship, we recognized, would "[depart] radically from the established doctrine that duty arises from a specific relationship between two parties" and would amount to "recognizing a general duty between all participants in market transactions to forgo actions based on material, nonpublic information."

*Id.*, at 232, 233. This requirement of a specific relationship between the shareholders and the individual trading on inside information has created analytical difficulties for the SEC and courts in policing tippees who trade on inside information. Unlike insiders who have independent fiduciary duties to both the corporation and its shareholders, the typical tippee has no such relationships.[2] In view of this absence, it has been unclear how a tippee acquires the *Cady, Roberts* duty to refrain from trading on inside information.

## A

The SEC's position, as stated in its opinion in this case, is that a tippee "inherits" the *Cady, Roberts* obligation to shareholders whenever he receives inside information from an insider:

> "In tipping potential traders, Dirks breached a duty which he had assumed as a result of knowingly receiving confidential information from [Equity Funding] insiders. Tippees such as Dirks who receive non-public, material information from insiders become 'subject to the same duty as [the] insiders.' *Shapiro v. Merrill Lynch, Pierce, Fenner & Smith, Inc.* [495 F.2d 228, 237 (2d Cir. 1974) (quoting *Ross v. Licht*, 263 F. Supp. 395, 410 (SDNY 1967))]. Such a tippee breaches the fiduciary duty which he assumes from the insider when the tippee knowingly transmits the information to someone who will probably trade on the basis thereof. . . . Presumably, Dirks' informants were entitled to disclose the [Equity Funding] fraud in order to bring it to light and its perpetrators to justice. However, Dirks — standing in their shoes — committed a breach of the fiduciary duty which he had assumed in dealing with them, when he passed the information on to traders." 21 S.E.C. Docket, at 1410, n.42.

This view differs little from the view that we rejected as inconsistent with congressional intent in *Chiarella*. In that case, the Court of Appeals agreed with the SEC and affirmed *Chiarella*'s conviction, holding that "[a]nyone — corporate insider or not — who regularly receives material nonpublic information may not use that information to trade in securities without incurring an affirmative duty to disclose." *United States v. Chiarella*, 588 F.2d 1358, 1365 (CA2 1978) (emphasis in original). Here, the SEC maintains that anyone who knowingly receives nonpublic material information from an insider has a fiduciary duty to disclose before trading.

In effect, the SEC's theory of tippee liability in both cases appears rooted in the idea that the antifraud provisions require equal information among all traders. This conflicts with the principle set forth in *Chiarella* that only some persons, under some circumstances, will be barred from trading while in possession of material nonpublic information. Judge Wright correctly read our opinion in *Chiarella* as

---

[2] [14] Under certain circumstances, such as where corporate information is revealed legitimately to an underwriter, accountant, lawyer, or consultant working for the corporation, these outsiders may become fiduciaries of the shareholders. The basis for recognizing this fiduciary duty is not simply that such persons acquired nonpublic corporate information, but rather that they have entered into a special confidential relationship in the conduct of the business of the enterprise and are given access to information solely for corporate purposes. . . .

repudiating any notion that all traders must enjoy equal information before trading: "[The] 'information' theory is rejected. Because the disclose-or-refrain duty is extraordinary, it attaches only when a party has legal obligations other than a mere duty to comply with the general antifraud proscriptions in the federal securities laws." 220 U.S. App. D. C., at 322, 681 F.2d, at 837. *See Chiarella*, 445 U.S., at 235, n.20. We reaffirm today that "[a] duty [to disclose] arises from the relationship between parties . . . and not merely from one's ability to acquire information because of his position in the market." *Id.*, at 231–232, n.14.

Imposing a duty to disclose or abstain solely because a person knowingly receives material nonpublic information from an insider and trades on it could have an inhibiting influence on the role of market analysts, which the SEC itself recognizes is necessary to the preservation of a healthy market. It is commonplace for analysts to "ferret out and analyze information," 21 S.E.C. Docket, at 1406, and this often is done by meeting with and questioning corporate officers and others who are insiders. And information that the analysts obtain normally may be the basis for judgments as to the market worth of a corporation's securities. The analyst's judgment in this respect is made available in market letters or otherwise to clients of the firm. It is the nature of this type of information, and indeed of the markets themselves, that such information cannot be made simultaneously available to all of the corporation's stockholders or the public generally.

## B

The conclusion that recipients of inside information do not invariably acquire a duty to disclose or abstain does not mean that such tippees always are free to trade on the information. The need for a ban on some tippee trading is clear. Not only are insiders forbidden by their fiduciary relationship from personally using undisclosed corporate information to their advantage, but they also may not give such information to an outsider for the same improper purpose of exploiting the information for their personal gain. *See* 15 U.S.C. § 78t(b) (making it unlawful to do indirectly "by means of any other person" any act made unlawful by the federal securities laws). cate with the fiduciary in such a breach are "as forbidden" as transactions "on behalf of the trustee himself." *Mosser v. Darrow*, 341 U.S. 267, 272 (1951). *See Jackson v. Smith*, 254 U.S. 586, 589 (1921); *Jackson v. Ludeling*, 21 Wall. 616, 631–632 (1874). As the Court explained in *Mosser*, a contrary rule "would open up opportunities for devious dealings in the name of others that the trustee could not conduct in his own." 341 U.S., at 271. *See SEC v. Texas Gulf Sulphur Co.*, 446 F.2d 1301, 1308 (CA2), *cert. denied*, 404 U.S. 1005 (1971). Thus, the tippee's duty to disclose or abstain is derivative from that of the insider's duty. *See* Tr. of Oral Arg. 38. *Cf. Chiarella*, 445 U.S., at 246, n.1 (BLACKMUN, J., dissenting). As we noted in *Chiarella*, "[the] tippee's obligation has been viewed as arising from his role as a participant after the fact in the insider's breach of a fiduciary duty." *Id.*, at 230, n.12.

Thus, some tippees must assume an insider's duty to the shareholders not because they receive inside information, but rather because it has been made available to them improperly. And for Rule 10b-5 purposes, the insider's disclosure is improper only where it would violate his *Cady, Roberts* duty. Thus, a tippee assumes a fiduciary duty to the shareholders of a corporation not to trade on material nonpublic information only when the insider has breached his fiduciary duty to the shareholders by disclosing the information to the tippee and the tippee knows or should know that there has been a breach. 20 As Commissioner Smith perceptively observed in *In re Investors Management Co.*, 44 S.E.C. 633 (1971): "[Tippee] responsibility must be related back to insider responsibility by a necessary finding that the tippee knew the information was given to him in breach of a duty by a person having a special relationship to the issuer not to disclose the information . . . ." *Id.*, at 651 (concurring in result). Tipping thus properly is viewed only as a means of indirectly violating the *Cady, Roberts* disclose-or-abstain rule.

## C

In determining whether a tippee is under an obligation to disclose or abstain, it thus is necessary to determine whether the insider's "tip" constituted a breach of the insider's fiduciary duty. All disclosures of confidential corporate information are not inconsistent with the duty insiders owe to shareholders. In contrast to the extraordinary facts of this case, the more typical situation in which there will be a question whether disclosure violates the insider's *Cady, Roberts* duty is when insiders disclose information to analysts. *See* n.16, *supra*. In some situations, the insider will act consistently with his fiduciary duty to shareholders, and yet release of the information may affect the market. For example, it may not be clear — either to the corporate insider or to the recipient analyst — whether the information will be viewed as material nonpublic information. Corporate officials may mistakenly think the information already has been disclosed or that it is not material enough to affect the market. Whether disclosure is a breach of duty therefore depends in large part on the purpose of the disclosure. This standard was identified by the SEC itself in *Cady, Roberts*: a purpose of the securities laws was to eliminate "use of inside information for personal advantage." 40 S.E.C., at 912, n.15. *See* n.10, *supra*. Thus, the test is whether the insider personally will benefit, directly or indirectly, from his disclosure. Absent some personal gain, there has been no breach of duty to stockholders. And absent a breach by the insider, there is no derivative breach. As Commissioner Smith stated in *Investors Management Co.*: "It is important in this type of case to focus on policing insiders and what they do . . . rather than on policing information per se and its possession. . . . " 44 S.E.C., at 648 (concurring in result).

The SEC argues that, if inside-trading liability does not exist when the information is transmitted for a proper purpose but is used for trading, it would be a rare situation when the parties could not fabricate some ostensibly legitimate business justification for transmitting the information. We think the SEC is unduly concerned. In determining whether the insider's purpose in making a particular disclosure is fraudulent, the SEC and the courts are not required to read the parties' minds. Scienter in some cases is relevant in determining whether the tipper has violated his *Cady, Roberts* duty. But to determine whether the disclosure itself "[deceives], [manipulates], or [defrauds]" shareholders, *Aaron v. SEC*, 446 U.S. 680, 686 (1980), the initial inquiry is whether there has been a breach of duty by the insider. This requires courts to focus on objective criteria, i.e., whether the insider receives a direct or indirect personal benefit from the disclosure, such as a pecuniary gain or a reputational benefit that will translate into future earnings. *Cf.*

40 S.E.C., at 912, n.15; Brudney, *Insiders, Outsiders, and Informational Advantages Under the Federal Securities Laws*, 93 Harv. L. Rev. 322, 348 (1979) ("The theory . . . is that the insider, by giving the information out selectively, is in effect selling the information to its recipient for cash, reciprocal information, or other things of value for himself . . . "). There are objective facts and circumstances that often justify such an inference. For example, there may be a relationship between the insider and the recipient that suggests a *quid pro quo* from the latter, or an intention to benefit the particular recipient. The elements of fiduciary duty and exploitation of nonpublic information also exist when an insider makes a gift of confidential information to a trading relative or friend. The tip and trade resemble trading by the insider himself followed by a gift of the profits to the recipient.

Determining whether an insider personally benefits from a particular disclosure, a question of fact, will not always be easy for courts. But it is essential, we think, to have a guiding principle for those whose daily activities must be limited and instructed by the SEC's inside-trading rules, and we believe that there must be a breach of the insider's fiduciary duty before the tippee inherits the duty to disclose or abstain. In contrast, the rule adopted by the SEC in this case would have no limiting principle.

## IV

Under the inside-trading and tipping rules set forth above, we find that there was no actionable violation by Dirks. It is undisputed that Dirks himself was a stranger to Equity Funding, with no pre-existing fiduciary duty to its shareholders. He took no action, directly or indirectly, that induced the shareholders or officers of Equity Funding to repose trust or confidence in him. There was no expectation by Dirks' sources that he would keep their information in confidence. Nor did Dirks misappropriate or illegally obtain the information about Equity Funding. Unless the insiders breached their *Cady, Roberts* duty to shareholders in disclosing the nonpublic information to Dirks, he breached no duty when he passed it on to investors as well as to the Wall Street Journal.

It is clear that neither Secrist nor the other Equity Funding employees violated their *Cady, Roberts* duty to the corporation's shareholders by providing information to Dirks. The tippers received no monetary or personal benefit for revealing Equity Funding's secrets, nor was their purpose to make a gift of valuable information to Dirks. As the facts of this case clearly indicate, the tippers were motivated by a desire to expose the fraud. *See supra.* In the absence of a breach of duty to shareholders by the insiders, there was no derivative breach by Dirks. *See* n.20, *supra.* Dirks therefore could not have been "a participant after the fact in [an] insider's breach of a fiduciary duty." *Chiarella*, 445 U.S., at 230, n.12.

## V

We conclude that Dirks, in the circumstances of this case, had no duty to abstain from use of the inside information that he obtained. The judgment of the Court of Appeals therefore is Reversed.

JUSTICE BLACKMUN, with whom JUSTICE BRENNAN and JUSTICE MARSHALL join, dissenting.

The Court today takes still another step to limit the protections provided investors by § 10(b) of the Securities Exchange Act of 1934. *See Chiarella v. United States*, 445 U.S. 222, 246 (1980) (dissenting opinion). The device employed in this case engrafts a special motivational requirement on the fiduciary duty doctrine. This innovation excuses a knowing and intentional violation of an insider's duty to shareholders if the insider does not act from a motive of personal gain. Even on the extraordinary facts of this case, such an innovation is not justified.

I

As the Court recognizes, . . . the facts here are unusual. After a meeting with Ronald Secrist, a former Equity Funding employee, on March 7, 1973, App. 226, petitioner Raymond Dirks found himself in possession of material nonpublic information of massive fraud within the company. In the Court's words, "[he] uncovered . . . startling information that required no analysis or exercise of judgment as to its market relevance." *Ibid.* In disclosing that information to Dirks, Secrist intended that Dirks would disseminate the information to his clients, those clients would unload their Equity Funding securities on the market, and the price would fall precipitously, thereby triggering a reaction from the authorities. App. 16, 25, 27.

Dirks complied with his informant's wishes. Instead of reporting that information to the Securities and Exchange Commission (SEC or Commission) or to other regulatory agencies, Dirks began to disseminate the information to his clients and undertook his own investigation. One of his first steps was to direct his associates at Delafield Childs to draw up a list of Delafield clients holding Equity Funding securities. On March 12, eight days before Dirks flew to Los Angeles to investigate Secrist's story, he reported the full allegations to Boston Company Institutional Investors, Inc., which on March 15 and 16 sold approximately $1.2 million of Equity securities. 4 *See id.*, at 199. As he gathered more information, he selectively disclosed it to his clients. To those holding Equity Funding securities he gave the "hard" story — all the allegations; others received the "soft" story — a recitation of vague factors that might reflect adversely on Equity Funding's management. *See id.*, at 211, n.24.

Dirks' attempts to disseminate the information to nonclients were feeble, at best. On March 12, he left a message for Herbert Lawson, the San Francisco bureau chief of The Wall Street Journal. Not until March 19 and 20 did he call Lawson again, and outline the situation. William Blundell, a Journal investigative reporter based in Los Angeles, got in touch with Dirks about his March 20 telephone call. On March 21, Dirks met with Blundell in Los Angeles. Blundell began his own investigation, relying in part on Dirks' contacts, and on March 23 telephoned Stanley Sporkin, the SEC's Deputy Director of Enforcement. On March 26, the next business day, Sporkin and his staff interviewed Blundell and asked to see Dirks the following morning. Trading was halted by the New York Stock Exchange at about the same time Dirks was talking to Los Angeles SEC personnel. The next day, March 28, the SEC suspended trading in Equity Funding securities. By that time, Dirks' clients had unloaded close to $15 million of Equity Funding stock and the price had plummeted from $26 to $15. The effect of Dirks' selective dissemination of Secrist's information was that Dirks' clients were able to shift the losses that were inevitable due to the Equity Funding fraud from themselves to uninformed market participants.

## II

### A

No one questions that Secrist himself could not trade on his inside information to the disadvantage of uninformed shareholders and purchasers of Equity Funding securities. See Brief for United States as Amicus Curiae 19, n.12. Unlike the printer in *Chiarella*, Secrist stood in a fiduciary relationship with these shareholders. As the Court states . . . corporate insiders have an affirmative duty of disclosure when trading with shareholders of the corporation. *See Chiarella*, 445 U.S., at 227. This duty extends as well to purchasers of the corporation's securities. *Id.*, at 227, n.8, citing *Gratz v Claughton*, 187 F.2d 46, 49 (CA2), *cert. denied*, 341 U.S. 920 (1951).

The Court also acknowledges that Secrist could not do by proxy what he was prohibited from doing personally * * * . *Mosser v. Darrow*, 341 U.S. 267, 272 (1951). But this is precisely what Secrist did. Secrist used Dirks to disseminate information to Dirks' clients, who in turn dumped stock on unknowing purchasers. Secrist thus intended Dirks to injure the purchasers of Equity Funding securities to whom Secrist had a duty to disclose. Accepting the Court's view of tippee liability, it appears that Dirks' knowledge of this breach makes him liable as a participant in the breach after the fact . . . . *Chiarella*, 445 U.S., at 230, n.12.

### B

The Court holds, however, that Dirks is not liable because Secrist did not violate his duty; according to the Court, this is so because Secrist did not have the improper purpose of personal gain. * * * In so doing, the Court imposes a new, subjective limitation on the scope of the duty owed by insiders to shareholders. The novelty of this limitation is reflected in the Court's lack of support for it.

The insider's duty is owed directly to the corporation's shareholders. *See* Langevoort, *Insider Trading and the Fiduciary Principle: A Post-*Chiarella *Restatement*, 70 Calif. L. Rev. 1, 5 (1982); 3 Aw. Fletcher, Cyclopedia of the Law of Private Corporations § 1168.2, pp. 288–289 (rev. ed. 1975). As *Chiarella* recognized, it is based on the relationship of trust and confidence between the insider and the shareholder. 445 U.S., at 228. That relationship assures the shareholder that the insider may not take actions that will harm him unfairly. The affirmative duty of disclosure protects against this injury. *See Pepper v. Litton*, 308 U.S. 295, 307, n.15 (1939); *Strong v. Repide*, 213 U.S. 419, 431–434 (1909); *see also Chiarella*, 445 U.S., at 228, n.10; *cf. Pepper*, 308 U.S., at 307 (fiduciary obligation to corporation exists for corporation's protection).

### C

The fact that the insider himself does not benefit from the breach does not eradicate the shareholder's injury. *Cf.* Restatement (Second) of Trusts § 205, Comments c and d (1959) (trustee liable for acts causing diminution of value of trust); 3 A. Scott, Law of Trusts § 205, p. 1665 (3d ed. 1967) (trustee liable for any losses to trust caused by his breach). It makes no difference to the shareholder whether the corporate insider gained or intended to gain personally from the transaction; the shareholder still has lost because of the insider's misuse of nonpublic information. The duty is addressed not to the insider's motives, but to his actions and their consequences on the shareholder. Personal gain is not an element of the breach of this duty.

\*     \*     \*

Although Secrist's general motive to expose the Equity Funding fraud was laudable, the means he chose were not. Moreover, even assuming that Dirks played a substantial role in exposing the fraud, he and his clients should not profit from the information they obtained from Secrist. . . .

\*     \*     \*

### IV

In my view, Secrist violated his duty to Equity Funding shareholders by transmitting material nonpublic information to Dirks with the intention that Dirks would cause his clients to trade on that information. Dirks, therefore, was under a duty to make the information publicly available or to refrain from actions that he knew would lead to trading. Because Dirks caused his clients to trade, he violated § 10(b) and Rule 10b-5. Any other result is a disservice to this country's attempt to provide fair and efficient capital markets. I dissent.

## NOTES

1.   Criminal prosecutions of insider trading frequently involve allegations that, in addition to violating Rule 10b-5, the defendants have committed mail fraud in violation of 18 U.S.C. § 1341, wire fraud in violation of 18 U.S.C. § 1343, and conspiracy in violation of 18 U.S.C. § 371.

Section 1341 provides:

> Whoever, having devised or intending to devise any scheme or artifice to defraud, or for obtaining money or property by means of false or fraudulent pretenses, representations, or promises, or to sell, dispose of, loan, exchange, alter, give away, distribute, supply, or furnish or procure for unlawful use any counterfeit or spurious coin, obligation, security, or other article, or anything represented to be or intimated or held out to be such counterfeit or spurious article, for the purpose of executing such scheme or artifice or attempting so to do, places in any post office or authorized depository for mail matter, any matter or thing whatever to be sent or delivered by the Postal Service, or takes or receives therefrom, any such

matter or thing, or knowingly causes to be delivered by mail according to the direction thereon, or at the place at which it is directed to be delivered by the person to whom it is addressed, any such matter or thing, shall be fined not more than $1,000 or imprisoned not more than five years, or both.

Section 1343 provides:

Whoever, having devised or intending to devise any scheme or artifice to defraud, or for obtaining money or property by means of false or fraudulent pretenses, representations, or promises, transmits or causes to be transmitted by means of wire, radio, or television communication in interstate or foreign commerce, any writings, signs, signals, pictures, or sounds for the purpose of executing such scheme or artifice, shall be fined not more than $1,000 or imprisoned not more than five years, or both.

Section 371 provides:

If two or more persons conspire either to commit any offense against the United States, or to defraud the United States, or any agency thereof in any manner or for any purpose, and one or more of such persons do any act to effect the object of the conspiracy, each shall be fined not more than $10,000 or imprisoned not more than five years, or both.

2.    With respect to conspiracy, courts have found that tippers are not liable to the extent that their tippees share the material nonpublic information with others without the knowledge and consent of the original tipper. Conspiracy requires a joint intent to commit a substantive offense. Although tippers and their tippees can be held liable for conspiracy where they jointly intend the purpose of trading on inside information, there is no joint intent among a tipper and remote tippees of whom he or she is unaware. *See U.S. v. Geibel*, 369 F.3d 682 (2d Cir. 2004), *U.S. v. McDermott*, 245 F.3d 133 (2d Cir. 2001), *U.S. v. Carpenter*, 791 F.2d 1024 (2d Cir. 1986).

## 3.    The Misappropriation Theory and Rule 14e-3

### a.    *Chiarella v. United States*

In *Chiarella v. United States*, 445 U.S. 222 (1980), Vincent Chiarella worked for Pandick Press, a financial printer. Pandick printed, among other things, documents relating to pending and potential corporate takeovers, mergers, and acquisitions. Pandick had a rule prohibiting its employees from trading on information that they acquired in the course of their employment. Although the documents were redacted to leave out the names of the corporations targeted for acquisition by Pandick's clients, Chiarella was able to figure out who some of the target companies were. He purchased stock in the targets before the offers were announced to the public, and made more than $30,000 in profits over a 14-month period. His trades were discovered, and he was indicted and convicted for criminal violations of Rule 10b-5. The Second Circuit affirmed, and he appealed his case to the Supreme Court. The Supreme Court reversed the conviction, holding that because Chiarella was not an insider of the companies in whose securities he traded, he owed those security holders no fiduciary duty to disclose his information or abstain from trading.

In this case, the petitioner was convicted of violating § 10 (b) although he was not a corporate insider and he received no confidential information from the target company. Moreover, the "market information" upon which he relied did not concern the earning power or operations of the target company, but only the plans of the acquiring company. Petitioner's use of that information was not a fraud under § 10 (b) unless he was subject to an affirmative duty to disclose it before trading. In this case, the jury instructions failed to specify any such duty. In effect, the trial court instructed the jury that petitioner owed a duty to everyone; to all sellers, indeed, to the market as a whole. The jury simply was told to decide whether petitioner used material, nonpublic information at a time when "he knew other people trading in the securities market did not have access to the same information." Record 677.

The Court of Appeals affirmed the conviction by holding that "[*anyone*] — corporate insider or not — who regularly receives material nonpublic information may not use that information to trade in securities without incurring an affirmative duty to disclose." * * * The Court of Appeals, like the trial court, failed to identify a relationship between petitioner and the sellers that could give rise to a duty. Its decision thus rested solely upon its belief that the federal securities laws have "created a system providing equal access to information necessary for reasoned and intelligent investment decisions." *Id.*, at 1362. The use by anyone of material information not generally available is fraudulent, this theory suggests, because such information gives certain buyers or sellers an unfair advantage over less informed buyers and sellers.

This reasoning suffers from two defects. First, not every instance of financial unfairness constitutes fraudulent activity under § 10 (b). See *Santa Fe Industries, Inc. v. Green*, 430 U.S. 462, 474–477 (1977). Second, the element required to make silence fraudulent — a duty to disclose — is absent in this case. No duty could arise from petitioner's relationship with the sellers of the target company's securities, for petitioner had no prior dealings with them. He was not their agent, he was not a fiduciary, he was not a person in whom the sellers had placed their trust and confidence. He was, in fact, a complete stranger who dealt with the sellers only through impersonal market transactions.

We cannot affirm petitioner's conviction without recognizing a general duty between all participants in market transactions to forgo actions based on material, nonpublic information. Formulation of such a broad duty, which departs radically from the established doctrine that duty arises from a specific relationship between two parties, see n.9, *supra*, should not be undertaken absent some explicit evidence of congressional intent.

As we have seen, no such evidence emerges from the language or legislative history of § 10 (b). Moreover, neither the Congress nor the Commission ever has adopted a parity-of-information rule. Instead the problems caused by misuse of market information have been addressed by detailed and sophisticated regulation that recognizes when use of market information may not harm operation of the securities markets. . . . Congress' careful action in this and other areas contrasts, and is in some tension, with the broad rule of liability we are asked to adopt in this case.

*Chiarella*, 445 U.S. at 232–34 (footnotes omitted).

In its brief to the Court, the United States suggested that, even though Chiarella did not owe a fiduciary duty to the target company or its shareholders, his conviction should be affirmed because he violated a duty to his employer and his employer's client, the acquiring company, by misappropriating information that belonged to the acquirer. The Court declined to consider this theory, because it had not been submitted to the jury. *See id.* at 235–36.

## b. *Carpenter v. United States*

In *Carpenter v. United States*, 484 U.S. 19 (1987), Foster Winans was a reporter for the Wall Street Journal. He wrote a popular column called "Heard on the Street," which commented on companies and their prospects. His opinion was influential, and stock prices tended to move up or down based on his recommendations. The Wall Street Journal had an employment policy that prohibited Winans from sharing or using information before publication. However, Winans provided information to his partner, David Carpenter, and to two of their friends, Brant and Felis, who were stock brokers. They and one of Brant's clients, Clark, traded on the information that Winans provided, and they made about $690,000 in profits over a 4-month period. The SEC got wind of what was going on and began an investigation. The conspirators had a falling out, and Winans and Carpenter went to the SEC and confessed the whole scheme.

Felis and Winans were convicted of violating Rule 10b-5, the mail fraud statute, the wire fraud statute, and the conspiracy statute. Carpenter was convicted for aiding and abetting. Brant pleaded guilty under an agreement that required him to testify against the others. The Second Circuit affirmed the convictions, and the defendants appealed to the Supreme Court.

The problem under Rule 10b-5 was that Winans was not a traditional insider; that is, he did not work for the companies he wrote about. He also was not prohibited from trading under a tippee theory, because he did not acquire the information he used in violation of a tipper's fiduciary duty. Some other theory thus was required to secure a conviction. The prosecution, therefore, alleged that Winans had misappropriated the information he used, in violation of a duty owed to his employer, the Wall Street Journal.

> The District Court found, and the Court of Appeals agreed, that Winans had knowingly breached a duty of confidentiality by misappropriating prepublication information regarding the timing and contents of the "Heard" column, information that had been gained in the course of his employment under the understanding that it would not be revealed in advance of publication and that if it were, he would report it to his employer. It was this appropriation of confidential information that underlay both the securities laws and mail and wire fraud counts. With respect to the § 10(b) charges, the courts below held that the deliberate breach of

Winans' duty of confidentiality and concealment of the scheme was a fraud and deceit on the Journal. Although the victim of the fraud, the Journal, was not a buyer or seller of the stocks traded in or otherwise a market participant, the fraud was nevertheless considered to be "in connection with" a purchase or sale of securities within the meaning of the statute and the rule. The courts reasoned that the scheme's sole purpose was to buy and sell securities at a profit based on advance information of the column's contents. The courts below rejected petitioners' submission, which is one of the two questions presented here, that criminal liability could not be imposed on petitioners under Rule 10b-5 because "the newspaper is the only alleged victim of fraud and has no interest in the securities traded."

*Carpenter*, 484 U.S. at 23–24.

The Supreme Court unanimously affirmed the lower court with respect to everything except the Rule 10b-5 count. With respect to that count, the Court was equally divided, four to four (Justice Powell had just retired, so only eight justices participated in the case). Therefore, the lower court's conviction stood, but the case did not establish conclusively whether the misappropriation theory was a valid theory for asserting a violation of Rule 10b-5.

# NOTE: RULE 14e-3

In 1980, The S.E.C. promulgated Rule 14e-3 under Section 14(e) of the 1934 Act, 15 U.S.C.A. § 78n(e). Section 14(e) prohibits fraud in connection with tender offers in language very similar to that found in Section 10(b). It reads as follows:

**e. Untrue statement of material fact or omission of fact with respect to tender offer.** It shall be unlawful for any person to make any untrue statement of a material fact or omit to state any material fact necessary in order to make the statements made, in the light of the circumstances under which they are made, not misleading, or to engage in any fraudulent, deceptive, or manipulative acts or practices, in connection with any tender offer or request or invitation for tenders, or any solicitation of security holders in opposition to or in favor of any such offer, request, or invitation. The Commission shall, for the purposes of this subsection, by rules and regulations define, and prescribe means reasonably designed to prevent, such acts and practices as are fraudulent, deceptive, or manipulative.

Rule 14e-3 prohibits trading based on material nonpublic information concerning a tender offer. It is more broadly worded than Rule 10b-5, in that it does not require that the defendant breach a fiduciary duty to be liable. The rule provides in part as follows:

Rule 14e-3.— Transactions in Securities on the Basis of Material, Nonpublic Information in the Context of Tender Offers

a. If any person has taken a substantial step or steps to commence, or has commenced, a tender offer (the "offering person"), it shall constitute a fraudulent, deceptive or manipulative act or practice within the meaning of section 14(e) of the Act for any other person who is in possession of material information relating to such tender offer which information he knows or has reason to know is nonpublic and which he knows or has reason to know has been acquired directly or indirectly from:

1. The offering person,

2. The issuer of the securities sought or to be sought by such tender offer, or

3. Any officer, director, partner or employee or any other person acting on behalf of the offering person or such issuer, to purchase or sell or cause to be purchased or sold any of such securities or any securities convertible into or exchangeable for any such securities or any option or right to obtain or to dispose of any of the foregoing securities, unless within a reasonable time prior to any purchase or sale such information and its source are publicly disclosed by press release or otherwise.

When the rule was adopted, there was some question as to whether it exceeded the SEC's rulemaking authority. Under Section 23(a) of the 1934 Act, the SEC has the power to make rules "as may be necessary or appropriate to implement the provisions of this title . . . ." A fraud action based on failure to speak requires breach of a duty to speak. Is it appropriate to try to prevent fraud with a rule that does not require a breach of duty? The Second Circuit considered this question in the *Chestman* case discussed below.

### c. *United States v. Chestman*

A stock broker named Robert Chestman was tried and convicted of, among other things, violating Rule 10b-5 and Rule 14e-3(a). The charges grew out of a transaction involving the acquisition of a New York grocery chain called Waldbaum, Inc. by a larger grocery company, The Great Atlantic and Pacific Tea Company. A&P had negotiated a deal with Ira Waldbaum, the company's president and controlling shareholder, as follows:

On November 21, 1986, Ira Waldbaum agreed to sell Waldbaum to the Great Atlantic and Pacific Tea Company (A & P). The resulting stock purchase agreement required Ira to tender a controlling block of Waldbaum shares to A & P at a price of $50 per share. Ira told three of his children, all employees of Waldbaum, about the pending sale two days later, admonishing them to keep the news quiet until a public announcement. He also told his sister, Shirley Witkin, and nephew, Robert Karin, about the sale, and offered to tender their shares along with his controlling block of shares to enable them to avoid the administrative difficulty of tendering after the public announcement. He cautioned them "that [the sale was] not to be discussed," that it was to remain confidential.

In spite of Ira's counsel, Shirley told her daughter, Susan Loeb, on November 24 that Ira was selling the company. Shirley warned Susan not to tell anyone except her husband, Keith Loeb, because disclosure could ruin the sale. The next day, Susan told her husband about the pending tender offer and cautioned him not to tell anyone because "it could possibly ruin the sale."

The following day, November 26, Keith Loeb telephoned [his stock broker] Robert Chestman at 8:59 a.m. Unable to reach Chestman, Loeb left a message asking Chestman to call him "ASAP." According to Loeb, he later spoke with Chestman between 9:00 a.m. and 10:30 a.m. that morning and told Chestman that he had "some definite, some accurate information" that Waldbaum was about to be sold at a "substantially higher" price than its market value. Loeb asked Chestman several times what he thought Loeb should do. Chestman responded that he could not advise Loeb what to do "in a situation like this" and that Loeb would have to make up his own mind.

That morning Chestman executed several purchases of Waldbaum stock. At 9:49 a.m., he bought 3,000 shares for his own account at $24.65 per share. Between 11:31 a.m. and 12:35 p.m., he purchased an additional 8,000 shares for his clients' discretionary accounts at prices ranging from $25.75 to $26.00 per share. One of the discretionary accounts was the Loeb account, for which Chestman bought 1,000 shares.

Before the market closed at 4:00 p.m., Loeb claims that he telephoned Chestman a second time. During their conversation Loeb again pressed Chestman for advice. Chestman repeated that he could not advise Loeb "in a situation like this," but then said that, based on his research, Waldbaum was a "buy." Loeb subsequently ordered 1,000 shares of Waldbaum stock.

*Chestman*, 947 F.2d at 555.

When the tender offer by A&P was publicly announced, Waldbaum's stock price shot up to $49 per share, and Chestman made a substantial profit. However, he soon found that he was being investigated for violating the securities and mail fraud statutes, and his trial and conviction followed. In his appeal, the Second Circuit considered two issues relevant to our current discussion. The first was whether the SEC had exceeded its rulemaking authority by promulgating Rule 14e-3.

The court noted that it was obligated to review the SEC's acts with a deferential standard, not substituting its judgment for that of the agency. It explained:

> The plain language of section 14(e) represents a broad delegation of rulemaking authority. The statute explicitly directs the SEC to "define" fraudulent practices and to "prescribe means reasonably designed to prevent" such practices. It is difficult to see how the power to "define" fraud could mean anything less than the power to "set forth the meaning of" fraud in the tender offer context. *See Webster's Third New International Dictionary* 592 (1971). This delegation of rulemaking responsibility becomes a hollow gesture if we cabin the SEC's rulemaking authority, as Chestman urges we should, by common law definitions of fraud. Under Chestman's construction of the statute, the separate grant of rulemaking power would be rendered superfluous because the SEC could never define as fraud anything not already prohibited by the self-operative provision. Such a narrow construction of the congressional grant of authority would

cramp the SEC's ability to define fraud flexibly in the context of the discrete and highly sensitive area of tender offers. And such a delegation of "power," paradoxically, would allow the SEC to limit, but not extend, a trader's duty to disclose.

Even if we were to accept the argument that the SEC's definitional authority is circumscribed by common law fraud, which we do not, the SEC's power to "prescribe means reasonably designed to prevent" fraud extends the agency's rulemaking authority further. The language of this portion of section 14(e) is clear. The verb "prevent" has a plain meaning: "To keep from happening or existing especially by precautionary measures." *Webster's New Third International Dictionary* 1798 (1971). A delegation of authority to enact rules "reasonably designed to prevent" fraud, then, necessarily encompasses the power to proscribe conduct outside the purview of fraud, be it common law or SEC-defined fraud. Because the operative words of the statute, "define" and "prevent," have clear connotations, the language of the statute is sufficiently clear to be dispositive here. *Chevron*, 467 U.S. at 842–43. . . .

*Id.* at 558.

The court discussed several other factors that bolster its analysis, and concluded that the rule was valid, upholding Chestman's conviction for violating Rule 14e-3.

With respect to the Rule 10b-5 charges, however, the court's conclusion might seem surprising. The government was proceeding on a misappropriation theory, accusing Keith Loeb of having misappropriated the information and passed it on to Chestman. Chestman, then, like Raymond Dirks, was a tippee. Therefore, the court had to determine whether Loeb had breached a fiduciary duty in giving the information to Chestman.

> The government agrees that Chestman's convictions cannot be sustained unless there was sufficient evidence to show that (1) Keith Loeb breached a duty owed to the Waldbaum family or Susan Loeb based on a fiduciary or similar relationship of trust and confidence, and (2) Chestman knew that Loeb had done so.

*Id.* at 564.

The court began with two propositions; first, that "a fiduciary duty cannot be imposed unilaterally by entrusting a person with confidential information," (*id.* at 567), and second, that "marriage does not, without more, create a fiduciary relationship." (*id.* at 568). The court noted that although marriage is a special, intimate relationship, it does not necessarily involve the sort of trust and confidence by one person that the other is acting in his or her best interests. The court found that the government had fallen short in proving that either the Waldbaum family or his wife had entrusted him with confidential business information in a way that created a fiduciary duty.

> Keith's status as Susan's husband could not itself establish fiduciary status. Nor, absent a pre-existing fiduciary relation or an express agreement of confidentiality, could the coda — "Don't tell." That leaves the unremarkable

testimony that Keith and Susan had shared and maintained generic confidences before. The jury was not told the nature of these past disclosures and therefore it could not reasonably find a relationship that inspired fiduciary, rather than normal marital, obligations.

*Id.* at 571.

As a consequence, Chestman's Rule 10b-5 convictions were overturned.

# NOTE: RULE 10b5-2

The SEC was understandably dismayed by the Second Circuit's conclusion that marriage does not of itself establish a fiduciary duty. In 2000, it promulgated Rule 10b5-2.

Rule 10b5-2 — Duties of Trust or Confidence in Misappropriation Insider Trading Cases

*Preliminary Note to § 240.10b5-2:*

This section provides a non-exclusive definition of circumstances in which a person has a duty of trust or confidence for purposes of the "misappropriation" theory of insider trading under Section 10(b) of the Act and Rule 10b-5. The law of insider trading is otherwise defined by judicial opinions construing Rule 10b-5, and Rule 10b5-2 does not modify the scope of insider trading law in any other respect.

    a.  *Scope of Rule.* This section shall apply to any violation of Section 10(b) of the Act and Rule 10b-5 thereunder that is based on the purchase or sale of securities on the basis of, or the communication of, material nonpublic information misappropriated in breach of a duty of trust or confidence.

    b.  *Enumerated "duties of trust or confidence."* For purposes of this section, a "duty of trust or confidence" exists in the following circumstances, among others:

        1.  Whenever a person agrees to maintain information in confidence;

        2.  Whenever the person communicating the material nonpublic information and the person to whom it is communicated have a history, pattern, or practice of sharing confidences, such that the recipient of the information knows or reasonably should know that the person communicating the material nonpublic information expects that the recipient will maintain its confidentiality; or

        3.  Whenever a person receives or obtains material nonpublic information from his or her spouse, parent, child, or sibling; provided, however, that the person receiving or obtaining the information may demonstrate that no duty of trust or confidence existed with respect to the information, by establishing

that he or she neither knew nor reasonably should have known that the person who was the source of the information expected that the person would keep the information confidential, because of the parties' history, pattern, or practice of sharing and maintaining confidences, and because there was no agreement or understanding to maintain the confidentiality of the information.

### d. *United States v. O'Hagan*

The Second Circuit determined in *Carpenter* that the misappropriation theory was a viable theory for prosecuting violations of Rule 10b-5. The Supreme Court did not overturn that holding, but its 4-4 decision also did not establish the theory as conclusively viable. In *Chestman*, the Second Circuit decided that Rule 14e-3 was a valid exercise of the SEC's rulemaking authority. The *O'Hagan* case originated in the U.S. District Court for the District of Minnesota. The defendant was convicted of violating both Rule 10b-5 and Rule 14e-3, and he appealed to the Eighth Circuit Court of Appeals. The Eighth Circuit concluded that the misappropriation theory was NOT a viable theory for prosecuting violations of Rule 10b-5, and also concluded that the SEC had exceeded its rulemaking authority in adopting Rule 14e-3. This split between the Second and Eighth Circuits led to the Supreme Court opinion that follows.

**UNITED STATES v. O'HAGAN**

Supreme Court of the United States

521 U.S. 642 (1997)

JUSTICE GINSBURG delivered the opinion of the Court.

This case concerns the interpretation and enforcement of § 10(b) and § 14(e) of the Securities Exchange Act of 1934, and rules made by the Securities and Exchange Commission pursuant to these provisions, Rule 10b-5 and Rule 14e-3(a). Two prime questions are presented. The first relates to the misappropriation of material, nonpublic information for securities trading; the second concerns fraudulent practices in the tender offer setting. In particular, we address and resolve these issues: (1) Is a person who trades in securities for personal profit, using confidential information misappropriated in breach of a fiduciary duty to the source of the information, guilty of violating § 10(b) and Rule 10b-5? (2) Did the Commission exceed its rulemaking authority by adopting Rule 14e-3(a), which proscribes trading on undisclosed information in the tender offer setting, even in the absence of a duty to disclose? Our answer to the first question is yes, and to the second question, viewed in the context of this case, no.

I

Respondent James Herman O'Hagan was a partner in the law firm of Dorsey & Whitney in Minneapolis, Minnesota. In July 1988, Grand Metropolitan PLC (Grand Met), a company based in London, England, retained Dorsey & Whitney as local counsel to represent Grand Met regarding a potential tender offer for the common stock of the Pillsbury Company, headquartered in Minneapolis. Both Grand Met and Dorsey & Whitney took precautions to protect the confidentiality of Grand Met's tender offer plans. O'Hagan did no work on the Grand Met representation. Dorsey & Whitney withdrew from representing Grand Met on September 9, 1988. Less than a month later, on October 4, 1988, Grand Met publicly announced its tender offer for Pillsbury stock.

On August 18, 1988, while Dorsey & Whitney was still representing Grand Met, O'Hagan began purchasing call options for Pillsbury stock. Each option gave him the right to purchase 100 shares of Pillsbury stock by a specified date in September 1988. Later in August and in September, O'Hagan made additional purchases of Pillsbury call options. By the end of September, he owned 2,500 unexpired Pillsbury options, apparently more than any other individual investor. See App. 85, 148. O'Hagan also purchased, in September 1988, some 5,000 shares of Pillsbury common stock, at a price just under $39 per share. When Grand Met announced its tender offer in October, the price of Pillsbury stock rose to nearly $60 per share. O'Hagan then sold his Pillsbury call options and common stock, making a profit of more than $4.3 million.

The Securities and Exchange Commission (SEC or Commission) initiated an investigation into O'Hagan's transactions, culminating in a 57-count indictment. The indictment alleged that O'Hagan defrauded his law firm and its client, Grand Met, by using for his own trading purposes material, nonpublic information regarding Grand Met's planned tender offer. *Id.*, at 8. According to the indictment, O'Hagan used the profits he gained through this trading to conceal his previous embezzlement and conversion of unrelated client trust funds. *Id.*, at 10. O'Hagan was charged with 20 counts of mail fraud, in violation of 18 U.S.C. § 1341; 17 counts of securities fraud, in violation of § 10(b) of the Securities Exchange Act of 1934 (Exchange Act), 48 Stat. 891, 15 U.S.C. § 78j(b), and SEC Rule 10b-5, 17 CFR § 240.10b-5 (1996); 17 counts of fraudulent trading in connection with a tender offer, in violation of § 14(e) of the Exchange Act, 15 U.S.C. § 78n(e), and SEC Rule 14e-3(a), 17 CFR § 240.14e-3(a) (1996); and 3 counts of violating federal money laundering statutes, 18 U.S.C. §§ 1956(a)(1)(B)(i), 1957. *See* App. 13-24. A jury convicted O'Hagan on all 57 counts, and he was sentenced to a 41-month term of imprisonment.

A divided panel of the Court of Appeals for the Eighth Circuit reversed all of O'Hagan's convictions. 92 F.3d 612 (1996). Liability under § 10(b) and Rule 10b-5, the Eighth Circuit held, may not be grounded on the "misappropriation theory" of securities fraud on which the prosecution relied. *Id.*, at 622. The Court of Appeals also held that Rule 14e-3(a) — which prohibits trading while in possession of material, nonpublic information relating to a tender offer — exceeds the SEC's § 14(e) rulemaking authority because the rule contains no breach of fiduciary duty requirement. *Id.*, at 627. The Eighth Circuit further concluded that O'Hagan's mail fraud and money laundering convictions rested on violations of the securities laws, and therefore could not stand once the securities fraud convictions were reversed. *Id.*, at 627–628. Judge Fagg, dissenting, stated that he would recognize and enforce the misappropriation theory, and would hold that the SEC did not exceed its rulemaking authority when it adopted Rule 14e-3(a) without requiring proof of a breach of fiduciary duty. *Id.*, at 628.

Decisions of the Courts of Appeals are in conflict on the propriety of the misappropriation theory under § 10(b) and Rule 10b-5, *see infra* and on the legitimacy of Rule 14e-3(a) under § 14(e), *see infra.* We granted certiorari, 519 U.S. 1087 (1997), 117 S. Ct. 759, 136 L. Ed. 2d 695 (1997) and now reverse the Eighth Circuit's judgment.

## II

We address first the Court of Appeals' reversal of O'Hagan's convictions under § 10(b) and Rule 10b-5. Following the Fourth Circuit's lead, see *United States v. Bryan*, 58 F.3d 933, 943–959 (1995), the Eighth Circuit rejected the misappropriation theory as a basis for § 10(b) liability. We hold, in accord with several other Courts of Appeals, that criminal liability under § 10(b) may be predicated on the misappropriation theory.

## A

In pertinent part, § 10(b) of the Exchange Act provides:

> "It shall be unlawful for any person, directly or indirectly, by the use of any means or instrumentality of interstate commerce or of the mails, or of any facility of any national securities exchange—

> * * *

> "(b)  To use or employ, in connection with the purchase or sale of any security registered on a national securities exchange or any security not so registered, any manipulative or deceptive device or contrivance in contravention of such rules and regulations as the [Securities and Exchange] Commission may prescribe as necessary or appropriate in the public interest or for the protection of investors."

15 U.S.C. § 78j(b).

The statute thus proscribes (1) using any deceptive device (2) in connection with the purchase or sale of securities, in contravention of rules prescribed by the Commission.

The provision, as written, does not confine its coverage to deception of a purchaser or seller of securities, *see United States v. Newman*, 664 F.2d 12, 17 (CA2 1981); rather, the statute reaches any deceptive device used "in connection with the purchase or sale of any security."

Pursuant to its § 10(b) rulemaking authority, the Commission has adopted Rule 10b-5, which, as relevant here, provides:

> "It shall be unlawful for any person, directly or indirectly, by the use of any means or instrumentality of interstate commerce, or of the mails or of any facility of any national securities exchange,

> "(a)  To employ any device, scheme, or artifice to defraud, [or]

> "(c)  To engage in any act, practice, or course of business which operates or would operate as a fraud or deceit upon any person, in

connection with the purchase or sale of any security."

17 CFR § 240.10b-5 (1996).

Liability under Rule 10b-5, our precedent indicates, does not extend beyond conduct encompassed by § 10(b)'s prohibition.

Under the "traditional" or "classical theory" of insider trading liability, § 10(b) and Rule 10b-5 are violated when a corporate insider trades in the securities of his corporation on the basis of material, nonpublic information. Trading on such information qualifies as a "deceptive device" under § 10(b), we have affirmed, because "a relationship of trust and confidence [exists] between the shareholders of a corporation and those insiders who have obtained confidential information by reason of their position with that corporation." *Chiarella v. United States*, 445 U.S. 222, 228 (1980). That relationship, we recognized, "gives rise to a duty to disclose [or to abstain from trading] because of the 'necessity of preventing a corporate insider from . . . taking unfair advantage of . . . uninformed . . . stockholders.'" *Id.*, at 228–229 (citation omitted). The classical theory applies not only to officers, directors, and other permanent insiders of a corporation, but also to attorneys, accountants, consultants, and others who temporarily become fiduciaries of a corporation. *See Dirks v. SEC*, 463 U.S. 646, 655, n.14 (1983).

The "misappropriation theory" holds that a person commits fraud "in connection with" a securities transaction, and thereby violates § 10(b) and Rule 10b-5, when he misappropriates confidential information for securities trading purposes, in breach of a duty owed to the source of the information. See Brief for United States 14. Under this theory, a fiduciary's undisclosed, self-serving use of a principal's information to purchase or sell securities, in breach of a duty of loyalty and confidentiality, defrauds the principal of the exclusive use of that information. In lieu of premising liability on a fiduciary relationship between company insider and purchaser or seller of the company's stock, the misappropriation theory premises liability on a fiduciary-turned-trader's deception of those who entrusted him with access to confidential information.

The two theories are complementary, each addressing efforts to capitalize on nonpublic information through the purchase or sale of securities. The classical theory targets a corporate insider's breach of duty to shareholders with whom the insider transacts; the misappropriation theory outlaws trading on the basis of nonpublic information by a corporate "outsider" in breach of a duty owed not to a trading party, but to the source of the information. The misappropriation theory is thus designed to "protect the integrity of the securities markets against abuses by 'outsiders' to a corporation who have access to confidential information that will affect the corporation's security price when revealed, but who owe no fiduciary or other duty to that corporation's shareholders." *Ibid.*

In this case, the indictment alleged that O'Hagan, in breach of a duty of trust and confidence he owed to his law firm, Dorsey & Whitney, and to its client, Grand Met, traded on the basis of nonpublic information regarding Grand Met's planned tender offer for Pillsbury common stock. App. 16. This conduct, the Government charged, constituted a fraudulent device in connection with the purchase and sale of securities.[3]

## B

We agree with the Government that misappropriation, as just defined, satisfies § 10(b)'s requirement that chargeable conduct involve a "deceptive device or contrivance" used "in connection with" the purchase or sale of securities. We observe, first, that misappropriators, as the Government describes them, deal in deception. A fiduciary who "[pretends] loyalty to the principal while secretly converting the principal's information for personal gain," Brief for United States 17, "dupes" or defrauds the principal. *See* Aldave, *Misappropriation: A General Theory of Liability for Trading on Nonpublic Information*, 13 Hofstra L. Rev. 101, 119 (1984).

We addressed fraud of the same species in *Carpenter v. United States*, 484 U.S. 19 (1987), which involved the mail fraud statute's proscription of "any scheme or artifice to defraud," 18 U.S.C. § 1341. Affirming convictions under that statute, we said in *Carpenter* that an employee's undertaking not to reveal his employer's confidential information "became a sham" when the employee provided the information to his coconspirators in a scheme to obtain trading profits. 484 U.S. at 27. A company's confidential information, we recognized in *Carpenter*, qualifies as property to which the company has a right of exclusive use. *Id.*, at 25–27. The undisclosed misappropriation of such information, in violation of a fiduciary duty, the Court said in *Carpenter*, constitutes fraud akin to embezzlement —" 'the fraudulent appropriation to one's own use of the money or goods entrusted to one's care by another.' " *Id.*, at 27 (quoting *Grin v. Shine*, 187 U.S. 181, 189 (1902)); *see* Aldave, 13 Hofstra L. Rev., at 119. *Carpenter*'s discussion of the fraudulent misuse of confidential information, the Government notes, "is a particularly apt source of guidance here, because [the mail fraud statute] (like Section 10(b)) has long been held to require deception, not merely the breach of a fiduciary duty." Brief for United States 18, n.9 (citation omitted).

Deception through nondisclosure is central to the theory of liability for which the Government seeks recognition. As counsel for the Government stated in explanation of the theory at oral argument: "To satisfy the common law rule that a trustee may not use the property that [has] been entrusted [to] him, there would have to be consent. To satisfy the requirement of the Securities Act that there be no deception, there would only have to be disclosure." Tr. of Oral Arg. 12; *see generally* Restatement (Second) of Agency §§ 390, 395 (1958) (agent's disclosure obligation regarding use of confidential information).[4]

---

   [3] [5] The Government could not have prosecuted O'Hagan under the classical theory, for O'Hagan was not an "insider" of Pillsbury, the corporation in whose stock he traded. Although an "outsider" with respect to Pillsbury, O'Hagan had an intimate association with, and was found to have traded on confidential information from, Dorsey & Whitney, counsel to tender offeror Grand Met. Under the misappropriation theory, O'Hagan's securities trading does not escape Exchange Act sanction, as it would under the dissent's reasoning, simply because he was associated with, and gained nonpublic information from, the bidder, rather than the target.

   [4] [6] Under the misappropriation theory urged in this case, the disclosure obligation runs to the source of the information, here, Dorsey & Whitney and Grand Met. Chief Justice Burger, dissenting in

The misappropriation theory advanced by the Government is consistent with *Santa Fe Industries, Inc. v. Green*, 430 U.S. 462 (1977), a decision underscoring that § 10(b) is not an all-purpose breach of fiduciary duty ban; rather, it trains on conduct involving manipulation or deception. *See id.*, at 473–476. In contrast to the Government's allegations in this case, in *Santa Fe Industries*, all pertinent facts were disclosed by the persons charged with violating § 10(b) and Rule 10b-5, *see id.*, at 474; therefore, there was no deception through nondisclosure to which liability under those provisions could attach, *see id.*, at 476. Similarly, full disclosure forecloses liability under the misappropriation theory: Because the deception essential to the misappropriation theory involves feigning fidelity to the source of information, if the fiduciary discloses to the source that he plans to trade on the nonpublic information, there is no "deceptive device" and thus no § 10(b) violation — although the fiduciary-turned-trader may remain liable under state law for breach of a duty of loyalty.

We turn next to the § 10(b) requirement that the misappropriator's deceptive use of information be "in connection with the purchase or sale of [a] security." This element is satisfied because the fiduciary's fraud is consummated, not when the fiduciary gains the confidential information, but when, without disclosure to his principal, he uses the information to purchase or sell securities. The securities transaction and the breach of duty thus coincide. This is so even though the person or entity defrauded is not the other party to the trade, but is, instead, the source of the nonpublic information. *See* Aldave, 13 Hofstra L. Rev., at 120 ("a fraud or deceit can be practiced on one person, with resultant harm to another person or group of persons"). A misappropriator who trades on the basis of material, nonpublic information, in short, gains his advantageous market position through deception; he deceives the source of the information and simultaneously harms members of the investing public. *See id.*, at 120–121, and n.107.

The misappropriation theory targets information of a sort that misappropriators ordinarily capitalize upon to gain no-risk profits through the purchase or embezzlement of sale of securities. Should a misappropriator put such information to other use, the statute's prohibition would not be implicated. The theory does not catch all conceivable forms of fraud involving confidential information; rather, it catches fraudulent means of capitalizing on such information through securities transactions.

The Government notes another limitation on the forms of fraud § 10(b) reaches: "The misappropriation theory would not . . . apply to a case in which a person defrauded a bank into giving him a loan or embezzled cash from another, and then used the proceeds of the misdeed to purchase securities." Brief for United States 24, n.13. In such a case, the Government states, "the proceeds would have value to the malefactor apart from their use in a securities transaction, and the fraud would be complete as soon as the money was obtained." *Ibid.* In other words, money can buy,

---

Chiarella, advanced a broader reading of § 10(b) and Rule 10b-5; the disclosure obligation, as he envisioned it, ran to those with whom the misappropriator trades. 445 U.S. at 240 ("a person who has misappropriated nonpublic information has an absolute duty to disclose that information or to refrain from trading"); *see also id.*, at 243, n.4. The Government does not propose that we adopt a misappropriation theory of that breadth.

if not anything, then at least many things; its misappropriation may thus be viewed as sufficiently detached from a subsequent securities transaction that § 10(b)'s "in connection with" requirement would not be met. *Ibid.*

The dissent's charge that the misappropriation theory is incoherent because information, like funds, can be put to multiple uses, *see post*, misses the point. The Exchange Act was enacted in part "to insure the maintenance of fair and honest markets," 15 U.S.C. § 78b, and there is no question that fraudulent uses of confidential information fall within § 10(b)'s prohibition if the fraud is "in connection with" a securities transaction. It is hardly remarkable that a rule suitably applied to the fraudulent uses of certain kinds of information would be stretched beyond reason were it applied to the fraudulent use of money.

The dissent does catch the Government in overstatement. Observing that money can be used for all manner of purposes and purchases, the Government urges that confidential information of the kind at issue derives its value only from its utility in securities trading. *See* Brief for United States 10, 21; *post* (several times emphasizing the word "only"). Substitute "ordinarily" for "only," and the Government is on the mark.

*  *  *

The misappropriation theory comports with § 10(b)'s language, which requires deception "in connection with the purchase or sale of any security," not deception of an identifiable purchaser or seller. The theory is also well-tuned to an animating purpose of the Exchange Act: to insure honest securities markets and thereby promote investor confidence. *See* 45 Fed. Reg. 60412 (1980) (trading on misappropriated information "undermines the integrity of, and investor confidence in, the securities markets"). Although informational disparity is inevitable in the securities markets, investors likely would hesitate to venture their capital in a market where trading based on misappropriated nonpublic information is unchecked by law. An investor's informational disadvantage vis-a-vis a misappropriator with material, nonpublic information stems from contrivance, not luck; it is a disadvantage that cannot be overcome with research or skill. *See* Brudney, *Insiders, Outsiders, and Informational Advantages Under the Federal Securities Laws*, 93 Harv. L. Rev. 322, 356 (1979) ("If the market is thought to be systematically populated with . . . transactors [trading on the basis of misappropriated information] some investors will refrain from dealing altogether, and others will incur costs to avoid dealing with such transactors or corruptly to overcome their unerodable informational advantages."); Aldave, 13 Hofstra L. Rev., at 122–123.

In sum, considering the inhibiting impact on market participation of trading on misappropriated information, and the congressional purposes underlying § 10(b), it makes scant sense to hold a lawyer like O'Hagan a § 10(b) violator if he works for a law firm representing the target of a tender offer, but not if he works for a law firm representing the bidder. The text of the statute requires no such result.[5] The

---

[5] [9] As noted earlier, however, *see supra*, the textual requirement of deception precludes § 10(b) liability when a person trading on the basis of nonpublic information has disclosed his trading plans to, or obtained authorization from, the principal — even though such conduct may affect the securities markets in the same manner as the conduct reached by the misappropriation theory. Contrary to the

misappropriation at issue here was properly made the subject of a § 10(b) charge because it meets the statutory requirement that there be "deceptive" conduct "in connection with" securities transactions.

## C

The Court of Appeals rejected the misappropriation theory primarily on two grounds. First, as the Eighth Circuit comprehended the theory, it requires neither misrepresentation nor nondisclosure. . . .

Second and "more obvious," the Court of Appeals said, the misappropriation theory is not moored to § 10(b)'s requirement that "the fraud be 'in connection with the purchase or sale of any security.' " . . . "Only a breach of a duty to parties to the securities transaction," the Court of Appeals concluded, "or, at the most, to other market participants such as investors, will be sufficient to give rise to § 10(b) liability." We read the statute and our precedent differently, and note again that § 10(b) refers to "the purchase or sale of any security," not to identifiable purchasers or sellers of securities.

*     *     *

In sum, the misappropriation theory, as we have examined and explained it in this opinion, is both consistent with the statute and with our precedent. Vital to our decision that criminal liability may be sustained under the misappropriation theory, we emphasize, are two sturdy safeguards Congress has provided regarding scienter. To establish a criminal violation of Rule 10b-5, the Government must prove that a person "willfully" violated the provision. Furthermore, a defendant may not be imprisoned for violating Rule 10b-5 if he proves that he had no knowledge of the rule. *See ibid.* O'Hagan's charge that the misappropriation theory is too indefinite to permit the imposition of criminal liability, see Brief for Respondent 30–33, thus fails not only because the theory is limited to those who breach a recognized duty. In addition, the statute's "requirement of the presence of culpable intent as a necessary element of the offense does much to destroy any force in the argument that application of the [statute]" in circumstances such as O'Hagan's is unjust. *Boyce Motor Lines, Inc. v. United States*, 342 U.S. 337, 342 (1952).

The Eighth Circuit erred in holding that the misappropriation theory is inconsistent with § 10(b). The Court of Appeals may address on remand O'Hagan's other challenges to his convictions under § 10(b) and Rule 10b-5.

## III

We consider next the ground on which the Court of Appeals reversed O'Hagan's convictions for fraudulent trading in connection with a tender offer, in violation of

---

dissent's suggestion, *see post*, the fact that § 10(b) is only a partial antidote to the problems it was designed to alleviate does not call into question its prohibition of conduct that falls within its textual proscription. Moreover, once a disloyal agent discloses his imminent breach of duty, his principal may seek appropriate equitable relief under state law. Furthermore, in the context of a tender offer, the principal who authorizes an agent's trading on confidential information may, in the Commission's view, incur liability for an Exchange Act violation under Rule 14e-3(a).

§ 14(e) of the Exchange Act and SEC Rule 14e-3(a). A sole question is before us as to these convictions: Did the Commission, as the Court of Appeals held, exceed its rulemaking authority under § 14(e) when it adopted Rule 14e-3(a) without requiring a showing that the trading at issue entailed a breach of fiduciary duty? We hold that the Commission, in this regard and to the extent relevant to this case, did not exceed its authority.

The governing statutory provision, § 14(e) of the Exchange Act, reads in relevant part:

> "It shall be unlawful for any person . . . to engage in any fraudulent, deceptive, or manipulative acts or practices, in connection with any tender offer. . . . The [SEC] shall, for the purposes of this subsection, by rules and regulations define, and prescribe means reasonably designed to prevent, such acts and practices as are fraudulent, deceptive, or manipulative." 15 U.S.C. § 78n(e).

Section 14(e)'s first sentence prohibits fraudulent acts in connection with a tender offer. This self-operating proscription was one of several provisions added to the Exchange Act in 1968 by the Williams Act, 82 Stat. 454. The section's second sentence delegates definitional and prophylactic rulemaking authority to the Commission. Congress added this rulemaking delegation to § 14(e) in 1970 amendments to the Williams Act. *See* § 5, 84 Stat. 1497.

Through § 14(e) and other provisions on disclosure in the Williams Act, Congress sought to ensure that shareholders "confronted by a cash tender offer for their stock [would] not be required to respond without adequate information." *Rondeau v. Mosinee Paper Corp.*, 422 U.S. 49 (1975); *see Lewis v. McGraw*, 619 F.2d 192, 195 (CA2 1980) (per curiam) ("very purpose" of Williams Act was "informed decision-making by shareholders"). As we recognized in *Schreiber v. Burlington Northern, Inc.*, 472 U.S. 1(1985), Congress designed the Williams Act to make "disclosure, rather than court imposed principles of 'fairness' or 'artificiality,' . . . the preferred method of market regulation." *Id.*, at 9, n.8. Section 14(e), we explained, "supplements the more precise disclosure provisions found elsewhere in the Williams Act, while requiring disclosure more explicitly addressed to the tender offer context than that required by § 10(b)." *Id.*, at 10–11.

Relying on § 14(e)'s rulemaking authorization, the Commission, in 1980, promulgated Rule 14e-3(a). That measure provides:

> "(a) If any person has taken a substantial step or steps to commence, or has commenced, a tender offer (the 'offering person'), it shall constitute a fraudulent, deceptive or manipulative act or practice within the meaning of section 14(e) of the [Exchange] Act for any other person who is in possession of material information relating to such tender offer which information he knows or has reason to know is nonpublic and which he knows or has reason to know has been acquired directly or indirectly from:
>
> (1)   The offering person,
>
> (2)   The issuer of the securities sought or to be sought by such tender offer, or

(3) Any officer, director, partner or employee or any other person acting on behalf of the offering person or such issuer, to purchase or sell or cause to be purchased or sold any of such securities or any securities convertible into or exchangeable for any such securities or any option or right to obtain or to dispose of any of the foregoing securities, unless within a reasonable time prior to any purchase or sale such information and its source are publicly disclosed by press release or otherwise." 17 CFR § 240.14e-3(a) (1996).

As characterized by the Commission, Rule 14e-3(a) is a "disclose or abstain from trading" requirement. 45 Fed. Reg. 60410 (1980). The Second Circuit concisely described the rule's thrust:

"One violates Rule 14e-3(a) if he trades on the basis of material nonpublic information concerning a pending tender offer that he knows or has reason to know has been acquired 'directly or indirectly' from an insider of the offeror or issuer, or someone working on their behalf. Rule 14e-3(a) is a disclosure provision. It creates a duty in those traders who fall within its ambit to abstain or disclose, *without regard to whether the trader owes a pre-existing fiduciary duty* to respect the confidentiality of the information."

*United States v. Chestman*, 947 F.2d 551, 557 (1991) (en banc) (emphasis added), *cert. denied*, 503 U.S. 1004 (1992).

* * *

We need not resolve in this case whether the Commission's authority under § 14(e) to "define . . . such acts and practices as are fraudulent" is broader than the Commission's fraud-defining authority under § 10(b), for we agree with the United States that Rule 14e-3(a), as applied to cases of this genre, qualifies under § 14(e) as a "means reasonably designed to prevent" fraudulent trading on material, nonpublic information in the tender offer context. A prophylactic measure, because its mission is to prevent, typically encompasses more than the core activity prohibited. As we noted in Schreiber,§ 14(e)'s rulemaking authorization gives the Commission "latitude," even in the context of a term of art like "manipulative," "to regulate nondeceptive activities as a 'reasonably designed' means of preventing manipulative acts, without suggesting any change in the meaning of the term 'manipulative' itself." 472 U.S. at 11, n.11. We hold, accordingly, that under § 14(e), the Commission may prohibit acts, not themselves fraudulent under the common law or § 10(b), if the prohibition is "reasonably designed to prevent . . . acts and practices [that] are fraudulent." 15 U. S. C. § 78n(e).

Because Congress has authorized the Commission, in § 14(e), to prescribe legislative rules, we owe the Commission's judgment "more than mere deference or weight." *Batterton v. Francis*, 432 U.S. 416, 424–426 (1977). Therefore, in determining whether Rule 14e-3(a)'s "disclose or abstain from trading" requirement is reasonably designed to prevent fraudulent acts, we must accord the Commission's assessment "controlling weight unless [it is] arbitrary, capricious, or manifestly contrary to the statute." *Chevron U.S.A. Inc. v. Natural Resources Defense Council,*

*Inc.*, 467 U.S. 837, 844 (1984). In this case, we conclude, the Commission's assessment is none of these.

\*   \*   \*

## IV

Based on its dispositions of the securities fraud convictions, the Court of Appeals also reversed O'Hagan's convictions, under 18 U.S.C. § 1341, for mail fraud. *See* 92 F.3d at 627–628. Reversal of the securities convictions, the Court of Appeals recognized, "did not as a matter of law require that the mail fraud convictions likewise be reversed." *Id.*, at 627 (citing *Carpenter*, 484 U.S. at 24, in which this Court unanimously affirmed mail and wire fraud convictions based on the same conduct that evenly divided· the Court on the defendants' securities fraud convictions). But in this case, the Court of Appeals said, the indictment was so structured that the mail fraud charges could not be disassociated ·from the securities fraud charges, and absent any securities fraud, "there was no fraud upon which to base the mail fraud charges." 92 F.3d at 627–628.

The United States urges that the Court of Appeals' position is irreconcilable with *Carpenter*: Just as in *Carpenter*, so here, the "mail fraud charges are independent of [the] securities fraud charges, even [though] both rest on the same set of facts." Brief for United States 46-47. We need not linger over this matter, for our rulings on the securities fraud issues require that we reverse the Court of Appeals judgment on the mail fraud counts as well.[6]

O'Hagan, we note, attacked the mail fraud convictions in the Court of Appeals on alternate grounds; his other arguments, not yet addressed by the Eighth Circuit, remain open for consideration on remand.

The judgment of the Court of Appeals for the Eighth Circuit is reversed, and the case is remanded for further proceedings consistent with this opinion.

It is so ordered.

JUSTICE SCALIA, concurring in part and dissenting in part.

I join Parts I, III, and IV of the Court's opinion. I do not agree, however, with Part II of the Court's opinion, containing its analysis of respondent's convictions under § 10(b) and Rule 10b-5.

I do not entirely agree with Justice Thomas's analysis of those convictions either, principally because it seems to me irrelevant whether the Government's theory of

---

[6] [25] The dissent finds O'Hagan's convictions on the mail fraud counts, but not on the securities fraud counts, sustainable. *Post.* Under the dissent's view, securities traders like O'Hagan would escape SEC civil actions and federal prosecutions under legislation targeting securities fraud, only to be caught for their trading activities in the broad mail fraud net. If misappropriation theory cases could proceed only under the federal mail and wire fraud statutes, practical consequences for individual defendants might not be large, *see* Aldave, 49 Ohio St. L.J., at 381, and n.60; however, "proportionally more persons accused of insider trading [might] be pursued by a U.S. Attorney, and proportionally fewer by the SEC," *id.*, at 382. Our decision, of course, does not rest on such enforcement policy considerations.

why respondent's acts were covered is "coherent and consistent," *post*. It is true that with respect to matters over which an agency has been accorded adjudicative authority or policymaking discretion, the agency's action must be supported by the reasons that the agency sets forth, *SEC v. Chenery Corp.*, 318 U.S. 80, 94 (1943); *see also SEC v. Chenery Corp.*, 332 U.S. 194 (1947), but I do not think an agency's unadorned application of the law need be, at least where (as here) no *Chevron* deference is being given to the agency's interpretation. In point of fact, respondent's actions either violated § 10(b) and Rule 10b-5, or they did not — regardless of the reasons the Government gave. And it is for us to decide.

While the Court's explanation of the scope of § 10(b) and Rule 10b-5 would be entirely reasonable in some other context, it does not seem to accord with the principle of lenity we apply to criminal statutes (which cannot be mitigated here by the Rule, which is no less ambiguous than the statute). *See Reno v. Koray*, 515 U.S. 50, 64–65 (1995) (explaining circumstances in which rule of lenity applies); *United States v. Bass*, 404 U.S. 336, 347–348 (1971) (discussing policies underlying rule of lenity). In light of that principle, it seems to me that the unelaborated statutory language: "to use or employ in connection with the purchase or sale of any security . . . any manipulative or deceptive device or contrivance," § 10(b), must be construed to require the manipulation or deception of a party to a securities transaction.

JUSTICE THOMAS, with whom THE CHIEF JUSTICE joins, concurring in the judgment in part and dissenting in part.

Today the majority upholds respondent's convictions for violating § 10(b) of the Securities Exchange Act of 1934, and Rule 10b-5 promulgated thereunder, based upon the Securities and Exchange Commission's "misappropriation theory." Central to the majority's holding is the need to interpret § 10(b)'s requirement that a deceptive device be "used or employed, in connection with the purchase or sale of any security." 15 U.S.C. § 78j(b). Because the Commission's misappropriation theory fails to provide a coherent and consistent interpretation of this essential requirement for liability under § 10(b), I dissent.

The majority also sustains respondent's convictions under § 14(e) of the Securities Exchange Act, and Rule 14e-3(a) promulgated thereunder, regardless of whether respondent violated a fiduciary duty to anybody. I dissent too from that holding because, while § 14(e) does allow regulations prohibiting nonfraudulent acts as a prophylactic against certain fraudulent acts, neither the majority nor the Commission identifies any relevant underlying fraud against which Rule 14e-3(a) reasonably provides prophylaxis. With regard to the respondent's mail fraud convictions, however, I concur in the judgment of the Court.

I

I do not take issue with the majority's determination that the undisclosed misappropriation of confidential information by a fiduciary can constitute a "deceptive device" within the meaning of § 10(b). Nondisclosure where there is a pre-existing duty to disclose satisfies our definitions of fraud and deceit for purposes of the securities laws. *See Chiarella v. United States*, 445 U.S. 222 (1980).

Unlike the majority, however, I cannot accept the Commission's interpretation of when a deceptive device is "used . . . in connection with" a securities transaction. Although the Commission and the majority at points seem to suggest that any relation to a securities transaction satisfies the "in connection with" requirement of § 10(b), both ultimately reject such an overly expansive construction and require a more integral connection between the fraud and the securities transaction. The majority states, for example, that the misappropriation theory applies to undis-closed misappropriation of confidential information "for securities trading pur-poses," . . . thus seeming to require a particular intent by the misappropriator in order to satisfy the "in connection with" language . . . (the "misappropriation theory targets information of a sort that *misappropriators ordinarily capitalize upon to gain no-risk profits* through the purchase or sale of securities") (emphasis added); . . . (distinguishing embezzlement of money used to buy securities as lacking the requisite connection). The Commission goes further, and argues that the misappropriation theory satisfies the "in connection with" requirement because it "depends on an inherent connection between the deceptive conduct and the purchase or sale of a security." . . .

The Commission's construction of the relevant language in § 10(b), and the incoherence of that construction, become evident as the majority attempts to describe why the fraudulent theft of information falls under the Commission's misappropriation theory, but the fraudulent theft of money does not. The majority correctly notes that confidential information "qualifies as property to which the company has a right of exclusive use." . . . It then observes that the "undisclosed misappropriation of such information, in violation of a fiduciary duty, . . . consti-tutes fraud akin to embezzlement — the fraudulent appropriation to one's own use of the money or goods entrusted to one's care by another." So far the majority's analogy to embezzlement is well taken, and adequately demonstrates that undis-closed misappropriation can be a fraud on the source of the information.

What the embezzlement analogy does not do, however, is explain how the relevant fraud is "used or employed, in connection with" a securities transaction. And when the majority seeks to distinguish the embezzlement of funds from the embezzlement of information, it becomes clear that neither the Commission nor the majority has a coherent theory regarding § 10(b)'s "in connection with" require-ment.

# NOTES

1.  The legitimacy of the "misappropriation theory" was one of the most widely debated issues involving SEC Rule 10b-5 liability in the decade following the Supreme Court decision in the *Carpenter* case where it deadlocked 4-4 on the issue. While leading to a result which most securities lawyers would consider equitable, *O'Hagan* does raise questions in squaring the misappropriation theory with the language of Rule 10b-5. The "in connection with" language of Rule 10b-5 is particularly troublesome to the dissent. Does the majority satisfactorily answer the dissent's argument that, if the misappropriation theory is accepted, a person who

embezzles funds and subsequently purchases securities in another corporation has violated Rule 10b-5?

**2.** The misappropriation theory leads to results which some would consider anomalous. Consider the following:

**a.** A wealthy individual formulates a plan to make a hostile tender offer at a premium price for shares in another corporation, the "Target." In the weeks before the offer, he quietly makes open market purchases of Target's stock at prices between $20 and $25 per share. Then, a tender offer is announced to purchase the remaining stock at a price of $35 per share. It is clear under the Williams Act that the Offeror has no duty to announce in advance his plan to conduct a tender offer, at least until he acquires five per cent of the securities of the Target and is required to file disclosure statements under section 13d-1 of the Williams Act.

**b.** Take the same facts as in "a" except that the purchaser of Target's stock is Offeror's secretary who learns of his plans to make a tender offer from reading documents which she has helped him prepare. She then purchases stock in Target for her own account. Secretary has misappropriated the information from Offeror and thus has violated Rule 10b-5 under the *O'Hagan* rule.

**c.** Same facts as in "a" except that Offeror tells "Secretary" and a few other trusted employees of his tender offer plans and authorizes them to quietly make purchases in Target for their own accounts in advance of public disclosure of the tender offer plans. Secretary has not misappropriated the information under the *O'Hagen* holding.

**d.** Suppose that Secretary is having lunch outside the office when she happens to overhear a conversation between two individuals whom she knows to be officers of Target discussing the fact that they have been approached by Offeror about the possibility of having a negotiated "friendly" tender offer for the shares of Target at a premium price. If Secretary purchases shares in Target based solely on her overhearing this conversation, would she be liable? *See SEC v. Switzer*, 590 F. Supp. 756 (W.D. Okla. 1984).

**e.** Suppose a psychiatrist's patient complains that her husband pays no attention to her because his company is being acquired and he is consumed with the deal. The psychiatrist then purchases stock in the husband's company. Would he be liable? *See United States v. Willis*, 737 F. Supp. 269 (S.D.N.Y. 1990).

**3.** The Court has repeatedly stated maintaining investor confidence in the securities markets is one of the most important reasons underlying Rule 10b-5's prohibition on insider trading. Given this rationale, does it make sense to distinguish between cases "a" through "d" above? Would an individual who had sold securities prior to public announcement of a take-over bid at a price significantly below the market price of Target's securities after the offer was announced feel any better about the transaction in the three cases where no Rule 10b-5 liability would probably result? If not why has the Court distinguished among them?

**4.** As the Court's opinion indicates, following the Court's decision in *Chiarella*, the SEC dealt with the most egregious cases of insider trading involving advance knowledge of corporate take-over bids by adopting Rule 14e-3, discussed in the

*O'Hagan* opinion. Given the inconsistencies in the misappropriation theory discussed by Justice Thomas' dissent, would the Court have been better off leaving further expansion of the scope of Rule 10b-5 to the SEC and Congress rather than proceeding to expand the coverage of the rule on a case by case basis? Should the fact that *O'Hagan* is a criminal case be relevant in making such a decision?

## SEC v. YUN
### United States Court of Appeals, Eleventh Circuit
### 327 F.3d 1263 (2003)

TJOFLAT, CIRCUIT JUDGE

This is an insider trading case, brought by the Securities and Exchange Commission ("SEC") under section 10(b) of the Securities Exchange Act of 1934 ("Exchange Act"), 15 U.S.C. § 78j(b), and (SEC) Rule 10b-5, 17 C.F.R. § 240.10b-5, against Donna Yun and Jerry Burch. Answering special verdicts, a jury found that the defendants had "violated Section 10(b)" under the "misappropriation theory" of liability. Acting on those verdicts, the district court entered judgment against the defendants, holding them "jointly liable" for $269,000, the profits generated by the prohibited trading, plus prejudgment interest, and individually liable for a penalty in the sum of $1,000. *SEC v. Yun*, 148 F. Supp. 2d 1287 (M.D. Fla. 2001).

Yun and Burch now appeal, contending that the district court erred in denying their motions for judgment as a matter of law and, alternatively, that the court erred in instructing the jury on elements of the misappropriation theory of liability.

I.

A.

Donna Yun is married to David Yun, the president of Scholastic Book Fairs, Inc., a subsidiary of Scholastic Corporation ("Scholastic"), a publisher and distributor of children's books whose stock is quoted on the NASDAQ National Market System and whose option contracts are traded on the Chicago Board Options Exchange. On January 27, 1997, David attended a senior management retreat at which Scholastic's chief financial officer revealed that the company would post a loss for the current quarter, and that before the quarter ended, the company would make a public announcement revising its earnings forecast downward. He cautioned the assembled executives not to sell any of their Scholastic holdings until after the announcement, which would likely result in a decline in the market price of Scholastic shares, and warned them to keep the matter confidential. Approximately two weeks later, on February 13, Scholastic's chief financial officer informed David that the negative earnings announcement would be made on February 20.

Over the weekend of February 15–16, David and Donna discussed a statement of assets that he had provided her in connection with their negotiation of a post-nuptial division of assets. David explained to Donna that he had assigned a $55 value to his Scholastic options listed on the asset statement, even though Scholastic's stock was then trading at $65 per share, because he believed that the price of the shares would drop following Scholastic's February 20 earnings announcement. He also told her not to disclose this information to anyone else, and she agreed to keep the information confidential. David anticipated that Donna would discuss this information with her attorney, but assumed her attorney would keep the information confidential.

The following Tuesday, February 18, Donna went to her place of work — a real estate office located in a nearby housing development. The office was a small sales trailer, approximately eleven by thirteen feet, that Donna shared with other real estate agents, including Jerry Burch. During the late morning or early afternoon, Donna telephoned Sam Weiss — the attorney assisting her in negotiating the post-nuptial division of assets — from her office to discuss David's statement of assets. While she was speaking to Weiss, Burch entered the office to gather materials for a real estate client. Standing three to four feet from Donna, Burch heard her tell Weiss what David had said about Scholastic's impending earnings announcement and that David expected the price of the company's shares to fall. As he testified at trial, Burch did not learn enough from what he overheard to feel "comfortable" trading in Scholastic's stock.

That evening, Donna and Burch attended a real estate awards banquet at the Isleworth Country Club. Donna, Burch, and another agent, Maryann Hartmann, carpooled to the reception. All three stayed at the reception for three hours and left together.

The next morning Burch called his broker and requested authority to purchase put options in Scholastic.[7] When the broker advised Burch that he knew of no new information indicating the price of Scholastic stock would decline, Burch stated that based on information he had obtained at a cocktail party, he nonetheless wanted to purchase the put options. The broker warned Burch of the risks of trading in options, and cautioned him about insider trading prohibitions. Despite these warnings, between the afternoon of February 19 and midday on February 20, Burch purchased $19,750 in Scholastic put options, which was equal to two-thirds of his total income for the previous year and nearly half the value of his entire investment portfolio.

After the stock market closed on February 20, Scholastic announced that its earnings would be well below the analysts' expectations. When the market opened the next day, the price of Scholastic shares had dropped approximately 40 percent to $36 per share. Burch then sold his Scholastic puts, realizing a profit of $269,000 — a 1,300 percent return on his investment. Within hours, the SEC commenced an investigation of Burch's trades, to determine whether insider trading had occurred. The investigation culminated in the present lawsuit. In a one-count complaint, the SEC alleged that Donna and Burch had violated section 10(b) of the Exchange Act and Rule 10b-5, and sought both legal and equitable relief.

---

[7] [6] A put option is an option contract that gives the holder of the option the right to sell a certain quantity of an underlying security to the writer of the option, at a specified price up to a specified date. The value of a put increases as the price of the stock decreases.

## B.

There are two theories of insider trading liability: the "classical theory" and the "misappropriation theory." The classical theory imposes liability on corporate "insiders" who trade on the basis of confidential information obtained by reason of their position with the corporation. The liability is based on the notion that a corporate insider breaches "a . . . [duty] of trust and confidence" to the shareholders of his corporation. *United States v. O'Hagan*, 521 U.S. 642, 652, 117, 138 L. Ed. 2d 724, 117 S. Ct. 2199 (1997). The misappropriation theory, on the other hand, imposes liability on "outsiders" who trade on the basis of confidential information obtained by reason of their relationship with the person possessing such information, usually an insider. The liability under the latter theory is based on the notion that the outsider breaches "a duty of loyalty and confidentiality" to the person who shared the confidential information with him. *Id.* at 652, 117 S. Ct. at 2207.

Not only are the insider and the outsider forbidden from trading on the basis of the confidential information they have received, they are forbidden from "tipping" such information to someone else, a "tippee," who, being fully aware that the information is confidential, does the trading. In other words, the insider and outsider are forbidden from doing indirectly what they are forbidden from doing. directly. To establish liability, however, the SEC need not show that the tippee actually traded for the tipper and gave him the profits of the trades; all the SEC needs to show is that the tipper received a "benefit," directly or indirectly, from his disclosure. *See Dirks*, 463 U.S. at 659–62, 103 S. Ct. at 3264–65.

This is a tipper-tippee case. The SEC prosecuted it under the "misappropriation theory" of insider trading liability. Its complaint alleged that Donna was an outsider who had a fiduciary relationship with David, and that she breached that duty when she divulged to Burch confidential information, which David had given her, "for her direct and/or indirect benefit because of her business relationship and friendship with . . . Burch." Under these circumstances, the complaint alleged, Donna was liable under section 10(b) of the Exchange Act and Rule 10b-5 to disgorge the profits Burch realized from the put options trades. Because Burch knew of Donna's breach of her fiduciary duty to David, but nonetheless traded on the confidential information she gave him, he, too, was liable under § 10(b) and Rule 10b-5.

\*    \*    \*

## II.

## A.

In assessing the district court's ruling on appellants' motions for judgment as a matter of law, we first consider whether Donna owed David a duty of loyalty and confidentiality not to disclose the revised earnings information he had received in confidence.

As stated *supra*, to prevail in an insider trading case, the SEC must establish that the misappropriator breached a duty of loyalty and confidentiality owed to the source of the confidential information. Certain business relationships, such as attorney-client or employer-employee, clearly provide the requisite duty of loyalty and confidentiality. On the other hand, it is unsettled whether non-business relationships, such as husband and wife, provide the duty of loyalty and confidentiality necessary to satisfy the misappropriation theory. The leading case on when a duty of loyalty and confidentiality exists in the context of family members — the case relied on by the parties and the district court for the elements of a confidential relationship — is *United States v. Chestman,* 947 F.2d 551 (2d Cir. 1991) (en banc).

In a divided en banc decision, the Second Circuit held that marriage alone does not create a relationship of loyalty and confidentiality. *Id.* at 568. Either an "express agreement of confidentiality" or the "functional equivalent" of a "fiduciary relationship" must exist between the spouses for a court to find a confidential relationship for purposes of § 10(b) and Rule 10b-5 liability. Since the spouses had not entered into a confidentiality agreement, the court turned its focus to determining what constitutes a fiduciary relationship or its functional equivalent. "At the heart of the fiduciary relationship," the court declared, "lies reliance, and de facto control and dominance." *Id.* at 568 (citations and internal quotation marks omitted). Having so concluded, the court explained that the functional equivalent of a fiduciary relationship "must share these qualities." *Id.* at 569. Applying the requisite qualities of reliance, control, and dominance to the husband and wife relationship at hand, the *Chestman* majority held that no fiduciary relationship or its functional equivalent existed. The spouses' sharing and maintaining of "generic confidences" in the past was insufficient to establish the functional equivalent of a fiduciary relationship. *Id.* at 571. Accordingly, the court decided that the defendants were not subject to sanctions for insider trading violations.

A lengthy dissent by Judge Winter, joined by four judges, took issue with the narrowness in which the majority would find a relationship of loyalty and confidentiality amongst family members, pointing out that under the majority's approach, the disclosure of sensitive corporate information essentially could be "avoided only by family members extracting formal, express promises of confidentiality." *Id.* at 580. Such an approach, in the view of the dissent, was "unrealistic in that it expects family members to behave like strangers toward each other." *Id.* Moreover, the normal reluctance to recognize obligations based on family relationships — the concern that intra-family litigation would exacerbate strained relationships and weaken the sense of mutual obligation underlying family relationships — was inapplicable in insider trading cases because the suits are brought by the government. *See id.* at 580. Given the circumstances of the case, the dissent concluded that a confidential relationship existed between the husband and wife which gave rise to a duty of loyalty and confidentiality on his part not to disclose the sensitive information.

We are inclined to accept the dissent's view that the *Chestman* decision too narrowly defined the circumstances in which a duty of loyalty and confidentiality is created between husband and wife. We think that the majority, by insisting on either an express agreement of confidentiality or a strictly defined fiduciary-like relationship, ignored the many instances in which a spouse has a reasonable expectation of confidentiality. In our view, a spouse who trades in breach of a reasonable and legitimate expectation of confidentiality held by the other spouse sufficiently subjects the former to insider trading liability. If the SEC can prove that the husband and wife had a history or practice of sharing business confidences, and those confidences generally were maintained by the spouse receiving the information, then in most instances the conveying spouse would have a reasonable expectation of confidentiality such that the breach of the expectation would suffice to yield insider trading liability. Of course, a breach of an agreement to maintain business confidences would also suffice.

For purposes of this case, then, the existence of a duty of loyalty and confidentiality turns on whether David Yun granted his wife, Donna, access to confidential information in reasonable reliance on a promise that she would safeguard the information. * * * If the SEC presented evidence that David and Donna had a history or pattern of sharing business confidences, which were generally kept, then Donna could have been found by the jury to have breached a duty of loyalty and confidentiality by disclosing to Burch the information regarding Scholastic's upcoming earnings announcement. Similarly, if the SEC presented evidence that Donna had agreed in this particular instance to keep the information confidential, then Donna could have been found to have committed the necessary breach of a duty of loyalty and confidentiality.

We conclude that the SEC provided sufficient evidence both that an agreement of confidentiality and a history or pattern of sharing and keeping of business confidences existed between David and Donna Yun such that David could have reasonably expected Donna to keep confidential what he told her about Scholastic's pending announcement. First, the SEC presented evidence that Donna explicitly accepted the duty to keep in confidence the business information she received. She testified that she considered the information confidential because, "David always told me, anything that he talks to me in regards to the company is confidential and can't go past he or I." That she fully understood and agreed to the understanding of confidentiality is further manifested by the fact that she declined to disclose any information about David's company to her attorney until she had "absolute certainty that there was confidentiality with everything [she] was sharing with him." Second, both David and Donna testified that David repeatedly shared confidential information about Scholastic with Donna, including information regarding its sales goals. This certainly qualified as a history or pattern of sharing business confidences. Overall, the SEC presented evidence upon which a jury could find that a duty of loyalty and confidentiality existed between David and Donna Yun; the SEC therefore established the first element of a "misappropriation theory" claim.

B.

Having reached this conclusion, we turn to the question of whether the evidence was sufficient to show that Donna breached her duty to David. . . . The SEC contends — contrary to the position it assumed in its complaint — that it did not have to prove that Donna divulged the information for her own benefit; all it had to show was that Donna acted with "severe recklessness." According to the SEC, the "intent to benefit" element only applies in cases brought under the classical theory of liability; the element has no application in cases brought under the misappropriation theory of liability. In other words, whether Donna expected to benefit from the disclosure of the confidential information is irrelevant.

Which position is correct — the one the SEC took in its complaint and the appellants essentially take in this appeal or the one the SEC advances now — is an issue we have not been called upon to decide. Several district courts have addressed the issue, though, with some requiring an expected benefit and others holding that no showing of an expected benefit is necessary. None of these courts, however, gave the issue more than perfunctory thought. After considering the policies underpinning the insider trading rules, we are led to the conclusion that the SEC must prove that a misappropriator expected to benefit from the tip.

The origin of the benefit requirement is the Supreme Court's decision in *Dirks v. SEC*, 463 U.S. 646, 103 S. Ct. 3255, 77 L. Ed. 2d 911 (1983). Addressing a case brought under the classical theory of insider trading liability, the Supreme Court held that for a tippee to be liable, the tipper (a corporate insider) would have to intend to benefit personally from his disclosure of the confidential information to the tippee. * * * Since the insiders (tippers) in *Dirks*, who disclosed the confidential information, did not do so for monetary benefit or to make a gift of valuable information, they did not personally gain, and the Court concluded that they and the tippees were not subject to insider trading liability. *Id.* at 667, 103 S. Ct. at 3267–68.

The SEC submits that an analysis of the rationale behind *Dirks*'s tipper benefit requirement demonstrates that the benefit requirement has no application in misappropriation cases. The SEC's argument proceeds in two steps. First, the SEC points out that the benefit requirement is inextricably linked to determining whether an insider has breached a duty to corporate shareholders. Second, the SEC notes that the distinguishing feature of misappropriation theory cases is that the outsider owes no fiduciary duty to the corporate shareholders. Put together, the SEC contends, it is unnecessary in misappropriation cases that it show that an outsider intended to benefit from his disclosure; since outsiders owe no duty to corporate shareholders to begin with, applying the *Dirks* test to determine if there was a breach of a duty to those same shareholders would be nonsensical.

We recognize the plausibility of the SEC's logic, but are not persuaded — mainly because it constructs an arbitrary fence between insider trading liability based upon classical and misappropriation theories. In other words, we think the SEC is unduly dichotomizing the two theories of insider trading liability. The SEC's approach essentially would allow the SEC and the courts to ignore precedent involving the classical theory of liability whenever the SEC brings its actions under a misappropriation theory, and vice versa. The Supreme Court, however, has indicated that we should attempt to synthesize, rather than polarize, insider trading law. *See O'Hagan*, 521 U.S. at 652, 117 S. Ct. at 2207 (stressing that the two theories "are complimentary, each addressing efforts to capitalize on nonpublic information through the purchase or sale of securities"). Our goal should be like that of the Court in *O'Hagan*, which sought to explain how the two theories work together to promote the policies underlying the securities laws. We believe . . . that requiring the SEC to establish that the misappropriator intended to benefit from his tip will develop consistency in insider trading caselaw.

* * *

Requiring an intent to benefit in both classical and misappropriation theory cases equalizes the positions of tippers and tippees and is also consistent with Supreme

Court precedent. Perhaps the simplest way to view potential insider trading liability is as follows: (1) an insider who trades is liable; (2) an insider who tips (rather than trades) is liable if he intends to benefit from the disclosure; (3) an outsider who trades is liable; (4) an outsider who tips (rather than trades) is liable if he intends to benefit from the disclosure.

Having concluded that the SEC must prove that Donna expected to benefit from disclosing the confidential information to Burch — the position the SEC took in its complaint — we now consider whether the SEC provided sufficient evidence for a jury reasonably to find such an expectation. Viewing the facts in the light most favorable to the SEC, we conclude that the SEC did so.

The showing needed to prove an intent to benefit is not extensive. The Supreme Court in *Dirks*, after establishing the tipper benefit requirement, proceeded to define "benefit" in very expansive terms. The Court declared that not only does an actual pecuniary gain, such as a kickback or an expectation of a reciprocal tip in the future, suffice to create a "benefit," but also cases where the tipper sought to enhance his reputation (which would translate into future earnings) or to make a gift to a trading relative or friend. *See Dirks*, 463 U.S. at 663–64, 103 S. Ct. at 3266.

In this case, the SEC presented evidence that the two appellants were "friendly," worked together for several years, and split commissions on various real estate transactions over the years. This evidence is sufficient for a jury reasonably to conclude that Donna expected to benefit from her tip to Burch by maintaining a good relationship between a friend and frequent partner in real estate deals. *See Sargent*, 229 F.2d at 77 (finding evidence of personal benefit when the tipper passed on information "to effect a reconciliation with his friend and to maintain a useful networking contact"). Accordingly, the SEC has sufficiently established the second element of a misappropriation theory claim — a breach of a duty of loyalty and confidentiality.

## III.

Having concluded that the evidence was sufficient to withstand appellants' motions for judgment as a matter of law, we turn to the question of whether the district court erred in instructing the jury on the elements of the SEC's claims and, if error occurred, whether it was harmless. The district court accepted the argument the SEC advances here: all it had to show to establish a breach of loyalty and confidentiality was that Donna acted with "severe recklessness" in letting Burch know what David had told her about Scholastic's anticipated earnings announcement. Over appellants' objections, the court instructed the jury as follows: (1) "the SEC must establish, by a preponderance of the evidence, that Mrs. Yun breached a fiduciary duty or other duty of trust and confidence to David Yun by disclosing to Mr. Burch material nonpublic information"; and (2) "the communication of such information must be intentional, or severely reckless." The court rejected the appellants' argument that the SEC had to prove that Donna acted out of a motive to benefit herself, and thus denied appellants' proposed instruction, which stated: "The disclosure has to be for the fiduciary's personal benefit to constitute a breach."

Our role "in reviewing a trial court's jury instructions [ ] is to assure that the instructions show no tendency to confuse or to mislead the jury with respect to the applicable principles of law." *Mosher*, 979 F.2d at 824 (internal quotation marks omitted). "We will not disturb a jury's verdict unless the charge, taken as a whole, is erroneous and prejudicial." *Id.* As our previous discussion makes clear, the district court erred in accepting the SEC's position that whether Donna anticipated a benefit was irrelevant. The question thus becomes whether the appellants were prejudiced.

The "severely reckless" instruction mentioned above, considered in the light of the court's overall charge on the SEC's burden of proof, permitted the SEC's counsel to tell the jury that the case turned on whether Donna tipped Burch "intentionally" or "severely recklessly." . . .

We have little difficulty in concluding that the "severely reckless" instruction materially prejudiced the appellants, such that they are entitled to a new trial. Given the court's improper instruction and the SEC's heavy reliance on that instruction in arguing its case to the jury, it is likely that the jury found against appellants on the ground that Donna acted with severe recklessness in disclosing the confidential information to Burch. *See Christopher v. Cutter Labs.*, 53 F.3d 1184, 1195 (11th Cir. 1995) (commenting that counsel's strong reliance on an erroneous instruction in closing argument "improperly guided [the jury] in its deliberations"). It is also likely that whether Donna disclosed the information for her personal benefit was not a factor in its deliberations.

*     *     *

IV.

In conclusion, we AFFIRM the district court's decisions denying appellants' motions for judgment as a matter of law. Because we find prejudicial error in the district court's instruction on the elements of the misappropriation theory of liability, we VACATE the court's judgment and REMAND the case for a new trial.

SO ORDERED.

---

The SEC's Rule 10b5-2, which provides that a marital relationship is a relationship of trust or confidence for purposes of the misappropriation theory, was adopted after the trades took place in the *Yun* case. The court noted in an omitted footnote that the rule had been adopted, but did not apply it here.

## NOTE: POSSESSION VS. USE OF INSIDE INFORMATION

In litigation, does the government or private plaintiff have to prove that the defendant actually traded based on inside information, or is it enough to prove that the defendant was in possession of the inside information at the time of the trade? The SEC adopted Rule 10b5-1 in 2000 to try to clarify this issue.

§ 240.10b5-1. Trading "on the basis of" material nonpublic information in insider trading cases.

(a) General. The "manipulative and deceptive devices" prohibited by Section 10(b) of the Act (15 U.S.C. 78j) and § 240.10b-5 thereunder include, among other things, the purchase or sale of a security of any issuer, on the basis of material nonpublic information about that security or issuer, in breach of a duty of trust or confidence that is owed directly, indirectly, or derivatively, to the issuer of that security or the shareholders of that issuer, or to any other person who is the source of the material nonpublic information.

(b) Definition of "on the basis of." Subject to the affirmative defenses in paragraph (c) of this section, a purchase or sale of a security of an issuer is "on the basis of" material nonpublic information about that security or issuer if the person making the purchase or sale was aware of the material nonpublic information when the person made the purchase or sale. . . .

Consider the following language from *Newby v. Lay (In re Enron Corp. Sec., Derivative & ERISA Litigation)*, 258 F. Supp. 2d 576 (S.D. Tex. 2003):

There has been a division among the Circuit Courts of Appeals regarding whether the language, "on the basis of material nonpublic information," employed in *O'Hagan, Chiarella, and Dirks*, in insider trading cases brought under § 10(b) and Rule 10b-5, requires a plaintiff to demonstrate that the insider defendant actually used the nonpublic information that he obtained through his position in the corporation in deciding whether to trade the securities, or whether the plaintiff need only show that the insider defendant merely possessed the nonpublic information at the time he traded the securities. The Ninth Circuit in a classic-theory, insider-trading criminal action held that the government had to show that the defendant not only had "knowing possession" of material inside information, but also that the defendant used that information in deciding to buy or sell securities, i.e., a causal connection. *United States v. Smith*, 155 F.3d 1051, 1066–69 (9th Cir. 1998), *cert. denied*, 525 U.S. 1071 (1999). Nevertheless the appellate court expressly did not decide whether that "use" standard would apply in a civil case. *Id.* at 1069 n.27. The Eleventh Circuit, in a civil enforcement action, held that while "use" of material, nonpublic information was the ultimate issue, evidence of "knowing possession" of such information raises a "strong inference" that the defendant did use it in trading, sufficient to make a *prima facie* case of liability, which the defendant would then have to rebut. *SEC v. Adler*, 137 F.3d 1325, 1337–39 (11th Cir. 1998). The Second Circuit had previously suggested that a plaintiff need only show that the insider defendant traded the securities while in "knowing possession" of material nonpublic information. *United States v. Teicher* 987 F.2d 112, 120–21 (2d Cir. 1993), *cert. denied*, 510 U.S. 976, 114 S. Ct. 467, 126 L. Ed. 2d 419 (1993).

To resolve this conflict, the SEC recently adopted a new rule, Rule 10b5-1 under the Exchange Act, effective October 23, 2000, 17 C.F.R.

§ 240.10b5-1(b), to address the question "what, if any, causal connection must be shown between the trader's possession of inside information and his or her trading." S.E.C. Release Nos. 7881, 43154, 33-7881, 34-43154, and IC-24599, 2000 SEC LEXIS 1672, 2000 WL 1201556, *21 (August 15, 2000). The rule largely adopts the Second Circuit's "knowing possession" test in *Teicher* but, as in *Adler*, employs it to create a rebuttable presumption: a plaintiff makes a *prima facie* case that the defendant is liable for insider trading merely by showing that the defendant was *"aware of the material nonpublic information"* when he made the purchase or sale of the securities. 17 C.F.R. § 240.10b5-1(b) (emphasis added). The rule establishes several affirmative defenses available to a defendant to rebut the presumption by showing that, in good faith and not as a part of a scheme to evade liability, he did not use material nonpublic information in entering into his trading decision. . . . [T]his Court defers to the SEC and adopts Rule 10b5-1's "awareness" standard.

*Id.* at 591–593.

# NOTE

The Private Securities Litigation Reform Act of 1995 was intended to remedy a perceived imbalance in favor of plaintiffs in private securities actions. Responding to plaintiffs' discovery requests can be extraordinarily expensive and, if plaintiffs achieve class certification, liability to a large number of plaintiffs could be ruinous. Therefore, Congress feared that even innocent defendants might pay to settle actions rather than litigate them and face the associated costs. The PSLRA requires plaintiffs in their initial complaints (before discovery) to specifically identify defendants' misstatements or omissions and explain why they were misleading. Plaintiffs must also state facts to establish a "strong inference" that defendants acted with scienter. In *Tellabs v. Makor*, 551 U.S. 308 (2007), the Supreme Court resolved a split in the circuits as to how plaintiffs establish such an inference.

This Court has long recognized that meritorious private actions to enforce federal antifraud securities laws are an essential supplement to criminal prosecutions and civil enforcement actions brought, respectively, by the Department of Justice and the Securities and Exchange Commission (SEC). See, *e.g., Dura Pharmaceuticals, Inc. v. Broudo*, 544 U.S. 336, 345, 125 S. Ct. 1627, 161 L. Ed. 2d 577 (2005); *J.I. Case Co. v. Borak*, 377 U.S. 426, 432, 84 S. Ct. 1555, 12 L. Ed. 2d 423 (1964). Private securities fraud actions, however, if not adequately contained, can be employed abusively to impose substantial costs on companies and individuals whose conduct conforms to the law. See *Merrill Lynch, Pierce, Fenner & Smith Inc. v. Dabit*, 547 U.S. 71, 81, 126 S. Ct. 1503, 164 L. Ed. 2d 179 (2006). As a check against abusive litigation by private parties, Congress enacted the Private Securities Litigation Reform Act of 1995 (PSLRA), 109 Stat. 737.

Exacting pleading requirements are among the control measures Congress included in the PSLRA. The Act requires plaintiffs to state with particularity both the facts constituting the alleged violation, and the facts evidencing scienter, *i.e.*, the defendant's intention "to deceive, manipulate, or defraud." *Ernst & Ernst v. Hochfelder*, 425 U.S. 185, 194, and n.12, 96 S. Ct. 1375, 47 L. Ed. 2d 668 (1976); see 15 U.S.C. § 78u-4(b)(1),(2). This case concerns the latter requirement. As set out in § 21D(b)(2) of the PSLRA, plaintiffs must "state with particularity facts giving rise to a strong inference that the defendant acted with the required state of mind." 15 U.S.C. § 78u-4(b)(2).

Congress left the key term "strong inference" undefined, and Courts of Appeals have divided on its meaning. In the case before us, the Court of Appeals for the Seventh Circuit held that the "strong inference" standard would be met if the complaint "allege[d] facts from which, if true, a reasonable person could infer that the defendant acted with the required intent." 437 F.3d 588, 602 (2006). That formulation, we conclude, does not capture the stricter demand Congress sought to convey in § 21D(b)(2). It does not suffice that a reasonable factfinder plausibly could infer from the complaint's allegations the requisite state of mind. Rather, to determine whether a complaint's scienter allegations can survive threshold inspection for sufficiency, a court governed by § 21D(b)(2) must engage in a comparative evaluation; it must consider, not only inferences urged by the plaintiff, as the Seventh Circuit did, but also competing inferences rationally drawn from the facts alleged. An inference of fraudulent intent may be plausible, yet less cogent than other, nonculpable explanations for the defendant's conduct. To qualify as "strong" within the intendment of § 21D(b)(2), we hold, an inference of scienter must be more than merely plausible or reasonable — it must be cogent and at least as compelling as any opposing inference of nonfraudulent intent.

*Tellabs*, 551 U.S. at 313–314.

The PSLRA also requires plaintiffs to establish that the defendant's actions caused the plaintiff to suffer financial loss. *See Dura Pharmaceuticals v. Broudo*, 544 U.S. 336 (2005) (plaintiff must both allege and prove loss causation). The *Halliburton* case following *Basic v. Levinson, supra*, details the impact on class certification of plaintiff's pleading obligation with respect to loss causation.

## C. SECTION 16(b): RECOVERY OF SHORT SWING PROFITS

### SECTION 16 OF THE SECURITIES EXCHANGE ACT OF 1934
15 U.S.C. § 78p (2011)

(a) *Disclosure Required.*

(1) *Directors, Officers, and Principal Stockholders Required to File.* Every person who is directly or indirectly the beneficial owner of more than 10 percent of any class of any equity security (other than an exempted security)which is registered pursuant to Section 12, or who is a director or an officer of the issuer of such security, shall file the statements required by this subsection with the Commission.

(2) *Time of Filing.* The statements required by this subsection shall be filed—

(A) at the time of the registration of such security on a national securities exchange or by the effective date of a registration statement filed pursuant to Section 12(g);

(B) within ten days after he or she becomes such beneficial owner, director, or officer, or within such shorter time as the Commission may establish by rule;

(C) if there has been a change in such ownership . . . involving such equity security, before the end of the second business day following the day on which the subject transaction has been executed, or at such other time as the Commission shall establish, by rule, in any case in which the Commission determines that such 2-day period is not feasible.

[The initial statement filed with the Commission under paragraph (A) or (B) must disclose the amount of all equity securities of the issuer of which the filer is the beneficial owner, and subsequent statements under paragraph (C) must disclose any changes in ownership.]

(b) *Profits from Purchase and Sale of Security Within Six Months.* For the purpose of preventing the unfair use of information which may have been obtained by such beneficial owner, director, or officer by reason of his relationship to the issuer, any profit realized by him from any purchase and sale, or any sale and purchase, of any equity security of such issuer (other than an exempted security) . . . within any period of less than six months, unless such security . . . was acquired in good faith in connection with a debt previously contracted, shall inure to and be recoverable by the issuer, irrespective of any intention on the part of such beneficial owner, director, or officer in entering into such transaction of holding the security . . . purchased or of not repurchasing the security . . . sold for a period exceeding six months. Suit to recover such profit may be instituted at law or in equity in any court of competent jurisdiction by the issuer, or by the owner of any security of the issuer in the name and in behalf of the issuer if the issuer shall fail or refuse to bring such suit within sixty days after request or shall fail diligently to prosecute the same thereafter; but no such suit shall be brought more than two years after the date such profit was realized. This subsection shall not be construed to cover any transaction where such beneficial owner was not such both at the time of the purchase and sale, or the sale and purchase, of the security involved, or any transaction or transactions which the Commission by rules and regulations may exempt as not comprehended within the purpose of this subsection.

A quick reading of the preceding statute should make it apparent that there are both substantial similarities and significant differences between section 10b-5 and section 16-b of the Securities Exchange Act of 1934. Both sections reflect a philosophy that insiders should not be able to reap profits from trading in the stock of a corporation where they have gained a significant informational advantage due to their position with such business. Both sections provide a means by which such insiders can be deprived of such profits in appropriate cases. However, there are significant differences in both the coverage and in the operation of the two provisions as well. Among the more significant differences are the following:

1. Section 16(b) applies only to corporations required to register with the SEC under section 12 of the 1934 Act. (Currently that means corporations with more than 500 shareholders and $10 million in net assets.) Section 10(b) and Rule 10b-5, on the other hand, reach all corporations engaged in interstate commerce and all transactions taking place on a national securities exchange, or through the mails or by interstate telephone transactions.

2. Section 16(b) applies only to "round trip" transactions, *i.e.*, a purchase and sale or a sale and purchase completed within a six-month time period. However, Rule 10b-5 applies to a single transaction, *i.e.*, either a purchase or sale is sufficient to invoke the statute.

3. Section 16(b) is a prophylactic rule which applies to all such transactions (unless exempted by the SEC pursuant to the rule making authority granted in the statute) regardless of whether non-public information was used in connection with the transaction. It applies even if the transaction occurs in good faith and without intent to profit based on the use of inside information. In contrast, Rule 10b-5 applies only if material inside information was used in connection with the purchase or sale of a security and if defendant had the requisite unlawful scienter.

4. Section 16(b) applies only to specified individuals: officers, directors, and owners of more than 10% of any class of equity security of the issuer. Rule 10b-5, on the other hand, can apply to anyone who receives material nonpublic information as either an insider, a tippee, or under circumstances where a duty is owed to the source of the information.

5. Recovery of unlawfully gained profits under section 16(b) accrues to the corporation, regardless of whether an action is brought by the corporation directly or in a shareholders' derivative action instituted by an individual shareholder. Also, attorney fees may be awarded to plaintiff's attorney, thereby giving her an incentive to discover and bring such actions. Under Rule 10b-5, individual shareholders may recover damages in their own right, either individually or in a class action.

6. Violations of section 16(b) are relatively easy to determine, since reports of purchases and sales of securities by covered individuals must be filed with the SEC within two days after the transaction. No such reporting requirement exists under Rule 10b-5.

# RELIANCE ELECTRIC CO. v. EMERSON ELECTRIC CO.
## Supreme Court of the United States
### 404 U.S. 418 (1972)

MR. JUSTICE STEWART delivered the opinion of the Court.

Section 16(b) of the Securities Exchange Act of 1934, 48 Stat. 896, 15 U.S.C. § 78p(b), provides, among other things, that a corporation may recover for itself the profits realized by an owner of more than 10% of its shares from a purchase and sale of its stock within any six-month period, provided that the owner held more than 10% "both at the time of the purchase and sale." In this case, the respondent, the owner of 13.2% of a corporation's shares, disposed of its entire holdings in two sales, both of them within six months of purchase. The first sale reduced the respondent's holdings to 9.96%, and the second disposed of the remainder. The question presented is whether the profits derived from the second sale are recoverable by the Corporation under § 16(b). We hold that they are not.

The term "such beneficial owner" refers to one who owns "more than 10 per centum of any class of any equity security (other than an exempted security) which is registered pursuant to section 12 of this title." Securities Exchange Act of 1934, § 16(a), 15 U.S.C. § 78p (a).

I

On June 16, 1967, the respondent, Emerson Electric Co., acquired 13.2% of the outstanding common stock of Dodge Manufacturing Co., pursuant to a tender offer made in an unsuccessful attempt to take over Dodge. The purchase price for this stock was $63 per share. Shortly thereafter, the shareholders of Dodge approved a merger with the petitioner, Reliance Electric Co. Faced with the certain failure of any further attempt to take over Dodge, and with the prospect of being forced to exchange its Dodge shares for stock in the merged corporation in the near future,[8] Emerson, following a plan outlined by its general counsel, decided to dispose of enough shares to bring its holdings below 10%, in order to immunize the disposal of the remainder of its shares from liability under § 16(b). Pursuant to counsel's recommendation, Emerson on August 28 sold 37,000 shares of Dodge common stock to a brokerage house at $68 per share. This sale reduced Emerson's holdings in Dodge to 9.96% of the outstanding common stock. The remaining shares were then sold to Dodge at $69 per share on September 11.

After a demand on it by Reliance for the profits realized on both sales, Emerson filed this action seeking a declaratory judgment as to its liability under § 16(b). Emerson first claimed that it was not liable at all, because it was not a 10% owner at the time of the purchase of the Dodge shares. The District Court disagreed, holding that a purchase of stock falls within § 16(b) where the purchaser becomes a 10% owner by virtue of the purchase. The Court of Appeals affirmed this holding,

---

[8] [2] The Court of Appeals for the Second Circuit has held that an exchange of shares in one corporation for those of another pursuant to a merger agreement constitutes a "sale" within the meaning of § 16(b). *Newmark v. RKO General, Inc.*, 425 F.2d 348, 354.

and Emerson did not cross-petition for certiorari. Thus that question is not before us.

Emerson alternatively argued to the District Court that, assuming it was a 10% stockholder at the time of the purchase, it was liable only for the profits on the August 28 sale of 37,000 shares, because after that time it was no longer a 10% owner within the meaning of § 16(b). After trial on the issue of liability alone, the District Court held Emerson liable for the entire amount of its profits. The court found that Emerson's sales of Dodge stock were "effected pursuant to a single predetermined plan of disposition with the overall intent and purpose of avoiding Section 16(b) liability," and construed the term "time of . . . sale" to include "the entire period during which a series of related transactions take place pursuant to a plan by which a 10% beneficial owner disposes of his stock holdings" 306 F. Supp. 588, 592.

On an interlocutory appeal under 28 U.S.C. § 1292(b), the Court of Appeals upheld the finding that Emerson "split" its sale of Dodge stock simply in order to avoid most of its potential liability under § 16(b), but it held this fact irrelevant under the statute so long as the two sales are "not legally tied to each other and [are] made at different times to different buyers . . . ." 434 F.2d 918, 926. Accordingly, the Court of Appeals reversed the District Court's judgment as to Emerson's liability for its profits on the September 11 sale, and remanded for a determination of the amount of Emerson's liability on the August 28 sale. Reliance filed a petition for certiorari, which we granted in order to consider an unresolved question under an important federal statute. 401 U.S. 1008.

II

The history and purpose of § 16(b) have been exhaustively reviewed by federal courts on several occasions since its enactment in 1934. *See, e.g., Smolowe v. Delendo Corp.*, 136 F.2d 231; *Adler v. Klawans*, 267 F.2d 840; *Blau v. Max Factor & Co.*, 342 F.2d 304. Those courts have recognized that the only method Congress deemed effective to curb the evils of insider trading was a flat rule taking the profits out of a class of transactions in which the possibility of abuse was believed to be intolerably great. As one court observed:

> "In order to achieve its goals, Congress chose a relatively arbitrary rule capable of easy administration. The objective standard of Section 16 (b)imposes strict liability upon substantially all transactions occurring within the statutory time period, regardless of the intent of the insider or the existence of actual speculation. This approach maximized the ability of the rule to eradicate speculative abuses by reducing difficulties in proof. Such arbitrary and sweeping coverage was deemed necessary to insure the optimum prophylactic effect." *Bershad v. McDonough*, 428 F.2d 693, 696.

Thus Congress did not reach every transaction in which an investor actually relies on inside information. Aperson avoids liability if he does not meet the statutory definition of an "insider," or if he sells more than six months after purchase. Liability cannot be imposed simply because the investor structured his transaction with the intent of avoiding liability under § 16(b). The question is, rather, whether the method used to "avoid" liability is one permitted by the statute.

Among the "objective standards" contained in § 16(b) is the requirement that a 10% owner be such "both at the time of the purchase and sale . . . of the security involved." Read literally, this language clearly contemplates that a statutory insider might sell enough shares to bring his holdings below 10%, and later — but still within six months — sell additional shares free from liability under the statute. Indeed, commentators on the securities laws have recommended this exact procedure for a 10% owner who, like Emerson, wishes to dispose of his holdings within six months of their purchase.

Under the approach urged by Reliance, and adopted by the District Court, the apparent immunity of profits derived from Emerson's second sale is lost where the two sales, though independent in every other respect, are "interrelated parts of a single plan." 306 F. Supp., at 592. But a "plan" to sell that is conceived within six months of purchase clearly would not fall within § 16(b) if the sale were made after the six months had expired, and we see no basis in the statute for a different result where the 10% requirement is involved rather than the six-month limitation.

The dissenting opinion reasons that "the 10% rule is based upon a conclusive statutory presumption that ownership of this quantity of stock suffices to provide access to inside information," and that it thus "follows that all sales by a more-than-10% owner within the six-month period carry the presumption of a taint, even if a prior transaction within the period has reduced the beneficial ownership to 10% or below." While there may be logic in this position, it was clearly rejected as a basis for liability when Congress included the proviso that a 10% owner must be such both at the time of the purchase and of the sale. Although the legislative history affords no explanation of the purpose of the proviso, it may be that Congress regarded one with a long-term investment of more than 10% as more likely to have access to inside information than one who moves in and out of the 10% category. But whatever the rationale of the proviso, it cannot be disregarded simply on the ground that it may be inconsistent with our assessment of the "wholesome purpose" of the Act.

To be sure, where alternative constructions of the terms of § 16(b) are possible, those terms are to be given the construction that best serves the congressional purpose of curbing short-swing speculation by corporate insiders.[9] But a construction of the term "at the time of . . . sale" that treats two sales as one upon proof of a pre-existing intent by the seller is scarcely in harmony with the congressional design of predicating liability upon an "objective measure of proof." *Smolowe v.*

---

　**9** [4] *See, e. g., Adler v. Klawans*, 267 F.2d 840 (one who is a director at the time of sale need not also have been a director at the time of purchase). In interpreting the terms "purchase" and "sale," courts have properly asked whether the particular type of transaction involved is one that gives rise to speculative abuse. *See, e. g., Bershad v. McDonough*, 428 F.2d 693 (granting of an option to purchase constitutes a "sale"). And in deciding whether an investor is an "officer" or "director" within the meaning of § 16(b), courts have allowed proof that the investor performed the functions of an officer or director even though not formally denominated as such. *Colby v. Klune*, 178 F.2d 872, 873; *cf. Feder v. Martin Marietta Corp.*, 406 F.2d 260, 262–263. The various tests employed in these cases are used to determine whether a transaction, objectively defined, falls within or without the terms of the statute. In no case is liability predicated upon "considerations of intent, lack of motive, or improper conduct" that are irrelevant in § 16(b) suits. *Blau v. Oppenheim*, 250 F. Supp. 881, 887.

*Delendo Corp., supra,* at 235. Were we to adopt the approach urged by Reliance, we could be sure that investors would not in the future provide such convenient proof of their intent as Emerson did in this case. If a "two-step" sale of a 10% owner's holdings within six months of purchase is thought to give rise to the kind of evil that Congress sought to correct through § 16(b), those transactions can be more effectively deterred by an amendment to the statute that preserves its mechanical quality than by a judicial search for the will-o'-the-wisp of an investor's "intent" in each litigated case.

* * *

The judgment is Affirmed.

[The dissent of Justice Douglas is omitted.]

## KERN COUNTY LAND CO. v. OCCIDENTAL PETROLEUM CORP.
### Supreme Court of the United States
### 411 U.S. 582 (1973)

Mr. Justice White delivered the opinion of the Court.

Section 16(b) of the Securities Exchange Act of 1934, 48 Stat. 896, 15 U.S.C. § 78p(b), provides that officers, directors, and holders of more than 10% of the listed stock of any company shall be liable to the company for any profits realized from any purchase and sale or sale and purchase of such stock occurring within a period of six months. Unquestionably, one or more statutory purchases occur when one company, seeking to gain control of another, acquires more than 10% of the stock of the latter through a tender offer made to its shareholders. But is it a § 16(b) "sale" when the target of the tender offer defends itself by merging into a third company and the tender offeror then exchanges his stock for the stock of the surviving company and also grants an option to purchase the latter stock that is not exercisable within the statutory six month period? This is the question before us in this case.

### I

On May 8, 1967, after unsuccessfully seeking to merge with Kern County Land Co. (Old Kern), Occidental Petroleum Corp. (Occidental) announced an offer, to expire on June 8, 1967, to purchase on a first-come, first-served basis 500,000 shares of Old Kern common stock at a price of $83.50 per share plus a brokerage commission of $1.50 per share. By May 10, 1967, 500,000 shares, more than 10% of the outstanding shares of Old Kern, had been tendered. On May 11, Occidental extended its offer to encompass an additional 500,000 shares. At the close of the tender offer, on June 8, 1967, Occidental owned 887,549 shares of Old Kern.

Immediately upon the announcement of Occidental's tender offer, the Old Kern management undertook to frustrate Occidental's takeover attempt. A management letter to all stockholders cautioned against tender and indicated that Occidental's offer might not be the best available, since the management was engaged in merger discussions with several companies. When Occidental extended its tender offer, the president of Old Kern sent a telegram to all stockholders again advising against tender. In addition, Old Kern undertook merger discussions with Tenneco, Inc. (Tenneco), and, on May 19, 1967, the Board of Directors of Old Kern announced that it had approved a merger proposal advanced by Tenneco. Under the terms of the merger, Tenneco would acquire the assets, property, and goodwill of Old Kern, subject to its liabilities, through "Kern County Land Co." (New Kern), a new corporation to be formed by Tenneco to receive the assets and carry on the business of Old Kern. The shareholders of Old Kern would receive a share of Tenneco cumulative convertible preference stock in exchange for each share of Old Kern common stock which they owned. On the same day, May 19, Occidental, in a quarterly report to stockholders, appraised the value of the new Tenneco stock at $105 per share.

Occidental, seeing its tender offer and takeover attempt being blocked by the Old Kern-Tenneco "defensive" merger, countered on May 25 and 31 with two mandamus actions in the California courts seeking to obtain extensive inspection of Old Kern books and records. Realizing that, if the Old Kern-Tenneco merger were approved and successfully closed, Occidental would have to exchange its Old Kern shares for Tenneco stock and would be locked into a minority position in Tenneco, Occidental took other steps to protect itself. Between May 30 and June 2, it negotiated an arrangement with Tenneco whereby Occidental granted Tenneco Corp., a subsidiary of Tenneco, an option to purchase at $105 per share all of the Tenneco preference stock to which Occidental would be entitled in exchange for its Old Kern stock when and if the Old Kern-Tenneco merger was closed. The premium to secure the option, at $10 per share, totaled $8,866,230 and was to be paid immediately upon the signing of the option agreement. If the option were exercised, the premium was to be applied to the purchase price. By the terms of the option agreement, the option could not be exercised prior to December 9, 1967, a date six months and one day after expiration of Occidental's tender offer. On June 2, 1967, within six months of the acquisition by Occidental of more than 10% ownership of Old Kern, Occidental and Tenneco Corp. executed the option. Soon thereafter, Occidental announced that it would not oppose the Old Kern-Tenneco merger and dismissed its state court suits against Old Kern.

The Old Kern-Tenneco merger plan was presented to and approved by Old Kern shareholders at their meeting on July 17, 1967. Occidental refrained from voting its Old Kern shares, but in a letter read at the meeting Occidental stated that it had determined prior to June 2 not to oppose the merger and that it did not consider the plan unfair or inequitable. Indeed, Occidental indicated that, had it been voting, it would have voted in favor of the merger.

Meanwhile, the Securities and Exchange Commission had refused Occidental's request to exempt from possible § 16(b) liability Occidental's exchange of its Old Kern stock for the Tenneco preference shares that would take place when and if the merger transaction were closed. Various Old Kern stockholders, with Occidental's interests in mind, thereupon sought to delay consummation of the merger by instituting various lawsuits in the state and federal courts. These attempts were unsuccessful, however, and preparations for the merger neared completion with an Internal Revenue Service ruling that consummation of the plan would result in a tax-free exchange with no taxable gain or loss to Old Kern shareholders, and with the issuance of the necessary approval of the merger closing by the California Commissioner of Corporations.

The Old Kern-Tenneco merger transaction was closed on August 30. Old Kern shareholders thereupon became irrevocably entitled to receive Tenneco preference stock, share for share in exchange for their Old Kern stock. Old Kern was dissolved and all of its assets, including "all claims, demands, rights and choses in action accrued or to accrue under and by virtue of the Securities Exchange Act of 1934 . . .," were transferred to New Kern.

The option granted by Occidental on June 2, 1967, was exercised on December 11, 1967. Occidental, not having previously availed itself of its right, exchanged certificates representing 887,549 shares of Old Kern stock for a certificate representing a like number of shares of Tenneco preference stock. The certificate was then endorsed over to the optionee-purchaser, and in return $84,229,185 was credited to Occidental's accounts at various banks. Adding to this amount the $8,886,230 premium paid in June, Occidental received $93,905,415 for its Old Kern stock (including the 1,900 shares acquired prior to issuance of its tender offer). In addition, Occidental received dividends totaling $1,793,439.22. Occidental's total profit was $19,506,419.22 on the shares obtained through its tender offer.

On October 17, 1967, New Kern instituted a suit under § 16(b) against Occidental to recover the profits which Occidental had realized as a result of its dealings in Old Kern stock. The complaint alleged that the execution of the Occidental-Tenneco option on June 2, 1967, and the exchange of Old Kern shares for shares of Tenneco to which Occidental became entitled pursuant to the merger closed on August 30, 1967, were both "sales" within the coverage of § 16(b). Since both acts took place within six months of the date on which Occidental became the owner of more than 10% of the stock of Old Kern, New Kern asserted that § 16(b) required surrender of the profits realized by Occidental. New Kern eventually moved for summary judgment, and, on December 27, 1970, the District Court granted summary judgment in favor of New Kern. *Abrams v. Occidental Petroleum Corp.*, 323 F. Supp. 570 (SDNY 1970). The District Court held that the execution of the option on June 2, 1967, and the exchange of Old Kern shares for shares of Tenneco on August 30, 1967, were "sales" under § 16(b). The Court ordered Occidental to disgorge its profits plus interest. In a supplemental opinion, Occidental was also ordered to refund the dividends which it had received plus interest.

On appeal, the Court of Appeals reversed and ordered summary judgment entered in favor of Occidental. *Abrams v. Occidental Petroleum Corp.*, 450 F.2d 157 (CA2 1971). The Court held that neither the option nor the exchange constituted a "sale" within the purview of § 16(b). We granted certiorari. 405 U.S. 1064 (1972). We affirm.

## II

Section 16(b) provides, inter alia, that a statutory insider must surrender to the issuing corporation "any profit realized by him from any purchase and sale, or any sale and purchase, of any equity security of such issuer . . . within any period of less than six months." As specified in its introductory clause, § 16(b) was enacted "for the purpose of preventing the unfair use of information which may have been obtained by [a statutory insider] . . . by reason of his relationship to the issuer." Congress recognized that short-swing speculation by stockholders with advance, inside information would threaten the goal of the Securities Exchange Act to "insure the maintenance of fair and honest markets." 15 U.S.C. § 78b. Insiders could exploit information not generally available to others to secure quick profits. As we have noted, "the only method Congress deemed effective to curb the evils of insider trading was a flat rule taking the profits out of a class of transactions in which the possibility of abuse was believed to be intolerably great." *Reliance Electric Co. v. Emerson Electric Co.*, 404 U.S. 418, 422 (1972). As stated in the report of the Senate Committee, the bill aimed at protecting the public "by preventing directors, officers, and principal stockholders of a corporation . . . from speculating in the stock on the basis of information not available to others." S. Rep. No. 792, 73d Cong., 2d Sess., 9 (1934).

Although traditional cash-for-stock transactions that result in a purchase and sale or a sale and purchase within the six-month, statutory period are clearly within the purview of § 16(b), the courts have wrestled with the question of inclusion or exclusion of certain "unorthodox" transactions. The statutory definitions of "purchase" and "sale" are broad and, at least arguably, reach many transactions not ordinarily deemed a sale or purchase. In deciding whether borderline transactions are within the reach of the statute, the courts have come to inquire whether the transaction may serve as a vehicle for the evil which Congress sought to prevent — the realization of short-swing profits based upon access to inside information — thereby endeavoring to implement congressional objectives without extending the reach of the statute beyond its intended limits. The statute requires the inside, short-swing trader to disgorge all profits realized on all "purchases" and "sales" within the specified time period, without proof of actual abuse of insider information, and without proof of intent to profit on the basis of such information. Under these strict terms, the prevailing view is to apply the statute only when its application would serve its goals. "Where alternative constructions of the terms of § 16(b) are possible, those terms are to be given the construction that best serves the congressional purpose of curbing short-swing speculation by corporate insiders." *Reliance Electric Co. v. Emerson Electric* Co., 404 U.S., at 424. *See Blau v. Lamb*, 363 F.2d 507 (CA2 1966), *cert. denied*, 385 U.S. 1002 (1967). Thus, "in interpreting the terms 'purchase' and 'sale,' courts have properly asked whether the particular type of transaction involved is one that gives rise to speculative abuse." *Reliance Electric Co. v. Emerson Electric Co., supra*, at 424 n.4.

In the present case, it is undisputed that Occidental became a "beneficial owner" within the terms of § 16(b) when, pursuant to its tender offer, it "purchased" more than 10% of the outstanding shares of Old Kern. We must decide, however, whether a "sale" within the ambit of the statute took place either when Occidental became irrevocably bound to exchange its shares of Old Kern for shares of Tenneco pursuant to the terms of the merger agreement between Old Kern and Tenneco or when Occidental gave an option to Tenneco to purchase from Occidental the Tenneco shares so acquired.

## III

On August 30, 1967, the Old Kern-Tenneco merger agreement was signed, and Occidental became irrevocably entitled to exchange its shares of Old Kern stock for shares of Tenneco preference stock. Concededly, the transaction must be viewed as though Occidental had made the exchange on that day. But, even so, did the exchange involve a "sale" of Old Kern shares within the meaning of § 16(b)? We agree with the Court of Appeals that it did not, for we think it totally unrealistic to assume or infer from the facts before us that Occidental either had or was likely to have access to inside information, by reason of its ownership of more than 10% of the outstanding shares of Old Kern, so as to afford it an opportunity to reap speculative, short-swing profits from its disposition within six months of its tender-offer purchases.

It cannot be contended that Occidental was an insider when, on May 8, 1967, it made an irrevocable offer to purchase 500,000 shares of Old Kern stock at a price substantially above market. At that time, it owned only 1,900 shares of Old Kern stock, far fewer than the 432,000 shares needed to constitute the 10% ownership required by the statute. There is no basis for finding that, at the time the tender offer was commenced, Occidental enjoyed an insider's opportunity to acquire information about Old Kern's affairs.

\* \* \*

By May 10, 1967, Occidental had acquired more than 10% of the outstanding shares of Old Kern. It was thus a statutory insider when, on May 11, it extended its tender offer to include another 500,000 shares. We are quite unconvinced, however, that the situation had changed materially with respect to the possibilities of speculative abuse of inside information by Occidental. Perhaps Occidental anticipated that extending its offer would increase the likelihood of the ultimate success of its takeover attempt or the occurrence of a defensive merger. But, again, the expectation of such benefits was unrelated to the use of information unavailable to other stockholders or members of the public with sufficient funds and the intention to make the purchases Occidental had offered to make before June 8, 1967.

The possibility that Occidental had, or had the opportunity to have, any confidential information about Old Kern before or after May 11, 1967, seems extremely remote. Occidental was, after all, a tender offeror, threatening to seize control of Old Kern, displace its management, and use the company for its own ends. The Old Kern management vigorously and immediately opposed Occidental's efforts. Twice it communicated with its stockholders, advising against acceptance of Occidental's offer and indicating prior to May 11 and prior to Occidental's extension of its offer, that there was a possibility of an imminent merger and a more profitable exchange. Old Kern's management refused to discuss with Occidental officials the subject of an Old Kern-Occidental merger. Instead, it undertook negotiations with Tenneco and forthwith concluded an agreement, announcing the merger terms on May 19. Requests by Occidental for inspection of Old Kern records were sufficiently frustrated by Old Kern's management to force Occidental to litigate to secure the information it desired.

There is, therefore, nothing in connection with Occidental's acquisition of Old

Kern stock pursuant to its tender offer to indicate either the possibility of inside information being available to Occidental by virtue of its stock ownership or the potential for speculative abuse of such inside information by Occidental. Much the same can be said of the events leading to the exchange of Occidental's Old Kern stock for Tenneco preferred, which is one of the transactions that is sought to be classified a "sale" under § 16(b). The critical fact is that the exchange took place and was required pursuant to a merger between Old Kern and Tenneco. That merger was not engineered by Occidental but was sought by Old Kern to frustrate the attempts of Occidental to gain control of Old Kern. Occidental obviously did not participate in or control the negotiations or the agreement between Old Kern and Tenneco. . . .

. . . We do not suggest that an exchange of stock pursuant to a merger may never result in § 16(b) liability. But the involuntary nature of Occidental's exchange, when coupled with the absence of the possibility of speculative abuse of inside information, convinces us that § 16(b) should not apply to transactions such as this one.

IV

Petitioner also claims that the Occidental-Tenneco option agreement should itself be considered a sale, either because it was the kind of transaction the statute was designed to prevent or because the agreement was an option in form but a sale in fact. But the mere execution of an option to sell is not generally regarded as a "sale." And we do not find in the execution of the Occidental-Tenneco option agreement a sufficient possibility for the speculative abuse of inside information with respect to Old Kern's affairs to warrant holding that the option agreement was itself a "sale" within the meaning of § 16(b). The mutual advantages of the arrangement appear quite clear. As the District Court found, Occidental wanted to avoid the position of a minority stockholder with a huge investment in a company over which it had no control and in which it had not chosen to invest. On the other hand, Tenneco did not want a potentially troublesome minority stockholder that had just been vanquished in a fight for the control of Old Kern. Motivations like these do not smack of insider trading; and it is not clear to us, as it was not to the Court of Appeals, how the negotiation and execution of the option agreement gave Occidental any possible opportunity to trade on inside information it might have obtained from its position as a major stockholder of Old Kern. Occidental wanted to get out, but only at a date more than six months thence. It was willing to get out at a price of $105 per share, a price at which it had publicly valued Tenneco preferred on May 19 when the Tenneco-Old Kern agreement was announced. In any event, Occidental was dealing with the putative new owners of Old Kern, who undoubtedly knew more about Old Kern and Tenneco's affairs than did Occidental. If Occidental had leverage in dealing with Tenneco, it is incredible that its source was inside information rather than the fact of its large stock ownership itself.

* * *

Nor can we agree that we must reverse the Court of Appeals on the ground that the option agreement was in fact a sale because the premium paid was so large as to make the exercise of the option almost inevitable, particularly when coupled with

Tenneco's desire to rid itself of a potentially troublesome stockholder. The argument has force, but resolution of the question is very much a matter of judgment, economic and otherwise, and the Court of Appeals rejected the argument. That court emphasized that the premium paid was what experts had said the option was worth, the possibility that the market might drop sufficiently in the six months following execution of the option to make exercise unlikely, and the fact that here, unlike the situation in *Bershad v. McDonough*, 428 F.2d 693 (CA7 1970), the option or did not surrender practically all emoluments of ownership by executing the option. Nor did any other special circumstances indicate that the parties understood and intended that the option was in fact a sale. We see no satisfactory basis or reason for disagreeing with the judgment of the Court of Appeals in this respect.

The judgment of the Court of Appeals is affirmed.

So ordered.

MR. JUSTICE DOUGLAS, with whom MR. JUSTICE BRENNAN and MR. JUSTICE STEWART concur, dissenting.

The Court, in resorting to an ad hoc analysis of the "possibility for the speculative abuse of inside information," charts a course for the interpretation of § 16 (b) of the Securities Exchange Act of 1934, 15 U. S. C. § 78p (b), that in my mind undermines the congressional purpose. I respectfully dissent.

I

"The statute is written broadly, and the liability it imposes is strict." *Reliance Electric Co. v. Emerson Electric Co.*, 404 U.S. 418, 431 (Douglas, J., dissenting). Except for narrowly drawn exceptions, it is all-inclusive. . . . By its own terms, the section subsumes all transactions that are technically purchases and sales and applies irrespective of any actual or potential use of inside information to gain a trading advantage. The conclusion seems inescapable that Occidental Petroleum Corp. (Occidental) purchased and sold shares of Kern County Land Co. (Old Kern) within a six-month period and that this "round trip" in Old Kern stock is covered by the literal terms of § 16 (b).

Occidental, pursuant to a cash tender offer, acquired in excess of 880,000 shares of Old Kern during May and June 1967. It is undisputed that these acquisitions were purchases within the meaning of the section. On August 30, 1967, Old Kern sold its assets to a newly formed subsidiary of Tenneco Corp., Kern County Land Co. (New Kern), in exchange for cumulative convertible preference stock of Tenneco, Inc. (Tenneco), Tenneco Corp.'s parent. Old Kern was dissolved in October 1967 (within six months of the tender offer), and each shareholder became irrevocably entitled to receive, share for share, for his Old Kern stock the cumulative convertible preference stock of Tenneco.

The question presented to us is whether this exchange of shares constituted a "sale" of the Old Kern shares. The term "sale," as used in the Securities Exchange Act, includes "any contract to sell or otherwise dispose of." 15 U.S.C. § 78c(a)(14). Clearly, Occidental "disposed" of its Old Kern shares through the Old Kern-

Tenneco consolidation. Its status as a shareholder of Old Kern terminated, and it became instead a shareholder of Tenneco, privy to all the rights conferred by the Tenneco shares. In my view, we need look no further. . . .

*  *  *

The very construction of § 16(b) reinforces the conclusion that the section is based in the first instance on a totally objective appraisal of the relevant transactions. *See Smolowe v. Delendo Corp., supra,* at 236. Had the draftsmen intended that the operation of the section hinge on abuse of access to inside information it would have been anomalous to limit the section to purchases and sales occurring within six months. Indeed, the purpose of the six-month limitation, coupled with the definition of an insider, was to create a conclusive presumption that an insider who turns a short-swing profit in the stock of his corporation had access to inside information and capitalized on that information by speculating in the stock. But, the majority departs from the benign effects of this presumption when it assumes that it is "totally unrealistic to assume or infer from the facts before us that Occidental either had or was likely to have access to inside information . . . ." *Ante.* The majority abides by this assumption even for that period after which Occidental became a 10% shareholder and then extended its tender offer in order to purchase additional Old Kern shares.

*  *  *

Thus, the courts will be caught up in an *ad hoc* analysis of each transaction, determining both from the economics of the transaction and the *modus operandi* of the insider whether there exists the possibility of speculative abuse of inside information. Instead of a section that is easy to administer and by its clear-cut terms discourages litigation, we have instead a section that fosters litigation because the Court's decision holds out the hope for the insider that he may avoid § 16(b) liability. In short, the majority destroys much of the section's prophylactic effect.

## C.R.A. REALTY CORP. v. FREMONT GENERAL CORP.
### United States Court of Appeals, Ninth Circuit
### 5 F.3d 1341 (1993)

NOONAN, CIRCUIT JUDGE:

C.R.A. Realty Corp. (C.R.A.) brought a stockholder's suit for the recovery of short-swing profits under § 16(b) of the Securities Exchange Act, 15 U.S.C. § 78p(b), against Fremont General Corp. (Fremont) and Lee Emerson McIntyre (McIntyre). The precise issue before the district court was one of first impression. That court gave judgment for McIntyre. We reverse and direct that judgment be entered for the plaintiff.

### FACTS

Fremont has issued 8,296,929 shares of common stock. McIntyre and his wife were co-settlors, and McIntyre the sole trustee, of an inter vivos trust of which he and his wife were joint life income beneficiaries with power to invade the corpus. As of January 1, 1991, the trust owned 1,400,000 shares of Fremont. McIntyre, therefore, was the beneficial owner of more than 10 percent of the stock of Fremont, whose securities were registered under the Securities Exchange Act of 1934, 15 U.S.C. § 78l(g). As such, McIntyre was subject to § 16(b)'s prohibition of short-swing insider trading of Fremont's stock.

On February 18, 1988 McIntyre and his wife through the L.E. McIntyre & Co.partnership loaned their son David $2 million, in return for which David executed a demand note and pledged 198,187 shares of Fremont.

In December 1989 David McIntyre's employment was terminated by Fremont, and he desired to sell all his stock in the company. On January 4, 1990 an agreement was made between him and his father's partnership by which he agreed to sell the 198,187 shares of Fremont to the partnership for a price of $19.835 per share or a total of $3,931,039.15. The larger portion of this amount was allocated by the agreement to the payment of the outstanding loan plus interest. In the nearly two years that had elapsed since the making of the loan, the value of the Fremont stock had risen, so in order to satisfy the preexisting debt of the son to the father, the son needed to sell only 141,193 shares. The remaining 56,694 shares were not acquired by McIntyre in satisfaction of any preexisting debt. The partnership agreed to pay the residue of the purchase price of $1,124,525.49 by a negotiable promissory note.

On March 28, 1990 McIntyre, through the partnership, sold 70,000 shares of Fremont on the open market. The price was $20.75.

## PROCEEDINGS

On April 13, 1990 C.R.A., a stockholder in Fremont, made demand upon Fremont to recover the short-swing profit allegedly made by McIntyre on the sale. Sixty days expired and Fremont did not respond. C.R.A. began this suit in the United States District Court for the Southern District of New York. By agreement of the parties it was discontinued without prejudice and reinstituted in the Central District of California.

Both parties moved for summary judgment. The district court found that the facts were not in dispute and that the shares received to retire the debt were clearly exempt from § 16(b) under the explicit provision of that statute exempting a security "acquired in good faith in connection with a debt previously contracted." The district court noted there was no precedent "in which the statutory insider acquired shares in part from the cancellation of the debt and in part for additional consideration." The court concluded that the transaction as a whole "did not clearly fall within or outside the purview" of § 16(b). The court then observed that the transaction did not seem to present "even the potential for abuse of insider information." The court treated the situation as one in which the loan was "over-collateralized." It concluded that McIntyre should not be penalized because of this fact and all of the stock sold should be treated as exempt. The court granted summary judgment in his favor.

C.R.A. appeals.

## ANALYSIS

The literal language of § 16(b) applies to the sale of the 56,694 shares that are the subject of this appeal. That number of shares was acquired by McIntyre by purchase on January 4, 1990 and that number of shares was not within the preexisting debt exemption when McIntyre sold 70,000 shares on March 28, 1990. The statute is peremptory in prescribing that "any profit realized" by a beneficial owner "from any purchase and sale" within "any period of less than six months" shall inure to the benefit of the issuer. 15 U.S.C. § 78p(b).

The statute has been glossed as not applying in the case of a purchase by a beneficial owner followed by a merger of the issuer effecting the disposition of its shares within the prohibited period. *Kern County Land Co. v. Occidental Corp.*, 411 U.S. 582 (1973). The Court recognized that such a situation was not an ordinary purchase and sale; in the jargon now current, it was an "unorthodox" transaction. *Id.* at 593. As the beneficial owner did not bring about the transaction by which its shares were disposed of, the Court was unwilling to construe the involuntary exchange at the time of merger as a "sale" within the meaning of § 16(b). *Id.* at 596, 93 S. Ct. at 1745.

It was in the spirit of *Kern County* that the district court interpreted § 16(b) in this case not to include the disposition of any of the shares acquired. The difficulty with this approach is that McIntyre acquired stock to settle the debt, and he acquired additional stock. McIntyre bought and sold on his own volition. There was nothing involuntary about either his purchase or his sale. *Kern County* has no application. *Colan v. Mesa Petroleum* Co., 951 F.2d 1512, 1522–1523 (9th Cir. 1991), *cert. denied*, 112 S. Ct. 1943 (1992).

The original loan may have been "over-collateralized," but at the time of the settlement the shares necessary to settle the debt were agreed by both parties to be less than the shares McIntyre agreed to purchase. These additional shares do not fit within the statutory exemption. True, the exemption has a certain vagueness, speaking of shares "acquired in good faith in connection with a debt previously contracted," a phrase slightly broader than in direct discharge of a debt. *Rheem Manufacturing Co. v. Rheem*, 295 F.2d 473, 476 (9th Cir. 1961). But the shares acquired must have a relation to the debt discharged. *Id.* Here is not a case where a lender obtained a security interest in shares worth more than the amount of a loan, then sold them when the debtor defaulted, making a profit because the sales proceeds exceeded the amount loaned plus interest. In the case before us, the agreement for purchase and sale of the stock, and the deposition testimony, demonstrated, and the parties agree, that in January 1990, L.E. McIntyre & Company acquired 141,493 shares in connection with the earlier loan as an offset against it, and an additional 56,694 shares for cash and a note. No contention is made that the 56,594 shares was acquired as security for the loan. The parties agree that 56,694 shares are not covered by the loan exemption, and 141,493 shares are. McIntyre's argument is that since he owned 141,493 exempt shares, and only sold 70,000 shares within six months of acquisition, the exemption should apply to the sale.

Here, McIntyre's good faith is not challenged. But we cannot construe the exemption as broadly as the district court did. The crux of the matter is that the potential for abuse of insider information was present. An insider could have known that Fremont stock was likely to go up and have wanted to acquire more stock to sell on the rise. Good faith in buying does not insulate McIntyre when he bought and sold within the forbidden period.

There can be no question of treating McIntyre's sale of 70,000 shares as a sale of only his exempt stock. That procedure is as inadmissible as supposing that he did not sell any of the stock acquired in January 1990 from his son but sold holdings of his own, acquired earlier. To analyze the transaction in that way would be, in effect, to earmark shares of stock and to let an insider decide which shares he was selling. Long ago the mistake in such an analysis was pointed out by Judge Learned Hand, *Gratz v. Claughton*, 187 F.2d 46, 50–51 (2d Cir. 1951), *cert. denied*, 341 U.S. 920 (1951). Shares of stock are as fungible as bushels of wheat. Because McIntyre purchased 56,694 non-exempt shares and then sold 70,000 shares within six months, he must disgorge his profit on all the non-exempt shares. In calculating the subtrahend and the minuend for purposes of § 16(b) a court must take non-exempt shares acquired within the prohibited six months and subtract their cost from the price of the minuend, the shares sold within the period, and so determine the profits realized, as follows:

| Sales proceeds | 56,694 shares x $20.75 | $1,176,400.50 |
| less cost | 56,694 shares x $19.835 | $1,124,525.49 |
| profit on non-exempt shares | | $51,875.01 |

This calculation leaves 13,306 shares of the 70,000 sold to be covered by the debt exemption, so, as the parties agree, no profit need be disgorged on those 13,306 shares.

As there is no dispute as to the facts, and as the law is here settled, the judgment is REVERSED and the case is REMANDED to the district court for entry of judgment in favor of C.R.A. in accordance with this opinion. C.R.A. may apply to the district court for attorney's fees.

# NOTES

**1.** The cases arising under section 16(b) of the Securities Exchange Act, 15 U.S.C. § 78p (1981), reflect a tension between, on the one hand, the desire to have an automatic, self-executing rule and, on the other hand, to avoid applying the rule to transactions not within its spirit. Given the fact that section 16(b) gives the SEC the power to exempt transactions not within the purpose of this section 16(b), should the courts properly consider granting any additional exemptions on their own?

**2.** In 1991, and again in 1996, the SEC adopted a comprehensive set of regulations designed to reduce significantly many of the ambiguities which had led to litigation under the rule. 17 C.F.R. §§ 240.16(a)-1 (1997) *et seq.*; Securities Exchange Act Release No. 34-28869, 56 Fed. Reg. 7241 (Feb. 8, 1991); Rel. No. 34-37260 (June 14, 1996). These rules deal with various matters, including the definition of "officers," "beneficial owners," the treatment of derivative securities such as options and warrants, and purchases and sales by employee benefit plans.

## PROBLEMS

The easiest way to learn Section 16 is through problems. Approach the following set of problems by asking these questions:

- Does section 16 apply?
- Is there a sale price that is higher than a purchase price?
- Are the purchase and sale within six months of each other? (It doesn't matter whether the sale or the purchase occurs first in time.)
- Is the trader a statutory defendant (an officer, director, or 10% shareholder)? Keep in mind that, if liability is asserted based on officer or director status, the defendant need only have that status at the time of EITHER the purchase or sale. If liability is asserted based on 10% shareholder status, the defendant must have that status at the time of BOTH the purchase and sale.

The statute is interpreted to find the largest possible amount of liability, so if there are several transactions within a 6-month period, the highest sale price will be matched with the lowest purchase price, and the court will work inward from there.

**1.** Jack and Jill form a corporation to deliver bottled water. Each owns 50 of the 100 shares outstanding. Each is a director and an officer of the corporation. On March 1, Jill buys 30 of Jack's shares for $50 per share. On April 1, she sells the shares back to him at $60 per share. Is Jill liable under § 16(b)?

**2.** Peter Piper is the Chairman and CEO of Pickled Peppers, Inc. ("PPI"), a corporation whose stock is listed on the New York Stock Exchange. For several years, Peter has owned 200,000 of the company's 3,000,000 outstanding shares. Peter had the following transactions in PPI stock:

**a.** On January 1, Peter bought 50,000 shares for $20 each. On May 1, he sold 50,000 shares for $30 each. Liability?

What if Peter had resigned from his positions with the company in March? Would that change your answer?

What if Peter said that the stock he sold in May was stock that he had held for several years, not the stock that he purchased in January?

What if Peter sold only 10,000 shares in May?

**b.** On January 1, Peter sold 50,000 shares of stock for $30 each. On May 1, he bought 50,000 shares for $20 each. Liability?

**c.** On January 1, Peter bought 50,000 shares at $20. In March, he sold 10,000 shares at $30. In April, he sold 40,000 shares at $10. Liability? Did Peter make a profit?

**d.** On January 1, Peter's wife, Petunia, bought 50,000 shares at $10. In March, she sold them for $40. Liability?

The statute speaks of "beneficial" ownership, a concept that is broader than record ownership. Beneficial ownership is defined in Rule 13d-3 to include sole or shared power to vote shares and/or buy or sell them. *See Jammies Int'l, Inc. v.*

*Lazarus*, 713 F. Supp. 83 (S.D.N.Y. 1989). Charles Lazarus was the Chairman and CEO of Toys "R" Us. His wife sold some of her Toys "R" Us stock within six months of his exercise of options to purchase Toys "R" Us stock at a price lower than her sale price. The plaintiff asserted that Lazarus should be considered the beneficial owner of his wife's shares, and thus his purchase and her sale should be matched. The court found, however, that Lazarus and his wife kept their finances entirely separate. He had no control over his wife's decision whether to buy or sell her own stock, and he received no financial benefit from her purchases or sales. Therefore, he was not the beneficial owner of her shares, and was not liable for short swing profits.

**3.** In December, Jenny Wren inherited 500,000 shares of PPI from her grandfather.

**a.** On May 1, she sold all 500,000 shares for $50 each. On June 1, she bought 100,000 shares for $30 each. Liability?

**b.** Same as a, except that she purchased 500,000 shares on June 1. Same result?

**c.** On January 1, Jenny bought 100 shares for $20 each. On May 1, she sold 500,000 shares for $50 each. Liability? If so, how much?

**d.** Jenny had the following transactions:

On January 1, she bought 100,000 shares for $20 per share.

On February 1, she sold 50,000 shares for $30.

On March 1, she sold 500,000 shares for $40.

On April 1, she bought 50,000 shares for $10.

On May 1, she bought 500,000 shares for $5.

Liability? If so, how much?

Securities that are convertible into equity securities (*e.g.*, debentures that are convertible into common stock) are also covered under section 16. To figure out liability problems involving convertible securities, it is sometimes necessary to calculate whether the holder counts as a 10% equity holder, and thus a statutory defendant. For this purpose, assume that the potential defendant has converted all of her securities into equity, but that no other convertible security holders have done so. Then determine her status based on the number of shares that would be outstanding following her conversion.

For instance, suppose that there are 900,000 shares of common stock outstanding. There are also 2,000 convertible debentures outstanding, and each debenture is convertible into 1,000 shares of common stock. Assume that Debra owns 100 debentures. When calculating her potential liability, we would first assume that Debra converted her debentures into common stock, resulting in ownership of 100,000 shares of stock (but that no other convertible debenture holders converted). Since there were 900,000 shares outstanding before she converted, her additional shares would result in there being 1,000,000 shares outstanding. She would own 10%, and would thus be a statutory defendant.

# Chapter 12

# PROXY REGULATION AND DISCLOSURE

## A. PROXY REGULATION

The corporation is managed by a board of directors. State law provides that the directors are elected by the shareholders, usually at the annual meeting of shareholders. The Securities Exchange Act of 1934 in section 14 requires compliance with rules promulgated by the Securities and Exchange Commission (SEC) when a corporation solicits proxies. Section 14 applies only to certain companies, at present those with assets of more than $10 million and a class of equity with 500 or more shareholders of record. Such corporations are commonly referred to as "reporting companies." Thus, when a reporting company desires to hold a shareholders' meeting and to obtain proxies to elect the board of directors, it must solicit its proxies in accordance with SEC rules. These rules require a great deal of disclosure about the company entirely apart from the names of the directors and their qualifications. Rule 14a-3 states the information that must be furnished to the shareholders. Rule 14a-4 states the requirements for the form of proxy. The document sent to the shareholders is generally called the Proxy Statement. State law requires notice of an annual meeting of shareholders. Generally the notice must be given at least 60 days before the meeting, and a record date must be set for the purpose of determining which shareholders are entitled to vote. For a publicly held company, complying with state law is an easy task. However, the solicitation of the proxies of shareholders makes the corporation subject to section 14 which imposes additional requirements as well as potential liabilities. Corporations must comply with the proxy rules not only in connection with the annual meeting of shareholders, but whenever they solicit their shareholders' votes, e.g., when the shareholders must vote to approve a merger pursuant to a state law requirement, or when the shareholders vote to approve a merger even when such vote is not required by state law. Two examples of why corporations would have their shareholders vote on a matter would be to comply with a rule of a stock exchange or to approve a stock option plan if federal tax law required such approval in order to obtain favorable tax treatment.

Violation of section 14 may create implied civil liabilities. *See J.I. Case Co. v. Borak*, 377 U.S. 426 (1964). That case, decided by the U.S. Supreme Court, concerns the judicial implication of a right of action from statutory provisions. The federal courts have created causes of action from federal securities statutes even in the absence of an express cause of action. The most far reaching effect of this doctrine is the jurisprudence developed under 10b-5. Note that Rule 10b-5 applies to any person who violates its terms. There is no requirement that limits its application to large publicly held corporations.

# MILLENCO L.P. v. MEVC DRAPER FISHER JURVETSON FUND I, INC.

Court of Chancery of Delaware

824 A.2d 11 (2002)

LAMB, VICE CHANCELLOR

I.

The plaintiff in this action is Millenco L.P., a privately owned company engaged in the business of investing for profit. Millenco is the largest stockholder of the defendant meVC Draper Fisher Jurvetson Fund I, Inc. (the "Fund"), owning over 6.3% of the Fund shares, purchased on the open market for a total purchase price of more than $10 million. Millenco has owned those shares continuously since before the record date of the Fund's 2001 Annual Meeting of Stockholders ("2001 Annual Meeting").

The Fund is a Delaware corporation organized as a closed-end mutual fund that has elected to be treated as a business development company under Section 54 the Investment Company Act of 1940, 15 U.S.C. § 80a, et seq. (the "1940 Act"). The Fund's stated investment objective is long-term capital appreciation from venture capital investments in information technology companies. In March 2000, the Fund conducted an initial public offering of its stock at $20 per share, realizing $311,650,000 of net proceeds. As of August 30, 2001, the closing price of the Fund's stock on the New York Stock Exchange had declined to $7.85 per share and the Fund's net asset value had declined to $12.35 per share.

The other defendants in this action are Larry J. Gerhard, Harold E. Hughes, Jr., Chauncey F. Lufkin and John Grillos, who are the current members of the Fund's board of directors. Before the IPO, the founders of the Fund appointed a five-member board of directors, consisting of the four individual defendants and Peter S. Freudenthal. Two of the five directors were representatives of the two Fund advisers: Freudenthal was a principal of MeVC Advisers, Inc. ("meVC Advisers") and defendant Grillos is a principal of Draper Fisher Jurvetson MeVC Management Co., LLC ("Draper Advisers"). Freudenthal was the Fund's President until he resigned in June 2002. Grillos has, at all times relevant to the complaint, been the Fund's CEO. Section 56(a) of the 1940 Act requires that a majority of the Fund's directors be independent. Gerhard, Hughes, and Lufkin were appointed to serve as the Fund's independent, disinterested directors. These three disinterested directors also comprised the Fund's three-member Audit Committee.

The directors' terms of office were staggered, with Freudenthal and Grillos designated to stand for reelection to three-year terms in 2001, Gerhard in 2002, and Hughes and Lufkin in 2003. Freudenthal and Grillos were reelected at the Fund's 2001 Annual Meeting. Gerhard was reelected in 2002.

## II.

This action was begun on April 3, 2002. In the second amended complaint, Millenco seeks, among other things, to invalidate the elections of directors at the 2001 and 2002 Annual Meetings on grounds that the proxy solicitations conducted in connection therewith were materially false and misleading. At the heart of this claim lies the Fund's failure to disclose the existence of certain relationships between and among Grillos, an inside director, and Gerhard and Hughes, two nominally independent directors. These relationships arise out of the involvement of all three (i.e., Grillos, Gerhard and Hughes) in an enterprise known as eVineyard, Inc. Millenco contends that full and accurate disclosure of the nature of those relationships was necessary for Fund stockholders to make an informed judgment about the "independence" of both Gerhard and Hughes.

### A. Grillos's Involvement in eVineyard

The business relationship of Grillos and Gerhard goes back for some years to a time when Grillos hired Gerhard as CEO of a company known as Test Systems Strategy, Inc. In 1999, Gerhard solicited Grillos to be an initial investor in eVineyard. Eventually, Grillos invested $256,000 personally, another $1,474,000 through iTech which Grillos managed as a principal, as well as additional sums as a limited partner in Osprey Ventures which invested approximately $1,500,000 in eVineyard.

In May 1999, Grillos was named to the eVineyard board of directors and also appointed as both Chairman of the Board and Chairman of the Compensation Committee. Pursuant to the eVineyard by-laws, the Chairman of the Board is an executive officer of the corporation. Moreover, Section 3.4 of those by-laws provides that "if the chief executive officer [i.e. Gerhard] is not also the chairman of the board, then the chief executive officer [Gerhard] shall report to the chairman of the board [i.e. Grillos]." Grillos continued to serve in these roles through November 6, 2001, when he resigned as Chairman of the Board, and January 28, 2002, when he resigned as a director and as Chairman of the Compensation Committee, but retained board visitation rights. While he was Chairman of the Board and Chairman of the Compensation Committee, eVineyard entered into a revised employment agreement with Gerhard. Grillos testified that he "took the lead" in terms of negotiating this contract with Gerhard.

Gerhard is a director of eVineyard and served as its CEO at all relevant times. Hughes is also a director of eVineyard and, for a time in 2001, served as COO /President. They are both substantial eVineyard stockholders.

### B. Grillos and Gerhard Propose a Fund Investment in eVineyard

On November 7, 2001, the day after Grillos's resignation as Chairman of eVineyard, Grillos and Gerhard proposed a transaction that Paul Wozniak, a principal of meVC Advisers and CFO of the Fund, described as one in which "the [F]und would wind up owning eVineyard stock in a deal that essentially boils down to a straight purchase of eVineyard stock [for $1 million] despite the machinations created to make it look otherwise." Wozniak also noted: "Even if this transaction proves technically legal (which is questionable at this juncture), the appearance of conflict is so great that we at meVC advisors do not wish for this deal to move forward."

## C. 2001 Proxy and Election

In 2001, Grillos and Freudenthal were up for reelection to the Board at the annual shareholders meeting. On March 1, 2001, the Fund filed a proxy statement with the SEC that included the Board's recommendation for the reelection of these two directors. The proxy statement disclosed Grillos's and Freudenthal's status as "interested persons" of the Fund due to their affiliation with the Fund's investment advisers. It also disclosed that Gerhard, Hughes and Lufkin were the Fund's "disinterested" directors. Grillos's biography included a description of his positions with the Fund and its sub-adviser and certain other positions he had held or was holding at the time. It did not disclose his positions with or investment in eVineyard or his relationships with Gerhard and Hughes. Grillos and Freudenthal ran unopposed and on April 21, 2001 were reelected to three-year terms.

## D. 2002 Proxy and Election

On February 25, 2002, the Fund filed with the SEC the proxy statement for the 2002 annual shareholders meeting. The proxy included two Board-recommended proposals for shareholder approval: (i) new advisory agreements with the Fund's investment adviser and sub-adviser,[1] and (ii) Gerhard's reelection to the Board. The proxy statement disclosed that Gerhard was not an "interested" person of the Fund. His biography included his position as Chairman of the Board of eVineyard (having succeeded Grillos), as well as his prior positions as President and CEO of that company. It did not, however, disclose Grillos's relationship to eVineyard. Gerhard ran unopposed and was reelected.

Millenco opposed the ratification of the new advisory agreements and successfully conducted a campaign to defeat them.

## III.

The parties have cross-moved for summary judgment on Millenco's claim seeking to invalidate the 2001 and 2002 elections of directors on grounds of breach of the directors' duty of disclosure. Pursuant to Court of Chancery Rule 56, summary judgment should be granted where there are no genuine issues of material fact and the moving party is entitled to judgment as a matter of law. In deciding a motion for summary judgment, the facts must be viewed in the light most favorable to the non-moving party, and the moving party has the burden of demonstrating that no material question of fact exists. "When a moving party has properly supported its motion, however, the non-moving party must submit admissible evidence sufficient

---

[1] [3] After the Fund's inception, meVC Advisers became the investment adviser to the Fund. Freudenthal was president, CEO and chairman of the board of directors of meVC Advisers. Additionally, Draper Advisers became the sub-adviser to the Fund. Grillos is the managing member and a 35% shareholder in Draper Advisers.

to generate a factual issue for trial or suffer an adverse judgment." Although the parties have crossed-moved for summary judgment, that fact "does not act per se as a concession that there is an absence of a factual issue." Here, there are no material issues of fact in dispute and the cross-motions present purely questions of law.

It is undisputed that no information relating to Grillos's association with eVineyard, Gerhard and Hughes was ever disclosed to the Fund's shareholders. Instead, the Fund's proxy statements have both disclosed that Gerhard, Hughes and Lufkin are "Independent Directors" who are not "interested persons" within the meaning of the 1940 Act. While the 2002 proxy statement discloses that Gerhard and Hughes are both affiliated with eVineyard, it does not disclose Grillos's past or current relationships with that company.

Millenco makes a plain and powerful argument that the omitted information about the Grillos/eVineyard connection was material. First, under Delaware law, the fiduciary duties of directors require that they disclose fully and with complete candor all material facts when they solicit proxies from stockholders. Second, that duty is "best discharged through a broad rather than a restrictive approach to disclosure," and mere technical compliance with a statutory mandate or relevant regulations does not create a safe harbor from liability for deceptive disclosures or material omissions. Third, "[a]n omitted fact is material if there is a substantial likelihood that a reasonable investor would consider it important in deciding how to vote." Finally, where, as here, the omitted information goes to the independence or disinterest of directors who are identified as the company's "independent" or "not interested" directors, the "relevant inquiry is not whether an actual conflict of interest exists, but rather whether full disclosure of potential conflicts of interest has been made." Applied to the facts presented, Millenco argues that the failure of either proxy statement to disclose or describe Grillos's relationship to eVineyard renders the proxy statements materially misleading and incomplete. A fund stockholder, Millenco suggests, would certainly have regarded the omitted information material in deciding how to vote on the election of directors in both 2001 and 2002.

The defendants make two arguments to avoid the result urged by Millenco. First, they argue that because the directors do not meet the definition of interestedness under the 1940 Act, the omitted information is immaterial as a matter of law. Second, the defendants argue that disclosure of the omitted information was not required because, when viewed in the context of the totality of information regarding Grillos's relationship to eVineyard, the omitted information does not bear materially on Gerhard's and Hughes's independence. These arguments are untenable.

With respect to the first argument, the defendants' obligation to disclose information that materially bears on Gerhard's and Hughes's qualifications to serve as disinterested directors of the Fund does not turn on some legal conclusion about their status under SEC rules and regulations. SEC publications in the area reinforce this point. On October 19, 1999, the SEC in a release titled "Interpretive

Matters Concerning Independent Directors of Investment Companies"[2] stressed the importance of the independent directors' role as "watchdogs" in investment companies. It concluded by issuing interpretive guidance concerning the situations under which a director would be deemed "interested" and therefore "not independent," as follows (bracketed material added):

> The staff believes that a fund director [i.e., Gerhard] who serves as a chief executive officer of any company [eVineyard] for which the chief executive officer of the fund's advisor [Grillos] serves as a director also may be treated as "interested." The relationship between the fund director and the adviser's chief executive officer may tend to impair the director's independence because the adviser's chief executive officer has the power to vote on matters that affect the director's compensation and status as chief executive officer of the company. In this instance, the fund director may act with respect to fund matters in a manner to preserve his or her relationship with the company and with the adviser's chief executive officer, rather than in the interest of the fund's shareholders.

The need to disclose relationships of this kind was reiterated by the SEC when it promulgated a new Item 22 to Schedule 14A to provide for a minimum threshold of disclosure obligations in proxy materials relating to the election of fund directors:

> (b) *Election of Directors*. If action is to be taken with respect to the election of directors of a Fund, furnish the following information in the proxy statement . . .
>
> (10) If an Officer of an investment advisor [Grillos] . . . of the Fund, serves, or has served since the beginning of the last two completed fiscal years of the Fund, on the board of directors of a company where a director of the Fund or nominee for election as director who is not or would not be an "interested person" of the Fund within the meaning of section 2(a)(19) of the Investment Company Act of 1940 . . . is, or was since the beginning of the last two completed fiscal years of the Fund, an officer [Gerhard and Hughes], identify:
>
> (i) The company;
>
> (ii) The individual who serves or has served as director of the company and the period of service as director;
>
> (iii) The investment advisor . . . where the individual . . . holds or held office and the office held; and
>
> (iv) The director of the Fund, nominee for election as director . . . who is or was an Officer of the company; the office held; and the period of holding the office.[3]

These amendments were effective as of January 31, 2002. Thus, when the 2002 proxy statement was issued, disclosure of these relationships appeared necessary as a matter of federal securities law.

---

[2] [14] Release No. IC-24083, 1999 SEC No-Act. LEXIS 844.

[3] [15] 17 C.F.R. § 240.14a-101(b)(10).

Even if the relationships of the defendants did not fit perfectly within the ambit of Section 14A requirements, nondisclosure of the relationships is not excused under federal law. The SEC emphasized as much when it noted that the disclosure requirements of Schedule 14A were minimum requirements and not safe harbor determinations of materiality:

> [W]e wish to emphasize that a fund's independent directors can vigilantly represent the interests of shareholders only when they are truly independent of those who operate and manage the fund. To that end, we encourage funds to examine any circumstances that could potentially impair the independence of independent directors, whether or not they fall within the scope of our disclosure requirements.

Defendants further attempt to argue disclosure is not required under the 1940 Act because the SEC has not exercised its administrative powers under Section 2(a)(19) of the Act to declare either Gerhard or Hughes to be interested persons. But, the SEC had no way of knowing about Grillos's involvement with eVineyard and its possible effect on the independence of Gerhard and Hughes because the defendants never publicly disclosed any of this information. Thus, the absence of action by the SEC is both understandable and irrelevant. The SEC realized that such a problem might arise under its disclosure regime and, in its commentary to the amendments to Item 22, stated the following:

> Our amendments regarding circumstances that may raise conflict of interest concerns for directors benefit investors by enabling investors to decide for themselves whether an independent director would be an effective advocate for shareholders. Disclosure of this type of information also results in its public dissemination, bringing these circumstances to the attention of the fund shareholders, and encouraging the selection of independent directors who are independent in the spirit of the Act. Finally, this information assists the Commission in determining whether to exercise its authority under section 2(a)(19) of the Act to find that a person is an interested person of a fund by reason of having had, at any time since the beginning of the last two completed years of the fund, a material business or professional relationship with the fund and certain persons related to the fund.

Finally, it must be said that a discussion of whether the supposedly independent directors were in fact independent under the 1940 Act is only of passing significance to the court's analysis. The real issue is whether the omission of the information in question violated the defendants' disclosure duties under Delaware law. In that sense, disclosure is necessary if a stockholder would have considered the information important in deciding how to vote. As the foregoing discussion illustrates, the omitted information would almost certainly be considered important in the context of an election of directors, especially in the context of a registered investment company.

Given the chance, the Fund's stockholders could have reasonably inferred, either from Grillos's de jure powers at eVineyard or from his de facto exercise of such powers, that his roles at eVineyard gave Grillos actual or potential influence over Gerhard and/or Hughes, which influence could be viewed as affecting their judgment as independent directors of the Fund. Further, the defendants' frequent references to Gerhard and Hughes as "independent" or "disinterested" directors of the Fund strongly implies that they were free to act with complete and undivided loyalty to the Fund. The Fund's stockholders were entitled to know the omitted information in order to judge for themselves Gerhard's and Hughes's independence and disinterestedness.

The defendants' second argument is that, even if the omitted information tended to show a lack of director independence, a complete understanding of Grillos's relationship with eVineyard shows that the undisclosed relationships could not have interfered with or diminished Gerhard's and Hughes's ability to act independently. This argument misconstrues the legal test to be applied. "Materiality is to be assessed from the viewpoint of the 'reasonable' stockholder, not from a director's subjective perspective." In other words, it does not matter whether Gerhard and Hughes each strongly held his ability to act independently of Grillos or whether the other defendants shared this view. What matters is how a reasonable stockholder would have regarded disclosure of the facts relating to Grillos's relationships to eVineyard, Gerhard and Hughes. Millenco correctly argues that the facts surrounding these relationships bore on the directors' independence and, because there is a substantial likelihood a reasonable investor would have wanted to know about these facts in deciding how to vote on the elections of each of Grillos, Freudenthal, and Gerhard, needed to be disclosed in the 2001 and 2002 proxy materials.

The defendants' efforts to explain away the omitted information by pointing to additional information that softens or mitigates the impact of the omission merely reinforces the conclusion that the Fund stockholders should have been given the chance to decide for themselves how things looked. The possibility that, with the benefit of complete disclosure, the stockholders would have allowed these men to run unopposed for election can hardly justify the omission of any information at all.

In the end, the defendants cannot escape the conclusion that they should have presented their explanations about the various relationships in the proxy statements in which they solicited votes for the election of directors at the 2001 and 2002 Annual Meetings. They were free to explain why they believed that the eVineyard relationships did not have the potential to impair the independence of either Gerhard or Hughes as directors of the Fund. Had they done so, the stockholders would have been able to decide for themselves what significance to attribute to such facts and the accompanying explanations.[4] What defendants were not free to do was to take the position that the stockholders had no right to know this information because they, the defendants, had determined it was not important.[5]

---

[4] [21] *Zirn*, 621 A.2d at 779 (materiality standard "does not contemplate the subjective views of the directors, nor does it require that the information be of such import that its revelation would cause an investor to change his vote").

[5] [22] In addition, the court notes that the defendants never discussed or considered whether disclosure of the omitted information was necessary. Surprisingly, the record shows that neither the Fund nor its counsel even distributed the normal questionnaires to officers and directors in order to ascertain the extent of each respondent's relationships with other directors, the Fund, its advisers or their affiliates.

## IV.

In view of the court's conclusion that the election of directors at both the 2001 and 2002 Annual Meetings was procured by the use of materially false and misleading proxy materials, the appropriate remedy is to order new elections to fill the three director seats that were up for election at those meetings. The record reflects that, if Millenco had been furnished with the omitted information in 2001 or 2002, it would have acted to oppose the elections. The courts of this state "have long held that inequitable conduct by directors that interferes with a fair voting process may be set aside in equity." Moreover, the "right of shareholders to participate in the voting process includes the right to nominate an opposing slate."[6]

The only remaining issue is whether to order a new election in advance of the 2003 annual meeting of stockholders. The answer to that question will turn on when that meeting is or will be scheduled to be held. If the court receives assurances that such a meeting will be held within 60 days of the date of this opinion, the court will be inclined to the view that only a single meeting needs to be conducted. If not, the court will order the convening of a special meeting no later than February 15, 2003 for the purpose of electing 3 directors.

## V.

For the foregoing reasons, Millenco's motion for summary judgment is GRANTED, and the defendants' cross-motion for summary judgment is DENIED.

## DESAIGOUDAR v. MEYERCORD
### United States Court of Appeals, Ninth Circuit
### 223 F.3d 1020 (2000)

SNEED, J.

The question in this appeal is whether the district court should have dismissed Desaigoudar's second amended complaint with prejudice for repeated failure to satisfy Federal Rule of Civil Procedure 9(b) and the Private Securities Litigation Reform Act of 1995 (the "PSLRA"). . . .

## I.

### A. PROCEDURAL HISTORY

Aarathi Desaigoudar, in her capacity as the trustee of the Chan Desaigoudar Charitable Foundation (the "Foundation"), sued officials of California Micro Devices Corporation ("CMD") 1 in 1997 for securities fraud. . . .

Desaigoudar subsequently filed what the district court labeled a "Second

---

**6**  [25] *Id.* (also noting that "[t]o set aside the election results on the basis of inequitable manipulation of the corporate machinery, it is not required that *scienter, i.e.,* actual subjective intent to impede the voting process be shown").

Amended Complaint." The entire complaint was dismissed with prejudice. Desaigoudar then filed this timely appeal.

## B. FACTUAL HISTORY

CMD sells microprocessors and related products. Its sales revenues reached $33 million in 1997. As of October 1998, the Foundation owned 72,580 shares of CMD stock, which were valued at approximately $372,000.

In September 1994, CMD entered into a one-year research and development contract with CellAccess, Inc., a company involved in developing asynchronous transfer mode technology.[7] In exchange for a 56% interest in CellAccess' technology and the option to renew the contract after the year, CMD agreed to make monthly payments of $90,000. CMD terminated these payments in April 1995 and relinquished its 56% interest. Sometime thereafter, for a reason not revealed by the record, CMD received a $1.5 million termination fee. In November 1995, CellAccess was acquired by FORE Systems, Inc. ("FORE Systems"), a Pittsburgh, Pennsylvania company. The purchase price was $60 million.

CMD held its 1995 Annual Shareholder Meeting on September 15th, prior to FORE Systems' purchase of CellAccess. The agenda included the re-election of the individual Appellees and a vote on a stock option plan for their benefit. A proxy solicitation in anticipation of these votes had been previously posted on June 12th, and a press release had followed on July 27th.[8] These materials explained that CMD had registered a quarterly profit for the first time in two years.

## II.

To repeat, the second amended complaint alleges that Appellees, as officers and directors of CMD, intentionally violated Exchange Act Section 14(a) and SEC Rule 14a-9. These disallow the solicitation of a proxy by a statement that contains either (1) a false or misleading declaration of material fact, or (2) an omission of material fact that makes any portion of the statement misleading. See 15 U.S.C. § 78j(b); 17 C.F.R. § 240.14a-9. In addition, a Section 14(a), Rule 14a-9 plaintiff must demonstrate that the misstatement or omission was made with the requisite level of culpability and that it was an essential link in the accomplishment of the proposed transaction.

The complaint clearly sounds in fraud.[9] Thus, Federal Rule of Civil Procedure 9(b) and the PSLRA require Desaigoudar to plead her case with a high degree of meticulousness. See Yourish v. California Amplifier, 191 F.3d 983, 993 (9th Cir.

---

[7] [2] This technology facilitates the electronic transference of data, voice, and other information.

[8] [3] We agree with the parties and the district court that the press release was part of a continuous plan to encourage a favorable vote by shareholders and was, therefore, a proxy solicitation. See 17 C.F.R. § 240.14a-1.

[9] [5] The district court rejected as "disingenuous" Desaigoudar's claim that the complaint also sounds in negligence. See Order Granting Defendants' Motion to Dismiss at 5 n.2 (Oct. 18, 1998). After carefully reviewing the complaint's language, which asserts "knowing[ ] and intentional[ ]" misconduct by the Appellees, we conclude that the rejection was proper. Second Amended Complaint at 14 (¶ 81).

1999) (noting applicability of Rule 9(b) to securities fraud claims); In re Silicon Graphics Inc. Securities Litigation, 183 F.3d 970, 996 (9th Cir. 1999) (describing heightened pleading standard of the PSLRA). Rule 9(b) mandates that "[i]n all averments of fraud or mistake, the circumstances constituting fraud or mistake shall be stated with particularity." The PSLRA modifies Rule 9(b), providing that a securities fraud plaintiff shall identify: (1) each statement alleged to have been misleading; (2) the reason or reasons why the statement is misleading; and (3) all facts on which that belief is formed. *See In re Silicon Graphics*, 183 F.3d at 996; 15 U.S.C. § 78u-4(b)(1). The district court found that Desaigoudar did not comply with these standards. We agree.

## III.

The complaint alleges that Appellees: (1) misled shareholders when they announced a quarterly profit in CMD's proxy materials; (2) failed to disclose that Appellee Jordan had a conflict of interest; and (3) misrepresented Jordan's qualifications for reelection as a director of CMD. None of these allegations, which we shall discuss seriatim, constitutes a valid claim.

## A. ALLEGATION ONE: MISREPRESENTATION OF "PROFIT"

Desaigoudar argues that the proxy statements the Appellees issued in June and July of 1995 misled shareholders because they described CMD's quarterly performance as "profitable." In her view, the shareholders should have been told that CMD's quarterly performance was a loss. She asserts that Appellees engineered the profit, in part, when they caused CMD to cancel monthly funding for CellAccess and thereby abandoned CMD's 56 percent interest in the venture. Desaigoudar reasons from FORE Systems' November 1995 purchase of CellAccess that the cancellation and abandonment of the venture caused CMD to forego 56 percent of a $60 million opportunity, or $36 million. She then alleges that the Appellees knowingly and intentionally failed to inform shareholders that CMD had forfeited an asset worth many millions of dollars in order to generate a portion of the profit that they claimed. Her argument is flawed.

Rule 14a-9 requires a complainant to demonstrate why a challenged proxy statement was misleading "at the time . . . made." 17 C.F.R. § 240.14a-9. Thus, the issue here is whether the Appellees could have known how much CellAccess was worth to CMD when it ceased funding for CellAccess. If there was no way to know, it is impossible to fault the Appellees. Failure to disclose information that does not yet exist cannot be the predicate for Rule 14a-9 liability. *See* 17 C.F.R. § 240.14a-9. Obviously Desaigoudar has suspicions, but that is not enough. We can therefore eliminate FORE Systems' purchase of CellAccess as a possible source for knowledge of the company's value. That transaction, which appears to be the only exchange that actually involved CellAccess, took place several months after the proxy statements were issued in the summer of 1995.

Desaigoudar relies on three other reasons why the Appellees would have known CellAccess' value at the time they posted the proxy statements. They are that: (1) Appellee Jordan performed a due diligence investigation of CellAccess in 1994; (2)

an unidentified "high technology publication" mentioned CellAccess as a "promising new company" in March 1995; and (3) sometime just prior to that favorable mention CISCO Systems paid $120 million for a company that, like CellAccess, was developing asynchronous transfer mode technology. We think these reasons are not enough to substantiate Desaigoudar's claim. Not one of the described events occurred contemporaneously with the proxy solicitations or CMD's cessation of the CellAccess project. There is also no indication that the Appellees knew about the "recognition" CellAccess received or about CISCO Systems' purchase of a CellAccess "competitor."

Ultimately, the greatest flaw in Desaigoudar's case is the fact that any estimate that the Appellees could have fabricated based on these events would have been utterly unreliable. The SEC has historically disfavored forecasts and value estimates in proxy statements. *See South Coast Services Corp. v. Santa Ana Valley Irrigation Co.*, 669 F.2d 1265, 1270 (9th Cir. 1982). An exception to this treatment has existed for estimates based on "objective, reasonably certain data, such as commodity prices prevailing in an active market." *See id.* at 1270–71. Here, the events upon which the complaint relies do not comprise the "objective, reasonably certain data" spoken of in the exception. Nothing in the complaint demonstrates that CellAccess was akin to a "commodity" traded in an "active market." Thus, we cannot fault the Appellees for omitting from the proxy statements an estimate based on those facts presented in the complaint. No *reasonable* shareholder would have considered such an estimate honestly presented important in deciding how to vote. Consequently, we agree with the district court that Desaigoudar failed to plead a material omission and that the Appellees are not liable under Section 14(a) and Rule 14a-9. *See TSC Industries, Inc. v. Northway, Inc.*, 426 U.S. at 449 [, 96 S. Ct. 2126] (noting that "[a]n omitted fact is material if there is a substantial likelihood that a reasonable shareholder would consider it important in deciding how to vote"); *Stahl v. Gibraltar Financial Corp.*, 967 F.2d 335, 337 (1992) (noting that materiality is the "touchstone of a [S]ection 14(a) violation").

Broadly read, Desaigoudar's complaint would require corporate officials to speculate about the value of potentially foregone opportunities and disclose the results whenever they might dissuade shareholders from adopting by proxy the officials' recommendations. However, Section 14(a) and Rule 14a-9 do not require corporate officials to predict such distant misfortunes. *See South Coast Services Corp.*, 669 F.2d at 1270. In a note appending Rule 14a-9, the SEC identifies "[p]redictions as to specific market values" as, depending on the facts of a particular case, possible examples of the very wrong that Rule 14a-9 was designed to prevent. 17 CFR § 240.14a-9. Since we conclude that a prediction based on the facts in the complaint would have been unreliable, we cannot conclude that omitting it from the proxy statements violated the law.

Section 14(a) and Rule 14a-9 do not obligate corporate officials to present, no matter how unlikely, every conceivable argument against their own recommendations. They instead require that officials divulge all known material facts so that shareholders can make informed choices. *See J.I. Case Co. v. Borak*, 377 U.S. 426, 431, 84 S. Ct. 1555, 12 L. Ed. 2d 423 (1964) (noting that Section 14(a) was designed to "prevent management or others from obtaining authorization for corporate action by means of deceptive or inadequate disclosure in proxy solicitation"). That is what the Appellees appear to have done.

Desaigoudar protests that the gravamen of the complaint was "self-dealing" by the Appellees and their "concealed mismanagement" of CMD, not their failure to provide an estimate of CellAccess' resale value. We find this interpretation unconvincing in light of the clear language of her complaint, which states: "The press release and proxy solicitation material were materially misleading as to the true general nature and terms of the quarterly profit, and as to whether Defendants merited stock options. Neither document disclosed that the modest quarterly profit . . . meant a $36 million loss . . . ." Moreover, the complaint makes no cognizable claim under Section 14(a) and Rule 14a-9 to the extent that it might allege something other than a material misstatement or omission in connection with a proxy statement. *See, e.g., Maher v. Zapata Corp.*, 714 F.2d 436, 444 n.16 (5th Cir. 1983) (noting inapplicability of Section 14(a) to claims of alleged mismanagement or breach of fiduciary duty).

Desaigoudar also contends that the Appellees failed to alert CMD shareholders that the heralded quarterly profit was not entirely from "operations," as the investors would likely presume. In her view, what was fatally absent from the proxy solicitations was an explanation that the Appellees generated a part of the quarterly profit by eliminating CMD's ties with CellAccess. That is, they should have disclosed that some portion of the quarterly profits came from abandoning CellAccess, collecting the termination fee, and not having to pay $90,000 per month to maintain CMD's interest in CellAccess.[10]

We are unable to agree. Desaigoudar cites no authority for the proposition that the Appellees misused the word "profit." Profit may be understood properly as "gain" or "[t]he excess of revenues over expenses in a business transaction." BLACK'S LAW DICTIONARY 1227 (7th ed. 1999). There is no dispute that CMD's revenue exceeded its expenses during the relevant fiscal quarter. Thus, it was not misleading to say that CMD turned a profit, and Appellees were entitled to disclose that favorable information to shareholders. Desaigoudar's theory that the ordinary CMD investor would think "profit" related only to "operations" does not provide the cause of action her complaint is otherwise lacking.

## B. ALLEGATION TWO: CONFLICT OF INTEREST

The second amended complaint also alleges that Appellees violated Section 14(a) when they did not disclose that Appellee Jordan had a conflict of interest. Jordan served as "Director Emeritus" of the Pittsburgh High Technology Council (the "Council") while he was a director of CMD. The Council's raison d'etre was to lure high technology businesses away from areas like California, where CMD resides, to Jordan's home town of Pittsburgh, Pennsylvania, where FORE Systems is located. Since the complaint contains no facts demonstrating that Jordan personally or financially benefitted from FORE Systems' purchase of CellAccess, the district court concluded that there was no conflict of interest.

---

[10] [6] Desaigoudar acknowledges that "other things" contributed to the quarterly profit. Second Amended Complaint at 8 (¶ 48).

Desaigoudar disagrees. She claims that a conflict can exist without a personal or financial benefit to the conflicted, such as when a "director appears on both sides of a transaction." In support, she cites a law review note[11] and the American Bar Association Model Business Corporation Act, ¶ 8.60 (3rd ed. 1997) (the "Model Act"). She makes no suggestion that either authority should be controlling.

Moreover, the complaint does not indicate how Jordan's presence on the Council placed him "on both sides" of CMD's dealings with CellAccess. While suspicions might be aroused by the fact that Jordan and the president of FORE Systems served together on the Council, suspicious circumstances alone cannot satisfy Rule 9(b) or the PSLRA. *See In re Silicon Graphics*, 183 F.3d 970. The facts as Desaigoudar presents them do not suggest that Jordan arranged for CMD to terminate funding for CellAccess so that, seven months later, FORE Systems could purchase the company. In addition, the Council was not a party to and never had any financial interest in either the termination or the purchase. Jordan therefore had no discernable conflict for Appellees to disclose in CMD's June and July 1995 proxy materials.

## C. ALLEGATION THREE: MISREPRESENTATION OF JORDAN'S BACK-GROUND

The second amended complaint further alleges that Appellees violated Section 14(a) when they falsely held out Jordan as a director of Keithley Instruments, Inc. ("Keithley").[12] However, the complaint does not suggest that Appellees' statements about Jordan and Keithley were material misrepresentations. There are, in other words, no facts to support the inference that it was substantially likely that a reasonable CMD shareholder would have considered the nature of Jordan's relationship with Keithley important in deciding how to vote. Since there can be no Section 14(a) liability without materiality, this allegation is defective. *See TSC Industries, Stahl.*

## IV.

We conclude that, even after three attempts, Desaigoudar has failed to state a claim because she failed to heed the district court's warning to comply with Rule 9(b) and the PSLRA. This subjected the complaint to the distinct possibility of dismissal with prejudice. *See Allen v. City of Beverly Hills*, 911 F.2d 367, 373 (9th Cir. 1990) ("The district court's discretion to deny leave to amend is particularly broad where plaintiff has previously amended the complaint.") (*quoting Ascon Properties, Inc. v. Mobil Oil Co.*, 866 F.2d 1149, 1160 (9th Cir. 1989)); 15 U.S.C. § 78u-4(b)(3)(A) (mandating dismissal under the PSLRA for failure to plead adequately a securities fraud claim). Nevertheless, this court has decided that "dismissal without leave to amend is improper unless it is clear, upon de novo review, that the complaint could not be saved by any amendment." *Griggs v. Pace*

---

[11] [7] Mary A. Jacobson, Note, *Interested Director Transactions and the (Equivocal) Effects of Shareholder Ratification*, 21 DEL. J. CORP. L. 981, 986 (1996).

[12] [8] Keithley described itself as "a measurement test company." *See* Second Amended Complaint at 4 (¶ 15).

*Am. Group, Inc.*, 170 F.3d 877, 879 (9th Cir. 1999). It is clear that no amendment could save Desaigoudar's complaint. The district court is therefore AFFIRMED.

## SHAEV v. SAPER
United States Court of Appeals, Third Circuit
320 F.3d 373 (2003)

ROSENN, J.

This case presents important questions pertaining to corporate governance and responsibility. They involve the application and alleged violations of Securities Exchange and Treasury Regulations with respect to shareholder proxy statements soliciting shareholder approval of executive incentive compensation plans. Datascope Corporation (Datascope or the Company), a corporation chartered under the laws of Delaware, has its principal place of business in Montvale, New Jersey, where it is engaged in the manufacture of complex cardiology, vascular, and other medical proprietary products. The Company's board of directors (Board) issued a proxy statement to its shareholders soliciting support for an amendment to its Management Incentive Plan (MIP) which determined the bonus compensation to be awarded to Datascope's president, Lawrence Saper.

Datascope shareholder David Shaev brought a derivative lawsuit under the Federal Securities Exchange Act of 1934 and applicable regulations alleging that the proxy statement made false and misleading statements regarding material facts. The District Court dismissed Shaev's claim on the pleadings and declined to exercise supplemental jurisdiction over Shaev's excessive compensation claim under Delaware law. Shaev timely appealed. We vacate and remand.

### I.

For the purposes of defendants' motion to dismiss, we must accept as true Shaev's allegations in his complaint and make all reasonable inferences in his favor. The defendant's motion to dismiss automatically halted discovery. Thus, Shaev has not had the opportunity to substantiate some of his allegations. Saper has been the Chief Executive Officer (CEO) and chairman of the Board of Datascope since 1964. Saper and his immediate family hold approximately 19% of Datascope's shares, which are traded on NASDAQ. As of July 1, 1996, Saper entered into an employment agreement with Datascope for a term of five years with an automatic extension, unless either party gave notice of an intent to terminate the contract. Saper receives an annual base salary with increases as determined by the Board or the Compensation Committee. On September 22, 1999, the Compensation Committee increased Saper's annual base salary to $1 million per year. Saper also became entitled to receive bonuses under various long-term and annual incentive compensation plans. On May 26, 1999, Saper received an immediately-exercisable option to purchase 70,000 shares of stock at an exercise price equal to the market price of the stock, expiring May 25, 2009. Using an option-pricing model, Shaev alleges that this option was worth $1,016,200. Additionally, the complaint alleges that Saper's annual lifetime retirement payments are worth approximately $1,406,400 per year and cost the company $10,000,000.

On December 7, 1999, Datascope adopted a supplemental Management Incentive Plan that provided for bonus payments to eligible executives. The payments were contingent on attainment of various corporate goals and some subjective criteria.[13] The December 7, 1999, supplement provides "the precise terms and provisions of the performance goals" to calculate Saper's bonus, based on Datascope's earnings per share measured before extraordinary and/or special items.

On May 16, 2000, the Board's Compensation Committee amended the 1999 supplement. The Board adopted the 2000 amendment for a nine-month performance period commencing October 1, 1999, and continuing through July 30, 2000. The performance goals for that nine-month performance period were adopted on December 7, 1999. However, as of December 7, 1999, the maximum Saper bonus was $2,225,000. In the May 16, 2000, amendment, the Board increased to $3,285,714 the amount of compensation that would be awarded to Saper if Datascope met the performance goals adopted five months earlier. The performance period ended approximately six weeks later.

Under the 2000 amendment, Saper could have received 83% of the increase in the earnings of the company at the high end of earnings per share. As a shareholder, Saper would also get 19% of the remaining 17% if dividends were issued, leaving only 14% of the remainder to the shareholders.

On October 27, 2000, the Board issued a proxy statement in connection with its annual meeting to be held on December 12, 2000. The proxy statement solicited shareholder approval of the 2000 amendment. However, the proxy statement did not include the material features of the 1999 supplement which it amended, and it did not mention the 1997 Plan which the 1999 MIP supplemented.

The proxy statement explained that the Board intended to administer the amendment in a way that would allow the Company to deduct bonuses and incentive payments for tax purposes. Furthermore, the proxy stated that "[s]hareholder approval of the Management Incentive Plan is required in order for the Management Incentive Plan to be effective and for bonuses payable thereunder to a 'covered employee' within the meaning of Section 162(m) . . . to be deductible under 162(m) of the Code."

Saper earned $3,285,714 in bonus compensation in FYE 2002. According to the proxy statement, $1,485,714 of that amount was subject to shareholder approval of the amendment. The proxy statement also stated that "[i]n the event that the Management Incentive Plan is not approved by the shareholders of the Corporation, the Compensation Committee may grant Mr. Saper another bonus for FYE 2000, a portion of which may not be deductible under Section 162(m) of the Code." On December 12, 2000, the Board submitted the amendment for shareholder

---

[13] [1] The MIP is described as a Supplemental Incentive Plan, but it does not specify what it supplements. Datascope explained at oral argument that it supplements the previous 1997 Plan, which is not in the record nor described in the disputed proxy. Because of this omission, it is difficult to evaluate the relevance and effect of the 1997 incentive Plan and its interaction with the 1999 supplement and the 2000 amendment to the supplement. Unlike the 1997 Plan, the 1999 supplement is part of the record, although neither it nor its material terms were included in the proxy statement.

approval at Datascope's annual meeting. The shareholders approved the amendment and the bonus payment to Saper.

Shaev filed a derivative action in the United States District Court for the District of New Jersey. Shaev did not make a demand on the Board prior to filing suit because he alleges that demand would have been futile and was, therefore, excused. Shaev asserts that the proxy statement erroneously stated that a bonus to Saper would be tax deductible to Datascope if it was approved by the shareholders. Shaev asserts that regardless of whether the shareholders voted for the Plan, the Company would not get the full deduction. Shaev also alleges that the proxy statement contained a material omission because it failed to include or even mention the original 1997 MIP that was being amended. Without the original 1997 MIP or a statement of the material terms of its 1999 supplement, Shaev alleges that the shareholders had no way of knowing that the proposed Saper bonus exceeded the amount to which he would have been entitled under the 1999 supplement's performance goals. Shaev also alleges that Saper's compensation was excessive under Delaware law.

\* \* \*

## II.

The threshold question we must decide is the validity of the defendants' challenge to the plaintiff's right to sue in behalf of the Company without first having made a demand upon its Board of Directors to take appropriate action for relief. In a derivative lawsuit, the shareholder must make a demand on the board of directors of the corporation to take action to correct the wrongdoing, or allege the reasons for the plaintiff's failure for not making the effort. *See* Fed. R. Civ. Proc. 23.1. The demand requirement ensures exhaustion of intra-corporate remedies, thereby possibly avoiding litigation in the first place.

Under *Rales v. Blasband*, 634 A.2d 927, 936–37 (Del. 1993), an interested director is one who receives a financial benefit from a corporate transaction. Saper, Altschiller and Grayzel are allegedly interested directors, and it is alleged that they constitute half of the Board. Shaev alleges that a demand on the directors for remedial action would have been futile. If so, demand would be excused because the interest of the Board in the situation was, at the very least, evenly divided. On remand, the parties can pursue the factual issues relevant to the futility of demand through the use of discovery.

There is no point, therefore, to discuss plaintiff's additional allegations that demand is excused under federal law, were we to decide that Delaware law was to the contrary.

## III.

Under the Securities Exchange Act, it is unlawful to solicit proxies in contravention of "such rules and regulations as the [Securities Exchange] Commission may prescribe as necessary or appropriate in the public interest or for the protection of investors." 15 U.S.C. § 78n(a). SEC Rule 14a-9 states in relevant part:

No solicitation subject to this regulation shall be made by means of any proxy statement . . . which, at the time . . . it is made, is false or misleading with respect to any material fact, or which omits to state any material fact necessary in order to make the statements therein not false or misleading or necessary to correct any statement in any earlier communication with respect to the solicitation of a proxy for the same meeting or subject matter which has become false or misleading.

Shareholders have an implied cause of action to seek relief when a false or misleading proxy statement interferes with "fair corporate suffrage." Section 14(a) seeks to prevent management or others from obtaining authorization for corporate actions by means of deceptive or inadequate disclosures in proxy solicitations. This is a highly important rule in the corporate life of this nation. A proxy statement should inform, not challenge the reader's critical wits. . . .

To state a claim under § 14(a), a plaintiff must allege that "(1) a proxy statement contained a material misrepresentation or omission which (2) caused the plaintiff injury and (3) that the proxy solicitation itself, rather than the particular defect in the solicitation materials, was 'an essential link in the accomplishment of the transaction.' " . . . An omitted fact is material if there is a substantial likelihood that a reasonable shareholder would consider it important in deciding how to vote. *See TSC Indus. Inc. v. Northway, Inc.*, 426 U.S. 438, 449, 96 S. Ct. 2126, 48 L. Ed. 2d 757 (1976); *Mills v. Elec. Auto-Lite Co.*, 396 U.S. 375, 384, 90 S. Ct. 616, 24 L. Ed. 2d 593 (1970).

The Internal Revenue Code (IRC) generally disallows deductions for employee remuneration in a publicly held corporation in excess of $1 million. IRC § 162(m)(1). However, the IRC contains exceptions for a narrow set of incentive programs, among which is a properly established employee incentive plan approved by the shareholders. The IRC provides in relevant part for the deductibility of remuneration to an applicable employee

only if — (i) the performance goals are determined by a compensation committee of the board of directors of the taxpayer which is comprised solely of 2 or more outside directors, (ii) the material terms under which the remuneration is to be paid, including the performance goals, are disclosed to shareholders and approved by a majority of the vote in a separate shareholder vote before the payment of such remuneration.

IRC § 162(m)(4)(C).

Likewise, the Treasury Regulations elaborate on the exception for the $1 million deduction limit under IRC § 162(m) when a compensation plan meets certain criteria for qualified performance-based compensation. *See* 26 C.F.R. § 1.162-27(e).[14]

---

[14] [3] The Treasury Regulations require: "Qualified performance-based compensation must be paid solely on account of the attainment of one or more preestablished, objective performance goals. A performance goal is considered preestablished if it is established in writing by the compensation committee not later than 90 days after the commencement of the period of service to which the performance goal relates, provided that the outcome is substantially uncertain at the time the compensation committee actually establishes the goal. However, in no event will a performance goal be

Companies may only deduct annual compensation in excess of $1 million pursuant to a Plan that is performance-based and approved by the company's stockholders. Here, the plaintiff alleges that the proxy statement falsely represents that the Saper bonus would qualify for an income tax deduction for the Company if the stockholders approved it. This statement is false or misleading, the complaint alleges, because the deduction was unavailable, regardless of the shareholders' approval because: (1) the 2000 amendment to the Plan was established too late for the performance goals to comply with the Regulations; (2) deductibility is destroyed if the bonus amount could be increased during the performance period; and (3) the Board's threat to take the deduction regardless of shareholder approval obviates its deductibility, even if approved.

Shaev's complaint that the 2000 amendment to the Plan was established too late to qualify for a deduction is well made. The Regulations require that a qualified performance goal be established not later than the ninetieth day of the performance period or before twenty-five percent of the performance period has elapsed. The supplement was adopted in December 1999, halfway through Datascope's fiscal year, and then restated in May 2000. December was too late to establish the necessary performance goals to receive the deduction because the Company's fiscal year ended in June 2000. By adjusting the amount of the incentive compensation in May 2000 and shortening the time period to less than a year, Datascope's Board hoped to circumvent the Regulations which allow corporations to create incentives for executives to meet objective, uncertain goals. As an incentive, the outcome of a performance goal, of course, must be substantially uncertain at the time the compensation committee establishes the goal. 26 C.F.R. § 1.162-27(e)(2)(i). The Company's alleged manipulation of the performance goals undermined the goals' character as "preestablished" and "objective." The performance period for the 1997 incentive plan was "a 12-month performance period that is adopted each year going forward." The nine-month performance period was adopted for the 2000 year plan "[b]ecause the Company wanted to be able to take advantage of the tax deduction that it was entitled to receive if it were a nine-month performance period."

In the absence of special circumstances, such as when a new company is formed or when an established company changes its fiscal year in good faith, a performance period shorter than one year makes it much less likely that the MIP will meet this requirement. On the facts as alleged. Datascope's performance period was too short to meet the Treasury Regulations requirements and improperly impaired their purpose. The incentive plan was only an exception to the general rule that salaries exceeding $1 million were not tax deductible. Therefore, an incentive program that allowed in excess of $1 million must comply strictly with the performance requirements set down by the Treasury Regulations.

Furthermore, even if the Company had established a long enough performance

---

considered to be preestablished if it is established after 25 percent of the period of service (as scheduled in good faith at the time the goal is established) has elapsed." 26 C.F.R. § 1.162-27(e)(2). *"(4) Shareholder approval requirement — (i) General rule.* The material terms of the performance goal under which the compensation is to be paid must be disclosed to and subsequently approved by the shareholders of the publicly held corporation before the compensation is paid. The requirements of this paragraph . . . are not satisfied if the compensation would be paid regardless of whether the material terms are approved by shareholders."

period, the existence of discretion to increase the amount of the bonus so late in the performance period undermined its deductibility. Under the Treasury Regulations, if there is discretion to increase the calculated bonus, the deduction is lost. See 26 C.F.R. § 1.162-27(e)(2)(iii)(A) ("The terms of an objective formula or standard must preclude discretion to increase the amount of compensation payable that would otherwise be due upon attainment of the goal") (emphasis added). Even though the performance goals were set in December, 1999, the amount of the compensation was changed on May 16, 2000, thereby undermining deductibility.[15]

Payments of the Saper bonus, even if the shareholders voted against it, also precluded the deduction. The Regulations state that "[t]he material terms of the performance goal under which the compensation is to be paid must be disclosed to and subsequently approved by the shareholders of the publicly held corporation before the compensation is paid. The requirements of this paragraph . . . are not satisfied if the compensation would be paid regardless of whether the material terms are approved by shareholders." 26 C.F.R. § 1.162-27(e)(4)(i). The Board's threat undermines the deductibility of the bonus even if the shareholders approved it.

The complaint accurately alleges that Datascope's Board made a materially false statement in the proxy statement when it stated that the bonus would be deductible if the shareholders approved it. Regardless of the shareholders' approval, the bonus would not have been deductible under the Treasury Regulations, and the alleged false statement in the proxy statement is actionable.[16]

## IV.

The allegations in the complaint that the Board failed to include the 1999 supplement in the proxy statement amounted to a material omission under SEC Rule 14a-9. Similarly, it was a material omission for the Board to fail even to mention the existence of the 1997 Plan. Counsel for the defendants concedes that the proxy statement would not have informed a hypothetical investor who bought Datascope stock on December 31, 1999, about the existence of the 1997 Plan. He argues, however, that this was not a material omission because the hypothetical investor would have been advised by the proxy statement that there was a separate bonus other than the MIP; the hypothetical investor could have contacted "the investor relations department at the Company to obtain past filings."

We hold that the cryptic references in the proxy statement were insufficient to satisfy Datascope's disclosure obligations under Rule 14a-9. Material not included in

---

[15] [4] The defendants argue that there was no discretion because the shareholders, not the Board, made the relevant changes to the performance goals. The problem with this reasoning is the timing. If the MIP could be changed retroactively, the terms are not pre-established. If they can only be changed prospectively, the time period would be six and a half weeks, altogether too short to comply with the Treasury Regulations. 26 C.F.R. § 1.162-27(e)(2).

[16] [5] Judge Sloviter notes that the District Court's conclusion that a one-year period is not required by the regulations is supported by an IRS private letter ruling by Robert Misner which recognizes that a performance period under a deductible plan "may be as short as a single calendar quarter." Private Letter Ruling, PLR 1999 50021 . . . (Dec. 17, 1999). Although a private letter ruling may not be cited as precedent, IRC § 6110(k)(3), the District Court may have deemed it instructive.

the proxy statement is generally not charged to the knowledge of the stockholder. *Cf. Koppel v. 4987 Corp.*, 167 F.3d 125, 132 (2d Cir. 1999) (document that was only available at defendants' offices during business hours, but not incorporated by reference in the proxy statement, was not treated as part of the "total mix" of information available to participants for 14a-9 purposes). That an investor could hypothetically conduct research to clarify ambiguities and discover omissions in the proxy statement does not relieve the Board of its obligations under Rule 14a-9. Defendant's counsel conceded at oral argument that the proxy statement "may not be the model of clarity and in hindsight it could have been drafted differently to lay out additional information . . . " We agree. A proxy statement should inform, not challenge a shareholder's critical wits. *See Virginia Bankshares*, 501 U.S. at 1097, 111 S. Ct. 2749.

The Proxy Statement's omission of the performance goals is material because the stockholders had no way of knowing that Saper had not earned the $3,285,714 bonus under the terms of the currently existing plan. The Proxy Statement contains no discussion of the 1997 Plan or how the 2000 amendment compares with the 1999 supplement or the 1997 Plan. The defendants respond that the two Plans have little to do with one another: "there was no need to publish the 1997 Plan again in the Proxy Statement nor was there a need to compare it to the 2000 Plan since both were to be in effect if the shareholders approved the 2000 Plan." This argument is sophistical because the 2000 amendment was not a stand-alone Plan. On the contrary, it was an amendment to an unstated supplement. To determine the overall incentive effects, stockholders would have had to read the three documents together, and they did not have them.

The terms of the 1997 Plan and the 1999 supplement are also relevant to the stockholders' assessment of the truth of the statement that the bonus would be tax deductible if approved. Assuming arguendo that the IRS treatment of the bonus was uncertain at the time of the proxy statement, a reasonable investor might take this uncertainty into account in deciding whether to vote to authorize the bonus. The risk that the bonus might not be tax deductible and the information necessary to determine whether it was deductible were material to the average investor's action at the time of the proxy statement, even if the IRS or a court should ultimately reject Shaev's argument.

The 1997 Plan and the 1999 supplement were also relevant to the shareholders' consideration of the 2000 proxy because the Board was asking the shareholders to approve a retroactive increase in Saper's bonus. There is no authority that the Board has the power to increase Saper's bonus retroactively. By failing to include the 1999 supplement in the proxy, the Board effectively asked the shareholders to do what the Board itself could not do, and without any notice to stockholders that they were doing it.

The District Court erred in concluding that 26 C.F.R. § 1.162-27(e)(4) insulates Datascope's Board from a claim under 15 U.S.C. § 78n(a) and Rule 14a-9. The District Court held that "applicable regulations clearly state the proxy statement need not disclose exactly that information which plaintiff claims Datascope share-holders were entitled [sic] so that they could determine whether executives merit the bonuses the Board intends to award." *See* Dist. Ct. op. at A 11. Even though the proxy statement did not have to reveal "specific business criteria" it does not follow that the proxy statement did not have to disclose the material terms of the existing incentive plan which would have demonstrated to the shareholders that the proposed bonus substantially would exceed the amount to which Saper would have been entitled under the extant MIP and to what extent.

The District Court misread the federal regulations when it concluded that Shaev's complaint demanded access to specific business criteria that the Board was not required to disclose. It is true that under 26 C.F.R. § 1.162-27(e)(4)(iii)(A), the specific business criteria upon which bonuses are contingent need not be disclosed in proxy statements. *See* Dist. Ct. op. at A 12. However, the material terms of the incentive plan and general performance goals on which the executive's compensation is based must, at a minimum, be disclosed. This position is supported by the Legislative History of the IRC § 162(m), which states:

> In order to meet the shareholder approval requirement, the material terms under which the compensation is to be paid must be disclosed . . . It is intended that not all the details of a plan (or agreement) need be disclosed in all cases . . . To the extent consistent with [the SEC] rules, however, disclosure should be as specific as possible. It is expected that shareholders will, at a minimum, be made aware of the general performance goals on which the executive's compensation is based and the maximum amount that could be paid to the executive if such performance goals were met.

We conclude that pertinent information in the 1997 Plan and notice that the proposed bonus substantially would exceed the amount to which Saper would have been entitled under the 1999 supplement were "material" within the meaning of IRC § 162(m)(4)(C)(ii), even though the "specific business criteria" discussed in 26 C.F.R. § 1.162-27(e)(4) are not.[17] We, therefore, hold that a proxy soliciting shareholders' approval of a proposed executive incentive compensation plan, which refers to an existing incentive plan, must disclose the material features of both plans. It must also state, if determinable, the amount of the increased benefits and performance goals under the proposed plan.

The District Court erred when it held on a Rule 12(b)(6) motion that the existence of the prior bonus Plan was not material. The allegations in the complaint were material unless the alleged misrepresentations and omissions were "so obviously unimportant to an investor that reasonable minds cannot differ on the question of materiality." *Shapiro v. UJB Financial Corp.*, 964 F.2d 272, 280–81 n.11 (3d Cir. 1992). The defendants argue that whether the bonus was tax deductible was immaterial because the deduction would represent a small figure in comparison with the $300 million revenues of the company. *See In re Westinghouse Sec. Litig.*, 90 F.3d 696, 715 (3d Cir. 1996) (holding that a write-down of .54% of net income was not material). Although the potential deduction is small in relation to the overall budget, the deduction is nevertheless material because the Treasury Regulations

---

[17] [8] 17 C.F.R. § 240.14a-101 and Fed. Sec. L. Rep. (CCH), Reg. S-K § 229.402(k) are not to the contrary. Regulation S-K applies to "specific quantitative and qualitative performance-related factors considered by the committee (or board) . . . " Again, the use of the term "specific" limits the scope of the exclusion to the specific details of the Plan, but does not address whether weightier issues such as the existence of a former plan or non-fulfillment of its requirements need to be disclosed.

required management disclosure and stockholder approval of the principal features of the incentive plan in order to qualify for the deduction. Thus, materiality of the required disclosure is not dependent on the quantity of money involved but on its purpose of informing the stockholders.[18]

## V.

The District Court may decline to exercise supplemental jurisdiction over state law claims when the District Court has dismissed all claims over which it has original jurisdiction. *See* 28 U.S.C. § 1367(c); Dist. Ct. op. at A 12. Because the District Court erred in dismissing the federal securities claims, we vacate the District Court's dismissal of Shaev's state law claims under 28 U.S.C. § 1367(c) and remand for its consideration in light of the decision we reach on this appeal.

## VI.

To recapitulate, the plaintiff has stated a cause of action on the following grounds: (1) the proxy statement failed to disclose the existence and material terms of the 1997 Plan; (2) the proxy statement failed to disclose the material terms of the 1999 supplement. Importantly, it did not disclose that the amount of compensation to which Saper would be entitled under the 2000 amendment exceeded the $2,225,000 compensation maximum established under the 1999 supplement; (3) the proxy statement omitted the number of eligible executive participants under the Plan, in violation of the Securities Exchange Regulations, 17 C.F.R. § 240.14a-101; (4) the proxy statement contained affirmative statements that were false or misleading in violation of Rule 14a-9 when it stated that a bonus to Saper would be tax deductible to Datascope if it was approved by the shareholders. This statement was false or misleading because (a) the 2000 amendment to the Plan was established too late for the performance goals to comply with the Treasury Regulations; (b) deductibility is destroyed if the bonus amount could be increased during the performance period; and (c) the Board's threat to take the deduction regardless of shareholder approval obviates its deductibility even if approved. 26 C.F.R. § 1.162-27(e)(2); *id.* at § 1.162-27(e)(4).

Accordingly, the District Court's order dismissing Shaev's securities claim will be vacated and the case remanded to the District Court for further proceedings consistent with this opinion. Costs taxed against the appellees.

---

[18] [10] The complaint alleges that among the material omissions in the proxy were reasonable estimates of the bonus payable and the number of eligible executive participants under the Plan. The Security Regulations provide that proxies soliciting shareholder approval for compensation plans must "[d]escribe briefly the material features of the plan being acted upon, identify each class of person who will be eligible to participate therein, indicate the approximate number of persons in each such class, and state the basis of such participation." 17 C.F.R. § 240.14a-101 (Item 10(a)(1)). These allegations raise important questions pertaining to material violations of the Securities Exchange Commission's Regulations.

# SEINFELD v. BARTZ

United States Court of Appeals, Ninth Circuit

322 F.3d 693 (2003)

TASHIMA, J.

Plaintiff-Appellant Greg Seinfeld appeals an order of the district court dismissing his action for failure to state a claim pursuant to Federal Rule of Civil Procedure 12(b)(6). Seinfeld, a shareholder of Cisco Systems, Inc., filed a derivative action against Appellees, the company and its board of directors. In his complaint, Seinfeld alleged that Appellees violated § 14(a) of the Securities Exchange Act of 1934 (the "Exchange Act"), 15 U.S.C. § 78n(a), and Rule 14a-9, 17 C.F.R. § 240.14a-9, by issuing a proxy statement that violated the proxy rules of the Securities and Exchange Commission ("SEC"). Specifically, Seinfeld contends that the proxy statement should have included the value of stock options granted to outside (non-employee) directors. The district court dismissed the complaint. We have jurisdiction pursuant to 28 U.S.C. § 1291, and we affirm.

## BACKGROUND

Seinfeld has been a stockholder of Cisco since August 20, 1998. In 1999, the board of directors sought to amend Cisco's Automatic Option Grant Program for outside directors, which is part of the company's 1996 Stock Incentive Plan. As the district court summarized it:

> The amendment, which was approved by shareholder vote at the November 1999 annual meeting, raised the number of stock options granted to outside directors upon joining the board from 20,000 shares to 30,000 shares. Additionally, the amendment raised the number of options granted annually to each continuing outside director from 10,000 shares to 15,000 shares.

Seinfeld filed a complaint in the United States District Court for the Southern District of New York, alleging that the proxy statement contained "materially false and misleading statements and omit[ted] material facts," in violation of SEC proxy rules. He contended that the proxy statement should have included the value of the option grants based on the Black-Scholes option pricing model, a model allegedly used by Cisco in its annual financial statements and used by the Financial Accounting Standards Board ("FASB"), the SEC, and the Internal Revenue Service ("IRS"). According to the complaint, the Black-Scholes model "measures the cost to the grantor to grant the stock option, . . . commonly referred to as the fair value or the Black-Scholes value of the option," relying on values such as "the volatility of the underlying stock, the risk-free rate of interest, the expiry of the option, the dividends on the underlying stock, the exercise price of the option, and the market price of the underlying stock." According to Seinfeld's calculations, the value of the annual stock option granted to each director on September 27, 1999, the date of the proxy statement, was $1,020,600, and the value on November 10, 1999, the date of the grant, was $630,900. The proxy statement stated that each director was paid an annual retainer of $32,000, plus stock options. Seinfeld alleged that this statement was materially false and misleading because, according to his calculations, the directors actually received annual compensation of $410,500.

Seinfeld also challenged a representation in the proxy statement that, " '[u]nless the market price of the Common Stock appreciates over the option term, no value will be realized from the option grants made to the executive officers.' " Seinfeld alleged that this statement was materially false and misleading because "the grant of stock options results in the immediate realization of value," which is best determined under the Black-Scholes model. Seinfeld further alleged that the proxy statement's representation of the tax consequences of the option grant was false because it failed to explain that stock options are taxable for federal estate tax, gift tax, and generation-skipping transfer tax purposes and are valued using the Black-Scholes model.

The district court held that the Black-Scholes valuations of the option grants are not material facts that were required to have been contained in the proxy statement. The court further rejected Seinfeld's allegation that the proxy statement was misleading because it failed to disclose all federal tax consequences of the options. It therefore dismissed the complaint with prejudice in its entirety, pursuant to Rule 12(b)(6).

\*     \*     \*

## DISCUSSION

Section 14(a) of the Exchange Act makes it unlawful to solicit a proxy "in contravention of such rules and regulations as the Commission may prescribe as necessary or appropriate in the public interest or for the protection of investors." 15 U.S.C. § 78n(a). Rule 14a-9 prohibits the solicitation of a proxy by means of a proxy statement that contains a statement that "is false or misleading with respect to any material fact, or which omits to state any material fact necessary in order to make the statements therein not false or misleading." 17 C.F.R. § 240.14a-9(a). "An omitted fact is material if there is a substantial likelihood that a reasonable shareholder would consider it important in deciding how to vote." *TSC Indus., Inc. v. Northway, Inc.*, 426 U.S. 438, 449, 96 S. Ct. 2126, 48 L. Ed. 2d 757 (1976). "In addition, a Section 14(a), Rule 14a-9 plaintiff must demonstrate that the misstatement or omission was made with the requisite level of culpability and that it was an essential link in the accomplishment of the proposed transaction." *Desaigoudar*, 223 F.3d at 1022 (footnote and citation omitted).

The essence of Seinfeld's complaint is that the proxy statement was misleading because it did not include the Black-Scholes valuation of the options granted to the non-employee directors. He makes several different arguments in advocating the use of Black-Scholes. We conclude that SEC regulations do not require the use of the Black-Scholes valuation and that the proxy statement is not materially false and misleading. In so holding, we agree with the Second Circuit, which faced the same issue in *Resnik v. Swartz*, 303 F.3d 147 (2d Cir. 2002).

Seinfeld's first argument is that the district court erred in relying on four lower court cases to reject the use of the Black-Scholes valuation model because this is inconsistent with our "holding" in *Custom Chrome, Inc. v. Comm'r*, 217 F.3d 1117 (9th Cir. 2000), that Black-Scholes is reliable. We reject this argument because, not only is *Custom Chrome* inapposite, but this was not even a holding in *Custom Chrome*.

The issue in *Custom Chrome* was the value, for federal income tax purposes, of warrants, which are, "in essence, options," that were issued in connection with a loan transaction. *Id.* at 1120. In that case, we were required to determine, under the Internal Revenue Code, when the warrants should be valued and what their value should be for original issue discount ("OID") purposes. Id. at 1121–23. We stated in a footnote that Black-Scholes is one of several "well-established and reliable methods" of valuing options for OID purposes.[19] Id. at 1124 n.10. The issue was the value of warrants for OID purposes in the federal income tax context. Custom Chrome in no way endorses the use of Black-Scholes to value options granted to outside directors, and it certainly does not require the use of Black-Scholes to value options for purposes of a proxy statement. Its reasoning simply is inapposite to the issue presented here.

Seinfeld's second approach is to rely on FASB Statement No. 123, *Accounting for Stock-Based Compensation*, to argue that Black-Scholes is a reliable pricing model. FASB Statement No. 123 deals with the reporting of employee stock options in a company's financial statements for purposes of "arriving at reported earnings." *FASB's Plans Regarding the Accounting for Employee Stock Options (July 31, 2002), available at http://www.fasb.org/news/nr073102.shtml.* "There are salient differences, however, between financial statement disclosure of an estimated value of stock options under a plan and disclosure for the purpose of shareholder ratification of adoption of the plan." *Lewis v. Vogelstein*, 699 A.2d 327, 332 (Del. Ch. 1997); *see also Resnik*, 303 F.3d at 153 (stating that FASB Statement No. 123 recommends recognizing "options' grant-date value as part of compensation expense" in financial statements but "does not purport to address the requirements for reporting proposed compensation in a proxy statement"). FASB Statement No. 123 is not pertinent.

Seinfeld also contends that director compensation is a material fact required to be disclosed under § 14(a) and that the proxy statement fails to comply with SEC regulation disclosure standards. These contentions fail. First, the proxy statement did disclose director compensation.

Second, the proxy statement does comply with SEC regulation disclosure standards. Item 8 of Schedule 14A, 17 C.F.R. § 240.14a-101, dealing with the compensation of directors and executive officers, requires a proxy statement to furnish the information required by Item 402 of Regulation S-K, 17 C.F.R. § 229.402, if action is to be taken with regard to a compensation plan. Item 402(g) addresses the compensation of directors and requires the disclosure of compensation amounts, "including amounts payable for committee participation or special assignments," and "any other arrangements pursuant to which any director of the registrant was compensated." 17 C.F.R. § 229.402(g). As in *Resnik*, "[t]he description of the directors' standard fees and the options proposed to be awarded, as

---

[19] [2] "When a loan is provided at a face value higher than the amount actually loaned, the debtor is allowed to deduct the difference over the life of the loan as [OID], while the creditor realizes the OID as ordinary income." *Custom Chrome*, 217 F.3d at 1121.

disclosed in the proxy statement . . . , plainly meets this basic requirement." 303 F.3d at 152. The proxy statement thus complies with SEC regulation disclosure standards.

Moreover, contrary to Seinfeld's contention, "neither subsection (g), nor any other provision of Item 402 expressly requires disclosure of the grant-date value of stock options proposed to be provided to the directors." *Id.* The court in *Resnik* compared subsection (g) with subsection (c) of Item 402, which requires the disclosure of the value of options granted to certain executive officers and specifically states that Black-Scholes is one possible way of calculating the value of the grant on the grant-date. *Id.*; *see* 17 C.F.R. § 229.402(c). "The absence of any mention of option values or of valuation methods from subsection (g), Compensation of Directors, is persuasive evidence that the Commission did not intend subsection (g) to require disclosure of grant-date value calculation for the options proposed to be awarded to non-employee directors."

Seinfeld contends that the regulations are only minimum disclosure standards and that compliance with the regulations does not necessarily guarantee compliance with Rule 14a-9. He relies on *Zell v. InterCapital Income Sec., Inc.*, 675 F.2d 1041 (9th Cir. 1982), in which we stated that " 'Schedule 14A sets minimum disclosure standards. Compliance with this schedule does not necessarily guarantee that a proxy statement satisfied Rule 14a-9.' " *Id.* at 1044 (quoting *Maldonado v. Flynn*, 597 F.2d 789, 796 n.9 (2d Cir. 1979)).

In support of his argument, Seinfeld repeats the allegations of his complaint that the following representation in the proxy statement was materially false and misleading: "Unless the market price of the Common Stock appreciates over the option term, no value will be realized from the option grants made to the executive officers." Seinfeld's only argument that this is false and misleading, however, is that, according to FASB Statement No. 123, the options are best evaluated by the use of Black-Scholes. As discussed above, this FASB statement concerns financial statements, not proxy statements, and is not relevant to the issue presented here.

More importantly, the statement Seinfeld challenges is contained in a footnote to a table that lists option grants made in the last fiscal year to executive officers of the company, as required by Item 402(c), 17 C.F.R. § 229.402(c). Option grants that have already been made to executive officers are completely unrelated to the amendments to the plan Seinfeld is challenging, which concerned options proposed to be granted to outside directors. *Cf. Resnik*, 303 F.3d at 153–54 (rejecting a challenge to a similar statement, in part because, as here, the statement was contained in a footnote to a table describing options already granted to executives who were not covered by the plan at issue).

The facts of *Zell* are quite different from those presented here. In *Zell*, the plaintiffs charged the defendants, an investment fund, the investment manager, and the parent organization, with violations of § 14(a) and Rule 14a-9 by failing to disclose material information in two proxy statements. The proxy statements recommended approval of an agreement between the fund and a subsidiary of the parent, based in part on the parent's responsible management, financial strength, and investment skills. The proxy statements, however, failed to disclose that there were numerous lawsuits pending against the parent and the subsidiary charging violations of state and federal securities laws. We concluded that "it cannot be said that the omitted information was so obviously unimportant that no reasonable Fund stockholders would consider it of actual significance in determining whether to approve" the agreement and therefore reversed the district court's grant of summary judgment in favor of the defendants. *Id.* at 1049. In finding the omitted information material, we reasoned that the proxy statements expressly relied on the corporations' financial stability and quality of management, that prior breaches of fiduciary duties or violations of securities laws "may have a direct bearing on managerial integrity," and that "[l]itigation involving substantial exposure to damages may affect a corporation's financial status." *Id.* at 1045–46.

The instant case does not present facts as compelling as those in *Zell.* In fact, the statement Seinfeld challenges as misleading is accurate; that is, the option grants made to the executive officers do not have value if the market price of the shares does not appreciate over the option term. *Cf. Resnik,* 303 F.3d at 154 (stating that a somewhat similar statement "accurately describes how value is realized when options are actually exercised").

Finally, Seinfeld contends that the proxy statement was misleading because it did not disclose federal estate, gift, and generation-skipping transfer tax conse-quences of the option grants. He argues that the IRS uses Black-Scholes to value stock options, citing in his complaint Rev. Rul. 98-21, 1998-1 C.B. 975, and Rev. Proc. 98-34, 1998-1 C.B. 983. The IRS publications to which Seinfeld refers deal with the valuation of stock options for federal transfer tax purposes; they have nothing to do with the valuation of options for purposes of disclosures in a proxy statement. *See* Rev. Rul. 98-21 (describing the issue as the time that "the transfer of a nonstatutory stock option . . . by the optionee to a family member, for no consideration" becomes a "completed gift" under the Internal Revenue Code); Rev. Proc. 98-34 § 3 ("This revenue procedure applies only to the valuation for transfer tax purposes of nonpublicly traded compensatory stock options . . . ."). Seinfeld cites no law or SEC regulation that requires the disclosure in a proxy statement of federal transfer tax consequences of option grants to outside directors. Nor does he explain how the failure to discuss federal transfer tax consequences was a material omission. As the district court also reasoned, Appellees have not "falsely stated that the options have no consequences under these three tax schemes."

## CONCLUSION

Even if we take all of the well-pleaded allegations of material fact as true and construe them in the light most favorable to Seinfeld, *see Desaigoudar,* 223 F.3d at 1021, he has not shown that the proxy statement made materially false or misleading statements or contained any material omission. The proxy statement complies with SEC regulations. "If appellant believes that Black-Scholes value disclosure should be mandatory whenever shareholders' approval is sought for a proposed option grant [to outside directors], his remedy is to advocate a change in the regulations before the [SEC]." *Resnik,* 303 F.3d at 155; *cf.* Rob Norton, *The Cure for Lavish Pay? Shame It to Death,* Wash. Post, Sept. 29, 2002, at B1, available at 2002 WL 101064666 (suggesting that the SEC could enact tougher standards for disclosure of corporate pay).

The judgment of the district court is Affirmed.

## NOTES

1.   Why would a shareholder be interested in how many options the officers or directors owned?

2.   Why would a shareholder be interested in the estimated values of the options owned by the officers or directors?

3.   Why do the SEC regulations require less disclosure for non-employee directors?

## B.   REGULATION OF COMMUNICATIONS AMONG SHAREHOLDERS

### SEC RELEASE NO. 34-31326
(Oct. 16, 1992)

SUMMARY: The Securities and Exchange Commission ("Commission") today announces the adoption of amendments to its proxy rules promulgated under Section 14(a) of the Securities Exchange Act of 1934 ("Exchange Act"). By removing unnecessary government interference in discussions among shareholders of corporate performance and other matters of direct interest to all shareholders, these rules should reduce the cost of regulation to both the government and to shareholders. The amendments eliminate unnecessary regulatory obstacles to the exchange of views and opinions by shareholders and others concerning management performance and initiatives presented for a vote of shareholders. The amendments also lower the regulatory costs of conducting a regulated solicitation by management, shareholders and others by minimizing regulatory costs related to the dissemination of soliciting materials. The rules also remove unnecessary limitations on shareholders' use of their voting rights, and improve disclosure to shareholders in the context of a solicitation as well as in the reporting of voting results.

\* \* \*

These changes include:

(1) Rule 14a-2(b) has been amended to create an exemption from the proxy statement delivery and disclosure requirements for communications with shareholders, where the person soliciting is not seeking proxy authority and does not have a substantial interest in the matter subject to a vote or is otherwise ineligible for the exemption. Public notice of written soliciting activity will be required by beneficial owners of more than $5 million of the registrant's securities through publication, broadcast or submission to the Commission of the written soliciting materials;

(3) Rule 14a-3 [FN3] has been amended to add a new paragraph (f), exempting solicitations conveyed by public broadcast or speech or publication from the proxy

statement delivery requirements, provided a definitive proxy statement is on file with the Commission;

(4) Rules 14a-3(a) and 14a-4 have been amended to allow registrants and other soliciting parties to commence a solicitation on the basis of a preliminary proxy statement publicly filed with the Commission, so long as no form of proxy is provided to the solicited shareholders until the dissemination of a definitive proxy statement;

\* \* \*

(8) Rule 14a-4(d) [FN8] has been amended to allow shareholders who seek minority representation on the board of directors to seek proxy authority to vote for one or more of management's nominees, so long as the names of non-consenting nominees do not appear on the dissident's form of proxy or in the dissident's proxy statement;

## I. INTRODUCTION

The amendments to the proxy rules and other disclosure provisions adopted today follow upon an extensive three-year examination by the Commission of the effectiveness of the proxy-voting process and its effect on the corporate governance system in this country.

\* \* \*

Within the overall scope of this broad examination, the Commission has focused particularly on the role of its proxy and disclosure rules in impeding shareholder communication and participation in the corporate governance process. This demonstrated effect of the current rules is contrary to Congress's intent that the rules assure fair, and effective shareholder suffrage. Apart from attempts to obtain proxy voting authority, to the degree the current rules inhibit the ability of shareholders not seeking proxy authority to analyze and discuss issues pertaining to the operation of a company and its performance, these rules may in fact run exactly contrary to the best interests of shareholders.

The amendments adopted today reflect a Commission determination that the federal proxy rules have created unnecessary regulatory impediments to communication among shareholders and others and to the effective use of shareholder voting rights. The Commission has also determined that modifications in the current rules are desirable to reduce these burdens and to achieve the purposes set forth in the Exchange Act.

\* \* \*

Thus, the description of the matters to be brought before a meeting for a vote (including the election of directors), the material information related to all such matters (including any substantial interest the soliciting person has in the subject matter of the vote), and the specifics on how the proxy recipient proposes to vote on behalf of the proxy giver unless otherwise instructed are core information critical to shareholders as part of the proxy process. Likewise, the terms of the proxy authority solicited and the ability of soliciting shareholders to reach other shareholders are key elements in assuring the fairness of the solicitation of proxy authority. On the whole, the regulatory scheme adopted by the Commission pursuant to the broad authority granted by Section 14(a) has been designed to make sure that management and others who solicit shareholder proxies provide this needed information to shareholders, allow them to instruct the specific use of their proxy and provide them access to other shareholders through mailing or by access to a shareholder list.

Originally, the definition of "solicitation" of a proxy reflected this principal focus of the proxy rules, by limiting the reach of those rules to any "request" for a proxy or the furnishing of a proxy, consent, or authorization to security holders. Thereafter, the definition was broadened to make clear that any communication by a person soliciting proxy authority, not just the communication delivered with the form of proxy, was a solicitation. However, in 1942, without explanation, the Commission expanded the definition of "solicitation" of a proxy to include "any request to revoke or not execute a proxy . . . .

In 1956, the Commission significantly expanded the definition of "solicitation" of a proxy to embrace "any communication" which could be viewed as being "reasonably calculated" to influence a shareholder to give, deny or revoke a proxy. In adopting the sweeping 1956 definition, the Commission sought to address abuses by persons who were actually engaging in solicitations of proxy authority in connection with election contests. The Commission does not seem to have been aware, or to have intended, that the new definition might also sweep within all the regulatory requirements persons who did not "request" a shareholder to grant or to revoke or deny a proxy, but whose expressed opinions might be found to have been reasonably calculated to affect the views of other shareholders positively or negatively toward a particular company and its management or directors. Since any such persuasion — even if unintended — could affect the decision of shareholders even many months later to give or withhold a proxy, such communications at least literally could fall within the new definition.

The literal breadth of the new definition of solicitation was so great as potentially to turn almost every expression of opinion concerning a publicly-traded corporation into a regulated proxy solicitation. Thus, newspaper op-ed articles, public speeches or television commentary on a specific company could all later be alleged to have been proxy solicitations in connection with the election of directors, as could private conversations among more than 10 shareholders. This created a basis upon which claims that the proxy rules, including the mandatory disclosure, filing and dissemination provisions of those rules, could be brought to bear not only on persons seeking authority to vote another's shares, but also on those persons merely expressing a view or opinion on management performance or on initiatives presented by management and others for a shareholder vote.

\* \* \*

*See* Letter re College Retirement Equities Fund, dated November 12, 1986 (no action relief with respect to op-ed piece submitted by employees of shareholder proponent of proposals on same issue, so long as article was solicited by newspaper, constituted a general discussion and did not refer to specific proposal, and appeared three months prior to meeting). *Cf.* Letter from the Director of the Division of

Corporation Finance to the American Newspaper Association, dated September 27, 1955 (addressing concern that proxy rules could apply to newspaper's own editorials relating to a proxy contest, by stating that rules, as well as proposed amendments then under construction, only apply to persons who solicit proxies from holders).

Since 192, conversations with not more than 10 shareholders have been exempt "solicitations." Exchange Act Rel. No. 3347 (Dec. 18, 1942) (exempting "less than 10").

If the current proxy rules apply to a communication, the effect can be very costly. Among other things, the person making the communication would be required to prepare a proxy statement and mail it to every shareholder of the company who is deemed to have been solicited. Where a communication appears in the public media, the Commission has taken the position that all shareholders have been solicited. In such a case, the cost of the mailing requirement alone could run into hundreds of thousands of dollars, and the decision on whether a solicitation occurred will be judged purely in hindsight. Thus, shareholders can be deterred from discussing management and corporate performance by the prospect of being found after the fact to have engaged in a proxy solicitation. The costs of complying with those rules also has meant that, unless they have substantial financial backing, shareholders and other interested persons may effectively be cut out of the debate regarding proposals presented by management or shareholders for a vote.

To correct this distortion of the purposes of the proxy rules, initially highlighted in petitions and other requests from the shareholder community for reform, the Commission proposed several revisions to the proxy rules intended to deregulate constraints on communications by persons who do not seek to obtain proxy authority from any other shareholders, and who do not have a substantial interest in the subject matter of the communication beyond the interest of such person as a shareholder. The original rule proposal was intended to allow such "disinterested" persons who are not seeking proxy authority to express their views freely, without any requirement to file materials with, or otherwise to notify, the Commission. Under this proposal, all communications would have remained subject to antifraud standards, but the excessive regulatory reach of "solicitation" would have been narrowed significantly. The Commission also proposed to remove some of the unnecessary regulatory costs from the regulated proxy solicitation process, such as by eliminating the requirement to obtain preclearance of all soliciting materials from the Commission's staff before their dissemination.

These proposals elicited widespread approval by the shareholder community and further suggestions for reform. Many commenters expressed the view that the proxy rules created both costs and a chilling effect on attempts to participate in the governance process by expressing their views.

The corporate community raised numerous objections to the proposals. Many corporate commenters argued that absent a filing obligation in connection with all communications among shareholders, the reforms would "further the disturbing trend toward the determination of the outcome of shareholder voting by secret back-room lobbying of and negotiations with institutional investors, rather than in open and public proxy campaigns." However, these comments did not provide examples of cases in which the outcome of a proposal submitted for a shareholder vote had been determined through secret actions of institutional investors. These comments also did not explain why any shareholder seeking to assemble majority voting support for a proposal would wish to keep the arguments in favor of the shareholder's position secret. Maximizing the knowledge of a shareholder's views rather than concealing them would seem the more likely approach.

When and under what circumstances a large shareholder, or group of shareholders acting together, must reveal to the SEC, the company, other shareholders, and the market its plans and proposals regarding the company has been addressed by Congress, but not through the provisions governing proxy solicitations. Section 13(d) of the Exchange Act, as implemented by the Commission in its regulations adopted thereunder, sets forth the circumstances when public disclosure of plans and proposals by significant shareholders, as well as agreements among shareholders to act together with respect to voting matters, must be disclosed to the market.

Corporate commenters also argued that disclosure of communications among shareholders is necessary to allow management "a role to play" in rebutting any misstatements or mischaracterizations, to the benefit of shareholders as a whole in ensuring that proxies are executed on the basis of "correct" information. Of course, much commentary concerning corporate performance, management capability or directorial qualifications or the desirability of a particular initiative subject to a shareholder vote is by its nature judgmental. As to such opinions, there typically is not a "correct" viewpoint.

While voting rights are valuable assets and an uninformed exercise of those rights could represent a wasted opportunity for the voting shareholder, that concern does not justify the government's requiring that all private conversations on matters subject to a shareholder vote be reported to the government. In the Commission's view, the antifraud provisions provide adequate protection against fraudulent and deceptive communications to shareholders on matters presented for a vote by persons not seeking proxy authority and not in the classes of persons ineligible for the exemption.

A regulatory scheme that inserted the Commission staff and corporate management into every exchange and conversation among shareholders, their advisors and other parties on matters subject to a vote certainly would raise serious questions under the free speech clause of the First Amendment, particularly where no proxy authority is being solicited by such persons. This is especially true where such intrusion is not necessary to achieve the goals of the federal securities laws.

The purposes of the proxy rules themselves are better served by promoting free discussion, debate and learning among shareholders and interested persons, than by placing restraints on that process to ensure that management has the ability to address every point raised in the exchange of views. Indeed, the Commission has not perceived, and the comments have not demonstrated, shareholder abuses where proxy authority is not being sought by the person engaged in the communications. However, there have been situations in which discontented shareholders have been subjected to legal threats based on the possibility the shareholder might have triggered proxy filing requirements by expressing disagreement to other shareholders.

In the amendments adopted today, the Commission has also attempted to remove unnecessary impediments to the solicitation of proxy authority to allow management and other persons seeking proxy authority more efficiently and effectively to get their case to the shareholders. The rules as adopted today reflect views expressed both by shareholders that some of the proposed restrictions would have had significant deterrent effect to the expression of views, and by management commenters that certain unnecessary restraints on their communications with shareholders remained under the reproposals.

## UNITED STATES v. MATTHEWS
United States Court of Appeals, Second Circuit
787 F.2d 38 (1986)

VAN GRAAFEILAND, J.

Clark J. Matthews, II, appeals from a judgment of the United States District Court for the Eastern District of New York (Sifton, J.) convicting Matthews of violating section 14(a) of the Securities Exchange Act of 1934, 15 U.S.C. § 78n(a) and SEC's Implementing Rule 14a-9, 17 C.F.R. 240.14a-9. This conviction was based on the second count of a two-count indictment. The first count charged that Matthews and S. Richmond Dole conspired with each other and with others to bribe members of the New York State Tax Commission in order to obtain favorable rulings on tax matters of interest to the defendants' employer, The Southland Corporation, and to file United States income tax returns for Southland which falsely listed the bribe payment as a legal fee. Both defendants were acquitted on this count.

The second count, which was against Matthews alone, charged in substance that Matthews' election to the Southland Board of Directors in 1981 was accomplished by means of a proxy statement which failed to disclose, among other things, that he was a member of the conspiracy alleged in Count I. For the reasons that follow, we reverse the judgment of conviction and remand to the district court with instructions to dismiss the indictment.

Prior to his conviction in this case, Clark Matthews had had an honorable career. . . . [He had been] a staff attorney for the Southland Corporation, a large commercial company with headquarters in Dallas. He subsequently became Southland's General Counsel and is now its Executive Vice President and Chief Financial Officer.

In 1972 Southland became involved in litigation with the New York State Department of Taxation and Finance regarding Southland's asserted obligation to pay sales taxes owed by some of its franchised stores. Eugene DeFalco, then manager of Southland's Northeastern Division, who was the Government's principal witness and an admitted liar and thief, testified under grant of immunity that he inquired of one John Kelly, another immunized thief and liar, whether Kelly knew of anyone who could help in resolving the tax problem. Kelly arranged for DeFalco to meet with a New York attorney and City Councilman, Eugene Mastropieri.

According to DeFalco, Mastropieri informed him that the matter might require "heavy entertainment," which DeFalco took to mean a bribe. DeFalco testified that he told S. Richmond Dole, Southland's Vice President for Franchise Stores, that, in his opinion, somebody was going to be paid off. This testimony was denied by Dole. DeFalco also testified that, when Dole refused Mastropieri's request that he be paid in cash, Kelly suggested payment by way of a bill purporting to cover the lease of an airplane. This proposal brought Matthews into the picture for the first time. When Dole conveyed the lease proposal to Matthews with the explanation that Mastropieri wanted to conceal the legal fee from his law partner, Matthews telephoned DeFalco and told him that "Southland doesn't pay legal bills in the form of airplane leases [and] he did not want to see any more funny proposals coming through like the airplane lease . . . ." When DeFalco assured Matthews that the payment to Mastropieri was in fact a legal fee, Matthews replied that "if it's a legal fee, we are going to pay it as a legal fee, not as something else."

In July 1977 DeFalco sent Dole a bill from Mastropieri for legal services in the amount of $96,500, which Dole processed for payment. The bill neither was seen nor approved by Matthews. Southland's check in payment was delivered to Mastropieri by Kelly who, upon instructions from DeFalco, secured a blank check from Mastropieri in exchange, which Kelly filled out in the same amount as the Southland check. Kelly promptly deposited Mastropieri's check in a Toronto bank where "nobody would know about it". On August 8, 1977 DeFalco arranged to have $10,000 transferred from Kelly's Toronto account to DeFalco's account at The Chase Manhattan Bank. Thereafter, on August 23rd, DeFalco opened an account in his own name at the Toronto bank and had Kelly transfer $20,000 into that account. He also had five checks totalling $18,500 issued for his own personal use. On March 22, 1978 DeFalco started drawing from his Toronto account, and, by August 16, 1979, the account was closed. In all, DeFalco stole $48,500 of Southland's money. The balance of $48,000 was taken by Kelly, $20,000 on September 21, 1977 and $28,000 on July 10, 1979. Not a penny was used to bribe anyone.

\* \* \*

### Testimony of Matthews

Q:  Now, at the conclusion of all this, what was the decision that was reached at the audit committee level there by yourself, Mr. Davis, the outside expert, Fedders, and the audit committee as to the Mastropieri matter?

A:  We concluded that we had no proof that there had been a bribe or any improper use of the money.

We took into consideration our concerns, but we also took into consideration that there were continuing sales tax cases filed and that there had been no unusual activity in those cases or no resolution during this period of time.

And based on the fact that we did not have any proof we determined that it would be inappropriate on a sensitive matter of this nature to include it in the written report, but that we would make an oral report on the matter to the board. . . .

Testimony of John Fedders

Q:          Would you tell us what were the reasons that were discussed and the
            conclusions that were reached as to why it shouldn't be put in the
            document?

A:          As I said, we didn't have proof. It was a matter of concern, but there
            was not sufficient proof.

We are not at all surprised that the jury acquitted Matthews of the charges in
Count I, and we are not completely comfortable with the Government's contention
that the acquittal was based on the running of the statute of limitations. The
Government argues that we must assume the jury followed the district court's
instruction not to convict Matthews on Count II unless it either found him guilty of
the crime charged in Count I or not guilty by reason of the statute of limitations.
Although this argument states generally sound doctrine, *United States v. Kaplan*,
510 F.2d 606, 611 (2d Cir. 1974), it comes with poor grace from a prosecution team
which successfully opposed Matthews' request for a special verdict or jury
interrogatory that would have precluded the making of the argument. This
interrogatory, which was requested not once, but twice, would have asked the jurors
to state whether, if they found a verdict of not guilty on Count I, that verdict was
based on the running of the statute of limitations. It would have been quite proper
for the district court to have submitted this query to the jury. . . .

Of course, the issue on this appeal is not whether the jury found Matthews guilty
of conspiracy in 1985, but whether Matthews should have publicly pronounced
himself guilty in 1981. We have expressed our misgivings concerning the assumed
finding of guilt by the jury simply because the greater the uncertainty that exists
today, the less reason there was for Matthews to confess seven years ago that he
was guilty. However, regardless of the merits of the Government's contentions
concerning the basis of the jury's verdict on Count I, we find no merit in the
Government's argument that Matthews violated section 14a and Rule 14a-9 by not
confessing that he was guilty of conspiracy three years before he was indicted on
that charge.

Section 14(a) makes it unlawful for any person to solicit or to permit the use of
his name to solicit any proxy "in contravention of such rules and regulations as the
Commission may prescribe as necessary or appropriate in the public interest or for
the protection of investors."

\*   \*   \*

The Commission also has promulgated rules dealing specifically with proxy
statements. *See* Schedule 14A, 17 C.F.R. § 240.14a-101. Item 6 of this section covers
statements used in the election of directors and executive officers, and incorporates
the disclosure requirements of Item 401 of Regulation S-K, 17 C.F.R. § 229.401.
Item 401 provides that a candidate for director must disclose whether he has been
"convicted in a criminal proceeding or is a named subject of a pending criminal
proceeding (excluding traffic violations and other minor offenses)" providing that
the incident in question occurred during the preceding five years and disclosure is
material to an evaluation of the candidate's ability or integrity.

In November 1980 attorneys at Arnold and Porter were informed that the federal prosecutor who had been presenting evidence to a grand jury during the preceding six months concerning possible criminal activities of Councilman Mastropieri now regarded Southland and DeFalco as targets of the investigation and Matthews and Dole as subjects.[20] On January 23, 1981 four Arnold and Porter partners, including Peter Bleakley, the partner with principal responsibility for the Southland account, attended a meeting of Southland's Board of Directors and reported this change of events to them. The Board was told that this involved the same matter that Vieth and Fedders had reported three years before. The minutes of the January 28, 1981 meeting state:

> Mr. Vieth then described the scope of an investigation by a Federal Grand Jury sitting in the Eastern District of New York. There followed a discussion of the investigation.

With full knowledge of Matthews' status as a "subject" of the grand jury's investigation, the Chairman of the Board nonetheless asked Matthews if he would run for election to the Board. Matthews inquired of Bleakley if, under the circumstances, he should run, and Bleakley told Matthews that there was no reason for him not to do so. Upon further inquiry by Matthews concerning disclosure, Bleakley told Matthews that Bleakley and his partners did not believe that the federal securities laws required Matthews to disclose that he was a subject of the investigation. Matthews ran and was elected.

\* \* \*

Although "[t]raditionally, there has been a close working relationship between the Justice Department and the SEC," H.R.Rep. No. 95-650, 95th Cong., 1st Sess. 10 (September 28, 1977), quoted in *United States v. Fields*, 592 F.2d 638, 646 n. 19 (2d Cir. 1978), *cert. denied*, 442 U.S. 917, 99 S. Ct. 2838, 61 L. Ed. 2d 284 (1979), in the instant case, the United States Attorney's office proceeded on its own. In fact, both the then local SEC Administrator and a former SEC General Counsel publicly questioned the wisdom of trying Matthews on the securities count. *See* WALL ST. J., February 5, 1985, at 20, col. 1.[21] The results of proceeding without the benefit of

---

[20] [3] There is a clear distinction between the "subject" of a grand jury investigation and the "target" of such an investigation. One about whom a grand jury seeks information in an investigation of possible wrongdoing that not yet has focused on the individual involved is a "subject" of the investigation. The Department of Justice guidelines define a "target" as a "person as to whom the prosecutor or the grand jury has substantial evidence linking him/her to the commission of a crime and who, in the judgment of the prosecutor, is a putative defendant." United States Attorney's Manual § 9-11.260 (June 15, 1984); *see United States v. Winter*, 348 F.2d 204, 207–08 (2d Cir.), *cert. denied*, 382 U.S. 955, 86 S. Ct. 429, 15 L. Ed. 2d 360 (1965); *People v. Steuding*, 6 N.Y.2d 214, 216, 189 N.Y.S.2d 166, 160 N.E.2d 468 (1959). In accordance with longstanding practice in this Circuit, if a grand jury witness is considered to be a "target", he must be informed of that fact. *United States v. Jacobs*, 547 F.2d 772, 774 (2d Cir. 1976), cert. dismissed, 436 U.S. 31, 98 S. Ct. 1873, 56 L. Ed. 2d 53 (1978).

[21] [4] Regional Director Ira Sorkin said "I don't know of any other case where someone is accused of failing to disclose a crime they haven't been convicted of." He said that prosecutors in the instant case were pushing "an expansion of the concept" of an executive's liability in failing to disclose pertinent information and concluded "It's a new approach."

Former General Counsel Harvey L. Pitt said "To ask people to accuse themselves and indict and convict themselves is silly. So why should that be required in proxy statements?" Such a disclosure statement,

SEC expertise are evident throughout the proceedings, beginning with the indictment itself.

The Proxy Statement upon which the Government's charges were based was for Southland's 1981 Annual Shareholders Meeting, at which eleven unopposed candidates for directorships, including Matthews, were elected. The Statement gave only basic information concerning each candidate. Insofar as Matthews was concerned, the Statement said that Matthews was forty-four years of age, that he served as Vice President and General Counsel from 1973 to 1979 and as Executive Vice President and Chief Financial Officer since 1979. The Statement also set forth Matthews' "Cash and cash-equivalent forms of remuneration" and the extent of his "Security Ownership." The Government contends that this simple recital was made false and misleading in violation of Rule 14a-9(a) because it (1) failed to disclose that Matthews had engaged in a conspiracy to bribe New York public officials and to defraud the United States by preventing the IRS from determining the true nature of the business expense deductions and (2) failed to disclose that Matthews had failed to disclose to the audit committee of the Board of Directors, Southland's independent auditors, outside tax counsel, the IRS, the SEC, the FBI and others that he was engaged in the conspiracy.

The Government argued under Count I that Matthews became a member of the conspiracy on the day he submitted his Business Ethics Review report to the Board of Directors, when, according to the prosecutor, "he held the truth and the lie in each hand and decided to give the lie to the Board of Directors." When the prosecutor thereafter turned to Count II, he argued that Matthews'failure to disclose to the shareholders that he had failed to disclose to the Board put him in violation of Rule 14a-9. We note as a preliminary matter that the evidence does not clarify precisely what facts Matthews should have told the shareholders he failed to disclose to the Board.

"Liability under Rule 14a-9 is predicated upon a showing that an allegedly omitted fact is true." Overstatement can be as seriously misleading as understatement. *Electronic Specialty Co. v. International Controls Corp.*, 409 F.2d 937, 948 (2d Cir. 1969). Although the prosecutor managed to incorporate the words "bribe", "bribery", and "slush fund" into every possible question, and prominently displayed one or more of these words in his blown-up summary charts, DeFalco testified that he neither heard nor used any of these words until they were spoken to him in the United States Attorneys Office in 1980, some two to three years after his alleged conversations with Matthews. Moreover, although it is undisputed that not a penny of bribe money was paid to anyone, the Government, even at this late date, argues that Matthews "never even asked the Board to approve the bribe, but instead misled it into believing that no bribe had been paid." . . .

Although Matthews hardly could have confessed to membership in a phantom conspiracy, the Government is equally vague concerning whom Matthews should have identified as his co-conspirators. The SEC disapproves of attacks on character without complete and adequate supporting data, the Commission's position being that such attacks are contrary to the standards of fair disclosure unless they are in

---

he continued "runs counter to what the Fifth Amendment is all about."

fact true. II Loss, Securities Regulation 913 (1961). In a note to Rule 14a-9, 17 C.F.R. § 240.14a-9, the Commission describes as examples of misleading statements under that section:

> Material which directly or indirectly impugns character, integrity or personal reputation, or directly or indirectly makes charges concerning improper, illegal or immoral conduct or associations, without factual foundation.

The courts agree. *See, e.g., Kass v. Arden-Mayfair, Inc.*, 431 F. Supp. 1037, 1045 (C.D. Calif. 1977) ("[A] 'puffed-up' accusation may constitute the presentation of an untrue statement.").

. . . The Government likewise makes no mention of the furor that would have resulted had Matthews "impugn[ed]" the "character, integrity or personal reputation" of the members of the New York State Tax Commission by falsely stating that one of them had received a bribe of $5,000 and that $35,000 more was to be spread among the other Commission members. *See* Note, *Disclosure of Payments to Foreign Government Officials Under the Securities Acts*, 89 Harv. L. REV. 1848, 1870 (1976) ("The State Department has warned that uncorroborated allegations that foreign officials have accepted improper payments have done grave harm to American foreign relations.").

The issue with the most far-reaching implications in the field of federal securities law, however, is not what "true" facts Matthews should have disclosed, but whether section 14a of the Exchange Act and the SEC rules enacted pursuant thereto required Matthews to state to all the world that he was guilty of the uncharged crime of conspiracy. This query, we are satisfied, must be answered in the negative.

When Congress created the SEC in the 1934 Exchange Act, it was its intention to give the Commission "complete discretion . . . to require in corporate reports only such information as it deems necessary or appropriate in the public interest or to protect investors." S.Rep. No. 792, 73d Cong., 2d Sess. 5 (1934), quoted in *Natural Resources Defense Council, Inc. v. SEC, supra*, 606 F.2d at 1051. Although we have held in a number of civil cases that Schedule 14A sets only minimum disclosure standards and that compliance with this Schedule does not guarantee that a proxy statement contains no false or misleading statements, *Maldonado v. Flynn*, 597 F.2d 789, 796 n. 9 (2d Cir. 1979), a discussion of criminal liability should begin at least with the rules and regulations that the Commission has enacted. *See* Herlands, *Criminal Law Aspects of the Securities Exchange Act of 1934*, 21 Va. L. REV. 139, 140 (1934). Schedule 14A provides us "with the Commission's expert view of the types of involvement in legal proceedings that are most likely to be matters of concern to shareholders in a proxy contest." *GAF Corp. v. Heyman*, 724 F.2d 727, 739 (2d Cir. 1983). We take cognizance of this "expert view" as disclosed in the Commission's Rules, knowing that it was arrived at in general compliance with the provisions of the Administrative Procedure Act, 5 U.S.C. § 551 et seq., and only after every feasible effort has been made to secure the views of persons to be affected. III Loss, Securities Regulation 1936–44 (1961); see Natural Resources Defense Council, Inc. v. SEC, supra, 606 F.2d at 1036–42.

The provisions of Item 6 of Schedule 14A, which require disclosure of only criminal convictions or pending criminal proceedings, were proposed in 1976, Securities Act Release No. 5758 [1976–77 Transfer Binder] Fed. Sec. L. Rep. (CCH) ¶ 80,783 and adopted in 1978, Securities Act Release No. 5949 [1978 Transfer Binder] Fed. Sec. L. Rep. (CCH) ¶ 81,649. In adopting the specifically articulated disclosure provisions of Item 6, the Commission said:

> Because information reflecting on management ability and integrity is, in part, subjective, it is difficult to articulate a meaningful, well-functioning objective disclosure requirement which will elicit it. The Commission believes that the categories of information about officers' and directors' involvement in litigation proposed in Release 5758 are material to investors. They represent factual indicia of past management performance in areas of investor concern.

Securities Act Release No. 5949, *supra*, at p. 80,618.

It is significant that, although the Commission gave consideration to amending Schedule 14A so as to require disclosure of questionable or illegal payments, *see* Securities Exchange Act Release No. 13185 [1976–77 Transfer Binder] Fed. Sec. L. Rep. (CCH) ¶ 80,896 at 87,382–84, it did so knowing that this area is "difficult and complex," and it failed to adopt the proposals.

\* \* \*

The Commission has not promulgated specific disclosure requirements relating to all qualitative conduct, or, to the extent necessary, articulated a policy for law enforcement when information about such conduct has not been disclosed. The full extent of the obligation to disclose such information is uncertain in light of existing cases. In this limited area, there is little guidance for issuers or practitioners for resolving materiality and disclosure problems.

We deem it significant that those courts which have spoken in this area in the years following Matthews' asserted violations almost universally have rejected efforts to require that management make qualitative disclosures that were not at least implicit in the Commission's rules.

\* \* \*

Absent credible allegations of self-dealing by the directors or dishonesty or deceit which inures to the direct, personal benefit of the directors — a fact that demonstrates a betrayal of trust to the corporation and shareholders and the director's essential unfitness for corporate stewardship — we hold that director misconduct of the type traditionally regulated by state corporate law need not be disclosed in proxy solicitations for director elections. This type of mismanagement, unadorned by self-dealing, is simply not material or otherwise within the ambit of the federal securities laws.

\* \* \*

We are satisfied, however, that Matthews was not legally required to confess that he was guilty of an uncharged crime in order that Southland's shareholders could determine the morality of his conduct.

We hold that at least so long as uncharged criminal conduct is not required to be disclosed by any rule lawfully promulgated by the SEC, nondisclosure of such conduct cannot be the basis of a criminal prosecution. Our unwillingness to permit section 14(a) to be used as expansively as the Government has done in this case rests not only on the history of the Commission's approach to the problem of qualitative disclosures and the case law that has developed on this subject but also on the obvious due process implications that would arise from permitting a conviction to stand in the absence of clearer notice as to what disclosures are required in this uncertain area.

\*    \*    \*

Were we to face the issue directly, we are not certain we would find persuasive the argument that Matthews' self-incrimination privilege was not violated because he was not compelled to run for the office of director. Coercion associated with a person's livelihood, professional standing and reputation may, in some circumstances, be too powerful to ignore when Fifth Amendment rights are at issue.

For all the reasons above discussed, the judgment of the district court is reversed, and the matter is remanded to the district court with instructions to dismiss the indictment.

## NOTE

This case illustrates the difficulty imposed on those corporations subject to the proxy rules. The type of disclosure required by the proxy rules is generally interpreted as a minimum. If literally following the rule results in a misleading statement, one must supplement it with the information that will make it "not misleading." That doctrine certainly had an impact on this case. Secondly, the principal case faces the problem of how to handle rumor, hearsay, or innuendo. Should the shareholders be entitled to learn of the allegations against Mr. Matthews? If the type of allegations discussed in the case must be disclosed to the shareholders, would the corporation be benefited or harmed?

## ROYAL BUSINESS GROUP, INC. v. REALIST, INC.
### United States Court of Appeals, First Circuit
### 933 F.2d 1056 (1991)

SELYA, J.

This case requires us to consider whether a proxy contestant has standing to sue under Section 14(a) of the Securities Exchange Act of 1934, 15 U.S.C. § 78n(a), for allegedly false and misleading statements contained in management's proxy materials. Because we are convinced that Congress did not intend proxy contestants to have a private right of action as such under Section 14(a), and because the complaint before us does not state a cognizable claim for common law fraud, we affirm the district court's dismissal of plaintiffs' suit.

## I. BACKGROUND

The proxy contest at issue involved Realist, Inc., a Delaware corporation having its principal place of business in Wisconsin. The plaintiffs, Royal Business Group, Inc. (Royal) and its wholly owned subsidiary, American Business Group, Inc. (ABG), New Hampshire corporations headquartered in Massachusetts, contend that, but for Realist's failure to disclose certain material information in the course of soliciting proxies, they would never have waged the proxy war, thus saving hundreds of thousands of dollars. We limn the relevant circumstances in accordance with the protocol which Fed.R.Civ.P. 12(b)(6) demands. *See, e.g., Correa-Martinez v. Arrillaga-Belendez*, 903 F.2d 49, 51 (1st Cir. 1990) (on motion to dismiss, reviewing court must accept all well-pleaded facts as they appear in the complaint and indulge all reasonable inferences in the plaintiffs' favor); *Dartmouth Review v. Dartmouth College*, 889 F.2d 13, 16 (1st Cir. 1989) (same).

In March 1988, ABG began to acquire Realist stock, ultimately buying 55,010 shares (8% of the issued and outstanding voting stock). In May of that year, Royal sent Realist the first of a series of letters declaring its intention to acquire all Realist's outstanding shares at an above-market premium. Realist repulsed the plaintiffs serial overtures, reaffirming its intention to remain independent and essaying a variety of defensive actions to thwart a hostile takeover. The directors reduced the size of the board.[22] They also began wooing a Swiss-based company, Ammann Laser Technik AG (Ammann). Although negotiations with Ammann were already well underway by the spring of 1989, Realist's proxy solicitation materials for the annual meeting, mailed on April 27, 1989, made no mention of them.[23]

Meanwhile, rebuffed by management and unaware of Realist's negotiations with Ammann, Royal instituted a proxy contest seeking, indirectly, a shareholder referendum on its offer to acquire Realist. As part of the battle plan, ABG notified the defendant of the plaintiffs' intention to nominate candidates for the two directorships to be filled at the June 6, 1989 annual meeting. The plaintiffs' proxy materials emphasized that their nominees, if elected, would actively pursue the sale of Realist to Royal. Five days before the annual meeting, two Realist directors purchased 26,000 shares of Realist stock. Although the seller had theretofore signed a proxy in favor of the plaintiffs' nominees, that proxy was revoked at the time of the sale and replaced by a proxy favoring the incumbent slate.

To make a tedious tale tolerably terse, the annual meeting took place as scheduled. The insurgents prevailed. The defeated incumbents challenged the election results in the Delaware Chancery Court. On June 30, 1989, Realist announced its acquisition of Ammann. In response to the announcement, Royal

---

[22] [2] Because of the directors' staggered terms, the change (from seven directors to six) had the effect of shrinking the number of seats to be filled at the 1989 annual meeting from three to two.

[23] [3] The planned acquisition of Ammann was potentially important to the proxy context in a variety of ways. It was to be financed partially by issuing stock, thus diluting the plaintiffs' stake in Realist, and partially by a cash payment, thus depleting Realist's liquid reserves. Consummation of the deal would also make Realist a less attractive takeover candidate since Ammann was likely, in the short run, to be a drag on earnings. Lastly, the planned transaction was designed to resurrect the newly eliminated board seat, see supra note 2, confer it on Ammann's president, Hans-Rudolph Ammann, and further strengthen management's hand by giving 68,000 shares of Realist stock to Mr. Ammann.

immediately withdrew its offer to acquire Realist.[24]

Invoking both federal question and diversity jurisdiction, 28 U.S.C. §§ 1331, 1332, the plaintiffs filed this civil action in the United States District Court for the District of Massachusetts. In their complaint, they alleged that Realist, in the proxy materials sent to shareholders prior to the annual meeting, had failed to disclose important matters (e.g., the negotiations to acquire Ammann; the planned acquisition of the 26,000-share block of stock) and that this failure constituted both a violation of Section 14(a) (count 1) and common law fraud (count 2). The complaint sought money damages of $350,000, more or less, representing the expenses incurred in connection with the proxy contest, election, and ensuing Delaware litigation. The gravamen of the suit lay in the idea that, had Realist complied with its disclosure obligations, the plaintiffs would have withdrawn their acquisition offer and eschewed the costly proxy contest.

The defendants moved to dismiss the complaint for failure to state a claim upon which relief could be granted.

\* \* \*

Section 14(a) of the Securities Exchange Act prohibits any person from soliciting proxies "in contravention of such rules and regulations as the Commission may prescribe as necessary or appropriate in the public interest or for protection of investors." 15 U.S.C. § 78n(a). The SEC promulgated Rule 14a-9 thereunder, which provides:

> No solicitation subject to this regulation shall be made by means of any proxy statement, form of proxy, notice of meeting or other communication, written or oral, containing any statement which, at the time and in the light of the circumstances under which it is made, is false or misleading with respect to any material fact, or which omits to state any material fact necessary in order to correct any statement therein not false or misleading or necessary to correct any statement in any earlier communication with respect to the solicitation of a proxy for the same meeting or subject matter which has become false or misleading.

It is well established that shareholders have a private right of action under Section 14(a) and Rule 14a-9 against issuers of allegedly false or misleading proxy materials. *See J.I. Case Co. v. Borak*, 377 U.S. 426 (1964). As the *Borak* Court reasoned: "While [Section 14(a)'s] language makes no specific reference to a private right of action, among its chief purposes is the 'protection of investors,' which certainly implies the availability of judicial relief to achieve that result." *Id.* at 432.

To say that shareholders have a private right of action under Section 14(a) is not necessarily to say that shareholders may unleash Section 14(a) even without a meaningful link between the claimed proxy violation and the shareholder's role qua shareholder. This case, then, tests the margins of the *Borak* doctrine. Plaintiffs claim that their status as shareholders of Realist gives them carte blanche under

---

[24] [4] On September 19, 1989, the Delaware court sustained the incumbents' challenge and ordered a new election. *See Parshalle v. Roy*, 567 A.2d 19 (Del. Ch. 1989). Royal did not contest either of the seats when the election was replayed on December 15, 1989.

Section 14(a) to seek damages for the expenses they incurred in a materially different capacity: as proxy contestants.[25] Thus, the issue before us is not whether there is a private remedy, or even who may invoke that remedy, *cf. Piper v. Chris-Craft Industries, Inc.*, 430 U.S. 1, 55 n.4, 97 (1977) (Stevens, J. dissenting), but when or, put another way, under what circumstances, that remedy may be invoked.

## Standing

A formidable obstacle confronts litigants who attempt to assert implied rights of action. *See Arroyo-Torres v. Ponce Federal Bank*, 918 F.2d 276, 278 (1st Cir. 1990). That obstacle does not loom only where the issue is whether a private right of action exists at all; it is equally forbidding in cases where an implied right of action exists but its scope is uncertain. In either event, unless congressional intent to allow the private right of action "can be inferred from the language of the statute, the statutory structure, or some other source, the essential predicate for implication of a private remedy simply does not exist." *Thompson v. Thompson*, 484 U.S. 174, 179 (1988) (quoting *Northwest Airlines, Inc. v. Transport Workers Union*, 451 U.S. 77, 94 (1981)). Hence, our determination of the remedial reach must focus on Congress' intent in enacting the statute.

This said, we turn to *Borak*. There, the Court, having examined the legislative history of Section 14(a), concluded that Congress' primary purpose in enacting the statute was to promote and protect shareholder democracy. *See, e.g., Borak*, 377 U.S. at 431 ("The section stemmed from the congressional belief that '[f]air corporate suffrage is an important right that should attach to every equity security bought on a public exchange.' ") (quoting H.R.Rep. No. 1383, 73d Cong., 2d Sess. 13 (1934)). As the Court later explained, Section 14(a) "was intended to promote 'the free exercise of the voting rights of stockholders' by ensuring that proxies would be solicited with an 'explanation to the stockholder of the real nature of the questions for which authority to cast his vote is sought.' " *Mills v. Electric Auto-Lite Co.*, 396 U.S. 375, 381 (1970) (quoting H.R. Rep. No. 1383, *supra*, and S. Rep. No. 792, 73d Cong., 2d Sess. 12 (1934)). Thus, the existence of a private right of action under Section 14(a) was inferred from the legislative history evidencing congressional concern to vindicate the voting rights of shareholders.

In determining whether the reach of the private remedy under Section 14(a) encompasses the claims asserted by Royal, we deem it appropriate to seek guidance in *Cort v. Ash*, 422 U.S. 66 (1975). The *Cort* approach contemplates that we will ask four questions: Is the plaintiff a member of the class for whose "especial benefit" the statute was passed? Is there any cogent indication of legislative intent to create or deny the remedy sought? Would recognition of the remedy be "consistent with the underlying purposes" of the statutory scheme? Would it be inappropriate to infer a federal remedy because "the cause of action [is] one traditionally relegated to state

---

[25] [6] The plaintiffs, of course, incurred the expenses in question in their twofold capacity as proxy contestants and tender-offerors. This appeal does not require that we distinguish between those closely related capacities. For simplicity's sake, we use the term "proxy contestant" to describe the whole of the dual roles.

law . . . ?" *Id.* at 78. These questions, although clearly subordinate to the "central inquiry" into congressional intent, *see Touche Ross & Co. v. Redington*, 442 U.S. 560 (1979), remain useful "[a]s guides to discerning that intent," *Thompson*, 484 U.S. at 179; and in this case, we find them to be especially well adapted to mapping the perimeter of an established private right of action.

Here, the claim of standing produces less than satisfactory answers to at least three of the four *Cort* questions. In the first place, it is crystal clear that, although appellants were shareholders of Realist, they did not initiate suit in that capacity. They do not complain that they (or any other Realist stockholders, for that matter) were denied the right to vote their shares knowledgeably. They sue instead in their role as disappointed proxy contestants. As such, they do not come within the class for whose particular benefit Section 14(a) was enacted. In the second place, there is absolutely no hint in the language or structure of the statute, or in the legislative history, that Congress was concerned with the rights of proxy contestants as opposed to the rights of shareholders. *See, e.g., Klaus v. Hi-Shear Corp.*, 528 F.2d 225, 232 (9th Cir. 1975) ("In enacting section 14(a), Congress intended to guarantee the integrity of the processes of corporate democracy."). In the third place, the remedy sought — reimbursement of the expenses Royal incurred in the abortive proxy contest — does not dovetail in any discernible way with Section 14(a)'s underlying purpose. We are utterly at a loss to see how, under these circumstances, the voting rights of shareholders would be furthered by implying a private right of action under Section 14(a) in favor of regretful proxy contestants. We think that the Court's elision of *Cort* and *Borak* is peculiarly apt in describing the result we must reach: "[W]hile 'it is the duty of the courts to be alert to provide such remedies as are necessary to make effective the congressional purpose,' in this instance the remedy sought would not aid the primary congressional goal." *Cort*, 422 U.S. at 84 (quoting *Borak*, 377 U.S. at 433).

Let us be perfectly clear: our holding is not that a shareholder who also happens to be a proxy contestant might never have an actionable claim under Section 14(a). Rather, we hold that where, as here, a plaintiff's specific claim arises from its role as a proxy contestant, not from its role as a shareholder, the relief sought would not serve the statutory purpose of safeguarding the corporate voting process; and therefore, implying a private right of action would in no way promote Congress' intent. Hence, because the plaintiffs' role in the contest and the remedy they seek do not further the objectives which Section 14(a) was designed to achieve, they cannot clear the "high hurdle," *Arroyo-Torres*, 918 F.2d at 278, which must be vaulted.

*     *     *

To summarize, under *Borak* and *Thompson*, any role to be played by proxy contestants must be limited to circumstances consistent with Section 14(a)'s underlying purpose of "promot[ing] the free exercise of the voting rights of shareholders." *Mills*, 396 U.S. at 381. Although in some situations standing for proxy contestants might help to promote the efficacy of shareholder democracy, *cf. Ameribanc Investors Group v. Zwart*, 706 F. Supp. 1248, 1253 (E.D. Va. 1989) (discussing standing for target companies as a means of guaranteeing shareholder rights), this is hardly one of them. Given plaintiffs' own statement of their claims, it would be poppycock to infer that this suit was brought in the interest of ensuring other shareholders a fairer, better informed proxy contest. To imply a private right of action in favor of a disappointed proxy contestant seeking to recover damages for an election contest that, in retrospect, it would have preferred not to wage would stretch Section 14(a) beyond any reasonable limit. We find the statute's language not to be so elastic and Congress' intent not to be so unfocused.

There is little more that can constructively be said. Shareholders, like other folk, routinely wear a multitude of hats. The fact that a proxy contestant is also a shareholder does not mean that every action it undertakes falls within its capacity as a shareholder. *Cf. Sheinkopf v. Stone*, 927 F.2d 1259, 1265 (1st Cir. 1991) ("The fact that a person is a lawyer . . . does not mean that every relationship he undertakes is, or reasonably can be perceived as being, in his professional capacity."). Whether or not a proxy contestant who also happens to be a shareholder should be able to sue in the latter capacity depends on an analysis, under the particular circumstances of each case, of the rights being asserted. Here, the plaintiffs' posture is that of proxy contestants — nothing more. The rights being asserted and the damages being sought have nothing to do with the purposes which animate Section 14(a). Mindful of these realities, we do not believe that standing can be conferred, without more, by the mere coincidence that a proxy contestant also enjoys shareholder status.[26]

## Transactional Nexus

Apart from standing, the plaintiffs face still another insuperable obstacle in their attempt to construct a claim under Section 14(a): their complaint fails to establish a causal nexus between their alleged injury and some corporate transaction authorized (or defeated) as a result of the allegedly false and misleading proxy statements.

The need to plead and prove a transactional nexus in a proxy solicitation case is not legitimately in doubt. . . . ("Where there has been a finding of materiality, a shareholder has made a sufficient showing of causal relationship between the violation and the injury for which he seeks redress if . . . he proves that the proxy solicitation itself, rather than the particular defect in the solicitation materials, was

---

[26] [8] We agree for the most part with the thoughtful analyses employed by the court below and by the district court in *Bolton v. Gramlich*, 540 F. Supp. 822 (S.D.N.Y. 1982), a case which, like this one, involved a demand for reimbursement of proxy expenses by "disappointed tender-offerors who strain to find protection in federal law." *Id.* at 827. We do, however, interject a caveat: to the extent that these cases stand for the proposition that a tender-offeror, per se, as a person "Congress intended to regulate, not to protect," *RBG I*, 751 F. Supp. at 313, quoting *Bolton*, 540 F. Supp. at 833–34, lacks standing to sue under Section 14(a), we believe they go too far. While the legislative history of the Williams Act has been interpreted by the Court to deny a takeover bidder standing to sue for damages under Section 14(e), *see Chris-Craft*, 430 U.S. at 35–37, there is no reason to extrapolate this analysis to Section 14(a), the legislative history of which indicates no particular concern for regulating tender-offerors. Furthermore, we note that the *Chris-Craft* Court, in denying standing, emphasized that the damages claimed were related to the plaintiff's "status as a contestant for control of a corporation," not to "its status as a [ ] shareholder," *id.* at 35, thus leaving open the possibility that, under other circumstances, a tender-offeror might be able to sue in its capacity as a shareholder under Section 14(e). *See id.*

an essential link in the accomplishment of the transaction.").[27] Indeed, the requirement's pedigree is impeccable; its lineage can be traced to the root purposes of Section 14(a), viz., "prevent[ing] management or others from obtaining authorization for corporate action by means of deceptive or inadequate disclosure in proxy solicitation," *Borak*, 377 U.S. at 431, and ensuring that proxies will be solicited with an "explanation to the stockholder of the real nature of the questions for which authority to cast his vote is sought," *Mills*, 396 U.S. at 381. Thus, we agree entirely with the Ninth Circuit that "[t]his 'transactional causation' is an essential element of a [§ ] 14(a) action." Gaines, 645 F.2d at 776 (quoting *In re Tenneco Secur. Litigation*, 449 F. Supp. 528, 531 (S.D. Texas 1978)).

In this instance, the proxy solicitation was geared toward only one corporate transaction: the election of directors. The plaintiffs can make no viable claim that they, as shareholders, were harmed by that transaction, since the candidates they nominated achieved at least a paper victory. The only "injury" that plaintiffs suffered was caused by their involvement as combatants in an election they won — but one where, in retrospect, they would rather not have entered the lists. It is simply too much of a stretch to bring such a claim within the causative sphere required for viability under Section 14(a). The plaintiffs did not plead, and are unable on the facts as disclosed to prove, that the expense of their now lamented proxy contest resulted from any transaction that the shareholders authorized (or defeated) in consequence of management's allegedly improper proxy materials. Accordingly, the required element of transactional causation was utterly lacking.

\* \* \*

AFFIRMED. Costs in favor of appellees.

# VIRGINIA BANKSHARES, INC. v. SANDBERG
### Supreme Court of the United States
### 501 U.S. 1083 (1991)

JUSTICE SOUTER delivered the opinion of the Court.

Section 14(a) of the Securities Exchange Act of 1934, 48 Stat. 895, 15 U.S.C. § 78n(a), authorizes the Securities and Exchange Commission (SEC) to adopt rules for the solicitation of proxies, and prohibits their violation. In *J.I. Case Co. v. Borak*, 377 U.S. 426, 84 S. Ct. 1555, 12 L. Ed. 2d 423 (1964), we first recognized an implied private right of action for the breach of § 14(a) as implemented by SEC Rule 14a-9, which prohibits the solicitation of proxies by means of materially false or misleading statements.

The questions before us are whether a statement couched in conclusory or

---

[27] [9] We note that the Court has lately agreed to review the question left open in *Mills*, 396 U.S. at 385 n.7 "whether causation would be shown where management controls a sufficient number of shares to approve the transaction without any vote from the minority." *Sandberg v. Virginia Bankshares, Inc.*, 891 F.2d 1112, 1120–21 (4th Cir. 1989), *cert. granted*, 495 U.S. 903 (1990). While it is possible that the Court's resolution of Sandberg may touch upon the issue here, the markedly dissimilar facts render it unlikely that any holding in that case would cast added light on the situation at bar. We see no reason to stay our hand.

qualitative terms purporting to explain directors' reasons for recommending certain corporate action can be materially misleading within the meaning of Rule 14a-9, and whether causation of damages compensable under § 14(a) can be shown by a member of a class of minority shareholders whose votes are not required by law or corporate bylaw to authorize the corporate action subject to the proxy solicitation. We hold that knowingly false statements of reasons may be actionable even though conclusory in form, but that respondents have failed to demonstrate the equitable basis required to extend the § 14(a) private action to such shareholders when any indication of congressional intent to do so is lacking.

I

In December 1986, First American Bankshares, Inc. (FABI), a bank holding company, began a "freeze-out" merger, in which the First American Bank of Virginia (Bank) eventually merged into Virginia Bankshares, Inc. (VBI), a wholly owned subsidiary of FABI. VBI owned 85% of the Bank's shares, the remaining 15% being in the hands of some 2,000 minority shareholders. FABI hired the investment banking firm of Keefe, Bruyette & Woods (KBW) to give an opinion on the appropriate price for shares of the minority holders, who would lose their interests in the Bank as a result of the merger. Based on market quotations and unverified information from FABI, KBW gave the Bank's executive committee an opinion that $42 a share would be a fair price for the minority stock. The executive committee approved the merger proposal at that price, and the full board followed suit.

Although Virginia law required only that such a merger proposal be submitted to a vote at a shareholders' meeting, and that the meeting be preceded by circulation of a statement of information to the shareholders, the directors nevertheless solicited proxies for voting on the proposal at the annual meeting set for April 21, 1987. In their solicitation, the directors urged the proposals adoption and stated they had approved the plan because of its opportunity for the minority shareholders to achieve a "high" value, which they elsewhere described as a "fair" price, for their stock.

Although most minority shareholders gave the proxies requested, respondent Sandberg did not, and after approval of the merger she sought damages in the United States District Court for the Eastern District of Virginia from VBI, FABI, and the directors of the Bank. She pleaded two counts, one for soliciting proxies in violation of § 14(a) and Rule 14a-9, and the other for breaching fiduciary duties owed to the minority shareholders under state law. Under the first count, Sandberg alleged, among other things, that the directors had not believed that the price offered was high or that the terms of the merger were fair, but had recommended the merger only because they believed they had no alternative if they wished to remain on the board. At trial, Sandberg invoked language from this Court's opinion in *Mills v. Electric Auto-Lite Co.*, 396 U.S. 375, 385 (1970), to obtain an instruction that the jury could find for her without a showing of her own reliance on the alleged misstatements, so long as they were material and the proxy solicitation was an "essential link" in the merger process.

The jury's verdicts were for Sandberg on both counts, after finding violations of Rule 14a-9 by all defendants and a breach of fiduciary duties by the Bank's directors. The jury awarded Sandberg $18 a share, having found that she would have received $60 if her stock had been valued adequately.

While Sandberg's case was pending, a separate action on similar allegations was brought against petitioners in the United States District Court for the District of Columbia by several other minority shareholders including respondent Weinstein, who, like Sandberg, had withheld his proxy. This case was transferred to the Eastern District of Virginia. After Sandberg's action had been tried, the Weinstein respondents successfully pleaded collateral estoppel to get summary judgment on liability.

On appeal, the United States Court of Appeals for the Fourth Circuit affirmed the judgments, holding that certain statements in the proxy solicitation were materially misleading for purposes of the Rule, and that respondents could maintain their action even though their votes had not been needed to effectuate the merger. 891 F.2d 1112 (1989). We granted certiorari because of the importance of the issues presented. 495 U.S. 903 (1990).

## II

The Court of Appeals affirmed petitioners' liability for two statements found to have been materially misleading in violation of § 14(a) of the Act, one of which was that "The Plan of Merger has been approved by the Board of Directors because it provides an opportunity for the Bank's public shareholders to achieve a high value for their shares." App. to Pet. for Cert. 53a. Petitioners argue that statements of opinion or belief incorporating indefinite and unverifiable expressions cannot be actionable as misstatements of material fact within the meaning of Rule 14a-9, and that such a declaration of opinion or belief should never be actionable when placed in a proxy solicitation incorporating statements of fact sufficient to enable readers to draw their own, independent conclusions.

## A

We consider first the actionability per se of statements of reasons, opinion, or belief. Because such a statement by definition purports to express what is consciously on the speaker's mind, we interpret the jury verdict as finding that the directors' statements of belief and opinion were made with knowledge that the directors did not hold the beliefs or opinions expressed, and we confine our discussion to statements so made.[28] That such statements may be materially significant raises no serious question. The meaning of the materiality requirement for liability under § 14(a) was discussed at some length in *TSC Industries, Inc. v. Northway, Inc.*, 426 U.S. 438 (1976), where we held a fact to be material "if there is a substantial likelihood that a reasonable shareholder would consider it important in deciding how to vote." *Id.*, at 449. We think there is no room to deny that a statement of belief by corporate directors about a recommended course of action, or

---

[28] [5] In *TSC Industries, Inc. v. Northway, Inc.*, 426 U.S. 438, 444, n. 7, 96 S. Ct. 2126, 2130, n. 7, 48 L. Ed. 2d 757 (1976), we reserved the question whether scienter was necessary for liability generally under § 14(a). We reserve it still.

an explanation of their reasons for recommending it, can take on just that importance. Shareholders know that directors usually have knowledge and expertness far exceeding the normal investor's resources, and the directors' perceived superiority is magnified even further by the common knowledge that state law customarily obliges them to exercise their judgment in the shareholders' interest. *Cf. Day v. Avery*, 179 U.S. App. D.C. 63, 71, 548 F.2d 1018, 1026 (1976) (action for misrepresentation). Naturally, then, the shareowner faced with a proxy request will think it important to know the directors' beliefs about the course they recommend and their specific reasons for urging the stockholders to embrace it.

## B

### 1

But, assuming materiality, the question remains whether statements of reasons, opinions, or beliefs are statements "with respect to . . . material fact [s]" so as to fall within the strictures of the Rule. Petitioners argue that we would invite wasteful litigation of amorphous issues outside the readily provable realm of fact if we were to recognize liability here on proof that the directors did not recommend the merger for the stated reason, and they cite the authority of *Blue Chip Stamps v. Manor Drug Stores*, 421 U.S. 723 (1975), in urging us to recognize sound policy grounds for placing such statements outside the scope of the Rule.

\* \* \*

Attacks on the truth of directors' statements of reasons or belief, however, need carry no such threats. Such statements are factual in two senses: as statements that the directors do act for the reasons given or hold the belief stated and as statements about the subject matter of the reason or belief expressed. In neither sense does the proof or disproof of such statements implicate the concerns expressed in *Blue Chip Stamps*. The root of those concerns was a plaintiff's capacity to manufacture claims of hypothetical action, unconstrained by independent evidence. Reasons for directors' recommendations or statements of belief are, in contrast, characteristically matters of corporate record subject to documentation, to be supported or attacked by evidence of historical fact outside a plaintiff's control. Such evidence would include not only corporate minutes and other statements of the directors themselves, but circumstantial evidence bearing on the facts that would reasonably underlie the reasons claimed and the honesty of any statement that those reasons are the basis for a recommendation or other action, a point that becomes especially clear when the reasons or beliefs go to valuations in dollars and cents.

\* \* \*

Respondents adduced evidence for just such facts in proving that the statement was misleading about its subject matter and a false expression of the directors' reasons. Whereas the proxy statement described the $42 price as offering a premium above both book value and market price, the evidence indicated that a calculation of the book figure based on the appreciated value of the Bank's real estate holdings eliminated any such premium. The evidence on the significance of market price showed that KBW had conceded that the market was closed, thin, and dominated by FABI, facts omitted from the statement. There was, indeed, evidence of a "going concern" value for the Bank in excess of $60 per share of common stock, another fact never disclosed. However conclusory the directors' statement may have been, then, it was open to attack by garden-variety evidence, subject neither to a plaintiff's control nor ready manufacture, and there was no undue risk of open-ended liability or uncontrollable litigation in allowing respondents the opportunity for recovery on the allegation that it was misleading to call $42 "high." This analysis comports with the holding that marked our nearest prior approach to the issue faced here, in *TSC Industries*, 426 U.S., at 454–455. There, to be sure, we reversed summary judgment for a *Borak* plaintiff who had sued on a description of proposed compensation for minority shareholders as offering a "substantial premium over current market values." But we held only that on the case's undisputed facts the conclusory adjective "substantial" was not materially misleading as a necessary matter of law, and our remand for trial assumed that such a description could be both materially misleading within the meaning of Rule 14a-9 and actionable under § 14(a). *See TSC Industries, supra*, at 458–460, 463–464.

2

Under § 14(a), then, a plaintiff is permitted to prove a specific statement of reason knowingly false or misleadingly incomplete, even when stated in conclusory terms. In reaching this conclusion we have considered statements of reasons of the sort exemplified here, which misstate the speaker's reasons and also mislead about the stated subject matter (e.g., the value of the shares). A statement of belief may be open to objection only in the former respect, however, solely as a misstatement of the psychological fact of the speaker's belief in what he says. In this case, for example, the Court of Appeals alluded to just such limited falsity in observing that "the jury was certainly justified in believing that the directors did not believe a merger at $42 per share was in the minority stockholders' interest but, rather, that they voted as they did for other reasons, e.g., retaining their seats on the board." 891 F.2d, at 1121.

The question arises, then, whether disbelief, or undisclosed belief or motivation, standing alone, should be a sufficient basis to sustain an action under § 14(a), absent proof by the sort of objective evidence described above that the statement also expressly or impliedly asserted something false or misleading about its subject matter. We think that proof of mere disbelief or belief undisclosed should not suffice for liability under § 14(a), and if nothing more had been required or proven in this case, we would reverse for that reason.

On the one hand, it would be rare to find a case with evidence solely of disbelief or undisclosed motivation without further proof that the statement was defective as to its subject matter. While we certainly would not hold a director's naked admission of disbelief incompetent evidence of a proxy statement's false or misleading character, such an unusual admission will not very often stand alone, and we do not substantially narrow the cause of action by requiring a plaintiff to demonstrate something false or misleading in what the statement expressly or impliedly declared about its subject.

On the other hand, to recognize liability on mere disbelief or undisclosed motive without any demonstration that the proxy statement was false or misleading about its subject would authorize § 14(a) litigation confined solely to what one skeptical court spoke of as the "impurities" of a director's "unclean heart." *Stedman v. Storer*, 308 F. Supp. 881, 887 (SDNY 1969) (dealing with § 10(b)). This, we think, would cross the line that *Blue Chip Stamps* sought to draw. While it is true that the liability, if recognized, would rest on an actual, not hypothetical, psychological fact, the temptation to rest an otherwise nonexistent § 14(a) action on psychological enquiry alone would threaten just the sort of strike suits and attrition by discovery that *Blue Chip Stamps* sought to discourage. We therefore hold disbelief or undisclosed motivation, standing alone, insufficient to satisfy the element of fact that must be established under § 14(a).

### C

\* \* \*

The answer to this argument rests on the difference between a merely misleading statement and one that is materially so. While a misleading statement will not always lose its deceptive edge simply by joinder with others that are true, the true statements may discredit the other one so obviously that the risk of real deception drops to nil. Since liability under § 14(a) must rest not only on deceptiveness but materiality as well (i.e., it has to be significant enough to be important to a reasonable investor deciding how to vote, *see TSC Industries*, 426 U.S., at 449), petitioners are on perfectly firm ground insofar as they argue that publishing accurate facts in a proxy statement can render a misleading proposition too unimportant to ground liability.

But not every mixture with the true will neutralize the deceptive. If it would take a financial analyst to spot the tension between the one and the other, whatever is misleading will remain materially so, and liability should follow. . . .

### III

The second issue before us, left open in *Mills v. Electric Auto-Lite Co.*, 396 U.S. at 385, n. 7, is whether causation of damages compensable through the implied private right of action under § 14(a) can be demonstrated by a member of a class of minority shareholders whose votes are not required by law or corporate bylaw to authorize the transaction giving rise to the claim. *J.I. Case Co. v. Borak*, 377 U.S. 426 (1964), did not itself address the requisites of causation, as such, or define the class of plaintiffs eligible to sue under § 14(a). But its general holding, that a private cause of action was available to some shareholder class, acquired greater clarity with a more definite concept of causation in Mills, where we addressed the sufficiency of proof that misstatements in a proxy solicitation were responsible for damages claimed from the merger subject to complaint.

Although a majority stockholder in *Mills* controlled just over half the corporation's shares, a two-thirds vote was needed to approve the merger proposal. After proxies had been obtained, and the merger had carried, minority shareholders brought a *Borak* action. *Mills*, 396 U.S., at 379. The question arose whether the plaintiffs burden to demonstrate causation of their damages traceable to the § 14(a) violation required proof that the defect in the proxy solicitation had had "a decisive effect on the voting." *Id.*, at 385. The *Mills* Court avoided the evidentiary morass that would have followed from requiring individualized proof that enough minority shareholders had relied upon the misstatements to swing the vote. Instead, it held that causation of damages by a material proxy misstatement could be established by showing that minority proxies necessary and sufficient to authorize the corporate acts had been given in accordance with the tenor of the solicitation, and the Court described such a causal relationship by calling the proxy solicitation an "essential link in the accomplishment of the transaction." *Ibid.* In the case before it, the Court found the solicitation essential, as contrasted with one addressed to a class of minority shareholders without votes required by law or by law to authorize the action proposed, and left it for another day to decide whether such a minority shareholder could demonstrate causation. *Id.*, 396 U.S., at 385, n. 7.

In this case, respondents address Mills' open question by proffering two theories that the proxy solicitation addressed to them was an "essential link" under the Mills causation test. They argue, first, that a link existed and was essential simply because VBI and FABI would have been unwilling to proceed with the merger without the approval manifested by the minority shareholders' proxies, which would not have been obtained without the solicitation's express misstatements and misleading omissions. On this reasoning, the causal connection would depend on a desire to avoid bad shareholder or public relations, and the essential character of the causal link would stem not from the enforceable terms of the parties' corporate relationship, but from one party's apprehension of the ill will of the other.

\* \* \*

Although respondents have proffered each of these theories as establishing a chain of causal connection in which the proxy statement is claimed to have been an "essential link," neither theory presents the proxy solicitation as essential in the sense of Mills' causal sequence, in which the solicitation links a directors' proposal with the votes legally required to authorize the action proposed. As a consequence, each theory would, if adopted, extend the scope of *Borak* actions beyond the ambit of Mills and expand the class of plaintiffs entitled to bring Borak actions to include shareholders whose initial authorization of the transaction prompting the proxy solicitation is unnecessary.

Assessing the legitimacy of any such extension or expansion calls for the application of some fundamental principles governing recognition of a right of action implied by a federal statute, the first of which was not, in fact, the considered focus of the *Borak* opinion. The rule that has emerged in the years since *Borak* and *Mills* came down is that recognition of any private right of action for violating a federal statute must ultimately rest on congressional intent to provide a private remedy, *Touche Ross & Co. v. Redington*, 442 U.S. 560, 575. From this the corollary follows that the breadth of the right once recognized should not, as a general matter, grow beyond the scope congressionally intended.

\* \* \*

## A

*Blue Chip Stamps* set an example worth recalling as a preface to specific policy analysis of the consequences of recognizing respondents' first theory, that a desire to avoid minority shareholders' ill will should suffice to justify recognizing the requisite causality of a proxy statement needed to garner that minority support. It will be recalled that in *Blue Chip Stamps* we raised concerns about the practical consequences of allowing recovery, under § 10(b) of the Act and Rule 10b-5, on evidence of what a merely hypothetical buyer or seller might have done on a set of facts that never occurred, and foresaw that any such expanded liability would turn on "hazy" issues inviting self-serving testimony, strike suits, and protracted discovery, with little chance of reasonable resolution by pretrial process. *Id.*, [421 U.S.] at 742–743. These were good reasons to deny recognition to such claims in the absence of any apparent contrary congressional intent.

The same threats of speculative claims and procedural intractability are inherent in respondents' theory of causation linked through the directors' desire for a cosmetic vote. Causation would turn on inferences about what the corporate directors would have thought and done without the minority shareholder approval unneeded to authorize action. A subsequently dissatisfied minority shareholder would have virtual license to allege that managerial timidity would have doomed corporate action but for the ostensible approval induced by a misleading statement, and opposing claims of hypothetical diffidence and hypothetical boldness on the part of directors would probably provide enough depositions in the usual case to preclude any judicial resolution short of the credibility judgments that can only come after trial. Reliable evidence would seldom exist. Directors would understand the prudence of making a few statements about plans to proceed even without minority endorsement, and discovery would be a quest for recollections of oral conversations at odds with the official pronouncements, in hopes of finding support for ex post facto guesses about how much heat the directors would have stood in the absence of minority approval. The issues would be hazy, their litigation protracted, and their resolution unreliable. Given a choice, we would reject any theory of causation that raised such prospects, and we reject this one.

## B

The theory of causal necessity derived from the requirements of Virginia law dealing with postmerger ratification seeks to identify the essential character of the proxy solicitation from its function in obtaining the minority approval that would preclude a minority suit attacking the merger. Since the link is said to be a step in the process of barring a class of shareholders from resort to a state remedy otherwise available, this theory of causation rests upon the proposition of policy that § 14(a) should provide a federal remedy whenever a false or misleading proxy statement results in the loss under state law of a shareholder plaintiff's state remedy for the enforcement of a state right. Respondents agree with the suggestions of counsel for the SEC and FDIC that causation be recognized, for example, when a minority shareholder has been induced by a misleading proxy statement to forfeit a state-law right to an appraisal remedy by voting to approve a transaction, cf. *Swanson v. American Consumers Industries, Inc.*, 475 F.2d 516, 520–521 (CA7

1973), or when such a shareholder has been deterred from obtaining an order enjoining a damaging transaction by a proxy solicitation that misrepresents the facts on which an injunction could properly have been issued. *Cf. Healey v. Catalyst Recovery of Pennsylvania, Inc.*, 616 F.2d 641, 647–648 (CA3 1980); *Alabama Farm Bureau Mutual Casualty Co. v. American Fidelity Life Ins. Co.*, 606 F.2d 602, 614 (CA5 1979), *cert. denied*, 449 U.S. 820 (1980). Respondents claim that in this case a predicate for recognizing just such a causal link exists in Va. Code Ann. § 13.1-691(A)(2) (1989), which sets the conditions under which the merger may be insulated from suit by a minority shareholder seeking to void it on account of Beddow's conflict.

This case does not, however, require us to decide whether § 14(a) provides a cause of action for lost state remedies, since there is no indication in the law or facts before us that the proxy solicitation resulted in any such loss. The contrary appears to be the case. Assuming the soundness of respondents' characterization of the proxy statement as materially misleading, the very terms of the Virginia statute indicate that a favorable minority vote induced by the solicitation would not suffice to render the merger invulnerable to later attack on the ground of the conflict. The statute bars a shareholder from seeking to avoid a transaction tainted by a director's conflict if, inter alia, the minority shareholders ratified the transaction following disclosure of the material facts of the transaction and the conflict. Va. Code Ann. § 13.1-691(A)(2) (1989). Assuming that the material facts about the merger and Beddow's interests were not accurately disclosed, the minority votes were inadequate to ratify the merger under state law, and there was no loss of state remedy to connect the proxy solicitation with harm to minority shareholders irredressable under state law. Nor is there a claim here that the statement misled respondents into entertaining a false belief that they had no chance to upset the merger, until the time for bringing suit had run out.

The judgment of the Court of Appeals is reversed.

It is so ordered.

JUSTICE SCALIA, concurring in part and concurring in the judgment.

I

As I understand the Court's opinion, the statement "In the opinion of the Directors, this is a high value for the shares" would produce liability if in fact it was not a high value and the directors knew that. It would not produce liability if in fact it was not a high value but the directors honestly believed otherwise. The statement "The Directors voted to accept the proposal because they believe it offers a high value" would not produce liability if in fact the directors' genuine motive was quite different — except that it would produce liability if the proposal in fact did not offer a high value and the Directors knew that.

I agree with all of this. However, not every sentence that has the word "opinion" in it, or that refers to motivation for directors' actions, leads us into this psychic thicket. Sometimes such a sentence actually represents facts as facts rather than opinions — and in that event no more need be done than apply the normal rules for

§ 14(a) liability. I think that is the situation here. In my view, the statement at issue in this case is most fairly read as affirming separately both the fact of the Directors' opinion and the accuracy of the facts upon which the opinion was assertedly based. It reads as follows:

> "The Plan of Merger has been approved by the Board of Directors because it provides an opportunity for the Bank's public shareholders to achieve a high value for their shares." App. to Pet. for Cert. 53a.

Had it read "because in their estimation it provides an opportunity, etc.," it would have set forth nothing but an opinion. As written, however, it asserts both that the board of directors acted for a particular reason and that that reason is correct. This interpretation is made clear by what immediately follows: "The price to be paid is about 30% higher than the [last traded price immediately before announcement of the proposal] . . . . [T]he $42 per share that will be paid to public holders of the common stock represents a premium of approximately 26% over the book value . . . . [T]he bank earned $24,767,000 in the year ended December 31, 1986 . . . ." *Id.*, at 53a–54a. These are all facts that support and that are obviously introduced for the purpose of supporting-the factual truth of the "because" clause, i.e., that the proposal gives shareholders a "high value."

If the present case were to proceed, therefore, I think the normal § 14(a) principles governing misrepresentation of fact would apply.

## II

I recognize that the Court's disallowance (in Part II-B-2) of an action for misrepresentation of belief is entirely contrary to the modern law of torts, as authorities cited by the Court make plain. *See Vulcan Metals Co. v. Simmons Mfg. Co.*, 248 F. 853, 856 (CA2 1918); W. KEETON, D. DOBBS, R. KEETON, & D. OWEN, PROSSER AND KEETON ON LAW OF TORTS § 109 (5th ed. 1984), cited ante, at 2759. I have no problem with departing from modern tort law in this regard, because I think the federal cause of action at issue here was never enacted by Congress, *see Thompson v. Thompson*, 484 U.S. 174, 190–192 (1988) (SCALIA, J., concurring in judgment), and hence the more narrow we make it (within the bounds of rationality) the more faithful we are to our task.

\*     \*     \*

I concur in the judgment of the Court, and join all of its opinion except Part II.

JUSTICE STEVENS, with whom JUSTICE MARSHALL joins, concurring in part and dissenting in part.

While I agree in substance with Parts I and II of the Court's opinion, I do not agree with the reasoning in Part III.

\*     \*     \*

The case before us today involves a merger that has been found by a jury to be unfair, not fair. The interest in providing a remedy to the injured minority shareholders therefore is stronger, not weaker, than in *Mills*. The interest in avoiding speculative controversy about the actual importance of the proxy solicitation is the same as in *Mills*. Moreover, as in *Mills*, these matters can be taken into account at the remedy stage in appropriate cases. Accordingly, I do not believe that it constitutes an unwarranted extension of the rationale of *Mills* to conclude that because management found it necessary — whether for "legal or practical reasons" — to solicit proxies from minority shareholders to obtain their approval of the merger, that solicitation "was an essential link in the accomplishment of the transaction." *Id.*, [396 U.S.] at 385, and n. 7. In my opinion, shareholders may bring an action for damages under § 14(a) of the Securities Exchange Act of 1934, 48 Stat. 895, 15 U.S.C. § 78n(a), whenever materially false or misleading statements are made in proxy statements. That the solicitation of proxies is not required by law or by the bylaws of a corporation does not authorize corporate officers, once they have decided for whatever reason to solicit proxies, to avoid the constraints of the statute. I would therefore affirm the judgment of the Court of Appeals.

JUSTICE KENNEDY, with whom JUSTICE MARSHALL, JUSTICE BLACKMUN, and JUSTICE STEVENS join, concurring in part and dissenting in part.

I am in general agreement with Parts I and II of the majority opinion, but do not agree with the views expressed in Part III regarding the proof of causation required to establish a violation of § 14(a). With respect, I dissent from Part III of the Court's opinion.

\* \* \*

According to the Court, acceptance of non-voting causation theories would "extend the scope of *Borak* actions beyond the ambit of *Mills*." *Ante*, at 2763. But *Mills v. Electric Auto-Lite Co.*, 396 U.S. 375 (1970), did not purport to limit the scope of *Borak* actions, and as footnote 7 of Mills indicates, some courts have applied nonvoting causation theories to *Borak* actions for at least the past 25 years. *See also* L. LOSS, FUNDAMENTALS OF SECURITIES REGULATION 948, n. 81 (2d ed. 1988).

To the extent the Court's analysis considers the purposes underlying § 14(a), it does so with the avowed aim to limit the cause of action and with undue emphasis upon fears of "speculative claims and procedural intractability." *Ante*, at 2765. The result is a sort of guerrilla warfare to restrict a well-established implied right of action. If the analysis adopted by the Court today is any guide, Congress and those charged with enforcement of the securities laws stand forewarned that unresolved questions concerning the scope of those causes of action are likely to be answered by the Court in favor of defendants.

B

The Court seems to assume, based upon the footnote in *Mills* reserving the question, that Sandberg bears a special burden to demonstrate causation because the public shareholders held only 15 percent of the stock of First American Bank of Virginia (Bank). JUSTICE STEVENS is right to reject this theory. Here, First American Bankshares, Inc. (FABI), and Virginia Bankshares, Inc. (VBI), retained the option to back out of the transaction if dissatisfied with the reaction of the minority shareholders, or if concerned that the merger would result in liability for violation of duties to the minority shareholders. The merger agreement was conditioned upon approval by two-thirds of the shareholders, App. 463, and VBI could have voted its shares against the merger if it so decided. To this extent, the Court's distinction between cases where the "minority" shareholders could have voted down the transaction and those where causation must be proved by nonvoting theories is suspect. Minority shareholders are identified only by a post hoc inquiry. The real question ought to be whether an injury was shown by the effect the nondisclosure had on the entire merger process, including the period before votes are cast.

The Court's distinction presumes that a majority shareholder will vote in favor of management's proposal even if proxy disclosure suggests that the transaction is unfair to minority shareholders or that the board of directors or majority shareholder is in breach of fiduciary duties to the minority. If the majority shareholder votes against the transaction in order to comply with its state-law duties, or out of fear of liability, or upon concluding that the transaction will injure the reputation of the business, this ought not to be characterized as nonvoting causation. Of course, when the majority shareholder dominates the voting process, as was the case here, it may prefer to avoid the embarrassment of voting against its own proposal and so may cancel the meeting of shareholders at which the vote was to have been taken. For practical purposes, the result is the same: Because of full disclosure the transaction does not go forward and the resulting injury to minority shareholders is avoided. The Court's distinction between voting and nonvoting causation does not create clear legal categories.

## III

Our decision in *Mills v. Electric Auto-Lite Co.*, *supra*, at 385, 90 S. Ct., at 622, rested upon the impracticality of attempting to determine the extent of reliance by thousands of shareholders on alleged misrepresentations or omissions. A misstatement or an omission in a proxy statement does not violate § 14(a) unless "there is a substantial likelihood that a reasonable shareholder would consider it important in deciding how to vote." *TSC Industries, Inc. v. Northway, Inc.*, 426 U.S. 438 (1976). If minority shareholders hold sufficient votes to defeat a management proposal and if the misstatement or omission is likely to be considered important in deciding how to vote, then there exists a likely causal link between the proxy violation and the enactment of the proposal; and one can justify recovery by minority shareholders for damages resulting from enactment of management's proposal.

If, for sake of argument, we accept a distinction between voting and nonvoting causation, we must determine whether the Mills essential link theory applies where a majority shareholder holds sufficient votes to force adoption of a proposal. The merit of the essential link formulation is that it rests upon the likelihood of causation and eliminates the difficulty of proof. Even where a minority lacks votes to defeat a proposal, both these factors weigh in favor of finding causation so long as the solicitation of proxies is an essential link in the transaction.

## A

The Court argues that a nonvoting causation theory would "turn on 'hazy' issues inviting self-serving testimony, strike suits, and protracted discovery, with little chance of reasonable resolution by pretrial process." *Ante*, at 2765 (citing *Blue Chip Stamps*, 421 U.S., at 742–743). The Court's description does not fit this case and is not a sound objection in any event. Any causation inquiry under § 14(a) requires a court to consider a hypothetical universe in which adequate disclosure is made. Indeed, the analysis is inevitable in almost any suit when we are invited to compare what was with what ought to have been. The causation inquiry is not intractable. On balance, I am convinced that the likelihood that causation exists supports elimination of any requirement that the plaintiff prove the material misstatement or omission caused the transaction to go forward when it otherwise would have been halted or voted down. This is the usual rule under *Mills*, and the difficulties of proving or disproving causation are, if anything, greater where the minority lacks sufficient votes to defeat the proposal. A presumption will assist courts in managing a circumstance in which direct proof is rendered difficult. *See Basic Inc. v. Levinson*, 485 U.S. 224, 245 (1988) (discussing presumptions in securities law).

## B

There is no authority whatsoever for limiting § 14(a) to protecting those minority shareholders whose numerical strength could permit them to vote down a proposal. One of § 14(a)'s "chief purposes is 'the protection of investors.' " *J.I. Case Co. v. Borak*, 377 U.S. at 432. Those who lack the strength to vote down a proposal have all the more need of disclosure. The voting process involves not only casting ballots but also the formulation and withdrawal of proposals, the minority's right to block a vote through court action or the threat of adverse consequences, or the negotiation of an increase in price. The proxy rules support this deliberative process. These practicalities can result in causation sufficient to support recovery.

The facts in the case before us prove this point. Sandberg argues that had all the material facts been disclosed, FABI or the Bank likely would have withdrawn or revised the merger proposal. The evidence in the record, and more that might be available upon remand, *see infra*, at 2772, meets any reasonable requirement of specific and nonspeculative proof.

FABI wanted a "friendly transaction" with a price viewed as "so high that any reasonable shareholder will accept it." Management expressed concern that the transaction result in "no loss of support for the bank out in the community, which was important." Although FABI had the votes to push through any proposal, it wanted a favorable response from the minority shareholders. Because of the "human element involved in a transaction of this nature," FABI attempted to "show those minority shareholders that [it was] being fair."

The theory that FABI would not have pursued the transaction if full disclosure had been provided and the shareholders had realized the inadequacy of the price is supported not only by the trial testimony but also by notes of the meeting of the Bank's board, which approved the merger.

\* \* \*

Though I would not require a shareholder to present such evidence of causation, this case itself demonstrates that nonvoting causation theories are quite plausible where the misstatement or omission is material and the damages sustained by minority shareholders is serious. As Professor Loss summarized the holdings of a "substantial number of cases," even if the minority cannot alone vote down a transaction,

> "minority stockholders will be in a better position to protect their interests with full disclosure and . . . an unfavorable minority vote might influence the majority to modify or reconsider the transaction in question."

I would affirm the judgment of the Court of Appeals.

# NOTE

This case involves an implied right of action under Section 14. The *Borak* case established that right of action, but the required elements have not yet been completely determined by the courts. Clearly fraud or deception as defined in Rule 14(a)(9) is required. Further, the fraudulent statement must be material. What is materiality? The definitive statement occurs in a case cited by the court, *TSC Industries, Inc. v. Northway*. A fact is material "if there is substantial likelihood that a reasonable shareholder would consider it important in deciding how to vote."

Does the court change the definition of fraud? Why should a misrepresentation of belief be treated differently from other kinds of misrepresentation? Why does Justice Scalia agree with the court?

## NEW YORK CITY EMPLOYEES'
## RETIREMENT SYSTEM v. SEC
### United States Court of Appeals, Second Circuit
### 45 F.3d 7 (1995)

McLAUGHLIN, J.

The plaintiffs, New York City Employees' Retirement System ("NYCERS") and two other institutional investors, sued the Securities and Exchange Commission ("SEC") in the United States District Court for the Southern District of New York (Kimba M. Wood, Judge), to enjoin the SEC from violating section 553(b) of the Administrative Procedure Act ("APA"). The lawsuit stemmed from an SEC "no-action" letter, in which the SEC announced that it was changing its interpretation of SEC Rule 14a-8(c)(7). *See* 17 C.F.R. § 240.14a-8(c)(7) (1994) ("Rule 14a-8(c)(7)"). The plaintiffs claimed that the old interpretation of Rule 14a-8(c)(7) was subjected to notice and comment before it was adopted, and, accordingly, the new interpretation had to follow the same procedures. The plaintiffs also challenged the new interpretation as arbitrary and capricious.

The district court, on plaintiffs' motion for summary judgment determined that the SEC's no-action letter announced a "legislative rule," as that term is used in the

APA. *See NYCERS v. SEC*, 843 F. Supp. 858 (S.D.N.Y. 1994). The court therefore enjoined the SEC from issuing any no-action letter inconsistent with the SEC's previous understanding of Rule 14a-8(c)(7) without first submitting the rule for notice and comment. The district court saw no need to address whether the rule was arbitrary and capricious.

The SEC now appeals, arguing that the no-action letter was "interpretive," not legislative, and, as such, was not subject to the APA's notice and comment requirements. The SEC also urges us to dismiss the arbitrary and capricious claim because the plaintiffs may obtain this relief without suing the agency.

We agree with the SEC. Accordingly, we vacate the injunction, reverse the order granting summary judgment, and dismiss the claim that the letter was arbitrary and capricious.

## BACKGROUND

All three plaintiffs are major institutional shareholders, sharing a common sensitivity to their social responsibility. After investing in a company, the plaintiffs regularly use their shareholder status as a bully pulpit to promote non-discriminatory policies in the workplace.

The plaintiffs' powder and shot are proxy materials and shareholder proposals. When the plaintiffs want to change a company policy, they put their idea up for a shareholder vote by submitting a shareholder proposal to the board of directors. Then, the plaintiffs ask the board to include the proposal in the proxy materials that are sent to all shareholders before meetings.

In 1991, Cracker Barrel Old Country Store, Inc. attracted the plaintiffs' ire. That January, Cracker Barrel, a restaurant chain, issued a press release:

> Cracker Barrel is founded upon a concept of traditional American values, quality in all we do, and a philosophy of 100% guest satisfaction. It is inconsistent with our concept and values, and is perceived to be inconsistent with those of our customer base, to continue to employ individuals . . . whose sexual preferences fail to demonstrate normal heterosexual values which have been the foundation of families in our society.

Upon the heels of this release, Cracker Barrel fired several gay employees.

Cracker Barrel's actions triggered public protests, boycotts, and negative media coverage. To defuse the furor, Cracker Barrel rescinded the anti-gay policy. It did not, however, rehire the former employees. Neither did it expressly include "sexual orientation" among the inappropriate criteria for employment decisions in its published anti-discrimination policy.

In November 1991, plaintiff NYCERS, a Cracker Barrel shareholder, proposed to Cracker Barrel's board of directors that the company expressly prohibit discrimination on the basis of sexual orientation. NYCERS called for a shareholder vote and asked Cracker Barrel to include the proposal in the proxy materials for the 1992 annual shareholder meeting.

Cracker Barrel wanted no part of this proposal, and did not even want to include it in the proxy materials. Under Rule 14a-8, however, Cracker Barrel had to include the proposal in the proxy materials unless the proposal dealt with "ordinary business operations." *See* Rule 14a-8(c)(7). The construction of that term lies at the heart of the controversy, and it requires some exegesis.

In 1976, the SEC proposed to revise various parts of Rule 14a-8. It wanted to tighten the exception for "ordinary business operations" in subsection (c)(7) — then subsection (c)(5) — so that only proposals regarding "routine, day to day matters relating to the conduct of the ordinary business operations" could be excluded from proxy materials. *See* Proposals by Security Holders: Notice of Proposed Amendments to Rule, Exchange Act Release No. 12,598 (July 7, 1976), 41 Fed. Reg. 29,982, 29,984 (the "Proposed Amendments"). This way, the SEC believed, corporations could not exclude proposals regarding policies important to shareholders just because they also happened to concern "ordinary business operations."

After reviewing comments on the proposed revision, the SEC decided not to change the subsection in any material way. *See* Adoption of Amendments Relating to Proposals by Security Holders, Exchange Act Release No. 12,999 (Nov. 22, 1976), 41 Fed. Reg. 52,994, 52,997 (1976) (the "1976 Adoption"). Instead, the 1976 Adoption indicated that the Rule would retain the historical "ordinary business operations" language, but that the SEC staff would thereafter interpret it so that corporations could not exclude proposals regarding "matters which have significant policy, economic or other implications inherent in them."

Befuddled by the 1976 Adoption, Cracker Barrel wrote to the SEC's Corporation Finance Division (the "Division") in 1991, to find out whether the SEC would bring an enforcement action if Cracker Barrel left NYCERS's sexual orientation proposal out of the proxy materials for the 1992 meeting. The letter argued that Rule 14a-8(c)(7) allowed Cracker Barrel to omit NYCERS's proposal because it related to employment policies, and these fell within the ambit of "ordinary business operations."

NYCERS wrote its own letter to the Division, relying upon the "significant policy implications" language in the 1976 Adoption. Contending that employment discrimination is an important policy issue, NYCERS argued that Cracker Barrel had no right to omit NYCERS's proposal.

In October 1992, the Division issued a no-action letter, stating that the SEC would not bring an enforcement action against Cracker Barrel. *See Cracker Barrel Old Country Store, Inc.*, SEC No-Action Letter, 1992 WL 289095 (SEC) (October 13, 1992) (the "Cracker Barrel no-action letter"). The letter conceded that the Division's staff had already experienced difficulty trying to discern when a proposal involved significant policy issues. It also acknowledged that the opaqueness of the standard had led to decisions "characterized by many as tenuous, without substance and effectively nullifying the application of the ordinary business exclusion to employment related proposals." The letter continued:

> The Division has reconsidered the application of Rule 14a-8(c)(7) to employment-related proposals in light of these concerns and the staff's experience with these proposals in recent years. As a result, the Division has determined that the fact that a shareholder proposal concerning a

company's employment policies and practices for the general workforce is tied to a social issue will no longer be viewed as removing the proposal from the realm of ordinary business operations of the registrant. Rather, determinations with respect to any such proposals are properly governed by the employment-based nature of the proposal.

NYCERS petitioned the SEC to reverse the Cracker Barrel no-action letter; the SEC reviewed it, and affirmed.

NYCERS and two other institutional investors feared that the Cracker Barrel no-action letter would frustrate any future attempts by them to change employment policies. So, they three sued the SEC in the Southern District of New York, seeking a declaration that the no-action letter's jettison of the "significant policy implications" rule was invalid because: (1) the SEC did not submit it for notice and comment, as required by section 553 of the APA; and (2) it was arbitrary and capricious. NYCERS also petitioned the court to enjoin the SEC from following the policy announced in the no-action letter.

\*    \*    \*

The district court denied the SEC's motion, granted the plaintiffs' motion, and entered judgment for plaintiffs. Acknowledging that agency decisions not to prosecute are not judicially reviewable, the court noted that NYCERS claimed the SEC violated the APA itself, not that the SEC wrongly abstained from enforcing Rule 14a-8. Thus, the court found that it had jurisdiction to hear the plaintiffs' claims.

On the merits, the district court ruled that the SEC had violated the APA by abandoning the "significant policy implications" rule without providing notice and comment. The court found, first, that the statement in the Cracker Barrel no-action letter was a "rule" as defined by section 551(4) of the APA. The court then characterized the letter as a "legislative," as opposed to "interpretive," rule because it amended the 1976 Adoption's "significant policy implications" rule, which was promulgated after notice and comment procedures. Since the APA requires that legislative rules undergo notice and comment before adoption, the district court ruled that the statement in the no-action letter was invalid. Having done so, the court did not find it necessary to decide whether the rule was arbitrary and capricious.

The district court granted the plaintiffs' request for an injunction, and barred the SEC from issuing any no-action letter inconsistent with the "significant policy implications" rule set out in the 1976 Adoption, unless the agency changed that rule by notice and comment.

The SEC appeals.

## DISCUSSION

Attacking the district court's holding that the Cracker Barrel no-action letter announced a legislative rule, the SEC contends that the rule was interpretive only, and, thus, was not subject to the APA's notice and comment requirements. The SEC also maintains that the plaintiffs may not challenge the no-action letter as arbitrary and capricious because adequate alternative remedies are available.

Preliminarily, we must consider whether we have jurisdiction to hear NYCERS's claim that the no-action letter violated the APA's notice and comment procedures. It is true that agency decisions not to prosecute are not reviewable because they are "generally committed to an agency's absolute discretion." *Heckler v. Chaney*, 470 U.S. 821, 831 (1985). But it is equally true that "[a] person . . . adversely affected or aggrieved by agency action within the meaning of a relevant statute, is entitled to judicial review thereof." 5 U.S.C. § 702.

As the district court recognized, the marrow of NYCERS's claim is that the SEC announced a new rule without following the statutory notice and comment procedures. We therefore have jurisdiction under section 702 to hear the plaintiffs' notice and comment claim. That said, we turn to the merits.

\* \* \*

A "rule," under the APA, is statutorily defined as "the whole or a part of an agency statement of general or particular applicability and future effect designed to implement, interpret, or prescribe law or policy." *Id.* § 551(4). Under this sweeping definition, the Cracker Barrel no-action letter's statement that the SEC would no longer follow the "significant policy implications" exception was a rule: it stated generally that the Division staff was making a sea change and that it was abandoning its former policy regarding proxy inclusion requirements.

There are two types of rules, legislative and interpretive. Legislative rules are those that "create new law, rights, or duties, in what amounts to a legislative act." *White*, 7 F.3d at 303. Legislative rules have the force of law. *See Batterton v. Francis*, 432 U.S. 416, 425 n.9 (1977). Interpretive rules, on the other hand, do not create rights, but merely "clarify an existing statute or regulation." *White*, 7 F.3d at 303. Since they only clarify existing law, interpretive rules need not go through notice and comment. 5 U.S.C. § 553(b)(3)(A). These rules do not have force of law, though they are entitled to deference from the courts.

To divine the nature of the Cracker Barrel rule, it is helpful to understand the nature of no-action letters generally. The no-action process works as follows: Whenever a corporation decides to exclude a shareholder proposal from its proxy materials, it "shall file" a letter with the Division explaining the legal basis for its decision. *See* Rule 14a-8(d)(3). If the Division staff agrees that the proposal is excludable, it may issue a no-action letter, stating that, based on the facts presented by the corporation, the staff will not recommend that the SEC sue the corporation for violating Rule 14a-8. . . .

No-action letters are deemed interpretive because they do not impose or fix a legal relationship upon any of the parties. *See Amalgamated Clothing & Textile Workers Union v. SEC*, 15 F.3d 254, 257 (2d Cir. 1994) ("*ACTWU*"). . . .

Under *ACTWU*, the Cracker Barrel no-action letter is interpretive because it does not create or destroy any legal rights. The casus belli of the Cracker Barrel letter is the statement that the SEC staff would no longer distinguish shareholder proposals concerning employment-related social issues from those involving ordinary business operations. *See* Cracker Barrel no-action letter at \*18. But this interpretation binds no one: The SEC may still bring an enforcement action against Cracker Barrel (or any other company) based on its failure to include a proposal regarding an employment-related social issue. *See id.* As the SEC has noted, "no-action . . . responses by the staff are subject to reconsideration and should not be regarded as precedents binding on the [SEC]."

The Cracker Barrel no-action letter certainly does not bind the parties.

\* \* \*

Finally, the Cracker Barrel no-action letter does not bind the courts. Should NYCERS bring a federal suit against Cracker Barrel under Rule 14a-8, the court may find a Rule 14a-8 violation despite the no-action letter. While the court would treat the no-action letter as persuasive, the court need not give it the same high level of deference that is accorded formal policy statements or rule-making orders. . . .

Thus, insofar as the Cracker Barrel no-action letter does not affix any legal relationships, it is an interpretive rule. As the district court noted, however, this is not a garden variety no-action letter. While most no-action letters merely state that the Division staff will not recommend an enforcement action, the Cracker Barrel no-action letter went further: it expressly abandoned a previous SEC rule. The district court, relying chiefly upon *American Mining Congress v. Mine Safety & Health Admin.*, 995 F.2d 1106 (D.C. Cir. 1993), concluded that renouncing the former SEC rule transubstantiated the no-action letter from interpretive to legislative. We do not agree.

\* \* \*

The rule enunciated in the Cracker Barrel no-action letter manifestly does not fit in any of the first three *American Mining Congress* categories: (1) it does not create a basis for an SEC enforcement action; (2) the SEC did not publish the letter in the C.F.R.; and (3) the SEC did not expressly invoke legislative authority.

The fourth factor — whether the rule effectively amends a prior legislative rule — requires deeper analysis. . . .

The district court surmised from these facts that the Cracker Barrel no-action letter "effectively amended" a legislative rule (viz., the legislative portion of the 1976 Adoption), and was thus itself legislative. This conclusion is untenable in light of *ACTWU*. As *ACTWU* held, no-action letters are nonbinding statements of the SEC's intent not to prosecute a potential rule violation; they do not oblige or prevent action by the SEC, the parties, or the courts. *See ACTWU*, 15 F.3d at 257. *Accord Roosevelt*, 958 F.2d at 427 n.19 (no-action letters concerning shareholder proposals are neither agency adjudication nor rulemaking). A necessary corollary of this proposition is that rules announced in no-action letters also have no binding authority. Thus, the Cracker Barrel no-action letter did not effectively amend the 1976 Adoption within the meaning of American Mining Congress, and did not contain a legislative rule. Rather, the letter merely expressed the view of the Division's staff that it lacks the necessary expertise in identifying issues as having "significant policy implications," and that the staff does not expect to allocate its limited resources to making such subjective determinations.

In so holding, we are mindful of the plaintiffs' warning that the SEC might be able to skirt the entire notice and comment process by using no-action letters to amend legislative rules. We are not persuaded by their prophecy of doom. * * * Consequently, because the Cracker Barrel no-action letter did not go through notice and comment, and was only an informal statement by the SEC, courts will not accord great deference to it.

Summing up: Because the Cracker Barrel no-action letter was not legislative, the APA did not require notice and comment. Thus, we reverse the district court's grant of summary judgment, and vacate the injunction.

*NYCERS* also wants us to set aside the rule announced in the Cracker Barrel no-action letter as arbitrary and capricious.

Section 706 of the APA permits a court to reverse an agency action that is arbitrary or capricious. *See* 5 U.S.C. § 706(2)(A). We may not even entertain the claim against the agency, however, if the plaintiffs have an adequate alternative legal remedy against someone else. . . .

Here, the plaintiffs have an effective alternative to suing the SEC: They can sue Cracker Barrel, or any other offending company under Rule 14a-8, to enjoin the board to include their proposal in the proxy materials. In that suit, should the company offer the rule espoused in the Cracker Barrel no-action letter to show compliance, the plaintiffs may counter that the rule is arbitrary and capricious. If the plaintiffs prevail in that suit, they would then get all the relief they now seek from the SEC on their claim of arbitrary and capricious agency action. Thus, we dismiss this claim under section 704.

### CONCLUSION

In light of the foregoing, we vacate the injunction, reverse the order of summary judgment, and dismiss the plaintiffs' claim that the no-action letter was arbitrary and capricious.

## SEC AMENDMENTS TO RULES
## ON SHAREHOLDER PROPOSALS
(May 21, 1998)

"Exchange Act"

### I. Executive Summary

With modifications, we are adopting some of the amendments to our rules on shareholder proposals that we initially proposed on September 18, 1997. As explained more fully in this release, we modified our original proposals based on our consideration of the more than 2,000 comment letters we received from the public.

Our proposed changes evoked considerable public controversy, as have our earlier efforts to reform these rules. Some shareholders and companies expressed overall support for our proposals. Certain of our proposals, however, were viewed as especially controversial, and generated strong comments in favor, as well as heavy opposition.

The amendments adopted today:

- recast rule 14a-8 into a Question & Answer format that is easier to read;
- reverse the Cracker Barrel no-action letter on employment-related proposals raising social policy issues;
- adopt other less significant amendments to rule 14a-8; and
- amend rule 14a-4 to provide shareholders and companies with clearer guidance on companies' exercise of discretionary voting authority.

These reforms, in our view, will help to improve the operation of the rules governing shareholder proposals and will address some of the concerns raised by shareholders and companies over the last several years on the operation of the proxy process.

\*    \*    \*

## II. Plain-English Question & Answer Format

We had proposed to recast rule 14a-8 into a more plain-English Question & Answer format. We are adopting that proposal, and the amended rule will be the Commission's first in question and answer format. Most commenters who addressed this proposal expressed favorable views, believing that it would make the rule easier for shareholders and companies to understand and follow.

\*    \*    \*

## III. The Interpretation Of Rule 14a-8(c)(7):
### The "Ordinary Business" Exclusion

We proposed to reverse the position announced in the 1992 Cracker Barrel no-action letter concerning the Division's approach to employment-related shareholder proposals raising social policy issues. In that letter, the Division announced that

> [T]he fact that a shareholder proposal concerning a company's employment policies and practices for the general workforce is tied to a social issue will no longer be viewed as removing the proposal from the realm of ordinary business operations of the registrant. Rather, determinations with respect to any such proposals are properly governed by the employment-based nature of the proposal.

We are adopting our proposal to reverse the Cracker Barrel position, which provided that all employment-related shareholder proposals raising social policy issues would be excludable under the "ordinary business" exclusion. The Division will return to its case-by-case approach that prevailed prior to the Cracker Barrel no-action letter.

In applying the "ordinary business" exclusion to proposals that raise social policy issues, the Division seeks to use the most well-reasoned and consistent standards possible, given the inherent complexity of the task. From time to time, in light of experience dealing with proposals in specific subject areas, and reflecting changing societal views, the Division adjusts its view with respect to "social policy" proposals involving ordinary business. Over the years, the Division has reversed its position on the excludability of a number of types of proposals, including plant closings, the manufacture of tobacco products, executive compensation, and golden parachutes.

We believe that reversal of the Division's Cracker Barrel no-action letter, which the Commission had subsequently affirmed, is warranted. Since 1992, the relative importance of certain social issues relating to employment matters has reemerged as a consistent topic of widespread public debate. In addition, as a result of the extensive policy discussions that the Cracker Barrel position engendered, and through the rulemaking notice and comment process, we have gained a better understanding of the depth of interest among shareholders in having an opportunity to express their views to company management on employment-related proposals that raise sufficiently significant social policy issues.

Reversal of the Cracker Barrel no-action position will result in a return to a case-by-case analytical approach. In making distinctions in this area, the Division and the Commission will continue to apply the applicable standard for determining when a proposal relates to "ordinary business." The standard, originally articulated in the Commission's 1976 release, provided an exception for certain proposals that raise significant social policy issues.

While we acknowledge that there is no bright-line test to determine when employment-related shareholder proposals raising social issues fall within the scope of the "ordinary business" exclusion, the staff will make reasoned distinctions in deciding whether to furnish "no-action" relief. Although a few of the distinctions made in those cases may be somewhat tenuous, we believe that on the whole the benefit to shareholders and companies in providing guidance and informal resolutions will outweigh the problematic aspects of the few decisions in the middle ground.

Nearly all commenters from the shareholder community who addressed the matter supported the reversal of this position. Most commenters from the corporate community did not favor the proposal to reverse Cracker Barrel, though many indicated that the change would be acceptable as part of a broader set of reforms.

Going forward, companies and shareholders should bear in mind that the Cracker Barrel position relates only to employment-related proposals raising certain social policy issues. Reversal of the position does not affect the Division's analysis of any other category of proposals under the exclusion, such as proposals on general business operations.

Finally, we believe that it would be useful to summarize the principal considerations in the Division's application, under the Commission's oversight, of the "ordinary business" exclusion. The general underlying policy of this exclusion is consistent with the policy of most state corporate laws: to confine the resolution of ordinary business problems to management and the board of directors, since it is impracticable for shareholders to decide how to solve such problems at an annual shareholders meeting.

The policy underlying the ordinary business exclusion rests on two central considerations. The first relates to the subject matter of the proposal. Certain tasks are so fundamental to management's ability to run a company on a day-to-day basis that they could not, as a practical matter, be subject to direct shareholder oversight. Examples include the management of the workforce, such as the hiring, promotion, and termination of employees, decisions on production quality and quantity, and the retention of suppliers. However, proposals relating to such matters but focusing on sufficiently significant social policy issues (e.g., significant discrimination matters) generally would not be considered to be excludable, because the proposals would transcend the day-to-day business matters and raise policy issues so significant that it would be appropriate for a shareholder vote.

The second consideration relates to the degree to which the proposal seeks to "micro-manage" the company by probing too deeply into matters of a complex nature upon which shareholders, as a group, would not be in a position to make an informed judgment. This consideration may come into play in a number of circumstances, such as where the proposal involves intricate detail, or seeks to impose specific time-frames or methods for implementing complex policies.

A similar discussion in the Proposing Release of the primary considerations underlying our interpretation of the "ordinary business" exclusion as applied to such proposals raised some questions and concerns among some of the commenters. Because of that concern, we are providing clarification of that position. One aspect of that discussion was the basis for some commenters' concern that the reversal of Cracker Barrel might be only a partial one. More specifically, in the Proposing Release we explained that one of the considerations in making the ordinary business determination was the degree to which the proposal seeks to micro-manage the company. We cited examples such as where the proposal seeks intricate detail, or seeks to impose specific time-frames or to impose specific methods for implementing complex policies. Some commenters thought that the examples cited seemed to imply that all proposals seeking detail, or seeking to promote time-frames or methods, necessarily amount to "ordinary business." We did not intend such an implication. Timing questions, for instance, could involve significant policy where large differences are at stake, and proposals may seek a reasonable level of detail without running afoul of these considerations.

Further, in a footnote to the same sentence citing examples of "micro-management," we included a citation to Capital Cities/ABC, Inc., (Apr. 4, 1991) involving a proposal on the company's affirmative action policies and practices. Some commenters were concerned that the citation might imply that proposals similar to the Capital Cities proposal today would automatically be excludable under "ordinary business" on grounds that they seek excessive detail. Such a position, in their view, might offset the impact of reversing the Cracker Barrel position. However, we cited Capital Cities/ABC, Inc. only to support the general proposition that some proposals may intrude unduly on a company's "ordinary business" operations by virtue of the level of detail that they seek. We did not intend to imply that the proposal addressed in Capital Cities, or similar proposals, would automatically amount to "ordinary business." Those determinations will be made on a case-by-case basis, taking into account factors such as the nature of the proposal and the circumstances of the company to which it is directed.

\*    \*    \*

(a) Question 1: What is a proposal?

A shareholder proposal is your recommendation or requirement that the company and/or its board of directors take action, which you intend to present at a meeting of the company's shareholders. Your proposal should state as clearly as possible the course of action that you believe the company should follow. If your proposal is placed on the company's proxy card, the company must also provide in the form of proxy means for shareholders to specify by boxes a choice between approval or disapproval, or abstention. Unless otherwise indicated, the word "proposal" as used in this section refers both to your proposal, and to your corresponding statement in support of your proposal (if any).

(b) Question 2: Who is eligible to submit a proposal, and how do I demonstrate to the company that I am eligible?

(1) In order to be eligible to submit a proposal, you must have continuously held at least $2,000 in market value, or 1%, of the company's securities entitled to be voted on the proposal at the meeting for at least one year by the date you submit the proposal. You must continue to hold those securities through the date of the meeting.

(2) If you are the registered holder of your securities, which means that your name appears in the company's records as a shareholder, the company can verify your eligibility on its own, although you will still have to provide the company with a written statement that you intend to continue to hold the securities through the date of the meeting of shareholders. However, if like many shareholders you are not a registered holder, the company likely does not know that you are a shareholder, or how many shares you own. In this case, at the time you submit your proposal, you must prove your eligibility to the company in one of two ways:

(i) The first way is to submit to the company a written statement from the "record" holder of your securities (usually a broker or bank) verifying that, at the time you submitted your proposal, you continuously held the securities for at least one year. You must also include your own written statement that you intend to continue to hold the securities through the date of the meeting of shareholders; or

(ii) The second way to prove ownership applies only if you have filed a Schedule 13D (§ 240.13d-101), Schedule 13G (§ 240.13d-102), Form 3 (§ 249.103 of this chapter), Form 4 (§ 249.104 of this chapter) and/or Form 5 (§ 249.105 of this chapter), or amendments to those documents or updated forms, reflecting your ownership of the shares as of or before the date on which the one-year eligibility period begins. If you have filed one of these documents with the SEC, you may demonstrate your eligibility by submitting to the company: (A) A copy of the schedule and/or form, and any subsequent amendments reporting a change in your ownership level; (B) Your written statement that you continuously held the required number of shares for the one-year period as of the date of the statement; and (C) Your written statement that you intend to continue ownership of the shares through the date of the company's annual or special meeting.

(c) Question 3: How many proposals may I submit?

Each shareholder may submit no more than one proposal to a company for a particular shareholders' meeting.

(d) Question 4: How long can my proposal be?

The proposal, including any accompanying supporting statement, may not exceed 500 words.

(e) Question 5: What is the deadline for submitting a proposal?

(1) If you are submitting your proposal for the company's annual meeting, you can in most cases find the deadline in last year's proxy statement. However, if the company did not hold an annual meeting last year, or has changed the date of its meeting for this year more than 30 days from last year's meeting, you can usually find the deadline in one of the company's quarterly reports on Form 10-Q (§ 249.308a of this chapter) or 10-QSB (§ 249.308b of this chapter), or in shareholder reports of investment companies under § 270.30d-1 of this chapter of the Investment Company Act of 1940. In order to avoid controversy, shareholders should submit their proposals by means, including electronic means, that permit them to prove the date of delivery.

(2) The deadline is calculated in the following manner if the proposal is submitted for a regularly scheduled annual meeting. The proposal must be received at the company's principal executive offices not less than 120 calendar days before the date of the company's proxy statement released to shareholders in connection with the previous year's annual meeting. However, if the company did not hold an annual meeting the previous year, or if the date of this year's annual meeting has been changed by more than 30 days from the date of the previous year's meeting, then the deadline is a reasonable time before the company begins to print and mail its proxy materials.

(3) If you are submitting your proposal for a meeting of shareholders other than a regularly scheduled annual meeting, the deadline is a reasonable time before the company begins to print and mail its proxy materials.

(f) Question 6: What if I fail to follow one of the eligibility or procedural requirements explained in answers to Questions 1 through 4 of this section?

(1) The company may exclude your proposal, but only after it has notified you of the problem, and you have failed adequately to correct it. Within 14 calendar days of receiving your proposal, the company must notify you in writing of any procedural or eligibility deficiencies, as well as of the time frame for your response. Your response must be postmarked, or transmitted electronically, no later than 14 days from the date you received the company's notification. A company need not provide you such notice of a deficiency if the deficiency cannot be remedied, such as if you fail to submit a proposal by the company's properly determined deadline. If the company intends to exclude the proposal, it will later have to make a submission under § 240.14a-8 and provide you with a copy under Question 10 below, § 240.14a-8(j).

(2) If you fail in your promise to hold the required number of securities through the date of the meeting of shareholders, then the company will be permitted to exclude all of your proposals from its proxy materials for any meeting held in the following two calendar years.

(g) Question 7: Who has the burden of persuading the Commission or its staff that my proposal can be excluded?

Except as otherwise noted, the burden is on the company to demonstrate that it is entitled to exclude a proposal.

(h) Question 8: Must I appear personally at the shareholders' meeting to present the proposal?

(1) Either you, or your representative who is qualified under state law to present the proposal on your behalf, must attend the meeting to present the proposal. Whether you attend the meeting yourself or send a qualified representative to the meeting in your place, you should make sure that you, or your representative, follow the proper state law procedures for attending the meeting and/or presenting your proposal.

(2) If the company holds its shareholder meeting in whole or in part via electronic media, and the company permits you or your representative to present your proposal via such media, then you may appear through electronic media rather than traveling to the meeting to appear in person.

(3) If you or your qualified representative fail to appear and present the proposal, without good cause, the company will be permitted to exclude all of your proposals from its proxy materials for any meetings held in the following two calendar years.

(i) Question 9: If I have complied with the procedural requirements, on what other bases may a company rely to exclude my proposal?

(1) Improper under state law: If the proposal is not a proper subject for action by shareholders under the laws of the jurisdiction of the company's organization;

Note to paragraph (i)(1): Depending on the subject matter, some proposals are not considered proper under state law if they would be binding on the company if approved by shareholders. In our experience, most proposals that are cast as recommendations or requests that the board of directors take specified action are proper under state law. Accordingly, we will assume that a proposal drafted as a recommendation or suggestion is proper unless the company demonstrates otherwise.

(2) Violation of law: If the proposal would, if implemented, cause the company to violate any state, federal, or foreign law to which it is subject;

Note to paragraph (i)(2): We will not apply this basis for exclusion to permit exclusion of a proposal on grounds that it would violate foreign law if compliance with the foreign law would result in a violation of any state or federal law.

(3) Violation of proxy rules: If the proposal or supporting statement is contrary to any of the Commission's proxy rules, including § 240.14a-9, which prohibits materially false or misleading statements in proxy soliciting materials;

(4) Personal grievance; special interest: If the proposal relates to the redress of a personal claim or grievance against the company or any other person, or if it is designed to result in a benefit to you, or to further a personal interest, which is not shared by the other shareholders at large;

(5) Relevance: If the proposal relates to operations which account for less than 5 percent of the company's total assets at the end of its most recent fiscal year, and for less than 5 percent of its net earnings and gross sales for its most recent fiscal year, and is not otherwise significantly related to the company's business;

(6) Absence of power/authority: If the company would lack the power or authority to implement the proposal;

(7) Management functions: If the proposal deals with a matter relating to the company's ordinary business operations;

(8) Relates to election: If the proposal relates to an election for membership on the company's board of directors or analogous governing body;

(9) Conflicts with company's proposal: If the proposal directly conflicts with one of the company's own proposals to be submitted to shareholders at the same meeting;

Note to paragraph (i)(9): A company's submission to the Commission under this section should specify the points of conflict with the company's proposal.

(10) Substantially implemented: If the company has already substantially implemented the proposal;

(11) Duplication: If the proposal substantially duplicates another proposal previously submitted to the company by another proponent that will be included in the company's proxy materials for the same meeting;

(12) Resubmissions: If the proposal deals with substantially the same subject matter as another proposal or proposals that has or have been previously included in the company's proxy materials within the preceding 5 calendar years, a company may exclude it from its proxy materials for any meeting held within 3 calendar years of the last time it was included if the proposal received:

> (i) Less than 3% of the vote if proposed once within the preceding 5 calendar years;

> (ii) Less than 6% of the vote on its last submission to shareholders if proposed twice previously within the preceding 5 calendar years; or

> (iii) Less than 10% of the vote on its last submission to shareholders if proposed three times or more previously within the preceding 5 calendar years; and

(13) Specific amount of dividends: If the proposal relates to specific amounts of cash or stock dividends.

(j) Question 10: What procedures must the company follow if it intends to exclude my proposal?

(1) If the company intends to exclude a proposal from its proxy materials, it must file its reasons with the Commission no later than 80 calendar days before it files its definitive proxy statement and form of proxy with the Commission. The company must simultaneously provide you with a copy of its submission. The Commission staff may permit the company to make its submission later than 80 days before the company files its definitive proxy statement and form of proxy, if the company demonstrates good cause for missing the deadline.

(2) The company must file six paper copies of the following:

> (i) The proposal;

> (ii) An explanation of why the company believes that it may exclude the proposal, which should, if possible, refer to the most recent applicable authority, such as prior Division letters issued under the rule; and

> (iii) A supporting opinion of counsel when such reasons are based on matters of state or foreign law.

(k) Question 11: May I submit my own statement to the Commission responding to the company's arguments?

Yes, you may submit a response, but it is not required. You should try to submit any response to us, with a copy to the company, as soon as possible after the company makes its submission. This way, the Commission staff will have time to consider fully your submission before it issues its response. You should submit six paper copies of your response.

(l) Question 12: If the company includes my shareholder proposal in its proxy materials, what information about me must it include along with the proposal itself?

(1) The company's proxy statement must include your name and address, as well as the number of the company's voting securities that you hold. However, instead of providing that information, the company may instead include a statement that it will provide the information to shareholders promptly upon receiving an oral or written request.

(2) The company is not responsible for the contents of your proposal or supporting statement.

(m) Question 13: What can I do if the company includes in its proxy statement reasons why it believes shareholders should not vote in favor of my proposal, and I disagree with some of its statements?

(1) The company may elect to include in its proxy statement reasons why it believes shareholders should vote against your proposal. The company is allowed to make arguments reflecting its own point of view, just as you may express your own point of view in your proposal's supporting statement.

(2) However, if you believe that the company's opposition to your proposal contains materially false or misleading statements that may violate our anti-fraud rule, § 240.14a-9, you should promptly send to the Commission staff and the company a letter explaining the reasons for your view, along with a copy of the company's statements opposing your proposal. To the extent possible, your letter should include specific factual information demonstrating the inaccuracy of the company's claims. Time permitting, you may wish to try to work out your differences with the company by yourself before contacting the Commission staff.

(3) We require the company to send you a copy of its statements opposing your proposal before it mails its proxy materials, so that you may bring to our attention any materially false or misleading statements, under the following timeframes:

(i) If our no-action response requires that you make revisions to your proposal or supporting statement as a condition to requiring the company to include it in its proxy materials, then the company must provide you with a copy of its opposition statements no later than 5 calendar days after the company receives a copy of your revised proposal.

(ii) In all other cases, the company must provide you with a copy of its opposition statements no later than 30 calendar days before its files definitive copies of its proxy

## LONG ISLAND LIGHTING CO. v. BARBASH
United States Court of Appeals, Second Circuit
779 F.2d 793 (1985)

CARDAMONE, J.

A Long Island utility furnishing that area with power has scheduled a stock-holders meeting for Thursday December 12, 1985. It has been embroiled in public controversy over its construction of the Shoreham Nuclear Power Plant and adverse publicity intensified recently because of extended loss of service to customers arising from damages to the transmission system caused by Hurricane Gloria.

In this setting, the company, believing that several groups had begun to solicit proxies during October in anticipation of the upcoming stockholders meeting, brought suit to enjoin them. The district court judge first slowed the matter by adjourning the case until the fall election was over, and then speeded it up by directing discovery to be completed in one day. Such handling only demonstrates again that in the law it is wise — even when expeditious action is required — to make haste slowly.

Long Island Lighting Company (LILCO) brings this expedited appeal from a November 8, 1985 order of the United States District Court for the Eastern District of New York (Weinstein, Ch.J.) that granted summary judgment dismissing LILCO's complaint against the Steering Committee of Citizens to Replace LILCO (the Citizens Committee), John W. Matthews and Island Insulation Corp. LILCO brought this action to enjoin defendants' alleged violations of § 14(a) of the Securities Exchange Act of 1934 and Rules 14a-9, 17 C.F.R. § 240.14a-9 and 14a-11, 17 C.F.R. 240.14a-11, promulgated under that statute, that govern proxy solicitations. The complaint alleges that defendants have committed such violations by publishing a false and misleading advertisement in connection with a special meeting of LILCO's shareholders scheduled for the purpose of electing a new LILCO Board of Directors. For the reasons explained below, this matter is remanded to the district court.

Plaintiff LILCO is a New York electric company serving Nassau and Suffolk Counties on Long Island, New York. Its common and preferred stocks are registered in accordance with Section 12(b) of the Securities Exchange Act and are traded on the New York Stock Exchange. Defendant John W. Matthews was an unsuccessful candidate for Nassau County Executive in the election held November 5, 1985. During the campaign he strongly opposed LILCO and its operation of the Shoreham Nuclear Power Plant. As an owner of 100 shares of LILCO's preferred stock and a manager of an additional 100 shares of common stock held by his company, Island Insulation Corp., Matthews initiated a proxy contest for the purpose of electing a majority of LILCO's Board of Directors. The stated purpose of the other defendants, the Citizens Committee, is to replace LILCO with a municipally owned utility company. The Citizens Committee was formed prior to this litigation, in order to challenge LILCO's construction of the Shoreham atomic energy plant, its service and its rates.

LILCO filed its complaint on October 21, 1985 alleging that defendants published a materially false and misleading advertisement in Newsday, a Long Island newspaper, and ran false and misleading radio advertisements throughout the New York area. The ads criticized LILCO's management and encouraged citizens to replace LILCO with a state-run company. The complaint sought an injunction against further alleged solicitation of LILCO shareholders until the claimed false and misleading statements had been corrected and a Schedule 14B had been filed. The district court granted LILCO an expedited hearing on its appeal from Magistrate Scheindlin's decision . . . .

LILCO argues first, that in view of the necessity in every case to determine whether a communication constitutes a "solicitation" under the proxy rates, the district court abused its discretion by limiting LILCO's opportunity for discovery. Second, LILCO asserts that the district court erroneously held that communications to shareholders through general and indirect publications can in no circumstances constitute "solicitations" under the proxy rules. Finally, LILCO contests the district court's view that this construction of the proxy rules is necessary to render them compatible with the First Amendment.

*    *    *

### Rules Governing Proxy Solicitation

In our view the district court further erred in holding that the proxy rules cannot cover communications appearing in publications of general circulation and that are indirectly addressed to shareholders. Regulation 14(a) of the Securities Exchange Act governs the solicitation of proxies with respect to the securities of publicly held companies, with enumerated exceptions set forth in the rules. 17 C.F.R. § 240.14a-1 et seq. Proxy rules promulgated by the Securities Exchange Commission (SEC) regulate as proxy solicitations:

> (1) any request for a proxy whether or not accompanied by or included in a form of proxy;

> (2) any request to execute or not to execute, or to revoke, a proxy; or

> (3) the furnishing of a form of proxy or other communications to security holders under circumstances reasonably calculated to result in the procurement, withholding or revocation of a proxy.

Rule 14a-1, 17 C.F.R. § 240.14a-1.

These rules apply not only to direct requests to furnish, revoke or withhold proxies, but also to communications which may indirectly accomplish such a result or constitute a step in a chain of communications designed ultimately to accomplish such a result. *Securities and Exchange Commission v. Okin*, 132 F.2d 784, 786 (2d Cir. 1943) (letter to shareholders was within the scope of the proxy rules where it was alleged that it was "a step in a campaign whose purpose it was to get [defendant] elected an officer of the company; it was to pave the way for an out-and-out solicitation later.")

The question in every case is whether the challenged communication, seen in the totality of circumstances, is "reasonably calculated" to influence the shareholders' votes. *See id.*; *Trans. World Corp. v. Odyssey Partners*, 561 F. Supp. 1311, 1320 (S.D.N.Y. 1983). Determination of the purpose of the communication depends upon the nature of the communication and the circumstances under which it was distributed. *Brown v. Chicago, Rock Island & Pacific R.R.*, 328 F.2d 122 (7th Cir. 1964). In *Studebaker Corporation v. Gittlin*, 360 F.2d 692, 694 (2d Cir. 1966), the defendant solicited authorizations from shareholders to obtain a shareholder list in the course of a proxy fight. Because the authorizations were sought only for the purpose of seeking future proxies, the court held that the authorizations were also covered by the proxy rules. *Id.* at 696.

Deciding whether a communication is a proxy solicitation does not depend upon whether it is "targeted directly" at shareholders. See Rule 14a-6(g), 17 C.F.R. § 240.14a-6(g) (requiring that solicitations in the form of "speeches, press releases, and television scripts" be filed with the SEC). As the SEC correctly notes in its amicus brief, it would "permit easy evasion of the proxy rules" to exempt all general and indirect communications to shareholders, and this is true whether or not the communication purports to address matters of "public interest." *See Medical Comm. for Human Rights v. SEC*, 432 F.2d 659 (D.C. Cir. 1970) (applying proxy rules to shareholder's proposal to prohibit company from manufacturing napalm during the Vietnam War). The SEC's authority to regulate proxy solicitations has traditionally extended into matters of public interest.

### First Amendment Concerns

The extent to which the activities of the defendants amount to a solicitation of the proxies of shareholders of LILCO may determine whether or not their actions are protected by the First Amendment. Therefore, it is unnecessary to express an opinion on any claim of privilege under the First Amendment until there has been a determination of the "solicitation" issue as a result of further proceedings in the district court.

Because discovery here was so abbreviated and the district court's determination was predicated on a mistaken notion of what constitutes a proxy solicitation and on the relationship between the proxy rules and the First Amendment, the case must be remanded to the district court. . . .

In consideration of the time constraints, the mandate of the Court shall issue forthwith.

WINTER, J., dissenting:

In order to avoid a serious first amendment issue, I would construe the federal regulations governing the solicitation of proxies as inapplicable to the newspaper advertisement in question. *See Lowe v. Securities and Exchange Commission*, 472

U.S. 181 (1985). Further discovery would then be unnecessary, and I therefore respectfully dissent.

\*    \*    \*

One of LILCO's principal antagonists is John W. Matthews, a defendant in this litigation. During the fall of 1985, Matthews was the Democratic candidate for County Executive in Nassau County and appears to have focused much of his campaign upon LILCO issues. During this campaign, Matthews purchased a sufficient number of shares of LILCO's preferred stock to force a special shareholders' meeting pursuant to its Charter. On October 9, 1985, he made a demand for such a meeting. The next day, a corporation that is controlled by Matthews and owns LILCO common stock asked to inspect and copy LILCO's list of common stockholders. The stated purpose of this request was to enable it and Matthews to communicate with LILCO shareholders with regard to the election of LILCO's Board and to whether LILCO should be sold to Nassau and Suffolk Counties.

\*    \*    \*

The content of the Committee's advertisement is of critical importance. First, it is on its face addressed solely to the public. Second, it makes no mention either of proxies or of the shareholders' meeting demanded by Matthews. Third, the issues the ad addresses are quintessentially matters of public political debate, namely, whether a public power authority would provide cheaper electricity than LILCO. Claims of LILCO mismanagement are discussed solely in the context of their effect on its customers. Finally, the ad was published in the middle of an election campaign in which LILCO's future was an issue.

On these facts, therefore, LILCO's claim raises a constitutional issue of the first magnitude. It asks nothing less than that a federal court act as a censor, empowered to determine the truth or falsity of the ad's claims about the merits of public power and to enjoin further advocacy containing false claims. We need not resolve this constitutional issue, however.

Where advertisements are critical of corporate conduct but are facially directed solely to the public, in no way mention the exercise of proxies, and debate only matters of conceded public concern, I would construe federal proxy regulation as inapplicable, whatever the motive of those who purchase them. This position, which is strongly suggested by relevant case law, see infra, maximizes public debate, avoids embroiling the federal judiciary in determining the rightness or wrongness of conflicting positions on public policy, and does not significantly impede achievement of Congress' goal that shareholders exercise proxy rights on the basis of accurate information.

It is of course true that LILCO shareholders may be concerned about public allegations of mismanagement on LILCO's part. However, shareholders are most unlikely to be misled into thinking that advertisements of this kind, particularly when purchased in the name of a committee so obviously disinterested in the return on investment to LILCO's shareholders, are either necessarily accurate or authoritative sources of information about LILCO's management. Such advertisements, which in no way suggest internal reforms shareholders might bring about through the exercise of their proxies, are sheer political advocacy and would be so recognized by any reasonable shareholder.

To be sure, the fact that a corporation has become a target of political advocacy might well justify unease among shareholders. No one seriously asserts, however, that the right to criticize corporate behavior as a matter of public concern diminishes as shareholders' meetings become imminent.

Potential conflicts between first amendment values and federal regulatory goals have arisen before and have been resolved by the Supreme Court by construing the particular regulatory scheme not to reach activities which clearly implicate the first amendment. . . .

This very year, in the *Lowe* case, the Supreme Court construed the Investment Advisors' Act not to reach non-personalized investment advice in an investment newsletter even where the source of that advice was a person barred from being a professional investment advisor because of past criminal conduct. In *Lowe*, the congressional purpose of protecting the public from investment advice by persons determined to be untrustworthy was far more deeply implicated by the newsletter than are the purposes of federal proxy regulation implicated by the advertisement at issue in the present case. *Lowe* actually involved the giving of investment advice by one barred from the profession by the Investment Advisors' Act, whereas the relationship of the advertisement in this case to the exercise of shareholder proxies is on its face very attenuated.

## ROSENFELD v. FAIRCHILD ENGINE AND AIRPLANE CORP.
### Court of Appeals of New York
### 128 N.E. 2d 291 (1955)

FROSSEL, J.

In a stockholder's derivative action brought by plaintiff, an attorney, who owns 25 out of the company's over 2,300,000 shares, he seeks to compel the return of $261,522, paid out of the corporate treasury to reimburse both sides in a proxy contest for their expenses. The Appellate Division has unanimously affirmed a judgment of an Official Referee dismissing plaintiff's complaint on the merits, and we agree. Exhaustive opinions were written by both courts below, and it will serve no useful purpose to review the facts again.

Of the amount in controversy $106,000 were spent out of corporate funds by the old board of directors while still in office in defense of their position in said contest; $28,000 were paid to the old board by the new board after the change of management following the proxy contest, to compensate the former directors for such of the remaining expenses of their unsuccessful defense as the new board found was fair and reasonable; payment of $127,000, representing reimbursement of expenses to members of the prevailing group, was expressly ratified by a 16 to 1 majority vote of the stockholders.

. . . The Appellate Division found that the difference between plaintiff's group and the old board "went deep into the policies of the company," and that among these Ward's contract was one of the "main points of contention." The Official Referee found that the controversy "was based on an understandable difference in policy between the two groups, at the very bottom of which was the Ward employment contract."

By way of contrast with the findings here, in *Lawyers' Advertising Co. v. Consolidated Ry., Lighting & Refrigerating Co.* [187 N.Y. 395], which was an action to recover for the cost of publishing newspaper notices not authorized by the board of directors, it was expressly found that the proxy contest there involved was "by one faction in its contest with another for the control of the corporation . . . a contest for the perpetuation of their offices and control." We there said by way of dicta that under such circumstances the publication of certain notices on behalf of the management faction was not a corporate expenditure which the directors had the power to authorize.

Other jurisdictions and our own lower courts have held that management may look to the corporate treasury for the reasonable expenses of soliciting proxies to defend its position in a bona fide policy contest.

It should be noted that plaintiff does not argue that the aforementioned sums were fraudulently extracted from the corporation; indeed, his counsel conceded that "the charges were fair and reasonable," but denied "they were legal charges which may be reimbursed for." This is therefore not a case where a stockholder challenges specific items, which, on examination, the trial court may find unwarranted, excessive or otherwise improper. Had plaintiff made such objections here, the trial court would have been required to examine the items challenged.

If directors of a corporation may not in good faith incur reasonable and proper expenses in soliciting proxies in these days of giant corporations with vast numbers of stockholders, the corporate business might be seriously interfered with because of stockholder indifference and the difficulty of procuring a quorum, where there is no contest. In the event of a proxy contest, if the directors may not freely answer the challenges of outside groups and in good faith defend their actions with respect to corporate policy for the information of the stockholders, they and the corporation may be at the mercy of persons seeking to wrest control for their own purposes, so long as such persons have ample funds to conduct a proxy contest. The test is clear. When the directors act in good faith in a contest over policy, they have the right to incur reasonable and proper expenses for solicitation of proxies and in defense of their corporate policies, and are not obliged to sit idly by. The courts are entirely competent to pass upon their bona fides in any given case, as well as the nature of their expenditures when duly challenged.

It is also our view that the members of the so-called new group could be reimbursed by the corporation for their expenditures in this contest by affirmative vote of the stokholders. With regard to these ultimately successful contestants, as the Appellate Division below has noted, there was, of course, "no duty . . . to set forth the facts, with corresponding obligation of the corporation to pay for such expense." However, where a majority of the stockholders chose in this case by a vote of 16 to 1 to reimburse the successful contestants for achieving the very end sought and voted for by them as owners of the corporation, we see no reason to deny the effect of their ratification nor to hold the corporate body powerless to determine how its own moneys shall be spent.

The rule then which we adopt is simply this: In a contest over policy, as compared to a purely personal power contest, corporate directors have the right to make reasonable and proper expenditures, subject to the scrutiny of the courts when duly challenged, from the corporate treasury for the purpose of persuading the stockholders of the correctness of their position and soliciting their support for policies which the directors believe, in all good faith, are in the best interests of the corporation. The stockholders, moreover, have the right to reimburse successful contestants for the reasonable and bona fide expenses incurred by them in any such policy contest, subject to like court scrutiny. That is not to say, however, that corporate directors can, under any circumstances, disport themselves in a proxy contest with the corporation's moneys to an unlimited extent. Where it is established that such moneys have been spent for personal power, individual gain or private advantage, and not in the belief that such expenditures are in the best interests of the stockholders and the corporation, or where the fairness and reasonableness of the amounts allegedly expended are duly and successfully challenged, the courts will not hesitate to disallow them.

The judgment of the Appellate Division should be affirmed, without costs.

DESMOND, J. (concurring).

We granted leave to appeal in an effort to pass, and in the expectation of passing, on this question, highly important in modern-day corporation law: is it lawful for a corporation, on consent of a majority of its stockholders, to pay, out of its funds, the expenses of a "proxy fight," incurred by competing candidates for election as directors? Now that the appeal has been argued, I doubt that the question is presented by this record. The defendants served were Allis who was on the old board but was re-elected to the new board, McComas and Wilson, defeated members of the old board, and Fairchild, leader of the victorious group and largest stockholder in the corporation. The expenses of the old board, or management group, in the proxy fight, were about $134,000, and those of the victorious Fairchild group amounted to about $127,500. In the end, the corporation paid both those sums, and it is for the reimbursement thereof, to the corporation, that this stockholder's derivative action is brought. Of the proxy fight expenses of the management slate, about $106,000 was paid out on authorization of the old board while the old directors were still in office. The balance of those charges, as well as the whole of the expenses of the new and successful, Fairchild group, was paid by the corporation after the new directors had taken over and after a majority of stockholders had approved such expenditures. The election had been fought out on a number of issues, chief of which concerned a contract which Ward (a defendant not served), who was a director and the principal executive officer of the company, had obtained from the corporation, covering compensation for, and other conditions of, his own services. Each side, in the campaign for proxies, charged the other with seeking to perpetuate, or grasp, control of the corporation. The Fairchild group won the election by a stock vote of about two-to-one, and obtained, at the next annual stockholders' meeting and by a much larger vote, authorization to make the payments above described.

Plaintiff asserts that it was illegal for the directors (unless by unanimous consent of stockholders) to expend corporate moneys in the proxy contest beyond the amounts necessary to give to stockholders bare notice of the meeting and of the matters to be voted on thereat. Defendants say that the proxy contest revolved around disputes over corporate policies and that it was, accordingly, proper not only to assess against the corporation the expense of serving formal notices and of routine proxy solicitation, but to go further and spend corporate moneys, on behalf of each group, thoroughly to inform the stockholders. The reason why that important question is, perhaps, not directly before us in this lawsuit is because, as the Appellate Division properly held, plaintiff failed "to urge liability as to specific expenditures." The cost of giving routinely necessary notice is, of course, chargeable to the corporation. It is just as clear, we think, that payment by a corporation of the expense of "proceedings by one faction in its contest with another for the control of the corporation" is ultra vires, and unlawful. (*Lawyers' Advertising Co. v. Consolidated Ry., Lighting & Refrigerating Co.*, 187 N.Y. 395, 399). Approval by directors or by a majority stock vote could not validate such gratuitous expenditures. (*Continental Securities Co. v. Belmont*, 206 N.Y. 7). Some of the payments attacked in this suit were, on their face, for lawful purposes and apparently reasonable in amount but, as to others, the record simply does not contain evidentiary bases for a determination as to either lawfulness or reasonableness. Surely, the burden was on plaintiff to go forward to some extent with such particularization and proof. It failed to do so, and so failed to make out a prima facie case.

We are, therefore, reaching the same result as did the Appellate Division but on one only of the grounds listed by that court, that is, failure of proof. . . .

> "The custom has become common upon the part of corporations to mail proxies to their respective stockholders, often accompanied by a brief circular of directions, and such custom when accompanied by no unreasonable expenditure, is not without merit in so far as it encourages voting by stockholders, through making it convenient and ready at hand. The notice in question, however, was not published until after proxies had been sent out. It simply amounted to an urgent solicitation that these proxies should be executed and returned for use by one faction in its contest, and we think there is no authority for imposing the expense of its publication upon the company. . . . [I]t would be altogether too dangerous a rule to permit directors in control of a corporation and engaged in a contest for the perpetuation of their offices and control, to impose upon the corporation the unusual expense of publishing advertisements or, by analogy, of dispatching special messengers for the purpose of procuring proxies in their behalf."

A final comment: since expenditures which do not meet that test of propriety are intrinsically unlawful, it could not be any answer to such a claim as plaintiff makes here that the stockholder vote which purported to authorize them was heavy or that the change in management turned out to be beneficial to the corporation.

The judgment should be affirmed, without costs.

VAN VOORHIS, J. (dissenting).

The decision of this appeal is of far-reaching importance insofar as concerns payment by corporations of campaign expenses by stockholders in proxy contests for control. This is a stockholder's derivative action to require directors to restore to a corporation moneys paid to defray expenses of this nature, incurred both by an incumbent faction and by an insurgent faction of stockholders. The insurgents prevailed at the annual meeting, and payments of their own campaign expenses were attempted to be ratified by majority vote. It was a large majority, but the stockholders were not unanimous. Regardless of the merits of this contest, we are called upon to decide whether it was a corporate purpose (1) to make the expenditures which were disbursed by the incumbent or management group in defense of their acts and to remain in control of the corporation, and (2) to defray expenditures made by the insurgent group, which succeeded in convincing a majority of the stockholders. The Appellate Division held that stockholder authorization or ratification was not necessary to reasonable expenditures by the management group, the purpose of which was to inform the stockholders concerning the affairs of the corporation, and that, although these incumbents spent or incurred obligations of $133,966 (the previous expenses of annual meetings of this corporation ranging between $7,000 and $28,000), plaintiff must fail for having omitted to distinguish item by item between which of these expenditures were warranted and which ones were not; and the Appellate Division held that the insurgents also should be reimbursed, but subject to the qualification that "The expenses of those who were seeking to displace the management should not be reimbursed by the corporation except upon approval by the stockholders." It was held that the stockholders had approved.

No resolution was passed by the stockholders approving payment to the management group. It has been recognized that not all of the $133,966 in obligations paid or incurred by the management group was designed merely for information of stockholders. This outlay included payment for all of the activities of a strenuous campaign to persuade and cajole in a hard-fought contest for control of this corporation. It included, for example, expenses for entertainment, chartered airplanes and limousines, public relations counsel and proxy solicitors. However legitimate such measures may be on behalf of stockholders themselves in such a controversy, most of them do not pertain to a corporate function but are part of the familiar apparatus of aggressive factions in corporate contests. In *Lawyers' Advertising Co. v. Consolidated Ry., Lighting & Refrigerating Co.* (187 N.Y. 395, 399), this court said:

> "The notice in question, however, was not published until after proxies had been sent out. It simply amounted to an urgent solicitation that these proxies should be executed and returned for use by one faction in its contest, and we think there is no authority for imposing the expense of its publication upon the company. It may be conceded that the directors who caused this publication acted in good faith, and felt that they were serving the best interests of the stockholders; but it would be altogether too dangerous a rule to permit directors in control of a corporation and engaged in a contest for the perpetuation of their offices and control, to

impose upon the corporation the unusual expense of publishing advertisements, or, by analogy, of dispatching special messengers for the purpose of procuring proxies in their behalf."

The Appellate Division acknowledged in the instant case that "[i]t is obvious that the management group here incurred a substantial amount of needless expense which was charged to the corporation," but this conclusion should have led to a direction that those defendants who were incumbent directors should be required to come forward with an explanation of their expenditures under the familiar rule that where it has been established that directors have expended corporate money for their own purposes, the burden of going forward with evidence of the propriety and reasonableness of specific items rests upon the directors. The complaint should not have been dismissed as against incumbent directors due to failure of plaintiff to segregate the specific expenditures which are ultra vires, but, once plaintiff had proved facts from which an inference of impropriety might be drawn, the duty of making an explanation was laid upon the directors to explain and justify their conduct.

The second ground assigned by the Appellate Division for dismissing the complaint against incumbent directors is stockholder ratification of reimbursement to the insurgent group. Whatever effect or lack of it this resolution had upon expenditures by the insurgent group, clearly the stockholders who voted to pay the insurgents entertained no intention of reimbursing the management group for their expenditures. The insurgent group succeeded as a result of arousing the indignation of these very stockholders against the management group; nothing in the resolution to pay the expenses of the insurgent group purported to authorize or ratify payment of the campaign expenses of their adversaries, and certainly no inference should be drawn that the stockholders who voted to pay the insurgents intended that the incumbent group should also be paid. Upon the contrary, they were removing the incumbents from control mainly for the reason that they were charged with having mulcted the corporation by a long-term salary and pension contract to one of their number, J. Carlton Ward, Jr. If these stockholders had been presented with a resolution to pay the expenses of that group, it would almost certainly have been voted down. The stockholders should not be deemed to have authorized or ratified reimbursement of the incumbents.

There is no doubt that the management was entitled and under a duty to take reasonable steps to acquaint the stockholders with essential facts concerning the management of the corporation, and it may well be that the existence of a contest warranted them in circularizing the stockholders with more than ordinarily detailed information.

\* \* \*

What expenses of the incumbent group should be allowed and what should be disallowed should be remitted to the trial court to ascertain, after taking evidence, in accordance with the rule that the incumbent directors were required to assume the burden of going forward in the first instance with evidence explaining and justifying their expenditures. Only such as were reasonably related to informing the stockholders fully and fairly concerning the corporate affairs should be allowed. The concession by plaintiff that such expenditures as were made were reasonable in amount does not decide this question. By way of illustration, the costs of entertainment for stockholders may have been, and it is stipulated that they were, at the going rates for providing similar entertainment. That does not signify that entertaining stockholders is reasonably related to the purposes of the corporation. The Appellate Division, as above stated, found that the management group incurred a substantial amount of needless expense. That fact being established, it became the duty of the incumbent directors to unravel and explain these payments.

Regarding the $127,556 paid by the new management to the insurgent group for their campaign expenditures, the question immediately arises whether that was for a corporate purpose. The Appellate Division has recognized that upon no theory could such expenditures be reimbursed except by approval of the stockholders and, as has been said, it is the insurgents' expenditures alone to which the stockholders' resolution of ratification was addressed. If unanimous stockholder approval had been obtained and no rights of creditors or of the public intervened, it would make no practical difference whether the purpose were ultra vires i.e., not a corporate purpose. Upon the other hand, an act which is ultra vires cannot be ratified merely by a majority of the stockholders of a corporation.

\* \* \*

The familiar rule, applied in those and other decisions, is that merely voidable acts of the directors of a corporation can be ratified by majority stockholder approval, such as contracts between corporations having interlocking directorates (*Continental Ins. Co. v. New York & H. R. Co.*, 187 N.Y. 225), loans of surplus funds by a trading corporation (*Murray v. Smith*, 166 App. Div. 528 — although not in the case of loans to stockholders in violation of the Stock Corporation Law, Consol. Laws, § 59), and other irregularities involving acts which are neither ultra vires, fraudulent or illegal.

In considering this issue, as in the case of the expenses of the incumbents, we begin with the proposition that this court has already held that it is beyond the power of a corporation to authorize the expenditure of mere campaign expenses in a proxy contest.

\* \* \*

In our view, the impracticability of such a distinction is illustrated by the statement in the *Hall* [*v. Trans-Lux Daylight Picture Screen Corp.*, 20 Del. Ch. 78, 171 A. 226, *supra*, p. 85] case that "It is impossible in many cases of intracorporate contests over directors, to sever questions of policy from those of persons." This circumstance is stressed in Judge RIFKIND's opinion in the *Steinberg* [*v. Adams*, 90 F. Supp. 604 (D.D.C.) *supra*, p. 608] case: "The simple fact, of course, is that generally policy and personnel do not exist in separate compartments. A change in personnel is sometimes indispensable to a change of policy. A new board may be the symbol of the shift in policy as well as the means of obtaining it."

That may be all very well, but the upshot of this reasoning is that inasmuch as it is generally impossible to distinguish whether "policy" or "personnel" is the dominant factor, any averments must be accepted at their face value that questions of policy are dominant. Nowhere do these opinions mention that the converse is equally true and more pervasive, that neither the "ins" nor the "outs" ever say that they have no program to offer to the shareholders, but just want to acquire or to retain control, as the case may be. In common experience, this distinction is unreal.

\* \* \*

The main question of "policy" in the instant corporate election, as is stated in the opinions below and frankly admitted, concerns the long-term contract with pension rights of a former officer and director, Mr. J. Carlton Ward, Jr. The insurgents' chief claim of benefit to the corporation from their victory consists in the termination of that agreement, resulting in an alleged actuarial saving of $350,000 to $825,000 to the corporation, and the reduction of other salaries and rent by more than $300,000 per year. The insurgents had contended in the proxy contest that these payments should be substantially reduced so that members of the incumbent group would not continue to profit personally at the expense of the corporation. If these charges were true, which appear to have been believed by a majority of the shareholders, then the disbursements by the management group in the proxy contest fall under the condemnation of the English and the Delaware rule.

\* \* \*

Some expenditures may concededly be made by a corporation represented by its management so as to inform the stockholders, but there is a clear distinction between such expenditures by management and by mere groups of stockholders. The latter are under no legal obligation to assume duties of managing the corporation. They may endeavor to supersede the management for any reason, regardless of whether it be advantageous or detrimental to the corporation but, if they succeed, that is not a determination that the company was previously mismanaged or that it may not be mismanaged in the future. A change in control is in no sense analogous to an adjudication that the former directors have been guilty of misconduct. . . .

The questions involved in this case assume mounting importance as the capital stock of corporations becomes more widely distributed. To an enlarged extent the campaign methods consequently come more to resemble those of political campaigns, but, as in the latter, campaign expenses should be borne by those who are waging the campaign and their followers, instead of being met out of the corporate or the public treasury. Especially is this true when campaign promises have been made that the expenses would not be charged to the corporation.

Nothing which is said in this opinion is intended as any reflection upon the motives of the insurgent group in instigating this corporate contest, nor upon the management group. Questions of law are involved which extend beyond the persons and the corporation presently before the court. It is the established law of this State that expenditures may be incurred by management limited to informing the stockholders fully and fairly concerning the affairs and policies of the corporation, which may well include an explanation of the reasons on account of which its policies have been undertaken, nor is there any reason on account of which stockholders who have neglected to sign proxies through apathy may not be solicited so as to insure a quorum, which would ordinarily occur in instances where there is no contest, but beyond measures of this character, the purely campaign expenses of a management group do not serve a corporate purpose, and paying them is ultra vires. The same is true of all of the expenses of insurgent stockholders.

## NOTE

Should the incumbent management be permitted to pay their expenses with corporate funds? Should the existing rules be changed to reimburse dissident shareholders for their expenses if they obtain a reasonable percentage of votes at the annual meeting? Assume that such a law might require the dissidents to obtain at least 30% of the votes cast. Will corporations be better run if the election of directors is similar to political elections? Who should have the burden of proof as to whether the expenses were reasonable? Are expenses for entertainment and chartered airplanes reasonable? When the insurgents won, why were they so generous in reimbursing the old management?

## CHAMBERS v. BRIGGS & STRATTON CORP.
United States District Court, Eastern District of Wisconsin
863 F. Supp. 900 (1994)

GORDON, J.

The plaintiff, Joseph G. Chambers, a shareholder of 17 shares of stock in the defendant corporation, Briggs & Stratton Corporation, commenced this action for declaratory and injunctive relief on September 14, 1994. Along with his complaint, Mr. Chambers filed a "Motion for Temporary Restraining Order/Preliminary Injunction." At an oral hearing held on September 27, 1994, counsel for both sides addressed the plaintiff's motion which was treated by consent of the parties as one for a preliminary injunction.

Counsel for the parties have been informed by telephone on the morning of Friday, September 30, 1994, that the plaintiff's motion was granted in part and denied in part. The reasons for that determination are explained herein.

The defendant's annual meeting is scheduled to be held on October 19, 1994. On September 8, 1994, the defendant sent to shareholders a "Notice of Annual Meeting of Shareholders," a "Proxy Statement" and a form of proxy. One of the items of business identified in the notice and proxy statement is the election of directors. Three of the nine seats on the defendant's board of directors are now up for election.

The proxy statement identifies the three candidates put forth as nominees by the current directors, but it omits the name of William P. Dixon, who the plaintiff claims he nominated pursuant to Article II, Section 2.01 of the defendant's by-laws. Mr. Dixon is described by the plaintiff as a lawyer who has formerly served as commissioner of banking of Wisconsin, chief of staff to United States Senator Gary Hart, and United States alternative executive director to the World Bank.

Under Article II, Section 2.01 of the defendant's bylaws a shareholder must comply with the following requirements in order properly to nominate a candidate to the board of directors: (1) provide written notice to the secretary no later than 90 days before the anniversary date of the annual meeting of shareholders in the immediately preceding year; (2) represent in the notice that the nominator is a shareholder of record and will remain so throughout the date of the meeting; (3) state the nominator's name and address and the class and number of shares held by that person; (4) represent that the nominator intends to appear in person or by proxy at the meeting to make such nomination; (5) identify the name and address of the nominee and disclose the nature of any agreements or understandings, if any, between the nominator and the nominee; (6) provide the written consent of the nominee to serve as a director if so elected. It is undisputed that Mr. Chambers has complied with all six of these requirements.

Notwithstanding the fact that Mr. Dixon had been properly nominated in accordance with Article II, Section 2.01, his name was not included in the proxy statement or the form of proxy that was mailed to the shareholders by the defendant on September 8, 1994. Mr. Chambers alleges that this omission renders the proxy materials materially false and misleading under the regulations of the Securities and Exchange Commission ["SEC"], namely, 17 C.F.R. § 240.14a-9. As a result of such material omission, the plaintiff contends that the defendant may acquire a sufficient number of proxies such that Mr. Dixon will not gain election to the board of directors.

Subsequent to the filing of this lawsuit, the Wisconsin Coalition for Responsible Investment ["WCRI"], an entity financially backed by the United Paperworkers International Union Local 7232 ["Union"], disseminated proxy materials to some of the defendant's shareholders in support of Mr. Dixon's candidacy. Mr. Chambers is the treasurer of the Union. Mr. Chambers' counsel, Richard G. McCracken, also represents the WCRI.

In his motion for a preliminary injunction, the plaintiff seeks the following relief: (1) an order requiring the defendant to issue a supplemental proxy statement which cures the material omission contained therein to each shareholder who received the misleading information; (2) an order requiring the defendant to issue a new proxy card which includes Mr. Dixon's name as a nominee; and (3) an order invalidating any proxy or voting instruction card cast by any shareholder relating to the election of directors which were distributed to shareholders with the unlawful proxy material.

\*    \*    \*

In order to obtain a preliminary injunction, the plaintiff has the burden to show "some likelihood of success" on its claim. See Roland Machinery Co. v. Dresser Industries, Inc., 749 F.2d 380, 387 (7th Cir. 1984). The plaintiff claims that the defendant's proxy materials violate Section 14(a) of the Securities Exchange Act, 15 U.S.C. § 78n(a), and the regulations promulgated thereunder in that they contain a material omission — namely, the materials do not disclose that Mr. Dixon is a candidate for director.

\*    \*    \*

The inclusion of any false or misleading statements in connection with a solicitation is proscribed by SEC Rule 14a-9(a), 17 C.F.R. § 240.14a-9 which states:

> No solicitation subject to this regulation shall be made by means of any proxy statement, form of proxy, notice of meeting . . . containing any statement which, at the time and in the light of circumstances under which it is made, is false or misleading with respect to any material fact, or which omits to state any material fact necessary in order to make the statements therein not false or misleading . . . .

Thus, in order to succeed on the merits of his claim, the plaintiff must establish that Mr. Dixon's candidacy for director was a material fact such that its omission in the proxy materials violated Rule 14a-9(a).

The United States Supreme Court has held that "an omitted fact is material if there is a substantial likelihood that a reasonable shareholder would consider it important in deciding how to vote." This standard

> does not require proof of a substantial likelihood that disclosure of the omitted fact would have caused the reasonable investor to change his vote. What the standard does contemplate is a showing of a substantial likelihood that, under all of the circumstances, the omitted fact would have assumed actual significance in the deliberations of the reasonable shareholder. Put another way, there must be a substantial likelihood that disclosure of the omitted fact would have been viewed by the reasonable investor as having significantly altered the "total mix" of information made available.

*TSC Industries, Inc. v. Northway, Inc.*, 426 U.S. 438, 449 (1976). The plaintiff argues that the above standard is met by the omission of Mr. Dixon's name in the defendant's proxy statement and form of proxy as a candidate for director because the omission makes the shareholders think that they have only three choices (the three candidates nominated by the board) for the three open seats on the board of directors.

In response, the defendant argues that Mr. Chambers has no likelihood of succeeding on the merits because the relief he seeks is contrary to the regulatory scheme embodied in the SEC's rules which place upon Mr. Chambers — not the company — the responsibility of disseminating information concerning opposition candidates. Specifically, the defendant contends that the following regulations support his position: (1) 17 C.F.R. § 240.14a-101; (2) 17 C.F.R. § 229.401(a)(5); and (3) 17 C.F.R. § 240.14a-8(c)(8).

17 C.F.R. § 240.14a-101 identifies the information to be included in a proxy statement. Note B of this section explains that

> [w]here any item calls for information with respect to any matter to be acted upon at the meeting, such item need be answered in the registrant's soliciting material only with respect to *proposals* to be made by or on behalf of the registrant. (Emphasis added.)

If action is to be taken with respect to the election of directors, Item 7(b) of 17 C.F.R. § 240.14a-101, obligates the party making a solicitation to furnish "information required by Items 401, . . . of Regulation S-K (§ 229.401, . . . ). Item 7 also provides that "If, . . . the solicitation is made on behalf of persons *other than the registrant*, the information required need be furnished only as to nominees of the persons making the solicitation." (Emphasis added.)

Under 17 C.F.R. § 229.401(a), a proxy statement is to "[l]ist the names and ages of all directors of the registrant and all persons nominated or chosen by management to become directors; . . . ." The accompanying Instruction 5 to § 229.401(a) specifies that:

> if the solicitation is made by persons *other than management*, information shall be given as to nominees of the persons making the solicitation. In all other instances, information shall be given as to directors and persons nominated for election or chosen by management. (Emphasis added.)

Contrary to the defendant's reading, I believe that these regulations place upon the defendant the obligation of disclosing in its proxy statement the existence of candidates who are not nominated by management. In instances involving the election of directors, persons other than management are obligated to disclose information only concerning their own nominees under Instruction 5 to § 229.401(a) and Item 7 of § 240.14a-101. However, this same limitation does not apply to solicitations by management. Rather, the express language of Instruction 5 to § 229.401(a) and Item 7 of § 240.14a-101 requires management to provide information as to (1) directors, (2) persons nominated for election; and (3) persons chosen by management. Had the SEC intended the same limitation to apply to solicitations by both management and persons other than management, it would not have distinguished between the two types of solicitations as it did in these regulations.

With respect to Note B of 17 C.F.R. § 240.14a-101, I find that rule to be inapplicable to the case at hand as that provision relates to proposals to be acted upon at the annual meeting and not specifically to the election of directors.

Accordingly, I reject the defendant's contention that the regulatory scheme developed by the SEC obligated Mr. Chambers — and not the company — to disclose Mr. Dixon's candidacy.

The defendant also maintains that the general principles of materiality under § 240.14a-9 establish that Mr. Chambers has no likelihood of succeeding on the merits of his claim. Both parties cite *Bertoglio v. Texas International Company*, 488 F. Supp. 630 (D. Del. 1980), in support for their respective positions on the issue of the materiality of Mr. Dixon's candidacy.

While the holding in *Bertoglio* is not binding on this court, I believe it is instructive. In *Bertoglio*, a Delaware district court determined that a verbal notification to management from the opposition in an ensuing proxy contest that proxy materials would be filed with the SEC opposing certain incumbent directors did not "trigger the obligation to disclose the existence of a proxy contest that had not yet materialized." *Bertoglio*, 488 F. Supp. at 654. The district court reasoned that "prior to its written formalization, and resting solely on the incomplete oral notification . . . opposition was not yet a 'fact' requiring disclosure." *Bertoglio*, 488 F. Supp. at 655 n.21. The district court recognized, however, that the "materiality of actual opposition to the election of directors cannot be questioned." *Bertoglio*, 488 F. Supp. at 655 n.21.

I agree with the district court's conclusion in *Bertoglio* that actual opposition to the election of directors is a material fact under 17 C.F.R. § 240.14a-9. This is so because there is a substantial likelihood that a reasonable shareholder would regard the existence of opposition to the board's nominees for director important in deciding how to vote.

Here, unlike the situation in *Bertoglio*, opposition to the board of directors' candidates was a fact made known to the defendant well in advance of its initial solicitation on September 8, 1994. Mr. Chambers notified the defendant, in writing, and in compliance with the nominating procedure established under Article II, Section 2.01 of the defendant's bylaws of his nomination of Mr. Dixon. I find that upon receipt of Mr. Chambers' written notification of nomination, the defendant was required to disclose the nomination in its proxy statement. This conclusion is consistent with my determination that the regulatory scheme enacted by the SEC obligates management to disclose in its proxy statement the names of persons nominated for election. I decline to accept the defendant's position that *Bertoglio* requires a full-blown proxy contest as a prerequisite to activation of a company's obligation to disclose opposition.

For these reasons, I conclude that Mr. Chambers has a likelihood of succeeding on the merits of his claim that the defendant's failure to disclose Mr. Dixon's candidacy was a material omission under 17 C.F.R. § 240.14a-9.

The plaintiff also contends that the defendant's failure to include Mr. Dixon's name in its form of proxy (as distinguished from the proxy statement) was a material omission. Mr. Chambers cites no authority to support this proposition nor has the court found any.

A form of proxy, when executed by a shareholder, provides to the party soliciting the proxy the authority to act for the shareholder. In the context of an election contest, the soliciting party is seeking authority to vote the shareholder's shares in a manner favorable to the soliciting party. In other words, the soliciting party wants the shareholder's authority to vote for its own candidate; the soliciting party does not seek the authority to vote for the opposition's candidate. If the shareholder does not wish to give his authority to vote to a particular soliciting party, or if he desires to vote for an opposition candidate, he can either inform the soliciting party that he intends to withhold his authority to vote or he can simply refuse to execute the proxy form. In this case, there is no allegation that the defendant's form of proxy did not allow a shareholder to withhold his authority to vote for any of the defendant's candidates.

I find that the absence of the name of an opposition candidate on a soliciting party's form of proxy cannot, without more, be said to alter significantly the "total mix" of information available to shareholders. Indeed, counsel for Mr. Chambers concedes as much, as evidenced by the fact that the form of proxy mailed to shareholders by his client, the WCRI, contains only the name of WCRI's candidate — Mr. Dixon — and omits any reference to the defendant's three nominees.

Accordingly, Mr. Chambers has not met his burden of demonstrating that he has some likelihood of succeeding on the merits of his claim that the omission of Mr. Dixon's name from the form of proxy was a material omission in violation of 17 C.F.R. § 240.14a-9.

Since the defendant's proxy statement contained a material omission, the shareholder vote will go forward on the basis of potentially misleading information unless the court grants the plaintiff's request for injunctive relief. The Supreme Court has recognized that "use of solicitation which is materially misleading poses the kind of irreparable injury to stockholders which can justify injunctive relief prior to a shareholder's meeting."

That the court could later undo the damage caused by an illegal proxy — by voiding the results of the election — is not an adequate alternative where, as here, the court can prevent in advance a shareholder vote to be taken on potentially misleading and incomplete information. Moreover, while a separate solicitation on Mr. Dixon's behalf could inform the shareholders of the existence of opposition to the defendant's nominees, that option does not excuse the defendant's failure to disclose this material fact.

The court is persuaded that the plaintiff has established that he would suffer irreparable harm if the injunction is not issued and that it has no adequate remedy at law.

In balancing the harms, the court is to consider the threatened harm to the shareholders who are intended to be protected by § 14(a) of the Securities Exchange Act, 15 U.S.C. § 78n(a). *See Klaus v. Hi-Shear Corporation*, 528 F.2d 225, 232 (9th Cir. 1975). A court order granting a preliminary injunction will prevent a shareholder vote to be taken pursuant to potentially misleading and incomplete information, and the right of informed corporate suffrage will be protected by the order rather than denied.

The defendant maintains that the balance of harms does not favor Mr. Chambers. According to the defendant, the fact that Mr. Chambers waited until after the defendant had expended $100,000 in mailing out its proxy materials on September 8, 1994, to file the present action despite the fact that he knew no later than August 25, 1994, that the defendant was not including Mr. Dixon's name in its proxy statement demonstrates Mr. Chambers'"unclean hands." Hence, the defendant maintains that Mr. Chambers is not entitled to equitable relief.

While Mr. Chambers does not offer an explanation for his delay, I do not believe that the delay, standing alone, negates his entitlement to equitable relief. The delay was not a lengthy one. Further, there is no evidence that the delay was based on Mr. Chambers' bad faith or was occasioned merely for the purpose of increasing the defendant's costs.

The defendant's contention that it will incur unnecessary additional costs if the injunction is issued is without merit in view of its admission that it is independently obligated to disseminate supplemental information in accordance with 17 C.F.R. § 240.14a-101 Items 4(b) and 5(b) and 17 C.F.R. § 240.14a-11 due to the recent distribution of proxy materials by WCRI. The defendant could include a supplemental statement curing its material omission along with the supplemental materials it is independently obligated to circulate under 17 C.F.R. § 240.14a-101 Items 4(b) and 5(b) and 17 C.F.R. § 240.14a-11 and thereby avoid additional costs.

The defendant also suggests that the issuance of an injunction would cause it to suffer great harm if the shareholders learn of the injunction as that information may influence the decision making process of individual shareholders. The described harm is too speculative to be accorded any weight. The balance of harms favors the plaintiff.

Given the overriding public interest in the full and accurate disclosure of information to shareholders of public corporations to ensure that a shareholder's vote is based upon accurate and complete information, I believe that this factor weighs in favor of granting a preliminary injunction. Allowing a shareholder vote based on incomplete and inaccurate information undermines the purpose underlying SEC Rule 14a-9.

The plaintiff has demonstrated all of the prerequisites for preliminary injunctive relief in connection with the defendant's failure to identify Mr. Dixon as a candidate in its proxy statement. I have determined that this constituted a material omission under 17 C.F.R. § 240.14a-9. I conclude that the plaintiff's request for a preliminary injunction must be granted in part. I have considered the several forms of relief sought by the plaintiff in this action and have determined that the equitable course is to require the defendant to cure the material omission in its proxy statement. In addition, the defendant will be directed not to vote any proxy it solicited prior to October 1, 1994, at the annual meeting of its shareholders.

Consistent with the identification of its own nominees in the initial proxy statement, Briggs & Stratton Corporation's revised proxy statement should name Mr. Dixon and include the following information: (1) Mr. Dixon's age (50); (2) that he is presently a partner in the law firm of Davis, Miner, Barnhill & Galland, P.D. in Madison, Wisconsin; (3) that he served as the commissioner of banking of Wisconsin from 1983 to 1985; (4) that he served as chief of staff to United States Senator Gary Hart in 1987; and (5) that he served as the alternative executive director to the World Bank from 1977 to 1979.

I decline Mr. Chambers' invitation to require Briggs & Stratton Corporation to disseminate a new proxy form that identifies Mr. Dixon as a candidate. Mr. Chambers is entitled to have Briggs & Stratton Corporation correct its proxy statement, but the corporation does not have to provide its shareholders with the form which solicits an actual proxy for Mr. Chambers' nominee. In other words, after (or simultaneously with) the transmission of a corrected proxy statement, the defendant is free to submit to its shareholders a proxy form which invites shareholders to select the nominees favored by Briggs & Stratton Corporation. If Mr. Chambers chooses to seek proxies from shareholders, he has to do so at his own expense.

# NOTE

The federal proxy rules permit the use of a Soviet style ballot. The only names on the ballot are those nominated by management. Of course, as the case indicates, the proxy statement must disclose Mr. Dixon's candidacy. Is this of much value, if he has to pay his own costs of mailing a form of proxy to all the shareholders?

# MONY GROUP, INC. v. HIGHFIELDS CAPITAL MANAGEMENT, L.P.

United States Court of Appeals, Second Circuit
368 F.3d 138 (2004)

Jacobs, J.

This expedited appeal pursuant to 28 U.S.C. § 1292(a)(1) arises against the backdrop of a proxy vote among shareholders of Plaintiff-Appellant MONY Group, Inc. ("MONY"), whose management seeks shareholder approval of a proposed merger of MONY with French insurance conglomerate AXA Financial, Inc. ("AXA"). Defendants-Appellees are institutional shareholders of MONY that oppose the merger and seek to distribute an exempt proxy solicitation to MONY shareholders under Rule 14a-2(b)(1) ("Rule 14a-2(b)(1)"), 17 C.F.R. § 240.14a-2(b)(1). This solicitation consisted of (i) a letter urging MONY shareholders to withhold their approval of the proposed merger, and (ii) a duplicate copy of the proxy card that had been sent to shareholders by MONY management after MONY had filed a proxy statement to the Securities and Exchange Commission ("SEC") under Rule 14a-3(a) ("Rule 14a-3(a)"), 17 C.F.R. § 240.14a-3(a).

> Rule 14a–2(b)(1) exempts from SEC proxy regulations "[a]ny solicitation by . . . any person who does not . . . seek . . . the power to act as proxy . . . and does not furnish . . . a form of revocation" to a company's shareholders as part of the solicitation. MONY argues that the duplicate proxy card is a "form of revocation" within the meaning of Rule 14a-2(b)(1), and sought a preliminary injunction in the United States District Court for the Southern District of New York (Holwell, J.) barring Appellees from including the duplicate card with their solicitations. On February 11, 2004, the district court denied MONY's request, concluding that it was unlikely to succeed on the merits of its claim against Appellees under Section 14(a) of the Exchange Act of 1934 ("Section 14(a)").

We conclude that, in the circumstances of this case — a proxy vote to authorize a proposed merger under Delaware law — a duplicate of management's proxy card, when included in a mailing opposing a proposed merger, is a "form of revocation" under Rule 14a-2(b)(1). We also conclude that MONY will suffer irreparable harm if Appellees enclose the duplicate card in their solicitations to MONY shareholders without first satisfying the disclosure regulations promulgated under Section 14(a).

## Background

MONY is a New York-based life insurance and financial services company incorporated in Delaware and registered under the Exchange Act. Defendants-Appellees Highfields Capital Management ("Highfields"), Longleaf Partners Small-Cap Fund ("Longleaf"), and Southeastern Asset Management ("Southeastern") collectively own approximately eight percent of MONY stock. On September 17, 2003, MONY (through its management) agreed to be acquired by AXA, a French life insurance and financial services conglomerate, in an all-cash merger valued at approximately $1.5 billion. Under the merger terms, MONY shareholders were to receive $31 per share of MONY common stock and a dividend to be paid by AXA based on MONY's earnings in the second half of 2003. After a full review by the SEC, MONY issued its definitive proxy statement on January 8, 2004 and scheduled a shareholder vote for February 24, 2004. Under Delaware law, a merger agreement is binding only if a majority of all issued and outstanding company shares approve it. *See* 8 Del. C. § 251(c).

Reaction to the merger announcement was mixed; many shareholders argued that AXA's offer (representing 75 percent of MONY's book value) substantially undervalued the company and that the $90 million severance payments for MONY's management were excessive and suggestive of a conflict-of-interest. The MONY/AXA merger announcement also spawned numerous lawsuits;[29] this appeal arises from MONY's action challenging Appellees' proxy solicitations.

In late January 2004, Appellees began considering a proxy solicitation to MONY shareholders that would be exempt under Rule 14a-2(b)(1) from the proxy regulations promulgated by the SEC. On January 22, 2004, Southeastern announced its intention to vote its MONY shares against the AXA merger, urged other MONY shareholders to do likewise, and indicated that Southeastern would further communicate its views "by means of an exempt solicitation under the federal proxy rules." By January 27, 2004, Highfields had begun exploring a similar shareholder communication and sought advice from SEC staff on any constraints imposed by the Exchange Act, particularly on whether an exempt solicitation under Rule 14a-2(b)(1) could "include a copy of MONY's proxy card in its mailing for the convenience of MONY shareholders to facilitate . . . voting [against the merger]."

Highfields was advised by SEC staff that "although it [had] not been released formally, the Office of Mergers and Acquisitions at the SEC had considered and adopted a 'nonpublished position'" in an informal April 1993 interpretation (circulated internally among SEC staff) that gave qualified approval to shareholders seeking to mail duplicates of management proxy cards as part of an exempt proxy solicitation under Rule 14a-2(b)(1). On the basis of these discussions with SEC staff, Highfields planned an exempt proxy solicitation to MONY shareholders that included duplicates of MONY's proxy card and conformed to the restrictions described in the April 1993 opinion.[30]

---

[29] [2] Several shareholder lawsuits against MONY, AXA, and MONY's board in Delaware Chancery Court were consolidated into one class action on November 4, 2003. On January 16, 2004, the class-action plaintiffs were granted leave to file a consolidated amended complaint. MONY, AXA, and MONY's board were also named in two class-action lawsuits (alleging similar claims) brought in New York State Supreme Court in Manhattan. Appellees have so far not joined these actions but have issued a number of public statements in various media denouncing the terms of the merger and urging its rejection by MONY shareholders.

[30] [3] In its informal discussions with Highfields, SEC staff said that Appellees could send out a duplicate copy of MONY's proxy card with its solicitation so long as: (1) the sender's solicitation materials stated that the sender opposed the merger, and was asking the shareholder to oppose it; (2) the sender's solicitation materials stated that the proxy card was being furnished by the sender, not by MONY; (3) the sender's solicitation materials stated that the proxy card was being furnished by the sender for the convenience of the shareholder; (4) the sender provided the copy of the proxy card without seeking proxy authority from the shareholder; and (5) the proxy card was returned directly to MONY, not to the sender. A sixth apparent requirement was that the sender never have "possession or control of or access to the proxy card."

MONY commenced an action on February 3, 2004 in the United States District Court for the Southern District (Preska, J.) seeking a temporary restraining order and a preliminary injunction blocking Appellees from sending the duplicate proxy cards without first filing a proxy statement under Rule 14a-3(a). After a hearing on February 3, 2004, Judge Preska granted MONY's request for a restraining order, stating that "[t]he exemption set out in Rule 14a-2(b)(1)] does not apply here because [Appellees'] solicitation 'furnishes or otherwise requests a form of revocation.' " Judge Preska also noted that a few votes changed by reason of the possibly invalid proxy solicitation would cause irreparable harm to MONY "[b]ecause of the requirement that 51% of [MONY] shareholders vote in favor of the proposal . . . ."

Judge Preska ordered Appellees to show cause on February 6, 2004 as to why a preliminary injunction should not issue prohibiting Appellees from sending the duplicate cards. In the interim, Highfields and Longleaf sent solicitation letters to MONY shareholders (without the duplicate proxy cards) that detailed how shareholders could vote, change, or revoke their proxies.

The case was assigned to Judge Holwell, who extended the restraining order "for the reasons set forth in Judge Preska's initial order" until he had considered the arguments of all of the parties. Judge Holwell also invited the SEC to submit an *amicus* letter brief setting forth its position on

> whether a party is entitled to the [Rule 14a-2(b)(1)] exemption if
>
> > (1) the party sends shareholders a proxy solicitation that includes a proxy voting card which is an exact duplicate of a card previously sent to shareholders as part of a proxy solicitation by a non-exempt party who complied with the SEC's disclosure rules;
> >
> > (2) the party solicits the shareholders to use the duplicate proxy card to vote against the proposal recommended by the company's Board of Directors and thereby to revoke any proxy previously given;
> >
> > (3) this duplicate card is sent with instructions that, once marked, it be returned to the party (or agent thereof) who sent the original proxy card; and
> >
> > (4) the duplicate card does not provide for any exercise of authority by the party who sent it, nor does it ever come back into the possession or under the control of the party who sent it.

By fax on February 10, 2004, Alan L. Beller, Director of the SEC's Division of Corporation Finance, and Giovanni P. Prezioso, General Counsel of the SEC, declined to take a formal position on behalf of the Commission: "In light of [the] short time frame, we have not had an opportunity to seek the view of the Commission with respect to the specific question raised by your letter." The letter-brief instead provided "background to Rule 14a-2(b)(1) and positions that the [SEC had] taken historically," noting that, in an informal April 1993 internal opinion, the SEC had considered whether

> a person otherwise qualified to rely on [the exemptions of Rule 14a-2(b)(1) could] provide a solicited shareholder with a copy of management's proxy

card for the purposes of facilitating the shareholder's revocation of a previous card or a vote in favor of a proposal supported by the soliciting party

The SEC's letter summarized this internal April 1993 opinion[31] as follows:

- the provision of Rule 14a-2(b)(1) would not be violated since providing a copy of management's proxy card — which would be returned directly to management — does not create any proxy authority in the soliciting party; and

- although management's proxy card could have the *effect* of a revocation of an earlier dated proxy submitted by the same shareholder, this should not constitute a "*form* of revocation" envisioned by Rule 14a-2(b)(1).

(emphases added).

In an Opinion and Order entered February 11, 2004, Judge Holwell denied MONY's motion for a preliminary injunction on the ground that MONY was unlikely to succeed on the merits of its claim because, as a matter of law, a duplicate of the issuer's proxy card was not a "form of revocation" under Rule 14a-2(b)(1). The district court invoked policy considerations and cited the SEC's informal April 1993 opinion (as summarized in the SEC's letter brief).

As to irreparable harm, the court ruled that, although many of MONY's assertions were "for the most part too speculative and causally tenuous to support a preliminary injunction . . . . there is support for plaintiff's showing that a misinformed shareholder vote may result in irreparable harm." However, in light of its ruling that MONY was unlikely to succeed on the merits of its claim, the court dissolved the restraining order and denied MONY's motion for a preliminary injunction. In the alternative, the district court ruled that MONY had failed to show "serious questions going to the merits of its claim" and "a balance of hardships tipping decidedly in its favor."

On February 22, 2004, MONY's Board voted (i) to sweeten the terms of the merger agreement by issuing a special dividend of a dime a share to MONY shareholders of record at the closing of the merger, and (ii) to postpone the shareholder vote to May 18, 2004 (with a record date of April 8, 2004). MONY appealed the district court's denial of the preliminary injunction, claiming in its brief to this Court that it "has every reason to believe that, once the date nears and MONY has mailed its proxy voting card, [Appellees] will again seek to engage in solicitations of the type which led to the filing of this action." Nothing in Appellees' briefs to this Court disavows that intention; and at oral argument, Appellees made clear that, unless enjoined, they will (after the April 8, 2004 record date) distribute proxy solicitations that include the duplicate proxy cards.

The appeal of the district court's denial of a preliminary injunction was heard by this Court on April 1, 2004. The parties agree on appeal that (i) the mailings are "solicitations" and (ii) the solicitations do not seek proxy authority from MONY

---

[31] [4] A second informal opinion from 2001 considered whether a duplicate proxy card where the vote had been pre-marked was a "form of revocation," and is therefore factually distinguishable from this case.

shareholders. The viability of the Rule 14a-2(b)(1) exemption therefore turns on one issue — whether the proxy card duplicate was a "form of revocation."[32] *See* 17 C.F.R. § 240.14a-2(b)(1). After deliberations, we reversed from the bench and issued an order later that day directing the district court to grant MONY's motion for a preliminary injunction, and reciting that an opinion would follow.

## Discussion

To secure a preliminary injunction in district court, the moving party must demonstrate "(1) that it will be irreparably harmed in the absence of an injunction, and (2) either (a) a likelihood of success on the merits or (b) sufficiently serious questions going to the merits of the case to make it a fair ground for litigation, and a balance of hardships tipping decidedly in its favor." *Forest City Daly Hous., Inc. v. Town of North Hempstead*, 175 F.3d 144, 149 (2d Cir. 1999). We evaluate MONY's request for a preliminary injunction under the "likelihood of success on the merits" prong because MONY does not appeal the district court's alternative holding that it failed to meet the more lenient standard of showing "sufficiently serious questions going to the merits of the case" and "a balance of hardships tipping decidedly in its favor."

It is settled that "a district court's decision to grant or deny a preliminary injunction is not generally reviewed de novo [but rather] for abuse of discretion." *Zervos v. Verizon N.Y., Inc.*, 252 F.3d 163, 171 (2d Cir. 2001). At the same time,

> [a] district court 'abuses' or 'exceeds' the discretion accorded to it when (1) *its decision rests on an error of law (such as application of the wrong legal principle)* or a clearly erroneous factual finding, or (2) its decision — though not necessarily the product of a legal error or a clearly erroneous factual finding — cannot be located within the range of permissible decisions. *Id.* at 169 (emphasis added).

Rule 14a-2(b)(1) is part of a comprehensive proxy regulation scheme promulgated by the SEC pursuant to Section 14(a) of the Exchange Act. See 15 U.S.C. § 78n(a); 17 C.F.R. § 240.14a-1, et seq.; see also 17 C.F.R. § 240.13d-1, et seq. Rule 14a-3(a) states (in relevant part) that

> [n]o solicitation subject to this regulation shall be made unless each person solicited is . . . furnished . . . with a publicly-filed . . . written proxy statement containing the information specified in Schedule 14A . . . or with a preliminary or definitive written proxy statement included in a registration statement filed under the Securities Act of 1933 on Form S-4 or F-4 . . . or Form N-14 . . . and containing the information specified in such Form.

---

[32] [5] On March 22, 2004, this Court invited SEC staff to submit to the Court its views on the issue of whether a proxy card duplicate constitutes a "form of revocation" under Rule 14a-2(b)(1). On March 25, 2004, SEC staff indicated in a faxed letter to this Court that it "does not wish to express any additional views beyond those set forth" in its February 10, 2004 letter-brief to the district court. Staff also informed this Court that "it has not been possible to seek the view of the Commission with respect to the interpretation of Rule 14a-2(b)(1) . . . "

17 C.F.R. § 240.14a-3(a). Appellees elected not to file proxy statements under Rule 14a-3(a).

In 1992, the SEC modified its proxy regulations to encourage "free discussion, debate and learning among shareholders." Regulation of Communications Among Shareholders, Exchange Act Release No. 31,326, 1992 SEC LEXIS 2470, at (October 22, 1992) (the "1992 Amendments.") As modified by the 1992 Amendments, Rule 14a-2(b)(1) exempted from SEC proxy regulations

> *any solicitation* by or on behalf of *any person who does not*, at any time during such solicitation, seek directly or indirectly, either on its own or another's behalf, the power to act as proxy for a security holder and does not furnish or otherwise request, or act on behalf of a person who furnishes or requests, a form of revocation, abstention, consent, or authorization . . .

17 C.F.R. § 240.14a-2(b)(1) (emphases added). Thus, any communication that meets the Rule 14a-2(b)(1) exemption need not comply with, inter alia, the proxy statement disclosure requirement of Rule 14a-3(a).[33] According to the SEC, this exemption sought to balance the policy goal of open shareholder communication with the "potential for abuse both by insurgents and by management" — especially in a proxy fight. 1992 Amendments at *27.

Until the events underlying this appeal, no federal court had addressed whether a proxy card duplicate is a "form of revocation" under Rule 14a-2(b)(1). We agree with Judge Holwell that "where a shareholder has previously submitted a proxy," transmission of a duplicate proxy card could legally have the "effect of a revocation," but that revocation "is not a necessary effect inherent in the card and does not transform management's proxy card into a form of revocation that places [Appellees] outside the ambit of the exemption." We further agree that, in some proxy voting situations, the submission of a subsequent proxy card may be something other or more than a "revocation" of a previous vote. For example, a shareholder might use a duplicate proxy card to "substitute" a new vote for one slate of director candidates in place of a prior vote for a slate.

We conclude, however, that the district court gave insufficient consideration to the particular circumstances of this case as affected by the mechanics of Delaware corporate law. Under Delaware law, any "merger or consolidation of domestic corporations" must meet a number of statutory requirements, including that, at a "special meeting for the purpose of acting on the [merger] agreement . . . a majority of the outstanding stock of the corporation entitled to vote thereon shall be voted for the adoption of the agreement." 8 Del. C. § 251(c). Thus, in the context of a proxy vote to approve a merger agreement under Delaware law, a majority of all outstanding shares must vote "yes" in order to approve the merger; an abstention (or any vote other than "yes") is tantamount to a "no" vote. *See* id. Moreover, "when two proxies are offered bearing the same name, then the proxy that appears . . . to have been last executed will be accepted and counted under the theory that the latter — that is, more recent — proxy constitutes a revocation of the former." *Standard Power & Light Corp. v. Investment Associates, Inc.*, 51 A.2d 572, 580 (Del.

---

[33] [6] Rule 14a-2(b)(1) excludes several categories of persons and restricts its use in certain situations; none of those exclusions or restrictions apply to this appeal.

1947). The duplicate proxy cards would thus operate as a "revocation" only when returned by MONY shareholders who previously voted in support of the merger with AXA.

Appellees vigorously argue on appeal that duplicates of MONY's proxy card may be used by persons other than the MONY shareholders who have already voted and seek to revoke their votes. Most obviously, such duplicates are handy for shareholders who have lost or discarded their original proxy cards. Here, however, Appellees' own solicitations reflect that they intend the duplicate proxy card to be a "form of revocation" for MONY shareholders who have already voted. For example, the text of Highfields' first proposed proxy solicitation (in part) sought to inform MONY shareholders that "[w]hen properly signed and returned this proxy card shall revoke any proxy previously given in connection with the special meeting."

Revocation is the only likely use for such a duplicate proxy because: (i) undecided MONY shareholders presumably retain blank copies of their (original) management proxy cards, and (ii) other than the (presumably few) MONY shareholders who have lost or discarded the multiple proxy cards that have been sent to them by MONY and who cannot otherwise obtain new copies, the only MONY shareholders who truly "need" proxy card duplicates are those who have already sent their proxy cards and want to revoke their votes. There is no indication that the term "revocation" in Rule 14a-2(b)(1) has an unconventional legal meaning. *See Standard Power & Light*, 51 A.2d at 580 (a later proxy "constitutes a revocation" of an earlier one); Letter from Alan L. Beller, Dir., SEC Div. of Corp. Fin., and Giovanni P. Prezioso, SEC Gen. Counsel, 3 (Feb. 10, 2004) (conceding that a duplicate proxy card has "the effect of a revocation"). Absent such a special meaning of the term "revocation," the factual and legal circumstances of this case clearly suggest that Appellees' proxy duplicate would operate as a "form of revocation" when distributed in the context of a vote on a merger governed by Delaware law, and that it is intended as such by Appellees.

## II

The 1992 Amendments emphasized that Rule 14a-2(b)(1) must be administered with an eye to the encouragement of a variety of policy goals. Highfields argues that paramount among these goals is preventing proxy voting from being a "one-sided discussion of the merits." 1992 Amendments at *23. Longleaf claims that another important goal of the Amendments is to encourage the "effective use of shareholder voting rights." 1992 Amendments at *8. According to Longleaf, reversal of the district court's ruling would contradict the goals of the 1992 Amendments because it would "make it more difficult and impractical for [such] shareholders to exercise their voting rights." Appellees also argue that subsequent informal opinions by SEC staff support the district court's view that allowing Appellees to distribute duplicate proxy cards would be "consistent with the policies underlying the adoption of the rule in 1992." In short, Appellees contend that the only way that dissident solicitors can communicate "effectively" with undecided shareholders is by sending a proxy solicitation that includes a duplicate proxy card.[34]

The SEC recognized that, if the 1992 Amendments (including Rule 14a-2(b)(1)) were construed too broadly, they could create the "potential for abuse both by insurgents and by management." 1992 Amendments at *27. The plain text of Rule 14a-2(b)(1) shows that the easy revocation of proxies was one such potential abuse. Moreover, in this case, participatory shareholder democracy is well-protected by Delaware law, which requires a majority of all MONY shareholders to approve the AXA merger for it to be binding. MONY management has every incentive to ensure that all company shareholders vote (and has sent multiple proxy cards to achieve that goal) — every proxy card that MONY shareholders lost, discarded, or simply did not bother to exercise is effectively a vote "against" the merger opposed by Appellees. Assuming Appellees are shrewd proxy tacticians, their only goal in sending out the duplicate proxy cards must be to encourage shareholders who have already voted for the merger to revoke their votes. The plain text of Rule 14a-2(b)(1) forbids the inclusion of such a "form of revocation" in an otherwise exempt solicitation.

We acknowledge that our conclusion on this issue could be viewed as contrary to the informal SEC opinion issued in April 1993. This Court has said that it

> must defer to the SEC's interpretations of its own regulations in its amicus briefs unless they are plainly erroneous or inconsistent with the regulations [and that informal opinions such as] SEC no-action letters constitute neither agency rule-making nor adjudication and thus are entitled to no deference beyond whatever persuasive value they might have.

*Gryl ex rel. Shire Pharms. Group PLC v. Shire Pharms. Group PLC*, 298 F.3d 136, 145 (2d Cir. 2002) (citations omitted). Here, the SEC's letter briefs to the district court (and this Court) expressly declined to offer formal support to its informal, unpublished April 1993 opinion. We therefore decline, for the reasons already stated in the context of this Delaware merger, to defer to the view expressed in the April 1993 opinion of the SEC.

As we first announced on April 1, 2004, we hold that MONY has demonstrated a likelihood that it will succeed on its claim that Appellees' use of duplicate proxy cards was outside the Rule 14a-2(b)(1) exemption and that, absent full compliance with SEC proxy regulations by Appellees, MONY will likely succeed in its claim against Appellees under Section 14(a).

## III

In its Opinion and Order addressing whether MONY had shown it would suffer irreparable harm without a preliminary injunction, the district court conceded "there is support for [MONY's] showing that a misinformed shareholder vote may result in irreparable harm." The district court concluded, however, that "even this showing of irreparable injury is unavailing in light of [MONY's] failure to show a

---

[34] [7] However, MONY concedes that, by itself, a letter giving shareholders detailed instructions on how to vote or how to revoke a vote is exempt under Rule 14a-2(b)(1). Brief for MONY at 30.

likelihood of success on the merits, and provides insufficient support for a preliminary injunction."

Rule 14a-3(a) requires that "[n]o solicitation subject to this regulation shall be made unless each person solicited is . . . furnished . . . with a publicly-filed . . . written proxy statement . . . " 17 C.F.R. § 240.14a-3(a). Both Highfields and Longleaf have elected not to file such proxy statements under Rule 14a-3(a).

It is well-established that a transaction — particularly a change-of-control transaction — that is influenced by noncompliance with the disclosure provisions of the various federal securities laws can constitute irreparable harm.[35] We decline to hold that a transaction influenced by noncompliance with the securities laws always results in irreparable harm because there are a number of circumstances that arguably could defeat such a broad rule, including those involving acts of bad faith, securities law infractions on both sides of a transaction, a situation where an injunction would suppress the only voice opposing a transaction, or other circumstances that we need not try to anticipate today.

In this case, we conclude that allowing Highfields and Longleaf to distribute duplicate proxy cards to MONY shareholders during a closely contested shareholder vote without complying with Rule 14a-3(a) would cause MONY irreparable harm. In passing Section 14(a), Congress sought to avoid a very particular harm — the solicitation of shareholder proxies without adequate disclosure. The SEC rules promulgated under Section 14(a) are intended to level somewhat the playing field for proxy contestants and to force disclosures that promote informed shareholder voting. In terms of MONY's interest as a proxy contestant, defeat of this transaction could spell the loss of a business opportunity that (by its nature) can only exist at one point in time and cannot be recovered or repaired with money damages.[36] In terms of adequate disclosure, we observe that at least one of the

---

[35] [9] *See ICN Pharmaceuticals, Inc. v. Khan*, 2 F.3d 484, 489 (2d Cir. 1993) ("[A]n injunction will issue for a violation of § 13(d) only on a showing of irreparable harm to the interests which that section seeks to protect. Those interests are fully satisfied when the shareholders receive the information required to be filed.") (internal citations and quotation marks omitted); *MAI Basic Four, Inc. v. Prime Computer, Inc.*, 871 F.2d 212, 218 (1st Cir. 1989) (noting "the utility of injunctive relief to prevent violations of disclosure requirements . . . to the extent . . . shareholders may be deprived of material information required to be disclosed" in change-of-control transactions); *Polaroid Corp. v. Disney*, 862 F.2d 987, 1006 (3d Cir. 1988) ("The purpose of the Williams Act is to insure that public shareholders . . . will not be required to respond without adequate information . . . . The theory of the Act is that shareholders are unable to protect their interests fully in making these decisions if the tender offeror fails to provide all material information regarding the offer. Irreparable harm arises because of the difficulty of proving money damages in a suit based upon material misrepresentations by the tender offeror. While Congress has determined that accurate disclosure is important to shareholders, it would often be impossible for shareholders to prove that on the facts of their particular tender offer accurate disclosure would have affected their decision making in a particular way with concomitant quantifiable monetary loss. The inadequacy of a remedy at law and the importance that Congress has attached to accurate disclosure of material information establishes irreparable harm.") (internal citations and quotation marks omitted); *Marshall Field & Co. v. Icahn*, 537 F. Supp. 413, 416 (S.D.N.Y. 1982) (concluding that "irreparable harm" exists in a change-of-control transaction if shareholders are denied "important and legally required information as to [a group's] intentions which may affect their judgment as to whether the stock should be sold, bought, or held").

[36] [10] It may be true, of course, that the interests of MONY's management have been served as well (or better) through the injunction of the proxy solicitations containing duplicate proxy cards. If so, that

Appellees, Highfields, has a "short" derivative position in bonds issued by AXA that has only recently been partially disclosed and that may or may not be in sync with the interests of other MONY shareholders.[37]

From either perspective, the possible harm is one that Congress has proscribed and that may easily transpire in a vote that (both sides concede) is likely to be close. The use of duplicate proxy cards to influence this vote therefore is inappropriate and amounts to the sort of irreparable harm that the securities laws and regulations were intended to prevent.

\*     \*     \*

For the foregoing reasons, we reverse the judgment of the district court, and, consistent with our April 1, 2004 Order, direct the district court to issue a preliminary injunction consistent with this opinion.

---

is merely an irony that stems from the initial tactical decision of Highfields and Longleaf not to make disclosures under the proxy regulations.

[37] [11] In the cases mentioned in Note 9, the refusals to comply with the securities rules were intended to help advance disputed transactions. Here, the refusal to comply with the securities rules arguably was intended to help block a disputed transaction. In light of the clear congressional intent of Section 14(a), we see no practical distinction between the harms inherent in these two situations.

# Chapter 13

# FUNDAMENTAL CHANGES

## A. MERGERS

### OMNICARE, INC. v. NCS HEALTHCARE, INC.
Supreme Court of Delaware
818 A.2d 914 (2003)

Before VEASEY, CHIEF JUSTICE, WALSH, HOLLAND, BERGER AND STEELE, JUSTICES, constituting the court en banc.

HOLLAND, J. for the majority:

NCS Healthcare, Inc. ("NCS"), a Delaware corporation, was the object of competing acquisition bids, one by Genesis Health Ventures, Inc. ("Genesis"), a Pennsylvania corporation, and the other by Omnicare, Inc. ("Omnicare"), a Delaware corporation. The proceedings before this Court were expedited due to exigent circumstances, including the pendency of the stockholders' meeting to consider the NCS/Genesis merger agreement. The determinations of this Court were set forth in a summary manner following oral argument to provide clarity and certainty to the parties going forward. Those determinations are explicated in this opinion.

### Overview of Opinion

The board of directors of NCS, an insolvent publicly traded Delaware corporation, agreed to the terms of a merger with Genesis. Pursuant to that agreement, all of the NCS creditors would be paid in full and the corporation's stockholders would exchange their shares for the shares of Genesis, a publicly traded Pennsylvania corporation. Several months after approving the merger agreement, but before the stockholder vote was scheduled, the NCS board of directors withdrew its prior recommendation in favor of the Genesis merger.

In fact, the NCS board recommended that the stockholders reject the Genesis transaction after deciding that a competing proposal from Omnicare was a superior transaction. The competing Omnicare bid offered the NCS stockholders an amount of cash equal to more than twice the then current market value of the shares to be received in the Genesis merger. The transaction offered by Omnicare also treated the NCS corporation's other stakeholders on equal terms with the Genesis agreement.

The merger agreement between Genesis and NCS contained a provision authorized by Section 251(c) of Delaware's corporation law. It required that the Genesis agreement be placed before the corporation's stockholders for a vote, even if the NCS board of directors no longer recommended it. At the insistence of Genesis, the NCS board also agreed to omit any effective fiduciary clause from the merger agreement. In connection with the Genesis merger agreement, two stockholders of NCS, who held a majority of the voting power, agreed unconditionally to vote all of their shares in favor of the Genesis merger. Thus, the combined terms of the voting agreements and merger agreement guaranteed, ab initio, that the transaction proposed by Genesis would obtain NCS stockholder's approval.

The Court of Chancery ruled that the voting agreements, when coupled with the provision in the Genesis merger agreement requiring that it be presented to the stockholders for a vote . . . , constituted defensive measures within the meaning of *Unocal Corp. v. Mesa Petroleum Co.* After applying the *Unocal* standard of enhanced judicial scrutiny, the Court of Chancery held that those defensive measures were reasonable. We have concluded that, in the absence of an effective fiduciary out clause, those defensive measures are both preclusive and coercive. Therefore, we hold that those defensive measures are invalid and unenforceable.

### The Parties

The defendant, NCS, is a Delaware corporation headquartered in Beachwood, Ohio. NCS is a leading independent provider of pharmacy services to long-term care institutions including skilled nursing facilities, assisted living facilities and other institutional healthcare facilities. NCS common stock consists of Class A shares and Class B shares. The Class B shares are entitled to ten votes per share and the Class A shares are entitled to one vote per share. The shares are virtually identical in every other respect.

The defendant Jon H. Outcalt is Chairman of the NCS board of directors. Outcalt owns 202,063 shares of NCS Class A common stock and 3,476,086 shares of Class B common stock. The defendant Kevin B. Shaw is President, CEO and a director of NCS. At the time the merger agreement at issue in this dispute was executed with Genesis, Shaw owned 28,905 shares of NCS Class A common stock and 1,141,134 shares of Class B common stock.

The NCS board has two other members, defendants Boake A. Sells and Richard L. Osborne. Sells is a graduate of the Harvard Business School. He was Chairman and CEO at Revco Drugstores in Cleveland, Ohio from 1987 to 1992, when he was replaced by new owners. Sells currently sits on the boards of both public and private companies. Osborne is a full-time professor at the Weatherhead School of Management at Case Western Reserve University. He has been at the university for over thirty years. Osborne currently sits on at least seven corporate boards other than NCS.

The defendant Genesis is a Pennsylvania corporation with its principal place of business in Kennett Square, Pennsylvania. It is a leading provider of healthcare and support services to the elderly. The defendant Geneva Sub, Inc., a wholly owned subsidiary of Genesis, is a Delaware corporation formed by Genesis to acquire NCS.

The plaintiffs in the class action own an unspecified number of shares of NCS Class A common stock. They represent a class consisting of all holders of Class A common stock. As of July 28, 2002, NCS had 18,461,599 Class A shares and 5,255,210 Class B shares outstanding.

Omnicare is a Delaware corporation with its principal place of business in Covington, Kentucky. Omnicare is in the institutional pharmacy business, with annual sales in excess of $2.1 billion during its last fiscal year. Omnicare purchased 1000 shares of NCS Class A common stock on July 30, 2002.

\* \* \*

### Fiduciary Duty Decision

A class action to enjoin the merger was brought by certain stockholders of NCS in the Court of chancery in C.A. No. 19786. The Court of Chancery denied a preliminary injunction in a decision and order dated November 22, 2002, and revised November 25, 2002 (the "Fiduciary Duty Decision"). That decision is now before this Court upon interlocutory review in Appeal No. 649, 2002. The standing of these stockholders to seek injunctive relief based on alleged violations of fiduciary duties by the NCS directors in approving the proposed merger is apparently not challenged by the defendants. Accordingly, the fiduciary duty claims, including those claims Omnicare sought to assert are being asserted by the class action plaintiffs.

### FACTUAL BACKGROUND

The parties are in substantial agreement regarding the operative facts. They disagree, however, about the legal implications. This recitation of facts is taken primarily from the opinion by the Court of Chancery.

### NCS Seeks Restructuring Alternatives

Beginning in late 1999, changes in the timing and level of reimbursements by government and third-party providers adversely affected market conditions in the health care industry. As a result, NCS began to experience greater difficulty in collecting accounts receivables, which led to a precipitous decline in the market value of its stock. NCS common shares that traded above $20 in January 1999 were worth as little as $5 at the end of that year. By early 2001, NCS was in default on approximately $350 million in debt, including $206 million in senior bank debt and $102 million of its 5 ¾ % Convertible Subordinated Debentures (the "Notes"). After these defaults, NCS common stock traded in a range of $0.09 to $0.50 per share until days before the announcement of the transaction at issue in this case.

NCS began to explore strategic alternatives that might address the problems it was confronting. As part of this effort, in February 2000, NCS retained UBS Warburg, L.L.C. to identify potential acquirers and possible equity investors. UBS Warburg contacted over fifty different entities to solicit their interest in a variety of transactions with NCS. UBS Warburg had marginal success in its efforts. By

October 2000, NCS had only received one non-binding indication of interest valued at $190 million, substantially less than the face value of NCS's senior debt. This proposal was reduced by 20% after the offeror conducted its due diligence review.

### NCS Financial Deterioration

In December 2000, NCS terminated its relationship with UBS Warburg and retained Brown, Gibbons, Lang & Company as its exclusive financial advisor. During this period, NCS's financial condition continued to deteriorate. In April 2001, NCS received a formal notice of default and acceleration from the trustee for holders of the Notes. As NCS's financial condition worsened, the Noteholders formed a committee to represent their financial interests (the "Ad Hoc Committee"). At about that time, NCS began discussions with various investor groups regarding a restructuring in a "pre-packaged" bankruptcy. NCS did not receive any proposal that it believed provided adequate consideration for its stakeholders. At that time, full recovery for NCS's creditors was a remote prospect, and any recovery for NCS stockholders seemed impossible.

### Omnicare's Initial Negotiations

In the summer of 2001, NCS invited Omnicare, Inc. to begin discussions with Brown Gibbons regarding a possible transaction. On July 20, Joel Gemunder, Omnicare's President and CEO, sent Shaw a written proposal to acquire NCS in a bankruptcy sale under Section 363 of the Bankruptcy Code. This proposal was for $225 million subject to satisfactory completion of due diligence. NCS asked Omnicare to execute a confidentiality agreement so that more detailed discussions could take place.[1]

In August 2001, Omnicare increased its bid to $270 million, but still proposed to structure the deal as an asset sale in bankruptcy. Even at $270 million, Omnicare's proposal was substantially lower than the face value of NCS's outstanding debt. It would have provided only a small recovery for Omnicare's Noteholders and no recovery for its stockholders. In October 2001, NCS sent Glen Pollack of Brown Gibbons to meet with Omnicare's financial advisor, Merrill Lynch, to discuss Omnicare's interest in NCS. Omnicare responded that it was not interested in any transaction other than an asset sale in bankruptcy.

There was no further contact between Omnicare and NCS between November 2001 and January 2002. Instead, Omnicare began secret discussions with Judy K. Mencher, a representative of the Ad Hoc Committee. In these discussions, Omnicare continued to pursue a transaction structured as a sale of assets in bankruptcy. In February 2002, the Ad Hoc Committee notified the NCS board that Omnicare had proposed an asset sale in bankruptcy for $313,750,000.

---

[1] [3] Discovery had revealed that, at the same time, Omnicare was attempting to lure away NCS's customers through what it characterized as the "NCS Blitz." The "NCS Blitz" was an effort by Omnicare to target NCS's customers. Omnicare has engaged in an "NCS Blitz" a number of times, most recently while NCS and Omnicare were in discussions in July and August 2001.

## NCS Independent Board Committee

In January 2002, Genesis was contacted by members of the Ad Hoc Committee concerning a possible transaction with NCS. Genesis executed NCS's standard confidentiality agreement and began a due diligence review. Genesis had recently emerged from bankruptcy because, like NCS, it was suffering from dwindling government reimbursements.

Genesis previously lost a bidding war to Omnicare in a different transaction. This led to bitter feelings between the principals of both companies. More importantly, this bitter experience for Genesis led to its insistence on exclusivity agreements and lock-ups in any potential transaction with NCS.

## NCS Financial Improvement

NCS's operating performance was improving by early 2002. As NCS's performance improved, the NCS directors began to believe that it might be possible for NCS to enter into a transaction that would provide some recovery for NCS stockholders' equity. In March 2002, NCS decided to form an independent committee of board members who were neither NCS employees nor major NCS stockholders (the "Independent Committee"). The NCS board thought this was necessary because, due to NCS's precarious financial condition, it felt that fiduciary duties were owed to the enterprise as a whole rather than solely to NCS stockholders.

Sells and Osborne were selected as the members of the committee, and given authority to consider and negotiate possible transactions for NCS. The entire four member NCS board, however, retained authority to approve any transaction. The Independent Committee retained the same legal and financial counsel as the NCS board.

The Independent Committee met for the first time on May 14, 2002. At that meeting Pollack suggested that NCS seek a "stalking-horse merger partner" to obtain the highest possible value in any transaction. The Independent Committee agreed with the suggestion.

## Genesis Initial Proposal

Two days later, on May 16, 2002, Scott Berlin of Brown Gibbons, Glen Pollack and Boake Sells met with George Hager, CFO of Genesis, and Michael Walker, who was Genesis's CEO. At that meeting, Genesis made it clear that if it were going to engage in any negotiations with NCS, it would not do so as a "stalking horse." As one of its advisors testified, "We didn't want to be someone who set forth a valuation for NCS which would only result in that valuation . . . being publicly disclosed, and thereby creating an environment where Omnicare felt to maintain its competitive monopolistic positions, that they had to match and exceed that level." Thus, Genesis "wanted a degree of certainty that to the extent [it] w[as] willing to pursue a negotiated merger agreement . . . , [it] would be able to consummate the transaction [it] negotiated and executed."

In June 2002, Genesis proposed a transaction that would take place outside the bankruptcy context. Although it did not provide full recovery for NCS's Noteholders, it provided the possibility that NCS stockholders would be able to recover something for their investment. As discussions continued, the terms proposed by Genesis continued to improve. On June 25, the economic terms of the Genesis proposal included repayment of the NCS senior debt in full, full assumption of trade credit obligations, an exchange offer or direct purchase of the NCS Notes providing NCS Noteholders with a combination of cash and Genesis common stock equal to the par value of the NCS Notes (not including accrued interest), and $20 million in value for the NCS common stock. Structurally, the Genesis proposal continued to include consents from a significant majority of the Noteholders as well as support agreements from stockholders owning a majority of the NCS voting power.

## Genesis Exclusivity Agreement

NCS's financial advisors and legal counsel met again with Genesis and its legal counsel on June 26, 2002, to discuss a number of transaction-related issues. At this meeting, Pollack asked Genesis to increase its offer to NCS stockholders. Genesis agreed to consider this request. Thereafter, Pollack and Hager had further conversations. Genesis agreed to offer a total of $24 million in consideration for the NCS common stock, or an additional $4 million, in the form of Genesis common stock.

At the June 26 meeting, Genesis's representatives demanded that, before any further negotiations take place, NCS agree to enter into an exclusivity agreement with it. As Hager from Genesis explained it: "[I]f they wished us to continue to try to move this process to a definitive agreement, that they would need to do it on an exclusive basis with us. We were going to, and already had incurred significant expense, but we would incur additional expenses . . . , both internal and external, to bring this transaction to a definitive signing. We wanted them to work with us on an exclusive basis for a short period of time to see if we could reach agreement." On June 27, 2002, Genesis's legal counsel delivered a draft form of exclusivity agreement for review and consideration by NCS's legal counsel.

The Independent Committee met on July 3, 2002, to consider the proposed exclusivity agreement. Pollack presented a summary of the terms of a possible Genesis merger, which had continued to improve. The then-current Genesis proposal included (1) repayment of the NCS senior debt in full, (2) payment of par value for the Notes (without accrued interest) in the form of a combination of cash and Genesis stock, (3) payment to NCS stockholders in the form of $24 million in Genesis stock, plus (4) the assumption, because the transaction was to be structured as a merger, of additional liabilities to trade and other unsecured creditors.

NCS director Sells testified, Pollack told the Independent Committee at a July 3, 2002 meeting that Genesis wanted the Exclusivity Agreement to be the first step towards a completely locked up transaction that would preclude a higher bid from Omnicare:

A.          [Pollack] explained that Genesis felt that they had suffered at the hands of Omnicare and others. I guess maybe just Omnicare. I don't know much about Genesis [sic] acquisition history. But they had suffered before at the 11:59:59 and that they wanted to have a pretty much bulletproof deal or they were not going to go forward.

Q.          When you say they suffered at the hands of Omnicare, what do you mean?

A.          Well, my expression is that that was related to — a deal that was related to me or explained to me that they, Genesis, had tried to acquire, I suppose, an institutional pharmacy, I don't remember the name of it. Thought they had a deal and then at the last minute, Omnicare outbid them for the company in a like 11:59 kind of thing, and that they were unhappy about that. And once burned, twice shy.

After NCS executed the exclusivity agreement, Genesis provided NCS with a draft merger agreement, a draft Noteholders' support agreement, and draft voting agreements for Outcalt and Shaw, who together held a majority of the voting power of the NCS common stock. Genesis and NCS negotiated the terms of the merger agreement over the next three weeks. During those negotiations, the Independent Committee and the Ad Hoc Committee persuaded Genesis to improve the terms of its merger.

The parties were still negotiating by July 19, and the exclusivity period was automatically extended to July 26. At that point, NCS and Genesis were close to executing a merger agreement and related voting agreements. Genesis proposed a short extension of the exclusivity agreement so a deal could be finalized. On the morning of July 26, 2002, the Independent Committee authorized an extension of the exclusivity period through July 31.

### Omnicare Proposes Negotiations

By late July 2002, Omnicare came to believe that NCS was negotiating a transaction, possibly with Genesis or another of Omnicare's competitors, that would potentially present a competitive threat to Omnicare. Omnicare also came to believe, in light of a run-up in the price of NCS common stock, that whatever transaction NCS was negotiating probably included a payment for its stock. Thus, the Omnicare board of directors met on the morning of July 26 and, on the recommendation of its management, authorized a proposal to acquire NCS that did not involve a sale of assets in bankruptcy.

On the afternoon of July 26, 2002, Omnicare faxed to NCS a letter outlining a proposed acquisition. The letter suggested a transaction in which Omnicare would retire NCS's senior and subordinated debt at par plus accrued interest, and pay the NCS stockholders $3 cash for their shares. Omnicare's proposal, however, was expressly conditioned on negotiating a merger agreement, obtaining certain third party consents, and completing its due diligence.

Mencher saw the July 26 Omnicare letter and realized that, while its economic terms were attractive, the "due diligence" condition substantially undercut its strength. In an effort to get a better proposal from Omnicare, Mencher telephoned Gemunder and told him that Omnicare was unlikely to succeed in its bid unless it dropped the "due diligence outs." She explained this was the only way a bid at the last minute would be able to succeed. Gemunder considered Mencher's warning "very real," and followed up with his advisors. They, however, insisted that he retain the due diligence condition "to protect [him] from doing something foolish." Taking this advice to heart, Gemunder decided not to drop the due diligence condition.

Late in the afternoon of July 26, 2002, NCS representatives received voicemail messages from Omnicare asking to discuss the letter. The exclusivity agreement prevented NCS from returning those calls. In relevant part, that agreement precluded NCS from "engag[ing] or particpat[ing] in any discussions or negotiations with respect to a Competing Transaction or a proposal for one." The July 26 letter from Omnicare met the definition of a "Competing Transaction."

Despite the exclusivity agreement, the Independent Committee met to consider a response to Omnicare. It concluded that discussions with Omnicare about its July 26 letter presented an unacceptable risk that Genesis would abandon merger discussions. The Independent Committee believed that, given Omnicare's past bankruptcy proposals and unwillingness to consider a merger, as well as its decision to negotiate exclusively with the Ad Hoc Committee, the risk of losing the Genesis proposal was too substantial. Nevertheless, the Independent Committee instructed Pollack to use Omnicare's letter to negotiate for improved terms with Genesis.

### Genesis Merger Agreement and Voting Agreements

Genesis responded to the NCS request to improve its offer as a result of the Omnicare fax the next day. On July 27, Genesis proposed substantially improved terms. First, it proposed to retire the Notes in accordance with the terms of the indenture, thus eliminating the need for Noteholders to consent to the transaction. This change involved paying all accrued interest plus a small redemption premium. Second, Genesis increased the exchange ratio for NCS common stock to one-tenth of a Genesis common share for each NCS common share, an 80% increase. Third, it agreed to lower the proposed termination fee in the merger agreement from $10 million to $6 million. In return for these concessions, Genesis stipulated that the transaction had to be approved by midnight the next day, July 28, or else Genesis would terminate discussions and withdraw its offer.

The Independent Committee and the NCS board both scheduled meetings for July 28. The committee met first. Although that meeting lasted less than an hour, the Court of Chancery determined the minutes reflect that the directors were fully informed of all material facts relating to the proposed transaction. After concluding that Genesis was sincere in establishing the midnight deadline, the committee voted unanimously to recommend the transaction to the full board.

The full board met thereafter. After receiving similar reports and advice from its legal and financial advisors, the board concluded that "balancing the potential loss of the Genesis deal against the uncertainty of Omnicare's letter, results in the conclusion that the only reasonable alternative for the Board of Directors is to approve the Genesis transaction." The board first voted to authorize the voting agreements with Outcalt and Shaw, for purposes of Section 203 of the Delaware General Corporation Law ("DGCL"). The board was advised by its legal counsel that "under the terms of the merger agreement and because NCS shareholders representing in excess of 50% of the outstanding voting power would be required by Genesis to enter into stockholder voting agreements contemporaneously with the signing of the merger agreement, and would agree to vote their shares in favor of the merger agreement, shareholder approval of the merger would be assured even if the NCS Board were to withdraw or change its recommendation. These facts would prevent NCS from engaging in any alternative or superior transaction in the future." (emphasis added).

After listening to a summary of the merger terms, the board then resolved that the merger agreement and the transactions contemplated thereby were advisable and fair and in the best interests of all the NCS stakeholders. The NCS board further resolved to recommend the transactions to the stockholders for their approval and adoption. A definitive merger agreement between NCS and Genesis and the stockholder voting agreements were executed later that day. The Court of Chancery held that it was not a per se breach of fiduciary duty that the NCS board never read the NCS/Genesis merger agreement word for word.[2]

### NCS/Genesis Merger Agreement

Among other things, the NCS/Genesis merger agreement provided the following:

- NCS stockholders would receive 1 share of Genesis common stock in exchange for every 10 shares of NCS common stock held;
- NCS stockholders could exercise appraisal rights under 8 Del. C. § 262;
- NCS would redeem NCS's Notes in accordance with their terms;
- NCS would submit the merger agreement to NCS stockholders regardless of whether the NCS board continued to recommend the merger;
- NCS would not enter into discussions with third parties concerning an alternative acquisition of NCS, or provide non-public information to such parties, unless (1) the third party provided an unsolicited, bona fide written proposal documenting the terms of the acquisition; (2) the NCS board believed in good faith that the proposal was or was likely to result in an acquisition on terms superior to those contemplated by the NCS/Genesis merger agreement; and (3) before providing non-public information to that third party, the third party would execute a confidentiality agreement at least as restrictive as the one in place between NCS and Genesis; and
- If the merger agreement were to be terminated, under certain circumstances NCS would be required to pay Genesis a $6 million termination fee and/or Genesis's documented expenses, up to $5 million.

### Voting Agreements

Outcalt and Shaw, in their capacity as NCS stockholders, entered into voting agreements with Genesis. NCS was also required to be a party to the voting

---

[2] [4] *See, e.g., Smith v. Van Gorkom*, 488 A.2d 858, 883 n. 25 (Del. 1985).

agreements by Genesis. Those agreements provided, among other things, that:

- Outcalt and Shaw were acting in their capacity as NCS stockholders in executing the agreements, not in their capacity as NCS directors or officers;

- Neither Outcalt nor Shaw would transfer their shares prior to the stockholder vote on the merger agreement;

- Outcalt and Shaw agreed to vote all of their shares in favor of the merger agreement; and

- Outcalt and Shaw granted to Genesis an irrevocable proxy to vote their shares in favor of the merger agreement.

- The voting agreement was specifically enforceable by Genesis.

The merger agreement further provided that if either Outcalt or Shaw breached the terms of the voting agreements, Genesis would be entitled to terminate the merger agreement and potentially receive a $6 million termination fee from NCS. Such a breach was impossible since Section 6 provided that the voting agreements were specifically enforceable by Genesis.

### Omnicare's Superior Proposal

On July 29, 2002, hours after the NCS/Genesis transaction was executed, Omnicare faxed a letter to NCS restating its conditional proposal and attaching a draft merger agreement. Later that morning, Omnicare issued a press release publicly disclosing the proposal.

On August 1, 2002, Omnicare filed a lawsuit attempting to enjoin the NCS/Genesis merger, and announced that it intended to launch a tender offer for NCS's shares at a price of $3.50 per share. On August 8, 2002, Omnicare began its tender offer. By letter dated that same day, Omnicare expressed a desire to discuss the terms of the offer with NCS. Omnicare's letter continued to condition its proposal on satisfactory completion of a due diligence investigation of NCS.

On August 8, 2002, and again on August 19, 2002, the NCS Independent Committee and full board of directors met separately to consider the Omnicare tender offer in light of the Genesis merger agreement. NCS's outside legal counsel and NCS's financial advisor attended both meetings. The board was unable to determine that Omnicare's expressions of interest were likely to lead to a "Superior Proposal," as the term was defined in the NCS/Genesis merger agreement. On September 10, 2002, NCS requested and received a waiver from Genesis allowing NCS to enter into discussions with Omnicare without first having to determine that Omnicare's proposal was a "Superior Proposal."

On October 6, 2002, Omnicare irrevocably committed itself to a transaction with NCS. Pursuant to the terms of its proposal, Omnicare agreed to acquire all the outstanding NCS Class A and Class B shares at a price of $3.50 per share in cash. As a result of this irrevocable offer, on October 21, 2002, the NCS board withdrew its recommendation that the stockholders vote in favor of the NCS/Genesis merger agreement. NCS's financial advisor withdrew its fairness opinion of the NCS/Genesis merger agreement as well.

### Genesis Rejection Impossible

The Genesis merger agreement permits the NCS directors to furnish non-public information to, or enter into discussions with, "any Person in connection with an unsolicited bona fide written Acquisition Proposal by such person" that the board deems likely to constitute a "Superior Proposal." That provision has absolutely no effect on the Genesis merger agreement. Even if the NCS board "changes, withdraws or modifies" its recommendation, as it did, it must still submit the merger to a stockholder vote.

A subsequent filing with the Securities and Exchange Commission ("SEC") states: "the NCS independent committee and the NCS board of directors have determined to withdraw their recommendations of the Genesis merger agreement and recommend that the NCS stockholders vote against the approval and adoption of the Genesis merger." In that same SEC filing, however, the NCS board explained why the success of the Genesis merger had already been predetermined. "Notwithstanding the foregoing, the NCS independent committee and the NCS board of directors recognize that (1) the existing contractual obligations to Genesis currently prevent NCS from accepting the Omnicare irrevocable merger proposal; and (2) the existence of the voting agreements entered into by Messrs. Outcalt and Shaw, whereby Messrs. Outcalt and Shaw agreed to vote their shares of NCS Class A common stock and NCS Class B common stock in favor of the Genesis merger, ensure NCS stockholder approval of the Genesis merger." This litigation was commenced to prevent the consummation of the inferior Genesis transaction.

## LEGAL ANALYSIS

### Business Judgment or Enhanced Scrutiny

The "defining tension" in corporate governance today has been characterized as "the tension between deference to directors' decisions and the scope of judicial review." The appropriate standard of judicial review is dispositive of which party has the burden of proof as any litigation proceeds from stage to stage until there is a substantive determination on the merits. Accordingly, identification of the correct analytical framework is essential to a proper judicial review of challenges to the decision-making process of a corporation's board of directors.

"The business judgment rule, as a standard of judicial review, is a common-law recognition of the statutory authority to manage a corporation that is vested in the board of directors."[3] The business judgment rule is a "presumption that in making a business decision the directors of a corporation acted on an informed basis, in good faith and in the honest belief that the action taken was in the best interests of the company." "An application of the traditional business judgment rule places the burden on the 'party challenging the [board's] decision to establish facts rebutting the presumption.'" The effect of a proper invocation of the business judgment rule, as a standard of judicial review, is powerful because it operates deferentially. Unless the procedural presumption of the business judgment rule is rebutted, a "court will

---

[3] [8] *MM Companies v. Liquid Audio, Inc.*, 813 A.2d 1118, 1127 (Del. 2003).

not substitute its judgment for that of the board if the [board's] decision can be 'attributed to any rational business purpose.'"

The business judgment rule embodies the deference that is accorded to managerial decisions of a board of directors. "Under normal circumstances, neither the courts nor the stockholders should interfere with the managerial decision of the directors." There are certain circumstances, however, "which mandate that a court take a more direct and active role in overseeing the decisions made and actions taken by directors. In these situations, a court subjects the directors' conduct to enhanced scrutiny to ensure that it is reasonable," "before the protections of the business judgment rule may be conferred."

The prior decisions of this Court have identified the circumstances where board action must be subjected to enhanced judicial scrutiny before the presumptive protection of the business judgment rule can be invoked. One of those circumstances was described in *Unocal*: when a board adopts defensive measures in response to a hostile takeover proposal that the board reasonably determines is a threat to corporate policy and effectiveness. In *Moran v. Household*, we explained why a *Unocal* analysis also was applied to the adoption of a stockholder's rights plan, even in the absence of an immediate threat. Other circumstances requiring enhanced judicial scrutiny give rise to what are known as *Revlon* duties, such as when the board enters into a merger transaction that will cause a change in corporate control, initiates an active bidding process seeking to sell the corporation, or makes a break-up of the corporate entity inevitable.

### Merger Decision Review Standard

The first issue decided by the Court of Chancery addressed the standard of judicial review that should be applied to the decision by the NCS board to merge with Genesis. This Court has held that a board's decision to enter into a merger transaction that does not involve a change in control is entitled to judicial deference pursuant to the procedural and substantive operation of the business judgment rule.When a board decides to enter into a merger transaction that will result in a change of control, however, enhanced judicial scrutiny under *Revlon* is the standard of review.

The Court of Chancery concluded that, because the stock-for-stock merger between Genesis and NCS did not result in a change of control, the NCS directors' duties under *Revlon* were not triggered by the decision to merge with Genesis. The Court of Chancery also recognized, however, that *Revlon* duties are imposed "when a corporation initiates an active bidding process seeking to sell itself." The Court of Chancery then concluded, alternatively, that *Revlon* duties had not been triggered because NCS did not start an active bidding process, and the NCS board "abandoned" its efforts to sell the company when it entered into an exclusivity agreement with Genesis.

After concluding that the *Revlon* standard of enhanced judicial review was completely inapplicable, the Court of Chancery then held that it would examine the decision of the NCS board of directors to approve the Genesis merger pursuant to the business judgment rule standard. After completing its business judgment rule review, the Court of Chancery held that the NCS board of directors had not breached their duty of care by entering into the exclusivity and merger agreements with Genesis. The Court of Chancery also held, however, that "even applying the more exacting *Revlon* standard, the directors acted in conformity with their fiduciary duties in seeking to achieve the highest and best transaction that was reasonably available to [the stockholders]."

The appellants argue that the Court of Chancery's *Revlon* conclusions are without factual support in the record and contrary to Delaware law for at least two reasons. First, they submit that NCS did initiate an active bidding process. Second, they submit that NCS did not "abandon" its efforts to sell itself by entering into the exclusivity agreement with Genesis. The appellants contend that once NCS decided "to initiate a bidding process seeking to maximize short-term stockholder value, it cannot avoid enhanced judicial scrutiny under Revlon simply because the bidder it selected [Genesis] happens to have proposed a merger transaction that does not involve a change of control."

The Court of Chancery's decision to review the NCS board's decision to merge with Genesis under the business judgment rule rather than the enhanced scrutiny standard of Revlon is not outcome determinative for the purposes of deciding this appeal. We have assumed arguendo that the business judgment rule applied to the decision by the NCS board to merge with Genesis. We have also assumed arguendo that the NCS board exercised due care when it: abandoned the Independent Committee's recommendation to pursue a stalking horse strategy, without even trying to implement it; executed an exclusivity agreement with Genesis; acceded to Genesis' twenty-four hour ultimatum for making a final merger decision; and executed a merger agreement that was summarized but never completely read by the NCS board of directors.

### Deal Protection Devices Require Enhanced Scrutiny

The dispositive issues in this appeal involve the defensive devices that protected the Genesis merger agreement. The Delaware corporation statute provides that the board's management decision to enter into and recommend a merger transaction can become final only when ownership action is taken by a vote of the stockholders. Thus, the Delaware corporation law expressly provides for a balance of power between boards and stockholders which makes merger transactions a shared enterprise and ownership decision. Consequently, a board of directors' decision to adopt defensive devices to protect a merger agreement may implicate the stockholders' right to effectively vote contrary to the initial recommendation of the board in favor of the transaction.[4]

It is well established that conflicts of interest arise when a board of directors acts to prevent stockholders from effectively exercising their right to vote contrary to the will of the board. The "omnipresent specter" of such conflict may be present whenever a board adopts defensive devices to protect a merger agreement. The stockholders' ability to effectively reject a merger agreement is likely to bear an

---

[4] [25] *See MM Companies v. Liquid Audio, Inc.*, 813 A.2d 1118, 1120 (Del. 2003).

inversely proportionate relationship to the structural and economic devices that the board has approved to protect the transaction.

In *Paramount v. Time*, the original merger agreement between Time and Warner did not constitute a "change of control." The plaintiffs in *Paramount v. Time* argued that, although the original Time and Warner merger agreement did not involve a change of control, the use of a lock-up, no-shop clause, and "dry-up" provisions violated the Time board's *Revlon* duties. This Court held that "[t]he adoption of structural safety devices alone does not trigger *Revlon*. Rather, as the Chancellor stated, such devices are properly subject to a Unocal analysis."

In footnote 15 of *Paramount v. Time*, we stated that legality of the structural safety devices adopted to protect the original merger agreement between Time and Warner were not a central issue on appeal. That is because the issue on appeal involved the "Time's board [decision] to recast its consolidation with Warner into an outright cash and securities acquisition of Warner by Time." Nevertheless, we determined that there was substantial evidence on the record to support the conclusions reached by the Chancellor in applying a *Unocal* analysis to each of the structural devices contained in the original merger agreement between Time and Warner.

There are inherent conflicts between a board's interest in protecting a merger transaction it has approved, the stockholders' statutory right to make the final decision to either approve or not approve a merger, and the board's continuing responsibility to effectively exercise its fiduciary duties at all times after the merger agreement is executed. These competing considerations require a threshold determination that board-approved defensive devices protecting a merger transaction are within the limitations of its statutory authority and consistent with the directors' fiduciary duties. Accordingly, in *Paramount v. Time*, we held that the business judgment rule applied to the Time board's original decision to merge with Warner. We further held, however, that defensive devices adopted by the board to protect the original merger transaction must withstand enhanced judicial scrutiny under the Unocal standard of review, even when that merger transaction does not result in a change of control.

## Enhanced Scrutiny Generally

In *Paramount v. QVC*, this Court identified the key features of an enhanced judicial scrutiny test. The first feature is a "judicial determination regarding the adequacy of the decisionmaking process employed by the directors, including the information on which the directors based their decision." The second feature is "a judicial examination of the reasonableness of the directors' action in light of the circumstances then existing." We also held that "the directors have the burden of proving that they were adequately informed and acted reasonably."

In *QVC*, we explained that the application of an enhanced judicial scrutiny test involves a judicial "review of the reasonableness of the substantive merits of the board's actions." In applying that standard, we held that "a court should not ignore the complexity of the directors' task" in the context in which action was taken. Accordingly, we concluded that a court applying enhanced judicial scrutiny should not decide whether the directors made a perfect decision but instead should decide whether "the directors' decision was, on balance, within a range of reasonableness."

In *Unitrin*, we explained the "ratio decidendi for the 'range of reasonableness' standard" when a court applies enhanced judicial scrutiny to director action pursuant to our holding in Unocal. It is a recognition that a board of directors needs "latitude in discharging its fiduciary duties to the corporation and its shareholders when defending against perceived threats." "The concomitant requirement is for judicial restraint." Therefore, if the board of directors' collective defensive responses are not draconian (preclusive or coercive) and are "within a 'range of reasonableness,' a court must not substitute its judgment for the board's [judgment]." The same ratio decidendi applies to the "range of reasonableness" when courts apply *Unocal*'s enhanced judicial scrutiny standard to defensive devices intended to protect a merger agreement that will not result in a change of control.

A board's decision to protect its decision to enter a merger agreement with defensive devices against uninvited competing transactions that may emerge is analogous to a board's decision to protect against dangers to corporate policy and effectiveness when it adopts defensive measures in a hostile takeover contest. In applying *Unocal*'s enhanced judicial scrutiny in assessing a challenge to defensive actions taken by a target corporation's board of directors in a takeover context, this Court held that the board "does not have unbridled discretion to defeat perceived threats by any Draconian means available". Similarly, just as a board's statutory power with regard to a merger decision is not absolute, a board does not have unbridled discretion to defeat any perceived threat to a merger by protecting it with any draconian means available.

Since *Unocal*, "this Court has consistently recognized that defensive measures which are either preclusive or coercive are included within the common law definition of draconian."[5] In applying enhanced judicial scrutiny to defensive actions under *Unocal*, a court must "evaluate the board's overall response, including the justification for each contested defensive measure, and the results achieved thereby."[6] If a "board's defensive actions are inextricably related, the principles of *Unocal* require that such actions be scrutinized collectively as a unitary response to the perceived threat."[7]

Therefore, in applying enhanced judicial scrutiny to defensive devices designed to protect a merger agreement, a court must first determine that those measures are not preclusive or coercive before its focus shifts to the "range of reasonableness" in making a proportionality determination. If the trial court determines that the defensive devices protecting a merger are not preclusive or coercive, the proportionality paradigm of *Unocal* is applicable. The board must demonstrate that it has reasonable grounds for believing that a danger to the corporation and its stockholders exists if the merger transaction is not consummated. That burden is satisfied "by showing good faith and reasonable investigation." Such proof is materially enhanced if it is approved by a board comprised of a majority of outside

---

[5] [47] *Unitrin, Inc. v. Am. Gen. Corp.*, 651 A.2d at 1387.

[6] [48] *Id.*

[7] [49] *Id.* (citation omitted).

directors or by an independent committee.

When the focus of judicial scrutiny shifts to the range of reasonableness, *Unocal* requires that any defensive devices must be proportionate to the perceived threat to the corporation and its stockholders if the merger transaction is not consummated. Defensive devices taken to protect a merger agreement executed by a board of directors are intended to give that agreement an advantage over any subsequent transactions that materialize before the merger is approved by the stockholders and consummated. This is analogous to the favored treatment that a board of directors may properly give to encourage an initial bidder when it discharges its fiduciary duties under *Revlon*.

Therefore, in the context of a merger that does not involve a change of control, when defensive devices in the executed merger agreement are challenged vis-à-vis their effect on a subsequent competing alternative merger transaction, this Court's analysis in *Macmillan* is didactic. In the context of a case of defensive measures taken against an existing bidder, we stated in *Macmillan*:

> In the face of disparate treatment, the trial court must first examine whether the directors properly perceived that shareholder interests were enhanced. In any event the board's action must be reasonable in relation to the advantage sought to be achieved [by the merger it approved], or conversely, to the threat which a [competing transaction] poses to stockholder interests. If on the basis of this enhanced *Unocal* scrutiny the trial court is satisfied that the test has been met, then the directors' actions necessarily are entitled to the protections of the business judgment rule.

The latitude a board will have in either maintaining or using the defensive devices it has adopted to protect the merger it approved will vary according to the degree of benefit or detriment to the stockholders' interests that is presented by the value or terms of the subsequent competing transaction.

### Genesis' One Day Ultimatum

The record reflects that two of the four NCS board members, Shaw and Outcalt, were also the same two NCS stockholders who combined to control a majority of the stockholder voting power. Genesis gave the four person NCS board less than twenty-four hours to vote in favor of its proposed merger agreement. Genesis insisted the merger agreement include a Section 251(c) clause, mandating its submission for a stockholder vote even if the board's recommendation was withdrawn. Genesis further insisted that the merger agreement omit any effective fiduciary out clause.

Genesis also gave the two stockholder members of the NCS board, Shaw and Outcalt, the same accelerated time table to personally sign the proposed voting agreements. These voting agreements committed them irrevocably to vote their majority power in favor of the merger and further provided in Section 6 that the voting agreements be specifically enforceable. Genesis also required that NCS execute the voting agreements.

Genesis' twenty-four hour ultimatum was that, unless both the merger agreement and the voting agreements were signed with the terms it requested, its offer was going to be withdrawn. According to Genesis' attorneys, these "were unalterable conditions to Genesis' willingness to proceed." Genesis insisted on the execution of the interlocking voting rights and merger agreements because it feared that Omnicare would make a superior merger proposal. The NCS board signed the voting rights and merger agreements, without any effective fiduciary out clause, to expressly guarantee that the Genesis merger would be approved, even if a superior merger transaction was presented from Omnicare or any other entity.

### Deal Protection Devices

Defensive devices, as that term is used in this opinion, is a synonym for what are frequently referred to as "deal protection devices." Both terms are used interchangeably to describe any measure or combination of measures that are intended to protect the consummation of a merger transaction. Defensive devices can be economic, structural, or both.

Deal protection devices need not all be in the merger agreement itself. In this case, for example, the Section 251(c) provision in the merger agreement was combined with the separate voting agreements to provide a structural defense for the Genesis merger agreement against any subsequent superior transaction. Genesis made the NCS board's defense of its transaction absolute by insisting on the omission of any effective fiduciary out clause in the NCS merger agreement.

Genesis argues that stockholder voting agreements cannot be construed as deal protection devices taken by a board of directors because stockholders are entitled to vote in their own interest. Genesis cites *Williams v. Geier* and *Stroud v. Grace* for the proposition that voting agreements are not subject to the Unocal standard of review. Neither of those cases, however, holds that the operative effect of a voting agreement must be disregarded per se when a Unocal analysis is applied to a comprehensive and combined merger defense plan.

In this case, the stockholder voting agreements were inextricably intertwined with the defensive aspects of the Genesis merger agreement. In fact, the voting agreements with Shaw and Outcalt were the linchpin of Genesis' proposed tripartite defense. Therefore, Genesis made the execution of those voting agreements a non-negotiable condition precedent to its execution of the merger agreement. In the case before us, the Court of Chancery held that the acts which locked-up the Genesis transaction were the Section 251(c) provision and "the execution of the voting agreement by Outcalt and Shaw."

With the assurance that Outcalt and Shaw would irrevocably agree to exercise their majority voting power in favor of its transaction, Genesis insisted that the merger agreement reflect the other two aspects of its concerted defense, i.e., the inclusion of a Section 251(c) provision and the omission of any effective fiduciary out clause. Those dual aspects of the merger agreement would not have provided Genesis with a complete defense in the absence of the voting agreements with Shaw and Outcalt.

### These Deal Protection Devices Unenforceable

In this case, the Court of Chancery correctly held that the NCS directors' decision to adopt defensive devices to completely "lock up" the Genesis merger mandated "special scrutiny" under the two-part test set forth in *Unocal.* That conclusion is consistent with our holding in *Paramount v. Time* that "safety devices" adopted to protect a transaction that did not result in a change of control are subject to enhanced judicial scrutiny under a *Unocal* analysis. The record does not, however, support the Court of Chancery's conclusion that the defensive devices adopted by the NCS board to protect the Genesis merger were reasonable and proportionate to the threat that NCS perceived from the potential loss of the Genesis transaction.

Pursuant to the judicial scrutiny required under *Unocal*'s two-stage analysis, the NCS directors must first demonstrate "that they had reasonable grounds for believing that a danger to corporate policy and effectiveness existed . . . ." To satisfy that burden, the NCS directors are required to show they acted in good faith after conducting a reasonable investigation. The threat identified by the NCS board was the possibility of losing the Genesis offer and being left with no comparable alternative transaction.

The second stage of the *Unocal* test requires the NCS directors to demonstrate that their defensive response was "reasonable in relation to the threat posed." This inquiry involves a two-step analysis. The NCS directors must first establish that the merger deal protection devices adopted in response to the threat were not "coercive" or "preclusive," and then demonstrate that their response was within a "range of reasonable responses" to the threat perceived. In *Unitrin*, we stated:

- A response is "coercive" if it is aimed at forcing upon stockholders a management-sponsored alternative to a hostile offer.

- A response is "preclusive" if it deprives stockholders of the right to receive all tender offers or precludes a bidder from seeking control by fundamentally restricting proxy contests or otherwise.

This aspect of the *Unocal* standard provides for a disjunctive analysis. If defensive measures are either preclusive or coercive they are draconian and impermissible. In this case, the deal protection devices of the NCS board were both preclusive and coercive.

This Court enunciated the standard for determining stockholder coercion in the case of *Williams v. Geier*. A stockholder vote may be nullified by wrongful coercion "where the board or some other party takes actions which have the effect of causing the stockholders to vote in favor of the proposed transaction for some reason other than the merits of that transaction." In *Brazen v. Bell Atlantic Corporation*, we applied that test for stockholder coercion and held "that although the termination fee provision may have influenced the stockholder vote, there were 'no structurally or situationally coercive factors' that made an otherwise valid fee provision impermissibly coercive" under the facts presented.

In *Brazen*, we concluded "the determination of whether a particular stockholder vote has been robbed of its effectiveness by impermissible coercion depends on the facts of the case." In this case, the Court of Chancery did not expressly address the issue of "coercion" in its *Unocal* analysis. It did find as a fact, however, that NCS's public stockholders (who owned 80% of NCS and overwhelmingly supported Omnicare's offer) will be forced to accept the Genesis merger because of the structural defenses approved by the NCS board. Consequently, the record reflects that any stockholder vote would have been robbed of its effectiveness by the impermissible coercion that predetermined the outcome of the merger without regard to the merits of the Genesis transaction at the time the vote was scheduled to be taken. Deal protection devices that result in such coercion cannot withstand *Unocal*'s enhanced judicial scrutiny standard of review because they are not within the range of reasonableness.

Although the minority stockholders were not forced to vote for the Genesis merger, they were required to accept it because it was a fait accompli. The record reflects that the defensive devices employed by the NCS board are preclusive and coercive in the sense that they accomplished a fait accompli. In this case, despite the fact that the NCS board has withdrawn its recommendation for the Genesis transaction and recommended its rejection by the stockholders, the deal protection devices approved by the NCS board operated in concert to have a preclusive and coercive effect. Those tripartite defensive measures — the Section 251(c) provision, the voting agreements, and the absence of an effective fiduciary out clause — made it "mathematically impossible" and "realistically unattainable" for the Omnicare transaction or any other proposal to succeed, no matter how superior the proposal.

The deal protection devices adopted by the NCS board were designed to coerce the consummation of the Genesis merger and preclude the consideration of any superior transaction. The NCS directors' defensive devices are not within a reasonable range of responses to the perceived threat of losing the Genesis offer because they are preclusive and coercive. Accordingly, we hold that those deal protection devices are unenforceable.

### Effective Fiduciary Out Required

The defensive measures that protected the merger transaction are unenforceable not only because they are preclusive and coercive but, alternatively, they are unenforceable because they are invalid as they operate in this case. Given the specifically enforceable irrevocable voting agreements, the provision in the merger agreement requiring the board to submit the transaction for a stockholder vote and the omission of a fiduciary out clause in the merger agreement completely prevented the board from discharging its fiduciary responsibilities to the minority stockholders when Omnicare presented its superior transaction. "To the extent that a [merger] contract, or a provision thereof, purports to require a board to act or not act in such a fashion as to limit the exercise of fiduciary duties, it is invalid and unenforceable."[8]

---

[8] [74] *Paramount Communications Inc. v. QVC Network Inc.*, 637 A.2d 34, 51 (Del. 1993) (citation omitted). Restatement (Second) of Contracts § 193 explicitly provides that a "promise by a fiduciary to violate his fiduciary duty or a promise that tends to induce such a violation is unenforceable on grounds of public policy." The comments to that section indicate that "[d]irectors and other officials of a

In *QVC*, this Court recognized that "[w]hen a majority of a corporation's voting shares are acquired by a single person or entity, or by a cohesive group acting together [as in this case], there is a significant diminution in the voting power of those who thereby become minority stockholders." Therefore, we acknowledged that "[i]n the absence of devices protecting the minority stockholders, stockholder votes are likely to become mere formalities," where a cohesive group acting together to exercise majority voting powers have already decided the outcome. Consequently, we concluded that since the minority stockholders lost the power to influence corporate direction through the ballot, "minority stockholders must rely for protection solely on the fiduciary duties owed to them by the directors."

Under the circumstances presented in this case, where a cohesive group of stockholders with majority voting power was irrevocably committed to the merger transaction, "[e]ffective representation of the financial interests of the minority shareholders imposed upon the [NCS board] an affirmative responsibility to protect those minority shareholders' interests." The NCS board could not abdicate its fiduciary duties to the minority by leaving it to the stockholders alone to approve or disapprove the merger agreement because two stockholders had already combined to establish a majority of the voting power that made the outcome of the stockholder vote a foregone conclusion.

The Court of Chancery noted that Section 251(c) of the Delaware General Corporation Law now permits boards to agree to submit a merger agreement for a stockholder vote, even if the Board later withdraws its support for that agreement and recommends that the stockholders reject it.[9] The Court of Chancery also noted that stockholder voting agreements are permitted by Delaware law. In refusing to certify this interlocutory appeal, the Court of Chancery stated "it is simply nonsensical to say that a board of directors abdicates its duties to manage the 'business and affairs' of a corporation under Section 141(a) of the DGCL by agreeing to the inclusion in a merger agreement of a term authorized by § 251(c) of the same statute."

Taking action that is otherwise legally possible, however, does not ipso facto comport with the fiduciary responsibilities of directors in all circumstances.[10] The synopsis to the amendments that resulted in the enactment of Section 251(c) in the Delaware corporation law statute specifically provides: "the amendments are not intended to address the question of whether such a submission requirement is appropriate in any particular set of factual circumstances." Section 251 provisions, like the no-shop provision examined in *QVC*, are "presumptively valid in the abstract." Such provisions in a merger agreement may not, however, "validly define or limit the directors' fiduciary duties under Delaware law or prevent the [NCS]

---

corporation act in a fiduciary capacity and are subject to the rule stated in this Section." Restatement (Second) of Contracts § 193 (1981) (emphasis added).

[9] [80] Section 251(c) was amended in 1998 to allow for the inclusion in a merger agreement of a term requiring that the agreement be put to a vote of stockholders whether or not their directors continue to recommend the transaction. Before this amendment, Section 251 was interpreted as precluding a stockholder vote if the board of directors, after approving the merger agreement but before the stockholder vote, decided no longer to recommend it. *See Smith v. Van Gorkom*, 488 A.2d 858, 887–88 (Del. 1985).

[10] [81] *MM Companies v. Liquid Audio, Inc.*, 813 A.2d 1118, 1132 (Del. 2003) (citation omitted).

directors from carrying out their fiduciary duties under Delaware law."

Genesis admits that when the NCS board agreed to its merger conditions, the NCS board was seeking to assure that the NCS creditors were paid in full and that the NCS stockholders received the highest value available for their stock. In fact, Genesis defends its "bulletproof" merger agreement on that basis. We hold that the NCS board did not have authority to accede to the Genesis demand for an absolute "lock-up."

The directors of a Delaware corporation have a continuing obligation to discharge their fiduciary responsibilities, as future circumstances develop, after a merger agreement is announced. Genesis anticipated the likelihood of a superior offer after its merger agreement was announced and demanded defensive measures from the NCS board that completely protected its transaction.[11] Instead of agreeing to the absolute defense of the Genesis merger from a superior offer, however, the NCS board was required to negotiate a fiduciary out clause to protect the NCS stockholders if the Genesis transaction became an inferior offer. By acceding to Genesis' ultimatum for complete protection in futuro, the NCS board disabled itself from exercising its own fiduciary obligations at a time when the board's own judgment is most important,[12] i.e. receipt of a subsequent superior offer.

Any board has authority to give the proponent of a recommended merger agreement reasonable structural and economic defenses, incentives, and fair compensation if the transaction is not completed. To the extent that defensive measures are economic and reasonable, they may become an increased cost to the proponent of any subsequent transaction. Just as defensive measures cannot be draconian, however, they cannot limit or circumscribe the directors' fiduciary duties. Notwithstanding the corporation's insolvent condition, the NCS board had no authority to execute a merger agreement that subsequently prevented it from effectively discharging its ongoing fiduciary responsibilities.

The stockholders of a Delaware corporation are entitled to rely upon the board to discharge its fiduciary duties at all times. The fiduciary duties of a director are unremitting and must be effectively discharged in the specific context of the actions that are required with regard to the corporation or its stockholders as circumstances change. The stockholders with majority voting power, Shaw and Outcalt, had an absolute right to sell or exchange their shares with a third party at any price. This right was not only known to the other directors of NCS, it became an integral part of the Genesis agreement. In its answering brief, Genesis candidly states that its offer "came with a condition — Genesis would not be a stalking horse and would not agree to a transaction to which NCS's controlling shareholders were not committed."

The NCS board was required to contract for an effective fiduciary out clause to

---

[11] [84] The marked improvements in NCS's financial situation during the negotiations with Genesis strongly suggests that the NCS board should have been alert to the prospect of competing offers or, as eventually occurred, a bidding contest.

[12] [85] *See Malone v. Brincat*, 722 A.2d 5, 10 (Del. 1998) (directors' fiduciary duties do not operate intermittently). *See also Moran v. Household Int'l, Inc.*, 500 A.2d 1346 (Del. 1985).

exercise its continuing fiduciary responsibilities to the minority stockholders.[13] The issues in this appeal do not involve the general validity of either stockholder voting agreements or the authority of directors to insert a Section 251(c) provision in a merger agreement. In this case, the NCS board combined those two otherwise valid actions and caused them to operate in concert as an absolute lock up, in the absence of an effective fiduciary out clause in the Genesis merger agreement.

In the context of this preclusive and coercive lock up case, the protection of Genesis' contractual expectations must yield to the supervening responsibility of the directors to discharge their fiduciary duties on a continuing basis. The merger agreement and voting agreements, as they were combined to operate in concert in this case, are inconsistent with the NCS directors' fiduciary duties. To that extent, we hold that they are invalid and unenforceable.

## Conclusion

With respect to the Fiduciary Duty Decision, the order of the Court of Chancery dated November 22, 2002, denying plaintiffs' application for a preliminary injunction is reversed. With respect to the Voting Agreements Decision, the order of the Court of Chancery dated October 29, 2002 is reversed to the extent that decision permits the implementation of the Voting Agreements contrary to this Court's ruling on the Fiduciary Duty claims. With respect to the appeal to this Court of that portion of the Standing Decision constituting the order of the Court of Chancery dated October 25, 2002, that granted the motion to dismiss the remainder of the Omnicare complaint, holding that Omnicare lacked standing to assert fiduciary duty claims arising out of the action of the board of directors that preceded the date on which Omnicare acquired its stock, the appeal is dismissed as moot.

The mandate shall issue immediately.

VEASEY, CHIEF JUSTICE, with whom STEELE, JUSTICE, joins dissenting.

The beauty of the Delaware corporation law, and the reason it has worked so well for stockholders, directors and officers, is that the framework is based on an enabling statute with the Court of Chancery and the Supreme Court applying principles of fiduciary duty in a common law mode on a case-by-case basis. Fiduciary duty cases are inherently fact-intensive and, therefore, unique. This case is unique in two important respects. First, the peculiar facts presented render this case an unlikely candidate for substantial repetition. Second, this is a rare 3-2 split decision of the Supreme Court.[14]

---

[13] [88] *See Paramount Communications Inc. v. QVC Network Inc.*, 637 A.2d at 42–43. Merger agreements involve an ownership decision and, therefore, cannot become final without stockholder approval. Other contracts do not require a fiduciary out clause because they involve business judgments that are within the exclusive province of the board of directors' power to manage the affairs of the corporation. *See Grimes v. Donald*, 673 A.2d 1207, 1214–15 (Del. 1996).

[14] [90] Split decisions by this Court, especially in the field of corporation law, are few and far between. One example is our decision in *Smith v. Van Gorkom*, 488 A.2d 858 (Del. 1985), where only three Justices supported reversing the Court of Chancery's decision. As Justice Holland and David Skeel recently noted, while our decisionmaking process fosters consensus, dissenting opinions "illustrate that principled

In the present case, we are faced with a merger agreement and controlling stockholders' commitment that assured stockholder approval of the merger before the emergence of a subsequent transaction offering greater value to the stockholders. This does not adequately summarize the unique facts before us, however. Reference is made to the Vice Chancellor's opinion and the factual summary in the Majority Opinion that adopts the Vice Chancellor's findings.

The process by which this merger agreement came about involved a joint decision by the controlling stockholders and the board of directors to secure what appeared to be the only value-enhancing transaction available for a company on the brink of bankruptcy. The Majority adopts a new rule of law that imposes a prohibition on the NCS board's ability to act in concert with controlling stockholders to lock up this merger. The Majority reaches this conclusion by analyzing the challenged deal protection measures as isolated board actions. The Majority concludes that the board owed a duty to the NCS minority stockholders to refrain from acceding to the Genesis demand for an irrevocable lock-up notwithstanding the compelling circumstances confronting the board and the board's disinterested, informed, good faith exercise of its business judgment.

Because we believe this Court must respect the reasoned judgment of the board of directors and give effect to the wishes of the controlling stockholders, we respectfully disagree with the Majority's reasoning that results in a holding that the confluence of board and stockholder action constitutes a breach of fiduciary duty. The essential fact that must always be remembered is that this agreement and the voting commitments of Outcalt and Shaw concluded a lengthy search and intense negotiation process in the context of insolvency and creditor pressure where no other viable bid had emerged. Accordingly, we endorse the Vice Chancellor's well-reasoned analysis that the NCS board's action before the hostile bid emerged was within the bounds of its fiduciary duties under these facts.

We share with the Majority and the independent NCS board of directors the motivation to serve carefully and in good faith the best interests of the corporate enterprise and, thereby, the stockholders of NCS. It is now known, of course, after the case is over, that the stockholders of NCS will receive substantially more by tendering their shares into the topping bid of Omnicare than they would have received in the Genesis merger, as a result of the post-agreement Omnicare bid and the injunctive relief ordered by the Majority of this Court. Our jurisprudence cannot, however, be seen as turning on such ex post felicitous results. Rather, the NCS board's good faith decision must be subject to a real-time review of the board action before the NCS-Genesis merger agreement was entered into.

\* \* \*

When Omnicare submitted its conditional eleventh-hour bid, the NCS board had to weigh the economic terms of the proposal against the uncertainty of completing a deal with Omnicare. Importantly, because Omnicare's bid was conditioned on its satisfactorily completing its due diligence review of NCS, the NCS board saw this as a crippling condition, as did the Ad Hoc Committee. As a matter of business

---

differences of opinion about the law [are] . . . never compromised for the sake of unanimity." Randy J. Holland & David A. Skeel, Jr., *Deciding Cases Without Controversy*, 5 Del. L. Rev. 115, 118 (2002).

judgment, the risk of negotiating with Omnicare and losing Genesis at that point outweighed the possible benefits. The lock-up was indisputably a sine qua non to any deal with Genesis.

A lock-up permits a target board and a bidder to "exchange certainties." Certainty itself has value. The acquirer may pay a higher price for the target if the acquirer is assured consummation of the transaction. The target company also benefits from the certainty of completing a transaction with a bidder because losing an acquirer creates the perception that a target is damaged goods, thus reducing its value.

\* \* \*

While the present case does not involve an attempt to hold on to only one interested bidder, the NCS board was equally concerned about "exchanging certainties" with Genesis. If the creditors decided to force NCS into bankruptcy, which could have happened at any time as NCS was unable to service its obligations, the stockholders would have received nothing. The NCS board also did not know if the NCS business prospects would have declined again, leaving NCS less attractive to other bidders, including Omnicare, which could have changed its mind and again insisted on an asset sale in bankruptcy.

Situations will arise where business realities demand a lock-up so that wealth-enhancing transactions may go forward. Accordingly, any bright-line rule prohibiting lock-ups could, in circumstances such as these, chill otherwise permissible conduct.

### Our Jurisprudence Does Not Compel This Court to Invalidate the Joint Action of the Board and the Controlling Stockholders

The Majority invalidates the NCS board's action by announcing a new rule that represents an extension of our jurisprudence. That new rule can be narrowly stated as follows: A merger agreement entered into after a market search, before any prospect of a topping bid has emerged, which locks up stockholder approval and does not contain a "fiduciary out" provision, is per se invalid when a later significant topping bid emerges. As we have noted, this bright-line, per se rule would apply regardless of (1) the circumstances leading up to the agreement and (2) the fact that stockholders who control voting power had irrevocably committed themselves, as stockholders, to vote for the merger. Narrowly stated, this new rule is a judicially-created "third rail" that now becomes one of the given "rules of the game," to be taken into account by the negotiators and drafters of merger agreements. In our view, this new rule is an unwise extension of existing precedent.

\* \* \*

The Vice Chancellor held that the NCS directors satisfied *Unocal*. He even held that they would have satisfied *Revlon*, if it had applied, which it did not. Indeed, he concluded — based on the undisputed record and his considerable experience — that: "The overall quality of testimony given by the NCS directors is among the strongest this court has ever seen. All four NCS directors were deposed, and each deposition makes manifest the care and attention given to this project by every member of the board." We agree fully with the Vice Chancellor's findings and conclusions, and we would have affirmed the judgment of the Court of Chancery on that basis.

\* \* \*

The Majority — incorrectly, in our view — relies on *Unitrin* to advance its analysis. The discussion of "draconian" measures in *Unitrin* dealt with unilateral board action, a repurchase program, designed to fend off an existing hostile offer by American General. In *Unitrin* we recognized the need to police preclusive and coercive actions initiated by the board to delay or retard an existing hostile bid so as to ensure that the stockholders can benefit from the board's negotiations with the bidder or others and to exercise effectively the franchise as the ultimate check on board action. *Unitrin* polices the effect of board action on existing tender offers and proxy contests to ensure that the board cannot permanently impose its will on the stockholders, leaving the stockholders no recourse to their voting rights.

The very measures the Majority cites as "coercive" were approved by Shaw and Outcalt through the lens of their independent assessment of the merits of the transaction. The proper inquiry in this case is whether the NCS board had taken actions that "have the effect of causing the stockholders to vote in favor of the proposed transaction for some reason other than the merits of that transaction." Like the termination fee upheld as a valid liquidated damages clause against a claim of coercion in *Brazen v. Bell Atlantic Corp.*, the deal protection measures at issue here were "an integral part of the merits of the transaction" as the NCS board struggled to secure — and did secure — the only deal available.

Outcalt and Shaw were fully informed stockholders. As the NCS controlling stockholders, they made an informed choice to commit their voting power to the merger. The minority stockholders were deemed to know that when controlling stockholders have 65% of the vote they can approve a merger without the need for the minority votes. Moreover, to the extent a minority stockholder may have felt "coerced" to vote for the merger, which was already a fait accompli, it was a meaningless coercion — or no coercion at all — because the controlling votes, those of Outcalt and Shaw, were already "cast." Although the fact that the controlling votes were committed to the merger "precluded" an overriding vote against the merger by the Class A stockholders, the pejorative "preclusive" label applicable in a *Unitrin* fact situation has no application here. Therefore, there was no meaningful minority stockholder voting decision to coerce.

In applying *Unocal* scrutiny, we believe the Majority incorrectly preempted the proportionality inquiry. In our view, the proportionality inquiry must account for the reality that the contractual measures protecting this merger agreement were necessary to obtain the Genesis deal. The Majority has not demonstrated that the director action was a disproportionate response to the threat posed. Indeed, it is clear to us that the board action to negotiate the best deal reasonably available with the only viable merger partner (Genesis) who could satisfy the creditors and benefit the stockholders, was reasonable in relation to the threat, by any practical yardstick.

### An Absolute Lock-up is Not a Per Se Violation of Fiduciary Duty

We respectfully disagree with the Majority's conclusion that the NCS board breached its fiduciary duties to the Class A stockholders by failing to negotiate a "fiduciary out" in the Genesis merger agreement. What is the practical import of a "fiduciary out?" It is a contractual provision, articulated in a manner to be negotiated, that would permit the board of the corporation being acquired to exit without breaching the merger agreement in the event of a superior offer.

In this case, Genesis made it abundantly clear early on that it was willing to negotiate a deal with NCS but only on the condition that it would not be a "stalking horse." Thus, it wanted to be certain that a third party could not use its deal with NCS as a floor against which to begin a bidding war. As a result of this negotiating position, a "fiduciary out" was not acceptable to Genesis. The Majority Opinion holds that such a negotiating position, if implemented in the agreement, is invalid per se where there is an absolute lock-up. We know of no authority in our jurisprudence supporting this new rule, and we believe it is unwise and unwarranted.

*     *     *

The Majority also mistakenly relies on our decision in *QVC* to support the notion that the NCS board should have retained a fiduciary out to save the minority stockholder from Shaw's and Outcalt's voting agreements. Our reasoning in *QVC*, which recognizes that minority stockholders must rely for protection on the fiduciary duties owed to them by directors, does not create a special duty to protect the minority stockholders from the consequences of a controlling stockholder's ultimate decision unless the controlling stockholder stands on both sides of the transaction, which is certainly not the case here. Indeed, the discussion of a minority stockholders' lack of voting power in *QVC* notes the importance of enhanced scrutiny in change of control transactions precisely because the minority stockholders' interest in the newly merged entity thereafter will hinge on the course set by the controlling stockholder. In *QVC*, Sumner Redstone owned 85% of the voting stock of Viacom, the surviving corporation. Unlike the stockholders who are confronted with a transaction that will relegate them to a minority status in the corporation, the Class A stockholders of NCS purchased stock knowing that the Charter provided Class B stockholders voting control.

### Conclusion

It is regrettable that the Court is split in this important case. One hopes that the Majority rule announced here — though clearly erroneous in our view — will be interpreted narrowly and will be seen as sui generis. By deterring bidders from engaging in negotiations like those present here and requiring that there must always be a fiduciary out, the universe of potential bidders who could reasonably be expected to benefit stockholders could shrink or disappear. Nevertheless, if the holding is confined to these unique facts, negotiators may be able to navigate around this new hazard.

Accordingly, we respectfully dissent.

STEELE, JUSTICE, dissenting.

I respectfully dissent from the majority opinion, join the Chief Justice's dissent in all respects and dissent separately in order to crystallize the central focus of my objection to the majority view.

I would affirm the Vice Chancellor's holding denying injunctive relief.

Here the board of directors acted selflessly pursuant to a careful, fair process and determined in good faith that the benefits to the stockholders and corporation flowing from a merger agreement containing reasonable deal protection provisions outweigh any speculative benefits that might result from entertaining a putative higher offer. A court asked to examine the decisionmaking process of the board should decline to interfere with the consummation and execution of an otherwise valid contract.

In my view, the Vice Chancellor's unimpeachable factual findings preclude further judicial scrutiny of the NCS board's business judgment that the hotly negotiated terms of its merger agreement were necessary in order to save the company from financial collapse, repay creditors and provide some benefits to NCS stockholders.

*     *     *

In my opinion, Delaware law mandates deference under the business judgment rule to a board of directors' decision that is free from self interest, made with due care and in good faith.

> Under Delaware law, the business judgment rule is the offspring of the fundamental principle, codified in § 141(a), that the business and affairs of a Delaware corporation are managed by or under its board of directors . . . . The business judgment rule exists to protect and promote the full and free exercise of the managerial power granted to Delaware directors.[15]

Importantly, *Smith v. Van Gorkom*, correctly casts the focus on any court review of board action challenged for alleged breach of the fiduciary duty of care "only upon the basis of the information then reasonably available to the directors and relevant to their decision . . . ." Though criticized particularly for the imposition of personal liability on directors for a breach of the duty of care, *Van Gorkom* still stands for the importance of recognizing the limited circumstances for court intervention and the importance of focusing on the timing of the decision attacked.

The majority concludes that *Unocal*'s intermediate standard of review compels judicial interference to determine whether contract terms, that the majority refers to at various times as "deal protection devices," "defensive devices," "defensive measures" or "structural safety devices," are preclusive and coercive. The majority's conclusion substantially departs from both a common sense appraisal of the contextual landscape of this case and Delaware case law applying the *Unocal* standard.

*     *     *

---

[15] [117] Smith v. Van Gorkom, 488 A.2d 858, 872 (Del. 1985).

We should not encourage proscriptive rules that invalidate or render unenforceable precommitment strategies negotiated between two parties to a contract who will presumably, in the absence of conflicted interest, bargain intensely over every meaningful provision of a contract after a careful cost benefit analysis. Where could this plain common sense approach be more wisely invoked than where a board, free of conflict, fully informed, supported by the equally conflict-free holders of the largest economic interest in the transaction, reaches the conclusion that a voting lockup strategy is the best course to obtain the most benefit for all stockholders?

This fundamental principle of Delaware law so eloquently put in the Chief Justice's dissent, is particularly applicable here where the NCS board had no alternative if the company were to be saved. If attorneys counseling well motivated, careful, and well-advised boards cannot be assured that their clients' decision — sound at the time but later less economically beneficial only because of post-decision, unforeseeable events — will be respected by the courts, Delaware law, and the courts that expound it, may well be questioned. I would not shame the NCS board, which acted in accordance with every fine instinct that we wish to encourage, by invalidating their action approving the Genesis merger because they failed to insist upon a fiduciary out. I use "shame" here because the majority finds no breach of loyalty or care but nonetheless sanctions these directors for their failure to insist upon a fiduciary out as if those directors had no regard for the effect of their otherwise disinterested, careful decision on others. The majority seeks to deter future boards from similar conduct by declaring that agreements negotiated under similar circumstances will be unenforceable.

Delaware corporate citizens now face the prospect that in every circumstance, boards must obtain the highest price, even if that requires breaching a contract entered into at a time when no one could have reasonably foreseen a truly "Superior Proposal." The majority's proscriptive rule limits the scope of a board's cost benefit analysis by taking the bargaining chip of foregoing a fiduciary out "off the table" in all circumstances. For that new principle to arise from the context of this case, when Omnicare, after striving to buy NCS on the cheap by buying off its creditors, slinked back into the fray, reversed its historic antagonistic strategy and offered a conditional "Superior Proposal" seems entirely counterintuitive.

*    *    *

Lockup provisions attempt to assure parties that have lost business opportunities and incurred substantial costs that their deal will close. I am concerned that the majority decision will remove the certainty that adds value to any rational business plan. Perhaps transactions that include "force-the-vote" and voting agreement provisions that make approval a foregone conclusion will be the only deals invalidated prospectively. Even so, therein lies the problem. Instead of thoughtful, retrospective, restrained flexibility focused on the circumstances existing at the time of the decision, have we now moved to a bright line regulatory alternative?

For the majority to articulate and adopt an inflexible rule where a board has discharged both its fiduciary duty of loyalty and care in good faith seems a most unfortunate turn. Does the majority mean to signal a mandatory, bright line, per se efficient breach analysis ex post to all challenged merger agreements? Knowing the majority's general, genuine concern to do equity, I trust not. If so, our courts and the structure of our law that we have strived so hard to develop and perfect will prevent a board, responsible under Delaware law to make precisely the kind of decision made here, in good faith, free of self-interest, after exercising scrupulous due care from honoring its contract obligations.

Therefore, I respectfully dissent.

## STAR CELLULAR TELEPHONE CO., INC. v. BATON ROUGE CGSA, INC.
### Court of Chancery of Delaware
### 1993 Del. Ch. LEXIS 158 (July 30, 1993)

JACOBS, VICE CHANCELLOR

The plaintiffs, Star Cellular Telephone Company, Inc. ("Star") and Capitol Cellular, Inc. ("Capitol"), are limited partners in Baton Rouge MSA Limited Partnership, a Delaware limited partnership formed in 1984 (the "Partnership"). The original general partner (and a limited partner) of the Partnership was Baton Rouge CGSA Inc. ("Baton Rouge Inc."), formerly a wholly owned subsidiary of BellSouth Mobility Inc. ("BellSouth"). In December 1991, Baton Rouge Inc. was merged into Louisiana CGSA Inc. ("Louisiana Inc."), another wholly owned subsidiary of BellSouth. On April 3, 1992, the plaintiffs brought this action against Baton Rouge Inc. and Louisiana Inc., claiming that the merger effected an impermissible transfer of Baton Rouge Inc.'s general partnership interest under the Partnership's limited partnership agreement. The plaintiffs contend that as a consequence Capitol is now the validly elected general partner. They seek an injunction directing the defendants to cooperate in the transfer of control of the Partnership's assets from Louisiana Inc. to Capitol.

On August 14, 1992, the plaintiffs moved for summary judgment, and the defendants cross-moved for summary judgment on January 12, 1993. Oral argument was heard on April 30, 1993. This is the Opinion of the Court on the cross-motions for summary judgment.

\*     \*     \*

The seeds of this dispute were planted in 1987, when United States Cellular Corporation ("USCC"), a principal competitor of BellSouth, gained control of the limited partnership interests of East Ascension and StarTel. Originally, Baton Rouge Inc. owned a 40% general partnership interest and an 8% limited partnership interest in the Partnership, while East Ascension owned a 27.5% limited partnership interest and StarTel owned a 24.5% limited partnership interest. USCC acquired East Ascension's interest in the Partnership through Capitol, an indirect subsidiary of East Ascension, in a series of transactions. East Ascension transferred its limited partnership interest to Capitol in 1987, and in 1988, USCC acquired all of the stock of Capitol's parent, Data and Telecommunications, Inc. By a similarly complex series of transactions, USCC also gained control of the limited partnership interest formerly owned by StarTel. On September 28, 1987, the Agreement was amended to reflect East Ascension's and StarTel's withdrawal from the Partnership, and the substitution of plaintiffs Capitol and Star as limited partners.

## The Merger

Through 1991 the Partnership operated without controversy. On December 9, 1991, BellSouth, motivated by tax considerations, decided to merge three of its subsidiaries that provided cellular telephone service in Louisiana: New Orleans CGSA, Inc. ("New Orleans Inc."); Lafayette CGSA, Inc. ("Lafayette Inc."); and Baton Rouge Inc. Both Lafayette Inc. and Baton Rouge Inc. were general partners in partnerships that had received FCC licenses, while New Orleans Inc. had received (and held) its license directly. All three BellSouth subsidiaries were incorporated in Georgia, and their merger became effective on December 31, 1991 (the "Merger"). In the Merger, Lafayette Inc. changed its name to Louisiana Inc., which became the surviving entity.

Before the Merger, all three subsidiaries had previously contracted with BellSouth for BellSouth to operate their respective cellular telephone businesses. After the Merger, those contracts remained in force. Before the Merger, the officers and directors of all three subsidiaries were identical, and all but one were officers and directors of BellSouth. After the Merger, those same officers and directors continued to serve in the same respective capacities on behalf of Louisiana Inc. No change in the business practices, policies, or procedures governing the three service areas was contemplated, and after the Merger no such changes have occurred.

## Post-Merger Events

The defendants never sought the plaintiffs' advance approval of the Merger. Not until January 24, 1993 did BellSouth and the defendants directly notify the plaintiffs and USCC that the Merger had taken place. On that date, BellSouth's counsel sent to Mr. Randy Jenkins of USCC a letter referencing "a merger effected on December 31, 1991 which merged Baton Rouge CGSA, Inc. with and into its affiliate Louisiana CGSA, Inc. . . . ." (Jenkins Aff. Ex. A). BellSouth's letter requested that Capitol and Star sign an attached proposed Amendment #2 to the Agreement, which reflected the Merger and the substitution of Louisiana Inc. as general partner. Mr. Jenkins did not respond to BellSouth's letter. BellSouth sent a similar letter to USCC on March 9, 1992, but again received no response.

Instead, Capitol sent a letter to the defendants on March 30, 1992, informing them that Star and Capitol, as the Partnership's remaining partners, had "unanimously voted not to permit a transfer or assignment of Baton Rouge CGSA Inc.'s partnership interest to Louisiana CGSA Inc." (App. of Exs., Ex. 40.) The letter stated that Star and Capitol had voted not to continue the business of the Partnership with Louisiana Inc. as general partner, but instead had appointed and designated Capitol as the new general partner. Capitol also offered to purchase the partnership interests previously held by Baton Rouge Inc., noted that it may not be required to compensate the defendants under the Agreement, and demanded that BellSouth and its affiliates (including the defendants) turn over all records relating to the Partnership.

The defendants and BellSouth rejected that request. The plaintiffs then filed this action to compel the defendants' cooperation in the transfer of control of the Partnership assets, including the FCC license, from Louisiana Inc. to Capitol.

## THE CONTENTIONS AND APPLICABLE STANDARD

Central to this case is the plaintiffs' claim that the Merger constituted a prohibited "transfer" of Baton Rouge's general partnership interest under the Agreement and the Delaware Revised Uniform Limited Partnership Act. Plaintiffs contend that the legal effect of the Merger was to trigger the withdrawal of Baton Rouge Inc. from the Partnership, and the plaintiffs'right to elect Capitol as the new general partner. In support of their claim, the plaintiffs rely principally on Sections 13.1 and 13.2 of the Agreement, which state as follows:

13.1 Assignment. The General Partner may transfer or assign its General Partner's Interest only after written notice to all the other Partners and the unanimous vote of all the other Partners to permit such transfer and to continue the business of the Partnership with the assignee of the General Partner as General Partner. Any such transfer or assignment shall be subject to required regulatory approval. The General Partner shall not admit any additional General Partner into the Partnership without the unanimous approval of all Limited Partners.

13.2 Withdrawal. Withdrawal of the General Partner (which will also be deemed its withdrawal as a Limited Partner) will cause the dissolution and termination of the Partnership in accordance with the terms of Article XIV except in the case of assignments as provided in Sections 3.1 and 13.1 unless it is continued by the unanimous consent of the remaining Partners given within ninety days thereafter . . . .

The defendants respond that the Merger was permissible under the Agreement, because (i) under Georgia law the Merger did not constitute a "transfer"; (ii) even if the Merger was a "transfer," it was authorized under Section 11.1 of the Agreement; (iii) Section 13.1 cannot be enforced against a transfer that has no adverse effect on the other contracting party; and (iv) 6 Del. C. § 17-705 authorized Louisiana Inc., as legal successor to Baton Rouge Inc., to exercise the Baton Rouge's powers as general partner. The defendants also advance several reasons why, from a procedural standpoint, the plaintiffs are not entitled to summary judgment. They argue that they should be given additional time to discover facts pertaining to the affirmative defenses of estoppel, waiver, and laches. They contend also that USCC's past inequitable conduct, specifically its surreptitious acquisition of the limited partnership interests in 1987 and 1988, bars the plaintiffs from summary judgment relief. Lastly, the defendants urge the Court to invoke the doctrine of primary jurisdiction and stay its hand until the FCC first determines whether USCC violated federal law when it acquired the limited partnership interests in 1987.

Summary judgment will be granted where the pleadings, affidavits, and other proofs show that there is no genuine issue as to any material fact and the moving party is entitled to judgment as a matter of law. Ch. Ct. R. 56(c). All factual inferences must be taken against the moving party who bears the burden of proving clearly the absence of any genuine issue of fact. *Brown v. Ocean Drilling & Exploration Co.*, Del. Supr., 403 A.2d 1114, 1115 (1979); *Nash v. Connell*, Del. Ch., 99 A.2d 242, 243 (1953). Because the Court concludes that the plaintiffs have failed to establish a legal basis for their claim, the plaintiffs' summary judgment motion must be denied and the defendants' cross-motion for summary judgment must be granted. It therefore becomes unnecessary to address the defendants' affirmative defenses and related procedural arguments.

## THE APPLICABILITY OF THE ANTITRANSFER CLAUSE

### A.

In arguing that the Merger violated the anti-transfer clause of the Agreement, the plaintiffs reason as follows: Section 13.1 of the Agreement forbids a "transfer" of the general partner's partnership interest without the approval of the other partners;[16] the Merger is a transfer; the other partners' approval was neither sought nor obtained; therefore, the Agreement was violated. That argument fails, in my opinion, because under applicable principles of contract interpretation, the word "transfer" cannot be read to encompass the Merger.

The plaintiffs' claim rests entirely upon their position that "transfer" must be given its broadest possible construction. All mergers are "transfers," plaintiffs say, because "transfer" includes any and all transactions whereby title passes from one party to another, regardless of the transaction's form (e.g., whether it be a merger or a sale of assets), and irrespective of whether the transaction adversely affects the other contracting parties. Both sides agree that the outcome turns on the meaning to be given the word "transfer" as used in Section 13.1 of the Agreement, and specifically, whether "transfer" includes the Merger. To arrive at an answer, the Court must analyze Section 13.1's anti-transfer clause in light of applicable contract principles. The Agreement provides that its interpretation will be governed by Delaware law.

Under Delaware law, when interpreting a contractual provision, a court must direct its "attention . . . to the meaning of the written terms in light of the surrounding circumstances." *Klair v. Reese*, Del. Supr., 531 A.2d 219, 223 (1987). "The primary search is for the common meaning of the parties, not a meaning imposed on them by law." *Id.* The starting point must be the language of the Agreement itself. *Citadel Holding Corp. v. Roven*, Del. Supr., 60 A.2d 818, 822 (1992). "If a writing is plain or clear on its face, there is no room for interpretation, construction, or a search for the intent of the parties." *Klair v. Reese*, 531 A.2d at 223. The "plain meaning" of a contract is its "generally prevailing meaning." *Id.* Thus, the Court must first determine whether the term "transfer" has a plain or generally prevailing meaning. If it does, then no other evidence need be considered.

Because I conclude that "transfer" has no generally prevailing meaning, I next turn to other provisions of the Agreement, including its recitals, to divine the

---

[16] [7] Section 13.1 of the Agreement employs the phrase "transfer or assign." The litigants do not distinguish between "transfers" and "assignments," but they focus solely upon whether the Merger was a "transfer." The plaintiffs also cite 6 Del. C. §§ 17-402, 17-702, and 17-801, which concern the withdrawal of the general partner and the assignment of the general partner's interest in a limited partnership. For the same reasons that the merger is not a "transfer" under Section 13.1, I find that the Merger did not effect an "assignment" within the meaning of § 17-702. Therefore, no "event of withdrawal" occurred under § 17-402 or § 17-801, such as would permit the election of a new general partner.

parties' intent. *Citadel Holding Corp.*, 603 A.2d at 823; *see E.I. du Pont de Nemours & Co., Inc. v. Shell Oil Co.*, Del. Supr., 498 A.2d 1108, 1113 (1985). I also examine the extrinsic evidence upon which the parties rely. *See Klair v. Reese*, 531 A.2d at 223. Those avenues likewise turn out to be unhelpful. As later discussed, the extrinsic evidence does not support either the plaintiffs' broad reading, or the defendants' narrower interpretation, of the word "transfer." Therefore, and lastly, the Court attempts to determine the contracting parties' likely intent by resorting to an interpretation of Section 13.1 grounded on principles fundamental to the law of assignments. *See id.*, 531 A.2d at 223–24. Based on that analysis I conclude that the plaintiffs' broad reading of "transfer" cannot be accepted, and that Section 13.1's prohibition against "transfers" cannot be interpreted to encompass the Merger.

### B.

The critical language of Section 13.1 is that which states that the general partner (Baton Rouge Inc.) may "transfer" its interest as a general partner "only after written notice to all the other Partners and the unanimous vote of all the other Partners to permit such transfer[.]" The dictionary definitions of "transfer," the differing judicial interpretations given to that word, and the scholarly commentary, all lead me to conclude that the word "transfer" has no plain or generally prevailing meaning.

The dictionary definition of "transfer" (when used as a verb) is:

> To convey or remove from one place, person, etc., to another; pass or hand over from one to another; specifically, to change over the possession or control of (as, to transfer a title to land).To sell or give.

BLACK'S LAW DICTIONARY 1497 (6th ed. 1990). The dictionary definition of "transfer" (when used as a noun) is more expansive:

> An act of the parties, or of the law, by which the title to property is conveyed from one person to another. The sale and every other method, direct or indirect, of disposing of or parting with property or with an interest therein . . . . The word is one of general meaning and may include the act of giving property by will.

*Id.* The principal difference between these definitions is that only the latter one includes the concept that transfers may occur by operation of law, such as a merger, as well as by voluntary acts, such as a sale or gift.

In this particular case, when Baton Rouge Inc. merged into Louisiana Inc., its interest in the Partnership passed to the surviving corporation by operation of law (Ga. Code. Ann. § 14-2-1106(a)(2) (Michie 1989)), as distinguished from passage of title by an express act such as a sale or gift. The distinction between an express transfer by sale or gift and a transfer by operation of law is significant in the realm of corporate law. *See Sterling v. Mayflower Hotel Corp.*, Del. Supr., 93 A.2d 107, 112 (1952) (merger "something quite distinct" from a sale of assets); *Torrey Delivery Inc. v. Chautauqua Truck Sales and Service, Inc.*, N.Y. Supr., 366 N.Y.S.2d 506, 510–11 (1975) (merger not a "sale" since corporate property not affected). And it has ramifications here, because if "transfer" were construed to mean only "to sell" or "to give" or any similar voluntary act, then Section 13.1 would not prohibit a transfer by operation of law, such as the Merger. On the other hand, if "transfer" were given the plaintiffs' broad meaning, it would encompass transfers by operation of law, including mergers. That distinction has generated a conflict in the decisions.

When interpreting the scope of so-called "anti-assignment" clauses in contracts, some courts have distinguished between transfers that occur by express, voluntary act and those that occur by operation of law. Other courts have not. *Compare, e.g., Dodier Realty & Inv. Co. v. St. Louis Nat'l Baseball Club, Inc.*, Mo. Supr., 238 S.W.2d 321, 325 (1951) (en banc) ("The merged corporation having succeeded to the rights of the original lessee by operation of law, it follows that there was no assignment [or transfer] within the prohibition of the covenant in question[.]") *with PPG Indus., Inc. v. Guardian Indus. Corp.*, 6th Cir., 597 F.2d 1090, 1096 ("A transfer is no less a transfer because it takes place by operation of law rather than by a particular act of the parties. The merger was effected by the parties and the transfer was a result of their act of merging."), *cert. denied*, 444 U.S. 930 (1979).[17] Some scholars have criticized those decisions that mechanically interpret "transfer" to include all mergers. *See* Ballew, *The Assignment of Rights, Franchises, and Obligations of the Disappearing Corporation in a Merger*, 38 Bus. Law. 45, 59 (1982); Note, *Effect of Merger and Consolidation on Property, Rights and Franchises of the Constituent Corporations* 38 Va. L. Rev. 496, 510 (1952) [hereinafter Virginia Note]; Note, *Effect of Corporate Reorganization on Nonassignable Contracts*, 74 Harv. L. Rev. 393, 394–96 (1960) [hereinafter Harvard Note].

Even under Georgia law, which governs the legal effect of the Merger upon the property and other rights of the three merged BellSouth subsidiaries, the legal status of a merger under an anti-assignment clause is less than clear. One Georgia court noted a split of authority regarding whether a Georgia merger breached a covenant barring assignments, but decided the case on other grounds. *See Albemarle, Inc. v. Eaton Corp.*, Ga. Ct. App., 357 S.E.2d 887, 888 (1987). The current Georgia merger statute, § 14-2-1106(a)(2), does not employ the term "transfer." Rather, it provides that the property of the disappearing corporation "is vested in the surviving corporation," and the unofficial comment to that section states that "[a] merger is not a conveyance or transfer[.]" However, the comment also purports not to substantially change the prior, superseded merger statute (§ 14-2-216 of the 1982 Georgia Code), which provided that all property of the merged corporation "shall be taken and deemed to be transferred to and vested in the surviving corporation without further act or deed[.]" *Imperial Enters., Inc. v. Fireman's Fund Ins. Co.*, 5th Cir., 535 F.2d 287, 291 (1976), further evidences the unsettled state of the law on this question. There the Fifth Circuit, applying Georgia law, held that a transfer of an insurance policy pursuant to a Georgia statutory merger did not violate an anti-assignment clause in the policy, and did not thereby defeat

---

[17] [8] Plaintiffs argue that these differing results may be explained in terms of the substantive rights in dispute. They contend that for public policy reasons courts strictly construe anti-transfer provisions in real estate leases (such as in Dodier, but loosely construe identical provisions in all other contracts (such as the patent license in PPG). However, that distinction does not easily harmonize all the cases. *See, e.g., Farmland Irrigation Co. v. Dopplmaier*, Cal. Supr., 308 P.2d 732, 740 (1957) (rejecting the presumption that patent licenses are not transferable unless the license explicitly so states and favoring the transferability of all types of property.)

coverage. The Court stated that it was "unable to conclude that the no-assignment provision unambiguously and unquestionably applied to this transfer [by operation of law]." *Id.* at 292–93.

Because of the existing uncertainty in the law when the Agreement was drafted, the word "transfer" did not then (and does not now) have a plain or generally prevailing meaning. It therefore must be inferred that had the parties contemplated this specific dispute and intended to prohibit all mergers under Section 13.1, they would likely have not chosen the unaided term "transfer" to express that intent. Rather, they would have specifically addressed mergers, or they would have provided by appropriate language that "transfer" means all transfers, including those arising by operation of law. In either case the Merger would fall within Section 13.1's prohibitory scope. *Citizens Bank & Trust Co. of Md. v. Barlow Corp.*, Md. Ct. App., 456 A.2d 1283, 1289 (1983). *Cf. Standard Operations, Inc. v. Montague*, Mo. Supr., 758 S.W.2d 442, 444 (1988) (en banc). However, as actually written, Section 13.1 does not plainly and unambiguously include mergers within the category of prohibited "transfers."

Arguing the contrary, the plaintiffs suggest that because the "whereas" recitals in the Agreement refer to the FCC, the Court ought to consider the FCC Application for Transfer of Control, which evidences that the parties to the Merger regarded it as a "transfer." But nothing in the Agreement's recitals persuasively establishes that the parties intended to define "transfer" in Section 13.1 by reference to the federal regulatory concept of "transfer of control."

In addition to the provisions of the Agreement, the Court has considered the extrinsic evidence, but that evidence also does not aid the plaintiffs' cause.

*　*　*

Anti-assignment clauses are normally included in contracts to prevent the introduction of a stranger into the contracting parties' relationship and to assure performance by the original contracting parties. In some business relationships the continued personal involvement of an original contracting party is a material premise of the contract itself. In such cases any assignment is problematic. In other cases the parties fear that the assignee will either not perform or will perform inadequately, in which case what is problematic is not the assignment per se but the identity of the assignee. The Restatement addresses both concerns:

> Unless otherwise agreed, a promise requires performance by a particular person only to the extent that the obligee has a substantial interest in having that person perform or control the acts promised.

Courts that have addressed whether a merger violates an anti-assignment clause have looked to these assignment law principles either explicitly or implicitly. *See* Ballew, *supra*, at 55, 59; 6 AM. JUR. 2d *Assignments* § 22 (1963). From those principles it may reasonably be concluded that where an anti-transfer clause in a contract does not explicitly prohibit a transfer of property rights to a new entity by a merger, and where performance by the original contracting party is not a material condition and the transfer itself creates no unreasonable risks for the other contracting parties, the court should not presume that the parties intended to prohibit the merger.

The interpretation of "transfer" which results from this analysis makes no bright-line distinction between permissible and impermissible transfers. The distinction does not rest upon whether the transaction occurred by operation of law, or upon whether the operative transaction was (or was not) a merger. Nor can the distinction be expressed in a single word or phrase. Some mergers would be permitted, while others would not be. To express it in terms of this case, for the Merger not to be a "transfer" prohibited by Section 13.1, it must not create unreasonable risks for the plaintiffs, and performance by Baton Rouge Inc. must not have been a material premise of the Agreement. The question is whether the Merger satisfies these criteria. I find that it does.

The plaintiffs urge that had the parties to the Agreement contemplated the Merger, they would have intended to prohibit it, because the performance obligations of the general partner are inherently personal and because the Merger would cause "a significant change." (Pls. Op. Br., 14, n.10.) They argue that partnership law prevents a third party from becoming a partner without the express approval of the other partners. But neither the law nor the evidence supports the absolute application of that principle in all cases. Here, the Merger did not materially affect the plaintiffs' position in the Partnership or their rights under the Agreement. In such a case, and absent contract language expressly treating the point, the law should not conclusively presume that a general partner's identity is invariably a factor so inherently material that under no circumstances would the parties have intended to permit any change in that identity, however nominal or substantively inconsequential that change might be. . . .

The record establishes that the Merger did not adversely impact the plaintiffs' position or rights. After the Merger, operational control of the Partnership remained in the hands of BellSouth, which made no material changes in the Partnership's management.

\* \* \*

In short, the Merger created no material change in the control of the general partner or in the operations of the Partnership. The change was purely formal — the substitution of a new corporate entity for the entity that was the original general partner. That effected a change, to be sure, but one of legal form, not of substance. It altered none of the pre-Merger realities that were crucial to the limited partners' economic interests.

## CONCLUSION

The drafters of the Agreement could have provided that the anti-transfer clause of Section 13.1 would apply to all transfers, including those (such as the Merger) arising by operation of law. They did not. Instead, they used, with no modification, a term ("transfer") that has no plain, settled meaning. No relevant extrinsic evidence persuasively establishes that the contracting parties intended for that word to be all inclusive. In these circumstances, the Court will not attribute to the contracting parties an intent to prohibit the Merger where the transaction did not materially increase the risks to or otherwise harm the limited partners.

# NOTE

This case illustrates a common problem with mergers. One or both of the corporations may have valuable contract rights, franchises, leases, or the like. Frequently there will be non-assignment clauses. The Delaware court's analysis is quite perceptive. The court noted that the old and new MBCAs were not helpful. In fact, the Georgia Code provisions illustrate the dilemma. The old version transfers and vests the property of the merged corporation in the surviving corporation. The new version does not use the word transfer but vests the property in the surviving corporation. The comment to the new version says no change was intended. The sensible interpretation of these merger statutes is that the property is transferred, but by operation of law. We still have the problem of determining whether a non-assignment clause applies. The court looks at the intent of the parties and whether the relationship was personal or whether the merger would cause a significant change. These factors appear far more relevant than the particular words in the merger statute. If the property interest is real estate such as a leasehold, some jurisdictions interpret anti-assignment clauses strictly based on the free alienation of real property doctrine. Those statutes would interpret the anti-assignment clause not to apply to transfers by operation of law unless the lease specifically stated so. In drafting leases with an anti-assignment clause, transfer by operation of law should always be considered. The parties should consider whether a merger into another corporation would trigger the clause.

## CODE OF LAWS OF SOUTH CAROLINA
### Title 33. Corporations, Partnerships, and Associations
### Chapter 11. Merger and Share Exchange
### S.C. Code Ann. § 33-11-106 (1996)

§ 33-11-106. Effect of merger or share exchange.

(a) When a merger takes effect:

   (1)  every other corporation party to the merger merges into the surviving entity and the separate existence of every corporation except the surviving entity ceases;

   (2)  the title to all real estate and other property owned by each corporation party to the merger is vested in the surviving entity without reversion or impairment;

   (3)  the surviving entity has all liabilities of each corporation party to the merger;

   (4)  a proceeding pending against a corporation party to the merger may be continued as if the merger did not occur or the surviving entity may be substituted in the proceeding for the corporation whose existence ceased;

   (5)  the articles of organization of the surviving entity are amended to the extent provided in the plan of merger; and

   (6)  the shares of each corporation party to the merger are converted into shares, obligations, or other securities of the surviving entity or into cash

or other property as appropriate, and the former holders of the shares are entitled only to the rights provided in the articles of merger or to their rights pursuant to Chapter 13.

(b) When a share exchange takes effect, the shares of each acquired corporation are exchanged as provided in the plan, and the former holders of the shares are entitled only to the exchange rights provided in the articles of share exchange or to their rights under Chapter 13.

## OFFICIAL COMMENT

Section 11.06 (Section 33-11-106) describes the legal consequences of a merger or share exchange on its effective date. Section 11.06(a) (Section 33-11-106(a)) describes the effect of a merger. On the effective date every disappearing corporation that is a party to the merger disappears into the surviving corporation and the surviving corporation automatically becomes the owner of all real and personal property and becomes subject to all liabilities, actual or contingent, of each disappearing corporation. A merger is not a conveyance or transfer, and does not give rise to claims of reverter or impairment of title based on a prohibited conveyance or transfer. See section 11.06(a)(2) (Section 33-11-106(a)(2)). Further, all pending litigation is continued; the name of the surviving corporation may, but need not be, substituted for the name of a disappearing corporation that is a party to litigation.

Section 11.06(a)(6) (Section 33-11-106(a)(6)) provides that if any shareholders to any party to the merger are to receive different shares or cash or property under the plan of merger, the rights of those shareholders after the articles of merger are filed are limited to their rights under the plan of merger or their rights under chapter 13 of this Act. The articles of incorporation of the surviving corporation are amended as provided in the plan of merger on the effective date of the merger. See section 11.06(a)(5) (Section 33-11-106(a)(5)).

Section 11.06(b) (Section 33-11-106(b)) describes the effect of a share exchange. On the effective date, the shareholders of the acquired class of shares cease to be shareholders of the acquired corporation. On that date they are entitled to receive only the consideration provided in the plan of share exchange, or the rights of dissenting shareholders under chapter 13.

## SOUTH CAROLINA REPORTERS' COMMENTS

The 1984 Model Act provision (Section 11.06) has been adopted unchanged. It represents no significant substantive change from Section 33-17-60 of the 1981 South Carolina Business Corporation Act.

## B.  SALE OF ASSETS

### KATZ v. BREGMAN
Court of Chancery of Delaware
431 A.2d 1274 (1981)

MARVEL, CHANCELLOR

The complaint herein seeks the entry of an order preliminarily enjoining the proposed sale of the Canadian assets of Plant Industries, Inc. to Vulcan Industrial Packaging, Ltd., the plaintiff Hyman Katz allegedly being the owner of approximately 170,000 shares of common stock of the defendant Plant Industries, Inc., on whose behalf he has brought this action, suing not only for his own benefit as a stockholder but for the alleged benefit of all other record owners of common stock of the defendant Plant Industries, Inc. However, it is contended by defendants that Mr. Katz having been a former chief executive officer of Plant Industries, Inc. and allegedly involved in litigation with present management of the corporate defendant is accordingly disqualified to sue derivatively or for a class. Nonetheless, he would appear to be qualified to sue individually as a stockholder of Plant Industries, Inc. for the relief sought. Significantly, at common law, a sale of all or substantially all of the assets of a corporation required the unanimous vote of the stockholders.

The complaint alleges that during the last six months of 1980, the board of directors of Plant Industries, Inc., under the guidance of the individual defendant Robert B. Bregman, the present chief executive officer of such corporation, embarked on a course of action which resulted in the disposal of several unprofitable subsidiaries of the corporate defendant located in the United States, namely Louisiana Foliage Inc., a horticultural business, Sunaid Food Products, Inc., a Florida packaging business, and Plant Industries (Texas), Inc., a business concerned with the manufacture of woven synthetic cloth. As a result of these sales Plant Industries, Inc. by the end of 1980 had disposed of a significant part of its unprofitable assets.

According to the complaint, Mr. Bregman thereupon proceeded on a course of action designed to dispose of a subsidiary of the corporate defendant known as Plant National (Quebec) Ltd., a business which constitutes Plant Industries, Inc.'s entire business operation in Canada and has allegedly constituted Plant's only income producing facility during the past four years. The professed principal purpose of such proposed sale is to raise needed cash and thus improve Plant's balance sheets. And while interest in purchasing the corporate defendant's Canadian plant was thereafter evinced not only by Vulcan Industrial Packaging, Ltd. but also by Universal Drum Reconditioning Co., which latter corporation originally undertook to match or approximate and recently to top Vulcan's bid, a formal contract was entered into between Plant Industries, Inc. and Vulcan on April 2, 1981 for the purchase and sale of Plant National (Quebec) despite the constantly increasing bids for the same property being made by Universal. One reason advanced by Plant's management for declining to negotiate with Universal is that a firm undertaking having been entered into with Vulcan that the board of directors of Plant may not legally or ethically negotiate with Universal. . . .

In seeking injunctive relief, as prayed for, plaintiff relies on two principles, one that found in 8 Del. C. § 271 to the effect that a decision of a Delaware corporation to sell "* * * all or substantially all of its property and assets * * *" requires not only the approval of such corporation's board of directors but also a resolution adopted by a majority of the outstanding stockholders of the corporation entitled to vote thereon at a meeting duly called upon at least twenty days' notice.

Support for the other principle relied on by plaintiff for the relief sought, namely an alleged breach of fiduciary duty on the part of the board of directors of Plant Industries, Inc. allegedly found in such board's studied refusal to consider a potentially higher bid for the assets in question which is being advanced by Universal, *Thomas v. Kempner, supra.*

Turning to the possible application of 8 Del. C. § 271 to the proposed sale of substantial corporate assets of National to Vulcan, it is stated in *Gimbel v. Signal Companies, Inc.*, Del. Ch., 316 A.2d 599 (1974) as follows:

> "If the sale is of assets quantitatively vital to the operation of the corporation and is out of the ordinary and substantially affects the existence and purpose of the corporation then it is beyond the power of the Board of Directors."

According to Plant's 1980 10K form, it appears that at the end of 1980, Plant's Canadian operations represented 51% of Plant's remaining assets. Defendants also concede that National represents 44.9% of Plant's sales' revenues and 52.4% of its pre-tax net operating income. Furthermore, such report by Plant discloses, in rough figures that while National made a profit in 1978 of $2,900,000, the profit from the United States businesses in that year was only $770,000. In 1979, the Canadian business profit was $3,500,000 while the loss of the United States businesses was $344,000. Furthermore, in 1980, while the Canadian business profit was $5,300,000, the corporate loss in the United States was $4,500,000. And while these figures may be somewhat distorted by the allocation of overhead expenses and taxes, they are significant. In any event, defendants concede that "* * * National accounted for 34.9% of Plant's pre-tax income in 1976, 36.9% in 1977, 42% in 1978, 51% in 1979 and 52.4% in 1980."

\* \* \*

> "While no pertinent Pennsylvania case is cited, the critical factor in determining the character of a sale of assets is generally considered not the amount of property sold but whether the sale is in fact an unusual transaction or one made in the regular course of business of the seller \* \* \*".

Furthermore, in the case of *Wingate v. Bercut* (C.A. 9) 146 F.2d 725 (1945), in which the Court declined to apply the provisions of 8 Del. C. § 271, it was noted that the transfer of shares of stock there involved, being a dealing in securities, constituted an ordinary business transaction.

In the case at bar, I am first of all satisfied that historically the principal business of Plant Industries, Inc. has not been to buy and sell industrial facilities but rather to manufacture steel drums for use in bulk shipping as well as for the storage of petroleum products, chemicals, food, paint, adhesives and cleaning agents, a business which has been profitably performed by National of Quebec. Furthermore, the proposal, after the sale of National, to embark on the manufacture of plastic drums represents a radical departure from Plant's historically successful line of business, namely steel drums. I therefore conclude that the proposed sale of Plant's Canadian operations, which constitute over 51% of Plant's total assets and in which are generated approximately 45% of Plant's 1980 net sales, would, if consummated, constitute a sale of substantially all of Plant's assets. By way of contrast, the proposed sale of Signal Oil in *Gimbel v. Signal Companies, Inc., supra,* represented only about 26% of the total assets of Signal Companies, Inc. And while Signal Oil represented 41% of Signal Companies, Inc. total net worth, it generated only about 15% of Signal Companies, Inc. revenue and earnings.

I conclude that because the proposed sale of Plant National (Quebec) Ltd. would, if consummated, constitute a sale of substantially all of the assets of Plant Industries, Inc., as presently constituted, that an injunction should issue preventing the consummation of such sale at least until it has been approved by a majority of the outstanding stockholders of Plant Industries, Inc., entitled to vote at a meeting duly called on at least twenty days' notice.

\* \* \*

Being persuaded for the reasons stated that plaintiff has demonstrated a reasonable probability of ultimate success on final hearing in the absence of stockholder approval of the proposed sale of the corporate assets here in issue to Vulcan, a preliminary injunction against the consummation of such transaction, at least until stockholder approval is obtained, will be granted.

## C.  DE FACTO MERGERS

### HARITON v. ARCO ELECTRONICS, INC.
Supreme Court of Delaware
188 A.2d 123 (1963)

SOUTHERLAND, CHIEF JUSTICE:

This case involves a sale of assets under § 271 of the corporation law, 8 Del. C. It presents for decision the question presented, but not decided, in *Heilbrunn v. Sun Chemical Corporation*, Del., 150 A.2d 755. It may be stated as follows:

A sale of assets is effected under § 271 in consideration of shares of stock of the purchasing corporation. The agreement of sale embodies also a plan to dissolve the selling corporation and distribute the shares so received to the stockholders of the seller, so as to accomplish the same result as would be accomplished by a merger of the seller into the purchaser. Is the sale legal?

The facts are these:

The defendant Arco and Loral Electronics Corporation, a New York corporation, are both engaged, in somewhat different forms, in the electronic equipment business. In the summer of 1961 they negotiated for an amalgamation of the companies. As of October 27, 1961, they entered into a "Reorganization Agreement and Plan." The provisions of this Plan pertinent here are in substance as follows:

1. Arco agrees to sell all its assets to Loral in consideration (inter alia) of the issuance to it of 283,000 shares of Loral.

2. Arco agrees to call a stockholders meeting for the purpose of approving the Plan and the voluntary dissolution.

3. Arco agrees to distribute to its stockholders all the Loral shares received by it as a part of the complete liquidation of Arco.

At the Arco meeting all the stockholders voting (about 80%) approved the Plan. It was thereafter consummated.

Plaintiff, a stockholder who did not vote at the meeting, sued to enjoin the comsummation of the Plan on the grounds (1) that it was illegal, and (2) that it was unfair. The second ground was abandoned. Affidavits and documentary evidence were filed, and defendant moved for summary judgment and dismissal of the complaint. The Vice Chancellor granted the motion and plaintiff appeals.

The question before us we have stated above. Plaintiff's argument that the sale is illegal runs as follows:

The several steps taken here accomplish the same result as a merger of Arco into Loral. In a "true" sale of assets, the stockholder of the seller retains the right to elect whether the selling company shall continue as a holding company. Moreover, the stockholder of the selling company is forced to accept an investment in a new enterprise without the right of appraisal granted under the merger statute. § 271 cannot therefore be legally combined with a dissolution proceeding under § 275 and a consequent distribution of the purchaser's stock. Such a proceeding is a misuse of the power granted under § 271, and a de facto merger results.

The foregoing is a brief summary of plaintiff's contention.

Plaintiff's contention that this sale has achieved the same result as a merger is plainly correct. The same contention was made to us in *Heilbrunn v. Sun Chemical Corporation*, Del., 150 A.2d 755. Accepting it as correct, we noted that this result is made possible by the overlapping scope of the merger statute and section 271, mentioned in *Sterling v. Mayflower Hotel Corporation*, 33 Del. Ch. 293, 93 A.2d 107. We also adverted to the increased use, in connection with corporate reorganization plans, of § 271 instead of the merger statute. Further, we observed that no Delaware case has held such procedure to be improper, and that two cases appear to assume its legality. *Finch v. Warrior Cement Corporation*, 16 Del. Ch. 44, 141 A. 54, and *Argenbright v. Phoenix Finance Co.*, 21 Del. Ch. 288, 187 A. 124. But we were not required in the *Heilbrunn* case to decide the point.

We now hold that the reorganization here accomplished through § 271 and a mandatory plan of dissolution and distribution is legal. This is so because the sale-of-assets statute and the merger statute are independent of each other. They are, so to speak, of equal dignity, and the framers of a reorganization plan may resort to either type of corporate mechanics to achieve the desired end. This is not an anomalous result in our corporation law. As the Vice Chancellor pointed out, the elimination of accrued dividends, though forbidden under a charter amendment (*Keller v. Wilson & Co.*, 21 Del. Ch. 391, 190 A. 115) may be accomplished by a merger. *Federal United Corporation v. Havender*, 24 Del. Ch. 318, 11 A.2d 331.

In *Langfelder v. Universal Laboratories*, D.C., 68 F. Supp. 209, Judge Leahy commented upon "the general theory of the Delaware Corporation Law that action taken pursuant to the authority of the various sections of that law constitute acts of independent legal significance and their validity is not dependent on other sections of the Act." 68 F. Supp. 211, footnote.

In support of his contentions of a de facto merger plaintiff cites *Finch v. Warrior Cement Corporation*, 16 Del. Ch. 44, 141 A. 54, and *Drug Inc. v. Hunt*, (5 Harr.) 339, 168 A. 87. They are patently inapplicable. Each involved a disregard of the statutory provisions governing sales of assets. Here it is admitted that the provisions of the statute were fully complied with.

Plaintiff concedes, as we read his brief, that if the several steps taken in this case had been taken separately they would have been legal. That is, he concedes that a sale of assets, followed by a separate proceeding to dissolve and distribute, would be legal, even though the same result would follow. This concession exposes the weakness of his contention. To attempt to make any such distinction between sales under § 271 would be to create uncertainty in the law and invite litigation.

We are in accord with the Vice Chancellor's ruling, and the judgment below is affirmed.

# D.   TENDER OFFERS AND LEVERAGED BUY-OUTS

A tender offer is simply an offer to buy stock, usually by one corporation for a controlling interest in another corporation. The offeror must offer a price high enough to attract tenders. A federal statute, the Williams Act, governs tender offers. The Williams Act forces the offeror to disclose certain information about the tender offer. This makes perfect sense if the tender offer is not all cash. But many tender offers are all cash. Why would a sensible shareholder care who will buy his stock, and what the offer will do with the company afterwards? One answer is that if the tender offer is for 51% of the stock, and everyone tenders, the Williams Act compels a pro-rata purchase of all of the tenders. Thus, even if you wish to sell all of your stock, you may not accomplish that, and your remaining shares may decline in value, or you may be cashed out in a second tier merger at an unfavorable price.

The term leveraged buy-out (LBO) is virtually synonymous with a tender offer. The term *leverage* refers to the fact that most tender offers load the acquired corporation with substantial debt once the tender is over. Some LBOs that have ended in bankruptcy suggest that those in control of the corporation may incur substantial liabilities if the end result of the LBO is a debt-heavy corporation without adequate working capital. Nonetheless, tender offers have had a generally beneficial effect for most shareholders, especially institutional investors. Corporations that have substantial liquid assets are often desirable targets for takeover. Further, corporations that might increase their stock market price under new (and possibly better) management will be targets as well.

Once a corporation is "in play," the Delaware courts have suggested that the board of directors has an obligation to "auction" the corporation to the highest bidder in order to maximize shareholder value. It is clear that the directors cannot place their interests of incumbency above the interests of the shareholders. However, the courts have frequently approved transactions that had the effect of blocking tender offers or of making them more difficult.

The Williams Act amended the 1934 Act by adding sections 13(d) and (e) and 14(d), (e), and (f). Section 13(d) requires the filing of a statement with the SEC if a person acquires more than 5% of any equity security registered pursuant to section 12 of the Act. The statement must be filed within 10 days.

Section 14(d) requires that a statement be filed with the SEC for any tender offer if, after consummation, the offeror would be the beneficial owner of more than 5% of any equity security registered pursuant to section 12 of the Act.

Section 14(d)(5), (6), and (7) contain rules that regulate the terms of the tender offer. In general, the rules mandate that (1) the tender offer permit withdrawal of securities tendered for specified periods, (2) the securities be purchased pro-rata if the offer is oversubscribed, and (3) that any increase in price be paid to all shareholders tendering in the event the price is raised.

What is the purpose of these rules?

## UNOCAL CORPORATION v. MESA PETROLEUM CO.
### Supreme Court of Delaware
### 493 A.2d 946 (1985)

MOORE, J.

We confront an issue of first impression in Delaware — the validity of a corporation's self-tender for its own shares which excludes from participation a stockholder making a hostile tender offer for the company's stock.

The Court of Chancery granted a preliminary injunction to the plaintiffs, Mesa Petroleum Co., Mesa Asset Co., Mesa Partners II, and Mesa Eastern, Inc. (collectively "Mesa")[18], enjoining an exchange offer of the defendant, Unocal Corporation (Unocal) for its own stock. The trial court concluded that a selective exchange offer, excluding Mesa, was legally impermissible. We cannot agree with such a blanket rule. The factual findings of the Vice Chancellor, fully supported by the record, establish that Unocal's board, consisting of a majority of independent directors, acted in good faith, and after reasonable investigation found that Mesa's tender offer was both inadequate and coercive. Under the circumstances the board had both the power and duty to oppose a bid it perceived to be harmful to the corporate enterprise. On this record we are satisfied that the device Unocal adopted is reasonable in relation to the threat posed, and that the board acted in the proper

---

[18] [1] T. Boone Pickens, Jr., is President and Chairman of the Board of Mesa Petroleum and President of Mesa Asset and controls the related Mesa entities.

exercise of sound business judgment. We will not substitute our views for those of the board if the latter's decision can be "attributed to any rational business purpose." *Sinclair Oil Corp. v. Levien*, Del. Supr., 280 A.2d 717, 720 (1971). Accordingly, we reverse the decision of the Court of Chancery and order the preliminary injunction vacated.[19]

## I.

The factual background of this matter bears a significant relationship to its ultimate outcome.

On April 8, 1985, Mesa, the owner of approximately 13% of Unocal's stock, commenced a two-tier "front loaded" cash tender offer for 64 million shares, or approximately 37%, of Unocal's outstanding stock at a price of $54 per share. The "back-end" was designed to eliminate the remaining publicly held shares by an exchange of securities purportedly worth $54 per share. However, pursuant to an order entered by the United States District Court for the Central District of California on April 26, 1985, Mesa issued a supplemental proxy statement to Unocal's stockholders disclosing that the securities offered in the second-step merger would be highly subordinated, and that Unocal's capitalization would differ significantly from its present structure. Unocal has rather aptly termed such securities "junk bonds."

Unocal's board consists of eight independent outside directors and six insiders. It met on April 13, 1985, to consider the Mesa tender offer. Thirteen directors were present, and the meeting lasted nine and one-half hours. The directors were given no agenda or written materials prior to the session. However, detailed presentations were made by legal counsel regarding the board's obligations under both Delaware corporate law and the federal securities laws. The board then received a presentation from Peter Sachs on behalf of Goldman Sachs & Co. (Goldman Sachs) and Dillon, Read & Co. (Dillon Read) discussing the bases for their opinions that the Mesa proposal was wholly inadequate. Mr. Sachs opined that the minimum cash value that could be expected from a sale or orderly liquidation for 100% of Unocal's stock was in excess of $60 per share. In making his presentation, Mr. Sachs showed slides outlining the valuation techniques used by the financial advisors, and others, depicting recent business combinations in the oil and gas industry. The Court of Chancery found that the Sachs presentation was designed to apprise the directors of the scope of the analyses performed rather than the facts and numbers used in reaching the conclusion that Mesa's tender offer price was inadequate.

Mr. Sachs also presented various defensive strategies available to the board if it concluded that Mesa's two-step tender offer was inadequate and should be opposed. One of the devices outlined was a self-tender by Unocal for its own stock with a reasonable price range of $70 to $75 per share. The cost of such a proposal would cause the company to incur $6.1–6.5 billion of additional debt, and a presentation was made informing the board of Unocal's ability to handle it. The directors were

---

[19] [2] This appeal was heard on an expedited basis in light of the pending Mesa tender offer and Unocal exchange offer. We announced our decision to reverse in an oral ruling in open court on May 17, 1985 with the further statement that this opinion would follow shortly thereafter. *See infra* n.5.

told that the primary effect of this obligation would be to reduce exploratory drilling, but that the company would nonetheless remain a viable entity.

The eight outside directors, comprising a clear majority of the thirteen members present, then met separately with Unocal's financial advisors and attorneys. Thereafter, they unanimously agreed to advise the board that it should reject Mesa's tender offer as inadequate, and that Unocal should pursue a self-tender to provide the stockholders with a fairly priced alternative to the Mesa proposal. The board then reconvened and unanimously adopted a resolution rejecting as grossly inadequate Mesa's tender offer. Despite the nine and one-half hour length of the meeting, no formal decision was made on the proposed defensive self-tender.

On April 15, the board met again with four of the directors present by telephone and one member still absent. This session lasted two hours. Unocal's Vice President of Finance and its Assistant General Counsel made a detailed presentation of the proposed terms of the exchange offer. A price range between $70 and $80 per share was considered, and ultimately the directors agreed upon $72. The board was also advised about the debt securities that would be issued, and the necessity of placing restrictive covenants upon certain corporate activities until the obligations were paid. The board's decisions were made in reliance on the advice of its investment bankers, including the terms and conditions upon which the securities were to be issued. Based upon this advice, and the board's own deliberations, the directors unanimously approved the exchange offer. Their resolution provided that if Mesa acquired 64 million shares of Unocal stock through its own offer (the Mesa Purchase Condition), Unocal would buy the remaining 49% outstanding for an exchange of debt securities having an aggregate par value of $72 per share. The board resolution also stated that the offer would be subject to other conditions that had been described to the board at the meeting, or which were deemed necessary by Unocal's officers, including the exclusion of Mesa from the proposal (the Mesa exclusion). Any such conditions were required to be in accordance with the "purport and intent" of the offer.

Unocal's exchange offer was commenced on April 17, 1985, and Mesa promptly challenged it by filing this suit in the Court of Chancery. On April 22, the Unocal board met again and was advised by Goldman Sachs and Dillon Read to waive the Mesa Purchase Condition as to 50 million shares. This recommendation was in response to a perceived concern of the shareholders that, if shares were tendered to Unocal, no shares would be purchased by either offeror. The directors were also advised that they should tender their own Unocal stock into the exchange offer as a mark of their confidence in it.

Another focus of the board was the Mesa exclusion. Legal counsel advised that under Delaware law Mesa could only be excluded for what the directors reasonably believed to be a valid corporate purpose. The directors' discussion centered on the objective of adequately compensating shareholders at the "back-end" of Mesa's proposal, which the latter would finance with "junk bonds". To include Mesa would defeat that goal, because under the proration aspect of the exchange offer (49%) every Mesa share accepted by Unocal would displace one held by another stockholder. Further, if Mesa were permitted to tender to Unocal, the latter would in effect be financing Mesa's own inadequate proposal.

On April 24, 1985 Unocal issued a supplement to the exchange offer describing the partial waiver of the Mesa Purchase Condition. On May 1, 1985, in another supplement, Unocal extended the withdrawal, proration and expiration dates of its exchange offer to May 17, 1985.

Meanwhile, on April 22, 1985, Mesa amended its complaint in this action to challenge the Mesa exclusion. A preliminary injunction hearing was scheduled for May 8, 1985. However, on April 23, 1985, Mesa moved for a temporary restraining order in response to Unocal's announcement that it was partially waiving the Mesa Purchase Condition. After expedited briefing, the Court of Chancery heard Mesa's motion on April 26.

On April 29, 1985, the Vice Chancellor temporarily restrained Unocal from proceeding with the exchange offer unless it included Mesa. The trial court recognized that directors could oppose, and attempt to defeat, a hostile takeover which they considered adverse to the best interests of the corporation. However, the Vice Chancellor decided that in a selective purchase of the company's stock, the corporation bears the burden of showing: (1) a valid corporate purpose, and (2) that the transaction was fair to all of the stockholders, including those excluded.

Unocal immediately sought certification of an interlocutory appeal to this Court pursuant to Supreme Court Rule 42(b). On May 1, 1985, the Vice Chancellor declined to certify the appeal on the grounds that the decision granting a temporary restraining order did not decide a legal issue of first impression, and was not a matter to which the decisions of the Court of Chancery were in conflict.

*   *   *

III.

We begin with the basic issue of the power of a board of directors of a Delaware corporation to adopt a defensive measure of this type. Absent such authority, all other questions are moot. Neither issues of fairness nor business judgment are pertinent without the basic underpinning of a board's legal power to act.

The board has a large reservoir of authority upon which to draw. Its duties and responsibilities proceed from the inherent powers conferred by 8 Del. C. § 141(a), respecting management of the corporation's "business and affairs". Additionally, the powers here being exercised derive from 8 Del. C. § 160(a), conferring broad authority upon a corporation to deal in its own stock. From this it is now well established that in the acquisition of its shares a Delaware corporation may deal selectively with its stockholders, provided the directors have not acted out of a sole or primary purpose to entrench themselves in office.

Finally, the board's power to act derives from its fundamental duty and obligation to protect the corporate enterprise, which includes stockholders, from harm reasonably perceived, irrespective of its source.

Thus, we are satisfied that in the broad context of corporate governance, including issues of fundamental corporate change, a board of directors is not a passive instrumentality.[20]

Given the foregoing principles, we turn to the standards by which director action is to be measured. In *Pogostin v. Rice*, Del. Supr., 480 A.2d 619 (1984), we held that the business judgment rule, including the standards by which director conduct is judged, is applicable in the context of a takeover. *Id.* at 627. The business judgment rule is a "presumption that in making a business decision the directors of a corporation acted on an informed basis, in good faith and in the honest belief that the action taken was in the best interests of the company." *Aronson v. Lewis*, Del. Supr., 473 A.2d 805, 812 (1984) (citations omitted). A hallmark of the business judgment rule is that a court will not substitute its judgment for that of the board if the latter's decision can be "attributed to any rational business purpose." *Sinclair Oil Corp. v. Levien*, Del. Supr., 280 A.2d 717, 720 (1971).

When a board addresses a pending takeover bid it has an obligation to determine whether the offer is in the best interests of the corporation and its shareholders. In that respect a board's duty is no different from any other responsibility it shoulders, and its decisions should be no less entitled to the respect they otherwise would be accorded in the realm of business judgment. *See also Johnson v. Trueblood*, 629 F.2d 287, 292–293 (3d Cir. 1980). There are, however, certain caveats to a proper exercise of this function. Because of the omnipresent specter that a board may be acting primarily in its own interests, rather than those of the corporation and its shareholders, there is an enhanced duty which calls for judicial examination at the threshold before the protections of the business judgment rule may be conferred.

This Court has long recognized that:

> We must bear in mind the inherent danger in the purchase of shares with corporate funds to remove a threat to corporate policy when a threat to control is involved. The directors are of necessity confronted with a conflict of interest, and an objective decision is difficult.

*Bennett v. Propp*, Del. Supr., 187 A.2d 405, 409 (1962). In the face of this inherent conflict directors must show that they had reasonable grounds for believing that a danger to corporate policy and effectiveness existed because of another person's stock ownership. *Cheff v. Mathes*, 199 A.2d at 554–55. However, they satisfy that burden "by showing good faith and reasonable investigation . . . ." *Id.* at 555. Furthermore, such proof is materially enhanced, as here, by the approval of a board comprised of a majority of outside independent directors who have acted in accordance with the foregoing standards.

---

[20] [8] Even in the traditional areas of fundamental corporate change, i.e., charter, amendments [8 Del. C. § 242(b)], mergers [8 Del. C. §§ 251(b), 252(c), 253(a), and 254(d)], sale of assets [8 Del. C. § 271(a)], and dissolution [8 Del. C. § 275(a)], director action is a prerequisite to the ultimate disposition of such matters. *See also, Smith v. Van Gorkom*, Del. Supr., 488 A.2d 858, 888 (1985).

## IV.

## A.

In the board's exercise of corporate power to forestall a takeover bid our analysis begins with the basic principle that corporate directors have a fiduciary duty to act in the best interests of the corporation's stockholders. *Guth v. Loft, Inc.*, Del. Supr., 5 A.2d 503, 510 (1939). As we have noted, their duty of care extends to protecting the corporation and its owners from perceived harm whether a threat originates from third parties or other shareholders.[21] But such powers are not absolute. A corporation does not have unbridled discretion to defeat any perceived threat by any Draconian means available.

The restriction placed upon a selective stock repurchase is that the directors may not have acted solely or primarily out of a desire to perpetuate themselves in office. See *Cheff v. Mathes*, 199 A.2d at 556; *Kors v. Carey*, 158 A.2d at 140. Of course, to this is added the further caveat that inequitable action may not be taken under the guise of law. *Schnell v. Chris-Craft Industries*, Inc., Del. Supr., 285 A.2d 437, 439 (1971). The standard of proof established in *Cheff v. Mathes* and discussed supra at page 16, is designed to ensure that a defensive measure to thwart or impede a takeover is indeed motivated by a good faith concern for the welfare of the corporation and its stockholders, which in all circumstances must be free of any fraud or other misconduct. *Cheff v. Mathes*, 199 A.2d at 554–55. However, this does not end the inquiry.

## B.

A further aspect is the element of balance. If a defensive measure is to come within the ambit of the business judgment rule, it must be reasonable in relation to the threat posed. This entails an analysis by the directors of the nature of the takeover bid and its effect on the corporate enterprise. Examples of such concerns may include: inadequacy of the price offered, nature and timing of the offer, questions of illegality, the impact on "constituencies" other than shareholders (i.e., creditors, customers, employees, and perhaps even the community generally), the risk of nonconsummation, and the quality of securities being offered in the exchange. *See* Lipton and Brownstein, *Takeover Responses and Directors' Responsibilities: An Update*, p. 7, ABA National Institute on the Dynamics of Corporate Control (December 8, 1983). While not a controlling factor, it also seems to us that a board may reasonably consider the basic stockholder interests at stake, including those of short term speculators, whose actions may have fueled the coercive aspect of the offer at the expense of the long term investor.[22] Here, the threat posed was

---

[21] [10] It has been suggested that a board's response to a takeover threat should be a passive one. Easterbrook & Fischel, supra, 36 Bus. Law. at 1750. However, that clearly is not the law of Delaware, and as the proponents of this rule of passivity readily concede, it has not been adopted either by courts or state legislatures. Easterbrook & Fischel, supra, 94 Harv. L. Rev. at 1194.

[22] [11] There has been much debate respecting such stockholder interests. One rather impressive study indicates that the stock of over 50 percent of target companies, who resisted hostile takeovers, later traded at higher market prices than the rejected offer price, or were acquired after the tender offer

viewed by the Unocal board as a grossly inadequate two-tier coercive tender offer coupled with the threat of greenmail.

Specifically, the Unocal directors had concluded that the value of Unocal was substantially above the $54 per share offered in cash at the front end. Furthermore, they determined that the subordinated securities to be exchanged in Mesa's announced squeeze out of the remaining shareholders in the "back-end" merger were "junk bonds" worth far less than $54. It is now well recognized that such offers are a classic coercive measure designed to stampede shareholders into tendering at the first tier, even if the price is inadequate, out of fear of what they will receive at the back end of the transaction. Wholly beyond the coercive aspect of an inadequate two-tier tender offer, the threat was posed by a corporate raider with a national reputation as a "greenmailer".[23]

In adopting the selective exchange offer, the board stated that its objective was either to defeat the inadequate Mesa offer or, should the offer still succeed, provide the 49% of its stockholders, who would otherwise be forced to accept "junk bonds," with $72 worth of senior debt. We find that both purposes are valid.

However, such efforts would have been thwarted by Mesa's participation in the exchange offer. First, if Mesa could tender its shares, Unocal would effectively be subsidizing the former's continuing effort to buy Unocal stock at $54 per share. Second, Mesa could not, by definition, fit within the class of shareholders being protected from its own coercive and inadequate tender offer.

Thus, we are satisfied that the selective exchange offer is reasonably related to the threats posed. It is consistent with the principle that "the minority stockholder shall receive the substantial equivalent in value of what he had before." *Sterling v. Mayflower Hotel Corp.*, Del. Supr., 93 A.2d 107, 114 (1952). *See also Rosenblatt v. Getty Oil Co.*, Del. Supr., 493 A.2d 929, 940 (1985). This concept of fairness, while stated in the merger context, is also relevant in the area of tender offer law. Thus, the board's decision to offer what it determined to be the fair value of the corporation to the 49% of its shareholders, who would otherwise be forced to accept highly subordinated "junk bonds," is reasonable and consistent with the directors' duty to ensure that the minority stockholders receive equal value for their shares.

---

was defeated by another company at a price higher than the offer price. *See* Lipton, *supra* 35 Bus. Law. at 106–109, 132–133. Moreover, an update by Kidder Peabody & Company of this study, involving the stock prices of target companies that have defeated hostile tender offers during the period from 1973 to 1982 demonstrates that in a majority of cases the target's shareholders benefited from the defeat. The stock of 81% of the targets studied has, since the tender offer, sold at prices higher than the tender offer price. When adjusted for the time value of money, the figure is 64%. *See* Lipton & Brownstein, *supra* ABA Institute at 10. The thesis being that this strongly supports application of the business judgment rule in response to takeover threats. There is, however, a rather vehement contrary view. *See* Easterbrook & Fischel, *supra* 36 Bus. Law. at 1739–1745.

[23] [13] The term "greenmail" refers to the practice of buying out a takeover bidder's stock at a premium that is not available to other shareholders in order to prevent the takeover. The Chancery Court noted that "Mesa has made tremendous profits from its takeover activities although in the past few years it has not been successful in acquiring any of the target companies on an unfriendly basis." Moreover, the trial court specifically found that the actions of the Unocal board were taken in good faith to eliminate both the inadequacies of the tender offer and to forestall the payment of "greenmail".

## V.

Mesa contends that it is unlawful, and the trial court agreed, for a corporation to discriminate in this fashion against one shareholder. It argues correctly that no case has ever sanctioned a device that precludes a raider from sharing in a benefit available to all other stockholders. However, as we have noted earlier, the principle of selective stock repurchases by a Delaware corporation is neither unknown nor unauthorized. *Cheff v. Mathes*, 199 A.2d at 554; *Bennett v. Propp*, 187 A.2d at 408; *Martin v. American Potash & Chemical Corporation*, 92 A.2d at 302; *Kaplan v. Goldsamt*, 380 A.2d at 568–569; *Kors v. Carey*, 158 A.2d at 140–141; 8 Del. C. § 160. The only difference is that heretofore the approved transaction was the payment of "greenmail" to a raider or dissident posing a threat to the corporate enterprise. All other stockholders were denied such favored treatment, and given Mesa's past history of greenmail, its claims here are rather ironic.

However, our corporate law is not static. It must grow and develop in response to, indeed in anticipation of, evolving concepts and needs. Merely because the General Corporation Law is silent as to a specific matter does not mean that it is prohibited. *See Providence and Worcester Co. v. Baker*, Del. Supr., 378 A.2d 121, 123–124 (1977). In the days when *Cheff, Bennett, Martin* and *Kors* were decided, the tender offer, while not an unknown device, was virtually unused, and little was known of such methods as two-tier "front-end" loaded offers with their coercive effects. Then, the favored attack of a raider was stock acquisition followed by a proxy contest. Various defensive tactics, which provided no benefit whatever to the raider, evolved. Thus, the use of corporate funds by management to counter a proxy battle was approved. *Hall v. Trans-Lux Daylight Picture Screen Corp.*, Del. Ch., 171 A. 226 (1934); *Hibbert v. Hollywood Park, Inc.*, Del. Supr., 457 A.2d 339 (1983). Litigation, supported by corporate funds, aimed at the raider has long been a popular device.

More recently, as the sophistication of both raiders and targets has developed, a host of other defensive measures to counter such ever mounting threats has evolved and received judicial sanction. These include defensive charter amendments and other devices bearing some rather exotic, but apt, names: Crown Jewel, White Knight, Pac Man, and Golden Parachute. Each has highly selective features, the object of which is to deter or defeat the raider.

Thus, while the exchange offer is a form of selective treatment, given the nature of the threat posed here the response is neither unlawful nor unreasonable. If the board of directors is disinterested, has acted in good faith and with due care, its decision in the absence of an abuse of discretion will be upheld as a proper exercise of business judgment.

To this Mesa responds that the board is not disinterested, because the directors are receiving a benefit from the tender of their own shares, which because of the Mesa exclusion, does not devolve upon all stockholders equally. *See Aronson v. Lewis*, Del. Supr., 473 A.2d 805, 812 (1984). However, Mesa concedes that if the exclusion is valid, then the directors and all other stockholders share the same benefit. The answer of course is that the exclusion is valid, and the directors' participation in the exchange offer does not rise to the level of a disqualifying interest. The excellent discussion in *Johnson v. Trueblood*, 629 F.2d at 292–293, of the use of the business judgment rule in takeover contests also seems pertinent here.

Nor does this become an "interested" director transaction merely because certain board members are large stockholders. As this Court has previously noted, that fact alone does not create a disqualifying "personal pecuniary interest" to defeat the operation of the business judgment rule. *Cheff v. Mathes*, 199 A.2d at 554.

Mesa also argues that the exclusion permits the directors to abdicate the fiduciary duties they owe it. However, that is not so. The board continues to owe Mesa the duties of due care and loyalty. But in the face of the destructive threat Mesa's tender offer was perceived to pose, the board had a supervening duty to protect the corporate enterprise, which includes the other shareholders, from threatened harm.

Mesa contends that the basis of this action is punitive, and solely in response to the exercise of its rights of corporate democracy. Nothing precludes Mesa, as a stockholder, from acting in its own self-interest.

However, Mesa, while pursuing its own interests, has acted in a manner which a board consisting of a majority of independent directors has reasonably determined to be contrary to the best interests of Unocal and its other shareholders. In this situation, there is no support in Delaware law for the proposition that, when responding to a perceived harm, a corporation must guarantee a benefit to a stockholder who is deliberately provoking the danger being addressed. There is no obligation of self-sacrifice by a corporation and its shareholders in the face of such a challenge.

Here, the Court of Chancery specifically found that the "directors' decision [to oppose the Mesa tender offer] was made in the good faith belief that the Mesa tender offer is inadequate." Given our standard of review under *Levitt v. Bouvier*, Del. Supr., 287 A.2d 671, 673 (1972), and *Application of Delaware Racing Association*, Del. Supr., 213 A.2d 203, 207 (1965), we are satisfied that Unocal's board has met its burden of proof.

## VI.

In conclusion, there was directorial power to oppose the Mesa tender offer, and to undertake a selective stock exchange made in good faith and upon a reasonable investigation pursuant to a clear duty to protect the corporate enterprise. Further, the selective stock repurchase plan chosen by Unocal is reasonable in relation to the threat that the board rationally and reasonably believed was posed by Mesa's inadequate and coercive two-tier tender offer. Under those circumstances the board's action is entitled to be measured by the standards of the business judgment rule. Thus, unless it is shown by a preponderance of the evidence that the directors'decisions were primarily based on perpetuating themselves in office, or some other breach of fiduciary duty such as fraud, overreaching, lack of good faith, or being uninformed, a Court will not substitute its judgment for that of the board.

In this case that protection is not lost merely because Unocal's directors have tendered their shares in the exchange offer. Given the validity of the Mesa exclusion, they are receiving a benefit shared generally by all other stockholders except Mesa. In this circumstance the test of *Aronson v. Lewis*, 473 A.2d at 812, is satisfied. *See also Cheff v. Mathes*, 199 A.2d at 554. If the stockholders are displeased with the action of their elected representatives, the powers of corporate democracy are at their disposal to turn the board out.

With the Court of Chancery's findings that the exchange offer was based on the board's good faith belief that the Mesa offer was inadequate, that the board's action was informed and taken with due care, that Mesa's prior activities justify a reasonable inference that its principle objective was greenmail, and implicitly, that the substance of the offer itself was reasonable and fair to the corporation and its stockholders if Mesa were included, we cannot say that the Unocal directors have acted in such a manner as to have passed an "unintelligent and unadvised judgment". *Mitchell v. Highland-Western Glass Co.*, Del. Ch., 167 A. 831, 833 (1933). The decision of the Court of Chancery is therefore REVERSED, and the preliminary injunction is VACATED.

# REVLON, INC. v. MACANDREWS & FORBES HOLDINGS, INC.
## Supreme Court of Delaware
## 506 A.2d 173 (1986)

MOORE, J.

In this battle for corporate control of Revlon, Inc. (Revlon), the Court of Chancery enjoined certain transactions designed to thwart the efforts of Pantry Pride, Inc. (Pantry Pride) to acquire Revlon.[24] The defendants are Revlon, its board of directors, and Forstmann Little & Co. and the latter's affiliated limited partnership (collectively, Forstmann). The injunction barred consummation of an option granted Forstmann to purchase certain Revlon assets (the lock-up option), a promise by Revlon to deal exclusively with Forstmann in the face of a takeover (the no-shop provision), and the payment of a $25 million cancellation fee to Forstmann if the transaction was aborted. The Court of Chancery found that the Revlon directors had breached their duty of care by entering into the foregoing transactions and effectively ending an active auction for the company. The trial court ruled that such arrangements are not illegal per se under Delaware law, but that their use under the circumstances here was impermissible. We agree. *See MacAndrews & Forbes Holdings, Inc. v. Revlon, Inc.*, Del. Ch., 501 A.2d 1239 (1985). Thus, we granted this expedited interlocutory appeal to consider for the first time the validity of such defensive measures in the face of an active bidding contest for corporate control. Additionally, we address for the first time the extent to which a corporation may consider the impact of a takeover threat on constituencies other than shareholders. *See Unocal Corp. v. Mesa Petroleum Co.*, Del. Supr., 493 A.2d 946, 955 (1985).

---

[24] [1] The nominal plaintiff, MacAndrews & Forbes Holdings, Inc., is the controlling stockholder of Pantry Pride. For all practical purposes their interests in this litigation are virtually identical, and we hereafter will refer to Pantry Pride as the plaintiff.

In our view, lock-ups and related agreements are permitted under Delaware law where their adoption is untainted by director interest or other breaches of fiduciary duty. The actions taken by the Revlon directors, however, did not meet this standard. Moreover, while concern for various corporate constituencies is proper when addressing a takeover threat, that principle is limited by the requirement that there be some rationally related benefit accruing to the stockholders. We find no such benefit here.

Thus, under all the circumstances we must agree with the Court of Chancery that the enjoined Revlon defensive measures were inconsistent with the directors' duties to the stockholders. Accordingly, we affirm.

## I.

The somewhat complex maneuvers of the parties necessitate a rather detailed examination of the facts. The prelude to this controversy began in June 1985, when Ronald O. Perelman, chairman of the board and chief executive officer of Pantry Pride, met with his counterpart at Revlon, Michel C. Bergerac, to discuss a friendly acquisition of Revlon by Pantry Pride. Perelman suggested a price in the range of $40–50 per share, but the meeting ended with Bergerac dismissing those figures as considerably below Revlon's intrinsic value. All subsequent Pantry Pride overtures were rebuffed, perhaps in part based on Mr. Bergerac's strong personal antipathy to Mr. Perelman.

Thus, on August 14, Pantry Pride's board authorized Perelman to acquire Revlon, either through negotiation in the $42–$43 per share range, or by making a hostile tender offer at $45. Perelman then met with Bergerac and outlined Pantry Pride's alternate approaches. Bergerac remained adamantly opposed to such schemes and conditioned any further discussions of the matter on Pantry Pride executing a standstill agreement prohibiting it from acquiring Revlon without the latter's prior approval.

On August 19, the Revlon board met specially to consider the impending threat of a hostile bid by Pantry Pride.[25] At the meeting, Lazard Freres, Revlon's investment banker, advised the directors that $45 per share was a grossly inadequate price for the company. Felix Rohatyn and William Loomis of Lazard Freres explained to the board that Pantry Pride's financial strategy for acquiring Revlon would be through "junk bond" financing followed by a break-up of Revlon and the disposition of its assets. With proper timing, according to the experts, such transactions could produce a return to Pantry Pride of $60 to $70 per share, while a sale of the company as a whole would be in the "mid 50" dollar range. Martin Lipton, special counsel for Revlon, recommended two defensive measures: first, that the company repurchase up to 5 million of its nearly 30 million outstanding shares;

---

[25] [3] There were 14 directors on the Revlon board. Six of them held senior management positions with the company, and two others held significant blocks of its stock. Four of the remaining six directors were associated at some point with entities that had various business relationships with Revlon. On the basis of this limited record, however, we cannot conclude that this board is entitled to certain presumptions that generally attach to the decisions of a board whose majority consists of truly outside independent directors.

and second, that it adopt a Note Purchase Rights Plan. Under this plan, each Revlon shareholder would receive as a dividend one Note Purchase Right (the Rights) for each share of common stock, with the Rights entitling the holder to exchange one common share for a $65 principal Revlon note at 12% interest with a one-year maturity. The Rights would become effective whenever anyone acquired beneficial ownership of 20% or more of Revlon's shares, unless the purchaser acquired all the company's stock for cash at $65 or more per share. In addition, the Rights would not be available to the acquiror, and prior to the 20% triggering event the Revlon board could redeem the rights for 10 cents each. Both proposals were unanimously adopted.

Pantry Pride made its first hostile move on August 23 with a cash tender offer for any and all shares of Revlon at $47.50 per common share and $26.67 per preferred share, subject to (1) Pantry Pride's obtaining financing for the purchase, and (2) the Rights being redeemed, rescinded or voided.

The Revlon board met again on August 26. The directors advised the stockholders to reject the offer. Further defensive measures also were planned. On August 29, Revlon commenced its own offer for up to 10 million shares, exchanging for each share of common stock tendered one Senior Subordinated Note (the Notes) of $47.50 principal at 11.75% interest, due 1995, and one-tenth of a share of $9.00 Cumulative Convertible Exchangeable Preferred Stock valued at $100 per share. Lazard Freres opined that the notes would trade at their face value on a fully distributed basis.[26] Revlon stockholders tendered 87 percent of the outstanding shares (approximately 33 million), and the company accepted the full 10 million shares on a pro rata basis. The new Notes contained covenants which limited Revlon's ability to incur additional debt, sell assets, or pay dividends unless otherwise approved by the "independent" (non-management) members of the board.

At this point, both the Rights and the Note covenants stymied Pantry Pride's attempted takeover. The next move came on September 16, when Pantry Pride announced a new tender offer at $42 per share, conditioned upon receiving at least 90% of the outstanding stock. Pantry Pride also indicated that it would consider buying less than 90%, and at an increased price, if Revlon removed the impeding Rights. While this offer was lower on its face than the earlier $47.50 proposal, Revlon's investment banker, Lazard Freres, described the two bids as essentially equal in view of the completed exchange offer.

The Revlon board held a regularly scheduled meeting on September 24. The directors rejected the latest Pantry Pride offer and authorized management to negotiate with other parties interested in acquiring Revlon. Pantry Pride remained determined in its efforts and continued to make cash bids for the company, offering $50 per share on September 27, and raising its bid to $53 on October 1, and then to $56.25 on October 7.

---

[26] [4] Like bonds, the Notes actually were issued in denominations of $1,000 and integral multiples thereof. A separate certificate was issued in a total principal amount equal to the remaining sum to which a stockholder was entitled. Likewise, in the esoteric parlance of bond dealers, a Note trading at par ($1,000) would be quoted on the market at 100.

In the meantime, Revlon's negotiations with Forstmann and the investment group Adler & Shaykin had produced results. The Revlon directors met on October 3 to consider Pantry Pride's $53 bid and to examine possible alternatives to the offer. Both Forstmann and Adler & Shaykin made certain proposals to the board. As a result, the directors unanimously agreed to a leveraged buyout by Forstmann. The terms of this accord were as follows: each stockholder would get $56 cash per share; management would purchase stock in the new company by the exercise of their Revlon "golden parachutes";[27] Forstmann would assume Revlon's $475 million debt incurred by the issuance of the Notes; and Revlon would redeem the Rights and waive the Notes covenants for Forstmann or in connection with any other offer superior to Forstmann's. The board did not actually remove the covenants at the October 3 meeting, because Forstmann then lacked a firm commitment on its financing, but accepted the Forstmann capital structure, and indicated that the outside directors would waive the covenants in due course. Part of Forstmann's plan was to sell Revlon's Norcliff Thayer and Reheis divisions to American Home Products for $335 million. Before the merger, Revlon was to sell its cosmetics and fragrance division to Adler & Shaykin for $905 million. These transactions would facilitate the purchase by Forstmann or any other acquiror of Revlon.

When the merger, and thus the waiver of the Notes covenants, was announced, the market value of these securities began to fall. The Notes, which originally traded near par, around 100, dropped to 87.50 by October 8. One director later reported (at the October 12 meeting) a "deluge" of telephone calls from irate noteholders, and on October 10 the Wall Street Journal reported threats of litigation by these creditors.

Pantry Pride countered with a new proposal on October 7, raising its $53 offer to $56.25, subject to nullification of the Rights, a waiver of the Notes covenants, and the election of three Pantry Pride directors to the Revlon board. On October 9, representatives of Pantry Pride, Forstmann and Revlon conferred in an attempt to negotiate the fate of Revlon, but could not reach agreement. At this meeting Pantry Pride announced that it would engage in fractional bidding and top any Forstmann offer by a slightly higher one. It is also significant that Forstmann, to Pantry Pride's exclusion, had been made privy to certain Revlon financial data. Thus, the parties were not negotiating on equal terms.

Again privately armed with Revlon data, Forstmann met on October 11 with Revlon's special counsel and investment banker. On October 12, Forstmann made a new $57.25 per share offer, based on several conditions.[28] The principal demand was a lock-up option to purchase Revlon's Vision Care and National Health Laboratories divisions for $525 million, some $100–$175 million below the value ascribed to them by Lazard Freres, if another acquiror got 40% of Revlon's shares. Revlon also was

---

**27** [5] In the takeover context "golden parachutes" generally are understood to be termination agreements providing substantial bonuses and other benefits for managers and certain directors upon a change in control of a company.

**28** [6] Forstmann's $57.25 offer ostensibly is worth $1 more than Pantry Pride's $56.25 bid. However, the Pantry Pride offer was immediate, while the Forstmann proposal must be discounted for the time value of money because of the delay in approving the merger and consummating the transaction. The exact difference between the two bids was an unsettled point of contention even at oral argument.

required to accept a no-shop provision. The Rights and Notes covenants had to be removed as in the October 3 agreement. There would be a $25 million cancellation fee to be placed in escrow, and released to Forstmann if the new agreement terminated or if another acquiror got more than 19.9% of Revlon's stock. Finally, there would be no participation by Revlon management in the merger. In return, Forstmann agreed to support the par value of the Notes, which had faltered in the market, by an exchange of new notes. Forstmann also demanded immediate acceptance of its offer, or it would be withdrawn. The board unanimously approved Forstmann's proposal because: (1) it was for a higher price than the Pantry Pride bid, (2) it protected the noteholders, and (3) Forstmann's financing was firmly in place.[29] The board further agreed to redeem the rights and waive the covenants on the preferred stock in response to any offer above $57 cash per share. The covenants were waived, contingent upon receipt of an investment banking opinion that the Notes would trade near par value once the offer was consummated.

Pantry Pride, which had initially sought injunctive relief from the Rights plan on August 22, filed an amended complaint on October 14 challenging the lock-up, the cancellation fee, and the exercise of the Rights and the Notes covenants. Pantry Pride also sought a temporary restraining order to prevent Revlon from placing any assets in escrow or transferring them to Forstmann. Moreover, on October 22, Pantry Pride again raised its bid, with a cash offer of $58 per share conditioned upon nullification of the Rights, waiver of the covenants, and an injunction of the Forstmann lock-up.

On October 15, the Court of Chancery prohibited the further transfer of assets, and eight days later enjoined the lock-up, no-shop, and cancellation fee provisions of the agreement. The trial court concluded that the Revlon directors had breached their duty of loyalty by making concessions to Forstmann, out of concern for their liability to the noteholders, rather than maximizing the sale price of the company for the stockholders' benefit. *MacAndrews & Forbes Holdings, Inc. v. Revlon, Inc.*, 501 A.2d at 1249–50.

## II.

\* \* \*

## A.

We turn first to Pantry Pride's probability of success on the merits. The ultimate responsibility for managing the business and affairs of a corporation falls on its board of directors. 8 Del. C. § 141(a). In discharging this function the directors owe fiduciary duties of care and loyalty to the corporation and its shareholders. *Guth v. Loft, Inc.*, 23 Del. Supr. 255, 5 A.2d 503, 510 (1939); *Aronson v. Lewis*, Del. Supr., 473

---

[29] [7] Actually, at this time about $400 million of Forstmann's funding was still subject to two investment banks using their "best efforts" to organize a syndicate to provide the balance. Pantry Pride's entire financing was not firmly committed at this point either, although Pantry Pride represented in an October 11 letter to Lazard Freres that its investment banker, Drexel Burnham Lambert, was highly confident of its ability to raise the balance of $350 million. Drexel Burnham had a firm commitment for this sum by October 18.

A.2d 805, 811 (1984). These principles apply with equal force when a board approves a corporate merger pursuant to 8 Del. C. § 251(b); *Smith v. Van Gorkom*, Del. Supr., 488 A.2d 858, 873 (1985); and of course they are the bedrock of our law regarding corporate takeover issues. *Pogostin v. Rice*, Del. Supr., 480 A.2d 619, 624 (1984); *Unocal Corp. v. Mesa Petroleum Co.*, Del. Supr., 493 A.2d 946, 953, 955 (1985); *Moran v. Household International, Inc.*, Del. Supr., 500 A.2d 1346, 1350 (1985). While the business judgment rule may be applicable to the actions of corporate directors responding to takeover threats, the principles upon which it is founded — care, loyalty and independence — must first be satisfied.

If the business judgment rule applies, there is a "presumption that in making a business decision the directors of a corporation acted on an informed basis, in good faith and in the honest belief that the action taken was in the best interests of the company." *Aronson v. Lewis*, 473 A.2d at 812. However, when a board implements anti-takeover measures there arises "the omnipresent specter that a board may be acting primarily in its own interests, rather than those of the corporation and its shareholders . . . " *Unocal Corp. v. Mesa Petroleum Co.*, 493 A.2d at 954. This potential for conflict places upon the directors the burden of proving that they had reasonable grounds for believing there was a danger to corporate policy and effectiveness, a burden satisfied by a showing of good faith and reasonable investigation. *Id.* at 955. In addition, the directors must analyze the nature of the takeover and its effect on the corporation in order to ensure balance — that the responsive action taken is reasonable in relation to the threat posed.

## B.

The first relevant defensive measure adopted by the Revlon board was the Rights Plan, which would be considered a "poison pill" in the current language of corporate takeovers — a plan by which shareholders receive the right to be bought out by the corporation at a substantial premium on the occurrence of a stated triggering event. *See generally Moran v. Household International, Inc.*, Del. Supr., 500 A.2d 1346 (1985). By 8 Del. C. §§ 141 and 122(13),[30] the board clearly had the power to adopt the measure. *See Moran v. Household International, Inc.*, 500 A.2d at 1351. Thus, the focus becomes one of reasonableness and purpose.

The Revlon board approved the Rights Plan in the face of an impending hostile takeover bid by Pantry Pride at $45 per share, a price which Revlon reasonably concluded was grossly inadequate. Lazard Freres had so advised the directors, and had also informed them that Pantry Pride was a small, highly leveraged company bent on a "bust-up" takeover by using "junk bond" financing to buy Revlon cheaply,

---

[30] [11] The relevant provision of Section 122 is:

Every corporation created under this chapter shall have power to: (13) Make contracts, including contracts of guaranty and suretyship, incur liabilities, borrow money at such rates of interest as the corporation may determine, issue its notes, bonds and other obligations, and secure any of its obligations by mortgage, pledge or other encumbrance of all or any of its property, franchises and income, . . . ". 8 Del. C. § 122(13).

*See* Section 141(a) in n. 8, supra. *See also* Section 160(a), n. 13, *infra*.

sell the acquired assets to pay the debts incurred, and retain the profit for itself.[31] In adopting the Plan, the board protected the shareholders from a hostile takeover at a price below the company's intrinsic value, while retaining sufficient flexibility to address any proposal deemed to be in the stockholders' best interests.

To that extent the board acted in good faith and upon reasonable investigation. Under the circumstances it cannot be said that the Rights Plan as employed was unreasonable, considering the threat posed. Indeed, the Plan was a factor in causing Pantry Pride to raise its bids from a low of $42 to an eventual high of $58. At the time of its adoption the Rights Plan afforded a measure of protection consistent with the directors' fiduciary duty in facing a takeover threat perceived as detrimental to corporate interests. *Unocal*, 493 A.2d at 954–55. Far from being a "showstopper," as the plaintiffs had contended in Moran, the measure spurred the bidding to new heights, a proper result of its implementation.

Although we consider adoption of the Plan to have been valid under the circumstances, its continued usefulness was rendered moot by the directors' actions on October 3 and October 12. At the October 3 meeting the board redeemed the Rights conditioned upon consummation of a merger with Forstmann, but further acknowledged that they would also be redeemed to facilitate any more favorable offer. On October 12, the board unanimously passed a resolution redeeming the Rights in connection with any cash proposal of $57.25 or more per share. Because all the pertinent offers eventually equalled or surpassed that amount, the Rights clearly were no longer any impediment in the contest for Revlon. This mooted any question of their propriety under Moran or Unocal.

## C.

The second defensive measure adopted by Revlon to thwart a Pantry Pride takeover was the company's own exchange offer for 10 million of its shares. The directors' general broad powers to manage the business and affairs of the corporation are augmented by the specific authority conferred under 8 Del. C. § 160(a), permitting the company to deal in its own stock.[32] *Unocal*, 493 A.2d at 953–54; *Cheff v. Mathes*, 41 Del. Supr. 494, 199 A.2d 548, 554 (1964); *Kors v. Carey*, 39 Del. Ch. 47, 158 A.2d 136, 140 (1960). However, when exercising that power in an effort to forestall a hostile takeover, the board's actions are strictly held to the fiduciary standards outlined in *Unocal*. These standards require the directors to determine the best interests of the corporation and its stockholders, and impose an enhanced duty to abjure any action that is motivated by considerations other than a good faith concern for such interests. *Unocal*, 493 A.2d at 954–55; *see Bennett v. Propp*, 41 Del. Supr. 14, 187 A.2d 405, 409 (1962).

---

[31] [12] As we noted in *Moran*, a "bust-up" takeover generally refers to a situation in which one seeks to finance an acquisition by selling off pieces of the acquired company, presumably at a substantial profit. *See Moran*, 500 A.2d at 1349, n. 4.

[32] [13] The pertinent provision of this statute is:

(a) Every corporation may purchase, redeem, receive, take or otherwise acquire, own and hold, sell, lend, exchange, transfer or otherwise dispose of, pledge, use and otherwise deal in and with its own shares. 8 Del. C. § 160(a).

The Revlon directors concluded that Pantry Pride's $47.50 offer was grossly inadequate. In that regard the board acted in good faith, and on an informed basis, with reasonable grounds to believe that there existed a harmful threat to the corporate enterprise. The adoption of a defensive measure, reasonable in relation to the threat posed, was proper and fully accorded with the powers, duties, and responsibilities conferred upon directors under our law. *Unocal*, 493 A.2d at 954; *Pogostin v. Rice*, 480 A.2d at 627.

However, when Pantry Pride increased its offer to $50 per share, and then to $53, it became apparent to all that the break-up of the company was inevitable. The Revlon board's authorization permitting management to negotiate a merger or buyout with a third party was a recognition that the company was for sale. The duty of the board had thus changed from the preservation of Revlon as a corporate entity to the maximization of the company's value at a sale for the stockholders' benefit. This significantly altered the board's responsibilities under the *Unocal* standards. It no longer faced threats to corporate policy and effectiveness, or to the stockholders' interests, from a grossly inadequate bid. The whole question of defensive measures became moot. The directors' role changed from defenders of the corporate bastion to auctioneers charged with getting the best price for the stockholders at a sale of the company.

### III.

This brings us to the lock-up with Forstmann and its emphasis on shoring up the sagging market value of the Notes in the face of threatened litigation by their holders. Such a focus was inconsistent with the changed concept of the directors' responsibilities at this stage of the developments. The impending waiver of the Notes covenants had caused the value of the Notes to fall, and the board was aware of the noteholders' ire as well as their subsequent threats of suit. The directors thus made support of the Notes an integral part of the company's dealings with Forstmann, even though their primary responsibility at this stage was to the equity owners.

The original threat posed by Pantry Pride — the break-up of the company — had become a reality which even the directors embraced. Selective dealing to fend off a hostile but determined bidder was no longer a proper objective. Instead, obtaining the highest price for the benefit of the stockholders should have been the central theme guiding director action. Thus, the Revlon board could not make the requisite showing of good faith by preferring the noteholders and ignoring its duty of loyalty to the shareholders. The rights of the former already were fixed by contract. *Wolfensohn v. Madison Fund, Inc.*, Del. Supr., 253 A.2d 72, 75 (1969); *Harff v. Kerkorian*, Del. Ch., 324 A.2d 215 (1974). The noteholders required no further protection, and when the Revlon board entered into an auction-ending lock-up agreement with Forstmann on the basis of impermissible considerations at the expense of the shareholders, the directors breached their primary duty of loyalty.

The Revlon board argued that it acted in good faith in protecting the noteholders because *Unocal* permits consideration of other corporate constituencies. Although such considerations may be permissible, there are fundamental limitations upon that prerogative. A board may have regard for various constituencies in discharging its responsibilities, provided there are rationally related benefits accruing to the stockholders. *Unocal*, 493 A.2d at 955. However, such concern for non-stockholder interests is inappropriate when an auction among active bidders is in progress, and the object no longer is to protect or maintain the corporate enterprise but to sell it to the highest bidder.

Revlon also contended that *by Gilbert v. El Paso Co.*, Del. Ch., 490 A.2d 1050, 1054–55 (1984), it had contractual and good faith obligations to consider the noteholders. However, any such duties are limited to the principle that one may not interfere with contractual relationships by improper actions. Here, the rights of the noteholders were fixed by agreement, and there is nothing of substance to suggest that any of those terms were violated. The Notes covenants specifically contemplated a waiver to permit sale of the company at a fair price. The Notes were accepted by the holders on that basis, including the risk of an adverse market effect stemming from a waiver. Thus, nothing remained for Revlon to legitimately protect, and no rationally related benefit thereby accrued to the stockholders. Under such circumstances we must conclude that the merger agreement with Forstmann was unreasonable in relation to the threat posed.

A lock-up is not per se illegal under Delaware law. Its use has been approved in an earlier case. *Thompson v. Enstar Corp.*, Del. Ch., 509 A.2d 578 (1984). Such options can entice other bidders to enter a contest for control of the corporation, creating an auction for the company and maximizing shareholder profit. Current economic conditions in the takeover market are such that a "white knight" like Forstmann might only enter the bidding for the target company if it receives some form of compensation to cover the risks and costs involved. Note, *Corporations-Mergers — "Lock-up" Enjoined Under Section 14(e) of Securities Exchange Act — Mobil Corp. v. Marathon Oil Co.*, 669 F.2d 366 (6th Cir. 1981), 12 Seton Hall L. Rev. 881, 892 (1982). However, while those lock-ups which draw bidders into the battle benefit shareholders, similar measures which end an active auction and foreclose further bidding operate to the shareholders' detriment.

Recently, the United States Court of Appeals for the Second Circuit invalidated a lock-up on fiduciary duty grounds similar to those here.[33] *Hanson Trust PLC, et al. v. ML SCM Acquisition Inc.*, et al., 781 F.2d 264 (2nd Cir. 1986). *Citing Thompson v. Enstar Corp., supra*, with approval, the court stated:

> In this regard, we are especially mindful that some lock-up options may be beneficial to the shareholders, such as those that induce a bidder to compete for control of a corporation, while others may be harmful, such as those that effectively preclude bidders from competing with the optionee bidder.

In *Hanson Trust*, the bidder, Hanson, sought control of SCM by a hostile cash

---

[33] [15] The federal courts generally have declined to enjoin lock-up options despite arguments that lock-ups constitute impermissible "manipulative" conduct forbidden by Section 14(e) of the Williams Act [15 U.S.C. § 78n(e)]. *See Buffalo Forge Co. v. Ogden Corp.*, 717 F.2d 757 (2nd Cir. 1983), cert. denied, 464 U.S. 1018, 104 S.Ct. 550, 78 L. Ed. 2d 724 (1983); *Data Probe Acquisition Corp. v. Datatab, Inc.*, 722 F.2d 1 (2nd Cir. 1983); *cert. denied* 465 U.S. 1052, 104 S.Ct. 1326, 79 L. Ed. 2d 722 (1984); *but see Mobil Corp. v. Marathon Oil Co.*, 669 F.2d 366 (6th Cir. 1981). The cases are all federal in nature and were not decided on state law grounds.

tender offer. SCM management joined with Merrill Lynch to propose a leveraged buy-out of the company at a higher price, and Hanson in turn increased its offer. Then, despite very little improvement in its subsequent bid, the management group sought a lock-up option to purchase SCM's two main assets at a substantial discount. The SCM directors granted the lock-up without adequate information as to the size of the discount or the effect the transaction would have on the company. Their action effectively ended a competitive bidding situation. The Hanson Court invalidated the lock-up because the directors failed to fully inform themselves about the value of a transaction in which management had a strong self-interest. "In short, the Board appears to have failed to ensure that negotiations for alternative bids were conducted by those whose only loyalty was to the shareholders."

The Forstmann option had a similar destructive effect on the auction process. Forstmann had already been drawn into the contest on a preferred basis, so the result of the lock-up was not to foster bidding, but to destroy it. The board's stated reasons for approving the transactions were: (1) better financing, (2) noteholder protection, and (3) higher price. As the Court of Chancery found, and we agree, any distinctions between the rival bidders' methods of financing the proposal were nominal at best, and such a consideration has little or no significance in a cash offer for any and all shares. The principal object, contrary to the board's duty of care, appears to have been protection of the noteholders over the shareholders' interests.

$57.25 offer was objectively higher than Pantry Pride's $56.25 ...eriority is less when the Forstmann price is adjusted for the In reality, the Revlon board ended the auction in return for ...rovement in the final bid. The principal benefit went to the ...l personal liability to a class of creditors to whom the board ...under the circumstances. Thus, when a board ends an intense ...nsubstantial basis, and where a significant by-product of that ...e directors against a perceived threat of personal liability for ...ng from the adoption of previous defensive measures, the ...d the enhanced scrutiny which *Unocal* requires of director ...93 A.2d at 954–55.

...ock-up option, the Court of Chancery enjoined the no-shop ...he attempt to foreclose further bidding by Pantry Pride. ...*Holdings, Inc. v. Revlon, Inc.*, 501 A.2d at 1251. The no-shop ...up option, while not per se illegal, is impermissible under the ...en a board's primary duty becomes that of an auctioneer ...g the company to the highest bidder. The agreement to negotiate only with Forstmann ended rather than intensified the board's involvement in the bidding contest.

It is ironic that the parties even considered a no-shop agreement when Revlon had dealt preferentially, and almost exclusively, with Forstmann throughout the contest. After the directors authorized management to negotiate with other parties, Forstmann was given every negotiating advantage that Pantry Pride had been denied: cooperation from management, access to financial data, and the exclusive opportunity to present merger proposals directly to the board of directors. Favoritism for a white knight to the total exclusion of a hostile bidder might be justifiable when the latter's offer adversely affects shareholder interests, but when bidders make relatively similar offers, or dissolution of the company becomes inevitable, the directors cannot fulfill their enhanced Unocal duties by playing favorites with the contending factions. Market forces must be allowed to operate freely to bring the target's shareholders the best price available for their equity.[34] Thus, as the trial court ruled, the shareholders' interests necessitated that the board remain free to negotiate in the fulfillment of that duty.

The court below similarly enjoined the payment of the cancellation fee, pending a resolution of the merits, because the fee was part of the overall plan to thwart Pantry Pride's efforts. We find no abuse of discretion in that ruling.

*   *   *

In conclusion, the Revlon board was confronted with a situation not uncommon in the current wave of corporate takeovers. A hostile and determined bidder sought the company at a price the board was convinced was inadequate. The initial defensive tactics worked to the benefit of the shareholders, and thus the board was able to sustain its *Unocal* burdens in justifying those measures. However, in granting an asset option lock-up to Forstmann, we must conclude that under all the circumstances the directors allowed considerations other than the maximization of shareholder profit to affect their judgment, and followed a course that ended the auction for Revlon, absent court intervention, to the ultimate detriment of its shareholders. No such defensive measure can be sustained when it represents a breach of the directors' fundamental duty of care. *See Smith v. Van Gorkom*, Del. Supr., 488 A.2d 858, 874 (1985). In that context the board's action is not entitled to the deference accorded it by the business judgment rule. The measures were properly enjoined. The decision of the Court of Chancery, therefore, is AFFIRMED.

## CARMODY v. TOLL BROTHERS, INC.
Court of Chancery of Delaware<br>723 A.2d 1180 (1998)

JACOBS, VICE CHANCELLOR

At issue on this Rule 12(b)(6) motion to dismiss is whether a most recent innovation in corporate antitakeover measures — the so-called "dead hand" poison pill rights plan — is subject to legal challenge on the basis that it violates the Delaware General Corporation Law and/or the fiduciary duties of the board of directors who adopted the plan. As explained more fully below, a "dead hand" rights plan is one that cannot be redeemed except by the incumbent directors who adopted the plan or their designated successors. As discussed below, the Court finds that the "dead hand" feature of the rights plan as described in the complaint (the "Rights Plan") is subject to legal challenge on both statutory and fiduciary grounds, and that

---

[34] [16] By this we do not embrace the "passivity" thesis rejected in *Unocal. See* 493 A.2d at 954–55, nn. 8–10. The directors' role remains an active one, changed only in the respect that they are charged with the duty of selling the company at the highest price attainable for the stockholders' benefit.

because the complaint states legally cognizable claims for relief, the pending motion to dismiss must be denied.

## A. Background Leading to Adoption of the Plan

The firm whose rights plan is being challenged is Toll Brothers (sometimes referred to as "the company"), a Pennsylvania-based Delaware corporation that designs, builds, and markets single family luxury homes in thirteen states and five regions in the United States. The company was founded in 1967 by brothers Bruce and Robert Toll, who are its Chief Executive and Chief Operating Officers, respectively, and who own approximately 37.5% of Toll Brothers' common stock. The company's board of directors has nine members, four of whom (including Bruce and Robert Toll) are senior executive officers. The remaining five members of the board are "outside" independent directors.

From its inception in 1967, Toll Brothers has performed very successfully, and "went public" in 1986. As of June 3, 1997, the company had issued and outstanding 34,196,473 common shares that are traded on the New York Stock Exchange. After going public, Toll Brothers continued to enjoy increasing revenue growth, and it expects that trend to continue into 1998, based on the company's ongoing expansion, its backlog of home contracts, and a continuing strong industry demand for luxury housing in the regions it serves.

The home building industry of which the company is a part is highly competitive. For some time that industry has been undergoing consolidation through the acquisition process, and over the last ten years it has evolved from one where companies served purely local and regional markets to one where regional companies have expanded to serve markets throughout the country. That was accomplished by home builders in one region acquiring firms located in other regions. Inherent in any such expansion-through-acquisition environment is the risk of a hostile takeover. To protect against that risk, the company's board of directors adopted the Rights Plan.

## B. The Rights Plan

The Rights Plan was adopted on June 12, 1997, at which point Toll Brothers' stock was trading at approximately $18 per share — near the low end of its established price range of $16 3/8 to $25 3/16 per share. After considering the industry economic and financial environment and other factors, the Toll Brothers board concluded that other companies engaged in its lines of business might perceive the company as a potential target for an acquisition. The Rights Plan was adopted with that problem in mind, but not in response to any specific takeover proposal or threat. The company announced that it had done that to protect its stockholders from "coercive or unfair tactics to gain control of the Company" by placing the stockholders in a position of having to accept or reject an unsolicited offer without adequate time.

## 1. The Rights Plan's "Flip In" and "Flip Over" Features

The Rights Plan would operate as follows: there would be a dividend distribution of one preferred stock purchase right (a "Right") for each outstanding share of common stock as of July 11, 1997. Initially the Rights would attach to the company's outstanding common shares, and each Right would initially entitle the holder to purchase one thousandth of a share of a newly registered series Junior A Preferred Stock for $100. The Rights would become exercisable, and would trade separately from the common shares, after the "Distribution Date," which is defined as the earlier of (a) ten business days following a public announcement that an acquiror has acquired, or obtained the right to acquire, beneficial ownership of 15% or more of the company's outstanding common shares (the "Stock Acquisition Date"), or (b) ten business days after the commencement of a tender offer or exchange offer that would result in a person or group beneficially owning 15% or more of the company's outstanding common shares. Once exercisable, the Rights remain exercisable until their Final Expiration Date (June 12, 2007, ten years after the adoption of the Plan), unless the Rights are earlier redeemed by the company.

The dilutive mechanism of the Rights is "triggered" by certain defined events. One such event is the acquisition of 15% or more of Toll Brothers' stock by any person or group of affiliated or associated persons. Should that occur, each Rights holder (except the acquiror and its affiliates and associates) becomes entitled to buy two shares of Toll Brothers common stock or other securities at half price. That is, the value of the stock received when the Right is exercised is equal to two times the exercise price of the Right. In that manner, this so-called "flip in" feature of the Rights Plan would massively dilute the value of the holdings of the unwanted acquiror.[35]

The Rights also have a standard "flip over" feature, which is triggered if after the Stock Acquisition Date, the company is made a party to a merger in which Toll Brothers is not the surviving corporation, or in which it is the surviving corporation and its common stock is changed or exchanged. In either event, each Rights holder becomes entitled to purchase common stock of the acquiring company, again at half-price, thereby impairing the acquiror's capital structure and drastically diluting the interest of the acquiror's other stockholders.

The complaint alleges that the purpose and effect of the company's Rights Plan, as with most poison pills, is to make any hostile acquisition of Toll Brothers prohibitively expensive, and thereby to deter such acquisitions unless the target company's board first approves the acquisition proposal. The target board's

---

[35] [5] The "flip-in" feature of a rights plan is triggered when the acquiror crosses the specified ownership threshold, regardless of the acquiror's intentions with respect to the use of the shares. At that point, rights vest in all shareholders other than the acquiror, and as a result, those holders become entitled to acquire additional shares of voting stock at a substantially discounted price, usually 50% of the market price. Commonly, rights plans also contain a "flip-over" feature entitling target company shareholders (again, other than the acquiror) to purchase shares of the acquiring company at a reduced price. That feature is activated when, after a "flip-in" triggering event, the acquiror initiates a triggering event, such as a merger, self-dealing transaction, or sale of assets. *See* Shawn C. Lese, Note, *Preventing Control From the Grave: A Proposal for Judicial Treatment of Dead Hand Provisions in Poison Pills*, 96 COLUM. L. REV. 2175, 2180–81 (1996).

"leverage" derives from another critical feature found in most rights plans: the directors' power to redeem the Rights at any time before they expire, on such conditions as the directors "in their sole discretion" may establish. To this extent there is little to distinguish the company's Rights Plan from the "standard model." What is distinctive about the Rights Plan is that it authorizes only a specific, defined category of directors — the "Continuing Directors" — to redeem the Rights. The dispute over the legality of this "Continuing Director" or "dead hand" feature of the Rights Plan is what drives this lawsuit.

### 2. The "Dead Hand" Feature of the Rights Plan

In substance, the "dead hand" provision operates to prevent any directors of Toll Brothers, except those who were in office as of the date of the Rights Plan's adoption (June 12, 1997) or their designated successors, from redeeming the Rights until they expire on June 12, 2007. That consequence flows directly from the Rights Agreement's definition of a "Continuing Director," which is:

> (i) any member of the Board of Directors of the Company, while such person is a member of the Board, who is not an Acquiring Person, or an Affiliate [as defined] or Associate [as defined] of an Acquiring Person, or a representative or nominee of an Acquiring Person or of any such Affiliate or Associate, and was a member of the Board prior to the date of this agreement, or (ii) any Person who subsequently becomes a member of the Board, while such Person is a member of the Board, who is not an Acquiring Person, or an Affiliate [as defined] or Associate [as defined] of an Acquiring Person, or a representative or nominee of an Acquiring Person or of any such Affiliate or Associate, if such Person's nomination for election or election to the Board is recommended or approved by a majority of the Continuing Directors.

According to the complaint, this "dead hand" provision has a twofold practical effect. First, it makes an unsolicited offer for the company more unlikely by eliminating a proxy contest as a useful way for a hostile acquiror to gain control, because even if the acquiror wins the contest, its newly-elected director representatives could not redeem the Rights. Second, the "dead hand" provision disenfranchises, in a proxy contest, all shareholders that wish the company to be managed by a board empowered to redeem the Rights, by depriving those shareholders of any practical choice except to vote for the incumbent directors. Given these effects, the plaintiff claims that the only purpose that the "dead hand" provision could serve is to discourage future acquisition activity by making any proxy contest to replace incumbent board members an exercise in futility.

\* \* \*

The critical issue on this motion is whether a "dead hand" provision in a "poison pill" rights plan is subject to legal challenge on the basis that it is invalid as ultra vires, or as a breach of fiduciary duty, or both. Although that issue has been the subject of scholarly comment, it has yet to be decided under Delaware law, and to date it has been addressed by only two courts applying the law of other jurisdictions.[36]

Some history may elucidate the issue by locating its relevance within the dynamic of state corporate takeover jurisprudence. Since the 1980s, that body of law, largely judge-made, has been racing to keep abreast of the ever-evolving and novel tactical and strategic developments so characteristic of this important area of economic endeavor that is swiftly becoming a permanent part of our national (and international) economic landscape.

For our purposes, the relevant history begins in the early 1980s with the advent of the "poison pill" as an antitakeover measure. That innovation generated litigation focused upon the issue of whether any poison pill rights plan could validly be adopted under state corporation law. The seminal case, *Moran v. Household International, Inc.*, answered that question in the affirmative.

In *Moran*, this Court and the Supreme Court upheld the "flip over" rights plan in issue there based on three distinct factual findings. The first was that the poison pill would not erode fundamental shareholder rights, because the target board would not have unfettered discretion arbitrarily to reject a hostile offer or to refuse to redeem the pill. Rather, the board's judgment not to redeem the pill would be subject to judicially enforceable fiduciary standards. The second finding was that even if the board refused to redeem the pill (thereby preventing the shareholders from receiving the unsolicited offer), that would not preclude the acquiror from gaining control of the target company, because the offeror could "form a group of up to 19.9% and solicit proxies for consents to remove the Board and redeem the Rights." Third, even if the hostile offer was precluded, the target company's stockholders could always exercise their ultimate prerogative — wage a proxy contest to remove the board. On this basis, the Supreme Court concluded that "the Rights Plan will not have a severe impact upon proxy contests and it will not preclude all hostile acquisitions of Household."

It being settled that a corporate board could permissibly adopt a poison pill, the next litigated question became: under what circumstances would the directors' fiduciary duties require the board to redeem the rights in the face of a hostile takeover proposal? That issue was litigated, in Delaware and elsewhere, during the second half of the 1980s. The lesson taught by that experience was that courts were extremely reluctant to order the redemption of poison pills on fiduciary grounds. The reason was the prudent deployment of the pill proved to be largely beneficial to shareholder interests: it often resulted in a bidding contest that culminated in an

---

[36] [10] The jurisdictions that have directly addressed the legality of the dead hand poison pill are New York, *see Bank of New York Co., Inc. v. Irving Bank Corp., et. al.*, N.Y. Sup. Ct., 139 Misc.2d 665, 528 N.Y.S.2d 482 (1988), and the United States District Court for the Northern District of Georgia, *see Invacare Corp. v. Healthdyne Technologies. Inc.*, N.D. Ga., 968 F. Supp. 1578 (1997) (applying Georgia law). In Delaware, the issue arose in *Davis Acquisition, Inc. v. NWA, Inc.*, Del. Ch., C.A. No. 10761, Allen, C., 1989 WL 40845 (Apr. 25, 1989), but was not decided because the preliminary injunction motion was resolved on other grounds. In *Sutton Holding Corp. v. DeSoto, Inc.*, Del. Ch., C.A. No. 12051, Allen, C, 1991 WL 80223 (May 13, 1991) the validity of a "continuing director" provision was presented indirectly (but again was not decided) in the context of an amendment to a pension plan prohibiting its termination or a reduction of benefits in the event of a "change of control." That term was defined as a new, substantial shareholder becoming the beneficial owner of 35% or more of the corporation's voting stock without the prior approval of two thirds of the board and a majority of the "continuing directors."

acquisition on terms superior to the initial hostile offer.

Once it became clear that the prospects were unlikely for obtaining judicial relief mandating a redemption of the poison pill, a different response to the pill was needed. That response, which echoed the Supreme Court's suggestion in Moran, was the foreseeable next step in the evolution of takeover strategy: a tender offer coupled with a solicitation for shareholder proxies to remove and replace the incumbent board with the acquiror's nominees who, upon assuming office, would redeem the pill.[37] Because that strategy, if unopposed, would enable hostile offerors to effect an "end run" around the poison pill, it again was predictable and only a matter of time that target company boards would develop counter-strategies. With one exception — the "dead hand" pill — these counterstrategies proved "successful" only in cases where the purpose was to delay the process to enable the board to develop alternatives to the hostile offer. The counterstrategies were largely unsuccessful, however, where the goal was to stop the proxy contest (and as a consequence, the hostile offer) altogether.

For example, in cases where the target board's response was either to (i) amend the by-laws to delay a shareholders meeting to elect directors, or (ii) delay an annual meeting to a later date permitted under the bylaws, so that the board and management would be able to explore alternatives to the hostile offer (but not entrench themselves), those responses were upheld.[38] On the other hand, where the target board's response to a proxy contest (coupled with a hostile offer) was (i) to move the shareholders meeting to a later date to enable the incumbent board to solicit revocations of proxies to defeat the apparently victorious dissident group, or (ii) to expand the size of the board, and then fill the newly created positions so the incumbents would retain control of the board irrespective of the outcome of the proxy contest, those responses were declared invalid.

This litigation experience taught that a target board, facing a proxy contest joined with a hostile tender offer, could, in good faith, employ non-preclusive defensive measures to give the board time to explore transactional alternatives. The target board could not, however, erect defenses that would either preclude a proxy contest altogether or improperly bend the rules to favor the board's continued incumbency.

In this environment, the only defensive measure that promised to be a "show stopper" (i.e., had the potential to deter a proxy contest altogether) was a poison pill with a "dead hand" feature. The reason is that if only the incumbent directors or their designated successors could redeem the pill, it would make little sense for shareholders or the hostile bidder to wage a proxy contest to replace the incumbent board. Doing that would eliminate from the scene the only group of persons having

---

[37] [15] See, Unitrin, Inc. v. American General Corp., Del. Supr., 651 A.2d 1361, 1379 (1995); Kidsco, Inc. v. Dinsmore, Del. Ch., 674 A.2d 483, 490 (1995), aff'd, 670 A.2d 1338 (1995).

[38] [16] See, e.g., Stahl v. Apple Bancorp, Inc., Del. Ch., 579 A.2d 1115 (1990) (upholding postponement of annual meeting to a later date permitted by bylaws to enable target board to explore alternatives to hostile offer); Kidsco Inc. v. Dinsmore, n.15, supra, (upholding amendment of bylaws to give target board an additional 25 days before calling a shareholder-initiated special meeting, to enable shareholders to vote on a pending merger proposal, and, if the proposal were defeated, to enable the board to explore other alternatives).

the power to give the hostile bidder and target company shareholders what they desired: control of the target company (in the case of the hostile bidder) and the opportunity to obtain an attractive price for their shares (in the case of the target company stockholders). It is against that backdrop that the legal issues presented here, which concern the validity of the "dead hand" feature, attain significance.

\* \* \*

Here, as in *Moran*, the plaintiff complains of the Rights Plan's (specifically, its "dead hand" feature's) present depressing and deterrent effect upon the shareholders' interests, in particular, the shareholders' present entitlement to receive and consider takeover proposals and to vote for a board of directors capable of exercising the full array of powers provided by statute, including the power to redeem the poison pill. Because of their alleged current adverse impact, the plaintiff's claims of statutory and equitable invalidity are ripe for adjudication, for the reasons articulated by the Supreme Court in *Moran*.

### 2. The "Derivative Claim" Defense

\* \* \*

Our Supreme Court has recognized that in litigation involving a challenge to defensive takeover tactics, the line between derivative and individual actions is often vague. Pivotal to the analysis here are the plaintiff's allegations that the "dead hand" provision has both the effect and purpose of deterring proxy contests to replace the incumbent board, thereby entrenching the incumbents in control. Although entrenchment claims may be either individual or derivative, "[a]n entrenchment claim . . . [is] . . . individual . . . when the shareholder alleges that the entrenching activity directly impairs some right she possesses as a sharholder." The complaint alleges an entrenching activity that directly impairs the shareholders' voting rights. Specifically, it claims that by rendering any shareholder vote to replace the board an exercise in futility insofar as the goal of redeeming the Rights is concerned, the "dead hand" provision purposefully interferes with the shareholders' right to elect a new board having the full array of powers authorized by statute and the corporation's charter. Because the right to vote is a contractual right and an attribute of the Toll Brothers shares, the claimed wrongful interference with that right states an individual cause of action.

Even if the claims were regarded as derivative, the complaint's entrenchment allegations are sufficient to excuse compliance with the demand requirement.

\* \* \*

The defendants further argue that the Rights Plan does not violate any fiduciary duty under Unocal/Unitrin or *Blasius*, because a majority of the company's board were independent directors who reasonably perceived a threat to Toll Brothers' ability to carry out its business objectives if the company remained vulnerable to a hostile takeover. They also contend that adopting the Rights Plan was a proportionate response that the "dead hand" feature did not render disproportionate, because the Rights Plan does not preclude offers that are fair and noncoercive. Finally, the defendants argue that the Rights Plan does not prevent the shareholders from electing a new board, and even though that board may be unable to redeem the Rights, that violates no fiduciary duty, because even *Blasius* permits a board to interfere with the voting process in sufficiently compelling circumstances. Because the Rights Plan survives scrutiny under *Unocal/Unitrin* and *Blasius*, the defendants conclude that the Plan is protected by the "powerful presumption" of validity conferred by the business judgment rule, which the complaint's allegations have failed to overcome as a matter of law.

For the reasons next discussed, the Court determines that the defendants' pro-dismissal arguments must be rejected.

\* \* \*

First, it cannot be disputed that the Rights Plan confers the power to redeem the pill only upon some, but not all, of the directors. But under § 141(d), the power to create voting power distinctions among directors exists only where there is a classified board, and where those voting power distinctions are expressed in the certificate of incorporation. Section 141(d) pertinently provides:

> . . . The certificate of incorporation may confer upon holders of any class or series of stock the right to elect 1 or more directors who shall serve for such term, and have such voting powers as shall be stated in the certificate of incorporation. The terms of office and voting powers of the directors elected in the manner so provided in the certificate of incorporation may be greater than or less than those of any other director or class of directors.
> . . . (emphasis added)

The plain, unambiguous meaning of the quoted language is that if one category or group of directors is given distinctive voting rights not shared by the other directors, those distinctive voting rights must be set forth in the certificate of incorporation. In the case of Toll Brothers (the complaint alleges), they are not.

Second, § 141(d) mandates that the "right to elect 1 or more directors who shall . . . have such [greater] voting powers" is reserved to the stockholders, not to the directors or a subset thereof. Absent express language in the charter, nothing in Delaware law suggests that some directors of a public corporation may be created less equal than other directors, and certainly not by unilateral board action. Vesting the pill redemption power exclusively in the Continuing Directors transgresses the statutorily protected shareholder right to elect the directors who would be so empowered. For that reason, and because it is claimed that the Rights Plan's allocation of voting power to redeem the Rights is nowhere found in the Toll Brothers certificate of incorporation, the complaint states a claim that the "dead hand" feature of the Rights Plan is ultra vires, and hence, statutorily invalid under Delaware law.

Third, the complaint states a claim that the "dead hand" provision would impermissibly interfere with the directors' statutory power to manage the business and affairs of the corporation. That power is conferred by 8 Del. C. § 141(a), which mandates:

> The business and affairs of every corporation organized under this chapter shall be managed by or under the direction of a board of directors, except

as may be otherwise provided in this chapter or in its certificate of incorporation. . . . (emphasis added)

The "dead hand" poison pill is intended to thwart hostile bids by vesting shareholders with preclusive rights that cannot be redeemed except by the Continuing Directors. Thus, the one action that could make it practically possible to redeem the pill — replacing the entire board — could make that pill redemption legally impossible to achieve. The "dead hand" provision would jeopardize a newly-elected future board's ability to achieve a business combination by depriving that board of the power to redeem the pill without obtaining the consent of the "Continuing Directors," who (it may be assumed) would constitute a minority of the board. In this manner, it is claimed, the "dead hand" provision would interfere with the board's power to protect fully the corporation's (and its shareholders') interests in a transaction that is one of the most fundamental and important in the life of a business enterprise.

The statutory analysis employed, and the result reached here, are consistent with and supported by *Bank of New York Co. v. Irving Bank Corp.* There, the New York Supreme Court invalidated a "continuing director" provision that the target company board had adopted as an amendment to a preexisting rights plan, as a defense against a tender offer/proxy contest initiated by a hostile bidder. The New York court observed that the continuing director provision at issue there created several different classes of directors having different powers, and that it also

> effectively limits the powers of the future board which is not a continuation of the present board or which is not approved by it, while still leaving those powers to a board which is approved. For example, the present board, or one approved by it, may redeem the rights. A future board, properly elected by a fifty-one percent majority, but not approved by the present board, may not redeem the shares.

Those observations apply equally here.

In *Bank of New York*, the court found that the continuing director provision violated the New York Business Corporation Law requirement that restrictions upon the board's powers are invalid, unless all the incorporators or all shareholders of record authorize the inclusion of the limitations or restrictions in the certificate of incorporation. Although the relevant language of the Delaware and New York statutes is not identical, their underlying intent is the same: both statutes require that limitations upon the directors' power be expressed in the corporation's charter. In *Bank of New York*, the rights plan was determined to be invalid because the target company's certificate of incorporation contained no such limitation. Neither (it is alleged) does the Toll Brothers certificate.

\* \* \*

On the other hand, the Toll Brothers "dead hand" provision, if legally valid, would embed structural power-related distinctions between groups of directors that no successor board could abolish until after the Rights expire in 2007.

\* \* \*

### 3. The Fiduciary Duty Invalidity Claims

Because the plaintiff's statutory invalidity claims have been found legally cognizable, the analysis arguably could end at this point. But the plaintiff also alleges that the board's adoption of the "dead hand" feature violated its fiduciary duty of loyalty. For the sake of completeness, that claim is addressed as well.

The duty of loyalty claim, to reiterate, has two prongs. The first is that the "dead hand" provision purposefully interferes with the shareholder voting franchise without any compelling justification, and is therefore unlawful under *Blasius*. The second is that the "dead hand" provision is a "disproportionate" defensive measure, because it either precludes or materially abridges the shareholders' rights to receive tender offers and to wage a proxy contest to replace the board. Under *Unocal/Unitrin*, in such circumstances the board's approval of the "dead hand" provision would not enjoy the presumption of validity conferred by the business judgment review standard, and therefore would be found to constitute a breach of fiduciary duty.

I conclude, for the reasons next discussed, that both fiduciary duty claims are cognizable under Delaware law.

#### a) The *Blasius* Fiduciary Duty Claim

The validity of antitakeover measures is normally evaluated under the *Unocal/Unitrin* standard. But where the defensive measures purposefully disenfranchise shareholders, the board will be required to satisfy the more exacting *Blasius* standard, which our Supreme Court has articulated as follows:

> A board's unilateral decision to adopt a defensive measure touching "upon issues of control" that purposefully disenfranchises its shareholders is strongly suspect under Unocal, and cannot be sustained without a "compelling justification."

The complaint alleges that the "dead hand" provision purposefully disenfranchises the company's shareholders without any compelling justification. The disenfranchisement would occur because even in an election contest fought over the issue of the hostile bid, the shareholders will be powerless to elect a board that is both willing and able to accept the bid, and they "may be forced to vote for [incumbent] directors whose policies they reject because only those directors have the power to change them."

A claim that the directors have unilaterally "create[d] a structure in which shareholder voting is either impotent or self defeating" is necessarily a claim of purposeful disenfranchisement. Given the Supreme Court's rationale for upholding the validity of the poison pill in *Moran*, and the primacy of the shareholder vote in our scheme of corporate jurisprudence, any contrary view is difficult to justify. In *Moran*, the Supreme Court upheld the adoption of a poison pill, in part because its effect upon a proxy contest would be "minimal," but also because if the board refused to redeem the plan, the shareholders could exercise their prerogative to remove and replace the board. In *Unocal* the Supreme Court reiterated that view — that the safety valve which justifies a board being allowed to resist a hostile offer a majority of shareholders might prefer, is that the shareholders always have their ultimate recourse to the ballot box. Those observations reflect the fundamental value that the shareholder vote has primacy in our system of corporate governance because it is the "ideological underpinning upon which the legitimacy of directorial power rests." As former Chancellor Allen stated in *Sutton Holding Corp. v. DeSoto, Inc.*:

> Provisions in corporate instruments that are intended principally to restrain or coerce the free exercise of the stockholder franchise are deeply suspect. The shareholder vote is the basis upon which an individual serving as a corporate director must rest his or her claim to legitimacy. Absent quite extraordinary circumstances, in my opinion, it constitutes a fundamental offense to the dignity of this corporate office for a director to use corporate power to seek to coerce shareholders in the exercise of the vote.

The defendants contend that the complaint fails to allege a valid stockholder disenfranchisement claim, because the Rights Plan does not on its face limit a dissident's ability to propose a slate or the shareholders' ability to cast a vote. The defendants also urge that even if the Plan might arguably have that effect, it could occur only in a very specific and unlikely context, namely, where (i) the hostile bidder makes a fair offer that it is willing to keep open for more than one year, (ii) the current board refuses to redeem the Rights, and (iii) the offeror wages two successful proxy fights and is committed to wage a third.

This argument, in my opinion, begs the issue and is specious. It begs the issue because the complaint does not claim that the Rights Plan facially restricts the shareholders' voting rights. What the complaint alleges is that the "dead hand" provision will either preclude a hostile bidder from waging a proxy contest altogether, or, if there should be a contest, it will coerce those shareholders who desire the hostile offer to succeed to vote for those directors who oppose it — the incumbent (and "Continuing") directors. Besides missing the point, the argument is also specious, because the hypothetical case the defendants argue must exist for any disenfranchisement to occur, rests upon the unlikely assumption that the hostile bidder will keep its offer open for more than one year. Given the market risks inherent in financed hostile bids for public corporations, it is unrealistic to assume that many bidders would be willing to do that.

For these reasons, the plaintiff's *Blasius*-based breach of fiduciary duty claim is cognizable under Delaware law.

### b) The *Unocal/Unitrin* Fiduciary Duty Claim

The final issue is whether the complaint states a legally cognizable claim that the inclusion of the "dead hand" provision in the Rights Plan was an unreasonable defensive measure within the meaning of *Unocal*. I conclude that it does.

As a procedural matter, it merits emphasis that a claim under *Unocal* requires enhanced judicial scrutiny. In that context, the board has the burden to satisfy the Court that the board (1) "had reasonable grounds for believing that a danger to corporate policy and effectiveness existed," and (2) that its "defensive response was reasonable in relation to the threat posed." Such scrutiny is, by its nature, fact-driven and requires a factual record. For that reason, as the Supreme Court recently observed, enhanced scrutiny "will usually not be satisfied by resting on a defense motion merely attacking the pleadings." Only "conclusory complaints without well-pleaded facts [may] be dismissed early under Chancery Rule 12."

The complaint at issue here is far from conclusory. Under *Unitrin*, a defensive measure is disproportionate (i.e., unreasonable) if it is either coercive or preclusive. The complaint alleges that the "dead hand" provision "disenfranchises shareholders by forcing them to vote for incumbent directors or their designees if shareholders want to be represented by a board entitled to exercise its full statutory prerogatives." That is sufficient to claim that the "dead hand" provision is coercive. The complaint also alleges that that provision "makes an offer for the Company much more unlikely since it eliminates use of a proxy contest as a possible means to gain control . . . [because] . . . any directors elected in such a contest would still be unable to vote to redeem the pill;" and the provision "renders future contests for corporate control of Toll Brothers prohibitively expensive and effectively impossible." A defensive measure is preclusive if it makes a bidder's ability to wage a successful proxy contest and gain control either "mathematically impossible" or "realistically unattainable." These allegations are sufficient to state a claim that the "dead hand" provision makes a proxy contest "realistically unattainable," and therefore, disproportionate and unreasonable under Unocal.

## CONCLUSION

The Court concludes that for the reasons discussed above, the complaint states claims under Delaware law upon which relief can be granted. Accordingly, the defendants' motion to dismiss is denied. IT IS SO ORDERED.

## AZURITE CORP. v. AMSTER & CO.
United States Court of Appeals, Second Circuit
52 F.3d 15 (1995)

LUMBARD, J.

On February 1, 1989, Azurite Corp. Ltd. brought an action in the Southern District under section 10(b) of the Securities Exchange Act of 1934, 15 U.S.C. § 78j(b), to recover damages from the defendants, Amster & Co., then known as Lafer, Amster & Co. ("LACO"), and its partners Arnold Marvin Amster, Barry Stuart Lafer, and Joel Richard Packer. Azurite claimed that the defendants made false disclosures and omissions in their Schedule 13D amendments filed under section 13(d) of the Exchange Act, 15 U.S.C. § 78m(d), thereby causing Azurite and other investors to sell their shares in Graphic Scanning Corp. in the period between February 3 and March 3, 1986 at prices lower than they would have sold the shares had there been proper disclosure. The defendants allegedly decided to wage a proxy contest for control of Graphic no later than February 3, 1986, but misrepresented the extent and timing of their plans under Item 4 of their Schedule 13D Amendments 5, 6, and 7 filed on February 10, February 18, and March 6, respectively.

This action followed the Securities and Exchange Commission's institution of a virtually identical action on December 5, 1988. The parties agreed to suspend proceedings pending disposition of the SEC action. Judge Haight granted summary judgment for the defendants and dismissed the complaint in the SEC action, *SEC v. Amster & Co.*, 762 F. Supp. 604 (S.D.N.Y. 1991), ruling,

> [D]efendants were under no duty to report preliminary considerations of a proxy contest for Graphic, any more than they were required to report other options under consideration. The duty to report arises only when a shareholder forms the purpose, which is to say the intention, of acquiring control of the company.

* * *

I agree with Judge Haight's interpretation of the law and that of Judge Milton Pollack in *Todd Shipyards Corp. v. Madison Fund, Inc.*, 547 F. Supp. 1383, 1387 (S.D.N.Y. 1982), that § 13(d) does not require a party filing a Schedule 13D statement to disclose preliminary considerations, exploratory work or tentative plans to wage a proxy battle and that it only requires disclosure of definite plans.

She found no genuine issue of fact as to whether the Schedule 13D filings were deficient or whether insider trading occurred. Azurite appeals from the order of summary judgment dismissing the complaint and denial of leave to amend the complaint. LACO, Amster, and Packer cross-appeal the denial of sanctions.

The facts of this case are more fully set out in the two district court opinions. A summary follows. After accumulating over 5% of the Graphic stock outstanding, on August 19, 1985 the defendants filed with the SEC a Schedule 13D, in which they stated that they had acquired Graphic stock "for the purpose of making an investment" and "not with the present intention of acquiring control of the Company's business." Because LACO, a partnership engaged in risk arbitrage, based its investment on the anticipated liquidation of Graphic's assets, it was disturbed by Graphic's SEC Form S-1 filing on January 28, 1986, which indicated that Graphic might not sell all of its assets if the offers to purchase were too low.

Over the next few weeks, LACO consulted with others to consider its options in dealing with the situation. On February 3, 1986, defendants met with Elaine Ruege and Scott Bessent of the Olayan Group, a Graphic institutional investor. Ruege wrote a memorandum dated February 6, documenting that "Lafer Amster is proposing that the shareholders group together in a proxy fight and force Mr. Yampol to liquidate [Graphic]" — Barry Yampol was the chairman of Graphic, as well as the president and sole shareholder of Azurite. The memo briefly sketched some aspects of the proposal. At deposition, Bessent explained that the proxy contest was "one of their [LACO's] options." The Olayan Group decided not to pursue this course of action, and a week or two later communicated this to Amster. A possible proxy contest also was mentioned at a February 4 meeting between Amster and Lafer and representatives of the General Electric Investor Corporation, LACO's largest limited partner.

Meanwhile, LACO increased its holdings in Graphic. On February 3, it purchased non-voting convertible debentures with a face value of $1.7 million for $1,466,250. Over the next four days, it purchased 205,000 additional shares of common stock for $1,410,000. Lafer and Amster as individuals each bought 25,000 shares on February 14.

Graphic then filed with the SEC a Form 8-K dated February 7, a Friday, stating that it was transferring certain valuable assets to Yampol. On Monday, February 10, LACO filed Amendment 5 to its Schedule 13D, not indicating any change in its investment purpose. According to Arnold Jacobs, LACO's outside counsel, midday on February 10, after LACO first heard of the 8-K filing, they engaged in "exploratory conversations" that included discussion of a proxy contest.

LACO met with John A. Morgan, managing director of the investment firm Morgan Lewis Githens & Ahn, and a general partner of LACO, on February 10 or 11, and with John J. McAtee, Jr. of the law firm of Davis Polk & Wardwell on February 12, to consider the alternatives, discussing "all of the normal possibilities" with regards to Graphic; a proxy fight was an "option."

On February 13 or 14, LACO consulted the law firm of Willkie Farr & Gallagher, which they retained as counsel. On February 18, LACO filed Amendment 6, which stated under "Item 4. Purpose of Transaction" that in light of Graphic's Form 8-K it "will not necessarily hold the shares of [Graphic] solely for the purpose of making an investment," and that it "is now giving consideration on a preliminary basis to various courses of action . . . including . . . a proxy contest." On March 3, it filed Amendment 7, declaring, "LACO and [others] . . . have decided to join a group to engage in a proxy contest to oust the present Board." The defendants eventually gained control of Graphic with the help of Drexel, which then conducted the liquidation.

\*     \*     \*

Regarding the legal standard of disclosure, Azurite argues that the district court improperly tied disclosure of "plans or proposals" to the formation of a control purpose. Further, Azurite contends that given the 1978 rule amendment to Item 4 and the Supreme Court decision in *Basic Inc. v. Levinson*, 485 U.S. 224, 108 S. Ct. 978, 99 L. Ed. 2d 194 (1988), materiality is the standard governing the disclosure of plans.

Pursuant to section 13(d), the SEC requires the beneficial owner of more than 5% of a class of stock to make certain disclosures on a Schedule 13D. 17 C.F.R. § 240.13d-101. Item 4 of the Schedule as amended in 1978 requires the disclosure of two things: (1) the purpose of the acquisition of securities, including a purpose to acquire control, and (2) certain enumerated types of plans or proposals, such as those relating to a liquidation or change in management of the issuer, regardless of an intent to acquire control; prior to 1978 plans needed to be disclosed only if there was a control purpose. A control purpose includes any intention to acquire control. *GAF Corp. v. Milstein*, 453 F.2d 709, 714 (2d Cir. 1971), *cert. denied*, 406 U.S. 910 (1972). Such an intention is a determination made with an element of resolve.

We also have construed a "plan" as something more definite than vaguely formed thoughts for the future. *Electronic Specialty Co. v. International Controls Corp.*, 409 F.2d 937, 948 (2d Cir. 1969) ("It would be as serious an infringement of these regulations to overstate the definiteness of the plans as to understate them.").

. . . "[D]isclosure is to be made of all definite plans and there is no requirement to make predictions, for example, of future behavior; or to disclose tentative plans; or inchoate plans. It is sufficient to merely identify those matters not fully determined." (Internal citations omitted). Thus, unless a course of action is decided upon or intended, it need not be disclosed as a plan or proposal under Item 4.

The 1978 amendment to Item 4 does not affect the standard established in our earlier decisions; it eliminates the condition that an acquiror must disclose the purpose of its acquisition only if it has a control intent, but it does not alter the "fixed plan" standard for disclosure of a plan or proposal.

Azurite's reliance on the Supreme Court decision in *Basic Inc. v. Levinson*, 485 U.S. 224 (1988), is misplaced. The Court in *Basic* decided that merger negotiations may be a "material fact" under Rule 10b-5, applying to section 10(b) the standard of materiality it adopted for section 14(a) in *TSC Industries, Inc. v. Northway, Inc.*, 426 U.S. 438 (1976). Whether a plan or proposal is material is not relevant to determining whether it is sufficiently "fixed" to require disclosure as a "plan or proposal" under Item 4; and if a plan need not be disclosed under Item 4, such an omission does not support a section 10(b) claim founded solely upon an alleged section 13(d) violation.

\*    \*    \*

We agree with Judges Sotomayor and Haight that the record, which is based on extensive discovery, indicates only that LACO was exploring many possibilities during the month of February. LACO's advisors all stated that their discussions were preliminary.

Azurite also argues that the purchase of 205,000 Graphic shares between February 3 and 7, and of the debentures convertible to 160,000 voting shares prove defendants' intent to acquire control, since LACO had stated on January 28 that it was an "unhappy shareholder." These purchases, however, represent only an increase in holdings consistent with the intent of "keeping all alternatives open,"

In sum, the evidence in the record as a whole, including the allegations contained in the proposed amended complaint, is insufficient as a matter of law to prove that an intent to acquire control, or a plan to wage a proxy contest or to liquidate Graphic had been formed before it was disclosed. The evidence indicates that Amendment 5 was permissibly silent, and that Amendment 6 reported a change in purpose and Amendment 7 reported the decision to engage in a proxy battle in an adequate and timely fashion.

\*    \*    \*

Judgment affirmed.

# NOTE

*Azurite* does not deal with a proxy statement but with the requirements of filing a Schedule 13D which is filed pursuant to Section 13(d) of the Securities Exchange Act of 1934, 15 U.S.C. § 78m(d). The Williams Act enacted by the Congress in 1968 regulates tender offers. It consists of Section 13(d) and (e) and Section 14(d).

Section 13(d) compels disclosure when a change of control is contemplated. The contemplated change of control may be by proxy fight rather than tender offer.

## E.  SALE OF CONTROL

### GERDES v. REYNOLDS
Supreme Court of New York
28 N.Y.S.2d 622 (1941)

WALTER, J.

At the conclusion of the trial herein I stated upon the record my views as to the facts and the law and invited all counsel to submit their suggestions respecting possible inaccuracies and omissions. Such suggestions have been received and considered, and I now make the decision required by Section 440 of the Civil Practice Act, stating such facts as I deem essential.

Defendants Clarence K. Reynolds and William F. Woodward, together with Richard S. Reynolds and Richard S. Reynolds, Jr., who are named as defendants but have not been served, were the officers and directors of Reynolds Investing Company, Inc., a Delaware corporation of the kind commonly known as an investment trust. They were also stockholders, and, with members of their families, owned a majority of its common stock, which was the only stock having voting power and was junior to debentures and preferred stock outstanding in the hands of the public. Ownership of such majority of the common stock was sold, and the persons just named resigned their offices and directorships and elected as their successors four persons designated by the purchaser. Assets of the company were then wasted and improperly applied, and the plaintiffs in the suit first above entitled, trustees of the company appointed in a proceeding under the Federal Bankruptcy Act, 11 U.S.C.A. § 1 *et seq.*, here seek to hold accountable therefor both those who sold and those who bought and those who aided the transaction.

\* \* \*

The negotiations which resulted in the transaction here complained of began in New York City about December 15, 1937, when defendant Mayer told defendant Woodward that he had a buyer "for the Reynolds Investing Company," and asked if the Reynolds family owned a majority of its stock and would sell it. Mayer knew, at least in large part, what assets Reynolds Investing Company had, such information being obtainable from regularly published statistics, and on that and the succeeding day he and Woodward discussed those assets at some length, and Mayer said his principal would pay $1.25 per share.

\* \* \*

The agreement as signed is stated to be between C. K. and R. S. Reynolds and Woodward "individually and as agents for certain other stockholders hereinafter specified," and F. E. Mayer, and provides for a sale of not less than 1,035,000 shares and not in excess of 1,055,000 shares at $2 per share. Performance by Mayer was guaranteed by Prentice & Brady, the firm of which Prentice was a member, and performance by the other parties was guaranteed by Granberry & Co., the firm of which C. K. Reynolds was a member.

\*    \*    \*

Coincident with that C. K. Reynolds, Woodward, R. S. Reynolds, Jr., and R. S. Reynolds, met as directors of Reynolds Investing Company and successively presented their resignations. When the resignation of C. K. Reynolds was accepted, the remaining directors elected Mayer to fill the vacancy so created. When the resignation of Woodward was accepted the remaining directors elected defendant Clayton B. Davis to fill the vacancy so created. When the resignation of R. S. Reynolds, Jr., was accepted, the remaining directors, who were then Mayer and Davis and R. S. Reynolds, elected defendant Alexander H. McLanahan to fill the vacancy so created. When the resignation of R. S. Reynolds was accepted the remaining directors, who were then defendants Mayer, Davis and McLanahan, elected defendant Prentice to fill the vacancy so created. At the same meeting Prentice was elected as president, Mayer was elected as vice-president, and Davis was elected as secretary and treasurer.

No notice of an intention to resign was given to other stockholders or to the debenture holders, and no substantial investigation of the character or ability of the persons so elected had been made by any of the resigning directors. Such persons were elected solely because the purchaser nominated them. Neither had the resigning directors made any investigation of the financial resources of Prentice other than the bank inquiry above mentioned. Further investigation would have disclosed that he bore an unblemished reputation among many social acquaintances but that such capital as he had in the firm of Prentice & Brady was borrowed and that he had practically no property other than that capital and no sources of income other than his share of the earnings of that firm and the income of a small trust.

The securities owned by Reynolds Investing Company, constituting substantially all its assets, were then located partly in a safe deposit box in the bank in Jersey City where the meeting was held and partly in a bank in New York City with which certain thereof had been pledged as collateral for a loan of $486,815.32, and to the knowledge of the resigning directors they were for the most part readily saleable and in practically negotiable form and of a value of over $5,000,000.

\*    \*    \*

To the extent of the difference between the total purchase price of $2,110,000 and the sum of the $1,106,175.77 and the $151,216.20, viz., to the extent of $852,608.03, Prentice & Brady in effect advanced the money for the acquisition of the 1,055,000 shares (precisely as the other brokers had done in the acquisition of First Income and Continental), and when they charged the check for $882,500 against a credit balance created by their sale of securities of Reynolds Investing Company they in effect repaid themselves that advance out of the proceeds of such sales of securities of Reynolds Investing Company. As in the case of First Income and Continental, therefore, the purchase price of the stock of Reynolds Investing Company was, to the extent stated, paid out of its own treasury.

\*   \*   \*

It now becomes necessary to determine who among the various participants in the transactions are legally accountable therefor in these suits. . . . [A]djudication is now to be made as to any defendant in the Ballantine suit other than those as to whom an adjudication can be made in the Gerdes suit. The result thus is that those as to whom an adjudication is now to be made are: Clarence K. Reynolds, William F. Woodward, the partners of the firm of Granberry & Co., the partners of the firm of Prentice & Brady, George H. Clayton, Vincent E. Ferretti, Franklin E. Mayer, Calmur & Co., Inc., Alexander H. McLanahan, Conroy & Co., Inc., Walter A. Galvin, George K. Hyslop, William B. Boehm, and Continental Securities Corporation.

\*   \*   \*

As regards defendant Mayer, the questions of fact involved are difficult. That he could have done all the things that he did in the innocent belief that he was merely an honest broker bringing honest buyers and sellers together, borders upon the incredible. Nevertheless, it was largely through what he did after the end of January, 1938, that further spoliation was prevented and the wrongdoing was uncovered, and after observing him upon the witness stand for several days I feel no strong conviction that his participation was with guilty knowledge. I consequently find that guilty knowledge on his part has not been established by a fair preponderance of the evidence, and that he is chargeable with negligence only. Negligent he certainly was. I cannot say, in view of all the circumstances, that he was negligent in not more closely guarding the safe deposit box between December 31, 1937, and January 8, 1938, and therefore the use made between those dates of the securities taken therefrom cannot be charged to him; but he was negligent in endorsing the check for $882,500. His conduct in that regard fell far below the standard of care required of a vice-president and director situated as he was . . . and he cannot excuse himself by urging that he was ignorant or that he acted in what his counsel describes as a state of "mental lethargy" induced by confidence in or reliance upon or domination by others.

\*   \*   \*

There remains for consideration the liability of the so-called "Reynolds group" of defendants, consisting of (a) those who sold their stock and resigned as officers and directors, and (b) the members of the firm of Granberry & Co. who, for a substantial consideration, guaranteed performance of the contract of sale by the sellers and received and disbursed the proceeds of sale. As already noted, no adjudication can be made with respect to R. S. Reynolds and R. S. Reynolds, Jr., because they were not served with process; but the liability of C. K. Reynolds and Woodward must be determined on the basis of the four together being sellers of stock and the officers and directors who resigned.

\*   \*   \*

Liability is asserted against them upon the grounds (a) that the sale of the stock, accompanied by their resignations and the election of successors nominated by the purchaser, was itself an illegal transaction because in violation of fiduciary duties owed to the corporation and the holders of its debentures and preferred stock and its minority common stockholders; and (b) that even if the transaction were not illegal in itself, it is made so because the selling defendants negligently or in bad faith failed to make proper investigation of the purchaser or to give advance notice to the other stockholders of an impending change of management, especially so inasmuch as what is claimed to be the excessive price paid was itself sufficient to put those defendants upon notice that some wrongful act was intended. Those contentions present interesting and important and difficult questions of law.

Inherent in the very nature of stock corporations as constituted by our law are the settled principles that the shares of stock are the property of the stockholders, that the stockholders may sell their shares when and to whom they please and for such price as they can get, that they may sell to buyers of whose identity and integrity and responsibility they are unaware (as is the common practice in the multitudinous sales through brokers on and off exchanges), that the purchase price paid upon such sales belongs to the sellers, and that these same rights exist even where the stockholders hold a majority of the stock and where the sellers are a group who together own and sell such a majority. Equally inherent is the further principle that the holders of a majority (or other statutorily fixed percentage) of the voting shares elect the directors who are to manage the business affairs of the corporation, and in that sense and to that extent control the corporation and its assets. Equally inherent is the further principle that, in the absence of some statutory restriction, officers and directors may resign when they please; and in the case of this particular corporation, as in many others, the remaining directors were specifically authorized to fill vacancies. Over against these principles and rules there is the principle that officers and directors of a corporation, and under certain circumstances and for some purposes the majority stockholders, whether one or many, stand in a fiduciary relation to the corporation and to the minority stockholders, and must observe the high standards of diligence, good faith and loyalty required of all fiduciaries. These principles are not destructive one of the other. They are complementary to each other, and are merely misinterpreted when thought to be otherwise. The fact that a certain case states one without referring to the others thus affords no ground for supposing that those not stated are rejected. (Compare *Rodkinson v. Haecker*, 248 N.Y. 480, 488, 489, 162 N.E. 493, where the ever-present necessity for considering principles in the light of the facts of particular cases is emphasized.)

\* \* \*

In this case, however, it indisputably was a condition of the sale that all the officers and directors then in office should forthwith resign and that under their power to fill vacancies they should forthwith elect an entirely new directorate chosen wholly by the purchaser of the stock, and all the officers and directors then in office did so resign and did so elect as directors persons designated by the purchaser. Furthermore, the brief submitted on behalf of this group of defendants accurately portrays the situation where it specifically states that the purchaser "insisted that on the closing date sufficient stock to constitute a majority should be actually delivered or placed in escrow beyond the control of the sellers,' and 'made certain that the purchaser was bound to get delivery of enough shares to constitute a clear majority contemporaneously with the closing on December 31st," and the contract was so arranged as to insure the purchaser that "the majority block was irrevocably within his control the minute the deal closed on the 31st of December." Immediate and complete control in advance of payment of the entire purchase price was thus specifically bargained for and accorded. The officers and directors were made specifically aware of the fact that what the purchaser or purchasers wanted was immediate and actual control, and not merely the right to elect directors which incidentally follows from a sale of a majority of voting stock.

Officers and directors always and necessarily stand in a fiduciary relation to the corporation and to its stockholders and creditors. They undoubtedly may free themselves of that fiduciary relationship by ceasing to be officers and directors, but their right to resign, although sometimes stated with seeming absoluteness (*Bruce v. Platt*, 80 N.Y. 379, 383), is qualified by their fiduciary obligations to others. "Rights are never absolute and independent of those of others."

*   *   *

It is obvious, of course that it would be illegal for officers and directors to resign and elect as their successors persons who they knew intended to loot the corporation's treasury. Even stockholders, despite their right to sell their stock to whom they please, could not legally do that. Liability for such an act would not have to be predicated upon breach of a fiduciary relation, for the act would amount to a willful and malicious injury to property, tortious in its very nature. . . . I here find as a fact that none of the sellers of the stock of Reynolds Investing Company had any knowledge that the purchasers thereof, or any one acting for them, had any intention to loot the corporation or to pay any part of the purchase price out of the corporation's own assets. Whether or not the resigning officers and directors nevertheless are chargeable with notice of such an intention — whether or not it was, under all the circumstances, a risk reasonably to be perceived — is, of course, another question.

The questions determinative of the liability of corporate officers and directors in such a situation as is here disclosed thus appear to me to be these: (1) Are the circumstances such that, despite actual ignorance of unlawful plans and designs on the part of the purchasers, they are chargeable with notice of such plans and designs, or, perhaps more accurately, with notice that unlawful plans and designs are a risk reasonably to be perceived? "The risk reasonably to be perceived defines the duty to be obeyed." *Palsgraf v. Long Island R. R. Co.*, 248 N.Y. 339, 344, 162 N.E. 99, 100, 59 A.L.R. 1253. (2) Is the price paid in reality a price paid for the stock, or is it, in part at least, a price paid for the resignations of the existing officers and directors and the election of the buyer's nominees? And the principal factors which must supply the answers to these questions are the nature of the assets which are to pass into the possession and control of the purchasers by reason of the transaction, the method by which the transaction is to be consummated, and the relation of the price paid to the value of the stock.

The immediate consequence of the resignation of the entire body of officers and directors of a corporation obviously is at least potentially different where the corporation's assets are land and buildings and where they are securities which to all intents and purposes are practically negotiable, and such potential difference must be taken into account, both by the officers and directors and by a court judging their conduct, in considering whether their en masse resignations would leave the assets without proper care and protection, because the risk of dissipation or speedy misapplication obviously is greater. Such difference in the nature of the assets must be considered, also, in gauging the significance of the purchaser's conceded requirement that custody and possession of the assets be accorded before payment of a substantial part of the purchase price. An assumption that the officers and directors of Reynolds Investing Company fully performed the fiduciary duty resting upon them thus requires an assumption that they realized that by doing what they did they were placing in the hands of those whom they elected as their successors the custody and possession of practically negotiable securities of a value of more than double the amount of the agreed purchase price, and were so placing such custody and possession at a time when a large part of the purchase price (over $600,000) still remained unpaid. For fiduciaries confronted with such a realization, I gravely doubt whether it is sufficient that they truthfully can say that they actually knew nothing against the character of the purchasers or of their nominees, or even that they had affirmative evidence that the purchasers were of good reputation. A man dealing with his own affairs may be as confiding and trusting as he pleases, and may be grossly negligent without being guilty of bad faith; but a fiduciary charged with the care of the property of others must be reasonably vigilant, and will not be heard to say that he did not know what the circumstances plainly indicated or that his faith in people was such that obvious opportunities for wrongdoing gave him no inkling that wrongdoing might be done, and schemes to acquire the stock of corporations by using assets of the corporation to pay the purchase price did not originate in the year 1937.

Precisely what would be the situation of directors who, by resignation and election, turned practically negotiable securities over to strangers who had not completed payment, need not be here determined, however, because here there is the added element that in connection with the same transaction a price was paid which is claimed to be grossly in excess of the value of the stock, and the situation of these directors must be considered in connection with that additional element.

Gross inadequacy of price long and frequently has been regarded as important evidence upon the question of good faith, and sometimes is sufficient in itself to charge a buyer with notice of fraudulent intent on the part of a seller.

*     *     *

A feature which I regard as of great importance in considering the particular problems here involved is the almost complete lack of any distinctiveness in the assets of the company. It owned no land of special adaptability — in fact, no land at all. It owned no plant or structures or machinery which would take a long time to assemble. It had no clientele or customers, the mere existence of which sometimes gives great value to the stock of a company. It had no specially trained personnel or organization of any kind. Such position as it had in the canning industry of the country by reason of its holdings of the Stokely stocks could be duplicated by the purchase of the stocks of other canning companies. Therefore, with the exception of its holdings in United States Foil and Reynolds Metals Company, its entire assets could have been substantially duplicated by anyone in a very few days, by the simple device of giving some buying orders to a broker. Not even the sagacity and acumen displayed in selecting and assembling its portfolio was an element of value, because its portfolio was publicly disclosed in published statistics, and any admirer of the genius for security selection displayed by the company's managers could appropriate that genius for himself by examining printed volumes of security manuals which any broker expecting an order would have been only too glad to make available free of charge. Furthermore, there is no showing that the company's portfolio exhibited any exceptionally high character as an assemblage of securities. On the contrary, there is considerable evidence that in times of rising security prices it had advanced less than certain averages looked upon as fair standards of comparison, and in times of declining security prices it had receded greater than such averages.

Assuming, therefore, that in December, 1937, there was an investor with $2,110,000 in cash which he desired to invest in such a portfolio as was then owned by Reynolds Investing Company, and assuming that such investor shared to the fullest extent the optimistic viewpoint as to the future which defendants' expert says was justified, it is to my mind most improbable, if not inconceivable, that he would have put his $2,110,000 in a block of common stock which had ahead of it senior securities and obligations of $5,312,847. . . .

\* \* \*

The situation thus bore not the slightest resemblance to a railway, public utility, or industrial plant, or any other assemblage of tangible assets, going business, and trained organization, where there is room for wide divergence of honest and reasonably entertained opinion as to what wonders may be worked by a sagacious buyer who places himself in control.

Some trouble and expense undoubtedly would be saved by acquiring an existing investment trust instead of creating a new one, and I am willing to make the somewhat difficult assumption that an existing trust may have something in the nature of good-will or name which is valuable to the owner of the common stock, even though it be what is called a "closed-end" trust, i.e., one not engaged in selling additional stock or other securities. Such items, however, necessarily are small.

Viewing all the elements which the fiduciary obligations of the officers and directors of Reynolds Investing Company required them to view I am convinced that $2,110,000 was so grossly in excess of the value of the stock that it carried upon its face a plain indication that it was not for the stock alone but partly for immediate en masse resignations and immediate election of the purchasers' nominees as successors. The transaction was not one in which there was merely a sale of stock, with the right to elect directors passing to the purchasers as a legal incident of the sale, and I think it proper to add that these officers and directors did not submit to the lawyers whom they retained in the matter the question of the price paid or its significance. They had their eyes and minds so centered upon the personal interests of themselves and their families and associates as stockholders and upon a desire to get what they could for what they regarded as theirs, that they failed to consider their position as officers and directors, and the consequent duty they owed as such to the corporation itself and its creditors and other stockholders.

It thus becomes necessary to determine what part of the $2,110,000 was paid for the 1,055,000 shares of stock, and what part was paid for resignations and election of successors. . . . [A] matter of fact which the trier of facts must find, and with due allowance for all elements I think that 75 cents per share is as liberal a finding as the evidence warrants. That gives $791,250 as the price paid for 1,055,000 shares of stock, and $1,318,750 as the price paid for the resignations of the officers and directors and their election of the buyer's nominees as their successors, or, in other words, for what is termed the turning over of control.

The conclusion ordinarily to be drawn from the foregoing is that, having violated their fiduciary duty, these officers and directors must account to the corporation or to its duly appointed trustees for the sum of $1,318,750, and for all damages naturally resulting from their official misconduct.

*   *   *

The situation thus being that $1,106,175.77 of Continental's money has been wrongfully diverted from it, there can be no doubt of the right of its trustee to recover the same unless recovery is prevented by rules applicable to bona fide purchasers.

The officers and directors whom I have just said would be accountable to the trustees of Reynolds Investing Company for the $1,318,750 but for the fact that $1,106,175.77 of the total purchase price came from Continental had no knowledge or notice that the money of Continental was being used or was being wrongfully diverted from it. They know nothing of Continental. They were engaged, however, in a transaction which I have held involved a breach of fiduciary duty on their part, and was hence illegal at least in that sense.

*   *   *

The substance of my holding, as I think already has been plainly indicated, is that the four officers and directors of Reynolds Investing Company arranged a transaction under which $791,250 was paid as the purchase price for 1,055,000 shares of stock and $1,318,750 was paid as a price for their resignations and the election of another's nominees as their successors. The $791,250 cannot be recovered from any one because it was a lawful price paid for what the owners of the stock had a right to sell, and as the sale of the stock is not being either rescinded or treated as void it also follows that those who received the stock need not return it, unless, for reasons hereafter to be discussed, such return becomes necessary for a proper adjustment of equities. The $1,318,750 must be returned because it was an unlawful price paid for what no one had any right to sell and the proceeds of which, if sold, are treated, for remedial purposes, as the property of the corporation (*Bosworth v. Allen, supra,* 168 N.Y. at page 167, 61 N.E. 163, 55 L.R.A. 751, 85 Am. St. Rep. 667), and the persons who must return it are those who arranged the transaction and gave the illegal consideration for it, viz., the four officers who so resigned and elected the successors. The basis of their liability for its return is their participation in a breach of fiduciary duty, and their liability is joint and several. . . .

I am not unmindful of the fact that those four officers and directors did not keep the entire $1,318,750 for themselves, or of the fact that under the form which they caused the transaction to take much of it never passed into or through their hands. That I regard as immaterial, irrespective of whether such officers and directors be regarded as agents of or as trustees for the other sellers of the stock. Such other sellers sold stock, whereas these officers and directors sold control, and liability for that breach of trust cannot be varied by or made dependent upon the accidental and fortuitous circumstance of whose stock was delivered on the different dates upon which deliveries of stock were made under the contract. Even an ordinary agent is personally liable for his own wrongs, and if he illegally receive money to which, to his knowledge, neither he nor his principal is entitled he does not free himself of liability by paying the money over to his principal.

\* \* \*

Submit judgments accordingly.

# NOTE

This case illustrates the sale of office theory. If control of the corporation is sold, the directors and officers are considered to be selling their offices as well. This theory is based on breach of fiduciary duty. Although a director is free to resign at any time, he must do so in a manner that protects the shareholders. In the principal case the assets of the corporation could be stolen easily, so the negligence of the directors was obvious. The stock of the Reynolds Investing Company was purchased at a premium price. Why was it so easy for the court to determine this? Could there be any explanation for the premium price other than an intent to loot the corporation? What could the directors have done to sell the stock at the premium price and also protect shareholders?

Could this problem occur today? *See* section 14(f) of the 1934 Act. It requires information about the new directors prior to their taking office if they were elected otherwise than at a meeting of the shareholders. The information must be filed with the SEC and transmitted to the shareholders.

## PERLMAN v. FELDMANN
United States Court of Appeals, Second Circuit
219 F.2d 173 (1955)

CLARK, J.

This is a derivative action brought by minority stockholders of Newport Steel Corporation to compel accounting for, and restitution of, allegedly illegal gains which accrued to defendants as a result of the sale in August, 1950, of their controlling interest in the corporation. The principal defendant, C. Russell Feldmann, who represented and acted for the others, members of his family[39], was at that time not only the dominant stockholder, but also the chairman of the board of directors and the president of the corporation. Newport, an Indiana corporation,

---

[39] [1] The stock was not held personally by Feldmann in his own name, but was held by the members of his family and by personal corporations. The aggregate of stock thus had amounted to 33% of the outstanding Newport stock and gave working control to the holder. The actual sale included 55,552 additional shares held by friends and associates of Feldmann, so that a total of 37% of the Newport stock was transferred.

operated mills for the production of steel sheets for sale to manufacturers of steel products, first at Newport, Kentucky, and later also at other places in Kentucky and Ohio. The buyers, a syndicate organized as Wilport Company, a Delaware corporation, consisted of end-users of steel who were interested in securing a source of supply in a market becoming ever tighter in the Korean War. Plaintiffs contend that the consideration paid for the stock included compensation for the sale of a corporate asset, a power held in trust for the corporation by Feldmann as its fiduciary. This power was the ability to control the allocation of the corporate product in a time of short supply, through control of the board of directors; and it was effectively transferred in this sale by having Feldmann procure the resignation of his own board and the election of Wilport's nominees immediately upon consummation of the sale.

The present action represents the consolidation of three pending stockholders' actions in which yet another stockholder has been permitted to intervene. Jurisdiction below was based upon the diverse citizenship of the parties. Plaintiffs argue here, as they did in the court below, that in the situation here disclosed the vendors must account to the non-participating minority stockholders for that share of their profit which is attributable to the sale of the corporate power. Judge Hincks denied the validity of the premise, holding that the rights involved in the sale were only those normally incident to the possession of a controlling block of shares, with which a dominant stockholder, in the absence of fraud or foreseeable looting, was entitled to deal according to his own best interests. Furthermore, he held that plaintiffs had failed to satisfy their burden of proving that the sales price was not a fair price for the stock per se. Plaintiffs appeal from these rulings of law which resulted in the dismissal of their complaint.

The essential facts found by the trial judge are not in dispute. Newport was a relative newcomer in the steel industry with predominantly old installations which were in the process of being supplemented by more modern facilities. Except in times of extreme shortage Newport was not in a position to compete profitably with other steel mills for customers not in its immediate geographical area. Wilport, the purchasing syndicate, consisted of geographically remote end-users of steel who were interested in buying more steel from Newport than they had been able to obtain during recent periods of tight supply. The price of $20 per share was found by Judge Hincks to be a fair one for a control block of stock, although the over-the-counter market price had not exceeded $12 and the book value per share was $17.03. But this finding was limited by Judge Hincks' statement that "what value the block would have had if shorn of its appurtenant power to control distribution of the corporate product, the evidence does not show." It was also conditioned by his earlier ruling that the burden was on plaintiffs to prove a lesser value for the stock.

Both as director and as dominant stockholder, Feldmann stood in a fiduciary relationship to the corporation and to the minority stockholders as beneficiaries thereof. . . . When a director deals with his corporation, his acts will be closely scrutinized. *Bossert v. Geis*, 1914, 57 Ind. App. 384, 107 N.E. 95. "Directors of a corporation are its agents, and they are governed by the rules of law applicable to other agents, and, as between themselves and their principal, the rules relating to honesty and fair dealing in the management of the affairs of their principal are applicable. They must not, in any degree, allow their official conduct to be swayed by their private interest, which must yield to official duty. *Leader Publishing Co. v. Grant Trust Co.*, 1915, 182 Ind. 651, 108 N.E. 121. In a transaction between a director and his corporation, where he acts for himself and his principal at the same time in a matter connected with the relation between them, it is presumed, where he is thus potential on both sides of the contract, that self-interest will overcome his fidelity to his principal, to his own benefit and to his principal's hurt." And the judge added: "Absolute and most scrupulous good faith is the very essence of a director's obligation to his corporation. The first principal duty arising from his official relation is to act in all things of trust wholly for the benefit of his corporation."

In Indiana, then, as elsewhere, the responsibility of the fiduciary is not limited to a proper regard for the tangible balance sheet assets of the corporation, but includes the dedication of his uncorrupted business judgment for the sole benefit of the corporation, in any dealings which may adversely affect it. Although the Indiana case is particularly relevant to Feldmann as a director, the same rule should apply to his fiduciary duties as majority stockholder, for in that capacity he chooses and controls the directors, and thus is held to have assumed their liability. *Pepper v. Litton, supra*, 308 U.S. 295, 60 S.Ct. 238. This, therefore, is the standard to which Feldmann was by law required to conform in his activities here under scrutiny.

It is true, as defendants have been at pains to point out, that this is not the ordinary case of breach of fiduciary duty. We have here no fraud, no misuse of confidential information, no outright looting of a helpless corporation. But on the other hand, we do not find compliance with that high standard which we have just stated and which we and other courts have come to expect and demand of corporate fiduciaries. In the often-quoted words of Judge Cardozo: "Many forms of conduct permissible in a workaday world for those acting at arm's length, are forbidden to those bound by fiduciary ties. A trustee is held to something stricter than the morals of the market place. Not honesty alone, but the punctilio of an honor the most sensitive, is then the standard of behavior. As to this there has developed a tradition that is unbending and inveterate. Uncompromising rigidity has been the attitude of courts of equity when petitioned to undermine the rule of undivided loyalty by the 'disintegrating erosion' of particular exceptions." *Meinhard v. Salmon, supra*, 249 N.Y. 458, 464, 164 N.E. 545, 546, 62 A.L.R. 1. The actions of defendants in siphoning off for personal gain corporate advantages to be derived from a favorable market situation do not betoken the necessary undivided loyalty owed by the fiduciary to his principal.

The corporate opportunities of whose misappropriation the minority stockholders complain need not have been an absolute certainty in order to support this action against Feldmann. . . . And in *Irving Trust Co. v. Deutsch, supra*, 2 Cir., 73 F.2d 121, 124, an accounting was required of corporate directors who bought stock for themselves for corporate use, even though there was an affirmative showing that the corporation did not have the finances itself to acquire the stock. Judge Swan speaking for the court pointed out that "The defendants' argument, contrary to *Wing v. Dillingham* (5 Cir., 239 F. 54), that the equitable rule that fiduciaries should not be permitted to assume a position in which their individual interests might be in conflict with those of the corporation can have no application where the corporation is unable to undertake the venture, is not convincing. If directors are permitted to justify their conduct on such a theory, there will be a temptation to refrain from exerting their strongest efforts on behalf of the corporation since, if it does not meet the obligations, an opportunity of profit will be open to them personally."

This rationale is equally appropriate to a consideration of the benefits which Newport might have derived from the steel shortage. In the past Newport had used and profited by its market leverage by operation of what the industry had come to call the "Feldmann Plan." This consisted of securing interest-free advances from prospective purchasers of steel in return for firm commitments to them from future production. The funds thus acquired were used to finance improvements in existing plants and to acquire new installations. In the summer of 1950 Newport had been negotiating for cold-rolling facilities which it needed for a more fully integrated operation and a more marketable product, and Feldmann plan funds might well have been used toward this end.

Further, as plaintiffs alternatively suggest, Newport might have used the period of short supply to build up patronage in the geographical area in which it could compete profitably even when steel was more abundant. Either of these opportunities was Newport's, to be used to its advantage only. Only if defendants had been able to negate completely any possibility of gain by Newport could they have prevailed. It is true that a trial court finding states: "Whether or not, in August, 1950, Newport's position was such that it could have entered into "Feldmann Plan" type transactions to procure funds and financing for the further expansion and integration of its steel facilities and whether such expansion would have been desirable for Newport, the evidence does not show." This, however, cannot avail the defendants, who — contrary to the ruling below — had the burden of proof on this issue, since fiduciaries always have the burden of proof in establishing the fairness of their dealings with trust property.

Defendants seek to categorize the corporate opportunities which might have accrued to Newport as too unethical to warrant further consideration. It is true that reputable steel producers were not participating in the gray market brought about by the Korean War and were refraining from advancing their prices, although to do so would not have been illegal. But Feldmann plan transactions were not considered within this self-imposed interdiction; the trial court found that around the time of the Feldmann sale Jones & Laughlin Steel Corporation, Republic Steel Company, and Pittsburgh Steel Corporation were all participating in such arrangements. In any event, it ill becomes the defendants to disparage as unethical the market advantages from which they themselves reaped rich benefits.

We do not mean to suggest that a majority stockholder cannot dispose of his controlling block of stock to outsiders without having to account to his corporation for profits or even never do this with impunity when the buyer is an interested customer, actual or potential, for the corporation's product. But when the sale necessarily results in a sacrifice of this element of corporate good will and consequent unusual profit to the fiduciary who has caused the sacrifice, he should account for his gains. So in a time of market shortage, where a call on a corporation's product commands an unusually large premium, in one form or another, we think it sound law that a fiduciary may not appropriate to himself the value of this premium. Such personal gain at the expense of his coventurers seems particularly reprehensible when made by the trusted president and director of his company. In this case the violation of duty seems to be all the clearer because of this triple role in which Feldmann appears, though we are unwilling to say, and are not to be understood as saying, that we should accept a lesser obligation for any one of his roles alone.

Hence to the extent that the price received by Feldmann and his codefendants included such a bonus, he is accountable to the minority stockholders who sue here. RESTATEMENT, RESTITUTION §§ 190, 197 (1937); *Seagrave Corp. v. Mount, supra,* 6 Cir., 212 F.2d 389. And plaintiffs, as they contend, are entitled to a recovery in their own right, instead of in right of the corporation (as in the usual derivative actions), since neither Wilport nor their successors in interest should share in any judgment which may be rendered. *See Southern Pacific Co. v. Bogert,* 250 U.S. 483, 39 S.Ct. 533, 63 L. Ed. 1099. Defendants cannot well object to this form of recovery, since the only alternative, recovery for the corporation as a whole, would subject them to a greater total liability.

The case will therefore be remanded to the district court for a determination of the question expressly left open below, namely, the value of defendants' stock without the appurtenant control over the corporation's output of steel.

\* \* \*

The judgment is therefore reversed and the action remanded for further proceedings pursuant to this opinion.

SWAN, CIRCUIT JUDGE (dissenting).

With the general principles enunciated in the majority opinion as to the duties of fiduciaries I am, of course, in thorough accord. But, as Mr. Justice Frankfurter stated in *Securities and Exchange Comm. v. Chenery Corp.,* 318 U.S. 80, 85, 63 S.Ct. 454, 458, 87 L. Ed. 626, "to say that a man is a fiduciary only begins analysis; it gives direction to further inquiry. To whom is he a fiduciary? What obligations does he owe as a fiduciary? In what respect has he failed to discharge these obligations?" My brothers' opinion does not specify precisely what fiduciary duty Feldmann is held to have violated or whether it was a duty imposed upon him as the dominant stockholder or as a director of Newport. Without such specification I think that both the legal profession and the business world will find the decision confusing and will be unable to foretell the extent of its impact upon customary practices in the sale of stock.

The power to control the management of a corporation, that is, to elect directors to manage its affairs, is an inseparable incident to the ownership of a majority of its stock, or sometimes, as in the present instance, to the ownership of enough shares, less than a majority, to control an election. Concededly a majority or dominant shareholder is ordinarily privileged to sell his stock at the best price obtainable from the purchaser. In so doing he acts on his own behalf, not as an agent of the corporation. If he knows or has reason to believe that the purchaser intends to exercise to the detriment of the corporation the power of management acquired by the purchase, such knowledge or reasonable suspicion will terminate the dominant shareholder's privilege to sell and will create a duty not to transfer the power of management to such purchaser. The duty seems to me to resemble the obligation which everyone is under not to assist another to commit a tort rather than the obligation of a fiduciary. But whatever the nature of the duty, a violation of it will subject the violator to liability for damages sustained by the corporation. Judge Hincks found that Feldmann had no reason to think that Wilport would use the power of management it would acquire by the purchase to injure Newport, and that there was no proof that it ever was so used. Feldmann did know, it is true, that the reason Wilport wanted the stock was to put in a board of directors who would be likely to permit Wilport's members to purchase more of Newport's steel than they might otherwise be able to get. But there is nothing illegal in a dominant shareholder purchasing from his own corporation at the same prices it offers to other customers. That is what the members of Wilport did, and there is no proof that Newport suffered any detriment therefrom.

*  *  *

Feldmann was also a director of Newport. Perhaps the quoted statement means that as a director he violated his fiduciary duty in voting to elect Wilport's nominees to fill the vacancies created by the resignations of the former directors of Newport. As a director Feldmann was under a fiduciary duty to use an honest judgment in acting on the corporation's behalf. A director is privileged to resign, but so long as he remains a director he must be faithful to his fiduciary duties and must not make a personal gain from performing them. Consequently, if the price paid for Feldmann's stock included a payment for voting to elect the new directors, he must account to the corporation for such payment, even though he honestly believed that the men he voted to elect were well qualified to serve as directors. He cannot take pay for performing his fiduciary duty. There is no suggestion that he did do so, unless the price paid for his stock was more than its value. So it seems to me that decision must turn on whether finding 120 and conclusion 5 of the district judge are supportable on the evidence. They are set out in the margin.[40]

Judge Hincks went into the matter of valuation of the stock with his customary care and thoroughness. He made no error of law in applying the principles relating to valuation of stock. Concededly a controlling block of stock has greater sale value than a small lot. While the spread between $10 per share for small lots and $20 per share for the controlling block seems rather extraordinarily wide, the $20 valuation was supported by the expert testimony of Dr. Badger, whom the district judge said he could not find to be wrong. I see no justification for upsetting the valuation as clearly erroneous. Nor can I agree with my brothers that the $20 valuation "was limited" by the last sentence in finding 120. The controlling block could not by any possibility be shorn of its appurtenant power to elect directors and through them to control distribution of the corporate product. It is this "appurtenant power" which gives a controlling block its value as such block. What evidence could be adduced to show the value of the block "if shorn" of such appurtenant power, I cannot conceive, for it cannot be shorn of it.

---

[40] [1] "120. The 398,927 shares of Newport stock sold to Wilport as of August 31, 1950, had a fair value as a control block of $20 per share. What value the block would have had if shorn of its appurtenant power to control distribution of the corporate product, the evidence does not show."

\* \* \*

I would affirm the judgment on appeal.

## NOTE

Why is control stock worth more than non-control stock? Why didn't Mr. Feldmann negotiate a merger between Wilport and Newport? Why didn't he insist that all shareholders be offered the same price? What if Mr. Feldmann resigned as an officer and director and then voted into office neutral directors and officers, would he then be free to sell his own stock for the best price he could get?

Is the reasoning of the court the sale of office theory of *Gerdes v. Reynolds, supra,* or is it based on another theory?

## F. STOCK SPLITS

### APPLEBAUM v. AVAYA, INC.
Supreme Court of Delaware
812 A.2d 880 (2002)

VEASEY, J.

In this appeal, we affirm the judgment of the Court of Chancery holding that a corporation could validly initiate a reverse stock split and selectively dispose of the fractional interests held by stockholders who no longer hold whole shares. The Vice Chancellor interpreted Section 155 of the Delaware General Corporation Law to permit the corporation, as part of a reverse/forward stock split, to treat its stockholders unequally by cashing out the stockholders who own only fractional interests while opting not to dispose of fractional interests of stockholders who will end up holding whole shares of stock as well as fractional interests. In the latter instance the fractional shares would be reconverted to whole shares in an accompanying forward stock split.

We hold that neither the language of Section 155 nor the principles guiding our interpretation of statutes dictate a prohibition against the disparate treatment of stockholders, for this purpose. We also hold that the corporation may dispose of those fractional interests pursuant to Section 155(1) by aggregating the fractional interests and selling them on behalf of the cashed-out stockholders where this method of disposition has a rational business purpose of saving needless transaction costs.

A further issue we address is whether, as an alternative method of compensation, the corporation may satisfy the "fair price" requirement of Section 155(2) by paying the stockholders an amount based on the average trading price of the corporation's stock. Here, the Vice Chancellor properly held that the trading price of actively-traded stock of a corporation, the stock of which is widely-held, will provide an adequate measure of fair value for the stockholders' fractional interests for purposes of a reverse stock split under Section 155.

## Facts

*[handwritten margin note: T → LU → Avaya Oct 2000]*

Avaya, Inc. is a Delaware corporation that designs and manages communications networks for business organizations and large non-profit agencies. The enterprise is a descendant of the industry standard-bearer, AT & T. Avaya was established as an independent company in October of 2000 when it was spun off from Lucent Technologies. Lucent itself is a spin-off of AT & T. Because its capital structure is the product of two spin-off transactions, the outstanding stock of Avaya is one of the most widely-held on the New York Stock Exchange. Over 3.3 million common stockholders own fewer than 90 shares of Avaya stock each. *[margin: 3.3 mill s/h < 90 sh]*

Although a large number of stockholders hold a small stake in the corporation, Avaya incurs heavy expenses to maintain their accounts. Avaya spends almost $4 million per year to print and mail proxy statements and annual reports to each stockholder as well as to pay transfer agents and other miscellaneous fees. Stockholders who own their stock in street names cost Avaya an additional $3.4 million in similar administrative fees. *[margin: cost to the corp to maintain]*

Since the cost of maintaining a stockholder's account is the same regardless of the number of shares held, Avaya could reduce its administrative burden, and thereby save money for its stockholders, by decreasing its stockholder base. In February of 2001, at the corporation's annual meeting, the Avaya board of directors presented the stockholders with a transaction designed to accomplish this result. The Avaya board asked the stockholders to grant the directors authorization to engage in one of three alternative transactions: *[margin: save $]*

   (1)   a reverse 1-for-30 stock split followed immediately by a forward 30-for-1 stock split of the Common stock

   (2)   a reverse 1-for-40 stock split followed immediately by a forward 40-for-1 stock split of the Common stock

   (3)   a reverse 1-for-50 stock split followed immediately by a forward 50-for-1 stock split of the Common stock.

*[margin: options presented to s/h]*

We refer in this opinion to all three of these alternative transactions as the "Proposed Transaction" or the "Reverse/Forward Split." Regardless of the particular ratio the board chooses, at some future date the Reverse Split will occur at 6:00 p.m., followed by a Forward Split one minute later. Once selected, the effective date of the Split will be posted on Avaya's website. *[margin: mechanics]*

The transaction will cash out stockholders who own stock below the minimum number ultimately selected by the directors for the Reverse/Forward Split pursuant to those three alternative options. Stockholders who do not hold the minimum number of shares necessary to survive the initial Reverse Split will be cashed out and receive payment for their resulting fractional interests (the "cashed-out stockholders" or "targeted stockholders"). Stockholders who own a sufficient amount of stock to survive the Reverse Split will not have their fractional interests cashed out. Once the Forward Split occurs, their fractional holdings will be converted back into whole shares of stock.

Avaya will compensate the cashed-out stockholders through one of two possible methods. Avaya may combine the fractional interests and sell them as whole shares *[margin: pymt 1. aggr/ and sell 2. avg ovr 10 days]* on the open market. In the alternative, the corporation will pay the stockholders the value of their fractional interests based on the trading price of the stock averaged over a ten-day period preceding the Reverse Split. Stockholders who hold their Avaya stock in street names have been advised to contact their nominees to see that they receive the same consideration as stockholders who have their interests registered in their own names.[41]

To illustrate the Proposed Transaction through a hypothetical, assume Stockholder A owns fifteen shares of stock and Stockholder B owns forty-five shares of stock. If Avaya chooses to initiate a Reverse 1-for-30 Stock Split, Stockholder A will possess a fractional interest equivalent to one-half a share of stock. Stockholder B will hold one whole share of Avaya stock and a fractional interest equivalent to one-half a share. Using the provisions of Section 155(1) or (2) of the Delaware General Corporation Law, Avaya would cash out Stockholder A since he no longer possesses a whole share of stock. Stockholder A would no longer be an Avaya stockholder. Stockholder B will remain a stockholder because Avaya will not cash out the fractional interest held by her. Stockholder B's fractional interest remains attached to a whole share of stock. When Avaya executes the accompanying Forward 30-for-1 Stock Split, Stockholder B's interest in one and one-half shares will be converted into forty-five shares of stock, the same amount that she held prior to the Transaction.

At the annual meeting, Avaya stockholders voted to authorize the board to proceed with any one of the three alternative transactions. Applebaum, a holder of twenty-seven shares of Avaya stock, filed an action in the Court of Chancery to enjoin the Reverse/Forward Split. Under any one of the three alternatives Applebaum would be cashed out because he holds less than thirty shares.

### Proceedings in the Court of Chancery

Applebaum asked the Court of Chancery to enjoin the Proposed Transaction, alleging that Avaya's treatment of fractional interests will not comport with the requirements set forward in Title 8, Section 155 of the Delaware Code. Applebaum argued that Section 155 does not permit Avaya to issue fractional shares to some stockholders but not to others in the same transaction. Even if Avaya could issue fractional shares selectively, Applebaum contended that the methods by which Avaya plans to cash-out the smaller stockholders do not comply with subsections (1) and (2) of Section 155.

After considering cross-motions for summary judgment, the Court of Chancery denied Applebaum's request for an injunction and held that the Reverse/Forward Split would comply with Section 155 and dispose of the cashed-out stockholders' interests in a fair and efficient manner. Applebaum appeals the final judgment entered for the defendants. We affirm.

---

[41] [1] In the Proxy Statement the Board explains that "Avaya intends for the Reverse/Forward Split to treat shareholders holding Common Stock in street name through a nominee . . . in the same manner as shareholders whose shares are registered in their names. Nominees will be instructed to effect the Reverse/Forward Split for their beneficial holders. However, nominees may have different procedures and shareholders holding shares in street name should contact their nominees."

## Issues on Appeal

Applebaum claims the Court of Chancery erred by: (1) holding that Title 8, Section 155 permits Avaya to issue fractional shares to the surviving stockholders but not issue fractional shares to the cashed-out stockholders; (2) holding that Avaya can combine the fractional interests and sell them on the open market; (3) holding that Avaya can instruct nominees to participate in the Split even if a particular nominee holds a sufficient amount of stock on behalf of all of its beneficial holders to survive the Split; (4) granting summary judgment and holding that the payment of cash for fractional interests based on a ten-day average of the trading price of Avaya stock constitutes "fair value" under Section 155; and (5) holding that the meaning of "fair value" in Sections 155(2) is different from Section 262 and thus failing to value the fractional shares as proportionate interests in a going concern.

### Section 155 Does Not Prevent Avaya From Disposing of Fractional Interests Selectively

Applebaum questions the board's authority to treat stockholders differently by disposing of the fractional interests of some stockholders but not others. Applebaum contends that Avaya will issue fractional shares in violation of Section 155. According to this view of the transaction, during the one minute interval between the two stock splits the corporation will not issue fractional shares to stockholders who possess holdings below the minimum amount. Those stockholders will be cashed out. Stockholders who hold stock above the minimum amount, by contrast, will be issued fractional shares that will be reconverted in the Forward Split into the same number of whole shares owned by those stockholders before the Reverse Split.

Applebaum argues that Section 155 prevents Avaya from achieving this disparate result by providing that:

> A corporation may, but shall not be required to, issue fractions of a share. If it does not issue fractions of a share, it shall (1) arrange for the disposition of fractional interests by those entitled thereto, (2) pay in cash the fair value of fractions of a share as of the time when those entitled to receive such fractions are determined . . . .

Applebaum reads Section 155 to mean that Avaya can employ the cash-out methods provided in Section 155 only if the corporation "does not issue fractions of a share."

This Court reviews de novo the Court of Chancery's decision to grant Avaya's motion for summary judgment. We need not reach the merits of Applebaum's interpretation of Section 155 because he has based his argument on the flawed assumption that Avaya will issue fractional shares. Since the Reverse/Forward Split is an integrated transaction, Avaya need not issue any fractional shares. The initial Reverse Split creates a combination of whole shares and fractional interests. Avaya will use either Section 155(1) or (2) to cash out the fractional interests of stockholders who no longer possess a whole share of stock. Fractional interests that are attached to whole shares will not be disposed of. Nor will they be represented by fractions of a share. Fractional shares are unnecessary because the surviving fractional interests will be reconverted into whole shares in the Forward Split.[42]

Applebaum correctly notes that Avaya stockholders are not treated equally in the Proposed Transaction. The disparate treatment, however, does not arise by issuing fractional shares selectively. It occurs through the selective disposition of some fractional interests but not others. The provisions of Section 155 do not forbid this disparate treatment. While principles of equity permit this Court to intervene when technical compliance with a statute produces an unfair result, equity and equality are not synonymous concepts in the Delaware General Corporation Law.[43] Moreover, this Court should not create a safeguard against stockholder inequality that does not appear in the statute.[44] Here there is no showing that Applebaum was treated inequitably. From all that appears on this record, the proposed transaction was designed in good faith to accomplish a rational business purpose — saving transaction costs.[45]

Our jurisprudence does not prevent Avaya from properly using Section 155 in a creative fashion that is designed to meet its needs as an on-going enterprise.[46] The subsections listed in Section 155 merely require the corporation to compensate its stockholders when it chooses not to recognize their fractional interests in the form of fractional shares.[47] Based upon this record, we conclude that Avaya is free to recognize the fractional interests of some stockholders but not others so long as the corporation follows the procedures set forth in Section 155.

---

[42] [7] Shares of stock are issued to provide a verifiable property interest for the residual claimants of the corporation. *See Kalageorgi v. Victor Kamkin, Inc.*, 750 A.2d 531, 538 (Del. Ch. 1999) (stating that "Corporate securities are a species of property right") *aff'd*, 748 A.2d 913 (Del. 2000). We do not believe Avaya must issue fractional shares to recognize a property interest that, by the terms of the transaction, will last only sixty seconds.

[43] [9] *See Nixon v. Blackwell*, 626 A.2d 1366, 1376 (Del. 1993) ("It is well established in our jurisprudence that stockholders need not always be treated equally for all purposes."); *see also Unocal Corp. v. Mesa Petroleum Co.*, 493 A.2d 946, 957 (Del. 1985); *Cheff v. Mathes*, 199 A.2d 548, 554–56 (Del. 1964).

[44] [10] *See, e.g., Williams v. Geier*, 671 A.2d 1368, 1385 n. 36 (Del. 1996) (noting "Directors and investors must be able to rely on the stability and absence of judicial interference with the State's statutory prescriptions"); *Nixon*, 626 A.2d at 1379–81 (absent legislation there should be no "special, judicially-created rules for minority investors"); *American Hardware Corp. v. Savage Arms. Corp.*, 136 A.2d 690, 693 (Del. 1957) (rejecting argument based on an interpretation that would "import serious confusion and uncertainty into corporate procedure").

[45] [11] *See Sinclair v. Levien*, 280 A.2d 717, 720 (Del. 1971) (board action presumed valid if it "can be attributed to any rational business purpose"); *see also Williams*, 671 A.2d at 1377–78 (board action in recommending charter amendment for stockholder action covered by business judgment rule in the absence of rebuttal demonstrating violation of fiduciary duty).

[46] [12] *See Grimes v. Alteon Inc.*, 804 A.2d 256, 266 (Del. 2002) (noting that corporations "should have the freedom to enter into new and different forms of transactions") (citations omitted).

[47] [13] *See* WARD, WELCH & TUREZYN, FOLK ON THE DELAWARE GENERAL CORPORATION LAW § 155.1 (4th ed. 2002) (stating "a corporation may refuse to issue share fractions . . . [but] If the corporation chooses to ignore share fractions, it must elect one of the three alternatives authorized by Section 155 . . . ").

### Avaya May Proceed with Any of Its Alternative Plans to Dispose of the Fractional Interests

The balance of Applebaum's appeal challenges the alternative methods by which Avaya proposes to dispose of the fractional interests. The Court of Chancery concluded that Avaya could proceed under Section 155(1) by aggregating the fractional interests and selling them on behalf of the cashed-out stockholders. The Court also held that Avaya could employ Section 155(2), which requires payment of the "fair value" of the fractional interests, by paying the cashed-out stockholders an amount based on the average trading price of Avaya stock. We agree with the decision of the Court of Chancery and address separately the issues based on each subsection of the statute.

### Section 155(1) Permits Avaya to Sell the Factional Interest on Behalf of the Stockholders

The stockholders have authorized Avaya to compensate the cashed-out stockholders by combining their fractional interests into whole shares and then selling them on the stockholders' behalf. Section 155(1) permits Avaya to "arrange for the disposition of fractional interests by those entitled thereto."

Applebaum claims that Avaya cannot use Section 155(1) because the corporation will sell whole shares rather than "fractional interests." According to this rendition of the transaction, the fractional interests held by the targeted stockholders must be reconverted into whole shares in the Forward Split. Otherwise, their fractional interests will be diluted.[48] Avaya must reconvert the interests back to their initial value as whole shares in order to sell the combined fractional interests. Thus, Avaya would be selling whole shares rather than fractional interests.

Applebaum's argument incorrectly assumes that Avaya must issue fractions of a share in the Proposed Transaction. After the Reverse Split takes place, the stockholders holding shares below the minimum amount will be cashed out. The fractional interests will not be represented as shares and are therefore not involved in the Forward Split. Avaya will then aggregate the fractional interests and repackage them as whole shares which the corporation will sell on the open market. The statute does not mandate any set procedure by which the fractional interests must be disposed of so long as those interests are sold in a manner that secures the proportionate value of the cashed-out holdings.

Applebaum also contends that Avaya cannot sell the fractional interests on behalf of the cashed-out stockholders. If Avaya sells the interests for the stockholders, Applebaum argues that the corporation will not comply with Section 155(1) because the interests are not disposed of by "those entitled thereto." As the Vice Chancellor noted, Applebaum presents a strained reading of Section 155(1). The Court of

---

[48] [15] Applebaum provides the following example: "[I]f the Minimum Number is 30, a holder of 10 pre-split shares will have a fractional interest of 1/3 of a share upon consummation of the Reverse Split. One minute later, the whole shares with their attendant fractional shares are multiplied by 30 in the Forward Split. If the 1/3 share fractional interest is not also multiplied by 30 in the Forward Split, it would be reduced to 1/90th of a post-Forward Split share." Appellant's Br. at 23 n. 10.

Chancery correctly reasoned that "In the eyes of equity, such sales would be 'by'" the stockholders.

Applebaum's interpretation also ignores the corporation's responsibility under Section 155(1) to "arrange" for the disposition of fractional interests. Since fractional shares cannot be listed on the major stock exchanges, the corporation must arrange for their aggregation in order to sell them. Aggregation is normally performed by affording to the stockholder an election to sell the fractional share or to purchase an additional fraction sufficient to make up a whole share. The elections are forwarded to a trust company or other agent of the corporation who matches up the purchases and sales and issues certificates for the whole shares or checks for payment of the fractional shares. . . . "

The general practice requires the corporation to act as an intermediary to package the fractional interests into marketable shares. If the corporation were not permitted to do so, the fractional interests of the cashed-out stockholders would be dissipated through the transaction costs of finding other fractional holders with whom to combine and sell fractional interests in the market.

 Avaya May Instruct Nominees to Execute the Proposed
Transaction on Behalf of the Beneficial Owners

To execute the Reverse/Forward Split, Avaya stated in its proxy statement that "Nominees will be instructed to effect the Reverse/Forward Split for their beneficial holders." Applebaum argues that nominees cannot be forced to elect to receive cash in exchange for the fractional interests held by their beneficial holders if the nominee's combined holdings for all of its beneficial holders exceeds the minimum amount of stock necessary to survive the Reverse Split.

Applebaum misstates the responsibility of a corporation to stockholders who hold their interests through nominees and brokers. Nominees, as agents of the beneficial owners, owe a duty to take the necessary steps to afford the true owners the opportunity to realize the benefits of the Proposed Transaction. The Court of Chancery properly held that the Reverse/Forward Split could operate at the level of the corporate ledger. Avaya is not required to take any additional actions to effect the transaction for stockholders who own their stock through a nominee.[49] The beneficial stockholders are responsible for making proper arrangements with their agents.[50]

Applebaum also raises a disclosure issue related to the instructions for beneficial owners. The proxy statement informs stockholders that nominees "will be instructed to effect" the transaction. Applebaum argues that this statement is misleading because, as explained above, he contends that a nominee has the option

---

[49] [24] *See Enstar Corp. v. Senouf*, 535 A.2d 1351, 1354 (Del. 1987) ("The legal and practical effects of having one's stock registered in street name cannot be visited upon the issuer. The attendant risks are those of the stockholder . . . .").

[50] [25] *See, e.g., Enstar*, 535 A.2d at 1354 (stating that the holder of record must demand appraisal rights); see also 8 Del. C. § 219(c) ("The stock ledger shall be the only evidence as to who are the stockholders entitled to examine the stock ledger, the list required by this section or the books of the corporation, or to vote in person or by proxy at any meeting of stockholders.").

either to effect the split or refrain from doing so if the aggregate amount of the beneficial holders' stock is sufficient to survive the Reverse Split. The proxy statement places the beneficial owners on notice that they must make arrangements with their nominees to receive payment from the transaction. The proxy statement is not misleading because it accurately states that the nominees must execute the transaction on behalf of the beneficial holders.

### The Ten-Day Trading Average by which Avaya Proposes to Compensate the Cashed-Out Stockholders Constitutes "Fair Value" under Section 155(2)

As an alternative to selling the fractional interests on behalf of the stockholders, Avaya may opt to pay the stockholders cash in an amount based on the trading price of Avaya stock averaged over a ten-day period preceding the Proposed Transaction. To do so, Avaya relies on Section 155(2), which provides that a corporation may "pay in cash the fair value of fractions of a share as of the time when those entitled to receive such fractions are determined."

The corporation owes its cashed-out stockholders payment representing the "fair value" of their fractional interests. The cashed-out stockholders will receive fair value if Avaya compensates them with payment based on the price of Avaya stock averaged over a ten-day period preceding the Proposed Transaction. While market price is not employed in all valuation contexts,[51] our jurisprudence recognizes that in many circumstances a property interest is best valued by the amount a buyer will pay for it.[52] The Vice Chancellor correctly concluded that a well-informed, liquid trading market will provide a measure of fair value superior to any estimate the court could impose.

Applebaum relies on two instances where the Court of Chancery intimated that a Section 155(2) valuation may be similar to a going concern valuation employed in an appraisal proceeding. In *Chalfin v. Hart Holdings Co.*, the Court of Chancery rejected a market price offered by a majority stockholder because the stock was not traded in an active market. In *Metropolitan Life Ins. Co. v. Aramark Corp.*, the Court of Chancery declined to apply a private company discount presented by a controlling stockholder seeking to squeeze out the minority stockholders. Neither case applies here.

The court cannot defer to market price as a measure of fair value if the stock has not been traded actively in a liquid market. In *Chalfin*, for example, the Court of

---

[51] [28] *See e.g.*, 8 Del. C. § 262(h) ("In determining . . . fair value," in an appraisal proceeding, "the Court shall take into account all relevant factors."); *Smith v. Van Gorkom*, 488 A.2d 858, 876 (Del. 1985) (holding that a decision by the board of directors to approve a merger did not fall within the proper exercise of business judgment because the directors failed to consider the intrinsic worth of the corporation where the stock traded at a depressed market value).

[52] [29] *Cf.* 8 Del. C. § 262(b)(1) (denying appraisal rights for stock listed on a national securities exchange, interdealer quotation system by the National Association of Securities Dealers, Inc. or held of record by more than 2,000 holders); *Revlon, Inc. v. MacAndrews & Forbes Holdings*, 506 A.2d 173, 182 (Del. 1986) (noting that an auction for the sale of a corporation is an appropriate method by which to secure the best price for the stockholders); *Baron v. Pressed Metals of America, Inc.*, 123 A.2d 848, 854 (Del. 1956) (noting that the "best price" a corporation could hope to obtain for the sale of a corporate asset "was what someone would be willing to pay" for it).

Chancery held that the controlling stockholder could not offer as "fair value" in a reverse stock split the same amount alleged to be the past trading value because the stock had not been publicly traded for "some time." The "market price" offered by the controlling stockholder was based on stale information.[53] An active trading market did not exist to monitor the corporation's performance. Thus, a more thorough valuation would have been necessary.

Avaya stock, by contrast, is actively traded on the NYSE. The concerns noted in *Chalfin* are not pertinent to the Proposed Transaction because the market continues to digest information currently known about the company. The value of Avaya's stock is tested daily through the purchase and sale of the stock on the open market.

In a related argument, Applebaum contends that the trading price cannot represent fair value because the stock price is volatile, trading at a range of prices from $13.70 per share to $1.12 per share over the past year. The volatility in trading does not necessarily mean that the market price is not an accurate indicator of fair value. Avaya stock is widely-held and actively traded in the market. The ten-day average has been recognized as a fair compromise that will hedge against the risk of fluctuation. Corporations often cash out fractional interests in an amount based on the average price over a given trading period.[54]

Applebaum also misunderstands the appropriate context for which a going-concern valuation may be necessary under Section 155(2). In both Chalfin and Aramark, the Court of Chancery recognized that a transaction employing Section 155 may warrant a searching inquiry of fair value if a controlling stockholder initiates the transaction.[55] When a controlling stockholder presents a transaction that will free it from future dealings with the minority stockholders, opportunism becomes a concern.[56] Any shortfall imposed on the minority stockholders will result in a transfer of value to the controlling stockholder. The discount in value could be imposed deliberately[57] or could be the result of an information asymmetry where the controlling stockholder possesses material facts that are not known in the

---

[53] [35] *See Seagraves v. Urstadt Prop. Co.*, 1996 WL 159626 (Del. Ch.) at *7 ("To be reliable, market price must be established in an active market."); *Cf. Gimbel v. Signal Companies, Inc.*, 316 A.2d 599, 615, (Del. Ch. 1974) (holding that an expert valuation of oil and gas properties should have been updated to account for market fluctuations) *aff'd* 316 A.2d 619 (Del. 1974).

[54] [37] *See* DREXLER et. al. *supra* n. 18 § 17.04 (2001) (stating "Merger agreements frequently provide for the payment of cash based on trading prices during an agreed period. While this technically may not key to an exact time when the persons entitled to fractions are determined . . . it is thought to better reflect fair values.").

[55] [38] *Chalfin*, 1990 WL 181958 at *3 n. 3 (noting that market price might satisfy the fair value requirement under Section 155(2) but not "where the market price was set by the issuer company, acting as the primary (if not the sole) buyer"); *Aramark*, 1998 Del. Ch. LEXIS 70 at *8 (going concern valuation is necessary when the controlling stockholder is performing the "functional equivalent" of a squeeze-out merger).

[56] [39] *Weinberger v. UOP, Inc.*, 457 A.2d 701, 710 (Del. 1983), ("Given the absence of any attempt to structure this transaction on an arm's length basis, [the controlling stockholder] . . . cannot escape the effects of the conflicts it faced . . . ").

[57] [40] *Chalfin*, 1990 WL 181958 at *3 n. 3. *Cf. Van Gorkom*, 488 A.2d at 877 (holding that merger price offered by CEO in a leveraged buyout could not be accepted as adequate without further investigation since the offer only calculated the amount that would allow the CEO to perform the transaction);

market.[58] Thus, a Section 155(2) inquiry may resemble a Section 262 valuation if the controlling stockholder will benefit from presenting a suspect measure of valuation, such as an out-dated trading price, or a wrongfully imposed private company discount.

Although the Reverse/Forward Split will cash out smaller stockholders, the transaction will not allow the corporation to realize a gain at their expense. Unlike the more typical "freeze-out" context, the cashed-out Avaya stockholders may continue to share in the value of the enterprise. Avaya stockholders can avoid the effects of the proposed transaction either by purchasing a sufficient amount of stock to survive the initial Reverse Split or by simply using the payment provided under Section 155(2) to repurchase the same amount of Avaya stock that they held before the transaction.

The Reverse/Forward Split merely forces the stockholders to choose affirmatively to remain in the corporation. Avaya will succeed in saving administrative costs only if the board has assumed correctly that the stockholders who received a small interest in the corporation through the Lucent spin off would prefer to receive payment, free of transaction costs, rather than continue with the corporation. The Transaction is not structured to prevent the cashed-out stockholders from maintaining their stakes in the company. A payment based on market price is appropriate because it will permit the stockholders to reinvest in Avaya, should they wish to do so.

The Meaning of "Fair Value" under Section 155(2) Is not Identical
to the Concept of "Fair Value" in Section 262

The Court of Chancery correctly interpreted "fair value" in Section 155 to have a meaning independent of the definition of "fair value" in Section 262 of the Delaware General Corporation Law.[59] Relying on the maxim that the same words used in different sections must be construed to have the same meaning, Applebaum argues that "fair value" under Section 155(2) requires the court to perform a valuation similar to an appraisal proceeding. Borrowing from appraisal concepts

---

*Weinberger* 457 A.2d at 711 (holding that outside directors for subsidiary company could not rely solely on fairness report prepared by individuals associated with the parent corporation to determine a fair price for the subsidiary's stock in a squeeze-out merger).

[58] [41] *See, e.g., Glassman v. Unocal Exploration Corp.*, 777 A.2d 242, 248 (De. 2001) (a fair value determination must be based on "all relevant factors" in a short-form merger because the transaction presented by the controlling stockholder may be "timed to take advantage of a depressed market, or a low point in the company's cyclical earnings, or to precede an anticipated positive development . . . ."). *See also* Robert B. Thompson, *Exit, Liquidity, and Majority Rule: Appraisal's Role in Corporate Law,* 84 Geo. L.J. 1, 36 (1995) (arguing that an appraisal valuation may be necessary in a squeeze-out context if "the minority does not have a choice and is being forced out, perhaps because of an anticipated increase in value that will only become visible after the transaction, [in which case] exclusion [of the minority stockholders] can easily become a basis for oppression of the minority").

[59] [44] 8 Del. C. § 262(a) (providing that "Any stockholder of a corporation of this State who holds shares of stock on the date of the making of a demand pursuant to subsection (d) . . . who continuously holds such shares through the effective date of the merger or consolidation . . . who has neither voted in favor of the merger or consolidation nor consented thereto . . . shall be entitled to an appraisal by the Court of Chancery of the fair value of the stockholder's shares of stock. . . . ).

that require that shares of stock be valued as proportionate interests in a going concern, Applebaum contends that the average trading price would be inadequate because the market price possesses an inherent discount that accounts for the holder's minority stake in the company.

The Delaware General Assembly could not have intended Section 155(2) to have the same meaning as the fair value concept employed in Section 262.[60] The reference to fair value in Section 155 first appeared in 1967. The General Assembly did not place the term fair value in Section 262 until 1976. Furthermore, the case law developing the concept of fair value under the appraisal statute did not acquire its present form until this Court discarded the Delaware block method and underscored the necessity of valuing a corporation as a going concern. This Court has not suggested similar valuation guidelines for the right to receive "fair value" under Section 155(2). Finally, Section 262(b)(2)(c) expressly excludes fractional interests from the appraisal remedy when the stock is traded on a national exchange. When applied in the context of a merger or consolidation, Applebaum's interpretation of "fair value" under Section 155(2) would accord the stockholder of a constituent corporation an appraisal of fractional interests to which the stockholder is not entitled under the "market out" exception provided in Section 262.[61]

As this Court noted in *Alabama By-Products v. Cede & Co.*, the right to an appraisal is a narrow statutory right that seeks to redress the loss of the stockholder's ability under the common law to stop a merger.[62] The Reverse/ Forward Split permitted under Section 155 does not present the same problem and is ill-suited for the same solution provided for in Section 262.

The valuation of a stockholder's interest as a "going concern" is necessary only when the board's proposal will alter the nature of the corporation through a merger. When a corporation merges with another corporation, the dissenting stockholder is entitled to the value of the company as a going concern because the nature of the corporation's future "concern" will be vastly different.[63] In a merger requiring an appraisal, the dissenting stockholder's share must be measured as a proportionate interest in a going concern because the proponents of the merger will realize the full

---

[60] [47] *Hariton v. Arco Electronics, Inc.*, 188 A.2d 123, 124 (Del. 1963) ("[t]he general theory of the Delaware Corporation Law that action taken pursuant to the authority of the various sections of that law constitute acts of independent legal significance and their validity is not dependent on other sections of the Act.") (quoting *Langfelder v. Universal Laboratories*, 68 F. Supp. 209, 211 (D.Del. 1946)).

[61] [51] Section 262(b)(1) denies appraisal rights to stockholders of a merging corporation if their stock is listed on a national securities exchange, interdealer quotation system, or held of record by more than 2,000 holders. 8 Del. C. § 262(b)(1). Similarly, under Section 262(b)(2)(c), those same stockholders are not afforded an appraisal right for cash they receive "in lieu of fractional shares" of the stock. 8 Del. C. § 262(b)(2)(c).

[62] [52] 657 A.2d 254, 258 (Del. 1995); *see also* WARD et. al. *supra* n. 13 § 262.1 ("Delaware recognizes the stockholders' appraisal right only in the case of a merger or consolidation."); *see also Glassman*, 777 A.2d at 247 (discussing short-form mergers authorized by Title 8, Section 253 of the Delaware Code and noting that appraisal is the appropriate remedy for the inability to block the transaction).

[63] [53] *See Paskill Corp. v. Alcoma Corp.*, 747 A.2d 549, 553 (Del. 2000) (discussing a recent analysis that justifies appraisal rights as a method by which proponents of a merger are forced to internalize the net benefits and costs of engaging in a "risk altering transaction") (quoting Peter V. Letsou, The Role of Appraisal in Corporate Law, 39 B.C. L. REV. 1121, 1123–24 (1998)).

intrinsic worth of the company rather than simply the market price of the stock. Thus, when a minority stockholder is confronted with a freeze-out merger, the Section 262 appraisal process will prevent the proponents of the merger from "reaping a windfall" by placing the full value of the company as a going concern into the merged entity while compensating the dissenting stockholder with discounted consideration.[64]

Avaya will not capture its full going-concern value in the Reverse/Forward Split. As the Vice Chancellor noted, if the cashed-out stockholders were awarded the value of the company as a going concern, they, rather than the corporation, would receive a windfall. The cashed-out stockholders could capture the full proportionate value of the fractional interest, return to the market and buy the reissued stock at the market price, and realize the going concern value a second time should Avaya ever merge or otherwise become subject to a change of control transaction.

The judgment of the Court of Chancery is affirmed.

## GADDY v. PHELPS COUNTY BANK
### Supreme Court of Missouri
### 20 S.W.3d 511 (2000)

PER CURIAM

A majority of Phelps County Bank shareholders approved an amendment of the Bank's articles of agreement. Under the amended articles, a reverse stock split was authorized. As required by section 362.325, the Missouri director of finance approved the amended articles and the reverse stock split. Various shareholders filed this action seeking relief primarily on the basis that the reverse stock split violated article I, section 28, of the Missouri Constitution. Respondents, Phelps County Bank and Phelps County Bancshares, as well as the Appellant shareholders, moved for summary judgment. The trial court entered summary judgment for the Bank and Bancshares. After opinion by the court of appeals, the case was transferred to this Court. Mo. Const. art.V, sec. 10. The judgment is affirmed.

Phelps County Bank is a private Missouri banking corporation with its principal place of business in Rolla, Missouri, Phelps County Bancshares, Inc., is a private Missouri corporation organized as a bank holding company. As of November 1997, Bancshares owned 25,856 shares (95.4%) of Bank's outstanding stock. On the same date, 66 minority shareholders, including Appellants, owned the remaining 1,244 shares of Bank's stock. Appellants owned a total of 92.5 shares, or 0.3%, of Bank's outstanding stock.

The amended articles and reverse stock split increased Bank's capital and, in effect, provided for a one-share-for-1,000-shares reverse stock split. The amendment also prohibited Bank from issuing any fractional shares. However, as to

---

[64] [54] *See Cavalier Oil*, 564 A.2d at 1145 ("[T]o fail to accord to a minority shareholder the full proportionate value of his shares imposes a penalty for lack of control, and unfairly enriches the majority shareholder who may reap a windfall from the appraisal process by cashing out a dissenting shareholder, a clearly undesirable result.").

shareholders whose interest would be less than one share, the amendment provided a payment of $560 per share for each share of stock held immediately prior to the amendment's effective date.[65]

Appellants' first amended petition contained three counts seeking, respectively, injunctive relief, rescission, and damages. Each remedy was based upon the theory that the reverse stock split violated article I, section 28, of the Constitution in that the stock split constituted the taking of private property for private use without the consent of the owner. Appellant shareholders also raise in this Court contentions that the reverse stock split violated "fundamental principles of equity, fair dealing, and shareholder protection," that these transactions contravene section 362.170, which prohibits a bank from purchasing its own stock, and that neither section 362.325 nor any other statute governing Missouri banks authorizes a reverse stock split.

"When considering appeals from summary judgments, this Court will review the record in the light most favorable to the party against whom judgment was entered." *ITT Commercial Fin. v. Mid-Am Marine Supply Corp.*, 854 S.W.2d 371, 376 (Mo. Banc 1993). "Our review is essentially de novo." *Id.* "The propriety of summary judgment is purely an issue of law. As the trial court's judgment is founded on the record submitted and the law, an appellate court need not defer to the trial court's order granting summary judgment."

Appellants' argument rests on that part of article I, section 28, stating: "That private property shall not be taken for private use with or without compensation, unless by consent of the owner . . . ." The only case Appellants cite to support their argument is *In re Doe Run Lead Co.*, 283 Mo. 646, 223 S.W. 600 (1920), which was a proceeding for the dissolution of the Doe Run Lead Company. This Court reversed the judgment of dissolution after deciding that the result was a "pretended dissolution" (rather than a "real dissolution") under the statute providing for a voluntary dissolution of a corporation.

The facts in *Doe Run* are vastly different from the instant case. There, the majority shareholders of Doe Run actually proposed a consolidation (as opposed to dissolution) of Doe Run with the St. Joseph Company. *Id.* at 609. Both corporations were engaged in the business of mining. At that time, a statute (section 3362, RSMo 1909) — long since repealed — granted the right of consolidation only to manufacturing corporations. *Id.* at 610. In effect, the "pretended dissolution" was an effort to circumvent the consolidation statute then in effect. The appellants in *Doe Run* were minority shareholders in that corporation. The majority shareholders proposed to permit all Doe Run shareholders to become shareholders in the St. Joseph Company or to receive fair value for their Doe Run shares. In either event, the St. Joseph Company would become the owner of the stock.

As Appellants in this case correctly note, in *Doe Run* this Court relied on the predecessor section to article I, section 28, and said: "The stock which belongs to appellants is their private property, and private property (with certain exceptions not here invoked) cannot, without the owner's consent, be taken for private use by any majority, however great, nor by the payment of any price, however large." *Id.*

---

[65]  [3] Appellants make no claim that the offering price of $560 per share is inadequate.

at 609. However, this statement seems only to be an emphatic restatement of the constitutional language. The claim of error in *Doe Run* alleged only "that this is not a bona fide dissolution proceeding such as is contemplated by the statute upon which this proceeding is based . . . ." *Id.* Deciding the dissolution was "pretended" rather than "real," this Court answered the issue raised and granted relief on that basis.

Appellants argue that article I, section 28, and *Doe Run* articulate a fundamental rule that, except for condemnation due to public necessity, a person's private property, such as bank stock, cannot be taken without that person's consent. In this case no such taking occurred. Upon purchasing their bank stock, Appellants consented to the majority shareholders' right to amend Bank's articles of agreement under section 362.325. This statute allows amendment of a bank's articles of agreement, with approval of a majority of the shareholders, to "increase . . . its capital stock to any amount" or "in any way not inconsistent with the provisions of this chapter." Such an amendment becomes effective after the director of finance is satisfied "that there has been a compliance in good faith with all the requirements of the law . . . ." Section 362.325.6. We reject Appellants' narrow reading of section 362.325; under Appellants' interpretation a reverse stock split would not be allowed unless specifically authorized by the statute. However, the plain words of the statute authorize capital changes unless specifically inconsistent with the statute. The reverse stock split does not seem to be inconsistent with any provision of chapter 362 or any other statute.

Appellants also argue that the transactions here violate section 362.170, which bars a bank from purchasing its own stock. Although the bank paid appellants for their fractional shares, the bank did not hold its own shares. It is difficult to see how a bank could effect an amendment of its articles to increase or decrease the bank's capitalization in these circumstances, as authorized by section 362.325, without some transactions of cash for shares. Reading the two sections together, it is clear that the bank has not purchased its own shares for a purpose that would violate section 362.170, and the capital changes are authorized by section 362.325.

"A shareholder in a corporation tacitly consents to any subsequent amendment of articles of incorporation designed to enable the corporation to conduct its business in a more profitable manner." *Midland Truck Lines v. Atwood*, 362 Mo. 397, 241 S.W.2d 903, 907 (1951). Applicable state laws are embodied in the charter of a corporation. *Id.* at 906. *See Shapiro v. Tropicana Lanes, Inc.*, 371 S.W.2d 237, 241 (Mo. 1963) (stating that corporations are subject to the requirements of the Missouri Constitution and statutory law and such laws become part of the corporation's charter).

In *State v. Holekamp Lumber Co.*, 340 S.W.2d 678, 681 (Mo. banc 1960), this Court explained the nature of share ownership:

> "The charter of a corporation having a capital stock is a contract between three parties, and forms the basis of three distinct contracts. The charter is a contract between the state and the corporation; second, it is a contract between the corporation and the stockholders; third, it is a contract between the stockholders and the state." Cook on Corporations, Sec. 492. The third is also described as a contract of the stockholders inter sese.

As early as the *Doe Run* case, this Court recognized the above principles and said that a "real dissolution," as allowed by the voluntary dissolution statute then in effect, "is one of the incidents contemplated when the stock was bought," was "a part of the implied contract between the stockholders," and that such a dissolution "is not a violation of the contract." 223 S.W. at 610. Thus, if the majority shareholders in *Doe Run* had pursued an actual dissolution under the statute in question, the minority shareholders' stock would have been "taken" with their consent on the theory that they contemplated the possibility of statutory dissolution when the stock was purchased. In this respect, *Doe Run* differs little from the instant case.

It is clear that chapter 362 was part of Bank's articles of agreement when Appellants purchased their stock. Appellants tacitly consented to any subsequent amendment of the articles of agreement under section 362.325.1. *Midland Truck Lines*, 241 S.W.2d at 907. Article I, section 28, is not implicated under the facts of this case because the reverse stock split did not take Appellants' stock without their consent.

Because these transactions were authorized by law, we reject Appellants' claim that the trial court's grant of summary judgment violated "fundamental principles of equity, fair dealing, and shareholder protection."

The judgment is affirmed.

All concur.

## G. APPRAISAL REMEDY

### PIEMONTE v. NEW BOSTON GARDEN CORP.
Supreme Judicial Court of Massachusetts
387 N.E. 2d 1145 (1979)

WILKINS, J.

The plaintiffs[66] were stockholders in Boston Garden Arena Corporation (Garden Arena), a Massachusetts corporation whose stockholders voted on July 19, 1973, to merge with the defendant corporation in circumstances which entitled each plaintiff to "demand payment for his stock from the resulting or surviving corporation and an appraisal in accordance with the provisions of (G.L. c. 156B, §§ 86–98)." G.L. c. 156B, § 85, as amended by St. 1969, c. 392, § 22. The plaintiffs commenced this action under G.L. c. 156B, § 90, seeking a judicial determination of the "fair value" of their shares "as of the day preceding the date of the vote approving the proposed corporate action." G.L. c. 156B, § 92, inserted by St. 1964, c. 723, § 1. Each party has appealed from a judgment determining the fair value of the plaintiffs' stock. We granted the defendant's application for direct appellate review.

On July 18, 1973, Garden Arena owned all the stock in a subsidiary corporation

---

66 [1] The fifteen plaintiffs collectively owned 6,289 shares in Garden Arena Corporation, representing approximately 2.8% of its 224, 892 shares of outstanding stock.

that owned both a franchise in the National Hockey League (NHL), known as the Boston Bruins, and a corporation that held a franchise in the American Hockey League (AHL), known as the Boston Braves. Garden Arena also owned and operated Boston Garden Sports Arena (Boston Garden), an indoor auditorium with facilities for the exhibition of sporting and other entertainment events, and a corporation that operated the food and beverage concession at the Boston Garden. A considerable volume of documentary material was introduced in evidence concerning the value of the stock of Garden Arena on July 18, 1973, the day before Garden Arena's stockholders approved the merger. Each side presented expert testimony. The judge gave consideration to the market value of the Garden Arena stock, to the value of its stock based on its earnings, and to the net asset value of Garden Arena's assets. Weighting these factors, the judge arrived at a total, per share value of $75.27.[67]

. . . We conclude that the judge followed acceptable procedures in valuing the Garden Arena stock; that his determinations were generally within the range of discretion accorded a fact finder; but that, in three instances, the judge's treatment of the evidence was or may have been in error and, accordingly, the case should be remanded to him for further consideration of those three points.

The statutory provisions applicable to this case were enacted in 1964 as part of the Massachusetts Business Corporation Law. St. 1964, c. 723, § 1. The appraisal provisions (G.L. c. 156B, §§ 86–98) were based on a similar, but not identical, Delaware statute . . . . In these circumstances, consideration of the Delaware law, including judicial decisions, is appropriate, but in no sense should we feel compelled to adhere without question to that law, which has been in the process of development since our enactment of G.L. c. 156B in 1964. We do not perceive a legislative intent to adopt judicial determinations of Delaware law made prior to the enactment of G.L. c. 156B and certainly no such intent as to judicial interpretations made since that date.

The Delaware courts have adopted a general approach to the appraisal of stock which a Massachusetts judge might appropriately follow, as did the judge in this case. The Delaware procedure, known as the "Delaware block approach," calls for a determination of the market value, the earnings value, and the net asset value of the stock, followed by the assignment of a percentage weight to each of the elements of value.

There have been no appellate decisions in this State concerning the appraisal of stock since the present appraisal statute was enacted, and there were few under the previously applicable, somewhat similar, statute.

---

[67] [3] The judge determined the market value, earnings value, and net asset value of the stock and then weighted these values as follows:

|                  | Value    | Weight    |   | Result   |
|------------------|----------|-----------|---|----------|
| Market Value:    | $26.50   | X   10%   | = | $2.65    |
| Earnings Value:  | $52.60   | X   40%   | = | $21.04   |
| Net Asset Value: | $103.16  | X   50%   | = | $51.58   |
|                  |          | Total Value Per Share: | | $75.27 |

\* \* \*

## Market Value

The judge was acting within reasonable limits when he determined that the market value of Garden Arena stock on July 18, 1973, was $26.50 a share. Each party challenges this determination. The plaintiffs' contention is that market value should be disregarded because it was not ascertainable due to the limited trading in Garden Arena stock.[68] The defendant argues that the judge was obliged to reconstruct market value based on comparable companies, and, in doing so, should have arrived at a market value of $22 a share.

Market value may be a significant factor, even the dominant factor, in determining the "fair value" of shares of a particular corporation under G.L. c. 156B, § 92. Shares regularly traded on a recognized stock exchange are particularly susceptible to valuation on the basis of their market price, although even in such cases the market value may well not be conclusive. See Martignette v. Sagamore Mfg. Co., 340 Mass. 136, 141–142, 163 N.E.2d 9 (1959). On the other hand, where there is no established market for a particular stock, actual market value cannot be used. In such cases, a judge might undertake to "reconstruct" market value, but he is not obliged to do so.[69] Indeed, the process of the reconstruction of market value may actually be no more than a variation on the valuation of corporate assets and corporate earnings.

In this case, Garden Arena stock was traded on the Boston Stock Exchange, but rarely. Approximately ninety per cent of the company's stock was held by the controlling interests and not traded. Between January 1, 1968, and December 4, 1972, 16,741 shares were traded. During this period, an annual average of approximately 1.5% of the outstanding stock changed hands. In 1972, 4,372 shares were traded at prices ranging from $20.50 a share to $29 a share. The public announcement of the proposed merger was made on December 7, 1972. The last prior sale of 200 shares on December 4, 1972, was made at $26.50 a share. The judge accepted that sale price as the market price to be used in his determination of value.

The judge concluded that the volume of trading was sufficient to permit a determination of market value and expressed a preference for the actual sale price over any reconstruction of a market value, which he concluded would place "undue reliance on corporations, factors, and circumstances not applicable to Garden Arena stock." The decision to consider market value and the market value selected were within the judge's discretion.

---

[68] [6] This argument also bears on the relative weight to be assigned to market value as against net asset value and earnings value, a subject we shall consider subsequently.

[69] [7] The Delaware cases require the reconstruction of market value only when the actual market value cannot be determined and a hypothetical market value can be reconstructed. Compare Application of Del. Racing Ass'n, 213 A.2d 203, 211–212 (Del. 1965), with Universal City Studios, Inc. v. Francis I. duPont & Co., 334 A.2d 216, 222 (Del. 1975).

## Valuation Based on Earnings

The judge determined that the average per share earnings of Garden Arena for the five-fiscal-year period which ended June 30, 1973, was $5.26. To this amount he applied a factor, or multiplier, of 10 to arrive at $52.60 as the per share value based on earnings.

Each party objects to certain aspects of this process. We reject the plaintiffs' argument that the judge could not properly use any value based on earnings, and also reject the parties' various challenges to the judge's method of determining value based on earnings.

Delaware case law, which, as we have said, we regard as instructive but not binding, has established a method of computing value based on corporate earnings. The appraiser generally starts by computing the average earnings of the corporation for the past five years. *Universal City Studios, Inc. v. Francis I. duPont & Co.*, 334 A.2d 216, 218 (Del. 1975); *Application of Del. Racing Ass'n*, 213 A.2d 203, 212 (Del. 1965). Extraordinary gains and losses are excluded from the average earnings calculation. *Gibbons v. Schenley Indus., Inc.*, 339 A.2d 460, 468–470 (Del. Ch. 1975); *Felder v. Anderson, Clayton & Co.*, 39 Del. Ch. 76, 86–87, 159 A.2d 278 (1960). The appraiser then selects a multiplier (to be applied to the average earnings) which reflects the prospective financial condition of the corporation and the risk factor inherent in the corporation and the industry. *Universal City Studios, Inc. v. Francis I. duPont & Co., supra*. In selecting a multiplier, the appraiser generally looks to other comparable corporations. *Universal City Studios, Inc. v. Francis I. duPont & Co., supra* at 219–221 (averaging price-earnings ratios of nine other motion picture companies as of date of merger); *Gibbons v. Schenley Indus., Inc., supra* at 471 (using Standard & Poor's Distiller's Index as of date of merger); *Felder v. Anderson, Clayton & Co., supra*, 39 Del. Ch. at 87, 159 A.2d 278 (averaging price-earnings ratios of representative stocks over previous five-year period because of recent boom in industry). The appraiser's choice of a multiplier is largely discretionary and will be upheld if it is "within the range of reason." *Universal City Studios, Inc. v. Francis I. duPont & Co., supra* at 219 (approving multiplier of 16.1); *Application of Del. Racing Ass'n, supra* at 213 (approving multiplier of 10); *Swanton v. State Guar. Corp.*, 42 Del. Ch. 477, 483, 215 A.2d 242 (1965) (approving multiplier of 14).

The judge chose not to place "singular reliance on comparative data preferring to choose a multiplier based on the specific situation and prospects of the Garden Arena." He weighed the favorable financial prospects of the Bruins: the popularity and success of the team, the relatively low average age of its players, the popularity of Bobby Orr and Phil Esposito, the high attendance record at home games (each home team retained all gate receipts), and the advantageous radio and television contracts. On the other hand, he recognized certain risks, the negative prospects: the existence of the World Hockey Association with its potential, favorable impact on players' bargaining positions, and legal threats to the players' reserve clause. He concluded that a multiplier of 10 was appropriate. There was ample evidentiary support for his conclusion. He might have looked to and relied on price-earnings ratios of other corporations, but he was not obliged to.

The judge did not have to consider the dividend record of Garden Arena, as the defendant urges. Dividends tend to reflect the same factors as earnings and, therefore, need not be valued separately. *See Felder v. Anderson, Clayton & Co.*, 39 Del. Ch. 76, 88–89, 159 A.2d 278 (1960). And since dividend policy is usually reflected in market value, the use of market value as a factor in the valuation process permitted the low and sporadic dividend rate to be given some weight in the process. Beyond that, the value of the plaintiffs' stock should not be depreciated because the controlling interests often chose to declare low dividends or none at all.

The judge did not abuse his discretion in including expansion income (payments from teams newly admitted to the NHL) received during two of the five recent fiscal years. His conclusion was well within the guidelines of decided cases. *See Gibbons v. Schenley Indus., Inc.*, 339 A.2d 460, 470 (Del. Ch. 1975) (gain from sale of real estate not extraordinary where corporation often sold such assets); *Felder v. Anderson, Clayton & Co.*, 39 Del. Ch. 76, 86–87, 159 A.2d 278 (1960) (loss attributable to a drought not extraordinary). The Bruins first received expansion income ($2,000,000) during the fiscal year which ended on June 30, 1967, a year not included in the five-year average. The franchise received almost $1,000,000 more in 1970 and approximately $860,000 in 1972. This 1970 and 1972 income was reflected in the computation of earnings. Expansion income did not have to be treated as extraordinary income. The judge concluded that it did not distort "an accurate projection of the earnings value of Garden Arena" and noted, as of July 18, 1973, an NHL expansion plan for the admission of two more teams in 1974–1975 and for expansion thereafter.

## Valuation Based on Net Asset Value

The judge determined total net asset value by first valuing the net assets of Garden Arena apart from the Bruins franchise and the concession operations at Boston Garden. He selected $9,400,000 (the June 30, 1973, book value of Garden Arena) as representing that net asset value. Then, he added his valuations of the Bruins franchise ($9,600,000) and the concession operation ($4,200,000) to arrive at a total asset value of $23,200,000, or $103.16 a share.[70]

The parties raise various objections to these determinations. The defendant argues that the judge included certain items twice in his valuation of the net assets of Garden Arena and that he should have given no separate value to the concession operation. The plaintiff argues that the judge undervalued both the Boston Garden and the value of the Bruins franchise.

The defendant objects to the judge's refusal to deduct $1,116,000 from the $9,400,000 that represented the net asset value of Garden Arena (exclusive of the net asset value of the Bruins franchise and the concession operation). The defendant's expert testified that the $9,400,000 figure included $1,116,000 attributable to the goodwill of the Bruins, net player investment, and the value of the AHL franchise. The judge recognized that the items included in the $1,116,000 should not be valued twice and seemingly agreed that they would be more appropriately included in the value of the Bruins franchise than in the $9,400,000. He was not

---

[70] [10] $23,200,000 / 224,892 (the number of outstanding shares).

plainly wrong, however, in declining to deduct them from the $9,400,000, because, as is fully warranted from the testimony of the defendant's expert, the judge concluded that the defendant's expert did not include these items in his determination of the value of the Bruins franchise. The defendant's expert, whose determination the judge accepted, arrived at his value of the Bruins franchise by adding certain items to the cost of a new NHL franchise, but none of those items included goodwill, net player investment, or the value of an AHL franchise. Acceptance of the defendant's argument would have resulted in these items' being entirely omitted from the net asset valuation of Garden Arena.

The plaintiffs object that the judge did not explicitly determine the value of the Boston Garden and implicitly undervalued it. Garden Arena had purchased the Boston Garden on May 25, 1973, for $4,000,000, and accounted for it on the June 30, 1973, balance sheet as a $4,000,000 asset with a corresponding mortgage liability of $3,437,065. Prior to the purchase, Garden Arena had held a long-term lease which was unfavorable to the owner of the Boston Garden.[71] The existence of the lease would tend to depress the purchase price.

The judge stated that the $9,400,000 book value "*includes* a reasonable value for Boston Garden" (emphasis supplied). He did not indicate whether, if he had meant to value the Boston Garden at its purchase price (with an adjustment for the mortgage liabilities), he had considered the effect the lease would have had on that price. While we recognize that the fact-finding role of the judge permits him to reject the opinions of the various experts, we conclude, in the absence of an explanation of his reasons, that it is possible that the judge did not give adequate consideration to the value of the Garden property. The judge should consider this subject further on remand.

A major area of dispute was the value of the Bruins franchise. The judge rejected the value advanced by the plaintiffs' expert ($18,000,000), stating that "(a)lthough the defendant's figure of ($9,600,000) seems somewhat low in comparison with the cost of expansion team franchises, *The Court is constrained to accept* defendant's value as it is the more creditable and legally appropriate expert opinion in the record" (emphasis supplied). Although the choice of the word "constrained" may have been inadvertent, it connotes a sense of obligation. As the trier of fact, the judge was not bound to accept the valuation of either one expert or the other. He was entitled to reach his own conclusion as to value.

Because the judge may have felt bound to accept the value placed on the Bruins franchise by the defendant's expert, we shall remand this case for him to arrive at his own determination of the value of the Bruins franchise. He would be warranted in arriving at the same valuation as that advanced on behalf of the defendant, but he is not obliged to do so.

The defendant argues that, in arriving at the value of the assets of Garden Arena, the judge improperly placed a separate value on the right to operate concessions at the Boston Garden. We agree with the judge. The fact that earnings from

---

[71] [13] The lease, which ran until June 1, 1986, contained a fixed maximum rent and an obligation on the lessee to pay only two-thirds of any increase in local real estate taxes. In a period of inflation and rising local real estate taxes, the value of the lease to the lessor was decreasing annually.

concessions were included in the computation of earnings value, one component in the formula, does not mean that the value of the concessions should have been excluded from the computation of net asset value, another such component.

The value of the concession operation was not reflected in the value of the real estate. Real estate may be valued on the basis of rental income, but it is not valued on the basis of the profitability of business operations within the premises. Moreover, it is manifest that the value of the concession operation was not included in the value placed on the Boston Garden. The record indicates that Garden Arena already owned the concession rights when it purchased the Boston Garden. The conclusion that the value of the concession operation was not reflected in the value of the Boston Garden is particularly warranted because the determined value of the right to operate the concessions ($4,200,000) was higher than the May 25, 1973, purchase price ($4,000,000) of the Boston Garden.

We do conclude, however, that the judge may have felt unnecessarily bound to accept the plaintiffs' evidence of the value of the concession operation. He stated that "since the defendant did not submit evidence on this issue, the Court will accept plaintiffs' expert appraisal of the value of the concession operation." Although the judge did not express the view that he was "constrained" to accept the plaintiffs' valuation, as he did concerning the defendant's valuation of the Bruins franchise, he may have misconstrued his authority on this issue. The judge was not obliged to accept the plaintiffs' evidence at face value merely because no other evidence was offered.

On remand, the judge should reconsider his determination of the value of the concession operation and exercise his own judgment concerning the bases for the conclusion arrived at by the plaintiffs' expert. However, the evidence did warrant the value selected by the judge, and no reduction in that value is required on this record.

### Weighting of Valuations

The judge weighted the three valuations as follows:

Market Value — 10%

Earnings Value — 40%

Net Asset Value — 50%

We accept these allocations as reasonable and within the range of the judge's discretion.

Any determination of the weight to be given the various elements involved in the valuation of a stock must be based on the circumstances. *Heller v. Munsingwear, Inc.*, 33 Del. Ch. 593, 598, 98 A.2d 774 (1953). The decision to weight market value at only 10% was appropriate, considering the thin trading in the stock of Garden Arena. The decision to attribute 50% weight to net asset value was reasonably founded. The judge concluded that, because of tax reasons, the value of a sports franchise, unlike many corporate activities, depends more on its assets than on its earnings; that Garden Arena had been largely a family corporation in which earnings were of little significance; that Garden Arena had approximately $5,000,000 in excess liquid assets; and that the Garden property was a substantial real estate holding in an excellent location.

The judge might have reached different conclusions on this record. He was not obliged, however, to reconstruct market value and, as the defendant urges, attribute 50% weight to it. Nor was he obliged, as the plaintiffs argue, to consider only net asset value. *See Martignette v. Sagamore Mfg. Co.*, 340 Mass. 136, 142, 163 N.E.2d 9 (1959). Market value and earnings value properly could be considered in these circumstances.

Although we would have found no fault with a determination to give even greater weight to the price per share based on the net asset value of Garden Arena, the judge was acting within an acceptable range of discretion in selecting the weights he gave to the various factors.

*       *       *

### Interest Allowance

The defendant objects to the judge's determination to award interest at 8% Per annum. It does not object to the judge's decision to award interest, a matter within his discretion, nor to his decision to compound interest annually. The judge heard evidence specifically directed toward the question of the appropriate rate of interest. The defendant's own witness testified on cross-examination that a prudent investment in corporate bonds, rated AAA by Moody's, would have yielded interest in excess of 8% uncompounded. The amount selected fairly compensated the plaintiffs for their inability to use the money during the period in question, a factor which the judge fairly could consider, and the judge reasonably could have concluded that 8% Per annum reflected "the rate of interest at which a prudent investor could have invested money."

We have concluded that the judge's method of valuing the Garden Arena stock was essentially correct. In this opinion, we have indicated, however, that the case should be remanded to him for clarification and further consideration on the record of three matters: his valuation of the Boston Garden, the Bruins franchise, and the concession operation.

So ordered.

# NOTE

Many states use the Delaware block method although it is no longer mandatory in Delaware. Should that fact be relevant? In *Weinberger v. UOP*, 457 A.2d 701 (Del. 1983), the Delaware court described the Delaware block method as "clearly outmoded." It is no longer the exclusive method in Delaware and evidence of value may be given by methods accepted in the financial community.

Many states grant appraisal rights to shareholders who dissent from mergers. Is this policy rational if the securities are traded on the NYSE or NASDAQ? Shouldn't the market value be conclusive in that case?

Market value: Shouldn't the judge have valued the market value at zero? Was the Boston Stock Exchange a real market? Is it relevant that 90% of the stock was held by "controlling interests?"

Earnings value: Why are the earnings averaged over a 5-year period? Isn't this an irrational rule? Do experts in finance place great weight on past earnings? What are extraordinary gains or losses? Should expansion income be included in "earnings?" Was the judge's decision correct as to a multiplier of 10? Price earnings ratios of similar companies provide a guideline for expert appraisers. Is this corporation of a nature that comparable companies would be easy to find?

Net assets: Should real estate be valued at book value? Shouldn't the judge have valued the net assets as 100%? If the net asset value is the highest and the minority shareholders are being bought out, aren't their assets being purchased? Isn't the Delaware block method certain to produce an unjust valuation every time?

Was interest at 8% uncompounded fair to the plaintiffs? Is the fact that AAA rated bonds paid 8% relevant?

## ARNAUD v. STOCKGROWERS STATE BANK OF ASHLAND, KANSAS
### Supreme Court of Kansas
### 992 P.2d 216 (1999)

ABBOTT, J.

This case is before the court on a question certified by the United States District Court for the District of Kansas pursuant to the Uniform Certification of Questions of Law Act, K.S.A. 60-3201 *et seq.*

The plaintiffs were minority shareholders in the Stockgrowers State Bank of Ashland, Kansas (Bank). The majority shareholders formed the Stockgrowers Banc Corp., a holding company, and when the plaintiffs refused to transfer their bank stock to the holding company, the Bank initiated a reverse stock split (1 for 400). The reverse stock split reduced the Bank's outstanding shares from 4,000 to 10. The purpose of the reverse stock split was to leave the plaintiffs with a fractional share and eliminate them as shareholders by invoking K.S.A. 17-6405.

K.S.A. 17-6405 authorizes, among other things, a corporation to refuse to issue fractional shares and "pay in cash the fair value of fractions of a share as of the time when those entitled to receive such fractions are determined." The defendants determined what they claimed was the fair value of plaintiffs' stock based on the average of two appraisals they commissioned. The defendants, in order to arrive at a "fair value," employed appraisers who started with a valuation, which they then reduced by a "minority" discount and then further reduced for a "marketability" discount. The plaintiffs objected to the valuations and brought this action in the United States District Court.

The Honorable Monti L. Belot, on his own motion, certified the following question to this court for determination:

"Is it proper for a corporation to determine the 'fair value' of a fractional share pursuant to K.S.A. § 17-6405 by applying minority and marketability discounts when the fractional share resulted from a reverse stock split intended to eliminate the minority shareholder's interest in the corporation?"

The Bank's board of directors employed two appraisal firms to determine fair value. One firm determined the fair market minority value of each prereverse stock split share as $2,175. It then reduced the value by a 35% marketability factor, arriving at a "fair value" of $1,414 per prereverse stock split share. The second firm appraised the fair market value of each prereverse stock split share at approximately $2,562.61. It then reduced the market value by a minority discount of 23.1% and a marketability discount of 25%, arriving at a "fair value" of $1,330 per prereverse stock split share. It appears the Bank's board of directors then averaged the two appraisals and paid $1.50 more than the average ($1,372).

A minority discount allows an appraiser to adjust for a lack of control over the corporation on the theory that the minority shares of stock are not worth the same as the majority holdings due to the lack of voting power. A marketability discount, on the other hand, allows an appraiser to adjust for a lack of liquidity in the stock itself on the theory that there is a limited supply of purchasers of that stock. *See* Hood *et al.*, *Valuation of Closely Held Business Interests*, 65 UMKC L. Rev. 399, 438 (1997).

This court has previously approved the procedure that the defendants have used to force the buy out of the plaintiffs' minority share holdings. *See Achey v. Linn County Bank*, 261 Kan. 669, 931 P.2d 16 (1997) (allowing the corporation to initiate a reverse stock split and force the buy-out of the minority shareholders' stock in order to prevent any fractional share holdings). We did not, however, discuss whether minority or marketability discounts should be applied in determining the "fair value" that was to be paid to the minority shareholders. 261 Kan. at 682, 931 P.2d 16.

There is no Kansas case law which interprets the meaning of "fair value" as set forth in K.S.A. 17-6405. Kansas courts have a long history, however, of looking to the decisions of the Delaware courts involving corporation law, as the Kansas Corporation Code was modeled after the Delaware Code. *See Achey*, 261 Kan. at 676, 931 P.2d 16 (the decisions of the Delaware courts involving corporation law are persuasive); *In re Hesston Corp.*, 254 Kan. 941, 980, 870 P.2d 17 (1994) (the Kansas provisions of the Corporation Code are "nearly identical" to the Delaware model); *Norton v. National Research Foundation*, 141 F.R.D. 510, 513 (D. Kan. 1992) (Kansas courts often look to Delaware case law for guidance regarding the Kansas Corporation Code); and *Vogel v. Missouri Valley Steel, Inc.*, 229 Kan. 492, 496, 625 P.2d 1123 (1981) (the Kansas Corporation Code was patterned after the Delaware Corporation Code and the decisions of the Delaware courts are considered persuasive). K.S.A. 17-6405 is based on a similar Delaware statute. *See* Del. Code Ann. tit. 8, § 155 (1991). Unfortunately, there are no Delaware cases which have discussed the meaning of "fair value" under Del. Code Ann tit. 8, § 155. The meaning of "fair value" has, however, been evaluated in other actions.

\* \* \*

Cases and commentators suggest that the majority of states have not applied minority and marketability discounts when determining the fair value of stock in similar cases. *See Lawson Mardon Wheaton Inc. v. Smith*, 160 N.J. 383, 401, 734 A.2d 738 (1999) (the majority of jurisdictions has held that shares should not be discounted and that the shareholder is entitled to his proportionate share of the fair market value of the corporation); *Charland v. Country View Golf Club, Inc.*, 588 A.2d 609, 611 (R.I. 1991) (most courts have held that no minority discount should be applied when a corporation is buying back the stock owned by its minority shareholders); Wertheimer, *The Shareholders' Appraisal Remedy and How Courts Determine Fair Value*, 47 Duke L.J. 613, 641–42 (1998) (a majority of courts have disallowed a minority discount); and Oitzinger, *Fair Price and Fair Play Under the Montana Business Corporation Act*, 58 MONT. L. REV. 407, 420–21 (1997) (a majority of courts have held that minority discounts should not be applied where the minority shareholder is selling his shares to the corporation).

The leading case in this area is *Cavalier Oil Corp. v. Harnett*, 564 A.2d 1137 (Del. 1989). Although Cavalier deals with a forced buy-out of a shareholder who objected to a merger and asserted appraisal rights pursuant to a statute similar to K.S.A. 17-6712, the policy rationale is sound and the holding persuasive. In Cavalier, the minority shareholder asserted appraisal rights following a short form merger pursuant to Del. Code Ann. tit. 8, § 253. The Court of Chancery of Delaware entered judgment fixing the value of the minority-owned stock at $347,000. The Court of Chancery did not apply either a minority discount or a marketability discount in determining the value of the minority owned stock. The Delaware Supreme Court affirmed and noted:

> "Discounting individual share holdings injects into the appraisal process speculation on the various factors which may dictate the marketability of minority share holdings. More important, to fail to accord to a minority shareholder the full proportionate value of his shares imposes a penalty for lack of control, and unfairly enriches the majority shareholders who may reap a windfall from the appraisal process by cashing out a dissenting shareholder, a clearly undesirable result." 564 A.2d at 1145.

The *Cavalier* court further noted that in performing an appraisal, the company should be viewed as a "going concern." 564 A.2d at 1145. The rationale set forth in *Cavalier* is sound.

Other courts have similarly held. *See Brown v. Allied Corrugated Box Co.*, 91 Cal. App. 3d 477, 486, 154 Cal. Rptr. 170 (1979) (holding that minority discounts should not have been applied and noting that minority discounts have "little validity" when the purchaser is someone who is already in control of the corporation); *Security State Bank v. Ziegeldorf*, 554 N.W.2d 884, 889–90 (Iowa 1996) (disallowing a marketability discount and holding that a marketability or minority discount would prevent a minority shareholder from receiving the fair value of their pro rata share); *Richardson v. Palmer Broadcasting Co.*, 353 N.W.2d 374, 379 (Iowa 1984) (holding that the application of a minority discount is "contrary to the spirit of 'fair value' determinations"); *Rigel Corp. v. Cutchall*, 245 Neb. 118, 130, 511 N.W.2d 519 (1994) (citing *Cavalier* and holding that neither a minority discount nor a marketability discount should be given in an action for appraisal of the dissenting shareholder's interests); *Lawson*, 160 N.J. at 402, 734 A.2d 738 (following the majority rule as set forth in *Cavalier* and holding that marketability discounts should not be applied); *Fisher v. Fisher*, 568 N.W.2d 728, 732 (N.D. 1997) (following *Cavalier* and holding that minority discounts should not be considered in valuing the minority shareholder's interests); *In re McLoon Oil Co.*, 565 A.2d 997, 1005 (Me. 1989) (citing *Cavalier* and holding that minority discounts and marketability discounts should not be applied as they would be bound to encourage "corporate squeezeouts"); *MT Properties v. CMC Real Estate Corp.*, 481 N.W.2d 383, 387–88 (Minn. App. 1992) (following the reasoning of Cavalier and holding that a minority discount is inappropriate as it penalizes the minority shareholder while allowing the corporation to purchase the minority interest "cheaply"); *Hansen v. 75 Ranch Co.*, 288 Mont. 310, 957 P.2d 32, 41–42 (1998) (finding the majority rationale "compelling"); *Woolf v. Universal Fidelity Life Ins.*, 849 P.2d 1093, 1095 (Okla. App. 1992) (decisions of the Delaware courts are "very persuasive" and holding that the trial court erred when it applied a minority discount); *Charland*, 588 A.2d at 612–13 (R.I.) (holding that the minority and marketability discounts should not be applied when a corporation is purchasing the stock from its minority shareholders); and *HMO-W Inc. v. SSM Health Care System*, 228 Wis.2d 815, 598 N.W.2d 577, 582–83 (Wis. App. 1999) (following *Cavalier* and holding that minority discounts are not appropriate when determining the value of minority shares in an appraisal action).

The American Law Institute has come to a similar conclusion. Section 7.22, Standards for Determining Fair Value, states:

> "(a) The fair value of shares under § 7.21 (Corporate Transactions Giving Rise to Appraisal Rights) should be the value of the [holders] proportionate interest in the corporation, without any discount for minority status or, absent extraordinary circumstances, lack of marketability." A.L.I., *Principles of Corporate Governance*, § 7.22, pp. 314–15.

A handful of courts have held, however, that minority and marketability discounts should be applied. All but one of these decisions precede the 1989 Delaware Supreme Court decision in Cavalier. *See Hernando Bank v. Huff*, 609 F. Supp. 1124, 1126 (N.D. Miss. 1985) (holding that a minority discount should be applied when determining the value of the minority shareholder's interests); *Perlman v. Permonite Mfg. Co.*, 568 F. Supp. 222, 231–32 (N.D. Ind. 1983) (allowing a trial court expert witness to apply minority and marketability discounts); *Atlantic States Construction v. Beavers*, 169 Ga. App. 584, 589–90, 314 S.E.2d 245 (1984) (holding that it is not against public policy to apply a minority or marketability discount but that it should be done with "caution"); *Stanton v. Republic Bank*, 144 Ill. 2d 472, 480, 163 Ill. Dec. 524, 581 N.E.2d 678 (1991) (holding that the trial court did not abuse its discretion when it applied a minority and marketability discount); *King v. F.T.J., Inc.*, 765 S.W.2d 301, 306 (Mo. App. 1988) (holding that it was appropriate for the trial court to apply a 7% minority discount); and *McCauley v. Tom McCauley & Son, Inc.*, 104 N.M. 523, 535, 724 P.2d 232 (Ct. App. 1986) (holding that the trial court properly exercised its discretion when it applied a minority discount of 25%).

In *Hansen*, the Montana Supreme Court set forth the rationale for refusing to apply minority or marketability discounts when the purchaser is the corporation:

"Applying a discount is inappropriate when the shareholder is selling her shares to a majority shareholder or to the corporation. The sale differs from a sale to a third party and, thus, different interests must be recognized. When selling to a third party, the value of the shares is either the same as or less than it was in the hands of the transferor because the third party gains no right to control or manage the corporation. However, a sale to a majority shareholder or to the corporation simply consolidates or increases the interests of those already in control. Therefore, requiring the application of a minority discount when selling to an 'insider' would result in a windfall to the transferee. This is particularly true since the transferring shareholder would expect that the shares would have at least the same value in her hands as in the hands of the transferee." 288 Mont. at 325, 957 P.2d at 41.

Indeed, in the present case, the defendants also stand to reap substantial tax benefits pursuant to IRC § 1361(b)(3)(B)(i) (S corporation must hold 100% of the stock of the "qualified subchapter S subsidiary").

To allow a discount under the facts of this case would discourage investments in corporations by persons who would acquire a minority interest because it would enable the majority shareholders to seize the minority shareholders' interest in the corporation to the extent a minority or marketability discount is allowed. Investments should be encouraged, not discouraged.

We hold that minority and marketability discounts are not appropriate when the purchaser of the stock is either the majority shareholder or the corporation itself.

The defendants have noted that one previous Kansas decision holds that minority discounts should be applied in an action for appraisal. *Moore v. New Ammest, Inc.*, 6 Kan. App. 2d 461, 475, 630 P.2d 167 (1981). To the extent that the opinion in *Moore* is inconsistent with the present opinion, it is hereby overruled.

In answering the certified question before us, we hold that minority and marketability discounts should not be applied when the fractional share resulted from a reverse stock split intended to eliminate a minority shareholder's interest in the corporation.

## MAGNER v. ONE SECURITIES CORPORATION
Court of Appeals of Georgia
574 S.E.2d 555 (2002)

ELLINGTON, J.

Richard E. Magner and the Magner Family, LLC appeal from the superior court order granting summary judgment to One Securities Corporation ("OSC") and Benefit Plan Services, Inc. ("BPS") in this declaratory judgment action. Appellees OSC and BPS sought a declaration establishing whether Magner or the LLC preserved any right of dissent to mergers which cashed out Magner's minority shareholder interest in the corporations. In the event the court concluded such dissenters' rights existed, OSC and BPS asked for a judicial appraisal of the value of that interest. Magner and the LLC counterclaimed, challenging the validity of the mergers and seeking rescission. OSC and BPS moved for summary judgment on whether Magner or the LLC had dissenters' rights. The parties filed cross-motions for summary judgment on Magner's and the LLC's counterclaim regarding the validity of the mergers. The court entered summary judgment in favor of the corporations on both motions, concluding the mergers were valid and that neither Magner nor the LLC had dissenters' rights. Finding no reversible error, we affirm.

Summary judgment is appropriate under OCGA § 9-11-56 "when there is no genuine issue of material fact and the movant is entitled to judgment as a matter of law."

Viewed in this light, the record reveals the following relevant facts. OSC and BPS are private, closely held Subchapter S corporations that designed, sold, and administered employee compensation and benefit plans. Barbara and Ronald Balser owned two-thirds of the corporations; Magner owned one-third. The boards of both corporations comprised the Balsers, O.C. Russell, and Stephen Berman.[72] On March 22, 1999, the corporations held a joint board of directors meeting. Each of the directors received or waived notice of the meeting. At this meeting, the directors approved a plan to merge OSC and BPS into Giotto, Inc. and Giotto Administrative Services, Inc., respectively, shell corporations created for this purpose a year before. The purpose of the mergers, which the directors had been discussing for several months before the meeting, was to cash out Magner's interest in the corporations. The directors agreed to pay Magner the "fair value" of his stock, an amount that had been determined by an independent appraiser.[73] The directors determined that OSC and BPS would be the corporate entities surviving the mergers and the Balsers would remain as the sole shareholders of the merged corporations. The directors set the record date for shareholders entitled to vote on the mergers as March 25, 1999. Finally, the directors authorized the senior management of both corporations to work with legal counsel to effect the mergers.

On March 26, 1999, the boards notified Magner in writing that a special shareholders' meeting of both corporations would be held on April 6, 1999, to vote on the merger plans. The notices set the record date, named the merging and surviving corporations, and advised Magner of his dissenters' rights. A plan of merger was attached to the notices. The attached plan of merger, however, contained a typographical error listing the fair value of all of Magner's stock as the price per share. Consequently, on April 3, 1999, the boards sent Magner a corrected notice and rescheduled the meeting for April 15, 1999.

On April 9, 1999, Magner wrote the corporations instructing them to cancel his shares in OSC and BPS and to reissue them to the LLC effective April 14. Although

---

[72] [1] Magner was not a board member during the relevant time period. He was removed as a director in 1997.

[73] [2] The corporations retained Phillips Hitchner Group, Inc. to establish the fair value of Magner's stock as of March 12, 1999. Prior to the March 22 meeting, the appraisers, in a draft report, set the value of Magner's 100 shares of OSC at $715,000 and 100 shares of BPS at $216,667. This draft report was either delivered to, or the substance of it was communicated to, each board member prior to the March 22 meeting.

Magner asserted he did this "for estate planning and asset protection purposes,"[74] it appears everyone understood that transferring Magner's stock into a limited liability company could destroy the corporations' Subchapter S status and result in increased tax liability. Through counsel, the corporations wrote Magner and asked him not to make the transfer, informing him of the tax consequences of that act. The corporations assert that Magner, through his attorney, agreed to postpone the decision to cancel his shares and to reissue the stock to the LLC. Magner, however, claims the corporations simply failed to honor his request to make the transfer. In any event, the corporations sought legal and tax advice and determined an argument existed for preserving Subchapter S status if the direction of the mergers was reversed, allowing the Giotto shell corporations to be the surviving entities. Consequently, on April 15, 1999, the board reissued its notice of meeting to Magner, stating that the shell entities would survive the merger, and rescheduled the meeting to April 26, 1999. The notice, like all previous notices, was attached to a plan of merger.

On April 26, 1999, OSC and BPS held a special meeting of shareholders. The Balsers, representing the majority of the shareholders, approved and adopted the merger agreements between the corporations and the shell entities as proposed. Magner, who attended the meeting through counsel, did not vote on either merger. During the meeting, the Balsers' stock was retired and Magner's stock was converted into the right to receive cash in the amount previously established as the stock's fair value. The mergers became effective on April 27, 1999, when the Certificates of Merger and Name Change were filed with the Secretary of State.

On May 4, OSC and BPS notified Magner of his dissenters' rights, offered him the established fair value of his stock, and directed him to demand payment and tender his shares to the corporations by June 7, 1999, if he intended to perfect his dissenters' rights. Instead, on May 12, Magner demanded that his stock in both corporations be recorded as having been transferred to the LLC as of April 14, 1999. The corporations complied with Magner's request, reissuing the stock of OSC and BPS to the Magner Family, LLC, as of April 14, 1999. On June 7, both Magner and the LLC delivered to the corporations documents entitled "Dissenter's Demand for Payment" and tendered the LLC's stock certificates. On June 11, OSC and BPS informed Magner and the LLC that because Magner canceled his shares, he forfeited his dissenters' rights. Moreover, because the LLC was not a shareholder of record in either corporation on March 25, 1999, it was not entitled to dissent. Again, the corporations offered to pay Magner the appraised fair value of his interest. Magner rejected the offer and, instead, demanded over $16 million for his combined interest in both corporations. On September 3, 1999, the corporations filed the instant declaratory judgment action, or, in the alternative, sought a judicial appraisal pursuant to OCGA § 14-2-1330.

---

[74] [3] In a summary judgment brief, Magner admitted a different motive for the stock transfer: "[By] eliminating the Subchapter S status for OSC and BPS, Magner hoped to create tax disincentives for the Balsers to transfer assets and income from MCG and FDS ([other] companies in which Magner retained an interest) to OSC and BPS (companies from which the Balsers were attempting to squeeze-out Magner)."

1. Magner and the LLC contend the trial court erred in failing to declare the mergers void.

First, in the absence of fraud or illegality, Magner's exclusive remedy with respect to the cash-out mergers was to dissent and seek payment for the fair value of his shares in accordance with the Code. OCGA § 14-2-1302(b). *See Grace Bros. v. Farley Indus.*, 264 Ga. 817, 821(3), 450 S.E.2d 814 (1995); *Lewis v. Turner Broadcasting System, Inc.*, 232 Ga. App. 831, 833(3), 503 S.E.2d 81 (1998). As the commentary to this Code section explains:

> [W]hen a majority of shareholders has approved a corporate change, the corporation should be permitted to proceed even if a minority considers the change unwise or disadvantageous, and persuades a court that this is correct. Since dissenting shareholders can obtain the fair value of their shares, they are protected from pecuniary loss. Thus in general terms an exclusivity principle is justified.

Commentary to OCGA § 14-2-1302(b). Magner, who failed to perfect his dissenters' rights, *see* Division 2, infra, seeks to rescind the mergers and avoid the consequences of his election. He does so by contending the directors failed to comply with the statutory requirements for merger in a number of ways. We find each of these arguments without merit.

(a) *The Boards of Directors Properly Adopted the Plans of Merger.* Contrary to Magner's contention, the evidence adduced demonstrates that the boards complied with the requirements for adopting the proposed plans of merger. OCGA § 14-2-1101 provides, in relevant part:

> (a) One or more corporations may merge into another corporation if the board of directors of each corporation adopts and its shareholders (if required by Code Section 14-2-1103) approve a plan of merger. (b) The plan of merger must set forth: (1) The name of each corporation planning to merge and the name of the surviving corporation into which each other corporation plans to merge; (2) The terms and conditions of the merger; and (3) The manner and basis of converting the shares of each corporation into shares, obligations, or other securities of the surviving or any other corporation or into cash or other property in whole or in part.

The evidence adduced demonstrates that the boards of directors of OSC and BPS met jointly on March 22, 1999, to consider the cash-out mergers. The corporate minutes[75] from this meeting, the March 24 unanimous consents[76] and the affidavit

---

[75] [4] Magner contends the official minutes of the March 22 meeting are "false" because they were reduced to writing after the meeting. We have found no law, nor has Magner cited any, suggesting that minutes must be put into a final, written form contemporaneously with the events they memorialize. Absent a credible challenge to the reliability and validity of the minutes, the trial court did not err in considering them. This is especially so since official minutes of corporate meetings are generally considered the best evidence of corporate business transacted. *See South Ga. Trust Co. v. Crandall*, 47 Ga. App. 328(1), 170 S.E. 333 (1933); *Lucas v. Bechtel Corp.*, 800 F.2d 839, 849(2)(B)(1) (9th Cir. 1986).

[76] [5] Magner complains the consent documents purportedly signed on March 24 were ineffective to adopt the plan of merger since they were drafted after the April 26 shareholders' meeting and "back dated." Pretermitting whether they were sufficient to effect action without a meeting, pursuant to OCGA

and deposition testimony of the directors all abundantly demonstrate: (1) that a meeting occurred on March 22, 1999, (2) that the directors received or waived notice of it, (3) that the directors discussed merging OSC and BPS into the Giotto entities, with the original corporations surviving, (4) that the terms and conditions of the mergers[77] were discussed, (5) that the directors agreed to convert Magner's shares to cash in the amounts recommended by the appraiser, (6) that a record date for shareholders entitled to vote was set, and (7) that the plans of merger were adopted by a majority vote. The evidence adduced demonstrates that the boards of OSC and BPS complied with the procedural requirements of OCGA § 14-2-1101(a), (b).

(b) *The Record Date Was Properly Set.* Magner also contends the record date was improper because it was not a "future" date as required by OCGA § 14-2-707(a). The evidence shows that on March 22, 1999, the combined boards set the record date as March 25, 1999 — a date that was, at that point, three days in the future. We see no merit to Magner's argument that the boards' rescheduling of the shareholders' meeting in some way made the record date "retroactive." This Code section limits to 70 days the period of time that may transpire between the record date and the meeting or action requiring the determination of shareholders. *See* OCGA § 14-2-707(b). Implicitly, a meeting may be scheduled — or rescheduled — at any time within the time limits set by the Code, so long as proper notice is given. In fact, OCGA § 14-2-707(c) even permits a meeting to be adjourned to a future date without setting a new record date so long as the meeting is not "adjourned to a date more than 120 days after the date fixed for the original meeting." *Id.* See OCGA § 14-2-707(d) (setting record date when a meeting adjourned beyond the 120-day period).

(c) *The Final Plans of Merger Were Materially the Same as Those Proposed.* Magner contends the mergers should be rescinded because the plans of merger changed twice between the March 22, 1999 joint board meeting and the shareholders' April 26, 1999 meeting. Interestingly, however, he makes no legal argument in his brief explaining how any change violated Georgia law, was material to the mergers, or affected his rights. Magner argues that OCGA § 14-2-1103(a) requires that the plans of merger adopted by the boards be identical in every respect to the ones submitted to the shareholders. However, that statute, in relevant part, provides:

> After adopting a plan of merger or share exchange, the board of directors of each corporation party to the merger and the board of directors of the corporation whose shares will be acquired in the share exchange shall submit the plan of merger (except as provided in subsection (h) of this Code section) or share exchange for approval by its shareholders.

---

§ 14-2-821, they are, nevertheless, some evidence of the merger plan and its terms.

[77] [6] Magner asserts that a plan of merger was not adopted during the March 22 meeting because it had not been reduced to final form before the meeting and presented to the directors for their approval at that time. We see nothing in OCGA § 14-2-1101 requiring such a formality. It appears from the record that the board members were each fully apprised of the essential terms of the plan of merger, that they discussed those terms, and that they adopted a plan which was shortly thereafter reduced to writing and attached to the meeting minutes. This plan was mailed to Magner as an attachment to his Notice of Shareholder Meeting.

OCGA § 14-2-1103(a). We see nothing in this Code section or in the cases cited by Magner that forbids a board from correcting typographical errors or making nonmaterial changes to the merger plans prior to their submission to the shareholders for a vote.

The merger plans, as far as we can deduce from the briefs and the record before us, changed in only two respects: (1) A typographical error was corrected; and, (2) the direction of the mergers was changed so that the Giotto shell corporations would survive. Under the circumstances of this case, we fail to see (nor has Magner explained) how these changes materially affected the substance of the mergers or Magner's rights. Correcting a typographical error in the price per share did not change the fact that the mergers were intended to cash out the fair value of Magner's ownership interest. Reversing the direction of the mergers resulted only in a change of corporate name. The parties to the merger never changed. The Giotto entities were shell corporations with no assets of their own. Allowing the shell corporations to survive may have, at the most, resulted in some potential tax benefit to the corporations. Clearly, however, this change did not materially affect Magner since he was never entitled to participate in the surviving corporations. More importantly, however, Magner received notice of all of these changes prior to the shareholders' meeting. Not only has Magner failed to show any illegality, he has failed to show that he was in any way harmed. *See* 15 Fletcher Cyc. Corp. § 7159 (rescission of merger generally requires a showing of both irreparable injury and inadequate remedy at law).

2. Magner contends he and the LLC properly perfected dissenters' rights and are, therefore, entitled to a judicial appraisal. We disagree.

OCGA § 14-2-1302(a) provides that a "record shareholder of the corporation is entitled to dissent from, and obtain payment of the fair value of his shares in the event of" certain enumerated events, including the "[c]onsummation of a plan of merger." OCGA § 14-2-1302(a)(1). The procedure for perfecting dissenters' rights is "extremely technical and must be . . . followed within the time [limits] provided; otherwise the shareholder risks losing such appraisal right[s]." Kaplan's Nadler Ga. Corporation Law (2001 ed.), § 12–20.

To perfect these rights following the merger, Magner, as the record shareholder, was required to "demand payment and deposit his certificates in accordance with the terms of the [dissenters'] notice" he was sent. OCGA § 14-2-1323(a). See also OCGA § 14-2-1301(4) (a dissenter is a shareholder who exercises his rights in accordance with OCGA §§ 14-2-1320 through 14-2-1327). If Magner failed to do as instructed in the dissenters' notice, the Code states he "is not entitled to payment for his shares under [the dissenters' rights] article." OCGA § 14-2-1323(c).

Magner did not tender his stock certificates and demand payment as required by the Code. Instead, he cancelled his certificates and had new certificates issued to another legal entity. By this act, Magner placed his certificates beyond his power to tender to the corporation. *See Graves v. Pittsburgh Consolidation Coal Co.*, 355 Pa. 224, 225, 49 A.2d 344 (1946). Consequently, Magner gave up his right to dissent, a right which attached to the possession of those particular stock certificates. *Id.* at 225, 49 A.2d 344.

The LLC has no dissenters' rights because it was not a record shareholder on the record date, March 25, 1999. A "record shareholder" is defined in the Code, in relevant part, as "the person in whose name [the] shares are registered in the records of a corporation." OCGA § 14-2-1301(7). Moreover, a record shareholder, as that term is used in the dissenters' rights provisions, contemplates a shareholder who also held shares on the "record date" for purposes of a particular corporate transaction or event. *See* OCGA §§ 14-2-707; 14-2-1302; 14-2-1320 through 14-2-1323. For example, OCGA § 14-2-707 allows the directors to fix a record date so that the corporation may determine, with some degree of certainty, the shareholders entitled to notice, to make demands, to vote, and to take any other action. The commentary to OCGA § 14-2-1323 explains that the record date "is the cut-off date for determining who has dissenters' rights under this article" and "the demand for payment . . . is the definitive statement by the dissenter." In cases like the instant one, the Code contemplates a demand for payment being made by one who previously received notice of the corporate action and properly expressed an intent to dissent prior to the shareholders' vote. *See* OCGA §§ 14-2-1321; 14-2-1322. As the commentary to OCGA § 14-2-1323 explains, the demand is "confirmation of the 'intention' expressed earlier."

In this case, the LLC was not a record shareholder in either OSC or BPS on the record date set by the corporation. As such, it was not entitled to participate in the event at issue: the mergers. *See Graves*, 355 Pa. at 225, 49 A.2d at 345. It had no right to dissent and obtain payment for its shares under the dissenters' rights statutes. *Id.* For these reasons, the trial court properly granted summary judgment in favor of OSC and BPS.

Judgment affirmed.

# Chapter 14

# DERIVATIVE LAWSUITS

The derivative suit developed over the years as an equitable remedy because there was no common law remedy for shareholders who were the victims of careless or dishonest directors or officers. Most of the cases involve fraud or breach of fiduciary duty, but the action is not limited to those situations. The theory of the derivative suit is that the corporation has a good cause of action against someone and has failed to assert it. The derivative suit is a mechanism under which a concerned shareholder can assert the right of the corporation if the directors have failed to do so. This theoretical basis is the spring from which all the procedural complexity flows. A derivative suit requires at least one shareholder to bring it. The corporation is normally an indispensable party, and thus is usually sued as a nominal defendant along with other defendants, frequently the directors or officers of the corporation. The plaintiff generally must make a demand on the board of directors. Although the MBCA always requires a demand before initiating a derivative suit, several important jurisdictions, including Delaware and New York, provide exceptions if demand would be futile. A common reason for not making a demand on the board of directors was the fact that a majority of the directors had participated in the conduct that was the basis of the derivative suit. That reason seems less persuasive today since many jurisdictions permit a special litigation committee composed of independent directors to decide whether the potential derivative suit has merit. The special litigation committee was a mechanism that evolved from two cases, *Auerbach v. Bennett*, 393 N.E.2d 994 (N.Y. 1979), and *Zapata v. Maldanado*, 430 A.2d 779 (Del. 1981). The concept of the special litigation committee has developed quite rapidly since that time. In addition to the demand requirement, the plaintiff must meet the contemporaneous ownership requirement, and the complaint must plead the facts of the case with particularity.

The following excerpt (a portion of Justice Jackson's majority opinion) from *Cohen v. Beneficial Industrial Loan Corp.*, 337 U.S. 541 (1948), provides some background on the historical development of the derivative action. The case involved the constitutionality of the New Jersey security for expenses statute.

> The background of stockholder litigation with which this statute deals requires no more than general notice. As business enterprise increasingly sought the advantages of incorporation, management became vested with almost uncontrolled discretion in handling other people's money. The vast aggregate of funds committed to corporate control came to be drawn to a considerable extent from numerous and scattered holders of small interests. The director was not subject to an effective accountability. That created strong temptation for managers to profit personally at expense of their trust. The business code became all too tolerant of such practices.

Corporate laws were lax and were not self-enforcing, and stockholders, in face of gravest abuses, were singularly impotent in obtaining redress of abuses of trust.

Equity came to the relief of the stockholder, who had no standing to bring civil action at law against faithless directors and managers. Equity, however, allowed him to step into the corporation's shoes and to seek in its right the restitution he could not demand in his own. It required him first to demand that the corporation vindicate its own rights but when, as was usual, those who perpetrated the wrongs also were able to obstruct any remedy, equity would hear and adjudge the corporation's cause through its stockholder with the corporation as a defendant, albeit a rather nominal one. This remedy born of stockholder helplessness was long the chief regulator of corporate management and has afforded no small incentive to avoid at least grosser forms of betrayal of stockholders' interests. It is argued, and not without reason, that without it there would be little practical check on such abuses.

Unfortunately, the remedy itself provided opportunity for abuse which was not neglected. Suits sometimes were brought not to redress real wrongs, but to realize upon their nuisance value. They were bought off by secret settlements in which any wrongs to the general body of share owners were compounded by the suing stockholder, who was mollified by payments from corporate assets. These litigations were aptly characterized in professional slang as "strike suits." And it was said that these suits were more commonly brought by small and irresponsible than by large stockholders, because the former put less to risk and a small interest was more often within the capacity and readiness of management to compromise than a large one.

\* \* \*

The very nature of the stockholder's derivative action makes it one in the regulation of which the legislature of a state has wide powers. Whatever theory one may hold as to the nature of the corporate entity, it remains a wholly artificial creation whose internal relations between management and stockholders are dependent upon state law and may be subject to most complete and penetrating regulation, either by public authority or by some form of stockholder action. Directors and managers, if not technically trustees, occupy positions of a fiduciary nature, and nothing in the Federal Constitution prohibits a state from imposing on them the strictest measure of responsibility, liability and accountability, either as a condition of assuming office or as a consequence of holding it.

Likewise, a stockholder who brings suit on a cause of action derived from the corporation assumes a position, not technically as a trustee perhaps, but one of a fiduciary character. He sues, not for himself alone, but as representative of a class comprising all who are similarly situated. The interests of all in the redress of the wrongs are taken into his hands, dependent upon his diligence, wisdom and integrity. And while the stockholders have chosen the corporate director or manager, they have no such election as to a plaintiff who steps forward to represent them. He is a self-chosen representative and a volunteer champion. The Federal Constitution does not oblige the State to place its litigating and adjudicating processes at the disposal of such a representative, at least without imposing standards of responsibility, liability and accountability which it considers will protect the interests he elects himself to represent. It is not without significance that this Court has found it necessary long ago in the Equity Rules and now in the Federal Rules of Civil Procedure to impose procedural regulations of the class action not applicable to any other. We conclude that the state has plenary power over this type of litigation.

\*   \*   \*

In considering whether the statute offends the Due Process Clause we can judge it only by its own terms, for it has had no interpretation or application as yet. It imposes liability and requires security for "the reasonable expenses, including counsel fees which may be incurred" (emphasis supplied) by the corporation and by other parties defendant. The amount of security is subject to increase if the progress of the litigation reveals that it is inadequate or to decrease if it is proved to be excessive. A state may set the terms on which it will permit litigations in its courts. No type of litigation is more susceptible of regulation than that of a fiduciary nature. And it cannot seriously be said that a state makes such unreasonable use of its power as to violate the Constitution when it provides liability and security for payment of reasonable expenses if a litigation of this character is adjudged to be unsustainable. It is urged that such a requirement will foreclose resort by most stockholders to the only available judicial remedy for the protection of their rights. Of course, to require security for the payment of any kind of costs or the necessity for bearing any kind of expense of litigation has a deterring effect. But we deal with power, not wisdom; and we think, notwithstanding this tendency, it is within the power of a state to close its courts to this type of litigation if the condition of reasonable security is not met.

337 U.S. at 547–552.

## A.   DIRECT VS. DERIVATIVE

### GUENTHER v. PACIFIC TELECOM, INC.
United States District Court, District of Oregon
123 F.R.D. 341 (1988)

Malcom F. Marsh, United States District Judge

Plaintiffs, former minority shareholders of American Network, Inc. (AmNet), originally brought this action asserting direct and derivative claims against Pacific Telecom, Inc. (PTI) and its directors; Price Waterhouse & Co., Inc., and its accountant Donald Irving; and AmNet and its directors. Since the filing of this action, AmNet and United States Transmissions Systems, Inc. (USTS), have entered into an Agreement and Plan of Exchange. The result of this Exchange Agreement was to automatically exchange all of plaintiffs' shares of AmNet for the right to receive $.25 in cash without interest.

Defendants now seek to dismiss plaintiffs' derivative claims on the basis that plaintiffs are no longer shareholders of AmNet. Plaintiffs oppose the motion and seek to assert their claim for breach of fiduciary duty directly. For the reasons set forth below, defendants' motions to dismiss are granted.

## DISCUSSION

It is well established that Fed. R. Civ. P. 23.1 implies that plaintiffs asserting a derivative claim must be shareholders at the time of the alleged wrong and must retain ownership for the duration of the lawsuit. *Lewis v. Chiles*, 719 F.2d 1044, 1047 (9th Cir. 1983). Consequently, plaintiffs only viable argument in opposition to defendants' motions to dismiss is that they should be allowed to bring their claim for breach of fiduciary duty directly.

The proper resolution of this issue depends upon the interpretation of three Ninth Circuit cases. While all three cases acknowledge the general rule that a claim for breach of fiduciary duty is derivative in nature, two of the cases appear to allow such a claim to be brought in directly.

In *Watson v. Button*, 235 F.2d 235 (9th Cir. 1956) the court allowed an individual plaintiff to recover from the former general manager of a corporation for the misappropriation of corporate funds. Prior to bringing the action, all of the stock of the sale was sold to third parties. In connection with the sale, the general manager secured an agreement from the purchasers to release and discharge him from any claims existing against him in favor of the corporation. In allowing the plaintiff's recovery, the court noted:

> Appellant and appellee were the only stockholders at the time of the misappropriation. The corporate creditors are adequately protected since appellant and appellee are jointly responsible for the corporate liabilities. It is doubtful, in any event, whether under Oregon law the creditors could sue appellant for his misappropriation. The only right apparently would be to enforce the corporate cause of action, but that was given up by the present owners of the corporation when they purchased it from appellant and appellee.

The District Court did not err in concluding that the Oregon court would follow these decisions from other states which allow an individual recovery in this situation, at least in a case where the rights of creditors and other shareholders are not prejudiced. Suits against directors for violations of fiduciary duties are equitable in nature. It is unlikely that the Oregon courts would allow a director to misappropriate funds and leave those injured without a remedy.

In contrast, in *Lewis v. Chiles*, 719 F.2d at 1048, the court held that an individual plaintiff could not bring a direct claim for breach of fiduciary duty despite his claim that the officers and directors of the corporation sold the corporate assets as a means of insulating themselves from liability. The court held that in light of the fact that the shareholders approved the sale of assets with knowledge of plaintiff's claim and of the potential conflict of interest of officers and directors, the plaintiff could not bring his claim individually. *Id.*

Finally, in *Eagle v. American Tel. and Tel. Co.*, 769 F.2d 541 (9th Cir. 1985) *cert. denied* 475 U.S. 1084 (1986), the court "assumed" former shareholders could bring a direct claim against majority shareholders for breach of fiduciary duty because a corporate recovery "would not compensate the former minority shareholders for any loss they may have suffered as a result of the injury to" the corporation. The court's holding, however, must be tempered by the fact that the court was addressing a jurisdictional issue as opposed to the merits of the particular claim. Thus, the court did not address the relative merits of *Watson* and *Lewis* and made only passing reference to the holding in *Watson.*

Having reviewed the above cases, I conclude that the present case is more akin to *Lewis* and does not present the factual basis which supported the *Watson* holding. In *Watson,* the court addressed the three factors which support derivative recovery as opposed to direct recovery. The court concluded that each factor was missing.235 F.2d at 237. In the present case, I cannot reach the same conclusion.

The first factor favoring derivative recovery is that it avoids a multiplicity of suits. *Id.* The *Watson* court concluded that such a factor was lacking in that case because there were only two shareholders, the plaintiff and the defendant. In the present case, however, the potential of a multiplicity of suits exists. This conclusion is evidence by the existence of *Numrich v. Gleason*, Civ. No. 88-140-MA, and by the court's denial of class certification.

The second factor favoring derivative recovery is that it protects the corporate creditor. *Id.* Again, the *Watson* court concluded that such a factor was lacking in that case because the two shareholders were jointly liable for corporate liabilities. In the present case, there is no similar indemnity agreement.

Finally, the third factor favoring derivative recovery is that it protects all shareholders of the corporation since the corporation recovers the benefit. The *Watson* court disregarded this factor on the basis that the only two shareholders were parties to the case. In contrast, the present case does not involve all shareholders or even all former minority shareholders.

Based on the foregoing, I conclude that *Watson* is not controlling in this case and that the facts of this case dictate against the allowance of direct recovery for plaintiffs' claim of breach of fiduciary duty. Accordingly, defendant PTI's Rule 23.1 motion #284, defendant AmNet's Rule 23.1 motion #281 and defendant Price Waterhouse and Irving's Rule 23.1 motion #295 are GRANTED.

## TOOLEY v. DONALDSON, LUFKIN & JENRETTE, INC.
### Supreme Court of Delaware
### 845 A.2d 1031 (2004)

VEASEY, J.

Plaintiff-stockholders brought a purported class action in the Court of Chancery, alleging that the members of the board of directors of their corporation breached their fiduciary duties by agreeing to a 22-day delay in closing a proposed merger. Plaintiffs contend that the delay harmed them due to the lost time-value of the cash paid for their shares. The Court of Chancery granted the defendants' motion to dismiss on the sole ground that the claims were, "at most," claims of the corporation being asserted derivatively. They were, thus, held not to be direct claims of the stockholders, individually. Thereupon, the Court held that the plaintiffs lost their standing to bring this action when they tendered their shares in connection with the merger.

Although the trial court's legal analysis of whether the complaint alleges a direct or derivative claim reflects some concepts in our prior jurisprudence, we believe those concepts are not helpful and should be regarded as erroneous. We set forth in this Opinion the law to be applied henceforth in determining whether a stockholder's claim is derivative or direct. That issue must turn *solely* on the following questions: (1) who suffered the alleged harm (the corporation or the suing stockholders, individually); and (2) who would receive the benefit of any recovery or other remedy (the corporation or the stockholders, individually)?

To the extent we have concluded that the trial court's analysis of the direct vs. derivative dichotomy should be regarded as erroneous, we view the error as harmless in this case because the complaint does not set forth *any* claim upon which relief can be granted. In its opinion, the Court of Chancery properly found on the facts pleaded that the plaintiffs have no separate contractual right to the alleged lost time-value of money arising out of extensions in the closing of a tender offer. These extensions were made in connection with a merger where the plaintiffs' right to any payment of the merger consideration had not ripened at the time the extensions were granted. No other individual right of these stockholders having been asserted in the complaint, it was correctly dismissed.

In affirming the judgment of the trial court as having correctly dismissed the complaint, we reverse only its dismissal with prejudice. We remand this action to the Court of Chancery with directions to amend its order of dismissal to provide that: (a) the action is dismissed for failure to state a claim upon which relief can be granted; and (b) that the dismissal is without prejudice. Thus, plaintiffs will have an opportunity to replead, if warranted under Court of Chancery Rule 11.

### Facts

Patrick Tooley and Kevin Lewis are former minority stockholders of Donaldson, Lufkin & Jenrette, Inc. (DLJ), a Delaware corporation engaged in investment banking. DLJ was acquired by Credit Suisse Group (Credit Suisse) in the Fall of

2000. Before that acquisition, AXA Financial, Inc. (AXA), which owned 71% of DLJ stock, controlled DLJ. Pursuant to a stockholder agreement between AXA and Credit Suisse, AXA agreed to exchange with Credit Suisse its DLJ stockholdings for a mix of stock and cash. The consideration received by AXA consisted primarily of stock. Cash made up one-third of the purchase price. Credit Suisse intended to acquire the remaining minority interests of publicly-held DLJ stock through a cash tender offer, followed by a merger of DLJ into a Credit Suisse subsidiary.

The tender offer price was set at $90 per share in cash. The tender offer was to expire 20 days after its commencement. The merger agreement, however, authorized two types of extensions. First, Credit Suisse could unilaterally extend the tender offer if certain conditions were not met, such as SEC regulatory approvals or certain payment obligations. Alternatively, DLJ and Credit Suisse could agree to postpone acceptance by Credit Suisse of DLJ stock tendered by the minority stockholders.

Credit Suisse availed itself of both types of extensions to postpone the closing of the tender offer. The tender offer was initially set to expire on October 5, 2000, but Credit Suisse invoked the five-day unilateral extension provided in the agreement. Later, by agreement between DLJ and Credit Suisse, it postponed the merger a second time so that it was then set to close on November 2, 2000.

Plaintiffs challenge the second extension that resulted in a 22-day delay. They contend that this delay was not properly authorized and harmed minority stockholders while improperly benefitting AXA. They claim damages representing the time-value of money lost through the delay.

## The Decision of the Court of Chancery

The order of the Court of Chancery dismissing the complaint, and the Memorandum Opinion upon which it is based, state that the dismissal is based on the plaintiffs' lack of standing to bring the claims asserted therein. Thus, when plaintiffs tendered their shares, they lost standing under Court of Chancery Rule 23.1, the contemporaneous holding rule. The ruling before us on appeal is that the plaintiffs' claim is derivative, purportedly brought on behalf of DLJ. The Court of Chancery, relying upon our confusing jurisprudence on the direct/derivative dichotomy, based its dismissal on the following ground: "Because this delay affected all DLJ shareholders equally, plaintiffs' injury was not a special injury, and this action is, thus, a derivative action, at most."

Plaintiffs argue that they have suffered a "special injury" because they had an alleged contractual right to receive the merger consideration of $90 per share without suffering the 22-day delay arising out of the extensions under the merger agreement. But the trial court's opinion convincingly demonstrates that plaintiffs had no such contractual right that had ripened at the time the extensions were entered into:

> *Here, it is clear that plaintiffs have no separate contractual right to bring a direct claim, and they do not assert contractual rights under the merger agreement.* First, the merger agreement specifically disclaims any persons as being third party beneficiaries to the contract. Second, any contractual

shareholder right to payment of the merger consideration did not ripen until the conditions of the agreement were met. The agreement stated that Credit Suisse Group was not required to accept any shares for tender, or could extend the offer, under certain conditions-one condition of which included an extension or termination by agreement between Credit Suisse Group and DLJ. *Because Credit Suisse Group and DLJ did in fact agree to extend the tender offer period, any right to payment plaintiffs could have did not ripen until this newly negotiated period was over. The merger agreement only became binding and mutually enforceable at the time the tendered shares ultimately were accepted for payment by Credit Suisse Group.* It is at that moment in time, November 3, 2000, that the company became bound to purchase the tendered shares, making the contract mutually enforceable. *DLJ stockholders had no individual contractual right to payment until November 3, 2000, when their tendered shares were accepted for payment.* Thus, they have no contractual basis to challenge a delay in the closing of the tender offer up until November 3. *Because this is the date the tendered shares were accepted for payment, the contract was not breached and plaintiffs do not have a contractual basis to bring a direct suit.*

Moreover, no other individual right of these stockholder-plaintiffs was alleged to have been violated by the extensions.

That conclusion could have ended the case because it portended a definitive ruling that plaintiffs have no claim whatsoever on the facts alleged. But the defendants chose to argue, and the trial court chose to decide, the standing issue, which is predicated on an assertion that this claim is a derivative one asserted on behalf of the corporation, DLJ.

The Court of Chancery correctly noted that "[t]he Court will independently examine the nature of the wrong alleged and any potential relief to make its own determination of the suit's classification. . . . Plaintiffs' classification of the suit is not binding." The trial court's analysis was hindered, however, because it focused on the confusing concept of "special injury" as the test for determining whether a claim is derivative or direct. The trial court's premise was as follows:

> In order to bring a *direct* claim, a plaintiff must have experienced some "special injury." [citing *Lipton v. News Int'l*, 514 A.2d 1075, 1079 (Del. 1986)]. A special injury is a wrong that "is separate and distinct from that suffered by other shareholders, . . . or a wrong involving a contractual right of a shareholder, such as the right to vote, or to assert majority control, which exists independently of any right of the corporation." [citing *Moran v. Household Int'l. Inc.*, 490 A.2d 1059, 1070 (Del. Ch. 1985), *aff'd* 500 A.2d 1346 (Del. 1986 [1985])].

In our view, the concept of "special injury" that appears in some Supreme Court and Court of Chancery cases is not helpful to a proper analytical distinction between direct and derivative actions. We now disapprove the use of the concept of "special injury" as a tool in that analysis.

### The Proper Analysis to Distinguish Between Direct and Derivative Actions

The analysis must be based solely on the following questions: Who suffered the alleged harm-the corporation or the suing stockholder individually-and who would receive the benefit of the recovery or other remedy? This simple analysis is well imbedded in our jurisprudence[1], but some cases have complicated it by injection of the amorphous and confusing concept of "special injury."

The Chancellor, in the very recent *Agostino* case[2], correctly points this out and strongly suggests that we should disavow the concept of "special injury." In a scholarly analysis of this area of the law, he also suggests that the inquiry should be whether the stockholder has demonstrated that he or she has suffered an injury that is not dependent on an injury to the corporation. In the context of a claim for breach of fiduciary duty, the Chancellor articulated the inquiry as follows: "Looking at the body of the complaint and considering the nature of the wrong alleged and the relief requested, has the plaintiff demonstrated that he or she can prevail without showing an injury to the corporation?"[3] We believe that this approach is helpful in analyzing the first prong of the analysis: what person or entity has suffered the alleged harm? The second prong of the analysis should logically follow.

### A Brief History of Our Jurisprudence

The derivative suit has been generally described as "one of the most interesting and ingenious of accountability mechanisms for large formal organizations." It enables a stockholder to bring suit on behalf of the corporation for harm done to the corporation. Because a derivative suit is being brought on behalf of the corporation, the recovery, if any, must go to the corporation. A stockholder who is directly injured, however, does retain the right to bring an individual action for injuries affecting his or her legal rights as a stockholder. Such a claim is distinct from an injury caused to the corporation alone. In such individual suits, the recovery or other relief flows directly to the stockholders, not to the corporation.

Determining whether an action is derivative or direct is sometimes difficult and has many legal consequences, some of which may have an expensive impact on the parties to the action. For example, if an action is derivative, the plaintiffs are then required to comply with the requirements of Court of Chancery Rule 23.1, that the

---

[1] [7] *See, e.g., Kramer v. Western Pacific Industries, Inc.*, 546 A.2d 348 (Del. 1988).

[2] [8] *Agostino v. Hicks*, No. Civ. A. 20020-NC, 2004 WL 443987 (Del. Ch. March 11, 2004).

[3] [9] *Agostino*, 2004 WL 443987, at * 7. The Chancellor further explains that the focus should be on the person or entity to whom the relevant duty is owed. *Id.* at *7 n. 54. As noted in *Agostino, id.*, this test is similar to that articulated by the American Law Institute (ALI), a test that we cited with approval in *Grimes v. Donald*, 673 A.2d 1207 (Del. 1996). The ALI test is as follows:

> A direct action may be brought in the name and right of a holder to redress an injury sustained by, or enforce a duty owed to, the holder. An action in which the holder can prevail without showing an injury or breach of duty to the corporation should be treated as a direct action that may be maintained by the holder in an individual capacity.

2 American Law Institute, Principles of Corporate Governance: Analysis and Recommendations § 7.01(b) at 17.

stockholder: (a) retain ownership of the shares throughout the litigation; (b) make presuit demand on the board; and (c) obtain court approval of any settlement. Further, the recovery, if any, flows only to the corporation. The decision whether a suit is direct or derivative may be outcome-determinative. Therefore, it is necessary that a standard to distinguish such actions be clear, simple and consistently articulated and applied by our courts.

In *Elster v. American Airlines, Inc.*, the stockholder sought to enjoin the grant and exercise of stock options because they would result in a dilution of her stock personally. In *Elster*, the alleged injury was found to be derivative, not direct, because it was essentially a claim of mismanagement of corporate assets. Then came the complication in the analysis: The Court held that where the alleged injury is to both the corporation *and* to the stockholder, the stockholder must allege a "special injury" to maintain a direct action. The Court did not define "special injury," however. By implication, decisions in later cases have interpreted *Elster* to mean that a "special injury" is alleged where the wrong is inflicted upon the stockholder alone or where the stockholder complains of a wrong affecting a particular right. Examples would be a preemptive right as a stockholder, rights involving control of the corporation or a wrong affecting the stockholder, qua individual holder, and not the corporation.[4]

In *Bokat v. Getty Oil Co.*, a stockholder of a subsidiary brought suit against the director of the parent corporation for causing the subsidiary to invest its resources wastefully, resulting in a loss to the subsidiary. The claim in *Bokat* was essentially for mismanagement of corporate assets. Therefore, the Court held that any recovery must be sought on behalf of the corporation, and the claim was, thus, found to be derivative.

In describing how a court may distinguish direct and derivative actions, the *Bokat* Court stated that a suit must be maintained derivatively if the injury falls equally upon all stockholders. Experience has shown this concept to be confusing and inaccurate. It is confusing because it appears to have been intended to address the fact that an injury to the corporation tends to diminish each share of stock equally because corporate assets or their value are diminished. In that sense, the *indirect* injury to the stockholders arising out of the harm to the corporation comes about solely by virtue of their stockholdings. It does not arise out of any independent or direct harm to the stockholders, individually. That concept is also inaccurate because a direct, individual claim of stockholders that does not depend on harm to the corporation can also fall on all stockholders equally, without the claim thereby becoming a derivative claim.

In *Lipton v. News International, Plc.*, this Court applied the "special injury" test. There, a stockholder began acquiring shares in the defendant corporation presumably to gain control of the corporation. In response, the defendant corporation agreed to an exchange of its shares with a friendly buyer. Due to the exchange and a supermajority voting requirement on certain stockholder actions,

---

[4] [14] See *Lipton v. News International, Plc.*, 514 A.2d 1075, 1078 (Del. 1986); *Moran v. Household International Inc.*, 490 A.2d 1059, 1069–70 (Del. Ch. 1985) (to distinguish a direct and derivative action, injury must be separate and distinct from that suffered by other stockholders or involve a contractual right independent of the corporation).

the management of the defendant corporation acquired a veto power over any change in management.

The *Lipton* Court concluded that the critical analytical issue in distinguishing direct and derivative actions is whether a "special injury" has been alleged. There, the Court found a "special injury" because the board's manipulation worked an injury upon the plaintiff-stockholder unlike the injury suffered by other stockholders. That was because the plaintiff-stockholder was actively seeking to gain control of the defendant corporation. Therefore, the Court found that the claim was direct. Ironically, the Court could have reached the same correct result by simply concluding that the manipulation directly and individually harmed the stockholders, without injuring the corporation.

In *Kramer v. Western Pacific Industries, Inc.*, this Court found to be derivative a stockholder's challenge to corporate transactions that occurred six months immediately preceding a buy-out merger. The stockholders challenged the decision by the board of directors to grant stock options and golden parachutes to management. The stockholders argued that the claim was direct because their share of the proceeds from the buy-out sale was reduced by the resources used to pay for the options and golden parachutes. Once again, our analysis was that to bring a direct action, the stockholder must allege something other than an injury resulting from a wrong to the corporation. We interpreted *Elster* to require the court to determine the nature of the action based on the "nature of the wrong alleged" and the relief that could result. That was, and is, the correct test. The claim in *Kramer* was essentially for mismanagement of corporate assets. Therefore, we found the claims to be derivative. That was the correct outcome.[5]

In *Grimes v. Donald*, we sought to distinguish between direct and derivative actions in the context of employment agreements granted to certain officers that allegedly caused the board to abdicate its authority. Relying on the *Elster* and *Kramer* precedents that the court must look to the nature of the wrong and to whom the relief will go, we concluded that the plaintiff was not seeking to recover any damages for injury to the corporation. Rather, the plaintiff was seeking a declaration of the invalidity of the agreements on the ground that the board had abdicated its responsibility to the stockholders. Thus, based on the relief requested, we affirmed the judgment of the Court of Chancery that the plaintiff was entitled to pursue a direct action.

*Grimes* was followed by *Parnes v. Bally Entertainment Corp.*, which held, among other things, that the injury to the stockholders must be "independent of any injury to the corporation." As the Chancellor correctly noted in *Agostino*, neither *Grimes* nor *Parnes* applies the purported "special injury" test.

Thus, two confusing propositions have encumbered our caselaw governing the direct/derivative distinction. The "special injury" concept, applied in cases such as *Lipton*, can be confusing in identifying the nature of the action. The same is true of the proposition that stems from *Bokat* — that an action cannot be direct if all stockholders are equally affected or unless the stockholder's injury is separate and

---

[5] [21] In the *Tri-Star* case, however, this Court lapsed back into the "special injury" concept, which we now discard. *In re Tri-Star Pictures, Inc. Litigation*, 634 A.2d 319, 330 (1993).

distinct from that suffered by other stockholders. The proper analysis has been and should remain that stated in *Grimes; Kramer* and *Parnes*. That is, a court should look to the nature of the wrong and to whom the relief should go. The stockholder's claimed direct injury must be independent of any alleged injury to the corporation. The stockholder must demonstrate that the duty breached was owed to the stockholder and that he or she can prevail without showing an injury to the corporation.

### Standard to Be Applied in This Case

In this case it cannot be concluded that the complaint alleges a derivative claim. There is no derivative claim asserting injury to the corporate entity. There is no relief that would go the corporation. Accordingly, there is no basis to hold that the complaint states a derivative claim.

But, it does not necessarily follow that the complaint states a direct, individual claim. While the complaint purports to set forth a direct claim, in reality, it states no claim at all. The trial court analyzed the complaint and correctly concluded that it does not claim that the plaintiffs have any rights that have been injured. Their rights have not yet ripened. The contractual claim is nonexistent until it is ripe, and that claim will not be ripe until the terms of the merger are fulfilled, including the extensions of the closing at issue here. Therefore, there is no direct claim stated in the complaint before us.

Accordingly, the complaint was properly dismissed. But, due to the reliance on the concept of "special injury" by the Court of Chancery, the ground set forth for the dismissal is erroneous, there being no derivative claim. That error is harmless, however, because, in our view, there is no direct claim either.

### Conclusion

For purposes of distinguishing between derivative and direct claims, we expressly disapprove both the concept of "special injury" and the concept that a claim is necessarily derivative if it affects all stockholders equally. In our view, the tests going forward should rest on those set forth in this opinion.

We affirm the judgment of the Court of Chancery dismissing the complaint, although on a different ground from that decided by the Court of Chancery. We reverse the dismissal with prejudice and remand this matter to the Court of Chancery to amend the order of dismissal: (a) to state that the complaint is dismissed on the ground that it does not state a claim upon which relief can be granted; and (b) that the dismissal is without prejudice.

Because our determination that there is no valid claim whatsoever in the complaint before us was not argued[6] by the defendants and was not the basis of the

---

[6] [28] As we have noted, the opinion of the trial court clearly stated that plaintiffs did not have a contractual right that had ripened. *Tooley,* 2003 WL 203060, at \*3. On appeal, appellees cited twice to the trial court's conclusion that there was no contractual right, but it was in the context of the derivative/direct claim issue. (Appellees' Answering Brief at pp. 3, 17–18). On appeal, plaintiffs-appellants

ruling of the Court of Chancery[7], the interests of justice will be best served if the dismissal is without prejudice, and plaintiffs have an opportunity to replead if they have a basis for doing so under Court of Chancery Rule 11. This result — permitting plaintiffs to replead — is unusual, but not unprecedented.[8]

# IN RE EBAY, INC. SHAREHOLDERS LITIGATION
### Court of Chancery of Delaware
### 2004 Del. Ch. LEXIS 4 (Feb. 11, 2004)

*MEMORANDUM OPINION*

CHANDLER, J.

Shareholders of eBay, Inc. filed these consolidated derivative actions against certain eBay directors and officers for usurping corporate opportunities. Plaintiffs allege that eBay's investment banking advisor, Goldman Sachs Group, engaged in "spinning," a practice that involves allocating shares of lucrative initial public offerings of stock to favored clients. In effect, the plaintiff shareholders allege that Goldman Sachs bribed certain eBay insiders, using the currency of highly profitable investment opportunities-opportunities that should have been offered to, or provided for the benefit of, eBay rather than the favored insiders. Plaintiffs accuse Goldman Sachs of aiding and abetting the corporate insiders breach of their fiduciary duty of loyalty to eBay.

The individual eBay defendants, as well as Goldman Sachs, have moved to dismiss these consolidated actions for failure to state a claim and for failure to make a pre-suit demand on eBay's board of directors as required under Chancery Court Rule 23.1. For reasons I briefly discuss below, I deny all of the defendants' motions to dismiss.

## I. BACKGROUND FACTS

The facts, as alleged in the complaint, are straightforward. In 1995, defendants Pierre M. Omidyar and Jeffrey Skoll founded nominal defendant eBay, a Delaware corporation, as a sole proprietorship. eBay is a pioneer in online trading platforms, providing a virtual auction community for buyers and sellers to list items for sale and to bid on items of interest. In 1998, eBay retained Goldman Sachs and other investment banks to underwrite an initial public offering of common stock. Goldman Sachs was the lead underwriter. The stock was priced at $18 per share. Goldman Sachs purchased about 1.2 million shares. Shares of eBay stock became immensely

---

do not challenge the trial court's finding. Moreover, inexplicably, plaintiffs-appellants filed no reply brief in this Court.

[7] [29] See, *Unitrin, Inc. v. American General Corp.*, 651 A.2d 1361, 1390 (Del. 1995) (decision of Supreme Court reversing trial court based on different grounds than that argued on appeal).

[8] [30] *Compare Brehm v. Eisner*, 746 A.2d 244, 267 (Del. 1999) (permitting plaintiffs to proceed because of the unique circumstances noted there), with *White v. Panic*, 783 A.2d 543, 556 (Del. 2001) (declining to permit plaintiffs to replead, there being no circumstances justifying such action).

valuable during 1998 and 1999, rising to $175 per share in early April 1999. Around that time, eBay made a secondary offering, issuing 6.5 million shares of common stock at $170 per share for a total of $1.1 billion. Goldman Sachs again served as lead underwriter. Goldman Sachs was asked in 2001 to serve as eBay's financial advisor in connection with an acquisition by eBay of PayPal, Inc. For these services, eBay has paid Goldman Sachs over $8 million.

During this same time period, Goldman Sachs "rewarded" the individual defendants by allocating to them thousands of IPO shares, managed by Goldman Sachs, at the initial offering price. Because the IPO market during this particular period of time was extremely active, prices of initial stock offerings often doubled or tripled in a single day. Investors who were well connected, either to Goldman Sachs or to similarly situated investment banks serving as IPO underwriters, were able to flip these investments into instant profit by selling the equities in a few days or even in a few hours after they were initially purchased.

The essential allegation of the complaint is that Goldman Sachs provided these IPO share allocations to the individual defendants to show appreciation for eBay's business and to enhance Goldman Sachs' chances of obtaining future eBay business. In addition to co-founding eBay, defendant Omidyar has been eBay's CEO, CFO and President. He is eBay's largest stockholder, owning more than 23% of the company's equity. Goldman Sachs allocated Omidyar shares in at least forty IPOs at the initial offering price. Omidyar resold these securities in the public market for millions of dollars in profit. Defendant Whitman owns 3.3% of eBay stock and has been President, CEO and a director since early 1998. Whitman also has been a director of Goldman Sachs since 2001. Goldman Sachs allocated Whitman shares in over a 100 IPOs at the initial offering price. Whitman sold these equities in the open market and reaped millions of dollars in profit. Defendant Skoll, in addition to co-founding eBay, has served in various positions at the company, including Vice-President of Strategic Planning and Analysis and President. He served as an eBay director from December 1996 to March 1998. Skoll is eBay's second largest stockholder, owning about 13% of the company. Goldman Sachs has allocated Skoll shares in at least 75 IPOs at the initial offering price, which Skoll promptly resold on the open market, allowing him to realize millions of dollars in profit. Finally, defendant Robert C. Kagle has served as an eBay director since June 1997. Goldman Sachs allocated Kagle shares in at least 25 IPOs at the initial offering price. Kagle promptly resold these equities, and recorded millions of dollars in profit.

## II. ANALYSIS

### A. Demand Futility

Plaintiffs bring these actions on behalf of nominal defendant eBay, seeking an accounting from the individual director defendants of their profits from the IPO transactions as well as compensatory damages from Goldman Sachs for its participation (aiding and abetting) in the eBay insiders' breach of fiduciary duty. Court of Chancery Rule 23.1 requires that a shareholder make a demand that the corporation's board pursue potential litigation before initiating such litigation on the corporation's behalf. When a plaintiff fails to make a demand on the board of directors, the plaintiff must plead with factual particularity why the demand is excused.

eBay's board of directors consists of seven members. Three are the individual defendants-Whitman, Omidyar and Kagle; defendant Skoll is not presently a director. All four of these individual defendants received IPO allocations from Goldman Sachs. As a result, the three current directors of eBay who received IPO allocations (Omidyar, Whitman and Kagle) are clearly interested in the transactions at the core of this controversy.

Although the other four directors of eBay (Cook, Lepore, Schultz and Bourguignon) did not participate in the "spinning," plaintiffs allege that they are not independent of the interested directors and, thus, demand is excused as futile. Since three of the seven present eBay directors are interested in the transactions that give rise to this litigation, plaintiffs need only demonstrate a reason to doubt the independence of one of the remaining four directors. Plaintiffs allege that directors Cook, Lepore, Schultz and Bourguignon all have "close business and personal ties with the individual defendants" and are incapable of exercising independent judgment to determine whether eBay should bring a breach of fiduciary duty action against the individual defendants. Plaintiffs allege, for example, that Schultz is a member of Maveron LLC, an investment advisory company in which Whitman has made significant personal investments. More significantly, plaintiffs allege that Cook, Lepore, Schultz and Bourguignon have received huge financial benefits as a result of their positions as eBay directors and, furthermore, that they owe their positions on the board to Omidyar, Whitman, Kagle and Skoll.

eBay pays no cash compensation to its directors, but it does award substantial stock options. For example, in 1998, when Cook joined eBay's board, it awarded him 900,000 options at an exercise price of $1.555. One fourth of these options (225,000) vested immediately, and an additional 2% vests each subsequent month so long as Cook remains a director. In 1998, after Cook had joined the board, eBay adopted a director's stock option plan pursuant to which each non-employee director was to be awarded 30,000 options each year (except for 1999, when no additional options were awarded). As of early 2002, Cook beneficially owned 903,750 currently exercisable options, and an additional 200,000 shares of eBay stock. The complaint notes that the exercise price on 900,000 of the options originally awarded to Cook is $1.555 per share. At the time the complaint was filed in this case, eBay stock was valued at $62.13 per share. At an exercise price of $1.555, Cook's original option grant is thus worth millions of dollars. In addition, the stock options awarded in 2000, 2001 and 2002, which are not yet fully Vested, and will never vest unless Cook retains his position as a director, are worth potentially millions of dollars.

The complaint further alleges that director Schultz, Lepore and Bourguignon are similarly situated. That is, the stock options granted to these directors, which are both vested and unvested, are so valuable that they create a financial incentive for these directors to retain their positions as directors and make them beholden to the defendant directors. As a result, plaintiffs contend that it is more than reasonable to assume that an individual who has already received, and who expects to receive still more, options of such significant value could not objectively decide whether to commence legal proceedings against fellow directors who are directly responsible for the outside directors'continuing positions on the board.

I need not address each of the four outside directors, as I agree with plaintiffs that the particularized allegations of the complaint are sufficient to raise a reasonable doubt as to Cook's independence from the eBay insider directors who accepted Goldman Sachs' IPO allocations. Defendants resist this conclusion by pointing out that Whitman, Kagle, Omidyar and Skoll, collectively with management, control 40% of eBay's common stock, which they argue is insufficient to allege control or domination. Defendants also contend that the options represent past compensation and would not effectively disable a director from acting fairly and impartially with respect to a demand. These arguments are unpersuasive in these circumstances.

First, defendants must concede that certain stockholders, executive officers and directors control eBay. For example, eBay's form 10-K for the fiscal year ending December 31, 2000 notes that eBay's executive officers and directors Whitman, Omidyar, Kagle and Skoll (and their affiliates) own about one-half of eBay's outstanding common stock.[9] As a result, these eBay officers and directors effectively have the ability to control eBay and to direct its affairs and business, including the election of directors and the approval of significant corporate transactions. Although the percentage of ownership may have decreased slightly from the time eBay filed the 2000 10-K, the decrease is insufficient to detract from the company's acknowledgement that these four individual defendants control the company and the election of directors.

Second, although many of the options awarded to Cook and the other purported outside directors have in fact vested, a significant number of options have not yet vested and will never vest unless the outside directors remain directors of eBay. Given that the value of the options for Cook (and allegedly for the other outside directors) potentially run into the millions of dollars, one cannot conclude realistically that Cook would be able to objectively and impartially consider a demand to bring litigation against those to whom he is beholden for his current position and future position on eBay's board. With the specific allegations of the complaint in mind, I conclude that plaintiffs have adequately demonstrated that demand on eBay's board should be excused as futile.

### B. Corporate Opportunity

Plaintiffs have stated a claim that defendants usurped a corporate opportunity of eBay. Defendants insist that Goldman Sachs' IPO allocations, to eBay's insider directors were "collateral investments opportunities" that arose by virtue of the inside directors status as wealthy individuals. They argue that this is not a corporate opportunity within the corporation's line of business or an opportunity in which the corporation had an interest or expectancy.[10] These arguments are

---

[9] [2] A 10-K is appropriately considered in ruling on a motion to dismiss, especially when referenced in the complaint.

[10] [3] See Broz v. Cellular Info. Sys. Inc., 673 A.2d 148, 155 (Del. 1996) (listing factors to find corporate opportunity).

unavailing.

First, no one disputes that eBay financially was able to exploit the opportunities in question. Second, eBay was in the business of investing in securities. The complaint alleges that eBay "consistently invested a portion of its cash on hand in marketable securities." According to eBay's 1999 10-K, for example, eBay had more than $550 million invested in equity and debt securities. eBay invested more than $181 million in "short-term investments" and $373 million in "long-term investments." Thus, investing was "a line of business" of eBay. Third, the facts alleged in the complaint suggest that investing was integral to eBay's cash management strategies and a significant part of its business. Finally, it is no answer to say, as do defendants, that IPOs are risky investments. It is undisputed that eBay was never given an opportunity to turn down the IPO allocations as too risky.[11]

Defendants also argue that to view the IPO allocations in question as corporate opportunities will mean that every advantageous investment opportunity that comes to an officer or director will be considered a corporate opportunity. On the contrary, the allegations in the complaint in this case indicate that unique, below-market price investment opportunities wereoffered by Goldman Sachs to the insider defendants as financial inducements to maintain and secure corporate business. This was not an instance where a broker offered advice to a director about an investment in a marketable security. The conduct challenged here involved a large investment bank that regularly did business with a company steering highly lucrative IPO allocations to select insider directors and officers at that company, allegedly both to reward them for past business and to induce them to direct future business to that investment bank. This is a far cry from the defendants' characterization of the conduct in question as merely "a broker's investment recommendations" to a wealthy client.

Nor can one seriously argue that this conduct did not place the insider defendants in a position of conflict with their duties to the corporation. One can realistically characterize these IPO allocations as a form of commercial discount or rebate for past or future investment banking services. Viewed pragmatically, it is easy to understand how steering such commercial rebates to certain insider directors places those directors in an obvious conflict between their self-interest and the corporation's interest. It is noteworthy, too, that the Securities and Exchange Commission has taken the position that "spinning" practices violate the obligations of broker-dealers under the "Free-riding and Withholding Interpretation" rules. As the SEC has explained, "the purpose of the interpretation is to protect the integrity of the public offering system by ensuring that members make a bona fide public distribution of 'hot issue' securities and do not withhold such securities for their own benefit or use the securities to reward other persons who are in a position to direct future business to the member."

Finally, even if one assumes that IPO allocations like those in question here do not constitute a corporate opportunity, a cognizable claim is nevertheless stated on

---

[11] [4] Defendants' counsel implied at oral argument that these investments were so risky that defendants may have lost money on some or all of them. That is a factual assertion that certainly contradicts allegations in the complaint, but of course I may not consider it on a motion to dismiss.

the common law ground that an agent is under a duty to account for profits obtained personally in connection with transactions related to his or her company. The complaint gives rise to a reasonable inference that the insider directors accepted a commission or gratuity that rightfully belonged to eBay but that was improperly diverted to them. Even if this conduct does not run afoul of the corporate opportunity doctrine, it may still constitute a breach of the fiduciary duty of loyalty. Thus, even if one does not consider Goldman Sachs' IPO allocations to these corporate insiders-allocations that generated millions of dollars in profit-to be a corporate opportunity, the defendant directors were nevertheless not free to accept this consideration from a company, Goldman Sachs, that was doing significant business with eBay and that arguably intended the consideration as an inducement to maintaining the business relationship in the future.[12]

## B. THE DEMAND REQUIREMENT

### ARONSON v. LEWIS
Supreme Court of Delaware
473 A.2d 805 (1984)

MOORE, JUSTICE:

In the wake of *Zapata Corp. v. Maldonado*, Del. Supr., 430 A.2d 779 (1981), this Court left a crucial issue unanswered: when is a stockholder's demand upon a board of directors, to redress an alleged wrong to the corporation, excused as futile prior to the filing of a derivative suit? We granted this interlocutory appeal to the defendants, Meyers Parking System, Inc. (Meyers), a Delaware corporation, and its directors, to review the Court of Chancery's denial of their motion to dismiss this action, pursuant to Chancery Rule 23.1, for the plaintiff's failure to make such a demand or otherwise demonstrate its futility.

\* \* \*

In our view demand can only be excused where facts are alleged with particularity which create a reasonable doubt that the directors' action was entitled to the protections of the business judgment rule. Because the plaintiff failed to make a demand, and to allege facts with particularity indicating that such demand would be futile, we reverse the Court of Chancery and remand with instructions that plaintiff be granted leave to amend the complaint.

### I.

The issues of demand futility rest upon the allegations of the complaint. The plaintiff, Harry Lewis, is a stockholder of Meyers. The defendants are Meyers and its ten directors, some of whom are also company officers.

\* \* \*

---

[12] [8] Restatement (Second) of Agency § 388 (1957).

This suit challenges certain transactions between Meyers and one of its directors, Leo Fink, who owns 47% of its outstanding stock. Plaintiff claims that these transactions were approved only because Fink personally selected each director and officer of Meyers.

\*    \*    \*

On January 1, 1981, [when Meyers was 75 years old,] the defendants approved an employment agreement between Meyers and Fink for a five year term with provision for automatic renewal each year thereafter, indefinitely. Meyers agreed to pay Fink $150,000 per year, plus a bonus of 5% of its pre-tax profits over $2,400,000. Fink could terminate the contract at any time, but Meyers could do so only upon six months' notice. At termination, Fink was to become a consultant to Meyers and be paid $150,000 per year for the first three years, $125,000 for the next three years, and $100,000 thereafter for life. Death benefits were also included. Fink agreed to devote his best efforts and substantially his entire business time to advancing Meyers' interests. The agreement also provided that Fink's compensation was not to be affected by any inability to perform services on Meyers' behalf.

\*    \*    \*

The complaint alleged that [demand on the Meyers board would have been futile because]:

(a)  All of the directors in office are named as defendants herein and they have participated in, expressly approved and/or acquiesced in, and are personally liable for, the wrongs complained of herein.

(b)  Defendant Fink, having selected each director, controls and dominates every member of the Board and every officer of Meyers.

(c)  Institution of this action by present directors would require the defendant-directors to sue themselves, thereby placing the conduct of this action in hostile hands and preventing its effective prosecution.

Complaint, at ¶ 13.

The relief sought included the cancellation of the Meyers-Fink employment contract and an accounting by the directors, including Fink, for all damage sustained by Meyers and for all profits derived by the directors and Fink.

## II.

Defendants moved to dismiss for plaintiff's failure to make demand on the Meyers board prior to suit, or to allege with factual particularity why demand is excused.

After recounting the allegations, the trial judge noted that the demand requirement of Rule 23.1 is a rule of substantive right designed to give a corporation the opportunity to rectify an alleged wrong without litigation, and to control any litigation which does arise. *Lewis v. Aronson*, 466 A.2d 375, 380. According to the Vice Chancellor, the test of futility is "whether the Board, at the time of the filing of the suit, could have impartially considered and acted upon the demand." *Id.* at

381.

As part of this formulation, the trial judge stated that interestedness is one factor affecting impartiality, and indicated that the business judgment rule is a potential defense to allegations of director interest, and hence, demand futility. However, the court observed that to establish demand futility, a plaintiff need not allege that the challenged transaction could never be deemed a product of business judgment. Rather, the Vice Chancellor maintained that a plaintiff "must only allege facts which, if true, show that there is a reasonable inference that the business judgment rule is not applicable for purposes of considering a pre-suit demand pursuant to Rule 23.1." *Id.* The court concluded that this transaction permitted such an inference.

Upon these formulations, the Court of Chancery addressed the plaintiff's arguments as to the futility of demand. The trial judge correctly noted that futility is gauged by the circumstances existing at the commencement of a derivative suit. This disposed of plaintiff's argument that defendants' motion to dismiss established board hostility and the futility of demand.

The Vice Chancellor then dealt with plaintiff's contention that Fink, as a 47% shareholder of Meyers, dominated and controlled each director, thereby making demand futile. Plaintiff also argued that Fink's interest, when combined with the shareholdings of four other defendants, amounted to 57.5% of Meyers' outstanding shares. After noting the presumptions under the business judgment rule that a board's actions are taken in good faith and in the best interests of the corporation, the Court of Chancery ruled that mere board approval of a transaction benefiting a substantial, but non-majority, shareholder will not overcome the presumption of propriety. Specifically, the court observed that:

> A plaintiff, to properly allege domination of the Board, particularly domination based on ownership of less than a majority of the corporation's stock, in order to excuse a pre-suit demand, must allege ownership plus other facts evidencing control to demonstrate that the Board could not have exercised its independent business judgment.

*Id.* at 382.

As to the combined 57.5% control claim, the court stated that there were no factual allegations regarding the alignment of the four directors with Fink, such as a claim that they were beneficiaries of the Meyers-Fink agreement. *Id.* at 382, 383. Because it was not alleged in the complaint, the court rejected plaintiff's argument that, as evidence of alignment with Fink, two of the directors have "similar" compensation agreements with Meyers.

Turning to plaintiff's allegations of board approval, participation in, and/or acquiescence in the wrong, the trial court focused on the underlying transaction to determine whether the board's action was wrongful and not protected by the business judgment rule. The Vice Chancellor indicated that if the underlying transaction supported a reasonable inference that the business judgment rule did not apply, then the directors who approved the transaction were potentially liable for a breach of their fiduciary duty, and thus, could not impartially consider a stockholder's demand.

The trial court then stated that board approval of the Meyers-Fink agreement, allowing Fink's consultant compensation to remain unaffected by his ability to perform any services, may have been a transaction wasteful on its face. Consequently, demand was excused as futile, because the Meyers' directors faced potential liability for waste and could not have impartially considered the demand.

## III.

The defendants make two arguments, one policy-oriented and the other, factual. First, they assert that the demand requirement embraces the policy that directors, rather than stockholders, manage the affairs of the corporation. They contend that this fundamental principle requires the strict construction and enforcement of Chancery Rule 23.1. Second, the defendants point to four of plaintiff's basic allegations and argue that they lack the factual particularity necessary to excuse demand. Concerning the allegation that Fink dominated and controlled the Meyers board, the defendants point to the absence of any facts explaining how he "selected each director." With respect to Fink's 47% stock interest, the defendants say that absent other facts this is insufficient to indicate domination and control. Regarding the claim of hostility to the plaintiff's suit, because defendants would have to sue themselves, the latter assert that this bootstrap argument ignores the possibility that the directors have other alternatives, such as cancelling the challenged agreement. As for the allegation that directorial approval of the agreement excused demand, the defendants reply that such a claim is insufficient, because it would obviate the demand requirement in almost every case. The effect would be to subvert the managerial power of a board of directors. Finally, as to the provision guaranteeing Fink's compensation, even if he is unable to perform any services, the defendants contend that the trial court read this out of context. Based upon the foregoing, the defendants conclude that the plaintiff's allegations fall far short of the factual particularity required by Rule 23.1.

## IV.

### A.

A cardinal precept of the General Corporation Law of the State of Delaware is that directors, rather than shareholders, manage the business and affairs of the corporation. 8 Del. C. § 141(a). Section 141(a) states in pertinent part:

> "The *business and affairs* of a corporation organized under this chapter *shall be managed by or under the direction* of a board of directors except as may be otherwise provided in this chapter or in its certificate of incorporation."

8 Del. C. § 141(a) (Emphasis added). The existence and exercise of this power carries with it certain fundamental fiduciary obligations to the corporation and its shareholders. *Loft, Inc. v. Guth*, Del. Ch., 2 A.2d 225 (1938), *aff'd*, Del. Supr., 5 A.2d 503 (1939). Moreover, a stockholder is not powerless to challenge director action which results in harm to the corporation. The machinery of corporate democracy and the derivative suit are potent tools to redress the conduct of a torpid or

unfaithful management. The derivative action developed in equity to enable shareholders to sue in the corporation's name where those in control of the company refused to assert a claim belonging to it. The nature of the action is two-fold. First, it is the equivalent of a suit by the shareholders to compel the corporation to sue. Second, it is a suit by the corporation, asserted by the shareholders on its behalf, against those liable to it.

By its very nature the derivative action impinges on the managerial freedom of directors. Hence, the demand requirement of Chancery Rule 23.1 exists at the threshold, first to insure that a stockholder exhausts his intracorporate remedies, and then to provide a safeguard against strike suits. Thus, by promoting this form of alternate dispute resolution, rather than immediate recourse to litigation, the demand requirement is a recognition of the fundamental precept that directors manage the business and affairs of corporations.

In our view the entire question of demand futility is inextricably bound to issues of business judgment and the standards of that doctrine's applicability. The business judgment rule is an acknowledgment of the managerial prerogatives of Delaware directors under Section 141(a). See *Zapata Corp. v. Maldonado*, 430 A.2d at 782. It is a presumption that in making a business decision the directors of a corporation acted on an informed basis, in good faith and in the honest belief that the action taken was in the best interests of the company. Absent an abuse of discretion, that judgment will be respected by the courts. The burden is on the party challenging the decision to establish facts rebutting the presumption.

The function of the business judgment rule is of paramount significance in the context of a derivative action. . . .

First, its protections can only be claimed by disinterested directors whose conduct otherwise meets the tests of business judgment. From the standpoint of interest, this means that directors can neither appear on both sides of a transaction nor expect to derive any personal financial benefit from it in the sense of self-dealing, as opposed to a benefit which devolves upon the corporation or all stockholders generally. Thus, if such director interest is present, and the transaction is not approved by a majority consisting of the disinterested directors, then the business judgment rule has no application whatever in determining demand futility.

Second, to invoke the rule's protection directors have a duty to inform themselves, prior to making a business decision, of all material information reasonably available to them. Having become so informed, they must then act with requisite care in the discharge of their duties. While the Delaware cases use a variety of terms to describe the applicable standard of care, our analysis satisfies us that under the business judgment rule director liability is predicated upon concepts of gross negligence.

However, it should be noted that the business judgment rule operates only in the context of director action. Technically speaking, it has no role where directors have either abdicated their functions, or absent a conscious decision, failed to act. But it also follows that under applicable principles, a conscious decision to refrain from acting may nonetheless be a valid exercise of business judgment and enjoy the protections of the rule.

The gap in our law, which we address today, arises from this Court's decision in *Zapata Corp. v. Maldonado*. There, the Court defined the limits of a board's managerial power granted by Section 141(a) and restricted application of the business judgment rule in a factual context similar to this action. *Zapata Corp. v. Maldonado*, 430 A.2d at 782–86, *rev'g, Maldonado v. Flynn*, Del. Ch., 413 A.2d 1251 (1980).

*   *   *

Delaware courts have addressed the issue of demand futility on several earlier occasions. The rule emerging from these decisions is that where officers and directors are under an influence which sterilizes their discretion, they cannot be considered proper persons to conduct litigation on behalf of the corporation. Thus, demand would be futile. . . .

However, those cases cannot be taken to mean that any board approval of a challenged transaction automatically connotes "hostile interest" and "guilty participation" by directors, or some other form of sterilizing influence upon them. Were that so, the demand requirements of our law would be meaningless, leaving the clear mandate of Chancery Rule 23.1 devoid of its purpose and substance.

The trial court correctly recognized that demand futility is inextricably bound to issues of business judgment, but stated the test to be based on allegations of fact, which, if true, "show that there is a reasonable inference" the business judgment rule is not applicable for purposes of a pre-suit demand. *Lewis*, 466 A.2d at 381.

The problem with this formulation is the concept of reasonable inferences to be drawn against a board of directors based on allegations in a complaint. As is clear from this case, and the conclusory allegations upon which the Vice Chancellor relied, demand futility becomes virtually automatic under such a test. Bearing in mind the presumptions with which director action is cloaked, we believe that the matter must be approached in a more balanced way.

Our view is that in determining demand futility the Court of Chancery in the proper exercise of its discretion must decide whether, under the particularized facts alleged, a reasonable doubt is created that: (1) the directors are disinterested and independent and (2) the challenged transaction was otherwise the product of a valid exercise of business judgment. Hence, the Court of Chancery must make two inquiries, one into the independence and disinterestedness of the directors and the other into the substantive nature of the challenged transaction and the board's approval thereof. As to the latter inquiry the court does not assume that the transaction is a wrong to the corporation requiring corrective steps by the board. Rather, the alleged wrong is substantively reviewed against the factual background alleged in the complaint. As to the former inquiry, directorial independence and disinterestedness, the court reviews the factual allegations to decide whether they raise a reasonable doubt, as a threshold matter, that the protections of the business judgment rule are available to the board. Certainly, if this is an "interested" director transaction, such that the business judgment rule is inapplicable to the board majority approving the transaction, then the inquiry ceases. In that event futility of demand has been established by any objective or subjective standard.

However, the mere threat of personal liability for approving a questioned transaction, standing alone, is insufficient to challenge either the independence or disinterestedness of directors, although in rare cases a transaction may be so egregious on its face that board approval cannot meet the test of business judgment, and a substantial likelihood of director liability therefore exists. In sum the entire review is factual in nature. The Court of Chancery in the exercise of its sound discretion must be satisfied that a plaintiff has alleged facts with particularity which, taken as true, support a reasonable doubt that the challenged transaction was the product of a valid exercise of business judgment. Only in that context is demand excused.

## B.

Having outlined the legal framework within which these issues are to be determined, we consider plaintiff's claims of futility here: Fink's domination and control of the directors, board approval of the Fink-Meyers employment agreement, and board hostility to the plaintiff's derivative action due to the directors' status as defendants.

Plaintiff's claim that Fink dominates and controls the Meyers' board is based on: (1) Fink's 47% ownership of Meyers' outstanding stock, and (2) that he "personally selected" each Meyers director. Plaintiff also alleges that mere approval of the employment agreement illustrates Fink's domination and control of the board. In addition, plaintiff argued on appeal that 47% stock ownership, though less than a majority, constituted control given the large number of shares outstanding, 1,245,745.

Such contentions do not support any claim under Delaware law that these directors lack independence. In *Kaplan v. Centex Corp.*, Del. Ch., 284 A.2d 119 (1971), the Court of Chancery stated that "[s]tock ownership alone, at least when it amounts to less than a majority, is not sufficient proof of domination or control." *Id.* at 123. Moreover, in the demand context even proof of majority ownership of a company does not strip the directors of the presumptions of independence, and that their acts have been taken in good faith and in the best interests of the corporation. There must be coupled with the allegation of control such facts as would demonstrate that through personal or other relationships the directors are beholden to the controlling person. To date the principal decisions dealing with the issue of control or domination arose only after a full trial on the merits. Thus, they are distinguishable in the demand context unless similar particularized facts are alleged to meet the test of Chancery Rule 23.1.

The requirement of director independence inheres in the conception and rationale of the business judgment rule. The presumption of propriety that flows from an exercise of business judgment is based in part on this unyielding precept. Independence means that a director's decision is based on the corporate merits of the subject before the board rather than extraneous considerations or influences. While directors may confer, debate, and resolve their differences through compromise, or by reasonable reliance upon the expertise of their colleagues and other qualified persons, the end result, nonetheless, must be that each director has brought his or her own informed business judgment to bear with specificity upon the corporate merits of the issues without regard for or succumbing to influences which convert an otherwise valid business decision into a faithless act.

Thus, it is not enough to charge that a director was nominated by or elected at the behest of those controlling the outcome of a corporate election. That is the usual way a person becomes a corporate director. It is the care, attention and sense of individual responsibility to the performance of one's duties, not the method of election, that generally touches on independence.

We conclude that in the demand-futile context a plaintiff charging domination and control of one or more directors must allege particularized facts manifesting "a direction of corporate conduct in such a way as to comport with the wishes or interests of the corporation (or persons) doing the controlling." *Kaplan*, 284 A.2d at 123. The shorthand shibboleth of "dominated and controlled directors" is insufficient. . . .

Here, plaintiff has not alleged any facts sufficient to support a claim of control. The personal-selection-of-directors allegation stands alone, unsupported. At best it is a conclusion devoid of factual support. The causal link between Fink's control and approval of the employment agreement is alluded to, but nowhere specified. The director's approval, alone, does not establish control, even in the face of Fink's 47% stock ownership. The claim that Fink is unlikely to perform any services under the agreement, because of his age, and his conflicting consultant work with Prudential, adds nothing to the control claim. Therefore, we cannot conclude that the complaint factually particularizes any circumstances of control and domination to overcome the presumption of board independence, and thus render the demand futile.

## C.

Turning to the board's approval of the Meyers-Fink employment agreement, plaintiff's argument is simple: all of the Meyers directors are named defendants, because they approved the wasteful agreement; if plaintiff prevails on the merits all the directors will be jointly and severally liable; therefore, the directors' interest in avoiding personal liability automatically and absolutely disqualifies them from passing on a shareholder's demand.

Such allegations are conclusory at best. In Delaware mere directorial approval of a transaction, absent particularized facts supporting a breach of fiduciary duty claim, or otherwise establishing the lack of independence or disinterestedness of a majority of the directors, is insufficient to excuse demand.

\*　\*　\*

## D.

Plaintiff's final argument is the incantation that demand is excused because the directors otherwise would have to sue themselves, thereby placing the conduct of the litigation in hostile hands and preventing its effective prosecution. This bootstrap argument has been made to and dismissed by other courts. Its acceptance would effectively abrogate Rule 23.1 and weaken the managerial power of directors. Unless facts are alleged with particularity to overcome the presumptions of independence and a proper exercise of business judgment, in which case the directors could not be expected to sue themselves, a bare claim of this sort raises no legally cognizable issue under Delaware corporate law.

### V.

In sum, we conclude that the plaintiff has failed to allege facts with particularity indicating that the Meyers directors were tainted by interest, lacked independence, or took action contrary to Meyers' best interests in order to create a reasonable doubt as to the applicability of the business judgment rule. Only in the presence of such a reasonable doubt may a demand be deemed futile. Hence, we reverse the Court of Chancery's denial of the motion to dismiss, and remand with instructions that plaintiff be granted leave to amend his complaint to bring it into compliance with Rule 23.1 based on the principles we have announced today.

Reversed and remanded.

### BEAM v. STEWART
#### Supreme Court of Delaware
#### 845 A.2d 1040 (2004)

VEASEY, J.

In this appeal we review and affirm the judgment of the Court of Chancery in dismissing under Rule 23.1 a claim in a derivative suit because the plaintiff failed to make presuit demand on the corporation's board of directors and failed to demonstrate demand futility. In his opinion, the Chancellor dealt with several issues and provided a detailed account of the facts of the case. We summarize only those facts most pertinent to this appeal. The single issue before us is that of demand futility, no appeal having been taken on the other issues.

The Chancellor analyzed in detail the plaintiff's demand futility allegations. We agree with the Chancellor's well-reasoned opinion. But, pursuant to our plenary appellate review, we undertake a further explication of certain points covered by the Chancellor, including the matter of director independence.

### Facts

The plaintiff, Monica A. Beam, owns shares of Martha Stewart Living Omnimedia, Inc. (MSO). Beam filed a derivative action in the Court of Chancery against Martha Stewart, the five other members of MSO's board of directors, and former board member L. John Doerr. In four counts, Beam's amended complaint (the "complaint") challenged three types of activity by Stewart and the MSO board. The Court of Chancery dismissed three of the four claims under Court of Chancery Rule 12(b)(6). Those dismissals were not appealed and are not before us.

In the single claim at issue on appeal (Count 1), Beam alleged that Stewart breached her fiduciary duties of loyalty and care by illegally selling ImClone stock in December of 2001 and by mishandling the media attention that followed, thereby jeopardizing the financial future of MSO. The Court of Chancery dismissed Count

1 under Court of Chancery Rule 23.1 because Beam failed to plead particularized facts demonstrating presuit demand futility.

When Beam filed the complaint in the Court of Chancery, the MSO board of directors consisted of six members: Stewart, Sharon L. Patrick, Arthur C. Martinez, Darla D. Moore, Naomi O. Seligman, and Jeffrey W. Ubben. The Chancellor concluded that the complaint alleged sufficient facts to support the conclusion that two of the directors, Stewart and Patrick, were not disinterested or independent for purposes of considering a presuit demand.

The Court of Chancery found that Stewart's potential civil and criminal liability for the acts underlying Beams claim rendered Stewart an interested party and therefore unable to consider demand.[13] The Court also found that Patrick's position as an officer and inside director,[14] together with the substantial compensation she receives from the company, raised a reasonable doubt as to her ability objectively to consider demand. The defendants do not challenge the Court's conclusions with respect to Patrick and Stewart.

We now address the plaintiff's allegations concerning the independence of the other board members. We must determine if the following allegations of the complaint, and the reasonable inferences that may flow from them, create a reasonable doubt of the independence of either Martinez, Moore or Seligman:

4. Defendant Arthur C. Martinez ("Martinez") is a director of the Company, a position that he has held since January 2001. Until December 2000, Martinez served as Chairman of the board of directors of Sears Roebuck and Co., and was its Chief Executive Officer from August 1995 until October 2000. Martinez joined Sears, Roebuck and Co. in September 1992 as the Chairman and Chief Executive Officer of Sears Merchandise Group, Sears's former retail arm. From 1990 to 1992, he was Vice Chairman of Saks Fifth Avenue and was a member of Saks Fifth Avenue's board of directors. Martinez is currently a member of the board of directors of PepsiCo, Inc., Liz Claiborne, Inc. and International Flavors & Fragrances, Inc., and is the Chairman of the Federal Reserve Bank of Chicago. Martinez is a longstanding personal friend of defendants Stewart and Patrick. While at Sears, Martinez established a relationship with the Company, which marketed a substantial volume of products through Sears. Martinez was recruited for the board by Stewart's longtime personal friend, Charlotte Beers. Defendant Patrick was quoted in an article dated March 22, 2001 appearing in Directors & Board as follows: "Arthur is an old friend to both me and Martha."

5. Defendant Darla D. Moore ("Moore") is a director of the Company, a position she has held since September 2001. Moore has been a partner of Rainwater, Inc., a private investment firm, since 1994. Before that, Moore was a Managing Director of Chase Bank. Moore is also a trustee of

---

[13] [3] Stewart was, at all relevant times, MSO's chairman and chief executive. She controls over 94% of the shareholder vote. *Beam*, 833 A.2d at 966. She also personifies MSO's brands and was its primary creative force. *Id.* at 968.

[14] [4] Patrick is the president and chief operating officer of MSO. *Id.* at 966.

Magellan Health Services, Inc. Moore is a longstanding friend of defendant Stewart. In November 1995, she attended a wedding reception hosted by Stewart's personal lawyer, Allen Grubman, for his daughter. Also in attendance were Stewart and Stewart's friend, Samuel Waksal. In August 1996, Fortune carried an article highlighting Moore's close personal relationship with Charlotte Beers and defendant Stewart. When Beers, a longtime friend and confidante to Stewart, resigned from the Company's board in September 2001, Moore was nominated to replace her.

6. Defendant Naomi O. Seligman ("Seligman") is a director of the Company, a position that she has held since September 1999. Seligman was a co-founder of Cassius Advisers, an e-commerce consultancy, where she has served as a senior partner since 1999, and is a co-founder of the Research Board, Inc., an information technology research group, where she served as a senior partner from 1975 until 1999. Seligman currently serves as a director of Akamai Technologies, Inc., The Dun & Bradstreet Corporation, John Wiley & Sons and Sun Microsystems, Inc. According to a story appearing on July 2, 2002 in The Wall Street Journal, Seligman contacted the Chief Executive Officer of John Wiley & Sons (a publishing house) at defendant Stewart's behest last year to express concern over its planned publication of a biography that was critical of Stewart.

\*   \*   \*

8. Martinez, Moore, Seligson [sic], and Ubben are hereinafter referred to collectively as the Director Defendants. By reason of Stewart's overwhelming voting control over the Company, each of the Director Defendants serves at her sufferance. Each of the Director Defendants receive [sic] valuable perquisites and benefits by reason of their service on the Company's Board.

\*   \*   \*

## DEMAND ALLEGATIONS

73. . . . No demand on the Board of Directors was made prior to institution of this action, as a majority of the Board of Directors is not independent or disinterested with respect to the claims asserted herein.

\*   \*   \*

77. Defendant Martinez is not disinterested in view of his longstanding personal friendship with both Patrick and Stewart.

78. Defendant Moore is not disinterested in view of her longstanding personal relationship with defendant Stewart.

79. Defendant Seligman is not disinterested; she has already shown that she will use her position as a director at another corporation to act at the behest of defendant Stewart when she contacted the Chief Executive Officer of John Wiley & Sons in an effort to dissuade the publishing house from publishing a biography that was critical of Stewart.

80. The Director Defendants are not disinterested as they are jointly and severally liable with Stewart in view of their failure to monitor Stewart's actions. Moreover, pursuit of these claims would imperil the substantial benefits that accrue to them by reason of their service on the Board, given Stewart's voting control.

### Decision of the Court of Chancery

The Chancellor found that Beam had not alleged sufficient facts to support the conclusion that demand was futile because he determined that the complaint failed to raise a reasonable doubt that these outside directors are independent of Stewart. Because Patrick and Stewart herself are not independent for demand purposes, all the plaintiff need show is that one of the remaining directors is not independent, there being only six board members.[15] The allegations relating to Moore, Seligman and Martinez are set forth above.

It is appropriate here to quote the Chancellor's analysis of the allegations regarding these three directors:

> The factual allegations regarding Stewart's friendship with Martinez are inadequate to raise a reasonable doubt of his independence. While employed by Sears, Martinez developed business ties to MSO due to Sears' marketing of a substantial quantity of MSO products. Martinez was recruited to serve on MSO's board of directors by Beers, who is described as Stewart's longtime personal friend and confidante and who was at that time an MSO director. Shortly after Martinez joined MSO's board, Patrick was quoted in a magazine article saying, "Arthur [Martinez] is an old friend to both me and Martha [Stewart]." Weighing against these factors, the amended complaint discloses that Martinez has been an executive and director for major corporations since at least 1990. At present he serves as a director for four prominent corporations, including MSO, and is the chairman of the Federal Reserve Bank of Chicago. One might say that Martinez's reputation for acting as a careful fiduciary is essential to his career — a matter in which he would surely have a material interest. Furthermore, the amended complaint does not give a single example of any action by Martinez that might be construed as evidence of even a slight inclination to disregard his duties as a fiduciary for any reason. In this context, I cannot reasonably infer, on the basis of several years of business interactions and a single affirmation of friendship by a third party, that the friendship between Stewart and Martinez raises a reasonable doubt of Martinez's ability to evaluate demand independently of Stewart's personal interests.

> The allegations regarding the friendship between Moore and Stewart are somewhat more detailed, yet still fall short of raising a reasonable

---

[15] [8] If three directors of a six person board are not independent and three directors are independent, there is not a majority of independent directors and demand would be futile. *See Beneville v. York,* 769 A.2d 80, 85–86 (Del. Ch. 2000) (holding that demand is excused where a board is evenly divided between interested and disinterested directors).

doubt about Moore's ability properly to consider demand on Count I. In 1995, Stewart's lawyer, Allen Grubman, hosted a wedding reception for his daughter. Among those in attendance at the reception were Moore, Stewart, and Waksal. In addition, Fortune magazine published an article in 1996 that focused on the close personal friendships among Moore, Stewart, and Beers. In September 2001, when Beers resigned from MSO's board of directors, Moore was selected to replace her. Although the amended complaint lists fewer positions of fiduciary responsibility for Moore than were listed for Martinez, it is clear that Moore's professional reputation similarly would be harmed if she failed to fulfill her fiduciary obligations. To my mind, this is quite a close call. Perhaps the balance could have been tipped by additional, more detailed allegations about the closeness or nature of the friendship, details of the business and social interactions between the two, or allegations raising additional considerations that might inappropriately affect Moore's ability to impartially consider pursuit of a lawsuit against Stewart. On the facts pled, however, I cannot say that I have a reasonable doubt of Moore's ability to properly consider demand.

No particular felicity is alleged to exist between Stewart and Seligman. The amended complaint reports in ominous tones, however, that Seligman, who is a director both for MSO and for JWS, contacted JWS' chief executive officer about an unflattering biography of Stewart slated for publication. From this, the Court is asked to infer that Seligman acted in a way that preferred the protection of Stewart over her fiduciary duties to one or both of these companies. Without details about the nature of the contact, other than Seligman's wish to "express concern," it is impossible reasonably to make this inference. Stewart's public image, as plaintiff persistently asserts, is critical to the fortunes of MSO and its shareholders. As a fiduciary of MSO, Seligman may have felt obligated to express concern and seek additional information about the publication before its release. As a fiduciary of JWS, she could well have anticipated some risk of liability if any of the unflattering characterizations of Stewart proved to be insufficiently researched or made carelessly. There is no allegation that Seligman made any inappropriate attempt to prevent the publication of the biography. Nor does the amended complaint indicate whether the biography was ultimately published and, if so, whether Seligman's inquiry is believed to have resulted in any changes to the content of the book. As alleged, this matter does not serve to raise a reasonable doubt of Seligman's independence or ability to consider demand on Count I.

In sum, plaintiff offers various theories to suggest reasons that the outside directors might be inappropriately swayed by Stewart's wishes or interests, but fails to plead sufficient facts that could permit the Court reasonably to infer that one or more of the theories could be accurate.[16]

---

[16] [9] *Beam*, 833 A.2d at 979–81 (footnotes omitted) (emphasis added).

## Demand Futility and Director Independence

This Court reviews de novo a decision of the Court of Chancery to dismiss a derivative suit under Rule 23.1. The scope of this Court's review is plenary. The Court should draw all reasonable inferences in the plaintiff's favor. Such reasonable inferences must logically flow from particularized facts alleged by the plaintiff. "[C]onclusory allegations are not considered as expressly pleaded facts or factual inferences." Likewise, inferences that are not objectively reasonable cannot be drawn in the plaintiff's favor.

Under the first prong of *Aronson*,[17] a stockholder may not pursue a derivative suit to assert a claim of the corporation unless: (a) she has first demanded that the directors pursue the corporate claim and they have wrongfully refused to do so; or (b) such demand is excused because the directors are deemed incapable of making an impartial decision regarding the pursuit of the litigation.[18] The issue in this case is the quantum of doubt about a director's independence that is "reasonable" in order to excuse a presuit demand. The parties argue opposite sides of that issue.

The key principle upon which this area of our jurisprudence is based is that the directors are entitled to a presumption that they were faithful to their fiduciary duties.[19] In the context of presuit demand, the burden is upon the plaintiff in a derivative action to overcome that presumption. The Court must determine whether a plaintiff has alleged particularized facts creating a reasonable doubt of a director's independence to rebut the presumption at the pleading stage. If the Court determines that the pleaded facts create a reasonable doubt that a majority of the board could have acted independently in responding to the demand, the presumption is rebutted for pleading purposes and demand will be excused as futile.

A director will be considered unable to act objectively with respect to a presuit demand if he or she is interested in the outcome of the litigation or is otherwise not independent. A director's interest may be shown by demonstrating a potential personal benefit or detriment to the director as a result of the decision.[20] "In such circumstances, a director cannot be expected to exercise his or her independent business judgment without being influenced by the . . . personal consequences resulting from the decision." The primary basis upon which a director's independence must be measured is whether the director's decision is based on the corporate merits of the subject before the board, rather than extraneous considerations or influences. This broad statement of the law requires an analysis of whether the

---

[17] [14] *See Aronson v. Lewis*, 473 A.2d 805, 814 (Del. 1984) (setting forth two steps of a demand futility analysis: whether (1) "the directors are disinterested and independent and (2) the challenged transaction was otherwise the product of a valid exercise of business judgment").

[18] [15] *Rales v. Blasband*, 634 A.2d 927, 932 (Del. 1993); see also Del. Ch. R. 23.1 (providing the demand requirements for initiation of derivative suits by stockholders).

[19] [16] *See Aronson*, 473 A.2d at 812 ("It is a presumption that in making a business decision the directors of a corporation acted on an informed basis, in good faith and in the honest belief that the action taken was in the best interests of the company.").

[20] [21] *Cf. Rales*, 634 A.2d at 936 ("A director is considered interested where he or she will receive a personal financial benefit from a transaction that is not equally shared by the stockholders. Directorial interest also exists where a corporate decision will have a materially detrimental impact on a director, but not on the corporation and the stockholders." (citation omitted)).

director is disinterested in the underlying transaction and, even if disinterested, whether the director is otherwise independent. More precisely in the context of the present case, the independence inquiry requires us to determine whether there is a reasonable doubt that any one of these three directors is capable of objectively making a business decision to assert or not assert a corporate claim against Stewart.

### Independence Is a Contextual Inquiry

Independence is a fact-specific determination made in the context of a particular case. The court must make that determination by answering the inquiries: independent from whom and independent for what purpose? To excuse presuit demand in this case, the plaintiff has the burden to plead particularized facts that create a reasonable doubt sufficient to rebut the presumption that either Moore, Seligman or Martinez was independent of defendant Stewart.

In order to show lack of independence, the complaint of a stockholder-plaintiff must create a reasonable doubt that a director is not so "beholden" to an interested director (in this case Stewart) that his or her "discretion would be sterilized." Our jurisprudence explicating the demand requirement

> is designed to create a balanced environment which will: (1) on the one hand, deter costly, baseless suits by creating a screening mechanism to eliminate claims where there is only a suspicion expressed solely in conclusory terms; and (2) on the other hand, permit suit by a stockholder who is able to articulate particularized facts showing that there is a reasonable doubt either that (a) a majority of the board is independent for purposes of responding to the demand, or (b) the underlying transaction is protected by the business judgment rule. The "reasonable doubt" standard "is sufficiently flexible and workable to provide the stockholder with "the keys to the courthouse" in an appropriate case where the claim is not based on mere suspicions or stated solely in conclusory terms."[21]

### Personal Friendship

A variety of motivations, including friendship, may influence the demand futility inquiry. But, to render a director unable to consider demand, a relationship must be of a bias-producing nature. Allegations of mere personal friendship or a mere outside business relationship, standing alone, are insufficient to raise a reasonable doubt about a director's independence. In this connection, we adopt as our own the Chancellor's analysis in this case:

---

[21] [26] *Id.* In her reply brief the plaintiff seemingly argues that our use of the phrases "reason to doubt" and "reasonable belief" in *Grimes* has somehow watered down the pleading threshold set forth in our jurisprudence. Reply Brief at 3–4. Nothing in *Grimes* was intended to weaken the traditional, objective reasonable doubt standard to be applied to the pleading threshold. *See Grimes*, 673 A.2d at 1217 n. 17 ("The concept of reasonable belief is an objective test and is found in various corporate contexts."); *see also Grobow v. Perot*, 539 A.2d 180, 186 (Del. 1988) (noting that determination of demand futility "[n]ecessarily . . . involves an objective analysis of the facts").

[S]ome professional or personal friendships, which may border on or even exceed familial loyalty and closeness, may raise a reasonable doubt whether a director can appropriately consider demand. This is particularly true when the allegations raise serious questions of either civil or criminal liability of such a close friend. Not all friendships, or even most of them, rise to this level and the Court cannot make a reasonable inference that a particular friendship does so without specific factual allegations to support such a conclusion.

The facts alleged by Beam regarding the relationships between Stewart and these other members of MSO's board of directors largely boil down to a "structural bias" argument, which presupposes that the professional and social relationships that naturally develop among members of a board impede independent decision making[22]. This Court addressed the structural bias argument in *Aronson v. Lewis:*

Critics will charge that [by requiring the independence of only a majority of the board] we are ignoring the structural bias common to corporate boards throughout America, as well as the other unseen socialization processes cutting against independent discussion and decision making in the boardroom. The difficulty with structural bias in a demand futile case is simply one of establishing it in the complaint for purposes of Rule 23.1. We are satisfied that discretionary review by the Court of Chancery of complaints alleging specific facts pointing to bias on a particular board will be sufficient for determining demand futility.

In the present case, the plaintiff attempted to plead affinity beyond mere friendship between Stewart and the other directors, but her attempt is not sufficient to demonstrate demand futility. Even if the alleged friendships may have preceded the directors' membership on MSO's board and did not necessarily arise out of that membership, these relationships are of the same nature as those giving rise to the structural bias argument.

Allegations that Stewart and the other directors moved in the same social circles, attended the same weddings, developed business relationships before joining the board, and described each other as "friends," even when coupled with Stewart's 94% voting power, are insufficient, without more, to rebut the presumption of independence. They do not provide a sufficient basis from which reasonably to infer that Martinez, Moore and Seligman may have been beholden to Stewart. Whether they arise before board membership or later as a result of collegial relationships among the board of directors, such affinities — standing alone — will not render presuit demand futile.

The Court of Chancery in the first instance, and this Court on appeal, must

---

[22] [29] *See* Dennis J. Block *et al.*, The Business Judgment Rule 1765 (5th ed. 1998) (describing the " 'structural bias' viewpoint . . . [as holding] that the judgment of seemingly disinterested directors — who are not defendants in a litigation or participants in wrongdoing alleged in a litigation — is inherently corrupted by the 'common cultural bond' and 'natural empathy and collegiality' shared by most directors"); Michael P. Dooley & E. Norman Veasey, The Role of the Board in Derivative Litigation: Delaware Law and the Current ALI Proposals Compared, 44 Bus. Law. 503, 534 (1989) ("As we understand the argument, it is that no professional colleague can be expected to be as neutral on questions of management misbehavior as a court to whom the alleged malefactor is a stranger.").

review the complaint on a case-by-case basis to determine whether it states with particularity facts indicating that a relationship — whether it preceded or followed board membership — is so close that the director's independence may reasonably be doubted. This doubt might arise either because of financial ties, familial affinity, a particularly close or intimate personal or business affinity or because of evidence that in the past the relationship caused the director to act non-independently vis à vis an interested director. No such allegations are made here. Mere allegations that they move in the same business and social circles, or a characterization that they are close friends, is not enough to negate independence for demand excusal purposes.

That is not to say that personal friendship is always irrelevant to the independence calculus. But, for presuit demand purposes, friendship must be accompanied by substantially more in the nature of serious allegations that would lead to a reasonable doubt as to a director's independence. That a much stronger relationship is necessary to overcome the presumption of independence at the demand futility stage becomes especially compelling when one considers the risks that directors would take by protecting their social acquaintances in the face of allegations that those friends engaged in misconduct.[23] To create a reasonable doubt about an outside director's independence, a plaintiff must plead facts that would support the inference that because of the nature of a relationship or additional circumstances other than the interested director's stock ownership or voting power, the non-interested director would be more willing to risk his or her reputation than risk the relationship with the interested director.[24]

---

[23] [31] *See Dooley & Veasey, supra* note 29, at 535 ("[O]utside directors tend to be men and women who have considerable investments in reputation but who have invested most of their human capital elsewhere.").

[24] [32] *See id.* ("The structural bias argument asks us to believe that outside directors generally are more willing to risk reputation and future income than they are to risk the social embarrassment of calling a colleague to account."); Bryan Ford, *In Whose Interest: An Examination of the Duties of Directors and Officers in Control Contests*, 26 ARIZ. ST. L.J. 91, 127 (1994) (recognizing that many factors — including personal integrity, honesty, concern about their business reputations, and the threat of liability to shareholders — may motivate directors to exercise their judgment independently of corporate executives); *cf. Cal. Pub. Employees' Ret. Sys. v. Coulter*, C.A. No. 19191, 2002 WL 31888343, at *9, 2002 Del. Ch. LEXIS 144, at *28–29 (Del. Ch. Dec. 18, 2002) (observing that an allegation of a lifelong friendship with an interested party is not alone sufficient to raise a reasonable doubt of a director's disinterest or independence); *Kohls v. Duthie*, 765 A.2d 1274, 1284 (Del. Ch. 2000) (holding that a personal friendship between a member of a special committee of the board and an interested party to the challenged transaction, as well as the fact that the interested party had once given the director a summer job, were insufficient to challenge the director's ability to exercise his independent judgment with respect to the transaction); *Benerofe v. Jung Woong Cha*, C.A. No. 14614, 1998 WL 83081, at *3, 1998 Del. Ch. LEXIS 28, at *9 (Del. Ch. Feb. 20, 1998) (stating that an allegation of a longtime friendship was not sufficient to raise a reasonable doubt about a director's ability to exercise his judgment independently of his friend); E. Norman Veasey, *The Defining Tension in Corporate Governance in America*, 52 BUS. LAW. 393, 406 (1997) ("Friendship, golf companionship, and social relationships are not factors that necessarily negate independence. . . . [T]here is nothing to suggest that, on an issue of questioning the loyalty of the CEO, the bridge partner of the CEO cannot act independently as a director. To make a blanket argument otherwise would create a dubious presumption that the director would sell his or her soul for friendship."); cf. also Lynn A. Stout, *On the Proper Motives of Corporate Directors (Or, Why You Don't Want to Invite Homo Economicus to Join Your Board)*, 28 DEL. J. CORP. L. 1, 8–9 (2003) (proposing an "other-regarding" theory of directorial behavior in which directors are motivated to "do a good job" not only by external pressures, but also by internal pressures such as "a director's sense of honor; her

Specific Allegations Concerning Seligman and Moore

## 1. Seligman

Beam's allegations concerning Seligman's lack of independence raise an additional issue not present in the Moore and Martinez relationships. Those allegations are not necessarily based on a purported friendship between Seligman and Stewart. Rather, they are based on a specific past act by Seligman that, Beam claims, indicates Seligman's lack of independence from Stewart. Beam alleges that Seligman called John Wiley & Sons (Wiley) at Stewart's request in order to prevent an unfavorable publication reference to Stewart. The Chancellor concluded, properly in our view, that this allegation does not provide particularized facts from which one may reasonably infer improper influence.

The bare fact that Seligman contacted Wiley, on whose board Seligman also served, to dissuade Wiley from publishing unfavorable references to Stewart, even if done at Stewart's request, is insufficient to create a reasonable doubt that Seligman is capable of considering presuit demand free of Stewart's influence. Although the court should draw all reasonable inferences in Beam's favor, neither improper influence by Stewart over Seligman nor that Seligman was beholden to Stewart is a reasonable inference from these allegations.

Indeed, the reasonable inference is that Seligman's purported intervention on Stewart's behalf was of benefit to MSO and its reputation, which is allegedly tied to Stewart's reputation, as the Chancellor noted. A motivation by Seligman to benefit the company every bit as much as Stewart herself is the only reasonable inference supported by the complaint, when all of its allegations are read in context.[25]

---

feelings of responsibility; her sense of obligation to the firm and its shareholders; and, her desire to 'do the right thing' ").

[25] [35] The complaint alleges:

16. The Company is highly dependent upon Stewart; as the Company's prospectus for the public offering indicated:

\*　\*　\*

We are highly dependent upon our founder, Chairman and Chief Executive Officer, Martha Stewart . . . . The diminution or loss of the services of Martha Stewart, and any negative market or industry perception arising from that diminution or loss, would have a material adverse effect on our business . . . . Martha Stewart remains the personification of our brands as well as our senior executive and primary creative force.

17. The prospectus for the public offering also warned that the Company's business would be affected adversely if "Martha Stewart's public image or reputation were to be tarnished. Martha Stewart, as well as her name, her image and the trademarks and other intellectual property rights relating to these, are integral to our marketing efforts and form the core of our brand name. Our continued success and the value of our brand name therefore depends, to a large degree, on the reputation of Martha Stewart."

Amended Complaint at paras. 16–17, *Beam*, 833 A.2d 961.

## 2. Moore

The Court of Chancery concluded that the plaintiff's allegations with respect to Moore's social relationship with Stewart presented "quite a close call" and suggested ways that the "balance could have been tipped." Although we agree that there are ways that the balance could be tipped[26] so that mere allegations of social relationships would become allegations casting reasonable doubt on independence, we do not agree that the facts as alleged present a "close call" with respect to Moore's independence. These allegations center on: (a) Moore's attendance at a wedding reception for the daughter of Stewart's lawyer where Stewart and Waksal were also present; (b) a Fortune magazine article focusing on the close personal relationships among Moore, Stewart and Beers; and (c) the fact that Moore replaced Beers on the MSO board. In our view, these bare social relationships clearly do not create a reasonable doubt of independence.

## 3. Stewart's 94% Stock Ownership

Beam attempts to bolster her allegations regarding the relationships between Stewart and Seligman and Moore by emphasizing Stewart's overwhelming voting control of MSO. That attempt also fails to create a reasonable doubt of independence. A stockholder's control of a corporation does not excuse presuit demand on the board without particularized allegations of relationships between the directors and the controlling stockholder demonstrating that the directors are beholden to the stockholder.[27] As noted earlier, the relationships alleged by Beam do not lead to the inference that the directors were beholden to Stewart and, thus, unable independently to consider demand. Coupling those relationships with Stewart's overwhelming voting control of MSO does not close that gap.[28]

---

[26] [36] The Chancellor concluded as follows:

To my mind, this is quite a close call. Perhaps the balance could have been tipped by additional, more detailed allegations about the closeness or nature of the friendship, details of the business and social interactions between the two, or allegations raising additional considerations that might inappropriately affect Moore's ability to impartially consider pursuit of a lawsuit against Stewart. On the facts pled, however, I cannot say that I have a reasonable doubt of Moore's ability to properly consider demand.

[27] [37] *See Aronson v. Lewis*, 473 A.2d 805, 815 (Del. 1984) ("[I]n the demand context even proof of majority ownership of a company does not strip the directors of the presumptions of independence, and that their acts have been taken in good faith and in the best interests of the corporation. There must be coupled with the allegation of control such facts as would demonstrate that through personal or other relationships the directors are beholden to the controlling person."); *Stroud v. Milliken Enters., Inc.*, 585 A.2d 1306, 1307 (Del. Ch. 1988) (stating that control of a corporation by a majority stockholder who nominates or elects the directors is not sufficient to raise a reasonable doubt about a director's independence; rather, the nature of the relationships between them must demonstrate that the director is beholden to the stockholder).

[28] [38] The plaintiff's counsel was asked at oral argument in this Court if she had any authority for the proposition that social friendship plus such strong voting power of the interested director was sufficient to create a reasonable doubt of independence alone. Counsel admitted that she could point to no such authority.

## A Word About the Oracle Case

In his opinion, the Chancellor referred several times to the Delaware Court of Chancery decision in *In re Oracle Corp. Derivative Litigation.* Indeed, the plaintiff relies on the *Oracle* case in this appeal. *Oracle* involved the issue of the independence of the Special Litigation Committee (SLC) appointed by the Oracle board to determine whether or not the corporation should cause the dismissal of a corporate claim by stockholder-plaintiffs against directors. The Court of Chancery undertook a searching inquiry of the relationships between the members of the SLC and Stanford University in the context of the financial support of Stanford by the corporation and its management. The Vice Chancellor concluded, after considering the SLC Report and the discovery record, that those relationships were too close for purposes of the SLC analysis of independence.[29]

An SLC is a unique creature that was introduced into Delaware law by *Zapata v. Maldonado* in 1981. The SLC procedure is a method sometimes employed where presuit demand has already been excused and the SLC is vested with the full power of the board to conduct an extensive investigation into the merits of the corporate claim with a view toward determining whether — in the SLC's business judgment — the corporate claim should be pursued. Unlike the demand-excusal context, where the board is presumed to be independent, the SLC has the burden of establishing its own independence by a yardstick that must be "like Caesar's wife" — "above reproach." Moreover, unlike the presuit demand context, the SLC analysis contemplates not only a shift in the burden of persuasion but also the availability of discovery into various issues, including independence.

We need not decide whether the substantive standard of independence in an SLC case differs from that in a presuit demand case. As a practical matter, the procedural distinction relating to the diametrically-opposed burdens and the availability of discovery into independence may be outcome-determinative on the issue of independence. Moreover, because the members of an SLC are vested with enormous power to seek dismissal of a derivative suit brought against their director-colleagues in a setting where presuit demand is already excused, the Court of Chancery must exercise careful oversight of the bona fides of the SLC and its process. Aside from the procedural distinctions, the Stanford connections in *Oracle* are factually distinct from the relationships present here.[30]

---

[29] [41] *Oracle*, 824 A.2d at 921. It is noteworthy that the Vice Chancellor was concerned and expressed "some shock" that the extent of the Stanford ties was not revealed in the Report of the SLC and was unearthed only in discovery. He noted that "the plain facts are a striking departure from the picture presented in the Report."

[30] [45] The analysis applied to determine the independence of a special committee in a merger case also has its own special procedural characteristics. In such cases, courts evaluate not only whether the relationships among members of the committee and interested parties placed them in a position objectively to consider a proposed transaction, but also whether the committee members in fact functioned independently. *See, e.g., Kahn v. Tremont Corp.*, 694 A.2d 422, 429–30 (Del. 1997) ("[T]he Special Committee . . . did not function independently. . . . From its inception, the Special Committee failed to operate in a manner which would create the appearance of objectivity in Tremont's decision to purchase the NL stock. As this Court has previously stated in defining director independence: 'it is the care, attention and sense of individual responsibility to the performance of one's duties . . . that generally touches on independence.' The record amply demonstrates that neither Stafford nor Boushka

Section 220

Beam's failure to plead sufficient facts to support her claim of demand futility may be due in part to her failure to exhaust all reasonably available means of gathering facts. As the Chancellor noted, had Beam first brought a Section 220 action seeking inspection of MSO's books and records, she might have uncovered facts that would have created a reasonable doubt. For example, irregularities or "cronyism" in MSO's process of nominating board members might possibly strengthen her claim concerning Stewart's control over MSO's directors. A books and records inspection might have revealed whether the board used a nominating committee to select directors and maintained a separation between the director-selection process and management. A books and records inspection might also have revealed whether Stewart unduly controlled the nominating process or whether the process incorporated procedural safeguards to ensure directors' independence.[31] Beam might also have reviewed the minutes of the board's meetings to determine how the directors handled Stewart's proposals or conduct in various contexts. Whether or not the result of this exploration might create a reasonable doubt would be sheer speculation at this stage. But the point is that it was within the plaintiff's power to explore these matters and she elected not to make the effort.

In general, derivative plaintiffs are not entitled to discovery in order to demonstrate demand futility. The general unavailability of discovery to assist plaintiffs with pleading demand futility does not leave plaintiffs without means of gathering information to support their allegations of demand futility, however. Both this Court and the Court of Chancery have continually advised plaintiffs who seek to plead facts establishing demand futility that the plaintiffs might successfully have used a Section 220 books and records inspection to uncover such facts.

Because Beam did not even attempt to use the fact-gathering tools available to her by seeking to review MSO's books and records in support of her demand futility claim, we cannot know if such an effort would have been fruitless, as Beam claimed on appeal. Beam's failure to seek a books and records inspection that may have uncovered the facts necessary to support a reasonable doubt of independence has resulted in substantial cost to the parties and the judiciary.

Conclusion

Because Beam did not plead facts sufficient to support a reasonable inference that at least one MSO director in addition to Stewart and Patrick was incapable of

---

possessed the 'care, attention and sense of responsibility' necessary to afford them the status of independent directors. The result was that Stein, arguably the least detached member of the Special Committee, became, de facto, a single member committee — a tenuous role." (fourth alteration in original) (citation omitted)).

[31] [48] Although not mandated by Delaware law, it is relevant to note that the New York Stock Exchange listing requirements, for example, require that listed companies have an independent and effective nominating committee. *See* New York Stock Exchange Corporate Governance Rule 303A.04 (2003), available at http://www.nyse.com/pdfs/finalcorpgovrules.pdf; Nat'l Ass'n Sec. Dealers Rule 4350(c)(4), NASD Manual Online (2003), http://cchwallstreet.com/NASD/NASD_Rules. Although these requirements may not have been in effect at times relevant to this complaint, it is relevant to note that MSO is an NYSE listed company.

considering demand, Beam was required to make demand on the board before pursuing a derivative suit. Hence, presuit demand was not excused. The Court of Chancery did not err by dismissing Count 1 under Rule 23.1. The judgment of the Court of Chancery is AFFIRMED.

# C.   THE SPECIAL LITIGATION COMMITTEE

The Special Litigation Committee was an innovation in the law. In the following case, the board of directors delegated the question of whether or not to pursue a lawsuit to an independent committee consisting of two independent directors. Since the committee members were not involved in the alleged wrongdoing, the business judgment rule should apply to whatever decision the independent committee makes. That is exactly the law of New York as decided by the case *Auerbach v. Bennett*, 393 N.E.2d 994 (N.Y. 1979). Delaware has a more stringent rule. It requires a two-step test as the case explains.

## ZAPATA CORP. v. MALDONADO
### Supreme Court of Delaware
### 430 A.2d 779 (1981)

QUILLEN, J.

This is an interlocutory appeal from an order entered on April 9, 1980, by the Court of Chancery denying appellant-defendant Zapata Corporation's (Zapata) alternative motions to dismiss the complaint or for summary judgment. The issue to be addressed has reached this Court by way of a rather convoluted path.

In June, 1975, William Maldonado, a stockholder of Zapata, instituted a derivative action in the Court of Chancery on behalf of Zapata against ten officers and/or directors of Zapata, alleging, essentially, breaches of fiduciary duty. Maldonado did not first demand that the board bring this action, stating instead such demand's futility because all directors were named as defendants and allegedly participated in the acts specified. In June, 1977, Maldonado commenced an action in the United States District Court for the Southern District of New York against the same defendants, save one, alleging federal security law violations as well as the same common law claims made previously in the Court of Chancery.

By June, 1979, four of the defendant-directors were no longer on the board, and the remaining directors appointed two new outside directors to the board. The board then created an "Independent Investigation Committee" (Committee), composed solely of the two new directors, to investigate Maldonado's actions, as well as a similar derivative action then pending in Texas, and to determine whether the corporation should continue any or all of the litigation. The Committee's determination was stated to be "final, . . . not . . . subject to review by the Board of Directors and . . . in all respects . . . binding upon the Corporation."

Following an investigation, the Committee concluded, in September, 1979, that each action should "be dismissed forthwith as their continued maintenance is inimical to the Company's best interests . . . ." Consequently, Zapata moved for dismissal or summary judgment in the three derivative actions. On January 24, 1980, the District Court for the Southern District of New York granted Zapata's motion for summary judgment, *Maldonado v. Flynn*, S.D.N.Y., 485 F. Supp. 274 (1980), holding, under its interpretation of Delaware law, that the Committee had the authority, under the "business judgment" rule, to require the termination of the derivative action. Maldonado appealed that decision to the Second Circuit Court of Appeals.

On March 18, 1980, the Court of Chancery, in a reported opinion, the basis for the order of April 9, 1980, denied Zapata's motions, holding that Delaware law does not sanction this means of dismissal. More specifically, it held that the "business judgment" rule is not a grant of authority to dismiss derivative actions and that a stockholder has an individual right to maintain derivative actions in certain instances. *Maldonado v. Flynn*, Del. Ch., 413 A.2d 1251 (1980) (herein *Maldonado*). Pursuant to the provisions of Supreme Court Rule 42, Zapata filed an interlocutory appeal with this Court shortly thereafter.

*   *   *

We begin with an examination of the carefully considered opinion of the Vice Chancellor which states, in part, that the "business judgment" rule does not confer power "to a corporate board of directors to terminate a derivative suit," 413 A.2d at 1257. His conclusion is particularly pertinent because several federal courts, applying Delaware law, have held that the business judgment rule enables boards (or their committees) to terminate derivative suits, decisions now in conflict with the holding below.

As the term is most commonly used, and given the disposition below, we can understand the Vice Chancellor's comment that "the business judgment rule is irrelevant to the question of whether the Committee has the authority to compel the dismissal of this suit." 413 A.2d at 1257. Corporations, existing because of legislative grace, possess authority as granted by the legislature. Directors of Delaware corporations derive their managerial decision making power, which encompasses decisions whether to initiate, or refrain from entering, litigation, from 8 Del. C. § 141 (a). This statute is the fount of directorial powers. The "business judgment" rule is a judicial creation that presumes propriety, under certain circumstances, in a board's decision. Viewed defensively, it does not create authority. In this sense the "business judgment" rule is not relevant in corporate decision making until after a decision is made. It is generally used as a defense to an attack on the decision's soundness. The board's managerial decision making power, however, comes from s 141(a). The judicial creation and legislative grant are related because the "business judgment" rule evolved to give recognition and deference to directors' business expertise when exercising their managerial power under s 141(a).

In the case before us, although the corporation's decision to move to dismiss or for summary judgment was, literally, a decision resulting from an exercise of the directors' (as delegated to the Committee) business judgment, the question of "business judgment", in a defensive sense, would not become relevant until and unless the decision to seek termination of the derivative lawsuit was attacked as improper. . . .

Thus, the focus in this case is on the power to speak for the corporation as to whether the lawsuit should be continued or terminated. As we see it, this issue in the current appellate posture of this case has three aspects: the conclusions of the Court below concerning the continuing right of a stockholder to maintain a derivative action; the corporate power under Delaware law of an authorized board committee to cause dismissal of litigation instituted for the benefit of the corporation; and the role of the Court of Chancery in resolving conflicts between the stockholder and the committee.

\* \* \*

Consistent with the purpose of requiring a demand, a board decision to cause a derivative suit to be dismissed as detrimental to the company, after demand has been made and refused, will be respected unless it was wrongful. A claim of a wrongful decision not to sue is thus the first exception and the first context of dispute. Absent a wrongful refusal, the stockholder in such a situation simply lacks legal managerial power.

[In other words, when stockholders, after making demand and having their suit rejected, attack the board's decision as improper, the board's decision falls under the "business judgment" rule and will be respected if the requirements of the rule are met. *See* Dent, *supra* note 5, 75 Nw. U. L. REV. at 100–01 & nn. 24–25. That situation should be distinguished from the instant case, where demand was not made, and the power of the board to seek a dismissal, due to disqualification, presents a threshold issue. For examples of what has been held to be a wrongful decision not to sue, *see* Stockholder Derivative Actions, *supra* note 5, 44 U. CHI. L. REV. at 193–98. We recognize that the two contexts can overlap in practice.]

\* \* \*

These conclusions, however, do not determine the question before us. Rather, they merely bring us to the question to be decided. It is here that we part company with the Court below. Derivative suits enforce corporate rights and any recovery obtained goes to the corporation. "The right of a stockholder to file a bill to litigate corporate rights is, therefore, solely for the purpose of preventing injustice where it is apparent that material corporate rights would not otherwise be protected." We see no inherent reason why the "two phases" of a derivative suit, the stockholder's suit to compel the corporation to sue and the corporation's suit (*see* 413 A.2d at 1261–62), should automatically result in the placement in the hands of the litigating stockholder sole control of the corporate right throughout the litigation. To the contrary, it seems to us that such an inflexible rule would recognize the interest of one person or group to the exclusion of all others within the corporate entity. Thus, we reject the view of the Vice Chancellor as to the first aspect of the issue on appeal.

The question to be decided becomes: When, if at all, should an authorized board committee be permitted to cause litigation, properly initiated by a derivative stockholder in his own right, to be dismissed? As noted above, a board has the power to choose not to pursue litigation when demand is made upon it, so long as the decision is not wrongful. If the board determines that a suit would be detrimental to the company, the board's determination prevails. Even when demand is excusable, circumstances may arise when continuation of the litigation would not be in the corporation's best interests. Our inquiry is whether, under such circumstances, there is a permissible procedure under § 141(a) by which a corporation can rid itself of detrimental litigation. If there is not, a single stockholder in an extreme case might control the destiny of the entire corporation. This concern was bluntly expressed by the Ninth Circuit in *Lewis v. Anderson*, 9th Cir., 615 F.2d 778, 783 (1979), *cert. denied*, 449 U.S. 869, 101 S. Ct. 206, 66 L. Ed. 2d 89 (1980): "To allow one shareholder to incapacitate an entire board of directors merely by leveling charges against them gives too much leverage to dissident shareholders." But, when examining the means, including the committee mechanism examined in this case, potentials for abuse must be recognized. This takes us to the second and third aspects of the issue on appeal.

Before we pass to equitable considerations as to the mechanism at issue here, it must be clear that an independent committee possesses the corporate power to seek the termination of a derivative suit. Section 141(c) allows a board to delegate all of its authority to a committee. Accordingly, a committee with properly delegated authority would have the power to move for dismissal or summary judgment if the entire board did.

Even though demand was not made in this case and the initial decision of whether to litigate was not placed before the board, Zapata's board, it seems to us, retained all of its corporate power concerning litigation decisions. If Maldonado had made demand on the board in this case, it could have refused to bring suit. Maldonado could then have asserted that the decision not to sue was wrongful and, if correct, would have been allowed to maintain the suit. The board, however, never would have lost its statutory managerial authority. The demand requirement itself evidences that the managerial power is retained by the board. When a derivative plaintiff is allowed to bring suit after a wrongful refusal, the board's authority to choose whether to pursue the litigation is not challenged although its conclusion reached through the exercise of that authority is not respected since it is wrongful. Similarly, Rule 23.1, by excusing demand in certain instances, does not strip the board of its corporate power. It merely saves the plaintiff the expense and delay of making a futile demand resulting in a probable tainted exercise of that authority in a refusal by the board or in giving control of litigation to the opposing side. But the board entity remains empowered under § 141(a) to make decisions regarding corporate litigation. The problem is one of member disqualification, not the absence of power in the board.

The corporate power inquiry then focuses on whether the board, tainted by the self-interest of a majority of its members, can legally delegate its authority to a committee of two disinterested directors. We find our statute clearly requires an affirmative answer to this question. . . .

We do not think that the interest taint of the board majority is per se a legal bar to the delegation of the board's power to an independent committee composed of disinterested board members. The committee can properly act for the corporation to move to dismiss derivative litigation that is believed to be detrimental to the corporation's best interest.

*          *          *

At the risk of stating the obvious, the problem is relatively simple. If, on the one hand, corporations can consistently wrest bona fide derivative actions away from well-meaning derivative plaintiffs through the use of the committee mechanism, the derivative suit will lose much, if not all, of its generally-recognized effectiveness as an intra-corporate means of policing boards of directors. If, on the other hand, corporations are unable to rid themselves of meritless or harmful litigation and strike suits, the derivative action, created to benefit the corporation, will produce the opposite, unintended result. It thus appears desirable to us to find a balancing point where bona fide stockholder power to bring corporate causes of action cannot be unfairly trampled on by the board of directors, but the corporation can rid itself of detrimental litigation.

As we noted, the question has been treated by other courts as one of the "business judgment" of the board committee. If a "committee, composed of independent and disinterested directors, conducted a proper review of the matters before it, considered a variety of factors and reached, in good faith, a business judgment that (the) action was not in the best interest of (the corporation)'" the action must be dismissed. *See, e.g.*, *Maldonado v. Flynn, supra*, 485 F. Supp. at 282, 286. The issues become solely independence, good faith, and reasonable investigation. The ultimate conclusion of the committee, under that view, is not subject to judicial review.

We are not satisfied, however, that acceptance of the "business judgment" rationale at this stage of derivative litigation is a proper balancing point. While we admit an analogy with a normal case respecting board judgment, it seems to us that there is sufficient risk in the realities of a situation like the one presented in this case to justify caution beyond adherence to the theory of business judgment.

The context here is a suit against directors where demand on the board is excused. We think some tribute must be paid to the fact that the lawsuit was properly initiated. It is not a board refusal case. Moreover, this complaint was filed in June of 1975 and, while the parties undoubtedly would take differing views on the degree of litigation activity, we have to be concerned about the creation of an "Independent Investigation Committee" four years later, after the election of two new outside directors. Situations could develop where such motions could be filed after years of vigorous litigation for reasons unconnected with the merits of the lawsuit.

Moreover, notwithstanding our conviction that Delaware law entrusts the corporate power to a properly authorized committee, we must be mindful that directors are passing judgment on fellow directors in the same corporation and fellow directors, in this instance, who designated them to serve both as directors and committee members. The question naturally arises whether a "there but for the grace of God go I" empathy might not play a role. And the further question arises whether inquiry as to independence, good faith and reasonable investigation is sufficient safeguard against abuse, perhaps subconscious abuse.

\*    \*    \*

After an objective and thorough investigation of a derivative suit, an independent committee may cause its corporation to file a pretrial motion to dismiss in the Court of Chancery. The basis of the motion is the best interests of the corporation, as determined by the committee. The motion should include a thorough written record of the investigation and its findings and recommendations. Under appropriate Court supervision, akin to proceedings on summary judgment, each side should have an opportunity to make a record on the motion. As to the limited issues presented by the motion noted below, the moving party should be prepared to meet the normal burden under Rule 56 that there is no genuine issue as to any material fact and that the moving party is entitled to dismiss as a matter of law. The Court should apply a two-step test to the motion.

First, the Court should inquire into the independence and good faith of the committee and the bases supporting its conclusions. Limited discovery may be ordered to facilitate such inquiries. The corporation should have the burden of proving independence, good faith and a reasonable investigation, rather than presuming independence, good faith and reasonableness. If the Court determines either that the committee is not independent or has not shown reasonable bases for its conclusions, or, if the Court is not satisfied for other reasons relating to the process, including but not limited to the good faith of the committee, the Court shall deny the corporation's motion. If, however, the Court is satisfied under Rule 56 standards that the committee was independent and showed reasonable bases for good faith findings and recommendations, the Court may proceed, in its discretion, to the next step.

The second step provides, we believe, the essential key in striking the balance between legitimate corporate claims as expressed in a derivative stockholder suit and a corporation's best interests as expressed by an independent investigating committee. The Court should determine, applying its own independent business judgment, whether the motion should be granted. This means, of course, that instances could arise where a committee can establish its independence and sound bases for its good faith decisions and still have the corporation's motion denied. The second step is intended to thwart instances where corporate actions meet the criteria of step one, but the result does not appear to satisfy its spirit, or where corporate actions would simply prematurely terminate a stockholder grievance deserving of further consideration in the corporation's interest. The Court of Chancery of course must carefully consider and weigh how compelling the corporate interest in dismissal is when faced with a non-frivolous lawsuit. The Court of Chancery should, when appropriate, give special consideration to matters of law and public policy in addition to the corporation's best interests.

If the Court's independent business judgment is satisfied, the Court may proceed to grant the motion, subject, of course, to any equitable terms or conditions the Court finds necessary or desirable.

The interlocutory order of the Court of Chancery is reversed and the cause is remanded for further proceedings consistent with this opinion.

# PELLER v. SOUTHERN COMPANY
United States Court of Appeals, Eleventh Circuit
911 F.2d 1532 (1990)

JOHNSON, J.

Georgia Power, a Georgia corporation, is a wholly owned subsidiary of Southern, a Delaware corporation. Georgia Power operates electric utilities and power-generating plants across the Southeast and provides most of Georgia's electrical power. Peller, an attorney and a shareholder of Southern, brought this derivative action for more than 800 million dollars against the Companies on April 30, 1986, contending that the Companies and their directors acted negligently and breached their fiduciary duties to the shareholders during the sixteen-year period since 1970. Peller's allegations focused specifically on a series of decisions by the Companies authorizing Georgia Power to begin and complete construction of the Alvin W. Vogtle nuclear power plant ("the Vogtle plant") and the Rocky Mountain Pumped Storage Facility ("Rocky Mountain"). Peller did not make a demand on the Boards of Directors of Southern or Georgia Power prior to commencing his lawsuit. On the contrary, he asserted that such a demand would have been futile because the defendant-directors were insiders who had participated in the conduct alleged in the complaint.

[Under Delaware law, which governs this litigation, before shareholders may sue on behalf of a corporation, they must make a demand on the board of directors asking it to redress the alleged wrong. There is, however, a notable exception to the demand requirement. When a shareholder demonstrates that the board is not capable of properly conducting the litigation (e.g., when the challenged wrong is self-dealing by the board), the court may excuse the demand as futile. *See Zapata v. Maldonado*, 430 A.2d 779, 783–84 (Del. 1981); *Aronson v. Lewis*, 473 A.2d 805 (Del. 1984).]

On July 18, 1986, the district court entered a consent order that stayed all aspects of this litigation pending the appointment and report of an independent litigation committee ("the Committee") to investigate Peller's claims. Initially the district court fixed December 31, 1986 as the deadline for the Committee's report. It eventually extended the deadline, however, to November 30, 1987. Established in September 1986, the Committee consisted of three directors chosen by the Companies who were not involved with them during the sixteen year period under dispute. The Companies gave the Committee the sole authority to evaluate the Peller litigation.

At the same time the Committee was undertaking its investigation, the Georgia Public Service Commission ("PSC") was considering a major rate case to determine whether to permit Georgia Power to recover the costs of constructing the Vogtle plant by increasing customer rates. By statute, the PSC was required to make its decision by October 2, 1987. After inspecting much of the same evidence reviewed by the Committee, the PSC found a number of imprudent management decisions by the Companies and disallowed approximately 300 million dollars from inclusion in the ratebase.

After reviewing the decisions challenged by Peller, the Committee issued its report dated October 1, 1987. It determined that all of the challenged decisions were either correct or at least reasonable business judgments at the times they were made. Furthermore, it found that the actions of the defendants were neither arbitrary nor self-interested. The Committee therefore concluded that, as a matter of business judgment, the derivative action was neither in the best interests of the Companies nor their shareholders and should be dismissed. By issuing its report on October 1, 1987, just one day before the PSC's decision and well before the November 30 deadline imposed by the district court, the Committee deliberately chose not to wait for the PSC's outcome.

On October 13, 1987, the Companies moved for dismissal or, alternatively, for summary judgment on Peller's suit arguing that because demand was not excused the business judgment rule required the district court to defer to the Committee's determination that the suit should be dismissed.[32] On March 25, 1988, the district court ruled that Peller was excused from making a demand on the Companies, but the court found the record insufficient at that stage to evaluate the Committee's recommendation. Limited discovery ensued, and the Committee filed a supplemental report. Following further briefing, on December 23, 1988, the district court denied the Companies' motion and ordered that the derivative suit go forward. On June 28, 1989, the district court denied the Companies' motion for reconsideration but clarified its December 1988 ruling in certain respects. The district court certified for interlocutory appeal its denial of the Companies' motion.

In this appeal, we address the following three issues: (a) whether the district court assumed correctly that all relevant aspects of Delaware corporate caselaw should be deemed adopted by the Georgia courts; (b) whether the district court properly found that Peller was excused from making a demand on the Companies; and (c) whether the district court properly exercised its discretion to reject the recommendation of the Committee and permit the derivative suit to proceed.

The Companies initiated their motion to dismiss or, alternatively, for summary judgment pursuant to Fed.R.Civ.P. 12(b)(6) and Fed. R. Civ. P. 56. However, shareholder derivative suits are governed by Fed. R. Civ. P. 23.1,[33] and the district court correctly reviewed the Companies' motion under this rule. Specifically, Rule 23.1 required the district court to resolve the preliminary question of whether a demand was excused before it could determine whether to grant the Companies'

---

[32] [3] Under Delaware law, the business judgment rule is a presumption that in making a business decision the directors of a corporation act on an informed basis, in good faith and in the honest belief that the action taken is in the best interests of the company. Absent an abuse of discretion, that judgment will be respected by the courts. When confronted with a derivative suit where demand is excused, however, Delaware courts are not bound by the business judgment rule. *Aronson v. Lewis*, 473 A.2d at 812–13.

[33] [5] Rule 23.1 provides in part:

In a derivative action brought by one or more shareholders or members to enforce a right of a corporation or of an unincorporated association, the corporation or association having failed to enforce a right which may properly be asserted by it, the complaint shall be verified and shall . . . allege with particularity the efforts, if any, made by the plaintiff to obtain the action the plaintiff desires from the directors or comparable authority and, if necessary, from the shareholders or members, and the reasons for the plaintiff's failure to obtain the action or for not making the effort.

motion. We review the district court's denial of the motion for dismissal pursuant to Rule 23.1 for abuse of discretion.

\* \* \*

Second, and more generally, the Companies dispute whether the Delaware case of *Zapata Corp. v. Maldonado*, 430 A.2d 779 (Del. 1981), should be deemed authoritative under Georgia law. As the district court found, there is no Georgia caselaw relating to the proper standard for dismissal of a shareholder derivative suit under the circumstances of this case. *See Peller I*, 1987–1988 Fed. Sec. L. Rep. (CCH) at 98,311, 1988 WL 90840. While the parties agree that Georgia law should incorporate the relevant parts of the far more extensively developed Delaware corporate caselaw, they debate whether *Zapata*, specifically, represents an innovation which has gained "majority" acceptance among the states. Resolution of this issue essentially requires an educated prediction as to what the Georgia courts would do in an area where there is no significant Georgia caselaw. The district court, relying on its experience interpreting and applying Georgia law, assumed that Georgia would follow Delaware caselaw. Because this Court recognizes the general principle that "a district court's interpretation of the law of the state where it sits . . . is entitled to deference," we accept the district court's determination of the status of Georgia law. *Shipes v. Hanover Ins. Co.*, 884 F.2d 1357, 1359 (11th Cir. 1989).

### The Demand-Excusal Issue

In determining whether a shareholder is excused from making a demand, Delaware courts examine the response of a challenged board when first confronted with a derivative suit. If a board responds to a derivative suit by appointing a special litigation committee with the sole authority to evaluate whether to pursue the litigation before making a motion to dismiss for failure to make a demand, then a court may conclude that the board has conceded its disqualification and therefore demand may be excused. *Abbey v. Computer & Communications Technology Corp.*, 457 A.2d 368, 374 (Del. Ch. 1983); *Spiegel v. Buntrock*, 571 A.2d 767, 776–77 (Del. 1990). By contrast, if a board responds to a derivative suit by filing a motion to dismiss for failure to make a demand before appointing a special litigation committee to evaluate the suit, a court may not find that such a board has conceded that demand is excused. *Spiegel v. Buntrock*, 571 A.2d at 776–77; *See Richardson v. Graves*, 1983 WL 21109 (Del. Ch.) (noting the importance of whether the challenged Board filed its motion to dismiss before or after appointing a special litigation committee in ruling whether a demand is excused). The district court found that by appointing the Committee and delegating to it the sole authority to evaluate whether to pursue the Peller litigation before seeking a motion to dismiss for failure to make a demand, the Companies effectively conceded that demand was excused.

On appeal, the Companies contend that the district court misread *Abbey*. Specifically, the Companies refer this Court to the recent decision of the Delaware Supreme Court in *Spiegel* which clarifies the holding in *Abbey*. In *Spiegel*, the Delaware Supreme Court held that "the decision of a board of directors to appoint a special litigation committee, with a delegation of complete authority to act on a demand, is not, *in all instances*, an acknowledgment that demand was excused and *ergo* that a shareholder's lawsuit was properly initiated as a derivative." *Spiegel v. Buntrock*, 571 A.2d at 777 (emphasis in original).

Contrary to the Companies' contention, the Delaware Supreme Court's clarification of *Abbey* supports the district court's finding that Peller was excused from making a demand because of futility. The facts in the *Abbey* and *Spiegel* cases differ sharply. In *Abbey*, the challenged board responded to a shareholder's derivative complaint alleging that demand was excused by appointing a special litigation committee with the sole authority to determine the board's response. The board in *Abbey* did not make a motion to dismiss for failure to make a demand until *after* it had appointed a special litigation committee. *Abbey v. Computer & Communications Technology Corp.*, 457 A.2d at 370–71. Under these circumstances, the Delaware court ruled that the board had conceded its disqualification, thereby excusing demand.

> By contrast, in *Spiegel*, the challenged board responded to a shareholder plaintiff's derivative complaint by filing a motion to dismiss for failure to make a demand. The shareholder plaintiff then reacted to the board's motion by making a demand, thereby prompting the board to appoint a special litigation committee. Thus, the board in *Spiegel* made a motion to dismiss before it appointed a special litigation committee. *Spiegel v. Buntrock*, 571 A.2d at 776. Under these circumstances, the Delaware court ruled that the board had not conceded its disqualification and therefore demand was not excused.

In the present case, the order of events is completely different from the order in *Spiegel* and virtually identical to the order in *Abbey*. When confronted with Peller's complaint, the Companies did not pursue a motion to dismiss. Rather, they appointed the Committee and delegated to it the sole authority to evaluate the merits of the suit and determine the Companies' response. The Companies then waited for the Committee to make its report and, upon the Committee's negative recommendation, filed a motion to dismiss with the district court. Like the board in *Abbey*, the Companies did not seek a motion to dismiss until *after* they had delegated sole authority to the Committee. Because the Companies, like the board in *Abbey*, did not file a motion to dismiss until after they appointed the Committee and delegated to it the sole authority to evaluate the Peller suit, we find that the district court did not abuse its discretion when it found that the Companies effectively acknowledged that Peller was excused from making a demand.

### Application of Zapata

The Delaware Supreme Court has held on numerous occasions that following an independent committee's recommendation to dismiss a derivative suit in a demand-excused case a court should apply the two-step "Zapata" test to the motion:

> First, the court must inquire into the independence and good faith of the committee and review the reasonableness and good faith of the committee's investigation. Second, the court must apply its own independent business judgment to decide whether the motion to dismiss should be granted.

In the present case, the district court found that the members of the Committee were independent, although it stated that it was not "completely comfortable" with their prior connections to the Companies. *Peller II*, 707 F. Supp. at 525, 528. As to good faith, the court noted the Committee's heavy reliance on its retained counsel and the fact that the interviews through which the Committee gathered its information were not recorded or transcribed but rather summarized by its counsel, which summaries the Committee refused at first to release to Peller. Concluded the court: "This is not good faith."[34]

The district court also found that the Committee's conclusions were not reasonable. The court noted that, by issuing its report only one day before the PSC's decision, the Committee rejected without adequate explanation the findings, made by technical consultants employed by the PSC, that several key decisions during the construction of the Vogtle plant were imprudent and cost the Companies several hundred million dollars.

The court found that the most substantial grounds for its rejection of the Committee's recommendation were the following: the Committee had implausibly blamed "middle management" personnel for the crucial decisions which cost the Companies hundreds of millions of dollars, given the Georgia PSC's exclusion of approximately 300 million dollars in misspent funds from the consumer ratebase, and the Committee had failed to conduct an adequate investigation of the damages sustained by the Companies. *Peller II*, 707 F. Supp. at 529–30. After reviewing this evidence, the district court invoked the "second step" of *Zapata* to hold that "even if . . . defendants had met their burden [as to independence, good faith, and reasonableness], the items enumerated above would be sufficiently troubling" to warrant denial of the Companies' motion to dismiss.

The Companies contend that, even under the *Zapata* test, the district court should have followed the Committee's recommendation. The Companies strenuously argue that the district court misapplied the "reasonableness" element of *Zapata* when it stated that "[the Companies] have not persuaded the court that the [Committee], as opposed to the PSC, arrived at the *correct* conclusion." *Id.* at 529–30. Although the Companies are correct that *Zapata* does not authorize *de novo* review of the *correctness* of a Committee's conclusions, the district court used that word only in passing. Indeed, the district court noted that the Committee had implausibly charged middle management for decisions costing the Companies several hundred million dollars and failed to investigate adequately the damages suffered by the Companies before the court held that the Companies had not "met their burden of establishing the good faith and reasonableness of the [Committee]."

---

[34] [6] In its order of·June 29, 1989, the court modified its finding in response to the Companies' challenge, stating:

> The court did not determine that the failure of defendants to provide [Peller] with the [Committee's] interview notes constituted a lack of good faith in the [Committee's] investigation. Rather, the court was concerned with the [Committee's] conducting its investigation in such a way that the only record prepared was considered "privileged."

The Companies construe this as a "finding" of good faith on the district court's part. This is inaccurate, but regardless of whether the district court renounced its earlier bad faith finding, it was clearly still concerned, in *Zapata*'s words, "for other reasons relating to the process, including but not limited to . . . good faith." *Zapata Corp. v. Maldonado*, 430 A.2d at 789.

The Companies' arguments on appeal largely come down to the contention that under the traditional "plain vanilla" business-judgment standard, the Committee's recommendation should not be disturbed. The Companies are obviously correct that if the proper standard was the "plain vanilla" business judgment rule, *Spiegel v. Buntrock*, 1988 WL 124324 (Del. Ch.), the district court would be obligated to defer to the Committee's judgment. Having determined, however, in its discretionary authority that demand was excused, the district court properly applied the *Zapata* test to the Committee's recommendation. In light of the foregoing analysis, we find that the district court did not abuse its discretion when it rejected the Committee's recommendation and permitted this litigation to proceed.

For the foregoing reasons, we Affirm the district court's denial of the Companies' motion to dismiss or, alternatively, for summary judgment.

## PROBLEM 14.1

Barry purchases 100% of the stock of Acme Corporation. After doing so, he learns that the former directors and officers had embezzled $10 million in cash and valuable assets. Barry brings a suit against the former wrongdoers. The lawsuit has two counts. In count I, he alleges a breach of fiduciary duty by the defendants and brings a cause of action derivatively. In count II, he alleges a direct cause of action. How should the court decide the case? Assume that Barry carefully investigated the value of the corporation prior to his purchase from the former stockholders. He determined that the price paid was a fair one.

## D.  OTHER PROCEDURAL ASPECTS

### 1.  Intervention

**FELZEN v. ANDREAS**
United States Court of Appeals, Seventh Circuit
134 F.3d 873 (1998)

Easterbrook, J.

"The rule that only parties to a lawsuit, or those that properly become parties, may appeal an adverse judgment, is well settled. . . . Following *Marino* we held that a class member in an action under Fed. R. Civ. P. 23 who has not become a party may not appeal from an order granting summary judgment to the defendant. *In re Brand Name Prescription Drugs Antitrust Litigation*, 115 F.3d 456 (7th Cir. 1997). Today we consider another proposed exception to the rule stated in *Marino*.

Courts have disagreed for several decades about whether class members (and shareholders, their counterparts in derivative actions under Rule 23.1) must intervene as parties in order to appeal from adverse decisions. See Comment, *The Appealability of Class Action Settlements by Unnamed Parties*, 60 U. Chi. L. Rev. 933 (1993). Until *Marino* this circuit permitted class members and stockholders to appeal, whether or not they had intervened, provided they had informed the district court of their objections to the decision that disadvantaged them. . . . But two shareholders who have appealed from the district court's approval of a settlement in this derivative action ask us to apply *Tryforos [v. Icarian Development Co.*, 518 F.2d 1258, 1263 n. 22 (7th Cir. 1975)] notwithstanding intervening precedent and the language of Rule 3(c).

*Tryforos* did not analyze the question now before us-whether shareholders who are not parties to a Rule 23.1 action nonetheless may appeal — but stated that their right to so do is "clear." Footnote 22 in *Tryforos* cites one case from the 1940s that permits such appeals, but that opinion did not give reasons. (*Tryforos* also cites one district court opinion from the 1960s, an odd reference for a rule of appellate jurisdiction.) An unexplained practice does not offer shelter from a later opinion of the Supreme Court holding that only parties may appeal, and withdrawing from the appellate courts any exception — making power. The two shareholder-appellants offer a number of arguments in support of appeal without intervention that boil down to a claim that erroneous decisions should be reversed, but arguments of this stripe do not justify omitting the step of intervening as a party. A court of appeals is not an ombudsman. Suppose the settlement of a derivative action induces the corporation to fire its CEO, or to curtail its purchases of fax machines, or to choose a different law firm. The affected employees, vendors, and lawyers could not appeal just because they believed the settlement improvident or the judge's action in approving it legally erroneous. Only parties may appeal. So too with shareholders, who have no more right to speak for the firm or control its litigation decisions than bondholders or banks or landlords, all of whom have contractual interests that may be affected by litigation. It may be, as appellants stress, that some district judges would not be receptive to attempts to intervene for the purpose of appeal, but the Supreme Court spoke to this in *Marino* when observing that a denial of a motion to intervene is itself appealable.

According to appellants, *[In re] Brand Name Prescription Drugs* did not actually jettison the approach of *Asgrow Seed* even for class actions. The question at issue in *Brand Name Prescription Drugs* was whether class members (other than the named representatives) could appeal from an order granting summary judgment, while *Asgrow Seed* and today's case involve an appeal from an order approving a settlement. *VMS Limited Partnership*, while dismissing the appeal at hand, remarked in a footnote that the decision did not disturb *Asgrow Seed*. 976 F.2d at 368 n. 8. That is technically so; neither *VMS Limited Partnership* nor *Brand Name Prescription Drugs* involved an appeal from an order approving a settlement. But the distinction is inconsequential for purposes of Rule 3(c), the rationale of *Marino*, and the rationale of *Brand Name Prescription Drugs*: that the court should not "fragment the control of the class action" (115 F.3d at 457) by allowing class members to usurp the role of the class representative without persuading the district judge that the representative is unfit or unfaithful, or that subclasses should be created. See also *Shults v. Champion International Corp.*, 35 F.3d 1056, 1060–61 (6th Cir. 1994); *Gottlieb v. Wiles*, 11 F.3d 1004, 1010–12 (10th Cir. 1993). Lest doubt linger, we now formally overrule *Asgrow Seed* and any other case in this circuit (including *Armstrong v. Board of School Directors*, 616 F.2d 305, 327–28 (7th Cir. 1980), and *Patterson v. Stovall*, 528 F.2d 108, 109 n. 1 (7th Cir. 1976)) that permits non-parties to appeal from a decision of any kind in a class action.

Well, then, is a shareholders' derivative action under Rule 23.1 different from a class action under Rule 23 in a way that permits appeal by non-parties? Not so far as Rule 3(c) or *Marino* is concerned. Although there are differences between class actions and derivative suits, these cut against the appellants' position. All class members are identical in entitlement to litigate; which injured persons become the representatives, and which the "mere" class members, is to a degree fortuitous and to a degree dependent on the entrepreneurial activity of the class counsel. It is the fact that each class member has a real grievance with the defendant that sets up at least an equitable argument for a class member who wants to appeal. But in a shareholders' derivative action, the individual investor is not an injured party and is not entitled to litigate. A derivative suit is brought by an investor in the corporation's (not the investor's) right to recover for injury to the corporation. *Frank v. Hadesman & Frank, Inc.*, 83 F.3d 158 (7th Cir. 1996); *Kagan v. Edison Brothers Stores, Inc.*, 907 F.2d 690 (7th Cir. 1990). The corporation obtains the damages; the investor-plaintiffs just get the ball rolling after the fashion of a *qui tam* action. Only when the corporation's board defaults in its duty to protect the interests of the investors is this step permitted, and even then many states permit the board to regain control of the litigation following a special investigation. *See Kamen v. Kemper Financial Services, Inc.*, 500 U.S. 90, 111 S. Ct. 1711, 114 L. Ed. 2d 152 (1991); American Law Institute, *Principles of Corporate Governance: Analysis and Recommendations* §§ 7.01, 7.03, 7.05 (1992). If in the course of managing or settling derivative litigation investors receive new injury, they do so only because the corporation becomes worse off-but loss to the corporation does not permit stockholders to sue directly. *See Mid-State Fertilizer Co. v. Exchange National Bank*, 877 F.2d 1333 (7th Cir. 1989). Once again the corporation holds the legal claim, and it acts through the board of directors. Stockholders may *replace* the board if dissatisfied with its performance, but they may not *displace* the board in litigation. So it cannot be surprising that stockholders other than the named plaintiffs are not treated as parties in derivative litigation-their citizenship is ignored when determining diversity, *see Smith v. Sperling*, 354 U.S. 91 (1957), and they are not allowed to opt out. Corporate management may affect the interests of stockholders without notifying them or obtaining their consent; by investing in stock, they placed their funds at the management's disposal and obtained, in exchange, the right to choose future managers. Shareholders have no more the attributes of parties when managers settle derivative litigation than when managers settle antitrust litigation. (This particular derivative suit arose out of claims that managers of Archer Daniels Midland Co. conspired with rival sellers and thus exposed the firm to criminal and treble-damages liability for conspiracy in restraint of trade.)

Rule 23.1 provides for notice to shareholders only in the event of dismissal or settlement, so that other investors may contest the faithfulness or honesty of the self-appointed plaintiffs; we do not doubt that this monitoring is often useful and that intervention to facilitate an appeal could be justified. Many thoughtful students of the subject conclude, with empirical support, that derivative actions do little to promote sound management and often hurt the firm by diverting the managers' time from running the business while diverting the firm's resources to the plaintiffs' lawyers without providing a corresponding benefit. Janet Cooper Alexander, *Do the Merits Matter? A Study of Settlements in Securities Class Actions*, 43 STAN. L. REV.

497 (1991); Reinier Kraakman, Hyun Park & Steven Shavell, *When are Shareholder Suits in Shareholder Interests?*, 82 Geo. L.J. 1733 (1994); Roberta Romano, *The Shareholder Suit: Litigation Without Foundation?*, 7 J.L. Econ. & Org. 55 (1991); Mark L. Cross, Wallace N. Davidson & John H. Thornton, *The Impact of Directors' and Officers' Liability Suits on Firm Value*, 56 J. Risk & Insurance 128 (1989); Daniel R. Fischel & Michael Bradley, *The Role of Liability Rules and the Derivative Suit in Corporate Law: A Theoretical and Empirical Analysis*, 71 Cornell L. Rev. 261 (1986). The two shareholder-appellants in this case believe that the modest settlement, half of which will be paid to counsel, exemplifies this problem. Their failure to become parties prevents us from considering this contention, for the possibility that a district court's judgment is erroneous does not dispense with the need for an appeal by a party.

One court of appeals has held, despite *Marino*, that a shareholder need not become a party in order to appeal from the final decision in derivative litigation. *Bell Atlantic Corp. v. Bolger*, 2 F.3d 1304, 1307–10 (3d Cir. 1993). The third circuit conceived of the question as whether the shareholder has standing, which is misleading. Standing means injury in fact, and a reduction in the market price of one's stock is injury. Parties are a subset of injured persons. Equating injury with party status is exactly the approach disapproved by *Marino*. The third circuit thought that shareholders in derivative actions should be treated like class members in class actions, and it permitted the shareholders to appeal because it permits class members to appeal. 2 F.3d at 1309–10; see also *Carlough v. Amchem Products, Inc.*, 5 F.3d 707, 714 (3d Cir. 1993). One does not follow from the other; for reasons we have discussed, shareholders have the weaker claim. But in this circuit, which requires class members to intervene if they want to appeal, similar treatment of shareholders is ordained. We overrule *Tryforos* to the extent it permits non-party shareholders to appeal in actions under Rule 23.1, and we disagree with the conclusion of *Bell Atlantic*.

\* \* \*

Because this opinion overrules some of our decisions and creates a conflict among the circuits, it was circulated before release to all judges in active service. No judge favored hearing the case en banc.

The appeal is dismissed for want of jurisdiction.

## 2. Counsel for the Officers

### LEWIS v. SHAFFER STORES CO.
United States District Court, Southern District of New York
218 F. Supp. 238 (1963)

McLean, J.

This is a derivative action by a stockholder of R. C. Williams & Company, Inc. ("Williams"), a New York corporation, in the right of that corporation against officers, directors and a majority stockholder of the corporation. Williams is made a nominal defendant. The complaint seeks recovery, pursuant to Section 16(b) of the Securities Exchange Act of 1934, of shortswing profits allegedly made by defendants in the purchase and sale of Williams securities. It also alleges that defendants acquired control of Williams in 1957 and that by reason of their domination and control, they caused Williams in 1957 and that by reason of which resulted in loss to Williams and which violated various sections of the Securities Act of 1933, the Securities Exchange Act of 1934, and the New York Stock Corporation Law, McKinney's Consol.Laws, c. 59. The complaint asks that defendants account to Williams for all profits allegedly made by defendants and that defendants pay all such profits and damages to Williams.

The law firm of Breed, Abbott & Morgan, which has been general counsel for Williams for many years, has appeared for Williams and also for the defendant officers, directors and majority stockholder. It has filed a joint answer on behalf of Williams and on behalf of the defendant officers, directors and majority stockholder which denies the allegations of wrongdoing and asks that the complaint be dismissed. Plaintiff now moves for an order striking the answer of Williams, striking the appearance of Breed, Abbott & Morgan as counsel for Williams, and "requiring the Corporation to appear by genuinely independent counsel whose answer shall be no more than an invitation to the plaintiff to prove his case to the end that the Corporation receive any benefits to which it is entitled."

The motion is timely, since the answer has only recently been filed. In this respect, the case is distinguishable from *Solomon v. Hirsch*, 35 Misc. 2d 716, 230 N.Y.S. 2d 625 (1962), in which a similar motion was denied on the ground that plaintiff had delayed for almost a year in making it.

The affidavit submitted by Breed, Abbott & Morgan states in substance that the firm feels an obligation to defend the officers and directors whom it has advised. This is understandable, and I see no impropriety in their doing so under the circumstances of this case. *Marco v. Dulles*, 169 F. Supp. 622 (S.D.N.Y. 1959), appeal dismissed 268 F.2d 192 (2d Cir. 1959).

Plaintiff indeed does not contend otherwise.

The question, however, is whether Breed, Abbott & Morgan should also appear for the corporation. The answer admits that the defendant stockholder owns a majority of Williams stock and that there are approximately 1,137 common stockholders of the corporation.

The interests of the officer, director and majority stockholder defendants in this action are clearly adverse, on the face of the complaint, to the interests of the stockholders of Williams other than defendants. I have no doubt that Breed, Abbott & Morgan believe in good faith that there is no merit to this action. Plaintiff, of course, vigorously contends to the contrary. The court cannot and should not attempt to pass upon the merits at this stage. Under all the circumstances, including the nature of the charges, and the vigor with which they are apparently being pressed and defended, I believe that it would be wise for the corporation to retain independent counsel, who have had no previous connection with the corporation, to advise it as to the position which it should take in this controversy.

*See Garlen v. Green Mansions, Inc.*, 9 A.D. 2d 760, 193 N.Y.S. 2d 116 (1st Dept. 1959); *Marco v. Dulles, supra*.

The fact that the selection of such independent counsel will necessarily be made by officers and directors who are defendants does not seem to me to present any insuperable difficulty. Plaintiff's motion is therefore granted to the extent of striking out the answer of Williams and the appearance of Breed, Abbott & Morgan as attorneys for Williams.

Plaintiff is not privileged to dictate the nature of the answer to be filed on behalf of the corporation. That is to be determined by the independent counsel to be selected. If, after investigation of the facts, they conclude that the action is without merit, that the corporation is not entitled to the relief sought by plaintiff, and that the action in any way threatens the best interests of the corporation, the answer to be filed by the corporation may be framed accordingly.

The order to be entered on this motion should contain appropriate provisions with respect to the time within which new counsel for the corporation are to be retained and the time when the corporation's new answer is to be filed.

## 3.  Conduct of Plaintiff

### LIKEN v. SHAFFER
United States District Court, Northern District of Iowa
64 F. Supp. 432 (1946)

GRAVEN, J.

\*    \*    \*

In a stockholder's derivative suit where recovery is allowed, the judgment is entered in favor of the corporation. *Smith v. Bramwell* [31 P.2d 647 (Or. 1934)], *supra; Hayden v. Perfection Water Cooler Co.*, 1917, 227 Mass. 589, 116 N.E. 871. The general rule is that no proportionate judgment can be allowed a stockholder in a derivative stockholder's suit. 13 Fletcher Cyclopedia Corporations, Perm. Ed., Sec. 6028; *Chicago Macaroni Mfg. Co. v. Boggiano*, 1903, 202 Ill. 312, 67 N.E. 17. One of the reasons why courts of equity have not allowed direct proportionate recoveries in stockholder's derivative suits, has been that the recovery is an asset of the corporation, and its creditors have first claim upon it; and that to award such recovery direct to the stockholders leaving any creditors unpaid, would be fraudulent as to them. *Smith v. Bramwell, supra; Hoyt v. Hampe*, 1927, 206 Iowa 206, 214 N.W. 718, 719, 220 N.W. 45. Another matter of increasing importance in recent years is the matter of state and federal taxes. Apart from the question of the recovery being needed to pay the unpaid claims of the state and federal government, is the fact that in a good many cases a substantial recovery by the corporation will require changes in tax reports previously made and result in additional tax liability.

While for certain purposes, as for instance, federal court jurisdiction, the stockholders instituting a stockholder's suit are technically regarded as parties (13

Cyclopedia Federal Procedure, Sec. 6892), yet so far as a court of equity is concerned, their status is that of those who set the judicial machinery in motion in behalf of the corporation. *Overfield v. Pennroad Corporation*, 3 Cir., 1944, 146 F.2d 889, 894; *Graham v. Dubuque Specialty Machine Works*, 1908, 138 Iowa 456, 114 N.W. 619, 15 L.R.A., N.S. 729. In the case of *Potter v. Walker*, 1937, 252 App. Div. 244, 293 N.Y.S. 161, 163, it is stated: "It has been well stated that in a representative derivative action a stockholder who brings the same is not the real plaintiff, but merely the 'instigator' of the action."

A stockholder's derivative suit is an invention of the courts of equity and is recognizable only in equity and cannot be maintained at law. * * *

In an ordinary action by a corporation on a claim, the conduct of a particular stockholder is not material. Stockholders have no power to act for or bind a corporation except at a corporate meeting. 13 Fletcher Cyclopedia Corporations, Perm. Ed., Sec. 5730. Courts of equity, in ordinary cases, will refuse relief to those suitors who do not come into equity with clean hands, or who have ratified or acquiesced in the wrong complained of. Both of these rules of law are applicable to stockholder's derivative suits. Where a claim is asserted in behalf of a corporation in a stockholder's derivative action in order for matters to be a bar to the claim, they must be such matters as relate to the corporation itself, and the conduct of a particular stockholder is not material. However, the conduct of a particular stockholder who seeks to maintain a stockholder's derivative suit might be so at variance with equitable principles, that a court of equity would abate the action.

Thus, a particular stockholder who institutes a stockholder's derivative suit, may have participated in the wrong complained of (*see Conners v. Conners Bros. Co.*, 1913, 110 Me. 428, 86 A. 843, 846), or may have ratified the wrong complained of or acquiesced in it, or have had knowledge of the wrong complained of under circumstances which would make him guilty of laches. In such cases, a court of equity will not recognize him as a proper suitor in a court of equity and will abate the action without reference to the merits of the claim sought to be asserted in behalf of the corporation. The fact that one stockholder has discovered fraud and is guilty of laches does not prevent another stockholder who is not guilty of laches from instituting a stockholder's derivative suit. 13 Fletcher Cyclopedia Corporations, Perm. Ed., Sec, 5886, p. 243, also Sec. 5874. Laches to be a matter of bar must be the laches of the corporation itself. *Daniels v. Briggs*, 1932, 279 Mass. 87, 180 N.E. 717; 13 Fletcher Cyclopedia Corporations, Perm. Ed., Sec. Perm. Ed., Sec. 5874, p, 226. Acquiescence of a stockholder in the wrong complained of, which prevents him from maintaining a stockholder's derivative suit, is distinct from the acquiescence on the part of a corporation which is a bar to the claim. 1 Morawetz Private Corporations, 2d Ed., Sec. 239, p. 255, and Sec. 262. In stockholder's derivative suits, matters in bar relate only to the claim of the corporation itself. Matters in abatement can relate to both the claim of the corporation and the particular stockholder instituting the action. A stockholder's derivative suit may be abated so far as the corporation itself is concerned because of lack of jurisdiction or because the claim was not due.

A stockholder's derivative suit may also be abated because of the conduct or situation of the particular stockholder or stockholders instituting the action.

However, the claim of the corporation cannot be barred by the conduct or situation of the particular stockholder or stockholders instituting the proceedings. If, however, a particular stockholder is suing in his own individual behalf for wrongs done in connection with corporate affairs, then his own conduct and situation could be a bar to his claim. The statute of limitations is a matter of positive bar. 37 C.J. p. 698. The knowledge or lack of knowledge of an individual stockholder not connected with a corporation other than as a stockholder is not material in considering the statute of limitations as a bar to the claim of the corporation itself. In such a situation it is the knowledge or lack of knowledge of those connected with the corporation whose knowledge is by law imputed to the corporation. Where those whose knowledge is ordinarily imputed to a corporation are the wrongdoers and they are in control of the corporation, the statute of limitations may be suspended until that situation is changed but that is not a matter having to do with the knowledge or lack of knowledge of a particular stockholder. The knowledge or lack of knowledge of an individual stockholder is material on the question of the statute of limitations as a matter of bar where such stockholder is asserting an individual right. The knowledge or lack of knowledge of an individual stockholder who institutes a stockholder's derivative suit is material on the matter of abatement of such a suit, because of the rule that equity will not grant relief as the behest of suitors whose conduct has offended equitable principles, but that is a matter of abatement and not of bar. . . .

### NOTE

The above excerpts illustrate the obscure origins and nature of the derivative suit. Although a derivative suit is brought in the name of the corporation, there must be at least one plaintiff shareholder unless the corporation itself brings the suit. If the shareholder himself is a wrongdoer, the suit will be abated if the technical equitable defense is raised, and ultimately the suit will be dismissed if a shareholder cannot be found to intervene who is not subject to the defense. Do any of these technical rules make any sense?

## 4.   Corporation as Indispensable Party

### DEAN v. KELLOGG
Supreme Court of Michigan
292 N.W. 704 (1940)

BUTZEL, J.

We are reviewing on one record the dismissal of a stockholders' derivative suit and the denial of a petition for discovery.

Plaintiffs filed a bill of complaint in chancery on behalf of themselves and any other stockholders and creditors of Seedtown Products, Inc., and Warren-Teed Seed Company, who might care to join in and contribute to the expense of the proceedings. The trial court granted a motion to dismiss on the grounds of lack of jurisdiction, laches and multifariousness. We shall summarize the allegations of the lengthy bill. Plaintiffs are the owners of over 130,000 shares in a Nevada corporation now known as the Warren-Teed Seed Company, hereinafter referred to as Warren-Teed. It is joined as a party defendant. Defendant Seedtown Products, Inc., was organized under the laws of Delaware, and shall hereafter be referred to as Seedtown. Defendant Kellogg Company, a Delaware corporation, maintains an office in Battle Creek, Michigan. Battle Creek is also the residence of defendant W. K. Kellogg. . . .

Shortly after December 1, 1930, after Seedtown had qualified its stock for sale in Illinois, an agreement was made by Warren-Teed and Seedtown whereby the stock of Seedtown was to be exchanged for the assets of Warren-Teed, and each stockholder of Warren-Teed was accorded the right to exchange his stock on a share for share basis for stock of a like class in Seedtown. It is charged that the shares of Seedtown were never issued and delivered to plaintiffs because of the persistent delay of John L. Kellogg.

A large block of Class A stock of Seedtown was exchanged for all the outstanding stock of Kellogg Terminal Warehouses, Inc., not a party to this suit.

Plaintiffs alleged that in 1924 John L. Kellogg began to acquire stock in Warren-Teed, and that by 1928 he had a majority interest therein. It is charged that through "all manner of intricacies and schemes known to corporate legerdemain" John L. Kellogg stripped both Warren-Teed and Seedtown of all their assets. He is alleged to have obtained by fraud in 1931 a default judgment in Illinois against Seedtown in the sum of $220,006.90.

*     *     *

The bill further alleged that a sale of the assets of Seedtown took place, resulting in the purchase by John L. Kellogg, as a judgment creditor, of all the assets. Although notice of dissolution was filed in Delaware, plaintiffs claim that Seedtown was never legally dissolved in a manner binding on plaintiffs or the other stockholders by a two-thirds vote as required by the laws of Delaware, and that the dissolution was brought about by false, fraudulent and illegal returns to the Secretary of State of Delaware, and that for this reason Seedtown is a de facto, if not a de jure, corporation doing business in Michigan.

It is further claimed that John L. Kellogg induced an inventor in the employ of Warren-Teed to become Kellogg's personal employee, and that valuable inventions and processes discovered were appropriated by Kellogg and other corporations controlled by him, in breach of his fiduciary duties to Warren-Teed. . . .

Plaintiffs prayed for an accounting, retransfer of the assets wrongfully misappropriated, an injunction, a receiver for Warren-Teed and Seedtown, and general relief. Plaintiffs' petition for discovery was denied without prejudice to a renewal thereof after defendants filed their plea or answer. The trial court granted a motion to dismiss on the grounds that it lacked jurisdiction of essential parties, that the bill was multifarious, and that plaintiffs' inexcusable laches barred equitable relief.

Only W. K. Kellogg and Kellogg Company were personally served with process in the State of Michigan; an order of publication was made as to defendants John

L. Kellogg, Warren-Teed Seed Company, and Seedtown Products, Inc. They have not appeared.

The question of jurisdiction over necessary parties to the suit or of the subject of action is controlling. Defendant John L. Kellogg, a resident of Illinois, is asked to account for alleged wrongs to Warren-Teed and Seedtown; he has not been personally served within the State, nor has he submitted to the jurisdiction of this court. We are powerless to render any personal decree against him; our process, personal or constructive, is confined to the limits of this State so far as acquiring personal jurisdiction over nonresidents. The dismissal of the bill was correct as to him.

A more difficult problem is presented as to our jurisdiction to adjudicate rights belonging to Warren-Teed and Seedtown. "There is no doubt of the power of a court of equity, in case of fraud, abuse of trust, or misappropriation of corporation funds, at the instance of a single stockholder, to grant relief, and compel a restitution." *Miner v. Belle Isle Ice Co.*, 93 Mich. 97, 53 N.W. 218, 223, 17 L.R.A. 412. In the usual stockholders' derivative suit, the stockholders as plaintiffs are permitted to instigate the action in a court of equity to enforce a claim of the corporation. *Foss v. Harbottle*, 2 Hare's Ch. 461, 67 Eng.Rep. 189; *Hawes v. Oakland*, 104 U.S. 450, 26 L. Ed. 827. Any recovery runs in favor of the corporation, for the shareholders do not sue in their own right. *Talbot v. Scripps*, 31 Mich. 268; *Horning v. Louis Peters & Co.*, 202 Mich. 140, 167 N.W. 874; *Curtiss v. Wilmarth*, 254 Mich. 242, 236 N.W. 773. They derive only an incidental benefit. *Davenport v. Dows*, 85 U.S. 626, 18 Wall. 626, 21 L. Ed. 938. If the defendants account, it must be to the corporation and not to the shareholders. As to the defendants charged with defrauding it, the corporation is an indispensable party. *Cicotte v. Anciaux*, 53 Mich. 227, 18 N.W. 793; *Coxe v. Hart*, 53 Mich. 557, 19 N.W. 183; *McMillan v. Miller*, 177 Mich. 511, 143 N.W. 631. Furthermore, the decree must protect the defendants against any further suit by the corporation, and this will not be true unless it properly be made a party to the action. *Davenport v. Dows, supra; Baltimore & O. R. Co. v. City of Parkersburg*, 268 U.S. 35, 45 S. Ct. 382, 69 L. Ed. 834; *Watts v. Vanderbilt*, 2 Cir., 45 F.2d 968; *Philipbar v. Derby*, 2 Cir., 85 F.2d 27. The usual American practice is to name the beneficiary corporation as a party defendant, although in substance it is a party plaintiff; the flexibility of equity procedure permits an affirmative judgment to be entered in favor of one defendant against other defendants. To be made a party so as to make the adjudication final, it must be subject to the jurisdiction and cannot be brought in the State by extraterritorial or constructive service. *Geer v. Mathieson Alkali Works*, 190 U.S. 428, 23 S. Ct. 807, 47 L. Ed. 1122; *Deming v. Beatty Oil Co.*, 72 Kan. 614, 84 P. 385; *Watts v. Vanderbilt, supra; Freeman v. Bean*, 266 N.Y. 657, 195 N.E. 368. *See also*, Winer, *Jurisdiction in Stockholders' Suits*, 22 VA. LAW REV. 153, at 160; *Necessity of Joinder of Corporation in Representative Suit against the Directors*, 44 YALE LAW JOURNAL, 1091. The beneficiary corporations are foreign corporations, and no agent doing business on its behalf in Michigan has been served. We think the suit fails for want of jurisdiction.

\*        \*        \*

In view of our holding on the jurisdictional question, we need not discuss the other questions raised in regard to the right of the court to interfere with the internal conduct of the affairs of a foreign corporation, the attack on the Illinois judgment for fraud in its procurement, the inquiry into the validity of the dissolution of the Delaware corporation, plaintiffs' laches, and the issue of multifariousness.

The judgment of dismissal is affirmed; the writ of mandamus to order the trial court to grant the petition for discovery is denied. Costs to defendants W. K. Kellogg and Kellogg Company.

## 5. Disqualification of Counsel

### CANNON v. U.S. ACOUSTICS CORP.
United States District Court, Northern District of Illinois
398 F. Supp. 209 (1975)

MARSHALL, J.

Charles B. Cannon, Richard L. Davis, John G. Marsh, and Jeffrey Ross brought this derivative shareholder's action, as well as personal claims, against the defendants, U.S. Acoustics Corporation (hereinafter "Acoustics"), a Florida corporation, and National Perlite Products, S.A., (hereinafter "Perlite"), a Panamanian Corporation. The six-count complaint alleges violations of the Securities Exchange Act of 1934, 15 U.S.C. § 78a et seq., and the common and statutory laws of Florida and Illinois. Jurisdiction of the federal claims exists under 28 U.S.C. § 1331 (1970), and 15 U.S.C. § 78aa (1970). The state claims which arise from the same transactional nucleus as the federal claims are here under the doctrine of pendent jurisdiction.

There are pending for decision cross-motions to disqualify counsel and a motion to disqualify Cannon as a party plaintiff. Shortly after Robert J. Gareis, Peter J. Mone and the firm of Baker & McKenzie filed their appearances on behalf of the corporate and individual defendants, plaintiffs moved to disqualify them from representing the corporate defendants and requested that the court appoint independent counsel.[35] Plaintiffs base their motion on the theory that dual representation in a shareholder derivative suit creates a conflict of interest that the court can order terminated.

Concomitant with filing their answer to the plaintiffs' motion, defendants moved to strike Cannon as a party plaintiff and to strike the appearances of N.A. Giambalvo and Boodell, Sears, Sugrue, Giambalvo & Crowley as counsel for the plaintiff.

Defendants argue that by virtue of Canon 4 of the American Bar Association's Code of Professional Responsibility (hereinafter "CPR"), Cannon (who is a lawyer), and the lawyers and law firm which represent him, cannot maintain the pending suit because each previously represented the corporate defendants in legal matters that are substantially related to the present litigation.

---

[35] [2] The motion was filed 16 days after Baker & McKenzie filed their appearance. Therefore the motion was timely.

Plaintiffs' motion to disqualify the lawyers from the firm of Baker & McKenzie from representing the corporate defendants raises fundamental questions of legal ethics and the extent to which a court should interfere with the right of any litigant to be represented by counsel of his own choosing. Furthermore, a motion to disqualify calls to question not only the probity of the individual lawyer, but the legal profession as a whole. *See Hull v. Celanese Corp.*, 513 F.2d 568 (2d Cir. 1975). Mindful of these problems and considerations we have reached the conclusion that independent counsel must be selected for the defendant corporations.

In substance, the plaintiffs' complaint is a shareholder's derivative suit. While no treatise exposition on the nature of these suits is necessary here, a few pertinent observations will be helpful in analyzing the ultimate issue presented by the motion: whether the same counsel can represent both the individual and corporate defendants in a derivative shareholders suit consistent with the ethical standards promulgated by the American Bar Association and adopted by this court. A derivative suit is, in legal effect, a suit brought by the corporation, but conducted by the shareholders. The corporation, although formally aligned as a defendant for historical reasons, is in actuality a plaintiff. . . .

The stockholder's suit (has) . . . a double aspect. The stockholders have a right in equity to compel the assertion of a corporate right of action against the directors or other wrongdoers when the corporation wrongfully refuses to sue. The suit is thus an action for specific enforcement of an obligation owed by the corporation to the stockholders to assert its rights of action when the corporation has been put in default by the wrongful refusal of the directors or management to take suitable measures for its protection.

The preceding paragraph delineates the anomalous position of the corporation; it is both a defendant and a plaintiff. An examination of plaintiffs' complaint amply reveals this position. Count 1 alleges that beginning in 1968 and continuing to the present, the individual defendants committed numerous violations of Rule 10b-5: illegal stock options were allegedly granted, stock was issued and purchased upon false representations that the stock was for services, rent, and other expenses, stock was issued for little or no consideration, corporate opportunities were usurped, illegal profits were retained by certain officers and directors, and illegal and excessive compensation was paid to Stedman.

The remaining derivative counts allege the same misconduct but seek recovery under Section 16(b) of the Securities Exchange Act of 1934, 15 U.S.C. § 78p(b) (1970), and the common law of Florida and Illinois.

Even a cursory examination of the foregoing allegations demonstrates that should they be established at trial, Acoustics and Perlite will benefit substantially. For this reason plaintiffs argue that Mone, Gareis, and the firm of Baker & McKenzie cannot represent the alleged wrongdoers and the ultimate beneficiaries of any judgment that might be obtained.

Defendants' position is that although there is a theoretical conflict of interest, no real conflict exists. They argue that the corporations are really inactive participants in the lawsuit, and that should any conflict arise they will withdraw their representation of the individual defendants and continue their representation of the corporations. Defendants further argue that their present position is that all the transactions complained of are legal and should be upheld.

\* \* \*

When a single lawyer or law firm undertakes to represent both the individual and corporate defendants in a derivative action, at least two potential ethical problems arise. First, there exists, as previously discussed, a potential conflict of interest between the individual and corporate defendants, and second, there is the threat that confidences and secrets obtained from each client may be jeopardized because of the dual nature of the representation. The CPR addresses each of these problems in varying degrees of particularity. No code of ethics could establish unalterable rules governing all possible eventualities. Ultimately, therefore, the resolution of these problems rests in the reasoned discretion of the court.

\* \* \*

In the instant case Gareis, Mone and their firm represent two clients with, at a minimum, potentially conflicting interests. The pleadings charge the individual defendants with serious corporate misconduct, and although counsel has in good faith represented there is no present conflict between the two sets of defendants, the subtle influences emanating from the representation of the individual defendants that might lead counsel to reach this position on behalf of the corporations are troubling.

Fortunately there are several other ethical considerations that deal more specifically with multiple clients. EC5-18 provides:

> A lawyer employed or retained by a corporation or similar entity owes his allegiance to the entity and not to a stockholder, director, officer, employee, representative, or other person connected with the entity. In advising the entity, a lawyer should keep paramount its interests and his professional judgment should not be influenced by the personal desires of any person or organization. Occasionally a lawyer for an entity is requested by a stockholder, director, officer, employee, representative, or other person connected with the entity to represent him in an individual capacity; in such case the lawyer may serve the individual only if the lawyer is convinced that differing interests are not present.

Admittedly the focus of this consideration is on the problem of corporate counsel representing corporate officials when the corporation is not also a party litigant. But its import is clear. The interest of the corporate client is paramount and should not be influenced by any interest of the individual corporate officials.

Although EC5-18 is persuasive authority for plaintiffs' position, EC5-15 is even more so:

> If a lawyer is requested to undertake or to continue representation of multiple clients having potentially differing interests, he must weigh carefully the possibility that his judgment may be impaired or his loyalty divided if he accepts or continues the employment. He should resolve all doubts against the propriety of the representation. A lawyer should never

represent in litigation multiple clients with differing interests; and there are few situations in which he would be justified in representing in litigation multiple clients with potentially differing interests. If a lawyer accepted such employment and the interests did become actually differing, he would have to withdraw from employment with likelihood of resulting hardship to the client; and for this reason it is preferable that he refuse the employment initially.

Taken together, these two ethical considerations convincingly establish that in a derivative suit the better course is for the corporation to be represented by independent counsel from the outset, even though counsel believes in good faith that no conflict of interest exists.

[Maintaining the independence of professional judgment required of a lawyer precludes his acceptance or continuation of employment that will adversely affect his judgment on behalf of or dilute his loyalty to a client. This problem arises whenever a lawyer is asked to represent two or more clients who may have differing interests, whether such interests be conflicting, inconsistent, diverse, or otherwise discordant.

EC 5-16 provides that in some circumstances multiple representation may be permissible if both clients are fully informed of potential conflict and the parties consent to the representation. This consent rationale seems peculiarly inapplicable to a derivative suit, because the corporation must consent through the directors, who, as in the present case, are the individual defendants. *See* Opinion 842, Association of the City of New York Committee on Professional Ethics (Jan. 4, 1960), 15 Record N.Y.C.B.A. 80 (1960).]

The exact question presented by the plaintiffs' motion was considered by the influential Association of the Bar of New York Committee on Professional Ethics, in Opinion 842. The Committee is in full agreement that if the corporation takes an active role in the litigation, independent counsel must be obtained. If the corporation's role is passive, a majority of the committee was still of the opinion that,

> a conflict of interests is inherent in any (derivative) action wherever relief is sought on behalf of the corporation against the individual director-officer defendants, and in such cases Canon 6 (presently Canon 5, EC5-14 n. 6 & 18) precludes one firm from representing both the corporation and the individual director-officer defendants except in unusual circumstances stemming from particular facts in a given case.

\*       \*       \*

Although there is not a wealth of cases dealing with the problem of dual representation in derivative shareholder's suits, the position of the federal courts has developed along two lines. The older cases have refused to disqualify counsel, while the more recent trend is to require the corporation to obtain independent counsel. This trend has also manifested itself in a number of cases under the Labor-Management Reporting and Disclosure Act, 29 U.S.C. § 501 et seq., (1970).

\*       \*       \*

The leading lower court decision requiring selection of independent counsel is *Lewis v. Shaffer Stores Co.*, 218 F. Supp. 238 (S.D.N.Y. 1963). There, plaintiff stockholder filed a derivative action alleging many of the same transgressions as are pleaded in the present action. One firm entered an appearance and filed an answer on behalf of the directors and the corporate defendant. Plaintiffs filed a timely motion to disqualify the firm from representing the corporation, asking that it be represented by truly independent counsel who would answer the complaint to the end that plaintiffs be invited to prove their case for the benefit of the corporation.

The court held:

> The interests of the officer, director, and majority stockholder defendants in this action are clearly adverse, on the face of the complaint, to the interests of the stockholders . . . other than the defendants. I have no doubt that . . . the law firm) believe(s) in good faith that there is no merit to this action. Plaintiff, of course, vigorously contends to the contrary. The court cannot and should not attempt to pass upon the merits at this stage. Under all the circumstances, including the nature of the charges, and the vigor with which they are apparently being pressed and defended, I believe that it would be wise for the corporation to retain independent counsel, who have no previous connection with the corporation, to advise it as to the position it should take in this controversy. *See Garlen v. Green Mansions, Inc.*, 9 A.D. 2d 760, 193 N.Y.S. 2d 116 (1st Dept. 1959), *Marco v. Dulles, supra.* 218 F. Supp. at 239–40.

The *Lewis* approach is the most advisable. On the face of plaintiffs' complaint there is a conflict of interest. It is unwise to assess the merits of the case now. . . .

A result similar to *Lewis* was reached in Murphy v. Washington American League Base Ball Club, Inc., 116 U.S. App. D.C. 362, 324 F.2d 394, (1963). Plaintiff brought a shareholder's derivative suit to challenge certain salary increases voted by the board of directors substantially for their own benefit. The corporation, a nominal defendant in the suit, was represented by the same firm that represented the individual officer-director defendants. The court held that dual representation was not proper because if the charges had substance, counsel chosen to represent both the wrongdoer and beneficiary of any judgment would not be able to guide the litigation in the best interest of the corporation.

\* \* \*

In summary, this is a derivative shareholder action against four officer-directors and two corporations. The complaint alleges that certain directors misappropriated monies of the corporation and violated federal and state securities laws. These are serious charges. If they are proved, the corporations stand to gain substantially. The CPR unquestionably prohibits one lawyer from representing multiple clients when their interests are in conflict. The code goes so far as to say that if the clients' interests are potentially differing, the preferable course is for the lawyer to refuse the employment initially. In addition, at least one influential bar association has issued an opinion stating that dual representation is subject to conflicts of interest even when the corporation takes a passive role in the litigation. The case law on the question is not consistent; older cases hold dual representation is not improper, while more recent decisions hold that it is, both in derivative shareholder suits and in suits under 29 U.S.C. § 501 (1970).

As previously discussed the court is bound to apply the CPR to lawyers practicing before it. The code is clear that multiple representation is improper when the client's interests are adverse. Nevertheless, defendants' counsel argue there is no present conflict and should one arise they will withdraw their representation of the individual defendants and represent only the corporations. There are a number of problems with this solution. First, the complaint on its face establishes a conflict that cannot be ignored despite counsel's good faith representations. Second, counsel overlooks the hardship on the court and the parties if in the middle of this litigation new counsel must be obtained because a conflict arises. Lastly, although counsel offers to withdraw its representation of the individual defendants and remain counsel for the corporations if a conflict should arise, the appropriate course, as suggested by Lewis and Murphy, is for the corporation to retain independent counsel. Under this procedure, once counsel has examined the evidence, a decision can be made regarding the role the corporation will play in the litigation. This decision will be made without the possibility of any influence emanating from the representation of the individual defendants, and will also eliminate the potential problem of confidences and secrets reposed by the individual defendants being used adverse to their interests by former counsel should new counsel have had to have been selected under the approach suggested by defense counsel. This solution, concededly, is not without its disabilities.

\* \* \*

Two questions remain. The first is how new counsel should be selected. Plaintiffs urge the court to make the selection because the individual defendants still serve as the board of directors and thus will make the selection unless prevented from doing so. There is no precedent in the reported decisions to support plaintiffs' suggestion. In *Lewis*, the court specifically held the problem of selecting counsel was not insurmountable and allowed the board to select new counsel.

The defendant corporations may select their own counsel. Certainly new counsel will recognize their duty to represent solely the interests of the corporate entities. And should difficulties arise, the parties or counsel may apply to the court for additional relief.

The final question is whether the corporations' answer should be stricken and new pleadings filed. Although this relief was not specifically requested, it is implied in the motion to strike the appearance of the corporations' counsel. *See Lewis v. Shaffer Stores Company*, 218 F. Supp. 238, 240 (S.D.N.Y. 1963); *Teamsters v. Hoffa*, 242 F. Supp. 246, 257 (D.D.C. 1965). The answer filed on behalf of the corporate defendants will be stricken with leave to new counsel to refile within 20 days of this order.

In accord with the foregoing, plaintiffs' motion to strike the appearance of Gareis, Mone and the firm of Baker & McKenzie as counsel for defendants Acoustics and Perlite, is granted, and the answer of these defendants is stricken with leave to new counsel to answer anew within 20 days.

## 6. Attorney Client Privilege

### GARNER v. WOLFINBARGER
United States Court of Appeals, Fifth Circuit
430 F.2d 1093 (1970)

GODBOLD, J.

This case presents the important question of the availability to a corporation of the privilege against disclosure of communications between it and its attorney, when access to the communications is sought by stockholders of the corporation in litigation brought by them against the corporation charging the corporation and its officers with acts injurious to their interests as stockholders. Also we are asked to review the correctness of an order of the District Court transferring the case to another district.

Stockholders of First American Life Insurance Company of Alabama (FAL) brought, in the Northern District of Alabama, a class action alleging violations of the Securities Act of 1933, the Securities Exchange Act of 1934, SEC Rule 10(b)(5), the Investment Company Act of 1940, the Alabama Securities Act and common law fraud, seeking to recover the purchase price which they and others similarly situated paid for their stock in FAL. The defendants are FAL and various of its directors, officers and controlling persons. The plaintiffs also claim that FAL was itself damaged by alleged fraud in the purchase and sale of securities, and they assert against various individual defendants a derivative action on behalf of the corporation.

FAL filed a cross-claim against all other defendants, asserting in its own behalf the rights the plaintiff shareholders had claimed in the derivative aspect of their complaint.

R. Richard Schweitzer served as attorney for the corporation in connection with the issuance of the FAL stock here involved. After the transactions sued upon were complete he became its president. On deposition Schweitzer was asked numerous questions concerning advice given by him to the corporation about various aspects of the issuance and sale of the stock and related matters. Other questions went into the content of discussions at meetings attended by him and company officials and information furnished to him by the corporation. All questions related to times at which Schweitzer acted solely as attorney, before he became an officer of the company and before the filing of suit. Objections were made by counsel for the corporation and by Schweitzer himself that the attorney-client privilege barred his revealing both communications to him by the corporation and the advice which he gave to the corporation.

The objection is the client's to invoke, not the attorney's. Since FAL counsel objected we need not inquire into the effectiveness of Schweitzer's objection. The parties make no distinction between the client's communications to the attorney and the attorney's communications to the client, and it is not necessary that we do so.

\*    \*    \*

Turning to the merits, there is no contention by plaintiffs that FAL is outside the ambit of the attorney-client privilege because a corporation is not a client.[36] Their argument is that the privilege is not available to FAL in the circumstances of this case against the demands of the corporate stockholders for access to the communications. The corporation says that its right to assert the privilege is absolute and of special importance where disclosure is sought in a suit brought by the shareholders against the corporation. The American Bar Association appears as amicus curiae and supports the view of an absolute privilege.

The privilege does not arise from the position of the corporation as a party but its status as a client. However, in this instance plaintiffs deny the availability to the corporation of the otherwise existent privilege because of the role of the corporation as a party defending against claims of its stockholders.

We do not consider the privilege to be so inflexibly absolute as contended by the corporation, nor to be so totally unavailable against the stockholders as thought by the District Court. We conclude that the correct rule is between these two extreme positions.

The availability *vel non* of the privilege involves a complex problem of choice of law. 2B Barron & Holtzoff, Federal Practice & Procedure, 967 at 241–44 (Wright ed. 1961). The order of the District Court appears to treat Alabama standards as controlling. We conclude that the choice of law cannot be settled by reference to any simple talisman, but can be arrived at only after a consideration of state and federal interests that are inseparable from the factors bearing on the availability of the privilege itself.

*   *   *

The privilege must be placed in perspective. The beginning point is the fundamental principle that the public has the right to every man's evidence, and exemptions from the general duty to give testimony that one is capable of giving are distinctly exceptional. 8 Wigmore, Evidence, § 2192 at 70. An exception is justified if — and only if — policy requires it be recognized when measured against the fundamental responsibility of every person to give testimony. *Id.*, § 2285 at 527. Professor Wigmore describes four conditions, the existence of all of which is prerequisite to the establishment of a privilege of any kind against the disclosure of communications:

§ 2285. General principle of privileged communications.

Looking back upon the principle of privilege, as an exception to the general liability of every person to give testimony upon all facts inquired of in a court of justice, and keeping in view that preponderance of extrinsic policy

---

[36] [10] Numerous cases sustain the proposition that a corporation is a client for the purpose of invoking the privilege. *E.g., United States v. Louisville & N. R.R.*, 236 U.S. 318, 35 S. Ct. 363, 59 L.Ed. 598 (1915); *Schwimmer v. United States*, 232 F.2d 855 (8th Cir.), *cert. denied*, 352 U.S. 833, 77 S. Ct. 48, 1 L. Ed. 2d 52 (1956); *Belanger v. Alton Box Board Co.*, 180 F.2d 87 (7th Cir. 1950). A decision to the contrary, *Radiant Burners, Inc. v. American Gas Ass'n*, 207 F. Supp. 771 (N.D. Ill. 1962) was reversed by the Seventh Circuit, 320 F.2d 314 (7th Cir.), *cert. denied*, 375 U.S. 929, 84 S. Ct. 330, 11 L. Ed. 2d 262 (1963).

which alone can justify the recognition of any such exception (§§ 2192 and 2197 supra), four fundamental conditions are recognized as necessary to the establishment of a privilege against the disclosure of communications:

(1) The communications must originate in a confidence that they will not be disclosed.

(2) This element of confidentiality must be essential to the full and satisfactory maintenance of the relation between the parties.

(3) The relation must be one which in the opinion of the community ought to be sedulously fostered.

(4) The injury that would inure to the relation by the disclosure of the communications must be greater than the benefit thereby gained for the correct disposal of litigation.

Only if these four conditions are present should a privilege be recognized.

And he points out that in the case of communications between attorney and client all four conditions are present, with the only condition open to dispute being the fourth. As to this particular type of privileged communication:

. . . the privilege remains an exception to the general duty to disclose. Its benefits are all indirect and speculative; its obstruction is plain and concrete . . . . It is worth preserving for the sake of a general policy, but is nonetheless an obstacle to the investigation of the truth. It ought to be strictly confined within the narrowest possible limits, consistent with the logic of its principle.

The policy of the privilege has been plainly grounded since the latter part of the 1700s on subjective considerations. In order to promote freedom of consultation of legal advisers by clients, the apprehension of compelled disclosure by the legal advisers must be removed; hence the law must prohibit such disclosure except on the client's consent. Such is the modern theory.

The problem before us concerns Wigmore's fourth condition, a balancing of interests between injury resulting from disclosure and the benefit gained in the correct disposal of litigation. We consider it in a particularized context: where the client asserting the privilege is an entity which in the performance of its functions acts wholly or partly in the interests of others, and those others, or some of them, seek access to the subject matter of the communications.

It is urged that disclosure is injurious to both the corporation and the attorney. Corporate management must manage. It has the duty to do so and requires the tools to do so. Part of the managerial task is to seek legal counsel when desirable, and, obviously, management prefers that it confer with counsel without the risk of having the communications revealed at the instance of one or more dissatisfied stockholders. The managerial preference is a rational one, because it is difficult to envision the management of any sizeable corporation pleasing all of its stockholders all of the time, and management desires protection from those who might second-guess or even harass in matters purely of judgment.

But in assessing management assertions of injury to the corporation it must be borne in mind that management does not manage for itself and that the beneficiaries of its action are the stockholders. Conceptualistic phrases describing the corporation as an entity separate from its stockholders are not useful tools of analysis. They serve only to obscure the fact that management has duties which run to the benefit ultimately of the stockholders. For example, it is difficult to rationally defend the assertion of the privilege if all, or substantially all, stockholders desire to inquire into the attorney's communications with corporate representatives who have only nominal ownership interests, or even none at all. There may be reasonable differences over the manner of characterizing in legal terminology the duties of management, and over the extent to which corporate management is less of a fiduciary than the common law trustee. There may be many situations in which the corporate entity or its management, or both, have interests adverse to those of some or all stockholders. But when all is said and done management is not managing for itself.

The representative and the represented have a mutuality of interest in the representative's freely seeking advice when needed and putting it to use when received. This is not to say that management does not have allowable judgment in putting advice to use. But management judgment must stand on its merits, not behind an ironclad veil of secrecy which under all circumstances preserves it from being questioned by those for whom it is, at least in part, exercised.

\*    \*    \*

The ABA urges that the privilege is most necessary where the corporation has sought advice about a prospective transaction, where counsel in good faith has stated his opinion that it is not lawful, but the corporation has proceeded in total or partial disregard of counsel's advice. The ABA urges that the cause of justice requires that counsel be free to state his opinion as fully and forthrightly as possible without fear of later disclosure to persons who might attack the transaction, and that without the cloak of the privilege counsel may be "required by the threat of future discovery to hedge or soften their opinions."

\*    \*    \*

Two traditional exceptions are also persuasive in negativing any absolute privilege in a corporation in the circumstances of this case. These are the exceptions for communications in contemplation of a crime or fraud, and for communications to a joint attorney.

Communications made by a client to his attorney during or before the commission of a crime or fraud for the purpose of being guided or assisted in its commission are not privileged. The stockholders claim to have been the victims of improprieties in the issuance and sale of FAL's stock. The questions, and the documents sought, concerned those alleged improprieties, with particular regard to whether the attorney advised the corporation that proposals it had in mind were not legal and that statements to be put in its prospectus were misleading.

The plaintiffs say that some of the matter claimed to be privileged concerned prospective criminal transactions, including issuance by FAL of a misleading prospectus, the circulation of which it is said was a criminal offense under federal securities law, and the granting of options (allegedly as bribes) for securing state registrations of FAL's stock and of its broker-dealer and salesmen. In considering the interplay of interest of management, of stockholders, and of the lawsuit, it must be recognized that management has an obligation to the corporation, to the stockholders and to the public to do what is lawful. But we do not consider unavailability of the privilege to be confined to the narrow ground of prospective criminal transactions. The differences between prospective crime and prospective action of questionable legality, or prospective fraud, are differences of degree, not of principle.

\*   \*   \*

In summary, we say this. The attorney-client privilege still has viability for the corporate client. The corporation is not barred from asserting it merely because those demanding information enjoy the status of stockholders. But where the corporation is in suit against its stockholders on charges of acting inimically to stockholder interests, protection of those interests as well as those of the corporation and of the public require that the availability of the privilege be subject to the right of the stockholders to show cause why it should not be invoked in the particular instance.

There are many indicia that may contribute to a decision of presence or absence of good cause, among them the number of shareholders and the percentage of stock they represent; the bona fides of the shareholders; the nature of the shareholders' claim and whether it is obviously colorable; the apparent necessity or desirability of the shareholders having the information and the availability of it from other sources; whether, if the shareholders' claim is of wrongful action by the corporation, it is of action criminal, or illegal but not criminal, or of doubtful legality; whether the communication related to past or to prospective actions; whether the communication is of advice concerning the litigation itself; the extent to which the communication is identified versus the extent to which the shareholders are blindly fishing; the risk of revelation of trade secrets or other information in whose confidentiality the corporation has an interest for independent reasons. The court can freely use in camera inspection or oral examination and freely avail itself of protective orders, a familiar device to preserve confidentiality in trade secret and other cases where the impact of revelation may be as great as in revealing a communication with counsel.

The order relating to availability of the attorney-client privilege is vacated. The cause is remanded for further proceedings not inconsistent with this opinion.

## PROBLEM 14.2

You are the general counsel to Gigantic Corp. Its President, Mr. Gee, asks your advice about his plan to avoid a tender offer. He will propose to the board of directors that a special dividend will be paid to all of the existing shareholders. The corporation does not have the funds to pay the dividend but can borrow the necessary amount. He is of the belief that loading the corporation with debt will make it unattractive as a target. He also tells you that he is worried whether the corporation can make payments on the new debt without having to file for bankruptcy in the near future. Also, he expresses some doubt about the accuracy of the corporation's balance sheet. He tells you that he believes that some assets are overvalued and that he has not pointed this out to the auditors because it would only cause trouble. You advise him against his plan pointing out the obvious risks. You also point out that under the law of the state of incorporation payment of a dividend that results in insolvency will make him personally liable. He replies that he is not concerned with personal liability because he has substantial off-shore accounts. The board of directors adopts Mr. Gee's plan in spite of your advice. Within three months, the corporation files for Chapter 7 bankruptcy. Mr. Gee then comes to you and asks whether you can be compelled to testify as to his conversations with you. What do you tell him?

## E.  ATTORNEY FEES

### TANDYCRAFTS, INC. v. INITIO PARTNERS
Supreme Court of Delaware
562 A.2d 1162 (1989)

WALSH, J.

This is an appeal from a Court of Chancery decision which awarded counsel fees to a plaintiff shareholder who voluntarily dismissed an individual action against a corporation and its directors after certain corrective action was taken by the corporation during a proxy contest. The Court of Chancery determined that the litigation, although moot, conferred a significant benefit upon all shareholders and granted plaintiff's application for fees in the amount of $180,000. The corporation asserts that the Vice Chancellor abused his discretion in awarding counsel fees for litigation which conferred no benefit on the corporation. It is also asserted that, since plaintiff did not purport to sue derivatively or on behalf of a class, plaintiff is not entitled to an award of counsel fees.

We hold that, under certain circumstances, counsel fees may be awarded to an individual shareholder whose litigation effort confers a benefit upon the corporation, or its shareholders, notwithstanding the absence of a class or derivative component. We further conclude that, under the circumstances of this case, the Court of Chancery did not abuse its discretion in making an award of counsel fees to an individual shareholder or in fixing the amount of the award.

Plaintiff, Initio Partners ("Initio"), a limited partnership, was, at the time of the commencement of this litigation, the largest single independent shareholder of Tandycrafts, Inc. ("Tandycrafts"), owning approximately 9.9% of the company's common stock. In the spring of 1986 Initio approached Tandycrafts' management with the prospect of Initio acquiring a larger, and perhaps controlling, interest in the company through a cooperative effort between the parties. Apparently, this approach was rebuffed and Tandycrafts' management determined to place before its shareholders, for consideration at its next annual meeting, two charter amendments which would limit any future takeover effort. The effect of the proposed amendment was to impose an 80% supermajority voting requirement for takeover proposals made without director approval.

On October 27, 1986, Initio filed a complaint in the Court of Chancery which sought a preliminary injunction to enjoin the holding of Tandycrafts' annual meeting, scheduled for November 12, 1986. The complaint alleged that the proxy material issued in connection with the proposed charter amendments was materially misleading. . . .

In addition to seeking injunctive relief, Initio also launched its own proxy campaign in which it sought to counter what it viewed as distortions in Tandycrafts' proxy material. In the meantime, while discovery was proceeding on an expedited basis, Tandycrafts prepared and distributed to its shareholders a supplement to its proxy statement. This supplemental statement, dated November 1, 1986, disclosed the combined holdings of the employee benefit plans and the management controlled shares. It also clarified the proposed amendments' limitation on the participation of an "Interested Stockholder" and an "Interested Officer."

In ruling on Initio's request for a preliminary injunction, the Vice Chancellor noted the corrective action taken by Tandycrafts through the Supplemental Proxy Statement. While acknowledging Initio's continued objection to the proxy material as modified, and after finding that the proxy material "could be clearer," the court ruled that the proxy material provided sufficient information on matters deemed important to shareholders. Injunctive relief was accordingly denied and the annual meeting ensued as scheduled. At the meeting, the proposed charter amendments were soundly defeated.

In the light of the defeat of the proposed charter amendments and viewing the litigation as moot, Initio filed a motion to dismiss the action together with an application for attorneys' fees and expenses, in the amount of $180,000, to be assessed against Tandycrafts. Tandycrafts vigorously opposed the request for counsel fees, contending that its action in making "technical corrective changes" in its proxy material was not attributable to Initio's litigation and that such corrections would have been made regardless of whether Initio, or any other shareholder, had sought such clarification. . . .

On appeal, Tandycrafts, in addition to disputing the reasonableness of the fees sought by Initio, argues that the Vice Chancellor erred in his implicit finding that a party suing directly for his own benefit, and not on behalf of a class or derivatively, is entitled to an award of counsel fees against the corporation. The latter issue poses a question of first impression in this Court.

The standards which control the award of counsel fees in shareholder litigation in the Court of Chancery have become fairly well established. The starting principle is recognition of the so-called American Rule, under which a prevailing party is responsible for the payment of his own counsel fees in the absence of statutory authority or contractual undertaking to the contrary.

\* \* \*

In the realm of corporate litigation, the Court may order the payment of counsel fees and related expenses to a plaintiff whose efforts result in the creation of a common fund, or the conferring of a corporate benefit. Typically, successful derivative or class action suits which result in the recovery of money or property wrongfully diverted from the corporation, or which result in the imposition of changes in internal operating procedures that are designed to produce such monetary savings in the future, are viewed as fund creating actions.

The definition of a corporate benefit, however, is much more elastic. While the benefit achieved may have an indirect economic effect on the corporation, in the sense that the interests of the plaintiff class reflect a value not theretofore apparent, the benefit need not be measurable in economic terms. Changes in corporate policy or, as here, a heightened level of corporate disclosure, if attributable to the filing of a meritorious suit, may justify an award of counsel fees.

\*   \*   \*

Tandycrafts' claim that an award of counsel fees to an individual shareholder is unprecedented under Delaware decisional law is correct in the sense that it appears that neither this Court nor the Court of Chancery has precisely so held. But a close reading of the Court of Chancery decision in *Baron v. Allied Artists Pictures Corp.*, Del. Ch., 395 A.2d 375 (1978), *aff'd.* Del. Supr., 413 A.2d 876 (1980), indicates that the plaintiff in that action sued as an individual stockholder challenging the election of directors under 8 Del. C. §§ 225 and 227. Id. at 383 n. The corporation and the director defendants did not raise the plaintiff's individual status as a bar to the counsel fee application. The Court of Chancery, while noting plaintiff's individual stance, nonetheless proceeded to apply the standards which govern fee awards in derivative actions. On appeal, this Court, in affirming the award of counsel fees, noted that the claimed benefit to the corporation was to be measured at the time of the filing of the action even though the suit was mooted by a later event, a corporate merger, which arguably produced the benefit independent of the litigation.

\*   \*   \*

Although this Court has not adopted an expansive approach to fee shifting in corporate litigation, the critical inquiry is not the status of the plaintiff but the nature of the corporate or class benefit which is causally related to the filing of suit. It is to be expected that litigation to force compliance with fiduciary standards or statutory duties will be initiated by a shareholder who has standing to sue for the benefit of the corporation. For the most part, such claims are clearly derivative, or class based. But where the shareholder's individual interests are directly and equally implicated, as in proxy contests, the distinction between individual and representative claims may become blurred. Indeed, the same wrong may give rise to both an individual and derivative action. . . .

The standard which governs the allowance of counsel fees in equity is not inclusive of all occasions when such fees may be sought. The concept is a flexible one based on the historic power of the Court of Chancery to do equity in particular situations. *Maurer v. Int'l Re-Insurance Corp.*, 95 A.2d at 831. If, as here, the shareholder commences an individual action with consequential benefit for all other members of a class, or for the corporation itself, there is no justification for denying recourse to the fee shifting standard which has evolved for the therapeutic purpose of rewarding individual effort which flows to a class. We believe the better reasoned approach to be that there is no class action or derivative suit prerequisite to an award of attorneys' fees under the common benefit exception. *See Reiser v. Del Monte Properties Co.*, 9th Cir., 605 F.2d 1135, 1139 (1979). We adopt the reasoning in *Reiser* that the "[i]mposition of a class action requirement would be inconsistent with the equitable foundations of the common benefit exception. . . . The form of suit is not a deciding factor; rather, the question to be determined is whether a plaintiff, in bringing a suit either individually or representatively, has conferred a benefit on others." *Id.* at 1139–40.

Tandycrafts also contends that permitting an individual plaintiff to seek the allowance of counsel fees creates the potential for abuse since such an individual will have initiated litigation without compliance with the demand requirements of Court of Chancery Rule 23.1, or without the usual class obligations assumed in a representative capacity. This concern is legitimate. An individual plaintiff may not seek to circumvent the standards which restrict the pursuit of derivative or class suits. These requirements are more than mere formalities of litigation but strictures of substantive law. While compliance is the norm, situations may arise, particularly in rapidly evolving contests for corporate control, including, as here, proxy contests, in which challenged transactions may become moot or superceded before appropriate demand can be made with any realistic hope of corrective action being taken by incumbent management. An individual shareholder in such circumstances is not foreclosed from commencement of an individual action to implement his right to informed participation in the corporate election process.

In the final analysis, however, the concern that individual plaintiffs may abuse the pre-suit and representative requirements and thereafter seek an award of counsel fees is offset by the plenary power of the Court of Chancery over the allowance of such fees. In this respect, an individual plaintiff is subject to essentially the same review process as would a derivative plaintiff who seeks the allowance of counsel fees incident to court approval of a derivative action pursuant to Court of Chancery Rule 23.1. . . .

Having concluded that, under these circumstances, Initio had standing to seek an award of counsel fees as an individual plaintiff, we summarily address Tandycrafts' claim that the Vice Chancellor abused his discretion in the fee allowance. The sequence of events is not in dispute and the correction or clarification of the proxy material chronologically followed the filing of the Initio suit attacking the accuracy of the material. It was thus incumbent upon Tandycrafts to demonstrate that there was no causal connection between the suit and the subsequent action. *See McDonnell Douglas Corp. v. Palley*, Del. Supr., 310 A.2d 635, 637 (1973). Although Tandycrafts argues that the corrective action would have been taken in any event, we are not persuaded that the Vice Chancellor abused his discretion in ruling to the contrary.

With respect to the amount of the fees allowed, the Vice Chancellor noted that Tandycrafts was "not seriously challenging the amount requested." In this Court, however, Tandycrafts mounts an attack on the amount of the allowance arguing that "the clarifying disclosures, while perhaps helpful, were not worth $180,000." Initio requested counsel fees of $180,000 plus $3,026.66 in expenses, an amount calculated by using accumulated hourly rates of Initio's counsel as the "lodestar" and applying a multiplier of 1.9 times.[37] As noted, the Vice Chancellor was apparently under the

---

[37] [1] A fee allowance based upon a time factor lodestar formulated in *Lindy Bros. Builders, Inc. of*

impression that the basis for the fee was not at issue, merely the entitlement to any award. In the absence of any finding validating the "lodestar" and multiplier components of the fee application we are unable to review the appropriateness of those elements. To the extent that on appeal Tandycrafts is seeking a proportionate reduction of the fee allowance based on an "other causes" contention, and given the limited scope of our review, we perceive of no basis in this record to disturb the conclusion of the Vice Chancellor awarding the full amount sought by Initio.

The decision of the Court of Chancery is affirmed.

## NOTE

The lodestar method starts with the hours worked by the attorney at her normal billable rate. A multiplier is then applied based on the risk involved in the case and the quality of the work done. Does this method tend to increase the hours spent working on the case? Is there any disincentive to an early settlement?

## F.  INDEMNIFICATION

### WASITOWSKI v. PALI HOLDINGS, INC.
United States District Court, Southern District of New York
2010 U.S. Dist. LEXIS 37802 (Apr. 7, 2010)

CASTEL, J.

Plaintiff David Wasitowski, a former director and officer of defendant Pali Holdings, Inc. ("Pali," or "the Company"), incurred more than $580,000 in legal fees in a state-court civil proceeding in which both he and Pali were defendants. Although it is not mentioned in the Complaint, the trial court denied a motion by Wasitowski seeking an order for the advancement of legal fees by Pali. Wasitowski now asserts that Pali is required to indemnify him pursuant to the New York Business Corporation Law (the "BCL") and Pali's own bylaws. Pali moves to dismiss or stay the action pursuant to Rules 12(b)(1) and 12(b)(6), Fed. R. Civ. P., and Wasitowski moves for summary judgment pursuant to Rule 56, Fed. R. Civ. P.

For the reasons explained below, the defendant's motion to dismiss is granted, the plaintiff's motion is denied, and the Complaint is dismissed.

### BACKGROUND

Plaintiff, a citizen of New Jersey, resigned as an officer and director of Pali in November 2008. Pali is organized under the laws of New York, where it also maintains its principal place of business. In June 2009, certain of Pali's shareholders commenced a proceeding [the "Berk Proceeding"] in the Supreme Court of the

---

*Phila. v. American Radiator and Standard Corp.*, 3d Cir., 487 F.2d 161 (1973), has not supplanted the multiple factors criteria including the nature of the benefit, the complexity of the litigation and the time, effort and skill of counsel. *Sugarland Industries, Inc. v. Thomas*, Del. Supr., 420 A.2d 142, 150 (1980).

State of New York. The Berk Proceeding arose under Article 78 of the New York Civil Practice Law and Rules. Broadly summarized, petitioners in the Berk Proceeding were Pali shareholders who alleged that Pali's board members, including Wasitowski, unlawfully pursued a scheme to dilute shareholder voting power in order to maintain their control over the Company.

Both Wasitowski and Pali were respondents in the Berk Proceeding. Wasitowski was named in his capacity as officer and director, and was not sued in his individual capacity. In an order dated July 27, 2009, the New York Supreme Court granted Wasitowski's motion to dismiss the petition's claims against him. No appeal was taken, and the order is final. During the Berk Proceeding, Wasitowski paid his own defense costs, which, by August 31, 2009, totaled $581,135.85.

According to the Complaint, pursuant to BCL § 723(a), a corporate officer or director is entitled to indemnification when he or she "has been successful, on the merits or otherwise, in the defense of a civil or criminal action or proceeding," provided that the individual has suffered no adverse judgment or finding of wrongdoing or bad faith. The plaintiff contends that his dismissal from the Berk Proceeding requires Pali to indemnify him for all costs incurred in that litigation. In addition, Pali's bylaws require indemnification to the "full extent permissible" under New York law.

According to the parties' submissions, legal proceedings involving Wasitowski and Pali remain ongoing. In addition to the Berk Proceeding, a subsidiary of Pali commenced a pending FINRA arbitration against Wasitowski and another former Pali officer for breach of fiduciary duty and abuse of control. Wasitowski also filed an application in the Berk Proceeding for advancement of legal fees, in a motion captioned as an order to show cause on a "Motion for Indemnification Pendente Lite." Justice Eileen Bransten denied Wasitowski's motion, holding that his dismissal did not preclude his "potential liability" and noting that "allegations of misconduct" against him remained unresolved.

\* \* \*

The BCL establishes a statutory framework for a corporation's indemnification of officers and directors, whether made voluntarily or by court order. I begin by discussing the BCL sections governing a corporation's voluntary indemnification. BCL § 722(c) states that a corporation may authorize indemnification if a "director or officer acted, in good faith, for a purpose which he reasonably believed to be in . . . the best interests of the corporation . . . ." Sections 722 "permits but does not require" a corporation's bylaws to provide for director and officer indemnification. Section 723 establishes the procedures by which shareholders or boards of directors may elect to provide indemnification. Although the text of section 722(a) is phrased permissively ("may"), BCL § 723(a) states that "[a] person who has been successful, on the merits or otherwise, in the defense of a civil or criminal action or proceeding of the character described in section 722 shall be entitled to indemnification as authorized in such section" (emphasis added). Thus, if a corporation provides for indemnification to its directors and officers consistent with section 722, section 723 binds the corporation to its promise to indemnify. *See Sequa Corp.*, 828 F. Supp. at 205 ("Quite apart from the corporation's bylaws, BCL § 723(a) mandates indemnification of officers or directors by the corporation if such individuals succeed defending against the kind of action covered by § 722."). Here, Pali's bylaws provide for voluntary indemnification to directors and officers.

Section 724 of the BCL establishes the procedures for court-ordered indemnification. In *Qantel Corp. v. Niemuller*, 771 F. Supp. 1372, 1374 (S.D.N.Y. 1991), Judge Leisure observed that sections 722 and 723 "merely permit the indemnification of directors and officers," while "[s]ection 724, in contrast, specifies the standards and procedures by which a court may order such indemnification under the BCL." (emphasis in original); *see also Brittania 54 Hotel Corp. v. Freid*, 251 A.D. 2d 49, 49, 673 N.Y.S.2d 668 (1st Dep't 1998) ("When a corporation declines to afford indemnification pursuant to Business Corporation Law § 722, the officer may apply to the court, which may direct that such payments be made 'if the court shall find that the defendant has by his pleadings or during the course of the litigation raised genuine issues of fact or law.' " (*quoting* BCL § 724(c)); *Mercado v. Coes FX. Inc.*, 12 Misc. 3d 766, 815 N.Y.S. 2d 806, 807 (N.Y. Sup. Ct. Nassau Cty 2006) ("[U]nder BCL § 724(c), courts are authorized to order indemnification of present or former corporate directors against litigation expenses, notwithstanding the corporation's refusal to do so.").

In applying section 724, the statute's "design is to authorize indemnification by judicial action to the full extent, subject to the same standards and qualifications where applicable as in the case of voluntary corporate indemnification." BCL § 724 cmt. (McKinney 2003). The relevant portions of section 724 state as follows:

> (a) Notwithstanding the failure of a corporation to provide indemnification, and despite any contrary resolution of the board or of the shareholders in the specific case under section 723 (Payment of indemnification other than by court award), indemnification shall be awarded by a court to the extent authorized under section 722 (Authorization for indemnification of directors and officers), and paragraph (a) of section 723. Application therefore may be made, in every case, either:
>
> (1) In the civil action or proceeding in which the expenses were incurred or other amounts were paid, or
>
> (2) To the supreme court in a separate proceeding, in which case the application shall set forth the disposition of any previous application made to any court for the same or similar relief and also reasonable cause for the failure to make application for such relief in the action or proceeding in which the expenses were incurred or other amounts were paid.

Thus, under section 724(a), a director or officer claiming indemnification may pursue one of two avenues for relief: 1.) application to the court presiding over the underlying proceeding, or 2.) commencing a separate proceeding, in which case, the applicant must set forth "reasonable cause" for any "failure" to seek indemnification as part of the underlying proceeding.

According to Pali, the Complaint should be dismissed because the plaintiff has not set forth "reasonable cause" for his "failure" to pursue indemnification in the underlying proceeding. See BCL § 724(a)(2). In opposition, Wasitowski argues that the motion should be denied because section 724 is not the only means to pursue court-ordered indemnification. That interpretation of section 724 is erroneous. . . .

The text of section 724(a)(2) unambiguously requires that a party seeking indemnification in a separate action must set forth "reasonable cause" as to why it did not raise the purported entitlement to indemnification in the underlying proceeding. When read jointly, sections 724(a)(1) and (a)(2) work to encourage a party seeking indemnification to raise the application as part of the original underlying case. For reasons of efficiency and judicial economy, this approach makes good sense: the court presiding over the underlying proceeding has familiarity with the director or officer's role in the action, and is best positioned to determine, pursuant to BCL § 722(c), whether the director or officer acted "in good faith" for a purpose he "reasonably believed" to be in "the best interests of the corporation," with "no reasonable cause to believe that his conduct was unlawful." *See generally Buffalo Forge Co. v. Ogden Corp.*, 595 F. Supp. 593 (W.D.N.Y. 1984) (ruling on timeliness, necessity and reasonableness of section 724 indemnification application brought after entry of judgment in that same court). For instance, in this case, the court presiding over the Berk Proceeding already has considered and rejected plaintiff's application for advancement of legal fees.

By contrast, a court entertaining a separate action for indemnification must familiarize itself with the facts and procedural history of the underlying case, potentially sitting in judgment of events that were, in the recent past, actively litigated before another tribunal. Perhaps this explains, at least in part, why section 724(a)(2) requires a showing of "reasonable cause for the failure" to raise indemnification in the underlying action, and why the action in which the fees were incurred is the statute's default tribunal for seeking indemnification. The plaintiff has not set forth a viable basis for the Court to ignore the "reasonable cause" requirement. The statute unambiguously requires this extra step as part of any indemnification application brought in a proceeding separate from the underlying action. Plaintiff's failure to allege "reasonable cause" warrants dismissal of the Complaint.

Plaintiff's other arguments for denying the motion are, to put it charitably, unpersuasive.

\* \* \*

[H]e asserts that the "reasonable cause" requirement applies only to a plaintiff already denied indemnification in the underlying action. This flatly misreads section 724(a)(2), which requires a party to set forth disposition of the underlying case "and also" reasonable cause for not seeking indemnification therein (emphasis added). Moreover, the court in the underlying proceeding unambiguously denied plaintiff's motion captioned "Motion for Indemnification Pendente Lite." The plaintiff's failure to set forth his application made to any court for . . . similar relief is yet another instance of noncompliance with BCL § 724(a)(2).

Third, plaintiff contends that enforcing the "reasonable cause" requirement amounts to a limitation on federal jurisdiction dictated by the New York legislature. This baseless argument overlooks the allegations of plaintiff's own Complaint, which seeks relief under the BCL. Further, under the plaintiff's novel approach to federalism and Article III, a federal court would be free to disregard any limiting language in a state statute as a purported affront to federal jurisdiction. The argument impliedly invites the court to disregard the long-accepted holding of *Erie*, 304 U.S. 64, and is without merit.

*   *   *

Because I conclude that the plaintiff has failed to state a claim for relief under the relevant provisions of the BCL, I need not reach the other arguments raised in the defendant's motion. The motion to dismiss is granted and the plaintiff's motion for summary judgment is denied.

<h2 style="text-align:center">WALTUCH v. CONTICOMMODITY SERVICES, INC.</h2>
United States Court of Appeals, Second Circuit<br>88 F.3d 87 (1996)

Jacobs, J.

Famed silver trader Norton Waltuch spent $2.2 million in unreimbursed legal fees to defend himself against numerous civil lawsuits and an enforcement proceeding brought by the Commodity Futures Trading Commission (CFTC). In this action under Delaware law, Waltuch seeks indemnification of his legal expenses from his former employer. The district court denied any indemnity, and Waltuch appeals.

As vice-president and chief metals trader for Conticommodity Services, Inc., Waltuch traded silver for the firm's clients, as well as for his own account. In late 1979 and early 1980, the silver price spiked upward as the then-billionaire Hunt brothers and several of Waltuch's foreign clients bought huge quantities of silver futures contracts. Just as rapidly, the price fell until (on a day remembered in trading circles as "Silver Thursday") the silver market crashed. Between 1981 and 1985, angry silver speculators filed numerous lawsuits against Waltuch and Conticommodity, alleging fraud, market manipulation, and antitrust violations. All of the suits eventually settled and were dismissed with prejudice, pursuant to settlements in which Conticommodity paid over $35 million to the various suitors. Waltuch himself was dismissed from the suits with no settlement contribution. His unreimbursed legal expenses in these actions total approximately $1.2 million.

Waltuch was also the subject of an enforcement proceeding brought by the CFTC, charging him with fraud and market manipulation. The proceeding was settled, with Waltuch agreeing to a penalty that included a $100,000 fine and a six-month ban on buying or selling futures contracts from any exchange floor. Waltuch spent $1 million in unreimbursed legal fees in the CFTC proceeding.

Waltuch brought suit in the United States District Court for the Southern District of New York (Lasker, J.) against Conticommodity and its parent company, Continental Grain Co. (together "Conti"), for indemnification of his unreimbursed expenses. Only two of Waltuch's claims reach us on appeal.

Waltuch first claims that Article Ninth of Conticommodity's articles of incorporation requires Conti to indemnify him for his expenses in both the private and CFTC actions. Conti responds that this claim is barred by subsection (a) of § 145 of

Delaware's General Corporation Law, which permits indemnification only if the corporate officer acted "in good faith," something that Waltuch has not established. Waltuch counters that subsection (f) of the same statute permits a corporation to grant indemnification rights outside the limits of subsection (a), and that Conticommodity did so with Article Ninth (which has no stated good-faith limitation). The district court held that, notwithstanding § 145(f), Waltuch could recover under Article Ninth only if Waltuch met the "good faith" requirement of § 145(a).[38] [*Watltuch v. Conticommodity Services, Inc.*,] 833 F. Supp. 302, 308–09 (S.D.N.Y. 1993). On the factual issue of whether Waltuch had acted "in good faith," the court denied Conti's summary judgment motion and cleared the way for trial. *Id.* at 313. The parties then stipulated that they would forgo trial on the issue of Waltuch's "good faith," agree to an entry of final judgment against Waltuch on his claim under Article Ninth and § 145(f), and allow Waltuch to take an immediate appeal of the judgment to this Court. Thus, as to Waltuch's first claim, the only question left is how to interpret §§ 145(a) and 145(f), assuming Waltuch acted with less than "good faith." As we explain in part I below, we affirm the district court's judgment as to this claim and hold that § 145(f) does not permit a corporation to bypass the "good faith" requirement of § 145(a).

Waltuch's second claim is that subsection (c) of § 145 requires Conti to indemnify him because he was "successful on the merits or otherwise" in the private lawsuits.[39] The district court ruled for Conti on this claim as well. The court explained that, even though all the suits against Waltuch were dismissed without his making any payment, he was not "successful on the merits or otherwise," because Conti's settlement payments to the plaintiffs were partially on Waltuch's behalf. *Id.* at 311. For the reasons stated in part II below, we reverse this portion of the district court's ruling, and hold that Conti must indemnify Waltuch under § 145(c) for the $1.2 million in unreimbursed legal fees he spent in defending the private lawsuits.

I

Article Ninth, on which Waltuch bases his first claim, is categorical and contains no requirement of "good faith":

> The Corporation shall indemnify and hold harmless each of its incumbent or former directors, officers, employees and agents . . . against expenses actually and necessarily incurred by him in connection with the defense of any action, suit or proceeding threatened, pending or completed, in which he is made a party, by reason of his serving in or having held such position

---

[38] [3] A Special Committee of Continental Grain Co.'s Board of Directors reached the same conclusion in November 1991. Waltuch filed his complaint two months later. In the district court, Conti argued that under the business judgment rule, the Special Committee's decision was immune from challenge, an argument the district court rejected. 833 F. Supp. at 305. Although the parties signed a stipulation preserving Conti's right to contest the district court's ruling on this issue, Conti has abandoned its business judgment rule argument on appeal.

[39] [4] The district court held that Waltuch was not successful "on the merits or otherwise" in the CFTC proceeding. 833 F. Supp. at 311. Waltuch does not appeal this aspect of the court's ruling.

or capacity, except in relation to matters as to which he shall be adjudged in such action, suit or proceeding to be liable for negligence or misconduct in the performance of duty.[40]

Conti argues that § 145(a) of Delaware's General Corporation Law, which does contain a "good faith" requirement, fixes the outer limits of a corporation's power to indemnify; Article Ninth is thus invalid under Delaware law, says Conti, to the extent that it requires indemnification of officers who have acted in bad faith. The affirmative grant of power in § 145(a) is as follows:

> A corporation shall have power to indemnify any person who was or is a party or is threatened to be made a party to any threatened, pending or completed action, suit or proceeding, whether civil, criminal, administrative or investigative (other than an action by or in the right of the corporation) by reason of the fact that he is or was a director, officer, employee or agent of the corporation, or is or was serving at the request of the corporation as a director, officer, employee or agent of another corporation, partnership, joint venture, trust or other enterprise, against expenses (including attorneys' fees), judgments, fines and amounts paid in settlement actually and reasonably incurred by him in connection with such action, suit or proceeding if he acted in good faith and in a manner he reasonably believed to be in or not opposed to the best interests of the corporation, and, with respect to any criminal action or proceeding, had no reasonable cause to believe his conduct was unlawful.

56 Del. Laws 50, § 1 at 170–71 (1967).

* * *

In order to escape the "good faith" clause of § 145(a), Waltuch argues that § 145(a) is not an exclusive grant of indemnification power, because § 145(f) expressly allows corporations to indemnify officers in a manner broader than that set out in § 145(a). The "nonexclusivity" language of § 145(f) provides:

> The indemnification and advancement of expenses provided by, or granted pursuant to, the other subsections of this section shall not be deemed exclusive of any other rights to which those seeking indemnification or advancement of expenses may be entitled under any bylaw, agreement, vote of stockholders or disinterested directors or otherwise, both as to action in his official capacity and as to action in another capacity while holding such office.

56 Del. Laws 50, § 1 at 172 (emphasis added), as amended and codified at 8 Del. Code Ann. tit. 8, § 145(f). Waltuch contends that the "nonexclusivity" language in § 145(f) is a separate grant of indemnification power, not limited by the good faith clause that governs the power granted in § 145(a). Conti on the other hand contends that § 145(f) must be limited by "public policies," one of which is that a corporation may indemnify its officers only if they act in "good faith."

---

[40] [5] Because the private suits and the CFTC proceeding were settled, it is undisputed that Waltuch was not "adjudged . . . to be liable for negligence or misconduct in the performance of duty."

In a thorough and scholarly opinion, Judge Lasker agreed with Conti's reading of § 145(f), writing that "it has been generally agreed that there are public policy limits on indemnification under Section 145(f)," although it was "difficult . . . to define precisely what limitations on indemnification public policy imposes." 833 F. Supp. at 307, 308. After reviewing cases from Delaware and elsewhere and finding that they provided no authoritative guidance, Judge Lasker surveyed the numerous commentators on this issue and found that they generally agreed with Conti's position. *Id.* at 308–09. He also found that Waltuch's reading of § 145(f) failed to make sense of the statute as a whole:

> [T]here would be no point to the carefully crafted provisions of Section 145 spelling out the permissible scope of indemnification under Delaware law if subsection (f) allowed indemnification in additional circumstances without regard to these limits. The exception would swallow the rule.

*Id.* at 309. The fact that § 145(f) was limited by § 145(a) did not make § 145(f) meaningless, wrote Judge Lasker, because § 145(f) "still 'may authorize the adoption of various procedures and presumptions to make the process of indemnification more favorable to the indemnitee without violating the statute.'" *Id.* at 309 (quoting 1 BALOTTI & FINKELSTEIN § 4.16 at 4-321). As will be evident from the discussion below, we adopt much of Judge Lasker's analysis.

## A. Delaware Cases

No Delaware court has decided the very issue presented here; but the applicable cases tend to support the proposition that a corporation's grant of indemnification rights cannot be inconsistent with the substantive statutory provisions of § 145, notwithstanding § 145(f). We draw this rule of "consistency" primarily from our reading of the Delaware Supreme Court's opinion in *Hibbert v. Hollywood Park, Inc.*, 457 A.2d 339 (Del. 1983). In that case, Hibbert and certain other directors sued the corporation and the remaining directors, and then demanded indemnification for their expenses and fees related to the litigation. The company refused indemnification on the ground that directors were entitled to indemnification only as defendants in legal proceedings. The court reversed the trial court and held that Hibbert was entitled to indemnification under the plain terms of a company bylaw that did not draw an express distinction between plaintiff directors and defendant directors. *Id.* at 343. The court then proceeded to test the bylaw for consistency with § 145(a):

> Furthermore, indemnification here is consistent with current Delaware law. Under 8 Del. C. § 145(a) . . . , "a corporation may indemnify any person who was or is a party or is threatened to be made a party to any threatened, pending or completed" derivative or third-party action. By this language, indemnity is not limited to only those who stand as a defendant in the main action. The corporation can also grant indemnification rights beyond those provided by statute. 8 Del. C. § 145(f).

*      *      *

This passage contains two complementary propositions. Under § 145(f), a corporation may provide indemnification rights that go "beyond" the rights provided by § 145(a) and the other substantive subsections of § 145. At the same time, any such indemnification rights provided by a corporation must be "consistent with" the substantive provisions of § 145, including § 145(a). In *Hibbert*, the corporate bylaw was "consistent with" § 145(a), because this subsection was "not limited to" suits in which directors were defendants. Hibbert's holding may support an inverse corollary that illuminates our case: if § 145(a) had been expressly limited to directors who were named as defendants, the bylaw could not have stood, regardless of § 145(f), because the bylaw would not have been "consistent with" the substantive statutory provision.[41]

A more recent opinion of the Delaware Supreme Court, analyzing a different provision of § 145, also supports the view that the express limits in § 145's substantive provisions are not subordinated to § 145(f). In *Citadel Holding Corp. v. Roven*, 603 A.2d 818, 823 (Del. 1992), a corporation's bylaws provided indemnification "to the full extent permitted by the General Corporation Law of Delaware." The corporation entered into an indemnification agreement with one of its directors, reciting the parties' intent to afford enhanced protection in some unspecified way. The director contended that the agreement was intended to afford mandatory advancement of expenses, and that this feature (when compared with the merely permissive advancement provision of § 145(e)) was the enhancement intended by the parties. The corporation, seeking to avoid advancement of expenses, argued instead that the agreement enhanced the director's protection only in the sense that the pre-contract indemnification rights were subject to statute, whereas his rights under the contract could not be diminished without his consent. *Id.*

In rejecting that argument, the court explained that indemnification rights provided by contract could not exceed the "scope" of a corporation's indemnification powers as set out by the statute:

> If the General Assembly were to amend Delaware's director indemnification statute with the effect of curtailing the scope of indemnification a corporation may grant a director, the fact that [the director's] rights were also secured by contract would be of little use to him. Private parties may not circumvent the legislative will simply by agreeing to do so.

*Id. Citadel* thus confirms the dual propositions stated in Hibbert: indemnification rights may be broader than those set out in the statute, but they cannot be inconsistent with the "scope" of the corporation's power to indemnify, as delineated

---

[41] [7] The *Hibbert* court cites to a 1978 article by Samuel Arsht, chairman of the committee of experts that drafted Delaware's General Corporation Law in 1967, *id.*, which supports our conclusion that indemnification rights permitted under § 145(f) must be consistent with the other substantive provisions of § 145. At the pages cited by the court, Arsht writes:

The question most frequently asked by practicing lawyers is what subsection (f), the non-exclusive clause, means . . . . The question which subsection (f) invariably raises is whether a corporation can adopt a by-law or make a contract with its directors providing that they will be indemnified for whatever they may have to pay if they are sued and lose or settle. The answer to this question is "no." Subsection (f) . . . permits additional rights to be created, but *it is not a blanket authorization to indemnify directors* against all expenses, fines, or settlements of whatever nature and *regardless of the directors' conduct.* The statutory language is circumscribed by limits of public policy . . . .

S. Samuel Arsht, *Indemnification Under Section 145 of Delaware General Corporation Law*, 3 Del. J. Corp. L. 176, 176–77 (1978). . . .

in the statute's substantive provisions. *See also Shearin v. E.F. Hutton Group, Inc.*, 652 A.2d 578, 593–94 & n. 19 (Del. Ch. 1994) (Allen, Ch.) (bylaw that provided indemnification "to the full extent permissible under Section 145" must be interpreted in way that is consistent with substantive provisions of § 145(a); nonexclusivity provision of § 145(f) not mentioned by the court); *Merritt-Chapman & Scott Corp. v. Wolfson*, 321 A.2d 138, 142 (Del. Super. Ct. 1974) (bylaw provided for mandatory entitlement to indemnification unless officer was "derelict in the performance of his duty"; although the court considered this entitlement to be "independent of any right under the statute," it did not hold that the bylaw was inconsistent with the "good faith" standard of § 145(a)).

## B. Statutory Reading.

The "consistency" rule suggested by these Delaware cases is reinforced by our reading of § 145 as a whole. Subsections (a) (indemnification for third-party actions) and (b) (similar indemnification for derivative suits) expressly grant a corporation the power to indemnify directors, officers, and others, if they "acted in good faith and in a manner reasonably believed to be in or not opposed to the best interest of the corporation." These provisions thus limit the scope of the power that they confer. They are permissive in the sense that a corporation may exercise less than its full power to grant the indemnification rights set out in these provisions. *See Essential Enter. Corp. v. Dorsey Corp.*, 182 A.2d 647, 653 (Del. Ch. 1962). By the same token, subsection (f) permits the corporation to grant additional rights: the rights provided in the rest of § 145 "shall not be deemed exclusive of any other rights to which those seeking indemnification may be entitled." But crucially, subsection (f) merely acknowledges that one seeking indemnification may be entitled to "other rights" (of indemnification or otherwise); it does not speak in terms of corporate power, and therefore cannot be read to free a corporation from the "good faith" limit explicitly imposed in subsections (a) and (b).

An alternative construction of these provisions would effectively force us to ignore certain explicit terms of the statute. Section 145(a) gives Conti the power to indemnify Waltuch "if he acted in good faith and in a manner reasonably believed to be in or not opposed to the best interest of the corporation." 56 Del. Laws 50, § 1 at 171 (emphasis added). This statutory limit must mean that there is no power to indemnify Waltuch if he did not act in good faith. Otherwise, as Judge Lasker pointed out, § 145(a) — and its good faith clause — would have no meaning: a corporation could indemnify whomever and however it wished regardless of the good faith clause or anything else the Delaware Legislature wrote into § 145(a).

When the Legislature intended a subsection of § 145 to augment the powers limited in subsection (a), it set out the additional powers expressly. Thus subsection (g) explicitly allows a corporation to circumvent the "good faith" clause of subsection (a) by purchasing a directors and officers liability insurance policy. Significantly, that subsection is framed as a grant of corporate power:

> A corporation shall have power to purchase and maintain insurance on behalf of any person who is or was a director, officer, employee or agent of the corporation . . . against any liability asserted against him and incurred

by him in any such capacity, or arising out of his status as such, whether or not the corporation would have the power to indemnify him against such liability under this section.

56 Del. Laws 50, § 1 at 172 (1967) (emphasis added), codified at 8 Del. Code Ann. tit. 8, § 145(g) (Michie 1991). The . . . passage reflects the principle that corporations have the power under § 145 to indemnify in some situations and not in others. Since § 145(f) is neither a grant of corporate power nor a limitation on such power, subsection (g) must be referring to the limitations set out in § 145(a) and the other provisions of § 145 that describe corporate power. If § 145 (through subsection (f) or another part of the statute) gave corporations unlimited power to indemnify directors and officers, then the final clause of subsection (g) would be unnecessary: that is, its grant of "power to purchase and maintain insurance" (exercisable regardless of whether the corporation itself would have the power to indemnify the loss directly) is meaningful only because, in some insurable situations, the corporation simply lacks the power to indemnify its directors and officers directly.

A contemporaneous account from the principal drafter of Delaware's General Corporation Law confirms what an integral reading of § 145 demonstrates: the statute's affirmative grants of power also impose limitations on the corporation's power to indemnify. Specifically, the good faith clause (unchanged since the Law's original enactment in 1967) was included in subsections (a) and (b) as a carefully calculated improvement on the prior indemnification provision and as an explicit limit on a corporation's power to indemnify:

> During the three years of the Revision Committee's study, no subject was more discussed among members of the corporate bar than the subject of indemnification of officers and directors. As far as Delaware law was concerned, the existing statutory provision on the subject had been found inadequate. Numerous by-laws and charter provisions had been adopted clarifying and extending its terms, but uncertainty existed in many instances as to whether such provisions transgressed the limits which the courts had indicated they would establish based on public policy.
>
> . . .
>
> It was . . . apparent that revision was appropriate with respect to the limitations which must necessarily be placed on the power to indemnify in order to prevent the statute from undermining the substantive provisions of the criminal law and corporation law . . . .
>
> [There was a] need for a . . . provision to protect the corporation law's requirement of loyalty to the corporation. . . . Ultimately, it was decided that the power to indemnify should not be granted unless it appeared that the person seeking indemnification had "acted in good faith and in a manner reasonably believed to be in or not opposed to the best interest of the corporation."

S. Samuel Arsht & Walter K. Stapleton, *Delaware's New General Corporation Law:*

*Substantive Changes*, 23 Bus. Law. 75, 77–78 (1967).[42] This passage supports Hibbert's rule of "consistency" and makes clear that a corporation has no power to transgress the indemnification limits set out in the substantive provisions of § 145.

Waltuch argues at length that reading § 145(a) to bar the indemnification of officers who acted in bad faith would render § 145(f) meaningless. This argument misreads § 145(f). That subsection refers to "any other rights to which those seeking indemnification or advancement of expenses may be entitled." Delaware commentators have identified various indemnification rights that are "beyond those provided by statute," *Hibbert*, 457 A.2d at 344, and that are at the same time consistent with the statute:

> [S]ubsection (f) provides general authorization for the adoption of various procedures and presumptions making the process of indemnification more favorable to the indemnitee. For example, indemnification agreements or by-laws could provide for: (i) mandatory indemnification unless prohibited by statute; (ii) mandatory advancement of expenses, which the indemnitee can, in many instances, obtain on demand; (iii) accelerated procedures for the "determination" required by section 145(d) to be made in the "specific case"; (iv) litigation "appeal" rights of the indemnitee in the event of an unfavorable determination; (v) procedures under which a favorable determination will be deemed to have been made under circumstances where the board fails or refuses to act; [and] (vi) reasonable funding mechanisms.

E. Norman Veasey, *et al.*, *Delaware Supports Directors With a Three-Legged Stool of Limited Liability, Indemnification, and Insurance*, 42 Bus. Law. 399, 415 (1987). Moreover, subsection (f) may reference non-indemnification rights, such as advancement rights or rights to other payments from the corporation that do not qualify as indemnification.

We need not decide in this case the precise scope of those "other rights" adverted to in § 145(f). We simply conclude that § 145(f) is not rendered meaningless or inoperative by the conclusion that a Delaware corporation lacks power to indemnify an officer or director "unless [he] 'acted in good faith and in a manner reasonably

---

[42] [9] Delaware commentators consider this article to be part of (if not all of) "[t]he legislative history of Section 145." A. Gilchrist Sparks, III, et al., *Indemnification, Directors and Officers Liability Insurance and Limitations of Director Liability Pursuant to Statutory Authorization: The Legal Framework Under Delaware Law*, 696 PLI/Corp 941 (1990) (at page 10 out of 123 on Westlaw).

Since it is clear that the 1967 statute changed the prior indemnification statute by making certain "public policy" limits explicit, we may easily distinguish the pre-1967 case, *Mooney v. Willys-Overland Motors, Inc.*, 204 F.2d 888 (3d Cir. 1953), on which Waltuch relies heavily. In *Mooney*, the court held that an indemnification agreement between corporation and director provided "an independent ground for the payment of litigation expenses," which was valid under the (prior) statute's nonexclusivity provision (similar to § 145(f)). *Id.* at 896. But the court did not see any inconsistency between this "independent" indemnification right and the "realistic limits [that the statutory provisions] set upon the right of indemnification," limits which the court said "met the requirements of public policy." *Id.*

As the Arsht and Stapleton article explains, the Legislature enacted the "good faith" clause after *Mooney* to make the State's "public policy" explicit: a corporation could not indemnify directors and officers who breached their duty of loyalty to the corporation. Because *Mooney* interpreted the pre-1967 statute, and because it does not contradict *Hibbert's* "consistency" rule, it therefore provides no support for Waltuch's contention that the good faith limit can be evaded by reference to the statute's nonexclusivity provision.

believed to be in or not opposed to the best interest of the corporation.' " *See* Arsht & Stapleton, 23 Bus. Law. at 78. As a result, we hold that Conti's Article Ninth, which would require indemnification of Waltuch even if he acted in bad faith, is inconsistent with § 145(a) and thus exceeds the scope of a Delaware corporation's power to indemnify. Since Waltuch has agreed to forgo his opportunity to prove at trial that he acted in good faith, he is not entitled to indemnification under Article Ninth for the $2.2 million he spent in connection with the private lawsuits and the CFTC proceeding. We therefore affirm the district court on this issue.

## II

Unlike § 145(a), which grants a discretionary indemnification power, § 145(c) affirmatively requires corporations to indemnify its officers and directors for the "successful" defense of certain claims:

> To the extent that a director, officer, employee or agent of a corporation has been successful on the merits or otherwise in defense of any action, suit or proceeding referred to in subsections (a) and (b) of this section, or in defense of any claim, issue or matter therein, he shall be indemnified against expenses (including attorneys' fees) actually and reasonably incurred by him in connection therewith.

56 Del. Laws 50, § 1 at 171 (1967), codified at 8 Del. Code Ann. tit. 8, § 145(c) (Michie 1991). Waltuch argues that he was "successful on the merits or otherwise" in the private lawsuits, because they were dismissed with prejudice without any payment or assumption of liability by him. Conti argues that the claims against Waltuch were dismissed only because of Conti's $35 million settlement payments, and that this payment was contributed, in part, "on behalf of Waltuch."

The district court agreed with Conti that "the successful settlements cannot be credited to Waltuch but are attributable solely to Conti's settlement payments. It was not Waltuch who was successful, but Conti who was successful for him." 833 F. Supp. at 311. The district court held that § 145(c) mandates indemnification when the director or officer "is vindicated," but that there was no vindication here:

> Vindication is also ordinarily associated with a dismissal with prejudice without any payment. However, a director or officer is not vindicated when the reason he did not have to make a settlement payment is because someone else assumed that liability. Being bailed out is not the same thing as being vindicated.

*Id.* We believe that this understanding and application of the "vindication" concept is overly broad and is inconsistent with a proper interpretation of § 145(c).

No Delaware court has applied § 145(c) in the context of indemnification stemming from the settlement of civil litigation. One lower court, however, has applied that subsection to an analogous case in the criminal context, and has illuminated the link between "vindication" and the statutory phrase, "successful on the merits or otherwise." In *Merritt-Chapman & Scott Corp. v. Wolfson*, 321 A.2d 138 (Del. Super. Ct. 1974), the corporation's agents were charged with several counts of criminal conduct. A jury found them guilty on some counts, but deadlocked on the others. The agents entered into a "settlement" with the prosecutor's office by pleading nolo contendere to one of the counts in exchange for the dropping of the rest. *Id.* at 140. The agents claimed entitlement to mandatory indemnification under § 145(c) as to the counts that were dismissed. In opposition, the corporation raised an argument similar to the argument raised by Conti:

> [The corporation] argues that the statute and sound public policy require indemnification only where there has been vindication by a finding or concession of innocence. It contends that the charges against [the agents] were dropped for practical reasons, not because of their innocence . . . .

The statute requires indemnification to the extent that the claimant "has been successful on the merits or otherwise." Success is vindication. In a criminal action, any result other than conviction must be considered success. Going behind the result, as [the corporation] attempts, is neither authorized by subsection (c) nor consistent with the presumption of innocence.

Although the underlying proceeding in *Merritt* was criminal, the court's analysis is instructive here. The agents in *Merritt* rendered consideration — their guilty plea on one count — to achieve the dismissal of the other counts. The court considered these dismissals both "success" and (therefore) "vindication," and refused to "go behind the result" or to appraise the reason for the success. In equating "success" with "vindication," the court thus rejected the more expansive view of vindication urged by the corporation. Under *Merritt*'s holding, then, vindication, when used as a synonym for "success" under § 145(c), does not mean moral exoneration. Escape from an adverse judgment or other detriment, for whatever reason, is determinative. According to *Merritt*, the only question a court may ask is what the result was, not why it was.[43]

Conti's contention that, because of its $35 million settlement payments, Waltuch's settlement without payment should not really count as settlement without payment, is inconsistent with the rule in *Merritt*. Here, Waltuch was sued, and the suit was dismissed without his having paid a settlement. Under the approach taken in *Merritt*, it is not our business to ask why this result was reached. Once Waltuch achieved his settlement gratis, he achieved success "on the merits or otherwise." And, as we know from *Merritt*, success is sufficient to constitute vindication (at least for the purposes of § 145(c)). Waltuch's settlement thus vindicated him.

---

[43] [12] Our adoption of *Merritt*'s interpretation of the statutory term "successful" does not necessarily signal our endorsement of the result in that case. The *Merritt* court sliced the case into individual counts, with indemnification pegged to each count independently of the others. We are not faced with a case in which the corporate officer claims to have been "successful" on some parts of the case but was clearly "unsuccessful" on others, and therefore take no position on this feature of the *Merritt* holding.

We also do not mean our discussion of *Merritt* to suggest that the line between success and failure in a criminal case may be drawn in the same way in the civil context. In a criminal case, conviction on a particular count is obvious failure, and dismissal of the charge is obvious success. In a civil suit for damages, however, there is a monetary continuum between complete success (dismissal of the suit without any payment) and complete failure (payment of the full amount of damages requested by the plaintiff). Because Waltuch made no payment in connection with the dismissal of the suits against him, we need not decide whether a defendant's settlement payment automatically renders that defendant "unsuccessful" under § 145(c).

The concept of "vindication" pressed by Conti is also inconsistent with the fact that a director or officer who is able to defeat an adversary's claim by asserting a technical defense is entitled to indemnification under § 145(c). *See* 1 Balotti & Finkelstein, § 4.13 at 4-302. In such cases, the indemnitee has been "successful" in the palpable sense that he has won, and the suit has been dismissed, whether or not the victory is deserved in merits terms. If a technical defense is deemed "vindication" under Delaware law, it cannot matter why Waltuch emerged unscathed, or whether Conti "bailed [him] out", or whether his success was deserved. Under § 145(c), mere success is vindication enough.

This conclusion comports with the reality that civil judgments and settlements are ordinarily expressed in terms of cash rather than moral victory. No doubt, it would make sense for Conti to buy the dismissal of the claims against Waltuch along with its own discharge from the case, perhaps to avoid further expense or participation as a non-party, potential cross-claims, or negative publicity. But Waltuch apparently did not accede to that arrangement, and Delaware law cannot allow an indemnifying corporation to escape the mandatory indemnification of subsection (c) by paying a sum in settlement on behalf of an unwilling indemnitee.

We note that two non-Delaware precedents (one from this Court) support our conclusion. In *Wisener v. Air Express Int'l Corp.*, 583 F.2d 579 (2d Cir. 1978), we construed an Illinois indemnification statute that was intentionally enacted as a copy of Delaware's § 145. *See id.* at 582 n. 3; 1 Balotti & Finkelstein, § 4.12 at 4-296 n. 1048 (§ 145 was the "prototype" for Illinois's indemnification statute). Our holding in that case is perfectly applicable here:

> It is contended that [the director] was not "successful" in the litigation, since the third-party claims against him never proceeded to trial. The statute, however, refers to success "on the merits or otherwise," which surely is broad enough to cover a termination of claims by agreement without any payment or assumption of liability.

583 F.2d at 583. It is undisputed that the private lawsuits against Conti and Waltuch were dismissed with prejudice, "without any payment of assumption of liability" by Waltuch. Applying the analysis of Wisener, Conti must indemnify Waltuch for his expenses in connection with the private lawsuits.

The second case, from the Eastern District of Pennsylvania, is almost on point. In *B & B Investment Club v. Kleinert's, Inc.*, 472 F. Supp. 787 (E.D. Pa. 1979), suit had been brought against a corporation and two of its officers. The corporation settled the suit against it (on unspecified terms). One of the officers (Stephens) settled by paying $35,000, and the other (Brubaker) settled without paying anything. Brubaker claimed indemnification under a Pennsylvania statute that was virtually identical to § 145(c), *id.* at 789 n. 3, as the court noted, *id.* at 791 n. 5. The corporation argued that Brubaker was not "successful on the merits or otherwise," because his settlement was achieved only as a result of Stephens's $35,000 payment. The court rejected this argument, explaining that "[Brubaker] is entitled to indemnification because he made no monetary payment and the case was dismissed with prejudice as to him." *Id.* at 790 (emphasis added). Even though there was evidence that the plaintiffs dismissed their claims against Brubaker only because of Stephens's payment, this payment was irrelevant to the determination of "success":

> That the class plaintiffs at one point in the negotiations sought a cash payment from Brubaker but later settled with him for no monetary consideration does not render Brubaker any less successful than the plaintiff in Wisener. Nor is the extent of Brubaker's success affected by Stephens' having paid sufficient consideration to enable Brubaker to negotiate a dismissal with prejudice without making any payment. In short, Brubaker was "successful on the merits or otherwise" . . . .

*Id.* at 791. The same logic applies to our case. "[T]he extent of [Waltuch's] success" is not lessened by Conti's payments, even if it is true (as it stands to reason) that his success was achieved because Conti was willing to pay. Whatever the impetus for the plaintiffs' dismissal of their claims against Waltuch, he still walked away without liability and without making a payment. This constitutes a success that is untarnished by the process that achieved it.

For all of these reasons, we agree with Waltuch that he is entitled to indemnification under § 145(c) for his expenses pertaining to the private lawsuits.

## NOTE

What is success on the merits? If the law were changed to permit indemnification only if a court made an alternative finding of "moral exoneration" would that undermine the policies behind indemnification? What are the policy reasons for indemnification of officers and directors? Note that the Delaware statute and many others permit the corporation to advance expenses of litigation to the officer or director. Is this going too far? *See* Diane H. Mazur, *Indemnification of Directors in Actions Directly by the Corporation: Must the Corporation Finance its Opponent's Defense?*, 19 J. CORP. L. 201 (1994).

## FASCIANA v. ELECTRONIC DATA SYSTEMS CORP.
### Court of Chancery of Delaware
### 829 A.2d 178 (2003)

STRINE, VICE CHANCELLOR

In this decision, I resolve plaintiff John E. Fasciana's request for indemnification of litigation expenses incurred bringing this action pursuant to § 145 of the Delaware General Corporation Law to enforce his contractual right to obtain an advancement of litigation expenses from defendant Electronic Data Systems Corporation ("EDS").

Fasciana served as outside counsel to EDS. In 2001, a federal grand jury returned an indictment against Fasciana, which in simple terms alleged that Fasciana had conspired with certain EDS insiders in a conscious scheme to defraud EDS. EDS, for its part, filed a civil action against Fasciana in a Texas federal court. EDS predicated its civil action on the same factual background that formed the basis for the federal indictment. Fasciana then filed this suit seeking an advancement of litigation expenses to defend himself against the federal indictment and the EDS civil action. In an earlier memorandum opinion, I partially granted Fasciana's request for an advancement. Indeed, although I found that Fasciana was entitled to a partial advancement, in major part his advancement request was denied.

Presently before me is Fasciana's request for an award of litigation expenses incurred in the process of bringing his § 145 claim. Fasciana argues that his partial success should lead to a full award of attorneys' fees and expenses incurred in the process of bringing this action. For the reasons stated below, I disagree. Fasciana is entitled to an award of litigation expenses for bringing his § 145 action under the teaching of the Delaware Supreme Court's *Stifel Financial Corp. v. Cochran* decision. But the "fees on fees" award he should receive must be proportionate to the success he achieved and the efforts required to obtain that success. In this case, Fasciana obtained quite limited — as opposed to substantial — success. To achieve that success, however, Fasciana did have to address certain across-the-board defenses that EDS asserted in order to secure the limited victory he achieved. After considering that factor and the other record evidence bearing on the appropriate award, I exercise my discretion to award fees on fees equal to one-third of the litigation expenses Fasciana incurred.

*     *     *

In May 1995, defendant Electronic Data Systems Corporation ("EDS") purchased FACS Incorporated ("FCI"). Among other things, FCI performed asset recovery services for clients involving the identification of client funds that had been erroneously escheated as abandoned property. John E. Fasciana, a New York attorney, represented FCI and its stockholders in selling FCI to EDS. After the acquisition, Fasciana continued to perform legal work for FCI — which was then operated as Global Financial Markets Group ("GFMG"), a division of EDS. In other words, as GFMG's attorney, Fasciana functioned as an attorney for EDS.

Under the terms of a purchase agreement, EDS agreed to purchase FCI for an initial cash payment of $6 million to FCI's stockholders. In addition to this cash payment, EDS placed $3 million into an escrow account that was to be controlled by Fasciana's law firm — Fasciana & Associates, P.C. — as escrow agent. Of that $3 million held in escrow, $2 million could be earned by the former FCI stockholders based on FCI's performance during the remainder of 1995. The other $1 million could be earned if certain performance targets were achieved and certain outstanding receivables of FCI were collected. Finally, EDS agreed to make up to $14 million in payments under an incentive compensation plan to certain former FCI stockholders provided that GFMG met specified earnings targets during a three-year period beginning in 1996.

In December 2001, Fasciana was indicted by a federal grand jury in the Southern District of New York on various counts of conspiracy, mail fraud, and wire fraud. Additionally, EDS filed a civil action against Fasciana in the United States District Court for the Eastern District of Texas. The causes of action recited in the civil action are: (1) attorney malpractice and negligence; (2) gross negligence; (3) breach of fiduciary duty; (4) fraud; and (5) breach of contract. Without getting lost in the details, the crux of both the criminal indictment and the civil action can be stated thusly: Fasciana participated in a scheme to defraud EDS by inducing EDS to make certain contingent payments under the escrow agreement and the incentive compensation plan when, in fact, the requisite contingencies had not occurred. As part of the scheme, Fasciana received kickbacks from the recipients of the fraudulent contingent payments — i.e., Fasciana received kickbacks from his co-conspirators.

In both the federal indictment and the civil complaint it is alleged that Fasciana — in furtherance of his and his co-conspirators' scheme to defraud EDS — made certain material misrepresentations on behalf of EDS to two GFMG clients — Kidder, Peabody & Co. ("Kidder") and Kidder's parent company, General Electric Capital Co. ("GECC"). Fasciana allegedly made these material misrepresentations to GECC and Kidder as part of the scheme to induce EDS to make the $2 million payment under the escrow agreement.

In response to the federal indictment and EDS's civil action, Fasciana filed an action against EDS in this court seeking an advancement of litigation expenses pursuant to 8 Del. C. § 145. Both Fasciana and EDS filed motions for summary judgment. For reasons that do not warrant full repetition, in my February 27 decision I granted in part and denied in part each side's summary judgment motion. As a result, EDS was only required to advance *some* of the litigation expenses for which Fasciana sought advancement.

In fact, Fasciana's victory — if it can be called that — was an exceedingly limited one. EDS was only required to advance litigation expenses necessary for Fasciana to respond to a narrow subset of the claims made against him by the federal government and EDS — i.e., for the most part Fasciana's request for advancement was denied.[44] Specifically, EDS was only required to advance litigation expenses necessary for Fasciana to respond to charges related to his dealings with certain third parties — i.e., GECC and Kidder — on behalf of EDS. In other words, Fasciana was only eligible for an advancement to respond to allegations that he acted improperly as EDS's agent.[45] This distinction between Fasciana's activities as an EDS agent and his non-agent activities is an important one because EDS's bylaws only mandated advancement of litigation expenses for directors, officers, employees, and agents.

What I did not address in my February 27 opinion was whether, and to what extent, EDS was liable to indemnify Fasciana for litigation expenses incurred in the process of bringing this § 145 advancement action. Instead, I ordered the parties to provide briefing on the issue of the extent of EDS's liability for these so-called "fees on fees."[46] In this memorandum opinion, I resolve this issue.

\* \* \*

---

**44** [10] *See id.* at \*8 (stating that Fasciana is eligible to receive an advancement to respond to allegations that he made misrepresentations to certain EDS clients, but not to respond to allegations merely involving his conduct as EDS's legal advisor).

**45** [11] *Cf. Fisher v. Townsends, Inc.*, 695 A.2d 53, 57–58 (Del. 1997) ("An agency relationship is created when one party consents to have another act on its behalf, with the principal controlling and directing the acts of the agent." (citations and internal quotation marks omitted)).

**46** [13] "Fees on fees" is a term of art that refers to an award of litigation expenses (including attorneys' fees) incurred in the process of obtaining another award of litigation expenses pursuant to some statutory or contractual authority. *Cf. Stifel Fin. Corp. v. Cochran*, 809 A.2d 555, 561–62 (Del. 2002) (using the term "fees on fees" in that context).

As an initial matter, I find that EDS is obligated to indemnify Fasciana for fees on fees incurred to the full extent permitted by § 145. EDS's bylaws contain the following provision:

> Each person who at any time shall serve or shall have served as a Director, officer, employee, or agent of the Corporation . . . shall be entitled to (a) indemnification and (b) advancement of expenses incurred by such person from the Corporation as, and to the fullest extent, permitted by Section 145 of the [Delaware General Corporation Law] or any successor statutory provision, as from time to time amended.

In my February 27, 2003 memorandum opinion in this matter, I decided that by adopting this bylaw, "EDS has bound itself to provide [Fasciana] with advancement for claims against him in the capacity of an agent for EDS if § 145 of the [Delaware General Corporation Law] would allow." Under the mandate of the Delaware Supreme Court's decision in *Stifel Financial Corp. v. Cochran*, this bylaw requires an award to Fasciana of the fees he incurred in vindicating his advancement rights. In *Cochran*, the Delaware Supreme Court overturned a line of Chancery Court authority holding that "fees on fees" were not due under maximal by laws like EDS's. It did so based on the policy judgment that "the corporation itself is responsible for putting the [corporate official] through the . . . [§ 145] litigation" and that by allowing for fees on fees corporations will be prevented "from using [their] 'deep pockets' to wear down a former [corporate official]."

Because EDS's bylaws clearly require EDS to provide indemnification to a corporate agent to the fullest extent permitted by § 145, Cochran requires that EDS's bylaw be read as requiring it to indemnify Fasciana for any reasonable fees on fees incurred by him, but only to the extent permitted by § 145.[47]

EDS disputes this reading of Cochran and contends that an award of fees on fees is not available because the underlying suit for which Fasciana seeks attorneys' fees is an advancement action, as opposed to an indemnification action. I disagree.

It is, of course, true that a § 145 advancement can be thought of as an extension of credit, the final repayment of which is conditioned on whether a corporate official is ultimately entitled to indemnification. That said, the right to an advancement pursuant to § 145 and a corporate bylaw is an important one for the corporate official who is faced with expensive litigation relating to his conduct on behalf of the corporation. Any rational corporate official faced with the choice of after-the-fact indemnification or up-front advancement would surely choose the latter. When a corporate official is entitled to an advancement of litigation expenses, the corporation wrongfully refuses to honor the official's advancement request, and, as a result, the official needs to bring a § 145 claim to enforce his contractual right, then it seems plain under the teaching of Cochran that reasonable fees on fees are in order. The fact is that the right to advancement is no less of a § 145 right than the ultimate right to indemnification. And, the reasoning of Cochran (that the public policy

---

[47] [20] *Cf. Cochran*, 809 A.2d at 561–62 ("[Corporations] remain free to tailor their indemnification bylaws to exclude 'fees on fees,' if that is a desirable goal."); R. Franklin Balotti & Jesse A. Finkelstein, *Delaware Law of Corporations and Business Organizations* § 4.23 (2003) ("[A] corporation must explicitly tailor its by-laws to exclude 'fees on fees' if it seeks to preclude such recovery.").

purposes of the rights authorized by § 145 would be incompletely vindicated if a corporate official had to bear the expense of enforcing that right) is, therefore, no less applicable to the advancement right than to the indemnification right.

In fact, in a later case, Reddy v. Electronic Data Systems Corp., this court held that EDS's bylaw — per Cochran — entitled an officer to "fees on fees" for prevailing in an advancement action. On appeal, the Supreme Court affirmed that ruling. The *Reddy* holding applies here.

### Fasciana's Request for Fees on Fees is a Request for Indemnification, Not a Request for Advancement

In its answering brief, EDS contends that "[i]f Fasciana is ultimately required to repay the substantive amounts advanced to him, he would also be required to repay any amounts advanced to him for pursuing advancement." In making this statement, EDS reveals its misunderstanding of the current procedural posture. In the present fees on fees litigation, Fasciana is actually seeking indemnification and not an advancement. He is partially entitled to that indemnification because he has already partially succeeded in litigation in which he was a party. Cochran makes clear that the "in any action" language of § 145(a) is broad enough "to encompass the [§ 145] action itself."

Thus, Fasciana's present predicament should be conceived of as involving three separate and independent litigations: the federal indictment, the EDS civil action, and the § 145 action. Ultimate lack of success on the first two would not alter the fact that he was partially successful on the third — and for that partial success he is entitled to a partial indemnification, not a partial advancement. No matter what eventuates in the criminal action and the civil action, Fasciana's partial victory in the § 145 action brought him a real benefit: the interest-free use of EDS's money until his entitlement to indemnification for the criminal action and the civil action is finally determined. Fasciana is being awarded fees on fees per Cochran because EDS was at least partially wrong in denying Fasciana his requested advancement. Even if Fasciana is ultimately adjudged not to be entitled to indemnification for the criminal action and the civil action, that fact would not cure EDS's wrongful denial of Fasciana's advancement rights and the harm that denial caused to Fasciana.

### Because of His Very Limited Success on His Advancement Claim, Fasciana is Only Entitled to a Partial Award of Fees on Fees

The more difficult question in this case is how to give life to Cochran in a case in which the party seeking advancement prevailed on less than all of his claims; indeed, when he prevailed on a small portion of the relief he sought. Cochran provides only a starting point, by conditioning the right to fees on fees on success. But what is the scope of the entitlement that flows from partial success rather than substantial success?

Naturally, Fasciana urges me to take a black or white approach to the concept of success — *i.e.*, if Fasciana achieved any success, then he is entitled to a full award of fees on fees. He says this generous approach best implements the policy articulated in Cochran. EDS, for its part, argues that any award of fees on fees must be limited to reflect the fact that Fasciana only achieved a partial victory in his underlying advancement action.

For the reasons stated below, I opt for an approach closer to the one pressed by EDS. Both § 145 and bylaw provisions like that adopted by EDS are subject to an implied reasonableness requirement. That reasonableness requirement, as well as Cochran's admonition that awards of fees on fees are conditioned on the successful prosecution of an underlying § 145 action, lead me to conclude that Fasciana should only be entitled to an indemnification of those expenses reasonably proportionate to the level of success he achieved.

\* . \* \*

The idea that an award of attorneys' fees should be reduced to reflect the fact that a party only achieved limited or partial success is not a novel one. . . .

Section 145 jurisprudence also points in this same direction. In *Merritt-Chapman & Scott Corp. v. Wolfson*, the Delaware Superior Court concluded that a § 145 claimant is entitled to a partial indemnification if he successfully defends himself against one count of a criminal indictment but is convicted on another count. Likewise, in *MCI Telecommunications Corp. v. Wanzer*, the Superior Court held that a former corporate director was entitled to a partial § 145 indemnification when he successfully defended against three of the four counts of a civil complaint filed against him. Indeed, this court has itself endorsed the approach taken by *Merritt-Chapman* and *MCI Telecommunications*.

\* \* \*

Clearly, the public policy underlying the advancement and indemnification provisions of § 145 is an important one. By enacting § 145, our General Assembly helped ensure that capable persons would be willing to serve as directors, officers, employees, and agents of Delaware corporations. But those indemnification and advancement provisions are not a blank check for corporate officials. The costs of indemnification are borne by corporations and ultimately by their stockholders. Fasciana's right to obtain fees on fees for the arguments raised in his § 145 action that were unsuccessful does not outweigh the right of EDS's stockholders to resist having to bankroll that part of Fasciana's claim that EDS was correct to oppose.

### *What Award is Reasonable in View of Fasciana's Level of Success?*

In the underlying § 145 litigation, Fasciana sought a full advancement of litigation expenses to respond to charges made against him in a criminal indictment and a civil action. In order to achieve that result, Fasciana needed to convince me that he was responding to charges brought against him for actions he took in the capacity of an agent for EDS. In his attempt to convince me that his actions were those of an agent (and therefore within the ambit of § 145 and EDS's bylaws), Fasciana pressed two principal arguments: (1) that a corporation's outside counsel is an agent of that corporation because a lawyer is always the agent of his client and (2) that a lawyer who acts as an escrow agent is an agent of the party that places the subject funds into the escrow account.

I rejected both of these arguments and instead concluded that "the General Assembly [in drafting § 145] intended that the term [agent] be used in its most traditional sense as involving action by a person (an agent) acting on behalf of another (the principal) as to third parties." As such, I held that Fasciana was only entitled to an advancement of litigation expenses to respond to a narrow subset of the claims made against him — i.e., those claims involving Fasciana's dealings (specifically, making false representations) with a third party (specifically, GECC or Kidder) on behalf of EDS. It is helpful to quantify what this holding meant in light of the charges made against Fasciana by the federal government and EDS. The federal indictment contained thirty-nine paragraphs. When asked by me to point to those parts of the federal indictment relating to Fasciana's false representations to GECC or Kidder, Fasciana's counsel was only able to identify three — paragraphs 20, 34(a), and 35(e).47 And, when Fasciana's counsel was asked to perform a similar analysis with respect to EDS's sixty-one-paragraph complaint, again, his counsel could only single out three paragraphs — paragraphs 23 through 25.

Of course, this attempt on my part to quantify Fasciana's level of success is only a rough one — i.e., there are some parts of the federal indictment and the EDS complaint that are not specific to any underlying facts and are, in a sense, of a more general character. And, there are some litigation expenses that Fasciana would have incurred even if he had merely sought advancement for the claims that I ultimately found to be advanceable. The reason for this is that EDS asserted some across-the-board defenses like laches, that applied to Fasciana's claim for any relief at all. Fasciana had to address these claims in order to obtain the success he did. Even so, those across-the-board issues were not the predominant focus of the briefs in this case. The bulk of the briefing addressed arguments on which Fasciana suffered defeat. The precise argument on which he succeeded involved a miniscule amount of the overall work, as his counsel admitted. Thus, summarized fairly, two facts emerge as critical: (1) Fasciana's success was very limited in light of the relief he sought and (2) the bulk of Fasciana's briefing in the underlying § 145 action was spent advancing arguments that I ultimately rejected.

To turn these key facts into an award necessarily involves a discretionary judgment that is not mathematically precise. That exercise of discretion is guided, however, by the policies underlying Cochran. Thus, I err towards generosity by awarding Fasciana one-third of his litigation expenses.

## IN RE LANDMARK LAND CO. OF CAROLINA, INC.
United States Court of Appeals, Fourth Circuit
76 F.3d 553 (1996)

RUSSELL, J.

This case comes before this Court at the twilight of the Debtors' bankruptcy proceedings. The Resolution Trust Corporation ("RTC") has already taken control of the Debtors and has liquidated their assets. The bankruptcy proceedings have proven to be successful, with the debtors-in-possession paying each claim in full. On this appeal, the second to this Court, we consider only whether the debtors' estates must indemnify several of the Debtors' former directors, officers, and employees for their costs in defending themselves against civil proceedings brought by the Office of Thrift Supervision ("OTS") in connection with the bankruptcy filings. The district court found that the Debtors'estates must indemnify these directors, officers, and employees for their defense costs. We affirm in part and reverse in part.

## I.

### A. The OTS Charges

On October 11, 1991, the Debtors (with one exception) filed for bankruptcy. The Debtors were first- and second-tier subsidiaries of Oak Tree Savings Bank, S.S.B. ("Bank"). At the top of the corporate structure was Landmark Land Company, Inc. ("Landmark Land"), a publicly traded company. It was a holding company and whole owner of the Bank, which was the whole owner of Clock Tower, which in turn was the holding company and whole owner of Landmark Carolina, Landmark Oklahoma, Landmark Florida, Landmark Louisiana, and Landmark California.

Gerald G. Barton and William W. Vaughan, III, were prominent figures in the Landmark corporations. Barton was the chairman of the board of directors of Landmark Land, the Bank, and all of the subsidiaries. He was also the chief executive officer of Landmark Land and the Bank, and a 29% shareholder of Landmark Land. Vaughan, Barton's son-in-law, was a director and officer of the Bank and most of the subsidiaries. An attorney, he was the general counsel to the subsidiaries. Joe W. Walser played a less prominent role in the Landmark hierarchy, but he served as a director of the Bank and some of the subsidiaries. Bernard G. Ille served as a director of only the Bank, but he did not participate actively in the management of the Bank or the subsidiaries. He was employed by First Life Assurance Company, a subsidiary of Landmark Oklahoma.

Prior to the bankruptcy filings, the subsidiary companies invested profitably in real estate using the Bank's funds to finance their operations. They developed, owned, and managed residential resort communities, complete with golf courses, tennis courts, and polo facilities. During this time, the Bank loaned the subsidiaries more than $986 million.

The financial position of the Landmark organization eventually deteriorated. An OTS investigation on June 4, 1990 revealed that the Bank was undercapitalized and had demonstrated a pattern of consistent losses. Despite several attempts, the Bank was unable to submit to the OTS an acceptable plan for meeting the minimum capital requirements. On January 15, 1991, the directors of the Bank signed a Consent Agreement with the OTS in which they agreed that the Bank's subsidiaries would not enter into any material transaction without prior approval from the OTS. The Consent Agreement indicated that the Bank was near failure and that an OTS takeover was imminent.

Despite the terms of the Consent Agreement, the subsidiaries filed for bankruptcy. Anticipating that the OTS would act quickly to take control of the Bank, the Debtors immediately sought and obtained from the bankruptcy court a temporary restraining order preventing the Bank from exercising its shareholder rights to remove and replace the management of the Debtors.

The bankruptcy filings did not receive a pleasant reception from the OTS. On October 13, 1991, as expected, the OTS took control of the Bank and appointed the Resolution Trust Corporation ("RTC") to act as receiver for the Bank. *See* Financial Institutions Reform, Recovery, and Enforcement Act of 1989 ("FIRREA"), Pub.L. No. 101-73, 103 Stat. 183 (1989) (codified in scattered sections of 12 U.S.C.). More importantly, the OTS filed civil administrative charges against Barton, Vaughan, Walser, and Ille (collectively, the "Directors"). The OTS alleged that the Directors breached their fiduciary duties to the Bank because they knew that the bankruptcy filings would have a substantially adverse effect on the Bank's ability to collect on the secured and unsecured lines of credit to the Debtors. The OTS also charged the Directors with violating the terms of the Consent Agreement by having the Debtors enter into a material transaction — the filing for bankruptcy — without receiving OTS approval. The OTS assessed a fine of one million dollars against the Directors, and it fined Landmark Land $500,000 for each day it failed to seek dismissal of the bankruptcy proceedings. On November 18, 1991, the OTS amended its charges to add allegations that the Directors had mishandled certain large loans. The Directors hired attorneys to defend themselves against the OTS charges.

As the OTS continued its investigation into the Bank's affairs, several members of the Bank's accounting department became subjects of investigation. D. Scott Cone, although he was an officer and director of Landmark Louisiana, headed the Bank's accounting department. Mohamed Motahari was a vice-president and the comptroller of the Bank. Gina Trapani was a vice-president, assistant comptroller, and tax manager of the Bank. Gary Braun was an accountant for the Bank. Motahari, Trapani, and Braun became employees of Landmark Louisiana soon after the Debtors' filed for bankruptcy.

By March or April 1992, Cone, Motahari, Trapani, and Braun (collectively, the "Employees"), believing that the OTS might take action against them, retained counsel. On April 21, 1992, the OTS filed civil administrative charges against Cone and Motahari. The OTS alleged that, in monthly reports to federal regulators, they had misrepresented that the Debtors' debt to the Bank was secured, even though it was actually unsecured. The OTS never brought charges against Trapani or Braun.

## B. The Reimbursement Motion

Although the RTC took control of the Bank, the original boards of directors remained in control of the Debtors until September 1992. Once the RTC was appointed conservator of the Bank, it immediately moved the district court to lift the temporary restraining order so that it could call a shareholders meeting and exercise its ownership rights over the Debtors. However, the district court, acting as the bankruptcy court, denied the RTC's motion and converted the temporary restraining order into a preliminary injunction. *See Landmark Land Co. of Carolina v. Resolution Trust Corp. (In re Landmark Land Co. of Okla.)*, 134 B.R. 557 (D.S.C. 1991), *rev'd* 973 F.2d 283 (4th Cir. 1992). The RTC was not able to take control of the subsidiaries until this Court lifted the injunction on August 18, 1992. *See In re Landmark Land Co. of Okla.*, 973 F.2d 283 (4th Cir. 1992). On September 12, 1992, the RTC took control of the Debtors, terminated the original boards of directors, and fired the Debtors' attorneys.

During the eleven-month interim when the original board controlled the Debtors, the Directors arranged for the Debtors to pay for the fees and costs of defending themselves against the OTS charges. On March 26, 1992, the Debtors filed a Reimbursement Motion requesting permission to fund the Directors' indemnification. After making the motion, several of the Debtors' boards of directors met to approve the indemnification.

On April 8, 1992, the board of directors for Landmark Oklahoma met to discuss and vote on indemnification for Walser and Ille. Landmark Oklahoma's board consisted of three members: Barton, Lowery Bea Roselle, and Bill D. Thompson. Only Roselle and Thompson were present, but the two constituted a quorum. They found that Walser and Ille "had acted in good faith and in a manner they reasonably believed to be in, or not opposed to, the best interests of [Landmark Oklahoma]." Accordingly, the board voted in favor of indemnification.

On April 21, 1992, the board of directors for Clock Tower met to discuss and vote on indemnification for Barton and Vaughan. Clock Tower's board consisted of five members: Barton, Vaughan, Roselle, Thompson, and a fifth director. At the time of the meeting, the fifth director had resigned and had not yet been replaced. The other four members of the board were present, constituting a quorum. The board found that Barton and Vaughan "had acted in good faith and in a manner they reasonably believed to be in, or not opposed to, the best interests of [Clock Tower]." Roselle and Thompson voted in favor of indemnification, and Barton and Vaughan abstained from the vote.

Although the Employees were not included in the Reimbursement Motion, the board of directors for Landmark Louisiana met on April 21, 1992 to discuss and vote on indemnification for the Employees. Landmark Louisiana's board consisted of five members: Barton, Vaughan, Cone, Roselle, and Thompson. Cone was not present, but the other four directors constituted a quorum. The board found that the Employees had acted in good faith and in the best interests of Landmark Louisiana, and they voted unanimously to indemnify the Employees for their expenses. Barton and Vaughan participated in the vote.

On June 3, 1992, the district court held a hearing on the Reimbursement Motion. The court did not rule on the motion at the time, and the motion remained dormant for almost two years.

On August 27, 1992, the Debtors amended their Reimbursement Motion to include the Employees' legal expenses. Even before this formal application, however, the Debtors had already begun indemnifying the Employees. In March 1992, Clock Tower paid $21,825 toward Motahari's legal expenses, and Landmark Louisiana paid $1,000 toward Braun's expenses. In June 1992, Clock Tower paid $35,398.48 toward Cone's, Motahari's, and Trapani's legal expenses. Thus, Clock Tower paid more than $57,000 toward the Employees' legal expenses, even though its board never voted to indemnify them. In total, the Debtors have paid $122,493.20 of the Employees' legal expenses.

## C. The RTC-controlled Debtors

The RTC took control of the Debtors on September 12, 1992, and replaced the boards of directors. On November 5, 1992, the RTC-controlled Debtors sought, by means of a consent order, to withdraw the Reimbursement Motion. The district court denied the withdrawal because it had already heard argument on the motion and had taken the motion under advisement. The district court also recognized that the beneficiaries of the Reimbursement Motion-namely, the Directors and the Employees-were not represented in the proposed consent order.

The RTC, once it took control of the Debtors, decided that it was advantageous to operate the Debtors in bankruptcy and chose not to withdraw the Debtors from the bankruptcy proceedings. The RTC even decided to place another Bank subsidiary, Carmel Valley Ranch, in bankruptcy. The RTC filed a reorganization plan for the Debtors that was approved by the district court.

Meanwhile, the OTS settled its civil administrative actions against some of the Directors and Employees. On October 30, 1992, the OTS dropped its charges against Cone and Motahari in exchange for their consent to orders (1) prohibiting them from participating in the affairs of any insured depository institution and (2) debarring them from practicing before the OTS. Although Cone and Motahari accepted prohibition and debarment, neither admitted, and both specifically disputed, the OTS charges.

On April 1, 1993, the OTS dropped the charges against Ille with only the mildest rebuke: Ille had to sign a cease and desist order, prohibiting him from engaging in unsafe and unsound banking practices and from breaching fiduciary duties to a federally insured depository institution. In other words, Ille agreed to follow diligently in the future the standard of conduct already required of him. Ille received this lenient treatment because he did not participate in the bankruptcy filings. He learned of the decision to place the Debtors in bankruptcy during a telephone call from Barton on the evening of October 10, 1991, the day before the bankruptcy filings; that same evening, he resigned from his position as a director of the Bank. At most, Ille failed only to follow the affairs of the Bank more diligently.

As of the date of this opinion, the OTS proceedings against Barton, Vaughan, and Walser remain unresolved.

## D. The District Court's Orders

On May 27, 1994, more than two years after the filing of the motion, the district court granted the Reimbursement Motion. The district court found that "the evidence demonstrates that the officers and directors of the Debtor companies sought the protection of the bankruptcy court in good faith." *In re Landmark Land Co. of Okla.*, Civ. Action No. 2:91-5286-1, order at 12 (D.S.C. May 27, 1994) (J.A. 1278). It also concluded that the RTC-controlled Debtors "ratified the decision to reorganize under the protection of the bankruptcy court, demonstrating that the placement of the Debtors into bankruptcy is reasonably viewed as being in the best interests of the Debtors." *Id.* Thus, the district court ordered the Debtors' estates to indemnify the Directors and Employees for their defense costs, and it granted the applications for payment from the Employees' attorneys.

The RTC-controlled Debtors filed a motion for reconsideration on June 6, 1994. When the Debtors filed this motion, the following parties moved to intervene:

1. the Directors;

2. McNair & Sanford, P.A. ("McNair"), the attorneys for the Debtors before the RTC took control;

3. Jones, Day, Reavis & Pogue ("Jones Day") and McGlinchey, Stafford & Lang ("McGlinchey"), the Directors' former OTS defense attorneys;

4. John W. Reed (of Glass & Reed), attorney for Cone; David Popper (of Popper & Popper), attorney for Motahari; Herbert V. Larson, Jr., attorney for Motahari; Robert H. Habans, attorney for Trapani; and William R. Campbell, Jr., attorney for Braun.

The district court granted their motions to intervene on August 31, 1994. The Employees themselves did not move to intervene.

On October 5, 1994, the district court denied the Debtors' motion for reconsideration with respect to the indemnification of the Directors. The district court did, however, grant the motion for reconsideration with respect to the applications of the Employees' attorneys. In a separate order on November 9, 1994, the district court approved the applications for payment from the Employees' attorneys.

The RTC and the RTC-controlled Debtors appeal from the district court's orders.

## II.

The RTC and the RTC-controlled Debtors raise a host of arguments challenging the district court's granting of the Reimbursement Motion. Rather than addressing all of their arguments, we address the issue most troubling to us about the district court's decision: the district court's finding that the Directors acted in good faith and in the best interests of the Debtors. We conclude that the district court clearly erred in finding that the Directors, with the exception of Ille, acted in good faith.[48]

## A.

California, Oklahoma, and Louisiana have similar statutes regarding the indemnification of officers and directors for the costs and expenses of legal proceedings.[49] Under the California statute (as well as the other statutes), indemnification is

---

[48] [4] At least one court has held that the good faith determination is a question of fact reviewed under a clearly erroneous standard. *Plate v. Sun-Diamond Growers of Calif.*, 225 Cal. App. 3d 1115, 275 Cal. Rptr. 667, 672 (1990) (holding that the "question of whether a corporate agent . . . acted in good faith and for the best interests of the corporation [ ] appears to be an essentially factual question for the trial court"). The good faith determination strikes us as a question of law, or at least a mixed question of law and fact; although the facts supporting the good faith determination should be reviewed for clear error, an appellate court should review *de novo* whether or not those facts lead to the conclusion that the agent acted in good faith. Nonetheless, we need not at this time decide the appropriate standard of review for the good faith determination because our reasoning applies under either standard.

[49] [5] California law applies to Barton and Vaughan, Oklahoma law to Walser and Ille, and Louisiana law to the Employees. Because the indemnification statutes are substantially similar, *compare* Cal. Corp.

mandatory if a corporate agent successfully defends himself in any proceeding. In such a case, the corporation has a duty to indemnify the agent for his costs and expenses, and the agent can sue the corporation if it fails to do so.

Even where the litigation does not result in a complete vindication for the agent, "[a] corporation shall have the power to indemnify any person who was or is a party or is threatened to be made a party to any proceeding . . . if that person acted in good faith and in a manner the person reasonably believed to be in the best interests of the corporation . . . ." Cal. Corp. Code § 317(b). Thus, the statute allows for indemnification even where the agent was negligent or committed some error, as long as the agent acted in good faith and in the best interests of the corporation. *Plate v. Sun-Diamond Growers of Calif.*, 225 Cal. App. 3d 1115, 275 Cal. Rptr. 667, 672 (1990). In such circumstances, indemnification is only permissive: the corporation does not have a duty to indemnify the agent but simply has the option to indemnify as long as the good faith requirement is satisfied.

Indemnification is never allowed where the agent acted in bad faith and against the best interests of the corporation. As one California court has stated:

> Indemnification, if permitted too broadly, may violate . . . basic tenets of public policy. It is inappropriate to permit management to use corporate funds to avoid the consequences of wrongful conduct or conduct involving bad faith. A director, officer, or employee who acted wrongfully or in bad faith should not expect to receive assistance from the corporation for legal or other expenses and should be required to satisfy not only any judgment entered against him but also expenses incurred in connection with the proceeding from his personal assets. Any other rule would tend to encourage socially undesirable conduct.

*   *   *

Thus, there are two requirements for permissive indemnification under § 317(b): (1) the corporation must authorize the indemnification, and (2) the agent must have acted in good faith and in the best interests of the corporation. It is not clear, however, whether the good faith determination should be made by a court or by the corporation itself. Section 317(e) provides that, before a corporation can authorize indemnification, the corporation must determine that the agent has acted in good faith and in the best interests of the corporation. The corporation can make this determination in any of the following ways:

(1)  A majority vote of a quorum consisting of directors who are not parties to such proceeding.

(2)  If such a quorum of directors is not obtainable, by independent legal counsel in a written opinion.

(3)  Approval of the shareholders . . . , with the shares owned by the person to be indemnified not being entitled to vote thereon.[50]

---

Code § 317 *with* Okla. Stat. tit. 18, § 1031 *and* La. Rev. Stat. Ann. § 12:83, we focus on the California statute for purposes of this discussion.

[50] [7] The California Code also provides a fourth way in which a corporation can determine that an agent has acted in good faith and in the best interests of the corporation:

Cal. Corp. Code § 317(e). At first glance, § 317(e) suggests that the corporation's finding of good faith settles the matter, and that the court's role is limited to ensuring that the corporation made its finding of good faith by proper procedures.

We do not agree that the court's role is so narrow. Although a corporation has to find that the agent acted in good faith before authorizing indemnification, nothing in § 317(e) restricts a court's authority under § 317(b) to make an independent assessment of the agent's good faith. Section 317(b) allows permissive indemnification where the agent has acted in good faith, not where the corporation finds that the agent has acted in good faith. Reading § 317(b) together with § 317(e), we conclude that the issue of an agent's good faith is a question for the courts to decide.

In making the good faith determination, however, a court cannot ignore the factual findings made during the underlying proceeding for which the agent seeks indemnification. If the court or administrative panel in the underlying litigation made factual findings relevant to the determination of the agent's good faith, the indemnification court cannot reevaluate the evidence and reach the opposite conclusion. Even the findings of an administrative agency have collateral estoppel effect on the indemnification court. As the Supreme Court has stated:

> When an administrative agency is acting in a judicial capacity and resolves disputed issues of fact properly before it which the parties have had an adequate opportunity to litigate, the courts have not hesitated to apply res judicata to enforce repose.

\* \* \*

Furthermore, where a court decides the question of indemnification before the completion of the underlying proceeding, the court must tread even more carefully. In determining whether or not the agent acted in good faith and in the best interests of the corporation, the indemnification court should not make any factual or legal determinations that are properly before the court or administrative panel in the underlying proceeding. The indemnification court should not base its good faith determination on its own conclusions about the merits of the charges in the underlying proceeding.

The indemnification court, however, does not need to postpone its determination until after the completion of the underlying proceeding. The indemnification court should consider whether the agent could have acted in good faith and in the best interests of the corporation if the charges against the agent turn out to be true.[51]

---

(4) The court in which the proceeding is or was pending upon application made by the corporation or the agent or the attorney or other person rendering services in connection with the defense, whether or not the application by the agent, attorney or other person is opposed by the corporation.

Cal. Corp. Code § 317(e)(4). This fourth option, which is not found in the Oklahoma or Louisiana statutes, is actually an exception. It provides that an agent can receive indemnification over the corporation's opposition if the court in the proceedings for which the agent seeks indemnification found that the agent acted in good faith and in the best interests of the corporation.

[51] [8] The indemnification court does not need to consider the agent's good faith if the charges turn out to be false. If the agent succeeds on the merits in the underlying proceeding, he is entitled to mandatory indemnification. *See* Cal. Corp. Code § 317(d). In such a situation, the issue of permissive

If the indemnification court finds that the agent could have acted in good faith even if the charges were true, it should grant indemnification because the indemnification determination is not contingent on the result of the underlying proceeding. On the other hand, if the indemnification court finds that the agent's alleged misconduct, if true, demonstrates that the agent acted in bad faith, the indemnification court should deny permissive indemnification; it should hold its indemnification decision in abeyance until the completion of the underlying proceedings and then grant indemnification only if the agent succeeds on the merits. For instance, an agent defending himself against charges of negligent conduct should receive indemnification if the indemnification court finds that the agent, even if he were negligent, acted in good faith. However, an agent defending himself against charges of intentionally wrongful conduct should receive indemnification only if he succeeds on the merits.

In the instant case, it is not clear whether the district court-the indemnification court in this case-recognized the proper scope of its "good faith" determination. In finding that the Directors acted in good faith and in the best interest of the Debtors when they filed the petitions for bankruptcy, the district court offered little explanation on how it reached its finding. In its May 27, 1994 order, it simply stated:

> [T]his court finds that the evidence demonstrates that the officers and directors of the Debtor companies sought the protection of the bankruptcy court in good faith. Further this court finds that the Debtors' new management ratified the decision to reorganize under the protection of the bankruptcy court, demonstrating that the placement of the Debtors into bankruptcy is reasonably viewed as being in the best interest of the Debtors.

*In re Landmark Land Co. of Okla.*, Civ. Action No. 2:91-5286-1, order at 12 (D.S.C. May 27, 1994) (J.A. 1278). Neither in this order nor in any of its subsequent orders did the district court articulate how the evidence demonstrated the Directors' good faith. More importantly, the district court did not explain how the Directors could have acted in good faith if the OTS charges filed against them were true.

Apparently, the district court's finding of the Directors' good faith stems from its belief that the OTS charges had no merit. From the very beginning of the bankruptcy proceedings, the district court found that the Directors "possesse[d] the requisite expertise to continue managing the debtors' estates in a manner most profitable for the preservation of corporate assets." *Landmark Land Co. of Carolina v. Resolution Trust Corp. (In re Landmark Land Co. of Okla.*, 134 B.R. 557, 560 (D.S.C. 1991), *rev'd* 973 F.2d 283 (4th Cir. 1992)). It found that "the RTC ha[d] acted with complete disregard of the efforts of management to keep the debtor companies afloat." *Id.* It seems that the district court believed that federal regulators were hampering the Directors' legitimate efforts to reorganize the companies, and that the Directors sought the protection of the bankruptcy code to protect themselves from an overrun bureaucracy. The district court thought little of the OTS charges, referring to them as an attempt by the OTS to "seek[ ] atonement from the named Debtor officers for placing the Debtor companies in bankruptcy." *In re Landmark Land Co. of Okla.*, Civ. Action No. 2:91-5286-1, order at 8 (D.S.C.

---

indemnification would be moot, thus rendering the good faith determination unnecessary.

Oct. 5, 1994) (J.A. 2452). Furthermore, it found that the Directors had the best interests of the Debtors in mind when they filed for bankruptcy because the RTC ratified the Directors' action by keeping the Debtors in bankruptcy once it obtained control over them.

Even if the district court was correct that the OTS was inept and overbearing, the Directors' action to file for bankruptcy was a deliberate attempt to circumvent the regulatory authority that Congress had clearly given to the OTS. Congress created the OTS in 1989 in response to the crisis in the savings and loan industry, which occurred when the insolvency of a large number of savings and loans bankrupted the Federal Savings and Loan Insurance Corporation. Although the majority of savings and loans were healthy financial institutions, Congress found that the thrift crisis was concentrated in the roughly twenty-five percent of the industry having capital, measured under generally accepted accounting principles, of less than three percent. H.R. Rep. No. 101-54(I), 101st Cong., 1st Sess. 303 (1989), reprinted in 1989 U.S.C.C.A.N. 86, 99. Congress found that, "[t]o a considerable extent, the size of the thrift crisis resulted from the utilization of capital gimmicks that masked the inadequate capitalization of thrifts . . . . [I]f a crisis of this nature is to be prevented from happening again, thrifts must be adequately capitalized against losses." H.R. Rep. No. 101-54(I), 101st Cong., 1st Sess. 310 (1989), reprinted in 1989 U.S.C.C.A.N. 86, 106. Congress invested the OTS with broad regulatory powers to oversee financial institutions and ensure that they were adequately capitalized.

By placing the Debtors in bankruptcy, the Directors intended to prevent the OTS from enforcing the minimum capitalization requirement against the Bank. According to the OTS charges, the OTS investigated the Bank on June 4, 1990 and found that the Bank was inadequately capitalized and had demonstrated a pattern of repeated losses. The OTS directed the Bank to infuse sufficient capital to meet the minimum capitalization requirement, but the Bank did not submit an acceptable plan. Because of the Bank's inability to meet the requirement, the OTS forced the Bank directors to sign a Consent Agreement on January 15, 1991, signalling to the Directors that an OTS takeover was imminent. Instead of working with the OTS to correct the Bank's capitalization problem, the Directors filed the bankruptcy petitions to prevent the OTS from exercising control of the Bank's subsidiaries.

We cannot conclude that the Directors' action was taken in good faith. If the OTS charges are accurate, the Director's action to place the Debtors in bankruptcy was a deliberate attempt to prevent the OTS from exercising control over the Bank's assets, thus hindering the OTS's ability to deal effectively with a failing savings and loan. Despite the district court's findings that the federal regulators had interfered with the Directors' efforts to keep the Debtors afloat, the fact remains that the Bank could not comply with the minimum capitalization requirement, and the OTS therefore had a statutory duty to force the Bank's management to comply with the capitalization requirement. The Directors acknowledged the OTS's regulatory authority when they signed the Consent Agreement and agreed that the Bank's subsidiaries would not enter into any material transaction without prior approval from the OTS. When the OTS threatened to take control of the Bank, however, the Directors' used the bankruptcy code to stymie the OTS, even though their action breached the Consent Agreement with the OTS and violated their fiduciary duties to the Bank. We cannot condone the Directors' blatant attempt to circumvent the OTS' regulatory authority by holding that they acted in good faith.

Even if the bankruptcy filings benefitted the Debtors, we still could not conclude that the Directors acted in good faith. An agent who has intentionally participated in illegal activity or wrongful conduct against third persons cannot be said to have acted in good faith, even if the conduct benefits the corporation. *Plate*, 275 Cal. Rptr. at 672. "For example, corporate executives who participate in a deliberate price-fixing conspiracy with competing firms could not be found to have acted in good faith, even though they may have reasonably believed that a deliberate flouting of the antitrust laws would increase the profits of the corporation." 1 Harold Marsh, Jr. and R. Roy Finkle, Marsh's California Corporation Law (3d ed.) § 10.43, at 751; *see Plate*, 275 Cal. Rptr. at 672 (citing same language from second edition). We recognize that the Directors did not break any law by filing the bankruptcy petitions, and that the OTS has not filed criminal charges against the Directors. Nonetheless, we find that a deliberate attempt to undermine the regulatory authority of a government agency cannot constitute good faith conduct, even if such actions benefit the corporation.

The Directors intentionally breached their fiduciary duties to the Bank and their Consent Agreement with the OTS in order to prevent the OTS from exercising the powers granted to it under FIRREA. The Directors knew the impropriety of their actions, and one of the Directors-Ille-resigned his position when he learned of the scheme. We therefore conclude that the Directors did not act in good faith when they placed the Debtors in bankruptcy.

### B.

We do not reach the same conclusion with respect to Ille. Because the OTS and Ille entered into a settlement and the OTS has dropped its charges against Ille, we have the benefit of the factual admissions contained in the settlement agreement. That agreement confirms that Ille had no part in the filing of the bankruptcy petitions. He learned of the decision to place the Debtors in bankruptcy on the evening of October 10, 1991, the day before the bankruptcy filings. Ille resigned his directorship later that same evening. In the settlement agreement, Ille admitted knowing of numerous serious underwriting deficiencies on loans approved by the Bank, and that he relied on representations by the Bank's management that these deficiencies were being addressed instead of his independently investigating the deficiencies known to him. At most, Ille failed only in his duties to follow the affairs of the Bank more diligently. The OTS, recognizing Ille's minimal participation, dropped the charges against him with only a mild punishment: it required Ille to sign a cease and desist order prohibiting him, in effect, from his breaching fiduciary duties in the future.

The terms of Ille's settlement agreement informs our decision regarding whether Ille acted in good faith and in the best interests of the corporation. The settlement agreement confirms that Ille committed no intentional wrongful act. Most importantly, upon realizing that the other Directors had schemed to circumvent the OTS's authority by placing the Debtors into bankruptcy, he immediately resigned from his position as a Bank director. We find that Ille acted in good faith and in the best interests of the Debtors.

We conclude, however, that Ille cannot receive indemnification from Landmark Oklahoma because he was not an agent of that corporation. Ille was not a member of the boards of directors of Landmark Oklahoma or any of the Bank's other subsidiaries. He was a director only of the Bank, and as the settlement agreement shows, he was not an active participant in the management of either the Bank or the subsidiaries. Ille's only connection to Landmark Oklahoma is that he was employed by First Life Assurance Company ("First Life"), a subsidiary of Landmark Oklahoma. His employment status, however, does not make him an agent of Landmark Oklahoma, especially because First Life has no involvement whatsoever in the bankruptcy filings or this litigation. Because Ille was not an agent of Landmark Oklahoma, he would have to seek indemnification from the Bank. Hence, Ille is not entitled to indemnification from Landmark Oklahoma.

Although Ille has not sought indemnification from the Bank, we note that, under Louisiana law, Ille would likely be entitled to mandatory indemnification from the Bank.9 The Louisiana indemnification statute provides for mandatory indemnification of an agent to the extent that he "has been successful on the merits or otherwise in defense" of the OTS charges. La. REV. Stat. Ann. § 12:83(B). Ille never received an adjudication on the merits, but courts in other jurisdictions have interpreted similar language to require indemnification when a settlement agreement demonstrates that the agent succeeded on the merits. *See Wisener v. Air Express Int'l Corp.*, 583 F.2d 579, 583 (2d Cir. 1978) (holding, under Illinois law, that the phrase "on the merits or otherwise" is "surely . . . broad enough to cover a termination of claims by agreement without any payment or assumption of liability."); *Waltuch v. Conticommodity Servs. Inc.*, 833 F. Supp. 302, 310–11 (S.D.N.Y. 1993) (following *Wisener* in interpreting Delaware law, although ultimately concluding that plaintiff was not successful on merits); *B & B Investment Club v. Kleinert's, Inc.*, 472 F. Supp. 787, 790-91 (E.D. Pa. 1979) (interpreting Pennsylvania law). *But see American Nat'l Bank & Trust Co. of Eau Claire, Wis. v. Schigur*, 83 Cal. App. 3d 790, 148 Cal. Rptr. 116, 117–18 (1978) (holding, under California law, that mandatory indemnification requires a judicial determination of the merits of the agent's defense).[52] The settlement agreement strongly suggests that Ille successfully defended himself against the OTS charges. Nevertheless, we cannot reach the issue of mandatory indemnification because the Bank is not a defendant and has not had an opportunity to argue against mandatory indemnification.[53]

---

[52] [10] The reasoning of the California court in *American Nat'l Bank & Trust* does not apply to Louisiana law. The mandatory indemnification provision in most states follows the language of the Model Business Corporations Act, which provides for mandatory indemnification of an agent who "has been successful on the merits or otherwise in defense" of any action. 1 Model Business Corporations Act Ann.2d § 5; *see, e.g.*, La. REV. Stat. Ann. § 12:83(B). The California statute, however, does not include the words "or otherwise," suggesting "a legislative intent that mandatory indemnification should depend upon a judicial determination of the actual merits of the agent's defense . . . ." *American Nat'l Bank & Trust*, 148 Cal. Rptr. at 118. Therefore, the *American Nat'l Bank & Trust* court's interpretation of California law has no bearing on Louisiana law.

[53] [11] We note that Ille has not paid any portion of his defense costs. In his deposition of April 9, 1992,

### III.

We next consider the district court's finding that the Employees acted in good faith and in the best interests of the Debtors. The district court found that:

> There is no evidence before this court that the employees had any reason to believe that their efforts in taking the company into bankruptcy were opposed to the best interests of the corporation. While Cone and Motahari were investigated for criminal conduct and the OTS brought administrative charges for breach of fiduciary duty against them, they were never found guilty of any charge. Braun and Trapani were never even named in any administrative or criminal proceeding. They were only questioned concerning actions taken in the discharge of their duties of employment.

*In re Landmark Land Co. of Okla.*, Civ. Action No. 2:91-5286-1, order at 5 (D.S.C. Nov. 9, 1994) (J.A. 2518) (footnote omitted). We find the district court's reasoning to be somewhat illogical. The Employees had no involvement in the Directors' decision to take the subsidiaries into bankruptcy. The OTS investigated the Employees to determine whether, in conducting the business of the Bank, they participated in unsafe and unsound business practices or violated banking laws and regulations. The charges brought against Cone and Motahari focused on their representations to federal regulators that the Debtors owed to the Bank over $950 million in secured debt, when in fact the debt was unsecured. The government has never alleged that any of the Employees participated in the decision to place the Debtors into bankruptcy.

We therefore conclude that the district court's holding that the Employees acted in good faith and in the best interests of the Debtors was clearly erroneous, at least with respect to Cone and Motahari. The OTS alleged that Cone and Motahari engaged in unsafe and unsound business practices by arranging for the Bank to loan over $950 million to its subsidiaries without securing the debt for the Bank. The OTS further alleged that they misrepresented to federal regulators that the loans were secured. Although Cone's and Motahari's settlement agreement stated that they continue to dispute the OTS charges against them, they accepted prohibition from practicing in the affairs of any insured depository institution and debarment from practicing before the OTS. In other words, the OTS kicked them out of the profession. Unlike the district court, which stated that the settlement agreement should not connote Cone's and Motahari's guilt, *In re Landmark Land Co. of Okla.*, Civ. Action No. 2:91-5286-1, order at 5 n. 4 (D.S.C. Nov. 9, 1994) (J.A. 2518 n. 4), we conclude that their punishment is strong evidence that they acted in bad faith.[54]

With respect to Trapani and Braun, we see little evidence in the record on which to base a "good faith" determination, and therefore conclude that the district court's

---

he testified that the Directors' attorneys represented him in defense of the OTS charges. Because his position was different from the other three Directors, he hired a personal attorney. He never received the bills from this attorney, who was paid by Barton. *See* J.A. 259-60.

[54] [12] We note that some of the subsidiaries have already indemnified Cone and Motahari for a substantial portion of their defense costs. The government represented at oral argument that it sought only prospective relief and that it was not demanding that Cone and Motahari repay the amounts already received.

finding of good faith was clearly erroneous. Nonetheless, Trapani and Braun have a right to mandatory indemnification because they succeeded on the merits. Like Cone and Motahari, the OTS investigated Trapani and Braun for possible violations of banking statutes and regulations and for any participation in unsafe or unsound business practices. After this investigation, the OTS subpoenaed Trapani and Braun and made them give depositions under circumstances that were clearly adversarial. The OTS never filed any charges against Trapani and Braun. Under these circumstances, we conclude that they succeeded on the merits in their defense and are thus entitled to mandatory indemnification under La. Rev. Stat. Ann. § 12:83(B).

We therefore reverse the district court's granting of the Reimbursement Motion with respect to Cone and Motahari, and we affirm on different grounds the district court's granting of the motion with respect to Trapani and Braun.

### IV.

We conclude that the district court erred in finding that Barton, Vaughan, Walser, Cone, and Motahari acted in good faith and in the best interests of the Debtors. Furthermore, we find that Ille, although he acted in good faith and in the best interests of the Bank, was not an agent of Landmark Oklahoma and could not receive indemnification from that entity. Therefore, we reverse the district court's granting of the Reimbursement Motion with respect to those parties. We conclude also that Trapani and Braun succeeded on the merits in their defense and were entitled to mandatory indemnification from their employer, Landmark Louisiana. We therefore affirm, on different grounds, the district court's granting of the Reimbursement Motion with respect to Trapani and Braun.

Because of the grounds upon which we base our conclusions, we need not reach the numerous other issues raised by the parties.

AFFIRMED in part and REVERSED in part.

## RIDDER v. CITYFED FINANCIAL CORP.
### United States Court of Appeals, Third Circuit
### 47 F. 3d 85 (1995)

FULLAM, J.

The appellants, Willem Ridder, Lyndon C. Merkle, John T. Hurst and Gregory DeVany, were employed by City Collateral and Financial Services, Inc. a wholly owned subsidiary of City Federal Savings Bank, which in turn was the wholly owned subsidiary of appellee CityFed Financial Corporation ("CityFed"), a Delaware corporation now in receivership. Resolution Trust Corporation ("RTC"), as receiver for CityFed, has sued the appellants in a companion case in the United States District Court for the District of New Jersey, *Resolution Trust Corp. v. Fidelity & Deposit Co. of Maryland*, et al., case No. 92-1003 (D.N.J.), asserting that the appellants committed various frauds and breaches of their fiduciary duty to their employer. Specifically, the RTC asserts that appellants (1) exceeded their authority by approving loans to Northwest Mortgage Co., Inc., (2) concealed

Northwest's default from CityFed's credit committee, (3) misrepresented to the credit committee the status of the Northwest line of credit, (4) misstated to the committee the risks associated with the Northwest loan, (5) concealed Northwest's criminal activity from CityFed, (6) falsified City Collateral records, and (7) improperly divulged confidential information for personal gain.

Upon being served with the complaint in the RTC action, appellants made demand upon CityFed to advance funds for attorneys fees they would incur in defending the RTC litigation. CityFed refused, whereupon appellants brought this action to compel CityFed to advance attorneys fees to them. Plaintiff sought a preliminary injunction to obtain immediate payment, and also filed a motion for summary judgment. After a hearing, the district court denied both motions, and appellants timely filed this appeal.

Article XI of CityFed's by-laws requires CityFed to indemnify and hold harmless all employees sued or threatened to be sued by reason of such employment by CityFed or any of its subsidiaries, "to the fullest extent authorized by the Delaware corporation law," and specifically provides that the right to indemnity "shall include the right to be paid the expenses incurred in defending any such proceeding in advance of its final disposition; provided, however that, if the Delaware Corporation Law so requires [it does] the payment of such expenses . . . shall be made only upon delivery to the corporation of an undertaking . . . to repay all amounts so advanced if it shall ultimately be determined that such employee is not entitled to be indemnified." [Emphasis added.] These by-law provisions are substantially identical to the provisions of the Delaware Corporation Law on the subject.

The district court denied the injunction sought by appellants for two reasons. Because of the perceived strength of the RTC's case against the appellants in the related litigation, the court concluded that appellants had failed to demonstrate a likelihood of success on the merits. And, in view of the fact that CityFed is in receivership and the rights of other creditors are implicated, the court felt that the harm to appellants from denial of the injunction was outweighed by the public interest in assuring equal treatment to all of CityFed's creditors, and that appellants' claim should not be accorded priority by the issuance of a preliminary injunction. 853 F. Supp. 131. We conclude that neither reason suffices to justify denial of the relief plainly mandated by the by-laws and the Delaware statute.

The issue before the district court was not whether appellants were likely to prevail in the RTC litigation, but whether they were likely to prevail in their assertion that CityFed should advance the costs of defense. Under Delaware law, appellants' right to receive the costs of defense in advance does not depend upon the merits of the claims asserted against them, and is separate and distinct from any right of indemnification they may later be able to establish. *Citadel Holding Corp. v. Roven*, 603 A.2d 818 (Del. 1992); *Salaman v. National Media Corp.*, No. C.A. 92 C-01-161, 1994 WL 465534 (Del. Super. July 22, 1994). *See* Joseph Warren Bishop, Jr., LAW OF CORPORATE OFFICERS AND DIRECTORS INDEMNIFICATION AND INSURANCE, ¶ 6.27 (1981 & Supp. 1993). Indeed, the provisions in both Article XI of CityFed's by-laws and § 145(e) of the Delaware corporation law, conditioning the obligation to advance defense costs upon an undertaking "to repay such amount if it shall ultimately be determined that [the officer] is not entitled to be indemnified by the corporation" leaves no room for argument on that score.

CityFed urges us to adopt the approach taken by the district court in *Fidelity Federal Savings & Loan Assn v. Felicetti*, 830 F. Supp. 262 (E.D. Pa. 1993), and rule that, notwithstanding the by-law provision, CityFed was justified in refusing to advance defense costs because of "the overriding duty of the directors to act in the best interests of the corporation." *Id.*, at 269. We respectfully disagree. Given a choice between decisions of the appellate courts of Delaware and courts of other jurisdictions, on issues of Delaware law, this court is plainly required to follow the decisions of the Delaware courts. Moreover, we find the reasoning in Felicetti unpersuasive. Rarely, if ever, could it be a breach of fiduciary duty on the part of corporate directors to comply with the requirements of the corporation's by-laws, as expressly authorized by statute.

The statutory provisions authorizing the advancement of defense costs, conditioned upon an agreement to repay if a right of indemnification is not later established, plainly reflect a legislative determination to avoid deterring qualified persons from accepting responsible positions with financial institutions for fear of incurring liabilities greatly in excess of their means, and to enhance the reliability of litigation-outcomes involving directors and officers of corporations by assuring a level playing field. It is not the province of judges to second-guess these policy determinations.

Appellants made a strong showing that, unless defense costs were advanced to them, their ability to defend the RTC action would be irreparably harmed. Appellee made no contrary showing, and the district court did not base its holding upon the absence of irreparable harm, but rather upon a comparison between the harm to appellants and the perceived harm to other creditors of CityFed. Here again, however, we conclude that the district court addressed the wrong issue. The only issue before the district court was whether appellants were entitled to advance payment of the cost of defense of the RTC action. The insolvency proceeding itself was not before the district court, and the impact, if any, of a grant of injunctive relief was not only a matter for other tribunals to decide, but, on this record, purely speculative.

We conclude that the appellants are entitled to have their costs of defense advanced to them, as a matter of law. The order appealed from will therefore be reversed, with instructions to issue an injunction requiring appellee to advance such defense costs as the parties by agreement, or the district court upon further proceedings, determines to be reasonable.

# CATERPILLAR, INC. v. GREAT AMERICAN INSURANCE COMPANY
United States Court of Appeals, Seventh Circuit
62 F.3d 955 (1995)

FLAUM, J.

Caterpillar, Inc. and Great American Insurance Company both appeal from a decision of the district court granting in part and denying in part Caterpillar's motion for summary judgment regarding the coverage afforded Caterpillar's directors and officers under a directors' and officers' liability insurance policy with respect to claims made against them in a federal class action securities suit. The district court determined that Caterpillar had not breached any conditions precedent in the policy in settling the suit but that Great American was entitled to attempt to allocate a portion of the settlement to uncovered claims or parties. We now affirm that decision but do so with modifications.

## I.

This insurance dispute derives from the Brazilian economic crises of the Spring of 1990. These crises substantially injured the Brazilian operations of Caterpillar, Inc., which in turn substantially reduced Caterpillar's profits. The disclosure of that decline in profits caused Caterpillar stock to lose 20% of its value over two days in June, 1990. That price drop subsequently inspired Caterpillar shareholders to sue Caterpillar and five of its directors. *See Kas v. Caterpillar, Inc.*, et al., No. 90-1238, and *Margolis v. Caterpillar, Inc., et al.*, No. 90-1242 (later consolidated as a class action as the *Kas* litigation).

The *Kas* complaint alleged several federal securities law (Sections 10(b) and 20 of the Securities Exchange Act of 1934, 15 U.S.C. §§ 78j(b), 78t and Rule 10b-5, 17 C.F.R. § 240.10b-5) and state law violations based on the defendants' failure to disclose the significance of Caterpillar's Brazilian operations, as well as the costs of a January, 1990 reorganization. Specifically, the *Kas* plaintiffs asserted that Caterpillar and its officers had indicated that the Brazilian plants accounted for only 5% of overall sales but had neglected to mention that these same plants generated 20% of Caterpillar's profits in 1989 and 30% in the first quarter of 1990. Thus, the plaintiffs argued, investors could not fully appreciate the potential impact of Brazil's economic woes on Caterpillar's bottom line.

At the time the *Kas* case was filed, Caterpillar held a directors' and officers' liability ("D & O") insurance policy purchased from Great American Insurance Company.[55] The policy in the present case requires Great American to reimburse Caterpillar's directors and officers (or Caterpillar itself if it had already indemnified the directors and officers) under certain circumstances:

> I.A. With the Directors or Officers of the Company that if, during the Policy Period or the Discovery Period, any Claim is first made against the Directors or Officers, individually or collectively, for a Wrongful Act the Insurer will pay on behalf of the Directors or Officers all Loss which the Directors or Officers shall be legally obligated to pay, except for such Loss which the Company actually pays as indemnification.

> I.B. With the Company that if, during the Policy Period or the Discovery Period, any Claim is first made against the Directors or Officers, individu-

---

[55] [1] D & O policies, which first became popular in the 1960s, protect directors and officers from the potential liability they might incur in performing their duties, thereby encouraging better directors and officers to accept responsibilities and allowing them to take management risks they might not otherwise take. *See* Roberta Romano, *What Went Wrong With Directors' and Officers' Liability Insurance?*, 14 DEL. J. CORP. L. 1, 3–5 (1989).

ally or collectively, for a Wrongful Act the Insurer will reimburse the Company for all Loss which the Company has to the extent permitted by law indemnified the Directors or Officers.

The policy also provides for payment of defense costs as well as indemnification above a $10 million retention but does not impose on Great American a duty to defend Caterpillar or its directors or officers against any claims.

The policy further includes a number of duties on the part of Caterpillar, of which two are relevant:

> VI.A. The Directors or Officers shall not admit liability for, or settle, any Claim or incur Costs of Defense in connection with any Claim, without the Insurer's prior written consent, which consent shall not be unreasonably withheld. The Insurer shall be entitled to full information and all particulars it may request in order to reach a decision as to such consent. Any Costs of Defense incurred, and/or settlements agreed to prior to the Insurer consent thereto shall not be covered.

> VI.C. The Insurer shall at all times have the right, but not the duty, to associate with the Directors or Officers in the investigation, defense or settlement of any Claim, to which this Policy may apply.

Another provision made Caterpillar's "full compliance . . . with all of the terms of this Policy" a condition precedent to any indemnification action against Great American.

*          *          *

Both before and after this letter, Caterpillar, through its in-house and outside counsel, promised to keep Great American "informed of developments as they occur." Letters from Caterpillar and its lawyers indicate that they provided Great American with notice of numerous motions and memoranda filed with the court and of accumulating defense costs. An October 10, 1991 letter sent to another of Caterpillar's insurers but copied to Great American stated that:

> [t]he possibility of settlement prior to finalization of the plaintiffs' complaint is being explored. No definitive offer has been made to, or received from, the plaintiffs. Whether or not an acceptable settlement can be reached will depend on a variety of factors, including the cooperation of Caterpillar's insurers. Needless to say we will keep you advised of developments in this area.

On March 30, 1992, the district court denied Caterpillar's motion to dismiss the *Kas* complaint for failure to allege scienter adequately. *Kas v. Caterpillar, Inc.*, et al., 815 F. Supp. 1158, 1165 (C.D. Ill. 1992). The next day, pursuant to a settlement between it and Caterpillar, the SEC issued an order concluding that Caterpillar had failed to comply with Section 13(a) of the Securities Exchange Act of 1934, 15 U.S.C. § 78m(a), as well as with certain rules promulgated thereunder.

During this same time period, Caterpillar, through its initial outside counsel, Orrick, Herrington & Sutcliffe, had discussed a settlement with the *Kas* plaintiffs that called for a cash payment of $5 million and stock warrants with a minimum value of $15 million and a maximum of $45 million.[56] Orrick, Herrington apparently mentioned the offer for the first time in November or December, 1991 and renewed it with reservations in a May 27, 1992 letter.[57] The offer apparently was made again on March 18, 1993, by Kirkland & Ellis, which by then had replaced Orrick, Herrington.[58]

Great American claims it received no notice of these negotiations until the Spring of 1993. A May 4, 1993 letter from Great American's attorneys to Caterpillar's in-house counsel reflected surprise and dismay that Caterpillar had made any previous settlement offers and professed a lack of prior knowledge of those negotiations. In that same letter, which foresaw many of the arguments Great American raises in the current litigation, Great American complained that Caterpillar was making offers well above what it should have and that these offers unreasonably raised the plaintiffs' expectations of settlement. The letter continued:

> We recognize that your decision to proceed without Great American's input was probably based on your conclusion that after allocating the settlement between the liability of the Company (uninsured) and the individual defendants, and applying the $10 million retention to the covered portion, Caterpillar would not be seeking reimbursement from Great American. However, given the magnitude of the plaintiffs' demands, we feel that all settlement proposals should be presented first to Great American, whether or not they are anticipated to involve the coverage.

Great American also responded to the news by engaging a settlement consultant, who issued a report on June 2, 1993, predicting that the *Kas* litigation should settle for approximately $10.6 million. Caterpillar's next settlement offer, made at a June 29, 1993 meeting, dropped to $4.5. After further negotiations, the parties agreed to a settlement worth between $17.25 and $23 million. Great American approved the settlement subject to certain reservations, and the district court entered the settlement on February 14, 1994.

Prior to the finalization of the settlement, Caterpillar filed the instant suit against Great American seeking a declaration that Great American was liable for the entire settlement amount and defense expenses in excess of the policy's $10 million retention. Before discovery had begun, Caterpillar moved for summary judgment on the declaratory judgment count without requesting a ruling on damages. Great American responded that it had no obligation to indemnify because Caterpillar had

---

[56] [2] The warrants, which were to number 3 million, were valued at a minimum of $5 each plus an additional dollar for every dollar Caterpillar's stock price exceeded $60 on the warrant's expiration date. The added value was capped at $70, so that each warrant would never be worth more than $15.

[57] [3] The letter hinted that Caterpillar might be more reluctant about the offer as of May 27, 1992, because the stock price was then around $59-5/8, much higher than its value in November and December of 1991. *See, e.g., Caterpillar Says Q4 Loss to Exceed 86 Million Dollars*, AFP-Extel News (November 14, 1991) (reporting Caterpillar's closing price at $48); Penny Britell, *U.S. Stocks Close Firm After Turbulent Session*, Reuters Newswire (December 11, 1991) (reporting Caterpillar's closing price at $39). Caterpillar disputes whether it ever authorized this renewed offer.

[58] [4] At this point, according to correspondence from the plaintiffs, Caterpillar's stock price had dropped to $58. The plaintiffs' attorneys rejected the offer, proposing instead that the case be settled for $115 million.

violated conditions precedent in the insurance contract by failing to inform it of the settlement negotiations prior to mid-1993. Alternatively, Great American argued, even if the policy did apply, it was entitled to an allocation for the portion of the settlement not attributable to the actions of Caterpillar's directors and officers.

The district court granted in part and denied in part Caterpillar's motion for summary judgment. *Caterpillar, Inc. v. Great American Ins. Co.*, 864 F. Supp. 849 (C.D. Ill. 1994). The court found that Caterpillar had not violated the terms of the insurance agreement and that the policy applied to the settlement and granted summary judgment to Caterpillar on that issue. The court also determined, however, that Great American was entitled to an allocation of some sort. Relying on our decision in *Harbor Ins. Co. v. Continental Bank Corp.*, 922 F.2d 357 (7th Cir. 1990), the district court concluded that Great American could try "to prove that all or part of those activities attributed to Caterpillar and its board in the *Kas* complaint were performed by uninsured persons or persons against whom no claims were made." *Caterpillar*, 864 F. Supp. at 854. The district court, again looking to *Harbor*, also indicated that in any allocation, Great American would not be permitted to exclude Caterpillar's potential liability. The *Harbor* court had stated that any corporate securities liability in that case would be entirely dependent on the activities of the directors and officers, thereby rendering those persons ultimately responsible for any liability the corporation faced. Notwithstanding the fact that *Harbor*'s comments on this issue were dicta, the district court thought that *Harbor* was "the best indication of how the Seventh Circuit would decide the issue" and that it would lead to the same result here. *Id.* at 857. Thus, while the district court refused to grant summary judgment on the issue, it markedly limited the scope of allocation.

Although the district court's ruling did not constitute a final order, the court certified its order for interlocutory appeal under 28 U.S.C. § 1292(b). Both parties filed timely petitions to this Court for leave to appeal, and we granted those petitions.

## II.

Great American and Caterpillar each appeal the district court's decision regarding allocation of liability under the policy. The district court held that Great American was entitled to an allocation, but only to the extent that the settlement was larger because of the activities of employees other than those directors and officers against whom claims were made. Great American asserts that allocation should be broader and should reflect Caterpillar's direct corporate liability. Caterpillar, in its cross-appeal, maintains that the district court, if anything, went too far and that no allocation for the acts of unnamed persons should be allowed. Both appeals are based on the district court's denial of summary judgment, a decision we review de novo. *United States v. Wisconsin Power and Light Co.*, 38 F. 3d 329, 332 (7th Cir. 1994). Summary judgment is appropriate "if the pleadings, depositions, answers to interrogatories, and admissions on file, together with the affidavits, if any, show that there is no genuine issue as to any material fact and that the moving party is entitled to judgment as a matter of law." Fed. R. Civ. P. 56(c); Celotex Corp. v. Catrett, 477 U.S. 317, 322, 106 S. Ct. 2548, 2552, 91 L. Ed. 2d 265

(1986). We view the record in the light most favorable to the non-moving party, noting that a genuine issue of material fact exists only where the potential evidence would permit a reasonable finder of fact to return a verdict for the non-moving party. *Anderson v. Liberty Lobby, Inc.*, 477 U.S. 242, 248–49, 106 S. Ct. 2505, 2510–11, 91 L. Ed. 2d 202 (1986).

## A.

We have addressed the allocation issue only once before, albeit as dicta. *Harbor Ins. Co. v. Continental Bank Corp.*, 922 F.2d 357 (7th Cir. 1990). In *Harbor*, a number of Continental Bank investors had filed securities fraud suits against Continental in the wake of its collapse following the Penn Square bank debacle. In two suits, investors claimed that Continental had concealed the nature of its Penn Square loans in order to inflate its stock price. The first suit, a class action, named as defendants Continental as well as twenty-five directors, officers, and employees of Continental, identified in the complaint only as "John Does." The second suit named Continental and five specific directors. Continental settled the cases for $17.5 million and then turned to its insurers, Allstate and Harbor, who refused to pay under D & O policies they had issued. *Id.* at 359–60.

*Harbor*'s holding primarily concerned the proper application of Illinois's "mend the hold" doctrine: prior to the settlement, Allstate and Harbor had argued that the directors' conduct had been so egregious that it placed them beyond coverage; after the settlement, the insurers reversed their position and contended that Continental had improperly paid out any money because the directors had done nothing wrong. Our ruling on that issue required remanding the case for a new trial, and in order to guide that proceeding, we discussed how damages should be calculated and liability allocated. We noted that "[t]o the extent that the amount for which Continental settled was larger than it would have been but for the misfeasance of these other persons — either noninsured persons or persons against whom no claim was made — Continental's entitlement to reimbursement in this suit would be cut down." *Id.* at 367. *Harbor* thus counseled an allocation of a settlement only where that settlement is larger because of the activities of uninsured persons who were sued or persons who were not sued but whose actions may have contributed to the suit, an approach other courts have referred to as the "larger settlement" rule. *See Nordstrom, Inc. v. Chubb & Son, Inc.*, 54 F.3d 1424, 1432–33 (9th Cir. 1995); *Raychem Corp. v. Federal Ins. Co.*, 853 F. Supp. 1170, 1180–82 (N.D. Cal. 1994).

Great American, as well as *Amici* Aetna Casualty and Surety Company, et al., argue that we should reject the larger settlement rule. They view the rule as an unfair rationing that allows uninsured defendants, usually the corporation, to piggy-back on D & O policies designed to insure only directors and officers. Even though the directors and officers might be theoretically liable for most if not all of what is commonly alleged in securities suits, they assert that it is unrealistic to assume that these suits and settlements could ever hinge on that liability alone. They also note that settlements provide a number of benefits to a corporate defendant and assert that directors and officers (and therefore their insurers) should not have to subsidize those benefits. Instead, they maintain, we should follow a "relative exposure" rule, a rule derived from the first reported D & O allocation case, *PepsiCo, Inc. v. Continental Cas. Co.*, 640 F. Supp. 656 (S.D.N.Y. 1986). In *PepsiCo*, PepsiCo had settled a number of claims stemming from a class action suit that had named as defendants PepsiCo, its directors and officers, a former officer, and its accounting firm. PepsiCo then sought complete indemnification for the suit under its D & O policy, which provided that "Loss shall mean any amount which the Directors and Officers are legally obligated to pay for . . . a claim or claims made against them for Wrongful Acts." *Id.* at 659. Interpreting the policy under New York law, the court held that it "require[d] the parties to allocate the settlement costs between those amounts attributable to the directors and officers and those attributable to PepsiCo and its accountants." *Id.* at 662. Thus, responsibility for the settlement bill should be allocated "according to the relative exposures of the respective parties to the [suit]." *Id.* A subsequent case, *Safeway Stores, Inc. v. National Union Fire Ins. Co.*, 1993 U.S. Dist. LEXIS 2006, 1993 WL 739643 (N.D. Cal. Feb. 4, 1993), in which both parties agreed "that the proper method of allocation is to determine the relative exposure of . . . officers and directors vis-à-vis uninsured defendants in the underlying shareholder actions," . . . provided an extensive list of what should be considered in allocation:

(1)    the identity, as an individual, an entity, or as a member of a group, of each beneficiary and the likelihood of an adverse judgment against each in the underlying action;

(2)    the risks and hazards to which each beneficiary of the settlement was exposed;

(3)    the ability of each beneficiary to respond to an adverse judgment;

(4)    the burden of litigation on each beneficiary;

(5)    the 'deep pocket' factor and its potential effect on the liability of each beneficiary;

(6)    the funding of the defense activity in the litigation and the burden of such funding;

(7)    the motivations and intentions of those who negotiated the settlement, as shown by their statements, the settlement documents and any other relevant evidence;

(8)    the benefits sought to be accomplished and accomplished by the settlement as to each beneficiary, as shown by the statements of the negotiators, the settlement documents and any other relevant evidence;

(9)    the source of the funds that paid the settlement sum;

(10)    the extent to which any individual defendants are exempted from liability by state statutes or corporate charter provisions; and

(11)    such other and similar matters as are peculiar to the particular litigation and settlement.

*Id.* at *5–6 (citing William E. Knepper & Dan A. Bailey, Liability of Corporate Officers and Directors § 17.06, Supp. at 248–49 (Michie, 4th ed.1988 & Supp.1992)). The relative exposure rule thus envisions a somewhat elaborate inquiry into what happened in a settlement and who really paid for what relief. *See also First Fidelity Bancorporation v. National Union Fire Ins. Co. of Pittsburgh*, 1994 WL 111363

(E.D. Pa. March 30, 1994); *Nodaway Valley Bank v. Continental Cas. Co.*, 715 F. Supp. 1458, 1465–67 (W.D. Mo. 1989), *aff'd* 916 F.2d 1362 (8th Cir. 1990); *Perini Corp. v. National Union Fire Ins. Co.*, 1988 WL 192453 (D. Mass. June 2, 1988).

In selecting one rule over the other, our role is to interpret the insurance contract between Caterpillar and Great American based on the applicable contract law, in this case that of Illinois. We do not sit to develop general canons of allocation for every conflict between D & O insurers and their insureds; rather we read a particular insurance contract and decide what method of allocation, if any, that contract envisions. *See Nordstrom*, 54 F. 3d at 1432.

We first note, as the district court indicated, that the insurance contract does not contain an allocation clause. However, the contract only requires Great American to indemnify Caterpillar to the extent Caterpillar paid to resolve claims actually made against its directors and officers. It does not obligate the insurer to do more. As such, assuming the possibility that the settlement did more than resolve these claims, some measure of allocation is appropriate.

Determining of how much allocation is appropriate depends on what the insured did in settling the complaint. *Raychem*, 853 F. Supp. at 1183; *cf. Hudson Ins. Co. v. City of Chicago Heights*, 48 F. 3d 234, 238 (7th Cir. 1995). Caterpillar paid money and offered warrants in exchange for dismissal with prejudice of all claims against the defendants named in the Kas complaint, as well as against a list of other Caterpillar affiliates, or any potential claims related to those made in the *Kas* complaint. The Great American policy provided coverage for "all Loss which the Directors or Officers shall be legally obligated to pay" where "any Claim is first made against the Directors or Officers, individually or collectively, for a Wrongful Act." That language implies a complete indemnity for claims regardless of who else might be at fault for similar actions. *Cf. Chicago Bd. of Options Exch., Inc. v. Harbor Ins. Co.*, 738 F. Supp. 1184, 1186 (N.D. Ill. 1990) ("The court is obliged to hold Harbor to the terms of its policy: any claim against an officer or director for a wrongful act, for which CBOE had to indemnify that officer or director, triggers Harbor's obligation to reimburse CBOE.").

Thus, in the instant case, we believe the larger settlement rule better suits the facts: the policy does not limit coverage because of the activities of others that might overlap the claims against the directors and officers. Furthermore, we note that Illinois disfavors pro rata allocation absent language in the insurance contract that so requires. *See Zurich Ins. Co. v. Raymark Industries*, 118 Ill. 2d 23, 112 Ill. Dec. 684, 699, 514 N.E. 2d 150, 165 (1987). We also believe that a protracted pursuit of the motivations underlying a settlement, as suggested in *Safeway* and by Great American and the *amici*, is not necessarily the best way to resolve coverage disputes: The question at issue is whether the insurance policy covered certain claims, not the metaphysical underpinnings of why a corporation or its directors and officers might have acted as they did. *See Nordstrom*, 54 F. 3d at 1433 n. 2.[59]

---

[59] [6] Our decision does not leave Great American "without recourse" against uninsured persons who participated in the alleged wrongful conduct but whose actions did not make the settlement larger. *Raychem*, 853 F. Supp. at 1182–83. The insurer, as subrogee of the directors and officers under Section VIII.E of the policy, may still pursue contribution claims against those other persons. *See Musick, Peeler*

## B.

We thus adopt *Harbor*'s dicta regarding the larger settlement rule as our holding today. Harbor also indicated, however, that corporate liability caused by the actions of directors should not come into the allocation calculus. Relying on the premise that Continental as a corporate entity only had liability derivative of the directors, *Harbor* stated that any allocation between the directors' liability and corporate derivative liability "would rob Continental of the insurance protection that it sought and bought." *Id.* at 368; *see also Nodaway*, 715 F. Supp. at 1466. In Harbor, we assumed that for almost any liability the corporation might have faced, it could have demanded reimbursement from its directors and officers.

Since *Harbor*, the Supreme Court has noted that corporations face direct liability under section 10(b) of the 1934 Act and Rule 10b-5. *Musick, Peeler & Garrett v. Employers' Ins. of Wausau*, 508 U.S. 286, 113 S. Ct. 2085, 2090–91, 124 L. Ed. 2d 194 (1993); *see also Central Bank of Denver v. First Interstate Bank of Denver*, 511 U.S. 164, 114 S. Ct. 1439, 1448, 128 L. Ed. 2d 119 (1994). The possibility of direct liability in these cases calls into question Harbor's premises regarding corporate liability. Indeed, there are conceivable situations where the individual actors would not be liable but their corporate employer would be, for example where a case depends on the collective scienter of its employees or where defenses are available to individuals but not the corporation. *See Nordstrom*, 54 F. 3d at 1435. If a corporation's liability in the face of a federal securities suit is possibly direct and not merely derivative, then Harbor's conjunction of officers and directors' liability and corporate liability loses some of its force.

The fact that a premise is incorrect, however, does not necessarily dictate that conclusions based on the premise are incorrect. The *Kas* complaint may have implicated direct claims against Caterpillar, but regardless of whether corporate liability is legally direct or derivative, a corporation still must act through its agents. If all those agents were directors and officers covered under the Great American policy, and Caterpillar incurred direct liability because of these individuals' actions, then perhaps the D & O policy should still cover claims based on those actions. . . . Furthermore, as Nordstrom noted, there is little case law supporting an independent corporate scienter theory. 54 F. 3d at 1435. *But cf. In re Warner Communications Securities Litigation*, 618 F. Supp. 735, 752–53 (S.D.N.Y. 1985) (noting that "the requisite degree of scienter is likely to be easier to attribute to [the corporation] than the individual defendants" and that "such proof would expose [the corporation] to infinitely greater liability than it would the individual defendants"), *aff'd*, 798 F.2d 35 (2d Cir. 1986); William M. Fletcher, Fletcher Cyclopedia of Private Corporations § 790 at 16 (perm. ed.). In other words, the differentiation between direct and derivative liability may well be a distinction without a difference.

In this case, we believe the distinction may matter. Caterpillar's policy obligates Great American to indemnify Caterpillar only to the extent Caterpillar must indemnify its directors and officers. Corporate derivative liability, which would essentially be a form of respondeat superior for these cases, entitles a corporation

---

*& Garrett v. Employers' Ins. of Wausau*, 508 U.S. 286, 113 S. Ct. 2085, 2086, 124 L. Ed. 2d 194 (1993); *Nordstrom*, 54 F.3d at 1436.

to indemnification from its officers and directors for liability those persons bring upon the corporation. *Cf. Steele v. Hartford Fire Ins. Co.*, 788 F.2d 441, 446 (7th Cir. 1986). But direct liability, as might have existed here,[60] ordinarily creates no such right of indemnification in the corporation, *see New Zealand Kiwifruit Marketing Board v. City of Wilmington*, 825 F. Supp. 1180, 1191 (D. Del. 1993), and section IV.K of the policy in question excludes coverage for "any Claim made against the Directors or Officers . . . by or at the behest of the Company." Moreover, we have held that federal securities law contains no implied right of indemnification under section 10(b), . . . although it allows contribution actions. . . . For whatever liability the corporation faced under § 10(b) and Rule 10b-5, it could not then turn to the responsible directors and officers for indemnification. Direct liability under section 10(b) was certainly a possibility in this case; the *Kas* complaint alleged actions by Caterpillar as a whole and named Caterpillar in the complaint, and the settlement contained language resolving any claims against the corporation and persons other than the directors and officers. Direct liability may also have arisen as the consequence of actions of persons other than officers and directors, something at which the SEC opinion and order hinted. Similarly, Caterpillar may well have incurred liability for the actions of its directors for which its directors and officers were themselves immune and could not have suffered any consequences.[61] To the extent the trier of fact determines that Caterpillar disposed of any direct action against it in settling the complaint and that that disposition increased the settlement figure, Caterpillar should not be entitled to recover from Great American.[62]

[As Great American notes, the claims in the *Kas* complaint against Caterpillar did not raise the issue of respondeat superior liability.]

In its cross-appeal, Caterpillar argues that the district court went too far in permitting an allocation to persons who were never named in the litigation. Caterpillar points out that the complaints in *Harbor* hinted at other, unnamed persons (the twenty-five "John Does") who might have been responsible for increasing the costs of the settlement. In the instant case, Caterpillar argues, that sort of argument is irrelevant because the *Kas* complaint explicitly alleged in paragraph 14 that "[e]ach of the individual defendants is liable as a direct participant in, an aider and abettor of, and co-conspirator with respect to the wrongs committed by all defendants complained of herein." Furthermore, the complaint stated in paragraph 46 that "[t]he name of each person and/or entity who

---

[60] [8] As Great American notes, the claims in the *Kas* complaint against Caterpillar did not raise the issue of *respondeat superior* liability.

[61] [9] *Nordstrom* rejected the possibility of finding corporate scienter without finding that scienter on the part of any particular director or officer: "On this record, we see no way that [the insurer] could show that the corporation, but not any individual defendants, had the requisite intent to defraud. Thus, any direct corporate liability would be derivative of, or concurrent with, D & O liability." 54 F.3d at 1436. *Nordstrom* thus differs from this case in its particulars, not in its analysis; in *Nordstrom*, extensive discovery was already underway (Nordstrom had produced over 100,000 pages of documents), *see id.* at 1429, whereas Caterpillar moved for partial summary judgment before discovery even began.

[62] [10] We reiterate that the fact that an allocation is permitted for the corporation's direct liability does not imply that Great American may go further. We believe the analysis of cases like *PepsiCo* and *Safeway* opens up more inquiry and exposure than the insurance policy in this case would permit.

is responsible for, participated in, conspired to bring about, or aided and abetted the fraud complained of herein, is set forth in this Complaint."

Contrary to Caterpillar's assertions, we believe the district court correctly interpreted Harbor on this point. The *Kas* plaintiffs named Caterpillar in the underlying suit, and some of its liability may well have stemmed from the actions of other persons, as hinted at in both the complaint and the settlement. While an insurer may not propose theories of liability never at issue in a complaint in addressing allocation, a court also need not assume the validity of every allegation in a settled complaint. In *Nordstrom*, the Ninth Circuit was able to look at the facts underlying the coverage and determine that this potential liability was not a problem because any liability was "wholly concurrent with D & O liability." *See* *Nordstrom*, 54 F. 3d at 1433. We are unable to make such an assessment at this time. That is not to say, however, that such liability exists; it still ultimately must be proven that Caterpillar might have incurred an independent liability from these actions and that these actions increased the final settlement value.[63]

Thus, as the district court noted, Great American is entitled to attempt some measure of allocation with regard to the settlement of the *Kas* litigation. That allocation may only reflect the extent to which the settlement was larger because of claims against uninsured persons or the actions of persons against whom no claims were made. Uninsured claims may include those made against the corporation for which the corporation would face direct liability and for which the insured directors and officers could not be held liable.

## III.

Great American also objects to the district court's decision granting Caterpillar partial summary judgment on the issue of notice regarding settlement offers made to the *Kas* plaintiffs by Caterpillar and its various attorneys. Great American contends that these unauthorized offers voided its obligations under the insurance contract. First, Great American argues that Caterpillar breached a condition precedent to its insurance policy by making settlement offers without Great American's prior knowledge or consent. Alternatively, Great American claims that Caterpillar breached a duty under Illinois law to defend the underlying litigation in

---

[63] [11] Although neither party directly raises the issue, there is an additional question regarding on whom the burden of proof in an allocation should fall. On the one hand, insurers are normally obligated to pay for any settlements negotiated in good faith. *PepsiCo*, 640 F. Supp. at 662 (placing the burden on the insurer). However, under many D & O policies, including the one in the instant case, the insureds control the underlying litigation. That renders them not only in possession of most information regarding the suit, *see Raychem*, 853 F. Supp. at 1175–76, but also gives them the opportunity, and the perverse incentive, to structure the underlying litigation so as to place all the fault on the backs of officers and directors and thereby ensure complete coverage. *See Slottow v. American Cas. Co.*, 10 F.3d 1355, 1359 (9th Cir. 1993) (remanding case under California law where settlement reflected an almost collusive attempt by parties to bring settlement within the terms of an insurance policy). Additionally, even if the insured is presumed covered for settlements negotiated in good faith, the insured should still have to show "the existence and extent of a loss covered by a policy." *Raychem*, 853 F. Supp. at 1176. We today express no view on the merits of this debate or application to this case and leave the resolution of this problem for a more appropriate time. *See also* 2 Knepper and Bailey, *supra*, § 21-10 at 274–76 (5th ed.1993) (discussing issue).

a reasonable and prudent manner. We disagree, for neither the insurance contract itself nor Illinois common law lend themselves to the results Great American desires.

First, Section VI.A. of the insurance contract provides that no settlement may be made without Great American's prior written consent and that the insurer "shall be entitled to full information and all particulars it may request in order to reach a decision as to such consent." Great American asserts that this language created a duty on the part of Caterpillar to inform Great American prior to making any settlement offers. Instead, Great American alleges, Caterpillar made repeated and unreasonably high settlement proposals to the *Kas* plaintiffs while falsely telling Great American that these proposals would not implicate its coverage. Great American points out that if the *Kas* plaintiffs had accepted one of Caterpillar's earlier offers without procuring Great American's assent, "Caterpillar's breach of a condition precedent would have been instantaneous and incurable."

As the district court correctly determined, Section VI.A does not help Great American. The plain and unambiguous language of that section only dictates that Caterpillar not settle or admit liability without Great American's consent. Caterpillar did neither. Caterpillar may have made offers without Great American's consent. . . . Although Great American alleges that it consented begrudgingly and only because circumstances left it little alternative, there is no question that it had the opportunity to say no. Great American had adequate knowledge of the circumstances surrounding the complaint at the time it consented; its consent was not coerced or based on fraudulent information.

\* \* \*

[Great American has presented an expert study indicating that the *Kas* litigation should have settled for approximately $10.6 million. Whatever its usefulness, the study is largely immaterial to any inquiry into Great American's rights in this case. If an insurance contract contains a duty of notice and a right of association on the part of the insurer as conditions precedent and the insured violates those conditions, the contract is void regardless of the consequences.]

\* \* \*

Caterpillar informed Great American of the *Kas* complaint, and Great American does not dispute this. That was enough. Great American's suggestion that we read into section VI.A's language an obligation to seek the insurer's advice and consent prior to making any offers of settlement thus derives little sustenance from *Keehn* [*v. Excess Ins., Co. of America*, 129 F.2d at 505 (7th Cir. 1942),] and is, we believe, inappropriate.

Section VI.C presents a closer issue. That section provides that although Great American had no duty to defend Caterpillar's directors and officers (section VI.B so stipulates), Great American had the right to associate with the directors and officers "in the investigation, defense or settlement of any Claim, to which this Policy may apply." As noted earlier, Caterpillar arguably engaged in a campaign of misinformation, hinting to Great American that the ultimate settlement would be lower than Caterpillar knew it would be. The question is whether this course of action violated section VI.C's "right to associate" language, thereby violating a condition precedent to any reimbursement.

The district court held, and we agree, that the right to associate language of the contract is ambiguous because the level of obligation it imposes on Caterpillar is uncertain. In the absence of other indications, the district court interpreted the contract against the insurance company. We are not persuaded by Great American's response that Caterpillar was hardly an ingenue faced with arcane language in an adhesion contract: Illinois law, in its majestic equality, requires us to construe ambiguities in insurance contracts in favor of insureds, great and small alike, and against insurers who draft the insurance policies. . . . Given that Great American had no duty to defend Caterpillar's directors and officers, Great American did not need to know everything about the suit, nor did it request such knowledge. The correspondence between the parties indicates that Great American requested "reports, investigations, pleadings, dispositive motions, briefs, court orders, and other pertinent documents on a current basis" and that Caterpillar promised in a number of letters to keep Great American apprised of "developments as they occur." There is no dispute that Caterpillar complied with the basic request. If Great American wanted information about settlement offers before they were made, it had an obligation to say so explicitly. That obligation renders *Keehn* equally inapposite to Caterpillar's duties under Section VI.C.

\*    \*    \*

Great American additionally contends that Caterpillar violated a common law duty to defend and settle the claim reasonably. Great American points to a number of cases in which the courts have held that an insurer's refusal to honor its duty to defend does not absolve the insured's obligation to act reasonably and in good faith in making its own settlement. . . .

Great American's argument has some appeal but is ultimately unpersuasive. The reasonable settlement rule permits insureds left in the lurch by their insurers to recover from these insurers defense and settlement costs regardless of policy limits. . . . The added common law protection simply ensures that this excess damage was in fact proximately caused by the insurers' refusal to defend. The instant situation did not place Great American in that jeopardy — Great American had no duty to defend. The district court thus correctly determined that the rule was inapplicable and that Caterpillar did not breach any common law duty to handle the underlying litigation in a reasonable and prudent manner.

For the foregoing reasons, the decision of the district court is affirmed as modified. AFFIRMED AS MODIFIED.

# TABLE OF CASES

[References are to pages.]

[References are to pages.]

# C

[References are to pages.]

[References are to pages.]

# H

[References are to pages.]

[References are to pages.]

[References are to pages.]

[References are to pages.]

[References are to pages.]

# INDEX

[References are to sections.]

[References are to sections.]

[References are to sections.]

[References are to sections.]

# V